MOORESTOWN LIBRARY
3 2030 00181 8615

D0900394

THE LOUISIANA PURCHASE

A Historical and Geographical Encyclopedia

THE LOUISIANA PURCHASE

A Historical and Geographical Encyclopedia

Junius P. Rodriguez, Editor

Santa Barbara, California—•—Denver, Colorado—•—Oxford, England

All images are from the Library of Congress unless otherwise noted.

Library of Congress Cataloging-in-Publication Data

The Louisiana Purchase: a historical and geographical encyclopedia
Junius P. Rodriguez, editor.
p. cm.
Includes bibliographical references (p.) and index.
ISBN 1-57607-188-X (alk. paper) — e-book ISBN 1-57607-738-1
1. Louisiana Purchase—Encyclopedias. I. Rodriguez, Junius P.
E333 .L69 2002
973.4'6—dc21

2002003228

06 05 04 03 —10 9 8 7 6 5 4 3

This book is also available on the World Wide Web as an e-book.
Visit abc-clio.com for details.
ABC-CLIO, Inc.
130 Cremona Drive, P.O. Box 1911
Santa Barbara, California 93116-1911

This book is printed on acid-free paper.
Manufactured in the United States of America

For my parents
Junius P. Rodriguez Sr. (1905–1978)
and Mildred D. Rodriguez (1914–)

Where we love is home,
Home that our feet may leave,
but not our hearts.

Oliver Wendell Holmes Sr.
(1809–1894)

CONTENTS

THE CONTRIBUTORS

Lisa Abney
Northwestern State University
Natchitoches, Louisiana

Elizabeth U. Alexander
Texas Wesleyan University
Fort Worth, Texas

Edward E. Baptist
University of Miami
Coral Gables, Florida

J. Herschel Barnhill
Yukon, Oklahoma

Adrienne W. Berney
Louisiana State Museum
New Orleans, Louisiana

Rachel Eden Black
Ecole Normale Supérieure de Lyon
Lyon, France

Christopher A. Blackburn
University of Louisiana at Monroe
Monroe, Louisiana

Jon L. Brudvig
University of Mary
Bismarck, North Dakota

Jay H. Buckley
Brigham Young University
Provo, Utah

Sean R. Busick
University of South Carolina
Columbia, South Carolina

Michael S. Casey
Graceland University
Lamoni, Iowa

Mark Cave
Williams Research Center
New Orleans, Louisiana

Roger Chapman
Bowling Green State University
Bowling Green, Ohio

Mark R. Cheathem
Mississippi State University
Mississippi State, Mississippi

Boyd Childress
Auburn University Library
Auburn, Alabama

Clarissa W. Confer
University of Florida
Gainesville, Florida

Rory T. Cornish
University of Louisiana at Monroe
Monroe, Louisiana

Dallas Cothrum
University of Texas at Tyler
Tyler, Texas

J. Wendel Cox
University of Minnesota, Morris
Morris, Minnesota

Jesus F. de la Teja
Southwest Texas State University
San Marcos, Texas

Chris Dennis
Fort Worth, Texas

Richard H. Dickerson
University of Houston Libraries
Houston, Texas

Douglas W. Dodd
California State University, Bakersfield
Bakersfield, California

Carrie E. Douthey
Texas Christian University
Fort Worth, Texas

Kathleen DuVal
University of California, Davis
Davis, California

J. Brent Etzel
Eureka College
Eureka, Illinois

Dean Fafoutis
Salisbury State University
Salisbury, Maryland

Elizabeth Field
Eureka College
Eureka, Illinois

Daniel L. Fountain
Louisiana School for Math, Science, and the Arts
Natchitoches, Louisiana

Steven M. Fountain
University of California, Davis
Davis, California

Andrew K. Frank
California State University, Los Angeles
Los Angeles, California

John K. Franklin
Texas Christian University
Fort Worth, Texas

Peter S. Genovese Jr.
Bowling Green State University
Bowling Green, Ohio

Henry H. Goldman
University of Phoenix
Phoenix, Arizona

Suzanne Disheroon Green
Northwestern State University
Natchitoches, Louisiana

Donald E. Heidenreich Jr.
Lindenwood University
St. Charles, Missouri

Ricardo A. Herrera
Texas Lutheran University
Seguin, Texas

John C. Jackson
Olympia, Washington

Melinda Marie Jette
University of British Columbia
Vancouver, British Columbia, Canada

Karen R. Jones
University of Bristol
Bristol, United Kingdom

Ari Kelman
University of Denver
Denver, Colorado

Todd Kerstetter
Texas Christian University
Fort Worth, Texas

Joseph Patrick Key
University of Arkansas, Fayetteville
Fayetteville, Arkansas

Michael Kimaid
Bowling Green State University
Bowling Green, Ohio

C. Richard King
Drake University
Des Moines, Iowa

Betje B. Klier
Austin, Texas

Christine Lambert
Emory University
Atlanta, Georgia

Derek R. Larson
St. John's University
Collegeville, Minnesota

Russell M. Lawson
Bacone College
Muskogee, Oklahoma

Alfred Lemmon
Williams Research Center
New Orleans, Louisiana

James W. Loewen
Washington, D.C.

Alecia P. Long
Louisiana State Museum
New Orleans, Louisiana

Brad D. Lookingbill
Columbia College
Columbia, Missouri

Mary F. McKenna
Quest College
Davenport, Iowa

Brian C. Melton
Texas Christian University
Fort Worth, Texas

Nathan R. Meyer
George Mason University
Fairfax, Virginia

Gene Mueller
Texas A& M University, Texarkana
Texarkana, Texas

Caryn E. Neumann
Ohio State University
Columbus, Ohio

Cynthia Clark Northrup
Texas Christian University
Fort Worth, Texas

Jeanne A. Ojala
University of Utah
Salt Lake City, Utah

Jerry L. Parker
Trunkee Meadows Community College
Reno, Nevada

Lisa Pruitt
Middle Tennessee State University
Murfreesboro, Tennessee

Elizabeth Pugliese
Rosetta Research
Austin, Texas

John David Rausch Jr.
West Texas A&M University
Canyon, Texas

Carey M. Roberts
University of South Carolina
Columbia, South Carolina

Alicia E. Rodriquez
California State University, Bakersfield
Bakersfield, California

Marie-Jeanne Rossignol
University Paris7-Denis Diderot
Institut Charles V
Paris, France

Loriene Roy
University of Texas at Austin
Austin, Texas

Margaret D. Sankey
Auburn University
Auburn, Alabama

Frank Schumacher
University of Erfurt
Erfurt, Germany

James L. Sledge III
Truett-McConnell College
Cleveland, Georgia

Gene A. Smith
Texas Christian University
Fort Worth, Texas

Robert W. Smith
University of Massachusetts, Boston
Boston, Massachusetts

Thomas C. Sosnowski
Kent State University, Stark
Canton, Ohio

Scott L. Stabler
Arizona State University
Tempe, Arizona

Christopher C. Strangeman
Southern Illinois University
Carbondale, Illinois

Amy H. Sturgis
Vanderbilt University
Nashville, Tennessee

Carol J. Terry
Texas Christian University
Fort Worth, Texas

George Thadathil
Paul Quinn College
Mesquite, Texas

Mark Thomason
Fort Worth, Texas

Matthew S. Warshauer
Central Connecticut State University
New Britain, Connecticut

Scott Wignall
Illinois Central College
East Peoria, Illinois

Lisa R. Williams
Washington State University
Pullman, Washington

John Wills
University of Bristol
Bristol, United Kingdom

Lisa-Kay Wolffe
Northwestern State University
Natchitoches, Louisiana

PREFACE

By their very nature defining moments in history often have inauspicious beginnings. The larger meaning of such events is generally recognized over the course of time once the ebb and flow of history have played out the consequences of actions both great and small upon the life of the nation. It is only then, after time and history provide the clarity of perspective, that we can comprehend the previously unseen connections that allow us to assess the importance of actions and policies in light of subsequent developments. Yet we of the modern era who are blessed with hindsight cannot help but wonder whether a few brave visionaries of the past truly understood the consequences of their actions. Was the history of the United States writ large by those who could envision the future of the nation?

Today it is abundantly clear that the decision of the United States to purchase the Louisiana Territory from France in 1803 was a defining moment in American national life. What began, ostensibly, as an effort to protect the commercial and economic interests of western farmers contained within itself the seminal essence of global realpolitik on the part of the young American republic. Neutralizing the French presence in North America had the added advantage of making the United States stronger in its diplomacy with Great Britain and Spain—the remaining European powers that sought hegemony in North America. Although it remains debated whether Thomas Jefferson's action in 1803 grew out of an incipient understanding of Manifest Destiny or simply was a fortunate occurrence, one cannot help but fathom that much of America's subsequent self-definition was largely influenced by the impact of that territorial acquisition.

The narrow definition of viewing the Louisiana Purchase as a mere diplomatic transaction involving the transfer of real estate belies the complete meaning of this event. What some might view as one story was a tale that contained many plots and an enormous cast of characters. The story of the Louisiana Purchase was America's story. Like the young republic that had acquired the vast wilderness expanse of the Louisiana Territory through purchase, there was something fervent and disquieting in both the nature of the possessor and its new possession. Through the transforming dynamic of the frontier experience, each would attempt to tame the other over time.

This work is designed to serve as a standard reference to the fully nuanced meaning of the Louisiana Purchase in the history and life of the United States. Within these pages one will find not only the diplomatic history of an 1803 event, but much more. The story of American expansionism is presented here through the stories of persons and peoples whose lives were changed by the economic, social, and cultural transformations wrought by Manifest Destiny. The story of the transformation of the land itself is also found within these pages. For good or for ill the changes foisted upon the natural landscape by American territorial growth and the economic regimen that followed had a profound impact upon the nation's history. Although the United States certainly benefited from this territorial acquisition, at many levels the nation continues to pay the costs of its stewardship two centuries after the diplomatic negotiations were finalized.

In 1803 the United States was a young nation with a population slightly larger than 5.3 million inhabitants who were primarily farmers. The acquisition of the Louisiana Territory provided the impetus for a national transformation that would affect all aspects of American society and culture. Through the dynamic of territorial growth the nation evolved in the nineteenth century into a more self-assured polity that would come to understand its purpose as being that of a continental power. That vision, once secured, would poise America upon the international stage as a world power. In time, the confident cosmopolitan republic peopled by millions that emerged would bear little resemblance to the young nation that existed two centuries prior.

Who we are today, and what we have been, emerged from the inauspicious beginnings of 1803 and the vagaries of frontier diplomacy. How we developed as a continental power stems from our efforts to reckon with the seemingly limitless resources of a vast national domain. Frontiers both past and present blur into historical obscurity as we trace the progression of the American experiment. For a nation that is forever a work in progress, the Louisiana Territory provided a canvas upon which the vivid colors of self-definition could be expressed. The hues, the texture, and the visual sense of that identity would come to be as varied as the land upon which it was established.

ACKNOWLEDGMENTS

It would have been certainly impossible to produce this volume without the assistance of many individuals, and I owe more appreciation than I can ever offer to all who helped to make this book a reality. I would like to thank the team of eighty-five scholars who contributed to this volume. Without their efforts in planning, researching, and writing the articles this work would have been impossible, and I cannot thank them sufficiently for their dedication to the task and for their professionalism. I owe special thanks to several contributors—Boyd Childress, Rory Cornish, Henry Goldman, and Gene Smith—who volunteered selflessly to write additional entries or to attract other scholars to the project. To all who contributed to this work I offer my heartfelt thanks.

I am also indebted to the expert staff of ABC-CLIO for their patience and counsel over the past two years. Alicia Merritt, Senior Acquisitions Editor, worked with me from the conception of this project, and her assistance has been invaluable. I thank her for believing in me and for agreeing that *The Louisiana Purchase* was a project worthy of development. Carol Smith, Production Editor, maintained oversight of the project and helped to make disparate articles come together into final form. Without Martin Hanft's copyediting this work would bear the scars of too many of my imperfections. I appreciate his keen eye and his perceptive queries that helped fashion this into a better book. I also appreciate the efforts of Liz Kincaid, Media Editor, who handled the details of obtaining the illustrations for this volume.

I treasure the understanding and support from my colleagues and my students who have helped me to remain focused to cope with the stress of looming deadlines and who have shared my joy in meeting the same—generally. Your encouragement and support along the way have meant much to me, and I will always remember your perception and kindness. I would also like to thank the Eureka College Faculty Development Committee for providing financial assistance to fund postage and duplicating costs when this project was just beginning. I owe a special debt of gratitude to several student assistants who worked with me as this volume developed. Seeff Grauer, Amanda Lampert, and Sarah Wilson all did an admirable job in helping to advance this work. Each of them has had a hand in the development of this volume, and I thank them for their service. I also appreciate the important contribution of a former student and good friend, Nathan Meyer, who listened intently to early conversations and offered valuable suggestions about this project when it was little more than a rough idea. As always, Joy Kinder offered secretarial assistance and helped to make sure that important mailings went out on time. Brent Etzel, Tony Glass, Ginny McCoy, Paul Lister, Ann Shoemaker, Eldrick Smith, and Kathy Whitson all pitched in to help when glitches of varying types appeared, and I appreciate their assistance.

As a Louisianian, I am especially proud to have been associated with the development of this reference work and take responsibility for its inevitable shortcomings. I hope that this encyclopedia will be valuable to students and researchers alike, and that this labor of love will serve as a valuable reference tool for years to come.

Junius P. Rodriguez
January 12, 2002

INTRODUCTION

In 2003, the people of the United States will celebrate the bicentennial of the Louisiana Purchase. The recognition of this historic event honors more than a simple real estate transfer between the government of the French Republic and that of the young United States of America. The acquisition of the Louisiana Territory was certainly one of the defining moments of American history, as it set the stage for many subsequent developments that would affect the course of American civilization and culture. Without the Louisiana Purchase, the concept of Manifest Destiny seems moot, the Free Soil controversy over the expansion of slavery into the territories is nonexistent, and the rise of an urban, industrial society built upon the economic resources of a vast national reserve appears less certain. Indeed, the United States redefined itself in 1803 by becoming a continental power, and that transformation unleashed forces, both positive and negative, the consequences of which have resonated throughout our national history.

Fifteen states owe either all or a portion of their territory to the acquisition from France in 1803. What was once viewed as wild, uncharted wilderness has been shaped by two centuries of American pioneers and their descendants, who have left their cultural marks upon the landscape in ways that are sometimes inconspicuous yet more often pronounced. The hand of man is evident as natural forms have been tamed by perpendicular township and range lines reflecting the imposition of a Cartesian grid system upon nature's disorder, thereby creating something that is surely less than natural. More disheartening is the depopulation of indigenous peoples that resulted from forced migrations and outright warfare as the U.S. government sought to tame the wilderness and its inhabitants through more insidious means. Environmental degradation has been another terrible cost of the past two centuries. The destruction of virgin forests and wild prairie grasses, the decimation of animal species, and the pollution of many rivers and streams have been brought about as a result of our unbridled national expansion.

The history of the Louisiana Purchase and the subsequent transformation of that region into a collection of American states tells an important story about the people of the United States. Our history has been characterized by both tremendous achievements and inglorious shortcomings. It is an important and sometimes painful history that certainly teaches the salient truth that American greatness has often been achieved at tremendous cost; it also reminds us, however, of the inescapable realization that it is *our* history, and we must reckon with it. Walt Whitman once observed that "the United States themselves are essentially the greatest poem." If that is so, the Louisiana Purchase of 1803 certainly provided a young nation that was itself a work in progress with much of the meter, rhythm, and rhyme of the poem that became America.

BEFORE THE BEGINNING

We often accept as a matter of fact that the Louisiana Purchase was simply a diplomatic arrangement whose consequence concerned only a few European royal courts and the government and people of the United States. What we fail to consider in such a view is that the entire region of the Louisiana Territory was inhabited by a host of Native American tribes who claimed the land as theirs by right of first possession. From the north woods of Minnesota to the Gulf Coast, and from the crest of the Rocky Mountains eastward across the high plains and on toward the Mississippi River, there existed a sophisticated network of indigenous peoples who inhabited the land and drew their sustenance from it. Each of these individual nations, based upon the Doctrine of Discovery (or the right of first ownership), actually owned the land upon which they lived, while Europeans—and later Americans—who purported to own the territory found themselves negotiating for and purchasing the land bit by bit from these groups over several centuries.

To claim that the French, the Spanish, or the Americans owned the Louisiana Territory at any given time actually means that they owned the *claim* to the territory, but not the land itself. Since the land was owned by individual tribes who resided upon it, the arduous process of converting one's claim into legal ownership would take countless treaties, seemingly endless negotiations, and much time. As a result, and because of frequent intransigence on the part of Native owners who cared not to negotiate, war and the outright seizure of territory were often the outcome.

Much of the legal system in the United States, as well as fundamental elements of free-market capitalism, is based upon the sanctity of contracts. Legal agreements are binding between individuals and groups when they enter into such arrangements willingly, bargain in good faith, and do not employ fraud or duplicity. Having said this, one would be hard-pressed to find circumstances in which the negotiated arrangements for the dispensation of Indian lands met the most basic standards of contract law. Despite this characteristic discrepancy, possession does have a powerfully symbolic meaning in the modern world, and how individuals came to acquire territory is often superseded by the physical reality that they are the de facto possessors of the land.

CONFLICTING CLAIMS

England and France entered the contest for colonial supremacy in North America on an equal footing and at about the same time. While the English established their first permanent settlement in North America at Jamestown in 1607, the French were close behind. In 1608, Samuel de Champlain established the French settlement of Quebec along the St. Lawrence River and created the nucleus for what became known as New France. Both outposts were small settlements whose survival seemed tenuous, at first, until the creation of a sustainable economy based upon either cash crops or trade goods made the colonies viable. For the English it was tobacco, cultivated for centuries by Native American peoples, that became the crop which first transformed Virginia, and later, many of the English Atlantic Seaboard settlements. For the inhabitants of New France, the pelts of fur-bearing animals that inhabited the Canadian wilderness and the Great Lakes region became the commodity that sustained French interest and investment in the North American colonial enterprise.

Neither New France nor the English colonies (with the exception of Massachusetts Bay) grew rapidly in population. It was characteristic in many of the earliest colonies that inhabitants experienced a "starving time" when the colonial populace struggled to produce enough food to sustain itself, while simultaneously needing to fend off epidemics, Indian attacks, and other natural difficulties created by exposure to the elements. Colonists in both the English and French areas had to develop an infrastructure that accommodated dwelling places, defensive structures, and the commercial sites needed to conduct the business activities that financed their continued existence. As a result, the geographical dispersion of colonists into hinterland regions was limited, because the physical labor of building a colony was intensive.

When opportunities for expansion did come, the French may have had an edge on their English counterparts. The French were connected by the St. Lawrence River and the Great Lakes system to numerous other rivers and streams that could take them farther and farther into the interior of North America. For a time, the French believed that they might well discover the elusive Northwest Passage, which was rumored to cross the continent. The English colonies established on the Atlantic Seaboard were settled primarily within the tidewater region, and nearly each of these colonies had an imposing western boundary outlined by the crests of the Appalachian Mountains. Since it was easier to traverse rivers than overland trails in colonial America, the French had access to superior avenues that might help expand the boundaries of New France. Also, by its very nature, the business of fur trapping involves the constant need to find new lakes, rivers, and streams to work while depleted trapping areas replenish their natural stock. To this purpose, French trappers and traders became the agents of empire.

French trappers and traders set out in the mid-seventeenth century to discover new lands where they might ply their trade. Most of these individual expeditions went unrecorded, but collectively these forays into the interior of North America expanded knowledge about the continent. The discoveries led to an improved cartography that began to depict North America more accurately. Two particular episodes of discovery from this period do stand out, for the sheer magnitude of the expeditions and the larger implications for the expansion of the empire. Both expeditions were predicated upon the mercantile desire to expand French trapping interests into yet unseen valleys.

In 1673, the Jesuit missionary Father Jacques Marquette and French-Canadian trapper Louis Joliet began an expedition that would take them farther into the North American interior than any Europeans had ventured since the expeditions of Spanish explorers Hernando DeSoto and Francisco Coronado in the early 1540s. Marquette, who was an expert linguist, was expected to serve as a translator as the explorers encountered new Indian tribes, and Joliet was to survey the regions he traversed for their potential as fur trapping lands. The Comte de Frontenac, the governor of New France, had authorized the expedition to travel from the Straits of Mackinac to seek the Mississippi River and follow that stream to its outlet, wherever that might lead. Marquette and Joliet, plus five *engagés* who supported their expedition, reached the upper Mississippi in May 1673 and traveled downriver for a month in two bark canoes. They traveled as far southward as the point where the Arkansas River joins the Mississippi. Having learned from the local tribes that the Mississippi does flow into the Gulf of Mexico and that Spanish settlements did exist farther south, Marquette and Joliet turned around and returned to New France with their information. Their expedition, which lasted four months and covered more than twenty-five hundred miles, brought a tremendous body of knowledge of the North American continent to French colonial fur trapping interests.

Nearly a decade later, in 1672, Robert Cavelier, Sieur de LaSalle, conducted an expedition that would continue the initial mission of Marquette and Joliet to explore the Mississippi River to its mouth. LaSalle paddled down the Mississippi for four months, and on August 9, 1682, he stood near the mouth of the river that the Choctaw called "The Father of Waters" and claimed for France the river and the entire basin that it drained. When LaSalle planted the fleur-de-lis banner, the flag of the French Bourbon monarchy, upon the land that he named Louisiana, he not only honored King Louis XIV but also raised the geopolitical stakes in the race for the North American empire, an achievement that certainly added luster to the "Sun King's" domain.

PRESERVING EMPIRE

France would hold all of Louisiana, as LaSalle had defined it, for ninety years. During that time the French would make a concerted effort to possess the territory that they had claimed, but after nearly a century, much of the Louisiana Territory was still a wilderness untouched by French habitation. The most successful effort taken by the French had been the establishment of a colony, aptly named Louisiana, on the Gulf Coast in 1699. This settlement was founded by the Le Moyne brothers, Iberville and Bienville. Although the colony originated near the site of present-day Mobile, Alabama, it gradually migrated westward until it was centered at the town of New Orleans, established along the Mississippi River in 1718. After the Louisiana colony was founded, the French began to construct a series of settlements in the North American interior in the hope that these isolated outposts would one day link Canadian New France with the Gulf Coast colony. French settlements at Ste. Genevieve, Kaskaskia, and Vincennes all resulted from this effort to expand French presence in North America.

LaSalle's decision to claim the entire basin of the Mississippi River for France would set the French on a collision course with English interests in North America. The English claim to all of North America was based upon the seafaring expedition of John Cabot in 1497. The English maintained that their Atlantic Seaboard colonies were, in reality, transcontinental colonies, since all of North America was English territory. Although such claims were hollow and not supported by the actual possession of territory, the government of Great Britain would press the issue during the eighteenth century once French settlements began to appear in the Ohio River Valley.

Much of the history of eighteenth-century relations between England (Great Britain after 1707) and France can be understood most clearly as being a century of conflict, or a "hundred years' war" centered upon the question of empire. According to their original plan, that was not supposed to be the case, but rivalry over North American empire did come to dominate relations between the two nations. Shortly before England's Glorious Revolution (1688), and not long after LaSalle's 1682 expedition, the leaders of England and France agreed to the Peace of Whitehall (1687), in which both powers pledged that they would never enter into a conflict with the other over a question concerning colonial matters. Nonetheless, despite their pledge of mutual amity, England and France soon found themselves at war, fighting King William's War (1689–1697), or the War of the Grand Alliance. During this conflict the English and the Iroquois fought against the French and their Indian allies over control of the upper Hudson River Valley. Neither side achieved its strategic goals during the war, as the English failed to conquer Quebec and the French were unable to take Boston. When the Peace of Ryswick (1697) ended the conflict, there were no colonial territorial adjustments made in North America.

A brief interlude of peace followed before the major European powers found themselves at war again. During Queen Anne's War (1702–1713), the North American phase of the War of the Spanish Succession (1701–1714), Great Britain and France again quarreled over colonial possessions in North America. The infamous Deerfield Massacre (February 29, 1704) occurred during this conflict, as French soldiers and their Indian allies burned a Puritan town in Massachusetts, killing 47 individuals and taking 109 others as captives. British forces were able to seize some strategic parts of New France, but were unable to capture either Quebec or Montreal. When the Treaty of Utrecht (1713) ended this conflict, there were territorial changes in North America. The French lost possession of Newfoundland, Hudson Bay, and Acadia (later named Nova Scotia). The British had diminished the size and influence of New France, but they had not eliminated their colonial rivals from North America.

A third colonial conflict would be fought in North America, as the British hoped to reduce New France further and the French hoped to reacquire lost possessions. King George's War (1744–1748) was the North American phase of the War of the Austrian Succession (1740–1748). Both the British and the French maintained similar goals, strategies, and tactics, which they had employed in the first two colonial wars, but the military exploits in North America proved inconclusive. The Treaty of Aix-la-Chapelle (1748), which ended the conflict, imposed status quo antebellum in North America, and the territorial integrity of each nation's colonial possessions remained intact.

The fourth colonial war between the British and the French would prove to be what many have called the Great War for Empire. The French and Indian War (1754–1763), known in Europe as the Seven Years' War (1756–1763), was truly a world war that witnessed fighting on three continents as well as naval battles on the high seas. In North America it was the expansion of French settlement into the Ohio Valley that triggered the conflict, as Great Britain maintained that such outposts were untenable and were meant to provoke another colonial conflict. Despite early setbacks, when British colonial and regular forces were twice rebuffed by the French at Fort Duquesne, British resolve only strengthened during the conflict. Under the leadership of Prime Minister William Pitt, British forces finally captured Fort Duquesne in 1758 and renamed the site Pittsburgh. In the final stages of the war, the British mounted sustained efforts to capture Quebec (1759) and Montreal (1760), which both fell. The French, realizing that they were on the verge of losing New France, sued for peace and stalled for time as they sought a diplomatic remedy to the situation before them.

A STRATEGIC ALLIANCE

On the verge of losing its North American colonial empire to the British, the French government sought a solution that might mitigate the harshness of their pending treaty losses. The French realized that if they were removed from New France, the Spanish, who possessed Mexico and a sprawling but sparsely populated territory in the American southwest, would be the only European power that could prevent British colonial hegemony in North America. Therefore, in 1761, the Bourbon monarchs of France and Spain agreed to a "Family Compact" in which each pledged to support one another's interests, colonial or otherwise. In the eyes of the French, this agreement was the first necessary step that had to be taken in order to effect a land transfer that would deny the British a significant portion of North American real estate while keeping the faint glimmer of a reestablished French empire alive.

In 1762 the nations of France and Spain negotiated and signed the Treaty of Fontainebleau. With this brilliant diplomatic move, the French divided the Louisiana Territory into two parts that were divided by the Mississippi River. France also identified the so-called Isle of Orleans as a separate area that was not a part of either territory, though it was contiguous to the western half of the Louisiana Territory. Since the British had shown a significant interest in the Ohio River Valley, the French believed that they would have to cede the eastern portion of Louisiana to the British in the Treaty of Paris (1763) that would end the French and Indian War. Since the British had not expressed an interest in the western portion of the Louisiana Territory, the French imagined that they might be able to transfer that territory, along with the Isle of Orleans, to the Spanish Bourbons. As fellow signatories to the "Family Compact" of 1761, the Spanish Bourbons were willing to support the interests and intentions of their French Bourbon cousins.

The Treaty of Fontainebleau (1762) did contain secret provisions that were advantageous to long-range French goals of reestablishing a North American empire. The Spanish were prevented from alienating the Louisiana Territory, and it was understood that if the French sought the retrocession of the territory at some point in the future, the Spanish were bound by their treaty obligations to surrender Louisiana and the Isle of Orleans. In the eyes of the French Bourbons, the transfer of Louisiana and the Isle of Orleans to the Spanish was a measure of strategic safe-keeping that would prevent the British from acquiring the region, while still allowing France to have ready access to the region at a later date.

Although the Spanish were willing to maintain their part of the "Family Compact" and accept Louisiana, they did not show an immediate interest in administering their new possession. The Spanish colonial possessions in the Western Hemisphere were vast and included most of South America (with the exception of Brazil), Central America, Mexico, the American Southwest, Cuba, and a host of other Caribbean islands. Spain had grown wealthy from her colonies by exploiting the wealth of precious metals—gold and silver—found in various parts of the vast Spanish empire. The seemingly mild interest that the Spanish showed for Louisiana was based upon two facts: the territory contained no known precious metals, and, for many years, Louisiana had been a financial burden to the French, rather than a profitable enterprise. For these reasons, the Spanish would wait for six years before finally establishing colonial authority in Louisiana in 1768.

During the interregnum between French and Spanish control, the French colonial inhabitants of Louisiana continued to operate as they had under French control. French inhabitants in the area of upper Louisiana (roughly the region around present-day Missouri) continued their work of expanding the fur trade by trapping new streams and founding new settlements. St. Louis, for example, was established in 1764 when the French trappers and traders in upper Louisiana realized that they needed to create an entrepôt on the western side of the Mississippi River once the British had come into possession of the eastern bank. Even under the period of Spanish control, very little change occurred in upper Louisiana.

Once the Spanish authorities had established themselves at New Orleans, they did begin a period of effective administration of the Louisiana colony. Within a decade the Spanish found themselves tenuously allied with the Americans living in the British Atlantic Seaboard colonies, who were then engaged in a struggle to win their independence from their colonial rulers. By being allies of the French through the Bourbon "Family Compact," the Spanish found themselves to be an associated ally of the Americans after France and the United States signed the Treaty of Alliance (1778). Ever careful not to send the signal that revolting against monarchial rule was proper behavior for its own colonial citizens, the Spanish did support the American cause by fighting against British possessions along the Gulf Coast. The military efforts of Louisiana governor Don Bernardo de Galvez were particularly praiseworthy in this regard.

After supporting the cause of American independence, the Spanish found themselves dissatisfied with their newly independent republican neighbors. First, it had been the understanding of the Spanish that the Americans were not to seek a separate peace with the British until all the wartime goals of the French and Spanish had been attained. In particular, the Spanish had hoped that they would be able to reacquire the island of Gibraltar from the British. When the Americans signed the Treaty of Paris in 1783, the Spanish believed that they had been double-crossed by their former ally. Secondly, the amorphous boundary of Spanish Florida as defined by the treaty also angered the court in Madrid. The Spanish had hoped to define the boundary of Florida at the so-called Yazoo Line of 32 degrees 28 minutes north latitude—far enough north to include the rich agricultural lands of the Natchez District—but the Americans supported a contrary line at 31 degrees north latitude. Contentious debate over these two questions would characterize relations between the United States and Spain for the next twelve years.

ECONOMIC WARFARE

After the United States became an independent nation with the Treaty of Paris in 1783, Spanish authorities in Mexico City reportedly felt confident that Spain's colonial possessions remained safe, because they believed that the trans-Appalachian West was too vast to permit rapid expansion by the Americans. Time would quickly prove that assumption false, as American settlers poured across the Appalachian Mountains and began to settle in the Ohio River Valley, where they established pioneer farmsteads. Since a good system of transmountain roads did not exist, the Western frontiersmen found themselves economically isolated from Eastern markets. If they desired to sell their produce, or to trade for necessary supplies, waterborne commerce along the Ohio and Mississippi Rivers seemed much more efficient, and more appealing, than attempting trans-Appalachian trade.

Spanish officials operating out of Madrid, Mexico City, and New Orleans began a concerted effort to conduct a campaign of economic warfare against the young American republic, and their plan had both covert and public elements. The Spanish began to wage a secret campaign against U.S. interests by privately encouraging the frontiersmen of the trans-Appalachian West to secede from the United States and ally themselves with Spanish Louisiana. Using the argument that both geography and economic necessity spoke to such an arrangement, the Spanish paid several leaders along the American frontier to foment discontent and to talk up the benefits of an alliance with the Spanish. Even though the Spanish Treasury was paying individuals such as James Wilkinson and John Sevier to advance Spanish interests in the region, the disinformation campaign proved to be ineffectual and only heightened anti-Spanish sentiment along the frontier.

A more public phase of the aggressive new Spanish policy involved efforts to deny Americans the right to navigate upon the Mississippi River or use warehouse facilities at the port of New Orleans. The Spanish believed that such a policy could cripple American commerce in the trans-Appalachian West, and might well achieve the goals that covert operations had failed to effect. The weight of the Spanish threat was so great that the U.S. Congress, under the Articles of Confederation government, appointed John Jay, who had served as secretary of foreign affairs for the Continental Congress, to serve as a special envoy to remedy the diplomatic impasse over the Florida boundary and the right of access to the Mississippi River and the port of New Orleans. Jay's Spanish counterpart in these negotiations was Don Diego de Gardoqui, who arrived in the United States in late 1784 to begin the talks. The Jay-Gardoqui negotiations would continue on and off over the course of two years, producing neither a satisfactory outcome for the American position nor a treaty that the Confederation Congress could ratify.

Gardoqui wanted Jay to agree that the United States would forgo commercial rights on the Mississippi River for a period of twenty-five to thirty years in exchange for special trading privileges that would be effected between the United States and the Spanish colonies of the Western Hemisphere. Gardoqui also wanted Jay to accept a Florida boundary that would keep the Natchez District in Spanish hands. Under pressure by Northeastern commercial interests, who felt that this was a good commercial arrangement, Jay was induced to accept the terms in a draft treaty, but the Confederation Congress would not ratify the arrangement; the impasse continued for nearly a decade more.

By 1795, Spain's views on these matters changed significantly in light of new alliances, both real and imaginary, that were changing the geopolitical landscape of the late-eighteenth-century world. When the Spanish learned of secret negotiations that were taking place between the United States and Great Britain in 1794, Spanish officials began to fear that the eventual outcome—Jay's Treaty (1794)—would produce an alliance between the two nations. Spanish officials imagined that the ultimate objective of such an alliance involved the seizure of Spanish colonial claims in North America and the valuable silver mines of northern Mexico. In an attempt to ingratiate themselves with the United States and forestall this worst-case scenario, Spanish officials in Madrid indicated a willingness to negotiate in good faith with the United States to settle the unresolved issues that remained from the failed Jay-Gardoqui talks.

The United States dispatched Thomas Pinckney to Spain, where he negotiated with Manuel de Godoy to produce the Treaty of San Lorenzo (1795), commonly known in U.S. history as Pinckney's Treaty. The United States received favorable outcomes on the two issues that had remained unresolved since the end of the American Revolution. The Spanish agreed to accept the U.S. position that 31 degrees north latitude was the northern boundary of the Floridas. In addition, the Spanish were willing to offer to the Americans the "right of deposit" at port and warehouse facilities in New Orleans. This commercial benefit was to exist for three years, and the terms were renewable thereafter.

The U.S. government staged a major commercial coup by attaining favorable terms in the Treaty of San Lorenzo (1795), but time would prove that the verities of international diplomacy often produced arrangements with a limited shelf life. The right to use the Mississippi River and benefit from special trade arrangements at New Orleans did benefit the United States greatly, but those opportunities only whet the national appetite for a more permanent arrangement. The "right of deposit" would be implemented in 1798, but soon the problems caused by the retrocession of Louisiana to the French would render all previous commercial arrangements related to Mississippi River navigation obsolete.

EARLY EFFORTS TO REESTABLISH EMPIRE

Starting with the fall of the Bastille in Paris in July 1789, the events of the French Revolution spiraled into a complex struggle that transformed a nation and ushered much of Europe into a generation of warfare. Within months France had transformed itself from a monarchy into a constitutional republic, and as the revolutionary cause grew more extreme, the French abolished the monarchy symbolically when they beheaded their Bourbon king Louis XVI in 1793. In such a world turned upside-down, the Bourbon "Family Compact" became a relatively insignificant arrangement, but nonetheless, France continued to have treaty obligations and requisite rites of diplomatic protocol that bound it to others within the family of nations.

The idea of reestablishing the former French empire in North America was one of the earliest foreign policy goals of the newly established French Republic. How it might achieve that goal—whether through diplomacy or conquest—was a matter that would be settled by time and circumstances. As early as 1793, when Edmond Charles Genêt arrived in America as the French minister to the United States, it seemed clear that finding an opportune means to wrest Louisiana away from Spain was a key objective of the French Republic. Genêt openly recruited American citizens to become mercenaries who would fight in behalf of the French Republic. He sought, and received, financial contributions that were used to outfit privateers to sail from American ports and engage British merchant vessels on the high seas.

Genêt never lost sight of his primary goal—"to germinate the principles of liberty and independence in Louisiana"—so that the French Republic might reacquire its former colonial possession and begin the process of recreating a French North American empire (DeConde 1976). To this end, Genêt had conversations with influential Americans who knew of the dissatisfaction present among Americans living in the trans-Appalachian West. Spain's refusal to allow Americans the right to use the Mississippi River and to trade their goods at New Orleans had created a furor among Western pioneers. Many of these settlers believed that they would have greater economic opportunities if the French, rather than the Spanish, possessed Louisiana.

French officials did attempt to negotiate the retrocession of Louisiana from the Spanish in the summer of 1795, but the terms that the Spanish demanded before they would agree to surrender Louisiana were unacceptable to the French, and the negotiations related to Louisiana stalled. These talks, associated with the negotiation of the Treaty of Basel (1795), demonstrated that Spain was willing to cede Louisiana, which it considered a liability, but the Spanish demand for the eastern half of the island of Hispaniola was far more than French negotiators were willing to accept.

Still, the French Republic used other means to act against Spanish interests in Louisiana. In 1796, French officials sent General Georges Henri Victor Collot, the former French colonial governor of Guadeloupe, as an observer who would travel throughout the Ohio and Mississippi River Valleys to gain insight into the popular mood of the day in Spanish Louisiana. Collot reported that the Spanish were intensely fearful of American expansionism, and he suggested that only France was strong enough to withhold such growth.

NAPOLEON AND EMPIRE

From 1795 onward, the French were aware that the Spanish Bourbons were willing to part with the Louisiana colony, provided that a suitable form of compensation could be found to sweeten the deal. Once Napoleon Bonaparte came to power in his coup of November 1799, he set in motion the diplomatic efforts that would result in the retrocession of Louisiana and the much-anticipated beginning of a new French empire in North America. Yet Napoleon realized that France would have to make peace with its former enemies in Europe to ensure that the legitimacy of the retrocession would be recognized.

Charles Maurice de Talleyrand-Périgord, the French minister of foreign relations, began the complicated and delicate task of engineering the diplomatic agreements that would be necessary to effect the retrocession. In the second Treaty of San Ildefonso (1800), Talleyrand was able to devise an understanding with the Spanish that would transfer Louisiana to France, but this treaty was contingent upon promises that other treaty agreements would have to support. In the Treaty of Lunéville, the French Republic made peace with the Austrian ruler, who represented the remnants of the old Holy Roman Empire. One of the terms of that treaty was that the French would acquire the Italian kingdom of Tuscany. This area would become a primary bartering chip between the French and the Spanish in their ongoing negotiations related to Louisiana.

In the second Treaty of San Ildefonso, Napoleon had promised to place the Duke of Parma on the throne of an Italian kingdom. Now that Napoleon had Tuscany, he could deliver on that promise, but he had second thoughts that complicated the delicate negotiations. Rather than place Fernando, the Duke of Parma, whom he detested, on the throne of Tuscany, Napoleon offered to make Luis, the Prince of Parma, king of Etruria (Napoleon's new name for Tuscany). These revisions would have to win the acceptance of King Charles IV, the Spanish Bourbon monarch, before the associated transfer of Louisiana could take place. These final negotiations resulted in the Convention of Aranjuez (1801), which affirmed the spirit of the Treaty of San Ildefonso (1800) and resulted in the retrocession of Louisiana from Spain to France.

NAPOLEON'S GRAND DESIGN

When First Consul Napoleon Bonaparte won the retrocession of the Louisiana Territory in 1801, he had every intention of reestablishing the French North American empire that had been destroyed by France's defeat in 1763. Although earlier colonial experiments in Louisiana—namely, the first French colony and the more recent Spanish colony—had proven to be financial failures, Napoleon had a grand design for a French empire in the Western Hemisphere that would incorporate all territorial components to maximize their value. The wilderness of Louisiana would, in Napoleon's view, become the breadbasket colony of the new French empire.

Central to Napoleon's plans was the reestablishment of French colonial control in the colony of St. Domingue on the Caribbean island of Hispaniola. A slave revolt that had begun in that colony in 1791 eventually led to the expulsion of the French; St. Domingue became an independent republic, governed by the former slaves who had previously harvested its crops. Napoleon recognized that the colony of St. Domingue had been one of the most valuable of French possessions prior to the 1791 rebellion, its annual sugar crop having been bountiful and immensely profitable. Napoleon hoped to re-create the halcyon days of sugar production on St. Domingue with the use of slave labor, so that his French Republic could once again reap the profits. Napoleon Bonaparte considered himself to be a product of the French Revolution and the spirit of republicanism associated with "liberty, equality, and fraternity," but his support of those values did not extend to the slaves of St. Domingue, who had rallied to the same cries of republicanism and overthrown the shackles of oppression. Napoleon equated St. Domingue with sugar and profits, and nothing more.

In January 1802, a French army of twenty thousand men arrived in St. Domingue to reconquer the colony and make it the jewel of the French empire in the Western Hemisphere. Napoleon's brother-in-law, General Charles-Victor-Emmanuel Leclerc, commanded the expedition and anticipated that a corps of elite French regulars would have little difficulty in suppressing an insurgent army consisting of former slaves. Neither Napoleon nor Leclerc, however, anticipated the impact that disease would have upon the troops. Yellow fever, a mosquito-borne disease, was rampant in the Caribbean basin region, and the French troops had no natural immunity. As a result, thousands died in an epidemic that decimated the French corps, claiming even the life of General Leclerc. The inability of French forces to reestablish authority in the prime sugar colony of St. Domingue certainly gave Napoleon reason to consider how his grand design for Louisiana—alone—would now generate profits for the French Republic.

Much as he had sent General Leclerc to St. Domingue, Napoleon named another French commander as captain general of Louisiana and authorized him to prepare an expedition to take control of the colony recently retroceded by the Spanish. General Claude P. Victor, Duc de Bellune, was advised to prepare an occupation force that would sail from Europe to accept possession of the Louisiana Territory at New Orleans. General Victor began the slow and methodical task of organizing the occupation force, but delays continued to push back the departure date. As the expedition prepared for departure in Helvoët Sluys, in the Netherlands, the winter of 1802–1803 arrived, and the expedition's ships became icebound in the harbor. Victor would have to wait until the spring thaw for nature to free his vessels before he could sail for Louisiana. Again, Napoleon had time to think and reconsider his options regarding Louisiana.

It may seem strange to think that mosquitoes and ice may have destroyed Napoleon Bonaparte's grand design for a new French empire in the Western Hemisphere, but unanticipated consequences did teach him valuable lessons and make him reconsider his initial plans. Another important element was that Napoleon needed ready cash, and quickly. Napoleon was enjoying a brief interlude of peace, but he knew that he would be at war with Great Britain—and perhaps with numerous British allies—soon. Since he knew it would be unwise to enter into a major European war without a significant supply of cash at hand, Napoleon pondered how much his North American wilderness might be worth, were he to sell it.

THE DEAL OF A LIFETIME

The retrocession of the Louisiana Territory from Spain to France in 1801 would have profound economic repercussions on America's commercial independence. The reacquisition of Louisiana by the French negated any commercial benefits that the United States held under the terms of the Treaty of San Lorenzo (1795), and the prospect of having to renegotiate those terms every time the Louisiana Territory changed hands was not appealing. From the earliest months of his presidential administration, Thomas Jefferson sought to devise a strategy whereby, through purchase, the United States might gain legal rights to navigate the Mississippi River and warehouse goods near its mouth.

President Jefferson's initial plan was to attempt to purchase either the Isle of Orleans or a portion of West Florida from the French. He advised Robert Livingston, the U.S. minister to France, to begin negotiating for this desired outcome, and he told Livingston that, in the event of failure to win the concessions sought, the United States should advise the French that it planned to join in an alliance with the British. Under such an arrangement, in the event of another European war, the United States could seize the Louisiana Territory as a wartime exigency. When it seemed as though Livingston's negotiations were not bearing fruit, Jefferson authorized James Monroe as an additional diplomat to the French Republic, to assist in the effort.

Neither Livingston nor Monroe—and certainly not Jefferson—was prepared for the real estate transfer that First Consul Napoleon Bonaparte offered the United States in the spring of 1803. Even though purchasing the entire Louisiana Territory exceeded the diplomatic charge with which they had been entrusted, Livingston and Monroe both realized that a quick response to the offer was key, lest Bonaparte change his mind on the matter. Both diplomats realized the magnitude of the opportunity, and they also understood the political repercussions that would result from their decision.

When President Jefferson learned of the decision that Livingston and Monroe had made, he supported the action of the diplomats, but he was still concerned about how the purchase of the entire Louisiana Territory would be accepted by the U.S. Senate and how foreign governments would view the American action. The ideology of Jeffersonian Republicanism was predicated upon the notion of small government. Jefferson and his political allies supported the doctrine of strict construction of the U.S. Constitution, whereby the government could claim only those rights that were specifically enumerated; the bulk of rights were reserved to the states and to the people. The idea of doubling the size of the nation by affixing signatures to one treaty was something that troubled Jefferson, because the diplomatic action did not have prior congressional authorization and he did not believe that the Constitution permitted the acquisition of such territory by treaty purchase. Privately, Jefferson pondered that an amendment to the Constitution would be necessary to make the arrangement legal, but he also understood that the likelihood of passing such a measure rapidly in the heated political climate of 1803 was unlikely. As a result, Jefferson set aside his views on small government and strict constructionism, for the moment, and became an advocate of a powerful, large federal government that drew its powers from a loose interpretation of the Constitution. Jefferson was being a pragmatist and putting the nation's interests ahead of partisan ideology.

REPERCUSSIONS

The Louisiana Purchase of 1803 was an extremely controversial event, in both an international geopolitical sense and also as a domestic policy matter within the United States. Beyond the United States and France, no other world powers recognized the legitimacy of the sale. Spain protested loudly that France had no legal right to sell the territory to the United States, and based the claim upon a stipulation in the second Treaty of San Ildefonso that did not permit France to alienate the territory or transfer it to a third party. Great Britain and other European powers did not recognize the legality of the Louisiana Purchase until after the end of the Napoleonic Era, when the Final Act of the Congress of Vienna (1814–1815) was signed. Until that time, most European leaders viewed the United States as possessing stolen goods to which it had no clear and legal title.

Additionally, most European powers believed that the Louisiana Purchase would prove to be the undoing of the American republic. It was inconceivable to most Europeans that a nation with territorial resources as vast as the United States could long survive without breaking into factions that would secede to represent their regional self-interests. By the European model, nations were small, compact political entities, and the idea that America's democracy within a republic could exist within a tremendously large territory was a notion that had few adherents in the early nineteenth century.

Even within the United States, many questioned the wisdom of acquiring such a vast territory. During the era of the American Founding, many had compared the United States to the Roman Republic, and much of the language of our political institutions reflects that, but the Roman Republic failed when it adopted imperial ambitions. Thus, some of the naysayers of 1803 based their arguments upon classical Roman antiquity. Many Federalists, who were members of the loyal opposition poised against Jeffersonian Republicans, were rather prescient when they opposed territorial expansion on the basis that it would reduce the political influence of New England Federalists within the government. The addition of each new Western state further reduced the power base of the Federalist Party.

AN ERRAND INTO THE WILDERNESS

Even before the opportunity to purchase the Louisiana Territory arose in 1803, President Jefferson had begun preparations for a major scientific expedition to travel overland to the Pacific Ocean. Jefferson had corresponded with friends who were major scientists and naturalists of the day, and he sought their advice as to what should be the areas of focus for such an expedition. As the experts responded to Jefferson's request, each was asked to tutor Meriwether Lewis, President Jefferson's personal secretary and the man whom he had selected to lead the proposed expedition. To that end, on January 18, 1803, Jefferson sent a secret message to the Congress calling for an expedition to explore the unknown regions of the West.

Captain Meriwether Lewis, having been selected to lead the expedition, was charged with all the details of preparing the Corps of Discovery. Lewis had to secure the party of explorers, draw up a budget, prepare a list of needed supplies, and make sure that everything worked according to schedule. One of his first decisions was to write to his friend William Clark, with whom he had served in the U.S. Army under the command of General "Mad" Anthony Wayne in 1795. Lewis, acting on his own initiative, invited Clark to join the expedition as coleader.

Lewis and Clark and the other members of their party witnessed the formal exchange of the upper part of the

Louisiana Territory at St. Louis on March 10, 1804. During the ceremony, the Spanish flag was lowered and replaced by the French tricolor, and shortly thereafter, that flag was lowered and replaced by the American flag. The final preparations for departure were then made, as Lewis and Clark and their Corps of Discovery set out from St. Louis, the "Gateway to the West," on May 14, 1804.

For twenty-eight months, Lewis and Clark and the Corps of Discovery ventured where no Anglo-Americans had traveled before. In encountering Indian tribes, many of whom had never before seen Americans, the members of the expedition were emissaries of American identity, but also early agents of Manifest Destiny and imperialism. By venturing beyond the crest of the Rocky Mountains, the Lewis and Clark Expedition suggested an early awareness that America's future might well be that of a continental power stretching from ocean to ocean.

The Lewis and Clark Expedition strengthened America's claim to the newly purchased Louisiana Territory, and it also provided a significant claim to the Oregon Country, which would be divided by a diplomatic agreement in the 1840s. The expedition produced a wealth of information about the flora, the fauna, and the ethnography of the West. The travels of Lewis and Clark also expanded our collective geographical sense of the West by providing more accurate maps, which confirmed the vastness of the region. In addition, the expedition disproved certain mythic falsehoods, such as the incredible hope that an easy, all-water route to the West might exist.

INADVERTENT DISCOVERERS

Although major explorations, like the Lewis and Clark Expedition, are justifiably much acclaimed, most of the discoveries that were made in the trans-Mississippi West were the result of individual acts of valor that were largely considered unhistoric in their time. Even before Lewis and Clark had returned from the Pacific, fur trappers and traders operating out of St. Louis had already begun to ascend the Missouri River. These individuals, the mountain men of Western myth and folklore, also became agents of empire who extended the American presence in the West as they wandered through obscure canyons and valleys.

The paths blazed and trails marked by the early fur trappers and traders were early avenues of commerce in the trans-Mississippi West, but these routes would later be used by emigrant pioneers as they traveled westward into the growing nation. In later years, when the golden age of the fur trade would fade, many of the former mountain men became guides to government expeditions and parties of emigrants who sought to follow the trails westward to new opportunities and adventure.

POSSESSION RATHER THAN CLAIM

In 1803 the U.S. government paid the French Republic $15 million to acquire the claim that France held upon the territory called Louisiana. At the time of the Louisiana Purchase, and for several decades thereafter, vast portions of the territory were occupied, and the land therein possessed, by several dozen Indian nations who had lived upon the land for centuries. It would be the job of the U.S. government as the new owner to make that claim real by acquiring the territory and possessing it, parcel by parcel. Achievement of this objective would take much of the nineteenth century, and the task would be achieved through a combination of methods, including negotiated treaties, federal laws, war, disease, theft, and duplicity.

Regardless of the method used to acquire Indian lands, the burden of defending the newly acquired possessions generally fell upon the U.S. Army. Shortly after the United States purchased Louisiana from France, plans were under way to establish a series of military outposts in those strategic frontier areas where the safe conduct of trade and commerce, and later of emigrant trains, was viewed as being in the national interest. Often the frontier forts themselves became the site of treaty negotiations with tribal bands as a sustained effort to reduce Indian lands continued throughout the nineteenth century.

The U.S. government's Indian policy in the nineteenth century was built around the idea of Indian removal. Large sections of Indian land were exchanged for smaller parcels of reservation land that was generally promised to a particular tribe in perpetuity. In addition, the tribe often received a cash annuity from the U.S. government for a period of years, and sometimes special trading privileges were also incorporated within the treaty's terms. The reasons for removal in particular situations varied. Tribes like the Sioux, for example, were moved away from the banks of the Missouri River, where it was believed that they might threaten river-borne commerce. Other groups, such as the Cheyenne and Arapaho, were removed to sites where they would be less likely to disrupt pioneer emigrant trains along the Oregon Trail. In still other cases, the discovery of precious metals or mineral deposits was used as the pretext for the removal of various tribes.

GROWING PAINS

As the United States began the process of populating the lands of the Louisiana Territory, there arose many controversies about how the nation should expand and what would be the most effective use of the Louisiana Purchase lands. The prospect that many new states would be carved out of the Louisiana Territory was a threat to many political leaders in already-existing Eastern states. Many realized that the addition of new states would merely dilute the political influence of the existing states, and they feared that the inordinate voting power of new, sparsely populated states in the trans-Mississippi West might negate the political influence of older, more populous Eastern states.

Occasionally, opponents of Western expansion defended ethnocentrism in their hope to maintain America for Americans. There was heated debate in 1812 when the Congress considered Louisiana's request for statehood. Many opponents of the measure believed that the French and Spanish heritage of the region's inhabitants, their Roman Catholicism, and their lack of awareness of American customs and traditions made them unfit candidates for admission into the Union. Still other opponents of Louisiana statehood argued that the presence of a large slave population in Louisiana made the region ripe for revolt, and that the cost of defending the area against such an uprising would be extravagant. In spite of these criticisms, Louisiana became a state in 1812, and its inhabitants proved themselves worthy citizens when they defended New Orleans against a British invasion during the War of 1812.

In the years during which the Louisiana Territory was still a relatively empty region, ideas were put forward as to the most effective use of the land. There were some who advocated that a large portion of the Louisiana Territory be set aside as Indian Territory, so that tribes from the Eastern half of the nation could be removed there. In such a fashion, the Louisiana Territory would become a safety valve for national expansion, thereby settling the "Indian question" that the nation faced in the early part of the nineteenth century. To a certain extent, the establishment of the region of present-day Oklahoma as Indian Territory, where members of various nations were resettled, was an effort to put this idea into practice. Still, by 1890 even Oklahoma lands were opened for white settlement.

Another idea that was put forward in the early nineteenth century was to establish a colony for freed slaves somewhere in the trans-Mississippi West. By 1817 organizations like the American Colonization Society were engaged in returning former slaves to the colony of Liberia in West Africa. (British abolitionists were doing the same in Sierra Leone.) Advocates for a colony of freed slaves in the Louisiana Territory maintained that the plan would eliminate one of the biggest problems in antebellum America—the presence of a free black population in a society that defined itself as being either slave or free. Despite support for the idea by some politicians and jurists, the plan was never enacted.

The question of slavery, and in particular the expansion of slavery, was one that would dominate political concerns in the antebellum era. How slavery should be allowed to expand into the Western territories was one of the key issues that brought the United States to civil war in 1861. In many respects, the first battle of that conflict may have been the congressional debates that surrounded Missouri's request for statehood in 1819. After nearly two years of rancorous debate, the Congress eventually allowed Missouri to enter the Union as a slave state. This was done through the congressional action that came to be known as the Missouri Compromise (1820). According to the doctrine established at the time of Missouri's admission to the Union, all lands in the Louisiana Territory that were north of 36 degrees 30 minutes north latitude (with the exception of Missouri) were to become free states, while states below that line were permitted slavery if they so desired. That policy would remain in effect until it was ignored by the Kansas-Nebraska Act (1854) and effectively overturned by the U.S. Supreme Court's *Dred Scott v. Sandford* decision in 1857.

The question of how America would grow in a manner that was equitable to all was an issue that would plague the nation for many years. Additional territorial expansion that occurred in the 1840s would only exacerbate the question and drive the slave states and the free states further apart as they debated the merits of expanding either slavery or freedom into an ever-expanding national domain.

CHANGES TO THE LAND

Today, much of the world's foodstuffs are produced upon the lands that were once a part of the Louisiana Purchase Territory. That a wilderness region has been converted in many respects to the breadbasket of much of the world is a modern marvel, but that tremendous human achievement has not been without its costs. The modern world has produced many benefits, but the original landscape has had to change in order to make our modern world possible.

Perhaps the greatest transformation that took place after the Louisiana Purchase was the dramatic environmental change that has occurred in the region over the past two centuries. Much of the wilderness area of the North American interior became farmland and ranches within the course of less than a century following 1803. The establishment of settlements in the Louisiana Territory corresponded with the rise of early industrialization in America, and not surprisingly, many of the farming and ranching implements were factory-produced marvels of modern technology. Steel plows were devised to turn the deep sod of the plains, and mechanical reapers were fashioned to harvest the rich soil's abundant yields. In the treeless expanse of the high plains, machine-made barbed wire marked out territorial property lines that forever erased the once common open range of an earlier era.

In those regions that were blessed with abundant hardwoods, pioneer settlers harvested the trees to build a nation, but paid little attention to the blighted landscapes they often left behind. In many areas the matchless bounty of the forests of the north woods was destroyed by aggressive logging practices that could have been averted. Even within the areas where renewable resources could be managed in a sustainable fashion, America's frontier settlers often acted only for the moment and thought little of the stewardship of the land.

In a rush to exploit the commercially ordained nature that we imposed upon the land, we often lost sight of the first nature, or original landscape, that we modified in the name of progress. While some lands were overplowed, others were overgrazed, but in the end the costs were similar: the tall grass prairies that had endured for millennia were destroyed within decades. Valuable topsoil was made vulnerable by overplowing, to the point where drainage runoff from fields and windstorms could carry away the richness of the land and leave behind a wasteland. Fresh water, a rare commodity in some parts of the trans-Mississippi West, was often exploited, and the hand of man often polluted streams to the point where they became virtually useless. Sites that contained rich mineral deposits were often mined in such a fashion that only the scars of an earlier prosperity remind us of what once existed.

Perhaps the most tragic example of environmental degradation occurred as animal species were driven to the point of extinction, or near-extinction. Although there was a time when millions of bison lived in herds that made seasonal migrations on the Great Plains, the wholesale slaughter of these animals nearly resulted in their extinction. At one point it was estimated that only one thousand bison survived in America, but as a result of twentieth-century conservation efforts and federal legislation, their population has increased.

PAST IS PROLOGUE

History speaks to us in an effort to instruct, but often we fail to heed its admonitions and reminders. So too the land speaks to us through the silent language of remembrance as we try to fathom the changes that the centuries have wrought. To cite Walt Whitman, we who live in "the greatest poem" have a series of obligations to the nation, to our fellow men, and to the land. We, like those who came before, must learn to comprehend the poetry that is America.

Thomas Jefferson was a visionary and a nationalist. He may have been the first American political leader to comprehend the coast-to-coast notion of American identity that by the 1840s would come to be called Manifest Destiny. Before he died in 1826, Jefferson saw two new states carved out of the lands that had been purchased during his administration. The admission of Louisiana (1812) and Missouri (1821) into the Union were historic occasions, but Jefferson the nationalist feared for the nation when the divisive issue of slavery—"a fire bell in the night"—surrounded the debate over Missouri's bid for statehood. Perhaps it was Jefferson's dream that the nation might be both expansive and united, but history would soon prove that these twin goals were mutually exclusive.

Jefferson's vision of America was rooted in the agrarian ideal of small, independent farmers who owned their own land, an image similar in purpose to that of the citizen-soldiers of the Roman Republic whom he admired. Although America's destiny would represent a departure from the Jeffersonian ideal, there are elements of the old agrarian notion that survive. In Jefferson's view, the people and the land were inextricably connected to one another in a symbiotic relationship. Free citizens needed to depend upon the bounty of the land to sustain themselves, but labor was required to husband the land and collect its many gifts. Yet, while we mark the passage of time in the small chronology of life spans, it is the land that endures, forever.

—Junius P. Rodriguez

MAPS

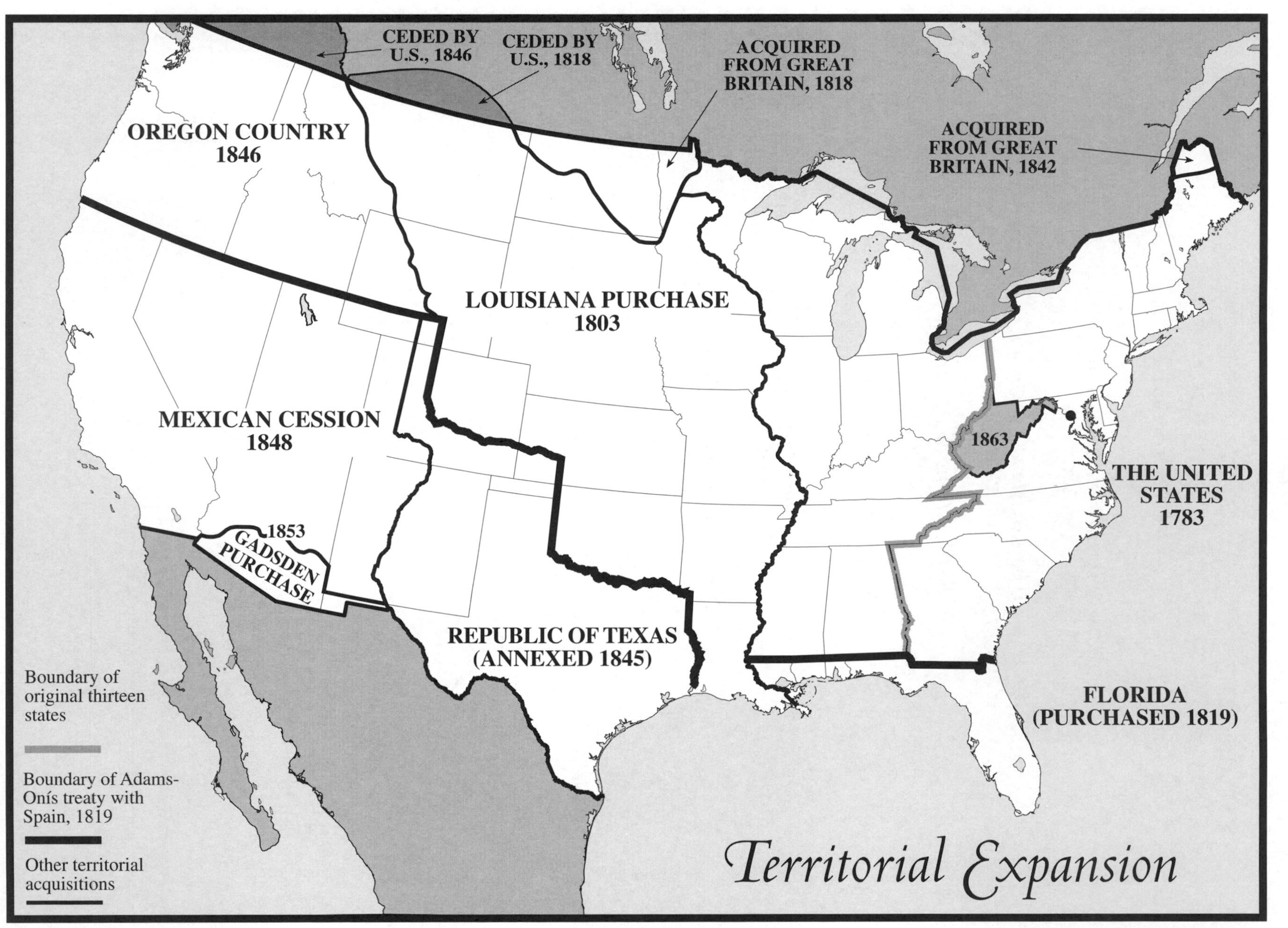

CEDED BY U.S., 1846
CEDED BY U.S., 1818
ACQUIRED FROM GREAT BRITAIN, 1818
ACQUIRED FROM GREAT BRITAIN, 1842
OREGON COUNTRY 1846
LOUISIANA PURCHASE 1803
MEXICAN CESSION 1848
1863
THE UNITED STATES 1783
1853
GADSDEN PURCHASE
REPUBLIC OF TEXAS (ANNEXED 1845)
FLORIDA (PURCHASED 1819)
Boundary of original thirteen states
Boundary of Adams-Onís treaty with Spain, 1819
Other territorial acquisitions
Territorial Expansion

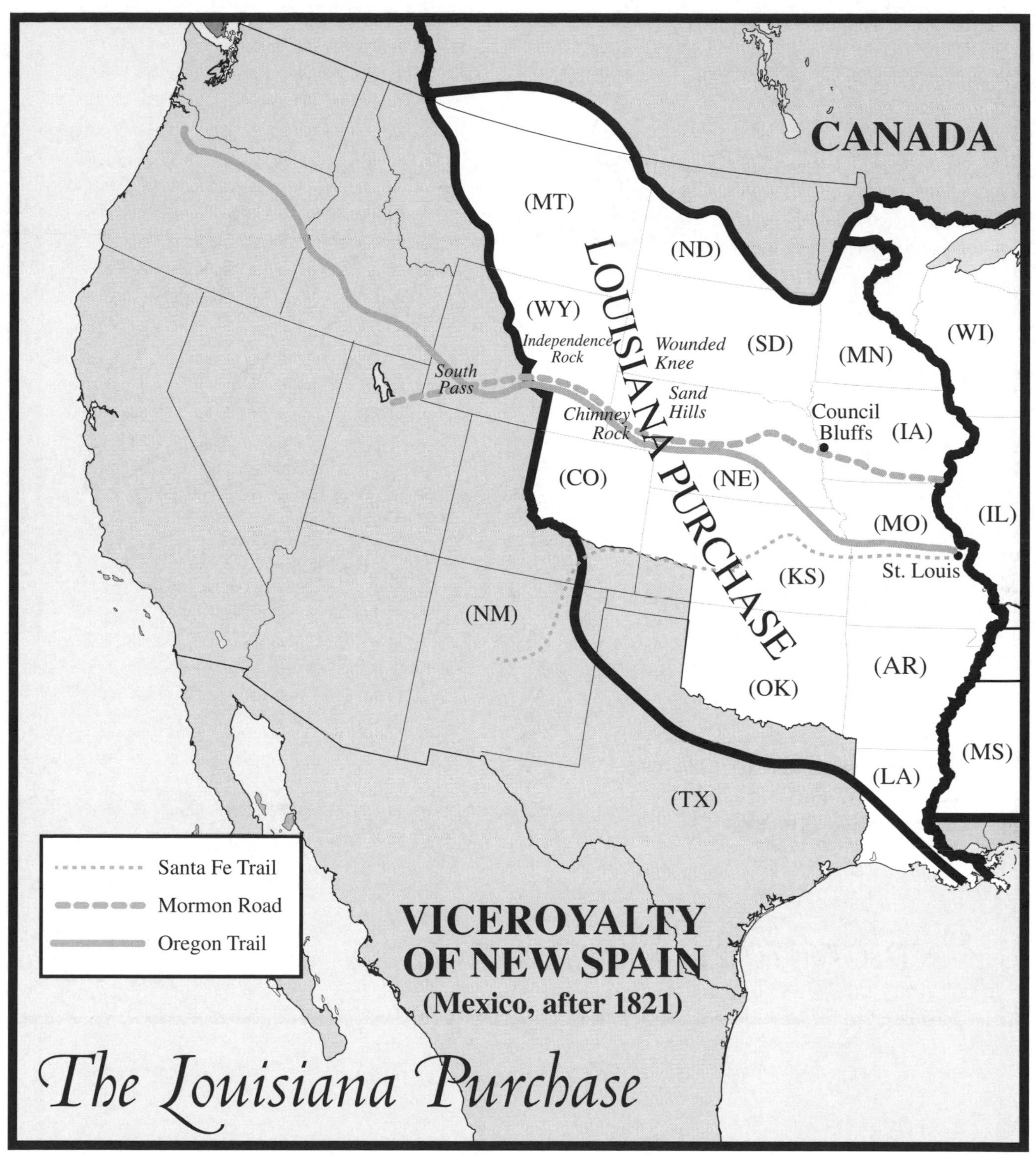

The Louisiana Purchase

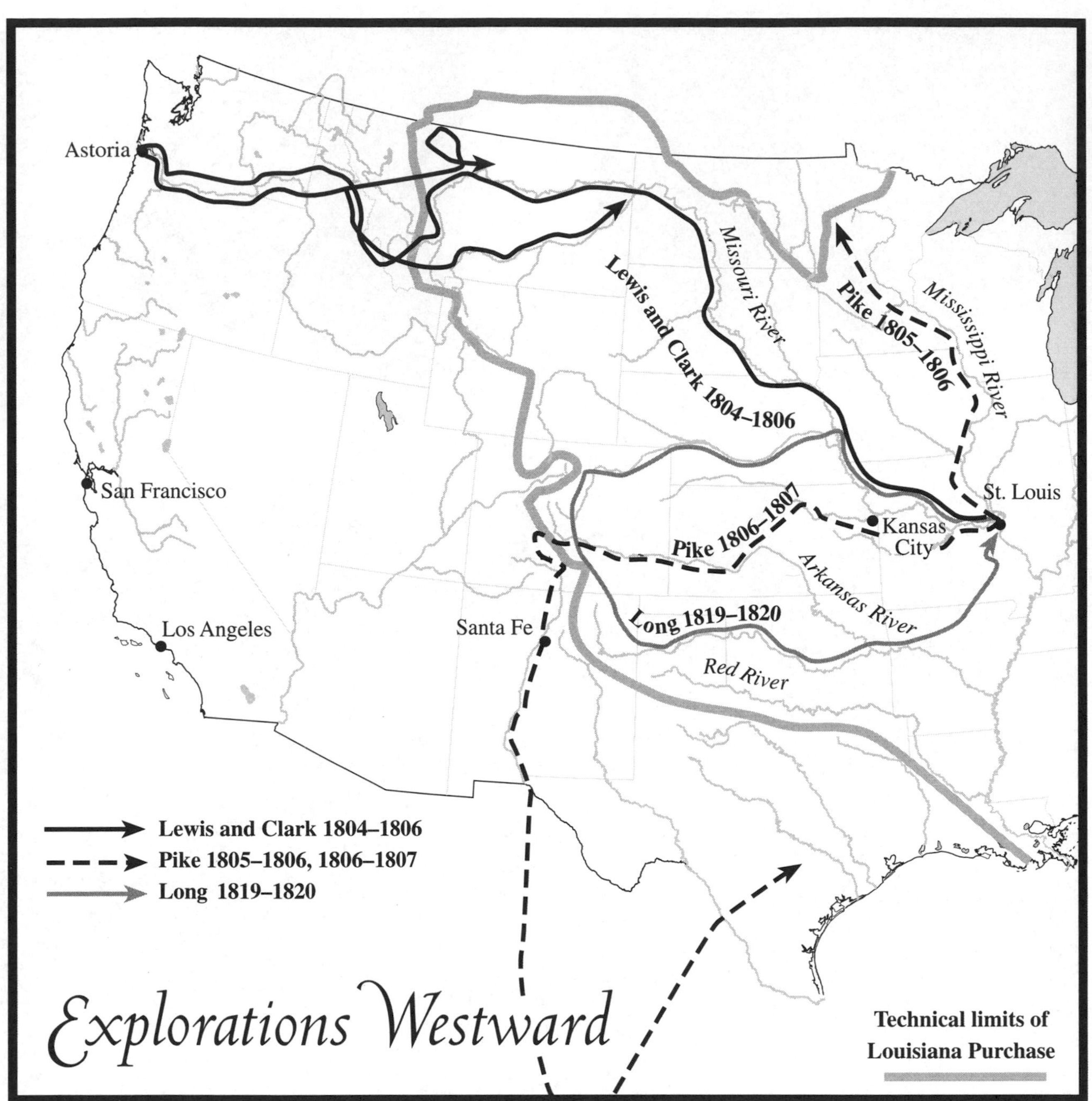
Astoria
Missouri River
Lewis and Clark 1804–1806
Pike 1805–1806
Mississippi River
San Francisco
St. Louis
Pike 1806–1807
Kansas City
Arkansas River
Long 1819–1820
Los Angeles
Santa Fe
Red River
Lewis and Clark 1804–1806
Pike 1805–1806, 1806–1807
Long 1819–1820
Explorations Westward
Technical limits of Louisiana Purchase

CREE
ASSINIBOINE
Astoria
BLACKFOOT
GROS VENTRE
MANDAN
HIDATSA
ARIKARA
FLATHEAD
CROW
NEZ PERCE
SHOSHONI
SANTEE
DAKOTA
(Sioux)
WINNEBAGO
TETON
DAKOTA
(Sioux)
OJIBWA
Missouri River
IOWAY
POTATWATOMI
CHEYENNE
PONCA
PAWNEE
KIOWA
SAUK
AND
FOX
San Francisco
KAW
ARAPAHO
OSAGE
COMANCHE
Arkansas River
WICHITA
Los Angeles
Santa Fe
QUAPAW
Red River
Mississippi River
Native American Peoples
Technical limits of
Louisiana Purchase

Fort Clark
Fort Mandan
Fort Snelling
Missouri River
Fort Caspar
Fort Armstrong
Fort Bridger
Fort Laramie
Fort Atkinson
Fort Kearny
Fort Leavenworth
Fort Riley
Fort Bellefontaine
Bent's Fort
Fort Osage
Fort de Chartres
Fort Scott
Arkansas River
Taos
Santa Fe
Fort Gibson
Fort Smith
Mississippi River
Fort Washita
Red River
Arkansas Post
Fort Towson
Fort Jesup
Fort Macomb
Fort Pike
Frontier Outposts
Technical limits of Louisiana Purchase

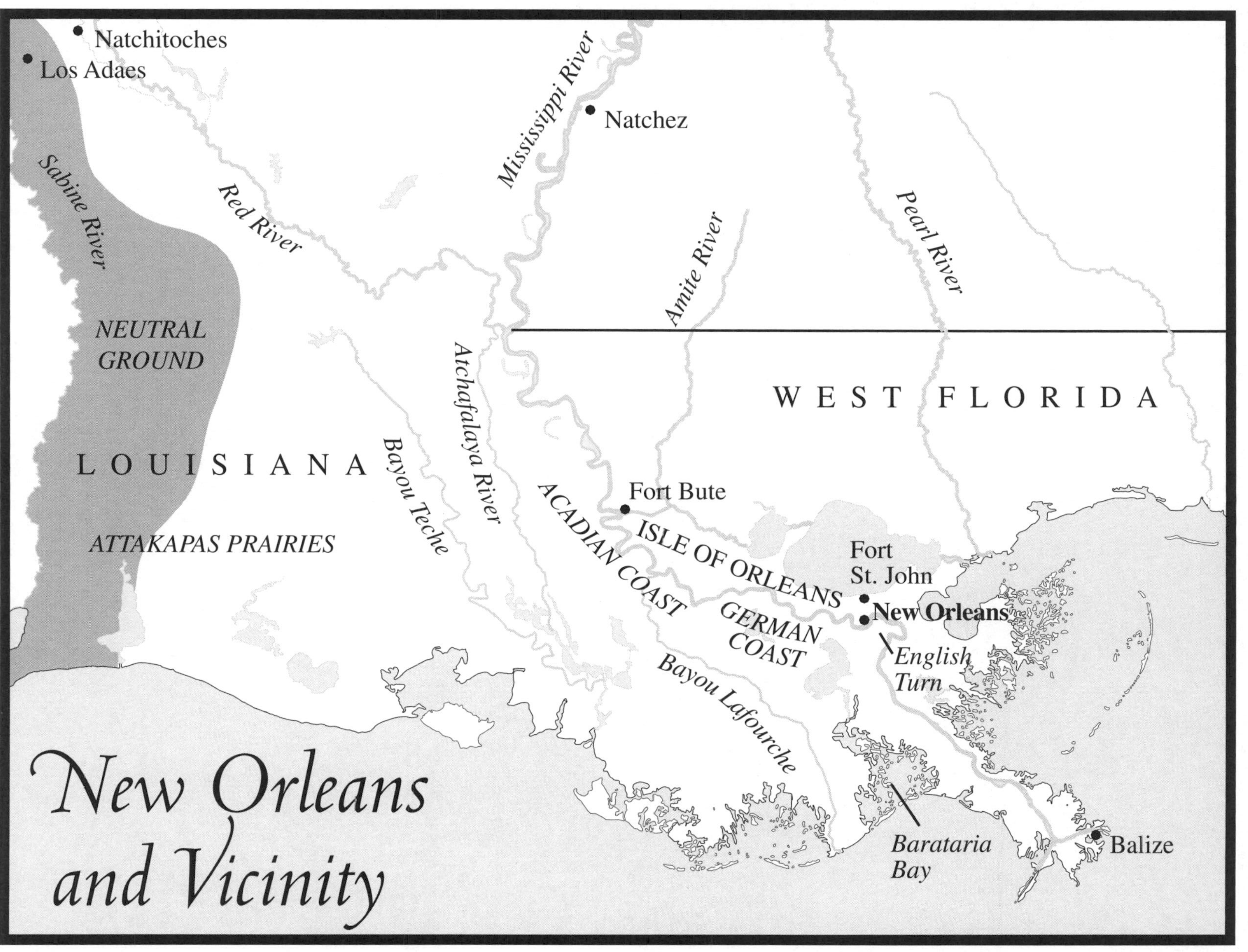
New Orleans and Vicinity
Natchitoches
Los Adaes
Mississippi River
Natchez
Sabine River
Red River
Amite River
Pearl River
NEUTRAL GROUND
WEST FLORIDA
LOUISIANA
Atchafalaya River
Bayou Teche
ATTAKAPAS PRAIRIES
Fort Bute
ACADIAN COAST
ISLE OF ORLEANS
Fort St. John
New Orleans
GERMAN COAST
English Turn
Bayou Lafourche
Barataria Bay
Balize

THE LOUISIANA PURCHASE

A Historical and Geographical Encyclopedia

ACADIANS
See Cajuns

ADAMS, JOHN QUINCY (1767–1848)

U.S. diplomat and the sixth president of the United States, Adams was born in Braintree, Massachusetts (in the part of town that is now Quincy), to John Adams, the second president of the United States, and Abigail Smith Adams. Before becoming president, John Quincy Adams was one of America's foremost diplomats and a noted secretary of state (1817–1824). He was responsible for negotiating the Adams-Onís (Transcontinental) Treaty of 1819, which finally established a western border for the Louisiana Purchase.

Adams spent much of his youth abroad with his father on diplomatic missions. Educated in Paris and the University of Leiden, he graduated from Harvard in 1787, read law, and established a legal practice in Boston. He wrote several anonymous articles for Northeastern newspapers supporting George Washington's policy of neutrality following the outbreak of war between Britain and France in 1793. Washington appointed him minister to the Netherlands in 1794, and his dispatches from The Hague, Europe's best diplomatic listening post, impressed Washington, who came to view the young Adams as perhaps the most able member of the republic's foreign service. He was appointed minister to Portugal in 1796, the year that his father became president, and was appointed minister to Prussia in 1797. He returned to Boston in 1801, was elected to the Massachusetts senate in 1802, and was later elected by the state legislature to the U.S. Senate as a Federalist in 1803.

Adams arrived too late to vote on the Louisiana Purchase Treaty, but made it known that if present he would have supported it. Never a strict party man (he disliked the Federalist Party's rather narrow views on foreign policy), he was the only Federalist senator to vote in favor of the appropriation bill to carry the purchase into effect. Believing that a constitutional amendment was necessary to incorporate the Louisiana Territory as a U.S. territory, and concerned with Jefferson's use of executive power to appoint territorial officers, he voted with other Federalists in opposing a bill delegating such powers to the president. He did, however, continue to support Jefferson's policy of neutrality, and he supported the Embargo Act (1807). These actions cost him his Senate seat in 1808. That year he attended the Republican congressional caucus that nominated James Madison, a man Adams greatly admired, as its candidate for president. Madison rewarded him with an appointment as minister to Russia in 1809.

While in Russia he became something of a friend to Tsar Alexander I and used his personal connections to improve Russo-American commercial relations. Adams believed that the success of the American Revolution was a providential sign that European colonialism on the American continent was an evil, and while in St. Petersburg he strongly opposed British trade restrictions as an attempt to revive colonialism. In 1812 war broke out between Britain and the United States, and Napoleon invaded Russia. In 1813, Tsar Alexander, wishing to help end the War of 1812 and thus free his ally Britain to concentrate her energies upon defeating Napoleon, offered to mediate a peace settlement between Britain and the United States. Madison accepted the offer, and in May 1813 he asked Congress to confirm the appointment of Adams, James A. Bayard, and Albert Gallatin as peace commissioners to Russia. Britain initially refused the offer of Russian mediation, but in the fall of 1813 the British foreign secretary, Lord Castlereagh, not wishing to appear unreasonable, accepted the tsar's offer. The American delegation, which now also included Henry Clay and Jonathan Russell, refused Castlereagh's offer to meet in London, insisting that they meet the British peace commissioners on neutral ground. Britain finally agreed, and the British commission, led by Admiral Lord Gambier, met the American commission, led by Adams, in Ghent, Belgium, in August 1814.

The peace commission was hampered by British arrogance and by Adams's dislike for a number of his fellow commissioners, especially Henry Clay. With the European powers meeting in Vienna to establish a new European status quo, Castlereagh became eager to end the American conflict; the Treaty of Ghent, signed on December 24, 1814, returned both nations to status quo antebellum. The treaty, which came about before General Andrew Jackson's victory at New Orleans in January

Generally considered the nation's greatest secretary of state, John Quincy Adams negotiated the Transcontinental Treaty (1819), which poised America for Western expansion.

1815, actually made no mention of the status of Louisiana. Britain had supported Spain's claim that under international law the purchase was invalid; Napoleon, it was argued, had ignored a clause in the Treaty of San Ildefonso (1800) stipulating that France could not dispose of Louisiana without first offering it back to Spain. However, the status quo antebellum clause of the Treaty of Ghent, first suggested by Adams, and Jackson's victory sealed the fate of Louisiana, and no more questions would be raised concerning the legality of the purchase.

In 1815, Madison appointed Adams the American minister to the Court of St. James in London. Together with Henry Clay and Albert Gallatin, Adams negotiated a new Anglo-American trade convention. Appointed secretary of state by President Monroe in 1817, Adams laid the foundations for two later treaties signed while he was in office. The Rush-Bagot Agreement (1817) demilitarized the Great Lakes, and the Convention of 1818 settled the northern limit of the Louisiana Purchase by extending the Canadian-American border along the forty-ninth parallel, west from the Lake of the Woods (Minnesota) to the crest of the Rocky Mountains. Although Adams's name will always be linked with the Monroe Doctrine (1823), his efforts to settle the question of the status of Florida led to his greatest coup, the Adams-Onís Treaty (1819).

The question of Florida was a familiar one to Adams, who, as a young senator, had insisted that the Louisiana Purchase include West Florida. At the time that Adams began negotiations with Luis de Onís y Gonzales, the Spanish representative in the United States, it was clear that Spain was in no position to dispute American occupation of West Florida, begun in 1811, or America's continued encroachments into East Florida; General Jackson made an unauthorized invasion of East Florida in 1818. Adams supported Jackson's actions, because they strengthened Adams's hand and led Spain to agree to the eventual purchase of Florida. During the negotiations Adams seized the opportunity to establish a western boundary line to the Louisiana Purchase, an issue of long dispute between the two countries and a problem made more difficult to resolve as diplomatic relations were severed between the United States and Spain in 1805.

Although Spain had insisted that the eastern boundary of Texas extended to the Arroyo Honda, a dry gulch just west of Natchitoches, the United States had claimed the Rio Grande as Louisiana's western boundary. The impasse resulted in a lawless "neutral strip" between the Arroyo Honda and the Sabine River. Adams gradually gave ground on the western boundary of Louisiana, accepting the Sabine River, but used the opportunity to insist upon a western boundary to the Louisiana Purchase extending along the Sabine, the Red River, the Arkansas River to its source, and north to the forty-second parallel and thence west to the Pacific coast. A delighted U.S. Senate immediately ratified the treaty in 1819, but disputed land claims held up Spanish ratification until February 1821.

Adams succeeded Monroe as president, following a disputed election in 1824. A one-term president, he himself was defeated by Andrew Jackson in 1828 following a nasty campaign that unfairly accused Adams of undertaking a "corrupt bargain" with his old nemesis Henry Clay, whom Adams had appointed his secretary of state in 1824. Elected to the House of Representatives in 1830, Adams had a notable second career in Congress, especially as a spokesman against the extension of slavery. Worn out by a long life in public service, he collapsed in the House on February 21, 1848, while rising to his feet to oppose an honorary grant of swords by Congress to the generals who had won victories in the ongoing Mexican War, a conflict he had strongly opposed. He died two days later and was buried in the family vault in Quincy, Massachusetts. John Quincy Adams may have lacked the common touch and, at times, proved to be obstinate, but he was one of the ablest, most hardworking, and most intellectual men to occupy American high office—not to mention the presidency.

—Rory T. Cornish

See also

Transcontinental Treaty

For Further Reading

Adams, John Quincy. 1874–1877. *Memoirs of John Quincy Adams: Comprising Portions of His Diary from*

1785 to 1848. Edited by Chauncey Worthington Ford. 7 vols. Philadelphia: J. B. Lippincourt; Bemis, Samuel Flagg. 1969. *John Quincy Adams and the Foundations of American Foreign Policy.* New York: Alfred A. Knopf; Brooks, Philip C. 1939. *Diplomacy and the Borderlands: The Adams-Onís Treaty of 1819*. Berkeley: University of California Press; Ford, Chauncey Worthington, ed. 1913–1917. *The Writings of John Quincy Adams*. 7 vols. New York: Macmillan; Johnson, Paul A. 1991. *The Birth of the Modern World Society, 1815–1830*. New York: Harper Collins; LaFeber, Walter, ed. 1965. *John Quincy Adams and the American Continental Empire: Letters, Speeches and Papers.* Chicago: Quadrangle Books; Nagel, Paul C. 1997. *John Quincy Adams: A Public Life, A Private Life.* New York: Alfred A. Knopf; Perkins, Bradford. 1964. *Castlereagh and Adams: England and the United States, 1812–1823*. Berkeley: University of California Press; Perkins, Dexter. 1928. "John Quincy Adams: Secretary of State, September 22, 1817, to March 4, 1825." In *The American Secretaries of State and Their Diplomacy,* vol. 3. Edited by Samuel Flagg Bemis. New York: Alfred A. Knopf; Russell, Greg. 1995. *John Quincy Adams and the Public Virtues of Diplomacy.* Columbia: University of Missouri Press.

ADAMS-ONÍS TREATY

***See* Transcontinental Treaty**

ADDINGTON, HENRY, FIRST VISCOUNT SIDMOUTH (1757–1844)

British politician who, as prime minister (1801–1804), was in power during the Louisiana Purchase. Addington was the son of Dr. Anthony Addington, the personal physician to the elder William Pitt, and his family connection and childhood friendship with the younger William Pitt (1759–1806) led to his political career. Genial and respected, Addington as a politician was slow to act; his harshest critic, William Cobbett, labeled him the "Doctor," a man who maintained the attitude of a physician looking at the tongue of a sick patient.

Educated at Oxford and trained as a lawyer, Addington was brought into the House of Commons in 1784 by Pitt, through whose influence he was elected speaker in 1789. When Pitt resigned in February 1801, over George III's refusal to grant Catholic emancipation to Ireland, the king, with Pitt's approval, asked Addington to form an administration. Something of a caretaker administration dependent upon Pitt's support, it was inexperienced—especially its foreign secretary, Robert Jenkinson, then known by his courtesy title, Lord Hawkesbury, later second Earl of Liverpool. The major achievement of the Addington government was the establishment of a temporary peace with France—the Peace of Amiens (1802)—which would briefly transform the diplomatic relationship between Britain and the United States.

Following secret negotiations with Louis Otto, the French representative in London, preliminary peace terms were signed in October 1801. Members of Pitt's previous administration had been concerned about the rumors that a secret treaty had been signed between Spain and France granting a retrocession of Louisiana to Napoleon. Eager to establish a lasting peace, Addington had refused to raise the question of Louisiana with Otto, and Hawkesbury convinced George III to ratify the final treaty in March 1802, with the argument that the territory was of no commercial importance, a wilderness that would take decades to develop. During the interim between the preliminaries and the final treaty, critics of the Peace of Amiens, including William Cobbett, William Windham, and, later, Lord Grenville, raised important questions about Louisiana, especially after Napoleon published the details of the Treaty of San Ildefonso in December 1801. Did Amiens, it was asked, technically confirm the retrocession, and what were the borders of this retrocession? Addington tended to ignore these questions. Throughout 1802 the British cabinet did not discuss Louisiana, and Hawkesbury made no serious mention of it in his dispatches to British ministers in America.

By early 1803, however, the warnings of Rufus King, the American minister in London, that the United States would not permit a French occupation of New Orleans were being taken seriously. Napoleon's insistence that Louisiana included the two Floridas raised serious concerns about British commercial interests in the Gulf of Mexico, the West Indies, and Latin America. The uncertainty of Louisiana's northern border raised similar concerns regarding the security of Canada. If Addington refused to listen to the opposition press, however, he was influenced by the publication in early 1803 of *The Possession of Louisiana by the French Considered,* by his staunch supporter George Orr. Orr reflected the persuasive reports arriving from Edward Thornton, the British minister in Washington, D.C. Both Orr and Thornton argued that a great diplomatic coup stared Britain in the face; if France intended to occupy New Orleans, Britain should launch a preemptive strike against the city, take it, and then present it as a gift to Jefferson. Such action would help create a new anti-French, Anglo-American understanding, and increase British influence in the United States.

In early March 1803, Addington was finally prodded into action. Hawkesbury sounded out King on such a plan, and Addington's ministry firmly supported the Spanish claim that the Floridas had not been included in the retrocession. Instructions were sent to Admiral Thornborough, commanding the naval squadron off the Dutch coast, to intercept any French troop ships heading out into the North Sea. Addington, however, had missed the diplomatic boat: war with France resumed that month, and in April 1803, Napoleon announced his wish to sell Louisiana to the United States. If the sale increased French prestige in the United States, as well as gaining millions of dollars for Napoleon's war chest, Addington at least played a last positive role. Against all the rules of war and existing British regulations, he gave permission for Baring Brothers to export the gold from Britain that helped make the Louisiana Purchase possible.

With the resumption of war and his growing unpopularity, Addington resigned in April 1804. Finally reconciled with Pitt in January 1805, he was included once again in the government and was created Viscount Sidmouth. He continued to serve in successive administrations, most noticeably as home secretary (1812–1822) in the Lord Liverpool government. His increasingly reactionary politics have won him, however, the odium of numerous British historians. A die-hard Tory to the last, he voted against Catholic emancipation in 1829 and the Great Reform Act of 1832. Viscount Sidmouth died on February 15, 1844.

—Rory T. Cornish

For Further Reading

Campbell, Charles S. 1974. *From Revolution to Rapprochement: The United States and Great Britain 1783–1900.* New York: John Wiley and Son; Ernst, Robert. 1968. *Rufus King: American Federalist.* Chapel Hill: University of North Carolina Press; Gash, Norman. 1984. *Lord Liverpool: The Life and Political Career of Robert Banks Jenkinson, Second Earl of Liverpool, 1770–1828.* Cambridge: Harvard University Press; Mayo, Bernard, ed. 1971. *Instructions to the British Ministers to the United States, 1791–1812.* New York: DaCapo Press; Pellew, George. 1847. *The Life and Correspondence of the Rt. Hon. Henry Addington, First Viscount Sidmouth.* 3 vols. London: Murray and Co.; Perkins, Bradford. 1967. *The First Rapprochement: England and the United States, 1795–1805.* Berkeley: University of California Press; Wright, J. Leita, Jr. 1975. *Britain and the American Frontier, 1783–1815.* Athens: University of Georgia Press; Ziegler, Philip. 1965. *Addington: A Life of Henry Addington, First Viscount Sidmouth.* New York: John Day and Company.

ADET, PIERRE AUGUSTE (1763–1834)

When George Washington warned of entangling alliances in his presidential Farewell Address, he aimed his remarks at French minister Pierre Auguste Adet, among others. Adet worked against approval of Jay's Treaty (1794), attempted to influence the election of 1796, and sent a spy mission to Louisiana in order to prepare for a French conquest of Spain's American empire.

Pierre August Adet was born at Nevers, France, in 1763. He was educated as a chemist but entered the diplomatic corps before he turned thirty-one as secretary of France's commission to St. Dominque, colonial administrator, member of the Marine Council, and finally, in October 1794, minister to the United States. He arrived in Philadelphia in June 1795 with instructions to ensure compliance with the commercial treaties and the alliance of 1778. He did not speak English. Adet was directed to work for a new commercial treaty, win the confidence of Congress and the president, and, more important, obtain a loan from the American government. From Europe, John Quincy Adams reported that the French administration considered Adet "a very able and very excellent man," and Federalist secretary of the treasury Oliver Wolcott, Jr., thought Adet well educated, mild tempered, and a minister who "will not be violent or troublesome" while still representing French interests (DeConde, 1958). Alexander Hamilton deemed Adet "more circumspect than either of his predecessors" (ibid.). Both proved to be badly mistaken in judgment, as Adet considered the American assignment distasteful and held all Americans in contempt—Adet wrote: "An American is the born enemy of all European peoples" (Turner, 1904).

Citizen Adet, as he became known, worked openly against Jay's Treaty after the Senate passage, pushing the House to defeat the passage of a bill for appropriations to execute the treaty. To Adet and the French, Jay's Treaty abrogated the French alliance of 1778 and threatened French commercial interests. He next meddled in the election of 1796, in which Adet worked to support Republican Thomas Jefferson's election as president. In November 1796, Adet penned four proclamations to Secretary of State Timothy Pickering, but had them published in Benjamin Franklin Bache's Philadelphia *Aurora,* a Republican newspaper. In the proclamations, Adet warned of the suspension of diplomatic relations and a toughened French policy on neutral shipping, and he reviewed Franco-American relations, blaming the current crisis on the Federalists. Adet also called upon Frenchmen in the country to wear the tricolored cockade as a symbol of French liberty; those who refused risked their access to the French consul. His actions infuriated the Federalists but had little bearing on John Adams's election to succeed Washington. In the words of one American, however, Adet "diminished that good will felt for his government and the people of France by most people here" (DeConde, 1958).

In the West, Adet was plotting for the French conquest of Louisiana—the true purpose of his mission. He saw the United States as a staging area for France's invasion army, and to that end he sent General Georges Henri Victor Collot on a reconnaissance mission to the Mississippi Valley. Collot was to report on the political, economic, and, foremost, the military situation in the region. In reality, Collot was sent as a spy to determine the potential for French military action against Spain; he also sought to ascertain the possibility of secession among the Western states (and those of the South as well), to form a coalition to take the Louisiana Territory for France. In addition, Adet was in contact with the Westerners George Rogers Clark and "Colonel" Samuel Fulton, who supplied the French minister with intelligence reports from the West. Fulton was especially useful as an agent—Adet sent him to Paris in April 1796 with information for the French government.

Victor Collot, like Adet, was contemptuous of the Americans, but, unlike the minister, he readily shared his feelings—he talked too much. Even before he left Philadelphia in March 1796, the American government knew of his objective, and the administration appropriated $500 for agents to shadow Collot and report on his plot. Collot noted that the Spanish fear of American expansion was so great that Spain attempted "to hide from the Americans whatever attractions the country might have for them" (ibid.). He reported to Adet a plan for defending Louisiana against the Americans and imagined a French territory spanning from the Alleghenies to the Rockies—parts of both Spain and America. His conclusions backed Adet's assertion that the Western states and Louisiana must be joined to fend off American advancement. Adet and Collot thus conspired to take Louisiana by military force if necessary, and American knowledge of their plans served only to further undermine relations. At Adet's instructions, Collot's mission also provided French officials with a blueprint for French policy—a frame of reference for Louisiana. Adet was recalled as minister in November 1796, and he left the United States in April of the following year.

Adet was a failure as a diplomat in America. Like his predecessors Genêt and Fauchet, his actions thwarted Franco-American relations, drove many Americans closer to the British as allies, angered politicians from both parties, and aggravated the British even more. Noted British journalist William Cobbett compared Adet to a blunderbuss and called him an "unprincipled shameless bully." Adet's career in America was one of intrigue that caused a serious setback between the two nations, but the underlying and clandestine object of his mission—gaining Louisiana—was important in the series of events leading up to the 1803 Louisiana Purchase.

—Boyd Childress

See also

Collot, Georges Henri Victor

For Further Reading

DeConde, Alexander. 1958. *Entangling Alliance: Politics & Diplomacy under George Washington.* Durham, NC: Duke University Press; Turner, Frederick Jackson. 1904. *Correspondence of the French Ministers to the United States, 1791–1797.* In *American Historical Association Annual Report: 1903,* vol. 2. Washington, DC: Government Printing Office.

AMANA COLONIES

The Amana Colonies were a planned religious community in east-central Iowa established by German Inspirationalists in 1855. German Inspirationalists, who formed in 1714 in southern Germany, believed that they received God's messages through certain individuals known as *Werkzeug.* They came to the United States in the 1840s to escape religious persecution in Germany. They first established a community in Ebenezer, New York, but after ten years decided that New York was too settled and expensive. The group decided to find a better location for their settlement.

Inspirationalists traveled west of Chicago looking for better land for their colony, and Iowa proved to be the perfect place. In 1855 the group purchased eighteen thousand acres along the Rock Island Railroad in east-central Iowa, including the town of Homestead, and laid out the six villages that formed the Amana Colonies. The original villages included Amana, Middle Amana, East Amana, West Amana, South Amana, and High Amana.

The group established woolen mills, sawmills, and meat-processing facilities; they also instituted large-scale agriculture and built fine furniture. The industries of the Amana Colonies proved very lucrative for the group. The group continued the communal lifestyle they had lived in Germany and New York. Single-family homes were built for individual families, but none of the original homes had kitchens. The Inspirationalists had a highly ordered distribution of jobs. Men worked in the fields or industries. Unmarried women worked in the communal kitchens. Married women worked in the gardens, and older women tended the nurseries. Every child in the Amana Colonies attended school through the eighth grade.

Amana residents attended church eleven times a week: three times on Sunday, every morning, and Wednesday evening. The church dominated all aspects of life, and the elders and the *Werkzeugs* maintained respected positions in the community. Throughout the nineteenth century, life was peaceful for the community.

In 1900, on account of their economic success, the elders found it more difficult to maintain the community's standards of religious and social behavior. In order to keep the group together, the elders started to relax rules regarding behavior and morality. The 1920s and 1930s were challenging for the group. A large flour mill and a gristmill burned in 1923. Neither building had been insured, and the loss created a hardship for the community. Additionally, during the 1920s sales at the various Amana industries decreased, causing financial difficulties. The hardships of the Great Depression further strained the colonies, and these financial troubles forced the group into a difficult decision. They could maintain their communal lifestyle or abandon the old ways.

In 1932 the entire adult population of the Amana Colonies voted on their future. The majority of the Amana residents voted to end communalism. The Amana colonies created a corporation to manage the various business enterprises. Every person in the group received one share of the new corporation. In all, the transition from communal lifestyle to corporation was relatively smooth. Today the Amana Colonies are a tourist attraction, drawing visitors to the old woolen mills, furniture shops, and numerous restaurants.

—*Mary F. McKenna*

See also
Iowa
For Further Reading

Bartel, Diane. 1984. *Amana: From Pietist Sect to American Community.* Lincoln: University of Nebraska Press; Shambaugh, Bertha M. H. 1971. *Amana that Was and Amana that Is.* New York: Benjamin Blom; Perkins, William Rufus. 1975. *History of the Amana Society.* New York: Arno Press.

AMERICAN FUR COMPANY

The American Fur Company became the dominant interest in the Western fur trade of the early nineteenth century. Started by German émigré John Jacob Astor, the company organization reflected its founder's considerable business skills and earned him a fortune. Astor had already amassed considerable wealth in the China trade before he turned his attention to monopolizing the fur supply coming out of the newly acquired Louisiana Territory. In 1808 he started the American Fur Company to pursue the fur trading enterprise that, until then, had been primarily in the hands of the British. A parallel venture, the Pacific Fur Company, used maritime and overland expeditions to establish a fort on the Pacific coast near the mouth of the Columbia River. This short-lived venture, Astoria, had to be released to British rivals during the War of 1812. However, its importance to the young nation lay in the routes that its employees pioneered, including South Pass, the only way to get a loaded wagon across the Rocky Mountains.

The nationalistic spirit of the country following the War of 1812 proved a welcome benefit to Astor's business plans. Congress enacted a law that forbade foreign operators from conducting trade operations on American soil. This removed British rivals, such as the North West Company, and allowed the American Fur Company to expand in a less competitive environment. Astor soon came to dominate the fur trade through the employment of hundreds of trappers, who covered the Missouri, Green, and Wind River systems.

The participation of these individuals was critical to the success of Astor's enterprise, and nineteenth-century fur trapping was certainly not a profession for everyone. The work demanded tough souls, for trapping was an arduous, solitary undertaking. The pursuit of beaver pelts took trappers far into remote areas, cut off from human contact. The white men involved in the trade forged an identity for themselves as "mountain men," and several individuals, such as Jim Bridger and Jedediah Smith, gained near legendary status in the annals of the West. Indeed, it was the men in the field, not the businessmen like Astor, who captured the American imagination. Much of the area of operation was unsettled by whites and still under the control of indigenous groups with considerable power. Native Americans often viewed the incursions of fur traders as a threat to their control. For their own part, white trappers often found the adaptations of native groups indispensable to survival in the harsh conditions; as a result, many adopted Indian modes of dress, travel, and food preparation, and some married into the tribes.

As companies struggled to deal with the power dynamics of the Rocky Mountain West, Astor's representatives established a relationship with the Blackfoot that opened rich territory to the company. This type of business acumen pushed the American Fur Company to the forefront of the fur trading business. By 1834 the American Fur Company so outclassed its competition that the rival Rocky Mountain Fur Company sold out to Astor. The combined forces of the trappers in the field and the businessmen in the cities proved a potent arrangement. The rendezvous system pioneered by William Ashley allowed the trappers to stay in the mountains all year and turn over their skins, at annual meetings, to supply trains sent from the settlements. This became the basis of the Rocky Mountain system, which ruled the West for a short time. At its height, the system employed more than one thousand men on the Missouri River drainage and Rocky Mountain streams. The fur supply began to dwindle under the pressure of heavy trapping at the same time that fashions veered toward silk. Astor sold the American Fur Company and retired with a personal fortune of $20 million. The fortunes of the company continued to decline until, in 1840, it called a halt to the annual rendezvous cycle.

The American Fur Company dominated the fur trade of the West for a seemingly brief span of four decades. In that time, however, it wrought several changes. The environmental effect on the beaver was obvious, and the animals could no longer be found over much of their former range. And the effect of the incursion of nonnatives on the indigenous people of the West was also devastating. Contact altered native life in countless ways, many of which would not be immediately felt, such as a desire for trade goods or an altered economic system. Other effects were immediately and painfully obvious. In 1837 an American Fur Company steamboat stopped at the Mandan villages on the Missouri River and inadvertently introduced a smallpox virus that decimated the villages.

—*Clarissa W. Confer*

See also
Astor, John Jacob
For Further Reading

Lavender, David. 1964. *A Fist in the Wilderness.* Garden City, NY: Doubleday; Sunder, John E. 1965. *The Fur Trade on the Upper Missouri, 1840–1865.* Norman: University of Oklahoma Press.

AMERICAN INSURANCE CO. V. CANTER (1828)

The question of the legality of the Louisiana Purchase (1803) was an issue that was debated both internationally and within the United States at the time and in subsequent years. At the international level, many European powers believed that the United States effectively concluded an illegal purchase in 1803, because in the transfer the French violated terms of the Treaty of San Ildefonso (1800) whereby the territory should have been returned to Spain rather than sold to a third power. In the eyes of some foreign leaders, the United States essentially was the possessor of "stolen goods." Within the United States, there was doubt associated with the exact timetable of the purchase, as opponents of territorial expansion maintained that the U.S. Senate, the body constitutionally mandated to ratify all treaties, was notified after the fact of the purchase. Even President Thomas Jefferson believed in 1803 that an amendment to the U.S. Constitution might be necessary in order to justify the legitimacy of the Louisiana Purchase.

In an odd fashion, the U.S. Supreme Court spoke to the issue of the legality of the Louisiana Purchase and other territorial acquisitions when it rendered a decision in the case of *American Insurance Co. v. Canter*, 1 Peters (26 U.S.) 511 (1828). The case was centered upon the question of what authority territorial courts possessed. In a larger sense, the case established a legal precedent that authorized the United States to annex territory and establish governments for the same, basing both legislative actions upon constitutional principles.

American Insurance Company sued for restitution associated with 356 cotton bales that had been a part of the cargo of the vessel *Point a Petre* that was wrecked just off the Florida Keys while on a voyage from New Orleans to the French port of Havre de Grace. A portion of the cargo had been salvaged, and it was taken to Key West. Under order of a Florida territorial court, the cotton was sold at auction to cover the costs of the salvage operation. American Insurance, having insured the cargo in question, challenged the action of what it considered an inferior court—one created by the Florida territorial legislature and not the U.S. Congress—to render a decision in a case that should have been heard by a higher court.

Article III of the Constitution of the United States does provide that "all cases of admiralty and maritime jurisdiction must be vested in the Supreme Court and in such inferior courts that Congress may establish." Chief Justice John Marshall, speaking for the Court in a unanimous 7–0 decision, maintained that the territorial court did have jurisdiction in the case because it had been legally established by a legislature that was created by congressional action. Chief Justice Marshall maintained that "[t]he Constitution confers absolutely on the government of the Union, the powers of making war, and of making treaties; consequently, that government possesses the power of acquiring territory, either by conquest or by treaty" (Keats). Therefore, it was the opinion of the Court that the Congress derived its plenary powers to acquire territories and to govern them in Article IV of the Constitution. In this fashion, the Court maintained that the right to annex territory, such as Florida or Louisiana, may be derived from either the stipulated powers to declare war or to conclude treaties. In 1857, Chief Justice Roger B. Taney would ignore this precedent when he rendered his decision in the case of *Dred Scott v. Sandford*.

—*Junius P. Rodriguez*

See also
International Law and the Louisiana Purchase Treaty; Marshall, John; Constitution of the United States

For Further Reading
Keats, John. 1973. *Eminent Domain: The Louisiana Purchase and the Making of America.* New York: Charterhouse; Kelly, Alfred H., and Winfred A. Harbison. 1970. *The American Constitution: Its Origins and Development.* New York: W. W. Norton.

AMES, FISHER (1758–1808)

Fisher Ames was one of the most eloquent and most outspoken critics of Jeffersonian democracy during the years of the early republic. He served in the House of Representatives (1789–1797) as a Massachusetts Federalist and constantly vilified his political opponents as being advocates of social anarchy and mob rule. It was Ames's belief that the democratic egalitarianism associated with the Jeffersonian Republicans was something akin to the Jacobin radicalism that had developed across the Atlantic as a result of the French Revolution. Ames wanted nothing of the sort to take root in the United States.

Ames was born in Dedham, Massachusetts, on April 9, 1758, and was raised in a strict New England household. His Calvinist upbringing influenced his later political ideology. Despite his father's death when he was a child, his mother made sure that her son received a classical education. He graduated from Harvard in 1774 when he was only sixteen years old and became a lawyer shortly thereafter. By 1787, Ames had become an accomplished solicitor, and he found himself elected to the convention called for the ratification of the U.S. Constitution in Massachusetts. Ames supported the idea of a strong national government, but the exact nature of that government was at odds with what others (who later called themselves Federalists) would see as the essential nature of federal authority.

As a member of the First Congress, Ames was involved in the debates associated with the drafting and passage of the Bill of Rights, the first ten amendments to the U.S. Constitution. Ames was especially associated with the language incorporated into the First Amendment. Ames strongly supported the administration of George Washington during his eight years in the House of Representatives.

Ames believed in the sanctity of contract and in inviolable property rights. He found comfort in the aristocratic airs of his fellow Federalists because he believed that the common sort could not govern themselves, despite the best intentions of democratic ideals. Although fellow Federalists, such as John Marshall and Alexander Hamilton, supported an expanding vision of America that incorporated economic nationalism and territorial growth, Ames would have nothing of such views.

Ames became one of the leading supporters of Jay's Treaty (1794) when it reached the Congress, despite widespread disapproval of it by the general public. He supported the measure for two clear reasons that were consistent with his political ideology: Ames believed that any treaty with Great Britain, however flawed it might be, would serve to punish the French, whom he despised. Also, Ames believed that the economic concessions that were given to the British in Jay's Treaty would halt the expansive desire of many who supported territorial growth and a strong national economy.

Ames believed—correctly, as time would prove—that the territorial expansion of the United States would further weaken the political power and influence of New England. Since Ames felt that the moral compass of the nation was defined by New England Calvinist values, only moral decay and national decline would follow in the wake of expansionist schemes. In 1804, shortly after the Louisiana Purchase had been accomplished, Ames described New England's waning influence as he wrote of the region's being "not as the guarded treasure of freemen, but as the pittance, which the disdain of conquerors has left to their captives" (Ames, 1969).

After retiring from political life, Ames was offered the presidency of Harvard University but was forced to decline the offer because of poor health. Despite his retirement from public life, Ames continued to correspond with leading national figures to ensure that the true ideology of the Federalists was always articulated. As such, Ames maintained his presence as the voice of the loyal opposition during the presidential administration of Thomas Jefferson. Ames died at his home in Dedham, Massachusetts, on July 4, 1808.

Ames's best-known work, *The Influences of Democracy on Liberty* (1835), was published after his death. In this work Ames describes popular democracy as "an illuminated hell, that in the midst of remorse, horror, and torture, rings with festivity" (Ames, 1835). Always the eloquent orator, even death could not silence the stinging language of Fisher Ames's critique of America's democratic experiment.

—Junius P. Rodriguez

See also

Federalist Party; Hamilton, Alexander; Jay's Treaty; Marshall, John

For Further Reading

Ames, Fisher. 1835. *The Influences of Democracy on Liberty, Property, and the Happiness of Society, Considered.* London: J. W. Parker; Ames, Fisher. 1969 [1854]. *Works of Fisher Ames: With a Selection from His Speeches and Correspondence.* Edited by Seth Ames. New York: DaCapo Press; Bernhard, Winfred E. A. 1965. *Fisher Ames: Federalist and Statesman, 1758–1808.* Chapel Hill: University of North Carolina Press.

AMIENS, PEACE OF (1802)

This treaty between the French republic, Great Britain, Spain, and the Batave republic (Holland) was concluded in Amiens, France, on March 27, 1802. The Peace of Amiens followed the signing of the Franco-Austrian Treaty of Lunéville (1801), which had brought peace to the European continent. Just prior to the conclusion of the Peace of Amiens, the British minister, William Pitt, was forced to resign on March 13, 1801. Pitt had been one of the key British officials opposed to negotiating with France. This political development helped create new possibilities for peace. Great Britain was isolated after Lunéville, and a Franco-British peace was opportune. On October 1, 1801, the preliminaries of this treaty were signed in London. After eight years of war, the British and the French welcomed the truce. In addition, the Peace of Amiens was essential for the re-establishment of a balance of power between France, Spain, and Great Britain in the colonies. This accord created a momentary respite from war and made it possible for France to negotiate the sale of Louisiana to the United States.

Joseph Bonaparte (France), Lord Cornwallis (Britain), Azzara (Spain), and Schimmel-Penninck (republic of Batave [Holland]) were the representatives who signed the Peace of Amiens. Under its conditions, Britain was to restore to France and her allies their colonies, with the exception of the Dutch possessions in Ceylon and the island of Trinity. In addition, the British had to evacuate Malta, the island of Elbe, and Egypt. In return, French troops were to leave Holland, Portugal, Naples, and the Roman states.

Without this period of peace, the first consul of the French government could not see any possibility of raising an empire in the Americas. At this point, Napoleon Bonaparte hoped that the peace would allow France the opportunity to deal with the slave rebellion in St. Domingue (Haiti). The French needed to regain control of St. Domingue, which was an important sugar colony. The Americans also hoped that the French would subdue the rebellion, because they feared that the crisis might spread to the United States.

The secret preparation of the Flessirque Expedition

confirms Bonaparte's initial intention of pursuing an American empire. The Peace of Amiens made conditions favorable to begin a Louisiana expedition. The Flessirque Expedition was preceded by General Leclerc's disastrous mission to St. Domingue. Leclerc, Napoleon Bonaparte's brother-in-law, and the majority of his troops died of yellow fever. At great expense to France, this disaster thwarted the plan to subdue the slave rebellion.

This time the mission had a different aim. Bonaparte ordered the mounting of troops and a large fleet, which were to sail from the Dutch port of Helvoët Sluys. Officially, the French fleet was to sail to St. Domingue. This ruse did not, however, deceive the British: informers speculated that the French intended to occupy Louisiana.

The Flessirque Expedition gravely jeopardized the Peace of Amiens. The French refused to remove their troops from Holland because the expedition was delayed by numerous setbacks. This increased the strain on Franco-British relations and revealed the fragility of the peace. And the Flessirque Expedition proved ill fated from the beginning. Delayed because of poor weather and supply, organizational, and reconnaissance problems, the French fleet never sailed. France sold Louisiana to the United States just before its departure.

In turn, the British were showing little intention of complying with the provisions of the Peace of Amiens. As a reaction to the French presence in Holland, the British refused to hand over the island of Malta to the French.

After the sale of Louisiana, Bonaparte wanted to end the Peace of Amiens and begin the war with England again. Given the circumstances, he knew he could not defend both Louisiana and St. Domingue. At this point, Bonaparte began to focus his energies on a Mediterranean empire, and he moved away from the expansion of French possessions in the Americas. He hoped to extend his territory with the conquest of Malta and Egypt. That was one of the essential factors in Napoleon's decision to sell Louisiana.

—Rachel Eden Black

See also
Haiti; Lunéville, Treaty of

For Further Reading

Peterson, Merrill D. 1998. "Louisiana!" In *The Louisiana Purchase Bicentennial Series in Louisiana History,* vol. 3. Edited by Dolores Egger Labbe. Lafayette: Center for Louisiana Studies.

ARANJUEZ, CONVENTION OF (1801)

The Convention of Aranjuez (March 21, 1801) was a negotiated arrangement between Napoleon Bonaparte's French republic and the Kingdom of Spain that further clarified and placed into effect the diplomatic agreements tentatively established between the two nations in the secret second Treaty of San Ildefonso (October 1, 1800). Lucien Bonaparte, the brother of the first consul and French ambassador at Madrid, negotiated on behalf of France, and Pedro de Cevallos, Spanish minister of foreign affairs, represented the interests of His Most Catholic Majesty Charles IV of Spain. It was through the Convention of Aranjuez that the retrocession of Louisiana from Spain to France actually took effect.

Napoleon Bonaparte had sent French General Louis Alexandre Berthier as his special envoy to Madrid to negotiate with the Spanish in the fall of 1800. Bonaparte was eager to re-establish a French empire in North America and desired the retrocession of Louisiana from the Spanish Bourbons. The first consul advised Berthier to seek from the Spanish the retrocession of Louisiana, the cession of the Floridas, and the provision of ten warships for which the French republic would guarantee a yet-undetermined kingdom on the Italian peninsula for the Duke of Parma. Spanish king Charles IV would not budge on the question of the Floridas, and he reduced the warship requisition down to six, but he was willing to transfer Louisiana, in principle, upon the acquisition of the promised Italian kingdom. Napoleon Bonaparte realized that he had to make his pledge of the Italian kingdom valid before the Spanish would surrender Louisiana.

French diplomats were quite busy in the months following the San Ildefonso negotiations. First, French and American negotiators completed their work drafting the Treaty of Mortefontaine (1800), which officially ended the Quasi-War (1798–1800) and attempted to re-establish a viable commercial relationship with the American republic. Other negotiators smoothed over differences between the French republic and the remnants of the Holy Roman Empire as they developed the Treaty of Lunéville. It was through this diplomacy that Napoleon acquired clear title to the kingdom of Tuscany in Italy, the region that he would use to satisfy his promise to Charles IV in the Treaty of San Ildefonso.

Once Napoleon acquired Tuscany, he had a few reservations about the promises made to the Spanish Bourbons. On a personal level, Napoleon did not care for Fernando, the Duke of Parma, and did not wish to see him inherit a kingdom. Napoleon believed that he might be able to live up to the spirit of the San Ildefonso negotiations if he guaranteed the Kingdom of Etruria (the new name given to the Grand Duchy of Tuscany) to Luis, the Prince of Parma, and the son of Fernando. The negotiations that took place at Aranjuez in early 1801 were aimed at getting the Spanish monarch to agree to the slight modification.

Spanish king Charles IV agreed to the changes. Since Luis was also his son-in-law, perhaps the thought of having his daughter serve as the queen of Etruria was an appealing prospect. In addition, the agreement signed at Aranjuez reiterated Spain's promise to retrocede Louisiana to the French. The Spanish also gave the island of Elba to the French.

Although it looked as though Napoleon Bonaparte had reclaimed Louisiana and set into motion the necessary steps to re-create a French North American empire, circumstances beyond his control would prevent that from happening. Still, the first consul was somewhat restricted by a pledge that he had made in the Treaty of San Ildefonso (1800), whereby the French promised the Spanish that the Louisiana Territory would never be traded or sold to a third party. For this reason, many European powers refused to recognize the legitimacy of the transfer of the Louisiana Territory when a cash-strapped Napoleon Bonaparte sold that region to the United States in 1803.

—Junius P. Rodriguez

See also

Bonaparte, Lucien; Charles IV; Fernando, Duke of Parma; Lunéville, Treaty of; Mortefontaine, Convention of; San Ildefonso, Treaty of; Tuscany

For Further Reading

DeConde, Alexander. 1976. *This Affair of Louisiana.* New York: Charles Scribner's Sons.

ARAPAHO

The Central Plains were home to the Arapaho and their allies, the Cheyenne. Both groups inhabited and hunted the region of present-day eastern Colorado and southeastern Wyoming. They lived primarily in the region between the Arkansas and North Platte Rivers. The Arapaho called themselves *Inuna-ina* or *Hinonoeino* ("our people"). Neighboring tribes that were favorably disposed toward the Arapaho referred to them as the "Blue Cloud People" because of their often-favorable temperament, but adversaries—such as the Sioux, Kiowa, Ute, and Pawnee—disparagingly called them "dog eaters."

The Arapaho spoke a language that stemmed from the Algonquian-Wakashan linguistic group. Although they had formerly been agriculturalists of the eastern woodlands of Minnesota, they migrated westward during the early seventeenth century. Settling in the Central Plains, they adopted the lifestyle of nomadic hunters who followed the vast herds of bison that inhabited the region. Because they were nomadic hunters, the Arapaho frequently came into contact with other tribes that maintained themselves in similar fashion. These frequent encounters generally led to clashes over rights to traditional hunting lands. The Arapaho often found themselves at war.

This often-warlike tribe came to be known as a peaceful people because they chose not to fight the Americans when they arrived on the Central Plains. The lands that the Arapaho occupied were of central importance to the course of the American empire because all major overland trails, such as the Oregon Trail and the Mormon Road—which would be traversed by emigrant pioneers, prospectors, and other trappers and traders—had to cross Arapaho country. The Arapaho agreed to a treaty with the U.S. government in which they promised to provide an open corridor that would allow for safe passage for overland travelers. Unfortunately, in making this decision, the Arapaho effectively divided their tribe.

The Southern Arapaho eventually merged with the Cheyenne and lived near the Arkansas River and its tributaries. This group eventually became the victims of the infamous Sand Creek Massacre (1864). The Southern Arapaho and Cheyenne who remained were eventually placed upon reservation land in Oklahoma. The Northern Arapaho lived along the North Platte River. Shortly after the Sand Creek Massacre, the Northern Arapaho signed the Treaty of Medicine Lodge (1867), in which they agreed to make peace with the Shoshone, their traditional enemy, and live among them on the Wind River Reservation in Wyoming.

One of the most ignoble events of U.S. history, the Sand Creek Massacre of November 29, 1864, became symbolic in Native American consciousness to the callous disregard that white Americans held for treaty obligations negotiated with Indian tribes. Colonel John M. Chivington and a contingent of the Colorado territorial militia deliberately attacked a village of Arapaho and Cheyenne who were flying an American flag—a clear sign that they were under treaty protection. In the wake of an artillery barrage and cavalry charge, more than 200 women and children were killed by Chivington's assault. A few Arapaho and Cheyenne warriors were also killed, but most of the men were participating in a hunt and were away from the encampment at the time of the attack.

Victimized by a treaty decision that served to divide and conquer, the Arapaho found themselves further marginalized by the pressures of Manifest Destiny. By 1867, the tribe had lost possession of all of its traditional hunting land. Even today the Arapaho remain a divided people with about 11,000 members living on reservations in Wyoming and Oklahoma.

—Junius P. Rodriguez

See also

Cheyenne; Colorado

For Further Reading

Berthrong, Donald J. 1976. *The Cheyenne and Arapaho Ordeal: Reservation and Agency Life in the Indian Territory.* Norman: University of Oklahoma Press; Fowler, Loretta. 1989. *The Arapaho.* New York: Chelsea House; Trenholm, Virginia Cole. 1970. *The Arapahoes, Our People.* Norman: University of Oklahoma Press.

ARIKARA

The Arikara are the northernmost of Caddoan-speaking villagers of the Plains, a language family also including the Pawnee, Wichita, Caddo, and Kitsai. Like their neighbors, the Mandan and

This group of Arikara were photographed as they participated in a medicine ceremony on reservation land in 1908.

the Hidatsa, the Arikara established villages along the Missouri River in the Dakotas, where they engaged in hunting, gathering, and a sophisticated agriculture that stood as the region's dominant mode of life before the rise of nomadic peoples.

Tribal tradition and archaeological study agree that the Arikara or their ancestors migrated from the Central Plains over a period of several centuries prior to contact with Europeans. Before the late eighteenth century, the Arikara were more numerous and diverse. Pre-epidemic populations are estimated to have been ten thousand or more, with twenty to forty villages associated in seven to a dozen bands. At least two major dialects were spoken, with early European traders observing still more subtle linguistic variation. After a series of late-eighteenth-century epidemics devastated the Arikara, survivors concentrated into a few autonomous villages under separate political leadership. When the Corps of Discovery arrived in 1804, two to three thousand Arikara lived in three villages located above the junction of the Grand and Missouri Rivers.

Like other Northern Plains villagers, the Arikara mixed seasonal gathering and hunting of small game, bison, and antelope with a varied agriculture, all made possible by the complex environment of river, floodplain, bluffs, and vast grasslands. Fortified villages often were located on bluffs above the Missouri River. Several dozen circular, domed earth-lodges, each thirty feet or more in diameter, served as residences, with prominent families near the village's center and its large Medicine Lodge, a seat of community and ceremonial life. Winter residences were located on the floodplain, which afforded plentiful game, access to wood for fuel, and protection from cold and wind. Villages were the focus of life for Arikara women, and a village's lodges, surrounding fields, and immediate environs were the setting for their efforts to sustain family and community. For men, the village was a place of origin and return from hunts and raids, and Arikara oral tradition describes immature young men as being unfamiliar with the world beyond the village.

Like other Northern Plains agriculturists, the Arikara masterfully adapted their plants and practices to aridity and a short growing season. Arikara fields, replete with sweet, flint, and flour corns, as well as beans, squashes, sunflowers, and melons, impressed many European and American visitors. Surpluses were exchanged with nomadic neighbors, who traded at Arikara villages or designated fairs elsewhere on the Plains.

By the mid-eighteenth century, Arikara trade also

involved the exchange of nonnative goods, including arms and horses. Although early-eighteenth-century maps may have relied on indirect information to situate Arikara villages, Canadian traders had arrived at the villages by the 1730s, followed by St. Louis–based traders in the 1790s. The presence of these newcomers also brought disease and recurrent epidemics in the eighteenth and nineteenth centuries, diminishing Arikara numbers and their ability to resist Sioux expansion.

Meriwether Lewis and William Clark, hoping to counter Sioux power and limit the influence of British traders, sought to broker an alliance between the Arikara and their fellow villagers, the Mandan and the Hidatsa. But Arikara economic ties to the Sioux, mutual suspicion among the erstwhile allies, and unproved American power precluded alliance. With the exception of a violent clash with William H. Ashley's trade expedition in 1823, and the subsequent military effort led by Colonel Henry Leavenworth, exchange between the Arikara and American traders remained a largely peaceful affair. Continued decline in their numbers, however, along with Sioux pressure, led the Arikara to seek mutual security with the Mandan and the Hidatsa on several occasions. Ultimately, they joined those peoples in 1862 at Like-A-Fishhook Village, just below the junction of the Missouri and Little Missouri Rivers; the place later became the seat of the Fort Berthold Reservation, established in 1870 by executive order.

Conflict on the Northern Plains during the 1860s and 1870s presented the Arikara with an opportunity to strike an alliance with the United States and secure a measure of protection from continued Sioux attack. With war at an end by the 1880s, the Arikara, like other Western Indian peoples, became subject to a systematic assimilation program. The allotment of tribal lands, an integral part of assimilation efforts, saw the Arikara begin to take individual homesteads in 1884, abandoning Like-A-Fishhook and establishing their own communities of Nishu and Elbowwoods east of the Missouri River. The Arikara, Mandan, and Hidatsa joined themselves as the Three Affiliated Tribes under terms of the Indian Reorganization Act of 1934.

—*J. Wendel Cox*

See also
Hidatsa; Mandan; Oglala Sioux; Pawnee; Santee Sioux

For Further Reading

Cash, Joseph H., and Gerald W. Wolff. 1974. *The Three Affiliated Tribes (Mandan, Arikara, and Hidatsa)*. Phoenix, AZ: Indian Tribal Series; Meyer, Roy W. 1977. *The Village Indians of the Upper Missouri: The Mandans, Hidatsas, and Arikaras.* Lincoln and London: University of Nebraska Press; Parks, Douglas R. 1996. *Myths and Traditions of the Arikara Indians.* Lincoln and London: University of Nebraska Press; Schneider, Mary Jane. 1986. *North Dakota Indians: An Introduction.* Dubuque, IA: Kendall Hunt.

ARKANSAS

On March 23, 1804, Captain Francisco Caso y Luengo of Spain relinquished command of Arkansas Post to Lieutenant James B. Many of the U.S. Army. The change of command occurred as the United States formally took possession of the former French and Spanish colony of Louisiana.

At the time of the American accession, Arkansas had a known population of less than five hundred, which included sixty enslaved blacks. The rest of the population consisted of French Creoles, métis (persons of mixed European and Indian ancestry), and Anglo-Americans. Most of these lived at Arkansas Post near three Quapaw villages that were estimated to have a population of 575. An unknown number of whites and Indians lived scattered throughout Arkansas. By 1820 there were only fourteen thousand people in the new territory, but there were more than fifty-two thousand by 1836, when Arkansas became a state. During the 1830s, Arkansas's population more than tripled, to ninety-eight thousand.

What became the state of Arkansas was first part of the District of Louisiana, established by Congress in 1804. A line run at 33 degrees north latitude divided the district from the Territory of Orleans and eventually became Arkansas's southern boundary.

The District of Arkansas was organized in 1806, only to be dissolved the next year and placed under the jurisdiction of the District of New Madrid. Then, in 1808, Governor Meriwether Lewis re-established the District of Arkansas in response to Arkansas citizens' complaints that New Madrid was too distant.

Arkansas took the next political step in 1813, when it became a county in the Territory of Missouri. Arkansas County was divided into four additional counties by 1819. That year the Territory of Arkansas was organized by Congress, with its northern boundary at 36 degrees 30 minutes north latitude, except for the so-called boot heel region of the new state of Missouri in northeastern Arkansas.

The western boundary of the territory was defined by several Indian treaties and federal government surveys as part of the creation of the Indian Territory. In 1820, the U.S. treaty with the Choctaw proposed to establish a reservation that would include the southwestern quarter of Arkansas. Because significant numbers of Arkansas residents lived there, the treaty was renegotiated in 1825. The southwest boundary of the territory was set on a line running from the Red River, west of the great bend, to the Arkansas River, just west of Fort Smith.

The northwest boundary was set in 1828 in a treaty with the Arkansas Cherokee. Many Cherokee had moved into Arkansas before 1803. Then, in 1817, about five thousand moved to a reservation in northwest Arkansas in exchange for their eastern lands. Eleven years later, a new treaty exchanged their Arkansas reservation for land in the northeast part of the Indian Territory. The line between the Cherokee reservation and Arkansas ran from Fort Smith to the southwestern corner of Missouri.

The Quapaw joined the Cherokee in the Indian Territory in 1833 after a series of treaties. In an 1818 treaty with the federal government, the Quapaw agreed to a reservation between the Ouachita and Arkansas Rivers. Six years later they were forced to sign another treaty that moved them to northwestern Louisiana. When they returned to Arkansas, a third treaty moved them to the Indian Territory in 1833.

The federal government quickly made its presence felt in ways other than the development of political geography. In 1805, John B. Treat established the first of three federally controlled Indian trading factories in Arkansas. Treat's factory was unsuccessful and closed in 1810, but two others were built soon after. In 1817 the Natchitoches trading factory was moved to the mouth of the Sulphur Fork of the Red River, just inside Arkansas. Two years later, a factory was built at Spadra Bluff, near present-day Russellville, for trade with the Cherokee. Then, in 1818, Fort Smith was built to bring peace to the frontier.

Expeditions, which began during President Thomas Jefferson's administration, explored, mapped, and gathered information about Arkansas and the Southwest. In 1804, the year in which Meriwether Lewis and William Clark set off for the West, William Dunbar and Dr. George Hunter traveled up the Ouachita River in Louisiana and Arkansas. Their destination was the famous hot springs. Two years later, Thomas Freeman and Peter Custis traveled up the Red River to find its source. Their expedition was turned back by a Spanish army contingent west of the great bend of the Red River. In 1819–1820, Major Stephen H. Long's expedition failed to find the source of the Red River, but it succeeded in traveling down the Arkansas River and recording information about the land and people of Arkansas.

The Territory of Arkansas was created in 1819, after Missouri petitioned for statehood. Arkansas was caught up in the debate over slavery during the admission of Missouri, and Congress permitted slavery in the territory upon its creation. James Miller was appointed the first territorial governor, and Robert Crittenden the first territorial secretary. Miller served, though he was not present in Arkansas for much of his term, until 1825. Crittenden, who frequently acted as governor, served until 1829. Miller was succeeded by George Izard, who served until his death in 1828. The new administration of Andrew Jackson appointed John Pope as governor in 1829, and William S. Fulton as secretary. Fulton succeeded Pope as governor in 1835.

Crittenden called the first legislative council together in 1819, before Miller arrived and without approval from Washington. Crittenden quickly became one of the most influential men in the territory. He supported the election of J. Woodson Bates as the first territorial delegate to Congress in 1819, but he broke with Bates in 1823. Henry Conway was elected that year with Crittenden's support. Four years later, Crittenden and Conway had become bitter enemies. The 1827 election for delegates was noted for mudslinging on both sides. After Conway defeated Crittenden's candidate, he unwisely challenged Crittenden to a duel—one in which Crittenden shot and killed Conway.

The duel symbolized political violence in territorial Arkansas and was the beginning of the end of Crittenden's political career in Arkansas. Conway had been a member of an extended family that was gaining political power in Arkansas. Known as "the family" or "the dynasty," it included judges, legislators, and federal officials and became associated with the Democratic Party. Among its members were Henry Conway's brother James, who was the surveyor-general of Arkansas Territory and later the first governor of the state, and his cousin Ambrose Sevier, who became the territorial delegate and then one of Arkansas's first U.S. senators. The family also included William Woodruff, who in 1819 published the first newspaper in Arkansas, the *Arkansas Gazette*.

Little Rock replaced Arkansas Post as the capital of the territory in 1821. Little Rock was located not only on the Arkansas River, at a famous landmark, but also on the Southwest Trail from Missouri to Texas. Migration and the growth of settlements on the trail had risen steadily since the Louisiana Purchase. As a result of these factors, Little Rock became an important depot; in addition, it was located closer than Arkansas Post to the center of the territory's population: nearly 70 percent lived in counties along the trail. Eventually, Little Rock became tied financially to the Arkansas lowlands, which were the leading slave-owning and cotton-producing section of the territory and state.

The lowlands, in fact, developed differently from the territory's highlands. In the 1820s, the lowlands of the Mississippi Delta and the Gulf Coastal Plain, which constituted the eastern and southern half of the territory, were moving into cotton production and increasing in the population of slaves. Slaves accounted for 15 percent of the population in 1830, only slightly higher than in 1810. Hempstead County on the Red River had the highest population of slaves, at 21 percent. Ten years later, one out of every five persons in Arkansas was a slave, and slavery had become more concentrated in the lowlands. Two new counties, Chicot in the southeast and Lafayette in the southwest, contained populations that were more than 70 percent slave. To control this expanding population, slave patrols began in 1825.

The highlands of the Ozark and Ouachita Mountains were home to subsistence farmers and herders. In this region, there were areas of slave ownership and cotton production, especially along the Arkansas River, and some farmers and herders produced corn and pork, two of the territory's most important products.

The 1820s were the transition period, when Arkansas gradually became economically tied to the southern United States. Before that decade, Arkansas's economy had been dominated by hunting and the trade in animal products (furs, skins, tallow, and buffalo tongues). Neither pursuit vanished, but they became less important to the economy.

The Louisiana Purchase resulted in a religious change in Arkansas. In the Colonial period, the white residents of Arkansas were Roman Catholic if they professed any religion. After 1803, whites in Arkansas were members of various Protestant denominations. They were Methodist, Presbyterian, Baptist (including Landmark and Primitive Baptists), Episcopalian, and Campbellites (Disciples of Christ), as well as Roman Catholic.

On June 25, 1836, Arkansas became the twenty-fifth state admitted to the Union—the third state created from the Louisiana Purchase.

—Joseph Patrick Key

See also
Dunbar-Hunter Expedition; Quapaw

For Further Reading

Bolton, S. Charles. 1998. *Arkansas: Remote and Restless, 1800–1860.* Fayetteville: University of Arkansas Press; Bolton, S. Charles. 1993. *Territorial Ambition: Land and Society in Arkansas, 1800–1840.* Fayetteville: University of Arkansas Press; Carter, Clarence, ed. 1934–1975. *The Territorial Paper of the United States.* Washington, DC: Government Printing Office; White, Lonnie J. 1964. *Politics on the Southwestern Frontier: Arkansas Territory, 1819–1838.* Memphis: Memphis State University Press.

ARKANSAS POST

Arkansas Post was founded in 1686 by Henri de Tonti, who assigned six men to trade with the Quapaw Indians and watch for the return of the expedition of Robert Cavelier, Sieur de la Salle, Tonti's business partner. La Salle, of course, never returned, and the post was abandoned by 1700. It was reestablished in 1721 as part of John Law's concession. The concession failed, but this time a few settlers and a garrison remained.

Arkansas Post had moved several times during the eighteenth century. By the time of the Louisiana Purchase, it was located about thirty-five miles upriver from the mouth of the Arkansas River at a place the French called Ecores Rouges ("Red Bluffs"). Arkansas Post was home to between sixty and seventy families. They consisted of French Creoles, métis (persons of mixed European and Indian ancestry), Anglo-Americans (some of whom were refugees from the American Revolutionary War), persons from various European backgrounds, and sixty black slaves.

Although some settlers farmed and herded cattle on the nearby Grand Prairie, a swath of grassland extending 150 miles to the northwest, most at Arkansas Post were merchants or hunters engaged in the trade of animal skins, tallow, and buffalo tongues. Once the Louisiana Purchase was successfully concluded, the U.S. government tried to regulate this trade, as it had elsewhere, and it established a factory in 1805 to trade with the Indians. Competing with entrenched merchants and long-established trade relationships, the factory failed and was closed in 1810.

Some Americans found quick success in the trade. Jacob Bright established a company with his New Orleans partner Benjamin Morgan. Bright broke into the trade thanks to a trading monopoly with the Osage granted by the War Department. The monopoly was soon rescinded, however, after lobbying by merchants with more experience in the Arkansas River trade and the government's own Indian trade factor. On Bright's death, the Scull brothers, James and Hewes, joined Morgan in the enterprise.

By the 1820s, many who began in the trade turned their investments to cotton. Frederick Notrebe and Antoine Barraque, both French natives who had immigrated to Arkansas after the Louisiana Purchase, started business in the fur trade. They later became cotton planters, and Notrebe acquired the first cotton gin on the Arkansas River.

In 1807, with the appointment of its first local judges, Arkansas Post became the administrative center for the District of Arkansas in the Louisiana Territory, and in 1813 for Arkansas County in the Missouri Territory. When the Territory of Arkansas was created in 1819, Arkansas Post became the first territorial capital. Still, Thomas Nuttall called it "an insignificant village containing three stores . . . and . . . about 20 houses" (Bolton, 1998). It was an observation that reflected the fact that most of the population in Arkansas was growing along the Southwest Trail. Only two years later, Little Rock, at the spot where the trail crossed the Arkansas River, became the capital.

—Joseph Patrick Key

See also
Arkansas

For Further Reading

Arnold, Morris. 1991. *Colonial Arkansas, 1686–1804: A Social and Cultural History.* Fayetteville: University of Arkansas Press; Bolton, S. Charles. 1998. *Arkansas, 1800–1860: Remote and Restless.* Fayetteville: University of Arkansas Press; Bolton, S. Charles. 1993. *Territorial Ambition: Land and Society in Arkansas, 1800–1840.* Fayetteville: University of Arkansas Press; Carter, Clarence, ed. 1934–1975. *The Territorial Papers of the United States.* Washington, D.C.: Government Printing Office.

ARMSTRONG, FORT

Fort Armstrong was a military outpost established on an island in the Mississippi River in 1816. The island is located between Rock Island, Illinois, and Davenport, Iowa. After President Thomas Jefferson bought Louisiana, he instructed Indiana territorial governor William Henry Harrison to negotiate with the Sauk and Fox Indians to purchase their land in western Illinois. In 1804 the Sauk and Fox ceded fifty million acres of land east of the Mississippi River in

Fort Armstrong was established to maintain an American military presence in the upper Mississippi River Valley in the region once occupied by the Sauk and Fox. (North Wind Picture Archives)

Illinois. However, Chief Black Hawk was not included in the negotiation and refused to accept the transfer. Because of increasing hostility with the Indians of the upper Mississippi, the U.S. Army decided to establish additional military posts north of St. Louis. The southern tip of Rock Island became a strategic location for the new fort, on account of the thirty-foot limestone cliffs that formed two sides of the new fort.

The soldiers stationed at Fort Armstrong remained busy chopping wood, constructing new buildings for the fort, and engaging in military drills. They shared the island with several thousand Indians. Over the next few years, several soldiers who had ventured too far from the fort were found murdered.

During the winter of 1828, the first white squatters moved into the Indian village, which is present-day Rock Island, Illinois. Some of the bolder whites even moved into Indians' homes. Black Hawk and his followers grew frustrated by the white encroachment on their land. He warned the settlers that he would forcibly remove them if they failed to leave. The settlers feared that other local Indians would join Black Hawk, so they raised a force of sixteen hundred volunteers. General Edmund Gaines and the Sixth U.S. Infantry from St. Louis joined the Illinois volunteers. Reluctantly, Black Hawk agreed to stay on the west side of the Mississippi. However, in 1832, Black Hawk broke the treaty, and the soldiers stationed at Fort Armstrong readied for war. Again reinforcements arrived from St. Louis, along with local volunteers ready to remove Black Hawk to the west of the Mississippi. The civilian volunteers included future presidents Abraham Lincoln and Zachary Taylor, Confederate president Jefferson Davis, presidential candidate Winfield Scott, as well as other notables. With Black Hawk's defeat, the threat of Indian conflict no longer existed, and the white settlers did not need protection. The soldiers at Fort Armstrong were relocated to Fort Snelling in the Minnesota Territory. From 1840 to 1845, the fort became an arms depot supplying soldiers on the frontier. In 1855, arsonists burned the buildings at the fort.

—Mary F. McKenna

See also
Black Hawk; Black Hawk Purchase; Black Hawk War; Fox; Sauk

For Further Reading
Jackson, Donald, ed. 1995. *Black Hawk: An Autobiography.* Champaign: University of Illinois Press; Rock Island Arsenal Historical Branch. 1966. *A Short History of Fort Armstrong.* Rock Island, IL: Rock Island Arsenal Historical Branch; Tillinghast, B. F. 1898. *Rock Island Arsenal in Peace and War.* Rock Island, IL: B. F. Tillinghast; U.S. Arsenal, Rock Island, IL. 1954. *A History of Rock Island and*

the Rock Island from the Earliest Times to 1954. Rock Island, IL: U.S. Army, Rock Island Arsenal.

ARMSTRONG, JOHN (1758–1843)

As American minister to France from 1804 to 1810, John Armstrong tried unsuccessfully to secure West Florida for the United States and define the western boundary of the Louisiana Purchase.

Being Robert R. Livingston's brother-in-law and a senator from New York, Armstrong was selected for this task to maintain an alliance between the Republicans of New York and Virginia. Armstrong was somewhat hampered in his mission by his limited finances, his inability to speak French, and his fear that Madison had spies planted among the American community in Paris.

Monroe and Livingston had concluded that, unbeknownst to France and Spain, West Florida was both part of the retrocession to France and the Louisiana Purchase. Jefferson accepted that theory, and it formed the basis for Madison's instructions to Armstrong. Armstrong expected French help in convincing Spain to cede West Florida, but the mission was doomed almost from the start, as Talleyrand denied the American claim on December 21, 1804. In response, Armstrong advised that the United States to seize the disputed territory. He would repeat this advice whenever negotiations deadlocked.

Napoleon's attitude toward the Armstrong mission and the West Florida question depended on French military fortunes. In September 1805 an unnamed agent presented Armstrong with several proposals in Talleyrand's handwriting. The agent said that France would ensure the delivery of West Florida if the United States granted commercial privileges to France and Spain in that territory, agreed to a boundary at the Rio Colorado and a thirty-league neutral zone on either side, agreed that claims against Spain would be paid by bills on the Spanish colonies, and paid $10 million to Spain. Armstrong objected to the concessions and balked at the purchase price. The agent lowered the price to $7 million, and Armstrong agreed to submit the proposals to Madison.

Before Armstrong's dispatch arrived, the cabinet agreed to offer $5 million for the Floridas. Jefferson presented Armstrong's letter on November 19, and the cabinet agreed to the proposals with the exception of the purchase price. Formal instructions to Armstrong and James Bowdoin, appointed as joint commissioners, were delayed until the passage of the Two Million Dollar Bill in February 1806. Instructions based on Armstrong's dispatch of September 1805 arrived in Paris on April 28, 1806.

As a result of a series of military victories, France no longer needed the money an arrangement with Spain might have produced, and thus took a harder line against the United States. When pressed by Armstrong, Talleyrand blamed the reversal of policy on the fact that Bowdoin's secretary had leaked the secret proposal to Spain. Armstrong attempted to reopen negotiations in May 1806, telling Talleyrand that the United States was willing to put the Florida matter at Napoleon's disposal. Talleyrand responded by showing Armstrong a note from Spain indicating that Spain would not cede the Floridas. A fitful round of back-channel negotiations ended when Talleyrand left for Prussia with Napoleon on September 25, 1806. By October, Armstrong was convinced that his mission would end in failure.

Armstrong, trying to revive negotiations on June 16, 1807, presented three "hypotheses" to Talleyrand. Under the first, the United States would accept the Rio Bravo and the Mississippi as the boundaries of Louisiana if Spain ceded the territory just east of the Mississippi. Under the second, the United States would exchange the territory between the Colorado and the Bravo for the land between the Mississippi and the Apalachicola. Under the third, Spain would cede the Floridas and the United States would pay an unspecified sum for the Sabine River as the western boundary, or a larger sum for the Colorado. Talleyrand gave no definite response. In August 1807, Armstrong pressed Champagny (later Duke of Cadore) for an answer on the western boundary, and received copies of the French treaty with Spain.

The growing conflict between the United States and Great Britain on the one hand, and France and Spain on the other, seemed to offer Armstrong an opening. In February 1808, Napoleon hinted that he would acquiesce in the American occupation of the Floridas if the United States declared war on Great Britain. When Armstrong sought a clarification, Napoleon criticized the United States for its supposed submission to Great Britain. Armstrong advised Madison that the United States should seize the Floridas, but Madison did not believe Napoleon would accept such a move.

Armstrong spent most of his last two years in France dealing with commercial regulations. He returned home to a hero's welcome, at least among Republicans, in 1810. As secretary of war in 1813, Armstrong directed the campaign to occupy Mobile and guarantee American possession of West Florida.

—*Robert W. Smith*

See also

Bonaparte, Napoleon; Jefferson, Thomas; Livingston, Robert R.; Madison, James; Mississippi River; Talleyrand-Perigord, Charles Maurice de; Texas; West Florida

For Further Reading

Cox, Isaac J. 1918. *The West Florida Controversy, 1798–1813: A Study in American Diplomacy.* Baltimore: Johns Hopkins Press; DeConde, Alexander. 1976. *This Affair of Louisiana.* New York: Charles Scribner's Sons; Egan, Clifford L. 1983. *Neither Peace nor War: Franco-American Relations, 1803–1812.* Baton Rouge: Louisiana State University Press; Skeen, C. Edward. 1981. *John Armstrong, Jr. 1758–1843: A Biography.* Syracuse, NY: Syracuse University Press.

ASHLEY, WILLIAM HENRY (1778?–1838)

Born in Virginia in approximately 1778, William Henry Ashley moved to Kentucky in 1798. He arrived in the Louisiana Territory in 1802 and had moved to St. Genevieve by 1805, where he became acquainted with Andrew Henry. Unsuccessful as a merchant, he joined with Henry in 1811 to operate lead and saltpeter mines.

Ashley gained leadership experience as a lieutenant colonel of the Missouri Territorial Militia during the War of 1812. He entered politics in 1820 in St. Louis, when he won election as lieutenant governor of the new state of Missouri. In 1821 he achieved the title of brigadier general of the state militia and decided to enter into the Rocky Mountain fur trade in partnership with Henry.

In 1822, Ashley and Henry ventured forth to establish a fort on the Yellowstone River. Their 1823 expedition brought west several new men who would eventually make their mark on the fur trade: Thomas Fitzpatrick, David Jackson, and William Sublette. Others, such as James Clyman and Jedediah Smith, were already connected to the Ashley-Henry enterprise.

Andrew Henry dissolved his partnership with Ashley in 1823, just as new discoveries promised success. Ashley had sent Jedediah Smith to explore the Green River country, a region he found to be thick with beaver. Ashley would move in coming years to exploit this new bonanza of "soft gold." In April 1825, Ashley divided his men into several smaller groups and sent them off to trap various sections of the Green River country. The groups of trappers would operate independently until early July, when they would all return to gather at a predetermined location on the Henry's Fork of the Green River for what Ashley termed a "randavoze."

Meanwhile, Ashley descended the Green River, passing through Flaming Gorge and Lodore Canyon. On a cliff in the canyon he carved his name and the date of his visit, a landmark that John Wesley Powell noted during his 1869 expedition. Below Lodore Canyon, Ashley met Taos-based trappers under Etienne Provost, who described the region downstream as poor in beaver. Armed with the information, Ashley and his men turned back north, trapping in and around the Uinta Mountains.

Returning to the appointed place on the Henry's Fork of the Green River in early July, Ashley found 120 men—his own and a number of former Hudson's Bay Company *engagés.* Ashley gathered some nine thousand beaver pelts at the rendezvous, and he and Smith undertook to return with them to St. Louis. On the Missouri they met an Army expedition, whose commanders they convinced to transport the cargo of furs to St. Louis aboard their keelboats.

Ashley's men remained in the mountains and continued to hunt beaver until the following summer. Meanwhile, Ashley and Smith assembled a new outfit and returned upriver for the second annual rendezvous, this time on the Weber River. During the summer of 1826, Ashley sold his business to Smith, Jackson, and Sublette. Ashley's involvement in the fur trade would now be to bring goods up from St. Louis to supply the trappers at their rendezvous, in trade for their furs, which he would then return to St. Louis to sell. Meanwhile, the trappers would remain in the mountains all year, trapping as independent operators—or "free trappers"—rather than as fur company employees. The rendezvous system pioneered by Ashley gave rise to the "golden age" of the mountain man.

Now a successful trader, Ashley revived his political career in Missouri. In 1831, he was elected to the U.S. House of Representatives as a Democrat. He served as a congressman until 1836, when he ran unsuccessfully for governor of Missouri (this time as a Whig, because of differences with Jackson over the Second Bank of the United States). Ashley died of pneumonia on March 26, 1838.

William Henry Ashley played an important role in the exploration of the West, being among the first to travel, along with Jedediah Smith, the Platte River route that eventually became the Oregon Trail. Ashley and his men contributed much to the geographical knowledge of the Mountain West. As an entrepreneur in the fur trade, Ashley's great innovation of the rendezvous system allowed trappers to remain in the field year-round and did away with the need to operate and maintain trading posts and forts. The rendezvous system made possible that icon of the far-Western fur trade: the mountain man.

—Douglas W. Dodd

See also

Fur Trapping; Missouri; Rendezvous System; Smith, Jedediah Strong.

For Further Reading

Carter, Harvey L. 1969. "William H. Ashley." In *The Mountain Men and the Fur Trade of the Far West,* vol. 7. Edited by LeRoy R. Hafen. Glendale, CA: A. H. Clark; Clokey, Richard M. 1980. *William H. Ashley: Enterprise and Politics in the Trans-Mississippi West.* Norman: University of Oklahoma Press; Wishart, David. 1999. "William Henry Ashley." In *American National Biography,* vol. 1. Edited by John A. Garraty and Mark Carnes. New York: Oxford University Press.

ASSINIBOINE

The Assiniboine, whose name derives from Cree or Ojibwa references to cooking with hot stones, are a Siouan-speaking people of the Northern Plains. Having split from the Sioux before 1640, the Assiniboine moved from the western Great Lakes to the western portion of the present-day Canadian province of Manitoba during the eighteenth century. By the early

After they signed treaties with U.S. authorities, the Assiniboine regularly exchanged trade goods with federal forces at Fort Union in present-day North Dakota.

nineteenth century, the Assiniboine lived between the Missouri and Assiniboine Rivers, with a substantial number later moving south to the upper Missouri River, east of the Milk River, in the present-day state of Montana.

Like many nomadic Plains peoples, the Assiniboine were organized in a loose alliance of largely autonomous bands, each with prominent leaders or headmen. Nevertheless, the people of these bands, of which there were a half-dozen to a dozen or more, considered themselves to be one people. In the seventeenth and eighteenth centuries, Assiniboine economic activities reflected their location on the boundary between the wooded northern parklands and vast southern plains of the present-day Canadian West. There they moved from season to season, trapping and fishing in spring along the parkland margin, turning to the Plains for raids, bison hunts, and trade with Missouri River villagers during the summer. With the approach of winter, they returned to the northern parklands. The Assiniboine adopted the horse late in the eighteenth century but never maintained large herds, even as they increasingly made bison hunting the focus of their economic activities.

In the early eighteenth century, the Assiniboine became middlemen in the bayside trade of the British Hudson Bay Company. They gained substantial advantage from that role and maintained this favorable position through their access to firearms and alliances with the Cree and Ojibwa. The advent of an inland trade in the mid–eighteenth century, with the establishment of posts throughout the interior of the present-day Canadian West, eventually eliminated the Assiniboine from their middleman role. But the inland trade also afforded a new opportunity. The posts of the Hudson Bay Company and the Montréal-based North West Company required vast amounts of food, and the Assiniboine became provisioners to the trade, supplying pemmican (a mixture of pulverized bison meat, fat, and berries) until displaced by the Red River Métis, the mixed-blood descendants of European traders and Indian peoples, in the mid–nineteenth century.

Trade provided material advantages to the Assiniboine, but in the eighteenth and nineteenth centuries it also brought alien diseases, often with disastrous consequences. For example, an 1818–1820 outbreak of whooping cough and measles devastated the Assiniboine, killing perhaps as many as half of their number and reducing their population to approximately three thousand. Other epidemics, such as the 1837–1838 outbreak of smallpox on the Northern Plains, further reduced their numbers. This, in combination with the expanding power and presence of the Sioux, left the Assiniboine in an increasingly precarious position as the nineteenth century advanced. Consequently, the Assiniboine sought new allies, even among former enemies such as the Gros Ventre. During the second half of the nineteenth century, some Assiniboine closely associated themselves with the Gros Ventre, and would later come to share the Fort Belknap reservation with them.

The expansion of the United States would also shape the future of many Assiniboine. But in the early nineteenth century, most Assiniboine lived at, or beyond, the limits of the Louisiana Purchase and maintained close contact with British traders. Although the Assiniboine figured in early American diplomatic efforts, their remove ensured a relationship conducted, at least initially, with little direct interaction. Meriwether Lewis and William Clark promised the Mandan and the Hidatsa that American trade would end their burdensome trade with the Assiniboine. But the Corps of Discovery made only a modest diplomatic initiative with a few Assiniboine bands, and otherwise avoided the Assiniboine for fear they might impede the expedition's progress.

For several decades after the Corps of Discovery's journey, the Assiniboine had little official contact with representatives of the United States, even as they came to participate directly in the American buffalo robe trade. Like many Northern Plains tribes, the Assiniboine viewed the newly arriving American traders and troops not as a enemies but as partners in trade and allies in defense against rival Indian nations. The Assiniboine in Canada would settle on several reserves in the Canadian provinces of Alberta and Saskatchewan. Those in the United States settled on two reservations in present-day Montana, Fort Peck and Fort Belknap, where despite the dramatic transformation of life during the late nineteenth and early twentieth centuries, they have displayed a remarkable continuity of culture and distinct identity as a people.

—J. Wendel Cox

See also
Gros Ventre; Hidatsa; Mandan; Oglala Sioux; Santee Sioux

For Further Reading
Denig, Edwin Thompson. 1961. *Five Indian Tribes of the Upper Missouri: Sioux, Arickaras, Assiniboines, Crees, Crows.* Edited by John C. Ewers. Norman and London: University of Oklahoma Press; Fowler, Loretta. 1987. *Shared Symbols, Contested Meanings: Gros Ventre Culture and History, 1778–1984.* Ithaca, NY: Cornell University Press; Ray, Arthur J. 1974. *Indians in the Fur Trade: Their Role as Trappers, Hunters, and Middlemen in the Lands Southwest of Hudson Bay, 1660–1870.* Toronto and Buffalo: University of Toronto Press.

ASTOR, JOHN JACOB (1763–1848)

A key figure in the Western expansion of the fur trade and the wealthiest man in America by the 1830s, John Jacob Astor was born to a butcher's family in Waldorf, Germany, on July 17, 1763. Following his older brothers, Astor made his way to London in 1779 and then to New York in 1784, initially hoping to establish a market for musical instruments made in his brother's London factory. He simultaneously pursued an interest in the fur trade, investing the proceeds from the sale of his first batch of sample flutes in furs, and was soon involved in the import-export business. Astor married Sarah Todd in 1785, and by the end of that year was advertising both imported musical instruments and furs for sale in New York. A growing network of business connections provided access to partners and capital that soon extended his reach to the fur-trading centers of Albany and Montreal, eventually allowing Astor to play a critical role in the North West Company's first trading venture to China in 1792, by sidestepping British trade regulations and shipping furs through his New York firm. He began to invest in New York real estate around that time as well.

Astor dramatically expanded his position in the fur trade after 1794, when Jay's Treaty removed barriers to his trade with Canadian trappers. He subsequently increased his investment in the China trade, exporting furs and importing tea and silks, and began to purchase his own ships in 1803 to reduce shipping costs. Always looking to diversify his investments, Astor also continued to purchase New York City real estate, and he moved his family (by now he had five children) to a fashionable Broadway residence that same year. Following the return of the Lewis and Clark Expedition in 1806, Astor became a driving force in the American conquest of the West, founding the American Fur Company in 1808 to challenge British-Canadian interests along the northern boundary of the Louisiana Purchase. Rising tensions with Britain, however, soon led to an embargo that made the China trade more attractive and prompted Astor to consider establishing an outpost on the Columbia River; such an outpost would provide access to the untapped resources beyond the Rocky Mountains as well as a more direct shipping route to the Orient. The Pacific Fur Company was created for that purpose in 1810, and a plan was developed to send two expeditions, one by land and one by sea, to establish the new post near the mouth of the Columbia. Although most of the sea party arrived safely to found the settlement of Astoria in the spring of 1811, the ship, its crew, and much of their supplies were destroyed soon after, when the ship's powder magazine exploded during an Indian attack brought on by the captain's incompetence. The overland party fared no better, getting lost and eventually splitting into three groups that arrived separately in the winter of 1812, having lost a quarter of their number. Astoria stood as a challenge to British claims to the Pacific Northwest only until the War of 1812 broke out. Then, despite Astor's pleas to the government for military assistance, the British exercised control over the region, and the American traders at Astoria sold the entire enterprise to the North West Company in October 1813, at a loss.

Despite the failure of the Astoria project, John Jacob Astor profited handsomely from the war. His real estate investments and purchase of government bonds secured his financial future, while the settlement of the conflict led directly to his control of the Mississippi trading networks of his former competitors. Consolidation in the fur trade continued as Astor's American Fur Company expanded up the Missouri River, moving quickly after his successful effort in 1821 to persuade Congress to abolish the government-sponsored factory system that had competed with private enterprise since 1796. After changing fashion reduced demand for beaver pelts and overtrapping made them harder to secure, declining profits led Astor to retire from the trade in 1834 to concentrate on managing his vast fortune and, in particular, his real estate holdings, which exceeded in value some $4 million at the beginning of the decade. Upon his death on March 29, 1848, his net worth was estimated at $8 million to $10 million, the bulk of which he left to his children, while less than $500,000 was dedicated to philanthropic causes. Remembered for his wealth, Astor was also a pioneer businessman whose innovative practices helped Americans penetrate the West and served as an example for the generation of capitalists that drove the Industrial Revolution.

—Derek R. Larson

See also

American Fur Company; Oregon Country

For Further Reading

Haeger, John Denis. 1991. *John Jacob Astor: Business and Finance in the Early Republic.* Detroit: Wayne State University Press; Lavender, David. 1964. *The Fist in the Wilderness.* Garden City, NY: Doubleday and Company; Ronda, James P. 1990. *Astoria & Empire.* Lincoln: University of Nebraska Press.

ATKINSON, FORT

In August 1804, the Lewis and Clark Expedition held council with the Oto and Missouri Indians beside the Missouri River in present-day Nebraska. They named this meeting place Council-bluff and believed it to be a most favorable location for a fort and trading post. Lewis and Clark proved correct, and at the Council-bluff site the Sixth Infantry, under the command of Colonel Henry Atkinson, built Camp Missouri in 1819. Camp Missouri was located approximately sixteen miles north of present-day Omaha, Nebraska.

However, Missouri River floodwaters inundated Camp Missouri in 1820, and a new fort was constructed on the top of a bluff overlooking the river. The post was named Fort Atkinson, in honor of Colonel Atkinson, who had commanded the first garrison. The Sixth Infantry set up post there, and with the promotion of Colonel Atkinson shortly thereafter, Colonel Henry Leavenworth assumed command.

At the time, Fort Atkinson was the westernmost military garrison of the United States. Its purpose was to offer protection for the fur trade. Following a previous period of decline, the fur trade was undergoing a revival during the 1820s in the lands out West, particularly on the upper Missouri and in the mountain West. Many famous mountain men and fur traders passed through Fort Atkinson as they made their way westward. These included Edward Rose, Louis Vasquez, Jim Bridger, Hugh Glass, and Jedediah Smith.

With a population of more than a thousand at the fort, a myriad of activities took place. There was a public library, a school (the first public school in Nebraska), and even amateur theatrical performances, with officers and their wives in leading roles.

For the most part, life at Fort Atkinson was tedious and boring. When soldiers were not drilling, they farmed their own crops, such as corn, potatoes, carrots, wheat, and hay, on large post farms. The day-to-day drudgery led to a problem with drunkenness, resulting in several courts-martial. As Colonel Leavenworth noted in one report, thirty-six men were court-martialed for drunkenness immediately following a payday.

The monotony of garrison life was suddenly interrupted in 1823 when General William H. Ashley (leader of a fur trading company on the upper Missouri) sent pleas for help to Colonel Leavenworth. The Arikara Indians had attacked Ashley's party near the mouth of the Grand River, inflicting several casualties. Ashley had retreated to a defensive position near present-day Chamberlain, South Dakota, and waited for help to punish the Arikara. Colonel Leavenworth, upon receiving Ashley's request, mustered the garrison. The colonel selected 220 men and led the Sixth Infantry Regiment, along with thirty trappers.

The Sixth Infantry headed up the Missouri River to do battle with the Arikara. Along the way, 80 additional trappers and 400 Sioux warriors—the Sioux being traditional enemies of the Arikara—joined them. After traveling several hundred miles, the force arrived at the Arikara village in South Dakota. The six-pounder cannon they had taken with them was set on a hill and fired lead balls into the Arikara village, while troopers and Sioux fought the Arikara outside the walls. In the ensuing battle, Chief Gray Eyes of the Arikara and forty warriors were killed. The Arikara sued for peace, thus ending the Arikara War of 1823. The action of the Sixth Infantry in this conflict is commemorated with a battle streamer attached to the group's regimental color. The streamer reads "South Dakota, 1823." It was during this war that six soldiers lost their lives by drowning in the mighty Missouri River—they were the first U.S. soldiers to die in the Indian wars of the West.

Only one other major expedition left Fort Atkinson. In 1825, approximately five hundred men went up the Missouri to make a show of force and conclude treaties with the Indian tribes on the upper Missouri. The mission proved successful when treaties were consummated with seventeen Indian tribes.

Following the expedition of 1825, life at Fort Atkinson returned to its usual drudgery. Isolated hundreds of miles from American civilian settlements, the fort had achieved its goals of protecting the local fur trade, representing the U.S. government in the West, and keeping peace with the Indians.

However, once the fur trade had shifted farther to the west, the War Department eventually questioned the need for Fort Atkinson. Inspector George Crogham went to Fort Atkinson in 1825 and declared the fort weak and the garrison poorly trained. Two years later Fort Atkinson was abandoned, and the Sixth Infantry was transferred to Jefferson Barracks near St. Louis.

—*Gene Mueller*

See also

Ashley, William Henry; Bridger, James; Council Bluffs, Iowa; Lewis and Clark Expedition

For Further Reading

Kivett, Marvin, and Sally Johnson. 1959. "Fort Atkinson on the Council Bluffs." *Nebraska History.* Lincoln: University of Nebraska Press; Ney, Virgil. 1977. "Daily Life at Fort Atkinson on the Missouri 1820–27." Parts 1 and 2. *Military* Review 57 (I/2): 1:36–48; 2:50–66; Olson, James. 1955. *History of Nebraska.* Lincoln: University of Nebraska Press; Wesley, Edgar B. 1939. "Life at a Frontier Post: Fort Atkinson, 1823–1826." *Journal of the American Military History Foundation* 3: 202–209.

Best known for producing The Birds of America, *the ornithologist and artist John James Audubon traveled through much of the Louisiana Territory and painted birds of the region. (North Wind Picture Archives)*

AUDUBON, JOHN JAMES (1785–1851)

A naturalist and artist, John James Audubon produced scientific illustrations of the birds of the Louisiana Purchase that helped foster an appreciation of wildlife. Although he claimed New Orleans as his birthplace, Audubon was born Jean Rabin Fougère in Les Cayes, St. Dominque, the illegitimate son of a sea captain and a servant. Formally adopted by Captain Audubon and his legal wife in 1794, the boy received the name Jean-Jacques Fougère Audubon. The beneficiary of only a brief formal education, Audubon would always find it difficult to express himself in writing, either in his native tongue or in English. His father encouraged his artistic talents, however, sending the boy to learn portraiture in the school of the French artist David. To avoid conscription in the Napoleonic Wars, Audubon left France for the United States in 1803 and began to sketch birds at his father's farm in the Philadelphia area. In that same year, he met Lucy Bakewell. The couple married in 1808 and produced four children, two of whom survived into adulthood.

Audubon did not at first consider an artistic career, and he made a number of attempts to become established in business. While his business partner in a general store in Louisville, Kentucky, stayed behind the counter, Audubon spent his days tramping through the woods drawing birds. By 1810, Audubon's portfolio contained more than two hundred pictures of American birds; even at that time he was painting them life-size, generally in pastel, and using watercolors for the eyes, bills, and feet. After the dissolution of the partnership in 1809, Audubon continued as a merchant for a few more years, by which time he had run through all of his money. Jailed for debt in 1819, Audubon began to draw portraits to raise cash, and he soon realized that he had found a new profession. With the aim of publishing a comprehensive collection of American birds in their natural surroundings, Audubon planned a journey down the Ohio and Mississippi Rivers, to New Orleans, and then east to the Florida Keys. En route, he would find new specimens, dissect and draw them, study the countryside and vegetation, and make notes for the text that would accompany the drawings.

In October 1820, Audubon reached New Orleans, combing it for commissions to sketch portraits. He remained in the city for five months and then took a job as a tutor at Bayou Sara, Louisiana. Many of the pictures that later established his fame were drawn there. Contemporary representations of birds were usually wooden-looking, since artists sketched birds from stuffed specimens. Audubon determined to infuse his paintings with energy by wiring up freshly killed birds. In Feliciana Parish, Audubon established certain characteristics that are unmistakably his own: a concern for the living animal and an unequaled sense of drama, color, and design. Although finances remained a concern as he bounced from job to job, Audubon did manage to establish a reputation as an ornithologist by publishing scientific papers in such works as the *Annals of the Lyceum of Natural History* and the *Edinburgh Journal of Science*.

Having antagonized prominent naturalists and engravers in the United States by criticizing another avian artist, Audubon concluded that he had to travel to Europe to seek out engravers and printers for his *Birds of America* volumes, ultimately illustrated with 435 plates. He arrived in Liverpool in 1826 and soon discovered the support and fame that had eluded him in the United States. Audubon returned to America and stayed in Feliciana Parish until the end of 1829, when he left again for England. He engaged the young Scots naturalist William MacGillivray to correct the errors in his grammar and to supply the necessary zoological detail for his *Ornithological Biography* volumes. Audubon spent much of the 1830s in England, supervising the completion of both publication projects.

In 1839, with his newly acquired wealth, Audubon bought land in Carmansville, now Washington Heights, in New York City. In 1843 he embarked on an eight-month journey up the Missouri River to seek out mammals for *The Viviparous Quadrupeds of North America*. Audubon habitually displayed a callous attitude toward animal suffering, and he would often shoot hundreds of specimens of a species to make one illustration. During the Missouri trip, however, his attitude changed as he disgustedly witnessed the wanton slaughter of buffalo, and he now expressed concern about the effects of indiscriminate killing of wildlife. After the trip his health failed, and Audubon died in Carmansville on January 27, 1851.

—Caryn E. Neumann

For Further Reading

Chancellor, John. 1978. *Audubon*. New York: Viking Press; McDermott, John Francis, ed. 1965. *Audubon in the West*. Norman: University of Oklahoma Press; Streshinsky, Shirley. 1993. *Audubon: Life and Art in the American Wilderness*. New York: Villard Books.

B

BADLANDS

The term "badlands" refers to arid barren lands found in several Great Plains states, the most well known being the South Dakota Badlands, located in the southwestern corner of that state near the Black Hills. The geological processes that created the South Dakota Badlands began nearly sixty-five million years ago with the draining of the ancient Pierre Sea. In the eons that followed, floods, sand drifts, and strong winds deposited various layers of mudstone, limestone, sandstone, and shale over the ancient seabed. Approximately 500,000 years ago, wind and water began to erode the sediments, gradually carving out a multihued landscape dotted with startling spires and other unique formations.

In historic times, the Arikara and the Sioux were the first known native peoples to venture through the South Dakota Badlands, the Sioux moving into the region during the late eighteenth century. Although Arikara and Sioux oral traditions relate stories set in the Badlands, both tribes viewed the area as a place best avoided, since the harsh climate and lack of food and water made it ill suited for human habitation. The term "Badlands" is a translation of the French phrase *mauvaises terres pour traverser* ("bad lands to cross"), itself a rendition of the original Lakota (Teton Sioux) name, *mako sica.*

During the 1780s, Anglo-Celtic and French-Canadian fur traders from the Hudson's Bay Company and the North West Company began trading with the various Indian groups in the Northern Plains. During their travels in the region, these newcomers were struck by the austere environment, strange shapes, and scattered fossils they found. The stories of fur traders of the period spoke of a

The desolate landscape of the South Dakota Badlands was unappealing to many pioneers who sought territory that was better suited to support farming or ranching.

place of ancient, ruined cities filled with bones, difficult to survive in but nonetheless awe-inspiring. By the 1850s these tales had begun attracting curious scientists and travelers to the Badlands, and in the succeeding decades, Black Hills gold miners and U.S. Army battalions also traveled through the area. Although the South Dakota Badlands were not a major site of Indian-white conflict, just prior to the Wounded Knee Massacre of 1890, five hundred Sioux evading the U.S. Army sought refuge on a grassy table in the area known as the Stronghold.

For nineteenth-century Euro-American visitors, the Badlands were a fascinating, mythical landscape. The metaphor of ancient ruined cities helped them make sense of an utterly alien environment. It also provided them with an enchanting fiction linking America to an ancient civilization, much like the antiquity of Europe. At the same time, however, the Badlands posed a unique challenge to the perception of the American frontier, particularly the West, as a bountiful paradise. The harsh, bone-dry region led some travelers to depict the Badlands as a spiritual wasteland, a manifestation of hell on earth.

Following the cessation of armed conflict between the Sioux and the U.S. Army in the late nineteenth century, the Badlands attracted a new breed of visitors, who sought to develop the grasslands in the surrounding area for ranching and farming; those ventures, however, were short-lived. South Dakota politicians, most notably Senator Peter Norbeck, then struck upon the idea of developing the Badlands as a tourist destination. Throughout the early decades of the twentieth century, promoters sought congressional approval to designate the area a national park. They faced considerable opposition because of lingering doubts about the Badlands' place in the national culture. Unlike Yosemite and Yellowstone, the Badlands contained few of the natural resources that would make it attractive to those who saw the National Park Service as the guardian of the nation's threatened flora, fauna, and waterways.

Through the perseverance of Senator Norbeck and others, Congress finally recognized the Badlands as a National Monument in 1939, acknowledging the scientific value of the region as an important depository of fossil remains. In 1978, Congress reclassified the area a National Park. Since taking charge of the South Dakota Badlands, the National Park Service has reintroduced the buffalo and mountain goat into the region, and constructed a two-lane highway, allowing more than a million visitors a year to visit the park. Modern travelers venture to the Badlands to experience the park's haunting beauty and to see for themselves the story it tells about America's natural history. In an increasingly urbanized, industrialized world, the Badlands have also become a sacred destination for Americans seeking both physical and spiritual renewal. In the 1980s the Sioux recognized the Stronghold as a sacred site, thereby adding their contemporary imprint to the curious landscape.

—Melinda Marie Jetté

See also
Black Hills; Oglala Sioux; Santee Sioux; South Dakota

For Further Reading

Froiland, Sven. 1990. *Natural History of the Black Hills and Badlands.* Sioux Falls, SD: Center for Western Studies; Hall, Philip S. 1993. *Reflections on the Badlands.* Vermillion: University of South Dakota Press; Hauk, Joy K. 1987. *Badlands: Its Life and Landscape.* Interior, SD: Badlands Natural History Association; Shuler, Jay. 1987. *A Revelation Called the Badlands: Building a National Park, 1909–1939.* Interior, SD: Badlands Natural History Association.

BARATARIANS

See **Laffite, Jean**

BARBÉ-MARBOIS, FRANÇOIS, MARQUIS DE (1745–1837)

François the Marquis of Barbé-Marbois was a distinguished politician, diplomat, and the minister of the French treasury. During the final stages of the negotiations of the Louisiana Purchase, Barbé-Marbois acted as the French representative.

Working as an important advisor to Napoleon Bonaparte, François Barbé-Marbois hoped that the sale of Louisiana would block the British from claiming the colony. Furthermore, he believed that French finances would benefit from the sale. Barbé-Marbois was opposed to France's holding on to this territory because he saw Louisiana as a failing colonial possession; it had continually run a deficit under Spanish rule. Because of the slave rebellions in St. Domingue (Haiti), Napoleon Bonaparte decided to invest his military forces in the protection of that important sugar colony. Barbé-Marbois personally warned Bonaparte that the British might try to retake Louisiana from Canada, by moving down through the Great Lakes region. He realized that it would be too expensive and difficult to protect both Louisiana and St. Domingue.

Although Bonaparte's decision to sell Louisiana was generally unpopular in France, Barbé-Marbois was a strong supporter of the sale. His previous experience in St. Domingue as a French official had made him aware of the volatility of the French situation in the Americas. He urged Bonaparte to focus on the diplomatic situation in Europe, rather than trying to redevelop an American empire.

On April 11, 1803, Bonaparte ordered the opening of secret negotiations with Robert Livingston, the American minister in Paris, for the sale of Louisiana. Charles Maurice de Talleyrand, the French foreign minister, began the negotiations, but he was relieved of this duty when his loyalty was drawn into question. Like Bonaparte's brothers, Joseph and Lucien, Talleyrand had been bribed to oppose the sale of Louisiana. Barbé-Marbois was chosen to complete this important transaction. Napoleon singled out Barbé-Marbois because he had a reputation for honesty. Eventually President Thomas Jefferson sent James Monroe to Paris in the spring of 1803 to aid in negotiating the purchase of Louisiana. Both parties initialed the treaty on April 30, 1803.

Bonaparte thought that Louisiana was worth only fifty million francs, but Barbé-Marbois asked for one hundred million. The American and French negotiators ultimately reached a compromise of eighty million francs ($15 million), of which sum three-fourths went to France and one-fourth to Americans with outstanding claims against France. Each party believed that it had stuck the better deal. Barbé-Marbois's shrewd business sense won him great favor from Bonaparte. The money from the sale of Louisiana was essential for financing costly military actions against Great Britain when war broke out once more between the two countries in May 1803.

Barbé-Marbois's service to France outlines his credentials and achievements. His career as a government official began under Louis XVI in 1785, when he was named the head quartermaster (*intendant générale*) in St. Domingue. Barbé-Marbois tried to put a number of financial reforms into place there. These changes were popular with the French government and colonists, but they caused further tension between the colonists and the slaves. This conflict continued after Barbé-Marbois fled the island. Later, the situation erupted into open rebellion.

Upon his return to France in 1789, Barbé-Marbois held a short-lived position in the department of foreign affairs. During the turbulent years of the French Revolution, Barbé-Marbois returned to his native Metz, where he became mayor. Slowly, he began once more to take part in national politics.

Barbé-Marbois's political career took a brief turn for the worse on September 4, 1797, when the French authorities deported him to Guyana. This retaliation was probably the result of Barbé-Marbois's vocal criticisms of the finance practices of the Directory (October 27, 1795–November 10, 1799), in particular the large profits being made by the individuals who supplied the army. He was deported on the grounds of antipatriotism and was falsely accused of collaborating on the Treaty of Pillnitz. Barbé-Marbois was freed two years later, on 18 Brummaire, year VII (November 9, 1798). The French government revoked the accusations against him.

Upon his return to France, Barbé-Marbois re-established his political career and quickly gained a reputation for being scrupulous and honest. In 1800 he was elected to Conseil d'Etat, the main governing body of the French state. The following year, he was named the councilor of the state and director of the public treasury. During this period, Barbé-Marbois played a role in securing the Treaty of San Ildefonso (1800) with Spain, in which Louisiana was returned to France.

Barbé-Marbois's political astuteness and his good fortune in the changing political tides helped him to survive a number of turbulent regimes. His role in negotiating the Louisiana Purchase was certainly one of the crowning achievements of his political and diplomatic career.

—*Rachel Eden Black*

See also

Diplomacy of the Louisiana Purchase; San Ildefonso, Treaty of

For Further Reading

Barbé-Marbois, François. 1829. *Histoire de la Louisiane et de la cession de cette colonie par la France aux Etats-Unis.* Paris; de Morembert, Tribout. 1958. "Une famille d'ancienne bourgeoisie messine et ses alliances: Barbé et Barbé de Marbois." *Cahiers lorrains.*

BARING BROTHERS

The bank founded in London in 1763 by John and Francis Baring would become one of the leading financial institutions in the world during the nineteenth century. Under the direction of Francis Baring, John and Francis Baring and Company, later Baring Brothers and Company, became heavily involved in the financial future of the young United States. In 1803, Baring Brothers, together with Hope and Company of Amsterdam, underwrote the financing of the loan for the Louisiana Purchase.

At the end of the American Revolution, Francis Baring had reestablished his family's links with several important financiers in Philadelphia, including Robert Morris and William (later Senator) Bingham, who was reputed to be the wealthiest man in the United States. Created a baronet in 1793 and becoming a member of the British House of Commons in 1794, Sir Francis dispatched his second son, Alexander Baring, to the United States in 1795 to oversee the development of the Baring interests in the vast Maine land holdings of Senator Bingham. In 1798, Alexander Baring married Bingham's daughter, Anna Louise, and their union produced nine children, creating in Baring an attachment to, and sympathy for, the young republic. The family bank frequently acted as the unofficial banker to the government of the United States; working with Rufus King, the American minister in London, Baring Brothers managed payments to the Barbary pirates, procured arms for the Adams administration, and helped President Jefferson liquidate the administration's holdings and debt to the Bank of the United States in 1802. When Bird, Savage, and Bird, the London banking agents for the U.S. government, failed in February 1803, Baring Brothers took up the appointment; until 1867 it remained the sole financial agent of the federal government in London.

Alexander Baring had returned to London by 1803, and when Napoleon Bonaparte refused to accept American securities for the purchase of Louisiana, demanding specie, Baring arranged to meet his brother-in-law, Pierce Cesar Labouchere, who was a partner of Hope and Company in Amsterdam, a bank associated with Baring Brothers and one in which Alexander had served his apprenticeship. An agreement was quickly made with the Marquis de Barbé-Marbois, who was acting for Napoleon, and the young Baring is credited with lowering French demands to just $15 million, $3.75 million of which was to be set aside to pay American claims against France. The two bankers promised to pay Napoleon the cash in three installments, as well as broker the bonds that underwrote the purchase. Although Sir Francis was initially concerned with the size of the transaction, the Barings' involvement in the management of the bonds, at 6 percent interest, eventually made Baring Brothers more than $3 million in commissions.

Elected to Parliament in 1806, Alexander Baring took over the main management of the bank following the death of his father in 1810. In Parliament he opposed the restrictive commercial practices then being followed by Britain toward the United States and published *An Inquiry into the Causes and Consequences of the Orders in Council* (1808). During the War of 1812, Baring maintained European financial confidence in the United States by providing funds to meet the interest payments of U.S. bond-holders. Created Baron Ashburton in 1842, he visited America to conclude the Wester-Ashburton Treaty (1842), which helped settle the American-Canadian border dispute.

Baring Brothers made many contributions to the financial infrastructure and commercial development of the state of Louisiana. In 1824 it helped Vincent Nolte and Company raise a loan to pave Rue Royale in New Orleans. Baring Brothers speculated in cotton bonds, especially those issued by the Consolidated Association of the Planters of Louisiana, and in 1832 it agreed to market the entire $7 million Louisiana state loan issue. In the same year, it helped charter and fund the Union Bank of Louisiana. The company had become so powerful by 1818 that the duc de Richelieu, Louis XVIII's chief minister, described Baring Brothers as one of the six great powers of Europe. The bank, however, oversaw the loan of vast amounts of British capital to the government of Argentina in the 1880s, and when Argentina defaulted, it involved Baring Brothers in a general financial crisis in 1890. Rescued by the Bank of England and reorganized as a limited company, it finally went bankrupt in 1995 when an employee lost $1.5 billion in unauthorized futures speculation.

—*Rory T. Cornish*

See also
Hope and Company

For Further Reading

Hidy, Ralph W. 1949. *The House of Baring in American Trade and Finance: English Merchant Bankers at Work, 1763–1861*. Cambridge: Harvard University Press; Perkins, Bradford. 1967. *The First Rapprochement: England and the United States 1795–1805*. Berkeley: University of California Press; Zegler, Philip. 1988. *The Sixth Great Power: Barings 1762–1929*. London: Collins.

BASTROP, BARON DE (1759–1827)

Baron de Bastrop was a land developer and Indian agent in Spanish Louisiana whose loss of influence following the Louisiana Purchase led to his removal to Texas and eventual partnership with Stephen F. Austin. Born Philip Hendrik Nering Bögel in Dutch Guiana, he grew up in the Netherlands, where he served in the military and as a tax collector. In 1782 he married Georgine Wolffeline Françoise Lijcklama à Nyeholt, with whom he had five children before accusations of embezzlement led him to abandon the family in 1793. He fled to North America, where he took up aristocratic airs and the pseudonym Baron de Bastrop.

Beginning in 1795, Bastrop was active on the Spanish-U.S. frontier, befriending Spanish officials, forming business partnerships in mercantile ventures, and promoting colonization schemes. The biggest plan with which Bastrop associated himself was the establishment of a large settlement in the Ouachita Valley of what is today northern Louisiana. In 1796 he signed a contract with Governor Baron de Carondelet for the settlement of European immigrant families in an area of approximately 850,000 acres on the east side of the Ouachita River. Bastrop hoped to secure the families in Louisville, Kentucky, offering each approximately 340 acres. For his effort, he was given exclusive milling and marketing privileges to all the wheat produced by the colonists. By May 1797, Bastrop had ninety-nine settlers—including seventeen families and eleven single men—clearing and planting land within the grant, and he had obtained permission to build two mills, on Bayous Siard and Bartholomew. The colonization project was suspended shortly thereafter, however, on the recommendation of Louisiana's financial officer, who declared the government without the funds necessary to meet its obligations to subsidize the travel and startup costs of the colonists. Although Bastrop retained trusteeship in the land, the project never resumed. Control of the land changed hands several times, and eventually part of it fell into the hands of Aaron Burr. The town of Bastrop, located within the boundaries of the colony, remains as a reminder of the Dutch entrepreneur's impact on late Spanish Louisiana.

With the suspension of the colonization enterprise, the baron turned to a series of commercial ventures in Louisiana and Kentucky. A partnership with John Nancarrow of Lexington, Kentucky, to operate a sailcloth factory lasted from 1799 to 1800 but fell victim to a rising number of lawsuits against Bastrop. The following year the baron obtained exclusive trading privileges with area Indians from Governor General Marqués de Casa Calvo, conducting the business out of his plantation at the mouth of Bayou Siard, just north of Fort Miró (now Monroe). He also operated a mill and warehouses on the property. The Louisiana Purchase brought an end to his lucrative monopoly over Indian trade and may have exposed the baron to renewed legal action regarding old debts in Kentucky.

By 1805, Bastrop had sold off his plantation, handed out deeds to some of the early settlers, and made his way to Texas under the Spanish Crown's offer to allow the migration of any subject wishing not to come under U.S. jurisdiction. Bastrop settled in San Antonio, where he advanced new colonization schemes, entered yet other mercantile partnerships, started a freighting business, and became a leading member of the community. Although his plan to establish a colony near the Trinity River came to nothing, Bastrop did become one of the most important actors in the Anglo-American colonization of Texas. In December 1820, when Moses Austin arrived in San Antonio seeking permission of the Spanish authorities to establish a colony of three hundred Catholic American families in Texas, it was the Baron de Bastrop who gained an audience for Austin with Governor Antonio Martínez. His previous experience with colonization under Spanish rule made him an invaluable ally to Stephen F. Austin, who carried out the first successful colonization effort in Texas during the 1820s. Bastrop not only acted as Austin's land commissioner during 1823–1826 but also served the cause of colonization in the Coahuila y Texas state legislature until his death at Saltillo, on February 23, 1827.

—Jesús F. de la Teja

See also
Burr, Aaron; Carondelet, Louis Francisco Hector de; Casa-Calvo, Sebastián Calvo de la Puerta y O'farrill, Marqués de

For Further Reading
Bacarisse, Charles A. 1955. "Baron de Bastrop." *Southwestern Historical Quarterly* 58, no. 3: 319–330; Moore, Richard W. 1948. "The Role of the Baron de Bastrop in the Anglo-American Settlement of the Spanish Southwest." *Louisiana Historical Quarterly* 31, no. 3: 606–681.

BECKNELL, WILLIAM (c. 1796–1865)

William Beckneil was born near Franklin, Missouri, about 1796. Little is known of his early life. He was twenty-five years of age when he undertook the events that were to earn him the title "Father of the Santa Fe Trail." Not only was he the "father" of the trail but he also was the founder of the Santa Fe trade. He led the first successful trading expedition to Santa Fe following the end of Spanish rule in Mexico. Spanish law did not permit U.S. citizens to trade in Mexico. That rule was promptly overturned as soon as Mexico declared her independence in 1821.

Becknell placed an advertisement in the June 20, 1821, issue of the [Franklin] *Missouri Intelligencer* calling for a company of seventy men "to go westward for the purpose of trading for horses and mules and catching wild animals of every description." Although Santa Fe is not mentioned by name, it is difficult to believe that the proposed expedition would have been headed anywhere else "westward." Yet recent scholarship has suggested that Becknell's original plan was to trade with the Indians, and that the movement to Santa Fe was an afterthought.

The party rendezvoused at the home of Ezekiel Williams, near Franklin, on August 4. The expedition was assembled and departed for the West shortly thereafter. It crossed the Missouri River at Arrow Rock on September 1, and the expedition reached the Great Bend of the Arkansas on September 24 and entered Santa Fe on November 16.

Becknell and his party of traders followed the trail laid out by mountain men en route to the fur-bearing regions of the Rocky Mountains. The trail followed the Arkansas River westward into the mountains where Becknell had intended to remain and trade with the Indians, but, having fallen in with a party of Mexicans, he was induced to take his party on to Santa Fe. There the traders sold all of their goods at a handsome profit.

Becknell, with a single companion (John McLoughlin, who is not otherwise described, but who had been a member of the westbound expedition), departed from San Miguel, New Mexico, on December 13. They reached Franklin, Missouri, on January 29, 1822.

The favorable report that he brought back led to another trading expedition in the spring of 1822. There were actually two separate parties that went west in 1822. The first left Franklin in April under the leadership of Broxton Cooper. That party made the journey safely and returned to Missouri the following autumn. Becknell and his trading group left Arrow Rock on May 22 with twenty-one men and three wagons. They encountered a band of Osage just west of the Missouri but well to the east of the Arkansas Crossing—probably at Pawnee Rock. After much negotiation, led by a member of the Chouteau family who spoke their language and had traded with the tribe in the past, the Osage permitted the party to pass.

The journey from the Arkansas to San Miguel, the first Spanish settlement in New Mexico, consumed twenty-two days. San Miguel is located about fifty miles northeast of Santa Fe. This particular journey is of historic importance in that it was the first expedition to use the Cimarron River instead of following the Arkansas to the mountains and over the Raton Pass. It was also the first trip to bring wagons to Santa Fe. It would have been quite difficult to bring the wagons over the pass and then to Santa Fe.

The Cimarron Crossing became the favored route of the Santa Fe traders; most of the subsequent expeditions used the new route. That route also permitted soldiers to meet and escort trading parties in both directions, with Mexican troops guiding the traders to San Miguel and U.S. troops picking up the traders as they left Mexico. Because the newer trail bypassed Taos, parties used both routes during the same trading season.

When Becknell returned to Missouri in January 1822, he carried with him a message from the governor of New Mexico, Facundo Melgares. That message was that American traders would be welcome in Santa Fe and the surrounding towns and villages. This information was sufficient to make the Santa Fe Trail, which Becknell had pioneered, a reality.

Becknell retired from the Santa Fe trade in 1834 and moved to Texas, where he died in 1865.

—Henry H. Goldman

For Further Reading

Becknell, Thomas. 1910. "The Journals of Thomas [William] Becknell from Boone's Lick to Santa Fe and from Santa Cruz to Green River." *Missouri Historical Review* 4: 76–79; Chittenden, Hiram Martin. 1954. *A History of the American Fur Trade of the Far West.* 2 vols. Stanford, CA: Academic Reprints; Hayes, A. A., Jr. 1880. "The Santa Fe Trail." *Harper's New Monthly Magazine* 61: 185–196; Oliva, Leo E. 1967. *Soldiers on the Santa Fe Trail.* Norman: University of Oklahoma Press.

BECKWOURTH, JAMES (1798–1866)

African American trapper, frontiersman, navigator, and Indian chief, Jim Beckwourth participated in the exploration and settlement of the Louisiana Purchase territory. The son of a slave mother and an English father, James Pierson Beckwourth (sometimes spelled Beckwith) was born on April 6, 1798, in Fredericksburg, Virginia. He was the third of thirteen children, and at the age of seven, Jim and his family moved to the Louisiana Territory to farm between the Missouri and Mississippi Rivers near St. Louis.

A voyage down the Mississippi River to New Orleans as a teenager inspired Beckwourth to join General William Ashley's Rocky Mountain Fur Company so that he could explore and travel the West. Beckwourth followed the Missouri and Arkansas Rivers to collect furs, and along the way he dealt with Indians, learned the importance of buffaloes, and stood at the Continental Divide. By virtue of sheer ability he soon overcame the prejudice of others to become one of the best and highest paid Rocky Mountain trappers. General Ashley honored him with a trading post of his own, where he learned Indian customs, culture, and languages. By 1827, however, Beckwourth decided to leave the fur company and to become a free trapper.

In 1828 a Crow woman mistook Beckwourth for the long-lost son of a tribal chieftain and adopted the mulatto trapper into the tribe. He rose to the rank of war chief, and, by his own account, he was named head chief of the Crow Nation. While living with the Crow, Beckwourth began to trap for John Jacob Astor's American Fur Company and, for his own profit, he encouraged Indians to do the same. Beckwourth spent eight years with the Crow, living a nomadic life and fighting in countless Indian wars across the Louisiana Territory. Beckwourth's career with the fur company and the Crow nation ended in the summer of 1836 because of his restlessness and longing to be rich and famous.

On a trip to St. Louis in 1837, Beckwourth learned of his father's death, and shortly thereafter he was ready for a change in his life. Recruited by General William Gaines, Beckwourth and several other mountain men, who were valuable because of their ability to track and their knowledge of Indian-style warfare, left Louisiana to fight in the Second Seminole War in Florida. Beckwourth went to war to become famous but instead found it boringly routine. After ten months of tracking and scouting, he returned to St. Louis in the summer of 1838.

Beckwourth immediately found employment trapping for Andrew Sublette and Louis Vaszquez along the Santa Fe Trail. By 1840 he had begun establishing trading posts for the brothers William and Charles Bent in the Southwest. Beckwourth quit his job with the Bent brothers and established a store in present-day Taos, New Mexico. Never a man to stay in one place too long, Beckwourth and twenty other families headed north to the Arkansas River. Beckwourth then built an adobe fortress and founded and named the city of Pueblo, Colorado. But once again, his stay was short. His former employers, the Bent brothers, saw him as unwelcome competition, and tension with Mexico made him leave the far-western reaches of the Louisiana Territory for California.

Beckwourth arrived in present-day Los Angeles in January 1844 to trade and soon found himself embroiled in a revolt of American settlers in California against Mexico. Beckwourth and five other families packed their belongings, took stray horses, and headed back to Pueblo to avoid war. He fled to Pueblo and then headed to Santa Fe to open a successful hotel. In Santa Fe he became involved in the Mexican War, in which he carried dispatches and offered horses to the U.S. Army. The Gold Rush in 1848 convinced him to return to California, where he noticed a break in the Sierra Nevada Mountains. Today, the route is called Beckwourth's Pass. Near the pass are the town of Beckwourth, California, and Beckwourth Mountain.

Jim Beckwourth continued his nomadic life by working as a merchant in Denver in 1859 and taking part in the Cheyenne War of 1864. In 1866 the U.S. government asked him to establish peace with the Crow nation. He met with the Crow for the first time in thirty years, and they asked him to be a tribal chief. Beckwourth declined the offer, and the Crow offered him a farewell dinner. The Crow then poisoned his meal, so they could have his spirit, and he died immediately thereafter. Much of James Beckwourth's life would have escaped written history had he not recited his self-admiring autobiography to T. D. Bonner in 1856.

—*Nathan R. Meyer*

See also
Bent's Fort; Crow

For Further Reading
Bonner, T. D. 1972. *The Life and Adventures of James P. Beckwourth*. Lincoln: University of Nebraska Press; Wilson, Elinor. 1972. *Jim Beckwourth*. Norman: University of Oklahoma Press.

BELLEFONTAINE, FORT

Fort Bellefontaine was the first U.S. military installation and Indian agency to be established in the Louisiana Purchase territory. It was located on the south bank of the Missouri River, four miles above its confluence with the Mississippi.

General James Wilkinson, the military commander and superintendent of Indian affairs of the Louisiana Territory, selected the site for the first U.S. military installation west of the Mississippi River. The army built the fort near a large spring on the southwest bank of the Missouri, at a site that the French called Belle Fontaine. The spring flowed from a cave near Cold Water Creek and had sufficient volume to provide enough fresh water to supply the army's needs.

The War Department authorized the construction of Fort Belle Fontaine (Bellefontaine) to accomplish two objectives: its primary purpose was to fulfill obligations to area tribes, some of which had signed a treaty in 1804 promising them a government trading house (factory) that would deliver goods in exchange for furs. The second objective was to provide a military fortification to protect the factory, to counter British intrigue among the Indians, and to protect St. Louis from possible invasion by the British or their Indian allies. The factory was placed under the supervision of French-speaking chief factor Rudolf Tiller and assistant factor George C. Sibley.

Beginning on July 23, 1805, Lieutenant Colonel Jacob Kingsbury of the First Infantry supervised the fort's construction. In addition to the company barracks, quartermaster's building, bake house, arsenal, and magazine, the two most impressive buildings within the palisades were the two-story storehouse and the head residence, both constructed of hewn logs atop a stonework foundation, with wood floors, shingled roofs, glass windows, and stone chimneys. Colonel Thomas Hunt served as the post's first commander of six companies of the First Infantry. He was succeeded by Captain James House in 1808 and by Lieutenant Colonel Daniel Bissell in 1809.

Several problems plagued the fort-factory complex. First, the post had been immensely expensive to build. The rights to the land and timber had not been cleared before construction, and Wilkinson was forced to purchase them from William Massey for several hundred dollars. Second, Tiller's salary of $1,250 plus $365 for subsistence, combined with Sibley's salary of $500 plus $180 for subsistence, were the highest among government factory workers. Moreover, the initial expense for goods totaled almost $45,000, indicating the importance of the trading establishment and its ability to accommodate a brisk trade with area tribes.

Locating the post on the Missouri's flood plain was a poor choice. Oppressive heat and disease-carrying insects incapacitated nearly half the men during the summer months. Although the post was only fifteen miles from St. Louis and provided access to both rivers, flooding and erosion caused the wooden buildings to rot quickly, and its distance from the Mississippi created inconveniences. Most unfortunate was the fact that the Indian factory did not serve the Missouri or Mississippi tribes particularly well. In addition, factor Tiller and his assistant, Sibley, did not get along. After an inspection, William Clark, principal Indian agent and brigadier general of upper Louisiana, wrote the secretary of war and gained approval for two new fort-factories, one farther up each river, to accommodate the tribes better. When these two forts were constructed in the fall of 1808, Sibley relocated to Fort Osage on the Missouri and the remaining goods were sent to Fort Madison on the Mississippi. Clark also received, in 1810, approval to relocate Fort Bellefontaine to command the higher ground atop Belle Mont, so the wooden fort would not deteriorate as quickly, the men could escape the muggy heat of the river bottom, and a slight breeze could provide relief from insects.

Although the Indian factory was not a success, the military post fared better. Representing one of the key frontier posts for almost two decades, the relocated Fort Bellefontaine operated as headquarters for the Department of Louisiana, which included Forts Madison, Osage, Massac, and Vincennes from 1809 to 1815. A large, well-provisioned garrison provided resources and manpower for building and staffing other posts along the Mississippi and the Missouri. Government expeditions into the Louisiana Purchase, including the Pike, Long, and Yellowstone expeditions, were launched or received assistance from the post. The fort assisted Indian delegations traveling to St. Louis or Washington, provided protection to Missouri settlements during the War of 1812, and helped maintain order at the signing of the peace treaties at nearby Portage des Sioux in 1815.

Bellefontaine continued as a military establishment until 1826, when the War Department asked Generals Henry Atkinson and Edmund Gaines to construct a large central garrison south of St. Louis, later named Jefferson

Barracks, that would be more convenient for distributing troops throughout the West. After Jefferson Barracks was completed, the troops at Bellefontaine, under the command of Stephen Watts Kearny, evacuated Fort Bellefontaine on July 10, 1826, and moved into their new location ten miles south of St. Louis. The army continued to utilize Bellefontaine's buildings for storage until the mid-1830s. Although the post's original site is gone, Fort Bellefontaine retains a prominent place in the early history of the Louisiana Purchase as perhaps the most important military post in the upper Mississippi Valley in the first two decades of the nineteenth century.

—Jay H. Buckley

See also
Clark, William; Osage, Fort; Saint Louis
For Further Reading
Gregg, Kate L. 1936. "Building of the First American Fort West of the Mississippi." *Missouri Historical Review* 30: 345–364; Magnaghi, Russell M. 1981. "The Belle Fontaine Indian Factory, 1805–1808." *Missouri Historical Review* 75: 396–416; Norton, W. T. 1911. "Old Fort Belle Fontaine." *Journal of the Illinois State Historical Society* 4: 334–339.

An ardent supporter of Western expansion, Thomas Hart Benton advocated preemption laws, which legalized the squatter's rights claimed by many pioneers along the frontier. (North Wind Picture Archives)

BENTON, THOMAS HART (1782–1858)

Thomas Hart Benton was born on March 14, 1782, in Hillsboro, North Carolina. After his father's death, Thomas's mother, Ann Gooch Benton, moved the family to an estate south of Nashville, Tennessee. Thomas attended the University of North Carolina for a short time, but funds ran short and required him to return to Tennessee. That state admitted Benton to the bar in 1806. He parlayed his law practice into a state senate seat in the 1809 legislative session.

The War of 1812 offered Benton an opportunity to better his position in Tennessee. He had joined the U.S. Army in 1810 and functioned as colonel during the war with Great Britain. In addition to serving as Andrew Jackson's aide-de-camp, Benton helped raise a regiment of volunteer soldiers. An unfortunate incident involving a duel between Thomas's brother, Jesse, and William Carroll, another Tennessee military officer and friend of Jackson, led to the estrangement of Benton and Jackson. The misunderstanding resulted in a sidewalk encounter and brawl between Jackson and the Benton brothers that left Jackson wounded and the Bentons' reputations marred. Thomas Benton continued in his military capacity until the war's end. In 1815, however, Benton decided that his prospects in Tennessee were meager, so he moved to St. Louis.

Benton's relocation to the Missouri Territory, which had been part of the Louisiana Purchase lands, marked the beginning of his long career in national politics. Once in St. Louis, Benton established a law practice and edited a newspaper, the *Missouri Enquirer.* His support of slavery during the Missouri statehood debates in 1819 and 1820 brought him appointment to the U.S. Senate when the territory became a state. Benton set out to assist settlers in gaining access to government lands. He also encouraged Western settlement by proposing a national road that would reach lands westward and encouraging the building of a transcontinental railroad.

The Jackson presidency gave Benton national recognition. Jackson and Benton had mended their relationship prior to the 1824 election, and that reconciliation proved fortuitous for both men from 1829 to 1837. Benton sided with Jackson against the South Carolina nullifiers, while the Bank War gave Benton a platform on which to advocate his hard money policy. Benton opposed the recharter of the Bank of the United States in 1831, defended Jackson's veto of the recharter passed by Congress, and supported the removal of government deposits from the financial institution. In 1836, Benton convinced Jackson to issue an executive order, known as the "Specie Circular," mandating payment in specie for public lands. Benton felt that payment in hard money for the lands would slow or stop the inflationary boom that had begun following the removal of government deposits in 1833. This decision unwittingly contributed to the financial panic of 1837.

Benton took a moderate course toward Western expansion during the 1840s, opposing American annexation of Texas because it violated Mexican interests. When President James K. Polk declared war on Mexico, however, Benton lent his support. On the Oregon question, Benton counseled compromise instead of war with Great Britain over the boundary debate.

Following the Mexican War (1846–1848), Benton began calling for moderation on the volatile issue of slavery. He viewed the Compromise of 1850 negatively because it benefited Southern secessionists. That stance cost him his seat in the Senate in 1850. Unwilling to retire, Benton won election to the House of Representatives in 1852. The new Missouri representative fought against both radical Southerners and Northerners. One biographer noted that Benton was "working for sectional peace, the Union, and the restriction of slavery" (Chambers, 1956). Benton, unfortunately for his career and the nation's future, lost his re-election bid in 1854, thus silencing another voice favorable to compromise.

Thomas Hart Benton died from cancer in 1858. He had devoted his life to securing benefits for Western settlers, but Benton's refusal to foster division over slavery led to his repudiation by the people of Missouri. Benton's achievements, however disappointingly his career ended, lay the foundation for successful Western expansion that he helped to create.

—Mark R. Cheathem

See also
Missouri
For Further Reading
Benton, Thomas Hart. 1854–56. *Thirty Years' View; or, A History of the Working of the American Government for Thirty Years, from 1820 to 1850.* New York: Appleton; Chambers, William N. 1956. *Old Bullion Benton: Senator from the New West.* Boston: Little, Brown and Co.; Meigs, William M. 1904. *The Life of Thomas Hart Benton.* Philadelphia: J. B. Lippincott; Roosevelt, Theodore. 1886. *Thomas Hart Benton.* Boston: Houghton Mifflin; Smith, Elbert B. 1958. *Magnificent Missourian: The Life of Thomas Hart Benton.* Philadelphia: J. B. Lippincott.

BENT'S FORT

There are two Colorado sites claiming the name of Bent's Fort. Bent's "Old" Fort was located seven miles east of present-day La Junta and was in use from 1832 to 1852. That is the site most historians identify with Bent's Fort.

Bent's Old Fort was founded and construction began in 1832, under the direction of William Bent (1809–1869), his brother Charles (1799–1847), and Ceran St. Vrain, William Bent's partner. The place was first known as Fort William, after William Bent. It was located on the north bank of the Arkansas River, on the Mountain Branch of the Santa Fe Trail. Bent's Old Fort participated in both the mountain fur trade and overland commerce to Santa Fe. It became the foremost trading post of the Southwest.

The place was rectangular in shape, measuring about 180 feet by 183 feet. The walls were constructed of gray adobe and were two to four feet thick and fifteen feet high. It was to this place that the Cheyenne and Arapaho brought buffalo robes and other furs for barter. From it, white traders carried their wares to Indian villages. An annual wagon train brought Indian furs to St. Louis, Missouri, and returned with trade goods.

Bent's Fort became a stopping place and a major point of reference for military expeditions, mountain men, and Santa Fe traders. The site was first visited by Lieutenant Zebulon M. Pike on his 1805–1807 expedition. His party reached the location of the future post on October 28, 1806. Bent's Fort became an informal depository for military supplies destined for several expeditions of the U.S. Topographical Engineers, including those of Stephen Watts Kearny, Philip St. George Cooke, and Stephen H. Long.

William Bent married a Cheyenne woman and raised his family at the fort. He is recognized as the first citizen of Colorado.

According to tradition, the U.S. government desired the fort but offered an inadequate price. Bent thereupon deserted the post and partially destroyed it in 1849. He constructed a new fort, Bent's "New" Fort, some forty miles downstream, which was completed in 1853. He leased that site to the government in 1859.

Bent's New Fort was located on the left bank of the Arkansas River, near the "Big Timbers." It was leased to the government and used as a storage facility for the new military post, first designated Fort Fauntleroy, on August 29, 1860. The new post was named in honor of Colonel Thomas T. Fauntleroy, First U.S. Dragoons, then renamed Fort Wise for Henry A. Wise, governor of Virginia. On June 25, 1862, the post's name was changed again, this time to Fort Lyon in honor of Brigadier General Nathaniel Lyon, killed on August 10, 1861, at the Battle of Wilson's Creek in Missouri.

Fort Bent–Fauntleroy–Wise–Lyon was abandoned on June 9, 1867, because of flooding along the Arkansas River. The post was replaced by a new Fort Lyon (generally regarded as Fort Lyon II). The military reservation was transferred to the Interior Department on July 22, 1884.

—Henry H. Goldman

See also
Colorado; Santa Fe Trail
For Further Reading
DeVoto, Bernard. 1947. *Across the Wide Missouri.* Boston: Houghton Mifflin; Goetzmann, William H. 1959. *Army Exploration in the American West, 1803–1863.* New Haven: Yale University Press; Hyde, George E. 1968. *A Life of George Bent, Written from His Letters.* Norman: University of Oklahoma Press; Utley, Robert M. 1997. *A Life Wild and Perilous: Mountain Men and Paths to the Pacific.* New York: Henry Holt and Company.

BERNADOTTE, JEAN BAPTISTE (1763–1844)

On October 1, 1800, Spain ceded Louisiana to the French consulate government of Napoleon Bonaparte in exchange for the Italian Duchy of Tuscany (renamed the Kingdom of Etruria). Two years later, Bonaparte offered the post of governor of Louisiana to General Jean Baptiste Bernadotte, a native of Gascony, who had achieved the rank of general of division at the age of thirty-one.

Having successfully served as military governor of Maastricht (1794), ambassador at Vienna (1798), and minister of war (1799), Bernadotte had earned a reputation for being an able administrator and a stern disciplinarian. Although often at odds with Bonaparte's increasingly absolutist regime (1800–1804), Bernadotte was attracted by the possibility of establishing a firm French foothold in North America; the Louisiana Territory was five times the size of France and numbered about eighty thousand inhabitants. Far from the political intrigues that flourished in Paris, Bernadotte hoped to pursue his goals of an independent career, personal advancement, and glory by developing commerce and promoting civilization in Louisiana.

To develop and defend this vast area, Bernadotte needed skilled workers and farmers and at least three thousand soldiers. He would also require financial support from France for at least two years; after that time, the colony would be self-sufficient. Bonaparte refused his requests, and Bernadotte declined the governorship. However, he accepted an appointment as ambassador plenipotentiary to the United States. In January 1803, Bonaparte ordered Bernadotte to leave for Washington.

Both Great Britain and the United States were suspicious of French imperial designs in Louisiana, viewing France as a potential military threat. President Thomas Jefferson did not want the French in control of the vital port of New Orleans. In fact, many Americans were in favor of acquiring Louisiana, by military force if necessary. Furthermore, Jefferson threatened to ally with Britain in the impending war if the French did not leave the area. By the spring of 1803, the first consul had resolved to sell Louisiana, and secret negotiations with the United States were under way. Bernadotte was unaware of these developments and prepared to sail from La Rochelle. On the day he was due to depart, April 12, 1803, the U.S. minister plenipotentiary, James Monroe, arrived in Paris with instructions to offer to purchase Louisiana from France. Bonaparte readily agreed, and the two governments signed the treaty on May 3, 1803; France would receive eighty million francs. After paying off an indemnity to the United States and a commission to Hope and Company and Baring Brothers, the bankers who handled the transaction, the French netted fifty-five million francs from the sale.

Bernadotte learned of the sale of Louisiana and resolved to abandon his new appointment. Without the vast French holdings that bordered the United States, Bernadotte considered the ambassadorship a less important post. He also read in the Paris newspapers that the British ambassador had left Paris and that France and Britain were at war. Bernadotte wrote to Bonaparte that he considered his diplomatic mission over, and he requested a military command. Through his brother-in-law, Joseph Bonaparte, Bernadotte tried to reconcile himself with Napoleon, who was displeased with his refusal to fulfill his diplomatic mission. For a year Bernadotte saw no active service, but when Napoleon declared the end of the consulate and the creation of the empire in 1804, he needed the support of his generals. Bernadotte acquiesced and was rewarded by being named a marshal of France. In June 1806, Napoleon bestowed on him the title of Prince de Ponte-Corvo, a former papal state that had been absorbed into the French empire.

When the heir of the Swedish king Charles XIII died in June 1810, the Swedes requested that Napoleon suggest a possible successor from his family or one of his marshals. Bernadotte, who was a relative of Napoleon by marriage and a marshal, met both criteria. As crown prince, Bernadotte relinquished his French nationality, was released from his oath of allegiance to his country, and converted to Lutheranism. On February 7, 1818, Bernadotte was crowned King of Sweden, taking the title Charles XIV John. He ruled for twenty-six years.

—Jeanne A. Ojala

For Further Reading

Barton, Sir Dunbar Plunkett. 1929. *The Amazing Career of Bernadotte, 1763–1844.* London: John Murray; Delderfield, Ronald F. 1962. *The March of the Twenty-Six: The Story of Napoleon's Marshals.* London: Hodder and Stoughton; Heathcote, T. A. 1987. "Bernadotte: Serjent Belle Jambe." In *Napoleon's Marshals.* Edited by David G. Chandler. New York: Macmillan; MacDonell, Archibald G. 1934. *Napoleon and His Marshals.* London: Macmillan; Young, Peter. 1973. *Napoleon's Marshals.* London: Hippocrene Books.

BINGHAM, GEORGE CALEB (1811–1879)

George Caleb Bingham was born in Augusta County, Virginia, in 1811. When he was eight, his family joined a caravan of Virginians moving to Missouri, where he grew up along the banks of the Missouri River. Although Bingham apprenticed to a cabinet-maker at sixteen, he abandoned the idea of becoming a woodworker in favor of becoming an artist after meeting an itinerant portrait painter. Primarily self-taught, Bingham studied briefly at the Pennsylvania Academy of the Fine Arts in Philadelphia and, in his later years, in Dusseldorf, Germany. He became such a prolific portrait painter that he had a reputation of being able to produce a portrait in a single day. Residing temporarily in

Washington, D.C., early in his career, he captured the crusty likeness of John Quincy Adams, in a work that greatly enhanced his reputation as an artist. Later he returned to Missouri, where he continued to paint portraits and began to study the effects of light in genre paintings (paintings of everyday life). Although Bingham produced nearly a thousand portraits during his lifetime, today he is more regarded for about two dozen genre paintings that established him as the first major American painter to reside in "the West" and record the images of ordinary people. These paintings were popular during his lifetime because they satisfied the Easterners' curiosity for visual information about the Louisiana Purchase territory and its inhabitants.

Deeply patriotic, Bingham expressed his passion for the democratic process and his love of his homeland through politics and art. The frontier life in Missouri fundamentally influenced his character and provided numerous subjects for his genre scenes, which generally pass for reportage even though they are actually highly ideological in content and purpose. One vivid example is *Daniel Boone Escorting Settlers through the Cumberland Gap* (1851–1852, George Washington University Gallery of Art, St. Louis, MO), which extols Manifest Destiny. Despite the ideological themes, his portrayal of middle- and lower-class subjects creates the impression that he is merely recording life around him in *Fur Traders Descending the Missouri* (1845, Metropolitan Museum, New York City) and *Boatmen on the Missouri* (1846, M. H. De Young Museum of Art, San Francisco). Despite their modern subjects, both are marked by a classical serenity and clarity. In his representations of the political process, Bingham idealized the American voting system, which provided for the participation of all social classes (of white males). He tried to capture the ongoing process of reconciliation in action scenes such as *The County Election* (1852, Boatmen's National Bank, St. Louis, MO) and *Campaigning for a Vote* (1851–1852, Nelson-Atkins Museum of Art, Kansas City, MO). His art demonstrates democracy's ability to accommodate the tensions inherent in imposing political control on the frontier, while creating political union in a society based on individual freedoms. All of his paintings set forth a rich and forgiving view of American democratic government and society, an optimistic view he chose to spread by having the election series reproduced.

George Caleb Bingham was also accommodating in his personal life. After his first two wives died, he married the widow of his best friend. After his death at age sixty-eight on July 7, 1879, Bingham was united in death to those he had loved in life. He was buried with his third wife and his best friend in the Union Cemetery in Kansas City, Missouri.

—Betje Black Klier

For Further Reading

Bloch, E. Maurice. 1986. *The Paintings of George Caleb Bingham: A Catalogue Raisonné*. Columbia: University of Missouri Press; Christ-Janer, Albert. 1940. *George Caleb Bingham of Missouri*. New York: Dodd, Mead and Company; Truettner, William H., ed. 1991. *The West as America*. Washington, DC: Smithsonian Institution Press for the National Museum of Art.

BISON

The largest plant-eating mammal left on the continent after the Ice Age, the North American bison roamed over most of the area of the Louisiana Purchase at the beginning of the nineteenth century. Although the number of bison is estimated to have been between thirty and two hundred million in 1800, excessive hunting and purposeful slaughter of the animal in the name of subduing Indians at war with the United States brought the bison to the brink of extinction. By the mid-1880s, fewer than one thousand bison remained.

The population of bison in North America is believed to have increased dramatically following the arrival of Europeans to the eastern shores of North America. Diseases from the Old World quickly spread westward, bringing massive mortality rates among North American Indians. As the native population decreased, reduced hunting led to expanded numbers of bison and other game.

Meriwether Lewis and William Clark wrote frequently of their observations of large herds of bison during their exploration of the Louisiana Territory. While traveling through present-day South Dakota in 1804, Lewis wrote: "This scenery already rich pleasing and beautiful was still farther heightened by immense herds of Buffalo, deer Elk and Antelopes which we saw in every direction feeding on the hills and plains. I do not think I exaggerate when I estimate the number of Buffalo which could be compre[hend]ed at one view to amount to 3000" (DeVoto).

In the early part of the nineteenth century, Indians were known to hunt bison on foot by surrounding a herd and leading them to charge off a cliff. Native hunters opted for bows and arrows once horses became available in the mid-1800s. Little was wasted of the animal—food, clothing, tools, and shelter could all be produced from its body and skin.

The seemingly limitless supply of bison combined with the arrival of American traders led to the unsustainable hunting of the animal. Trading companies offered manufactured goods and alcohol at inflated prices to Indians in exchange for bison skins and meat. By the late 1820s, the number of bison skins purchased from Indians numbered well over 100,000 per year.

As the United States warred with Plains Indian tribes in the 1860s and 1870s, American military lead-

The destruction of the bison herds that once populated the Great Plains hastened the departure of many tribal groups from the region.

ership identified Indian dependence on the bison as a weakness easily exploited. Using long-range rifles, buffalo hunters hired by the U.S. government were able to eliminate large numbers rapidly. At the same time, railroad companies employed hunters to shoot bison in order to clear the way for rail expansion. By the end of the nineteenth century, North American bison were all but gone.

The survival of the bison can be accredited to conservationists and zoologists who saw either economic or scientific opportunity in the animal's survival. In 1900 a few hundred bison remained, either at Yellowstone National Park or on private lands. The American Bison Society was formed in 1905 to promote the survival of the species. Largely through its work, the North American bison population is no longer endangered.

—J. Brent Etzel

For Further Reading
DeVoto, Bernard, ed. 1953. *The Journals of Lewis and Clark*. Boston: Houghton Mifflin Company; Isenberg, Andrew C. 2000. *The Destruction of the Bison: An Environmental History, 1750–1920*. Cambridge: Cambridge University Press.

BLACK HAWK (1767–1838)

Black Hawk (Ma-ka-tai-me-she-kia-kaik) led a struggle by a faction of the Sauk (also known as the Sak or Asakiwaki, the "People of the Yellow Earth") against the United States. These battles between the Sauk, in alliance with the Fox (or Mesquakie, the "People of the Red Earth"), and the United States culminated in the Black Hawk War (1832). Black Hawk's life illustrates the major changes that indigenous people of the Mississippi River Valley experienced after the Spanish loss of Louisiana to France and its subsequent sale to the United States and the British retreat into Canada.

Born in 1767, Black Hawk, like his father, grandfather, and great-grandfather, earned a position of respect as a war chief. He was a traditionalist and a proponent of resistance to settler encroachment onto tribal lands. He married once, consumed no alcohol, and stood for preserving the Sauk way of life at Saukenuk, the head village of the Sauk, near present-day Rock Island, Illinois. Upon his father's death, Black Hawk became keeper of the Sauk's medicine bundle. Also called Big Black Bird or

Black Sparrow Hawk, after his spirit guardian, Black Hawk favored the British, since, unlike the Americans, they did not seek to populate the frontier. Like the Shawnee leader Tecumseh, he tried to unify a dissident pan-tribal group. Black Hawk led more than two hundred Sauk and Fox warriors to Detroit, where they joined Tecumseh on the side of the British during the War of 1812. Because of that allegiance, his followers were called the British Band of Sauk and Fox. He may have been influenced by Winnebago (Ho Chunk) prophet White Cloud, who predicted that the British, along with other Indian tribes, would support the Sauks' efforts to return to Illinois.

Black Hawk spoke against the Treaty of St. Louis (1804), signed by the Sauk and Fox, which moved the tribes west of the Mississippi. He signed several subsequent treaties but indicated that he was unaware that they would result in the loss of his homelands.

Black Hawk returned in the spring of 1829 from the traditional fall hunt to find white squatters occupying Saukenuk. Instead of moving west, Black Hawk remained in the village. He repeated this pattern of leaving to hunt in the fall and returning to Saukenuk in the spring, in 1830 and 1831. In retaliation, the Illinois governor John Reynolds ordered the militia to march against the Sauk. When the Sauk did not leave Saukenuk in 1831, Reynolds ordered the village destroyed. Black Hawk did sign the Articles of Agreement and Capitulation (1831), agreeing not to return to Illinois, but he soon found that the Americans reneged on the promise to provide food to his hungry followers.

The militia followed him when he crossed the Mississippi in early April 1832, in search of fertile fields. The Black Hawk War, an engagement of fifteen weeks, had begun. It ended at the Battle of Bad Axe in August 1832.

Black Hawk surrendered at Prairie du Chien, Wisconsin, on August 27, 1832. The Ho Chunk delivered him to Zachary Taylor, the Indian agent at Fort Crawford. Along with five other men, he was transported to Fort Armstrong, Iowa, under the guard of Jefferson Davis. After several months of incarceration at Jefferson Barracks near St. Louis, he was taken to President Andrew Jackson, who ordered him imprisoned at Fort Monroe in Virginia. At the end of their confinement, the prisoners were taken on an Eastern tour, a common U.S. strategy used to subdue potential insurgents by demonstrating examples of American military strength and sheer volume of population. He returned to the Sauk on August 2, 1833, and was released on the condition that he be paroled to Keokuk. Black Hawk returned to Washington, D.C., for a second time in 1837, as part of a Sauk and Fox delegation. George Catlin and other artists of the day painted Black Hawk's portrait during his Eastern stays.

Black Hawk never regained his position of influence within his tribe. He moved to Iowa and died near Iowaville on October 3, 1838. Nine months later, his body was stolen. His skeleton was exhibited until the building where it was displayed, the Burlington (Iowa) Geological and Historical Society, was destroyed in a fire in the mid-1850s. Black Hawk's autobiography—dictated to Antoine LeClaire, an interpreter of mixed Indian-Anglo heritage, and edited by John B. Patterson, an Illinois newspaper publisher—was first published in 1833. Black Hawk had three children. His great-grandson was Jim Thorpe, to many the greatest American athlete of the twentieth century.

The Sauk warrior Black Hawk led an ill-fated attempt to reclaim his people's homeland after it had been ceded to American authorities by treaty.

—*Loriene Roy*

See also

Armstrong, Fort; Black Hawk War; Catlin, George; Fox; Indian Removal; Iowa; Manifest Destiny; Potawatomi; Sauk; War of 1812; Winnebago

For Further Reading

Black Hawk. 1999. *Life of Ma-Ka-Tai-Me-She-Kia-Kiak or Black Hawk*. Boston: Russell, Odiorne and Metcalf, 1833. Reprint: *Black Hawk's Autobiography.* Edited by Roger L. Nichols. Ames: Iowa State University Press; Eby, Cecil. 1973. *"That Disgraceful Affair," the Black Hawk War.* New York: W. W. Norton; Nichols, Roger L. 1992. *Black Hawk and the Warrior's Path*. Arlington Heights, IL: Harlan Davidson.

BLACK HAWK PURCHASE (1832)

General Winfield Scott and Governor John Reynolds of Illinois orchestrated the Black Hawk Purchase on September 21, 1832, at Fort Armstrong near present-day Rock Island, Illinois. The treaty, which concluded the Black Hawk War, ended nearly thirty years of hostile relations between westward-moving Americans and the Sauk and Fox aligned with Black Hawk, a prominent Sauk warrior chief who refused to surrender ancestral lands in northwestern Illinois and southwestern Wisconsin.

A surge of land-hungry pioneers into the region, combined with President Andrew Jackson's Indian removal policies, had precipitated the hostilities of 1832. Tensions, however, had first surfaced in 1804 when Sauk leaders traveled to St. Louis for peace talks. President Thomas Jefferson, eager to obtain Sauk and Fox lands in the newly acquired Louisiana Territory, authorized William Henry Harrison, governor of the Indiana Territory, to obtain title to tribal lands. Harrison, who plied the visitors with liquor and gifts, secured fifteen million acres of tribal lands from the compliant chiefs. Black Hawk and other Sauk leaders protested, however, arguing that the treaty was invalid because those who had signed it did not possess the authority to do so. Years of intermittent skirmishing followed, until government officials permitted the Sauk and Fox to inhabit the disputed cession until American settlers arrived.

When homesteaders swarmed into the region, American Indians found themselves forced from their productive fields and villages and, by 1829, driven westward across the Mississippi into Iowa Territory. Black Hawk and his followers, however, refused to submit without a fight. In the spring of 1831, they crossed the Mississippi and moved into their villages near Rock Island. General Edmund Gaines responded with military force but managed to avoid war by hashing out an agreement with the Sauk, who promised never again to cross to the eastern bank of the Mississippi without permission.

In April 1832, Black Hawk rallied about one thousand of his followers and crossed the Mississippi River into Illinois, a region from which they had been evicted the previous year. Illinois militiamen rushed to the scene in droves as General Henry Atkinson and his soldiers began arriving from Jefferson Barracks, St. Louis. Black Hawk responded to the news by arranging a truce. Excited militiamen, however, fired upon Black Hawk's emissaries, killing two of them.

The war had begun. Panic spread throughout the region as Black Hawk's starving followers fought their way through northern Illinois and southern Wisconsin in a desperate attempt to reach the Mississippi before General Henry Atkinson's soldiers caught them. Following yet another botched surrender attempt, the elusive rebels were crushed during a desperate attempt to cross the Mississippi at the mouth of the Bad Axe River. The resulting Battle of Bad Axe (August 1–2, 1832) destroyed the American Indian resistance. Black Hawk, who had escaped the bloodbath, surrendered a short time later.

In September 1832, General Scott and Governor Reynolds arrived at Rock Island, Illinois, to establish a lasting peace and firm friendship between the pioneers and disgruntled natives, by extracting a valuable land cession from American Indians who had sparked an "unprovoked war" upon unsuspecting and defenseless inhabitants of the region. To achieve this end, government negotiators demanded six million acres of tribal lands carved out of the Louisiana Purchase. The Treaty of Fort Armstrong required the tribes to cede a strip of land fifty miles wide running almost the entire length of the Mississippi River in the present state of Iowa. In return for their lands, the Sauk and Fox received a $20,000 annuity for thirty years and a small reservation along the Iowa River within the ceded territory. They also obtained assurances that the United States would provide additional blacksmith and gunsmith shops. Negotiators also promised to supply forty kegs of tobacco and salt and pay a $40,000 debt owed to traders. To prevent future misunderstandings, the Sauk and Fox were ordered to vacate permanently all lands east of the Mississippi before June 1, 1833.

Black Hawk, his two sons, and seven "turbulent spirits" were shipped east to Fort Monroe in Virginia. President Andrew Jackson informed them that their period of confinement depended upon the good behavior of their kinsmen. After a brief stay, the prisoners were released to Keokuk, the leader of the Sauk and Fox peace faction. After a whirlwind tour of Eastern cities designed to display the power and wealth of the United States, Black Hawk and the other prisoners arrived in Iowa Territory in 1833. The rebellious Sauk leader, who had devoted most of his adult life to stopping the westward-surging Americans, honored the peace terms and lived peacefully on a reservation near Fort Des Moines until his death in 1838.

—Jon L. Brudvig

See also

Armstrong, Fort; Black Hawk; Black Hawk War

For Further Reading

Hagan, William T. 1958. *The Sac and Fox Nation.* Norman: University of Oklahoma Press; Jackson, Donald, ed. 1955. *Black Hawk (Ma-Ka-Tai-Me-She-Kia-Kiak): An Autobiography.* Urbana: University of Illinois Press; Josephy, Alvin. 1958. *The Patriot Chiefs: A Chronicle of Indian Resistance.* New York: Viking Press; Prucha, Francis Paul. 1984. *The Great Father.* 2 vols. Lincoln: University of Nebraska Press.

BLACK HAWK WAR (1832)

The Black Hawk War, which lasted less than four months in 1832, was the last of the Indian wars of the old Northwest Territory. Associated with Sauk warrior Black Hawk, the conflict

An estimated 5,000 Indians representing the Ojibwa, Sac, Fox, Ioway, and others gathered at Prairie du Chien in August 1825 to sign a treaty with American authorities.

consisted of Sauk attacks on small groups of settlers with resultant military deployment. It ended with American troops and militia slaughtering Sauk men, women, and children who were attempting to return to Iowa under a white flag.

After the Louisiana Purchase in 1803, greater numbers of settlers moved into the Rock River Valley of northwestern Illinois and southwestern Wisconsin, displacing the Sauk. The American strategy to push the Sauk west was accomplished by negotiating treaties with subsets of the tribe and dividing tribal allegiance by supporting Black Hawk's intertribal opponents as well as the Sauk's traditional enemies, the Osage.

In August 1804, relatives of a Sauk woman insulted at a dance killed three settlers in an event called the Cuivre River Massacre. Four Sauk tribal leaders traveled twice to St. Louis to negotiate peace with William Henry Harrison, governor of the Indiana Territory. On the second visit they brought one of the killers, whom the Americans imprisoned. Without consulting other tribal members, and under the influence of the Americans' gifts of alcohol, the tribal representatives signed the Treaty of St. Louis on November 4, 1804, ceding fifty million acres of tribal lands east of the Mississippi River in exchange for an annuity of $1,000 plus $2,000 in supplies. The treaty heightened not only the stress between Indians and Americans but also stress between tribal groups.

When Black Hawk returned to Saukenuk from British service during the War of 1812, he discovered that a number of his tribespeople had moved to Iowa. Those remaining had elected his opponent, Keokuk (Watchful Fox)—an orator who supported the Americans—to be their spokesperson.

Black Hawk led numerous raids over the next two decades while his opponents continued to try to negotiate peace with the Americans. The Sauk signed treaties in 1815 and 1816 to affirm the 1804 treaty. The Treaty at Prairie du Chien on August 25, 1825, set tribal boundaries.

A lead "boom" near Galena, Illinois, in the 1820s resulted in white miners encroaching on traditional Sauk lead mines. Settlers moved into Sauk lodges at Saukenuk in 1827, and Sauk homeland was sold to U.S. citizens in October 1829. Secretary of War Lewis Cass assured the governor of Illinois that all Indians would be removed from the state by 1829. On July 25, 1830, Sauk and Fox leaders signed another Treaty at Prairie du Chien, again setting borders between tribes. Members of the British Band signed the Articles of Agreement and Capitulation on June 30, 1831, acknowledging Keokuk as tribal leader and restricting their movements to new lands in the West. Again, Black Hawk would not adhere to the treaty. He organized several attacks against settlers' villages in 1831 and 1832 and then moved west across the Mississippi.

When the Sauk found the prairie fields difficult to till and plant, Black Hawk returned to Illinois in April 1833 to seek a site on which to raise corn. The British Band, with one thousand men, half of whom were noncombatants, moved across the Mississippi and then north along the Rock River, carefully avoiding Saukenuk. The Sixth Infantry, under General Henry Atkinson, was ordered against Black Hawk and on April 8, 1832, started upriver to try to curtail Sauk movements.

When neither British nor sufficient Indian support materialized, Black Hawk's band attempted several times to negotiate a surrender, only to receive a hostile response from U.S. troops, or none at all. Early in the war, Black Hawk moved to surrender, sending three emissaries, followed by five scouts, to negotiate the terms. After Illinois volunteers killed two of the emissaries, Black Hawk retaliated on May 12, 1832. This exchange, the Battle of Stillman's Run, was named after Major Isaiah Stillman, leader of an unattached group of Illinois militia. The militia, numbering some 275, became disorganized and fled from battle. Three Sauk were killed, along with twelve Americans.

The Indians' victory was short lived. Black Hawk led other attacks on settlements, but his general movement turned to one of escape into inhospitable swampland. Militia located the British Band on July 21, 1832, killing a number of warriors at the Battle of Wisconsin Heights. Starving and exhausted, on August 1, 1832, Black Hawk's group of pan-tribal followers (consisting of Sauk, Fox, Kickapoo, and Ho Chunk/Winnebago), now some five hundred people, split when he proposed moving north to seek shelter with the Ho Chunk. A number of the band tried to forge the confluence of the Mississippi and Bad Axe Rivers, and started to construct rafts. When the steamboat *Warrior* came upon the Sauk the militia opened fire, even after the British Band raised a white flag. Atkinson was supported by four thousand volunteers under Henry Dodge and James Henry. The Battle of Bad Axe ended, on August 2, 1832, with the deaths of nearly all of the British Band. Many of the Sauk who escaped to the west bank of the Mississippi were killed by the waiting Sioux.

Black Hawk continued north into Wisconsin, where he surrendered on August 27, 1832. Black Hawk was imprisoned and eventually returned to the Sauk. The Black Hawk War resulted in some four hundred to six hundred Indian deaths, including many noncombatants, and seventy settler or military deaths. The war officially ended on September 21, 1832. In reparation, the Sauk lost most of eastern Iowa in exchange for an annuity of $20,000 a year for thirty years, an agreement referred to as the "Black Hawk Purchase." The Sauk sold their lands in Iowa in 1842, and in 1845 they, along with the Fox, were removed to a reservation in Kansas. They moved once more, in 1869, to Indian Territory, later Oklahoma. Abraham Lincoln was the most famous veteran of the Black Hawk War, having served as an Illinois volunteer. Other veterans profited from their service through acquisition of land, government payments, and advancement of military or political careers.

—Loriene Roy

See also

Black Hawk; Fox; Indian Removal; Indian Territory; Iowa; Kickapoo; Manifest Destiny, Osage; Saint Louis; Sauk; War of 1812; Winnebago

For Further Reading

Black Hawk. 1999. *Life of Ma-Ka-Tai-Me-She-Kia-Kiak or Black Hawk*. Boston: Russell, Odiorne and Metcalf, 1834. Reprint: *Black Hawk's Autobiography.* Edited by Roger L. Nichols. Ames: Iowa State University Press; Eby, Cecil. 1973. *"That Disgraceful Affair," the Black Hawk War.* New York: W. W. Norton; Nichols, Roger L. 1992. *Black Hawk and the Warrior's Path*. Arlington Heights, IL: Harlan Davidson.

BLACK HILLS

The Black Hills occupy a five-thousand-square-mile mountainous area south of the Belle Fourche River and west of the southern fork of the Cheyenne River. Two-thirds of the Black Hills lie in southwestern South Dakota, and the remainder in northeastern Wyoming. Acquired by the United States in the Louisiana Purchase, the pine- and spruce-forested granite outcroppings appear black at a distance. President Grover Cleveland established the Black Hills Forest Reserve, along with twelve other forest reserves, in 1897. In 1907 the Black Hills National Forest was established. The Hills, geologically classified as dome mountains, average 3,500 feet, while its Harney Peak, at 7,242 feet, is the tallest point east of the Rocky Mountains. General William S. Harney was remembered for his aggressive attack on the Brule Sioux in 1853, resulting in one hundred Indian men killed and one hundred women and children captured, and for his assistance in negotiating the Treaty of Fort Laramie.

The Lakota referred to the Black Hills as the Paha Sapa, or "the hills that are black." The Paha Sapa figure prominently in Sioux creation stories, in which the original people emerged from a life underground through Wind Cave and were saved by one of their own people, who transformed himself into a buffalo. These were sacred lands, used for solitary religious pursuits, and a shared ground that provided sanctuary in which warring nations met for council.

The first non-Indians to see the Black Hills were French explorers François and Louis-Joseph de la Verendrye, in January 1743. On October 1, 1804, Lewis and Clark were camped near the mouth of the Cheyenne River, where they heard reports of the Black Hills from Jean Valle, a trapper and trader. Valle relayed to them the legend of mysterious thunder heard in the Hills. Miners and trappers frequented the Hills during the 1830s. Father Pierre Jean De Smet visited in the 1840s and 1850s, exploring the region and advising the Indians to conceal the presence of gold. In 1861, Dakota Territory was created. The Treaty of Fort Laramie (1868) set aside the Black Hills for exclusive use by the Sioux as part of the Great Sioux Reservation. In 1874, Lieutenant Colonel George Armstrong Custer led a military exploration of the Black Hills, largely in part to confirm long-reported sightings of gold. His sixty-day excursion included one thousand men, 110 wagons, three Gatling guns, and a retinue of scientists (geologists, naturalists, and botanists), miners, photographers, journalists, guides, scouts, and a sixteen-piece band. Custer's reports to the press of gold findings initiated a gold rush and the development of large-scale mining ventures, such as the Homestake Mine. The path he followed to the Black Hills came to be called Thieves' Road by the Lakota and Freedom's Trail by the miners. The Black Hills are also repositories of other minerals: silver, copper, tin, mica, graphite, iron, lead, and nickel. In 1875 the United States sought to alter the 1868 treaty, offering to buy the Black Hills from the Sioux people. When the offer was not accepted, the government ordered the Lakota to report to agencies. An intertribal group of Cheyenne, Arapaho, and Sioux (Oglala, Brule, Minneconjou, and Hunkpapa) that remained off reservation forced General Crook's troops to retreat on June 17, 1876, and on June 25, 1876, they killed Custer's forces at the Battle of the Little Big Horn. The Great Sioux War of 1876–1877 ended with the surrender of the few surviving native people.

In 1877, the U.S. government confiscated the Black Hills and removed it from the Great Sioux Reservation, a decision still contested by the Lakota people. The Sioux bands were forced to relocate, and those that did not report to reservation lands by January 31, 1878, were declared hostile. Non-Indians were then free to move into the Black Hills. The state of South Dakota was established in 1889. The resources of the Black Hills were open to commercial exploitation, seen in the arrival of boom towns, cattlemen, and saw mills and the development of national Western icons such as Wild Bill Hickok and Calamity Jane. In the early twentieth century, the forests of the Black Hills were first decimated by timber interests and then subjected to experiments in government regulation over public land. In 1927, President Coolidge vacationed in the Black Hills, awakening a national interest in the area. Today, the Black Hills' rivers, valleys, and other natural wonders are a recreation area for many. Manmade attractions include Mount Rushmore National Memorial, Crazy Horse Monument, Deadwood, the Black Hills Passion Play, and the annual motorcycle rally at Sturgis.

—Loriene Roy

See also
Badlands; Cartography; Corps of Discovery; Laramie, Fort; Lewis and Clark Expedition; Manifest Destiny; Oglala Sioux; South Dakota; Vallé, Jean-Baptiste; Wyoming

For Further Reading

Greene, Jerome A. 1994. *Lakota and Cheyenne: Indian Views of the Great Sioux War, 1876–1877.* Norman: University of Oklahoma Press; Jackson, Donald. 1966. *Custer's Gold: The United States Cavalry Expedition.* New Haven: Yale University Press.

BLACKFOOT

The Blackfoot were one of the larger and more powerful tribes that inhabited the Northern Plains when Anglo-American explorers, trappers, and fur traders began to travel through the northern portion of the Louisiana Purchase Territory. The tribe inhabited the region north of the Upper Missouri River in present-day Montana and southern Alberta. Their lands were located just east of the Rocky Mountains, and two mountain tribes, the Shoshone and the Nez Perce, were their traditional enemies.

Like other peoples of the Great Plains—such as the Sioux, the Crow, the Cheyenne, and the Arapaho—the Blackfoot had originated in the eastern woodlands near the Great Lakes and had moved westward prior to the eighteenth century. They spoke a language called *Siksika,* which was part of the Algonquian-Wakashan linguistic group. Their geographic migration westward had also entailed a cultural transformation as they abandoned the sedentary agricultural lifestyle of the earth-lodge and became nomadic hunters on the Plains. They acquired horses from southern tribes and soon became known as some of the most expert hunters of the Plains.

Although the Blackfoot constituted one tribal group, they were organized into three different bands: the Siksika (or Blackfoot), the Piegan, and the Kainah (or Blood). Although these three bands had their own leaders and operated somewhat autonomously, the tribe always unified in time of warfare to defend its territory. This warfare-induced unity was quite common because the Blackfoot earned the reputation of being frequently hostile to their neighbors whenever they believed that tribal welfare was jeopardized by the incursions of others. This pattern of behavior persisted as whites began to trespass upon Blackfoot territory. During the entire Lewis and Clark Expedition (1804–1806), the only hostile encounter that the Corps of Discovery experienced was an ambush by a group of Blackfoot warriors who attempted to steal horses from the explorers when they traveled along the Marias River in northwestern Montana. Two Indians were killed in this attack.

The arrival of white Americans would bring many changes to the culture of the Blackfoot. They did acquire wealth by trading beaver pelts with merchants and traders from St. Louis who navigated the Missouri River annually to participate in the mountain rendezvous with the region's free trappers. But contact with Americans took its toll on the Blackfoot as they frequently suffered from epidemic diseases such as smallpox to which they had no immunity. Some accounts suggest that the tribe was presented with blankets that were infected with smallpox—a nineteenth-century version of ethnic cleansing that decimated the tribe. When the vast herds of bison began to vanish as a result of widespread slaughter by white hunters, it foreshadowed the decline of the Blackfoot, who had been so dependent upon the hunt as a means of survival.

The era of the Plains Indian Wars was also a difficult time for the Blackfoot. In 1870 the U.S. Army was seeking a hostile band of Blackfoot warriors under the leadership of Mountain Chief. By mistake, the American force came upon a peaceful encampment of Blackfoot—mostly women and children—who were under the protection of Heavy Runner. The U.S. forces attacked and more than 200 Blackfoot were killed. In the confusion, Mountain Chief and his band escaped by crossing the border into Canada.

War, disease, and the near extinction of the bison changed the Blackfoot. This realization was evident in the words spoken by Lame Bull, a chief of the Piegan band, as he informed a Presbyterian missionary of his new understanding of things. He said: "When we catch a wild animal on the prairie & attempt to tame him we sometimes find it very hard. . . . But almost any animal can be tamed by kindness and perseverance. We have been running wild on the prairie and now we want the white sons and daughters of our great Father to come to our country and tame us" (Ewers, 1967). It was clear that the pacification of the once-fierce warrior tribe was almost complete.

By the 1880s the Blackfoot living in the United States as well as those in Canada had been relocated to reservations. Today, an estimated 38,000 Blackfoot live in the United States, and more than 11,000 reside in Canada.

—Junius P. Rodriguez

See also
Crow; Montana

For Further Reading

Dempsey, Hugh A. 1972. *Crowfoot, Chief of the Blackfeet.* Norman: University of Oklahoma Press; Ewers, John C. 1967. *The Blackfeet: Raiders on the Northwestern Plains.* Norman: University of Oklahoma Press; McFee, Malcolm. 1972. *Modern Blackfeet; Montanans on a Reservation.* New York: Holt, Rinehart and Winston; Nettl, Bruno. 1989. *Blackfoot Musical Thought: Comparative Perspectives.* Kent, OH: Kent State University Press.

BLEEDING KANSAS

See **Kansas**

BODMER, CHARLES (1809–1893)

Charles Bodmer toured the American frontier, painting and sketching the sites to document the expedition of Prince Maximilian of Wied-Neuwied to the upper Missouri country in 1832–1834. His pictures of the frontier remained unequaled until the advent of photography. Born in Zurich, Switzerland, Bodmer was apprenticed to his uncle, Johann Jakob Meier, from whom he learned sketching, engraving, and watercolor. He demonstrated particular expertise as an aquatint engraver, showing a special interest in nature and landscapes. In 1828, Bodmer settled in the Rhine and Moselle regions of Germany, obtaining work as an illustrator for travel albums and publishing a book of Moselle Valley scenes. The book probably brought him to the attention of Prince Maximilian, a naturalist and explorer living nearby who planned a trip to North America to collect fauna and observe Native Americans. Needing an artist to record the images of Indians, Maximilian invited Bodmer to accompany him.

The expedition to America began on May 17, 1832, when Maximilian, Bodmer, and a servant, David Dreidoppel, set sail from Holland and landed at Boston on the Fourth of July. After spending late July through mid-September in Bethlehem, Pennsylvania, and the winter in New Harmony, Indiana, Bodmer left to take a trip down the Ohio and Mississippi Rivers to New Orleans. The artist had been executing watercolors to document the journey, and he continued to paint as he traveled solo. Rejoining Maximilian, the travelers reached St. Louis on March 24, 1833. The party went up the Missouri aboard one of the American Fur Company's new steamboats and reached Bellevue, near modern-day Omaha, Nebraska, in early May. At Bellevue, Bodmer began his first painting of Western Indians—two Omahas, a father and son, visiting the fur company's post. The trip resumed as the men pushed on along the Missouri to the Sioux Agency near the mouth of the White River. Particularly fascinated by the Sioux, Bodmer produced one of his most famous portraits, of Wahktägeli ("Big Soldier"). Bodmer had had no formal training in portraiture, and that proved to be a benefit, since he applied no European ideals of form or beauty to his paintings that might have distorted the likenesses.

By May 30 the party reached Fort Pierce, one of the largest of the fur company's posts. When they reached Fort Clark, the Europeans were fortunate to encounter a delegation of Crow Indians who had journeyed from as far west as the Big Horn Mountains, and Bodmer grabbed his chance to paint more portraits. The party next reached Fort Union, which stood on a plain at the junction of the Yellowstone and Missouri Rivers. The remainder of the trip now took place in keelboats as the group meandered through the Badlands. The group had intended simply to pass through Fort McKenzie, near present-day Great Falls, Montana, and continue to travel westward, but relations between whites and Indians had become severely strained in the vicinity of the post. Determining that further travel would be hazardous, the group nevertheless stayed long enough for Bodmer to become acquainted with the leading men of all three bands of the Blackfoot. Bodmer's portraits of these chiefs and shamans are among his outstanding works. The party spent the harsh winter of 1833–1834 at Fort Clark, near present-day Bismarck, North Dakota, and established warm relations with the Mandan and Hidatsa Indians. The Mandan would be nearly extinguished by smallpox a few years later, and Bodmer's works constitute an invaluable record of their lives, inasmuch as he typically included detailed renditions of the Indians' ornamentation, attire, and implements. Bodmer and Maximilian returned to Europe in July 1834. The artist never again visited the New World. He had completed nearly four hundred watercolors and sketches, mostly landscapes.

Maximilian decided to publish a deluxe account of the journey, with illustrations based on Bodmer's watercolors. Bodmer supervised the production of this multivolume narrative of the expedition, which sold but few copies because of its exorbitant price. A short and more affordable book, *North America in Pictures* (1846), also met with little success, but Bodmer's aquatints gained fame as being among the most significant contributions to the iconography of the Western frontier. In the 1840s, Bodmer moved between Cologne, Germany, and Paris as he painted in oils and exhibited landscapes. Best known in his day as a prolific engraver, Bodmer spent his remaining years illustrating magazines and books. By the time of his death, in 1893, his career had already slipped into a deep decline. His paintings were rediscovered after World War II and are now housed at the Joslyn Art Museum in Omaha.

—Caryn E. Neumann

See also

Mandan; Maximilian, Prince Alexander Philipp zu Wied-Neuwied.

For Further Reading

Goetzmann, William, et al. 1985. *Karl Bodmer's America.* Lincoln: Joslyn Art Museum and the University of Nebraska Press; Moore, Robert J. 1997. *Native Americans: The Art and Travels of Charles Bird King, George Catlin, and Karl Bodmer.* New York: Stewart, Tabori, and Chang.

BONAPARTE, JOSEPH (1768–1844)

Joseph Bonaparte conducted the 1800 negotiations with three American commissioners leading to the signing of the Convention of Mortefontaine, which re-established friendship and maritime peace between France and the United States after the Quasi-War (1798–1800), one of the steps necessary for Napoleon to carry out his dream of reconquering Louisiana. Joseph was not officially involved in the negotiations that were to lead to the Louisiana Purchase, but he was instrumental in conveying Robert R. Livingston's views to his brother before real negotiations got under way. He is also rumored to have been involved in a conspiracy with the British ambassador in Paris to maintain peace in Europe, which may partly explain why he protested Napoleon's sale of the vast colony without the French parliamentary chambers having been consulted, although to no avail.

Joseph Bonaparte was born in Ajaccio, Corsica, the eldest son of Charles Bonaparte and Letizia Ramolino. Benefiting from his brother's influence, Joseph was appointed *commissaire des guerres* in the French Army of Italy; then he was elected as representative for his native Corsica in the Council of the Five Hundred. He bought the magnificent estate of Mortefontaine, thirty miles north of Paris, in October 1798. He was not very active in the Council of the Five Hundred, but after his brother's Brumaire coup (November 1799), he joined the Tribunat, then the Counsel of State, preferring diplomatic missions such as re-establishing friendly relationships with the United States (Convention of Mortefontaine, October 3, 1800). On that occasion, Joseph headed the group of French commissioners, including Pierre-Louis Roederer and Charles de Fleurieu, who met the Americans Oliver Ellsworth, William Davie, and William Vans Murray in discussions on how to solve mutual grievances caused by the Quasi-War between France and the United States. As this was Joseph's first major diplomatic mission, he was keen on the discussions' succeeding—even though Napoleon would not hear of any indemnities for damage caused to American trade by French privateers during the Quasi-War, and Americans were adamant that some compensation had to be paid. Napoleon was not in a hurry to have the American treaty signed; he wanted to make peace in Europe first, so that he could dictate his terms to the Americans next. However, Joseph was allowed to have his way, and negotiations proceeded smoothly, although no solution could be found on the matter of indemnities for the prizes made by the French during the Quasi-War: that subject should be reserved for future negotiation. Thus could Joseph host the final signing ceremony in his Mortefontaine mansion (October 3, 1800), celebrating the renewed French-American friendship with a lavish party.

By that time negotiations in Spain on the retrocession of Louisiana to France, which had begun over the summer, had led to the signing of the Treaty of San Ildefonso (October 1).

Joseph Bonaparte went on to negotiate peace in 1801 with Austria (the Peace of Lunéville) and with Great Britain (the Peace of Amiens). Such successful results made Napoleon feel grateful, and he offered Joseph the Crown of Italy, which the latter declined.

Because Joseph was very close to his brother, he was

approached in the summer of 1802 by Robert R. Livingston, the American minister in Paris, who was trying to ingratiate himself with French officials by leading an active social life. Joseph informed him that Napoleon Bonaparte had not responded in any way when he had broached the subject of Livingston's recent memoir on Louisiana ("Whether it will be advantageous to France to take possession of Louisiana?"). Still, later in the fall, Joseph hinted at selling the Floridas or Louisiana to Livingston, but the eldest Bonaparte put an end to these informal discussions early in 1803, suggesting that the American minister turn again to Charles Maurice de Talleyrand as a proper diplomatic conduit.

By that time, Napoleon was faced with the failure of his policy to reconquer St. Domingue, and he decided that he would abandon his colonial system, keeping the secret to himself for the time being. Still, by early March, Napoleon started voicing his anti-British feelings publicly. The British ambassador wrote his government that he was in touch with people close to Lucien Bonaparte and was confident that Joseph especially might be bribed into pleading for peace with the first consul. There is an indication that by March 24, Joseph had been approached, and he met with Charles Whitworth, the British ambassador, on March 30. Yet he did not reassure Whitworth on the subject of peace, though Whitworth understood that this was just a preliminary discussion. There is no proof that any actual bribery took place, and the men later met within the general framework of the official negotiations.

By April 10, Napoleon had decided to sell Louisiana so that he could finance his coming war with Britain and keep that great colonial prize out of the hands of Britain. Negotiations between Barbé-Marbois, Monroe, and Livingston were well under way when Joseph learned of his brother's decision. Together with Lucien Bonaparte, they paid a visit to the first consul, firmly observing that he could not sell Louisiana without the consent of the chambers. Napoleon told them he would do so, which stirred the two brothers' anger but did nothing to change Napoleon's resolve.

Joseph became King of Naples on March 31, 1806. He was instrumental in bringing about administrative reforms and energizing the local economy. His record was marred, however, by reports of corruption and pillage of the kingdom. A much worse experience was to come when Joseph accepted the title of King of Spain, on April 18, 1808. After Napoleon was finally sent to the island of St. Helena, Joseph fled to the United States under the name of Count of Survilliers. For seventeen years, he was a popular citizen of Bordentown, New Jersey, and Philadelphia. He made friends in high places, was elected to the American Philosophical Society, and was received by President Andrew Jackson. He left for England in 1832, returning to the United States between 1837 and 1839 before moving to Florence, Italy, where he died on July 28, 1844.

—Marie-Jeanne Rossignol

See also

Barbé-Marbois, François, Marquis de; Bonaparte, Lucien; Bonaparte, Napoleon; Livingston, Robert R.; Mortefontaine, Convention of; Talleyrand-Perigord, Charles Maurice de

For Further Reading

Adams, Henry. 1986. *History of the United States of America during the Administrations of Jefferson and Madison.* New York: Literary Classics of America; DeConde, Alexander. 1966. *The Quasi-War: The Politics and Diplomacy of the Undeclared War with France, 1797–1801.* New York: Charles Scribner's Sons; Lokke, Carl Ludwig. 1943. "Secret Negotiations to Maintain the Peace of Amiens." *American Historical Review* 49: 55–64; Tulard, Jean, ed. 1989. *Dictionnaire Napoléon.* Paris: Fayard.

BONAPARTE, LUCIEN (1775–1840)

Lucien Bonaparte, Napoleon's younger brother and the third son of Charles Bonaparte and Letizia Ramolino, rounded off the negotiations with Spain that were to lead to the retrocession of Louisiana to France by signing the Convention of Aranjuez (1801). He was also indirectly involved in a conspiracy with Great Britain that might have prevented the sale of Louisiana in 1803.

Lucien Bonaparte was trained as a future infantry officer at the same military schools as his older brothers, Joseph and Napoleon, but then sent to the seminary on his father's death. He did not choose an ecclesiastical career, however, returning in 1789 to Corsica, where he became a leading member of the Jacobin Club. After a short stint in prison as a Jacobin, he was liberated by Napoleon and chose to start a political career as a representative for his native island. He was elected to the Council of Five Hundred in 1798 and became very active there, reaching the position of president of that assembly in October 1799, which enabled him to come to the rescue of his brother Napoleon during the latter's Coup of 18 Brumaire. All the while, Lucien proved to be a businessman of great acumen, quickly becoming rich on shrewd investments in privateering.

After 18 Brumaire, Lucien Bonaparte sat in the Tribunat, then was appointed an interior (police) minister. Once again, he betrayed his earlier republican principles by being instrumental in the falsification of the referendum on the Year VIII Constitution. He also intrigued against his brother, circulating in November 1800 a supposedly anonymous pamphlet about Napoleon's lack of an heir. The suggestion was that Lucien himself should be considered as Napoleon's successor. Napoleon had him resign and then appointed him as ambassador to Madrid. There he was to conclude the negotiations aimed at reestablishing the Family Compact between Spain and France, which involved the retrocession of Louisiana to France.

The new Family Compact had two goals: it was first aimed at destroying Britain's power in the Iberian peninsula and in the Mediterranean. Spain would provide France with its fleet, and, once victorious against the British, the thankful French would reward Spain with territory taken from Portugal, a steady British ally. The Family Compact also provided that the French would offer the kingdom of Tuscany to the Prince of Parma, the Spanish king's son-in-law, thanks to which they would be able to reach their second goal, the retrocession of Louisiana. The kingdom of Tuscany was the Queen of Spain's own ambitious invention; she insisted upon her daughter's reigning over an enlarged duchy, which involved dethroning the current duke and adding other territories to his possessions to form a bigger, newly created kingdom: Tuscany.

The first step of this complex diplomatic process had been the signing by General Louis-Alexandre Berthier of the secret Treaty of San Ildefonso on October 1, 1800, which provided that the Spanish would retrocede Louisiana "in exchange for the territorial aggrandizement of the Duchy of Parma." Six months after these conditions were met, the French would repossess Louisiana. This particular treaty had not been made public at the time, for fear that the British would invade Louisiana and secure it before the colony was returned to France; the American government could thus only rely on rumors as word began to spread that Louisiana had been retroceded.

Lucien's mission was to negotiate a new treaty closing the bargain in regard to Parma and Tuscany. As he now controlled Italy, Napoleon himself set about convincing the old Duke of Parma that he should leave his duchy. He soon informed Lucien that the duke was renouncing his rights to all his states, which were to become the sovereign possession of the Prince of Parma. The duke was to content himself with some financial compensation. Final discussions between Lucien and Manuel de Godoy, the Spanish negotiator, took place on March 20 and 21, 1801, leading to the Convention of Aranjuez on Parma and Tuscany: the convention provided that the duke renounce his hereditary rights on behalf of the French republic, which in turn conveyed them to the new "vassal" king. The Prince of Parma was created King of Tuscany, and the sixth article of the Convention provided that the retrocession of Louisiana at once be carried out. The convention was signed at Madrid on March 21, 1801. Copies of it were soon forwarded to Washington by Rufus King, the American minister in London. Now the American government could rely on facts, no longer on mere rumors, to protest the retrocession and ask for explanations or territorial arrangements.

Meanwhile, Lucien remained to make sure that the second goal of the Family Compact, the destruction of British power in the Iberian peninsula, was carried out. Lucien wrote to the Portuguese ambassador in Madrid, demanding that his country comply with a 1795 treaty with France. The treaty provided that Portugal shut its harbors to British ships and cede its northern provinces to Spain. Upon Portugal's refusal, war was declared by Spain and France and was rapidly won. Lucien was hurried by Godoy into signing a treaty that did not offer the military guarantees that Talleyrand and Napoleon eventually meant to request from Portugal (Treaty of Badajoz, June 5, 1801), which led to Napoleon's angry recall of his brother in October 1801. There is no denying that Lucien came back a rich man from his embassy in Madrid, his wealth the result of continual bribery on the part of the Spanish court, and then on the part of the Portuguese.

In 1802 he sat on the Tribunat again. One can find a connection between his career and Louisiana again in March 1803, at a time of renewed tensions with Britain. Then the British ambassador in Paris, Charles Whitworth, wrote the foreign secretary that a friend of Lucien's had approached him, suggesting that the Bonaparte family might be bribed into promoting a peace policy toward Great Britain in their discussions with the first consul. Peace in 1803 would have made the sale of Louisiana unnecessary for France. Fruitless negotiations were conducted with Joseph, but still, the two brothers did react angrily to Napoleon's decision to sell Louisiana without consulting the chambers—which also put an end to whatever conspiracy in which they may have been involved.

Lucien went into exile to Rome in April 1804. He reconciled himself with his brother Napoleon in 1815, believing that a new, constitutional empire would be established. His hopes defeated, he moved back to Italy and died in Viterbe in 1840.

—Marie-Jeanne Rossignol

See also

Aranjuez, Convention of; Bonaparte, Napoleon; Leclerc, Charles-Victor-Emmanuel; San Ildefonso, Treaty of; Talleyrand-Perigord, Charles Maurice de; Tuscany

For Further Reading

Adams, Henry. 1986. *History of the United States of America during the Administrations of Jefferson and Madison.* New York: Literary Classics of America; Barbé-Marbois, M. 1829. *Histoire de la Louisiane et de la cession de cette colonie par la France aux Etats-Unis de l'Amérique septentrionale.* Paris: Firmin Didot; Martineau, Gilbert. 1989. *Lucien Bonaparte, Prince de Canino.* Paris: Editions France-Empire; Tulard, Jean, ed. 1989. *Dictionnaire Napoléon.* Paris: Fayard.

BONAPARTE, NAPOLEON (1769–1821)

Following a series of failed attempts to expand French influence in the New World, First Consul Napoleon Bonaparte abandoned his ambitious colonial policy and approved the sale of Louisiana to the United States in April 1803.

Once he abandoned plans to reestablish a French empire in North America, Napoleon Bonaparte decided to sell the entire Louisiana Territory to the United States in 1803.

During the eighteenth century, the Louisiana Territory was held periodically by France and Spain. In accordance with the Treaty of Paris (1763), which brought an end to the Seven Years' War, France surrendered the vast Louisiana territories to Great Britain and Spain. In his typically charismatic style, Voltaire agonized over the loss of Louisiana in a letter to his friend the Count Argental. Voltaire wrote: "I have never conceived . . . how one abandoned the most beautiful climate of the earth, from which one may have tobacco, silk, indigo, a thousand useful products, and still carry on a more useful commerce with Mexico. I declare to you that if I had not built Ferney, I would go and establish myself in Louisiana."

As a voracious reader and patron of the French Enlightenment, Napoleon Bonaparte was no doubt acquainted with both Voltaire's writings on Louisiana and the intrinsic value of the former French colony. Thus it is not surprising that the loss of France's North American holdings proved a temporary arrangement as First Consul Napoleon Bonaparte worked at the close of the century to renew France's western colonial empire. After assuming the title of first consul following the Coup of 18–19 Brumaire (November 9–10, 1799), Napoleon worked to regain all the Louisiana territories west of the Mississippi River from Spain. Control over this enormous territory would halt the westward expansion of the United States and supply French colonies in the Caribbean with much-needed men and raw materials. Napoleon's plan called for Louisiana and the Caribbean basin to work together to increase their wealth for the benefit of France. The first consul envisioned Louisiana as the natural storehouse of the Caribbean, providing the area with a vast supply of furs, timber, salted meat, and grain. To that end, France regained Louisiana through the secret Treaty of San Ildefonso on October 1, 1800. The arrangement concluded that France would surrender Tuscany to the rule of the daughter and son-in-law of Spain's King Charles IV, and in return, Spain would restore Louisiana to France. Upon discovering the transfer of Louisiana from Spain to France in October 1802, President Thomas Jefferson dispatched Robert Livingston, U.S. minister to France, to Paris to attempt to purchase New Orleans from the French. Napoleon, however, continued to recognize the collective value of New Orleans and the French Caribbean holdings, and he declined the American offer.

Even as the first consul declined offers to purchase portions of the Louisiana Territory he worked to consolidate French control of the region. Napoleon sent explicit instructions as to who would serve as the colonial prefect, captain general, and botanical gardener for Louisiana's colonial administration. Furthermore, he ordered that navigation agreements along the Mississippi River remain as they had been under the Spanish, and that all French citizens be cordial to the bordering U.S. population. While decreeing official goodwill toward all American citizens, Bonaparte noted that the defense of Louisiana was paramount, and that the United States must be watched at all times. To help guard Louisiana's border, Napoleon ultimately sought to rekindle France's relationship with the Native American population of the region, as they had done during the French and Indian Wars.

Napoleon's imminent plan for an expanded French presence in the Western Hemisphere collapsed rapidly, however, as a revolt of slaves and free blacks in the French colony of St. Domingue enjoyed continued success. The French detachment sent to the island of Haiti totaled some thirty-three thousand men; the force under General Charles-Victor-Emmanuel Leclerc included a mixed group of French, Spanish, Creole, and Polish troops. Once ashore, Leclerc's army was instructed to occupy the western half of the island and to crush the revolt led by Toussaint L'Ouverture; however, most of the French manpower was squandered, as the potential combatants died of yellow fever and dysentery before ever entering the fight. The surviving French forces were eventually forced to surrender to the British or return in disgrace to France. Angered and disheartened by the disastrous loss of General Leclerc, Napoleon's brother-in-law, and his men, Napoleon exclaimed: "Damn sugar, damn coffee, damn colonies!" The Caribbean revolt proved costly for France and her allies, as they were forced to abandon the island of Hispaniola in 1802. This setback proved ultimately too difficult to overcome, as it prevented the French from reinforcing troops already dedicated to the defense of New Orleans and the greater Louisiana Territory. The French defeat in the Caribbean marked the end of Napoleon's North American dream: the loss of St. Domingue had made the Louisiana Territory both untenable and unimportant.

Subsequently, the disastrous Caribbean campaign coupled with the imminent threat of another war with Great Britain to weaken France's international position. With that in mind, President Jefferson made another attempt to purchase New Orleans from France. In response to both American public opinion and requests from U.S. negotiators, Jefferson bolstered the U.S. bargaining position on the eve of negotiations by letting it be known that if France remained in Louisiana, the United States would join Britain in the coming war. Jefferson then dispatched U.S. statesman James Monroe to Paris to assist Livingston in the 1803 negotiations. Monroe was instructed to negotiate at least one of the following items with France: the purchase of New Orleans, the purchase of West Florida and New Orleans, the purchase of land on the eastern bank of the Mississippi River, or the acquisition of the right of navigation along the Mississippi River. In April 1803, just days before Monroe arrived in Paris, Napoleon surprisingly offered to sell the United States the entire Louisiana Territory. Following the public announcement of the first consul's willingness to sell, an incident involving two of Napoleon's brothers occurred in his private quarters. According to contemporary accounts, Joseph and Lucien Bonaparte burst into Napoleon's bath and began shouting their displeasure over the possible sale of Louisiana, to which Napoleon responded by dousing them with water. With all opposition silenced, or at least soaked, the first consul authorized the final sale of all Louisiana Territories. Napoleon's pragmatic decision to transfer the entire territory to the United States reveals both his desire to secure a favorable relationship with the United States and his need to keep Louisiana out of British hands. In a meeting with his ministers on April 10, Napoleon clarified his position on the sale: "I think of ceding it to the United States. I can hardly say that I cede it to them, for it is not yet in our possession. If I leave the least time to our enemies, I will transmit only an empty title to those Republicans whose friendship I seek. They ask for only one town of Louisiana; but I already consider the Colony as completely lost, and it seems to me that in the hands of that growing power it will be more useful to the policy, and even to the commerce of France than if I should try to keep it." The resulting treaty of May 2, 1803, secured eighty million francs ($15 million) for the beleaguered French treasury, of which only fifty-five million francs ($11.3 million) remained after the price was adjusted for American civil claims "held against France for losses stemming from ship seizures and other damages sustained in the Anglo-French war." Like most decisions made by Napoleon Bonaparte, the agreement to sell Louisiana to the United States was pragmatic and expedient. After the costly campaign and the loss of the highly profitable island of Hispaniola, France no longer had the desire or resources to develop the unrefined Louisiana expanse into a profitable French outpost. The additional economic pressures associated with Napoleon's ongoing European wars also served to motivate France to sell Louisiana to supply much-needed monies to the French military. Ultimately, Napoleon's potential French empire in the New World proved unrealistic and was sold off to help finance the First French Empire of the Old World.

—Christopher Blackburn

For Further Reading
Lefebvre, Georges. 1969. *Napoleon: From 18 Brumaire to Tilsit, 1799–1807*. New York: Columbia University Press; Lyon, E. Wilson. 1974. *Louisiana in French Diplomacy: 1759–1804*. Norman: University of Oklahoma Press; Murat, Ines. 1981. *Napoleon and the American Dream*. Baton Rouge: Louisiana State University Press; Schom, Alan. 1997. *Napoleon Bonaparte*. New York: Harper Collins.

BONNEVILLE, BENJAMIN L. E. (1796–1878)

Benjamin Louis Eulalie de Bonneville was born near Paris on April 14, 1796. His father, a well-educated person, had gone a bit too far in discussing the issues of the times in a series of pamphlets that were published in Paris, and he had fallen under the displeasure of the government and was imprisoned. He sought permission to immigrate to the United States, but was not permitted to do so. He was, however, able to send his wife and son Benjamin with Thomas Paine, who had also found it expedient to leave France. The party sailed to North America under secrecy.

The Bonnevilles lived for a time with Paine in New Rochelle, New York. Through Paine's influence, Benjamin was appointed a cadet at the military academy at West Point, from which he graduated in 1819, ranked thirty-five in his class. He spent two years in France with Lafayette, who brought him back with him after his American tour. Upon his return to the United States in 1821, Bonneville was assigned to duty on the Western frontier as a first lieutenant, Seventh Infantry Regiment, and promoted to captain on October 4, 1825.

He became infatuated with the idea that there was a fortune to be made in the fur trade. These ideas culminated in his famous expedition of 1832–1833: Captain Bonneville requested and was granted a leave of absence from the War Department (from August 1831 to October

1833) for the purpose of spending time in the "unexplored regions of the Far West." The letter from the War Department authorizing that leave, signed by General Alexander Macomb, states that the reason the leave was granted was "for the purpose of carrying into execution your design of exploring the country to the Rocky mountains [*sic*] and beyond, with a view to ascertaining the nature and character of the several tribes inhabiting those regions." This expedition was clearly for the purpose of trade. Bonneville entered into agreement with Alfred Seton of New York, one of the Astorians, who, along with several associates, were to provide funding for the expedition.

To carry out this mission, Captain Bonneville recruited and organized a troop of 110 men with two principal assistants: Joseph Reddeford Walker, who would later earn fame in California, and Michael S. Cerre, a member of a St. Louis family well connected in the fur trade.

The expedition was well fitted out. "A fine assortment of goods was provided and the equipment was in all respects a splendid one. Wagons were used on the expedition, contrary to the practice of the mountain traders generally." There were twenty wagons, drawn by oxen and mules. The entire organization was based upon a code of strict military discipline. It was apparent to anyone seeing the group that it was a full military reconnaissance into foreign territory.

The expedition left Fort Osage, west of Independence, Missouri, on May 1, 1832. The route west followed the usual trail into the mountains: up the Platte and Sweetwater Rivers, through South Pass, and on to Green River, where Bonneville and his troop arrived on July 27.

Bonneville's travels through the mountains and high deserts are well documented. He met with several groups of mountain men and fur traders. His presence in those regions was of great concern to a number of people and organizations, most viewing Captain Bonneville as an interloper and refusing to give him much information.

Dr. John McLoughlin, chief factor for the Hudson's Bay Company and chief administrator for the British in the jointly held Oregon Country, feared that Bonneville was the advanced guard of what would become an American invasion. He also worried about increasing American influence in the fur trade. McLoughlin ordered Peter Skene Ogden into the mountains to create a "fur desert" so that the American trappers would come away empty handed.

There is considerable evidence that Bonneville's grand strategy was to take the expedition into California. Joseph R. Walker "was ordered to steer through an unknown country toward the Pacific and if he did not find beaver he should return to the Great Salt Lake in the following summer [1833]."

There is additional evidence that Captain Bonneville was under War Department orders. Clearly, he had objectives beyond merely fur trapping. "Instead of beaver, he pursued both grand adventure for himself and all the information about the West that he judged useful to his government."

—*Henry H. Goldman*

For Further Reading

Chittenden, Hiram Martin. 1954. *A History of the American Fur Trade of the Far West.* 2 vols. Stanford, CA: Academic Reprints; Goetzmann, William H. 1966. *Exploration and Empire: The Explorer and the Scientist in the Winning of the American West.* New York: Alfred A. Knopf; Irving, Washington. 1837. *The Adventures of Captain Bonneville; or Scenes, Incidents, and Adventure in the Far West.* Philadelphia: Carey, Lea, and Blanchard; Utley, Robert M. 1997. *A Life Wild and Perilous: Mountain Men and the Paths to the Pacific.* New York: Henry Holt and Company.

BOONE, DANIEL (1734–1820)

Daniel Boone's activities east of the Mississippi River earned his reputation as one of America's greatest frontiersmen. Never formally educated, he became a skilled hunter and trapper at an early age. Boone further honed his skills as an outdoorsman when his father moved the family from Pennsylvania to the North Carolina frontier in 1750. He first explored the Kentucky wilderness in 1767 and returned two years later with several others for an extended hunting trip. Boone was instrumental in promoting migration to this region. He moved his own family there in 1775 and opened a trail known as the Wilderness Road across Cumberland Gap, along which several settlements, including Boonesboro, soon sprung up.

In the following years, Boone defended Kentucky pioneers from Indian attacks. His success as a militia officer and dramatic capture and escape from the Shawnee made him a local hero. As his reputation grew, Boone served in other important posts, including terms as a Virginia state legislator and county sheriff. His fame grew to new heights with the publication of John Filson's account, *The Adventures of Col. Daniel Boone* (1784), which trumpeted the frontiersman's exploits in the wilderness and as an Indian fighter to readers across the nation and abroad.

Ironically, the man who had done so much to open the path for settlement across the Allegheny Mountains had little success in acquiring territory for himself. He engaged heavily in land speculation and filed claims amounting to tens of thousands of acres, but most were never validated. He was a poor businessman, and others often took advantage of him. Financial difficulties eventually forced him to sell much of the property he did have to satisfy his debts. Disillusioned by these failures and harassed by creditors, Boone looked for opportunities farther west.

During the late 1790s, Spanish officials in Louisiana

began to encourage American immigration into the territory. Fearful of a British invasion from Canada, they believed that increasing the population was essential for defense. With opportunities for settlers dwindling in Kentucky, the promise of generous land grants and no property taxes appealed to many. In 1797, Boone's son, Daniel Morgan, crossed into Spanish territory to look for a place to settle in Missouri. At his father's request, Morgan met with Lieutenant Governor Trudeau to inquire about land grants. Some Spaniards had reservations about inviting in the Boones, but Trudeau was enthusiastic over the prospect of the accomplished frontiersman's leading a number of families into the country.

Impressed by Boone's reputation, the lieutenant governor offered liberal terms, promising to exempt the famed pioneer from the usual restrictions on new settlers. He waived the limit on individual land grants, so Boone could receive one thousand arpents (over a square mile). Families accompanying Boone would be awarded six hundred arpents each. Trudeau also agreed to ignore the rule that they convert to Roman Catholicism, nor would the one-year residency and land-improvement requirement apply to their concessions. Boone requested a land grant on the Femme Osage in Missouri. Morgan had scouted the area and noted its fertile soil, plentiful game, and convenient river access.

In September 1799, Boone set out from Kentucky for Upper Louisiana, joined by a number of his relatives and other families and single men. He traveled by land, escorting the company's stock, while several boats carried tools, household goods, and other supplies. In early October they reached the Mississippi River. Boone rode into St. Louis to secure his land grant and that of fifteen other heads-of-household who traveled with him. The new lieutenant governor, Don Charles Dehault Delassus, treated him as an honored guest. The Spanish official agreed to respect all of Trudeau's promises, and even offered to enlarge the pioneer's tract if he could persuade more families to emigrate. Delassus set up the Femme Osage community as a separate administrative district, with Boone as its chief administrator, or "syndic," so the Americans could distribute the concessions themselves.

Life in Missouri for Boone was similar to his experiences on the Kentucky frontier years earlier. He immediately began to hunt and explore, earning much of his income from the fur and pelt trade. Declining health and old age, however, limited those activities, and the elder Boone increasingly relied upon his family. His previous dealings with Native Americans proved useful, as he once again had to deal with Indians hostile to an intrusion into their territory. He even reunited with some of his Shawnee friends (and former captors), who had also moved west. Still interested in acquiring land, he lured more families to Spanish Louisiana and earned thousands of arpents for his efforts. As syndic he also resumed his role as a community leader. He parceled out land to new immigrants and performed the duties of a justice of the peace. Holding court outdoors under the shade of an elm, Boone heard criminal cases and handed out punishments.

After the Louisiana Purchase, Boone suddenly found his land titles under question. The American commission investigating claims in Missouri required evidence of cultivation before certifying a concession as valid. Boone had not bothered to improve his holdings, because Spanish authorities had assured him that as syndic he was exempt from that requirement. Unfortunately, this had never been put in writing, and the commissioners ruled against him. Sympathy for the pioneer's plight prompted Congress to pass a special act in 1814, returning part of his tract.

Now in the last years of his life and in poor health, Boone sold this land to pay his remaining debts. In the decades following his death on September 26, 1820, the legend of Daniel Boone continued to grow. He is most remembered now for his activities east of the Mississippi River, but historians also recognize his contributions to the early American settlement of Missouri.

—*Christopher Dennis*

For Further Reading

Bakeless, John. 1965. *Daniel Boone.* Harrisburg, PA: Stackpole Company; Faragher, John Mack. 1992. *Daniel Boone: The Life and Times of an American Pioneer.* New York: Henry Holt and Company; Foley, William E. 1989. *The Genesis of Missouri: From Wilderness Outpost to Statehood.* Columbia: University of Missouri Press; Houck, Louis. 1908. *A History of Missouri from the Earliest Explorations and Settlements until the Admission of the State into the Union.* Vol. 2. Chicago: R. R. Donnelly and Sons.

BORE, JEAN ETIENNE (1741–1820)

On November 30, 1803, the French prefect Pierre Clément Laussat established a governing body in New Orleans and selected Jean Etienne Bore as mayor. Bore was a native of the Louisiana colony, having been born in Kaskasia in the Illinois country in 1741. He was educated in France and served in the French military before returning to Louisiana in 1776. Bore invested much of his capital in sugarcane production. His plantation succeeded in granulating sugar and proved that its production could be a profitable enterprise in Louisiana—holding out some promise for the economic viability of the colony.

Because of his success, Bore emerged as a leader of the French-speaking planter class. His political career was spent defending the interests of that class. When Laussat created the new municipal council, Bore was a natural choice. Following Louisiana's transfer to the United States, the council was re-established with most of the same members, and with Bore retaining his position as mayor. On December 24, 1803, in the presence of Governor William Charles Cole Claiborne, Mayor Bore and the members of the council took the oath of allegiance to the United States.

On March 26, 1804, Congress passed legislation that divided Louisiana into two parts: the Territory of Orleans, which included the land "south of the Mississippi Territory and of an east-and-west-line, to commence on the Mississippi River, at the thirty-third degree of north latitude, and to extend west to the western boundary of said cession" (Fortier, 1904); and the District of Louisiana, which included the rest of the purchase area. In addition, the act designated that the Territory of Orleans be administered by a governor appointed by the president for a period of three years. The legislative power was vested in a council of thirteen members appointed annually by the president, and the governor had the right to convene this council at any time. One of the most controversial elements of the act was that it forbade the importation of slaves from foreign countries, and it allowed the importation of slaves from the United States only if they were the property of citizens moving into the territory.

The reaction to the act in Louisiana was understandably negative. Article Three of the Treaty of Cession stated that "the inhabitants of the ceded territory shall be incorporated in the union of the United States, and admitted as soon as possible, according to the principles of the federal constitution, to the enjoyment of all the rights, advantages and immunities of citizens of the United States; and in the meantime they shall be protected in the free enjoyment of their liberty, property, and the religion which they profess." Many Louisianians felt that the congressional act was not only a violation of this article of the Treaty of Cession but also of their natural rights.

On May 16, 1804, Mayor Bore addressed the municipal council in New Orleans in the hope that the council would voice an official protest against the act. Bore stated that "the municipal body was formed under the French government: its powers are what they would [be] if it had remained under that government, Governor Claiborne having confirmed it, at the time of the transfer, with the same powers. It is proper, then, to protest against the constitution decreed by Congress on March 26, because it annihilates the rights of the Louisianians, of whom we form a part and of whom we are the only representative body. The American government, by the wisdom of its constitution, cannot and should not, without departing from its principles and its obligations, infringe our natural rights and article third of the treaty of cession" (ibid.). The council agreed that the act should be protested but would not voice an official protest as a municipal body.

As a result, Mayor Bore resigned on May 19, 1804. On June 1 a group of merchants and planters met in New Orleans and decided to petition Congress to repeal the act and admit Louisiana into the Union immediately. Bore was a leader in this movement for immediate statehood. The group was particularly upset with the division of Louisiana into two parts and the restrictions placed on the importation of slaves. On October 1, 1804, the act took effect despite their efforts. President Jefferson named Bore to the legislative council of the Territory of Orleans, but Bore refused to serve.

—Mark Cave

For Further Reading

Fortier, Alcée. 1904. *A History of Louisiana, Volume III: The American Domination, Part 1, 1803–1861.* New York: Goupil and Company of Paris, Manzi, Joyant, and Company, successors; Louisiana Legislature. 1816. "1803 Treaty of Cession," as found in *A General Digest of the Acts of the Legislatures of the Late Territory of Orleans and of the State of Louisiana.* New Orleans: Peter K. Wagner.

BOURBON FAMILY COMPACT

See **Family Compact**

BRECKINRIDGE, JOHN (1760–1806)

As spokesman for Western interests and leader of Jeffersonian Republicans in the U.S. Senate, John Breckinridge secured passage of the treaty of cession from France and sponsored bills for American occupation and territorial government of Louisiana.

After relocating to Kentucky from Virginia in 1793, Breckinridge became actively involved in the Lexington Democratic Society, where strong anti-Spanish and anti-British sentiment flourished. Antagonistic to arbitrary power exercised by distant governments and deeply concerned about the "Mississippi Question," Kentuckians insisted that free navigation of the Mississippi River depended upon the right to deposit and to transport cargo freely to oceangoing vessels in New Orleans. When news reached Washington that France reclaimed possession of Louisiana and that the Spanish intendant, still running the New Orleans port, abrogated the right of deposit for Americans, Breckinridge submitted a resolution by the Kentucky legislature calling for direct federal involvement, or Kentucky would act on its own.

After Thomas Jefferson requested Breckinridge's assistance in composing an amendment declaring the purchase constitutional, Breckinridge ignored Jefferson's anxiety and thought instead of the future bounties awaiting the West. As floor leader for the Republicans, he won passage of the treaty of cession by a vote of 24 to 7. On October 22, 1803, he introduced a bill, initially drafted by Albert Gallatin, authorizing the possession of the territory and providing the president with the necessary funds and military force to carry out the occupation.

Regarding the constitutionality of the purchase, Breckinridge continued to follow the principles of the Kentucky Resolutions he had helped draft in 1798. Although he conceded the ability of Congress to control migration to the territory, he hoped posterity would make that decision. Rather than seeing the U.S. Constitution as a narrow instrument confining the rights of the majority and entrusting governance to an enlightened elite, Breckinridge hoped that Congress would avoid legalistic squabbles and leave matters to "the good sense of the community" (Harrison, 1969). In short, Breckinridge interpreted the Constitution as a compact limiting the power of the federal government over matters best left to local majorities. Like other leading Jeffersonians, Breckinridge denied that federal land purchases were unconstitutional but denounced excessive federal interference after territorial governments were established. Contrary to other Jeffersonians, who later frowned upon Western migration, Breckinridge supported James Madison's idea of an extended Union based upon republican institutions.

After Spanish sovereignty was formally transferred to France on November 30, 1803, war fever in the West subsided and American occupation peacefully began. Breckinridge quickly submitted a bill on December 5 creating a temporary territorial government. Appointed to a select subcommittee charged with producing permanent political institutions, Breckinridge authored the final outline of territorial government, known as the "Breckinridge Bill."

The Breckinridge Bill divided the purchase between two territories at the line of 33 degrees north latitude. The area south of the line was the southern Territory of Orleans, ruled by a governor and secretary appointed by the president for three years and a thirteen-member legislative council. At the suggestion of Attorney General Levi Lincoln, Breckinridge reluctantly placed the northern land, known as the District of Louisiana, under the territorial government of Indiana. Rather than committing the unconstitutional action of acquiring new land, Lincoln believed that annexing the purchase to an existing territory merely extended the boundaries of the Union to encompass contiguous area.

Like most Republicans and Federalists, Breckinridge believed that since inhabitants of Louisiana had been subject to monarchical influences, a period of republican tutelage was necessary before they could preserve their self-government. Thus a discrepancy seemed to exist between Breckinridge's championing of natural rights and republican government and the centralized structure of Louisiana's territorial government. One such example figured prominently in congressional debate. Jury trials were possible only for civil cases involving $20 or more and in criminal cases involving capital punishment. Some Republicans balked at the stringency of the bill, while Federalists chided the Republicans as hypocrites.

Elsewhere in the bill it stated that slaves could not be imported from abroad, nor brought from other parts of the Union, if they were imported after May 1, 1798. Even then, only American citizens who planned to reside in the territory permanently could bring their slaves. Minor changes were made to the bill, and it passed in mid-February 1804.

Breckinridge resigned from the Senate in 1805 to become Jefferson's attorney general, leaving behind a dearth of Republican leadership in the Senate and prematurely jeopardizing the extension of the Republican Revolution of 1800.

—*Carey M. Roberts*

See also
Gallatin, Albert; Jefferson, Thomas; Loose Construction of the U.S. Constitution

For Further Reading
Dicken-Garcia, Hazel. 1991. *To Western Woods: The Breckinridge Family Moves to Kentucky in 1793.* Rutherford, NJ: Fairleigh Dickinson University Press; Harrison, Lowell H. 1969. *John Breckinridge: Jeffersonian Republican.* Louisville, KY: Filson Club.

BRIDGER, FORT

Fort Bridger was built in 1843 to assist immigrants along the Oregon-California and Mormon Trails, and it served as an army post after 1858 before being abandoned in 1890.

Constructed on Black's Fork of the Green River in present-day southwestern Wyoming by mountain men James Bridger and Louis Vasquez, Fort Bridger served as a trading, supply, and army post for nearly fifty years. With the decline of the Rocky Mountain fur trade in the late 1830s, Bridger built the fort to service immigrant trains along the Oregon-California and Mormon Trails, although he continued a brisk trade with fur trappers and the Shoshone for a number of years.

Nestled at the northern base of the Uinta Range, Fort Bridger's location on Black's Fork, a tributary of the Green River, made it one of the crossroads of the West. Immigrants on the overland trails stopped to replenish supplies, refresh stock, and gather information. The post was ideally suited for travelers exhausted from crossing the Great Plains and Continental Divide, and it marked the halfway point for travelers proceeding to Oregon or California. The valley had adequate wood, plentiful water, and abundant grass—all essential elements in the westward movement.

Although practical, the original post was not impressive. An eight-foot-high L-shaped palisade surrounded several log cabins with mud-filled cracks and enclosed a separate picket yard for livestock. A number of mountain men and Indians periodically pitched their tepees nearby, while a few, like John Robertson, built cabins in the vicinity.

The Mormon journey to the Great Basin that commenced in 1847 and continued for several decades brought

Federal forces en route westward to participate in the Mormon War (1858) established encampments at Fort Bridger.

seventy-five thousand immigrants to or near the fort. The Mormons, members of the Church of Jesus Christ of Latter-Day Saints, traveled by foot, wagon, and, later, handcarts. Many of them left detailed descriptions of the post. The Mormons also built a rival post and permanent colony at Fort Supply, twelve miles to the south, in 1853 to assist immigrants, provide Green River ferry operators, and proselytize Indians. Mormons and the Gold Rushers to California proved a boon to the fort during the first decade, and Bridger traded fresh stock for the immigrants' worn-out ones, augmenting his herds. In 1855 the Latter-Day Saints purchased Fort Bridger for $8,000. The Mormons made improvements to the fort, enclosing a hundred-square-foot area with cobblestone walls that were eighteen feet high. They used the two forts to control eastern access to Utah Territory, assist immigrants, and maintain friendly relations with the Shoshone and the Ute.

However, in 1857 the federal government sent an army expedition under the command of Colonel Albert Sidney Johnston to Utah Territory to force the Mormons to relinquish their hold upon the territory. As the Johnston Expedition approached, the Mormons abandoned and destroyed both forts. With Mormons hindering the army's progress and winter approaching, the army encamped near the charred remains of the fort. The following summer, Johnston issued orders to establish a U.S. military post at the location.

The army rented the fort and a twelve-square-mile reserve from Bridger, who presumably held a Mexican land grant despite the fact that he had already sold the fort to the Latter-Day Saints. The garrison built approximately fifty-seven buildings using a combination of logs, rock, and sun-dried bricks. The fort, with more than thirty pieces of artillery, fortified the trail, served the Overland Stage and telegraph, and operated as a stop for the Pony Express. From 1860 to 1868 relatively few troops were stationed at Fort Bridger. The Fourth Infantry Press's *Daily Telegraph,* Wyoming's first printing endeavor, brought Civil War news in 1863. The post continued operating as the Shoshone Indian Agency, and Eastern Shoshone and Bannocks signed several treaties there in 1863 and 1868. The following year, the Union Pacific completed the Transcontinental Railroad a dozen miles north of Fort Bridger at Carter Station. Judge William A. Carter served as sutler-general for the post and was its most prominent and influential resident throughout its military existence.

The post was vacated by the military in 1890, and the Latter-Day Saints settled Bridger Valley that decade; towns such as Lyman, Mountain View, and, to a lesser extent, Fort Bridger grew. In 1933 the fort became a Wyoming Historical Landmark and Museum, and later, a State Historic Site. An annual rendezvous is held there each fall. Fort Bridger's role as a trading/military establishment, Indian agency, Pony Express station, Overland Stage stop, and telegraph depot made it one of the most important fortifications on the western edge of the Louisiana Purchase.

—*Jay H. Buckley*

For Further Reading

Alter, J. Cecil. 1962 [1925]. *Jim Bridger.* Norman: University of Oklahoma Press; Davis, W. N. 1971. "The Sutler at Fort Bridger." *Western Historical Quarterly* 2: 37–54; Ellison, Robert S. 1981 [1931]. *Fort Bridger: A Brief History.* Cheyenne: Wyoming State Archives, Museums and Historical Department; Gowans, Fred R., and Eugene E. Campbell. 1975. *Fort Bridger: Island in the Wilderness.* Provo, UT: Brigham Young University Press.

BRIDGER, JAMES (1804–1881)

The legendary mountain man Jim Bridger was born on March 17, 1804, in Richmond, Virginia, and moved to St. Louis, Missouri, with his family in 1812. Following the death of his parents in 1817–1818 he became a blacksmith's apprentice, but when the illiterate Bridger learned in 1822 of an advertisement seeking one hundred young men who would ascend the Missouri River to its headwaters, there to be employed in the fur trade, he signed on as the youngest member of General William H. Ashley's trapping expedition to the Rockies. There Bridger assisted in the construction of the Fort Henry trading post, learned the rudiments of the beaver trade, and worked beside such well-known figures as keelboatman Mike Fink and explorer Jedediah Smith, who would later give Bridger the nickname "Old Gabe." When in 1823 conflict with the Arikara necessitated moving Fort Henry farther upstream into Crow territory, near the mouth of the Bighorn, Bridger went along. On the way, trapper Hugh Glass was mauled by a grizzly and seemingly mortally wounded; Bridger and John S. Fitzgerald agreed to stay with Glass until he died, bury him, and then rejoin the party upriver. After five days, when Glass refused to die, the two men abandoned him. Surprisingly, Glass survived and appeared at Fort Henry four months later to claim his revenge, sparing Bridger only because of his relative youth but leaving him with a psychological burden that some contemporaries believed drove Bridger to a period of recklessness.

Bridger first earned his credentials as an explorer in 1824 in order to settle a dispute, volunteering to float down the Bear River canyon to determine where it led and, in the process, becoming the first known white man to see the Great Salt Lake. As growing competition between British, French, and American trappers yielded new partnerships and consolidation in the fur industry over the following decades, Bridger moved from one company to another and survived adventures atypical even of rough-living mountain men of the period. Skirmishes with the hostile tribes of the region resulted in his capture by a band of Blackfoot in 1827 and his being shot in the back with two arrows in 1832; one arrowhead would remain there until the iron point was removed by Dr. Marcus Whitman three years later. Throughout his years in the fur trade Bridger repeatedly traversed the territory of present-day Montana, Wyoming, Colorado, Utah, and Idaho, gaining geographical knowledge that would prove essential to Bridger in his subsequent career as a guide. The decline of the fur trade and a rising tide of emigration prompted him to establish Fort Bridger in 1843 as the first trading post intended to sell goods and services to the wagon trains headed west, rather than deal primarily in furs.

In 1846, Bridger aided the Mormon pioneers led by Brigham Young, telling them that the Great Basin was in fact inhabitable and providing directions that would take them toward Salt Lake. For the next seven years he would serve as a guide to countless parties of immigrants and occasional government expeditions, always relying on what one newspaperman described as his "intuitive knowledge of the topography of the country" (Alter, 1962). Jealous of his command of the immigrant trade and suspicious of his relationship with Indians who had been attacking Mormon settlers, a Mormon militia attempted to arrest Bridger in 1853 and take control of his business; although they failed to do so, they did drive him from the area and loot his fort. Bridger subsequently returned to Missouri and settled briefly on a farm, but demand for his services as a guide for immigrants, hunting parties, and government expeditions soon drew him back West. He served as a guide for numerous parties in the years that followed, including federal troops during the Mormon War in 1857–1858, the expedition by the Army Corps of Engineers into the Yellowstone country in 1859–1860, the Berthoud survey of a new Denver–Salt Lake stage route in 1861, and the U.S. Army in its attempts to stop Cheyenne and Sioux attacks along the Powder River in 1865–1866.

Bridger was married three times, first to a Flathead woman who died in 1846, then to a Ute who died in childbirth in 1849, and finally to a Snake/Shoshone who died in 1858, and he had six children. Upon his retirement in 1868 he returned to his family in Missouri for the last time and lived there with his children until his death, on July 17, 1881. Immortalized through his own tales and the writings of his contemporaries, Jim Bridger became a figure of legend during his own lifetime and the archetype of the mountain man in early histories of the fur trade.

—Derek R. Larson

See also
Arikara; Ashley, William Henry; Mountain Men; Smith, Jedediah Strong

For Further Reading
Alter, J. Cecil. 1962. *Jim Bridger.* Norman: University of Oklahoma Press; Caesar, Gene. 1961. *King of the Mountain Men: The Life of Jim Bridger.* New York: E. P. Dutton Company; Vestal, Stanley. 1946. *Jim Bridger: Mountain Man.* Lincoln: University of Nebraska Press.

BUFFALO SOLDIERS

The Buffalo Soldiers were African American men who served in the U.S. military in the nineteenth century. When Native Americans encountered black cavalry soldiers on the Great Plains,

The African American soldiers who were members of the Ninth and Tenth Cavalries became known as the Buffalo Soldiers. (North Wind Picture Archives)

they began using the term "buffalo soldiers" because they thought that the African Americans' hair resembled the fur of a bison or buffalo. The soldiers did not seem to mind, but rather enjoyed the special distinction, and the Tenth Cavalry even put a buffalo on its regimental crest.

African Americans first received a chance to prove their bravery and commitment to the government when they enlisted in the U.S. Colored Troops during the Civil War. The experiment worked so well that some within the government remained committed to enlisting black soldiers at the end of that conflict. There was considerable opposition, but a bill made it through Congress on July 28, 1866, authorizing the creation of two cavalry and four infantry regiments composed entirely of African Americans. General Ulysses S. Grant ordered his seconds in command, Generals Philip Sheridan and William Tecumseh Sherman, to create the black regiments in their divisions. Initially established as the Thirty-eighth, Thirty-ninth, Fortieth, and Forty-first Infantry, under a consolidation plan the infantry became two units, the Twenty-fourth and Twenty-fifth, and the cavalry remained the Ninth and Tenth. At the time the army had ten cavalry and twenty-five infantry units, so these black regiments constituted a significant body of U.S. military forces. These units, like those in the Civil War, remained under the command of white officers. Many officers would not accept a position with these units, regarding it as demeaning to serve with nonwhites, even if it meant a promotion. (For example, George Armstrong Custer turned down an assignment.) Two trusted officers, Edward Hatch and Benjamin Grierson, took command of the Ninth and Tenth Cavalries, respectively. Receiving their first postings in the West, the buffalo soldiers remained there for more than twenty years, representing the United States in many of the former Louisiana Purchase territories.

Posted onto the frontier, the African American soldiers received responsibility for implementing the government's plan to force Plains Indians onto reservations. In this assignment they found themselves facing the formidable warriors of the Kiowa, Comanche, Cheyenne, and Apache, who were fighting to protect their homelands. Stationed at several Western forts from Wyoming to New Mexico, the Buffalo Soldiers rode out against Oklahoma boomers, the Apache leaders Victorio and Geronimo, and the Sioux Ghost Dancers. Such assignments exposed the men both to dangerous fighting and to grueling conditions—intense summer heat, bitter winter cold, and violent storms. In addition, the Buffalo Soldiers endured these hardships with inferior supplies. From the beginning, the black units had borne the brunt of a racism manifested in poorer quality food and quarters and even worse mounts than those supplied to white soldiers. Relegated to riding horses rejected by the Seventh Cavalry that often died soon after arrival, the Ninth Cavalry struggled to stay mounted. This subtle discrimination plagued the service of the regiments, as did the more blatant racism from those who refused to accept black men in uniform. Such discrimination ranged from recommendations to disband black troops to civilian violence in frontier towns. Despite these conditions, the Buffalo Soldiers exhibited excellent discipline and a lower desertion rate than white units. It could be that they had both more to prove to the nation and fewer opportunities outside the military.

The Buffalo Soldiers represent a unique intersection between minority groups in the growing country. Black soldiers using the military to gain a foothold in a white-dominated society were given the task of removing indigenous peoples from the West to ensure white expansion in the latter days of Manifest Destiny. Apparently respected by natives, the Buffalo Soldiers struggled to gain acceptance by whites. The men who enlisted came from a variety of backgrounds, from field hands to artisans, with widely varying literacy levels. They faced demanding military assignments in difficult conditions and with continued discrimination. The Buffalo Soldiers established an exceptional record of bravery and perseverance.

—Clarissa W. Confer

For Further Reading

Kenner, Charles. 1999. *Buffalo Soldiers and Officers of the Ninth Cavalry.* Norman: University of Oklahoma Press; Leckie, William. 1967. *The Buffalo Soldiers: A Narrative of the Negro Cavalry in the West.* Norman: University of Oklahoma Press.

BURR, AARON (1756–1836)

Aaron Burr was the third vice president of the United States, a New York politician, and one of the most controversial figures of the Revolutionary generation.

The son of Aaron Burr Sr., president of the College of New Jersey (now Princeton), and Esther Edwards, the daughter of the famous theologian Jonathan Edwards, Burr graduated from Princeton in 1772. During the American Revolution, Burr rose to the rank of lieutenant colonel and served on the staffs of both Benedict Arnold and George Washington. Having antagonized Washington, and realizing that future promotion would be withheld from him, Burr resigned from the army in 1779. Called to the New York bar in 1782, he entered state politics as an ally of Governor George Clinton, who made him state attorney general in 1789. In state politics he was a strong critic of General Philip Schuyler and his son-in-law, Alexander Hamilton. In 1791, Burr was elected to the U.S. Senate, and, although a loyal Republican Party man, he served without distinction and failed to gain reelection in 1797.

Returning to New York, Burr was again elected to the state legislature in 1798, and he did much to ensure a Republican victory in that state during the presidential election of 1800, thus helping to gain a national victory for the party. He was nominated as the vice presidential candidate on the Republican ticket, and under the procedures then prevailing, the electorate cast their votes for Jefferson and Burr without indicating a choice for president or vice president. The election resulted in a tie of seventy-three votes for each candidate in the Electoral College, and thus the election was thrown into the House of Representatives. Although it is clear that Burr did not attempt to influence the vote in the House, his ambiguous actions earned the distrust of both Thomas Jefferson and James Madison. On the thirty-sixth ballot the political deadlock in the House was broken only when Alexander Hamilton persuaded a fellow Federalist, Rep. James Bayard, to break Federalist ranks and vote for Jefferson; this single vote won the presidency for Jefferson. In 1804, continued distrust of Burr's ambitions led Jefferson to replace Burr on the Republican ticket with George Clinton.

In February 1804, Burr's friends in New York hoped to replace Clinton with Burr, but in a scurrilous gubernatorial campaign Burr was defeated, largely by the actions of Alexander Hamilton. Furious at Hamilton's denigrating remarks regarding his character, Burr challenged Hamilton to a duel, which took place at Weehawken, New Jersey, on July 11, 1804. Hamilton's death led to Burr's being indicted for murder in both New Jersey and New York, and he returned to Washington, D.C., as a wanted man, to preside over the Senate until his term expired in 1805. During impeachment proceedings in the Senate against the Federalist judge Samuel Chase (February–March 1805), Burr, by his rulings, frustrated the Republican campaign against the judiciary. An infuriated Jefferson refused to offer Burr a future office, and still a wanted man, Burr fled to Philadelphia, where the seeds of the "Burr Conspiracy" were firmly planted.

What exactly Burr's harebrained scheme entailed is hard to discover. One thing is certain, however: his plans to create a Western empire did include the assistance of General James Wilkinson, who, among other things, was a scoundrel, a paid agent in the service of Spain, and, more important, the governor of the recently acquired Louisiana Territory above the thirty-third parallel whose headquarters were situated in St. Louis. Before they met in Philadelphia in the spring of 1805, Wilkinson had sent a deputation of disgruntled Louisianians from New Orleans to Burr, who listened sympathetically to their criticism of Jefferson's administration of the Territory of Orleans and their wish for self-government. Burr entered into negotiations with the British minister in Washington, Anthony Merry, who sent a dispatch to London on March 29, 1805, suggesting British naval support for Burr's scheme to detach New Orleans, the Louisiana Territory, and the Western states from the Union.

When Wilkinson and Burr met in the Philadelphia home of Wilkinson's brother-in-law, Nicholas Biddle, they discussed Burr's future, his popularity in the West, and a campaign by a force of volunteers against Mexico with the intent to create a separate state. Whether these plans concluded a conspiracy to detach Louisiana and the Western states from the Union remains unclear. Nonetheless, Burr then undertook a much publicized Western trip from Pittsburgh to New Orleans, where he received great acclamation. Warmly welcomed in Tennessee, he gained the support of Andrew Jackson, who was keen to expel the "hated Dons" from the continent. By the time that Wilkinson and Burr met again, in St. Louis in September of 1805, Wilkinson was becoming lukewarm to the adventure, on account of the hostile accounts being published in the East regarding Burr's suspected activities.

Unconcerned about Wilkinson's reception and encouraged by his own popularity in the West, Burr returned to Washington, where he gained a final interview with Jefferson in March 1806. Disappointed by Jefferson's refusal to appoint him to office, Burr, encouraged by the possibility of war with Spain over the disputed western Louisiana border, pressed on with his plans. Raising financial backing, he returned to the West, raised more than a thousand volunteers, and proceeded down the Mississippi toward New Orleans, sending ahead a letter in cipher to Wilkinson instructing him to create a decisive border incident in Louisiana that would ignite war with Spain. Instead, Wilkinson, motivated always by his own financial interests, warned the viceroy in Mexico of Burr's activities and betrayed Burr to Jefferson, claiming that he had just discovered a sinister plot to revolutionize the West. Jefferson issued a presidential proclamation denouncing Burr as a traitor and ordering his arrest. Recognized at Natchez, Burr was arrested and sent to Richmond, Virginia, for trial on a charge of treason.

Burr was indicted by a grand jury on the charge in May 1807, and his trial began on August 10, 1807. If Jefferson was convinced of Burr's complete guilt, that was not a view shared by Chief Justice John Marshall, who presided over the trial and who intended to use it to embarrass the administration. Although Burr had clearly planned an invasion of Mexico, Marshall's rather narrow definition of treason aided Burr's defense, as did the rather circumstantial nature of the evidence and the growing suspicions of Wilkinson's part in the conspiracy. In one of the longest decisions of his career, Marshall ruled that the government had failed to prove that Burr had actually committed treason by an overt act, and therefore, dismissing all the collateral evidence, he instructed the jury to find Burr not guilty.

Burr's victory in court was short-lived. He would remain discredited forever, and under a cloud of suspicion and distrust, he left the United States for Europe in June 1808. Unable to persuade Napoleon to back his vision of conquering Mexico or his proposals that France should attempt to regain Canada or Louisiana, Burr continued to live in Europe, in increasing penury, for four years. Returning to New York in 1812, Burr practiced law with some success until his death in September 1836.

—Rory T. Cornish

For Further Reading

Abernethy, Thomas Perkins. 1954. *The Burr Conspiracy.* New York: Oxford University Press; Chidsey, Donald Barr. 1967. *The Great Conspiracy: Aaron Burr and His Strange Doings in the West.* New York: Crown Publishers; Fleming, Thomas. 1999. *Duel: Alexander Hamilton, Aaron Burr, and the Future of America.* New York: Basic Books; Klime, Mary-Jo, ed. 1983. *Political Correspondence and Public Papers of Aaron Burr.* 2 vols. Princeton: Princeton University Press; Lomask, Milton. 1982. *Aaron Burr.* 2 vols. New York: Farrar, Straus and Giroux.

CABOT, GEORGE (1751–1823)

As a former Massachusetts senator and unofficial leader of the Essex Junto, George Cabot was a staunch critic of Jeffersonian expansionism. He later served as president of the Hartford Convention (1814–1815).

Like his Federalist colleagues, Cabot believed that Jefferson's election as president in 1800 marked the beginning of the end of the American republic. The election was a herald of democracy, which Cabot considered "government of the worst" (Lodge, 1878). Cabot feared that the new spirit was infecting the Federalist Party itself, and he planned with Fisher Ames to establish a purely Federalist newspaper.

To Cabot, the Louisiana Purchase was both a symptom and a cause of the new democratic spirit. In foreign policy, the Louisiana Purchase was an example of Jefferson's strategic incompetence and reliance upon the good will and good word of France. "The cession of Louisiana is an excellent thing for France," Cabot wrote to Rufus King. "It puts into safekeeping what she could not keep herself; for England would take Louisiana in the first moment of war, without the loss of a man. France would neither settle it nor protect it" (ibid.). The true title, Cabot believed, rested on the force of arms and not law. Cabot considered opposition to the Louisiana Purchase a test of political loyalty and good sense. He lamented John Quincy Adams's support of the purchase as a sad example of how some formerly good Federalists were willing to pander to the new spirit and ruling powers. Cabot believed that Jefferson, in his rush to acquire new territory, had ignored the problem of how to protect it.

Politically, Cabot believed that each addition of new territory to the Union diminished the power and influence of New England. The new states carved out of the trans-Mississippi West would almost certainly vote with Jefferson, and the unabated rise of democracy would reduce New England to insignificance. The Louisiana Purchase led Cabot and other Federalists to dabble off and on in secession schemes until the end of the War of 1812. Cabot wrote Timothy Pickering in early 1804 that New England's separation from the Union was not far distant, although the time was not yet right. Cabot was convinced that the political crisis of New England and the nation would have to bottom out before New England would act. Cabot hoped that Aaron Burr would be elected governor of New York in 1804, and that would bring the final crisis. Cabot did not favor disunion, but he feared it would be necessary to preserve New England's interests. Cabot considered the spirit that produced the Louisiana Purchase as the same spirit that would continue to oppress New England, bringing the Embargo and eventually war with Great Britain.

The New England separatism created by the Louisiana Purchase flared up at the Embargo and then lay dormant until 1814. That year, the burning of Washington, invasion of New York, blockade of New England, and occupation of parts of Maine forced New England's leaders to plan for their own defense. A series of town meetings calling for a New England convention culminated in the Hartford Convention, which met from December 15, 1814, to January 5, 1815. Cabot attended to prevent rather than cause a crisis. Cabot hoped to put a damper on radical solutions from younger Federalists, and he believed that the ultimate result of the convention would be "A Great Pamphlet" (Banner, 1970). The convention unanimously elected Cabot president. One participant described Cabot as a man of "lofty Washingtonian dignity," and like Washington at the Constitutional Convention, Cabot did not lead debate, leaving that duty to Harrison Gray Otis (Morison, 1913). As there is no record of day-to-day debates, the final report is the only record of the convention's views. The convention did not endorse separation, but it did attack virtually every aspect of Republican foreign and domestic policy. One article condemned the admission of new states as destructive of the sectional balance of power. The second of seven proposed amendments to the Constitution prohibited the admission of new states without the approval of two-thirds of both houses of Congress. The end of the convention marked Cabot's exit from public life.

The arrival of the convention's report in Washington was overshadowed by the news of Jackson's victory at New Orleans and the successful conclusion of the war. Cabot's critique of expansionism, as tied to the rise of democracy and the rule of the South over the North, would form the basis for New England's opposition to the admission of other states carved out of the Louisiana Purchase territory and the acquisition of new lands.

—Robert W. Smith

See also
Adams, John Quincy; Ames, Fisher; Burr, Aaron; Essex Junto; Federalist Party; Jefferson, Thomas; King, Rufus; New Orleans, Battle of; Pickering, Timothy

For Further Reading
Banner, James M., Jr. 1970. *To the Hartford Convention: The Federalists and the Origins of Party Politics in Massachusetts.* New York: Alfred A. Knopf; Dwight, Theodore. 1970. *History of the Hartford Convention: With a Review of the Policy of the United States Government which Led to the War of 1812.* New York: DaCapo; Lodge, Henry Cabot. 1878. *Life and Letters of George Cabot.* Boston: Little, Brown; Morison, Samuel Eliot. 1913. *The Life and Letters of Harrison Gray Otis, Federalist 1765–1848.* 2 vols. Boston: Houghton Mifflin Company.

CAJUNS

The Cajuns are a distinct ethnic group in the United States, identified primarily with rural Louisiana since the last half of the eighteenth century. Until the late twentieth century they were regarded as quaint, perhaps a sort of American peasant whose unique culture was defined by many as primitive. However, with the civil rights movement of the twentieth century and the subsequent value placed on diversity in the United States, the Cajuns have attracted new interest and have gained respect. In parts of Louisiana they have dominated society and politics for some two centuries and have surprisingly thrived despite the onslaughts of the predominant American culture with both its mores and language.

The Cajun journey to a Louisiana homeland began in France in the seventeenth century with the migration of French Catholic peasants (Huguenots or Protestant dissenters were not permitted to settle in the new North American colony of Acadia, known today as Nova Scotia). Here they adapted themselves to a different terrain and climate and created a relatively comfortable existence, especially by contemporary peasant standards. This comfortable existence would end when the War of Spanish Succession (known in the Western Hemisphere as Queen Anne's War) resulted in the transfer of Acadia from France to Great Britain with the Treaty of Utrecht in 1713. The peasants' culture seemed an affront to the British government that claimed rule over them. The Acadian peasants refused to make an unconditional oath of allegiance to Great Britain and considered themselves neutrals. Their historical perspective taught them that future wars could change the political landscape again and possibly return them to French jurisdiction. After initial requests for submission, the British government became more tolerant of the Acadians until the middle of the century, prior to the commencement of the Seven Years' War (or French and Indian War as it is known in North America). The Acadians were still considered subversive elements by some colonial administrators because of their noncommitment to the British Crown. A hostile stance towards the Acadians became apparent under the new governor, Major Charles Lawrence, in 1754. He demanded an oath of allegiance, and when this policy was met with noncompliance, he organized the *Grand Dérangement,* or Great Migration, an exile that took Acadians to many foreign lands. The British confiscated Acadian property, and the Acadians were forced to move in small groups to other locations. Some returned to their ancestral homeland, others retreated to various British colonies to the south like Maryland, where the welcome was less than cordial, and some went to the French colony of St. Domingue (modern Haiti).

With the conclusion of the Seven Years' War at the Treaty of Paris (1763) and its requirement that Louisiana (that is, all French lands west of the Mississippi River) be transferred to Spanish control, some of these Acadian refugees applied for immigration to the new Spanish colony. After overcoming legal hurdles, many began to migrate from their various temporary settlements to Louisiana, where the initial welcome turned sour and resulted in Acadian support of an overthrow of the Spanish governor Antonio de Ulloa in 1768. The story of this migration was memorialized and romanticized by Henry Wadsworth Longfellow in his epic "Evangeline."

After the development of more cordial relations with the new colonial government, the Acadians adapted themselves to their new environment. Agriculture was a primary concern—the diet of a northern colony was not appropriate to semitropical Louisiana. Cabbages, turnips, and even wheat, staples of the Acadian diet, were not indigenous to the new climate, so these migrants turned to various beans and squash, as well as rice. Similarly their style of domestic architecture needed adaptation since heat, not frigid winds, was the norm in their new homeland—covered porches became a necessity. Even their clothing demanded modification in the subtropical climate, and this change developed rapidly and included shedding shoes during the summer. Nonetheless, their French peasant roots still dominated in their belief in the importance of the land, the farm, and the family. It was during these early resettlement years that the Cajun culture as it is perceived today developed. For at least a generation the Acadian refugees adapted to their new circumstances and developed some comfort with them. They succeeded in creating a new ethnicity that is called Cajun. In fact, the word *Cajun* is a corruption of the French *Acadien.* Those characteristics so familiar in Acadian culture predominated and, in turn, were complemented by others.

One significant aspect of their culture was religion. They practiced Catholicism but not with the unquestioning devotion that characterized their ancestors in France. Their Acadian experience with a paucity of clergy made them self-dependent and encouraged them to rely on the ordained for specifically sacerdotal functions like baptism, marriage, and burial. The occasional celebration of the mass was a relief to the tediousness of their lives and provided the necessary spiritual comfort, especially for the women and children, because the men, although professing Catholicism, did not often attend mass. Nonetheless, the clergy were expected to remain aloof from the quotidian aspects of the Cajuns' lives—they were to be present only when requested.

Other characteristics of their distinct culture that have been noted and researched are the importance of family and familial relationships, as well as attachment to the soil. Related to these traits was a spirit of fraternity with other ethnic brethren. Cajuns were not highly competitive in agricultural production and finances; they sought to maintain a level of friendliness and egalitarianism. To them it was most important to produce what was necessary to sustain life for the family throughout the year and to share what they could with their neighbors and extended family. However, some Cajuns became successful farmers and excelled in their agrarian pursuits, and even became slaveholders. They became, in a sense, a type of Cajun gentry during the nineteenth century. This status symbolized another noticeable characteristic of Cajun culture—a strong sense of individual independence. Nonetheless, they were able to maintain their own distinctive culture, including their French patois.

What is remarkable is that the Cajuns were able to maintain this distinct culture despite the pressures from the Spanish overseers at the time of their arrival in Louisiana, the brief French rule after the second Treaty of San Idelfonso (1800), and the American acquisition of the Cajun homeland with the Louisiana Purchase of 1803. Ironically, the Cajuns met with pressures from the Creoles, the descendants of the French settlers in Louisiana. Despite a similarity of language with the Cajuns, the Creoles did not share the same cultural background. An affinity of tongues was not sufficient to create a connective bond. However, throughout the nineteenth and even the twentieth centuries, these two groups have been brought closer together through marriage between their ranks. But it is interesting to note that the dominant culture in the region appears to be Cajun; non-Cajun spouses usually assimilate, and children are raised to follow Cajun customs. Moreover, this pattern is also apparent in marriages with anglophones, especially when the bride is Cajun. The familial and ethnic ties appear to be tightened by the maternal line and supersede that of the paternal. In many regions of Louisiana Cajun culture has been dominant and has quickly, if not easily, overcome other ethnicities.

—Tom Sosnowski

See also
Creoles

For Further Reading

Brasseaux, Carl A. 1987. *The Founding of New Acadia: The Beginnings of Acadian Life in Louisiana, 1765–1803.* Baton Rouge: Louisiana State University Press; Brasseaux, Carl A. 1992. *Acadian to Cajun: Transformation of a People, 1803–1877.* Jackson: University Press of Mississippi; Rushton, William Faulkner. 1979. *The Cajuns: From Acadia to Louisiana.* New York: Farrar Straus Giroux.

CAMEAHWAIT

When the Lewis and Clark Expedition advanced far into the Rocky Mountain region and crossed the Continental Divide at Lemhi Pass (in present-day Montana) in August 1805, the members of the Corps of Discovery knew that they were truly entering uncharted territory. It was clear that the exploring party would need to form alliances with friendly tribes in the region in order to obtain the horses, food, and other provisions necessary for continuing onward to the Pacific. Additionally, the support of friendly tribes would be of diplomatic assistance as the Corps of Discovery entered territory that was rumored to be hostile.

Prior to entering the region, Meriwether Lewis had written: "If we do not find [the Shoshoni], I fear the successful issue of our voyage will be very doubtful" (DeVoto, 1653). Uncertain of whether he would encounter the group and of how he would be received, Lewis realized that the success of the Corps of Discovery's efforts depended upon the assistance of the Shoshoni.

Captain Lewis and a small party encountered a band of Shoshoni women on August 13, 1805, members of the tribe led by Chief Cameahwait ("One Who Never Walks"). Lewis was able to convince the women that the expedition came in peace. He distributed trinkets (blue beads and vermilion) to the group and asked that they direct him toward their camp. Within two miles of the first encounter, Lewis and his party came upon sixty mounted Shoshoni warriors and Chief Cameahwait himself. Lewis distributed additional presents, including an American flag, and smoked peace pipes with the group.

The Shoshoni were fascinated by Lewis and his men, as they were the first white men that members of the tribe had ever seen. Cameahwait welcomed the group and provided food and a tipi for the party. Through the assistance of interpreter George Drouillard, Lewis was able to tell Cameahwait about the purpose and goals of the expedition. Cameahwait, in response, was able to inform Lewis of the challenge that the party faced in crossing the Bitterroot Mountain range that lay ahead. He also acknowledged that an all-water route to the Pacific did not exist.

Lewis convinced Cameahwait and some of his warriors to travel with him to join William Clark and the remainder of the Corps of Discovery. Lewis hoped that the group might be able to negotiate successfully for Shoshoni horses, since the tribe owned a herd of about seven hundred. These animals would be essential during the mountain crossings that lay ahead.

It was during this meeting that a fortuitous circumstance occurred. While Lewis and Clark were negotiating with Cameahwait, Sacagawea recognized the Shoshoni chief as her brother, whom she had not seen in four years. Having been raised as a Shoshoni, Sacagawea had been kidnapped by the Hidatsa. The two shared an emotional reunion during which Sacagawea discovered that all her family, except for her brother and her nephew, had died. Thereafter, as a result of the chance encounter, it was clear that Cameahwait would do everything within his power to assist the American explorers.

—Junius P. Rodriguez

See also
Sacagawea
For Further Reading
DeVoto, Bernard, ed. 1953. *The Journals of Lewis and Clark*. Boston: Houghton Mifflin Company.

CAMINO REAL, EL

El Camino Real, known variously as the Royal Road or the King's Highway, was a historically significant route in Spanish North America. As the limits of Spanish colonial America expanded—as they did after Spain acquired the Louisiana Territory from France in 1762—so too did *El Camino Real* extend itself to include the newly incorporated regions. Efforts were under consideration in the late eighteenth century to extend the route to the Natchez District.

Officials in Mexico City first expressed the need for such a roadway when they became concerned about foreign interest in the lands of eastern Texas. By 1691, after LaSalle's colony had been established along the Texas Gulf Coast, it became clear that a greater Spanish presence was necessary in the region, and the development of a road that served as a trade and communications corridor soon followed. In 1718, when St. Denis, the Frenchman who had established the Natchitoches settlement in Louisiana, wandered into eastern Texas seeking to establish a trade relationship, Spanish officials invested more time and energy into developing the roadway.

For nearly 150 years, *El Camino Real* was the primary road linking Mexico City with Los Adaes, now located near Natchitoches in northwestern Louisiana, but then the capital of Texas and Coahuila (until 1773). Along the route were linked the settlements of Saltillo, Monclova, Guerrero, and Coahuila, along with other presidios and missions scattered throughout the region. Whether large or small, these Spanish settlements and garrisons were linked by a secure route that seemingly reduced the vast expanse of territory separating these isolated outposts. Contemporary accounts described the roadway as consisting of pressed earth, and it was said to have been as wide as any of the finest roadways in Europe.

El Camino Real was a significant artery of both trade and communication that served multiple roles in Spanish America, including exploration, conquest, governance, missionary supply, settlement, cultural exchange, and military campaigns. The regular use and maintenance of the route carried both real and symbolic weight in keeping hostile Indian tribes from harming the isolated colonial outposts in eastern Texas.

Although the Spanish had been vigilant to protect eastern Texas from trade incursions that originated in French Louisiana, they relaxed that policy once Louisiana became a Spanish possession. At the time, the Spanish authorities in Mexico City believed it highly unlikely that citizens of the United States would settle the trans-Appalachian frontier and threaten Texas. Upon the recommendation of Baron de Rubi, the Spanish decided to limit their colonial defensive perimeter to the Rio Grande, thereby abandoning the East Texas missions and effectively returning the region to Indian Territory. With the New Regulation of the Presidos (1772), the Spanish authorities closed all of their missions and presidios beyond San Antonio. Accordingly, the use and influence of *El Camino Real,* once a powerful symbol of Spanish colonial authority, began to wane.

—Junius P. Rodriguez

See also
Los Adaes; Nacogdoches; Natchitoches; Texas
For Further Reading
Corle, Edwin. 1949. *The Royal Highway: El Camino Real.* New York: Bobbs-Merrill.

CARONDELET, LOUIS FRANCISCO HECTOR DE (1747–1807)

Baron de Carondelet was appointed governor of Louisiana and West Florida in 1791 and served during some of the most turbulent years in the Spanish colony.

Internal threats such as French Creole sedition and slave revolts, combined with the threat of invasion from France, Britain, or the United States, made the assignment a difficult one. Before arriving in Louisiana, Carondelet had served briefly as governor of San Salvador, and although he had participated in the siege of Pensacola in 1781, his knowledge of Mississippi Valley affairs was limited.

The colony was poorly defended and faced increasing expansionist pressures from the United States. Only one regiment was assigned to Louisiana, and its military posts needed significant repair. The Kentucky intrigue, a conspiracy to weaken the United States by dividing it into two rival republics, had subsided, and Kentuckians were absorbed in admission to statehood and war with northern Indians. In addition, a strategy to strengthen the colony through immigration was, at that time, not working. The plan allowed Protestants the rights of Spanish subjects in an attempt to depopulate Kentucky, Cumberland, and Holston. The attempt failed for several reasons: the rights granted as a Spanish subject were less than those they already enjoyed; a reduction in the amount of tobacco annually purchased by the Spanish government eliminated a waiting market for their agricultural products; and Spain proved unable to protect the settlers from Indian attacks.

The only apparent option for Carondelet regarding the defense of the colony appeared to be Indian alliances. Prior to his administration, the policy regarding Indians was one of maintaining a monopoly on Indian trade in order to create dependency. Carondelet's attempt to forge military alliances with the Indians was a blatant violation of the orders of the Spanish government. He probably felt that he had no choice, for he mistakenly interpreted the presence of U.S. forces on the Ohio River as a prelude to invasion. In reality, they were there to aid in the conflict against the northern Indians.

Carondelet asked representatives of the four southern Indian nations to assemble at Nogales to work out a treaty. The Spanish representative was Manuel Luis Gayoso de Lemos y Amorin, then governor of the Natchez district. Gayoso believed that the Indian tribes could not act as a unified force, and that they did not represent a sufficient defense for the colony. Carondelet wanted the treaty to provide for sending a delegation of Indian chiefs to the United States with the ultimatum of re-establishing the frontier line, as it had existed in 1772, or to face war. Carondelet felt that the Spanish had an adequate defense, with the Indian alliance, but Gayoso disagreed and ignored Carondelet's instructions regarding the delegation. A treaty was signed that created on paper a confederation of the four southern tribes under Spanish protection, with a mutual territorial guarantee. It also allowed for Spanish troops to enter the Indian country in order to establish additional posts.

Carondelet's attempts to secure disputed territories for Spain and discourage American expansion by controlling the Mississippi River were undermined by the Spanish government. On August 4, 1795, representatives of Spain signed a peace treaty with the French republic at Basel. This treaty was in direct violation of a previous treaty signed with Great Britain, and Spain expected British aggression as a result, with an attack probable somewhere in the Gulf of Mexico region. Spain was not in a position to be at war with both Britain and the United States, and it was determined to settle its dispute with the latter. On October 27, 1795, the Treaty of San Lorenzo was signed, surrendering the disputed territories to the United States and providing free navigation rights to the Mississippi.

The Treaty of San Lorenzo has been viewed by many as the beginning of the disintegration of the Spanish empire. This may have unjustly colored perceptions of Carondelet's administration. The events that led to the surrender of the territories were largely out of his control. Carondelet's term in Louisiana ended in 1796, after which he was reassigned as president of the Audiencia of Quito, where he died in 1807.

—Mark Cave

See also

Gayoso de Lemos, Manuel; San Lorenzo, Treaty of; West Florida

For Further Reading

Nasatir, Abraham P. 1976. *Borderland in Retreat: From Spanish Louisiana to the Far Southwest.* Albuquerque: University of New Mexico Press; Whitaker, Arthur Preston. 1927. *The Spanish-American Frontier, 1783–1795: Westward Movement and the Spanish Retreat in the Mississippi Valley.* Lincoln: University of Nebraska Press.

CARSON, CHRISTOPHER "KIT" (1809–1868)

Kit Carson, a true frontiersman and mountain man, is one of the most recognizable names in Western American history. He was quiet, unassuming, and unable to read or write until he was in his middle fifties, but he stands out as one of America's heroes.

Kit Carson moved with his family from Madison County, Kentucky, to the Boone's Lick region of Missouri in 1811 when he was but two years old. Nearly his entire career was spent living and working in the lands of the Louisiana Purchase.

A young Kit Carson joined a group of early Santa Fe traders in 1826. That single event defined his future life. In 1829, he joined a fur-trapping expedition out of Taos, crossed the Mojave Desert into California, and returned to Taos in 1831. From that experience Carson developed a reputation in the West that was to last throughout the rest of his life. He became known as "the bear that walked like a man" because of his well-known reluctance either to shave his beard or to cut his hair.

Kit Carson was heavily engaged in fur trapping from 1831 to 1841, usually in the northwestern mountains of present-day Utah, Colorado, Wyoming, Montana, and Idaho—states some or all of whose lands had been carved out of the Louisiana Purchase. The practical knowledge that he gained about the Rocky Mountains and the passes through them served him well as a guide to explorer John Charles Frémont, whom he met along the Santa Fe Trail early in 1842. Carson had been in St. Louis on business and was returning home to Taos when he overtook the Frémont Party. Frémont hired him to guide the group to California. That activity lasted from June through October. He then remained with Frémont and served as guide to both Frémont's Second (1843–1844) and Third (1846–1847) Expeditions. During the Third Expedition, Carson participated in Frémont's conquest of California.

Christopher "Kit" Carson was one of the most experienced trappers, traders, and scouts to operate along the southwestern frontier.

When the U.S. Senate declined to confirm a "battlefield" commission, Kit Carson returned to Taos, now in the U.S. Territory of New Mexico, and retired. He was thirty-nine years old. He came out of retirement, however, in 1853, to accept a federal appointment as Indian agent among the Ute, a position that he held until 1861, when he resigned to organize a volunteer infantry regiment to respond to President Lincoln's call for troops to fight in the Civil War. He led the First New Mexico Volunteer Infantry into battle against Texas soldiers under Confederate general Henry Hopkins Sibley at the Battle of Valverde. The First New Mexico Volunteer Infantry was subsequently attached to the California troops under the command of Major General James Henry Carleton after their arrival in the territory in 1862.

Kit Carson participated in several skirmishes with Native Americans, both in New Mexico and on the Western Plains. His most noted efforts were directed against the Navajo in the Canyon de Chelly, which resulted in the "Long Walk" of the Navajo from Fort Wingate to Fort Sumner in 1863, and the Battle of Adobe Walls in 1864. He also led an expedition against the Comanche, which resulted in a charge that he massacred an innocent Indian band.

Kit Carson was brevetted brigadier general in March 1865 and assigned as commander at Fort Garland. His health had begun to fail. He traveled east to seek medical help, but to no avail. Kit Carson died in May 1868, after returning to his newly built home in Boggsville, Colorado.

Every contemporary account characterizes Kit Carson as a man of exceptional honor and integrity. He was described by those who knew him as being plainspoken but unlettered. As a matter of fact, he did not learn to read or write until his New Mexico troops were joined to the California regiments. General Carleton took credit for teaching Colonel Carson reading, writing, and "military courtesy."

A number of places on the land have been named for Kit Carson, including Carson Pass, Carson River, Carson Sink, and Carson City, Nevada. Christopher "Kit" Carson remains one of the most important icons in American history, as well as in American folklore.

—Henry H. Goldman

For Further Reading

Carter, Harvey Lewis. 1968. *Dear Old Kit: The Historical Christopher Carson.* Norman: University of Oklahoma Press; Dunn, J. P. 1886. *Massacres of the Mountains: A History of the Indian Wars of the Far West, 1815–1875.* New York: Archer House; Unruh, John D., Jr. 1993. *The Plains Across: The Overland Immigrants and the Trans-Mississippi West, 1840–1860.* Urbana: University of Illinois Press.

CARTOGRAPHY

When the United States negotiated for the purchase of Louisiana from France, neither party could produce clearly defined boundaries to frame the conveyed territory. This problem was not only the result of a lack of human and financial resources on the part of the previous nations that had claimed title to Louisiana, but also a fundamental difference in understanding regarding the nature of the relationship between the land and the empires whose flags had flown over it since the seventeenth century. A lack of cartographic knowledge of the territory contributed to an unrealistic perception of the region's vastness. That perception left the remaining imperial powers on the continent ill prepared to counter the westward advance of the United States.

Key to early French claims to Louisiana was their knowledge of the Missouri River. Seeking the elusive Northwest Passage, the French had dominated trade in the trans-Mississippi West, using the Missouri as their main thoroughfare. This was made possible by Louis Joliet and Father Jacques Marquette, who, along with five others in their expedition, documented the course of the Missouri River in June 1673. Not long after, French *courers de bois* traveled up the Missouri, west of Lake Superior, bringing distant Indian nations into the French commercial sphere. These private enterprises pushed the borders of the amorphous Louisiana north and west, but only as far as the Missouri River and its offshoots allowed the traders to travel. The northern boundary of Louisiana was settled upon later with the British at the Treaty of Utrecht (1713), which set the dividing line between French Louisiana and British Canada north of the forty-ninth parallel (DeVoto, 1983).

The western boundary of Louisiana under the French became more clearly defined by Etienne Veniard de Bourgmont. Living among the Osage Indians, Bourgmont sent a detailed map of the Missouri River as far as the Arikara and Caricara villages (six hundred leagues from the confluence with the Mississippi) to Paris in 1717, noting that "by way of the Missouri commerce could be carried on with the Spaniards, who were not far distant from the branches of this river, according to the reports of the savages who trafficked with them" (Nasitir, 1952).

Farther south the boundary of Louisiana was equally contentious. War between France and Spain in 1719 gave France the opportunity to assert itself along the Red and Arkansas Rivers, where Spain claimed territorial sovereignty but was unable to enforce it. To the east, early eighteenth-century French claims to Louisiana stemmed from the juncture between the Mississippi and Ohio Rivers. The Ohio was a convenient waterway for moving furs and trade goods from the eastern Great Lakes region to New Orleans, and the river valley was protected from British encroachment by the Appalachian Mountain chain until the latter half of the century. This area was ceded to the British at the Treaty of Paris (1763), and France's empire west of the Mississippi had gone to Spain in the Treaty of Fontainebleau a year earlier, to prevent it from falling under British rule.

As the eighteenth century came to a close, France was waging war in Europe under Napoleon Bonaparte. Rumors that France sought to regain the North American empire it had lost at the Treaty of Paris (1763) had circulated since the presidential administration of John Adams, and Napoleon confirmed that France indeed sought to reclaim its North American empire after his decisive victory at Marengo. The victory served to punctuate his request that King Charles IV of Spain retrocede that part of Louisiana given to Spain.

The Treaty of San Ildefonso (1800) stipulated that the boundaries of the transfer from Spain to France were to be exactly as the French had ceded Louisiana to Spain in the Treaty of Fontainebleau (1762). A dispatch sent to the French captain-general of Louisiana from Minister Denis Duc de Decrés offers the clearest determination of what the French considered the boundaries of Louisiana: "The colony of Louisiana is a vast province located west of the Mississippi, which forms on that side its common boundary with the United States. On the west, it is bounded by New Mexico [Nouveau Mexique], on the south by the sea, and at the north by a limitless extent of lands scarcely known." This lack of a solid boundary with Spain along New Mexico's eastern perimeter would become the Achilles' heel of the Spanish empire once the Louisiana Territory was sold to the United States (Robertson, 1911).

Once the terms of the Louisiana Purchase were agreed upon, determining the boundaries of Louisiana then became the focus of the diplomatic proceedings. According to the final wording of the treaty signed on April 30, 1803, France transferred to the United States "the Colony or Province of Louisiana, with the same extent that it now has in the hands of Spain, & that it had when France possessed it; and Such as it Should be after the treaties subsequently entered into between Spain and other states." This wording was deliberately vague, designed to give the United States elasticity to its new claim, particularly in regards to the boundary with West Florida and the western boundary with New Mexico, both still under Spanish control (Lyon, 1934).

As the French understood it, the western boundary of Louisiana was the Rio Bravo, from its mouth at the Gulf of Mexico up to 30 degrees north latitude. After 30 degrees north latitude, Charles Maurice de Talleyrand admitted in a letter to Decrés that "from that last point, the line is less exact." He further admitted that "it does not appear that any convention of boundaries was ever held for that part of the frontier. The farther north one goes, the more vague is the demarcation" (ibid.). The terms of the Louisiana Purchase were deliberately vague. There was no set western or northern boundary to the territory. This allowed the United States to fill in the map as it saw fit. Although that incensed the Spanish Crown and ultimately led to the demise of its North American empire, it could offer no cartographic evidence that checked American westward expansion.

—Michael Kimaid

For Further Reading

DeVoto, Bernard. 1983. *The Course of Empire.* Lincoln: University of Nebraska Press; Lyon, E. Wilson. 1934. *Louisiana in French Diplomacy.* Norman: University of Oklahoma Press; Nasitir, Abraham P. 1952. *Before Lewis and Clark: Documents Illustrating the History of the Missouri 1785–1804.* St. Louis: St. Louis Historical Documents Foundation; Robertson, James Alexander, ed. 1911. *Louisiana under the Rule of Spain, France and the United States, 1785–1807.* Cleveland: Arthur C. Clark Company.

CASA-CALVO, SEBASTIÁN CALVO DE LA PUERTA Y O'FARRILL, MARQUÉS DE (c. 1754–1820)

Serving as acting military governor of Louisiana from 1799 to 1801, the Marqués de Casa-Calvo participated in the full range of Spain's activities in Louisiana, from early occupation and expansion to the surrender of the region to the French in 1803.

Casa-Calvo was a soldier during Spain's glory days in Louisiana. Born in Havana, he joined the Spanish army as a teenager. After France gave Louisiana to Spain in 1762, French residents of New Orleans rebelled against the imposition of Spanish rule. In 1769 the Spanish Crown sent General Alejandro O'Reilly to put down the rebellion. O'Reilly collected some two thousand troops in Havana, including the young cavalry officer Casa-Calvo. O'Reilly and his troops successfully reinstated Spanish rule over New Orleans and Louisiana.

During the American Revolution, Casa-Calvo helped Spain expand into West Florida. He fought with Bernardo de Gálvez in Spanish victories over the British at Mobile in 1780 and Pensacola in 1781. The Spanish military promoted Casa-Calvo to lieutenant colonel in 1786.

When Louisiana governor Manuel Gayoso de Lemos died in July 1799, the Crown appointed Casa-Calvo interim governor. By that time, Spanish Louisiana was endangered on many fronts. The British and their Indian allies threatened to invade the Mississippi Valley from Canada in 1800 and again in 1801. The British also periodically blockaded the port of New Orleans, preventing supplies and trade from flowing into and out of the colony. Most dangerously, American settlers and traders were increasingly encroaching on Spanish Louisiana. Casa-Calvo ordered the arrest and deportation of all Americans without Spanish passports, but their numbers continued to increase.

As interim governor, Casa-Calvo also faced troubles within the colony and with the Spanish Crown. Unlike previous governors, Casa-Calvo had power only over the military affairs of Louisiana. Another man, Nicolas María Vidal, was given authority over civil affairs. With neither the permanency nor the power of his predecessors, Casa-Calvo had to fight Vidal and other New Orleans officials every time he wanted to implement a policy. Spain's troubles in Europe deflected attention from Louisiana, resulting in a diminished military and insufficient funds for maintaining Indian alliances. The interim governor struggled to maintain control over the colony for two years, until the new governor, Manuel Juan de Salcedo, finally arrived from the Canary Islands in 1801. Casa-Calvo left for Cuba, but he was back in Louisiana two years later to oversee the Spanish retreat from the colony.

Casa-Calvo attended both the triumphal institution of Spanish rule over Louisiana in 1769 and the ceremony returning Louisiana to France in 1803. In that year, Casa-Calvo was appointed commissioner for handing over Louisiana to the French. Along with Governor Salcedo, Casa-Calvo officially surrendered Louisiana to the French on November 13. At the time, Casa-Calvo suspected that France would not keep its promise to prevent the colony from falling into the hands of the United States. In fact, in the spring of 1803, France had already sold Louisiana to the United States, and barely a month later, the French turned the colony over.

After Spain lost Louisiana, the Crown appointed Casa-Calvo commissioner of limits to determine the border between Spanish America and the United States. In 1805 and 1806 he led a secret, four-month mission to explore and map western Louisiana and eastern Texas. At issue was the border between Louisiana, which now belonged to the United States, and Spanish Texas. The Spanish had become alarmed when a French minister claimed that Louisiana extended to the Rio Grande, and Casa-Calvo set out to disprove that claim before American explorers, such as William Dunbar, could get there. Casa-Calvo needed to prove that the disputed area between the Rio Grande and the Sabine River had belonged to Spain before 1762, when France had given Louisiana to Spain. Casa-Calvo found records in Texas that allegedly proved that the San Miguel de los Adaes mission and presidio were founded by the Spanish in 1716. If the Los Adaes district was Spanish territory before 1762, then Spanish Texas extended at least to the Sabine River, and perhaps considerably farther east.

When word of Casa-Calvo's expedition spread, rumors flew among the Anglo-American population of Louisiana. Some said that Casa-Calvo was going to take command of three thousand Spanish troops in Texas to retake Louisiana by force. Others believed that he was fomenting rebellion among the Spanish, French, and Indian residents of Louisiana. As a result of these rumors, the first U.S. territorial governor of Louisiana, William C. C. Claiborne, persuaded President Jefferson to order all Spanish officials and military men in Louisiana either to accept U.S. citizenship or to leave U.S. soil. Immediately upon Casa-Calvo's return to New Orleans in February 1806, the governor expelled him from Louisiana.

As he left Louisiana, Casa-Calvo warned his superiors in Spain that the disputed and unprotected Texas-Louisiana border would expose Mexico to invasion by the United States, and he asked to lead a military force to reconquer Louisiana. The Crown refused his request, and U.S. westward expansion continued.

—Kathleen DuVal

See also

Claiborne, William Charles Cole; Los Adaes

For Further Reading

Din, Gilbert C. 1990. "Francisco Bouligny, Marqués de Casa-Calvo, Manuel Juan de Salcedo, Pierre Clément, Baron de Laussat, Colonial Governors, 1799–1803." In *The Louisiana Governors, from Iberville to Edwards.* Edited by Joseph G. Dawson III. Baton Rouge: Louisiana State University Press; Holmes, Jack D. L. 1966. "The Marqués de Casa-Calvo, Nicolás de Finiels, and the 1805 Spanish Expedition through East Texas and Louisiana." *Southwestern Historical Quarterly* 69: 324–339; Nasatir, Abraham P. 1976. *Borderland in Retreat: From Spanish Louisiana to the Far Southwest.* Albuquerque: University of New Mexico Press; Whitaker, Arthur Preston. 1934. *The Mississippi Question, 1795–1803: A Study in Trade, Politics, and Diplomacy.* New York: D. Appleton.

CASPAR, FORT

Fort Caspar (often spelled "Casper") was established in May 1862, on the south side of the North Platte River at the present-day site of Casper, Wyoming. The site had been in use since 1840, when the river crossing became known as Camp Platte and served as a convenient and natural crossing place for overland immigrants following the Oregon Trail. In June 1847, the Mormons established a ferry there, and for the next twelve years the place was known as Mormon Ferry. In 1858, Platte Bridge Station was constructed, consisting of several adobe buildings, located at the same site.

Troops from Companies D and E of the Fourth U.S. Artillery were stationed there from July 29, 1858, to April 20, 1859. These troops were under the command of Captain Joseph Roberts and Captain George W. Getty. There was a threefold purpose for locating troops there: to protect Oregon-bound immigrant trains, to facilitate the movement of supplies in support of the Utah expeditionary force, and to keep lines of communication open with Salt Lake City. During the brief lifetime of the Pony Express, the fort served as a relay station for express riders.

Louis Guinard constructed a thousand-foot bridge there in 1859, from which the camp derived its name—Platte Bridge Station. In May 1862, the camp was garrisoned by troops of the Sixth U.S. Volunteers, to protect from Indian attack the crossing and the newly installed telegraph line.

In the spring of 1865 the post, still called Platte River Station, was made a permanent post. The camp became unusually active that same year, when the Indians sought to halt all traffic along the Oregon Trail. On November 21, 1865, Major General John Pope, commanding the department, ordered that the camp be named Fort Caspar, in honor of First Lieutenant Caspar W. Collins, Eleventh Ohio Cavalry, killed in the Platte Bridge Station Battle on July 26, 1865. Collins had been killed while trying to rescue a fallen comrade during a battle with three thousand Sioux and Cheyenne who had attacked a wagon train. The post was first garrisoned by regular troops on June 28, 1866, under the command of Captain Richard L. Morris, Eighteenth U.S. Infantry.

The post was rebuilt and enlarged in 1866. It was abandoned, by order of the War Department, on October 19, 1867, when it was replaced by Fort Fetterman. As soon as it was closed and the troops had departed, the buildings and the bridge across the North Platte were burned by Indians. The fort has been reconstructed, and the site is now a state park.

—*Henry H. Goldman*

See also

Oregon Trail; Wyoming

For Further Reading

Frazer, Robert W. 1965. *Forts of the West.* Norman: University of Oklahoma Press; National Park Service. 1963. *Soldier and Brave: Indian and Military Affairs in the Trans-Mississippi West.* New York: Harper and Row; Utley, Robert M. 1984. *The Indian Frontier of the American West, 1846–1890.* Albuquerque: University of New Mexico Press; Young, Otis. 1955. *The West of Philip St. George Cooke, 1809–1895.* Glendale, CA: Arthur H. Clark Company.

CATLIN, GEORGE (1796–1872)

Born in Wilkes-Barre, Pennsylvania, George Catlin moved with his family to rural Broome County, New York, at the age of one year. He was schooled at home, and he enjoyed the outdoor life of hunting and fishing more than the academic one. He collected Indian relics, coming by his interest in Indians because his mother had been taken by Indians during the Wyoming Valley Massacre of 1778. He studied law in Litchfield, Connecticut, in 1817 and 1818, but he quickly abandoned the profession. A self-taught artist, by 1821 Catlin was working as a miniaturist in Philadelphia. He was elected to the Pennsylvania Academy of the Fine Arts in 1824. He painted portraits and miniatures in Washington, D.C., and Albany, New York, between 1824 and 1829.

George Catlin first encountered Indians in 1824, when a delegation passed through Philadelphia on its way to Washington, D.C. Catlin finished his first portrait of an Indian, Red Jacket, in 1826, two years after his friend, Charles Neagle, had painted the same individual.

Catlin's influences include Thomas Sully, who had a portrait studio, and Charles Wilson Peale, whose Philadelphia Museum taught Catlin the importance of natural history. From Samuel F. B. Morse, president of the National Academy of Design, Catlin learned that art must serve education.

Like many Americans of his time, Catlin caught the fever of cultural nationalism, a commitment to scientific accuracy, and the fear that progress was eroding the unique America represented by wilderness and the noble savage. Determined to paint the dying race and its environment before it was too late, he moved to St. Louis in 1830. There he met and became friends with General William Clark and painted the Indians who visited Clark's office. For five years he traveled throughout the Indian country, sketching and painting Indians in or near their natural homes. He was the first to paint the northern tribes, including the Sioux, Mandan, Crow, and Blackfoot. He also traveled to Fort Gibson in Indian Territory, and although he got sick and could not make the journey to Fort Sill to meet with the Comanche, he was first to paint them as well. He also painted other Southern Plains Indians, such as the Osage and Kiowa, as well as the relocated Civilized Tribes. In 1837, Catlin's Western phase ended. He presented paintings from the second

While traveling through the Dakotas in 1832, artist George Catlin had an opportunity to paint Four Bears, the second chief of the Mandan. (Smithsonian American Art Museum/Art Resource)

trip to Congress in 1838, but Congress rejected them. Catlin went to Europe, where his paintings were better received. He had success in London and Paris with "The Indian Gallery," a collection that he updated periodically. He continued traveling, through North America and, possibly, South America. Some claim that he fictionalized his account of his 1850s travel in South America.

Catlin was not the first to paint Indians, but he was the first to go to the Indians' homelands, the first to capture a fading civilization, the first to draw the contrast between the dignified native and the one corrupted by civilization. One set of two paintings of *The Light,* an Assiniboine, portrayed him in native dress on his way to meet the white man, and in an elaborate American uniform upon his return. The side-by-side representations were symbolic of the corrupting influence of civilization, a good romantic-era motif.

Catlin worked quickly and was highly prolific. After his Western travels he copied his original sketches in pencil and other media, often taking more pains than with the original, giving better quality at the expense of the freshness that characterized his best work. Catlin set the pattern of being an encyclopedist, attempting to capture every tribe and every type of landscape. His influence shows in the voluminous output of his successors, such as Seth Eastman, John Mix Stanley, Henry H. Cross, Joseph Henry Sharp, Elbridge Ayer Burbans, and Edward S. Curtis. He also set the tone of nostalgia for a lost time that characterizes the Western genre; after all, by the time he got to the pristine Indians, they had already been corrupted by earlier contact with white civilization. And it was his work that made the Plains Indian America's stereotypical Native American.

His work is characterized by strong and accurate depictions of facial expression; his weaknesses are in anatomy and proportion, and he sometimes takes liberties with perspective. After Catlin any artist who wanted to be taken seriously had to go out to the Indians instead of waiting for them to come to him.

Catlin's published works include *Manners, Customs, and Conditions of the North American Indians* (2 vols., 1841), *Catlin's North American Indian Portfolio* (1844), and *My Life among the Indians* (1867).

—J. Herschel Barnhill

For Further Reading

Ewers, John C. 1982. *Artists of the Old West.* New York: Promontory Press; Troccoli, Joan Carpenter. 1993. *First Artist of the West: George Catlin Paintings and Watercolors from the Collection of Gilcrease Museum.* Tulsa: Thomas Gilcrease Museum Association.

CHARBONNEAU, TOUSSAINT (c. 1759–c. 1840)

Toussaint Charbonneau and his wife, Sacagawea, served as interpreters for the Lewis and Clark Expedition (1804–1806). Originally from Montreal, Charbonneau worked as an *engagé* (a laborer) for the North West Company from 1793 to 1796, after which time he established himself as an independent fur trader among the Hidatsa and Mandan peoples of the Northern Plains. When the Lewis and Clark Expedition reached the mouth of the Knife River in present-day North Dakota in October 1804, Charbonneau was living in the area with two Shoshoni wives whom he had purchased from the Hidatsa, the younger one being Sacagawea.

Charbonneau offered his services as an interpreter to Lewis and Clark at Fort Mandan, and an agreement was later reached recognizing Charbonneau as one of the party's two official interpreters (George Drouillard being the other). Charbonneau, Sacagawea, and their infant son, Jean Baptiste, were three of only eight civilian members of the expedition, Sacagawea being the only woman. Lewis and Clark were inclined to hire Charbonneau because Sacagawea's people, the Shoshoni, lived farther along the route the expedition was to travel.

To succeed in its quest to cross the Rocky Mountains, the Corps of Discovery would need to negotiate with the Shoshoni, inasmuch as they were said to have an important supply of horses.

During the passage of the expedition through the territories of the Hidatsa and Shoshoni, Lewis and Clark relied on Charbonneau and Sacagawea to communicate with the local tribes, though the process was cumbersome. Sacagawea spoke Shoshoni and Hidatsa, while Charbonneau spoke Hidatsa and French, the final link in the chain being the translation from French to English by Private François Labiche. Upon their arrival among the Shoshoni, the party learned that Sacagawea's brother, Cameahwait, whom she had not seen since her capture by the Hidatsa in 1800, was a Shoshoni headman. He furnished the Corps of Discovery with horses and a guide to cross the Bitterroot Range through the present-day Lolo Pass. In addition to Charbonneau's and Sacagawea's invaluable service as interpreters for the Lewis and Clark Expedition, the presence of Sacagawea in the party served to defuse tensions with native peoples over the arrival of foreigners.

Toussaint, Sacagawea, and their son remained with the Corps of Discovery throughout its journey across the Rocky Mountains to the Pacific Coast and back to Fort Mandan. Upon the party's return to the fort in August 1806, Charbonneau ended his association with the expedition. He was given a voucher valued at $500.33 (a large sum at the time) and the cost of a horse and lodge. Upon Charbonneau and Sacagawea's visit to St. Louis in 1809, he was also awarded a land grant of 320 acres, as were all the enlisted men of the Lewis and Clark Expedition.

A fur trader all his life, Charbonneau had little interest in becoming a farmer. He eventually sold his acreage to William Clark and returned to live among the Mandan and the Hidatsa. Sacagawea died in 1812, and one year later, William Clark became guardian to Lizette and Jean Baptiste, Charbonneau's children by Sacagawea. For the next twenty-eight years, Charbonneau continued to work as an interpreter for government officials, artists, explorers, and other visitors. It is believed that he died in 1840, although his son, Jean Baptiste Charbonneau, did not settle Toussaint's estate until 1843.

—Melinda Marie Jetté

See also

Lewis and Clark Expedition; Sacagawea

For Further Reading

Anderson, Irving W. 1992. *A Charbonneau Family Portrait: Biographical Sketches of Sacagawea, Jean Baptiste, and Toussaint Charbonneau.* Astoria, OR: Fort Clatsop Historical Society; Moulton, Gary E., ed. 1987. *The Journals of the Lewis and Clark Expedition,* vol. 3. Lincoln: University of Nebraska Press; Ronda, James P. 1984. *Lewis and Clark among the Indians.* Lincoln: University of Nebraska Press.

CHARLES IV (1748–1819)

King Charles IV of Spain, who ruled from 1788 to 1808, was the fifth and most inept of the Spanish Bourbons. Carlos (in Spanish) reigned, with little vision or strength, over the approaching dissolution of Spain's American empire, starting with the retrocession of the Louisiana Territory to Napoleon's France in 1801. This disinterested monarch was the son of Charles III (1716–1788), perhaps the ablest and strongest of the Spanish Bourbons and Maria de Sajonia (1724–1760). In 1765, Carlos married his cousin, Maria Luisa of Parma (1751–1819). Their shared grandparents were Philip V of Spain (1683–1746) and Elisabetta (Isabela) Farnese of Parma (1692–1766). Charles was also a first cousin to the ill-fated Louis XVI of France, through their Saxon mothers. Finally, both these tragic and ill-suited Bourbon monarchs were, of course, descendants of France's Louis XIV, the Sun King. Charles and Maria Luisa were considered lazy and morally deficient by the demanding Charles III and, as a result, were largely ignored by him.

Early in their reign, this hapless royal pair fell under the influence of the clever and devious Manuel de Godoy, originally a guardsman of the royal household. This man, sixteen years Queen Maria Luisa's junior, was generally believed to have been her principal lover. It was even rumored that he sired two of the royal children. Charles IV, referred to as the "Royal Cuckold," never seemed aware of his wife's rampant libido or the situation with Godoy. He gave Godoy estates and royal titles, finally dubbing him the "Prince of the Peace" after he helped negotiate peace with the French Directory in 1795.

Intimidated by Napoleon and manipulated by Godoy and the queen, Charles was easily persuaded to return the title of Louisiana to France in 1801. This was accomplished in exchange for the throne of Tuscany (enlarged and created as the Kingdom of Etruria by Napoleon) for the queen's brother, Fernando, Duke of Parma. Eventually, however, Fernando's son, Luis, who had married the Spanish Infanta, his cousin Maria Luisa, occupied that throne.

Fernando de Bourbon, Charles's son and heir apparent, split with his father because of his distaste for the situation at court. Finally, after Spain's loss of Louisiana and Godoy's continued accommodations to and appeasement of Napoleon, Fernando overthrew his father in 1808 and ruled as Fernando VII for just a few days. Charles then appealed to Napoleon, who summoned father and son to France, where both were forced to abdicate in favor of Joseph Bonaparte, brother of the emperor, who ruled as José I.

After the abdication, Charles and Maria Luisa remained as pensioners of France, spending much of their time at the Chateau de Chambord. Their legacy was that of finally having reduced the once mightiest country on earth to a French satellite. The couple fled to Rome after the fall of Napoleon, in 1814. Charles was on a prolonged visit to his brother, Fernando IV of Naples, when his wife died on January 2, 1819, with Godoy at her side. Charles never left Naples and died there on January 19, 1819, of "fever and gout." Fernando VII, who had been restored to the Spanish throne in 1814, later allowed his parents to be buried in the Escorial. Fernando ruled Spain, even less ably than the preceding ménage à trois, until his own death in 1833.

Charles IV will always be remembered by the brutally realistic and insightful painting, *Charles IV and His Family,* by Francisco de Goya (1746–1828), who had been named court painter in 1800. The painting, which resides at the Museo del Prado in Madrid, clearly depicts the family's lack of intelligence and character. Goya made no attempt to hide his disdain and contempt for the pathetic group. The reign of Charles IV, Maria Luisa, and Godoy, together with the French Revolution and Napoleon's rise to power, was absolutely disastrous for the once mighty Spain.

—Richard H. Dickerson

See also

Bonaparte, Joseph; Bonaparte, Napoleon; Fernando, Duke of Parma; Godoy, Manuel de; San Ildefonso, Treaty of

For Further Reading

Bergamini, John D. 1974. *The Spanish Bourbons: The History of a Tenacious Dynasty.* New York: G. P. Putnam's Sons; Descola, Jean. 1963. *A History of Spain.* New York: Alfred A. Knopf; Kern, Robert W., ed. 1990. *Historical Dictionary of Modern Spain.* New York: Greenwood Press; Petrie, Sir Charles. 1956. *The History of Spain: Part II, from the Death of Philip II to 1945.* London: Eyre and Spottiswoode.

CHARTRES, FORT DE

Built in 1720 approximately fifteen miles northwest of Kaskaskia, Illinois, Fort de Chartres became the French colonial seat of government in Illinois. Today one can visit the reconstructed site located about twelve miles west of Ruma, between Prairie Du Rocher and Kidd, Illinois. A palisaded structure, Fort de Chartres became an important link for French trade from Quebec, Montreal, and Detroit in the north to New Orleans in the south. The fort was part of a series of outposts constructed by John Law's Company of the Indies that controlled the French Louisiana Territory until 1731. Illinois was one of nine military districts, and with troops stationed at Fort de Chartres, there grew a small, though fairly prosperous, French settlement in nearby villages—most notably at Kaskaskia.

Fort de Chartres's brief history (1720–1763) is marked by Indian wars, the desire to keep British traders from intruding into the Illinois country, and concern over the costs of maintaining the fort. From its earliest years, soldiers stationed at Fort de Chartres were involved in the Fox Indian Wars (1718–1730) and quickly realized that their fort was vulnerable to a massive Indian attack. Worse yet, built quite close to the Mississippi River, the fort was also in danger from possible flooding, which did occur in 1727. The palisades were completely destroyed that year, as were the wooden buildings within the grounds. The fort was rebuilt near the same site, though again with wood as the only construction material. Very soon this second fort became dilapidated. In view of the continued deterioration of the fort, its commander, Sieur de Bertet, moved most of the garrison to Kaskaskia in 1747. Finally, in 1753, a more serious effort was made to construct a permanent structure, using stone and earthen material. A more spacious fort was built, one that could house between three hundred and five hundred men.

The garrison at Fort de Chartres was never very large: sixty men in 1727 and three hundred men in 1751. Nonetheless, they were actively involved in controlling Indians, protecting French trade routes, and exploiting the lead mines in the area.

There was, for example, an ill-fated attack carried out against the Chickasaw in 1736. Troops from Fort de Chartres prepared to attack a Chickasaw village, only to be outflanked by the Chickasaw, who had been alerted to the impending attack by British traders. It was a total disaster: many of the French, including their commander, were killed. Alphonse de la Buissonniere took over command after the disaster and began immediate repairs to the fort to make it less vulnerable to Indian attack. Another threat to the Illinois country and the region around the fort came in 1752, when Fox Indians and their allies sent four hundred to five hundred warriors to raid an Illinois Indian (Cahokia) village, close to Fort de Chartres. Although the raiders destroyed much of the village and took scalps and captives, they did not present a real threat to the fort, which at that time had a garrison of only three hundred men.

Besides its military and political importance, the fort was an important contributor to regional economic development. Soldiers from the fort worked in lead mines nearby. Furthermore, several men, and occasionally patrols, set out from the fort into Missouri to gain Indian allies and explore the area west of the Mississippi. For example, Antoine Valentin de Guy set out in 1743 from Fort de Chartres and led an expedition to the Big River in Missouri, searching for lead mines. Later, in 1763, Pierre Laclède Liguest left from Fort de Chartres to establish a trading post at the mouth of the Missouri River, named the site St. Louis, in honor of the canonized French monarch Louis IX.

By the terms of the Treaty of Paris (1763), which concluded the French and Indian War (1755–1763), France ceded the Illinois country to the British. Although occupied by British troops in 1765, the fort's occupation was to be of short duration. Major General Thomas Gage, commander of British troops in North America, recommended to the British cabinet that Fort de Chartres be abandoned. Believing it to be too costly to maintain a garrison there, he asserted that the local (French) inhabitants could be gathered into one village for better defense, and they could establish their own militia for protection. His recommendation was approved in 1771, and General Gage subsequently had Fort de Chartres demolished.

—Gene Mueller

See also
Fox; Kaskaskia; Saint Louis

For Further Reading
Alvord, Clarence W. 1965. *The Illinois Country*. Chicago: Loyola University Press; Belting, Natalia Maree. 1975. *Kaskaskia under the French Regime*. New Orleans: Polyanthos; Brown, Margaret K. 1977. "Uncovering the Mystery of the Three Forts de Chartres." *Illinois Magazine* 16(9): 23–29; Brown, Margaret K., and Lawrie Cena Dean. 1995. *The French Colony in the Mid-Mississippi Valley*. Carbondale, IL: American Kestral Books; Hauser, Raymond. 1993. "The Fox Raid of 1752: Defensive Warfare and the Decline of the Illinois Indian Tribe." *Illinois Historical Journal* 86, no. 4: 210–224.

CHEYENNE

The Central Plains were home to the Cheyenne and their allies, the Arapaho. Both groups inhabited and hunted the region of present-day eastern Colorado and southeastern Wyoming. They lived primarily in the region between the Arkansas and North Platte Rivers just east of the Front Range of the Rockies.

The Cheyenne spoke a language that stemmed from the Algonquian-Wakashan linguistic group. Although they had formerly been sedentary farmers of the eastern woodlands near Lake Superior, they migrated westward during the early seventeenth century. It is likely that hostilities with rival tribes—especially the Santee Sioux and the Ojibwa, both of which possessed guns—were responsible for the departure of the Cheyenne from western Wisconsin and Minnesota. For a time they lived in present-day North Dakota in the valley of the Sheyenne River, but they continued to move west. Tribal folklore recalling how the Cheyenne "lost the corn" indicates the profound cultural transformation that took place as the tribal migration occurred.

Settling in the Central Plains, the Cheyenne adopted the lifestyle of nomadic hunters who followed the vast herds of bison that inhabited the region. Because they were nomadic hunters, the Cheyenne frequently came into contact with other tribes that maintained themselves in similar fashion. These frequent encounters generally led to clashes over rights to traditional hunting lands. As a result, the Cheyenne often found themselves at war against the Kiowa, Comanche, and Apache.

The Cheyenne split into Southern and Northern bands around 1830 when a large group decided to settle upon the headwaters of the Arkansas River, where they could engage in trade with Americans at Bent's Fort. This division was made more permanent when the Cheyenne and the Arapaho, two frequently warlike tribes, came to be known as a peaceful people because they chose not to fight the Americans who began to arrive on the Central Plains. The lands that the Cheyenne occupied were of central importance to the course of American empire because all major overland trails, such as the Oregon Trail and the Mormon Road—which would be traversed by emigrant pioneers, prospectors, and other trappers and traders—had to cross Cheyenne country. The Cheyenne agreed to a treaty with the U.S. government in which they promised to provide an open corridor that would allow for safe passage for overland travelers. Unfortunately, in making this decision, the Cheyenne effectively divided their tribe.

The Southern Cheyenne eventually merged with the Arapaho and lived near the Arkansas River and its tributaries. This group eventually became the victims of the infamous Sand Creek Massacre (1864). The Southern Cheyenne and Arapaho who remained were eventually placed upon reservation land in Oklahoma. The Northern Cheyenne lived along the North Platte River. Shortly after the Sand Creek Massacre, the Northern Cheyenne allied themselves with the Sioux. A large contingent of Northern Cheyenne would later fight along with the Sioux at the Battle of Little Bighorn (1876), where they would defeat General George A. Custer and his Seventh Cavalry. The following year the Northern Cheyenne were pacified and U.S. forces removed them to reservation land in Oklahoma, where they were rejoined with surviving elements of the Southern Cheyenne.

An increasingly large number of prospectors and settlers moved into the region of Colorado after gold was discovered near Pike's Peak in 1859. In the Treaty of Fort Lyon (1861) the Southern Cheyenne and their Arapaho allies agreed to live upon reservation land in southeastern Colorado, where they would not harass whites who traveled across their traditional hunting grounds. Several chiefs were taken to Washington to meet President Lincoln, and they received medallions and American flags as evidence of the good faith between U.S. authorities and tribal leaders. Unfortunately, this goodwill would not last very long.

One of the most ignoble events of U.S. history, the Sand Creek Massacre of November 29, 1864, became symbolic in Native American consciousness to the callous disregard that white Americans held for treaty obligations negotiated with Indian tribes. Colonel John M. Chivington and a contingent of the Colorado territorial militia deliberately attacked a village of Cheyenne and Southern Arapaho who were flying an American flag—a clear sign that they were under treaty protection. In the wake of an artillery barrage and cavalry charge, more than 200 women and children were killed by Chivington's assault. A few Cheyenne warriors were also killed, but most of the

Located along the Oregon Trail in western Nebraska, Chimney Rock was one of the most famous landmarks found along the emigrant trail.

men were participating in a hunt and were away from the encampment at the time of the attack.

Victimized by a treaty decision that served to divide and conquer, the Cheyenne found themselves further marginalized by the pressures of Manifest Destiny. By 1867, the tribe had lost possession of all of its traditional hunting land. Even today the Cheyenne remain a divided people, with about 12,000 members living on reservations in Montana and Oklahoma.

—*Junius P. Rodriguez*

See also
Arapaho; Bent's Fort; Colorado

For Further Reading

Berthrong, Donald J. 1976. *The Cheyenne and Arapaho Ordeal: Reservation and Agency Life in the Indian Territory.* Norman: University of Oklahoma Press; Grinnell, George Bird. 1956. *The Fighting Cheyennes.* Norman: University of Oklahoma Press; Grinnell, George Bird. 1972. *The Cheyenne Indians,* 2 vols. Lincoln: University of Nebraska Press; Hoebel, E. Adamson 1960. *The Cheyennes.* New York: Holt; Millard, Joseph. 1964. *The Cheyenne Wars.* Derby, CT: Monarch Books; Moore, John H. 1987. *The Cheyenne Nation.* Lincoln: University of Nebraska Press.

CHIMNEY ROCK

This formation of Brule clay and volcanic ash, known to American Indians as elk penis, rises about 325 feet above the North Platte River Valley in present-day western Nebraska and is most widely known as arguably the most famous landmark on the Oregon-California Trail.

Whites probably first saw Chimney Rock in 1813, when fur traders traveled the valley. Joshua Pilcher made the first recorded reference to Chimney Rock in his report on an 1827 trapping expedition. As the Platte River Road drew more and more American traffic during the ensuing decades, an estimated 500,000 westbound immigrants and travelers saw Chimney Rock, many welcoming it as a sign that their journey across the Plains was nearing an end and that they would soon be in the Rocky Mountains.

Although some early travelers thought that the formation resembled an inverted funnel, a lighthouse, or a shot-tower, most agreed that it most closely resembled the chimney ruins of a burned-down house or a factory chimney, and that it had been named appropriately. Regardless of how they described the formation, almost all who kept a diary of their journey mentioned the rock. One study of immigrants' diaries found Chimney Rock mentioned in ninety-seven of one hundred journals, a greater rate of occurrence than for any other landmark on the Oregon Trail. Furthermore, the diarists described it in greater detail and in greater length than the other landmarks. Some writers disdained Chimney Rock, but most praised it with terms such as "celebrated," "famous," and "the most remarkable object I ever saw." In 1837, artist Alfred Jacob Miller celebrated Chimney Rock by making the first known sketch of the landmark.

Given its prominence and the slow rate of travel along the trail, immigrants could see Chimney Rock for days before they reached it. After travel through the relatively featureless Platte Valley, the rock likely provided welcome relief. Many immigrants celebrated reaching this milestone by clambering up the rock's base to carve their initials on it. Although many journals mention that activity, virtually no carvings remain today, because of erosion.

By the 1860s, a mail, stage, and telegraph station had been established in the vicinity of Chimney Rock, possibly thanks to the water provided by a handful of springs. The presence of water, however, did not distinguish Chimney Rock from other points along the Oregon Trail. The formation's greatest significance rests in the psychological impact it had on early travelers in the Platte Valley. They welcomed the change in scenery and—especially after the trail had been well worn and publicized—enjoyed seeing a famous landmark that indicated their progress toward their destination.

—Todd M. Kerstetter

See also
Oregon Trail

For Further Reading

Mattes, Merrill J. 1955. "Chimney Rock on the Oregon Trail." *Nebraska History* 36: 1–26; Mattes, Merrill J. 1969. *The Great Platte River Road: The Covered Wagon Mainline via Fort Kearny to Fort Laramie.* Lincoln: Nebraska State Historical Society.

CHIPPEWA

See Ojibwa

CHOUTEAU, RENÉ AUGUSTE (1749–1829)

The noted frontiersman René Auguste Chouteau, an active entrepreneur in the fur trade and one of the founders of St. Louis, Missouri, was born in the city of New Orleans in colonial French Louisiana. After his parents separated when he was six years old, Chouteau was raised by his common-law stepfather, Pierre Laclède Liguest, and Marie Thérèse Chouteau, his mother. When the French and Indian War ended in 1763, Laclède (of Maxent, Laclède and Company) and his newly formed family moved from New Orleans to the Illinois Territory, where he hoped to become involved in frontier trade and commerce as an agent of the Louisiana Fur Trade Company.

Laclède had obtained an eight-year monopoly for the Missouri region fur trade in 1762. He had hoped to use Fort de Chartres as his primary trading post, but the transfer of that site to Britain in the Treaty of Paris (1763) forced him to change his plans. In 1764, work began on establishing a fur trading center on the western bank of the Mississippi River near the point where the Missouri River joins. Even as a teenager, Chouteau began serving as Laclède's trusted clerk and lieutenant, and when he was only fourteen years old Chouteau found himself in charge of thirty workers who were building the first crude structures in what soon became known as St. Louis, named in honor of the canonized French monarch Louis IX. The village quickly grew into a commercial hub, making the transition to Spanish rule in 1770 and American control in 1804.

Because of his efforts in establishing St. Louis, Laclède became one of the growing community's most influential citizens, and his family eventually became recognized as influential leaders in the economic and social life of the region. Although trading in furs was the primary interest of Laclède and Chouteau, the men eventually diversified their financial interests as they became involved in real estate and banking. Chouteau inherited his stepfather's wealth and social prominence when Laclède died in 1778. From that point forward Chouteau became quite wealthy, and he was soon recognized as the largest landowner and one of the most influential businessmen and civic leaders in the early community of St. Louis.

President Thomas Jefferson appointed Chouteau one of the three justices of the Territorial Court after the Louisiana Territory was sold to the United States in 1803. Having achieved such prominence, Chouteau would subsequently serve as the first chairman of the board of trustees when St. Louis was incorporated as a city in 1809. He also served as a colonel in the St. Louis militia, served a term as a judge on the Court of Common Pleas, and functioned as U.S. pension agent for the Missouri Territory. In addition, Chouteau worked as a negotiator in 1815 when he successfully concluded the Treaty of Portage des Sioux with the neighboring Sioux, Iowa, Sauk, and Fox peoples.

Chouteau had long recognized that success in the fur trade was predicated upon maintaining friendly relations with Native American peoples who could supply pelts and who could help maintain the peace that was necessary for the successful conduct of business on the frontier. Chouteau maintained friendly relations with the Osage that enabled him to extend his business considerably. From 1794 to 1802, during the era of Spanish colonial control, he held the lucrative monopoly on trade with the Osage—essentially a vast trading empire, and one that brought him great wealth.

Chouteau was the wealthiest citizen of St. Louis, the unofficial banker for the region, and the city's largest landowner. He used his wealth to promote business interests throughout the region. Chouteau helped finance several other individuals and companies that became involved in the fur trade throughout the Louisiana Purchase Territory.

—Junius P. Rodriguez

See also
Chartres, Fort de; Osage; Portage des Sioux, Treaty of; Saint Louis

For Further Reading

Wooldridge, Rhoda. 1975. *Chouteau and the Founding of Saint Louis*. Independence, MO: Independence Press.

CITIZEN GENÊT

See **Genêt, Edmond Charles**

CLAIBORNE, WILLIAM CHARLES COLE (1775–1817)

As a Tennessee congressman, territorial governor of Mississippi, governor of the Territory of Orleans, and governor of Louisiana, W. C. C. Claiborne enjoyed a distinguished political career that embodied the developing Western perspective and spirit of Jeffersonian Republicanism. William Charles Cole, son of Colonel William and Mary (Leigh) Claiborne, was born in Sussex County, Virginia, in 1775. He attended Richmond Academy and studied briefly at the College of William and Mary until financial difficulties ended his formal instruction at the age of fifteen. John Beckley, a fellow Virginian who was clerk of the U.S. House of Representatives, hired Claiborne as an assistant in his office. In that capacity, Claiborne met the leading statesmen of the period, including his mentor and later benefactor, Thomas Jefferson.

Claiborne decided to study law when North Carolina congressman John Sevier recognized the young clerk's talent and offered encouragement. He returned to Virginia for studies, and upon passing the bar moved to the frontier in 1794 to practice criminal law in Sullivan County, Tennessee. Representing his county in the 1796 statehood convention, Claiborne helped to draft the original Tennessee constitution. When Sevier became governor of Tennessee, he appointed Claiborne, then only twenty-one years old, to serve as a judge on the state supreme court. In August 1797, Tennessee voters chose Claiborne to complete Andrew Jackson's unexpired congressional term and re-elected him in subsequent elections, although he remained under the legal constitutional age to hold the office.

Claiborne chaired the congressional committee that supervised the Mississippi Territory, and in that capacity he investigated allegations of political impropriety leveled against Governor Winthrop Sargent. On May 25, 1801, President Jefferson replaced Sargent as governor of the Mississippi Territory with Claiborne, and he arrived at Natchez on November 23. Despite the intense rivalry of vying factions, Governor Claiborne maintained a moderate course, resulting in substantive progress for the territory and its inhabitants. The creation of new counties, the settlement of land claims, and reforms in public health, education, and internal security were provincial successes in Claiborne's tenure. Additionally, continuing negotiations with regional Indian tribes and with Spanish Louisiana trained the young governor in larger national policy issues.

Upon the purchase of Louisiana in 1803, Jefferson sent Claiborne and General James Wilkinson to New Orleans as his commissioners, to accept the orderly transfer from French to American authority. Jefferson's appointment of Claiborne as governor of the Territory of Orleans was implicit in this arrangement, and Claiborne remained at New Orleans to begin the challenge of making the recently purchased territory truly American. Conversant in neither French nor Spanish, unfamiliar with local customs and practices, and Protestant in a Roman Catholic region, Claiborne faced many cultural obstacles in governing this new territory. Creoles remained suspicious of the governor and leery of Americanization.

Claiborne was an enigmatic leader. Contemporaries sometimes mistook his prudence for indecision when facing difficulties, but he shunned rashness, frequently seeking instruction and approval from peers and superiors. During crises, most notably the Burr conspiracy and the Battle of New Orleans, Claiborne seemed weak by consigning extraordinary powers upon Generals Wilkinson and Jackson. Although his leadership and policies generated vociferous criticism, Claiborne was an honorable man who assumed responsibility for his actions. He even fought a duel in 1807 when Daniel Clark charged that Claiborne demonstrated incompetence by abdicating responsibilities during the Burr affair.

Criticism notwithstanding, Claiborne enjoyed certain accomplishments as a territorial governor. In 1810 he secured the Baton Rouge district as the United States annexed the West Florida parishes, joining them to the Territory of Orleans. In January 1811, he directed the effective military suppression of the German Coast slave insurrection, an uprising that threatened New Orleans. In 1812, Louisiana became the eighteenth state, with Claiborne its first elected governor.

The War of 1812 presented Louisiana with dual threats of internal unrest in plantation districts and external invasion by the British, but Claiborne remained confident. Despite low numbers of militia enlistments and few Creoles joining the Forty-fourth Infantry, newly created for coastal defense, Claiborne overestimated Louisiana's potential troop strength in official communications with General Jackson. When Jackson arrived in December 1814, he declared martial law and initiated active procedures for defending New Orleans from impending attack. Unlike Jackson's scornful assessment, Claiborne's faith in the valiant efforts of Louisiana militia and fervent civilian patriotism vindicated his earlier confidence in the loyalty of Louisiana's citizens.

In 1817, Louisiana residents elected Claiborne to the U.S. Senate, completing the cycle of his political journey, but he died before taking office. A competent emissary of

Jeffersonian Republicanism, Claiborne effectively administered demanding frontier regions and prepared diverse communities for statehood.

—*Junius P. Rodriguez*

See also
Clark, Daniel; Orleans, Territory of; Wilkinson, James

For Further Reading
Claiborne, Nathaniel Herbert. 1819. *Notes on the War in the South; with Biographical Sketches of the Lives of Montgomery, Jackson, Sevier, and Late Gov. Claiborne, and Others*. Richmond, VA: William Ramsay; Claiborne, W. C. C. 1917. *The Official Letter Books of W. C. C. Claiborne*. Edited by Dunbar Rowland. Jackson: Mississippi Department of Archives and History; Hatfield, Joseph T. 1976. *William Claiborne: Jeffersonian Centurion in the American Southwest*. Lafayette: University of Southwestern Louisiana.

CLARK, DANIEL (1766–1813)

Daniel Clark was born in the maritime province of Sligo on the west coast of Ireland in 1766. Clark was named after his uncle, the most successful member of the family. The elder Daniel Clark had immigrated to the Spanish province of Louisiana and established a thriving commercial house in New Orleans. Young Clark joined his uncle there in 1786.

The younger Clark obtained a position in the office of the provincial governor, Ésteban Rodriguez Miró, which enabled him to assist his uncle and learn valuable techniques for negotiating the confusing Spanish customs regulations. In 1793, Clark formed a partnership with a Philadelphia merchant, Daniel Coxe, whose contacts within the U.S. government complemented Clark's influence in New Orleans.

The lack of formal regulations for trade between the United States and the Spanish province of Louisiana was a persistent problem for American merchants like Daniel Clark. In 1795 the Treaty of San Lorenzo (Pinckney's Treaty) granted American merchants a place of deposit in New Orleans and recognized the right of free navigation of the Mississippi River for American shippers. The deposit did not actually open until 1798, and the first entry in the books kept by the customs officials lists seventy bags of cotton placed in deposit by Daniel Clark. Although he used the deposit at New Orleans, Clark believed that the Spanish taxes on goods imported into the province in American ships largely negated any advantage earned through the deposit. Clark proposed to the Spanish officials that American and Spanish ships pay the same taxes when exporting products from New Orleans to ports in the United States or other nations. In return, Spanish ships could take cargoes from the American deposit without payment of export duties. After the Spanish governor endorsed Clark's proposal, the colonial treasury adopted and even expanded Clark's recommendations.

Clark's successful negotiations with the Spanish government encouraged New Orleans merchants to urge President Thomas Jefferson to appoint Clark U.S. consul for the Orleans Territory. Some opposition to Clark's appointment arose among members of the Jefferson administration who questioned his loyalty to the United States. The commission nominating Clark indicated that he was a Spanish subject, but Clark insisted that he had never been a Spanish subject but had been naturalized, as an American citizen, in the latter part of 1798 in Natchez. Clark proved to be the most successful of U.S. appointees to the post in New Orleans.

When rumors of a possible transfer of the province of Louisiana from Spain to France appeared in New Orleans in 1802, Daniel Clark became the most important source of information about provincial conditions for President Jefferson. In 1802, Clark warned his government that the French would quickly end the American deposit in New Orleans, and the American merchant community in New Orleans credited Clark's information with convincing Jefferson that only the purchase of New Orleans would ensure American use of the port. One local resident concluded that the United States owed the acquisition of Louisiana to Daniel Clark.

Before the transfer of Louisiana from France to the United States actually occurred, Clark continued to relay information about conditions in New Orleans to the two commissioners, William C. C. Claiborne and General James Wilkinson, waiting to accept the territory. After the transfer, Clark apparently expected to be named permanent governor of Louisiana, but he was disappointed. Jefferson's unwillingness to name a former British subject and lingering doubts about his loyalty doomed his ambitions. Clark's failure poisoned his relations with Claiborne, the acting governor, and caused him to become the center of opposition to Claiborne's policies. Their mutual antipathy culminated in a duel fought in 1807 in which Claiborne was seriously injured.

From 1804 to 1808, Clark served as a territorial delegate to the U.S. Congress from the Territory of Orleans. As a delegate, he urged the immediate admission of Louisiana as a state and the removal of restrictions on the importation of slaves into the territory. The "Louisiana Memorial of 1804," presented by Clark to the Congress, detailed the opposition of the New Orleans merchants to Louisiana's uncertain status and the policies of its governor.

The extent of Clark's involvement in the Burr conspiracy of 1805–1806 is uncertain. Burr arrived in New Orleans on June 25, 1805, bearing letters of introduction from General Wilkinson to Governor Claiborne and Daniel Clark. Both men entertained Burr, their rivalry prompting them each to try to outdo the other. Wilkinson's letter to Clark contained a cryptic comment that Burr would "communicate to him many things improper" to write and which "he would not say to any other." If Burr did contemplate a plan to separate the Western states from the United States or a conquest of Mexican territory, Clark apparently feared being drawn into Burr's plots. He wrote to Wilkinson that "how the devil I have been lugged into the conspiracy or what assistance I can be of in it is to me incomprehensible." Clark's actions after Burr's visit only increased suspicions about his involvement. Two months after Burr left New Orleans, Clark set out on an extended journey that took him to several Mexican ports, including Vera Cruz. Many recent immigrants to Louisiana clamored for the conquest of Mexico and the other Spanish territories in North America. A group of three hundred prominent New Orleans citizens organized a "Mexican Association" for the purpose of collecting data on Mexico in case of a war with Spain. Clark certainly knew of the Mexican Association, and he may have introduced its leaders to Burr. Clark wrote a self-serving defense of his actions years later, in which he claimed that he never would have been "fool enough to expose a large fortune and a respectable standing to certain destruction on an impractible scheme." Instead, he claimed that he dissuaded his friends from participating in any venture of Burr's. At Burr's trial for treason in 1807, General Wilkinson and Clark each accused the other of complicity in Burr's plans. In 1809, Clark published his *Proofs of the Corruption of General James Wilkinson,* calling Wilkinson a "trembling coward [and a] sanguinary traitor." Wilkinson replied in his *Memoirs* (published in 1816, after Clark's death) that Clark was an "ostentatious, vain, vindictive, and ambitious" man.

Clark's possible connections with Burr and his duel with Governor Claiborne wrecked his political future in New Orleans and with the Democratic-Republican administrations of Jefferson and Madison. Clark was not re-elected as territorial delegate in 1808. He continued to manage his business until his sudden death from a fever on August 16, 1813. Twenty years after his death, his estate became embroiled in litigation over his rightful heir. Myra Clark Whitney Gaines claimed to be his legitimate daughter by a secret marriage to a young Frenchwoman, and the lawsuit she instigated tied up the Clark estate for the next sixty years. The "Great Gaines Case" was celebrated as the "true-life romance of the American courts" in the nineteenth century, and a justice of the U.S. Supreme Court called it "the most remarkable case" ever brought before that court.

—Elizabeth U. Alexander

See also

Burr, Aaron; Claiborne, William Charles Cole; Wilkinson, James

For Further Reading

Alexander, Elizabeth U. 2001. *Notorious Woman: The Celebrated Case of Myra Clark Gaines.* Baton Rouge: Louisiana State University Press; Clark, Daniel. 1970 [1809]. *Proofs of the Corruption of General James Wilkinson, and of his connexion with Aaron Burr.* Freeport, NY: Books for Libraries Press; Harmon, Nolan B. 1946. *The Famous Case of Myra Clark Gaines.* Baton Rouge: Louisiana State University Press.

CLARK, FORT

Fort Clark, located in present-day Mercer County, North Dakota, was an important fur trade outpost established on the west bank of the Missouri River by James Kipp in 1830. The rectangular fort, named in honor of the famous explorer William Clark, measured 120 by 160 feet. Kipp built the fort high on a bluff, at an angle in the river, on the side of the Missouri opposite from where Meriwether Lewis and William Clark spent the winter of 1804–1805 at Fort Mandan.

Fort Clark was the result of a corporate merger involving John Jacob Astor's American Fur Company with the Columbia Fur Company in 1827. Alexander MacKenzie, director of the western division of the American Fur Company, the Upper Missouri Outfit, attempted to monopolize the region's fur trade by building forts at strategic locations beginning in 1828. As part of this plan, MacKenzie instructed James Kipp, a company clerk fluent in Mandan, to cement a trading partnership with the Mandan who spent their summers at Mih-tutta-hang-kush, an earth-lodge village located next to the trading post. Kipp was also responsible for encouraging neighboring Arikara and Hidatsa to conduct business at Fort Clark. Kipp, like many of the trading post's employees, married a Mandan woman. The seasoned clerk also employed Toussaint Charbonneau, the guide who accompanied Lewis and Clark's Corps of Discovery, to help facilitate trade with the region's Indian inhabitants. The frontier post prospered, thanks to its strategic location at a historic crossroads where migrating bands of Sioux, Assiniboine, and Crow frequently came to trade.

The *Yellow Stone,* a steamboat carrying provisions to the forts along the upper Missouri, arrived at the trading post in 1832. After replenishing Fort Clark's supplies, the steamboat returned to St. Louis with one hundred packs of beaver pelts and bison robes. Pelts shipped downriver to St. Louis each summer were then counted, weighed, and shipped to New York. In return for their furs, Indians received brightly colored coarse woolen goods imported from England. They also traded for guns, powder and lead, tobacco, knives, flints, and kettles. Fort Clark's ban on the sale of alcohol suited the Mandan, who preferred water, tea, and coffee.

Trade along the upper Missouri thrived until June 19, 1837, when the American Fur Company's steamboat, *St. Peter's,* brought the deadly smallpox disease to Fort Clark and Fort Union. Neighboring Mandan villages were devastated by the end of summer. Those fortunate enough to survive the initial onslaught, approximately 125 residents from a village of 1,800 people, abandoned their village on August 11, 1837, to join the Hidatsa living farther north near the mouth of the Knife River. To accommodate these Indians, Francis Chardon, the clerk assigned to Fort Clark at the time, built Fort Berthold beside their village.

Arikara who lived near Fort Clark did not suffer as much as the Mandan. Those who survived the deadly epidemic occupied the abandoned Mandan village adjacent to Fort Clark in 1838 and resumed their dealings with traders assigned to Fort Clark. Unfortunately, however, the Arikara could not escape the diseases that ravaged native peoples. A cholera outbreak in 1851 and another smallpox epidemic in 1856 decimated the Arikara settlement. The weakened Arikara continued to use the village as a summer home until relocating to Fort Berthold in 1862.

In 1850 competitors built Primeau's Post, owned and operated by Harvey, Primeau, and Company of St. Louis, on the south side of the Arikara village. The two forts then vied for Indian customers until a fire destroyed the south half of Fort Clark in 1860. The trading post's owners, Pierre Chouteau, Jr., and Company, responded by purchasing Primeau's Post, which they operated until 1861. The post and nearby Arikara village were abandoned sometime before 1862, following repeated raids by warriors associated with Two Bears's band of Sioux.

Much is known about life at Fort Clark, thanks to Francis A. Chardon, head trader at the post, who kept a detailed journal from 1834 to 1839 concerning his experiences in the Dakota wilderness. Famous artists Karl Bodmer and George Catlin also left a rich legacy in their reproductions of the people and events associated with Fort Clark. Other notable visitors included Prince Maximilian of Weid-Neuweid and the famous naturalist John James Audubon.

Today the State Historical Society of North Dakota manages Fort Clark. The former trading post is an important archaeological site containing the remains of a Mandan earth-lodge village, foundations of the fort's structures, and a large Indian burial ground. It is listed on the National Register of Historic Places and has been nominated as a National Historic Landmark.

—*Jon L. Brudvig*

See also
Arikara; Mandan; North Dakota

For Further Reading

Athearn, Robert G. 1967. *Forts on the Upper Missouri.* Lincoln: University of Nebraska Press; Heidenreich, Virginia L., ed. 1990. *The Fur Trade in North Dakota.* Bismarck: State Historical Society of North Dakota; Meyer, Roy. 1977. *The Village Indians of the Upper Missouri.* Lincoln: University of Nebraska Press; Thomas, David, and Karin Ronnefeldt, eds. 1982. *People of the Flint: Life among the Plains Indians in Their Final Days of Glory.* New York: Promontory Press.

CLARK, GEORGE ROGERS (1752–1818)

Conqueror of the Old Northwest and founder of Louisville, Kentucky, George Rogers Clark, elder brother of William Clark, was born in Albemarle County, Virginia, two and a half miles northwest of Thomas Jefferson's birthplace at Shadwell. In January 1778, Clark was appointed by Governor Patrick Henry of Virginia to lead a military expedition against British forces in the West. Clark won fame when he defeated British garrisons and captured the frontier outposts of Kaskaskia in July 1778 and Vincennes in February 1779 in what would later become, respectively, the states of Illinois and Indiana. After the war he settled near the falls of the Ohio River.

Like many settlers in the trans-Appalachian West, Clark considered free navigation of the Mississippi River vital to the economic independence of Western settlers, and he therefore resented Spanish control of New Orleans and the mouth of the Mississippi. Because Westerners felt that the American government was neglecting their interests and concerns by not working hard enough to secure access to the Mississippi, many felt justified in taking matters into their own hands and were responsive to extralegal schemes to wrest possession of Louisiana from the Spaniards. In addition to these common complaints, Clark was further dissatisfied with the government because his claims incurred in his country's service dating back to the American Revolution remained unpaid, and he felt that his ser-vices were not adequately appreciated. Clark thus became active in many of these intrigues, and because of his fame as a military commander he was viewed as a natural leader.

Despairing over never receiving compensation for his claims from the U.S. government, in 1788 Clark petitioned Diego de Gardoqui, Spanish envoy to the United States, for a grant of approximately one hundred square miles of land opposite the mouth of the Ohio for the founding of a colony. Clark, however, refused to agree to the terms offered by the Spanish government, which did not include adequate political and religious freedom, and the plan died.

He again became involved in Western land intrigues in 1790–1791, this time with war seemingly imminent between Spain and Britain. James O'Fallon, general agent of the South Carolina Yazoo Company, hoped to take advantage of the situation by launching an expedition against Louisiana. The Yazoo Company was formed to settle territory granted by Georgia, but its plans were frustrated by Spain, which claimed jurisdiction over the area. O'Fallon enlisted Clark's support and placed him in command of an armed force, and he threatened Spanish governor Esteban Miró that he would send it against Natchez and New Orleans in 1791 with the goal of organizing a western confederation independent of both the United States and Spain if not allowed to settle the Yazoo land peacefully. By the end of the year the plan had collapsed, following President Washington's denunciation of the unlawful scheme.

In the summer of 1793, Clark was again at the center of an intrigue involving Louisiana. Citizen Edmond Genêt, newly arrived minister to the United States from France, was interested in separating Louisiana from Spain. Therefore he gladly accepted an offer from Clark to raise a force for the capture of New Orleans with assistance from the French navy, and he appointed Clark major general of the "Independent and Revolutionary Legion of the Mississippi." Afterward, Louisiana was to be made an independent state maintaining commercial relations with France and the United States. Upset with Genêt's violations of U.S. neutrality, Washington and his cabinet demanded his recall by the French government in August 1793. By March 1794 the planned attack on Louisiana had collapsed. The new French minister to the United States disavowed any further violations of American neutrality. Meanwhile Washington forbade Americans to participate in any future illegal designs on Louisiana and charged officers of the federal government with enforcement of the laws against filibusters.

France again planned for the conquest of Louisiana from Spain in 1798. As a general in the French army, Clark was called upon to raise a force of volunteers for that purpose from among settlers in the West, where pro-French sympathies ran high. Refusing an order of the U.S. government to relinquish his French commission, Clark fled to St. Louis.

In 1803 he moved into a cabin at Clarksville, across the Ohio River from Louisville. In 1809 poor health and the amputation of his right leg forced Clark to move in with his sister Lucy at her home, Locust Grove, near Louisville. There he died in 1818.

—*Sean R. Busick*

See also
Clark, William; Gardoqui, Diego María de; Genêt, Edmond Charles; Jefferson, Thomas; Kaskaskia

For Further Reading
James, James Alton. 1928. *The Life of George Rogers Clark*. Chicago: University of Chicago Press.

CLARK, WILLIAM (1770–1838)

Born the ninth of ten children to John and Ann (Rogers) Clark on August 1, 1770, William Clark spent the first fourteen years of his life on the family's Caroline County, Virginia, plantation. Drawn by brother George Rogers Clark's tales of the Ohio Valley, the Clark family relocated to a new plantation called Mulberry Hill near present-day Louisville, Kentucky.

Growing up a planter's son on the Virginia and Kentucky frontiers, William Clark had a rich military heritage. Following his brothers' examples, he engaged in military service, first in the militia and then the regular army. In 1792, President George Washington commissioned Clark a lieutenant of infantry. Under the command of General Anthony Wayne, Clark assisted in building and supplying a string of forts throughout Ohio before commanding an elite rifleman corps that saw action at the Battle of Fallen Timbers. Clark, a slaveowner, resigned his commission in 1796 to return home and care for his aging parents and to manage the family estate.

In 1803 he received his now-famous invitation to greatness by his friend Meriwether Lewis. Clark agreed to co-command an expedition envisioned by President Jefferson whose primary purposes included exploring the country west of the Mississippi and, if possible, ascertaining the feasibility of a commercial route to the Pacific. The Lewis and Clark Expedition traversed a continent and established U.S. claims from St. Louis to the Pacific. Although Captain Lewis was officially in charge of the Corps of Discovery, Clark trained the men and operated as the expedition's principal cartographer and waterman. He gained an appreciation for the tremendous diversity of Indian cultures and was often the more skillful of the co-commanders in Indian negotiations. President Bill Clinton granted Clark a posthumous captain's commission in the year 2000.

Following the expedition's return to St. Louis, President Jefferson appointed Clark a federal Indian agent. From 1807 to 1838, Clark served as the most important representative of the federal government to the Indian nations in the West. He was perhaps the most seasoned and accomplished person ever to serve in this position, personally signing thirty-seven (or one-tenth) of all treaties ratified between the Indians and the United States.

As principal Indian agent for the Louisiana Territory, Clark promoted the government factory system to provide Indians goods at cost and to establish friendships with tribes in the Midwest and on the Great Plains. Clark's efforts to quell hostilities during the War of 1812 by building a string of frontier blockhouses and patrolling the area with mounted rangers achieved moderate success. As brigadier general of the territorial militia, he rose to the challenge of reorganizing that body into a respectable fighting force. He sought to win over the allegiance of tribes along the upper Missouri and Mississippi by promoting the government factory system. He also promoted commercial fur trading far from white settlement and joined Manuel Lisa as a partner of the Missouri Fur Company in 1809.

Clark designed Fort Osage, the future starting point of the Santa Fe Trail. During the War of 1812, President James Monroe commissioned Clark as Missouri's first territorial governor, a position Clark occupied from 1813 to 1820. Governor Clark acted as ex officio superintendent of Indian affairs, and he kept Missouri's far-reaching frontier settlements relatively safe during the War of 1812. One of his first duties involved combating British forces among the Indians in the upper Mississippi Valley. He led a campaign up the Mississippi to capture Prairie du Chien, hoping to reduce British influence there. Clark's victory asserted American control over the upper Mississippi, but it was fleeting; a combined British and Indian force recaptured the area shortly thereafter. Despite the setback, Clark successfully elicited peace from the tribes represented at the 1815 Portage des Sioux Treaty Council.

Governor Clark supervised the removal of tribes located within the boundaries of the Missouri and Arkansas Territories. He helped land-grant holders protect their claims, and he assisted new immigrants by extinguishing Indian title through treaty and accurate surveys. Despite these efforts to establish peace and release Indian holdings, some Missourians felt him too sympathetic to the Indians, a perception that cost him the state's first governorship.

After being defeated by Alexander McNair in Missouri's inaugural gubernatorial election, Clark was appointed superintendent of Indian affairs in 1822 by President Monroe. In that new position he was headquartered at St. Louis, on the cusp of a colonial empire rapidly expanding and on the edge of threatened Indian civilizations. There Clark found a middle ground between the changing forces revolutionizing the frontier and the Indian nations already living there. Clark exercised jurisdiction over Western tribes and Eastern nations being removed west of the Mississippi River. He expressed great sympathy for those removed tribes and promoted their interests as he understood them. Nevertheless, Clark agreed with and helped implement Indian removal. His ethnocentrism caused him to reject the idea that Indians could maintain their identity and culture within the advancing frontier.

Clark's evolving Indian policy consisted of executing federal policy by being friendly but firm and helping Indians all that he could when they cooperated while punishing warlike or unreceptive nations. He endeavored to secure Indian friendship in a way he thought most beneficial to them and the most effectual and economical to the United States. Clark felt that commerce exercised a powerful influence on Indian actions. Therefore he promoted St. Louis's greatest commercial enterprise—the fur trade.

Superintendent Clark issued trading licenses, removed unauthorized persons from Indian country, and confiscated illegal alcohol. Clark extended patronage to American fur traders, artists, and explorers, who in turn assisted him in his mission by establishing friendly relations with numerous tribes. They gathered ethnographic and geographic information for Clark's monumental map of the West and assisted in transporting Indian delegations, visitors, and annuities up and down the river. Unfortunately, the fur trade brought harmful consequences, too. Unscrupulous traders found their way into Indian country, where they swindled, maligned, and debauched some Indians through the use of liquor and deceptive trading practices. Clark asked the government to revise the Trade and Intercourse Laws to give him and his agents real authority to take decisive action against the perpetrators.

Coleader of the Lewis and Clark Expedition, William Clark later served with distinction as the governor of Missouri Territory.

Perhaps it was in the realm of policy-making, however, that Clark made his greatest contributions. Clark was the most experienced and knowledgeable government official in the trans-Mississippi West. From the government's perspective, Clark served as an able administrator of federal policy who offered helpful suggestions in fine-tuning it to match the realities of the frontier. In a time of expanding bureaucratic control, he contributed to and modified portions of the Indian Civilization Act of 1819. His efforts to modify the factory system fell on deaf ears in Washington, and the system collapsed. Clark and Lewis Cass did, however, make significant contributions in efforts to modify the laws and regulations governing Indian affairs. Their report contributed to the Indian Removal Act of 1830, the revision of the Trade and Intercourse Laws, and the reorganization of the entire Indian Bureau in 1834. That year,

Clark retained his influential position in St. Louis despite being in his sixties.

In the controversial and often repulsive business of Indian removal, Clark was more involved than history has credited him. A Jeffersonian man in a Jacksonian world, he indeed thought it best to congregate the tribes in order to minimize Indian-white conflict. He tried to enforce the trade and intercourse laws to protect the tribes from the evils of alcohol and dishonest traders. He worked incessantly to establish clear Indian-white boundaries and even served a term as acting surveyor general of Illinois, Missouri, and the Arkansas Territory from 1824 to 1825. He sought to evict squatters on Indian lands and to keep settlers from rushing pell-mell into them by insisting that the government purchase the lands first.

More often than not, he was the one sent to negotiate the purchase. Over the course of his career, millions of acres passed from Indian to white ownership by his own hand. Whether the government took Indian land by treaty or by war, the results were often similar. Sometimes he used threats to accomplish the government's goals, but, unlike Jackson, he did not turn to force in evicting Indians from their lands. Clark was responsible for making things work out for the government at the least possible expense. To his credit, the Indians regarded Clark as their friend, and they gave him their highest respect. In return, he made the bitter pill of removal a little easier to swallow and did what he could to improve conditions during their removals and upon their arrival at their destination.

As an agent of empire, Clark promoted economic and political expansion of the republic, secured its western and northern borders, and assisted in the growth and expansion of the fur trade and the overland trails. He was a patron of the arts, and he supported the establishment of schools, the growth of banks, and the incorporation of cities. Clark invested in real estate, maintained one of the first museums in the West, and promoted other economic and cultural endeavors in St. Louis and the surrounding region.

William Clark was a devoted family man. His wife, Julie Hancock, bore him five children: Meriwether, William, Mary, George, and John. Following her death he married Harriet Kennerly Radford, a widow, and they had three children: Jefferson, Edmond, and Harriett. He also adopted Sacagawea's two children, Jean Baptiste and Lizette Charbonneau, and offered assistance to religious groups, missionaries, explorers, and travelers. He did much to expand the geographical knowledge of the continent.

Clark was one of America's great statesmen. For more than three decades, Clark's service as the federal government's official representative to Indian nations west of the Mississippi placed him in a key position to encourage expanding trade networks, temper white settlement, and oversee Indian affairs—important themes that affected Missouri, the West, and the entire nation. In addition to his contributions as coleader of America's most famous, and perhaps most important, expedition, Clark's tenure as superintendent of Indian affairs has created his legacy as antebellum America's most influential representative of Indian affairs.

—Jay H. Buckley

See also

Clark, George Rogers; Corps of Discovery; Lewis, Meriwether; Lewis and Clark Expedition; Missouri Fur Company; Osage, Fort; Portage des Sioux, Treaty of; Saint Louis

For Further Reading

Bakeless, John. 1947. *Lewis and Clark: Partners in Discovery.* New York: William Morrow; Buckley, Jay H. 2001. "William Clark: Superintendent of Indian Affairs at St. Louis, 1813–1838." Ph.D. diss., Department of History, University of Nebraska, Lincoln; Loos, John L. 1953. "A Biography of William Clark, 1770–1813." Ph.D. diss., Washington University, St. Louis, MO; Moulton, Gary E., ed. 1983–2001. *The Journals of the Lewis and Clark Expedition.* 13 vols. Lincoln: University of Nebraska Press; Steffen, Jerome O. 1977. *William Clark: Jeffersonian Man on the Frontier.* Norman: University of Oklahoma Press.

CLINTON, GEORGE (1739–1812)

Revolutionary War soldier, seven-term governor of New York, and twice-elected vice president, George Clinton was a member of one of New York's most powerful families. As vice president, Clinton found himself isolated from the Jefferson administration, yet he was elected again in 1808 when James Madison won the presidency. Clinton opposed the Constitution and a strong federal government, but he took no active role in the Louisiana Purchase.

Born in New York in 1739, Clinton served in the colonial militia, studied law, was admitted to the bar, sided with the revolutionary cause, rose to general, and was elected to the Second Continental Congress. He was a surprise victor in New York's gubernatorial race in 1777 and held the position for six successive terms. Clinton also enjoyed the support and friendship of New York's influential Livingston family. Yet for all of his patriotism and success as one of George Washington's brightest supporters, Clinton was an ardent opponent of the ratification of the Constitution. Clinton based his opposition to a strong federal government on two issues: the commerce power and a deep concern over the loss of state sovereignty. With New York City's natural harbor, Clinton was aware of the trade advantage New York had over neighboring states, an advantage he feared would be sacrificed to a federal government with the power to regulate commerce. No less of an issue was the potential loss of state sovereignty under the proposed constitution.

Given those factors, Clinton rallied support against state ratification of the federal charter.

Under the pseudonym "Cato," Clinton penned seven letters critical of the Constitution, citing opposition to biennial elections for a congress, state legislative election of upper-house (Senate) representatives, continuance of the slave trade, and a standing army. Published in the *New York Journal,* Clinton's comments drew rebuttal from Alexander Hamilton, who signed himself as "Caesar," in the *Daily Advertiser.* Despite Clinton's efforts, New York finally ratified the Constitution, but only after the required nine states had voted ratification and New Yorkers expressed fear of being left out of the newly formed federal government.

Under duress from a state legislature dominated by Federalists, Clinton declined to run for governor in 1795, but in 1800 he was elected for a seventh term. Clinton had greater ambitions at the national level, and in 1804 he was elected vice president when Thomas Jefferson won re-election. As vice president, an aging Clinton was generally ineffective, although he was again elected vice president under James Madison in 1808. Presiding over the Senate was his only contribution, and in that role, he did very little, but in 1811 Clinton cast the deciding vote against the recharter of the Bank of the United States, breaking a deadlocked Senate vote. New Hampshire Federalist senator William Plummer was Clinton's harshest critic, calling the vice president old, feeble, and awkward. Future president John Quincy Adams was also adamant about Clinton's ineptness, questioning the vice president's judgment and knowledge of Senate procedures. Adams concluded that "a worse choice than Mr. Clinton could scarcely have been made" for the second office. Plummer termed Clinton "uncapable" of presiding over the Senate and remarked that Clinton "has no mind—no intellect—no memory—He forgets the question—."

George Clinton was a poor choice for vice president, but his selection provided the balance necessary for Republican electoral success. Despite his ineptness at the national level, Clinton's stance against aristocratic leadership in his native New York in favor of the revolutionary yeoman solidified his standing among New Yorkers, who were not to be discounted in national elections. Even his great adversary Alexander Hamilton termed Clinton the leader of his party, and contemporaries referred to him as "Chief" or "Chairman" or "Pharaoh," all with the respect due a national leader.

To Clinton, the spread of the nation into the vast reaches of the Louisiana Territories meant loss of New York's trading power, a Federalist issue. Although for years as governor a bitter enemy of New York's aristocratic rulers, Clinton and his national views were more in line with the Federalist economic position on acquiring Louisiana. Clinton was certainly no ally of Jefferson, although he supported the administration. In December of 1803, William P. Van Ness, a supporter of Clinton's adversary Aaron Burr, published *An Examination of the Various Charges Exhibited against Aaron Burr.* Under the pseudonym of "Aristides," Van Ness quoted Clinton on Jefferson as "an accommodating trimmer, who would change with the times and bend to circumstances for the purpose of personal promotion." William Coleman published significant portions of the pamphlet in the New York *Evening Post,* delighting in the divisions among leading Republicans. Although Clinton denied his characterizations of Jefferson, and the president accepted the explanation, the rift between the two was concrete. This was not the first time that such criticisms had been aired publicly, and Jefferson dismissed Clinton in the 1808 election, favoring Madison. Although Clinton supporters campaigned ardently for their candidate, it was obvious that Madison was the party's choice. The decision to include Clinton was made to demonstrate solidarity, a step hardly necessary considering the rapid decline in Federalist support. Clinton was elected, but his second term proved no better than his first. In the spring of 1812, a month-long illness ended with the death of the vice president, the first to die in office.

—Boyd Childress

For Further Reading

Kaminski, John P. 1993. *George Clinton: Yeoman Politician of the New Republic.* Madison, WI: Madison House; Spaulding, Ernest W. 1938. *His Excellency George Clinton: Critic of the Constitution.* New York: Macmillan.

COLLOT, GEORGES HENRI VICTOR (1750–1805)

In October 1795 a new government, the Directory, took control of the revolutionary government of the French republic. Under this new administration, the French government took a decidedly active interest in efforts to re-establish a French North American empire. As a part of this strategy, the disposition of Louisiana became a matter of prime interest. In previous years, the French position on Louisiana had been, above all else, to keep the territory out of the hands of Great Britain. Under the Directory, the question became one of how the French might reacquire their former colony from Bourbon Spain.

Charles Delacroix, the Directory's minister of foreign relations, set in motion a plan that, if successful, might wrest Louisiana away from Spain. Delacroix directed Pierre Auguste Adet, the French minister to the United States, to begin a covert effort at seeking strategic information about Louisiana, such as its defensive capabilities and its readiness, that could assist the French in formulating a plan to recover the former colony. Additionally, Adet was to determine how the temperate American diplomatic mood might change if the French republic, rather than Bourbon Spain, possessed Louisiana.

Adet requested that General Georges Henri Victor Collot, the former French colonial governor of Guadeloupe, travel throughout the Ohio and Mississippi River Valleys to gain insight on the popular mood of the day. In his posthumously published two-volume *Journey in North America* (1826), Collot wrote that he traversed "the western imperium of the American continent" as he did Adet's and Delacroix's bidding. Collot discovered that the Spanish were intensely fearful of American expansionism (what he termed "the American phalanx"), and he suggested that only France was strong enough to withhold such growth. He further reported to his superiors that "as long as Spain remained in possession of Louisiana, one of her chief objects was to hide from the Americans whatever attractions the country might have for them" (Collot).

Collot also devised a plan of action that could prevent the Americans from acquiring Louisiana. It was Collot's opinion that the successful defense of Louisiana, regardless of whether Spain or France was the possessor, depended upon forming a strategic alliance with those U.S. settlers living in the trans-Appalachian regions of the Old Northwest and the Old Southwest. Such a policy was similar to the one that the Spanish had undertaken when they placed key American frontiersmen on the Spanish payroll and sought to encourage the formation of a confederation that would break with the United States and cast its allegiance with Spain.

Such a plan was not unrealistic. Since Thomas Pinckney and Manuel de Godoy had only recently negotiated the Treaty of San Lorenzo (1795), Spain's historic refusal to allow the Americans access to the Mississippi River and permission to trade their goods at the port of New Orleans was an economic weapon that, if used correctly, might drive the U.S. frontiersmen into the Spanish economic orbit. If the settlers of the Ohio Valley could be convinced that their economic interests were better suited by an arrangement with Louisiana, it followed that their political allegiance might be swayed as well. Collot maintained that "the Western states of the North American Republic must unite themselves with Louisiana and form in the future one single compact nation" if the Louisiana Territory hoped to endure as anything short of a U.S. possession (ibid.).

The report that Collot prepared after his 1795 journey continued to influence French policy with regard to Louisiana for several years. In July 1798, when the United States and France began an undeclared naval war, the Quasi-War, and the possibility of a full-scale conflict loomed, the French government took a measured response, drawing its policy from Collot's suggestions.

Joseph Philippe Létombe, the French consul general in the United States, advised the Directory not to declare war upon the Americans. It was his opinion, as it was Collot's, that the acquisition of Louisiana, and perhaps the Floridas, should remain the French goal. Fighting a war with the Americans would not serve to advance the French imperial agenda. Létombe urged that, if war was necessary in the Western Hemisphere, it should be fought against Great Britain for the reacquisition of Canada. Such a policy would win the hearty approval of the Americans, thereby allowing the French to acquire those lands "which the nature of things gives to us" (DeConde).

Napoleon Bonaparte would read Collot's report in 1800 and ponder its recommendations as he prepared to negotiate the secret, second Treaty of San Ildefonso (1800) that would lead to the retrocession of Louisiana from Spain to France. Unfortunately, not all of Collot's observations were readily understood or accepted at the time. He had warned in his report that no European power was likely strong enough "to maintain itself in Louisiana against the will of the United States" (Collot). Perhaps it was the final recognition of that reality that forced the first consul's hand in 1803 and convinced him to sell the Louisiana Territory to the United States.

—*Junius P. Rodriguez*

See also
Adet, Pierre Auguste

For Further Reading

Collot, Georges Henri Victor. 1974 [1826]. *Journey in North America*. New York: AMS Press; DeConde, Alexander. 1976. *This Affair of Louisiana*. New York: Charles Scribner's Sons; Echeverria, Durand, trans. 1952. "General Collot's Plan for a Reconnaissance of the Ohio and Mississippi Valleys, 1796." *William and Mary Quarterly* 9, no. 3: 518.

COLONY FOR FREED SLAVES

In the early nineteenth century, antislavery advocates proposed to establish a colony for freed slaves in the newly acquired Louisiana Territory. Proponents of the Louisiana scheme failed to receive sufficient political backing, however, and most colonization supporters viewed Africa and Haiti as more suitable sites.

Thomas Jefferson believed that colonization was an effective way to emancipate the slaves without precipitating a civil or race war. Although he was a slave owner who hesitated to speak out in behalf of emancipation, Jefferson favored abolition. After the successful slave revolt in St. Domingue (Haiti), he feared similar upheavals in the United States, and that reinforced his conviction that whites must dictate the terms of emancipation. He also believed that blacks could never be accepted into white society as equals because of white racial prejudices. In Jefferson's view, blacks and whites composed two separate nations, and colonization was the best means for blacks to attain liberty and equality. Not only would slavery end but, in addition, Virginia would be rid of its black population.

Some of Jefferson's contemporaries shared his view that colonization should be a vital component of any emancipation plan. In a 1789 memorandum, James Madison argued that Africa was the best location for a black colony: the interior wilderness of the United States was too close to the westward-moving white population, and such proximity might lead to renewed racial conflicts. After the acquisition of Louisiana, Jefferson never considered the territory a viable site for a black colony, and he favored Africa or newly independent Haiti. Haiti was especially appealing to Jefferson because the cost of transporting blacks would be lower. In his mind, the Haitians also shared the same skin color, and their congenial manner would allow the black colonists to enjoy the liberty and equality they could never attain in the United States. Most colonization advocates discounted Louisiana as a suitable location for a colony of freed slaves.

Some disagreed, however: St. George Tucker favored Louisiana as an ideal site for colonization. Tucker had a distinguished career as a federal judge and professor of law at the College of William and Mary. In an 1803 essay he called for the abolition of slavery and recommended a colonization project in southern Louisiana, because the climate suited blacks. Another supporter of colonization, James Monroe, believed that Louisiana would be a good location for a colony. In 1805 the Virginia state legislature passed a resolution to found a colony for freed slaves in upper Louisiana. They sent the resolution to the U.S. Congress for consideration, but the plan never went forward.

Thomas Branagan also preferred the Louisiana Territory for a colonization project. Branagan was born in Dublin, Ireland, in 1774, and went to sea at the age of fourteen before settling in Antigua in the 1790s to work as an overseer on a sugar plantation. After being exposed to slavery, in 1799 he moved to Philadelphia, where he worked as a preacher and wrote essays advocating social and moral reform. In an 1805 essay calling for emancipation and colonization, he concurred with Jefferson's belief that blacks could never hope to live as free and equal citizens in white society. If a colony were not established, emancipated blacks would inundate the North demanding social services and burdening white society. That would lead to greater social tension between blacks and whites, and Branagan feared the unleashing of an upheaval similar to the Haitian slave revolt. He selected Louisiana as an ideal place for a colony of freed slaves because of its availability of land, and he believed that the climate was congenial to the nature of blacks. As he envisioned it, each colonist would receive a plot of land, and the states would pay for the emigration costs. The federal government would appoint a black governor, judges, and magistrates to govern the colony. Branagan's plan failed to win backing, and the selection of Louisiana never enjoyed widespread support among colonization adherents.

Africa was more appealing because of its distance from the United States. Founded in 1816 and based in Washington, D.C., the American Colonization Society (ACS) bought land in Africa and named the colony Liberia. The ACS sent about twelve thousand African Americans to the colony over the next fifty years. In later years Abraham Lincoln focused on Haiti and Central America as possible locations for a colony of freed slaves. Efforts to colonize blacks in Haiti in 1860 and 1863 failed miserably, and U.S. negotiators never obtained consent from Central American governments to establish a colony. Passage of the Fourteenth Amendment put an end to serious colonization projects.

—*Mark Thomason*

See also

Jefferson, Thomas; Monroe, James

For Further Reading

Branagan, Thomas. 1805. *Serious remonstrances, addressed to the citizens of the northern states . . . being an appeal to their natural feelings & common sense . . . on the recent revival of the slave trade . . . .* Philadelphia: T. T. Stiles; Goodyear Freehling, Alison. 1982. *Drift toward Dissolution: The Virginia Slavery Debate of 1831–1832.* Baton Rouge and London: Louisiana State University Press; Staudenraus, P. J. 1961. *The African Colonization Movement, 1816–1865.* New York: Columbia University Press; Tucker, St. George. 1803. *Reflections on the Cession of Louisiana to the United States.* Washington, DC: Samuel Harrison Smith.

COLORADO

Organized as a territory in 1861, Colorado later became the thirty-eighth state of the Union on August 1, 1876, thus earning its nickname of "Centennial State." The territory shared the rectangular shape of the state, from 102 degrees longitude in the east over the Rockies to 109 degrees longitude, and from 37 degrees latitude in the south to 41 degrees in the north, encompassing 104,100 square miles. Early Coloradans achieved these boundaries at considerable cost to the neighboring territories of Utah, New Mexico, Kansas, and Nebraska, which each yielded land to create the near perfect rectangle of present-day Colorado. Although Colorado is usually regarded as a mountain state, one-third of the state actually falls within the Great Plains. The Rocky Mountains fill the central two-fifths of the state, while the Colorado Plateau, located along the state's western boundary, occupies about one-fifth.

Spain was the first European power to claim the region. Spaniards exploring northward from Santa Fe found a mighty river and named it Colorado ("ruddy") for the reddish silt burden it carried, and the name stuck to the area. Spanish influence remains in other romantic names, such as the Sangre de Christo ("Blood of Christ") Mountains and the Dolores River ("River of Sorrows"). Early Spanish explorers found a region that had been inhabited for thousands of years. The Anasazi had lived in southwestern Colorado for more than one thousand

The Pike's Peak gold rush of 1859 attracted many prospectors and settlers to relocate to Colorado.

years before Europeans arrived. These "ancient ones" made homes both on valley floors and later in unique cliff dwellings that remain preserved in Mesa Verde National Park and other historic sites. Their life as agriculturists in an arid region was often difficult. Perhaps because of climate changes that affected rainfall, these people abandoned the region abruptly, long before European contact.

Although the Pueblo peoples of the southwest count the Anasazi as their ancestors, people of entirely different ancestry and language lived in the Rocky Mountains. The Ute moved into Colorado from adjacent territory in Utah, migrating and living in small bands and leaving few permanent marks on the land. They hunted and gathered in the Rocky Mountains, often living at high elevations. When these groups later moved onto the Plains they found their expansion checked by recent arrivals coming in from the east—the Cheyenne and Arapaho. Indigenous peoples of both the mountains and the Plains would find the incursions of white men to be the greatest challenge to their existence.

Despite several expeditions, the Spanish never established permanent settlements in Colorado. The area did not loom large in European expansion until the Louisiana Purchase in 1803. When Thomas Jefferson bought Louisiana from Napoleon, he knew little about the western regions of the tract that would become the eastern half of Colorado. In 1806 an expedition under the command of Zebulon Pike set out from St. Louis in an attempt rectify this ignorance. By the time Spanish soldiers arrested Pike and his men on the Rio Grande, they had pushed into the Rocky Mountains, viewed (but not ascended) the famed peak later named for their leader, and found the source of the Arkansas River. In the face of what proved to be insatiable U.S. curiosity for the unknown West, Spain agreed to settle the disputed border of eastern Colorado at the Arkansas River in the Transcontinental Treaty (1819). Another U.S. expedition, led by Stephen Long, evaluated the region in 1820, named Long's Peak, and recorded the now famous assessment of the Central Plains as an uninhabitable "Great American Desert."

Perhaps because of such pronouncements, American

interest in the Colorado region did not really develop until the fur trapping period of the 1820s. During that brief but intense exploitation of the fur-bearing animals of the Rocky Mountains, hundreds of white men walked Indian trails through every river valley and mountain pass that might yield pelts. The trappers learned from the indigenous peoples both where to go and how to live. This intimate knowledge of the topography, along with the establishment of forts (for example, Bent's Fort, 1828), laid the foundation for the next stage of U.S. expansion in the region.

The exploits of adventurers like John C. Frémont sparked Eastern interest in the rugged West. By the time of the Mexican War (1846–1848), Frémont and guide Kit Carson had mapped northern Colorado up to Wyoming and the Oregon Trail. When war broke out, Stephen Kearny moved seventeen hundred soldiers from Kansas, through eastern Colorado, down to Santa Fe, which surrendered without a fight. Finally, the United States had all the pieces of what would become the state of Colorado.

People trickled into the region as they found profitable enterprises. By 1840 a few individuals from the New Mexico Territory were farming in southern Colorado. In 1851 they founded San Luis in the San Luis Valley, Colorado's first permanent settlement. However, Colorado remained scarcely settled by whites until the 1860s. Then, in one quick influx, thousands of Americans descended upon the region, altering its course forever. The impetus—gold. Once gold was found in the Pikes Peak area in 1859, it prompted a mass migration similar to California's a decade earlier. The mining boom created instant population centers, and, if they were not "civilized" towns, at least they had a veneer of U.S. culture. Mining camps sprang up overnight, and if the minerals held out they eventually developed the trappings of a town, including hotels, saloons, barbershops, and retail stores. No matter the topography, if there was gold, people would go. Thus Colorado boasted settlements throughout the Rockies. Leadville, Blackhawk, and Silver Plume are just a few of the colorful names that remain part of Colorado's landscape. By 1861 these newly arrived settlers had gained territorial status for 66,718,000 acres, and they settled upon the name Colorado.

The white population quickly surpassed both the Indian and Spanish residents, who would be relegated to minority status. The mixture of cultures present in Colorado from the beginnings of its political life ensured a diverse society, but also tensions. The indigenous residents felt the power of the Americans soon after their arrival. These residents faced a white population explosion that put pressure on their game resources, their land, and eventually their very existence. Location determined the time of the impact, but in the end all the indigenous peoples lost their land. The Plains dwellers felt keenly the destruction of the bison herds upon which they had lived and the encroachment of settlements. The Treaty of Fort Laramie (1851) purported to guarantee the Plains to the Cheyenne and Arapaho, but in a decade the next treaty stripped the territory from the tribes. Denver was built on lands that Congress had reserved for the Cheyenne and Arapaho peoples.

Viewed by whites as an obstacle to the civilization of the region that was demanded by Manifest Destiny, indigenous peoples bore unbearable pressure. Expansionist politicians like Governor John Evans and Colonel John M. Chivington openly advocated extermination as the only solution to the growing tensions between natives and white residents. In 1864, Chivington led his men in an attack on a sleeping Indian village at Sand Creek, where the peace chief Black Kettle flew a U.S. flag given to him by President Lincoln. The ensuing slaughter and dismemberment of men, women, and children forever stained Colorado's territorial history. The Ute, a group of loosely aligned bands living in the Rockies, also encountered the land hunger of whites. After removal efforts in the 1870s, by 1880 the Ute had been stripped of all but 1,650 square miles, which lasted only another two decades.

The removal of the indigenous peoples from Colorado left its white residents free to expand. Mining continued to be an important source of income in the territory, contributing to a boom and bust type of economy. The cattle industry, however, added a stabilizing influence after the Civil War. Texas longhorns fattened on Plains grasses in eastern Colorado could feed residents of Denver or be driven to the railheads of the rapidly expanding railroads. Technology grew to allow large-scale irrigation in the arid area, and agriculture increased in Colorado. The factors combined to push the population up to the level required for statehood in 1876, thus ending the era of the Colorado Territory and opening a new chapter in the region's development.

—Clarissa W. Confer

See also
Arapaho; Cheyenne

For Further Reading

Abbot, Carl, Stephen J. Leonard, and David McComb. 1994. *Colorado: A History of the Centennial State.* Boulder: University Press of Colorado; Limerick, Patricia. 1987. *Legacy of Conquest: The Unbroken Past of the American West.* New York: W. W. Norton; Sprague, Marshall. 1976. *Colorado: A Bicentennial History.* New York: W. W. Norton.

COLTER, JOHN (c. 1775–1813)

John Colter, one of the youngest members of Lewis and Clark's Corps of Discovery, often undertook hazardous and risky assignments during the expedition. At its end in 1806, Colter returned to the Rocky Mountains for four more years of exploring and trapping.

John Colter was born near Staunton, Virginia, and the first recorded mention of him is upon his recruitment by

Meriwether Lewis at Louisville, Kentucky, on October 15, 1803. His age was given as eighteen, making him the youngest member of the party except for George Shannon.

A typical young man, Colter had problems waiting for the expedition to begin. On March 3, 1804, he was confined to quarters for ten days for drunkenness. Later that month he was tried for mutiny for threatening to shoot Sergeant John Ordway. Promising to be better, Colter was released without punishment on March 29 and declared a full member of the party on March 31. Once the expedition began its trek, Colter's physical strength and enthusiasm stood him in good stead.

Colter's value to the expedition was especially noted when Private George Shannon failed to report back from a hunting trip on August 26. After two days, Colter was dispatched to search for him but was unsuccessful. Before giving up on Shannon, Colter was sent out again on September 3. Fortunately, Shannon was merely lost; he thought the expedition was ahead of him instead of behind him. They were soon reunited.

Colter performed his tasks well, with notable skill and bravery. He was mentioned often in the journals of the expedition. When William Clark finally determined the Snake River route to be impassable, it was John Colter who carried the information to Lewis.

As the expedition was returning in 1806, it met two men, Joseph Dickson and Forest Hancock, who had set out to explore the Yellowstone. John Colter requested permission to be released early from his enlistment, which would expire on October 10. On August 17 he was formally released, the only member of the party to be so honored. He set out guiding Dickson and Hancock upriver.

The spring of 1807 found John Colter floating down the Missouri River in a dugout canoe without Hancock or Dickson. Colter was met at the mouth of the Platte River by Manuel Lisa's trapping party. Lisa was thrilled to meet Colter, and he persuaded Colter to guide his trappers to the Big Horn River.

While Lisa was building Fort Raymond at the mouth of the Big Horn, Colter was sent to meet the Crow and other tribes south of the Yellowstone and invite them to trade. On foot with pack and gun, Colter plunged into country never before seen by white men. His route, while disputed, is traced on Clark's 1810 map. For five hundred miles John Colter explored what is now the Big Horn Basin. He penetrated southwest to Jackson Lake and traversed what is today Yellowstone Park. He saw the geysers and hot springs, called Colter's Hell, along the Stinking Waters (Shoshone) River in northern Wyoming.

The following spring, 1809, Colter explored the Three Forks of the Missouri. This rich beaver region was guarded by hostile Blackfoot. In a battle between the Blackfoot and a party of Crow and Flathead, Colter sided with the Crow and was seriously injured. He had no more than recovered from his injuries when he returned to the region and was captured by the Blackfoot. Stripped naked, he was turned loose to be run down by the Blackfoot warriors. Colter outran all but one of his pursuers; finally turning and seizing the warrior's spear, Colter killed him. Colter made his way to the Hidatsa village at the mouth of the Yellowstone and Missouri and recuperated there.

The great St. Louis Missouri Fur Company Expedition of 1809 reached the village. Recruited by Andrew Henry, Colter guided the party to Fort Raymond and then on to Three Forks. There, on April 3, 1810, a stockade was begun. Nine days later the site was attacked by Blackfoot. After escaping from this assault, Colter left the mountains never to return. He took up farming near Dundee, Missouri, married, and died in 1813 of jaundice. In a period of just six years, John Colter had lived a life of adventure that has rarely been duplicated.

—*Jerry L. Parker*

See also
Blackfoot; Corps of Discovery; Lisa, Manuel

For Further Reading
Bechdolt, Frederick Ritchie. 1969. *Giants of the Old West.* Freeport, NY: Books for Libraries Press; Harris, Burton. 1993 [1952]. *John Colter, His Years in the Rockies.* New York: Scribner. Reprint: Lincoln: University of Nebraska Press; Vinton, Stallo. 1926. *John Colter, Discoverer of Yellowstone Park* . . . . New York: E. Eberstadt.

COMANCHE

Although they are recognized as one of the earliest of the Plains Indian tribes to adopt the use of the horse for hunting bison, the Comanche were migrants who came from the West and adopted a new culture on the High Plains during the sixteenth century. Originally considered a branch of the Eastern Shoshoni, the group that came to be called the Comanche left the Great Basin region and initially settled in the valley of the Upper Platte River in southeastern Wyoming. For nearly a century the relatively small tribe hunted and remained unmolested within the vast range between the Front Range of the Rocky Mountains and the Black Hills. When other larger tribes migrating from the eastern woodlands began to enter the region in the seventeenth century, the pressure of these new arrivals—including the Arapaho, Cheyenne, and Sioux—caused the Comanche to move farther southward into the region of present-day New Mexico and Texas.

The Comanche were decidedly different from the other tribes that moved into the Southern Plains. They spoke a language that, like the Shoshoni language, stemmed from the Uto-Aztecan branch of the Aztec-Tanoan linguistic family. The former eastern woodlands folk who had relocated to the region all spoke languages associated with the Algonquian-Wakashan linguistic family. There is some uncertainty as to the origin of the name

Comanche, but one possible explanation is that it was a Spanish mispronunciation of the Ute name *Kohmahts* ("those who are against us"), which they had used to identify the Comanche.

In a fashion that indicated the Comanche's primacy to the Southern Plains, the other tribes of the region accepted the use of Comanche as the language of trade and commerce throughout the area. Also, because of their earlier adoption of the horse for hunting purposes, the Comanche had become talented horsemen and habitual raiders. They were also known as fierce warriors who resisted both neighboring tribes as well as the arrival of American settlers. It is believed that the Comanche killed more whites (in proportion to the size of their own tribe) than any other Native American group.

The Comanche were using horses by 1680, and the mobility provided by that form of transportation allowed the tribe to trade and raid throughout a vast region. On occasion the Comanche were know to have extended themselves as far as northern Mexico. A group of Comanche were present at a trading fair that took place in Taos in 1705. They soon became regular participants in trade fairs held at Taos, Santa Fe, and other points along the Spanish borderlands. The Comanche quickly earned a reputation of trading in items that had been taken during raids against other Plains Indian tribes. In addition to standard trade items, the Comanche often captured women and children who would be sold—or ransomed—at the regional trading fairs along the southwestern frontier.

Spanish authorities in Mexico revised their colonial policy in the 1770s when they realized that the vast Texas frontier could not be defended effectively by the limited military resources that were available. This retrenchment by the Spanish provided the Comanche with a free reign over much of northern Texas, where they quickly established a dominant presence that belied the small number of members who constituted the tribe. In later years, once Texas settlers revolted and formed the Republic of Texas (1836–1845), the Comanche continued to operate as a semiautonomous state within a state. There were regular skirmishes between Texans and Comanches throughout the nine-year-long history of the Texas Republic. At one point it was believed that the Comanche were holding as many as 200 captives whom they had kidnaped from Texas settlements.

Like other indigenous peoples of the Great Plains, the Comanche eventually lost most of their traditional hunting lands as they signed treaties with U.S. authorities. In the Treaty of the Little Arkansas River (1865) and the Treaty of Medicine Lodge Creek (1867) bands of Comanche signed away possession of their territory as they agreed to be relocated to reservation lands. By clearing the Comanche from the plains of northern Texas, the U.S. government fashioned a safe corridor that would soon be used by Texas cattlemen who drove herds of cattle to northern railheads in Kansas during the "golden age" of the American cowboy. All of the major cattle trails that would come into use made their way across territory that had formerly been controlled by the Comanche.

Today about 9,000 Comanche live in the United States on reservation land in Oklahoma.

—*Junius P. Rodriguez*

See also

Arapaho; Cheyenne; Kiowa; New Mexico; Taos; Texas

For Further Reading

Jones, Douglas C. 1966. *The Treaty of Medicine Lodge.* Norman: University of Oklahoma Press; Mayhall, Mildred P. 1965. *Indian Wars of Texas.* Waco, TX: Texian Press; Richardson, Rupert Norval. 1933. *The Comanche Barrier to South Plains Settlement.* Glendale, CA: Arthur H. Clark; Wallace, Ernest, and E. Adamson Hoebel. 1964. *The Comanches: Lords of the South Plains.* Norman: University of Oklahoma Press

CONSTITUTION OF THE UNITED STATES

The Louisiana Purchase was illegal, at least in the eyes of Thomas Jefferson and according to the Republican Party's notions of strict constitutional construction. Indeed, the Sage of Monticello had no qualms about his lack of authority for acquiring the territory, stating that "they will be obliged to ask from the People an amendment of the Constitution." He added later: "I had rather ask an enlargement of power from the nation . . . than to assume it by a constitution which would make our powers boundless." Then, expressing his ultimate concern over broad construction, the president declared: "Our peculiar security is in possession of a written Constitution. Let us not make it a blank paper by construction." Notwithstanding his professed constitutional scruples, Jefferson opted for political expediency rather than lose the highly prized Louisiana Purchase (Carson, 1992).

Jefferson had given thought to the question of its constitutionality before the purchase was ever negotiated. In January 1803, Attorney General Levi Lincoln asserted that the territory was so important to the United States that any action in acquiring it was justified. Additionally, he maintained that in an earlier treaty France had agreed to broaden the boundaries of the Mississippi and Georgia Territories, and thus the purchase could be tied to this earlier arrangement. In Lincoln's mind, such a strategy avoided constitutional difficulties regarding the acquisition of foreign territory. Shortly after Jefferson received this opinion, Secretary of the Treasury Albert Gallatin assured the president that the nation had "an inherent right to acquire territory" and that "the same constituted authorities in whom the treaty-making power is vested have a constitutional right to sanction the acquisition of territory." Both Lincoln's and Gallatin's views were decidedly broad in nature. There existed no specific language in the Constitution that sanctioned the purchase (Deutsch, 1967).

Still, even though Lincoln and Gallatin argued the purchase's legality, Jefferson worried about expanding the Constitution and informed his cabinet on July 16 of the need for an amendment. In the ensuing weeks he worked on two drafts, both of which authorized the purchase and defined Indian rights, in addition to creating an Indian zone above the thirty-first parallel. The second draft added a provision authorizing the future acquisition of Florida. Neither amendment was ever sent to Congress.

On August 17, Jefferson's constitutional ethics were laid aside when he received a letter from U.S. minister to France Robert Livingston stating that Napoleon had changed his mind and wanted to void the purchase agreement. Just five days later the president wrote to Gallatin, directing him to prepare for a transfer of stock in order to pay France, and added that "it will be well to say as little as possible on the constitutional difficulty, and that Congress should act on it without talking" (ibid.).

When Congress met on October 17, Jefferson delivered his third annual address and made the official announcement of the purchase treaty with France, impressing upon the Senate the importance of a speedy ratification. He never mentioned the issue of constitutionality. The Senate received the treaty the same day, and on October 20 ratified it by a vote of 24 to 7. On October 26 it passed legislation for taking control of the territory and setting up a government.

There was really little doubt of the treaty's approval. Republicans dominated both houses of Congress, and Jefferson had, as usual, worked behind the scenes to ensure party solidarity. The only people unhappy with the purchase were New England Federalists. One historian notes that it was not really the issue of constitutionality that upset Federalists—indeed, they were the architects of broad construction. Rather, it was Jefferson's and the South's plan to "force New England Federalism into a position of perpetual minority" (Brent, 1968).

Thus Federalists attacked every aspect of the purchase in an attempt to halt the floodwaters of ascendant Republicanism. During the treaty discussions in the Senate, Federalists William Wells and James Hillhouse questioned the legality of France's title to Louisiana. Napoleon had acquired the territory from Spain in the Treaty of San Ildefonso (1800), but it had clearly stipulated that France was not to cede Louisiana to another country. On November 1, Spain sent a letter of protest to the United States.

House Federalists attempted the same strategy when discussing the bill providing funds and authorizing the occupation and governing of the territory. Roger Griswold requested a copy of the San Ildefonso Treaty and any correspondence between the U.S. and Spanish governments. His strategy was not only clever but also effective. Fearing that they might spend $15 million for land they could never legally own, many Republicans voted in favor of looking at the French-Spanish treaty.

On October 25, House Federalists fired another salvo when Gaylord Griswold questioned the constitutionality of the purchase. In light of the fact that there existed no authority for the acquisition of foreign territory, he insisted that the House should refuse passing any measures connected to the purchase. Republicans rose to the challenge by advocating broad construction. John Randolph of Roanoke, an ultrastrict constructionist in earlier and later days, argued that the president had the right to expand the nation's territories through the treaty-making powers. Next, Caesar Rodney revealed the ultimate Republican betrayal of strict construction, insisting that the Constitution did not specifically prevent the acquisition of territory and that it could be authorized under the general welfare clause.

The House debates never endangered the Louisiana Purchase. Republicans easily passed the bill for purchasing, occupying, and governing the territory. Federalists, however, continued to grumble. Senator Timothy Pickering once again questioned the deal's constitutionality and declared that even an amendment would not authorize such a powerful act. Explaining the contractual nature of the Constitution, he argued that each member of the contract, the original states, would have to approve the purchase. Pickering's last-ditch effort to kill the most momentous piece of legislation in Jefferson's presidency was to no avail. Still, Pickering's enmity would not cease, and signifying the final role reversal in Federalist-Republican ideology, he turned to the Kentucky and Virginia Resolutions for a remedy. In a wave of letters to New England Federalists, he advocated the creation of a separate Northern confederacy. Pickering's plea represented the dying gasp of Federalist opposition to the purchase.

Few will doubt the importance of the Louisiana Purchase. But those who look for ideological consistency on the part of Jefferson and the Republicans will be disappointed. According to the dictates of strict construction, the Purchase was illegal. And as one critic has noted, Jefferson "had an utterly exquisite constitutional conscience when he was not in power" (ibid.).

—*Matthew S. Warshauer*

For Further Reading

Brent, Robert. 1968. "Puncturing Some Jeffersonian Mythology." *Southern Quarterly* 6, no. 2: 175–190; Carson, David A. 1992. "Blank Paper of the Constitution: The Louisiana Purchase Debates." *Historian* 54, no. 3: 477–490; Deutsch, Eberhard P. 1967. "The Constitutional Controversy over the Louisiana Purchase." *American Bar Association Journal* 53, no. 1: 50–57; Farnham, Thomas J. 1965. "The Federal-State Issue and the Louisiana Purchase." *Louisiana History* 6, no. 1: 5–25.

CONVENTIONS

***See* individual conventions listed by location**

CONVENTION OF 1818

This international agreement between the United States and Great Britain was the result of efforts to partition the Oregon Country, the territory on the northwestern flank of the Louisiana Purchase. The Oregon Country extended westward from the Rocky Mountains to the Pacific Coast and northward from the limit of Spanish California at the line of 42 degrees north latitude to Russian possessions in Alaska at 54 degrees 40 minutes north latitude. Following the War of 1812 and the Treaty of Ghent (1814), this was a significant test for Anglo-American relations in an era of colonial expansion by both parties. In negotiations leading up to the agreement, the crux of the territorial dispute was the region from the Lower Columbia River north to the line of 49 degrees north latitude (the northern boundary of present-day Washington state). Great Britain proposed the river as a demarcation line because it sought to safeguard the commercial interests of the Hudson's Bay Company in the region. The American delegation rejected this offer, because the United States coveted the harbors from the Strait of Juan de Fuca to Puget Sound, the only safely navigable harbor region north of Spanish Mexico (the entrance to the Columbia River being a treacherous bar harbor).

When both nations finally signed the Convention of 1818, they agreed to a ten-year joint occupancy, a compromise position that ensured citizens of both countries freedom of trade and movement in the Oregon Country. In the beginning the convention was primarily beneficial to the British, since the Hudson's Bay Company had a significant presence in the region. Following the War of 1812, which neutralized John Jacob Astor's Pacific Fur Company, and the acquisition of the Montreal-based North West Company in 1821, the Hudson's Bay Company retained a monopoly on the fur trade in the Oregon Country that lasted into the 1840s.

Near the end of the initial ten-year limit for the original convention, the United States and Great Britain returned to the bargaining table. However, for a second time they proved unable to reach a permanent settlement on the Oregon question, because the issue of territorial sovereignty remained unresolved. For their part, British negotiators sought to resist what they perceived as American aggression, while the Americans wished to curb British imperialism in the Western Hemisphere. As a result, in August 1827 both governments renewed the agreement for an indefinite period on the condition that it could be rescinded following a twelve-month notice by either nation. In the spirit of the original convention, both parties agreed that neither nation claimed exclusive jurisdiction, nor would either establish any type of territorial government in the region.

By the mid-1840s, historical realities had shifted, bolstering American claims to the region. In 1844, James K. Polk was elected to the presidency on the Democrats' expansionist platform, which called for the "reannexation of Texas and the reoccupation of Oregon." That same year, fifteen hundred Americans traveled to the Pacific Northwest on the Oregon Trail, and the following year another twenty-five hundred made the journey west. In 1845 the expansionist rhetoric reached a fever pitch following the popularization of the campaign slogan "54°40' or Fight," and the great congressional debate on Oregon that lasted for nearly five months, from December 1845 to April 1846.

These developments strengthened Polk's position at a time when the American claim on present-day Washington state was tenuous because of a lack of American settlement north of the Columbia. When the Hudson's Bay Company announced plans to relocate its Pacific headquarters from the Columbia to Vancouver Island, the British cabinet was willing to accept 49 degrees north latitude as the demarcation line. Great Britain and the United States reached a permanent settlement in June 1846, when the international boundary treaty was signed, establishing the current Canadian-American border. With this agreement each power acquired an outlet to the Pacific and each established territorial sovereignty over one-half of the approximately half a million square miles that had composed the original Oregon Country.

The Joint Occupancy Convention of 1818 must be understood in light of the history of British imperialism in North America; the Monroe Doctrine, which sought to limit European colonization in the Western Hemisphere; and U.S. westward expansionism. With the Louisiana Purchase, President Thomas Jefferson secured the vast tract of land in the central portion of the North American continent. In the Convention of 1818, the United States laid claim to the adjoining region that could give the nation territorial interests from coast to coast, with a harbor on the northern Pacific slope being a key component in the country's dreams of empire.

The Convention of 1818 also established the northern boundary of the Louisiana Purchase Territory when it fixed the boundary between the United States and Canada at 49 degrees north latitude, from Lake of the Woods, in present-day Minnesota, to the crest of the Rocky Mountains. This part of the agreement was an equitable land swap: portions of the Mississippi River drainage basin above 49 degrees north latitude were transferred to Canadian authority, and lands within the basin of the Red River of the North, which drained northward toward Hudson's Bay, became a part of U.S. territory.

—Melinda Marie Jetté

See also

Astor, John Jacob

For Further Reading

Merk, Frederick. 1967. *The Oregon Question: Essays in Anglo-American Diplomacy and Politics*. Cambridge: Harvard University Press; Stuart, Reginald. 1988. *United States Expansion and British North America, 1775–1871*. Charlotte: University of North Carolina Press.

CORDERO Y BUSTAMENTE, MANUEL ANTONIO (1753–1823)

Manuel Antonio Cordero y Bustamente, a learned gentleman, served Spain on the frontier of New Spain beginning in 1793, where he distinguished himself as an Indian fighter. As governor of Texas from 1805 to 1808, he was involved in issues surrounding the boundary between Louisiana and the province of Texas after the Louisiana Purchase. Arriving in San Antonio in the summer of 1805 as assistant to Governor Elquezabal, who was ill, one of his first assignments was an inspection tour of Spanish outposts in eastern Texas. Bayou Pierre (Arroyo Hondo) near Los Adaes (the capital of Spanish Texas until 1773) was the easternmost site. Cordero established the Villa Santísima Trinidad de Salcedo near Los Adaes (near present-day Robeline, Louisiana).

After the Louisiana Purchase (1803), it was readily apparent that problems would soon result, since the western limits of Louisiana had never been fixed. The United States contended that the boundary between Texas and Louisiana was the Sabine River. On February 5, 1806, U.S. troops appeared at Los Adaes and attempted to force Spanish troops to withdraw to the Sabine River. Although the soldiers at Los Adaes refused, the soldiers at the two smaller Spanish outposts east of the Sabine River, at Comichi and La Nana, did retreat to the western side of the River. As Spain did not want to engage in war with the United States, Cordero proposed an agreement designating the territory between the Arroyo Hondo and the Sabine a "neutral ground" until the boundary questions could be resolved. Nonetheless, in 1806, U.S. personnel did make exploratory trips up the Red River into Spanish territory. The U.S. expedition was successfully halted.

—Alfred Lemmon

See also

Los Adaes; Neutral Ground; Wilkinson, James

For Further Reading

Brandt, Penny S. 1988. "A Letter of Dr. John Sibley, Indian Agent." *Louisiana History* 29, no. 4: 365–387; Luettenegger, Benedict, trans. 1978. "Puelles' Report of 1827 on the Texas-Louisiana Boundary." Translated by Benedict Luettenegger, with annotations by Marion A. Habig. *Louisiana History* 19, no. 2: 133–180.

CORPS OF DISCOVERY

When President Thomas Jefferson won approval from Congress to fund a small expeditionary party to document the uncharted West, he first dubbed the faction the Corps of Discovery. Jefferson appointed his personal friend and secretary Captain Meriwether Lewis as the first corps member and named him to head the government expedition. Lewis followed up by asking his former military leader William Clark to co-command the expedition; Clark readily accepted. Lewis and Clark then selected men to compose the Corps of Discovery based on leadership and interpreting skills, hunting prowess, specialized craftsmanship, and frontier adeptness.

Secretary of War Henry Dearborn initially suggested only twelve members, because of the expedition's small budget and the fear that the presence of too many troops would provoke Indian hostility, but Lewis quickly discovered that more men were needed to navigate the boats on the voyage. When Lewis met Clark in Clarksville, Indiana (opposite Louisville), they recruited enlisted soldiers who volunteered from nearby army outposts and continued to register troops in St. Louis. By the spring of 1804, the corps voyaged up the Missouri River with forty-five members. Some military personnel and local boatmen were recruited to go only part of the way. Only thirty-three members would travel from Fort Mandan (North Dakota) to the Pacific Ocean and return in 1806: the thirty-three members plus Lewis's Newfoundland dog, Seaman, would form the permanent party.

The corps's permanent party had two captains, three sergeants, twenty-three privates, and five nonmilitary members. The group included members who were white, black, Native American, and of mixed ancestry. Among the nonmilitary members was William Clark's lifelong slave, York, who, among his other duties, voted when corps decisions were made and completely awed the Indian men, women, and children who had never before seen a black man. Jean Baptiste LePage and Toussaint Charbonneau, French-Canadian fur traders, joined the Corps of Discovery at Fort Mandan in 1804, after the dismissal of Privates Moses Reed and John Newman for desertion and mutinous acts. Charbonneau and his teenage Shoshoni wife, Sacagawea, who gave birth to a son at Fort Mandan named Jean Baptiste, were used as interpreters and guides. Sacagawea became an invaluable member by guiding the corps over the mountains and easing native hostility. Toussaint Charbonneau was the oldest corps member, at the age of forty-seven, while the youngest member was his son, who was only fifty-five days old when the group departed from Fort Mandan for the Pacific Ocean in April 1805. Another useful interpreter, hunter, and guide for the corps was George Drouillard, who was a métis, half French and half Shawnee.

Each private selected to the corps had a specific expertise plus frontier ingenuity. The privates came from all

Meriwether Lewis, who had formerly been personal secretary to president Thomas Jefferson, adapted to his new role as co-commander of the Corps of Discovery.

parts of the United States, and some were French-Canadian as well. Among the enlisted men was Private Pierre Cruzatte, who was a proficient waterman and interpreter, but also played the violin. John Shields was chosen by merit, but also by his capability as a gunsmith, blacksmith, and boat builder, while Private John Colter was a quick-minded frontiersman and hunter who later became the first white man to view Yellowstone Park and its geysers.

The only officers under Captains Lewis and Clark were sergeants. The only member to die on the Lewis and Clark Expedition was Sergeant Charles Floyd, Jr., who died near present-day Sioux City, Iowa, of a ruptured appendix. A carpenter from Pennsylvania, Patrick Gass, became a commissioned sergeant in Floyd's place. The two remaining sergeants, Nathaniel Pryor (Floyd's cousin) and John Ordway, issued provisions, appointed guards, kept journals, and were assigned army administration.

The sergeants, privates, and nonmilitary members cooked the meals, built the camps, manned the boats, interpreted the native languages, and portaged the supplies without fanfare. Captains Lewis and Clark molded unruly men to be tough, disciplined, and steadfastly loyal—all without protest. Even when morale was low or they disagreed with the captains' decisions, the corps never openly challenged them.

The tattered Corps of Discovery returned to St. Louis as national heroes, but they soon went their separate ways. Many stayed in the Louisiana Territory, while others headed to their homes in the East. Little is known about the corps after the expedition, except that numerous members died young. The Congress offered the corps's soldiers double pay plus 320 Louisiana acres, while Lewis and Clark received 1,600 acres each. Despite Jefferson's naming of the unit the Corps of Discovery, Sergeant Patrick Gass holds claim to popularizing the term "Corps of Discovery" by displaying it on his 1807 published journal.

—*Nathan R. Meyer*

See also
Lewis and Clark Expedition

For Further Reading

Ambrose, Stephen E. 1996. *Undaunted Courage: Meriwether Lewis, Thomas Jefferson, and the Opening of the American West.* New York: Simon and Schuster; DeVoto, Bernard. 1953. *The Journals of Lewis and Clark.* New York: Houghton Mifflin; Jackson, Donald, ed. 1978. *Letters of the Lewis and Clark Expedition, with Related Documents: 1783–1854.* Urbana: University of Illinois Press.

COUNCIL BLUFFS, IOWA

Located on the Missouri River in southwestern Iowa, across from Omaha, Nebraska, the city of Council Bluffs has served as an agriculture and railroad center since the mid–nineteenth century.

A village of Ioway Indians occupied the site of the present-day city when Meriwether Lewis and William Clark arrived in 1804. The U.S. explorers met with representatives of the Missouri and Otoe Indian tribes north of the present city at a bluff near present-day Fort Calhoun, Nebraska. This council with the Indians led Lewis and Clark to name the area Council Bluff. Early traders and government officials would later refer to the area between the mouth of the Platte River and Lewis and Clark's meeting site as "the Council Bluffs."

The first trading post in what is now Council Bluffs may have appeared as early as 1824, with the establishment of a post at "Hart's Bluffs." The United States secured the Council Bluffs area after several Indian tribes ceded their claim to the territory in an 1830 treaty. Pottawattamie Indians were assigned to this land after surrendering their territory in Indiana and Illinois in an 1833 treaty. Mistakes on the part of emigration agents of the Indian Bureau led to the tribe's settling briefly in western Missouri (near Fort Leavenworth) before being redirected to southwestern Iowa in 1837. In that year a blockhouse was constructed and a Pottawattamie village was established at the site of present-day Council Bluffs.

Father Pierre-Jean De Smet began a Jesuit mission at the blockhouse in May of 1838. De Smet was transferred a year later, and the mission was abandoned during the summer of 1841. In 1842 troops under Captain John H. K. Burgwin were sent to the area to defend the Potawattomi from the Sioux, who were threatening war. Burgwin established a cantonment about five miles south of the blockhouse. Originally named Camp Fenwick, it was renamed Fort Croghan before being abandoned in October 1843.

Mormons arrived in the area in June 1846 after being expelled from their settlement in Nauvoo, Illinois. A Mormon village established near the blockhouse was briefly named Miller's Hollow. By request of Brigham Young, a post office was established there in 1848, and by resolution the name of the village was changed to Kanesville. The name was in honor of Colonel Thomas Lieper Kane of Philadelphia. During their stay in Kanesville, hundreds of Mormons were recruited by the U.S. government to serve in the war with Mexico. As gold seekers headed west to California in 1849, the village became known as an important outfitting post. The population of the village got as high as seven thousand before most of the Mormon settlers left to continue their journey west.

Upon the incorporation of the city by act of the Iowa legislature in 1853, the city's name was changed from Kanesville to Council Bluffs, in honor of Lewis and Clark's council with the Indians. The city of Council Bluffs was also made the seat of Pottawattamie County. In 1859 the city was chosen as the eastern terminus of the Union Pacific Railroad—the first transcontinental railroad in the United States.

—*J. Brent Etzel*

See also
Ioway; Mormon Road; Potawatomi; Sioux.

For Further Reading
Dunbar, Jean. 2001. *Omaha, Council Bluffs, and Bellevue in the Nineteenth Century: A Photographic History.* Chicago: Arcadia Publishing.

COUREURS DE BOIS

Coureurs de bois is a French term that means "woods-runners." These were the men who secured furs from the American Indians and ordinarily sold them to government-licensed agents in Montreal, Quebec, and other designated points in New France. The fur trade in the seventeenth and eighteenth centuries was one of the most lucrative markets for investment in North America, because European clothing fashions demanded an extensive use of furs, not only for warmth but also for ornamentation. This style of adornment remained popular well into the nineteenth century.

The Louisiana Territory was not the first to face the onslaught of fur traders. The French had encouraged this economic activity since their arrival in the early 1600s and had organized it under mercantilistic principles of governmental control. By the end of the seventeenth century they created, or at least oversaw, a system that extended from the political and demographic centers of New France (that is, Montreal and Quebec) to the Rocky Mountains.

A certain hierarchy had become obvious by the end of that century. At the top, the *fermiers* directed distant posts with royal permits to underscore their political and economic position, and they could even call upon their allied Indians to assist them in wars against the British. Their position resembled that of the tax farms in Old Regime France. Under the "control" of the *fermiers* were the *coureurs de bois,* who ordinarily acted as middlemen by trading directly with the Indians. They, however, needed some capital or accessible credit, for they had to supply their canoes with merchandise that could be traded with the Indians for furs. It must be noted that a round-trip expedition often required more than a year, which time included the construction of special winter quarters. Many of the *coureurs de bois* were sons of *habitants,* settlers in New France, who were attracted by the freedom of action in the wilderness and the opportunities for wealth not apparent with the relatively poor soils of the St. Lawrence River Valley. These men were renowned for their independence of action, while those "beneath" them, the *voyageurs,* ordinarily had the skill and financial acumen of the *coureurs de bois* but lacked the financial support, depending heavily therefore on the more economically resourceful superiors in the hierarchy. They were regarded as agents of the government. The *coureurs de bois* and *voyageurs* were often looked upon as lawless and untrustworthy, especially to their creditors, since it was easy for them to slip into the woods and trade with the British, thereby avoiding them and government officials in Quebec. Catholic Church leaders also castigated them for immorality, because many of them developed intimate relationships with Indian women without religious approbation.

The *coureurs de bois* at first focused on the St. Lawrence River Valley, then on the Great Lakes basin, and eventually, by the early 1700s, on the Louisiana Territory. They were the first European explorers of that vast region, which stretched from Hudson Bay in the north to New Orleans, near the Gulf of Mexico. Although they worked usually without the aid of maps, they nonetheless charted the region through their diaries or logs and verbal testimony to their contemporaries. One of the most remarkable of this variety was Pierre de la Vérendrye, who not only created a successful fur trade network between the Saskatchewan and Missouri Rivers but also explored, via the river systems, what became two Canadian provinces, Manitoba and Saskatchewan, and at least three American states, North Dakota, South Dakota, and Minnesota. His hope was to find a route to the Pacific from the Northern Plains, a plan that eluded him and his successors for more than seven decades until the historic Lewis and Clark Expedition in the early nineteenth century. He died unexpectedly in December 1749 at the age of sixty-four while preparing for yet one more major expedition to the West. The activities of the *coureurs de bois* and the *voyageurs* remain apparent today with the survival of many place names in the Northern Plains, especially Montana.

Until the Seven Years' War, known in North America as the French and Indian War, the fur trade was the principal economic activity of the Louisiana Territory, especially in the north. The neighboring Spanish appeared uninterested in it and focused primarily on their historic centers of Mexico and Peru. Their northern territories, such as California and Santa Fe, experienced a version of benign neglect based primarily on their distance. The *coureurs de bois* and their assistants did not establish any significant relationships with these domains, but maintained close ties only with the French and the British, seeking, of course, the best financial arrangements for their furs. There were some slowdowns in this activity during the Anglo-French wars, which recommenced with the War of the League of Augsburg in 1689 and continued intermittently until the conclusion of the Napoleonic conflicts more than a century later in 1815. During the war years, the fur trade suffered a noticeable decline, only to be revived significantly upon the arrangement of peace. However, the most important blow to the fur traders was William Pitt the Elder's war for empire, the French and Indian War, which successfully chased the French from continental North America by the Treaty of Paris (1763). The *coureurs de bois,* as well as the American Indians, were left in an awkward situation with no competitors for their goods. The Spanish, aloof from this activity, found their subsequent takeover of Louisiana to be financially burdensome. And several years later, a new participant in continental affairs appeared after the successful War for American Independence. These new overlords of the Atlantic seaboard and Ohio River system would preside over the demise of the fur trade while becoming the new political masters of Louisiana in 1803.

—*Thomas C. Sosnowski*

For Further Reading

Crouse, Nellis M. 1956. *La Verendrye: Fur Trader and Explorer.* Ithaca: Cornell University Press; Phillips, Paul Chrisler, and J. W. Smurr. 1967. *The Fur Trade.* Norman: University of Oklahoma Press.

CREE

The Cree are a group of indigenous North Americans whose language is part of the Algonquian branch of the larger Algonquian-Wakashan family. As Canada's largest native group, the Cree were closely associated with the European (and later American) trappers and traders who traversed the uppermost portion of the Louisiana Purchase territory along the Canadian borderlands. Because of their large numbers, the extensive territory that they inhabited, and the means by which they coexisted and assimilated with white trappers and traders, the Cree managed to preserve their cultural identity during a time of great change.

The name *Cree* is a French term of unknown origin; it may have been derived from the name Cristino or Kenisteno, which the Ojibwa used to identify their woodland neighbors. When speaking of themselves in their own language, the Cree use the name Ayisiniwok (Eythinyuwuk), a word that means "true men." They formerly inhabited the area south of Hudson Bay and James Bay in what now constitutes the provinces of Quebec, Ontario, and the region of Manitoba south of the Churchill River. Members of one branch of the Cree, allying themselves with the Siouan Assiniboine, in the mid–eighteenth century moved southwestward into buffalo territory and became the Plains Cree. They may have introduced the method of hunting buffalo by driving them into enclosures, since the Woodland Cree used a similar method to hunt deer. The culture and language of the Woodland Cree greatly resembles that of the Ojibwa.

The Cree were originally forest dwellers, and as such they found sustenance by hunting rabbit, deer, beaver, caribou, moose, and bear in the subarctic forests that they inhabited. It was rumored that during times of famine they practiced cannibalism. The Cree generally lived in woodland lodges made of bent saplings that they covered with birch bark.

Considered by others—especially the neighboring Blackfoot and Sioux—to be a warlike tribe, the Cree were generally friendly toward French and British trappers and traders, and their history is closely connected with that of the fur trade—particularly with the Hudson's Bay and the North West Companies. Many of the European traders established strong ties when they took Ojibwa or Cree wives, and the mixed-race offspring (métis) from these unions became an influential population along the frontier. The Cree were powerful allies in the late eighteenth century as they traded furs to the Europeans for weapons, traps, and other items, until they were decimated by smallpox and measles epidemics that drastically reduced their numbers. In 1885 some of the Cree were involved in the second Riel Rebellion (the Northwest Rebellion) in Saskatchewan.

Today an estimated 120,000 Cree live in the provinces of Quebec, Ontario, Manitoba, Saskatchewan, and Alberta. They have the largest population and are spread over the largest area of any indigenous group in Canada. In 1990 there were more than 8,000 Cree who lived in the United States, many of whom shared reservation lands in Montana with the Ojibwa.

—*Junius P. Rodriguez*

See also
Fur Trapping; Ojibwa
For Further Reading
Denig, Edwin T. 1975. *Five Indians Tribes of the Upper Missouri: Sioux, Arickaras, Assiniboines, Crees, Crows.* Edited by John C. Ewers. Norman: University of Oklahoma Press; Mason, Leonard. 1967. *The Swampy Cree: A Study in Acculturation.* Ottawa: Queen's Printer.

CREOLES

The term *Creole* has been defined in many ways since its inception. Spanish colonials used the word to mean "born in the New World of European, specifically Iberian, heritage." As time passed, the term came to mean anything from or anyone born in Louisiana. The term was applied to farm produce, as in Creole tomatoes, and livestock, as in Creole ponies. Today the term is often defined as any person who is of French colonial or Spanish colonial ancestry who may or may not be of two or more races. Even within the state of Louisiana, people have had difficulty defining the term. In New Orleans, the term *Creole* was once used with accompanying words: Creole of Color. However, the *of color* was gradually dropped, and the term *Creole* came to mean biracial people living in New Orleans. Such people were indeed accomplished and often owned land, held vast amounts of cash, and were well-educated. In other parts of Louisiana, whites of colonial French descent called themselves Creoles and still do so.

One of the primary differences between Louisiana and the larger American South that derived from French rule may be seen in contemporary perceptions of racial categories. From the beginning of the colonial era, the French settlers did not operate within a binary racial system with the intent of disenfranchising people of color. Although the remainder of the Southern region viewed race as a binary proposition—an individual was either white and free, or black and enslaved—because of its unique colonial legacy, Louisiana's racial system had developed quite differently. A middle racial caste, consisting of free people of color or mixed race people, often called *gens de couleur libre,* frequently grew wealthy, purchasing substantial parcels of land that they developed into lucrative plantations.

In northwestern Louisiana, for example, a colony of *gens de couleur libre* grew and gained influence in the region as a result of the manumission of Marie Thérèze Coincoin. Coincoin was originally a slave owned by the St. Denis family of Natchitoches Parish, and she was granted her freedom as a result of her faithful service and her hand in saving her mistress's life. When (Western) medical techniques had failed to cure Mme. St. Denis of a terminal illness, Coincoin reportedly begged for the opportunity to try herbal remedies and methods of folk healing. Mme. St. Denis made a full recovery, and not only was Coincoin set free but, in addition, the St. Denis family assisted her in purchasing the initial parcel of land that became the Isle Brevelle colony, where Melrose plantation now stands. Coincoin started her plantation with the help of two slaves. As Gary Mills has reported in *The Forgotten People,* Coincoin "had worked hard as a slave and she continued to do so as a free woman . . . . She was the first in the area to recognize the suitability of Natchitoches soil for the cultivation of the lucrative indigo. Only this dye, it was said, produced the desired depth of blue for the uniforms of European armies" (Mills, 1977). Through the toil and foresight of Coincoin, the colony grew and prospered.

Coincoin devoted much of her energy in the first years to gaining the freedom of her children, eventually purchasing all of her offspring who were enslaved. Several of her children were born out of her relationship with the nobleman Claud Thomas Pierre Metoyer. Before her death, she divided her (by then) extensive land holdings among these children, and Mills asserts: "[F]or almost half a century following her death, the Metoyers of Cane River enjoyed a wealth and prestige that few whites of their era could match." Mills further points out that these children, too, married and had families of their own, often intermarrying with "*gens de couleur libre* from Haiti and New Orleans . . . whose background[s] passed inspection". As a result, the population of free people of color grew exponentially during the era leading up to the U.S. purchase of the Louisiana Territory.

One of the results of the intermarriage of this financially independent population of free people of color was the solidification of the tripartite racial system. As Mills has argued, despite their mixed racial heritage, "the men of the family were accepted and accorded equality in many ways by the white planters. It was not uncommon to find prominent white men at dinner in Metoyer homes, and the hospitality was returned". Clearly, this third, middle caste resulted in a more racially sophisticated society than that found throughout the rest of the South. Eugene Genovese has demonstrated, for example, that as late as the 1850s, free people of color were voting, albeit illegally, in elections in Rapides Parish. Further, as Charles Barthelemy Rousséve has argued, "French and Spanish colonists of Louisiana were more considerate of their mixed-blood children than were settlers in other parts of America . . . . [They] accepted them as members of their families, freed them, and educated them. Eventually, the descendants of many were totally absorbed into the white Creole group" (Rousséve, 1937). Gwendolyn Midlo Hall states that this "process of acculturation took place throughout lower Louisiana during the eighteenth century" and caused the incidents of passing to become common and, to a large extent, tacitly approved (Hall, 1992). Hence, when American law began to be enforced in the Louisiana Territory, it is not surprising that the free people of color were displeased at the prospect of seeing the tripartite caste system collapse into a binary distinction whereby they became members of a group that they had traditionally considered beneath them, the African American slaves.

—Suzanne Disheroon-Green and Lisa Abney

For Further Reading

Domínguez, Virginia. 1986. *White by Definition: Social Classification in Creole Louisiana.* New Brunswick, NJ: Rutgers University Press; Genovese, Eugene D. 1976. *Roll, Jordan, Roll: The World the Slaves Made.* New York: Vintage; Hall, Gwendolyn Midlo. 1992. *Africans in Colonial Louisiana: The Development of Afro-Creole Culture in the Eighteenth Century.* Baton Rouge: Louisiana State University Press; Mills, Gary B. 1977. *The Forgotten People: Cane River's Creoles of Color.* Baton Rouge: Louisiana State University Press; Rousséve, Charles Barthelemy. 1937. *The Negro in Louisiana: Aspects of His History and His Literature.* New Orleans: Xavier University Press.

CROW

The Crow refer to themselves as the "Apsaalooke" ("children of the large-beaked bird"). Their dialect was characteristic of the Siouan linguistic stock. This cultural clue indicates that the Crow originated somewhere to the east and relocated themselves westward in the early eighteenth century. The Crow are believed to have been a branch of the Hidatsa (sometimes called the "Minataree") that moved westward from the Dakotas. It is likely that they were drawn westward by their desire to hunt buffalo and trade the region's wild horses.

In their migration toward the eastern Rockies, the Crow abandoned the traditional earth-lodge dwelling of the woodlands and adopted the tipi, a home better suited to the nomadic life of hunters. In their new home on the Northern Plains, the Crow inhabited a vast expanse of hunting grounds extending along the Yellowstone and Cheyenne Rivers and their tributaries southward toward the Bighorn Mountains and the Black Hills. This region encompasses much of present-day southeastern Montana and northeastern Wyoming.

Since the Crow were one of the smaller tribes of the Northern Plains, they often strategically allied themselves with U.S. forces whom they believed could protect them against more powerful neighboring warrior nations—such as the Sioux, Cheyenne, Blackfoot, and Comanche—who were their traditional enemies. In 1825 the tribe signed a treaty of friendship with the U.S. government. Subsequently, the Crow were one of nine tribes that participated in the conference that produced the Treaty of Fort Laramie (1851). In this effort, the U.S. army became the "honest broker" that brought peace to the Plains, albeit temporarily, by specifically outlining the land-use rights of the region's inhabitants.

The Crow tended to cooperate with American authorities, and several Crow served as scouts for the U.S. army throughout much of the nineteenth century. Some whites became fluent in Crow as fur trapper Osborne Russell observed that the Crow language was "clear, distinct and not intermingled with guttural sounds, which renders it remarkably easy for a stranger to learn" (Russell, 1965). The Crow also demonstrated a remarkable degree of cultural assimilation. For many years the mulatto fur trapper and scout James Beckwourth lived among the Crow, who regarded him as a chief.

As hunters, the Crow were largely dependent upon the large herds of bison that were found on the Northern Plains. Food, shelter, and clothing—essentially the survival of the Crow—depended upon the success of the seasonal hunt. On occasion the Crow used a creative hunting practice that they borrowed from the Blackfoot in which a herd of bison were made to stampede only to be driven over cliffs and killed by the fall. When the bison herds were depleted almost to the point of extinction by the actions of white hunters, the loss foreshadowed the cultural subjugation of the Crow.

Like other Native American groups of the Great Plains, the Crow eventually lost possession of their vast traditional hunting grounds and were reduced to living upon reservation land located southeast of Billings, Montana. The effort to transform themselves from a nomadic hunting band to that of sedentary agriculturalists wreaked havoc with the cultural identity of the Crow. Describing the changes brought by reservation life, the former Crow warrior Two Leggings recounted, "Nothing happened after that. We just lived. There were no more war parties, no capturing of horses from the Piegans and the Sioux, no buffalo to hunt. There is nothing more to tell" (Nabokov, 1967).

—Junius P. Rodriguez

See also

Beckwourth, James; Hidatsa; Montana

For Further Reading

Andrist, Ralph K. 1964. *The Long Death: The Last Days of the Plains Indians.* New York: Macmillan; Nabokov, Peter. 1967. *Two Leggings: The Making of a Crow Warrior.* New York: Thomas Y. Crowell Co.; Russell, Osborne. 1965. *Journal of a Trapper.* Lincoln: University of Nebraska Press.

DEARBORN, HENRY (1751–1829)

Secretary of war throughout the Jefferson administration (1801–1809), Henry Dearborn oversaw American military activity related to the Louisiana Territory during the years immediately preceding its purchase through the end of his tenure in 1809. This included the occupation of key military posts, orchestrating early attempts at incorporating Indians into the republic, and eventually planning their removal beyond the Mississippi. Dearborn was a former physician and Continental Army officer who had served with distinction in the American Revolution (1775–1783). An intimate of General James Wilkinson, Dearborn was an important actor in Wilkinson's 1808 court martial in the wake of the Burr conspiracy.

Following the October 1802 Spanish denial of the American right of deposit at New Orleans by the acting intendant of Louisiana, Juan Ventura Morales, Dearborn ordered the reinforcement of Fort Adams (Mississippi Territory), thirty-eight miles south of Natchez, Mississippi, and alerted the militias of Tennessee and Kentucky in preparation for a possible forceful seizure of New Orleans by General Wilkinson. The American purchase of Louisiana, however, made an invasion unnecessary. Dearborn's friend Wilkinson, through the intervention of Vice President Aaron Burr, assumed the post of territorial governor in 1805. Although the details are unknown, it seems that Burr and Wilkinson, a corrupt officer and Spanish spy for many years, were co-conspirators in a scheme aiming at the separation of the Louisiana Territory from the United States so that they might establish an independent republic.

Following the end of Burr's term of office in 1805, the former vice president boarded a boat in Pittsburgh and sailed to Lexington, Kentucky, where he began recruiting followers in the summer of 1806. While Burr was in Kentucky, Wilkinson wrote to Jefferson, informing him of Burr's plot. Burr learned of this and Jefferson's order for his arrest in 1807, as he and his band approached Natchez en route to New Orleans. Burr fled for Pensacola, Florida, but was seized and brought to trial in Richmond, Virginia. Wilkinson's connection with Burr led to Virginia representative John Randolph's resolution for a congressional investigation of the general. Although the resolution was tabled, Wilkinson called for a court-martial to clear his name. In January 1808, Secretary of War Dearborn picked the members of the court, which met from January through June 1808. Wilkinson escaped censure and continued his military service through 1815.

Dearborn's role as secretary of war included executing Jefferson's Indian policies and overseeing the daily management of the federal government's nascent Indian relations bureaucracy. Before purchasing the Louisiana Territory, Jefferson and Dearborn envisioned incorporating the Indians into American society through education, trade, and other means that would supplant Indian cultural norms with those of the United States, particularly in private land ownership and intensive agriculture. Dearborn envisioned building a road from Nashville to Natchez with public establishments placed every twenty or thirty miles, jointly run by whites and Indians in partnership. He believed that this close contact would help effect Jefferson's dream. However, by 1803 this policy, for a variety of reasons, proved unrealistic; the Louisiana Territory, therefore, made Indian removal west of the Mississippi River a feasible option. Dearborn, with Jefferson's approval, encouraged the efforts of government negotiators to convince Indians living east of the Mississippi River who had not adopted American norms to exchange their lands for those west of the river. Jefferson's Indian initiatives were among the more significant antecedents for Andrew Jackson's Indian Removal. Dearborn was an able and conscientious administrator whose efforts clearly contributed to the successful implementation of Jefferson's plans for the new territory. His friendship with James Wilkinson, however, clouded his objectivity during the Burr conspiracy.

—Ricardo A. Herrera

See also

Burr, Aaron; Indian Removal; Jefferson, Thomas; Natchez Trace; Randolph, John; Right of Deposit; Wilkinson, James

For Further Reading

De Conde, Alexander. 1976. *This Affair of Louisiana*. New York: Charles Scribner's Sons; Erney, Richard A. 1979. *The Public Life of Henry Dearborn*. New York: Arno Press; Prucha, Francis Paul. 1969. *The Sword of the Republic: The United States Army on the Frontier, 1783–1846*. New York: Macmillan; Sheehan, Bernard W. 1973. *Seeds of Extinction: Jeffersonian Philanthropy and the American Indian*. Chapel Hill: University of North Carolina Press.

DE DECRÉS, DENIS DUC (1761–1820)

Denis Duc de Decrés entered the French navy in 1779 and rapidly distinguished himself. As a member of the nobility, he was arrested at the time of the French Revolution. Eventually he was reinstated, however, and in October 1801 he was appointed minister of the navy and colonies, a position he held until the fall of the empire.

As minister, Decrés was one of the most active supporters of Napoleon's North American policy. In responding to Napoleon's desire in 1802 for France to take possession of Louisiana as quickly as possible, he asked Charles Maurice de Talleyrand to secure from the Spaniards detailed information concerning the administration of the colony. In order to expedite the return of the governance of Louisiana to France, Decrés was willing to retain Spanish troops in the region until French forces could completely occupy the colony. Numerous delays, however, prevented the actual dispatchment of French troops to Louisiana. Chief among these was the delay of Spain in issuing the royal order that authorized France to take possession of the colony. In addition, the Spaniards withheld information concerning the military situation in Louisiana. Upon the arrival of royal orders from Spain authorizing the transfer of Louisiana to France, Decrés ordered an expedition to set sail at once. In Decrés's instructions (approved by the first consul) to General Claude Perrin Victor (1764–1841), the commander of the expedition and the military governor designated for Louisiana, all existing navigation agreements were to be honored, a friendly attitude toward the United States maintained, the residents of the western portions of the United States monitored, and the colony defended. The goal was to strengthen Louisiana to such a degree that it could be abandoned in the event of war. The abandoned colony was to be strong enough to inflict serious damage against any enemy.

The Louisiana Expedition, however, was delayed initially because of weather, and when the weather improved, British ships were blockading the coast of Holland, where the expedition was to have set sail. Therefore, during March 1803, with more delays awaiting the Louisiana Expedition, Napoleon began to consider using the troops amassed in Holland against the British Isles. Finally, as the troops seemed destined to sail for Louisiana at long last, word was received that Louisiana had been sold to the United States. Napoleon had allowed the expedition preparations to develop up to the point of his sudden announcement of the sale of Louisiana. However, Decrés, a strong believer in the colonial system and an ardent supporter of Napoleon, disagreed with Napoleon concerning the sale of Louisiana. Napoleon chose not to inform Decrés of the potential sale of Louisiana. He was not told to stop the Louisiana Expedition until word was received that the treaty authorizing the sale of Louisiana had been signed.

—Alfred Lemmon

See also

Bonaparte, Napoleon; Talleyrand-Perigord, Charles Maurice de; Victor, Claude Perrin

For Further Reading

Bush, Robert D. 1977. "Documents on the Louisiana Purchase: The Laussat Papers." *Louisiana History* 18, no. 1: 104–107; DeConde, Alexander. 1976. *This Affair of Louisiana*. New York: Charles Scribner's Sons; Lyon, E. Wilson. 1974. *Louisiana in French Diplomacy, 1759–1804*. Norman: University of Oklahoma Press; Robertson, James Alexander. 1911. *Louisiana under the Rule of Spain, France, and the United States, 1785–1807*. Cleveland: Arthur H. Clark Company; Smith, Ronald D. 1971. "Napoleon and Louisiana: Failure of the Proposed Expedition to Occupy and Defend Louisiana, 1801–1803." *Louisiana History* 12, no. 1: 21–40.

DESERET, STATE OF (1848–1896)

In July 1847, the first wagon train of Mormon pioneers reached the Salt Lake Valley. By the end of the year, the Mormon leader, Brigham Young, had sent "apostolic letters" to Mormons throughout the world, urging them to move to "Latter-Day Israel," which would be called Deseret. The name, taken from *The Book of Mormon,* meant "honeybee," signifying industriousness and communal effort.

The initial boundaries of the state of Deseret included most of present-day Utah, Nevada, and Arizona. Large areas of Wyoming, Idaho, Colorado, New Mexico, and Oregon, plus coastal lands in California from Los Angeles to the Mexican border, were claimed by Mormons who began to colonize the region. This vast territory was diminished by Congress when it created the Territory of Utah (named by a congressional committee after the Ute Indians) as part of the Compromise of 1850: the forty-second parallel formed the northern boundary, the thirty-seventh parallel the southern perimeter. Large areas of eastern and western Utah were lost to the Nevada, Colorado, and Nebraska Territories, which were established in 1861. By 1868, the Territory of Utah was reduced to its present size.

A provisional government was established by Brigham Young in 1848; he parceled out land, started public works projects, and levied a tax for public services and improvements. A year later a constitution was adopted, and voters chose Brigham Young as governor in March 1849. However, the state had been created without consulting or being authorized by the U.S. Congress. That same year, the petition seeking statehood was denied; between 1849 and 1887, the Mormons requested statehood six times and were denied admittance each time.

Several issues stood in the way of obtaining statehood. Mormons were accused of practicing polygamy and favoring a theocratic form of government, a "theodemocracy," as Mormon founder Joseph Smith had insisted. Finally, the question of slavery in the Western regions complicated matters for Congress. But in 1850, a geographically reduced state of Deseret was accepted as the Territory of Utah, and President Millard Fillmore named Brigham Young as governor and superintendent of Indian affairs. Young now headed both the civil and church governments, and "ruled Utah absolutely" (May, 1987). Federal officials in Utah found it difficult to deal with the Mormon church, which controlled all aspects of its followers' lives.

As leader of the church and governor, Brigham Young was assisted by a three-member First Presidency, the Quorum of Twelve Apostles, and the secretive Council of Fifty. In Utah and its colonies, the line between church and state was never clearly drawn. The state of Deseret was conceived as a model for an ideal society in which the new Kingdom of God (Zion) would flourish and expand. The Mormons were to become self-sufficient in all things political, social, and economic and to avoid contact with "gentiles" (non-Mormons). That was not possible, however, and conflict with the federal government ensued. In 1857, President James Buchanan sent federal troops to Utah to enforce national laws, and he appointed Alfred Cumming as governor; Brigham Young responded by creating the Nauvoo Legion to repel the "invasion." Unsympathetic to the peculiar ways of the Mormons, federal officials in Utah now had the backing of troops stationed at Fort Douglas, overlooking the Salt Lake Valley.

Contact with gentiles was discouraged, but the local Indian tribes were in a different category. Shoshonian tribes, the Northern Shoshoni, the Gosiutes, the Utes, and the Southern Paiutes, were already inhabiting Deseret when the Mormons arrived. The *Book of Mormon* spoke of people of Hebrew descent (the "Lamanites") whom the Mormons identified as American Indians. The Lamanites were ripe for conversion, and the Mormons set up "missions" among the various tribes. Mormon regard for the spiritual welfare of the Indians did not prevent frequent clashes over land and water rights, however, since the Mormon economy was largely based on agriculture. Moreover, thousands of newly arrived Mormon settlers increased pressure to expand into new regions of the West.

During the American Civil War, Mormons expected the national government to collapse, an event that would usher in the Kingdom of God that would eventually rule the world. In 1862 the Mormons drafted a new constitution for the state of Deseret and petitioned Congress for statehood, which was denied. At the end of the war, the issue of slavery was settled, and in 1890, Mormon president Wilford Woodruff was "inspired" to end polygamy and issued the Manifesto to that effect. The last major obstacle to statehood was thus removed, and six years later Utah was admitted to the Union.

—Jeanne A. Ojala

See also

Mormon Road

For Further Reading

Arrington, Leonard J., and Davis Bitton. 1979. *The Mormon Experience: A History of the Latter-Day Saints.* New York: Alfred A. Knopf; Campbell, Eugene E. 1988. *Establishing Zion: The Mormon Church in the American West, 1847–1869.* Salt Lake City: Signature Books; Lyman, Edward Leo. 1986. *Political Deliverance: The Mormon Quest for Utah Statehood.* Urbana: University of Illinois Press; May, Dean L. 1987. *Utah: A People's History.* Salt Lake City: University of Utah Press; Morgan, Dale L. 1987. *The State of Deseret.* Logan: Utah State University Press.

DIPLOMACY OF THE LOUISIANA PURCHASE

Diplomatic maneuvering involving the United States, Spain, Great Britain, and France resulted in the American purchase of the Louisiana Territory from France in 1803. The principal players were President Thomas Jefferson, minister to France Robert Livingston, statesman James Monroe, French minister for foreign affairs Charles Maurice de Talleyrand-Périgord, French treasurer François de Barbé-Marbois, and Napoleon Bonaparte. In the resulting treaty, France agreed to sell all of Louisiana to the United States for approximately $15 million.

Thomas Jefferson said that "there is on the globe one single spot, the possessor of which is our natural and habitual enemy. It is New Orleans" (McDonald, 1976). Originally settled by the French in the early eighteenth century, the huge province of Louisiana, including the port of New Orleans near the mouth of the Mississippi River, had been ceded to Spain by secret treaty in 1762 near the end of the French and Indian War. In 1795 the United States and Spain concluded the Treaty of San Lorenzo, or Pinckney's Treaty, which gave America the right to ship goods originating in American ports through the mouth of the Mississippi without paying duty, and also the right of deposit of American goods at New Orleans for transshipment. These concessions were vital to the survival of the United States as an economic entity west of the Appalachians. Since the founding of the nation, and especially after the signing of Jay's Treaty (1794), thousands of American settlers had crossed to the western side of the Appalachians and spread throughout the Ohio River valley to the Mississippi River. The economic survival of the settlements they founded depended upon the free use of the Mississippi River and the right of deposit at the port of New Orleans. As long as Spain, no longer a world power, held Louisiana, the United States felt secure in its continued use of the Mississippi and New Orleans.

However, Napoleon's accession to power in France altered the situation. Frustrated in his attempts to defeat

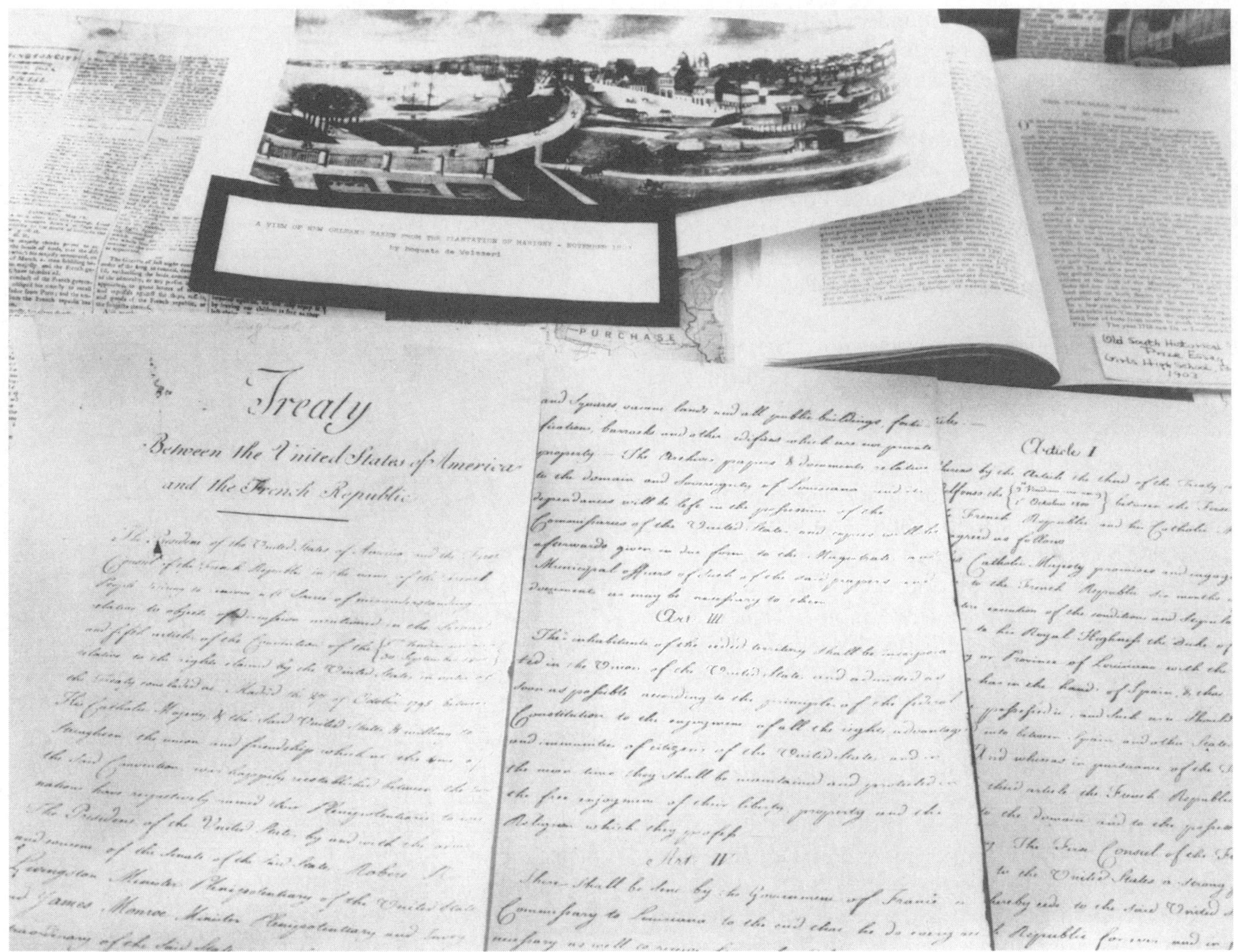

Although the United States and France both considered the Louisiana Purchase Treaty to be a legally binding document, other European powers were more skeptical about the transfer.

Great Britain decisively in Europe and the Mediterranean, especially the failed expedition to Egypt in 1798, Napoleon decided to shatter the British empire in North America. He undertook to establish a French empire centered on the sugar-producing islands in the Caribbean. Haiti, the western half of the sugar island of St. Domingue, which France had acquired from Spain in 1795, was to be the centerpiece. Louisiana was to be the breadbasket for these islands. Napoleon entered negotiations with Spain, offering a Bourbon kingdom in Tuscany in exchange for possession of Louisiana. In October 1800, under immense pressure from Napoleon, Spain ceded the Louisiana Territory back to France in the Treaty of San Ildefonso. Several years would pass, however, before the actual transfer took place.

Just prior to the retrocession of Louisiana, St. Domingue witnessed a violent slave revolt led by Toussaint L'Ouverture, who established a military dictatorship while nominally acknowledging allegiance to France. If Napoleon was to establish a new empire in North America, he must overthrow Toussaint, re-establish French rule in St. Domingue, and restore slavery on the island. However, he could not safely send an army to accomplish these tasks until peace had been made with Great Britain. When peace terms preliminary to the Peace of Amiens (1802) were made in October 1801, Napoleon sent an army of twenty thousand men under his brother-in-law, General Charles-Victor Leclerc, to St. Domingue. Once the island was restored to French control, another expedition was to take possession of Louisiana.

News of the Treaty of San Ildefonso and the French expedition to St. Domingue caused much concern in the United States. Clearly this was the beginning of French imperial aggression in the Western Hemisphere that threatened America's commercial interests. The United States had only recently concluded an unofficial naval war with France during the administration of John Adams; now it seemed that another war was likely. In 1802 two events brought the matter to a climax. In October, Juan Morales, the Spanish Intendant at New

Orleans, closed the port to foreign shipping and withdrew the American right of deposit. This was an outright violation of the Treaty of San Lorenzo (1795). America assumed that France was responsible, and much uproar ensued. Then France landed its army in St. Domingue to put down the slave rebellion. Word reached Jefferson that another French expedition was to occupy Louisiana once French rule was restored.

Jefferson believed that "[t]he day that France takes possession of N. Orleans . . . seals the union of two nations who in conjunction can maintain exclusive possession of the ocean. From that moment we must marry ourselves to the British fleet and nation" (ibid.). He understood, however, that it would be detrimental to the diplomatic position of the United States to become dependent upon Great Britain. Some way must be found to secure New Orleans and the Mississippi River for American commerce. France must not be allowed to shut the United States out of New Orleans, but Jefferson was not willing to ally America with the British to do so. In this atmosphere Jefferson sent special commissioner James Monroe to Paris to aid the U.S. minister to France, Robert R. Livingston, in an attempt to resolve the situation. The president instructed Monroe to negotiate with Talleyrand the purchase of New Orleans, the right to build an American port on the eastern bank of the Mississippi, or, at the very least, the perpetual rights of navigation and deposit. He was authorized to offer as much as $10 million. If he could not secure any such agreement, he was to submit the matter to Washington and await the decision of Congress. If France undertook hostilities against the United States or closed the Mississippi entirely to American commerce, Livingston and Madison were to proceed to London to seek out an alliance with the British: hence the marriage to the "British fleet and nation" that Jefferson so loathed was a last resort.

Meanwhile, the peace that France had secured with Great Britain at Amiens in 1802 was about to break. The French expedition to St. Domingue had failed despite initial victories and the capture of Toussaint: yellow fever ravaged the French army and even claimed Leclerc. St. Domingue was lost, and without it Louisiana was useless. Napoleon moreover realized that possession of Louisiana was a liability in the face of renewed war with Great Britain. The British navy was superior to that of the French, and it would quickly capture the distant province in the event of war. If he could sell Louisiana to the Americans for cash, he could thereby fund his military operations more fully, deny the British a potential prize in the Western Hemisphere, and help make the United States a maritime rival to Great Britain. If the British wanted Louisiana, they would have to fight the United States for it. He therefore sent Barbé-Marbois, the French treasurer, to assist Talleyrand in the ongoing negotiations with Livingston (Monroe's arrival was imminent), and he instructed him to sell New Orleans and everything attached to it to the Americans for as much as they could get.

Livingston was shocked at the sudden proposal and deferred an answer until Monroe's arrival. They had been commissioned only to purchase New Orleans and perhaps a bit of the Floridas; now they were offered all of Louisiana, including New Orleans. Negotiations commenced upon Monroe's arrival on April 12, 1803, and continued until the signing of the treaty on May 2. After much haggling, the negotiators finally agreed on a sum of $15 million, of which three-fourths was to be paid to France and the remainder to Americans holding damage claims against the French government. The final transfer of Louisiana came on December 20, 1803. France had been in actual possession of Louisiana for twenty days. The United States had taken advantage of Europe's problems to more than double its size in one moment. The Louisiana Purchase was the most amazing land deal in history.

There were two serious questions about the acquisition of Louisiana. First was the uncertainty of the exact composition of the territory. How far east did the territory extend? How far west? The exact boundaries were not known with certainty. The Louisiana treaty used the same vague language as the Treaty of San Ildefonso. However, the United States would later use Europe's preoccupation with the Napoleonic Wars to secure the most generous interpretation of Louisiana's boundaries. Second, Jefferson seriously doubted the constitutionality of the purchase. A strict constructionist, he believed that the U.S. Constitution did not authorize the president or the Senate to make such a purchase. Upon a careful study of the Louisiana treaty, Jefferson proposed a constitutional amendment validating the purchase. However he abandoned the idea when warned from Paris that any unnecessary delay might risk the loss of Louisiana. Despite the constitutional questions, the Senate ratified the treaty and passed a bill empowering the president to take possession of Louisiana and govern it until Congress established a territorial government. Both Jefferson and the Congress realized that an opportunity of such magnitude could not be squandered, regardless of legal or constitutional questions. Jefferson said that "the good sense of our country will correct the evil of construction when it shall produce ill effects" (ibid.).

—Scott D. Wignall

See also

Amiens, Peace of; Barbé-Marbois, François, Marquis de; Bonaparte, Napoleon; French and Indian War; Jay's Treaty; Jefferson, Thomas; Leclerc, Charles-Victor-Emmanuel; Livingston, Robert R.; L'Ouverture, Toussaint; Monroe, James; Right of Deposit; San Ildefonso, Treaty of; San Lorenzo, Treaty of; Talleyrand-Perigord, Charles Maurice de.

For Further Reading

Bemis, Samuel Flagg. 1959. *A Short History of American Foreign Policy and Diplomacy.* New York: Holt, Rinehart, and Winston; Ferrell, Robert H. 1969. *American Diplo-*

macy: A History. New York: W. W. Norton; McDonald, Forrest. 1976. *The Presidency of Thomas Jefferson.* Lawrence: University Press of Kansas; Pratt, Julius W. 1965. *A History of United States Foreign Policy.* Englewood Cliffs, NJ: Prentice-Hall.

DRY FARMING

When pioneer settlers began to inhabit the eastern portion of the Louisiana Purchase territory after the United States acquired the region from France in 1803, they carried with them the farming techniques that had worked successfully on earlier homesteads in the East. These pioneer farmers initially found themselves in a rich land where the well-watered prairie loam was an agriculturalist's dream, but as the farming frontier moved westward and settlers encountered marginally arable land, they were forced to develop new strategies and techniques. By the late nineteenth century, vast stretches of the original Louisiana Territory, especially the High Plains region beyond the one hundredth meridian, used the concept of dry farming to cultivate lands that might otherwise have been considered barren.

When Stephen H. Long crossed the Great Plains in 1820, he described the region as the "Great American Desert," and for nearly forty years that name, and the negative connotations it evoked, characterized the way that many viewed a vast region of the North American interior. For many the lure of gold, or at least adventure, in the far West was much more attractive than the burden that would be required to make the desert bloom; as a result, the region of the High Plains became an area to be crossed but not settled.

Several factors contributed to the transformation of the agricultural West and the eventual development of dry farming techniques. Research that came out of the agricultural and mechanical (A&M) schools that developed through the Morrill Land Grant Act (1862) became a boon to U.S. farmers in the West. The land-grant colleges and universities perfected technologies with mechanical engineering, such as the drilling of deep water wells, and used laboratory research in botany, chemistry, and later genetics to develop seed varieties for crops that were drought resistant. Additionally, new seed varieties, introduced by immigrant farmers from Northern Europe, produced good yields on the Northern Plains, and eventually hybrid forms took shape that had a high tolerance for the arid conditions found in parts of the West.

Dry farming is essentially a type of sustainable agriculture that attempts to draw the greatest benefit from scarce water resources. Methods of dry farming are most commonly practiced in those areas that receive between ten and twenty inches of rainfall per year. Among the Hopi, a primitive method of dry farming was used when farmers planted their crops in dry stream beds. Such areas were the most likely places where water would pool when infrequent rains fell. Other strategies of dry farming that developed through the years involve the keeping of crop stubble in the fields through the winter season so that drifting snow might be better held to produce meltwater with the spring thaw.

More sophisticated systems of dry farming employ the summer fallow method, whereby lands remain tilled and removed of weeds during the season when rainfall is most likely. Such systems incorporate fast-growing crops that can be cultivated in late summer and the fall before the onset of winter snows. For this reason, cultivation of winter wheat replaced spring wheat cultivation in many regions of the High Plains that faced chronic water shortages and were forced to depend upon dry farming methods. Other elements of dry farming involve careful crop selection, the effective management of runoff, and strategies to reduce water loss through transpiration by widespread use of mulch or no-till practices.

Dry farming methods, along with conservation efforts and water management systems, have helped to turn portions of the U.S. West once considered desert into productive farmland. Today the diet of millions in the United States and around the world consists of foodstuffs that originated on the North American High Plains, owing their very existence to the dry farming methods that were used for their cultivation.

—*Junius P. Rodriguez*

See also
Flora of the Louisiana Purchase

For Further Reading

Engelbert, Ernest A., ed. 1984. *Water Scarcity Impacts on Western Agriculture.* Berkeley: University of California Press; Hargreaves, Mary W. M. 1993. *Dry Farming in the Northern Great Plains: Years of Readjustment, 1920–1990.* Topeka: University Press of Kansas.

DU PONT DE NEMOURS, PIERRE SAMUEL (1739–1817)

Pierre Samuel Du Pont de Nemours was born in Paris to a prosperous and ambitious family. He trained for various occupations, including medicine and watch-making, but from the early 1770s he developed a career as an economic adviser.

In 1775, Du Pont began assisting Louis XVI's controller general, Anne-Robert-Jacques Turgot, in an official capacity. Du Pont is mainly remembered as a major developer of "physiocracy," as an early historian of economics, and as the editor and preserver of the works of Turgot and the physician-economist François Quesnay.

Webster defines "physiocrat" as a proponent of Quesnay's political and economic doctrines based on the supremacy of "natural order" as the only proper influence on the relations of society to industry.

Samuel Du Pont was a politically active advocate for reform before and during the French Revolution. Even though he was arrested in 1794, a timely end to the Reign of Terror allowed him to escape execution. Du Pont was subsequently elected to a position in the legislative assembly of the new government, but another shift in power and a second arrest prompted him to remove his family to the United States in 1799. He returned to Paris in 1802 and served later in the Paris Chamber of Commerce from 1803 to 1810.

Du Pont's final migration to the United States, in 1815, was to Wilmington, Delaware, where his son Irénée had started the gunpowder factory from which the mammoth Du Pont chemical conglomerate developed. He died there in 1817.

During his five-year stay as the American minister to France in the 1780s, Thomas Jefferson had befriended another of Samuel's sons, the diplomat Victor Du Pont. Later Jefferson's endorsement of Irénée's scheme to enter the U.S. gunpowder business won Samuel's reluctant agreement to the investment. Additionally, large government orders facilitated the mill's showing a substantial profit the first year in operation.

It seems only natural that—given this warm and trusting association and after years of correspondence—Jefferson, upon learning of his friend's planned return to France, would seek the elder Du Pont's assistance in his negotiations with Napoleon for the acquisition of Louisiana. Further, considering Du Pont's ambition, his connections within the French government, and his fondness for the United States, it is not surprising that he would offer Jefferson his assistance while on this trip back to Paris. Their letters crossed in the mail.

An urgency concerning Louisiana arose when news reached the United States that, by secret treaty in 1800, Napoleon had forced Spain to retrocede that vast territory to France. Jefferson was gravely concerned that if Louisiana, along with New Orleans (with its position at the convergence of the Mississippi River and the Gulf), fell under the control of a strong and aggressive country like France, war might result for the United States. The president's hopes lay in the fact that France had yet to take possession of either New Orleans or the rest of Louisiana. The U.S. government was not aware that, because of the decimation by yellow fever of a French expeditionary force to its American colonies as well as a deteriorating peace with England, Napoleon's plans to revive an empire in the Americas had begun to fade.

Even so, for an agonizingly long period during French and U.S. negotiations in 1802, Napoleon refused to commit himself on his future plans regarding Louisiana. Robert Livingston, the U.S. minister to France, endured months of frustration because of his inability to reach consensus with Charles Maurice de Talleyrand and other officials of the French consulate.

It was at this juncture, on April 25, 1802, that Jefferson sent Du Pont a package for delivery to Robert Livingston. Jefferson wrote to Du Pont: "I wish you to be possessed of the subject, because you may be able to impress upon the government of France the inevitable consequences of their taking possession of Louisiana." To this purpose, Jefferson left one of the missives to Livingston unsealed, so that Du Pont might be enlightened as to the progress of the negotiations. In his April 24 letter to Jefferson, Du Pont remarked that he had heard of a suggestion that the United States purchase Louisiana. If there were any truth in that rumor, he thought, the idea was "salutary and acceptable." He also pointed out that he knew personally the French officials, understood "the customs of that nation, and had resolved to entrust to America his children, his fortune, and his hopes for repose in his old age."

By October 1802 the situation was becoming critical, but Du Pont's optimism was unflagging. On October 4 he wrote to Thomas Jefferson expressing his belief that things were not nearly as bad as Livingston believed. It was obvious that Du Pont's optimism and foreknowledge were inspired by sources within the French government. This perception allowed Jefferson to remain relatively calm upon hearing the news that on October 16, Spanish officials, still in control of the territory, announced the revocation of the U.S. "right of deposit" at New Orleans. This right of deposit allowed U.S. producers and brokers to deposit their exports in New Orleans until the appropriate sale or passage was available.

It seems, in retrospect, that Samuel Du Pont was particularly useful in transferring ideas and suggestions, in an unofficial way, from the French to the Americans and back. In this way, after several more months of ministerial meetings and bargaining, Napoleon, for practical reasons, determined to sell the United States the whole of Louisiana. By treaty dated April 30, 1803, the United States paid some $15 million for Louisiana.

—Richard H. Dickerson

See also

Bonaparte, Napoleon; Diplomacy of the Louisiana Purchase; Jefferson, Thomas; Livingston, Robert R.; Monroe, James; Talleyrand-Perigord, Charles Maurice de.

For Further Reading

De Conde, Alexander. 1976. *This Affair of Louisiana.* New York: Charles Scribner's Sons; Lyon, E. Wilson. 1974. *Louisiana in French Diplomacy, 1759–1804.* Norman: University of Oklahoma Press; Saricks, Ambrose. 1965. *Pierre Samuel Du Pont de Nemours.* Lawrence: University of Kansas Press; Williams, Kenneth H. 1999. "Du Pont, Elèuthere Irénée." In *American National Biography.* Edited by John A. Garraty and Mark C. Carnes. New York: Oxford University Press.

DUANE, WILLIAM (1760–1835)

In 1789, William Duane began working as an assistant editor at a Philadelphia newspaper called the *Aurora*. In that same year the editor, Benjamin Franklin Bache, died. Before his death, Bache named Duane his successor, and Duane assumed control of the publication—a position he held until his retirement in 1822. Following the pattern established by Duane in previous journalistic enterprises in Ireland and India, the *Aurora* became more politicized and abrasive. Through the editor's constant and acrid criticism of Federalists, the newspaper became the leading Jeffersonian organ in the nation's capital. This influential position enabled Duane to become a confidant and friend of Thomas Jefferson, but it also made him a favorite target of political opponents. Recipients of Duane's caustic critiques sued him for libel on numerous occasions, and the editor was arrested under the Alien Act of 1798 but later acquitted. In 1799 he was arrested again, in violation of the Sedition Act, but upon Jefferson's ascendancy to the presidency, charges were dropped. With the transfer of the capital to Washington, D.C., the *Aurora* declined in national importance, but it still played a crucial role in local politics and continuously espoused a Jeffersonian position on matters related to expansion and the role of Western lands.

Both issues were essential to Duane's desire for the United States to become self-sufficient. The failure of the Embargo Act (1807) made Duane, and many others, realize the nation's economic dependence on foreign powers. Duane expressed this view in the debate that surrounded the rechartering of the Bank of the United States in 1816. Believing that the bank represented the interests of a moneyed and speculative elite, the editor espoused a redirection in American economic policy. Blaming the commercial interests for the flood of British goods and the nation's increasing indebtedness abroad, Duane argued for the development of an internal national market under the guidance of the national government. A reorganized national bank, internal improvements, and high tariffs were the centerpieces of his program.

According to Duane, in order to counteract the abusive and monopolistic policies of the Bank of the United States, a new banking institution would use Western lands as a form of capital. Based upon the land bank policies of many colonies in the eighteenth century, the plan required the government to back the bank's capital by granting farmers long-term mortgages at low interest. Duane believed that this was a much more democratic form of public credit. Although rejected by most political economists of the period, the plan demonstrated Duane's commitment to the belief that the future wealth of the U.S. lay in the West. Crucial to the increased capitalization of the bank was an expansion in the amount of—and a rise in the price of—land, two changes spurred by internal improvements.

A national system of transportation was an issue that Duane repeatedly advocated in the *Aurora*. Roads and canals were instrumental in connecting the frontier to the urban market. Duane, along with his Jeffersonian cronies, espoused the yeoman ideal, which dictated that the physical expansion of agriculture was the only method that ensured both an increase in economic wealth and the maintenance of a virtuous society. Because of the crucial role that improvements played, he believed that the national government should have complete control over the construction of the system. In order to complete this fully integrated domestic market, Duane supported high tariffs to protect manufacturing. In the view of most Jeffersonians, this industry was small-scale in nature, conceived as artisans providing only necessities not luxuries.

Duane further demonstrated his expansionist vision in his criticism of negotiations with Spain for Florida that preceded the Adams-Onís Treaty (1819) and of the Missouri Compromise (1820). Duane recommended a hard line toward the Spanish. Jubilantly supporting the revolutions occurring across South America at the time, he believed that the government should not negotiate with Spain but wait until South American revolutionaries had liberated Florida and offered it to the United States. For that reason, Duane enthusiastically supported General Andrew Jackson's expedition into Florida in 1818 to pacify the Seminole Indians, which eventually led to the defeat of a Spanish fort at Pensacola. Duane supported this aggression because it demonstrated the weakness of Spain and it undermined a passive policy that he believed was destined to fail. The Missouri Compromise (1820) also angered Duane because of his opposition to the expansion of slavery. The *Aurora* charged that rather than reaching an equitable agreement over the admission of the states, the government had bowed to the power and influence of the slave interests.

—*Peter S. Genovese, Jr.*

See also

Federalist Party; Missouri Compromise; Tertium Quids

For Further Reading

Philips, Kimberly T. 1968. "William Duane, Revolutionary Editor." Ph.D. diss., University of California, Berkeley; Shankman, Andrew. 1999. "Malcontents and Tertium Quids: The Battle to Define Democracy in Jeffersonian Philadelphia." *Journal of the Early Republic* 19: 43–72.

DUNBAR-HUNTER EXPEDITION (1804–1805)

The Dunbar-Hunter Expedition, in the fall and winter of 1804–1805 up the Ouachita River to the Hot Springs of Arkansas, provided one of the first scientific perspectives of the recently purchased Louisiana Territory. William Dunbar, a native of Scotland, was an immigrant living in Natchez, Mississippi—a Southern planter considered to be the best naturalist of the lower Mississippi Valley. In 1804, President Thomas Jefferson approached Dunbar with the idea of ascending the Red River to acquire precise knowledge about the southern border of Louisiana. Dunbar eventually would be the mastermind behind the Freeman Expedition up the Red River in 1806. But in 1804 the Red River Expedition was put on hold because of the anticipated objections of Spain. Dunbar—and Jefferson—had to be content with exploring the less significant, yet fascinating, Ouachita River.

Dunbar recruited Dr. George Hunter as the other scientist of the journey; Jefferson arranged for thirteen soldiers to escort the two scientists into the potentially hostile territory. They set forth from Natchez on October 16, 1804, in a large keel boat. The soldiers, manning twelve oars, ascended the Mississippi to the mouth of the Red River, which they followed to the mouth of the Black River, up which they rowed to the mouth of the Ouachita River. Along the way Dunbar kept a thorough scientific journal that included detailed descriptions of the surrounding landscape, the sporadic settlements, the variety of vegetation, the varying depths of the rivers, the speed of the current, the temperature of the air and water at dawn and dusk, and the distances between important locations. Each noon, if the weather permitted, Dunbar took the angle of the sun to ascertain the precise latitude; he also attempted to estimate longitude. He hoped to provide enough data for the production of accurate maps of the Ouachita valley.

A good part of the voyage was trial and error, hypothesis and experimentation. Dunbar and Hunter relied on their wits and observations. The soldiers were of little help, beyond providing muscles for transport. The scientists relied on local hunters to pilot the expedition day to day, upstream, against a variable current. It took them about four weeks to ascend the Ouachita to the Post of Washita in northern Louisiana. There they hired a flat-bottomed barge and a knowledgeable pilot to guide them the rest of the way to Hot Springs. The river narrowed as they ascended into Arkansas. Frequently they spent hours negotiating rapids and waterfalls. Sheer will and determination led them into the hilly elevations of the Hot Springs.

The unnamed pilot, whom Dunbar haughtily pronounced to be tolerably intelligent, taught the scientist about the mannerisms of the local squatters, their hunting techniques, the habits of the deer, and the ferocity of the black bear, which devours its prey alive. They passed a clearing in the forest where one French hunter suspended his skins over poles—the frontier inhabitants considered such contrivances to be sacred and untouchable. Local hunters passed along anecdotes about the Arkansas River Valley, its supposed silver mines, salt plains, and fertile lands, as well as ferocious Indian tribes: the Osage in particular were much feared. The locals assured Dunbar and Hunter that the Osage rarely left the Arkansas to tread over the watershed of hills leading to the Ouachita Valley. Perhaps the Crystal or Shining Mountain, reputedly made of glass, terrified the natives. Beyond to the west were massive prairies filled with countless buffalo, deer, beer, and elk. These endless prairies, according to one French hunter, "enclosed . . . the great chain of [Rocky] Mountains which separate the waters flowing into the Mississippi from those which discharge themselves into the Western pacific" (Rowland, 1930). The prodigious plain of prairie land was supposed to be 200 leagues in breadth due west.

The men stayed at Hot Springs for more than a month, during which time they passed Christmas and the New Year (1806) and saw some very cold weather. Dunbar made various experiments on the springs, recording their temperature, makeup, and the minerals and vegetation thereabouts. The men set out for the Mississippi River on January 9. The return voyage downstream was quick, lacking some of the troubles and adventures of the ascent. Dunbar took copious notes and prepared his journal for a report on the Ouachita River Valley to be presented to President Jefferson, in part to gain funding from Congress for further such scientific excursions into the new Louisiana Territory.

—Russell M. Lawson

See also
Arkansas; Osage

For Further Reading

Rowland, Mrs. Dunbar, ed. 1930. *Life, Letters and Papers of William Dunbar.* Jackson: Press of the Mississippi Historical Society.

EDITORIAL RESPONSE

See Newspapers (International) and the Louisiana Purchase; Newspapers (U.S.) and the Louisiana Purchase

ESSEX JUNTO

The Essex Junto was a Massachusetts association of high Federalists whose members opposed the changing nature of U.S. politics in the early republic. John Adams and Thomas Jefferson condemned the club for its real and imagined intrigues, including supporting Alexander Hamilton's nomination as senior major general of the army in 1798, scotching Adams's reelection in 1800, challenging Jefferson's embargo (1807–1809), and advocating New England's secession in 1803 and 1814. Similar but less well known or active Federalist organizations existed in seaboard cities and included Charleston's Mutton Chop Club and New York's Friendly Club and Sub-Rosa Society.

Timothy Pickering and fellow Essex Junto members Fisher Ames, George Cabot, Francis Dana, Nathan Dane, Benjamin Goodhue, Stephen Higginson, Jonathon Jackson, John Lowell, Theophilus Parsons, Israel Thorndike, and Nathaniel Tracy came of political age during the American Revolution. All were born between 1745 and 1758, from prosperous, old New England families. Most had graduated from Harvard College and had gone on to successful lives in commerce, the law, or public service. Thus these men shared common bonds of interest, kinship, and thought. Politically, they were conservatives: republicans, not democrats. Whereas the Jeffersonians conceived of society in highly individualistic terms, the Essex Junto clung to older notions of an organic society composed of distinctive leaders and followers linked together by the notions of deference and noblesse oblige. According to their political philosophy, some men were born or meant to rule and lead society. They viewed developing democratic norms in America as indicative of waning virtue and waxing corruption. Eschewing personal political campaigning as pandering to the mob, they wrote off as venal men those politicians who deviated from the practice of standing for office.

In 1803, Massachusetts senator Timothy Pickering and a group of like-minded Federalists in Congress suspected a Republican conspiracy bent on overthrowing the Federalist political order and ultimately aimed at establishing Thomas Jefferson as president for life. This group viewed the Louisiana Purchase as one step in a greater scheme that had already removed from office Federalist members of the judiciary and ratified the Twelfth Amendment. These Federalists believed that the purchase was a preliminary step toward increasing the number of slave states in the Union so that Jefferson's adherents might overturn Federalist and New England influence in national affairs. Pickering considered secession a viable alternative to the Republican ascendancy, one that might preserve for the Northeast the accomplishments of the American Revolution and the power of the Federalists. He envisioned a confederacy sponsored by Great Britain and composed of New England, New York, New Jersey, and Canada. To this end Pickering, along with Roger Griswold of Connecticut, supported Republican Aaron Burr's aspirations for governor of New York in 1804. Pickering and Griswold hoped that New York would lead the Northern confederation out of the Union and that Burr would head it. However, Alexander Hamilton disdained the idea of secession and saw the plan as ruinous to both the nation and the Federalist Party. He opposed the plan and strongly urged New York Federalists to throw their support behind Burr's Republican opponent, Morgan Lewis. Hamilton's campaign to prevent disunion and preserve the Federalists through public condemnations of Burr led to Burr's challenge and their duel on July 11, 1804, at Weehawken, New Jersey. Although the Essex Junto was not involved in the secessionist discussions, Pickering's leadership of that faction and his membership in the Essex Junto implicated the New England club through his association with it.

In 1814 the Essex Junto was once more suspected of involvement in a secessionist scheme involving the Hartford Convention. Ironically, it was at the time that these men were retiring from public life in the 1790s that the Essex Junto entered the American "political vocabulary."

—Ricardo A. Herrera

See also

Ames, Fisher; Burr, Aaron; Cabot, George; Federalist Party; Griswold, Roger; Hamilton, Alexander; Jefferson, Thomas; Pickering, Timothy

For Further Reading

Clarfield, Gerard H. 1969. *Timothy Pickering and American Diplomacy.* Columbia: University of Missouri Press; Clarfield, Gerard H. 1980. *Timothy Pickering and the American Republic.* Pittsburgh: University of Pittsburgh Press; Fischer, David Hackett. 1964. "The Myth of the Essex Junto." *William and Mary Quarterly* 21: 191–235; Fischer, David Hackett. 1965. *The Revolution of American Conservatism: The Federalist Party in the Era of Jeffersonian Democracy.* New York: Harper and Row.

FAMILY COMPACT (1761)

The Family Compact (1761) was the third in a series of secret treaties between the Bourbon monarchs of France and Spain, who were cousins through their common descent from Louis XIV of France. The first Family Compact had been signed in 1733, when the breakup of the Quadruple Alliance encouraged Spain, by the early eighteenth century a declining power, to link its resources to those of France as a defense against the British and the Austrians, especially to protect their colonial territory and interests in Italy. Despite gaining favored trade status and a promise of redress for losses in the Treaty of Utrecht (1713), the Spanish received little from the agreement except the possession of Parma. A renewal of the Family Compact was signed in 1743, when Spain's objective was to provoke the British and then involve the French in their defense in order to gain possession of Milan, Piacenza, and the strategic island of Gibraltar during the War of the Austrian Succession. Again, the Spanish received only Piacenza in the Treaty of Aix-la-Chapelle (1748), hardly the outcome the Spanish had hoped to achieve, and they turned their attention to colonial, rather than European, affairs.

In August 1761, while France was engaged in the Seven Years' War, a third and final version of the Family Contract was negotiated, between Charles III of Spain and Louis XV of France. The Spanish, represented by the Marquis of Grimaldi, wanted French protection in Europe so that they would have few expenses except coastal defense and supplying their colonies, allowing another assault on Gibraltar. Also, the new king, Charles III, personally disliked the British for their threats against Naples in the 1730s and had concerns about British logging in Honduras and Newfoundland fishing rights. The French, meanwhile, needed the Spanish to supply and defend their Caribbean islands and the Louisiana Territory against British incursion. Furthermore, the treaty specified that any territorial losses suffered by either France or Spain would be compensated by the other partner, and that Spain would declare war on Great Britain if a peace were not reached by May 1762. The treaty, intended to be secret, was leaked to the British, who promptly declared war on Spain in January 1762, dragging Spain into the Seven Years' War as Britain gained the advantage and was already in negotiations for peace with France.

With inadequate military resources and underestimating the British war machine, the Spanish immediately began to lose valuable property, including the ports of Havana and Manila. The Peace of Paris (1763), which ended the war, primarily benefited the British, who received all of Canada from France, as well as Spanish Florida east of the Mississippi. Although Havana and Manila were returned to Spain, Charles III had lost a major piece of the colonial empire, and he demanded compensation from France under the Family Compact. The French, whose already unprofitable Louisiana Territory was now threatened by the British in Canada and was dependent upon Caribbean supply, especially from Havana, offered it to Spain. In 1761, trying to raise a war loan, Louis XV had offered Louisiana to Spain for a loan of 3.6 million piasters, but negotiations had failed despite Spanish interest.

It was through the Family Compact that Spain gained control of Louisiana and the port of New Orleans, which the French cleverly negotiated to keep out of enemy hands by claiming that the Manchac River was a major tributary of the Mississippi and that thus the city was not actually included in the cession of land east of the Mississippi to the British. The cession of Louisiana took place in November 1763, and the first Spanish governor, Antonio de Ulloa, a veteran Spanish colonial administrator, arrived from Peru in October 1764. The Family Compact foundered over the Falklands crisis of 1770, when the French failed to back the Spanish against the British, but the agreement smoothed the way for Spanish assistance to the American rebels in conjunction with France in 1778. From their position in Louisiana, the Spanish under Bernardo de Galvez seized British Pensacola and Mobile, hoping to use them to bargain for Gibraltar, but they were again crossed by the French, who agreed to a treaty that violated the Family Compact.

The outbreak of the French Revolution in 1789 was the death knell of the Family Compact, as the Bourbon family was ousted from power in France and the new government began behaving belligerently toward Spain. The Family Compact, by which Spain had hoped to restore its European prestige by clinging to France's coattails, had at almost every juncture been ignored by the French, who regarded Spain as a poor and expendable relation. Save the acquisition of Louisiana, the entire series of treaties was a failed attempt by Spain to retrieve the glories of the old Spanish empire when armed neutrality might have served it far better.

—*Margaret D. Sankey*

See also
Fontainebleau, Treaty of
For Further Reading
Lynch, John. 1989. *Bourbon Spain; 1700–1808.* Oxford: Basil Blackwell; Lyon, Elijah Wilson. 1934. *Louisiana in French Diplomacy, 1759–1804.* Norman: University of Oklahoma Press; Wall, Bennett H., ed. 1984. *Louisiana: A History.* Arlington Heights, IL: Forum Press.

FEDERALIST PARTY

The party of Presidents George Washington and John Adams, the Federalists favored an energetic central government, public debt, veneration of national institutions, and, in general, federal support for manufacturing, commercial navigation, and internal improvements. Most Federalists went along with the Louisiana Purchase, although Louisiana's most vocal opposition emanated from Federalist ranks.

In the early 1790s, followers of George Washington and Alexander Hamilton began referring to themselves as Federalists, borrowing the same name assumed by supporters of the federal constitution. The term "federal men" had surfaced a few years earlier in the Confederation Congress to denote supporters of a stronger, central government and those with nationalistic ambitions. Primarily centered in the northeastern United States, the Federalist Party garnered support from every state until the presidential election of 1800, when they lost to the Republicans. The Federalist Party never again controlled the presidency or Congress, and it continued to diminish until its final extinction in the 1820s. Often attacked for their elitist tendencies and opposition to democratic politics, the Federalist political machine was actually quite sophisticated and pioneered partisan tactics used extensively throughout the nineteenth century.

In terms of a political platform, the Federalists divided along two fronts. The first, best exemplified by Alexander Hamilton and Gouverneur Morris, favored a program of economic nationalism, protective tariffs, central banking, and federally sponsored internal improvements. Other Federalists, particularly John Adams and Fisher Ames, followed a more ideological course, wishing to unite the country through institutional veneration and the promotion of a national common good.

The acquisition of Louisiana in 1803 proved to be the culmination of a decade-long battle between the Federalist and Republican Parties, the focus of which was differing interpretations of the federal compact. Articulated mainly by Southern Tidewater Jeffersonians, the Republicans described the events of 1787–1789 as the American people, through their sovereign states, strengthening the bonds of union while rigidly delineating federal jurisdiction. In their eyes, the Constitution exercised a negative influence over federal power. The Federalists painted a starkly different picture.

Unable to regain momentum after the election debacle of 1800, the Federalists could not create a common front against Louisiana and the westward migration that spelled their party's doom. Alexander Hamilton and John Quincy Adams favored the purchase, and Gouveneur Morris envisioned all of North America being incorporated into the Union one day. Most Federalists, however, perceived the West as both detrimental to the Union and to the kind of homogenous social order they supported. If the Federalists held one common principle, it was seeing American society as a social organism, a unified whole, in which each part was subordinated to the common good. Thus the federal compact they defended was strictly limited to the original thirteen states and territory extending to the Mississippi River in 1789. They condemned anything that might weaken communal ties, burden the economy, or otherwise contribute to centrifugal social forces. At the same time, many Federalists realized that Western migration would sap away what remained of their dwindling political strength.

Thomas Jefferson aside, it was to be expected that Federalists would be the first to raise constitutional objections to annexation. Led primarily by Uriah Tracy and Timothy Pickering, they attacked the purchase as overextending congressional and presidential powers, and as a violation of the original compact. Historians often refer to their reasoning as a strict interpretation of the constitutional text or as a dedication to the original intent of the thirteen states. However, the Federalists cleverly devised a dual compact wherein the original thirteen were superior to any additional states. Furthermore, the annexation of any new territory or state into the Union required the consent of the original thirteen. Such reasoning was most prevalent within the confines of New England, where political power rested less on majority rule than on reaching a consensus that preserved social unity.

The Federalists' animosity toward the West also reflected their dedication to a form of government that downplayed continuous popular participation. The people exercised their political power on election day, but that power was quickly transferred to the politician, who would ideally rule in the best interests of everyone, not just his constituents. But on the frontier, consent to virtuous statesmen, a central government that would determine national moral standards, and veneration of national institutions all seemed distant reminders of an old, aristocratic world. Furthermore, the Louisiana Purchase opened the way for other social malignancies, such as slavery, and increased foreign threats along an extended boundary. Ironically, it was not threats on the Western frontier that started the next American war in

1812, but conflict among foreign commercial interests, a part of the economy usually defended by Federalists.

Having lost the battle over Western expansion and their leading light (Alexander Hamilton) in 1803–1804, Federalist politicians saw little hope for the kind of American unity they had championed. They abandoned their beliefs about America's having a homogeneous culture and ideology and bitterly attacked national institutions now in Jeffersonian hands. Factions quickly developed within the party geographically and generationally. Feeling the full brunt of Jefferson's embargo policy, New England Federalists blamed Westerners for their problems and refused to sanction support for war against Great Britain. Not wishing to be the first casualty of what would become the American System, New England Federalists met in Hartford, Connecticut, in the winter of 1814–1815 to plot a strategy against Western expansion, anticommercial legislation, and the War of 1812. Although cooler heads prevailed to stop moves toward secession and the establishment of a New England Confederation, the Hartford Convention, in connection with New England reluctance to enforce Jefferson's embargo, stigmatized the Federalist Party as a band of traitors. Its adherents gradually migrated into Republican ranks until the Federalists were no more. Eventually those ideologically committed to a homogenous social order would come to terms with both democratic politics and Western settlement. Retreating from national political circles, they focused increasingly on cultural institutions and literary pursuits in order to "civilize" the masses.

—Carey M. Roberts

See also
Constitution of the United States; Loose Construction of the U.S. Constitution; Pickering, Timothy; Tracy, Uriah

For Further Reading
Adams, Henry. 1887. *Documents Relating to New-England Federalism, 1800–1815.* New York: Burt Franklin; Ben-Atar, Doron, and Barbara B. Oberg, eds. 1998. *Federalist Reconsidered.* Charlottesville: University Press of Virginia; Fischer, David Hackett. 1965. *The Revolution of American Conservatism: The Federalist Party in the Era of Jeffersonian Democracy.* New York: Harper and Row; Sheidley, Harlow. 1998. *Sectional Nationalism.* Cambridge: Harvard University Press.

FERNANDO, DUKE OF PARMA (1765–1802)

Fernando (Ferdinand in Spain) Farnese-Bourbon was the grandson of Elisabetta (Isabela in Spain) Farnese of Parma (1692–1766) and Felipe V (1683–1746), the first Bourbon king of Spain. Fernando was also the brother of Maria Luisa, queen and consort to their cousin, Carlos IV of Spain (1788–1808), another of Elisabetta's grandsons.

Parma was among the many northern and central Italian states that had been overrun by Napoleon by 1796. The Farnese family had ruled Parma and Piacenza since 1513, when Pope Paul III created the duchy for his son, Pier Luigi. It passed to the Spanish Bourbons through Elisabetta of Parma and Spain. During the Middle Ages, Parma was the home of a university and a center of learning and culture.

Spain under Carlos IV was in an exceedingly weakened and disadvantageous position. Not only was Spain intimidated by Napoleon but it had also begun to lose control of its empire in the Americas. Additionally, the corrupt and wily Don Manuel Godoy, prime minister and paramour of the queen, had created an air of intrigue and instability at the Spanish court.

Soon after Napoleon Bonaparte overthrew the Directory (1795–1799), a French revolutionary government succeeding the Reign of Terror (1793–1794), he reappointed Charles Maurice de Talleyrand-Perigord as minister of foreign relations, with a mandate to champion a revival of a true French empire in North America. In July 1800 he ordered Talleyrand to reopen negotiations in Madrid, as both considered quick repossession of Louisiana to be a matter of great importance. Spain's secretary of state for foreign affairs, Mariano Luis de Urquijo, expressed willingness to give up Louisiana for territory in Italy, as the Directory had earlier offered, if the European powers involved would consent. He did not wish to have the retrocession of Louisiana drag Spain into a war she could not handle. King Carlos IV of Spain, who admired Bonaparte, went along, especially because his queen, Maria Luisa, was eager to see her brother Fernando, the Duke of Parma, either securely in possession of the duchy or seated on some throne in central Italy.

After years of tedious bargaining, on March 21, 1801, Lucien Bonaparte, his brother's envoy to Madrid, negotiated at San Ildefonso, the residence of the Spanish court, a new convention. It did little more, however, than deepen and emphasize that of the preceding October. In return for the elevation of the Duke of Parma to the sovereignty of Tuscany, the retrocession of Louisiana to France was to be carried out at once. At the last minute, however, because of Napoleon's extreme distaste for Fernando, the Duke of Parma, he specified that Parma's son Luis (also Ludovic) would sit upon the throne of Tuscany instead. An enlarged Tuscany was then to be known as Etruria. This arrangement was finally deemed palatable to Queen Maria Luisa, as her daughter, also Maria Luisa, the Infanta of Spain, was married to Fernando's son (her cousin), this same Luis. Fernando Farnese-Bourbon remained the Duke of Parma, in name, until his death in 1802, when Napoleon completely dispossessed the Farnese dynasty of Parma.

Finally, by the Treaty of San Ildefonso, October 1, 1800, and the Convention of Aranjuez, March 21, 1801, Napoleon Bonaparte acquired Louisiana for France in return for placing the son-in-law of the Spanish king on the newly erected throne of Etruria. He and Talleyrand hoped to build a colonial empire in the West Indies and the heart of North America. The mainland colony would be a source of supplies for the Caribbean colonies, a market for France, and a large territory for settlement.

—*Richard H. Dickerson*

See also
Bonaparte, Lucien; Fontainebleau, Treaty of; Godoy, Manuel de; Paris, Treaty of; San Ildefonso, Treaty of; Talleyrand-Perigord, Charles Maurice de; Tuscany

For Further Reading
Bertrand, Louis, and Sir Charles Petrie. 1956. *The History of Spain, Part II.* London: Eyre and Spottiswoode; De Conde, Alexander. 1976. *This Affair of Louisiana.* New York: Charles Scribner's Sons.

FITZPATRICK, THOMAS (1799–1854)

Born in 1799 to a Catholic family in County Cavan, Ulster, Northern Ireland, Thomas Fitzpatrick immigrated to America when he was seventeen. Fitzpatrick answered William H. Ashley's 1823 call for "enterprising young men" to ascend the Missouri River and trap beaver. Ashley's men were stopped by the Arikara, however, near the Grand River, exchanged fire, and returned to St. Louis for reinforcements. That fall Fitzpatrick participated in the Leavenworth debacle, or "Arikara Campaign," aimed at punishing those Indians for thwarting the fur trade. In company with Jedediah Smith, he wintered with the Crow and, the following spring, helped rediscover South Pass. During the winter and spring of 1824–1825, Fitzpatrick guided Ashley's caravan to Rendezvous Creek (Henry's Fork of the Green River) for the first of the sixteen annual mountain man rendezvous. Over the next few years he led trapping brigades in Utah, Wyoming, Montana, and Idaho.

At the 1830 rendezvous, Fitzpatrick, Jim Bridger, Milton Sublette, Henry Fraeb, and Jean B. Gervais purchased the mountain fur interests of Jedediah Smith, William Sublette, and David Jackson. Fitzpatrick led the new firm, the Rocky Mountain Fur Company, sending out trapping brigades. He also transported furs to St. Louis and brought out the next year's supplies to the rendezvous. The company faced hard times, particularly when William Sublette forced Fitzpatrick to take an unexpected journey to Santa Fe before receiving the company's supplies. During the trip, Fitzpatrick found a young Arapaho boy he named Friday and became his guardian. The lateness in supplying his men, his restrictive agreement with Sublette to supply his company, and increased field competition by American Fur Company employees all depleted the company's profits. After narrowly escaping death at the hands of Atsina Indians near the Green River and at the Battle of Pierre's Hole in 1832, Fitzpatrick and his partners did a little better in 1833. In 1834, however, they were forced to dissolve their interests. Fitzpatrick, Bridger, and Milton Sublette joined Lucien Fontenelle and Andrew Dripps to form Fontenelle, Fitzpatrick and Company, apparently employed in part by the American Fur Company. That winter Fitzpatrick bought Fort William on the Laramie River from William Sublette and Robert Campbell. The following year, Joshua Pilcher and the American Fur Company bought Fontenelle, Fitzpatrick and Company and hired Fitzpatrick as an employee.

With the end of the beaver trade in 1840, Fitzpatrick entered service as a guide to the first immigrant trains bound for Oregon and California, such as the Bartleson-Bidwell, and missionary groups including those of Father Pierre De Smet and Elijah White in 1841 and 1842. He saved the lives of Lansford W. Hastings and missionary A. L. Lovejoy, who were captured by a Lakota party at Independence Rock. John C. Frémont hired him as a guide for his second expedition in 1843 to Oregon and California. Upon returning in 1845, he led Stephen Watts Kearny and the First Dragoons to the mountains for a show of military strength to the Indians, then led Lieutenant James W. Abert through Comanche country to explore the Canadian and Arkansas Rivers. The following year Colonel Kearny requested his services in guiding the Army of the West toward California during the Mexican War. He met Kit Carson at Socorro, from where Carson continued on with the army and Fitzpatrick was sent to Washington to report. Upon his arrival in Washington, the president commissioned him as an Indian agent for the tribes of the Upper Platte and Arkansas. He traveled to Fort Leavenworth, then up the South Platte, and resided among the Arapaho and Cheyenne on the upper Arkansas River at Bent's Fort. The Indians called him White Hair because of his harrowing fur trade experiences that had turned his hair white almost overnight, or Broken Hand because one of his hands, presumably the left, had been shattered in a rifle accident wherein he lost the use of several fingers. He settled down in what is today Colorado and married Margaret Poisal (1834–1875), a French-Canadian Arapaho. Thomas and Margaret had two children, Andrew Jackson (October 8, 1850) and Virginia Thomasine (May 13, 1854).

Fitzpatrick helped orchestrate, and served as a commissioner at, the influential Treaty of Fort Laramie (1851), the largest Indian council ever held in the West, which helped define tribal boundaries and open a corridor for Western travelers. After the council, Fitzpatrick escorted an Indian delegation to Washington. In the fall of 1853 he negotiated a treaty with the Comanche and Kiowa near present-day Dodge City, Kansas. That winter Fitzpatrick journeyed to Washington, where he died of pneumonia on February 7, 1854; he was buried in the congressional cemetery. His estate was valued at more than $10,000.

Fitzpatrick is hailed as one of the top frontiersmen of his day. His life as a fur trade entrepreneur, immigrant train guide, army expedition scout, and Indian agent gives evidence of his storied career.

—Jay H. Buckley

For Further Reading

Hafen, LeRoy R. 1929. "Tom Fitzpatrick and the First Indian Agency in Colorado." *Colorado Magazine* 6: 53–62; Hafen, LeRoy R., and W. J. Ghent. 1981 [1931]. *Broken Hand: The Life Story of Thomas Fitzpatrick, Mountain Man, Guide, and Indian Agent.* Lincoln: University of Nebraska Press; Hafen, LeRoy R., and Ann W. Hafen. 1969. "Thomas Fitzpatrick." In *The Mountain Men and the Fur Trade of the Far West,* 10 vols., 7: 87–105. Edited by Leroy R. Hafen. Glendale, CA: Arthur H. Clark Co.; Munkres, Robert. 1978. "Broken Hand and the Indians: A Case Study of Mid-19th Century White Attitudes." *Annals of Wyoming* 50, no. 1: 157–171.

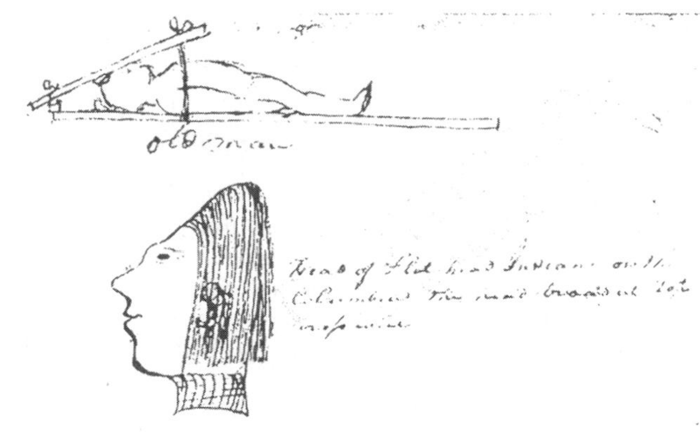

Curiosity about the physical appearance of the Flathead prompted William Clark to sketch these drawings while the Corps of Discovery wintered at Fort Clatsop in 1805 and 1806. (North Wind Picture Archives)

FLATHEAD

The Native American peoples of the plateau culture area in the northern Rocky Mountain region who came to be known as Flatheads spoke a variety of the Salish language, a branch of the Algonquian-Wakashan linguistic stock that is widely spoken by tribes throughout the Pacific Northwest. Although the Flathead today reside primarily in the mountainous area of western Montana, their ancestral territory was much larger, stretching from the crest of the Cascade Mountains eastward to the Continental Divide and centered along the headwaters region of the Clark Fork, a tributary of the Columbia River.

Although the name *Salish* was initially used by the tribe, the name *Flathead* has come into common usage since the early nineteenth century. Some of the slave captives who were owned by the Salish practiced a form of head-flattening, but the custom was not common among the Salish themselves. Nonetheless, when European and American trappers and traders first met the Salish, they called all whom they encountered Flathead.

The Flathead exhibit characteristics of a borderland people. Although they are the easternmost tribe of the plateau culture area, they display cultural characteristics and traits that are more common among the tribes of the Great Plains. For example, the Flathead owned vast herds of horses that they used for seasonal bison hunts on the Plains, and disputes over hunting rights and territoriality often put the Flathead at odds with neighbors to the east such as the Crow and Blackfoot. Additionally, many of the character traits associated with Plains Indian warrior culture were practiced or celebrated among the Flathead, including the staging of war dances, the scalping of enemies, horse stealing, and quick coups (touching enemies in order to humiliate them).

The influence of the Plains Indian culture was also evident in other aspects of Flathead life. Although they were mountain-dwelling folk, the Flathead used both the tipi, characteristic of Plains Indians, as well as sod-covered family lodges. They navigated streams in the mountain valleys using both dugout canoes and bullboats (framed vessels covered with bison hide).

Although the Flathead made war occasionally with the Shoshoni and Bannock, it was their extended conflict with the Blackfoot that posed the greatest threat to peace and security in the region. The Flathead fought several wars with the Blackfoot over hunting land, and these conflicts threatened the safety of overland travelers who hoped to follow secure trails through the northern Rockies.

To a certain extent, the spread of Christianity among the Flathead would help to pacify the region. In 1831 a delegation of Flathead and Nez Perce traveled all the way down the Missouri River to St. Louis to request that Christian missionaries be sent into their lands. Evidently the Flathead had learned of the white man's "medicine" by way of métis trappers from Canada. In response to the request, Jesuit missionary Pierre Jean De Smet established the mission of St. Mary among the Flathead in the Bitterroot Valley in 1841, and members of the tribe became some of the earliest Native Americans in the West to convert to Christianity. De Smet eventually persuaded the Flathead and the Blackfoot to agree to a truce. This was followed in 1842 by the opening of the Oregon Trail, which brought a steady stream of American pioneers through Flathead country. Many years later, in the Garfield Treaty (1872), the Flathead surrendered a sizable portion of their land and agreed to relocate northward into the valley of the Flathead Lake and River.

Today, many surviving Flathead live on the Flathead Indian Reservation, located just north of Missoula, Montana, which they share with a small band of Kootenai. Census figures from 1990 indicated that nearly five thousand Flathead and more than two thousand people of mixed Flathead and Kootenai descent live in the United States.

—*Junius P. Rodriguez*

For Further Reading
Johnson, Olga Weydemeyer. 1969. *Flathead and Kootenay: The Rivers, the Tribes, and the Region's Traders*. Glendale, CA: A. H. Clark Company; Jorgensen, Joseph G. 1969. *Salish Language and Culture: A Statistical Analysis of Internal Relationships, History, and Evolution*. Bloomington: Indiana University Press.

FLORA OF THE LOUISIANA PURCHASE

Exploration of the regions encompassed by the Louisiana Purchase greatly extended knowledge of the plant life of North America. Most expeditions included naturalists, whether amateur or formally trained. For several weeks prior to embarking on what historians now call the Lewis and Clark Expedition, for example, Meriwether Lewis studied botany in Philadelphia with the renowned botanist and physician Benjamin Smith Barton. Lewis and the naturalists who came after him wrote meticulous descriptions of plant life, often drew or painted illustrations of what they saw (or engaged artists to do so), and collected botanical specimens to send back to herbariums in the East or in Europe for further study, cataloging, and classification. Despite the fact that far more samples were lost to weather or circumstances than made it safely back, the efforts of these naturalist-explorers greatly expanded knowledge of the natural history of North America by adding hundreds of new species to the recorded flora of the continent. That knowledge ultimately had a significant impact on the disciplines of medical botany and horticulture.

Meriwether Lewis and William Clark explored the Louisiana Purchase from May 1804 until September 1806. Although their training was limited, they collected many plant samples and extensively described in their journals the flora that they encountered. In April 1805, Lewis shipped two groups of plant specimens from Fort Mandan, where the expedition had wintered. One shipment of sixty specimens arrived at the American Philosophical Society in November 1805. The second shipment, with sixty-seven specimens, went first to Thomas Jefferson at Monticello, who then forwarded the material to Benjamin Smith Barton in Philadelphia. Most of the other plant specimens collected by Lewis and Clark were either lost or destroyed in transit.

After the expedition was completed, William Clark returned to the East and signed Benjamin Smith Barton to a contract to study, describe, and classify the specimens and publish the botanical portion of the expedition's history. Many of the specimens ended up in Barton's possession, but he never completed the work. At some point, he apparently enlisted his protégé, Frederick Pursh, to assist in the project. Pursh left for England with at least some of the plant material. His descriptions appeared in his *Flora Americae Septentrionalis* (1814), the first detailed scientific description of the flora of North America to include discoveries from the Louisiana Purchase regions. It would be the early twentieth century before many of the scattered remnants of the botanical specimens of the Lewis and Clark Expedition were finally reassembled. Much of the herbarium of the expedition is now at the Academy of Natural Sciences in Philadelphia.

The first book-length description of the flora of North America had appeared in Paris in 1803. Andre Michaux's *Flora borealis-americana* recorded more than fifteen hundred species of plants. Eleven years later, Pursh's work revealed the impact on botanical knowledge of the opening of the Louisiana Territory. His work recorded more than three thousand indigenous plant species in North America. At least eighty-five species and four genera described by Pursh had been previously unknown in Western scientific literature.

Perhaps the first academically trained botanist to explore the regions of the Louisiana Purchase was Englishman John Bradbury, who arrived in St. Louis at the end of 1809. He and another Englishman and trained botanist, Thomas Nuttall, joined the 1810–1811 expedition funded by John Jacob Astor. When the War of 1812 loomed, Bradbury shipped his samples back to England. Bradbury himself, however, was stranded in the United States by the war. His specimens ended up in the hands of Frederick Pursh, who included descriptions of them (without permission) in his 1814 *Flora,* along with descriptions of the Lewis and Clark specimens and, apparently, purloined descriptions of some of Nuttall's discoveries. Nuttall published his own flora, *The Genera of North American Plants,* in 1818.

Following the war, Nuttall returned to the United States and continued his explorations of the Louisiana Territory. He spent 1819–1820 traveling through what later became Arkansas and Oklahoma. His botanical observations appeared in articles in the *Journal of the Academy of Natural Sciences* (1821–1822) and in the *Transactions of the American Philosophical Society* (1835–1836). He published a full-length account of the journey in 1821. In 1834, Nuttall joined Nathaniel Wyeth's expedition retracing the steps of Lewis and Clark from St. Louis to the Pacific Coast. From there, he continued down the coast of California and sailed across the Pacific to Hawaii. He reported his botanical discoveries and observations in the *Transactions of the American Philosophical Society* in 1841 and 1843. In honor of Nuttall's botanical discoveries, John Jacob Audubon named the Pacific dogwood—*Cornus nuttallii*—for him in 1836. Many of Nuttall's descriptions of his discoveries in the Louisiana Territory subsequently appeared in Asa

Detailed sketches of the flora that they encountered—in this case, the evergreen shrub—reflect the scientific value of the Lewis and Clark Expedition (1804–1806). (North Wind Picture Archives)

Gray and John Torrey's *Flora of the United States* (1838, 1840), a work that attempted to comprehend all of the botanical discoveries in North America up to that time. That work also represented the first major American botanical publication to abandon the Linnaean system for a modern system of classification.

The botanical discoveries of the explorers and naturalists who trekked the vast expanses of the Louisiana Territory greatly expanded the knowledge of the natural history of North America. Two disciplines in particular greatly benefited from those discoveries: medical botany and horticulture. Building on the observations and reports of explorers and naturalists, as well as his own botanical work, Jacob Bigelow published the first multivolume *American Medical Botany* between 1817 and 1820 and a *Pharmacopoeia of the United States* in 1820. These represented the first attempts to describe in a comprehensive way the medicinal uses of indigenous American plants. Many of those uses were drawn from Native American traditions. In the area of horticulture, many nurseries in the United States, England, and France received and began cultivating seeds collected by explorers and naturalists. Nurserymen such as Bernard M'Mahon of Philadelphia, through their plant and seed sales and their catalog descriptions, helped to extend the knowledge and cultivation of the plants of the Louisiana Territory throughout the nation and Europe, so that such American exotics as the Osage orange could be found growing in the gardens at Versailles in the nineteenth century. The dispersal of plant life by human agents also contributed to experimentation with hybridization and the development of new species of flowers, shrubs, trees, vegetables, and fruits.

—Lisa J. Pruitt

See also

Nuttall, Thomas

For Further Reading

Ewan, Joseph, ed. 1969. *A Short History of Botany in the United States*. New York: Hofner Publishing Company; McKelvey, Susan Delano. 1991 [1956]. *Botanical Exploration of the Trans-Mississippi West, 1790–1850*. Corvallis: Oregon State University Press; Moulton, Gary E., ed. *Herbarium of the Lewis and Clark Expedition: The Journals of the Lewis and Clark Expedition,* vol. 12. Lincoln: University of Nebraska Press; Reveal, James L. 1992. *Gentle Conquest: The Botanical Discovery of North America with Illustrations from the Library of Congress*. Washington, DC: Starwood Publishing.

FLOYD, CHARLES

Sergeant Charles Floyd occupies two unique positions in American frontier history. He was the first U.S. soldier to die west of the Mississippi River and the only member of Lewis and Clark's Corps of Discovery to lose his life during the expedition.

Sergeant Floyd was the son of Captain Charles Floyd, who served under George Rogers Clark in the frontier campaigns that followed the Revolutionary War. Clark recommended young Floyd to his brother, Captain William Clark, to serve on the expedition. Accordingly, young Floyd joined the Corps of Discovery in the summer of 1803, having been appointed by Clark at Louisville, Kentucky.

The Lewis and Clark Expedition fitted out at Pittsburgh, Pennsylvania, and Captain Lewis received quite a few applications from young men in Pittsburgh who wanted to join. There were so many, in fact, that the captains could select the best. The reward for serving would be a land grant similar to those given to the veterans of the Revolutionary War—a princely reward for frontiersmen.

Clark was a good judge of character. He had already hired seven of "the best woodsmen & Hunters in this part of the Countrey [sic]" (DeVoto, 1953). Charles Floyd was among that group.

Charles Floyd and Nathaniel Pryor were appointed sergeants. The men were sworn into the U.S. Army in a solemn ceremony in the presence of William Clark. The Corps of Discovery was born.

The expedition was augmented by the inclusion of additional personnel in March 1804, while at St. Louis. These soldiers were selected to be members of "the Detachment destined for the Expedition through the interior of the *Continent* of North America" (ibid.). A second group of five soldiers was designated to accompany the expedition to its winter quarters and then return to St. Louis with dispatches, communiqués, and specimens. The main group was divided into three squads, with Sergeant Floyd in command of one of these.

Little is mentioned of Floyd in the expedition's journals until August 1804, when the Corps of Discovery reached the site of present-day Sioux City, Iowa. It was there that Sergeant Floyd fell ill, suffering from what the captains called "Bilios Chorlick" (bilious colic). He died on Sunday, August 19, 1804, from what appears to have been a burst appendix. Given the limited medical technology of the time, it is unlikely that he could have survived such an attack, even if he had been back in the East.

Sergeant Floyd was buried with full military honors on a bluff overlooking an unnamed river. Meriwether Lewis read the funeral service over the grave. William Clark provided a fitting epitaph in his journal: "This Man at all times gave us proofs of his firmness and Determined resolution to doe [*sic*] service to his Countrey [*sic*] and honor to himself" (ibid.). The captains concluded the service by naming the river Floyd's River, and the bluff Sergeant Floyd's Bluff.

Today a granite shaft marks the grave site in Sioux City, Iowa.

—Henry H. Goldman

See also

Corps of Discovery; Lewis and Clark Expedition

For Further Reading

Ambrose, Stephen E. 1996. *Undaunted Courage: Meriwether Lewis, Thomas Jefferson and the Opening of the American West.* New York: Simon and Schuster; DeVoto, Bernard. 1953. *The Journals of Lewis and Clark.* Boston: Houghton and Mifflin Company; Goetzmann, William H. 1959. *Army Exploration in the American West, 1803–1863.* New Haven: Yale University Press; National Park Service. 1967. *Founders and Frontiersmen: Historic Places Commemorating Early Nationhood and the Westward Movement, 1783–1828.* Washington, DC: United States Department of the Interior.

FONTAINEBLEAU, TREATY OF (1762)

The Treaty of Fontainebleau transferred the part of the French colony of Louisiana located west of the Mississippi River and the Isle of Orleans to Spain. Great Britain received the remainder of the territory under the terms of the peace settlement to end the French and Indian War (1755–1763). As France's ally, Spain received the valuable city of New Orleans in order to keep it out of British hands. France deemed the rest of the ceded territory to be unimportant at the time. Although the cession seemed to be the best decision France could have made under the circumstances in 1762, after the French Revolution the decision would become one more symbol of the incompetence and shortsightedness of French royalty. Subsequent governments would negotiate for years seeking to regain the lost territory from Spain.

Great Britain and France fought what became known as the French and Indian War in the New World and the Seven Years' War in Europe. The reason for the war was the balance of power in Europe. Prime Minister William Pitt of Great Britain realized that the outcome of the colonial portion of the war would affect European politics through the acquisition of territory. Great Britain was determined to take as much of the French colonial territory as possible. Many Native American groups in the New World sided with France, but their aid was not enough to enable France to defeat Great Britain. The French recognized the need for another ally.

France looked closer to home for its second ally. Spain entered the war on the side of France as part of a series of agreements between the two nations. The treaty known as the Family Compact encompassed the main alliance between the two nations. Because many of the European royal families were related in one degree or another, this term might apply to almost any alliance among them, but, at this time, the French and Spanish were particularly close. King Louis XV of France and Charles III of Spain were both of the House of Bourbon and close cousins. In addition, they were both staunchly Catholic monarchs united in traditional hatred of the Protestant British. Spain further saw the war as a chance to gain more territory in the New World. Unfortunately, the additional ally did not help the French cause. Spain paid dearly in terms of power and prestige for this alliance.

Soon after entering the war to aid the French, Spain lost the city of Havana, Cuba, to British forces. This was a devastating blow, inasmuch as Havana was a major city in the Spanish empire. The terms of the Family Compact provided for the preservation of both kingdoms in their entirety and stated that any advantages gained by one power would be used to compensate any loss by the other. Spanish ministers soon joined the peace negotiations in Paris in an attempt to limit their losses, stating that Spain deserved compensation for the loss of Havana. This compensation could also constitute leverage in any negotiations with Great Britain for the return of the lost city.

Great Britain demanded all of the eastern part of the Louisiana Territory from France as part of the peace settlement. The British also demanded the Floridas from Spain, as punishment for allying with France. Further complicating France's efforts to end the war with some dignity, Spain maintained its historical right to object to any other nation colonizing the Gulf of Mexico. The Spanish definitely objected to the hated British gaining a foothold in the region.

The best solution to all of these complications for France seemed to be to transfer part of the Louisiana Territory to Spain. The city of New Orleans embodied a powerful bargaining chip for Spain to use in negotiating the return of Havana from the British or as compensation for the loss of the Floridas. The rest of the territory would enhance Spanish colonial holdings while simultaneously offsetting British encroachment in the Gulf. France would also have the satisfaction of keeping as much of the Louisiana Territory as possible out of British hands. The King of France wrote to the King of Spain on October 9, 1762, making the offer of the Isle of Orleans and the western part of the Louisiana Territory as compensation, if Spain would agree to Britain's peace terms.

The negotiations were conducted on two levels—the official, ministerial negotiations and the unofficial, royal negotiations. Charles III rejected the French offer on October 22, 1762. However, the next day the Spanish ambassador was instructed to sign the peace agreement and accept the Louisiana Territory. The signing formally took place on November 3, 1762. France relinquished Canada and eastern Louisiana; New Orleans and the western Louisiana Territory were ceded to Spain; Spain sacrificed the Floridas to Great Britain but received Havana back. Spain would hold on to its part of the Louisiana Territory until 1803, when France succeeded in having the territory returned.

The transfer of the territory further cemented relations between France and Spain, while relieving both nations of some of their most vexing colonial problems. By controlling New Orleans, Spain eliminated smuggling by the French through that port into the Spanish colonies. They also managed to keep Great Britain from controlling that important city and thus the entire Mississippi River. France no longer had the enormous drain on its treasury of supporting the Louisiana Territory. The colony had never been self-sufficient. It was very easy for France to cede what it considered worthless territory in return for the end of a disastrous war and continued good relations with Spain.

The final treaty dictated a change in the nationality of the inhabitants, but no change in individual rights. The British colonies, and later the United States, retained the commercial rights formerly enjoyed under the French. For some reason, however, Louisiana residents did not receive notification of the treaty and its terms until April 21, 1764. Spain was not prepared in 1762—or even 1764—to garrison the colony and govern it. Spain, in its usual slow, diplomatic fashion, did not actually take control of the territory until August 1769.

—Elizabeth Pugliese

See also
Family Compact; Isle of Orleans; Paris, Treaty of

For Further Reading
Lyon, E. Wilson. 1974. *Louisiana in French Diplomacy 1759–1804*. Norman: University of Oklahoma Press; Martin, Henri. 1866. *History of France from the Most Remote Period to 1789,* vol. 15. Translated by Mary L. Booth. Boston: Walker, Fuller, and Company.

FORTS

***See* individual forts listed by name**

FOX

Members of the Native American group known as the Fox refer to themselves as Meskwaki ("Red Earth People"). This name comes from the rich soil near early Fox farming villages. For much of their history, the Fox have been closely associated with the Sauk, to whom they are related. The two groups were often mistakenly referred to as the Sac and Fox. The Fox tribal group can be traced to the area around present-day Green Bay, Wisconsin, and along the eastern shore of Lake Michigan. Members of the Algonquian family, the Fox are sometimes characterized as "Prairie Algonquian" because of where they lived.

The Fox were seminomadic. During summer they lived in villages of permanent bark or cattail-covered houses called wickiups. The Fox raised corn, beans, squash, and tobacco. In winter they followed deer and buffalo. They made their clothing of buckskin.

Tribes were organized under a hereditary "peace chief" or magistrate, a "war chief" elected on merit when needed, and a ceremonial leader, or shaman, who was the main religious authority. Internal tribal organization was based on a clan system governing traditions and religious practices.

The Fox came into contact with French fur traders during the 1600s. The Frenchmen called them Fox, and the name persisted. Controlling key river "highways," the Fox extracted tolls from the French and the tribes who sold furs to the French. Although the practice brought them wealth, it also earned the Fox many enemies. The Fox were allied with the Iroquois Confederacy to the east, a major British ally.

The Fox fought repeatedly with various tribes, especially the Ojibwa, favorites of the French. Still, the French sought to improve relations and convinced the Fox to move closer to Detroit, a major trading hub, where they became embroiled in renewed conflict with their old enemies, the Ojibwa. The French, coldly calculating the situation, cast their support to the Ojibwa. Sporadic fighting ensued for decades, decimating the Fox. By 1730, French-Ojibwa forces had virtually exterminated the Fox. Facing utter destruction, the Fox allied with the Sauk in 1734.

The Fox moved south. Some joined with Sauk along the Illinois side of the Mississippi River. Others settled in the eastern portion of present-day Iowa. Each year, the two groups traveled north to collect maple syrup. Their historical lifestyle survived into the 1820s, when the last buffalo were driven out of eastern Iowa.

The Fox tried to get along with the U.S. government, but efforts proved ineffective after the Louisiana Purchase opened the area across the Mississippi to white settlement. U.S. insistence on treating the two tribes as one, the Sac and Fox, rather than recognizing two distinct groups, contributed to misunderstanding. In St. Louis in 1804, tribal leaders, mostly Sauk from Missouri, signed a treaty with the United States. Not representing other tribal groups, these chiefs ceded to the United States all Fox land in eastern Iowa, as well as all Sauk land in western Illinois.

Not having been consulted beforehand, all Fox and most Sauk were horrified by this treaty, but there was little legal recourse. During the War of 1812, many Sauk fought for the British. The federal government was then further disinclined to show sympathy for the "Sac and Fox," assuming both groups to be traitorous. A subsequent treaty in 1815 between the Fox and the United States failed to resolve the situation. Soon encroachment by settlers made the Fox positions in Illinois and Iowa untenable.

In 1829 both Fox and Sauk were ordered to depart disputed territory in Illinois. Both groups crossed the Mississippi, seeking a new home. In 1832, however, under pressure from the Sioux, the Sauk under the war chief Black Hawk returned to Illinois. In the subsequent Black Hawk War, the Fox avoided the fray. When the Sauk surrendered, however, the Fox were lumped into the punitive settlement.

The Fox had to vacate their easternmost lands in Iowa. Until 1845 they lived along the Des Moines River, but they were subsequently relocated outside Fort Des Moines. When settlement expanded, most of the Fox were moved to a reservation in Kansas, along the Osage River.

In the 1850s, unhappy with conditions in Kansas, some Fox returned to Iowa and purchased about three thousand acres of their former lands as private property. Today a large group of Fox reside near Tama, Iowa. Other Fox are located in Kansas and Oklahoma. A conservative people, the Fox have fought hard to maintain as many of their traditions as possible in the modern world.

—*Michael S. Casey*

See also

Black Hawk Purchase; Black Hawk War; Sauk

For Further Reading

Edmunds, R. David. 1993. *The Fox Wars: The Mesquakie Challenge to New France.* Civilization of the American Indian, vol. 211. Norman: University of Oklahoma Press; Hagan, William Thomas. 1958. *The Sac and Fox Indians.* Norman: University of Oklahoma Press.

FREDONIAN REBELLION (1826–1827)

The Fredonian Rebellion is the name given to an East Texas land dispute in late 1826 and early 1827, after the United States renounced its claims to Texas in the Louisiana Purchase. The dispute involved Mexican officials, American settlers, and the nearby Cherokee, who had come to Texas from their temporary refuge in Arkansas with the informal approval of the Mexican government, which was intent on establishing a buffer zone of Indians between Texas and the United States.

One of the Cherokee chiefs, Richard Fields, a mixed-race, English-speaking master Mason who styled himself "Captain general of the Indian tribes in the province of Texas," stated that the superior government had granted him "territory . . . and also a commission to command all the Indian tribes and nations that are in the four eastern provinces." An 1823 Bexar Archives document from Minister Lucas Alamán both confirms Fields's agreement with Colonel Trespalacios and undermines it (Winkler, 1903). Alamán advised the provisional governor that the agreement should "remain provisionally in force . . . [while] endeavoring to bring [Cherokee tribal settlements] toward the interior, at places least dangerous." Fields's aggressive efforts to organize the Indians in Texas threatened Mexican authorities, who denied that documents existed supporting either a commission or a land grant. Local authorities were instructed to prevent Fields from assembling his tribes, but he refused to submit to local authority.

Claims for the Cherokee land were further clouded by an 1825 grant for eight hundred families given to Haden Edwards that caused an influx of Anglo-Americans. Like all *empresarios* in the fledgling nation, Edwards was required to uphold all previous grants, whether Spanish or Mexican. In September 1825, he posted notices in Nacogdoches requiring landowners to present evidence of title or forfeit their lands to new settlers, thus polarizing the community between old and new settlers. The split was aggravated in December during the alcalde's election, when Edwards certified that his son-in-law had defeated the representative of the old settlers. When that certification was overturned by Mexican authorities, who subsequently nullified the grant of the uncooperative Edwards, the stage was set for a bloodier dispute.

The Edwards brothers organized a revolt against the Mexican government. Although outnumbered, they counted on the fighting strength of the disgruntled Cherokee and their Indian allies under Fields, with whom Benjamin Edwards had signed an agreement in December 1826 to fight a government considered faithless. Symbolically calling their new nation "Fredonia," the rebels declared their independence from Mexico. Over the Old Stone Fort, which became their capitol, they flew a flag with white and red bars, denoting a White-Indian alliance, and proclaiming "Independence, Liberty, and Justice." "Fredonia" would designate the place where liberty had been accomplished—*free*dom was *done* there.

The rebels signed a declaration of independence on December 21, 1826. Immediately thereafter they appealed to Stephen F. Austin and his colonists to join them, but Austin sided with the Mexican authorities, who feared a total conflagration from the alliance of Indians and Fredonians. Mexican troops were dispatched from San Antonio to Nacogdoches, supported by Austin and a mounted militia. As a counterrevolutionary strategy, the Indian agent for the Mexican government, Peter Ellis Bean, created dissension within the Cherokee confederation. When Chief Fields tried to muster his Cherokee allies against these loyalist forces, he discovered that Bean and his agents had been to the Cherokee village and promised them the land for which they contended. Cherokee under Bowles and Big Mush murdered Fields (and his colleague John Donne Hunter) and presented the Fredonian flag to the Mexican officials as a gesture of loyalty. This incident effectively eliminated the Cherokee as allies to the Fredonians, who were unable to fight by themselves.

On December 28, 1826, the Fredonian rebels evacuated Nacogdoches, crossing the Sabine shortly afterward. In response, the Mexican government sent troop reinforcements to Nacogdoches under the command of José de las Piedras, who secured the town. Five years later, the Battle of Nacogdoches, on August 2, 1832, resulted in the removal of Mexican troops from East Texas.

—Betje B. Klier

See also

Nacogdoches; Texas

For Further Reading

Aberbach, Alan D. 1971. "A Search for an American Identity." *Canadian Review of American Studies* 2, no. 2: 77–88; Everett, Dianna. 1990. *The Texas Cherokees: A People between Two Fires 1819–1840.* Norman: University of Oklahoma Press; Klier, Betje B. 1998. *Tales of the Sabine Borderlands.* College Station: Texas A&M University Press; McDonald, Archie P. 2000. "Fredonian Rebellion." In *The New Handbook of Texas.* Edited by Ron C. Tyler et al. Austin: Texas State Historical Association; Winkler, Ernest William. 1903. "The Cherokee Indians in Texas." *Quarterly of the Texas State Historical Association* 7, no. 2: 95–165.

FREE SOIL PARTY (1848)

Concern over the extension of slavery into the territories had been raised in 1818, when Missouri petitioned to enter the Union as a slave state. At that time the speaker of the House, Henry Clay of Kentucky, engineered the Missouri Compromise, which the North and South accepted. Under the compromise, slavery would not be permitted in the Louisiana Purchase territory north of the line of 36 degrees 30 minutes north latitude (with the exception of the state of Missouri). By 1846 the extension issue once again reached a critical level. The Free Soil Party was born out of the tensions that arose over the question of extending slavery to the territories acquired from Mexico.

In August 1846, Democratic congressman David Wilmot of Pennsylvania attached the Wilmot Proviso to a Mexican War appropriations bill. Although only in the third month of the war, the United States expected to win, and antiextension supporters prepared for a U.S. victory. Wilmot's proviso stated that slavery would not be allowed in any territories acquired from Mexico as a result of war. The bill passed in the House, where Northerners dominated, but failed in the Senate. Although the proviso never became law, it helped rally support for the cause of halting the extension of slavery into the territories and generated suspicion and distrust between Northerners and Southerners, thus setting the stage for the birth of the Free Soil Party. The debate over the proviso also served to divide further the Democratic Party, which since 1844 had found itself increasingly divided by section.

By the summer of 1848, the Whig and the Democratic Parties, well aware that the Northern and Southern wings of their parties were divided over the issue of slavery in the territories, had tried to avoid the issue in the presidential campaign. Democratic and Whig antiextensionists, however, found themselves unable to accept the presidential candidates nominated by their parties—Democrat Lewis Cass and Whig Zachary Taylor. Moreover, intraparty friction continued to drive wedges between extensionists and their opponents, eventually causing antiextension Whigs and Democrats to bolt their respective parties.

In August 1848, a convention of nonextension men organized the Free Soil Party. Among them were former members of the Liberty Party (founded in 1839 as an abolition party), Barnburner Democrats (Northerners upset with their party's domination by Southerners), and Conscience Whigs (Whigs opposed to slavery on moral grounds). Holding its national convention in Buffalo, New York, the party nominated former Democratic president Martin Van Buren of New York as its candidate for president and former Whig Charles Francis Adams of Massachusetts as his running mate. This third party, which found its strength in the Northeast and in parts of the Midwest, siphoned power from the leading parties and ultimately forced them to confront the extension issue in national politics.

The party opposed the extension of slavery into the territories, but it did not support equality for African Americans, nor did it advocate the abolition of slavery. Although there were a few abolitionists and egalitarians among the party's membership (such as the old Liberty Party men), the majority had little concern for the welfare of African Americans. The party adopted the slogan "Free Soil, Free Speech, Free Labor, and Free Men," but the slogan's message should not be interpreted as proabolition. Most Free Soil Party members were content with slavery remaining where it already existed.

Most party members opposed the extension of slavery for fear that it would damage white men's economic opportunities. This belief was grounded in the Free Labor ideology of the period. Those subscribing to this belief viewed free, wage labor as virtuous and slave labor as degrading. The mere presence of slave labor was an anathema. Free Soilers also argued that allowing slave labor to compete with free labor would result in stifled social mobility and poverty for white laborers and their families. Thus Free Soilers believed that slavery should be excluded from the territories.

Although the party elected men to Congress and exerted influence in politics, by 1851 many Barnburners returned to the Democratic Party. In 1854 the Kansas-Nebraska Act brought about the purely sectional Republican Party that opposed the extension of slavery into the territories, prompting the remaining Free Soilers to join the new party. Even though the Free Soil Party existed for only a short time, it succeeded in forcing nonextension into national politics and helped usher in the Second Party System (Democrats vs. Republicans).

—Alicia E. Rodriquez

For Further Reading

Blue, Fredrick J. 1973. *The Free Soilers: Third Party Politics, 1848–54*. Urbana: University of Illinois Press; Gienapp, William E. 1987. *The Origins of the Republican Party, 1852–1856*. New York: Oxford University Press; Holt, Michael F. 1999. *The Rise and Fall of the American Whig Party: Jacksonian Politics and the Onset of the Civil War*. New York: Oxford University Press; Mayfield, John. 1980. *Rehearsal for Republicanism: Free Soil and the Politics of Anti-Slavery*. Port Washington, WA: Kennikat Press.

FREEMAN EXPEDITION (1806)

The expedition that Thomas Freeman led into the Red River Valley in 1806 was primarily designed to expand knowledge about the southern portion of the recently purchased Louisiana Territory. On a more subtle level, the expedition might be viewed as a precursor to the ideology of Manifest Destiny that would characterize America's insatiable expansionist attitude in the nineteenth century. What few imagined at the time was that the Freeman Expedition (1806) would lead to an international incident largely precipitated by the conspiratorial designs of Aaron Burr and General James Wilkinson.

The Freeman Expedition, which President Thomas Jefferson described as his "Grand Excursion" to the Southwest, was a daunting effort to determine answers to important questions. Jefferson hoped that the party might identify a suitable river route that could provide direct commercial contact with Santa Fe that would enhance the trade and commerce of the United States. Another major purpose of the expedition was to trace and map the exact boundary between the Louisiana Territory and Spanish colonial possessions in the Southwest. Additionally, through the generous distribution of presents to the Indian tribes that the expedition encountered, Jefferson hoped to sway the allegiance of those groups away from the Spanish and toward the Americans. The hefty funding of $11,000 to finance this expedition, more than three times what the Congress had provided to fund the Lewis and Clark Expedition, suggests the serious nature of the work and the confidence that the government placed upon Freeman and his party.

Unlike other forays westward, such as the Lewis and Clark and Zebulon Pike Expeditions, the Freeman Expedition did not rely upon military men as explorers, but rather used civilian scientists and naturalists as trained observers of the West. Thomas Freeman, selected to lead the party, was an experienced astronomer and surveyor. Peter Custis, a University of Pennsylvania medical student who had studied under the noted naturalist Benjamin Barton Smith, served as the chief naturalist and ethnographer for the expedition. Captain Richard Sparks led a forty-five-man military contingent along with French and Indian guides to escort the scientists as they traveled westward.

The Freeman Expedition departed from Concordia Parish in Louisiana, following the Red River westward from its intersection with the Mississippi. The party officially commenced the expedition on May 2, 1806, and advanced toward Natchitoches. They left Natchitoches on June 2 and subsequently portaged their way around the Great Raft on the Red River as they made their way into the unknown Southwest. Eventually the group would advance as far as 615 miles up the Red River before being forced to abandon the expedition and turn around on July 28.

General James Wilkinson, the commander of the U.S. Army in the South, had informed Spanish authorities about the expedition that was planning to enter into the disputed territory that Spain claimed to be its own. At the time, Wilkinson and former vice president Aaron Burr were hoping to instigate an international incident between the United States and Spain that might precipitate the seizure of the Southwest, or perhaps, of Spanish Mexico. Thus alerted of the trespassers who were ascending the Red River, the Spanish sent Francisco Viana with a small force to intercept the Freeman Expedition and direct its members to remove themselves from Spanish Territory. That occurred, without incident, at a site that is today called Spanish Bluff, in Bowie County, Texas. Wilkinson's participation in what became known as Burr's Washita Conspiracy became evident many years later, when Spanish documents removed from Havana in 1898 revealed the exact nature of his complicity.

Despite the failure of the Freeman Expedition to complete its goals, the scientists and naturalists who did explore the Red River region, albeit briefly, were able to document and catalog a wealth of information about the flora, fauna, and ethnography of the region. The failure of the expedition did cause embarrassment to the Jefferson administration, but, fortunately, the type of incident for which Wilkinson and Burr had hoped never took place. The Freeman Expedition's failure also made the Congress more leery about expending large amounts of public revenue for Western exploration. A planned 1807 expedition into the Arkansas River Valley was canceled as a result of the political repercussions from the 1806 event.

—Junius P. Rodriguez

See also

Dunbar-Hunter Expedition; Wilkinson, James

For Further Reading

Flores, Dan L. 1984. "The Ecology of the Red River in 1806: Peter Custis and Early Southwestern Natural History." *Southwestern Historical Quarterly* 88: 1–42; Flores, Dan L., ed. 1984. *Jefferson and Southwestern Exploration: The Freeman and Custis Accounts of the Red River Expedition of 1806.* Norman: University of Oklahoma Press.

FRENCH AND INDIAN WAR (1754–1763)

The French and Indian War was the fourth and most decisive struggle between the European colonial powers to win mastery over North America. Initiated by a Franco-British territorial clash over the ownership of the upper Ohio Valley, the war would later become part of a more complex European struggle for dominance, the Seven Years' War (1756–1763), which aligned Britain, Prussia, Hanover, and Portugal against France, Spain, Austria, Russia, and Sweden. Fought upon four continents, hostilities were finally ended by the Peace of Paris (February 10, 1763) and the Treaty of Hubertsburg (February 15, 1763). Whereas Hubertusburg returned Europe to the prewar territorial status quo, the Peace of Paris rearranged the map of North America and had a tremendous impact upon the future of the continent, especially Louisiana.

In 1748, King George's War (the War of the Austrian Succession) was ended by the Treaty of Aix-la-Chapelle, which did little to settle the competing Franco-British territorial claims in North America. In 1749, the same year that George II granted 200,000 acres in the trans-Appalachian region to the Ohio Company of Virginia, the governor general of New France, the Comte de La Galissoniere, dispatched an expedition to the Ohio to establish the French claim to the region. His successor, the Marquis de Duquesne, initiated a policy of fort building in the area to establish an influence over the powerful indigenous tribes and, the British feared, to create a link between New France and Louisiana that would limit the westward expansion of the British colonies. In 1753 Governor Robert Dinwiddie of Virginia dispatched a young George Washington to the Ohio to demand a French evacuation from, it was claimed, British territory. When the request was politely refused and Fort Duquesne (now Pittsburgh) was erected on the forks of the Ohio River, Washington returned, clashed with the French at Great Meadows, and was finally forced to surrender at Fort Necessity, July 4, 1754. Alarmed at these developments on its colonial frontier, London dispatched two regiments under General Edward Braddock to dislodge the French.

Arriving in Virginia in April 1755, Braddock ignored all advice for caution and, reinforced by Virginia militia, began to hack a slow path through the wilderness to Fort Duquesne, only to be ambushed and killed by French regulars, Canadian militia, and their Native American allies in July 1755. In the following two years, Anglo-American forces suffered a series of defeats at Crown Point, Fort Oswego, and Fort William Henry. If these French victories had little impact upon Louisiana, British actions in Nova Scotia would have a lasting effect upon the future of the French southern colony.

The Treaty of Utrecht, which had ended Queen Anne's War (the War of the Spanish Succession, 1702–1713), ceded Nova Scotia to Britain and restricted the French in

Acadia to their "ancient limits"—limits that were never defined by common consent. British concerns over the refusal of the French Acadians living in Nova Scotia to take an oath of allegiance were magnified in 1750, when the French built Fort Beausejour, which dominated the peninsula joining Nova Scotia to the Canadian mainland. Following the outbreak of hostilities in Ohio, the British ministry dispatched to Nova Scotia the New England Regiment and a detachment of regulars to take Beausejour. After its capture, the British disarmed, detained, and finally deported the Acadians from the region, irrespective of whether they had borne arms or attempted to remain neutral, dispersing them among the British colonies and Europe. This "Grand Derangement," an action denounced by many historians as an atrocious act of barbarity, led many Acadians to settle in Louisiana. After the war, the Spanish governor of Louisiana, Antonio de Ulloa, encouraged their immigration to Louisiana, where their descendants have become known as Cajuns.

When a territorial dispute between Austria and Prussia over the possession of Silesia led to the outbreak of the Seven Years' War in Europe in 1756, continuing defeats led William Pitt to be included into the British ministry. Taking effective control of British war policy, Pitt reversed the trend of the war by blockading France and New France, and concentrating British energy toward winning the war in American while keeping Frederick the Great's Prussian armies in the field by providing large subsidies. Following the capture of Cape Breton and the formidable French bastion at Louisbourg in 1758, a series of remarkable British victories at Fort Niagara, Fort Frontenac, and Fort Duquesne, as well as the capture of the important French sugar island of Guadeloupe in April 1759, was capped in September 1759 by General James Wolfe's victory over the Marquis de Montcalm on the Plains of Abraham near Quebec. That victory forced the surrender of Quebec, and French power in Canada was effectively ended in September 1760, when the governor of New France, the Marquis de Vaudreuil, surrendered Montreal to Sir Jeffrey Amherst.

Louisiana, long neglected by France, had not escaped British attention. In 1756 and again in 1759, a military campaign had been planned, but not carried out, against Louisiana. However, the outbreak of a bitter British-Cherokee war in the autumn of 1759 refocused British attention on the south. Fears of continuing French influence among the Native Americans, fueled by rumors of a massive French migration from Canada to Louisiana, a province potentially vastly more useful to France than Canada had ever been, raised a British demand, first voiced in December 1759, that Louisiana be ceded to Britain at a peace treaty. Such demands received increasing support when it was realized that two of Britain's main war aims, to establish firm boundaries to her colonial possessions and to retain Canada, would be handicapped if no recognized boundary between France's northern possessions and Louisiana existed. Consequently, when Louis XV made a formal appeal for a peace conference in March 1761, an appeal that led to the unsuccessful Stanley-Bussey talks (May–September 1761), the British made their first official demands that France give up eastern Louisiana.

At this stage of negotiations, the French foreign minister, the Duc de Choiseul, maintained an equivocal attitude to both the success of the talks and the future of Louisiana. He first offered Louisiana to Spain as collateral for a loan with which to continue the war, and later as a prize to encourage Spain to join the war against Britain. When Pitt's own peace terms proved too imperious for France to accept, Choiseul, emboldened by a treaty of alliance with Spain (the Third Family Compact of August 15, 1761), broke off the negotiations in September 1761. Aware of the compact, Pitt demanded an immediate declaration of war against Spain; when that was refused by the British cabinet, he resigned on October 5, 1761, and became a vocal supporter for the escalation of the war, the need to retain all of Britain's conquests, and the launching of a campaign against Louisiana. The continuation of the war and Britain's declaration of war on Spain, on January 4, 1762, proved both ruinous to France and a disaster for Spain. In February 1762, General Robert Monckton captured Martinique, a victory followed by later British successes against St. Lucia, the Grenadines, Grenada, St. Vincent, and Dominica. While negotiations were again being held, the Earl of Albermarle captured Spanish Havana in August 1762, and only the deplorable condition of the British troops in Cuba prevented a planned invasion of Louisiana later that same year. Spain was further shocked when a surprise amphibious British strike force, launched from India under Admiral Cornish and Colonel Draper, captured Manila in the Philippines in October 1762. These latter two events embarrassed Lord Bute, Pitt's successor, who was attempting to bring a speedy end to the war. If, however, the French and Indian War proved disastrous to both the French and Spanish colonial empires, it also proved financially devastating to Britain itself.

Following secret Franco-British negotiations, begun in December 1761, the Spanish were shocked to learn by the summer of 1762 that their ally intended to cede all of Spain's southern territory east of the Mississippi, excluding New Orleans, to the British in a peace settlement. Concerned that this would allow the expansionist British access to the Gulf of Mexico, Spain protested and was only mollified by the cession of New Orleans and western Louisiana to Madrid in November 1762. Allowed to retain Manila, Spain was eventually forced to cede Florida to the British in exchange for the return of Havana. Grateful for France's cession of western Louisiana, Spain intended to use the province as a buffer to protect Mexico from British influence.

Britain's own new imperial responsibilities would, however, bring it to colonial disaster in the American Revolution, and although Spain would regain both East and West Florida, south of the thirty-second parallel, with the Treaty of Versailles (1783), Britain ceded the rest of its trans-Appalachian territory to the new United States. Whereas the Spanish would have to face the even more expansionist Americans across the Mississippi, the people of Louisiana, like the Acadians and Canadians before them, would continue to be used as imperial pawns. Following the French and Indian War, they, unconquered and not consulted, became either British or Spanish subjects. In 1800 the people of New Orleans and western Louisiana once again became French, only to learn three years later that they had been sold to the United States.

—Rory T. Cornish

For Further Reading

Anderson, Fred. 2000. *Crucible of War: The Seven Years' War and the Fate of Empire in British North America, 1754–1766.* New York: Alfred A. Knopf; Brasseaux, Carl. 1987. *The Founding of New Acadia: The Beginnings of Acadian Life in Louisiana, 1765–1803.* Baton Rouge: Louisiana State University Press; Christelow, Alan. 1946. "Economic Background of the Anglo-Spanish War of 1762." *Journal of Modern History* 18: 22–36; Cornish, Rory T. 1986. "A Vision of Empire: The Development of British Opinion Regarding the American Colonial Empire, 1730–1770." Ph.D. diss., University of London; Eccles, W. J. 1972. *France in America.* New York: Harper Torchbooks; Gipson, Lawrence Henry. 1968. *The Great War for the Empire. The Years of Defeat, 1754–1757: The British Empire before the American Revolution,* vol. 6. New York: Alfred A. Knopf; Jennings, Francis. 1998. *Empire of Fortune: Crowns, Colonies and Tribes in the Seven Years' War in America.* New York: W. W. Norton; McNeil, John Robert. 1985. *Atlantic Empires of France and Spain: Louisbourg and Havana, 1700–1763.* Chapel Hill: University of North Carolina Press; Peckham, Howard H. 1964. *The Colonial Wars, 1689–1762.* Chicago: University of Chicago Press; Steele, Ian. 1990. *Fort William Henry and the "Massacre."* New York: Oxford University Press; Winsor, Justin. 1895. *The Mississippi Basin: The Struggle in America between England and France, 1697–1763.* Boston and New York: Houghton, Mifflin, and Company.

FUR TRAPPING

Native Americans traded in animal skins prior to European conquest. Plains Indians exchanged antelope hides and deerskins for agricultural produce grown by Mandan and Wichita tribes. However, Europeans encouraged Native Americans to increase their hunting and trading activities. The Hudson's Bay Company collected furs from indigenous tribes as well as employing its own band of trappers, while along the Pacific Coast, British and Russian ships decimated otter populations. The Louisiana Purchase (1803) presented Americans with an opportunity to challenge the colonial fur trade in the West and, in so doing, weaken European claims to the continent. The Lewis and Clark Expedition (1804–1806) set out to foster amicable relations with native tribes and survey the Western territory for commercial gain. Lewis and Clark returned with news of a region rich in fur-bearers. Lewis declared the headwaters of the Missouri River to be "richer in beaver and otter than any country on earth" (Utley, 1997).

In 1807, Manuel Lisa traveled up the Missouri, establishing a trading post (Fort Raymond) at the mouth of the Bighorn River. Lisa initiated trade with Crow Indians, while employing a number of Euro-Americans to trap local streams. Two years later Lisa founded the St. Louis, Missouri, Fur Company (later renamed the Missouri Fur Company). In the early 1820s, five major companies competed for furs on the northern Great Plains. By the late 1820s, the American Fur Company had eclipsed its rivals, exercising dominance over the Plains-based fur economy until the 1860s. The hub of the American fur trade was St. Louis. The fast-growing city served as an entrepôt for supplies and furs traveling between Eastern markets and Western trapping grounds. In summer months, traders ferried their goods from St. Louis up the Missouri River, before it iced over in November. The Plains fur trade depended upon Native American labor. The hunters killed bison, beaver, and muskrats, while their Indian wives prepared skins and robes for trade. Native American women were experts in their craft, spending three days on each bison hide. In return for their wares, Plains tribes received American and European commodities, including alcohol, blankets, and cutlery. They also contracted smallpox.

In 1823, William Ashley suffered a number of setbacks on a trapping expedition up the Missouri. Two boats carrying $20,000 worth of provisions were lost on the river, while Arikara Indians, armed with British rifles, attacked his party. Ashley duly shifted his attention westward, toward the Rocky Mountains. Upon reaching mountainous terrain, his expeditionary force split up into smaller brigades to hunt for beaver, later regrouping at a rendezvous site on the banks of the Green River. Supplies were hastened from St. Louis. The "brigade-rendezvous" system brought early success, with Ashley accumulating furs worth in excess of $50,000. Ashley then sold his assets to three experienced trappers, Jedediah Smith, David Jackson, and William Sublette. For four years, Smith, Jackson, and Sublette supervised trapping operations in the Rockies. In 1830 they sold out to the Rocky Mountain Fur Company, an association managed by several veteran trappers. The lure of quick riches enticed Americans, Irish, Portuguese, French, and Canadians to the Rockies. "Free trappers" operated independently, selling their furs to the highest bidder. Others were outfitted by a company on a credit basis or worked as *engagés* with a fixed wage. Trappers combed the Rockies, laying traps in fall and spring when beavers sported their thickest coats. When beaver ponds iced over in November, trappers set up winter camps in sheltered valleys. During the summer, "mountain men"

Fur trappers and traders who plied the waters of the upper Missouri River lived perilous lives in which attacks by hostile Indians were frequent occurrences. (North Wind Picture Archives)

attended the annual rendezvous, reveling in its volatile mix of business and pleasure. Trappers, traders, and Native Americans bartered, brawled, drank, and gambled. They also exchanged tips and information regarding mountain terrain. Spending months, often years, in the Rockies, mountain men developed keen instincts for survival. Jim Bridger claimed that he could "smell his way where he could not see it" (ibid.). American trappers relied upon the advice given them by local Indians and often married Native American women who acted as mediators between the white and native communities. Their wilderness craft and manner of living situated mountain men outside the traditional confines of American society, and trappers were duly tagged the "white Indians" of the West.

The fur trade in the Rockies collapsed during the 1830s, as a result of the mass extermination of beaver combined with the change in fashion on the streets of New York and Paris from fur-lined to silk headwear. Trappers became guides and traders for immigrant parties moving westward in the 1840s and also scouted terrain for the U.S. Army. Although the fur trade furnished Americans with valuable data regarding land west of the Mississippi, it also cemented an exploitative attitude toward indigenous peoples and animals. Native Americans were bought off with alcohol and encouraged to abandon their traditional customs. In the 1870s and early 1880s, white hunters and settlers inflicted a devastating holocaust on the bison, with little regard for species conservation.

—*John Wills*

See also

Bison; Hudson's Bay Company; Missouri Fur Company; Rendezvous System; Rocky Mountain Fur Company

For Further Reading

Utley, Robert Marshall. 1997. *A Life Wild and Perilous: Mountain Men and the Paths to the Pacific.* New York: Henry Holt; Wishart, David J. 1979. *The Fur Trade of the American West, 1807–1840: A Geographical Synthesis.* London: Croom Helm.

GALLATIN, ALBERT (1761–1849)

In his capacity as U.S. treasurer under Jefferson and Madison, Albert Gallatin helped orchestrate the purchase of Louisiana and was the man chiefly responsible for paying the resulting federal debt.

Emigrating from Geneva, Switzerland, at the age of nineteen, Albert Gallatin might be considered an Eastern frontiersman, though he lived in the region from Boston to Washington during the course of his long life. Eventually settling in western Pennsylvania, Gallatin was an early defender of Western interests and a leader among Democratic-Republicans. Elected to the federal Congress in 1795, Gallatin quickly rose through the ranks of the Republican leadership, thanks to his insightful criticisms of Alexander Hamilton's financial schemes and his being an ardent foe to Federalist politics. He was also a leading defender of Western tax revolts like the Whiskey Rebellion (1794).

Appointed secretary of the treasury in 1802 by Thomas Jefferson, Gallatin served as the principal architect of the Republican "retrenchment and reform" campaign. He levied his chief complaint against Federalist financial policies and Hamilton's insistence that perpetual public debt could be a public blessing. Outlining his views on political economy in *A Sketch of the Finances of the United States* (1796), Gallatin challenged virtually every aspect of Hamiltonian finance. Gallatin proved how Hamilton, far from placing the federal and Revolutionary War debt on the road to extinction, had actually increased public debt about $1 million per year from 1789 to 1795. Undermining Hamilton's reputation for being an economic genius provided a crucial element in eroding Federalist political strength. Once the Republicans gained control of Congress and the presidency in 1800, Gallatin proceeded to implement his own plans for the national economy.

Assisted by John Randolph and Nathaniel Macon in the House, and Wilson Cary Nicholas and John Breckinridge in the Senate, Gallatin pushed through the most ambitious curtailment of federal power and expenditure to date. Some internal taxes were abolished, and federal expenditures suffered under extreme frugality. The military establishment was reduced, and efforts to sell Western land to increase federal revenue were encouraged. Congress began passing specific appropriations rather than the general expenditure bills favored by Federalists. The result was a drastic reduction of public debt and an increased soundness of the country's monetary and economic base. Complicating the success, however, were two unforeseen events. Jefferson's naval war against the Barbary pirates forced Gallatin to increase funding for the War Department and raise tariffs. But the most burdensome event was the purchase of Louisiana from France.

Gallatin always looked favorably at Western expansion, partly because of his attachments to western Pennsylvania and also because of his nationalistic tendencies. But he was well aware that Western war fever would remain intense as long as foreign governments controlled aspects of the Mississippi River. When word came that Napoleon was willing to sell New Orleans, Gallatin strongly encouraged the administration to act in an effort to buy peace for the West. Agreeing with Jefferson and other cabinet members that force was necessary if France or Spain refused peaceful delivery, the normally pacific Gallatin drafted a Senate bill authorizing military operations and pressuring War Department officials to direct troops and supplies to New Orleans.

Gallatin frowned upon the Creole civilization in the territory, seeing them "but one degree above the French West Indians" (Walters, 1957). He insisted that Anglo-Saxon liberties be imposed upon the French, especially trial by jury, freedom of religion, and freedom of the press.

When proposals for purchasing New Orleans first surfaced, few if any Republicans questioned the constitutional power of Congress to make the deal. Initial bills passed Congress with large margins and even garnered substantial Federalist support. Always fearful of providing precedents that might enlarge the scope of federal power, however, President Jefferson was among the first to raise the constitutional issue. Gallatin scoffed at Jefferson's and Levi Lincoln's attempt to "extend" the boundaries of the United States by annexing Louisiana to an existing state or territory. Such tactics could enable the president and Senate to annex "Cuba to Massachusetts or Bengal to Rhode Island" (ibid.). In effect, Gallatin, like his close friend John Randolph, worried that the Jeffersonians, in their effort to preserve a constitutional compact, would aggrandize executive power.

The Louisiana Purchase threatened to derail Gallatin's overriding concern for extinguishing the federal debt. Under the terms of the treaty of cession, the United States agreed to pay France $11,250,000 in 6 percent stock certificates to be redeemed in fifteen years. The remainder of the $15 million would be used to settle the claims of Americans against France. The French government arranged with two banks to handle the transaction: the British House of Baring Brothers and the Dutch Hope and Company. When the United States formally took control of the territory in January 1804, Gallatin turned over one-third of the stock to Alexander Baring. Gallatin then sent the other two-thirds of the certificates to Robert Livingston in Paris. He regretted the low price the two banks paid for the American stock, only 78.5 percent, believing that the price poorly reflected on U.S. public credit. He was also dissatisfied with the large amount expended to settle U.S. claims and the extended period of redemption. Nevertheless, Gallatin quickly formulated a plan to retire the enlarged federal debt as soon as possible. Thanks to a sizable treasury surplus created under Gallatin's frugal leadership, the United States paid more than one-quarter of the purchase price in cash. By increasing debt payments by approximately $1 million dollars per year, and with higher customs revenue from increased Western and foreign trade, Gallatin's plan to liquidate federal debt without increased taxes would have met his initial forecasts had the War of 1812 not intervened. Additional revenue came from Western land sales, which Gallatin strongly favored. He argued that the price of Western lands should be reduced by 25 percent in order to sell them off before Congress gave them away for purposes of patronage. Under Gallatin's financial leadership, the federal debt was reduced by half from 1801 to 1810.

Gallatin ended his treasury career in 1814, when Madison appointed him as a commissioner to negotiate the Treaty of Ghent. He then negotiated a limited commercial treaty with Great Britain in 1815. He served as the U.S. envoy to France from 1815 to 1823 and as minister plenipotentiary to Great Britain from 1826 to 1827. After returning to America, he settled in New York City to become the president of the National Bank of New York in 1831.

—*Carey M. Roberts*

See also

Breckinridge, John; Jefferson, Thomas; Randolph, John

For Further Reading

Ewing, Frank. 1959. *America's Forgotten Statesman: Albert Gallatin.* New York: Vantage Press; Ferguson, E. James, ed. 1967. *Selected Writings of Albert Gallatin.* Indianapolis: Bobbs-Merrill Company; Walters, Raymond, Jr. 1957. *Albert Gallatin: Jeffersonian Financier and Diplomat.* New York: Macmillan Company.

GARDOQUI, DIEGO MARÍA DE (1735–1798)

Although Spanish *encargado de negocios* to the United States (1784–1789) and minister of finance (1792–1795), Gardoqui failed to convince the U.S. government to yield its claims to navigate the Mississippi River and to fix its southern boundary with West Florida at 31 degrees north latitude, which Spain eventually recognized in Pinckney's Treaty (1795).

A scion of the commercial firm of Joseph Gardoqui and Sons who pursued a career in the Ministry of Finance, Gardoqui first defended Spanish claims in North America during the American Revolution. As an emissary of the Foreign Office in negotiations with U.S. commissioners Arthur Lee (1777) and John Jay (1780–1782), Gardoqui arranged for his family's merchant house to serve as the principal conduit for Spanish aid to the U.S. cause. In so doing, he tried unsuccessfully to secure U.S. recognition of Spain's claim of exclusive right to navigate the Mississippi River as consideration for such assistance.

Confusion created by the Treaty of Paris (1783) and rapid U.S. westward expansion threatened Spanish ownership of Louisiana (acquired from France in 1762). Spain opposed a provision in the treaty that granted Americans free use of the Mississippi River from its source to the Gulf of Mexico. Although the agreement remained silent on the limits of West Florida, Spain claimed the same border established by the British in 1764 (the junction of the Mississippi River with the Yazoo), in order to defend New Orleans. To force American acceptance of these claims, Spain closed the river to U.S. commerce in 1784. Later that year, it sent Gardoqui to America hopeful that both commercial inducements and his friendship with Jay, now secretary of state, would preserve Spanish power in North America.

The postwar economic depression in the United States and Gardoqui's craftiness in his dealings with Jay nearly produced a successful mission. In seeking U.S. recognition of its claim of exclusive right to navigate the Mississippi River, the sine qua non of the negotiation, Spain offered the United States most-favored-nation trade with Spanish peninsula ports and the Canary Islands, mediation of U.S.–Barbary pirate difficulties, and forgiveness of the U.S. war debt. Spain also abandoned its territorial claims in the West between the Ohio and Yazoo Rivers and offered to tender its good offices to remove Britain from the Northwest. To obtain Jay's assent, Gardoqui appealed to his vanity through gifts, dinners, entertainment, and constant attention to the secretary's wife.

In exchange for these concessions, Jay agreed to restrain U.S. use of the Mississippi River for twenty-five to thirty years, while reserving the right to navigate it until U.S. power could force Spanish concessions. That produced a firestorm of protest from Southern states and encouraged talk of secession in the West, stemming from the erroneous belief that Jay had forever surrendered the

U.S. right to use the river, in order to benefit Northern commercial interests. Gardoqui tried to save the negotiation by abandoning the Yazoo Line as the northern boundary of West Florida, but Jay realized that he could not muster the two-thirds vote necessary to ratify the agreement. Bowing to his critics, Jay reversed himself, recommending that Congress assert, by force if necessary, the right to navigate the river. He then ended his negotiation with Gardoqui to await the formation of the new federal government.

Once the Jay-Gardoqui talks collapsed, Gardoqui took an active role in the Spanish Conspiracy, an attempt to take advantage of Western discontent to defend Louisiana and West Florida against U.S. expansion. James White, superintendent of Indian affairs in the Southern District, James Sevier and James Robertson, leaders of settlements in the proposed state of Franklin, and John Brown and James Wilkinson of Kentucky each informed Gardoqui that Westerners deemed the right to navigate the Mississippi River as vital to their prosperity, and they were prepared to secede from the United States if their access to the river continued to be denied. Westerners also sought Spanish protection against Indian depredations. Hence, between 1787 and 1789 Gardoqui made overtures to Brown and Wilkinson, promising commercial access to the Mississippi River if Kentucky declared its independence and accepted Spanish protection. Similarly, he offered access to the river and protection against Indians as inducements to settlers in Franklin to leave the United States. He also encouraged efforts by frontier speculators George Morgan and James O'Fallon to establish colonies on both banks of the Mississippi River aligned with Spain. Each of these schemes fell victim to Madrid's vacillations, the manipulations of Wilkinson, and opposition from Esteban Miró, the Spanish governor at New Orleans.

When the Washington administration pressed Spain to resume negotiations in 1793, Foreign Minister Manuel de Godoy directed Gardoqui to discuss the matter with U.S. commissioners William Short and William Carmichael. Gardoqui pursued a policy of evasion and procrastination, hiding behind the Anglo-Spanish alliance against France to retain Louisiana and West Florida. He met the U.S. commissioners at irregular intervals, ridiculed their claims, and purposely delayed his replies to their notes. Meanwhile, he tried to force the Americans to moderate their demands to use the Mississippi River by excluding them from trade between New Orleans, Pensacola, and St. Augustine. He also supported Spanish alliances with the Creek, Choctaw, and Chickasaw Indians to secure a favorable boundary settlement regarding West Florida and thus protect New Orleans.

Changing circumstances in Europe and the United States forced Gardoqui to accept U.S. demands on the river and boundary questions in Pinckney's Treaty (October 1795). A proposed Franco-American assault against Louisiana demonstrated Spain's vulnerability there. Spain's decision to switch alliances during the Wars of the French Revolution and the Jay Mission to Great Britain caused it to fear a possible Anglo-American alliance in which a vengeful Britain would force open the Mississippi River and seize Louisiana. Furthermore, the U.S. government had satisfied Western demands for protection through treaties with the Creeks and Cherokees and several successful military campaigns, thus winning Western allegiance to the Union. Gardoqui's failure to secure a mutual guarantee of possessions in Pinckney's Treaty set the stage for the retrocession of Louisiana to France in 1800.

—Dean Fafoutis

See also

Genêt, Edmond Charles; Godoy, Manuel de; Jay-Gardoqui Negotiations; Jay's Treaty; Paris, Treaty of; San Ildefonso, Treaty of; San Lorenzo, Treaty of; West Florida; Wilkinson, James

For Further Reading

Bemis, Samuel Flagg. 1960 [1926]. *Pinckney's Treaty: A Study of America's Advantage from Europe's Distress.* Baltimore: Johns Hopkins Press. Reprint: New Haven: Yale University Press; Cava, María Jesús, y Begoña Cava. 1992. *Diego María de Gardoqui: Un Bilbaino en la Diplomacia del Siglo XVIII.* Bilbao, Spain: Bilbao Bizkaia Kutxa; Marks, Frederick W. 1973. *Independence on Trial: Foreign Affairs and the Making of the Constitution.* Baton Rouge: Louisiana University Press; Whitaker, Arthur Preston. 1962 [1927]. *The Spanish Frontier, 1783–1795: The Westward Movement and Spanish Retreat in the Mississippi Valley.* Lincoln: University of Nebraska Press. Reprint: Gloucester, MA: Peter Smith.

GATEWAY ARCH

The Gateway Arch symbolizes the strategic role that the city of St. Louis played as the "Gateway to the West" in nineteenth-century America. As the starting point for the Lewis and Clark Expedition, the place from which much of the business of the early fur trade was conducted, and the primary entrepôt that linked East and West, St. Louis played a crucial role in the exploration and development of the trans-Mississippi West. For these reasons, St. Louis was the most logical site that the National Park Service could select for establishing the Jefferson National Expansion Memorial. The memorial complex, which was first established in 1935, now consists of the Gateway Arch, the Museum of Westward Expansion, and the Old Courthouse that served St. Louis.

Finnish-born architect Eero Saarinen (1910–1961) designed the arch that would become the signature feature of the St. Louis skyline. Saarinen's design was selected the winner of the 1947–1948 Jefferson National Expansion Memorial Competition. The architect described the historical context of his visionary design when he said: "The major concern . . . was to create a monument which would have lasting significance and would be a landmark of our time . . . . Neither an obelisk nor a rectangular box nor a dome seemed right on this site or for this purpose. But here, at the edge of the Mississippi River, a great arch did seem right" (Brown, 1980).

Construction of the Gateway Arch began on February 12, 1963, and the monument was completed on October 28, 1965. On July 24, 1967, the facility was opened to the public when the north tram became operational; the south tram was completed the following year. The project was completed at a cost of $13 million. Of that amount, $11 million was required for construction of the arch, and $2 million was required for constructing the tram system. Costs for the facility were shared between the federal government and the state of Missouri.

The 630-foot-tall monument rises from an urban park along the banks of the Mississippi River. Seen from a distance, the ribbon of stainless-steel dominates the city skyline as an ever-present reminder of the historic role that St. Louis played in the nation's development. The Gateway Arch, with its inverted catenary design, is a sublime architectural expression of such simplicity and modernity that it seems avant-garde even by twenty-first century standards.

Thousands of visitors ascend the Gateway Arch each year to experience the panoramic view from the apex of the memorial. In a symbolic sense, the sweeping landscape set before them represents a before and after vision of America as defined by the Louisiana Purchase.

—Junius P. Rodriguez

For Further Reading

Brown, Sharon. 1980. "Jefferson National Expansion Memorial: The 1947–48 Competition." *Gateway Heritage: The Quarterly Journal of the Missouri Historical Society* 1, no. 3: 40–48; Brown, Sharon. 1985. *Administrative History: Jefferson National Expansion Memorial National Historic Site.* St. Louis: National Park Service, Jefferson National Expansion Memorial National Historic Site.

GAYOSO DE LEMOS, MANUEL (1747–1799)

Serving as governor of the Natchez District (1789–1797) and governor of Louisiana and West Florida (1797–1799), Manuel Gayoso de Lemos strengthened defenses in Louisiana and helped Spain protect its North American possessions from encroachment by the United States.

Gayoso was chosen to govern the Natchez District and, subsequently, all of Louisiana and West Florida. The Spanish Crown chose him for his diplomatic skill, his knowledge of military matters, and his fluency in French and English. Those assets served him well in diverse and contested late-eighteenth-century Louisiana.

Spain had seized Natchez from the British in 1779 during the American Revolution. Natchez had a predominantly Anglo-American population, and emigration from the United States continued in the region under Spanish rule. When Gayoso arrived at Natchez in 1789, the district bordered the United States, and Spanish fears of U.S. expansion were high. In 1781, Natchez settlers had revolted against Spain. Their revolt was unsuccessful, but Gayoso faced the difficult task of keeping them satisfied under Spanish rule. With Spanish resources strained to protect this large new empire, which stretched from New Orleans to Florida, the Natchez command had an insufficient budget and only a small number of soldiers. Recognizing the impracticability of governing by force, Gayoso gained the loyalty of the Anglo-American residents of Natchez with generous land grants and a reputation for fairness and openness. He forged family ties with Anglo-American residents by marrying into a U.S. family in Natchez. He made improvements to the city of Natchez in sanitation, created public spaces, and built roads to improve communications in the district.

Gayoso strongly opposed the Treaty of San Lorenzo (1795), in which Spain ceded to the United States its lands above 31 degrees north latitude and east of the Mississippi River, an area that included Natchez. He rightly predicted that the loss of that region (which became the states of Mississippi and Alabama) would not appease the expansionist United States but would instead foreshadow Spain's loss of Louisiana. But the Spanish Crown proceeded with the treaty and appointed Gayoso the seventh governor of Louisiana. As governor, Gayoso supervised the evacuation of West Florida and its forts to the United States.

In both gubernatorial positions, Gayoso strengthened Spanish defenses in Louisiana. As governor of the Natchez District, he advocated the Spanish plan of building new posts and reinforcing old ones up and down the Mississippi River and on an east-west line from Florida to the Texas border. He helped to design and build Nogales in what is now Mississippi. For his work on San Fernando de las Barrancas on Chickasaw Bluffs near the present-day Memphis, he was promoted to brigadier general in 1795. He rebuilt Natchez into a strong post, and to support Spanish troops stretched thinly across Louisiana and West Florida, Gayoso built up local militias. He recruited and conspired with Anglo-Americans in the western United States, including James Wilkinson, attempting to draw them into the Spanish sphere. As governor of Louisiana, Gayoso adjusted Spanish defenses to the reality of the Treaty of San Lorenzo. He strengthened forts, such as Baton Rouge and St. Louis, which sat on the new border, and he founded new settlements along that border. The governor reinforced the crews of the Spanish squadron patrolling the Mississippi River. He continually lobbied the Crown for increased funding, arguing for the importance of Louisiana in Spanish defenses in the Americas.

Gayoso's understanding of Indian diplomacy was an asset to Spanish control over Louisiana. Indian alliances were vital to protecting the region from the United States, and the governor cultivated a reputation for honesty and reasonableness among the tribes of Louisiana and West Florida. He understood the importance of careful diplomacy and generous presents to Indian alliances. He gained the allegiance of many Southeastern Indian peoples by promising them that the Spanish would not allow settlers to move onto their lands, while making it clear that the United States did not prevent its people from taking Indian lands. He negotiated peace treaties between the Spanish and various Indian tribes, as well as among tribes. His most important treaty was the Treaty of Nogales (1793), which allied Spain with the Chickasaw, Creek, Tallapoosa, Alibamon, Cherokee, and Choctaw.

During his career in Louisiana, Gayoso proved himself to be a capable administrator who strengthened colonial defenses in the waning years of Spanish control. Governor Gayoso died in New Orleans of a fever in 1799.

—Kathleen DuVal

For Further Reading

Holmes, Jack D. L. 1965. *Gayoso: The Life of a Spanish Governor in the Mississippi Valley, 1789–1799.* Baton Rouge: Louisiana State University Press.

An undiplomatic envoy, French minister Edmond Charles Genêt unceremoniously attempted to foment unrest that would wrest Louisiana away from Spanish control in the 1790s.

GENÊT, EDMOND CHARLES (1763–1834)

In November 1792, the government of the French republic, then under the control of the Girondin faction, named Edmond Charles Genêt to be the new French minister to the United States. Genêt received his official instructions, obtained his credentials, and departed for his new assignment, arriving in the United States in April 1793. What few Americans realized at the time was that a major charge assigned to the new young minister was to destabilize the Spanish colony of Louisiana so that it could be conquered by France.

Genêt's diplomatic sojourn in the United States would not be a pleasant one. Although the brash Frenchman's youth and inexperience might explain some aspects of his curious behavior, his inauspicious statements and calculated actions reflected a true commitment on his part to the republican ideology manifested in the principles of liberty, equality, and fraternity that had inspired the French Revolution. Rather than following diplomatic protocol and traveling to New York to present his credentials to appropriate individuals at the national capital, Genêt landed instead at Charleston, South Carolina, where he immediately took his ideological message directly to the American people.

Hailed as "Citizen Genêt," a representative of a free people who, like the Americans, had thrown off the shackles of monarchial rule and embraced republicanism, the new French minister was welcomed and feted in all of the towns that he visited on his journey northward from Charleston to New York. Sparing no one from his vitriol, Genêt chastised the Washington administration for its Proclamation of Neutrality (1793) and its failure to live up to the principles outlined in the Treaty of Alliance (1778) between the United States and France. Playing upon the sympathetic reminder that France had come to the aid of the American people during their recent struggle for independence, Genêt used every speaking opportunity to remind his U.S. audiences that it was still possible to return the favor.

In this endeavor, Genêt proved to be an undiplomatic emissary. He openly recruited U.S. citizens to become mercenaries who would fight in behalf of the French republic. He sought, and received, financial contributions that were used to outfit privateers that would sail from U.S. ports and engage British merchant vessels on the high seas. In one particular case, the French were allowed to bring a captured British brig, the *Little Sarah,* into port at Philadelphia, where the vessel was refitted, renamed *La Petite Démocrate,* and allowed back out to sea under the French tricolor.

Additionally, Citizen Genêt never lost sight of his primary goal—"to germinate the principles of liberty and independence in Louisiana"—so that the French republic might reacquire its former colonial possession and begin the process of re-creating a French North American empire (DeConde, 1976). To this end, Genêt had conversations with influential Americans who knew of the dissatisfaction present among Americans living in the trans-Appalachian West. Spain's refusal to allow Americans the right to use the Mississippi River and to trade their goods at New Orleans had created a furor among Western pioneers. Many of these settlers believed that they would have greater economic opportunities if the French, rather than the Spanish, possessed Louisiana.

The danger to Louisiana was more real than one might imagine. George Rogers Clark, the American military hero who had captured Vincennes during the American Revolution, informed Genêt that he could capture Louisiana with a force of twelve hundred men, who would be supported by Indian allies. At New Orleans, the Spanish governor of Louisiana, Baron de Carondelet, feared the French republic for its designs on Louisiana and pondered how he might defend the colony from such an attack if Genêt's recruiting efforts proved successful. Months later, after the threat of such an invasion had passed, Carondelet would write that "Genêt's coup against Louisiana . . . failed only because of lack of money" (ibid.).

U.S. politicians were vociferous in their calls for the French minister's recall. President George Washington believed that Genêt had acted improperly, and leading Federalists such as Alexander Hamilton, John Jay, and Rufus King found the minister's indiscretions inexcusable. Even Thomas Jefferson, the most pro-French member of the Washington cabinet, could not defend the actions that Genêt had taken, and he joined the chorus calling for Genêt's recall.

In the meantime, the ever-changing political situation in France had once again taken a new turn. By June 1793, the Jacobins had come to power in France, and Genêt's faction, the Girondins, were defeated and largely eliminated during the Reign of Terror. It became clear to officials in the United States that Genêt would face almost certain death if he were to return to France, and the thought of forcing the young diplomat to such a fate was unappealing to the sensibilities of the Washington administration.

Stripped of his diplomatic credentials by the new French government, Genêt was allowed to remain in the United States, where he eventually became an American citizen. He married the daughter of New York governor George Clinton and settled into life as a farmer in New York state.

—Junius P. Rodriguez

See also
Jay-Gardoqui Negotiations
For Further Reading
DeConde, Alexander. 1976. *This Affair of Louisiana.* New York: Charles Scribner's Sons.

GIBSON, FORT

Fort Gibson was established as Cantonment Gibson by Colonel Matthew Arbuckle in 1824. Following 1817, army troops stationed at Fort Smith in the Arkansas Territory had tried to end conflict between the Osage and the Western Cherokee in eastern Indian Territory. The troops also worked to protect the white and Indian settlers in western Arkansas. In 1824, Colonel Arbuckle, the commander at Fort Smith, received orders to move his garrison farther west. He established Cantonment Gibson on the banks of the Grand (or Neosho) River, three miles above its confluence with the Arkansas River. The new post was named after the commissary-general of the U.S. Army, Colonel George Gibson.

Fort Gibson became a key post in the resettlement of the Eastern tribes, leading some historians to call it the "Terminal on the Trail of Tears." A few members of the Creek nation came West voluntarily in the late 1820s. In a treaty signed in 1828, the Western Cherokee agreed to move farther west in exchange for their lands in western Arkansas. Fort Gibson was on the western edge of the new Cherokee lands.

In 1831, Cantonment Gibson became the headquarters of the Seventh Infantry. Cavalry troops were added to the garrison in 1832, and the post was renamed Fort Gibson. In 1833 the Regiment of Dragoons moved to the fort, and in 1834, Fort Gibson became headquarters of the southwestern frontier.

The forced removal of the Five Civilized Tribes from their homelands in the southeastern United States was the result of the Indian Removal Act of 1830. To prepare the region for the immigration of the Five Civilized Tribes, two expeditions set out from Fort Gibson to pacify the Plains tribes. The Expedition of 1832 traveled as far west as present-day Oklahoma City and did not encounter any Plains Indians. The Dragoon Expedition of 1834 was only slightly more successful, having reached the North Fork of the Red River, encountering both the Comanche and the Wichita. More than half of the expedition's members became ill with malaria. The noted Western artist George Catlin accompanied the expedition in 1834.

Fort Gibson served as a supply post for newly arrived

Indians from the East. The new arrivals were given rations, supplies, and equipment. During the late 1830s and into the 1840s, thousands of Creek, Cherokee, and Seminole stopped at Fort Gibson before moving into the Indian Territory.

In 1841, General Arbuckle was transferred from Fort Gibson, marking the end of the post's role in the army's mission of resettling and protecting the tribes removed from the East. Departmental headquarters were removed from the fort, but it continued as an active military post until 1857, when troops were withdrawn and the buildings and land were granted to the Cherokee Nation.

The fort was reactivated in 1863 and was the Union Army's key post in Indian Territory during the Civil War. A large Confederate force moved on the fort in 1863, but it was stopped by Union forces at the Battle of Honey Springs, near present-day Checotah, Oklahoma. During the Civil War, African Creeks and Seminoles of the First Indian Home Guard Regiment of the Indian Brigade under the command of William A. Phillips occupied Fort Gibson. These former slaves and free blacks from the Creek and Seminole Nations were the first African American soldiers mustered in the Union army and the first to participate in combat during the Civil War.

At the end of the Civil War, the U.S. Army decided to keep a contingent of black soldiers in the regular army. The Tenth U.S. Cavalry, the "Buffalo Soldiers," were stationed at Fort Gibson. The primary job of this unit was to protect horse and cattle herds from rustlers in Indian Territory. Soldiers from Fort Gibson rebuilt Fort Arbuckle and established Fort Sill in order to provide the army with more effective outposts in the West.

In 1871 the troops at Fort Gibson were withdrawn and the post was redesignated a commissary supply post. The fort was reactivated in 1872 to combat the problem of outlaws and squatters who traveled to the region on the new railroads. Troops remained at Fort Gibson through most of the 1870s and 1880s to help keep order and protect against intrusions on Indian lands. In 1890 the army recognized that maintaining a post in eastern Indian Territory was no longer necessary, and it closed Fort Gibson for the last time.

—*John David Rausch, Jr.*

See also

Buffalo Soldiers; Catlin, George; Indian Removal; Indian Territory; Osage; Smith, Fort; Towson, Fort; Washita, Fort

For Further Reading

Agnew, Brad. 1980. *Fort Gibson: Terminal on the Trail of Tears.* Norman: University of Oklahoma Press; Corbett, William P. 1982. "Rifles and Ruts: Army Road Builders in Indian Territory." *Chronicles of Oklahoma* 60: 294–309; Holcomb, Raymond L. 1990. *The Civil War in the Western Choctaw Nation, 1861–1865.* Atoka, OK: Atoka County Historical Society; West, C. W. 1974. *Fort Gibson: Gateway to the West.* Muskogee, OK: Muscogee Publishing Company.

GODOY, MANUEL DE (1767–1851)

Manuel de Godoy, Queen Maria Luisa's favorite courtier, rose through the ranks of the Spanish army to become the chief minister of Spain between 1792 and 1808 (except for a brief interlude between 1798 and 1801). Godoy reversed the policy to colonize North America that his predecessors advanced, scaled back Spanish expansion in the indefensible Mississippi River Valley, and granted the United States substantial concessions in that region as set forth in the Treaty of San Lorenzo (1795). All of these actions ultimately enabled the United States to purchase Louisiana from the French in 1803.

As a result of its defeat in the French and Indian War (1755–1763), France lost the territory that the French explorer La Salle had called Louisiana. The British acquired the territory east of the Mississippi in the Treaty of Paris (1763) while the Spanish had earlier received New Orleans and the territory west of the Mississippi in the Treaty of Fontainebleau (1762). In spite of their losses, the French always wanted to regain control of the territory they had ceded to Spain.

Godoy had concluded early that the Louisiana Territory was worthless and could not be easily defended against potential aggressors. The cost of defending the territory was more than the Spanish could afford since even the administration of Louisiana was becoming a serious drain on their national treasury. With fewer than fifty thousand inhabitants, the territory did not produce much revenue, especially because of the illegal smuggling activities carried on by Americans and others. New Orleans, the most important city in the territory, had become a seat of international intrigue. Additionally, possession of the territory embroiled Spain in serious disputes with Great Britain over fur trade in the Missouri River Valley and with the United States over navigation rights along the Mississippi. Therefore, as early as 1794 the Spanish court decided that it would not attempt to defend the Louisiana Territory against a great-power invasion. Meanwhile, Godoy hoped to use Louisiana as an aid in diplomacy and to gain from it when Spain finally decided to part with it.

This change in Spanish outlook was reflected in the Treaty of San Lorenzo (1795) between the United States and Spain. With the treaty, Godoy offered the United States significant concessions with respect to Louisiana and Florida. Previously Spain had claimed exclusive right of navigation on the lower Mississippi and sovereignty on the east bank of the river. The treaty allowed Americans free navigation on the entire Mississippi and the right of deposit at New Orleans. Godoy's dealings with the United States were shaped at least in part by European developments. In 1793 Spain had joined Great Britain in a war against the French republic. Spain fared badly in the war and was forced to sign the Treaty of Basel with

France. The next year, when Spain joined France against Britain, the British navy cut off communications between Spain and its colonial possessions in the Western Hemisphere, giving the Americans an opportunity to trade with Spanish colonies.

If Godoy could not befriend the United States, he hoped to at least neutralize it. That was why he resisted all French attempts to regain Louisiana so that America would not join Britain in attacking Spanish possessions. Nevertheless, a Spanish attempt to delay the implementation of the Treaty of San Lorenzo with America caused concern and suspicion in the United States regarding Godoy's motives in signing it.

Once he had signed the treaty with the Americans, Godoy was ready to part with the Louisiana Territory. The treaty, however, did not earn the friendship of the United States. Rather, the right of navigation and deposit gave rise to new disputes with the Americans. Therefore, Godoy sought to keep secret the negotiations with the French for the retrocession of Louisiana. He was cautious lest the Americans, sensing trouble, would seize the territory with or without British help before he could hand over the territory and the French had time to defend it. Although he signed a treaty with the French in 1796, the Directory refused to endorse it, saying that their negotiators offered to pay too much for the area. Negotiations for the sale continued until 1798. Meanwhile, Godoy changed his plans and withdrew from the negotiations. Later, with the change in government in Paris, negotiations picked up speed and by the Treaty of San Ildefonso (1800) Spain agreed to return Louisiana to France with the understanding that the French would not transfer the territory to another power.

Contrary to the understanding with Spain, France decided to sell Louisiana to the United States. The sale disappointed the Spanish and caused serious concern in Madrid for the safety and security of Florida and New Spain. The Spaniards rightly concluded that the cession would only increase the desire for expansion in the United States. They were concerned that it would be difficult to defend Mexico against American expansion. Nevertheless, although Godoy was angry about Napoleon's decision to sell, he did not think it wise to precipitate a crisis with the United States over the issue. He was concerned that it would cause a break with France and a war with the United States. He hoped to strengthen eastern frontier defenses with military colonies supported by the Spanish navy. Unfortunately for Godoy, Spain was dragged into an Anglo-French war yet again, its navy was devastated at Trafalgar, its royal dynasty was overthrown by Napoleon I, and Godoy had to go into exile in France, where he died in 1851. However, the loss of Louisiana was in keeping with Godoy's policy of strategic withdrawal from the indefensible Mississippi River Valley.

—George Thadathil

For Further Reading

Chastenet, Jacques. 1953. *Godoy: Master of Spain, 1792–1808*. London: Batchworth Press; DeConde, Alexander. 1976. *This Affair of Louisiana*. New York: Charles Scribner's Sons; Whitaker, Arthur Preston. 1949. *The Mississippi Question, 1795–1803: A Study in Trade, Politics and Diplomacy*. New York: Foreign Policy Association.

GRADUATION ACT (1854)

Passed in order to increase land sales in the West and to appease supporters of a fair price for poor-quality land, this act established a gradually descending price scale for less desirable public lands. The law lowered the price of land that remained unsold for ten years from the minimum of $1.25 to a fixed price of $1.00 per acre. After each additional five-year period, the price of the land would drop another 25 cents. The lowest level permitted was 12.5 cents per acre, after thirty years. Excluded from being purchased under this act were lands granted to the states for railroads or other internal improvements, or mineral lands. The act also stipulated that the buyer had to swear that the land would be used for settlement and cultivation, or for the use of a joining farm or plantation owned by the buyer, and that the buyer had not acquired under the act, or from previous purchases, more than 320 acres from the government.

Although graduation was an important issue in early national discussions over the sale of public lands, the topic had faded from consideration until 1820. That year, Senator Henry Johnson of Louisiana presented a motion before the Senate that provided for a reduction in prices based upon the length of time that land was on the market. From then on, numerous proposals were made in Congress to implement a graduated price scale for public lands. In addition, in 1826, 1832, and 1836, the House Committee on Public Lands recommended reducing prices. The issue also received support from Presidents Jackson, Van Buren, and Polk. Despite that approval, the issue faced strong sectional opposition and met repeated failures.

Proponents like Senator Thomas Hart Benton of Missouri believed that requiring the minimum price of $1.25 per acre was unjust for second- or third-rate lands. Advocates proposed that the price of land be dictated by its quality. Nearly every state that included public lands, except Michigan, supported graduated land prices. In addition to the Western states, the former frontier states of Ohio, Indiana, Illinois, Alabama, Mississippi, and Missouri especially favored graduation because, with the opening of more desirable land farther West, less attractive and marginal lands in these states went unsold and untaxed. Individual states saw the measure as a way to increase revenues, to lower the tax burden on their citizens, and to increase land use. In January 1854, Representative Williamson R. W. Cobb of Alabama introduced the bill that finally became the Graduation Act. It passed the House by a vote of 83 to 64 on April 14, and the Senate by viva voce vote on August 4, 1854. Although a popular matter, graduation drew criticism from many who believed that it sabotaged the passage of free land legislation in Congress.

A considerable land rush resulted from the passage of the act, which led to many problems that hampered the administration and enforcement of the law. The sheer number of applicants greatly overtaxed the capacity of local land offices, and, as with any massive land sale, fraud was common. Another major problem involved the classification of land. In several instances different parts of the same township or county offered land for sale at different times, which made it difficult for officials to arrive at the proper price. Also, as many opponents had feared, revenues were much lower than expected because the majority of the land purchased sold at 12.5 and 25 cents per acre. That price range represented more than 50 percent of all the land available under the act and accounted for 68 percent of the total land sold. More land sold for 12.5 cents an acre than was sold at the other prices combined. The act generated $8,207,000, for an average of about 32 cents per acre. Also, the percentage of land actually purchased was much lower than was available. Although some states did sell a high percentage of their designated lands—particularly Ohio (98 percent), Indiana (81 percent), Illinois (67 percent), and Missouri (64 percent)—the majority sold approximately 20 to 30 percent or less.

Despite these problems and shortcomings, the act was important because under it some states sold large amounts of land rather quickly. Arkansas sold the most land, 14,212,610 acres. Alabama followed with 14,039,502 acres, and the next largest seller was Missouri, with 13,850,020. Effectively replaced by the Homestead Act (1862), the Graduation Act (1854) allowed for the sale of 77,561,007 acres of land in eight years.

—Peter S. Genovese, Jr.

For Further Reading

Dick, Everett. 1970. *The Lure of the Land: A Social History of the Public Lands from the Articles of Confederation to the New Deal.* Lincoln: University of Nebraska Press; Gates, Paul W. 1979. *History of Public Land Law Development.* New York: Arno Press; Hibbard, Benjamin H. 1965. *A History of the Public Land Policies.* Madison: University of Wisconsin Press; Stephenson, George M. 1967. *The Political History of the Public Lands from 1840 to 1862: From Pre-emption to Homestead.* New York: Russell and Russell.

GREAT AMERICAN DESERT

The phrase "Great American Desert" was the nineteenth-century designation for the semiarid area between the 100 degree west meridian and the Rocky Mountains. Westward from a line varying from the 98 degree west to the 105 degree west meridian (for convenience, approximating the 100 degree west meridian) to the lee side of the western Rocky Mountains lies an area where the annual rainfall averages less than twenty inches. The area is now known as the Great Plains. For nineteenth-century Americans, however, coming out of the Eastern woodlands and the fertile prairies, this area appeared to be aptly named the Great American Desert.

When President Thomas Jefferson purchased the Louisiana Territory in 1803, he wanted the port of New Orleans and regarded upper Louisiana as a wasteland: sandy with a salt mountain 180 miles long and forty-five wide. The successful conclusion of Lewis and Clark's exploration three years later reinforced the belief in the area's desolation; the expedition's journalists frequently commented about the treeless and seemingly arid land with rivers mere trickles vanishing into the sand. Zebulon Pike crossed on the latitude of Kansas from the Missouri to the Rockies in 1806 and reported large areas of sandy desert blown into dunes, an area too dry for timber or for farming. Stephen H. Long crossed at the Nebraska level, and his expedition provided the map that formally named the Great Desert and defined it as incorporating the drainage basin of the Missouri, Arkansas, and a large area of western Kansas and Nebraska. U.S. maps kept this designation as late as 1870.

Initially the desert appeared to be a natural limit to the expansionist urge of Americans, and Washington Irving (after reading the reports of John Jacob Astor's agents) expected it to become a badlands inhabited by outlaws and savages—the dregs of society. Although travel over the Oregon, California, and Mormon trails exposed many people to the terrain, the idea persisted that the land was worthless. In the 1850s, Americans edged across the Missouri River and established river towns for trade across the desert—for instance, from Independence to Santa Fe. The farming frontier moved west, and the desert line moved to the 99 degree west meridian, two hundred miles to the west, by 1855. Still, those exploring railroad routes assumed that the railroad was necessary to get from the Missouri Valley across the desert and mountains to California. This assumption persisted into the 1860s. Encouraged by the Homestead Act (1862) and later railroad land grants, farmers ventured farther west onto the desert.

U.S. Geographical and Geological Survey director Ferdinand Hayden in 1867 expected that settlement would reduce prairie fires, decreased fires would increase the number of trees, and more trees would bring more rain. And into the 1870s the rainfall did increase, in some areas hitting an ample thirty-eight inches. Around 1880 immigrants moved into the Western areas of Nebraska, across the 100 degree west meridian. Then nature's cycle brought drought in the 1890s. Many settlers lost everything. Overcoming the desert and peopling the Plains were not easy.

In the twentieth century, the Great American Desert became the world's breadbasket. Harvesters moved from south to north, from Mexico to Canada, bringing in the crops. Making agriculture practical required government assistance through land sales or giveaways and changed laws. Dryland agriculture required larger acreages; a Nebraska family required at least one hundred cattle and one thousand acres plus the use of new technology and techniques including windmills, dry farming, and irrigation. The 100 degree west meridian remains the boundary between rainbelt and semiarid farming and grazing practices.

—J. Herschel Barnhill

See also

Dry Farming; Long (Stephen H.) Expedition

For Further Reading

Billington, Ray Allen. 1974. *Westward Expansion: A History of the American Frontier.* New York: Macmillan Publishing Company; Dick, Everett. 1975. *Conquering the Great American Desert: Nebraska.* Omaha: Nebraska State Historical Society; Merk, Frederick. 1978. *History of the Westward Movement.* New York: Borzoi Books; Webb, Walter Prescott. 1972. *The Great Plains.* New York: Grosset and Dunlap.

GRIFFIN, THOMAS (1773–1837)

A one-term representative to Congress from the state of Virginia, Thomas Griffin, a Federalist, opposed presidential and Senate authority to regulate commerce by granting France and Spain preferential treatment at the port of New Orleans by the terms of the treaty approving the Louisiana Purchase.

Thomas Griffin was a native Virginian from Yorktown, a traditionally strong Federalist region, in the eastern district of the state. He studied law, was admitted to the bar, and represented eastern Virginia in the state legislature. He was also appointed a local jurist but was elected to the Eighth Congress as a Federalist in 1803. Griffin served only one term, and his congressional career included few highlights. He was defeated when he ran for a second term on account of low voter turnout in the historically Federalist eastern shore.

On October 25, 1803, the House of Representatives met as a committee of the whole to discuss and vote on President Thomas Jefferson's message about the treaty centering on the Louisiana cession. Virginia's John Randolph of Roanoke carried the administration's banner favoring approval of the treaty and answered any and all opposing criticisms and charges. Connecticut's staunch Federalist Roger Griswold predictably led his party's opposition, but others in the House leveled serious concerns as well. One of those was Griffin, who questioned the authority of the president and Senate to make commercial treaties, as outlined in the seventh article of the treaty. Citing the Constitution, Griffin charged that the regulation of commerce was granted to the House, and thus the treaty was unconstitutional. Griffin and fellow Virginian Joseph Lewis, Jr., concluded that France and Spain would receive preferential treatment by having their duties for goods deposited at New Orleans reduced from 50 cents to 6 cents per ton, an obvious infringement on the rights of other states as stated in Article One, Section Nine of the U.S. Constitution. At this point Griffin argued against approval of the resolution approving the treaty and concluded by expressing his fear "that this Eden of the New World would prove a cemetery for the bodies of our citizens" (U.S. Congress, 1852). At the end of the day, Griffin and Lewis joined twenty-five other representatives, including fellow Virginians Thomas Lewis and James Stephenson and many Northern Federalists, in voting against the treaty resolution; yet the resolution easily carried, with ninety affirmative votes.

Griffin followed the lead of Joseph Lewis, Jr., and Federalists in the Senate over the charge of preferential treatment for ships of foreign nations at the port of New Orleans, but his contention that the House alone had the right to regulate commerce and that the president and Senate were infringing on a House issue was an idea that he himself had conceived. Griffin's only other significant contribution to House deliberations occurred over the impeachment of Judge Samuel Chase, and his brief congressional career is marked by little else. His objections to an infringement on House powers was obviously not economically motivated, as, unlike many of his Republican colleagues in the House, Griffin was not a planter but a lawyer. His motivation was political: he was one of a handful of Federalists who consistently voted against the administration's lead.

Griffin presented the House with a sound question of constitutionality, yet Randolph elected to ignore the issue that Griffin had raised. Also speaking in behalf of the administration, Samuel Mitchell of New York did refer to the arguments raised by Lewis and Griffin, but only with a derogatory comment; he concluded "that the apprehension and alarm expressed by the two gentlemen from Virginia were wholly unfounded" (ibid.). Like virtually all other members of Congress and historians of the constitutional issue surrounding the Louisiana Purchase, Randolph and Mitchell simply ignored Griffin's question of the House's proprietary right over commercial legislation. Historians do agree, however, that the actions and arguments of Griffin and other Federalists in Virginia sealed their re-election fate.

A survivor, after his one term Griffin returned to Yorktown, where he served on the bench in various courts until 1820. He was an officer in the War of 1812 and was twice elected to the Virginia House of Delegates (1819–1823 and 1827–1830). He died in Yorktown in 1837.

—Boyd Childress

For Further Reading
United States Congress. 1852. *The Debates and Proceedings in the Congress of the United States.* Eighth Congress, First session. Washington, DC: Gales and Seaton.

GRISWOLD, ROGER (1762–1812)

Declaring the Louisiana Purchase Treaty with France not only "void, but absurd," Roger Griswold, a Federalist representative from Connecticut, did everything in his power to stop the American acquisition. A seasoned legislator, he first argued upon procedural grounds, then ultimately attacked the treaty's constitutionality. In the process, he played a key role in the Federalist onslaught against the purchase. Moreover, his arguments characterized the Federalist reversal on the broad construction of the U.S. Constitution.

President Jefferson had little difficulty steering the purchase through the Senate. On October 20, 1803, the senior legislative branch voted 24 to 7 in favor of the treaty. The House of Representatives was another matter. When Republicans introduced a bill to provide for payment, occupation, and governing of the Louisiana Territory, Federalists threw up roadblocks. Roger Griswold devised the strategy.

Introducing a resolution on October 24, Griswold requested that the president provide the House with the Treaty of San Ildefonso (1800), which ceded the territory from Spain to France, as well as proof of such a cession, correspondence concerning Spain's view of the French sale to the United States, and any title that affirmed rightful possession of Louisiana by the United States. Griswold maintained that such information was necessary for the House to legislate properly on the bill, for if the acquisition were not official and "no new territory or subjects were acquired, it was perfectly idle to pass even temporary laws for the occupation of the one, or the government of the other" (U.S. Congress, 1851).

Griswold's preliminary strategy was simple. It was unclear whether Spain had actually ceded the land to France. It was therefore useless for the House to pass any legislation until that question was resolved. Such an argument was, however, merely the beginning of Griswold's attack. In answer to Republican criticism of his position, Griswold hinted at another problem. Reiterating once again the uncertainty of the treaty, he added that if it were "fairly and constitutionally made" (ibid.), the House was bound to execute it. Griswold used exactly the same language one more time in his speech, but he did not elaborate on the issue of constitutionality. He instead stuck to his original argument concerning the validity of the cession.

It is not entirely clear why Griswold attempted to stall the House bill rather than attack directly the constitutionality of the purchase. John Randolph, a Republican representative from Virginia, addressed this very issue: "Whilst he acknowledges an indispensable political obligation to carry treaties into effect," charged Randolph of Griswold, his only purpose is to "discover some real or apparent obscurity, should no Constitutional objections present themselves" (ibid.).

Perhaps Griswold was simply building steam. Whatever his purpose, it did not take long to unleash his full constitutional arguments. Although acknowledging the importance of American rights in regard to the use of the Mississippi River, Griswold declared: "I can never consent to secure this object, however desirable and important, by means which shall set at defiance the Constitution of my country." And if that is the case, he continued, Congress is "obliged, by their duty and their oath, to support the Constitution, and to refuse their assent to laws which go to infringe this great charter of our Government" (ibid.).

After expounding upon constitutionally strict construction, Griswold delivered his specific objection to the treaty: "The framers of the Constitution never intended that a power should reside in the President and Senate to form a treaty by which a foreign nation and the people shall be incorporated into the Union, and that this treaty, so far as it stipulates for such an incorporation, is void." Viewing the Constitution as a contract, Griswold insisted that adding new members without the individual consent of each original state was a "violation of the principles on which that compact was formed" (ibid.).

Griswold's ultimate concern was New England's diminishing power in the government. The addition of new Western, Republican states hurt the Federalists. "It is highly probable," he contended, that New England "would never have consented to such a connexion, if a new world was to be thrown into the scale, to weigh down the influence which they [New England states] might otherwise possess in the national councils" (ibid.).

Griswold's final constitutional argument focused on particulars of the House bill to occupy and govern the territory. The second section provided the president with full civil, military, and judicial authority. "I do not," declared Griswold, "understand that, according to the Constitution, we have a right to make him legislator, judge, and executive, in any territory belonging to the United States" (ibid.).

The arguments made by Federalists against the Louisiana Purchase Treaty were ultimately ineffective. Firmly in command of Congress, Republicans pushed the measure through. Still, Griswold and his fellow New Englanders had raised important constitutional discrepancies about a plan proposed by a president who prided himself on strict construction. The constitutional role reversal between the two parties could not have been more complete.

—*Matthew S. Warshauer*

See also
Federalist Party
For Further Reading
Farnham, Thomas J. 1965. "The Federal-State Issue and the Louisiana Purchase." *Louisiana History* 6: 5–25; Malone, Dumas, ed. 1932. *Dictionary of American Biography,* vol. 8. New York: Charles Scribner's Sons; United States Congress. 1851. *Annals of the Congress of the United States,* vol. 12. Washington, DC: Gale and Seaton.

GROS VENTRE

The Gros Ventre, or A'aninin, reside at the Fort Belknap reservation in north-central Montana. The designation Gros Ventre resulted from a gesture that tribes in the area made when they encountered French explorers. The A'aninin, identified as "The Water Falls People" or Atsina, were described with a sweeping downward motion, outward from the chest to the waist area. Although the gesture was intended to depict waterfalls along the Saskatchewan River, the French explorers misinterpreted the gesture to mean "Gros Ventre," or "Big Belly" in the French language. Tribal members prefer the name A'aninin, or the "People of the White Clay," a reference to their belief that they were made from the white clay that is found along the riverbottoms of their homeland. To complicate matters, careless observers also referred to the Hidatsa, Siouan speakers who lived in settled agricultural villages along the upper Missouri, as Gros Ventre. To distinguish them from the A'aninin, referred to as the Gros Ventre of the Prairies, Europeans identified the Hidatsa as the Gros Ventre of the River.

Gros Ventre oral tradition indicates that the A'aninin were part of the Arapaho Nation until around 1700, when, for reasons that remain unclear, the two groups divided. The Gros Ventre were nomadic big-game hunters and warriors who originally resided in the woodlands before migrating westward to Canada and Montana in the eighteenth and nineteenth centuries. After settling on the Northern Plains, the Gros Ventre allied themselves with the Blackfoot and followed the buffalo, the staff of life for the native peoples of the region.

During his travels, Meriwether Lewis noted that the Gros Ventre were grouped into two north-south divisions. One group, some twenty-five hundred "Falls Indians," lived in 260 tipis in the northern region of Canada and traded with the French. The "Stactan Indians," or southern bands, consisted of 40 tipis closely allied with the Arapaho. Although the Corps of Discovery spotted evidence of Gros Ventre hunters, they never encountered the "Minnetarees of Fort de Prairie," who preferred the acquaintance of Canadian traders. In July 1806, however, Lewis and three members of the expedition parleyed with eight Piegans who falsely identified themselves as Gros Ventre. The incident was significant because a bungled attempt to steal the expedition's horses and guns culminated in bloodshed.

Before the arrival of the Americans, English and French traders established economic relationships with the Gros Ventre during the eighteenth century. The demand for buffalo robes during the 1830s proved lucrative for the Gros Ventre, experts in procuring hides and making robes. By this time the Gros Ventre had also started trading with Americans who staffed a series of forts along the Missouri River. As a result of these economic ties, the Gros Ventre became increasingly dependent on the traders' guns and goods. The relationship also made the Gros Ventre susceptible to smallpox epidemics and reinforced the escalation of intertribal rivalry that had begun following the acquisition of the horse during the early eighteenth century. The military struggles of the era prompted the Gros Ventre to move south to the upper waters of the Missouri and ally with the Blackfoot groups, especially the Piegan. The migrations and frequent warfare with the Crow, Assiniboine, and Cree transformed the Gros Ventre into the most unified of the Northern Plains peoples.

By the mid–nineteenth century, the westward-moving frontier had driven the Teton Dakota into Montana. To retain their territory, the Gros Ventre allied themselves with the Assiniboine and Crow. Tribal leaders also recognized the need to win the support of American traders and U.S. government officials. As a result, the Gros Ventre signed their first treaty with the United States in 1855, when Isaac Stevens, governor of the Washington Territory, concluded the Fort Laramie Treaty with the Blackfoot, Flathead, and Nez Perce tribes. The Gros Ventre signed the treaty as part of the Blackfoot Nation, whose territory became common hunting grounds for all signatories. In 1888, Congress acquired 17,500,000 acres of tribal lands. In return for the native peoples' lands, government officials established three reservations: the Blackfoot, Fort Peck, and Fort Belknap. Following the agreement, the Gros Ventre and the Assiniboine relocated to Fort Belknap Reservation. In time, however, encroachers in search of gold in the Little Rockies invaded tribal lands. To avoid conflict, government officials pressured the tribes to cede the southern portion of their reservation in 1895.

Despite the dramatic changes that affected the A'aninin during the nineteenth and twentieth centuries, they eventually adjusted to reservation life. The Fort Belknap Indian Community was organized under the Wheeler Howard Act of 1934. The Fort Belknap Council Constitution and Bylaws were approved the following year, and a corporate charter was ratified in 1937. Today some fifty-one hundred Gros Ventre and Assiniboine remain united as one government. Although both tribes have experienced a number of changes in their rich history, they continue to nurture a way of life that has deep respect for its land, its culture, and its heritage.

—Jon L. Brudvig

For Further Reading
Fowler, Loretta. 1987. *Shared Symbols, Contested Meanings: Gros Ventre Culture and History, 1778–1984.* Ithaca: Cornell University Press; Horse Capture, George P. 1992. *The Seven Visions of Bull Lodge.* Lincoln: University of Nebraska Press; Ronda, James P. 1984. *Lewis and Clark among the Indians.* Lincoln: University of Nebraska Press; Ronda, James P. 1998. *Voyages of Discovery: Essays on the Lewis and Clark Expedition.* Helena: Montana Historical Society Press.

GUTIERREZ-MAGEE EXPEDITION (1812–1813)

The Gutierrez-Magee Expedition (1812–1813) was an early filibustering expedition against Spanish Texas. Jose Bernardo Gutierrez de Lara was a blacksmith and merchant from Revilla, Mexico, during the Hidalgo Revolt—a period of growing unrest in Mexico under Spanish rule. He traveled to Washington, D.C., where he was favorably received by officials in the U.S. Departments of War and State in 1811. After meetings with U.S. officials on behalf of the antiroyalists in New Spain, Gutierrez received only an unofficial blessing from Secretary of State James Monroe and vague promises of support for the antiroyalist cause. Gutierrez left Washington and sailed to New Orleans with a letter of introduction to William C. C. Claiborne, the territorial governor of the Orleans Territory. Upon his arrival, Governor Claiborne introduced Gutierrez to William Shaler, an officer seeking to enter New Spain and monitor antiroyalist activities. The men then proceeded to Natchitoches, where Gutierrez found numerous volunteers willing to join the expedition. Shaler eventually became the principal advisor of the campaign and enlisted the military assistance of Lieutenant William Augustus Magee, a graduate of West Point and member of the U.S. Army. East Texas Indians provided support for the expedition as well.

Although many Anglo-Americans and Indians had joined Gutierrez and Magee because of the possibilities for booty, the primary goal of their army was to bring Texas into the fold of Mexican revolutionaries. The expedition of 130 men grew to almost 300 after the fall of Nacogdoches on August 12, 1812. After learning that La Bahía was poorly defended, Gutierrez and Magee marched directly there and expelled the few defenders in the area on November 7. The Republican Army occupied a huge stone fort and a few cannons. Three days later, a royalist army under the command of Manuel de Salcedo and Simon de Herrera laid siege to La Bahia with only 200 men. After reinforcements had increased this force to almost 800 soldiers, Magee requested the terms of surrender from Salcedo. As a result of unsatisfactory terms, the republicans continued to fight and were eventually victorious. In early February 1813, Magee died under uncertain circumstances and Samuel Kemper succeeded to the command. Throughout the siege the republican forces had grown by means of volunteers in Nacogdoches and deserters from the Spanish army. Later that month, Salcedo and Herrera abandoned the offensive. Two days afterward, on February 21, the republicans defeated a royalist army of 1,200 men commanded by Herrera about eight miles east of San Antonio in the Battle of Salado. Anglo-Americans, Mexicans, and Indian allies defeated the royalists within twenty minutes, suffering only six killed and twenty-six wounded. Herrera, however, endured 330 killed and 60 captured. Following this battle, Salcedo and Herrera surrendered in San Antonio.

After his military success, Gutierrez proceeded to organize a provisional government in Texas and proclaimed himself governor. As a result of his new political authority, the governor ordered the release of royalist prisoners and organized a tribunal that found Salcedo and Herrera guilty of treason against the Hidalgo Revolt and condemned them to death. Anglo officers protested the decision and convinced Gutierrez to spare the royalists by sending them to prison. The governor complied and ordered Mexican rebel captain Antonio Delgado and his company to escort the captives to Matagorda Bay, where they would sail for points in southern Mexico or New Orleans. On their journey, the rebel company ordered the prisoners to dismount and disrobe. Delgado and his men then proceeded to stab and cut the throats of the royalists, including Governor Salcedo, Herrera, and twelve others, leaving them lying at the Salado battle site. When Delgado returned, his boastful remarks about the assassinations upset many volunteers in the Republican Army. As a result, several Anglo-Americans deserted the republicans, and the incident encouraged the deteriorating relations between Anglo-American and Mexican contingents. The murder of Governor Salcedo and his staff led to further attempts to reconquer Texas by the government of New Spain. Meanwhile, Texas remained under the trivial control of Gutierrez. On April 6 he declared the province indepen-dent of Spain, and on April 17, 1813, he proclaimed Texas's first constitution. This document called for a centralized rather than republican form of government. Although Gutierrez governed briefly as president protector of the state of Texas, he was soon removed from power and sent into exile by factions within the Republican Army. The Gutierrez-Magee Expedition intensified Spanish interest in Texas so much that peace could not be restored. The province remained the center of plots or the object of invasion until Mexico won its independence in 1821.

—*Carrie Douthey*

See also
Claiborne, William Charles Cole; Herrera, Simón de; Nacogdoches; Texas

For Further Reading
Chipman, Donald E. 1992. *Spanish Texas, 1519–1821.* Austin: University of Texas Press.

HAITI

The island of Hispaniola, of which Haiti occupies a part, was visited during Christopher Columbus's first voyage to the New World. In fact, the Spaniards built the first settlement on the island out of the remains of the foundered *Santa Maria*. The first Europeans, being Spanish, named the island Hispaniola, "Spanish Island." They soon established a colony there as a steppingstone to further conquests in the Gulf. At the time, the island was completely under Spanish control.

After the defeat of the Spanish Armada (1588) and Spain's subsequent reduction in her control of the high seas, both England and France began to enter the ports of Hispaniola to trade. This free trade undercut the Spaniards' controlled prices. Naturally the Spanish resented this intrusion, and by 1689, Spain and France were often fighting each other for control of the island. The Peace of Ryswick (1697) formally recognized French sovereignty over most of the western half of the island and ended the issue of control. Spain retained territory on the central plateau that jutted into the French territory. The French portion of the island, known as St. Domingue, would eventually (in 1804) take the name Haiti, the name coming from the Arawak word for "mountainous."

Prior to the American Revolution, France had fought its own devastating war with Great Britain in the French and Indian War (1755–1763). As a consequence of the Treaty of Paris (1763), which ended that war, France had to surrender large amounts of territory to Great Britain. This loss forced the French to evaluate the importance of each of their colonies in the New World in order to decide which to sacrifice. There were three from which to choose: French Canada, the Louisiana Territory, and St. Domingue. St. Domingue was never seriously considered for surrender; it was the keystone of the French colonial empire in the Caribbean by virtue of its strategic position. By the mid-1700s, St. Domingue dominated the European sugar market. One-third of France's foreign trade came from the colony. To save this valuable colony, the French gave the Louisiana Territory to Spain to keep it out of British hands and to compensate Spain for the loss of Havana. French Canada was turned over to Great Britain, completing that nation's control over all of the Canadian territory.

St. Domingue would remain nominally under French control, but the colony's slaves had another plan in mind. Part of the economic success of the sugar colony was its reliance on slave labor. The slaves soon outnumbered the white colonists by a ratio of at least twenty to one. The situation was never stable on the island, and there were several slave rebellions prior to France's defeat in the French and Indian War. When the French Revolution began in 1789, the slaves took to heart the slogan "liberty, fraternity, equality." The National Assembly in Paris encouraged this belief by extending suffrage in the colony to land-owning and tax-paying men of color. The majority of the black population, however, remained excluded.

The final slave revolt took place in 1791. With France distracted by the Reign of Terror at home, it could spare little attention to the out-of-control colony. Both Britain and Spain saw their chance and reached an informal agreement to divide St. Domingue between them. Great Britain landed troops and attempted to quell the uprising. Spain's tactic was to ally with the slaves. They bribed the rebels' cooperation by offering land and Spanish citizenship to those who helped Spain's cause. Both nations' plans collapsed when their troops began to sicken and die from tropical disease. The Americans repaid St. Domingue's aid in the American Revolution (1,550 soldiers from the island had been part of a French West Indian Force) by staying out of it and distracting Great Britain and France from the region by playing each against the other.

Throughout the revolt, the man who would become Haiti's founding father, Toussaint L'Ouverture, rose through the ranks of the rebel forces. His military strategy was so brilliant that historians have often referred to him as the "black Napoleon"—but that is slightly inaccurate, as L'Ouverture's first military successes preceded those of Napoleon Bonaparte. As L'Ouverture was consolidating the rebels' hold on Haiti, Bonaparte was consolidating his power in France.

Spain and France soon settled their differences by the Treaty of Basel (1795), in which Spain agreed to cede its holding on Hispaniola to France. That was not enough for Bonaparte; he envisioned a French empire in the New World to rival that of Spain. Bonaparte, after becoming first consul in Paris, began to negotiate for the return of the Louisiana Territory from Spain. L'Ouverture saw the negotiations as an encirclement of St. Domingue by

France. L'Ouverture took advantage of this lull and proclaimed a constitution for St. Domingue on July 7, 1801. This proclamation was tantamount to a declaration of independence, as colonies did not have constitutions of their own. Bonaparte could not ignore such a provocation. He fully intended to bring St. Domingue and its slaves back under complete French control. In late 1801 he ordered that plans be developed for an invasion of the island to return control to French colonial administration. On February 1, 1802, lookouts spotted French ships in the bay of Port-au-Prince, carrying between sixteen thousand and twenty thousand men, equal to L'Ouverture's army.

The slave rebels could not hold out against the better-trained force, and they knew it. Faced with desertions by his once loyal lieutenants, L'Ouverture surrendered to General Charles-Victor-Emmanuel Leclerc on May 5, 1802. Although he was promised his freedom on condition of retirement, the French seized him and sent him to France. He died in prison on April 7, 1803, never knowing a free St. Domingue.

But Haiti managed to secure its independence despite that loss. Needing money for his wars at home, Bonaparte sold the Louisiana Territory to the United States of America in 1803. This sale marked the end of Bonaparte's dreams for France in the New World. The slaves in Haiti had continued a guerrilla war, and without the rest of the French territories, there was no reason for France to continue fighting and losing men. Haiti declared its independence on January 1, 1804.

—Elizabeth Pugliese

For Further Reading
Haggerty, Richard A., ed. 1989. *Haiti: A Country Study.* Washington, D.C.: Federal Research Division, Library of Congress; Heinl, Robert Debs, Jr., and Nancy Gordon Heinl. 1978. *Written in Blood: The Story of the Haitian People 1492–1971.* Boston: Houghton Mifflin Company; Ros, Martin. 1994. *Night of Fire: The Black Napoleon and the Battle for Haiti.* New York: Sarpedon Publishers.

HAMILTON, ALEXANDER (1755–1804)

Alexander Hamilton was both a leading federalist and nationalist. He served as the secretary of the treasury (1789–1795) and an advisor to George Washington after leaving the treasury. He also served as the inspector general of the army and then as its senior officer during the crisis with the French. While a political opponent of Thomas Jefferson, he nonetheless supported the acquisition of Louisiana by the United States.

Hamilton was born on January 11, 1755, on the island of Nevis in the West Indies. He came to British North America in 1772 to attend school in New Jersey. In 1776 he was commissioned a captain of artillery, and then in 1777 he joined George Washington's staff. He left the staff in 1781 and went on to command an infantry regiment at Yorktown. In 1782 he returned to civilian life to practice law in New York, where he also became a leading politician and nationalist. In 1787 he attended the Constitutional Convention in Philadelphia, where he was the only New York delegate to sign the document. He became a leading advocate of the Constitution in New York and the predominant writer of the *Federalist Papers.*

In September 1789, Hamilton was appointed secretary of the treasury in Washington's administration, a position he would hold until January 1795. During his tenure at the treasury, he was responsible for the creation of the Bank of the United States, and the creation of the *Report on Public Credit* and the *Report on Manufactures.* His efforts played an important role in the organization of the national finances. Hamilton was concerned with both the economic and national security implications of who owned Louisiana.

On September 15, 1790, Hamilton wrote a reply to Washington about a British request for free passage of troops from Detroit to Mississippi. His thoughts reflected concern over the ownership of the vast Western lands: "An increase of the means of annoying us, in the same hands is a certain ill consequence of the acquisition of the Floridas and Louisiana by the British" (Hamilton, vol. VII). From Hamilton's perspective, the possibility of the British gaining Louisiana would cause a number of potential problems for the United States. He believed that the British would be more open to trade, leading many Western citizens to shift their allegiances. Their expanded presence on the continent would give them even greater influence over the Native American populations in the region. He also believed that Louisiana would soon become the chief supplier of Britain's Caribbean and Canadian colonies, thus removing the need for commerce with the East Coast states (ibid.). That a British conquest did not happen did not remove Louisiana as a point of concern for Hamilton. After leaving the administration, Hamilton continued on as an advisor to Washington and as a leader of the Federalists. He assisted Washington in the writing of his Farewell Address.

John Adams's presidency would see a continuation of Hamilton's concerns over Louisiana. As the problems with France grew, Hamilton become more concerned about the status of Louisiana. Hamilton favored the United States obtaining Louisiana from Spain if possible and voiced concern about the future if the French were to gain it. On April 12, 1798, he wrote about the possible effects of Louisiana's becoming French: "With the [French] acquisition of Louisiana, the foundation will be laid for stripping her [Spain] of South America and her mines; and perhaps for dismembering the United States. The magnitude of this mighty mischief is not easy to be calculated" (ibid., vol. XXI). Hamilton's distaste for

Adams was not hidden, and it became only worse during the Adams presidency. Still, as the French crisis grew, Washington insisted on Hamilton's being appointed the army's inspector general in the summer of 1798. He became the army's ranking officer upon Washington's death in December 1799, a position he gave up in the summer of 1800. In that same year he worked against the re-election of Adams and, through his efforts, unintentionally ended the Federalist rule. In the end he helped put Thomas Jefferson—whom he distrusted—in the presidency. As his biographer Broadus Mitchell noted, he was a good statesman and a poor politician.

When the cession of Louisiana to France finally did happen, it was a source of serious concern. In the *New York Evening Post* on February 8, 1803, he wrote that there were two possible solutions to the problem caused by the French acquisition of Louisiana. The first was to buy the region; the second was to take it by force, then negotiate. He considered the second course to be a better and likely more successful course. But he doubted Jefferson's ability to handle the problem of Louisiana (ibid., vol. XXVI). Hamilton wrote favorably of the purchase of Louisiana by the United States from France when it became known. In the *New York Evening Post* on July 5, 1803, he wrote that he saw it as "an important acquisition, not, indeed, as territory, but as being essential to the peace and prosperity of our Western country" (ibid.).

Hamilton favored the acquisition of Louisiana and saw it as a moment of good fortune for the United States, where the nation's needs and France's inability to extend its empire met, to the benefit of the American cause. Hamilton died on July 12, 1804, from wounds sustained in his famous duel with Aaron Burr the day before.

—Donald E. Heidenreich, Jr.

See also
Jefferson, Thomas; Nootka Sound crisis

For Further Reading
Brookhiser, Richard. 1999. *Alexander Hamilton, American*. New York: Free Press; Hamilton, Alexander. 1963–. *The Papers of Alexander Hamilton*. Edited by Harold Syrett. New York: Columbia University Press; Mitchell, Broadus. 1957–1962. *Alexander Hamilton*. 2 vols. New York: Macmillan; Mitchell, Broadus. 1976. *Alexander Hamilton: A Concise Biography*. New York: Oxford University Press.

HERRERA, SIMÓN DE (1754–1813)

Simón de Herrera is remembered for his role in establishing the Neutral Ground east of the Sabine River in 1806. The letters he exchanged with U.S. General James Wilkinson permitted Spain and the United States honorably to avoid armed conflict over the western boundary of the Louisiana Purchase.

Simón de Herrera was born in the Canary Islands. He began his distinguished military and governmental career in the service of the Spanish Crown as a sublieutenant in 1763, rising to the rank of lieutenant colonel by 1795. Herrera saw service in New Spain (Mexico), the United States, South America, France, and Spain. He served in the Army of Operations under Bernardo de Gálvez in 1782–1783 in support of General George Washington, whom he later met and venerated. In Mexico, Herrera served as commandant of several provincial militias and led a successful expedition against marauding Apache and Comanche in 1797.

Herrera would defend Spanish Texas against domestic and foreign enemies for more than seven years. In 1806, as a result of the Louisiana Purchase, the United States increased its troop strength in the Louisiana Territory. This development alarmed Spanish officials, who sent Herrera, then governor of Nuevo Leon, to Texas as commandant of the Louisiana frontier. Supported by more than six hundred troops, his mission was to reconnoiter the Spanish lands east of the Sabine as far as Natchitoches and Bayou Pierre, also patrolled by U.S. troops, which soon came under the command of General James Wilkinson. At that time Wilkinson was preoccupied with accusing his former partner, Aaron Burr, of treason and was anxious to leave the military camp on the Sabine for a confrontation in New Orleans. To avoid an armed conflict, Herrera and Wilkinson exchanged letters in November 1806. They designated a Neutral Ground that denied either country jurisdiction over the disputed land. Never ratified as a treaty, their agreement would nonetheless be observed by both sides during Napoleon's occupation of Spain, when diplomatic relations were suspended between the United States and Spain. After Waterloo, when boundary negotiations resumed, Herrera's and Wilkinson's letters were superseded by the Adams-Onís Treaty (1819).

After the showdown on the Sabine, Herrera devoted his efforts to improving the defenses of Texas. When Zebulon Pike was returning from his illegal foray into Mexico, he met Herrera in San Antonio and described him in his diary as "one of the most gallant and accomplished men I ever knew. He possesses a great knowledge of mankind from his experience in various countries and societies" (Coues, 1895). Pike attributed to "Governor Herrera's prudence that we are not now engaged in a war with Spain," stating that Herrera had received orders to engage in predatory warfare that he had disobeyed in favor of a peaceful withdrawal (ibid.). It is unknown whether Herrera knew then that Wilkinson was a Spanish spy.

Loyal to the royalists during the 1810 revolt led by Miguel Hidalgo y Costilla, Herrera was captured in January 1811 along with Texas governor Manuel María Salcedo. They were sent to Coahuila, to the hacienda of Ignacio Elizondo, for detention. However, the two prisoners regained their freedom by persuading Elizondo to desert the rebel cause led by Hidalgo, whom he killed shortly thereafter. This action prevented San Antonio from becoming the center of the rebellion in New Spain.

After the Hidalgo rebellion was suppressed, Herrera returned to San Antonio as interim governor until Salcedo reluctantly resumed the position in December 1811. Salcedo and Herrera were soon confronted with a new rebellion from the Neutral Ground. Known as the Gutierrez-Magee Expedition, the filibusters captured Nacogdoches and La Bahía by November 1812. Herrera and Salcedo laid siege to La Bahía, but a stalemate developed. Failing to dislodge the rebels, the governors withdrew toward San Antonio in February. On March 29, the two opposing forces engaged in the battle of Rosillo, resulting in a clear victory for the filibusters; Herrera and Salcedo surrendered as prisoners of war. San Antonio surrendered unconditionally on April 1. Two days later, Mexicans among the filibusters murdered Herrera, Salcedo, and a dozen other Spaniards. Anglo-Americans among the filibusters felt such revulsion at the decapitation of their prisoners that they abandoned the group. The governors' bodies were brought back to San Antonio for Christian burial after the decisive defeat of the remnant of the filibusters at the battle of Medina.

—Betje B. Klier

See also

Gutierrez-Magee Expedition; Neutral Ground; Wilkinson, James

For Further Reading

Coues, Elliot, ed. 1895. *The Expeditions of Zebulon Montgomery Pike. . . .* New York: Harper; Haggard, J. Villasana. 1945. "The Neutral Ground between Louisiana and Texas, 1806–1821." *Louisiana Historical Quarterly* 28: 1000–1003, 1082n, 1087, 1089, 1098, 1101; Holmes, Jack D. L. 1964. "Showdown on the Sabine: General James Wilkinson vs. Lieutenant-Colonel Simón de Herrera." *Louisiana Studies* 3: 46–76; Tyler, Ron C., et al., eds. 1996. *New Handbook of Texas.* Austin: Texas State Historical Association; Wallace, Earnest, David M. Vigness, and George B. Ward, eds. 1994. "The Neutral Ground Agreement: October 29 and November 4, 1806." In *Documents in Texas History.* Austin: State House Press.

HIDATSA

The Hidatsa resided in large, permanent villages and pursued intensive agriculture on the upper lengths of the Missouri River. At the time of the Louisiana Purchase, they lived in three villages at the junction of the Knife and Missouri Rivers, home to approximately two thousand people. The Hidatsa of this period were composed of three bands: the Awatixa, the Awaxawi, and the Hidatsa-proper. *Hidatsa,* a name of Hidatsa origin, refers to willows on sand bars; it later came to encompass the entire people. Although sharing a common Siouan language, each Hidatsa band spoke a distinct dialect. Archaeological evidence and oral traditions suggest that the Awaxawi and Hidatsa migrated from present-day eastern North Dakota, but Awatixa tradition claims a continuous residence on the Missouri River.

Hidatsa clans incorporated each individual and bound them in mutual obligation, providing community, identity, and care. The seven or eight Hidatsa clans active in the historical era were matrilineal and cut across the three bands. Clans ensured relatives in each village, while marriage, which joined men and women of different clans, further linked bands and villages. Societies for men and women provided peer groups, but unlike clans, whose membership lasted a lifetime, society membership was based on age and changed over time.

The Hidatsa located their permanent villages on bluffs above the Missouri River, with ready access to the environments and resources of river, floodplain, and open tablelands. Hidatsa villages were composed of several dozen domed earth-lodges. These semisubterranean and largely wooden structures, thirty or more feet in diameter, were covered with brush, grass, earth, and sod. The Hidatsa built lodges in two styles, flat and domed, the flat roof being the preferred place of leisure. In the early twentieth century, a Hidatsa woman recalled the excitement of moving to temporary winter villages on the floodplain, away from the wind and cold, but she also remarked that they considered the earth-lodge village to be their true home.

Hidatsa villages bustled with activity as people worked, played, and discharged their various obligations. Women owned homes and fields and cultivated crops, including nine varieties of corn and five varieties of beans. Men hunted, engaged in raids and warfare, and traveled extensively beyond the village's bounds. Surpluses from Hidatsa fields, as well as a fortuitous location, made for an extensive trade with other tribes, conducted in Hidatsa villages and at designated fairs elsewhere on the Plains. Initial meetings between the Hidatsa and French traders occurred early in the eighteenth century, and by the end of the century, French, Spanish, and British traders had traveled to Hidatsa villages to exchange furs, buffalo robes, food, and other provisions and services. American traders followed, after the Louisiana Purchase, and continued a trade with the Hidatsa for several decades.

Traders and travelers of this period provide a rich account of Hidatsa life, as well as a horrifying record of the consequences of disease, including the devastating smallpox epidemic in 1837 that took the lives of half the Hidatsa people within a few months. By 1845 the Hidatsa and the Mandan had moved some fifty miles north on the Missouri River to establish Like-A-Fishhook village, and they were joined there by the Arikara in 1862. This association addressed each tribe's declining numbers and their defense in long-standing conflict with the Sioux. In 1870 a strip of land containing Like-A-Fishhook village was added to lands described by earlier treaties, and the Fort Berthold reservation was established. The reservation's boundaries were revised several times over the next two decades, reducing it from some twelve million acres to a little more than one million acres in 1880.

The Hidatsa and their Mandan and Arikara neighbors, like other Western Indian peoples, were subject to a concerted assimilation effort during the last decades of the nineteenth century. Compulsory education, religious mission, and the encouragement of commercial agriculture were combined with a program to break tribal lands into individual possessions. This process led to Like-A-Fishhook's dispersal in the mid-1880s, with a formal allotment following in 1891. The Hidatsa, as well as the Mandan and the Arikara, were soon spread along fifty miles of the Missouri River. Each of the three tribes established distinct districts, with Hidatsa settling to the north, at the villages of Lucky Mound, Independence, and Shell Creek. Efforts at assimilation largely ended in the early 1930s, and the Hidatsa, the Mandan, and the Arikara would create their modern political form, the Three Affiliated Tribes, under the terms of the Indian Reorganization Act (1934).

—*J. Wendel Cox*

See also

Arikara; Catlin, George; Mandan; Maximilian, Prince Alexander Philipp zu Wied-Neuwied; Oglala Sioux

For Further Reading

Ahler, Stanley A., Thomas D. Thiessen, and Michael K. Trimble. 1991. *People of the Willows: The Prehistory and Early History of the Hidatsa Indians.* Grand Forks: University of North Dakota Press; Cash, Joseph H., and Gerald W. Wolff. 1974. *The Three Affiliated Tribes (Mandan, Arikara, and Hidatsa).* Phoenix: Indian Tribal Series; Gilman, Carolyn, and Mary Jane Schneider. 1987. *The Way to Independence: Memories of a Hidatsa Indian Family, 1840–1920.* St. Paul: Minnesota Historical Society Press; Meyer, Roy W. 1977. *The Village Indians of the Upper Missouri: The Mandans, Hidatsas, and Arikaras.* Lincoln and London: University of Nebraska Press.

HISTORIOGRAPHY OF THE LOUISIANA PURCHASE

At the end of the nineteenth century, interest in the Louisiana Purchase was stimulated by a changing political and cultural climate. New directions of historical inquiry, the Spanish American War (1898), and celebrations of the centennial of the purchase in 1903 inspired historians to evaluate the impact of the event in the young nation's history. The Louisiana Purchase has been the subject of countless popular and narrative histories. The scholarly debate surrounding the event, however, has centered upon the role and character of Thomas Jefferson and the nature of American expansionism.

In 1889, Henry Adams's influential *History of the United States during the Administrations of Thomas Jefferson and James Madison* was published. Drawing upon the record of Napoleon's minister François Barbé-Marbois, Adams paints a portrait of Jefferson paralyzed by indecision in the face of growing Western discontent during the Mississippi crisis and willing to put aside his constitutional scruples in order to complete a transaction that he had no part in creating. In Adams's version, Jefferson appears the craven opportunist, not the architect of the grandest real estate deal in American history.

In describing Jefferson's role in the purchase, Adams set the terms of the historiographical debate that would occupy later historians. Was Jefferson a hypocrite in abandoning his constitutional principles in order to complete the purchase, or was he a hero and mediator by pursuing a cautious diplomacy among European rivals? Some, such as James K. Hosmer in *History of the Louisiana Purchase* (1902) and Frederic Austin Ogg in *The Opening of the Mississippi: A Struggle for Supremacy in the American Interior* (1904), echo Adams's characterization of Jefferson as a fortuitous, if passive, beneficiary of the transaction, even as they reject Adams's harshest judgments of the president. Like Adams, Ogg and Hosmer focus on events in France and Europe to explain why Napoleon decided to relinquish his claim to Louisiana, taking Jefferson and the rest of the world by surprise. Although both authors agree that Jefferson had not been instrumental in completing the deal, they also describe Jefferson as a peacemaker who charted a difficult course through the geopolitics of the European imperial powers.

In 1893, Frederick Jackson Turner advanced the thesis that the Western frontier had been the genesis and incubator of American democracy. In "The Significance of the Frontier in American History," Turner argued that at the closing of the nineteenth century, the continent had effectively been conquered and the frontier had disappeared. This thesis, along with the Spanish-American War (1898), galvanized historians to explore the nature of American expansionism. They looked to the Louisiana Purchase for precedents and clues about how Americans had managed, in less than a century, to settle a continent and even to contemplate extending their reach to include Cuba and the Philippines. Thus James K. Hosmer describes the purchase as the event that marked the beginning of America's progress toward global power and preeminence. However, in describing Jefferson as a passive observer to the deal and in focusing upon events in Europe to explain it, Hosmer agrees with other historians of this era that Americans were set upon this path of expansion and conquest almost without their own volition.

Arthur Preston Whitaker in *The Mississippi Question, 1795–1803: A Study in Trade, Politics, and Diplomacy*

(1934) challenges this assumption. He argues that Americans had a longstanding interest in the Mississippi delta. In the years leading up to the Louisiana Purchase, American settlers, merchants, and speculators had increased their economic penetration of the region. Whitaker argues, however, that American economic interests could not fully explain why the country so enthusiastically embraced the Louisiana Purchase. He attempts to explain the "mental attitude" that transformed many Americans during the Mississippi crisis from economic opportunists into eager imperialists. Although Whitaker attributes this transformation to growing American antagonism toward the French and Spanish prior to the Louisiana Purchase, recent biographers of Thomas Jefferson have discovered more ideological motives.

Merrill D. Peterson in *Thomas Jefferson and the New Nation: A Biography* (1970) and Dumas Malone in his multivolume biography, *Jefferson and His Times* (1970), describe Jefferson and his contemporaries as enthusiastic expansionists. By transporting republican institutions and freedoms into the interior, however, American settlers were creating the groundwork for an expansive, orderly, and democratic nation. This argument is elaborated by Robert W. Tucker and David C. Hendrickson in *Empire of Liberty: The Statecraft of Thomas Jefferson* (1990), who argue that Jefferson inaugurated a new kind of diplomacy based on economic coercion and peaceful persuasion rather than the threat of military conquest. These authors join Peterson and Malone in describing Jefferson and his republican contemporaries as building a new type of empire. Thus these "empire of liberty" historians suggest that American expansionism was premised on the belief that republican institutions would be replicated as the nation advanced westward. The fact that Jefferson, in the process of completing the Louisiana Purchase, had to stretch the U.S. Constitution and thereby subvert his own belief in limited federal powers is downplayed by these historians, who accept Jefferson's defense that he acted for the greater good.

In *This Affair of Louisiana* (1976), Alexander DeConde disagrees with those historians who would mask American expansionism in the cloak of republican freedom and self-government. He argues that Americans were the inheritors of a Western European ideology of expansion and conquest. It was their destiny, Americans believed, to push farther into the interior of the continent and to claim new lands. This "imperial thrust," the author contends, meant that, long before the Louisiana Purchase, Americans had coveted the area and had contrived ways of possessing it. Thus when Napoleon suddenly offered it, Jefferson's emissaries in Paris did not hesitate to accept. Both DeConde and the "empire of liberty" historians agree that the Louisiana Purchase served as a precedent and example for America's inexorable march westward. DeConde argues, however, that American expansionism was not nearly as benign as Jefferson and his biographers have suggested. American settlers pushed ever westward, not because they were motivated by a democratic zeal to disseminate the blessings of republican self-government, but because they had a thirst for land and a drive to forge an empire. Conflict with Indians and European rivals was an accepted consequence of this momentum into the interior.

In arguing for the universal appeal of an ideology of expansion, however, DeConde discounts those voices that questioned the wisdom of pushing the boundaries of the young republic too rapidly and too far. At the time of the purchase, New England Federalists worried that the event had transformed the nature of the republic and the meaning of the U.S. Constitution. These dissenting voices appear more prominently in Everett S. Brown's *The Constitutional History of the Louisiana Purchase, 1803–1812* (1920). Although this is an exhaustive account of the congressional debates at the time of the purchase, the author adds little in the way of analysis to the interesting political narrative. Other historians who examine the reaction of New England Federalists to the purchase include Thomas J. Farnham in "The Federal-State Issue and the Louisiana Purchase" (*Louisiana History* 6 [winter 1965]: 5–25) and, representative of the many biographies of New England Federalists, Robert A. McCaughey's *Josiah Quincy, 1772–1864: The Last Federalist* (1974).

All of these histories have broken new ground in the historiographical discussion about the Louisiana Purchase. Rooted firmly in primary sources, they have contributed to our understanding of the purchase and its consequences upon the history of the nation.

—Christine Lambert

For Further Reading

Brown, Everett S. 1920. *The Constitutional History of the Louisiana Purchase, 1803–1812.* Berkeley: University of California Press; DeConde, Alexander. 1976. *This Affair of Louisiana.* New York: Charles Scribner's Sons; Ogg, Frederic Austin. 1904. *The Opening of the Mississippi: A Struggle for Supremacy in the American Interior.* New York: Greenwood Press; Whitaker, Arthur Preston. 1934. *The Mississippi Question, 1795–1803: A Study in Trade, Politics, and Diplomacy.* New York: D. Appleton.

HOMESTEAD ACT (1862)

Congress intended the Homestead Act (1862) to provide individuals settling west of the Mississippi with free land upon which they could settle as independent farmers. The act, however, did not produce the expected results. Poorly conceived and constructed, fraud and abuse undermined the intent of the act and resulted in large tracts of land being abandoned by settlers or acquired by speculators.

Prior to the passage of the Homestead Act (1862), the

Lured by the promise of free land for those settlers hardy enough to brave the unforgiving environment of the Western Plains, thousands became homesteaders after 1862. (North Wind Picture Archives)

federal government encouraged westward migration by helping Americans obtain public lands through sale or donation. In addition to helping settle the Western regions of the country, the sale of public lands generated much-needed revenue for the federal government in the early decades of the nineteenth century.

As Americans pushed west across the Mississippi River in increasing numbers, demands grew for making free public lands available for homesteading. Western lawmakers in particular, who hoped such a policy would facilitate growth, called for the distribution of free public lands to settlers. An increase in the number of small farms would not only help fulfill Thomas Jefferson's vision of an agrarian nation but also could mean increased congressional representation for new Western states.

Policymakers, however, faced great difficulties in devising a plan to distribute lands. Not only did they need to provide for land distribution on a large scale; they also wished to construct a law that would avoid the problems that allowed corruption to run rampant under earlier nineteenth-century land policies. Preemption (or squatter's rights) policies, which had long been recognized, allowed settlers to occupy unsurveyed federal lands and improve them. Squatters were later provided the opportunity to purchase those lands at auction. Too often, however, cash-poor frontier settlers were unable to purchase the lands they had improved, and thus those lands were often acquired by speculators rather than by the small farmers who had worked them. Attempts in the 1830s and early 1840s such as the Preemption Act (1841)—which gave squatters the opportunity to purchase 160 acres at $1.25 an acre prior to the land's being offered at auction—did not end the problems that had arisen under the preemption system.

By the mid–nineteenth century, as new territories were being carved from the Louisiana Territory, lawmakers introduced a number of homestead bills into Congress. None became law. Some congressmen opposed these bills, believing them to be unconstitutional. Others feared that opening lands in the West would create labor shortages in the East, as workers left industrial jobs to pursue livelihoods as independent freeholders. Southern congressmen were particularly disinclined to support homestead measures. They feared that the small, independent farmers who would settle the lands would oppose the expansion of slavery, thus undermining Southern congressional power and the interests of the slaveholding section.

By 1860, free land for homesteading had become a sectional issue. In that year, the new Republican Party adopted a platform with planks not only formally opposing the expansion of slavery but also favoring the distribution of land to support the expansion of small farms. That platform helped heighten the growing sectional crisis, which erupted after the strength of Northern voters elected Republican Abraham Lincoln to the presidency in November 1860.

In the summer of 1861, a new homestead bill was introduced during a special session of Congress. The bill passed both houses. Although many Southerners had retreated to their home states after the Civil War erupted, the majority of the votes cast against the bill came from those Southerners who had remained. On May 20, 1862, Abraham Lincoln signed the bill into law. Under the Homestead Act of 1862, approximately 84 million acres of public lands were set aside for homesteading. Although certainly an enormous amount, three times that many acres had been donated to the railroads by 1862, and 140 million acres had been donated to the states. Thus, by comparison, the amount of land available under the Homestead Act was relatively small.

Under the terms of the Homestead Act, any head of household or person at least twenty-one years of age who was a U.S. citizen, or who intended to become a citizen, could acquire surveyed federal lands. Specifically, settlers could obtain 160 acres of land, the equivalent of one-quarter square mile. Although the policy intended to promote the establishment of small farms, claimants need not have had any farming experience, nor were they required to own farm equipment. In order to prevent abuse of the law, claimants were, however, required to help fulfill a number of requirements before they were given clear title to the land.

The law stipulated that claimants swear that they were requesting land for themselves for the purpose of settlement and cultivation. Before taking title to the land, settlers had to prove that they had been in residence on the land for five years and that the land had been in cultivation. Claimants were also required to pay various filing and commission fees. Under the Homestead Act, settlers could also purchase land outright for the price of $1.25 an acre.

The act produced fewer small farms than had been expected. Some of the lands open to settlement were simply unsuitable for farming, such as those in parts of the Dakota Territory subject to frigid winters and dry summers. In other areas, farmers had their dreams destroyed by drought, blizzards, locusts, and prairie fires. Unable to make a living under those harsh circumstances, many farmers abandoned their claims.

Corruption also undermined the purpose and intent of the law, removing fertile land from legitimate homesteaders and placing it in the hands of speculators. Land office officials, with inside knowledge of the best lands, fraudulently claimed lands in excess of 160 acres for themselves. Wealthy speculators purchased lands from struggling farmers and acquired large tracts by various fraudulent methods.

Although the Homestead Act of 1862 did not produce the number of independent farmers it intended, it did facilitate the growth and development of the West.

—Alicia E. Rodriquez

See also
Dry Farming; Preemption Act; Squatter's Rights

For Further Reading
Gates, Paul W. 1968. *History of Public Land Law Development*. Washington, DC: Government Printing Office; Hibbard, Benjamin Horace. 1965. *A History of the Public Land Policies*. Madison: University of Wisconsin; Opie, John. 1987. *The Law of the Land: Two Hundred Years of American Farmland Policy*. Lincoln: University of Nebraska Press.

HOPE AND COMPANY

Founded in 1734 in Amsterdam, the Netherlands, the banking house of Hope and Company was considered one of Europe's preeminent financial institutions. Along with the British firm Baring Brothers and Company, headquartered in London, Hope and Company would provide the immediate loans to the United States that were needed to effect the terms of the Louisiana Purchase. Indirectly, the financial assistance that the houses of Baring and Hope provided to France in 1803 would help finance the series of Napoleonic Wars that would impact Europe for the decade that followed. Both Great Britain and Holland would feel the tragic effects of the Napoleonic Wars at many levels.

Once the last of the treaty agreements between France and the United States had been signed on May 9, 1803, Napoleon Bonaparte and U.S. diplomats Robert R. Livingston and James Monroe hoped to find a fast and efficient way to finance the Louisiana Purchase agreement. Since war between France and Great Britain seemed imminent, French banks did not wish to be burdened by possessing U.S. bonds that they could not market and convert into ready cash. The U.S. diplomats suggested the banking houses of Baring Brothers and Company of London and Hope and Company of Amsterdam as reputable establishments that could effect the particular financial demands of the transaction. Both of these companies had had previous experience in handling U.S. securities.

Napoleon agreed to the suggestion, and French treasury minister François Barbé-Marbois made the necessary arrangements with the banking houses to convert the bonds that France would receive into cash. Many of the bonds that were issued by the banks to finance the Louisiana Purchase were acquired by Russia. The two banking houses agreed upon the selection of Alexander Baring (later Lord Ashburton) as the official agent, with the powers of attorney for conducting negotiations with the United States and France. Putting all national allegiances aside, likely because they were able to earn $3 million in interest, both the British and the Dutch bankers were willing participants in the financial negotiations.

The amount secured by the American diplomats totaled $11,250,000 in the form of twenty-year bonds that promised a 6 percent return in interest. The U.S. Treasury redeemed all of the bonds between 1812 and 1823. Bondholders and the banking houses that financed the purchase earned $8,221,320 in interest as a result of the arrangement.

In 1804 the U.S. Congress would enact the appropriate legislation necessary to approve the financial arrangements that Livingston and Monroe had conducted the previous year with the European banking houses.

—Junius P. Rodriguez

See also
Baring Brothers

For Further Reading
DeConde, Alexander. 1976. *This Affair of Louisiana*. New York: Charles Scribner's Sons.

HUDSON'S BAY COMPANY

In 1670 the Gentlemen Adventurers of the English merchant vessel *Nonesuch* returned with a cargo of beaver pelts from the New World. The Adventurers promptly petitioned King Charles II for a charter to establish a company for exploiting the newly discovered riches. The monarch complied on May 2, 1670, with a royal charter granting to the Hudson's Bay Company "the whole trade" of the territory that encompassed those lands drained by waterways that emptied into Hudson's Bay. The members of the company were the "true and absolute lords and proprietors" of the territory. As a result, the Hudson's Bay Company held an absolute monopoly over, and independent governance of, a region of 1,486,000 square miles.

The company built a chain of forts at the mouths of the rivers flowing into Hudson's Bay to secure their claim. The forts provided a central trading area with the Native American tribes. Rather than send traders out to the tribes, the tribes came to the traders. At first, the traders negotiated the best price they could get for the pelts. Later, headquarters in London set the price, and the English could not change their prices without direct orders. The Indians often preferred to trade with the French rather than with the English, because they could get a better price for their pelts without the effort of travel.

The source of conflict between the British and French was not restricted to trading methods. The French felt encircled by the British, in Hudson's Bay to the north and west of French Canada and in the south by the Atlantic seaboard colonies. The overlap in trading areas—resulting from the fact that the French traders held monopolies issued by the French government while the Hudson's Bay Company held a monopoly issued by the British king—inevitably led to tensions. The conflicts often degenerated into military skirmishes or, worse, court battles. In court, the British tended to prevail, as the charter proved impossible to overturn. The court battles ended with the Treaty of Utrecht (1713), which ended the War of the Spanish Succession (1702–1714). Militarily, the British did not fare so well. The French burned British ships and forts, although, despite help from Native Americans, they never completely defeated the British in Hudson's Bay; the British always held at least one fort.

The military clashes blossomed into a full-scale war in the 1750s. The French and Indian War (1755–1763) doomed the French in the New World, but it also eventually doomed the Hudson's Bay Company's monopoly on the fur trade. At first it had seemed that the war would be helpful to the company's position: the fall of Quebec

Indians exchanged beaver pelts for other trade goods as part of a thriving barter economy at company stores operated by the Hudson's Bay Company. (North Wind Picture Archives)

in 1759 had ended the French-licensed monopoly, and the peace negotiations further raised the hopes of the company for continued power. The directors hoped to extract a cash settlement from the French as part of the terms of the Treaty of Paris (1763) as compensation for damages to company property over the years. Compensation to the Hudson's Bay Company, however, was not part of the final peace treaty. It was the first sign of the company's waning power.

With the end of the French trade in Quebec, it seemed that the company's monopoly was secure. The British enacted strict laws, such as the "Plan for the Regulation of the Fur Trade" in 1764, to counteract what French trade remained. It dictated that trade take place only at posts under license and bond—that is, British posts. The Indians naturally resented such restrictions and proceeded to move their trade away from the St. Lawrence River route and Hudson's Bay. The trade shifted to what would become the state of Michigan, specifically to the posts of Sault Ste. Marie and Mackinac Island. Although nominally British, there was a strong French presence in those areas. From Michigan, the French traders shipped the furs down the Mississippi to the port of New Orleans. Although that town was no longer in French hands, Spain had granted liberal trading rights to their allies upon taking over.

The Louisiana Purchase in 1803 allowed the Americans to compete against the company in the fur trade. The United States now controlled the trade down the Mississippi, and the Indians still preferred not to deal with the British. The best known of the companies that competed against Hudson's Bay Company was John Astor's American Fur Company. Astor became a very rich man from the trade.

The competition became too much for the Hudson's Bay Company, and there was growing resentment among the other British regions about the company's territorial sovereignty, granted in the original charter. In the 1870s, the company relinquished its territorial sovereignty to the British government and gave up its trading monopoly. But the company was not finished. It became a corporation, the only British corporation with its own flag, which it continues to use to this day. Although changed, it is still a trading company in that it maintains retail stores throughout the world.

—*Elizabeth Pugliese*

For Further Reading
McKay, Douglas. 1937. *The Honourable Company: A History of the Hudson's Bay Company.* London: Cassell and Company; Tharp, Louise Hall. 1946. *Company of Adventurers: The Story of the Hudson's Bay Company.* Boston: Little Brown and Company; Woodcock, George. 1970. *The Hudson's Bay Company.* New York: Crowell-Collier Press.

HUNT, WILSON PRICE (1783–1842)

As commander of the Pacific Fur Company's overland expedition to the Pacific Coast (1811–1812), Wilson Price Hunt assisted in securing the U.S. claim on the Oregon Country, the vast territory on the northwestern flank of the Louisiana Purchase. A native of New Jersey, Hunt migrated to St. Louis in 1803, establishing himself in the general-merchandise business. He harbored dreams of Western exploration, however, and in the fall of 1806 he met Meriwether Lewis in St. Louis upon the explorer's return to the city. This meeting heightened Hunt's desire to go West, and by 1809 he had secured a position as a senior partner in John Jacob Astor's Pacific Fur Company venture.

After a recruiting trip to Montreal to secure the much-sought-after French-Canadian *voyageurs,* the Astorians set out from St. Louis in October 1810. Their objective was to travel to the Pacific coast and establish a fur trading post on the Columbia River, thereby challenging the Montreal-based North West Company, which had recently begun expanding into the Oregon Country. After spending the winter of 1810–1811 near the Arikara villages in the north-central region of present-day South Dakota, Hunt turned the party south, as he wished to avoid the Blackfoot Indians of the Missouri River region. The Astorians trekked across Wyoming, establishing a route over the Continental Divide along the Wind River, thence following the Snake River to the mouth of the Columbia.

The Pacific Fur Company's overland expedition was an arduous and difficult journey beset by many hardships, including bad weather, hunger, illness, and ill-fated navigational decisions (Hunt had considerable difficulty locating the Columbia River). Although Hunt had believed that following the Snake River to the Columbia was the most practical course, the Astorians learned the hard lesson that the Snake River canyon was a hazardous desert unsuitable for overland travel. This information would prove invaluable for Oregon Trail migrants thirty-five years later.

The Pacific Fur Company's overland expedition arrived at Fort Astoria at the mouth of the Columbia River in February 1812. The fort had been established a year earlier in 1811, upon the arrival of the company's maritime expedition aboard the *Tonquin.* A well-functioning post by 1812, Astoria was strategically located for the American enterprise to challenge both the North West Company and the Hudson's Bay Company for control of the Northwest.

The Astorians set about securing trading links with local native peoples and expanding the company's operations into the interior. However, their commercial enterprise was short-lived because of the North West Company's strong presence and the Anglo-American War of 1812. Lacking supplies and reinforcements, the partners of the Pacific Fur Company sold out to the Nor'westers in the fall of 1813, and in December the officers of the British warship the *Raccoon* took formal possession of Fort Astoria, renaming it Fort George. That marked the end of John Jacob Astor's fur trade enterprise on the Pacific slope.

Although some Astorians returned to the East by land, and others remained in the West to work for the North West Company, Wilson Price Hunt returned to the United States by sea, finally reaching New York in 1816. Hunt's later life was as marked by stability and respectability as his earlier years had been by the challenges of exploration and travel. He resettled in St. Louis, becoming a successful merchant and landowner, and eventually marrying Anne L. Hunt, widow of his cousin Theodore. He also served as postmaster of St. Louis for eighteen years.

Although Astor's Pacific Fur Company venture proved a commercial failure, it had long-term historical consequences for the United States and Great Britain. In the Treaty of Ghent (1814), which concluded the War of 1812, all territories seized during the war were officially returned, including Fort Astoria. That allowed the United States to reaffirm its claim on the Oregon Country, which, in addition to the Louisiana Purchase, would make the country a national empire from coast to coast. In 1818 the United States and Great Britain agreed to a joint occupancy treaty for the region. Wilson Price Hunt's role in these events was to lead the overland expedition from St. Louis to Astoria, thereby reconnoitering possible overland routes and reinforcing the Pacific Fur Company's initial presence in the region.

—Melinda Marie Jetté

See also
Astor, John Jacob; Convention of 1818; Oregon Country
For Further Reading
Brandon, William. 1968. "Wilson Price Hunt." In *The Mountain Men and the Fur Trade of the Far West,* vol. 6. Edited by Le Roy Hafen. Glendale, CA: Arthur H. Clark; Elliot, T. C. 1931. "Wilson Price Hunt." *Oregon Historical Quarterly* 32: 130–135; Franchère, Gabriel. 1969. *Journal of a Voyage on the North West Coast of North America during the Years 1811, 1812, 1813, and 1814.* Toronto: Champlain Society; Ronda, James P. 1990. *Astoria and Empire.* Lincoln: University of Nebraska Press.

INDEPENDENCE ROCK

Independence Rock is an immense oblong granite block of oval but irregularly shaped stone lying just north of the Sweetwater River. The formation covers an area of more than twenty-seven acres, and its highest point is 155 feet above the level of the river. It is wholly isolated and looks as if it had been dropped there, in the midst of the High Plains. The massive formation is located in central Wyoming, about fifty miles southwest of Casper.

The Oregon Trail passed along the northern side of Independence Rock, and like Chimney Rock in Nebraska, the formation served as a familiar landmark to overland immigrants. Its naming shrouded in legend, this granite boulder on the north side of the Sweetwater River was a welcome sight to travelers along the Oregon Trail. Immigrants to the Pacific Slope stopped here for fresh water and trail information. Independence Rock is approximately two-fifths of the way from the trail's beginning at Independence, Missouri, to its western terminus at Fort Vancouver, Washington.

The rock from the first became a great and popular camping place, and the custom early arose of inscribing upon it the names of travelers who passed by. Thus it was, as Jesuit Father Pierre Jean De Smet justly observed, "the great register of the desert." No one is certain when the first passerby inscribed a name at the rock's base.

The name itself is of very early date, probably preceding 1830, and, if so, comes from the expeditions of General William H. Ashley and his Rocky Mountain Fur Company expeditions. "The incident which gives rise to it is fairly well known, from various references [and sources], all of which indicate that a party of hunters encamped at the base of the rock on a Fourth of July and there celebrated the anniversary of the country's independence." Rufus Sage says that "[the rock] derived its name from a party of Americans on their way to Oregon under the lead of one Tharp, who celebrated the [holiday] at this place—they being the first company of whites that ever made the journey from the States via South Pass." As Oregon then included everything west of South Pass, this may very likely refer to the first Ashley party, which followed this route probably as early as 1823.

—Henry H. Goldman

See also
Oregon Trail

For Further Reading

DeVoto, Bernard. 1947. *Across the Wide Missouri.* Boston: Houghton Mifflin Company; Masters, Joseph G. 1935. *Stories of the Far West: Heroic Tales of the Last Frontier.* Boston: Ginn and Company; Unruh, John D. 1993. *The Plains Across: The Overland Emigrants and the Trans-Mississippi West, 1840–1860.* Urbana: University of Illinois Press; Utley, Robert M. 1997. *A Life Wild and Perilous: Mountain Men and the Paths to the Pacific.* New York: Henry Holt.

INDIAN REMOVAL

Following the acquisition of the Louisiana Territory, federal Indian policy increasingly emphasized the removal of Indians residing in the Eastern United States, demanding their relocation west of the Mississippi River.

At the time of the Louisiana Purchase, the relocation of indigenous peoples to the newly acquired territory was little more than an appealing idea. Thomas Jefferson, who was taken with the idea of exchanging land held by Native Americans east of the Mississippi for comparable tracts in the West, never made removal central to his Indian policy. Within a quarter of a century, however, Indian removal would become the cornerstone of governmental relations with indigenous peoples. Indeed, during the first quarter of the nineteenth century, politicians and the American public more generally came to understand the relocation of indigenous peoples west of the Mississippi as a solution to a number of nagging problems they associated with the Indians.

Arguments advanced in support of removal ranged from the practical to the philanthropic, but almost invariably they were overtly racist. They included the promotion of national security, territorial expansion, defense of states' rights, access to resources on Indian-held lands, a burgeoning population, the assimilation of Native Americans, an end to persistent conflicts with native nations, and the salvation of indigenous cultures. Although quite popular, the idea of removal met with opposition throughout this period, fostering troubling debates about cultural differences, civilization, justice, and the rule of law.

Relocation began to mature as a policy within treaties made with native nations. Previous negotiations and compacts between the federal government and indigenous peoples had focused on pledges of friendship and cooperation, promises of peace, the termination of hostilities, the recognition of the authority of the United States, and the cession of territory. But once the dust had settled following the War of 1812, and no later than 1817, treaties first encouraged voluntary relocation and then demanded removal. The Treaty of Doak's Stand (1820), negotiated with the Choctaw, exemplified the new direction in federal policy. Under its terms, the Choctaw agreed to relinquish their claims to thirteen million acres and remove to the West, in exchange for a small annuity, material goods, a school, and comparable territory. Subsequent treaties made with native nations in the Southeast, Northeast, and trans-Mississippi West conformed to and refined this early model.

At the same time, spurred by increasing conflicts with Indians in the Southeast, politicians began to reformulate Indian policy around removal. In 1825 the Monroe administration advocated the establishment of an "Indian Line" in the Louisiana Territory, running along the western borders of Missouri and Arkansas to the headwaters of the Mississippi, the area being reserved exclusively for Indian settlement. Over the next five years, as tensions in the Southeast mounted, removal remained largely rhetorical and mostly voluntary.

With the election of Andrew Jackson, relocation became a priority and soon became law. Following a contentious debate, Congress narrowly passed the Indian Removal Act of 1830. The law did not stipulate that all Native Americans be removed, but rather, it established procedures and provided funds for relocation. It charged the federal government with assigning specific parcels of land as yet unclaimed by states to tribes and communities in exchange for their holdings east of the Mississippi. Moreover, it apportioned funds to reimburse Indian landowners for any improvements they had made to their property, and to pay for the transit westward and the transition to the new territory. Advocates of removal, particularly in the Southeast, seized upon the act and almost immediately began to set it in motion.

Despite the act's apparent momentum, two rulings by the Supreme Court challenged the legitimacy of removal. Both hinged on efforts by the state of Georgia to force the Cherokee off of their ancestral lands. First, in *Cherokee Nation v. Georgia* (1831), the court held that indigenous groups were "domestic dependent nations," or distinct sovereign peoples bound to and wards of the United States by treaty. A year later, in *Worcester v. Georgia* (1832), the court affirmed its earlier decision, underscoring that native nations were subject to federal not state laws. Together these decisions suggested that removal was unconstitutional; they did not, however, alter significantly either the objectives or the outcomes of Indian removal.

Removal necessitated that entire Indian communities abandon homes, agricultural plots, hunting grounds, and sacred sites, often located on ancestral land, and move to new areas, usually unknown to them. Demands for removal evoked a range of responses among Native Americans, including acceptance, anger, despair, disbelief, litigation, and armed resistance. In almost all cases, relocation destabilized indigenous groups, fostering disagreements, factionalism, and blood feuds. Worse, during their westward migrations, Native Americans suffered malnutrition, exposure, exhaustion, illness, and death. Some lived for periods in detention camps. Almost all endured exploitation by speculators and merchants, as well as abuse at the hands of officials and citizens alike. Thus the Cherokee came to refer to their forced removal as "the Trail of Tears."

Initially, Indian removal concentrated on those groups living in the Old Northwest. Most of the tribes of the Ohio River Valley and the Great Lakes region removed voluntarily, before the passage of the Indian Removal Act.

The Shawnee, for instance, agreed to remove in 1831 and traveled west in two groups: the majority relocated to a reservation in northeastern Kansas, and a smaller segment settled with the Quapaw in Indian Territory. Although many Northeastern tribes removed without incident, a few cases were marked by armed resistance rather than resigned acceptance. At about the same moment that the Shawnee were relocating, Black Hawk (Ma-ka-ta-i-me-she-kia-kiak) and a faction of Sauk Indians unsuccessfully rebelled against removal agreements signed by other Sauks and took up arms against the United States in a brief conflict known as the Black Hawk War (1832).

In the Southeast, removal began in earnest only after the passage of the Indian Removal Act (1830) and was largely forced, running from the early 1830s to the late 1840s. Complicating matters was the fact that the most prominent groups in the South—the Cherokee, the Chickasaw, the Choctaw, the Creek, and the Seminole, dubbed the Five Civilized Tribes—had endeavored to adopt many Euro-American conventions and institutions. They practiced agriculture, owned slaves, in some cases established constitutional democracy, and created written versions of their languages.

Removal in the Southeast began with the Choctaw, who signed the Treaty of Dancing Rabbit Creek (1830), in which they agreed to cede their remaining territory (some 10.5 million acres). They were removed in three waves (1831, 1832, and 1833). A large remnant remained in Mississippi, evading efforts to relocate them. Next, attention turned to the Creek. Following a brief conflict known as the Creek War (1836), the majority were taken to concentration camps and then removed to Indian Territory between 1837 and 1839. Around the same time, the Chickasaw were relocated over a ten-year period beginning in 1837, largely without incident. More problematic were efforts to remove the Cherokee. After years of refusing to relocate, a small faction of the Cherokee signed the Treaty of New Echota (1835), ceding eight million acres. A much larger segment (with more than fifteen thousand members) signed a petition opposing the treaty and refused to prepare for removal. As many as four thousand Cherokee died during the westward migration. Finally, the Seminole actively resisted removal, provoking the Second Seminole War (1835–1842). After a seven-year campaign, the United States had forcibly relocated more than thirty-five hundred Seminole west of the Mississippi, leaving behind fewer than five hundred renegades in the Florida swamps.

Removal also impacted Native Americans living west of the Mississippi. First, it required that many tribes cede territory for the incoming tribes. Second, many found their lives constrained by the terms of treaties that limited their hunting grounds, settled them on reservations, and introduced programs designed to "civilize" and assimilate them. Third, the presence of alien tribes increased both the competition for resources, such as game, and the conflicts within and between indigenous groups. Fourth, many Western tribes themselves eventually had to relocate. For instance, the Ioway moved first to an area along the Kansas-Nebraska state line, before a portion removed to Indian Territory; and the Kaw abandoned their homes in northeastern Kansas for a reservation near Council Grove, and later to a second reservation in Indian Territory.

Indian removal had a profound impact on the United States and the native nations with which it shared the eastern half of North America. In the years following the passage of the Indian Removal Act, more than forty-five thousand Native Americans were relocated west of the Mississippi. Fewer than ten thousand Indians, including the Eastern Cherokee and Seminole, remained in the Eastern United States. Removing the vast majority of indigenous peoples greatly increased the size of the young nation, for a relatively meager price. Removal added one hundred million acres to the territory of the United States at a cost of $68 million, as well as thirty-two million acres west of the Mississippi. The costs for Native Americans were much higher. Removal rapidly and irreversibly altered where and how indigenous peoples in the Northeast, Southeast, and trans-Mississippi West lived their lives.

—*C. Richard King*

See also
Black Hawk War; Indian Territory; Marshall, John; various tribes, by name

For Further Reading

Foreman, Grant. 1976. *Indian Removal.* Norman: University of Oklahoma Press.

INDIAN TERRITORY

From early colonial times, Indians were disadvantaged in their contacts with Europeans. By the time of the Louisiana Purchase, there were two compelling motives for removing Native American peoples from the United States. First, contact hurt Indian culture; second, Indian land use patterns interfered with American growth. The solution was to move the Indians west of the frontier, where they could live their own way in peace. Unfortunately for the Indians, the frontier kept moving west.

The 1804 law that divided the Louisiana Purchase into the District of Louisiana and the Territory of Orleans authorized President Thomas Jefferson to propose removal. Early exploration had established that the eastern area of the Great American Desert, the region from the Red River northward, was suitable for agriculture. Jefferson wanted to preserve Indian culture by moving the Indians away from the United States to the Permanent Indian Frontier, or Permanent Indian Barrier.

Some Cherokee, Choctaw, and Chickasaw were already west of the Mississippi River before the Louisiana Purchase. In 1808 the Western Cherokee, or Old Settlers, established themselves between the White and Arkansas Rivers in northwest Arkansas. They received an outlet to the west under 1818 and 1821 agreements.

The Osage, in northeastern Oklahoma since around 1796, lost their land in 1825 after violent confrontations with the original Cherokee, white settlers, and the federal government. They moved to Kansas, moved again when that territory organized, and by the 1870s were back in Indian Territory. Their land, which later became Osage County, was rich in oil, and they were at one point in the 1920s the richest people per capita in the United States.

An 1820 treaty gave the Choctaw land, ceded by the Quapaw, between the Red and Canadian Rivers. The Choctaw removal of 1820 was peaceful. However, the area they received included part of Arkansas that was already occupied by whites, so their border was shifted to the west to put the white-occupied area in Arkansas (whites in the Indian Territory were removed under an 1826 treaty).

In 1828, Southern Indian Territory was west of Arkansas, east of Spanish territory, and running from 37 degrees north latitude to the Red River. Its owners were primarily the civilized tribes, those who had adapted the white man's ways and intermarried. After the passage of the Indian Removal Act (1830), the last Cherokee to migrate moved across Missouri and Arkansas in the dead of winter. They called their trek the "Trail of Tears" because they lost many tribal members, who were buried along the way. Creek and Chickasaw followed. The final relocation of the Five Civilized Tribes was the Seminole trek in 1842.

The line of 37 degrees north latitude served as the boundary between Plains and agricultural Indians. Between 1829 and 1844, the government relocated Indians into the area stretching north from the modern north border of Oklahoma to the Platte River. Indians living in this area included Kiowa, Kaw, Shawnee, Kickapoo, Ottawa, Potawatomi, Munsee, Chippewa, Wea, Iiankesha, Peoria, Kaskaskia, Otoe, Missouri, Omaha, Pawnee,

Miami, Sac and Fox, and others. By 1844 all land from the Red to beyond the Platte belonged by treaty to Indians; land north of this Western Territory was controlled by untreatied Plains Indians. The federal government convinced the Eastern tribes to open their unoccupied lands in western Indian Territory to the Kiowa, Comanche, and Wichita, who had long regarded that land as their hunting territory anyway. The agreements also allowed access to this territory by licensed Indian traders.

In the 1830s, the northern Indian Territory, from the line of 37 degrees north latitude to the Niobrara River, was inhabited by whites or controlled by belligerent tribes such as the Sioux in the Dakotas. Pressure built in the 1840s for a railroad through this territory to the Pacific Ocean. Advocates included Stephen A. Douglas and Thomas Hart Benton. The Kansas-Nebraska Act (1854) cleared the way, by moving Indians into southern Indian Territory. Southerners began agitating for a route through Indian Territory. At the same time, there began a series of unsuccessful attempts to break up the Indian governments and allot their lands. The Civil War diverted American attention from Indian Territory, except as a theater of war.

The Civilized Tribes found out quickly that their new home was unlike what they had left in Mississippi and Georgia. Once they learned that semiarid conditions required a new style of agriculture, they developed a thriving economy based on agriculture, cattle and horse raising, and hunting. They established schools and political institutions, medical facilities, roads, and towns. Their relocated Southern-style slaveholding society included plantations, Southern-style architecture, and magnolia and pecan trees. The Choctaw police, the Lighthorsemen, policed much of the territory.

The Civil War divided the Civilized Tribes. Some wanted the Union, but others wanted the law and order that Confederates gave after the federal forces left. John Ross kept the Cherokee in the Union, but Brigadier General Stand Watie led Cherokee Confederate forces and became the last Confederate general to surrender. Bands of Choctaw and Chickasaw also joined the Confederates.

An 1862 law authorized abrogation of all treaties made with disloyal Indians. Even though the Cherokee and Creek tribal governments remained loyal, the federal government reduced all tribal lands and imposed a territorial governor over the once sovereign nations.

Empty land attracted occupants. As white pressure drove tribes from Kansas, they ended up in the Indian Territory. Among these were the Sac, Fox, and Pottawatomie (who gave up their tribal lands for citizenship and individual allotments).

By the late 1870s, efforts to add Indians from Arizona and New Mexico as well as some Sioux fell to defeat. There were new uses for the vacant lands. Freedmen, former slaves, wanted to move away from the South and their old masters. They established all-black towns throughout the territory, among them Taft, Boley, and Langston.

Over Indian resistance, the federal government promised the railroads Indian land, once all of the Indian nations were extinguished and a territorial government established. (Representative George C. McKee [D-MS] estimated in 1872 that organization would cause the Indians to lose twenty-three million acres to the railroads.) Lines built in the 1870s were the Missouri Kansas and Texas (MK&T), from north to south, and the Atlantic and Pacific, from Missouri to the MK&T. Railroads attracted exploiters of Indian coal lands, outlaws, and other undesirables. The Cherokee began selling grazing rights in their outlet to white cattlemen.

In 1872 executive orders replaced treaties as the federal method of dealing with Indians. By 1879 all attempts to organize a territorial government for Indian Territory ended, and Oklahoma (Choctaw for "home of the red man") was in disfavor as a name and a concept. In Sedalia, Missouri, David Payne, an attorney for the MK&T, insisted that if the government would not open the territory, the people would.

In 1879 the Indian Territory had 75,000 people on twenty-two reservations under eight federal Indian agencies. There were also 2,600 Chickasaw and 4,000 Choctaw freedmen, and 6,200 whites (1,200 railroaders and 5,000 illegals). In 1889 the total was still around 70,000 people, but the next year there were a quarter of a million.

The Black Hills gold rush of 1876 had shown the federal government's inability to enforce Indian treaties in the face of mass pressure, as also did successful white invasions of reservations at Malheur, Oregon, and Pyramid Lake, Nevada. In 1879 C. C. Carpenter, fresh from the Black Hills, organized the first invasion of Indian Territory's thirteen million "vacant" acres. Following Carpenter was David Payne, arrested the first time forty miles east of Fort Reno in the center of the state. Over the next several years, despite adverse court decisions and removal by military force, Payne and his Boomers persisted. Payne died unexpectedly, but his last foray, with six hundred Boomers in 1884, was the largest yet. Under William L. Couch, the Boomers re-entered in December 1884 and January 1885, the second time facing 350 troops of the Ninth Cavalry. Although Couch lost, in March, the Congress authorized negotiations with the Creek, Cherokee, and Seminole for the purchase of their unoccupied lands. The Dawes Act (1887) broke up the reservations; it authorized allotment of 160 acres to each family, eighty for each single person over eighteen or orphan, and forty for those under eighteen. Land was not to be mortgaged or sold for twenty-five years. Land freed by this law was for sale in 160-acre tracts to settlers who had to live on it for five years to establish title. Land was available in the western half of the territory only. Exempted because of their adamant disapproval were the Five Civilized Tribes; also exempt were the Osage, Peoria, Miami, Sac, and Fox.

Their turns would come in the five additional runs after the Land Run of 1889 that doomed Indian Territory.

In 1890, Congress organized Indian Territory and Oklahoma, the twin territories. Whites dominated Indian Territory through finagling, intermarriage, and migration that swamped the Indian populations. The last token effort to preserve the independent Indian state was the 1905 Sequoyah convention. In 1907 the twin territories merged. Indian Territory faded, absorbed into Oklahoma.

—J. Herschel Barnhill

For Further Reading
Gibson, Arrell. 1965. *Oklahoma: A History of Five Centuries.* Norman, OK: Harlow Publishing Corporation; Gittinger, Roy. 1917. *The Formation of the State of Oklahoma: 1803–1906.* Berkeley: University of California Press; Joyce, Davis D. 1994. *An Oklahoma I Had Never Seen Before: Alternative Views of Oklahoma History.* Norman: University of Oklahoma Press; McReynolds, Edwin C. 1964. *Oklahoma: A History of the Sooner State.* Norman: University of Oklahoma Press; Morgan, Anne Hodges, and H. Wayne Morgan, eds. 1982. *Oklahoma: New Views of the Forty-Sixth State.* Norman: University of Oklahoma Press; Otis, D. S. 1973. *The Dawes Act and the Allotment of Indian Lands.* Norman: University of Oklahoma Press; Scales, James R., and Danney Goble. 1982. *Oklahoma Politics: A History.* Norman: University of Oklahoma Press; Thompson, John. 1986. *Closing the Frontier: Radical Response in Oklahoma, 1889–1923.* Norman: University of Oklahoma Press; Thurman, Melvena, ed. 1982. *Women in Oklahoma: A Century of Change.* Oklahoma City: Oklahoma Historical Society.

INTERNATIONAL LAW AND THE LOUISIANA PURCHASE TREATY

International law is the body of rules and limitations that sovereign states agree to observe in their actions with each other. There are generally two types of law: *express,* such as treaties, formal declarations, or statutes enacted regarding common customs; and *tacit,* which consists of conformity to common, approved practices not formally embodied in laws. The 1803 purchase of the Louisiana Territory by the United States from France involved an express law, because the parties reduced the details of the sale to a formal, written treaty.

International law is made by sovereign nations, which are generally free to do as they wish in relation to other nations, except in instances when they agree to be bound by international law. Nations will usually agree to some curtailment of their absolute sovereignty for one main reason: national security. By regulating activities between nations, international law makes it easier for nations to anticipate what other nations may do, therefore making all feel safer. National security was also the main reason that the United States entered into the treaty with France to acquire the Louisiana Territory. By acquiring this territory, the United States would fully control the main artery through the country, the Mississippi River, and reduce the number of nations bordering the United States. Once France had surrendered its last colony in North America, the only colonies bordering the United States were those of Great Britain and Spain. Thomas Jefferson recognized this fact when he sent the treaty to the Senate for ratification with the message that this treaty "would secure the territory under conditions which, would ensure the secure exercise of U.S. rights" (*State Papers*).

Under international law, there are four ways of legally acquiring territory: occupation, prescription, cession, and accretion. The Louisiana Purchase involved cession of territory from Spain to France to the United States, and this double cession of territory casts some doubt on the legality of the transfer. As Spain slowly moved toward ceding the territory to France, President Jefferson sent James Monroe to France as a special envoy to aid the U.S. minister in the negotiations for the city of New Orleans and, if they could get them, the Floridas. The instructions were very specific. Because of slow travel across the Atlantic at that time, however, events surpassed these instructions. Before Monroe arrived in France, Napoleon had already decided to sell the entire Louisiana Territory to the United States in order to raise money for his wars. Livingston, who had already exceeded his instructions by asking for the left bank of the Mississippi as well as New Orleans, agreed readily to Napoleon's suggestion. Negotiations over the purchase price had already begun between Livingston and France's minister of finance, François Barbé-Marbois, before Monroe arrived. Ignoring instructions from the U.S. government, the two ministers proceeded to conclude a treaty for the purchase of the entire Louisiana Territory. Technically, ministers are not supposed to exceed their instructions, and if they do their nations may refuse to ratify the treaty. The U.S. Senate decided to overlook that small detail, however, realizing what a good deal this was for the United States; it decided to ratify the treaty anyway.

However, France was not yet in possession of the territory. Spain had yet to cede the territory to France by treaty. Spain agreed to the cession for certain considerations from France, among them that the Duke of Parma would receive a kingdom to rule, and that France would never cede the territory to anyone else. The ratified version of the treaty contained only the former condition; therefore, France's promise never to cede the territory was not a valid obligation under international law. However, France never gave the Duke of Parma any territory. This treaty was for a consideration, rendering its interpretation akin to that of the interpretation of a legal contract. In this case, France never tendered the consideration. Without the consideration, the treaty was, technically, not valid, and a legal transfer of the Louisiana Territory from Spain to France did not take place. If

France did not legally possess the territory, it had no sovereign rights in it, and therefore could not transfer it to any other country. Spain lacked the power to mount a challenge to the treaty's validity and chose instead to transfer the territory in spite of the lack of consideration. Spain's voluntary cession made the transfer legal under international law.

France, however, once in legal, if not actual, possession of the territory, proceeded to cede it to the United States under the Louisiana Purchase Treaty. Again, this cession was for a consideration, paid for through a complex arrangement of stock sales by Baring Brothers and Company. However, the mere signing of a treaty is not enough to make the treaty law. Each nation must ratify it according to its own procedures. In the United States, this procedure meant that the Senate needed to approve it by a two-thirds majority. It passed the Senate on October 19, 1803, by a vote of 24–7, ten more votes than were needed. France, nominally a constitutional republic, was supposed to submit the treaty for ratification to its legislature. Napoleon, however, knowing that the French legislature would never approve a treaty ceding territory that after years of negotiations was being returned, chose to ratify it himself. This was a violation of the French constitution, and thus, legally, France never ratified the treaty.

Fortunately, there is another rule of international law that allows for changes in international relations without the formality of treaties. Treaties are the best way to codify international law, as the parties write out the terms and conditions of the agreement, and reference to the clauses of the treaty can easily settle most disputes. However, there are times when there is no need for a formal written document. In such cases, accepted usage and custom suffice. With regard to the Louisiana Territory, the rest of the world has accepted the territorial sovereignty of the United States since 1803, rendering it legally part of the United States.

—Elizabeth Pugliese

For Further Reading

Brierly, J. L. 1963. *The Law of Nations: An Introduction to the International Law of Peace.* 6th ed. Edited by Humphrey Waldock. New York and Oxford: Oxford University Press; Lyon, E. Wilson. 1974. *Louisiana in French Diplomacy 1759–1804.* Norman: University of Oklahoma Press; United States Government. 1903. *State Papers and Correspondence Bearing upon the Purchase of the Territory of Louisiana.* Washington, DC: Government Printing Office.

IOWA

When Iowa was acquired as part of the Louisiana Purchase in 1803, it was the home and hunting grounds of the Sauk (or Sac) and Fox, the Sioux, the Winnebago, the Potawatomi, and the Ioway (after whom the land received its name). Louis Joliet and Jacques Marquette were the first Europeans to explore the area, in 1673; however, Iowa would remain largely uncharted and unsettled by American pioneers until the 1830s.

In the meantime, Congress began organizing and administering the vast extent of land encompassed by the Louisiana Purchase. Iowa was included in the Louisiana District, and when the Territory of Missouri was organized in 1812, Iowa was attached to it. When Missouri became a state in 1820, however, Congress failed to attach Iowa to another territory, and its status remained undefined for the next fourteen years.

The U.S. government used the competition and conflict between the resident Indian tribes to acquire gradually formal title to much of the land that would eventually make up the present state of Iowa. Between 1824 and 1851, the federal government negotiated treaties with the Sauk, Fox, Winnebago, Sioux, and Potawatomi, treaties in which the Indian tribes gave up their right to use or inhabit their traditional lands in Iowa.

Arguably, the most important treaty of this era was signed in the aftermath of the Black Hawk War (1832). It began when Black Hawk, a chief of the Sauk, refused to be relocated to the western side of the Mississippi River in accordance with the Indian Removal Act of 1830. Despite an initial victory, Black Hawk and his warriors were ultimately defeated by U.S. soldiers. As a result, U.S. agents demanded that the Sauk and Fox turn over a portion of their land west of the Mississippi as an indemnity for the losses suffered by the United States in the brief war. What became known as the "Black Hawk Purchase" formed the basis for the future state of Iowa. This triangular strip of land extended 195 miles north of Missouri's northern border and stretched from between forty to fifty miles wide, along the west bank of the Mississippi.

This Black Hawk cession was important because, for the first time, it opened up Iowa to full-scale white settlement. Farmers, speculators, miners, and traders flooded into the area after 1830. The population of the area in 1836 was estimated to be 10,500, but two years later it had already doubled.

In order to deal with the migration of settlers, the federal government had to clarify Iowa's territorial status. In 1834 the Territory of Michigan was extended to include Wisconsin, Iowa, much of Minnesota, and the Dakotas. In 1836, however, Iowa's status changed once again, when the lands west of Lake Michigan were organized to create a new territory. This territory, called Wisconsin, included the District of Iowa. As the population of Iowa grew, however, so did pressure from residents to divide the Territory of Wisconsin at the Mississippi River. In 1838 the federal government agreed to create the Territory of Iowa. The new territory included all the land of present-day Iowa, as well as much of Minnesota and the Dakotas. It possessed a population of 23,242.

The government of the new territory was identical to those of other new territories. The governor was appointed by the president to serve a term of three years. The legislative assembly consisted of an appointed legislative council of thirteen members and a house of representatives with twenty-six elected members. Elections for the first territorial legislature produced a body of men who reflected the character of the majority of white settlers. They were mostly young (under the age of thirty), and nineteen of the twenty-six seats were filled by farmers.

The first governor of the territory was Robert Lucas, a prominent Ohio Democrat who served from 1838 to 1841. Despite petty squabbles and political maneuvering between the governor and the legislature, the territorial government did manage to create a working administrative structure for the new territory. They agreed that the permanent capital for Iowa would be established in Iowa City, which, at the time, was on the western edge of white settlement in the area. They organized the first counties in the territory, all of which were located in the Black Hawk Purchase lands. And they negotiated a border dispute with Missouri concerning its northern boundary line.

At the beginning of the territorial period, most white settlements were located in eastern Iowa, near the Mississippi River or near other waterways that flowed into the Mississippi. Farmers and traders depended on the river as an easy and inexpensive way to transport their produce and goods to markets in the East Coast and Europe. During the 1840s, however, settlers pushed farther into the western half of Iowa. As migration to the trans-Mississippi West accelerated in the 1840s, Iowa became a way station for many of the people heading for the Oregon Trail. Iowa was particularly important for the westward movement of the Mormons during the 1840s. More than fifteen thousand Mormons trekked across southern Iowa on what became known as the Mormon Trail. Much of the internal development of Iowa occurred as a result of these westerly migrations. Towns and roads were built to take advantage of the traffic of overland migrants.

White settlements expanded despite the fact that the last treaties giving the federal government title to much of the western lands of Iowa were not signed until 1851. Once they were acquired, federal agents surveyed the land and opened land offices. White settlers could then purchase title to these newly surveyed lands. Treaties and titles were only formalities that many white settlers ignored during this era, however. Preemption or squatting was a common tactic that settlers used to stake their claims on desirable Iowa land, even before Indian tribes had relinquished their rights. Many of these squatters organized themselves into squatters' associations known as "claim clubs," which protected their collective property interests.

Slavery was barred from the territory according to the Missouri Compromise (1820). In 1839 and 1841 decisions, the territorial Supreme Court confirmed Iowa's status as a "free-soil" territory. The court upheld the rights of slaves to sue for their freedom once they were brought into Iowa. Despite its being a free-soil territory, however, black Iowans did not enjoy political or social equality with whites. They were not allowed to vote, and racial discrimination limited their economic opportunities. The population of black settlers in Iowa remained minuscule. According to the census of 1840, there were only 188 blacks in the territory. Despite those modest numbers, issues of slavery and black equality were raised again during the territory's application for statehood.

In 1844 a constitutional convention was assembled to draft a constitution as a preliminary to applying for statehood. A petition received by the convention raised the issue of black rights. It urged that blacks be admitted into the new state "on the same footing as white citizens." Upon consideration, the committee to whom the petition was referred decided that political and social equality for black Iowans, while a noble goal, was impractical. The committee's report expressed a fear that such a provision would make the new state a magnet for additional black settlers, which, according to the thinking of these white Iowans, was undesirable. One committee member even went so far as to suggest that all black settlers be barred from Iowa. That suggestion, however, along with the original petition, was tabled.

To keep the national balance between free and slave states, Congress paired Iowa's application for statehood with that of Florida, a slave state that had been waiting for admission to the Union since 1838. Northern congressmen wanted to be able to carve as many states as possible out of the territories north of the Missouri Compromise line in order to increase the number of free states in Congress. Southern Congressmen wanted to see Iowa admitted as a large state for the opposite reason. According to the provisions approved by the constitutional convention, the state's boundaries would have included all of the land included in present-day Iowa as well as the southern portion of Minnesota. On March 3, 1845, Congress admitted Iowa as a state, upon the condition that its boundaries be reduced. The new state borders, however, were rejected by the people of Iowa in a referendum.

The whole process had to be repeated, and a new constitutional conventional was assembled in 1846. This new convention agreed upon the state boundaries as they exist today. Iowa would be bounded by the Mississippi River on the east, the Missouri River on the west, and the state of Missouri to the south. The disputed northern border would now be set at the line of 43 degrees 30 minutes north latitude. Iowa was finally admitted as the twenty-ninth state of the Union on December 28, 1846.

—Christine Lambert

See also

Black Hawk; Black Hawk Purchase; Black Hawk War; Fox; Oglala Sioux; Potawatomi; Sauk; Winnebago

For Further Reading

Harlan, Edgar Rubey. 1931. *A Narrative History of the People of Iowa.* New York: American Historical Society; Sage, Leland L. 1974. *A History of Iowa.* Ames: Iowa State University Press.

IOWAY

The Ioway, or Iowa, Indians lived for much of their history in the river valleys of the state that now bears their name. In common with other woodland groups, the Ioway constructed semipermanent, bark longhouse villages. They cultivated a complex society rooted in an elaborate kinship system and translocal trade networks that was noteworthy for its agricultural innovations and its craft traditions. The coming of the Europeans and the subsequent U.S. presence dramatically altered that way of life.

Known to Europeans as the Ioway, who unknowingly adopted the playful name (meaning "the Sleepy Ones") from the Dakota in their Chiwere Sioux language, they called themselves Pa-ho-ja (alternately, Baxoje), which has been translated as "gray snow covered" and "dusty noses." Tribal tradition and ethnohistorical scholarship suggest that the Ioway and the Otoe, and likely the Missouri as well, were once a single cultural group. Moreover, linguistic, cultural, and archaeological evidence indicates that they share a deep historical connection with the Winnebago, or Ho Chunk, people.

Following a series of migrations southward from their ancestral homeland, the Ioway settled along the waterways in the state that would come to bear their name (particularly the Missouri, the Big Sioux, the Grand River, and the Des Moines River, as well as the Okoboji-Spirit Lakes). In time, they established villages throughout the region. Archaeological evidence and tribal tradition indicate that the Ioway dwelled in Minnesota, Wisconsin, Illinois, South Dakota, Nebraska, Kansas, and Missouri.

Initially the Ioway had rather sporadic interactions with Europeans. The French first made mention of the Ioway in 1650. A quarter of a century later, in 1676, a more detailed description concerning the Ioway appears in colonial reports. Finally, in 1685, the Ioway came into contact with French agent Nicholas Perrot in southern Minnesota. In subsequent years the combination of disease, the depletion of game, competition for commerce, and intertribal warfare devastated the Ioway, resulting in depopulation, a shrinking of their territory, forced migration, and the acceptance of other indigenous groups—namely, the Fox and Sauk—onto the eastern edges of their territory.

This pattern of conflict and loss took a turn for the better in the latter third of the eighteenth century. With the end of the French and Indian War (Seven Years' War) and the transfer of the Louisiana Territory to the Spanish, the Ioway enjoyed an extended period of peace and prosperity. They lived in relative freedom and conducted a profitable trade with the British.

The Louisiana Purchase marked an important turning point for the Ioway. It resulted in the encroachment of whites onto their traditional lands, the eventual loss of their territory, exploitation by traders and government representatives, and forced relocation. These circumstances, individually and collectively, produced increasing conflict within Ioway communities, political factionalism, crime, and interpersonal violence; they also fostered raids and hostilities between Indian communities and spawned disease and demoralization.

In 1837 the Ioway were relocated to a reservation straddling the Nebraska-Kansas border, near the Sauk and Fox. There they suffered arrogant and ethnocentric programs intended to remake them. These efforts to "civilize" the Ioway included the provision of housing and clothing and the introduction of education, Chritianity, and even farming. Making matters worse, given the quality of the land they occupied, the Ioway were pressured to negotiate and eventually agreed to accept treaties reducing their land holdings.

The reservation proved equally difficult for the Ioway. Many individuals despaired at their confinement and loss, and some turned to alcohol to escape from or cope with their circumstances. At the same time, the federal government and missionaries actively worked to undermine indigenous values and practices. And corrupt Euro-Americans, mainly agents and traders, continued to take advantage of the Ioway.

Nearly a half-century after settling on the reservation along the Kansas-Nebraska border, in the early 1880s, a number of Ioway petitioned the federal government for a new reservation in Indian Territory (later Oklahoma). After much debate, in which progressive Ioway argued against the move and more traditional Ioway argued for it, the government agreed to let a portion of the tribe move south in 1883. Following the move the northern community more or less thrived, but the southern community deteriorated. After 1890, both communities underwent allotment as provided for in the Dawes Act.

—*C. Richard King*

For Further Reading

Blaine, Martha Royce. 1995. *The Ioway Indians.* Norman: University of Oklahoma Press.

IRUJO, CARLOS MARTÍNEZ DE (MARQUIS DE CASA IRUJO)

As the Spanish minister to the United States, the Marquis de Casa Irujo had the responsibility of informing the Spanish government of the conditions concerning the Louisiana Purchase and informing both U.S. and French authorities that they were in violation of the second Treaty of San Ildefonso (1800). He felt that Louisiana had been a costly colony for Spain. Spain had not had sufficient contact with Louisiana by sea, and the products of the colony were far from being sufficient to offset the expenses of maintaining it. He contended that as a military barrier it was too extensive and too weak. The scattered number of Spanish troops in Upper Louisiana could offer no real resistance to aggression. Nevertheless, he was opposed to the Louisiana Purchase.

The Marquis de Casa Irujo contended that, in the event that the United States should try to penetrate the *provincias internas* (borderlands), a blockade of the mouth of the Mississippi River could be arranged by virtue of the strength of the Spanish presence in Havana. He believed that the Louisiana Purchase would not be advantageous for the United States. As a European accustomed to small landholdings, he could not conceive of a country having so much land available to its citizens. Further, he felt that while the United States would have the needed access to the mouth of the Mississippi River, regional rivalries and jealousies would result on account of the amount of produce (that is, cotton) that would suddenly be placed on the market.

He informed U.S. secretary of state James Madison that when Spain transferred Louisiana to France, it was clearly understood that France was never to alienate the province. The Marquis de Casa Irujo informed U.S. authorities on multiple occasions (September 4, September 27, and October 12, 1803) that Spain opposed the transfer, and he cited a letter dated July 22 from the French ambassador at Madrid to the Spanish secretary of state. The letter stated that "His Catholic Majesty" desired that France should not alienate the province of Louisiana, and that he was authorized to inform the King of Spain that France would not alienate it. Madison, however, in writing to Livingston in Paris, noted that the promise made by the French ambassador to Madrid did not form any part of the treaty of retrocession to France. He noted that Spain had informed the United States, on May 4, that if there were interest in acquiring Louisiana, inquiries should be made to the French government.

The opposition of the Marquis de Casa Irujo to the transfer of Louisiana to the United States was seen as a possible source of disruption to the ratification proceedings for the treaty in both the U.S. Senate and House of Representatives. The Marquis de Casa Irujo viewed the Louisiana Purchase as reason to be even more skeptical of the cession of Florida to the United States. He considered the ports of Florida to be of economic importance in the event of hostilities between the United States and Spain. They would be advantageous to either country in disrupting the economic well-being of the other. He also feared that if the United States owned Florida, an immense contraband trade would soon emerge with Cuba.

—*Alfred Lemmon*

See also

Charles IV; San Ildefonso, Treaty of; West Florida

For Further Reading

Gayarré, Charles. 1903. *History of Louisiana: The Spanish Domination*. New Orleans: F. F. Hansell and Brothers.

ISLE OF ORLEANS

The term "Isle of Orleans" exaggerated a geographical feature of the land in south Louisiana where the city of New Orleans had developed. One of the contested issues in the Treaty of Paris (1763), ending the French and Indian War, was access to the Mississippi River and, especially, the port of New Orleans. Duc de Choiseul, the French minister for foreign affairs, identified the land surrounding New Orleans as an island so that he could make an exception to the general border between British and French territory that the treaty established. Except for the "Isle of Orleans," the land east of a line drawn in the center of the Mississippi River became British territory; west of that line remained Spanish (Spain had acquired the land the previous year). The bodies of water bordering New Orleans included the Gulf of Mexico to the southeast, Lakes Ponchartrain and Maurepas to the north, and the Mississippi River to the southwest. By designating the small body of water that connects the lakes and the Mississippi as the Iberville River (known today as Bayou Manchac), the French could claim that the city existed on an island and take advantage of a diplomatic rule that allowed an island in a river to go to either country involved in a treaty. Choiseul erroneously defined this network of water as an alternate mouth of the Mississippi and promised the British navigation through this route. Because the port of New Orleans provided access to markets for the regions along the Mississippi and its tributaries, the primary value of the Louisiana colony lay in the city. Thus Choiseul's diplomatic maneuver had great significance.

The Treaty of Paris (1763) not only ensured that this portion of the east bank of the Mississippi would remain in Spanish control for the time being, but it also established the eastern boundary of Louisiana in subsequent treaties for the next four decades. Diplomats had considered the "Isle of Orleans" as part of the Louisiana colony and separate from West Florida when France ceded Louisiana to Spain in 1762, when Spain secretly retroceded Louisiana to France in 1800, and finally when France sold Louisiana to the United States in 1803.

The U.S. minister to France, Robert R. Livingston, had attempted to negotiate a purchase of Louisiana from the time he heard rumors of Spain's retrocession of the colony to France. Growing numbers of American settlers were relying on New Orleans trade for their livelihood. Moreover, one-third of the mercantile houses in the city belonged to U.S. citizens. The United States began its quest to acquire the Isle of Orleans more earnestly in 1802, after Spain revoked the U.S. right of deposit at New Orleans. In response, the Kentucky legislature threatened to attack the city and capture it for the United States. President Jefferson, however, pledged to find a peaceful route to acquisition through negotiation, even as Congress issued belligerent statements and the United States made defensive preparations. In March 1803, when Livingston was especially frustrated in his efforts to negotiate a purchase, he proposed the organization of the Isle of Orleans as an independent state under the shared protection of Spain, France, and the United States. Later, Jefferson sent James Monroe to Paris to assist Livingston with explicit instructions to purchase the Isle of Orleans and perhaps the Floridas (mistakenly believing that Spain had ceded that region to France as well). Jefferson intended to acquire only the port cities along the Gulf Coast for the United States, and he hoped to fix the Mississippi River as the boundary between French and U.S. possessions.

Napoleon Bonaparte considered the Isle of Orleans especially vulnerable as the most likely site of foreign attack. Not only had groups of Americans threatened to attack from the north, but as war resumed between Great Britain and France, Napoleon expected the British to attack from the Gulf. Wanting to keep the United States as an ally and prevent an Anglo-American alliance from developing further, Bonaparte decided to sell the entire Louisiana colony to the United States. Thus the fate of the Isle of Orleans became the fate of much of the trans-Mississippi West.

—Adrienne Berney

See also

New Orleans; Paris, Treaty of; Right of Deposit

For Further Reading

Carson, David A. 1998. "The Role of Congress in the Acquisition of the Louisiana Territory." In *The Louisiana Purchase and Its Aftermath.* Edited by Dolores Egger Labbe. Lafayette: Center for Louisiana Studies; Lyon, E. Wilson. 1974. *Louisiana in French Diplomacy, 1759–1804.* Norman: University of Oklahoma Press; Robertson, James Alexander. 1911. *Louisiana under the Rule of Spain, France, and the United States, 1785–1807.* Cleveland, OH: Arthur H. Clark Company.

JAY-GARDOQUI NEGOTIATIONS (1785–1786)

When the United States and Great Britain concluded negotiations over the Treaty of Paris (1783), ending the American Revolution, the newly established nation received much more than its independence alone. The British agreed to surrender the entire trans-Appalachian West to the United States but were careful to use vague language in defining the boundaries of this territorial windfall that would soon constitute the national domain of the fledgling American republic. It was clear that the Mississippi River formed the western boundary of the territory exchanged in the Treaty of Paris (1783), but the northern and southern boundaries were much less specific. Spanish Florida would border the United States to the south, while the Great Lakes and British Canada would form the northern boundary. It would take a series of subsequent treaties with Spain and Great Britain to determine the exact position of these boundaries, and the issue—particularly of the northern boundary—would remain in dispute well into the 1840s.

The Spanish found themselves in a precarious situation when the Americans reached a treaty settlement with the British in 1783. Spain had been an ally, once removed, of the Americans seeking independence. By being allies of the French through the Bourbon "Family Compact," the Spanish found themselves as an associated ally of the Americans after France and the United States had signed the Treaty of Alliance (1778). Ever careful not to send the signal that revolting against monarchial rule was the proper behavior for its own colonial citizens, the Spanish did however support the American cause by fighting against British possessions along the Gulf Coast. The military efforts of Louisiana governor Don Bernardo de Galvez were particularly praiseworthy in that regard.

The Spanish found themselves dissatisfied with the Americans in 1783 for two reasons. First, it was the understanding of the Spanish that the Americans were not to seek a separate peace with the British until all wartime goals of the French and the Spanish had been attained. In particular, the Spanish had hoped that they would be able to reacquire the island of Gibraltar from the British. When the Americans signed the Treaty of Paris (1783), the Spanish believed that they had been double-crossed by their former ally. Secondly, the amorphous boundary of Spanish Florida as defined by the Treaty of Paris (1783) also angered the court in Madrid. The Spanish hoped to define the boundary of Florida at the so-called Yazoo Line of 32 degrees 28 minutes north latitude—far enough north to include the rich agricultural lands of the Natchez District.

The Spanish decided to retaliate against both of these diplomatic indiscretions by using an effective form of economic warfare against the newly established American republic. Since the Spanish were in possession of both the Isle of Orleans and the Louisiana Territory in 1783, they held both banks of the Mississippi River at its mouth. By the standards of international law that had existed for centuries and were collected and published by Hugo Grotius in *De Jure Belli et Pacis* (1625), the Spanish were within their legal rights to determine who could and who could not transport their goods and commerce on the Mississippi River. They also were within their rights to restrict port privileges at New Orleans to the merchants and farmers from the United States who might have need of such facilities.

Although the Spanish were within their rights to prohibit the Americans from using the Mississippi River, the government of the United States under the Articles of Confederation sought a negotiated settlement of the question that might produce a more favorable outcome. The Confederation government appointed John Jay, who had served as secretary of foreign affairs for the Continental Congress, to serve as a special envoy to remedy the diplomatic impasse over the Florida boundary and the right of access to the Mississippi River and the port of New Orleans. Jay's Spanish counterpart in these negotiations was Don Diego de Gardoqui, who arrived in the United States in late 1784 to begin the talks. The Jay-Gardoqui negotiations would continue on and off over the course of two years, producing neither a satisfactory outcome for the American position nor a treaty that the Confederation Congress could ratify.

Gardoqui was an effective negotiator and a good judge of character. He recognized a certain strain of vanity in Jay, and thus played that fact to the advantage of the Spanish cause. Gardoqui even showered gifts and praise upon Jay's wife in an effort to ingratiate himself with the U.S. envoy. Gardoqui wanted Jay to agree that the United States would forgo commercial rights on the Mississippi River for a period of twenty-five to thirty years in exchange for special trading privileges that would be effected between the United States and the Spanish colonies in the Western Hemisphere. Gardoqui also wanted Jay to accept a Florida boundary that would keep the Natchez District in Spanish hands.

Although Eastern merchants believed that the potential value of special trading privileges would outweigh the value of the Mississippi River for trade and commerce, such sentiments were not shared by those Americans who were settling in the trans-Appalachian West and establishing farms and homesteads in the Ohio River Valley. There was vociferous opposition to what seemed the pending outcome of the Jay-Gardoqui negotiations, and this would render futile any efforts to reach the negotiated settlement that the Spanish hoped to achieve. Even though Jay believed that Gardoqui had negotiated in good faith and that the pending treaty was in the best interests of the United States, the concerted opposition from Southern and Western interests rendered the negotiations a failure. The Congress approved the proposed treaty by a vote of 7–5, but the Articles of Confederation required the support of nine states for official ratification.

The diplomatic impasse would remain until both nations negotiated the Treaty of San Lorenzo (1795)—or "Pinckney's Treaty"—which provided terms that were much more favorable to U.S. interests. In the 1795 treaty the United States received permission to use the Mississippi River and obtained the "right of deposit" at New Orleans for a period of three years, with the option of renewing the privilege thereafter. Additionally, the Spanish settled upon the line of 31 degrees north latitude as the northern boundary of Florida, thus turning the Natchez District over to the United States.

—Junius P. Rodriguez

See also

Gardoqui, Diego María de; Right of Deposit; San Lorenzo, Treaty of

For Further Reading

Bemis, Samuel Flagg. 1960 [1926]. *Pinckney's Treaty: A Study of America's Advantage from Europe's Distress*. Baltimore: Johns Hopkins Press. Reprint: New Haven: Yale University Press; Marks, Frederick W. 1973. *Independence on Trial: Foreign Affairs and the Making of the Constitution*. Baton Rouge: Louisiana University Press; Whitaker, Arthur Preston. 1962 [1927]. *The Spanish Frontier, 1783–1795: The Westward Movement and Spanish Retreat in the Mississippi Valley*. Lincoln: University of Nebraska Press. Reprint: Gloucester, MA: Peter Smith.

JAY'S TREATY (1794)

Also called the Treaty of Amity, Commerce, and Navigation, Jay's Treaty was signed on November 19, 1794, in London by U.S. chief justice John Jay and British foreign minister Lord Grenville. It was ratified by the United States on August 14, 1795, and by Great Britain on October 28, 1795. Ratifications were exchanged in London on October 28, 1795, and the treaty was officially proclaimed on February 29, 1796. The treaty settled most outstanding differences between the United States and Great Britain that had existed since the end of the American Revolution. Great Britain promised to remove its troops and garrisons from U.S. territory as defined in the Treaty of Paris (1783), to end discrimination against U.S. commerce, and to grant the United States a limited right to trade in the British West Indies. The Mississippi River was declared open to both countries. Great Britain also agreed to the establishment of a commission to investigate U.S. claims for damages and losses resulting from illegal British ship seizures. The treaty also prohibited the outfitting of privateers in the United States by Britain's enemies, and provided for the payment of debts incurred by Americans to British merchants before the American Revolution. Finally, the treaty called for the establishment of a commission to determine the boundaries between the United States and British North America in the Northwest and Northeast.

In the 1790s, the primary goal of the United States was survival. The British illegally maintained forts and trading posts on U.S. soil and continually incited Indian attacks on American settlements and provided the Indians with munitions. These actions were intended to prevent American settlement beyond the Ohio River, in order to create an Indian buffer state between U.S. and British territory that would be tributary to Britain. Thousands of U.S. settlers poured into the West, but few were able to settle north of the Ohio. As settlements grew, the economic existence of the United States west of the Appalachians came to depend on the use of the Mississippi River and the port of New Orleans, which was controlled at the time by Spain.

In 1793, Revolutionary France declared war on most of Europe, including Great Britain and Spain. The United States found itself in a delicate situation. Technically, the 1778 alliance with France was still in effect, but the United States could ill afford to get involved in a major war. President Washington quickly issued the Declaration of Neutrality (1793). About the same time, minister from France Edmond Charles Genêt arrived in the United States and undertook to commission U.S. vessels as French privateers to campaign against British commerce. Genêt also intrigued to form an army in the West to attack Spanish Florida and Louisiana and perhaps also British Canada.

Meanwhile, the war had given the United States a great commercial opportunity with the belligerents. France, however, bought more from the United States than did Britain, and U.S. trade with the revolutionary government boomed. In response, the British Navy seized hundreds of U.S. commercial vessels. With a wary eye on Genêt's activities in the United States, Britain increased the number of troops in Canada and began building a new fort on American soil in the Northwest. President Washington raised an army of thirteen thousand men. An Anglo-American war loomed on the horizon, despite Washington's condemnation of Genêt's activities.

In this tense atmosphere Washington sent Chief Justice John Jay to London in April 1794 to negotiate a settlement. The result was Jay's Treaty, an agreement that met much opposition in the United States but was most likely the best deal that the Americans could get, given the circumstances. Jay secured the territorial integrity of the United States, peace with Great Britain, and important trading rights. He failed, however, to win any significant victories on the issues of neutral rights or impressment, the hated British practice of seizing their own, and sometimes U.S., citizens from U.S. ships on the grounds that they had deserted the British Navy. Thus the treaty was met with opposition, especially in the commerce-driven Northeast and in the West. The limits placed on the West Indies trade were especially despised. Jay was burned in effigy on many occasions. In Philadelphia, mobs threatened Vice President John Adams's house and the office of the British minister. Westerners threatened to break away from the Union if the British tried to use the treaty to close the Mississippi to American trade. These protestations occurred even though the treaty did include provisions whereby both Great Britain and the British East Indies were opened to U.S. merchant vessels.

John Jay became one of the most hated men in America after negotiating Jay's Treaty with the British in 1794.

Political divisions in the United States made the ratification of Jay's Treaty difficult. Federalists, led by Alexander Hamilton, had always favored close ties with Great Britain and thus favored the treaty. Treasury Secretary Hamilton's National Bank needed much money and feared any measure that might reduce the flow of British capital into the United States. Republicans, led by Thomas Jefferson, favored a tougher approach to U.S.-British relations that would compel Britain to alter its discriminatory commercial policies; they saw the treaty as a surrender to Britain. Jefferson was especially concerned with U.S. obligations to France under the 1778 alliance. James Madison argued that the House of Representatives had an equal right to consider the treaty because monies would have to be appropriated to put many of its clauses into effect. President Washington denied that anything but the approval of the Senate was necessary for ratification under the Constitution.

Despite the outcry of its opponents and its narrow ratification, Jay's Treaty had a great impact upon subsequent U.S. history. British withdrawal from American territory in the Northwest and their cessation of assistance to the Indians opened up the lands beyond the Ohio River to American settlement; thousands soon established themselves all the way to the eastern banks of the Mississippi, ensuring that the river would become a vital part of U.S. economic life. The treaty averted war with Great Britain for eighteen years, giving the infant United States time to settle uncertain constitutional matters and strengthen its military establishment. Finally, the treaty created an atmosphere conducive to U.S.-Spanish relations. In 1795, Thomas Pinckney negotiated the Treaty of San Lorenzo with Spain, which settled the boundaries between the United States and Spanish Florida and gave American traders the right of deposit at New Orleans.

—Scott D. Wignall

See also
Diplomacy of the Louisiana Purchase; Genêt, Edmond Charles; Hamilton, Alexander; Jefferson, Thomas; Madison, James; Mississippi River; New Orleans; Pinckney, Thomas; Right of Deposit; San Lorenzo, Treaty of

For Further Reading

Bemis, Samuel Flagg. 1923. *Jay's Treaty: A Study in Commerce and Diplomacy.* New York: Macmillan; Ferrell, Robert H. 1969. *American Diplomacy: A History.* New York: W. W. Norton; Ogg, Frederic Austin. 1904. *The Opening of the Mississippi: A Struggle for Supremacy in the American Interior.* New York: Greenwood Press; Pratt, Julius W. 1965. *A History of United States Foreign Policy.* Englewood Cliffs, NJ: Prentice-Hall.

JEFFERSON EXPANSION NATIONAL MEMORIAL

***See* Gateway Arch**

JEFFERSON, THOMAS (1743–1826)

Perhaps best known as the primary author of the Declaration of Independence (1776), Thomas Jefferson also played a role as president of the United States in acquiring the Louisiana Purchase Territory and in shepherding the treaty to Senate ratification that did much to protect the commercial independence of the young republic he had helped to found a generation earlier. Jefferson may have been the one political leader of the era most ideally suited to conclude successfully the murky diplomacy associated with the Louisiana Purchase, and he certainly placed national interest above particular partisan ideology when he lobbied for acceptance of a singular decision—lacking congressional authorization—that effectively doubled the size of the young nation. A true renaissance man of many talents, Jefferson the scientist realized the wealth of knowledge that the Louisiana Territory contained, and he initiated the Lewis and Clark Expedition to explore the flora, fauna, and ethnography of the newly acquired region. But above all things, Jefferson the political realist understood the implications of his efforts as early as April 18, 1802, when in a letter to statesman Robert Livingston he wrote, "There is on the globe one single spot, the possessor of which is our natural and habitual enemy . . . it is New Orleans . . ." (DeConde 1976).

As a son of Virginia's Piedmont region, Thomas Jefferson reached adulthood as the French and Indian War was coming to a conclusion. In many respects the beginnings of his political education were influenced by two products of that earlier conflict: the transfer of French Louisiana to the Spanish Bourbons and the origins of anti-British colonial attitudes among fellow residents of the Atlantic seaboard colonies. In both of these episodes Jefferson would learn that even those who possess great power, whether political or economic, might be persuaded to yield that power when confronted by a sustained resistance.

Jefferson began his political career by serving in the Virginia House of Burgesses. He quickly became known for his well-reasoned arguments against British policies within the colonies, and he outlined these in the his treatise *Summary View of the Rights of British America* (1774). The Virginia colony sent Jefferson as a delegate to the Second Continental Congress in Philadelphia when that body met in 1775. At the age of thirty-three, Jefferson was selected by the assembled delegates to draft a declaration to support fellow Virginian Richard Henry Lee's call for U.S. independence that had been approved by the body. Working with a committee that included John Adams, Benjamin Franklin, Roger Sherman, and Robert Livingston, Jefferson borrowed heavily from the ideas of the English political philosopher John Locke and drafted a document that found support for revolution in the natural rights that were possessed by all.

After helping to inspire the American Revolution with his high-minded prose, Jefferson returned from the Second Continental Congress to Virginia where he served two terms as governor during the years of the American Revolution. Jefferson did not prove to be a tremendously successful administrator during his gubernatorial career. Many questioned the apparent ineffectiveness and timidity of his actions when British forces under the command of Lord Cornwallis invaded Virginia in 1780. Fortunately, the American victory at Yorktown (1781) sealed the fate of Britain's defeat and guaranteed the formation of the independent republic that Jefferson's words had asserted in 1776.

Immediately following the conclusion of the American Revolution, Jefferson began to serve the young nation as a diplomat. Jefferson traveled to Paris in 1783 where he had been assigned to assist Benjamin Franklin and John Adams who were already there negotiating a series of commercial agreements between the United States and the government of King Louis XVI. Upon Franklin's retirement from diplomatic service in 1785, Jefferson was appointed to succeed the aged diplomat as the United States Minister to France, a position that he held from 1785 to 1789. During his years in Paris, Jefferson came to admire the culture and tradition of the French people. He realized, perhaps better than most, that the success of the Continental Army against the British in the American Revolution was due, in large part, to generous support from France that flowed into American coffers after the Treaty of Alliance (1778) had been negotiated.

Jefferson's diplomatic stint in Paris and his admiration for the French made his political opponents in the United States view him as an incurable Francophile in subsequent years. Though he was a product of the Enlightenment, his republican rhetoric often made him sound like a budding romantic, and his words sometimes had a shocking resonance. For example, when Jefferson learned of the events associated with the Massachusetts uprising known as Shays' Rebellion (1786), he commented from Paris that "From time to time the tree of liberty needs to be watered with the blood of tyrants." Jefferson would leave Paris before the French Revolution began there in July 1789, but somehow by default, many of the republican excesses of that conflict came to be associated with the Jeffersonian ideology.

Jefferson returned to the United States in 1789 where he accepted the appointment to serve as secretary of state (1790–1793) during the first term of George Washington's presidency. In this capacity Jefferson was bedeviled by the appropriate response that the United States should take in response to the beginning of the French Revolution. The terms of the Treaty of Alliance (1778) did call upon the United States to support France in time of need, but the exact nature of how that obligation should be tendered was a point of great debate within President Washington's cabinet. Jefferson often disagreed with Secretary of the Treasury Alexander Hamilton, but neither man believed it wise for the United States to become engaged in a European conflict that could threaten America's security and freedom. Though some stereotyped Jefferson a Francophile, he was much more of a pragmatist than an ideologue. When Edmond Charles Genêt, the young minister of the French Republic, conducted himself as an agent provocateur of the French cause, even Jefferson joined in the chorus of political leaders calling for Genêt's recall.

American officials from the time of the Articles of Confederation Congress through the first three presidential administrations faced a common diplomatic concern that had lingered since the end of the American Revolution. Since the Treaty of Paris (1783) had inadequately defined the southern boundary between the United States and Spanish Florida, relations between the two nations were strained. As the issue festered, Spanish officials in the colony of Louisiana decided to close the Mississippi River to American commerce and they prevented frontiersmen from the United States from warehousing their trade goods at New Orleans. The Articles of Confederation government had attempted to settle this question with the Jay-Gardoqui negotiations, but those talks had proven ineffective. The matter did seem to subside when the American diplomat Thomas Pinckney was able to negotiate the Treaty of San Lorenzo (1795) that set the Florida boundary and gave Americans the right to navigate the river and claim the "right of deposit" (permission to use port and warehouse facilities) at New Orleans, but the issue would reappear later.

By the curious cause of constitutionally mandated voting practices, Thomas Jefferson found himself elected as vice president of the United States (1797–1801) during the presidential administration of John Adams. The Adams-Jefferson pairing was a true odd couple as the president was a strong Federalist while the vice president was a Democratic-Republican, or Jeffersonian Republican, and the two men seldom agreed with one another on matters of political or diplomatic importance. As vice president, Jefferson found himself part of an administration that waged an undeclared naval war against the French Republic—the so-called Quasi-War (1798–1800)—in response to the humiliating treatment that French officials had bestowed upon three American diplomats in the XYZ Affair. Yet, while Adams and Jefferson disagreed on policy matters, both men were neither political ideologues nor iconoclasts. President Adams fought against members of the Federalist Party to ensure that the conflict did not expand into a larger declared war that would threaten American interests. Thomas Jefferson, as president of the United States in 1801, would urge the Senate to ratify the Convention of Mortefontaine (1800) that his predecessor had engineered, to bring an end to the Quasi-War and establish a new commercial relationship between France and the United States.

The retrocession of the Louisiana Territory from Spain to France in 1800 would have profound economic repercussions on America's commercial independence. The reacquisition of Louisiana by the French negated any commercial benefits that the United States held under the terms of the Treaty of San Lorenzo (1795) and the prospect of having to renegotiate these terms every time that the Louisiana Territory changed hands was not an appealing prospect. From the earliest months of his presidential administration, Thomas Jefferson sought to devise a strategy whereby, through purchase, the United States might gain legal rights to navigate the Mississippi River and warehouse goods at a location somewhere near its mouth.

Thomas Jefferson effectively doubled the size of the United States in 1803 by purchasing the Louisiana Territory from France.

President Jefferson's initial plan was to attempt to purchase either the Isle of Orleans or a portion of West Florida from the French. He advised Robert Livingston, the United States Minister to France, to begin negotiating for this desired outcome and told Livingston that in the event of a failure to win the concessions sought, the United States should advise the French that it planned to join in an alliance with the British. Under such an arrangement, in the event of another European war, the United States could seize the Louisiana Territory as a wartime exigency. When it seemed as though Livingston's negotiations were not bearing fruit, Jefferson authorized James Monroe as an additional diplomat to the French Republic to assist in the effort.

Neither Livingston nor Monroe, and certainly not Jefferson, was prepared for the real estate transfer that First Consul Napoleon Bonaparte offered the United States in the spring of 1803. Even though the charge of purchasing the entire Louisiana Territory exceeded the diplomatic business with which they had been charged, Livingston and Monroe both realized that a quick response to the offer proffered by Bonaparte was key lest he change his mind on the matter. Both diplomats realized the enormity of the opportunity, but they also understood the political fallout that would result from their decision.

When President Jefferson learned of the decision that Livingston and Monroe had made, he supported the action of the diplomats, but he was still concerned about how the purchase of the entire Louisiana Territory would be accepted by the U. S. Senate and how foreign governments would view the American action. The ideology of Jeffersonian Republicanism was predicated upon the notion of small government. Jefferson and his political allies supported the doctrine of strict construction of the U.S. Constitution, whereby the government could only claim those rights that were specifically enumerated with the bulk of rights reserved to the states and to the people. The idea of doubling the size of the nation by affixing signatures to one treaty was something that troubled Jefferson because the diplomatic action did not have prior congressional authorization and he did not believe that the Constitution permitted the acquisition of such territory by treaty purchase. Privately, Jefferson pondered that an amendment to the Constitution would be necessary to make the arrangement legal, but he also understood that the likelihood of passing such a measure rapidly in the heated political climate of 1803 was unlikely. As a result, Jefferson set aside his views on small government and strict constructionism, for the moment, and became an advocate of a powerful large federal government that drew its powers from a loose interpretation of the Constitution. Jefferson was being a pragmatist and putting the national good ahead of partisan ideology.

Even before the opportunity to purchase the Louisiana Territory arose in 1803, President Jefferson had begun preparations for a major scientific expedition to travel overland to the Pacific Ocean. Jefferson had corresponded with friends who were major scientists and naturalists of the day, and he sought their advice as to what should be the areas of focus that such an expedition might take when it did occur. As the experts responded to Jefferson's requests, each was asked to tutor Meriwether Lewis, President Jefferson's personal secretary and the man whom he had selected to lead the proposed expedition to the West. On January 18, 1803, Jefferson sent a secret message to Congress calling for an expedition to explore the unknown regions of the West.

That Jefferson dispatched his personal secretary to lead the Corps of Discovery indicates how closely the president wanted to be connected to the expedition. Lewis was specifically instructed to send samples of rocks, flora, and fauna back to Jefferson so that he could view them and then send them along to other American scientists and other specialists who could study them. Upon the successful conclusion of the excursion in 1806, Meriwether Lewis reported directly to Jefferson before he began work on editing the official journals of the expedition.

Thomas Jefferson was a visionary and a nationalist. He may have been the first American political leader to comprehend the coast-to-coast notion of American identity that would come to be called Manifest Destiny by the 1840s. Before he died in 1826, Jefferson saw two new states carved out of the lands that had been purchased during his administration. The admission of Louisiana (1812) and Missouri (1821) into the Union were historic occasions, but Jefferson the nationalist feared for the nation when the divisive issue of slavery—"a fire bell in the night"—surrounded debate over Missouri's bid for statehood. Perhaps it was Jefferson's dream that the nation might be both expansive and united, but history would soon prove that these twin goals were mutually exclusive.

—Junius P. Rodriguez

See also

Genêt, Edmond Charles; Lewis, Meriwether; Lewis and Clark Expedition; Livingston, Robert; Missouri Compromise; Monroe, James; Right of Deposit; Slavery

For Further Reading

Banning, Lance. 1978. *The Jeffersonian Persuasion: Evolution of a Party Ideology.* Ithaca, NY: Cornell University Press; DeConde, Alexander. 1976. *This Affair of Louisiana.* New York: Scribner's; Kaplan, Lawrence S. 1999. *Thomas Jefferson: Westward the Course of Empire.* Wilmington, DE: Scholarly Resources; Peterson, Merrill D. 1960. *The Jefferson Image in the American Mind.* New York: Oxford University Press; Tucker, Robert W. and David C. Hendrickson. 1990. *Empire of Liberty: The Statecraft of Thomas Jefferson.* New York: Oxford University Press.

JESUP, FORT

When Jefferson purchased Louisiana from France in 1803, he also acquired an unresolved border dispute. France had claimed land as far west as the Brazos and Sabine Rivers, whereas Spain claimed that the border was east of there, at the Red River and Arroyo Hondo, a small creek four miles west of Natchitoches.

By 1805 the situation had deteriorated, and it looked as if Spain and the United States would go to war over the disputed territory. U.S. troops under Captain Turner headed west out of Natchitoches and met Spanish corporal Gonzales at Los Adaes. The Americans forced the Spanish to agree in writing to retire west of the Sabine, but that did not resolve the issue. By 1806 the Spanish were back in force under the leadership of General Simon Herrera, and General James Wilkinson rode out of Natchitoches to meet him. A battle seemed inevitable, but that evening Samuel Swartwout, an emissary from Aaron Burr, arrived and conferred in secret with General Wilkinson. The next day, Wilkinson and Herrera agreed to form a "Neutral Strip" that covered the disputed area.

The Neutral Strip was a no-man's land under the control of neither government and without any sort of police force. It became a refuge for outlaws, highwaymen, and fugitive slaves. Settlers heading for Texas were frequently robbed and murdered there, and nobody dared try to cross it unarmed or alone.

The boundary dispute was settled by the Adams-Onís Treaty (1819), when it was decided that the Sabine River would be the western boundary of Louisiana. The United States moved swiftly to control its new territory and to establish law and order.

Colonel Zachary Taylor and General Gaines arrived in March 1822 to make a personal inspection of the area. They selected the site for Fort Jesup (named in honor of Brigadier General Thomas Sidney Jesup) based on its location on the Camino Real at the crest of a high ridge between the Red River and the Sabine River. Water and timber were abundant, and the new border was only a short day's march away.

The first troops arrived in May 1822 and immediately set to work. At its height the post consisted of eighty-two structures built with stones quarried nearby and with timber harvested and turned into boards on the post. There were officers' quarters, soldiers' barracks, kitchens, a hospital, and a sawmill.

In May 1844, General Taylor was ordered back to Fort Jesup in order to take command of the Army of Observation encamped there. War was brewing between the United States and Mexico over the status of the settlers in Texas. Taylor received word from the Secretary of War that Texas would probably vote for annexation on July 4, 1845, and that he should prepare for any emergency. By July 1, 1845, Taylor had his men on the move and launched attacks by both land and water.

Fort Jesup was of vital importance during the war between Mexico and the United States, but the victory it helped to realize brought about the demise of the fort. The border moved farther west, and the post was no longer needed. It was abandoned in 1846 and left with only a caretaker and a handful of guards. These too were soon withdrawn, and the post began to fall into a state of disrepair. The people who were supposed to keep an eye on the buildings began to dismantle them and sell the pieces for personal profit. In a letter written January 30, 1847, to Colonel Stenton, the quartermaster general in Washington, D.C., A. Darling, the "post butler" complained about a man named Hamilton who was supposed to be taking care of the post and was, in fact, "stealing everything he could get his hands on" (Fort Jesup MSS).

It was decided to divide the fort into lots for sale to the general public. In April 1850, the government hired three local people to appraise the land, and most of it was sold for 25 cents an acre to two of them, William D. Stephens and George W. Thompson. Later that month in a letter to General Jesup, Thompson offered to buy the unsold lots for 10 cents an acre.

A small portion of the military grounds was preserved by Sabine Parish as a historical park, and the 1956 Louisiana State Legislature authorized the establishment of a Historic Park and National Reservation in memory of its military importance. In 1961 the fort was designated a National Historic Landmark by the U.S. Department of the Interior.

—Lisa-Kay Wolffe

See also
Camino Real, El; Los Adaes; Natchitoches; Neutral Ground; Texas

For Further Reading
Fort Jesup Collection. Microfilm Collection #206, reel 4. Northwestern State University Archives. Natchitoches, LA; Judge Jones Collection. Folder 39. Northwestern State University Archives. Natchitoches, LA; Ruth Cross Collection. Box 2, Folder 47. Northwestern State University Archives. Natchitoches, LA.

JONES, EVAN (1739–1813)

Evan Jones was born in New York City on August 17, 1739. He married Marie Ponponne Verret in Ascension Parish, Louisiana, and the couple raised a family of seven children.

By the time he was in his early thirties, Jones was working in a mercantile house in New York City that regularly did business along the Amite River, within the Spanish colony of Louisiana, and with Pensacola during the British interlude that followed the French and Indian War. The commercial ties that Jones had established were hampered by the years of the American Revolution, but the contacts that he had made across the Gulf Coast region would serve him well during the early years of American independence.

The Confederation Congress commissioned Jones as consul to the Spanish government at New Orleans, which then served as the colonial capital of Louisiana. Impressed with the young American consul, the Spanish appointed him to serve as commandant of Lafourche de Chitamachas ("The Fork of the Chitamachas"), a colonial district located southwest of New Orleans. The district followed the course of Bayou Lafourche, a distributary of the Mississippi River that runs through present-day Ascension and Lafourche Parishes in Louisiana. The name Chitamacha refers to an Indian tribe that populated the region.

In 1780, Jones purchased a tract of land for $1,200. This tract contained approximately 797 arpents. By 1787 the Spanish government rewarded Jones with an additional land grant of 1,713 arpents, thus giving the American 2,511 arpents of prime farmland. Jones made one additional purchase of land in 1809, after the region was possessed by the United States. Eventually Jones would use this vast land holding to establish the plantation that became known as Evan Hall.

When the United States purchased the Louisiana Territory in 1803, it became necessary to begin the process of establishing the forms and institutions of U.S. government upon a region that had known only colonial control at the hands of the French, and later the Spanish. Territorial governor William C. C. Claiborne appointed Evan Jones to serve on the legislative council of the Territory of Orleans. Jones would soon resign this post, however, because he believed that the Americans did not treat the former French and Spanish colonists with due respect for their customs and traditions. In 1804, Jones was named the president of the Louisiana Bank.

During the colonial era, under both French and Spanish rule, the Louisiana colonists had sought a suitable cash crop that could make the colony economically sustainable. In 1795, Etienne Bore made a remarkable advancement in the infant sugar industry by perfecting a means of processing the product. Bore earned an amazing $12,000 off a crop of sugar that he grew on a plantation near New Orleans. Lured by the promise of tremendous profits, Jones began to cultivate sugar cane at Evan Hall in 1807. Jones's industrial concept involved the manufacture of raw cane into sugar by using horse-powered mills and simple open kettles. Soon other plantations in the Lafourche region and points beyond were following Jones's lead.

Evan Jones died at New Orleans on May 11, 1813. He was first buried in Donaldsonville, in Ascension Parish, but his remains were later moved to a tomb in the historic St. Louis Cemetery No.1 in New Orleans.

—Junius P. Rodriguez

See also

Bore, Jean Etienne; Claiborne, William Charles Cole

For Further Reading

McCall, Henry. 1899. *History of Evan Hall Plantation.* Chapel Hill: Southern Historical Collection, University of North Carolina.

KANSAS

The Louisiana Purchase was controversial from the start. Federalists and Republicans battled over its constitutionality, Thomas Jefferson secretly admitted that an amendment was necessary to make the purchase legal, and many wondered how this vast territory would affect the new nation. Yet even those who argued over Louisiana in 1803 would have been surprised that some fifty years later, certain areas of the purchase were still at the center of controversy. The contention had to do with the spread of slavery. Antebellum politicians designed the Compromise of 1850 to quell the nation's increasing sectional agitation. Yet passage of the Kansas-Nebraska Act (1854) unleashed a firestorm that was extinguished only by the Civil War.

Senator Stephen A. Douglas, the "Little Giant" from Illinois, lit the Kansas fuse in January 1854. As chairman of the Senate Committee on Territories, he introduced a bill to organize Kansas. His motives were both economic and political. On the one hand, organization of the territory encouraged the creation of a transcontinental railroad that passed through Chicago. On the other lay a larger party goal. Douglas hoped that focusing on expansion in the West, and more particularly upon popular sovereignty, would help to unify a troubled Democratic Party shaken by sectional discord.

The difficulty in Douglas's plan was the Missouri Compromise (1820), which stipulated that all new territories and states carved out of the Louisiana Purchase above the line of 36 degrees 30 minutes north latitude were closed to slavery. In order to make the Kansas bill palatable to Southerners, Douglas ultimately advocated repeal of the Missouri Compromise and use of popular sovereignty instead. In this scenario, the people settling in the territory decided on the legality of slavery. This Democratic idea, though untested, had already been used in the Compromise of 1850 to settle the dispute over the newly established New Mexico and Utah territories.

The finalized Kansas-Nebraska Act passed on May 30, 1854. Instead of a single Kansas territory, the act split the area in two, both of which incorporated the notion of popular sovereignty. The repercussions that followed turned Kansas into a battleground, divided the Democratic Party, completed the destruction of the Whig Party, and aided in the creation of a sectional Republican Party. Moreover, tensions grew to such an extreme that blood was spilled on the floor of the U.S. Senate. Senator Douglas's plan to create a railroad and stabilize his party took a very wrong turn.

Rather than an example of democracy in action, popular sovereignty was a race. Anti- and proslavery advocates rushed to get their forces into Kansas so that a territorial government with the "proper" views would prevail in the referendum that would be conducted there. Amos Lawrence of Massachusetts organized the Emigrant Aid Company, which provided financial assistance to Northerners willing to leave for Kansas. Some 1,240 people took advantage of the offer.

The proslavery forces had, however, the advantage of geography. They needed to travel only a short distance in order to lay first claim to the plains of Kansas. Missouri "ruffians" crossed the state border and formed a government that legalized slavery. President Franklin Pierce, considered by many to be a "doughface"—a Northerner with Southern sympathies—quickly acknowledged the legitimacy of the proslavery territorial government. The new legislature enacted laws that safeguarded slavery: fines and imprisonment for expressing opinions about slavery; the death penalty for encouraging slave revolts or aiding escaped slaves; and requirements that all voters take an oath upholding these slave codes.

By September 1855, antislavery Northerners had arrived in sufficient numbers to challenge the proslavery government. Organizing a Free-State Party, Northerners called for a constitutional convention in Topeka. In October and November antislavery forces wrote a free-state constitution and elected both a governor and legislature. Kansas now had two territorial governments. One was proslavery and accepted by President Pierce, and subsequently by President James Buchanan. The other, though technically illegal, represented the majority of voters. With the political battle lines clearly drawn, it was merely a matter of time before anger and hatred resulted in bloodshed. One proslavery Kansas newspaper encouraged its supporters to raise the sword and pistol: "Let us purge ourselves of all abolition emissaries . . . and give distinct notice that all who do not leave immediately for the East, will leave for eternity!"

In the spring of 1856, proslavery forces heeded such advice. Acting on an indictment to arrest members of the free state government for treason, Missourians

The appearance of sod houses on the Great Plains of Kansas marked the arrival of homesteaders who settled in the more desolate parts of the state. (North Wind Picture Archives)

entered the town of Lawrence on May 21 with five cannon and a thirst for blood. After destroying two newspaper offices, the "ruffians" burned the hotel, along with the home of the free state governor, plundered shops, and ultimately killed five men. Kansas was bleeding. The sacking of Lawrence proved to Northerners that slavery advocates resorted to lawlessness and violence in order to force the peculiar institution down the nation's throat.

Nor was Kansas the only scene of bloodshed. The battle over the new territory raged in the halls of Congress as well. Kansas was a microcosm of the larger slavery debate and thus became a focal point for both sides. Leading the charge for antislavery forces in the Senate was Charles Sumner of Massachusetts. At the same time that proslavery forces prepared to invade Lawrence, Sumner, on May 19 and 20, delivered a speech entitled "The Crime against Kansas." Charging that a "slave-power" conspiracy existed, Sumner lambasted the actions of Southerners and singled out certain senators for special rebuke. Among them was Andrew P. Butler of South Carolina, who, Sumner charged, "has chosen a mistress to whom he has made his vows, and who, though ugly to others, is always lovely to him; though polluted in the sight of the world, is chaste in his sight—I mean the harlot, Slavery."

Such indecorous language was dangerous in light of the Southern regard for honor. And though Butler was not present to hear the insults, the South Carolinian's nephew, congressional representative Preston Brooks, learned of the affront. Dueling was out of the question because Brooks did not view Sumner as a social equal. A sound thrashing, however, was in order. Thus on May 22, Brooks entered the Senate chamber and beat Sumner unconscious with a cane. Bloody Kansas had reached Washington.

The attack in the Senate emboldened both sides. Northerners charged that slaveholders trampled upon democracy and free speech, turning to violence for victory. The South celebrated Brooks's vindication of Southern honor and showered him with gifts of canes. The acts of violence on the part of proslavery forces encouraged two things: retaliation, and the creation of a new anti-Southern Republican Party.

Retaliation came in the form of John Brown. An abolitionist with a messianic vision and enraged by both the Lawrence massacre and the caning of Charles Sumner, Brown exacted an eye for an eye. On May 24, with seven followers, four of whom were his sons, Brown rode into Pottawatomie, Kansas, and with a broadsword split the heads of five proslavery men.

The violence on the part of both sides also eroded loyalty to the Democratic and Whig Parties. Whereas Stephen A. Douglas and other Democrats worked hard to avoid a complete sectional split in the wake of the Kansas fiasco, the Whigs were not as successful. The party slowly disintegrated, and along with a number of disgruntled Democrats, politicians organized a new anti-Southern Republican Party that focused on stopping an aggressive "slave power" bent on tyrannizing the North.

The battle in Kansas was both a catalyst and a victim of the political maneuvering in Washington. The next challenge was the attempt by Kansas at statehood. In February 1857, the proslavery legislature called for a constitutional convention to meet in Lecompton in September. When antislavery forces protested the subsequent Lecompton Constitution and demanded that it be presented to voters for approval, the legislature refused. They instead offered voters the option of deciding only on the clause specifically legalizing slavery. The trick, however, was that the constitution contained ample safeguards for the protection of slavery even if the main clause was voided. When the antislavery forces refused to play such a game and boycotted the polls, the Lecompton Constitution passed easily in December.

Yet in the midst of this political game playing, free state forces took legal control of the legislature and called for a new vote on the constitution. On January 4, 1858, it suffered a crushing defeat, but the Buchanan administration had other plans. It succeeded in pushing the Lecompton Constitution through the Senate; the House of Representatives, however, was another matter. The House passed the Crittenden-Montgomery Amendment, stipulating that the entire constitution be resubmitted to Kansas voters. When the Senate refused to accept this change, a stalemate ensued. A resolution came in the English Bill. A shameless carrot-and-stick tactic, the bill offered Kansas a land grant if the Lecompton Constitution passed; if it failed, postponement of admission would result, until the territory's population reached 93,600.

Bribery and threats had no effect on the people of Kansas. The Lecompton Constitution was defeated by a whopping 12,000 to 1,900, and statehood was postponed until January 1861, by which time the question of slavery simply did not matter. War was already on the way.

The battle over Kansas was a key component in the coming of the Civil War. Yet Stephen A. Douglas had merely hoped to secure economic benefits to Illinois and help solidify the Democratic Party. What ultimately occurred was a battle over popular sovereignty, a weakening of the second U.S. party system, and the growth of a Northern, sectional party.

—*Matthew Warshauer*

For Further Reading

Holt, Michael F. 1978. *The Political Crisis of the 1850s.* New York: W. W. Norton; McPherson, James M. 1988. *Battle Cry of Freedom: The Civil War Era.* New York: Oxford University Press; Rawley, James A. 1969. *Race and Politics: Bleeding Kansas and the Coming of the Civil War.* Philadelphia: J. B. Lippincott.

KANSAS-NEBRASKA ACT (1854)

As early as the 1840s, Americans expressed interest in constructing a transcontinental railroad through the unorganized territory of the Louisiana Purchase to the Pacific coast. In 1853, eager to see the region opened to settlement and railroad construction, the federal government forced several groups of Plains Indians from the area. The desire to bridge East and West resulted in the Kansas-Nebraska Act (1854), and the political turmoil that followed served as the catalyst for the development of the Second Party System.

In January 1854, in an effort to open the region to official settlement, Democratic senator Stephen A. Douglas of Illinois proposed a bill that would organize the area into two territories, Kansas and Nebraska. To win Southern support, Douglas proposed that the question of slavery in the territories be decided by popular sovereignty. Thus if it became law, the Kansas-Nebraska Act would effectively repeal the Missouri Compromise (1820), which had "forever prohibited" slavery above the line of 36 degrees 30 minutes north latitude in the Louisiana Purchase territory.

Douglas's bill instantly created a political crisis in the North. Angry Free Soiler men denounced the bill as a violation of the Missouri Compromise and a capitulation to the slave interests. Despite the massive outcry from those opposed to the extension of slavery into new territory, the bill passed with the votes of many Northern Democratic congressmen.

Outrage over the bill prompted Northerners to form anti-Nebraska clubs to protest the law. As a result, the Democratic Party in the North found itself more factionalized than ever. Numerous Northern Democrats in Congress who had supported the bill found themselves voted out of office in the fall 1854 elections. By 1856, as anti- and proslavery Whigs could no longer tolerate each other, that party faced imminent dissolution. Eventually the Republican Party, born in 1854 as a Free Soil organization, absorbed the coalition of anti-Nebraska factions, former Northern Whigs, and Democrats and emerged as a sectional party on a platform that opposed the expansion of slavery.

Meanwhile, many contemporary observers presumed that the Kansas Territory, adjacent to the state of Missouri and with a climate suited for agriculture, would become a slave state by popular sovereignty, while the Nebraska Territory would remain free. Free Soil Northerners and proslavery Southerners were, however, determined that Kansas would be organized to reflect their own beliefs.

Northern Free Soil interests organized the New England Emigrant Aid Company to promote and finance settlement of Kansas by antislavery residents. Southerners, likewise, encouraged settlement of Kansas by proslavery forces. In March 1855, a territorial election was held to select a legislature for Kansas. Some five thousand Missourians crossed over into the territory on election day and fraudulently cast votes. The so-called border ruffians succeeded in helping the proslavery forces elect a proslavery legislature. The legislature quickly adopted measures hostile to antislavery residents. Opposition to slavery, for example, was made a felony, and the death penalty was the prescribed punishment for aiding a fugitive slave.

As chief sponsor of the Kansas-Nebraska Bill, Senator Stephen A. Douglas hoped that popular sovereignty would stem the divisive debate over slavery's expansion into the territories.

Furious antislavery forces responded by drafting a Free Soil territorial constitution and electing their own legislature. Indicative of their Free Soil stand but antiblack prejudices, the legislature not only banned slavery in Kansas but free blacks as well. With two legislatures in place, one elected fraudulently and the other established extralegally, Kansas was poised for a showdown between the two groups.

Sporadic skirmishes erupted in 1855, but the violence escalated in May 1856. On May 21, a group of proslavery men attacked the Free Soil stronghold of Lawrence, Kansas, destroying printing presses, buildings, and other property. Three days later, the radical abolitionist John Brown sought to avenge the crime and led a small band of men to a settlement near Pottawatamie Creek. Brown and his men dragged five proslavery men from their homes and attacked them with broadswords, splitting their skulls and hacking their bodies. As proslavery forces sought revenge and antislavery forces mounted their own attacks, Kansas erupted into civil war. More than two hundred people died in the fighting before federal troops dispatched to "Bleeding Kansas" put an end to the violence.

The fallout from the Kansas-Nebraska Act, and the violence that followed, split the Democrats and the Whigs along sectional lines. The turmoil ushered in the Republican Party and the Second Party System. By 1856, the new party became the purely sectional party of the North, as the Democratic Party moved closer to becoming a sectional party dominated by the South.

—Alicia E. Rodriquez

See also
Kansas; Missouri Compromise

For Further Reading
Foner, Eric. 1970. *Free Soil, Free Labor, Free Men: The Ideology of the Republican Party before the Civil War.* New York: Oxford University Press; Freehling, William W. 1990. *The Road to Disunion: Secessionists at Bay, 1776–1854.* New York: Oxford University Press; Gienapp, William E. 1987. *The Origins of the Republican Party, 1852–1856.* New York: Oxford University Press; Holt, Michael F. 1999. *The Rise and Fall of the American Whig Party: Jacksonian Politics and the Onset of the Civil War.* New York: Oxford University Press.

KASKASKIA

Located along the Mississippi River, the tiny settlement of Kaskaskia is considered by some to be the oldest town in the West—certainly it is the oldest white settlement located in the Mississippi Valley. The first Kaskaskia settlement was founded in 1675 by Father Jacques Marquette as a mission settlement among the Kaskaskia Indians near the site of present-day Utica, Illinois. A second Kaskaskia was founded (or relocated) by French Jesuits in 1703 as an Indian village for members of the Kaskaskia and Tamaroa Tribes, which had moved from central Illinois farther to the southwest as they sought to avoid hostilities with members of the Iroquois Confederation. Although the village started out primarily as a mission station, eventually French settlers began to live there, and soon the community assumed more and more of a French colonial appearance. By the 1720s the French began to fortify the area around Kaskaskia by establishing military outposts like Fort de Chartres.

Despite its French colonial origins, the settlement eventually changed hands and played a critical role in determining the geopolitical future of much of North America. Following the Treaty of Paris (1763) that ended the French and Indian War, the settlement at Kaskaskia, being located on the east side of the Mississippi River, became a possession of the British. The settlement served as a major base of British power in the West until it was captured without bloodshed by George Rogers Clark on July 4, 1778. This victory gave the American colonial forces titular control over the Northwest Territory and was largely responsible for the western boundary of the United States being placed at the Mississippi River in the Treaty of Paris (1783) at the end of the American Revolution. In subsequent years, the U.S. government selected Kaskaskia to be the capital of the Illinois Territory, and it also served as the capital of the newly created state of Illinois from 1818 to 1820. The economic and political influence of Kaskaskia declined after 1820 and so too did the population of the town.

The settlement is located in what is today Randolph County, Illinois, near the site where the Kaskaskia River joins with the Mississippi. The original village site was gradually inundated by flood waters after 1844 as the Mississippi River changed its course; by the early 1880s, this action had eventually created Kaskaskia Island. The island is today sparsely populated, as it still faces the threat of flooding from time to time.

—Junius P. Rodriguez

See also
Clark, George Rogers; Chartres, Fort de

For Further Reading
Belting, Natalia M. 1948. *Kaskaskia under the French Regime.* Urbana: University of Illinois Press.

KAW

Also known as the Kansa, or Konza, people, the Kaw typify the experience of indigenous peoples in the wake of the Louisiana Purchase. For much of their history, they lived as farmers in semisedentary villages throughout northeastern Kansas and portions of Missouri and Nebraska. They supplemented staple crops (such as corn, beans, pumpkin, and melons) with hunting (particularly of bison) and to a lesser extent fishing. Kaw social organization was grounded in kinship relations and loose political confederacies. Following the Louisiana Purchase, the Kaw, in common with other native nations in the trans-Mississippi West, endured intense and irreversible cultural modification.

The Kaw, along with the Osage, Ponca, Omaha, and Quapaw, lived as one people in the lower Ohio Valley before the arrival of the Europeans in the late fifteenth century. Together they constitute a division of the Hopewell cultures dubbed Dehegiha-Siouan. During the sixteenth century, pressured by native nations to their east and the depletion of game, this collective group migrated westward to the Mississippi Valley. Eventually the singular Dehegiha-Siouan people split into distinct ethnic groups. The Osage and Quapaw pushed south, with the former taking control of the Ozark plateau region; the

Omaha and Ponca moved north, settling in present-day Nebraska. The Kaw, in turn, occupied an extensive area centering around the Kansas River Valley in northeastern Kansas. Because their new homeland was claimed by other groups who often saw the newcomers as trespassers, the Kaw regularly came into conflict with their neighbors and for a time endured persistent migrations.

The Kaw first encountered Europeans in the early eighteenth century, and they rapidly found themselves in regular contact with Spanish, French, British, and later American traders and officials. Although these interactions opened novel economic opportunities for the Kaw, they brought with them many unforeseen and negative consequences. Trade disrupted the indigenous subsistence economy. Increased contact with Europeans and Americans spread epidemic diseases among the Kaw. Cholera and smallpox proved especially devastating during this period, causing massive depopulation, the breakdown of families, and individual despair. Conflicts with surrounding native nations became more common and pronounced, while factionalism and internal dissent marked Kaw social relations.

In spite of these difficulties, the Kaw remained an important impediment to U.S. efforts to realize the promise of the Louisiana Purchase. They occupied areas desirable for commercial and agricultural activities. And what was worse, both for many Americans and neighboring tribes, they continued to command the Kansas River Valley. The presence and vitality of the Kaw in the early nineteenth century also proved an obstacle to the emerging policy that advocated the relocation of Eastern Indian communities to reservations in Kansas.

The Louisiana Purchase set in motion processes that exacerbated existing social problems. Disease remained a constant threat, while individual despair and alcoholism increased. Violence, factionalism, and intertribal hostilities persisted, often marked by greater desperation and intensity. What was left of the internal economy collapsed and was replaced by poverty and dependence. And the near extinction of the bison and later poor provisioning on reservations made malnutrition common.

The Indian Removal Act (1830) relocated Eastern Indians west of the Mississippi. Many tribes were initially moved to areas in the Kansas Territory that the Kaw claimed as their own. The increasing presence of removed tribes introduced other problems. The Kaw felt crowded and threatened as the already scarce game was further depleted. More important, Indian removal combined with the desires of whites forced the Kaw to negotiate treaties and exchange large tracts of land for promises of money, education, and other assistance.

Beginning in 1825, the Kaw signed four treaties with the federal government. The first shrunk their domain from twenty million acres to two million acres, an exchange for which the Kaw received a small annuity, livestock, and schools. The second, in 1846, provided for the sale of the remainder of their original domain and relocated them to a reservation near Council Grove, Kansas. In a third treaty, negotiated in 1859, developers and speculators pressured the government to reduce the Kaw reservation by more than half. Finally, in 1872, the Kaw agreed, despite intense opposition, to sell their remaining holdings in Kansas and move to a larger reservation in Indian Territory.

In 1902, thirty years after settling in Oklahoma, Charles Curtis, a mixed-blood tribal member, Kansas congressman, and future vice president in the Hoover administration, guided the Kaw Allotment Act through Congress over the opposition of many full-blood Kaw.

The Kaw were reorganized in the late 1950s, becoming a federally recognized Indian tribe, the Kaw Nation of Oklahoma. Today, nearly twenty-five hundred enrolled members compose the tribe, which is headquartered in Kaw City, Oklahoma.

—*C. Richard King*

See also
Osage; Ponca; Quapaw

For Further Reading

Unrau, William E. 1971. *The Kansa Indians: A History of the Wind People, 1673–1873*. Norman: University of Oklahoma Press.

KEARNY, FORT

The U.S. Army first built Fort Kearny—named for Stephen Watts Kearny, who won fame in the Mexican War—on the banks of the Missouri River near present-day Nebraska City, Nebraska, in 1846, to protect travelers on the overland trails. Officials moved the fort westward to the south bank of the Platte River near present-day Kearney, Nebraska, in 1848. For the next twenty-three years, Fort Kearny stood guard over the Platte River Road, providing a federal presence that helped the nation expand across and into the Louisiana Purchase.

The first Fort Kearny contributed to growing traffic and settlement, which helped spawn Nebraska City, an important early shipping point on the Missouri River and a jumping-off place for overland emigrants. Army officials supposed that the location would allow it to protect overland travelers while at the same time receiving supplies by steamboat. The Mexican War drew soldiers from the fort soon after its establishment, leaving it with a skeleton garrison. Officials also recognized that the heaviest trail traffic went from Independence and St. Joseph in Missouri to the Platte River, and that a better location for the fort would be where the trails from the various Missouri River border towns converged to travel the main line of the Platte River Road. In 1848 they moved the fort to that location, about 180 miles to the west, on land ceded by the Pawnee in 1833 at the head of Grand Island.

Despite its humble appearance, the second Fort Kearny symbolized the gateway to the Great Plains and served various duties associated with U.S. continental expansion. For most of its career, the fort consisted of a cluster of buildings lacking any fortifications. During hostilities with the Lakota and Cheyenne in the mid-1860s, soldiers built a stockade, although Fort Kearny never experienced an Indian attack. The early collection of sod buildings inspired reactions from travelers ranging from "desolate" and "forbidding" to "an oasis in the desert." Later additions of frame structures and the hospitality rendered by officers and their wives led some to perceive it as an outpost of civilization. However travelers perceived it, Fort Kearny served as the most important link between the Missouri River and Fort Laramie.

As a military operation, Fort Kearny's most important roles included providing escorts for travelers and freighters and as an assembly point for campaigns against Indian nations in conflict with the United States. Expeditions against the Lakota and Cheyenne departed from Fort Kearny in 1855 and 1857, respectively. Also in 1857, the Utah Expedition passed through Fort Kearny on its way to enforce federal order in the Utah Territory, where U.S. officials believed Mormon leaders to be in rebellion. The Civil War diverted regular troops from the fort and saw them replaced by volunteer units, mostly from Nebraska and Iowa. Raids on travelers, freighters, ranchers, and stage stations in 1864 and 1865 by the Lakota and Cheyenne periodically stopped traffic on the Platte River Road and resulted in increased patrols from Fort Kearny and soldiers being assigned to garrison new posts along the trail.

Overland travelers often found the fort an important source of supplies. The commander could sell goods from the government warehouse to destitute travelers, which he sometimes did for promissory notes that often proved worthless. The post sutler and blacksmith also provided valuable goods and services for emigrants, as did the Fort Kearny post office. Neighboring settlements sprang up in the late 1850s just off the military reservation to provide services unavailable at the fort. Valley City and Kearney City, also known as Dogtown (after a nearby prairie dog colony) and Dobytown (after its adobe-style buildings), respectively, started as stage stations and evolved to include other diversions, such as liquor, gambling, and prostitution. The fort's protective presence also contributed to the cattle industry's development in the Platte Valley.

In addition to stage lines, other forms of travel and communications links followed the Platte River Road through Fort Kearny's jurisdiction. The Pony Express had stations in the vicinity during its brief existence. The Pacific Telegraph, which helped kill the Pony Express, passed through the fort on its way from Omaha to San Francisco. The Union Pacific Railroad reached the fort's vicinity in 1866, but on the north side of the Platte, marking the beginning of the end for Fort Kearny. Although soldiers from the fort guarded construction crews, the new transportation system and its location north of the Platte marked Fort Kearny's obsolescence. The army abandoned the fort in 1871.

Farmers plowed under portions of the site but preserved the parade ground and the foundations of some neighboring buildings. A state historical park now tells the fort's history, as does a nearby private monument to the Platte River Road, which remains a vital transcontinental transportation and communications corridor.

—Todd M. Kerstetter

See also
Nebraska
For Further Reading
Mantor, Lyle E. 1948. "Fort Kearny and the Westward Movement." *Nebraska History* 29: 175–207; Mattes, Merrill J. 1969. *The Great Platte River Road.* Lincoln: Nebraska State Historical Society; Vifquain, Sally. 2000. "Public History: A Case Study and Annotated Bibliography of Fort Kearny, 1848–1999." Master's thesis, University of Nebraska at Kearney.

KICKAPOO

The name "Kickapoo" evolved from an Algonquian word meaning "he stands or moves about." The Kickapoo spoke an Algonquian dialect originating in the southern Great Lakes area and closely related to the Shawnee tongue. According to legend, the Kickapoo and Shawnee were once one people who divided over a disagreement regarding a bear paw. The cultural and linguistic evidence suggests that the two groups did indeed develop in tandem.

Before the Columbian encounter of 1492, the Kickapoo inhabited the area between Lake Erie and Lake Michigan, today known as northwest Ohio and southern Michigan. Attacks in the mid–seventeenth century by other native nations, such as the Neutrals and Iroquois in the so-called Beaver Wars, forced the Kickapoo west. By the late–eighteenth century, the nation had settled in current-day central Illinois and spread through the Wabash Valley.

Like many Great Lakes Algonquian peoples, the Kickapoo lived in stable settlements with longhouses during the warm months, and broke into hunting camps during the winter. They were skilled farmers of squash, beans, and corn, and hunters of buffalo. They followed a patrilineal clan system to organize their society. Unlike neighboring native nations, however, the Kickapoo incorporated horses into their lives and economy very early. This became particularly important later, when they were removed to the plains of the Midwest and proved particularly adaptable to its challenges.

One repeating theme in the history of the Kickapoo is

their cultural purism. Early French traders rarely gained entrance to their villages—the Kickapoo fought with the French against the Chickasaw only in support of their traditional allies, the Miami and Illinois—and Jesuits characterized them as singularly uninterested in conversion. Other European groups met with similar resistance. By the mid–eighteenth century, the French still could only guess at their number, but estimated it at approximately three thousand.

By the time of Lewis and Clark, the Kickapoo had divided into two separate factions. The western group, or Prairie Band, grew closer to the Sauk and Fox, while the other band remained linked with the Miami. Both preferred to trade with U.S. citizens using other native nations as intermediaries, however, and they remained culturally exclusive. The Louisiana Purchase and its resulting promise of U.S. expansion west did little to reassure the Kickapoo that their lands, their lives, and their culture would remain safe.

It is no wonder, then, that on the heels of the Louisiana Purchase, the Kickapoo embraced a man known as "The Prophet" who preached unity, traditionalism, and resistance to the United States. He was the Shawnee brother of powerful chief Tecumseh, Tenskwatawa. With Tenskwatawa's spiritual leadership, bolstered by his successful prediction of a solar eclipse, and Tecumseh's reputation as a war leader and dynamic politician, the brothers called for all native peoples to stop ceding land to the United States. The Kickapoo, who had agreed to give up some land in the past, answered the call and, by 1809, had invited the two to relocate Tecumseh's capital (Prophetstown) to Tippecanoe Creek in western Indiana. Other native peoples followed suit, and the brothers gained impressive support.

The strength and violence of the Shawnee message was answered by the new owners of the Louisiana Territory. The resulting war climaxed with the Battle of Tippecanoe, which ended with a victory for the United States in November 1811. The Kickapoo, however, remained loyal to Tecumseh and his message until his death at the Battle of the Thames in 1813.

Skirmishes persisted, but the battered Kickapoo had lost. By 1819 they signed treaties at Edwardsville and Fort Harrison that surrendered all their lands in Illinois and Indiana, and they promised to relocate to Missouri. Those Kickapoo who did not go voluntarily were forcibly removed by the U.S. military in 1824. From Missouri, Kickapoo groups eventually spread through Kansas, Oklahoma, Texas, and Mexico.

Today, three federally recognized Kickapoo tribes remain: the Kickapoo of Kansas, the Kickapoo of Oklahoma, and the Kickapoo Traditional Kickapoo Tribe of Texas, which includes members in Mexico. Of the approximately twenty-five hundred Kickapoo, the vast majority reside in Oklahoma. The cultural purism that once marked the people continues. The Kickapoo language remains alive and in use, and the people boast one of the highest percentages of full-bloods of any native tribe in the United States.

—*Amy H. Sturgis*

See also
Fox; Sauk

For Further Reading

Gibson, Arrell Morgan. 1963. *The Kickapoos: Lords of the Middle Border.* Norman: University of Oklahoma Press; Latorre, Felipe A., and Dolores L. Latorre. 1976. *The Mexican Kickapoo Indians.* Austin: University of Texas Press; White, Phillip M., ed. 1999. *The Kickapoo Indians, Their History and Culture: An Annotated Bibliography.* Westport, CT: Greenwood Press.

KING, RUFUS (1755–1827)

As a U.S. senator from Massachusetts, in 1820 Rufus King strongly opposed the admission of Missouri as a slave state because he wanted to prevent an increase in the South's political power and because he believed that slavery went against natural law. Born in Scarborough, Maine, King attended Harvard and then studied law. But in August 1778, as the Revolutionary War spread northward, King served as a major during the recapture of Newport, Rhode Island. In 1780 he began the practice of law in Massachusetts and soon rose to serve as a delegate to the Massachusetts General Assembly in 1783. His experience in Congress during the period 1784–1786 convinced him of the wisdom of a strong central government.

King's interest in slavery was primarily political, but it was shaped by humanitarian considerations. His father had been a slaveholder, and King had been raised with slaves; he had freed his one known slave in 1812. He did not strongly oppose slavery in the states, because he saw it as a local matter. But the slavery in federal territory was an altogether different issue to King, and he continually denounced it beginning in 1785. In March of that year, he called for neither "slavery nor involuntary servitude" in the area to be known as the Northwest Territory. This phrase would later be incorporated in the Ordinance of 1787, which King helped to draft and which was introduced while he served in the Constitutional Convention in Philadelphia. As debate raged over the Constitution, King voiced distaste for the three-fifths clause that counted a slave as less than a free person. Four months after the convention disbanded, King served as a delegate to the Massachusetts convention that ratified the Constitution. In 1788, King moved with his wife and children to New York City; he abandoned the practice of law when he was elected to the state assembly. In July 1789, King was chosen as a U.S. senator. Throughout his political career King remained a moderate who desired stability and continuity in government while accepting property qualifications that limited democratic participation. A Federalist, King remained suspicious of the influence of Continental Europeans on American life but agreed to serve as U.S. minister to Great Britain. He proved to be a skilled diplomat, helping to prevent a break in severely strained Anglo-American relations. Weary of diplomacy and in disagreement with the Jefferson administration, King tendered his resignation in 1803. After the acquisition of Louisiana, King shared the view widely held by Northeastern Federalists that representation there should be limited to free inhabitants and that new states carved out from the territory should hold no slaves. In 1804, King became the Federalist candidate for the vice presidency. In 1816, he would make a bid for the presidency, becoming the last Federalist candidate for president.

Several months after the declaration of the War of 1812, the New York legislature selected King again as a U.S. senator. A critic of the war, King often led the Senate opposition to the Madison administration. He opposed a bill for the recovery of fugitive slaves and voted to exclude slavery from the Territory of Arkansas. Late in February 1819, as the Senate began debates over Missouri's petition for statehood, King made two powerful speeches urging the exclusion of slavery from Missouri. These remarks were the first lengthy public statements that the senator made on slavery, but they expressed ideas that he had held for some time. In a futile attempt to avoid inflaming passions, King barely touched on the morality of slavery, confining his attention to its impact upon national defense and public welfare. King argued that since all men are born free and entitled to life, liberty, and the pursuit of happiness, neither man nor the state could enslave a man—and hence Congress was bound to prohibit slavery in the territories. Slavery impaired the productivity and power of the nation, and experience seemed to show that slave labor did not make manufacturers prosper. If dependent upon slave labor, Missouri would be unable to recruit soldiers and seamen in wartime, and her slaves would be a liability in an exposed frontier area. King held that, if slaves were forbidden in all states admitted in the future, the slave markets would be destroyed, and free Americans could more easily resist foreign aggression and defend themselves against domestic insurrection. In his speeches, King argued for the constitutional right of Congress to set the conditions for the admission of new states to the Union. Congress had allowed Kentucky, Tennessee, Mississippi, and Alabama to hold slaves only because they had been created out of states in which slavery was legal. Missouri Territory was not within the confines of the original thirteen colonies, and King believed that Congress ought to act upon its right to bar slavery.

Torrents of abuse from supporters of slavery poured down upon King, who then sought to stir up a storm in the North. As a longtime supporter of Northern commerce, King was deeply concerned over the balance of power and hoped for an antislavery party aimed at strengthening Northern influence in Washington. After the session of Congress ended, he worked over his speeches and in November published them as a pamphlet that became a focus of agitation despite its sober legalism. King's words inspired newspaper essays and mass meetings. In 1820, he enlarged his argument to include human rights and liberties. King's conservative disposition, respect for property, and legal training led him to acquiesce in the definition of slaves as property where slavery was legal. He could not defend bondage, but he did not ardently pursue either colonization or emancipation.

Suffering from gout, King retired from the Senate in 1825. He was persuaded to serve again as minister to Great Britain, but ill health cut short his service and forced him to return to the United States in 1826. He died less than a year later in New York City.

—Caryn E. Neumann

See also

King-Hawkesbury Treaty; Missouri Compromise

For Further Reading

Ernst, Robert. 1968. *Rufus King: American Federalist.* Chapel Hill: University of North Carolina Press.

KING-HAWKESBURY TREATY (1803)

Negotiated and signed by Rufus King, U.S. minister plenipotentiary to England, and Lord Hawkesbury (Robert Banks Jenkinson), the British foreign secretary, this treaty sought to define the northern boundary between the United States and Canada all the way from the Mississippi River and Lake of the Woods in the west eastward to the Bay of Fundy. This treaty, signed on May 12, 1803, was received by the president of the Senate on October 24 of that year. The Senate ratified the document conditionally by excluding Article V, which specified the exact boundary. The British government refused to accept the modified treaty.

Talks between King and Hawkesbury concerning this treaty began in 1801. Initially King was reluctant to discuss the boundary issue because of his unfamiliarity with the vast territory in question. Finally British officials met with King and tried to arrange an agreement but failed. When negotiations stalled in 1802, King asked for additional instructions from Secretary of State James Madison. Madison suggested that the northwestern boundary should start at the source of the Mississippi River and continue to the western shore of the Lake of the Woods, where it would then continue along the banks to the northwestern corner of the lake. With regard to the eastern portion of the boundary dispute, Madison stressed that navigation of Passamaquoddy Bay was necessary to protect U.S. shipping. He also suggested that King ask for Campobello Island and any other island in the Bay of Fundy that the British would be willing to relinquish.

King was vacationing in France when Madison's instructions arrived in England. Upon his return he attended several meetings with Hawkesbury during which he proposed Madison's terms. The two men finally reached an agreement. Although the United States had no real claim to any of the islands in the bay except for Moose Island, the British agreed to draw the boundary so as to provide for U.S. access to a shipping channel north of Campobello Island, which remained under British control, for navigation during low tides. King believed that the Senate would quickly ratify the treaty, and, having asked to be replaced shortly after Jefferson took office, he finally returned to the United States confident that his diplomatic mission had been fruitful.

Congress delayed ratification hearings on the King-Hawkesbury Treaty until February 1804 because of a more pressing issue involving the Louisiana Purchase Treaty between the United States and France. While King and Hawkesbury had been engaged in discussions over the details of the treaty, Thomas Jefferson had instructed Robert Livingston and James Monroe to travel to France. Their mission focused on negotiating with the French government to purchase the mouth of the Mississippi River. Napoleon realized that the United States might ally with Great Britain if France proceeded to colonize Louisiana, and he subsequently agreed to sell the entire territory to the United States for $15 million.

The undefined boundaries of the acquisition created a problem for the Senate when debate over the King-Hawkesbury Treaty began a few days after the Louisiana Purchase Treaty was ratified. Many senators objected to Article V of the treaty, which defined the northwest boundary. It was strongly believed that if the United States accepted the proposed borders, future claims to any lands north or west of the Lake of the Woods might be compromised. John Quincy Adams, the Senate committee chairman, asked for clarification concerning the chronology of the treaty negotiations in an attempt to analyze British intentions. Madison inquired as to when the language of the treaty had been approved, and if the British knew of the Louisiana Purchase prior to or after the cession of Louisiana. King, then residing in New York, responded that the terms of the convention had been drafted weeks before news of the purchase reached Parliament. The Senate, unsatisfied, continued to object to Article V.

Some senators seized this opportunity to embarrass King and discredit his efforts, since it was rumored that he had political aspirations that included the presidency. King, a staunch Federalist, had reluctantly agreed to remain in England as the U.S. minister when the Republican administration under Jefferson took control of the government in 1801. By failing to ratify this treaty, the senators hoped to diminish King's national position and the possible goodwill of Republicans because of his service under Jefferson. In this manner they could reduce King's future chances of successfully running for the office of chief executive.

Congress finally ratified the treaty but excluded Article V. When Parliament received word of the restrictions placed on the agreement, the British government refused to accept the treaty. The Louisiana Purchase delayed the possibility of negotiating the northwestern boundary until Republican secretary of state John Quincy Adams signed the British-U.S. Convention of 1818 during James Monroe's administration.

—*Cynthia Clark Northrup*

See also

Convention of 1818; King, Rufus

For Further Reading

Ernst, Robert. 1968. *Rufus King: American Federalist.* Chapel Hill: University of North Carolina Press; King, Charles R., ed. 1971. *The Letters and Correspondence of Rufus King.* New York: DaCapo Press.

KIOWA

A Tanoan-speaking people, the Kiowa were one of the buffalo-hunting nations whose homeland was encompassed by the Louisiana Purchase. According to the oral tradition, their ancestors emerged from a hollow cottonwood log, escaping through a hole made by an owl. They were called the *K'uato,* which meant "pulling out people," but they later embraced the name Kiowa, or "principal people." Stories were told about a heroic sun-boy who brought the buffalo out of a subterranean cavern for their hunting expeditions. The oldest tribal medicine bundle, *talyi-da-i,* came from the transformed body of the sun-boy, whose twin brother of legend had walked into a magic lake and disappeared under its waters. The *pa-hy,* or the sun-father, also granted power to the people through the *tai-me,* a sacred medicine doll protecting generations from hunger and cold.

The Kiowa were a semisedentary people, dwelling in tipis constructed of buffalo hides. They lived in small, independent bands called *topadogas,* which included extended families of kin. Each was led by a group of brothers, who looked to the leadership of the most respected brother, or *topadok'i.* In addition to subtribes, which were organized for the conduct of sacred ceremonies, there were several shield societies in their social organization. Although the nation contained a number of main chiefs, the medicine men, or *ondedw,* possessed great power as warriors, healers, or visionaries.

The Kiowa spoke of a mysterious power called *dwdw,* a spirit force inhabiting the land, hills, rivers, plants, and animals. Indeed, its most powerful permutations were evident in the Sun, Moon, Stars, Air, and Buffalo. The great spirit constituted a mystery that was manifested through observable natural phenomena such as thunder, lightning, whirlwinds, and tornadoes. The return of the sun to a peak level in the sky each summer inspired them to offer a ritual celebration of thanksgiving called the *k-ado,* or sun dance. Like their kinsmen elsewhere, they ritually sought visions by gazing into the sky and by meditating in mountains or in secluded places away from their communities.

Although related to the Tiwa speakers of Taos pueblo, the Kiowa once occupied the territory near the Yellowstone River and the headwaters of the Missouri. When they migrated eastward to the Black Hills area, they befriended the Crow, who lived there in the sixteenth century. Driven out by the Sioux, the Cheyenne, and the Arapaho in the mid–eighteenth century, they moved southward along the front range of the Rocky Mountains and toward the Ouachita Mountains and the upper Arkansas River. By the end of the eighteenth century, the Kiowa were ranging across the southern limits of the territory that became the possession of France. They developed a sense of identity from the movements across the heart of the continent, and settled down to a difficult and harsh existence in a vast hunting domain north of the Red River.

Intertribal competition created potential dangers for the Kiowa, but they mastered diplomacy to form alliances with other Indian nations of the region. They counted as one of their bands a group of Apache known as the Kiowa-Apache, who retained their own Athabascan language. After forming ties with the Comanche around 1790, the allies established trade routes extending to the Spanish-controlled pueblos of the Southwest. They were also fierce and effective raiders, striking against the outposts of the Spanish empire in North America. Realizing the Spaniards' abundance of horses, and their advantages, trading and raiding became an important occupation. Later they struck alliances with both the Osage and the Southern Cheyenne to secure access to the majestic bison herds roaming the Great Plains.

Although the Kiowa interacted with the French and the Spanish for years, they remained relatively isolated from contact with Europeans. By the time the United States purchased the Louisiana Territory from France, they numbered approximately one thousand people. The Lewis and Clark Expedition in 1804 noted hearing about their villages but did not report seeing them. During another expedition a few years later, Zebulon Pike encountered a Kiowa party returning from a trading expedition. Later a division of Stephen Long's Expedition observed the Kiowa. Smallpox exacted a toll upon this indigenous nation, particularly during the epidemic of 1816.

By the twenty-first century, the Kiowa have come to embody one of the quintessential nations of Indian country. The tribe has some ten thousand enrolled members, about half of them living in Oklahoma near the communities of Anadarko, Ft. Cobb, and Carnegie.

—Brad D. Lookingbill

See also

Long (Stephen Harrriman) Expedition; Osage; Pike Expedition

For Further Reading

Kracht, Benjamin. 1996. "Kiowa." In *Encyclopedia of North American Indians.* Edited by Frederick Hoxie. Boston: Houghton Mifflin; Mayhall, Mildred. 1962. *The Kiowas.* Norman: University of Oklahoma Press; Mooney, James. 1979 [1898]. *Calendar History of the Kiowa Indians: Seventeenth Annual Report of the Bureau of American Ethnology, 1895–1896, Part 1.* Washington, DC: Government Printing Office. Reprint: Washington: Smithsonian Institution Press; Nye, Wilbur S. 1962. *Bad Medicine and Good: Tales of the Kiowas.* Norman: University of Oklahoma Press.

LAFITTE, JEAN (1780?–1826?)

The youngest of three boys (his brothers were Alexandre Frederic, 1771; Pierre, 1776), Jean Lafitte most likely was born in or near Bayonne, France. Some sources list Port-au-Prince, Haiti, as his birthplace, however, while others claim that he was born in the Spanish Pyrenees. The conflicting stories about his origins only compound the mystery of his early life. Accordingly, he may have resided in the West Indies with his grandmother and have been taught by tutors until he was fourteen; he supposedly attended a private school on Martinique and secured military training on the island of Saint Christopher. He married Christina Levine of St. Croix in 1800, and most likely he and Pierre migrated to Louisiana during the Creole exodus from St. Dominque in the aftermath of the 1804 slave rebellion. Some accounts claim that the Lafitte brothers arrived in Louisiana as early as 1802—they probably made privateering trips to the region as early as 1802—but the earliest confirmed report of Pierre Lafitte was as captain of an armed French privateer in 1804; Jean was not officially listed as a privateer until 1812.

The brothers supposedly opened a blacksmith shop in New Orleans after arriving. But if so, it only served as a front for their more profitable illegal operations. Between 1807 and 1810, Lafitte acquired control over warehouses in New Orleans, Donaldsonville, and Barataria. He also became the spokesman for the privateering-smuggling association based on the Louisiana island of Grand Terre, which by 1810 included forty warehouses, slave pens, a hospital, residences, a fort with cannon, and a force estimated at three thousand to five thousand men. The Baratarians plundered U.S., British, Spanish, and neutral merchantmen, as well as disregarding international neutrality laws and hijacking any vessel that could yield a profit. The organization's elaborate network consisted of ships, warehouses, and distribution depots that stretched from the Gulf of Mexico north to the city of New Orleans.

Lafitte's illegal businesses prospered prior to the War of 1812, generating enough wealth to build a sizable warehouse at the Temple—south of New Orleans—that became his distribution center. In fact, Lafitte's audacity prompted Louisiana Governor William C. C. Claiborne to authorize an expedition against the Baratarian operation. In November 1812, U.S. dragoons ambushed several Baratarian pirogues loaded with contraband, and during the struggle Lafitte was taken prisoner; he was later released on bond. The following year, in October 1813, revenue officials unsuccessfully attacked a Baratarian cargo vessel, and a federal agent was killed in the struggle. This brazen disrespect for U.S. law prompted Claiborne to issue a five-hundred-dollar reward for Lafitte's capture. Lafitte responded by advertising for the capture and delivery of Governor Claiborne. In January 1814, Lafitte boldly advertised for a slave auction to be held at the Temple; a customs agent was killed trying to stop the auction.

In early September 1814, Royal Navy captain Nicholas Lockyer, commanding the sloop *Sophie,* delivered dispatches to Lafitte at Barataria proposing an alliance between the privateers and the British. The offer promised Lafitte reward money, land, a British pardon for past offenses, and a captaincy in the Royal Army should he accept the alliance. Lafitte told the British that he needed time to consider the proposal and then secretly communicated the plans to Governor Claiborne, who forwarded copies to General Andrew Jackson. Despite Lafitte's apparent loyalty to the United States, two weeks later—on September 16, 1814—Master-Commandant Daniel Patterson and Colonel George T. Ross led a joint army-navy expedition against the privateer's encampment at Barataria; they encountered little resistance and seized several privateers, prizes, and eighty prisoners.

Although U.S. forces had sacked his base, Lafitte still refused to join the British. He chose instead to offer his assistance to the United States and Jackson. When Jackson learned of the December 14, 1814, defeat of the American gunboats on Lake Borgne, he realized that New Orleans needed defensive assistance. As British forces gathered south of the city, preparing for an assault, the Louisiana legislature granted amnesty for any Baratarian who aided in the defense of New Orleans; Lafitte served as a topographic advisor and guide on Jackson's volunteer staff. Lafitte also offered the Baratarians' stockpile of powder, shot, and flints, which provided Jackson the materials he needed to hold the British at bay. Although initially reluctant to use the Baratarians, Jackson later acknowledged their gallantry, loyalty, and devotion. He also recognized the "courage and fidelity" of the Lafitte brothers during the victory of January 8,

1815, which, without a doubt, ensured that the United States would retain the territory purchased from France.

The Lafitte brothers were pardoned by President James Madison in February 1815 in recognition for their services at the Battle of New Orleans. In 1816, Lafitte met with Spanish minister to the United States Luis de Onís, and most likely at that time agreed to work as an agent for King Ferdinand VII of Spain. Later that fall, Lafitte traveled throughout the Southwest, and along with Arsène Lacarrière Latour, he visited, surveyed, and helped prepare maps of the headwaters of the Red, Sabine, Arkansas, and Colorado Rivers. Latour's subsequent report warned Spain of continued U.S. expansion into the Southwest. Shortly thereafter, Lafitte again became involved in privateering and filibustering, using Galveston, Texas, as a base. But in 1819 several of Lafitte's Galveston associates were captured by the U.S. Navy, convicted of piracy, and hanged in New Orleans. Although tarnished by the accusations of piracy, he remained in charge at Galveston until being expelled in 1820.

The rumors of Lafitte's demise are as abundant as those of his early life. One story insists that Jean Lafitte moved to the Yucatan Peninsula in 1821 and died there of fever in 1826. Another claims that Lafitte, alias John Lafflin, traveled extensively in Europe and later lived a long life in the U.S. Midwest, supposedly dying on May 5, 1851, in Alton, Illinois. Regardless, Lafitte was characteristic of the raucous adventurers who arrived in Louisiana during the uncertain years before and after the purchase. His career along the lawless Louisiana frontier mirrored the development of the region, fading out once the state of Louisiana had been fully incorporated into the Union.

—*Gene A. Smith*

See also

Claiborne, William Charles Cole; New Orleans, Battle of

For Further Reading

De Grummond, Jane Lucas. 1961. *The Baratarians and the Battle of New Orleans.* Baton Rouge: Louisiana State University Press; De Grummond, Jane Lucas. 1983. *Renato Beluche: Smuggler, Privateer and Patriot, 1780–1860.* Baton Rouge: Louisiana State University Press; Faye, Stanley. 1940. "The Great Stroke of Pierre Laffite." *Louisiana Historical Quarterly* 23: 733–826; Gayarré, Charles. 1883. "Historical Sketch of Pierre and Jean Lafitte; The Famous Smugglers of Louisiana." *Magazine of American History* 10: 284–298, 389–396; Latour, Arsène Lacarrière. 1999 [1816]. *Historical Memoir of the War in West Florida and Louisiana in 1814–15: With an Atlas.* Edited by Gene A. Smith. Gainesville: Historic New Orleans Collection and the University Press of Florida.

LAND LAW OF 1820

On March 15, 1820, Congress debated the issue of land grants in the state of Louisiana and the territories of Missouri and Arkansas. After Senator Henry Johnson from Louisiana proposed the bill, a motion was made to defer the issue until other business had been conducted, but the motion was then waived. Rufus King of New York then asked for a second deferment in order to study the numerous provisions of the bill that would alter the land claims of a substantial portion of the region. He suggested the creation of a tribunal to examine the evidence and determine the validity of the claims. The members decided that Congress should continue along the present course and decide the matter of land claims in Louisiana.

After preceding through the appropriate committees in both the House and the Senate, "An act supplementary to the several acts for the adjustment of land claims in the state of Louisiana" became law on May 11, 1820. Congress confirmed the land claims in the eastern district of the state as reported to Congress by the register and receiver of the district, eliminating any future claim to the land by the United States. Addressing the issue of land claims west of the Mississippi, the area formerly owned by Spain prior to the Treaty of San Ildefonso (1800), Congress declared that any claims based on Spanish grants of land prior to U.S. acquisition of the territory must be filed, along with the appropriate evidence, with the district register between July 1 and December 31 of 1820. Any claim in which the party failed to comply with this measure within the specified time would be void and never again admitted in any court within the United States. Once all claims had been received, the register would be required to forward a report listing the claims, describing the evidence, and evaluating the validity of the supporting documentation to the secretary of the treasury. Congress also stipulated that even if the claims had previously been recorded with the register, claimants basing their rights of possession on any Spanish grants, concessions, or surveys must resubmit their claim within the same time period or they also would forfeit their claim to the land forever. After receiving the reports of the registers, Congress ordered the secretary of the treasury to examine the claims and report to the legislature those claims that he believed should be confirmed by the United States, accompanied by the supporting evidence. Congress imposed a restriction on the size of the grants that could be listed by the secretary of the treasury to portions of land under a league square. Congress further ordered that the registers be compensated $600 for their services by the treasury, in addition to the stipulated fee of twenty-five cents for each hundred words, paid by the claimant.

Congress then revived the fifth section of the act, passed on March 3, 1811, entitled "An act providing for the final adjustment of claims to lands, and for the sale of the public lands in the territories of Orleans and Louisiana," for a term of two years. Under this section, individuals who possessed confirmed grants of land became eligible to purchase public lands of the United States that bordered their property in Louisiana with a limit placed on the size of the purchase that equaled the amount of land currently owned, up to forty arpents, French measure, in depth. The property could be purchased at the current price designated by Congress for the sale of public lands, with the date of purchase corresponding to the date on which the claimant filed the original notice with the register. In any case where lakes, bayous, rivers, creeks, or other watercourses prevented the claiming of equal tracts of land contiguous to the claimant's property, or where two individuals both claimed property adjacent to their own lands that involved the same land, Congress authorized the principal deputy surveyor to divide the vacant land in the most equitable manner.

—*Cynthia Clark Northrup*

For Further Reading
Annals of Congress, 16th Congress, 1st Session.

LAND SPECULATION

The basic principle of land speculation is to buy land at a low price and sell it at a high one, and by 1803 implementation of this axiom had already shaped westward settlement in the United States. Speculation had also helped to shape French and Spanish Louisiana, reaching a peak in the brief but intense expansion driven by John Law's Compagnie des Indes (Company of the West), which went bankrupt in 1720. But Thomas Jefferson hoped that the Louisiana Purchase would make available enough low-priced land to ensure economic independence for generations of yeoman farmers.

Settlement of the trans-Appalachian West had only just begun in 1803, and west of the Mississippi, only lower Louisiana and a few river towns had even the smallest populations. Yet the desire to buy low and sell high was already strong. Along the Mississippi itself, colonial land grants created overlapping land claims that would need to be adjusted. Speculators rushed in and bought French and Spanish grants, both genuine and counterfeit, and then presented them to boards of commissioners in Orleans and Louisiana (later Missouri) Territories for confirmation.

Actual settlement of the Louisiana Purchase Territory began after the federal government drove Native Americans from their land, surveyed the public domain, and organized sales. Surveyors mapped the new territory in squares six miles on a side, dividing each one further into one-mile squares called sections. When the surveyors had plotted a sufficient number of sections, the sections were put up for auction at government land offices like the ones opened by 1816 in St. Louis, New Orleans, and Ouachita, and Opelousas, Louisiana. But in Missouri, settlers had already begun to clear farms before land sales began. To protect such farmers from wealthy bidders who threatened to acquire their "improvements," Congress sporadically enacted, and land offices sporadically enforced preemption laws that allowed settlers to pay the minimum price ($1.25 per acre) for small tracts that they actually cultivated. This measure sometimes provided another opportunity for speculators, who amassed scores of counterfeit preemption claims.

Migrants began to cross the Mississippi in number in 1815, when the end of war with Britain reopened overseas markets for American agriculture. Buying land on speculation, or land-jobbing, in the Louisiana Purchase focused on the lower Red River in Louisiana and central Missouri. This boom ended in 1819, when overproduction of cotton and overinvestment in land brought about a crash. Still, by the end of the 1820s, the government had created land offices for all of Arkansas and Missouri, preparing the way for a new wave of sales. In the next decade "planter banks" created by the governments of Louisiana and Arkansas diverted money from Northern and European investors into the pockets of plantation owners. Ready money drove high prices and high profits for those who speculated in cotton lands on the upper Red River and in northeastern Arkansas and the interior of Missouri, until the inevitable crash came again in 1837.

The next burst of speculation occurred to the north. Free-state settlers began to cross the Mississippi after 1850, and in Iowa and Minnesota, speculative companies like the Providence Land Company of Rhode Island bought up prime farmland along waterways at the minimum price, and resold it at forty and fifty dollars. Speculation also followed the lines—or the anticipated lines—of railroad construction. Despite the Homestead Act (1862), which gave away public land to farmers willing to cultivate it, other measures threw the weight of the federal government on the side of the land speculator. Congress granted one million acres to the Union Pacific Railroad, located along its proposed route; sale of this land financed the railroad's building project. The Morrill Act (1862) allowed land-grant institutions like Cornell University to net millions by gambling on the public domain. In other cases, cowboys posed as homesteading farmers to claim rangeland for the large cattle interests that employed them. The Desert Land Act (1877) provided more opportunity for both speculation and swindling, permitting investors to lay claim to large areas of the Dakotas and Montana, which they later sold to settlers.

Laws enacted by Congress could not eliminate speculation in the Louisiana Purchase Territory. Speculators large and small continued to squeeze money out of the public domain until well after the end of the nineteenth century. Legislators were torn between a desire to appeal to the large number of citizens who wanted cheap land, and a desire to protect their own interests as land speculators. The landscapes left in the wake of speculative booms and bust—dominated by commercialized farming, cotton plantations, and large-scale ranching—rarely resembled the Jeffersonian dream.

—*Edward E. Baptist*

See also
Homestead Act; Louisiana Land Law of 1804; Preemption Act; Squatter's Rights

For Further Reading
Dick, Everett. 1970. *The Lure of the Land: A Social History of the Public Lands from the Articles of Confederation to the New Deal.* Lincoln: University of Nebraska Press; Rohrbough, Malcolm J. 1968. *The Land Office Business: The Settlement and Administration of American Public Lands, 1789–1837.* New York: Oxford University Press.

LARAMIE, FORT

Fort Laramie was one of the largest and best known forts in the nineteenth century American West. It had a long career serving both civilians and soldiers, but it is remembered primarily as a military installation. Located in far eastern Wyoming at the junction of the Laramie and North Platte Rivers, the fort got its name from a little-known trapper, Jacques LaRamee, who was killed by the Arapaho in 1822.

The site originally held a small cottonwood structure built in 1834 by William Sublette and Robert Campbell. Named Fort William, the outpost represented the extension of the fur trade in the Rocky Mountains. The business changed rapidly in the 1830s, and in 1835, Jim Bridger, William Fitzpatrick, and Milton Sublette bought the fort. As larger firms out-competed smaller enterprises for the already dwindling resources, the large American Fur Company bought the entire company from Fort William's owners, including the fort. In 1841, spurred by a rival installation upriver, the company replaced the rotting log structure with one made of adobe and christened it Fort John. By this time the beaver trade had been greatly reduced, but the fort was well located to carry out the growing bison trade with Plains Indians, especially the Sioux. The traders invited the Brule and Oglala to move closer to the fort; many did, so many in fact that they soon outnumbered other tribes in the region.

The location of the fort became even more important as greater numbers of travelers used the Platte River Road. The fort then served in a new capacity as trading post for emigrants on the trail. There groups could resupply their outfits for the arduous mountain crossings ahead. In 1850, flour and sugar could be purchased for 50 cents/lb., and precious whiskey for $8/gallon, a considerable increase over the 50 cents/gallon it cost in the Midwest. Nearly everyone going West visited Laramie, including the infamous Donner Party, Brigham Young and the Mormons, and John C. Frémont. The traffic reached a peak in 1850, when fifty thousand people passed through the fort.

As emigrant traffic on the Oregon Trail increased, the possibility of conflict with the tribal groups whose homeland the trails bisected increased. In 1849 the U.S. government bought Fort Laramie for $4,000 in

Typical of the solitary military outposts of the Far West, locations like Fort Laramie were often used as the site of treaty negotiations with various tribes of Plains Indians.

response to fears of Indian uprisings. In an effort to instill a sense of military order on the Plains, the United States called for a treaty council at Fort Laramie in 1851. The government invited all the tribes of the northern High Plains and promised lavish presents in exchange for their participation. In September 1851, nearly ten thousand Brule, Oglala, Arapaho, and Cheyenne came—the largest assembly of Plains Indians in history. The gathering was so large that the group moved thirty-six miles down the Platte because there was not enough forage for all the horses at Fort Laramie. After the distribution of $50,000 in presents, the Indian signers accepted $50,000 annually for fifty years in return for permitting forts, posts, and roads in the region and keeping the peace. This marked the beginning of the government's efforts to make seminomadic hunters respect designated hunting grounds rather than their traditional means of foraging.

The Treaty of Fort Laramie (1851) became one in a long series of treaties that consistently robbed the Plains people of their homeland to feed the insatiable land hunger of white Americans. Naturally the tensions in the area also continued. To meet the challenges of expanding white settlement into the West, the army maintained troops at Fort Laramie. Between 1848 and 1868, the garrison varied from fifty to more than four thousand soldiers. The numbers were swelled by the support staff, including teamsters, laundresses, scouts, and woodcutters, to make the fort a small town. Indeed, as a major frontier installation Fort Laramie boasted all the elements of a town. By 1876 it had everything for a military post—officers, infantry and cavalry quarters, post headquarters, commissary storehouses—plus a post trader's store, a twelve-bed hospital, bakery, telegraph office, civilian housing, and a cemetery. It even had a three-span iron bridge across the Platte River.

Fort Laramie continued to hold an important responsibility on the ever-changing frontier as a base for communications. The short-lived Pony Express had a station at Fort Laramie during its eighteen months of operation, and later the telegraph lines were protected by Laramie troops. The fort provided a base for the ongoing conflicts on the Great Plains, such as the Grattan and Fetterman Incidents, and the Sioux War of 1876. The fort hosted another major treaty meeting with the Lakota and Arapaho in 1868. By the late 1880s the warfare had dwindled and with it the fort's useful life. In March 1890 the last troops left Fort Laramie, and the location resorted to civilian use. It is now a unit of the National Park Service.

—Clarissa W. Confer

For Further Reading

Lavender, David. 1982. *Fort Laramie.* Tucson, AZ: Patrice Printing; LeRoy, Reuben Hafen. 1984. *Fort Laramie and the Pageant of the West.* New York: Bison Books; Nadeau, Remi. 1967. *Fort Laramie and the Sioux Indians.* Englewood Cliffs, NJ: Prentice Hall.

LAUSSAT, PIERRE CLÉMENT DE (1756–1835)

Born in Pau, France, on November 23, 1756, Pierre Clément, Baron de Laussat, held diplomatic posts under Louis XVI, survived the revolution to serve in Napoleon's legislature, and continued to hold various posts under the Bourbon restoration. On August 20, 1802, Napoleon named him colonial prefect of Louisiana, following France's regaining of Louisiana from Spain. His role was to prepare Louisiana to receive its new captain-general, Claude Perrin Victor, one of Napoleon's most distinguished officers.

Laussat arrived in Louisiana in March 1803 but did not immediately move to take over the province. Rumors of a sale to the United States reached New Orleans in June, although Laussat received no official notification until August 17, 1803. His immediate reaction was to brand the news of the cession of Louisiana to the United States an "impudent lie," designed to encourage the French residents to flee the colony. The remainder of Laussat's brief stay in Louisiana was marked by dissension between French and Spanish government officials that often erupted at the balls and soirees held nightly in New Orleans.

In a retrocession ceremony held at noon on November 30, 1803, Laussat accepted possession of Louisiana for France. He served as colonial governor for only twenty days. During that time he abolished the Cabildo and replaced it with a municipal government patterned along French republican lines. This new government, consisting of a mayor, a municipal council of twelve members, and a recorder-secretary, governed the city until March 11, 1805, when a new mayor and conseil de ville were installed.

On December 20, Laussat represented France in the formal transfer of the colony to the United States. In his report to the French court, Laussat described a sullen populace who by their silence manifested their palpable disappointment at losing their newly regained French citizenship.

In 1804, Laussat left Louisiana to serve as prefect in Martinique, and later in Antwerp and Jemmapes. He became a member of the Chamber of Deputies during Napoleon's brief return to power in 1815. After the Bourbon restoration, Laussat was appointed governor of French Guiana. Rewarded with a baronage by King Louis Philippe, he retired to his home in Bernadets, where he died in 1835.

—Elizabeth U. Alexander

For Further Reading

De Laussat, Pierre Clément. 1978. *Memoirs of My Life to My Son during the Years 1803 and After . . . .* Edited by Robert D. Bush. Translated by Sister Agnes-Josephine Pastwa, Order of St. Francis. Baton Rouge: Published for the Historic New Orleans Collection by the Louisiana State University Press; Kukla, Jon, ed. 1993. *A Guide to the Papers of Pierre Clément Laussat, Napoleon's Prefect for the Colony of Louisiana, and of General Claude Perrin Victor at the Historic New Orleans Collection.* Baton Rouge: Louisiana University Press.

LEAVENWORTH, FORT

After the initial explorations of the Louisiana Purchase were completed, the door was opened to the possibility of trade with Mexico. On January 25, 1826, Missouri senator Thomas Hart Benton made a speech in the U.S. Senate calling for the promotion of such trade and its protection by the U.S. Army. Congress agreed and provided for a survey of what would become the Santa Fe Trail. Within a few years, caravans of mules regularly made the seven-hundred-mile trip to New Mexico, but the question of protection for these traders had not yet been settled.

With attacks by hostile Indians increasing on the smaller caravans, Benton intervened a second time. After several possible locations were considered and rejected, Congress decided to construct a fort at a site on the Missouri River, near the eastern terminus of the trail. The War Department then dispatched Colonel Henry Leavenworth with more than one hundred men to build it.

Leavenworth and his men arrived on May 18, 1827, but decided to move the building site to a better location on the right bank of the Missouri. Officials in Washington later confirmed this decision, and on September 19, 1827, it was named "Cantonment Leavenworth." On February 8, 1832, it was officially designated "Fort Leavenworth."

From its very inception, the fort was designed for convenience rather than defense. Over time, this proved to be worthwhile; not a single hostile action was ever fought there. Instead, Leavenworth served as a starting point and staging area for thousands of overland expeditions west, both civilian and military.

Early in the fort's existence, it served as base for many of the explorations of the territory acquired in the Louisiana Purchase. Many of these expeditions combined both martial and scientific elements. The first military force to pass through was headed by Captain Bennett Riley, who escorted a caravan to Santa Fe on June 5, 1829. Later expeditions sometimes became more exploratory in character, but they were nearly always conducted by military men with a few civilians accompanying them. Men permanently stationed at the fort often took command, as well as those who would later gain notoriety in the Civil War. These included W. W. Loring, Edwin "Bull" Sumner, Albert Sidney Johnston, and J. E. B. Stuart.

Although Santa Fe continued to be the destination of choice for traders, the goal of most emigrants to pass through Fort Leavenworth in the 1840s was either Oregon or California. Most followed a path originally blazed by "mountain men" that began at the fort and came to be called the "Oregon Trail." The first of many thousands to pass through on that road were the Bartleston Party, from Peoria, Illinois, in May 1841. As time progressed, the number of settlers passing through increased dramatically. For instance, in 1844 more than fourteen hundred emigrants went West, but later, as gold drew many on, 5,350 wagons passed in the month of May 1849 alone. As with the Santa Fe Trail, smaller trains were in danger of Indian attack, and Congress eventually established more forts along the route to protect them.

During the Mexican War (1846–1848), Fort Leavenworth served as the staging ground from which most of the forces sent West advanced. The first of these to leave was an army made up of mainly Missouri volunteers led by Colonel Stephen Watts Kearny. After taking Santa Fe and Chihuahua, this command saw action in California before returning to Fort Leavenworth on August 22, 1847. Other expeditions followed and were brought to successful conclusions.

In addition to seeing off the group that quelled the Mormon uprising in 1857, the fort also played an important role in the events leading up to the Civil War. It served as temporary capital when the territory was first opened to white settlement. Later, as events unfolded, troops from the fort saw limited action in the controversy over the state government. Although the fort was understaffed at the time of Fort Sumter (April 1861), the Confederate sympathizers in Kansas failed to attack it promptly, and the federal government bolstered the garrison. For the duration of the war, the fort was once again a staging area and training center.

After the war, Leavenworth again took its old mantle of "Gateway to the West," this time serving as a departure point for U.S. forces during the Indian Wars. When the dust settled, it went on to take its place as one of the army's major educational centers, becoming home to the Command and General Staff School. Still garrisoned today, it is the oldest U.S. fort west of the Mississippi River.

—Brian C. Melton

See also

Kansas; Oregon Trail; Santa Fe Trail

For Further Reading

Hunt, Elvid. 1937. *History of Fort Leavenworth, 1827–1927.* Fort Leavenworth, KS: General Staff School; Partin, John W., ed. 1983. *A Brief History of Fort Leavenworth, 1827–1983.* Fort Leavenworth, KS: U.S. Army Command and General Staff College; Walton, George. 1973. *Fort Leavenworth and the American West.* Edgewood Cliffs, N.J.: Prentice-Hall.

LECLERC, CHARLES-VICTOR-EMMANUEL (1772–1802)

In 1800, after intense negotiations with the Spanish government, the agents of First Consul Napoleon's French Republic secured the retrocession of Louisiana. Although not a productive colony to His Most Catholic Majesty Charles IV, Louisiana was perceived as a key in Napoleon's quest for empire. His legendary successes in Europe buoyed his confidence to follow a similar path in other parts of the world, thereby undermining British financial and naval power. A key to his colonial dream was St. Domingue, the eastern third of the Caribbean island of Hispaniola, which, until the rebellions commencing in 1790, was the gem in France's empire because of its sugar production. Here a small white planter population controlled a larger mulatto class and an especially large number of slaves (perhaps 90 percent), whose work provided the financial strength of the colony. However, included in the egalitarian rhetoric of the French Revolution was the abolition of slavery. By the mid-1790s, St. Domingue was in rebellion against its French masters with thousands of whites killed in the uprisings, and many others seeking refuge in other colonies or in the United States. The new leader of the colony was a former slave, the remarkable Toussaint L'Ouverture, who reorganized the island with a new constitution and administration, theoretically under French tutelage.

The reorganization of France under Napoleon that began in 1799 included a forcible suppression of the rebellion and a return of slavery. He expected St. Domingue to return quickly to its former agricultural glory in sugar production and planned Louisiana as a subsidiary that would produce the other agricultural goods needed on the island. He did not want to waste such precious land on food production. But to accomplish this task, he needed a strong military presence, and for that he turned to his brother-in-law, Charles-Victor Leclerc, the husband of his sister Pauline. This general had gained the confidence of the first consul in various battles in Europe, such as Toulon, and in a successful campaign against the Portuguese. A fleet of sixty-seven ships that carried more than twenty thousand soldiers set sail from several French ports late in 1801. Over half of the expeditionary force arrived in February 1802 and began an assault on L'Ouverture's forces, which resorted to a combination of guerrilla and scorched-earth tactics. Within weeks Leclerc had pushed the rebels to the mountains and by May forced them to surrender. Within a month, L'Ouverture was arrested and sent to France, where he died in prison a year later.

Following Napoleon's orders, Leclerc proceeded to pacify the island and prepared to re-establish slavery. However, as total military victory became apparent, he faced an outbreak of yellow fever. This mosquito-borne infection was complemented by another disease, malaria, and together they decimated the French troops. Despite reinforcements from France, more than three-quarters of the troops died of one disease or the other, but especially the former. Included among the dead was General Leclerc. By that time, the colony's black population heard about the reinstitution of slavery on nearby Guadeloupe and revived their almost moribund rebellion. When Napoleon heard about these developments and coupled them with the renewal of war with Great Britain, he decided to abandon his dreams of a Caribbean empire and concentrate on Europe. The last of the French troops pulled out in 1803 and abandoned St. Domingue to the former slaves and mulatto population. However, the defeat of France by St. Domingue's "Generals Yellow Fever and Malaria" meant that Louisiana was expendable. The death of Leclerc and much of the officer corps made the task of subduing the emancipated blacks impossible, especially with the formidable opposition of the British Navy. As a result, when diplomats of the United States arrived in Paris to discuss the purchase of New Orleans, they were greeted warmly with an offer of the whole colony instead. Militarily successful in both Europe and St. Domingue, General Leclerc was not able to fend off the ravages of yellow fever.

—Thomas Sosnowski

For Further Reading

Heinl, Robert Debs, and Nancy Gordon Heinl. 1996. *Written in Blood: The Story of the Haitian People, 1492–1995.* Lanham, MD: University Press of America; Leclerc, V.-L. 1937. *Lettres de Saint-Domingue.* Paris: Sociéte de l'histoire des colonies françaises; Markham, F. 1975. *The Bonapartes.* London: Weidenfeld and Nicolson; Nabonne, B. 1963. *Pauline Bonaparte.* Paris: Hachette.

LEDYARD, JOHN (1751–1789)

As an American sailing on James Cook's third voyage of exploration (1776–1781), John Ledyard became an early advocate for American trade in the North Pacific. In London, at age twenty-four, he enlisted in the British Royal Marines to join Captain Cook on his next voyage. When he sailed from England on board the *Resolution* in July 1776, Ledyard was unaware of the Declaration of Independence and the permanent rift between his native land and Great Britain. After voyaging around Cape Horn, Ledyard first viewed the shores of the Pacific Northwest in March 1778.

After landfall on Vancouver Island at Nootka Sound, Captain Cook began searching in earnest for the fabled Northwest Passage. Exploring north to the Arctic Ocean, Cook failed to find any waterway to the Atlantic. He did, however, find Russian traders among the Aleuts of southeastern Alaska. The mariners also traded for pelts to protect themselves against the Arctic climate, then neglected the furs as they sailed south to warmer seas.

The southern leg of the trip ended with Cook's death in Hawaii. An attempt to continue the previous years' explorations included trading at Kamchatka and Canton, where the remaining furs, which had been previously used, sold for enormous sums. As the crew threatened mutiny in order to return to Nootka Sound for more pelts, John Ledyard envisioned the potential profits of a North Pacific fur-trading concern. He believed the Northwest Passage to be nonexistent, and so envisioned reaching the region from the American colonies across the continent to the Pacific.

Cook's ships returned to Britain, where Ledyard refused to fight the American rebels. He later managed to steal away from a British frigate patrolling American waters and returned to his homeland. He quickly published an account of his journeys with Cook in 1783, thus becoming the first American to write authoritatively about the Pacific coast. More important, he described the astonishing profits that sea otter furs brought in Canton. Cook's exploration had also verified the proximity of Asia to the shores of North America, and Americans expressed concern about Russian expansion. France and Britain soon sent ships to the North Pacific, possibly to join the Russians on North America's western shore. Whether coincidental or not, it was at this time that Thomas Jefferson made his first suggestion of an American expedition west of the Mississippi River.

Meanwhile, Ledyard attempted to gather support for a transcontinental fur trading scheme. Financier Robert Morris encouraged Ledyard and for a time attempted to help him acquire a ship, but he abandoned the enterprise by early 1784. Ledyard then left for France to seek other backing. In the summer of 1785, Ledyard and Thomas Jefferson became friends in Paris. U.S. naval hero John Paul Jones briefly collaborated with Ledyard to establish a Pacific fur-trading post, but he eventually abandoned the plan.

As securing a ship appeared to be the downfall of Ledyard's plans, he determined to reach the Pacific by land. In November 1786, Ledyard embarked on a journey to reach the North Pacific by crossing Europe and Russia. His allies, Jefferson and the Marquis de Lafayette, simultaneously attempted to convince Catherine the Great to give Ledyard permission to travel across the Russian empire. Ledyard made his way through a Scandinavian winter to Saint Petersburg in June 1787. From there he traversed over four thousand miles to Yakutsk by September, stopping only when deterred by the local Russian commandant or the onset of winter.

With the Pacific nearly within reach, Ledyard was suddenly arrested in January 1788, under the direct orders of Catherine the Great. The Russian American Fur Company as well as a rival Russian exploring party (led by another of Cook's former sailors) were both aware of Ledyard's plans and likely played a role in halting him. The Russians quickly deported Ledyard west to the Polish border, ending his trans-Siberian scheme.

Shortly after his return to Europe, a British group hired Ledyard to explore the Niger River in Africa. Jefferson understood that, once this task was completed, Ledyard would then attempt a westward crossing of North America from the Kentucky frontier. With fur trade exploits on hold, Ledyard went to Cairo to arrange for the trip into the interior. There, extremely ill, he overdosed on an emetic and died on January 10, 1789.

Jefferson thereupon looked to others to take up the transcontinental scheme. The Lewis and Clark Expedition and John Jacob Astor's Pacific Fur Company both incorporated Ledyard's elusive plans and ideas. John Ledyard thus shaped the earliest visions of a continental United States and planted the seeds of U.S. expansion far beyond the Mississippi River.

—Steven M. Fountain

See also

Astor, John Jacob; Jefferson, Thomas; Lewis and Clark Expedition

For Further Reading

Augur, Helen. 1946. *Passage to Glory: John Ledyard's America.* Garden City, NY: Doubleday; Munford, James Kenneth, ed. 1963. *John Ledyard's Journal of Captain Cook's Last Voyage.* Corvallis: Oregon State University; Sparks, Jared. 1828. *The Life of John Ledyard, The American Traveler; Comprising Selections from His Journals and Correspondence.* Cambridge, MA: Hilliard and Brown; Watrous, Stephen D. 1966. *John Ledyard's Journey through Russia and Siberia, 1787–1788.* Madison: University of Wisconsin.

LEWIS, MERIWETHER (1774–1809)

Meriwether Lewis was born on August 18, 1774, the son of William Lewis and Lucy Meriwether. He was born in Albermarle County, Virginia, near the home of Thomas Jefferson, a neighbor and friend. The Lewis family was of Welsh ancestry and was a pioneer family of frontier Virginia, having braved the elements and settled in the Piedmont region.

William Lewis served as an officer in the Continental Army fighting against the British during the American Revolution, and he died of pneumonia during that conflict. Meriwether Lewis would always blame his father's death, an event that occurred when he was five years old, on the British, and he maintained a decidedly anti-British attitude throughout his life.

Meriwether Lewis moved to Georgia after his widowed mother married Captain John Marks, but the family held onto the Albermarle County property. As the eldest child in the family, Lewis would eventually inherit the substantial land holdings in Virginia and in Georgia. As a child, Meriwether Lewis had very little formal education, with only occasional tutors, but he learned much as a pupil of nature, developing a keen sense of survival skills in the wilderness tracts of Virginia and Georgia. At age sixteen, after his mother's second husband died, Lewis brought his family back to Virginia and began to farm the family property.

Four years later, Lewis abandoned farming for a career that promised more adventure. He volunteered to join the army that had been created to put down the Whiskey Rebellion (1794). Although there was no real military action involved in suppressing the uprising, Lewis realized that the military life suited him quite well. He remained in the army when his tour of duty ended, and in 1795, he found himself in General "Mad" Anthony Wayne's army at the Battle of Fallen Timbers. While Lewis was in the service of Wayne, so too was William Clark, Lewis's future partner in the exploration of the West.

In 1795, Lewis learned another side of military life. He was brought up for a general court-martial on charges of "provocative speech and gestures" and "conduct unbecoming an officer and a gentleman" (Dillon, 1988). He was cleared of the charges at his hearing, but perhaps because of his notoriety, Lewis began to impress his commanders. When General Wayne needed to get important dispatches from Detroit to Pittsburgh, he selected Lewis to carry out the mission. Lewis rose in prestige and rank within the army, and by 1801 he had been promoted to the rank of captain.

Shortly after Thomas Jefferson, Lewis's friend and neighbor, was elected president of the United States in 1800, he selected Captain Meriwether Lewis to be his personal secretary. It seems that Jefferson already had in mind a Western exploration project, and he had decided to have his young friend from Albermarle County command the expedition. As Jefferson's personal secretary, Lewis was exposed to the highest level information of a domestic and diplomatic nature pertaining to the Western lands. Like Jefferson, Lewis realized the significance of the Louisiana Territory and the importance of a Western expedition in world power politics.

Meriwether Lewis was personally selected by Thomas Jefferson to lead the Corps of Discovery on its expedition westward.

Even before the chance to purchase the Louisiana Territory came along, Jefferson had begun preparations for a major expedition to the Pacific. He had written to friends who were major scientists of the day and requested their opinion regarding the areas of focus of such an expedition. In time, these scientists and doctors would each serve to tutor Meriwether Lewis in the various areas of their specialization.

On January 18, 1803, Jefferson sent a secret message to Congress calling for an expedition to explore the unknown regions of the West. Congress authorized the funding for the Corps of Discovery that was to explore the West. Shortly thereafter, Meriwether Lewis was selected to lead the expedition.

Lewis was charged with all of the details of preparing the Corps of Discovery for its journey. In this capacity, he had to secure the party of explorers, draw up a budget, prepare a list of needed supplies, and make sure that everything worked according to schedule. One of his first decisions was to write to his old friend William Clark, whom he invited to come along on the journey as coleader.

At the time that Lewis and Clark arrived at St. Louis to begin their expedition, the final transfer of the Louisiana Territory, which had been purchased from France in 1803, was not yet official. Not wishing to stir international tensions, the party made their camp across the river from St. Louis in the Illinois country. Spanish colonial officials, fearing the purpose and scope of the intended expedition, sent word to Madrid that the explorers might really have their sights set upon the silver mines of northern Mexico.

Meriwether Lewis witnessed the formal exchange of the upper part of the Louisiana Territory at St. Louis. He saw the Spanish flag replaced by the tricolor of France, and then he saw that flag in turn lowered and replaced by the U.S. flag. Once Lewis had gathered all of his men and supplies, he set off on his voyage of discovery. The expedition began on Monday, May 14, 1804.

Lewis proved to be a competent and well-tempered leader during the arduous journey up the Missouri River, across the Rocky Mountains, and through the Columbia Basin toward the Pacific. Along the way Lewis learned that maintaining good relations with the Indian tribes that the Corps of Discovery encountered was key to the success of the mission. He negotiated in good faith and personified the firmness and the commitment of the United States to establishing true and legal claim to the territory acquired in the Louisiana Purchase. The tremendous success of the expedition was due, in no small part, to the leadership and character of Meriwether Lewis.

On September 23, 1806, the Corps of Discovery made its triumphant return to St. Louis. Meriwether Lewis wrote letters to Jefferson and to his family upon his return. There were celebrations, toasts, and speeches in every town that Lewis entered on his way eastward to Washington. Pro-Federalist authors wrote poems to try to play down the enthusiasm bestowed upon the "Republican" explorers whom Jefferson had sent into the West.

Lewis began to work on writing the official journal of the expedition. In an effort to do this, he attempted to get a monopoly of the reading market by publicly discrediting the works of some of the other members of the Corps of Discovery. According to Lewis, the journals of the others did not contain the high quality of scientific information that his journal would provide. This effort to destroy the literary competition did not make Lewis any more popular with the public, and if anything, it served to tarnish his reputation.

As a means of thanking his former secretary, Jefferson rewarded Lewis by naming him governor of the Louisiana Territory. Lewis made the critical mistake of remaining in the East for nearly a year and a half, while he tried to govern the territory from a distance. As a result, many of the immediate decisions within the region had to be made by the secretary of the territory, Frederick Bates, a man with whom Lewis often had disagreements. Regardless of the cause of the problems, whether it was Bates's incompetence or Lewis's long-distance management, it soon became clear that there were administrative concerns within the Louisiana Territory that needed to be addressed.

In 1809, Lewis decided to travel to Washington to get some of his business matters in order. He first went down the Mississippi River to New Orleans and subsequently traveled up the Natchez Trace to make his way northeastward, toward the nation's capital. On October 11, 1809, Lewis died at Grinder's Stand, a frontier inn along the Natchez Trace in Tennessee where he was lodging. Lewis died of gunshot wounds and slashes to his body inflicted either in a suicide attempt or in a murder-robbery. Even today, the exact nature of Meriwether Lewis's death remains one of the mysteries of U.S. frontier history.

—Junius P. Rodriguez

See also
Corps of Discovery; Jefferson, Thomas; Lewis and Clark Expedition

For Further Reading
Ambrose, Stephen E. 1996. *Undaunted Courage: Meriwether Lewis, Thomas Jefferson and the Opening of the American West.* New York: Simon and Schuster; Bakeless, John. 1947. *Lewis and Clark: Partners in Discovery.* New York: William Morrow; Dillon, Richard H. 1988. *Meriwether Lewis: A Biography.* Santa Cruz, CA: Western Tanager Press.

LEWIS AND CLARK EXPEDITION (1804–1806)

Even before the opportunity to purchase the Louisiana Territory arose in 1803, U.S. president Thomas Jefferson had begun preparations for a major scientific expedition to travel overland to the Pacific Ocean. Jefferson had corresponded with friends who were prominent scientists and naturalists of the day, and he sought their advice concerning the areas of focus that such an expedition might take when it did occur. As the experts responded to Jefferson's request, each was asked to tutor Meriwether Lewis, President Jefferson's personal secretary and the man whom he had selected to lead the proposed expedition to the West.

From the point in 1801 when he became Jefferson's personal secretary, Meriwether Lewis had been privy to the highest levels of information of a domestic and diplomatic nature regarding the Western lands. Like Jefferson, Lewis realized the importance that a Western expedition would play in the geopolitical climate of the day. Therefore, on January 18, 1803, Jefferson sent a secret message to the Congress calling for an expedition to explore the unknown regions of the West.

In 1792, Captain Robert Gray had found the mouth of the Columbia River. The purpose of the plan that Jefferson was requesting was to follow the Missouri River to its headwaters, to portage the mountains, and to follow the Columbia River from its headwaters to its mouth. Essentially, it was Jefferson's desire that this expedition would fill in the unknown "middle" of the West, an area that remained a mystery to cartographers of the day.

Congress authorized funding for the Corps of Discovery that was to explore the West. At the same time, Jefferson had the good fortune of being able to purchase the entire Louisiana Territory from the French in May 1803. In order to be on the safe side, the United States informed both the British and the French about the proposed expedition in order to get passports for the exploring party. In informing these nations, Jefferson stressed that this exploration was being made in the name of science and that there were no imperial designs involved. For unknown reasons, Jefferson failed to inform the Spanish government about the proposed expedition.

Captain Meriwether Lewis, having been selected to lead the expedition, was charged with all the details of preparing the Corps of Discovery. Lewis had to secure the party of explorers, draw up a budget, prepare a list of needed supplies, and make sure that everything worked according to schedule. One of his first decisions was to write to his friend William Clark, with whom he had served in the U.S. Army under the command of General "Mad" Anthony Wayne in 1795. Lewis, acting on his own initiative, invited Clark to join the expedition as coleader.

As far as the U.S. Congress was concerned, Lewis was the only commander of the Corps of Discovery and

Lewis and Clark held their first meeting with Indians of the Missouri River Valley at Council Bluffs in present-day Iowa. (North Wind Picture Archives)

William Clark was merely a subordinate officer. Lewis had made an effort to get a captain's position for Clark, but Secretary of War Henry Dearborn refused his request. This decision upset Lewis, and he responded by having the men in the Corps of Discovery all call Clark, Captain Clark. Over the years, Meriwether Lewis and William Clark have been recognized as equals in their leadership of the Corps of Discovery, but from an official bureaucratic perspective, that was not the case.

The start of the expedition was postponed because of construction delays. Lewis had designed a special boat made of an iron frame with animal hides. The boat weighed only ninety-six pounds, and it was believed that it would be outstanding in the "short portage" across the mountains. In time, reality would prove otherwise. Lewis had also designed a special type of flatboat that would be used in going up the Missouri River. This boat had front and rear cabins, and it had sides that could be raised in an effort to fortify the vessel in the event of an Indian attack. Once these state-of-the-art vessels were constructed, Lewis joined Clark at St. Louis to begin the mission.

At the time of their arrival at St. Louis, the transfer of the Louisiana Territory had not yet been made official. In order to prevent any type of international incident, the Corps of Discovery made its camp across the Mississippi River from St. Louis in the Illinois Territory. Meanwhile, Spanish officials who feared the purpose and scope of this expedition had sent word to Madrid that these American explorers might really have their sights on the silver mines of northern Mexico. (While Lewis and Clark would be traveling up the Missouri River, a group of Spanish officials were attempting to track them down and arrest them in the area around Santa Fe.) Lewis, who had previously contemplated going to Santa Fe, had been told by Jefferson to avoid taking the Corps of Discovery anywhere near Spanish territory.

Lewis and Clark witnessed the formal exchange of the upper part of the Louisiana Territory at St. Louis on March 10, 1804. During the ceremony, the Spanish flag was lowered and replaced by the French tricolor, and shortly thereafter, that flag was lowered and replaced by the U.S. flag. The final preparations for departure were then made as Lewis and Clark and their Corps of Discovery set out from St. Louis on May 14, 1804.

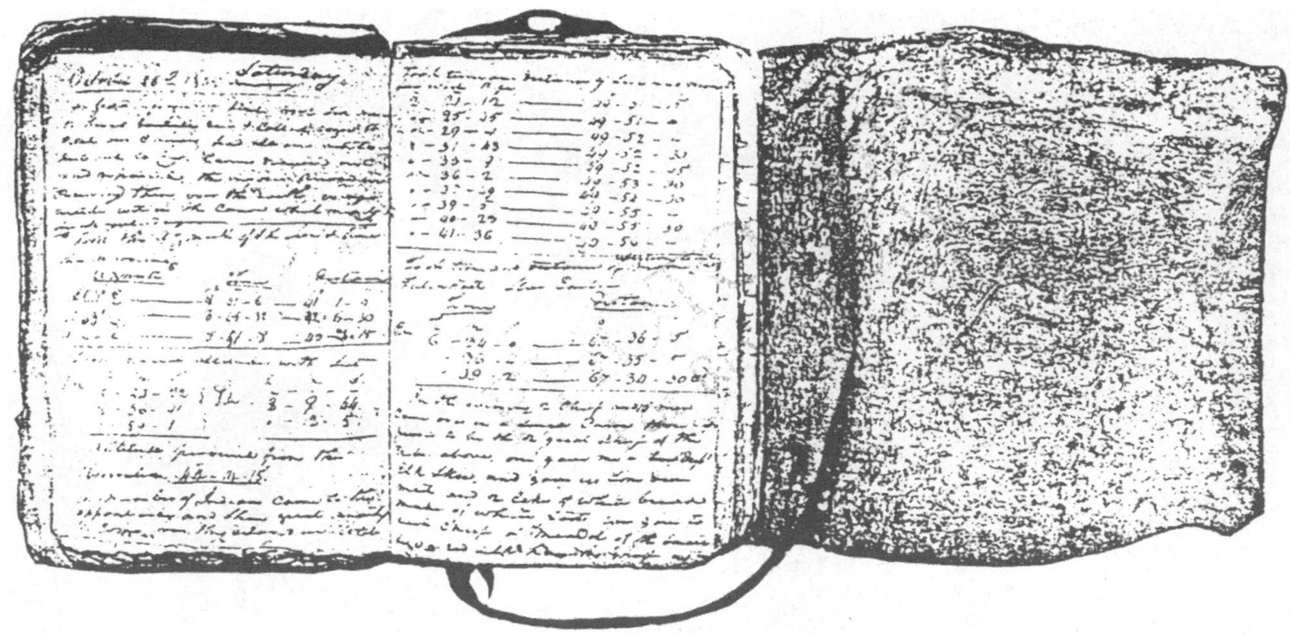

The diary carried by William Clark on the Lewis and Clark Expedition (1804–1806). (North Wind Picture Archives)

The Missouri River, sometimes called the "big muddy," is a large river that carries a huge volume of silt from its headwaters in the distant eroding mountains. Lewis and Clark were leading a group of thirty-three men aboard one flatboat and two pirogues into the vast unknown. Travel upriver was difficult in the early part of the expedition, as the men had to paddle and push-pole their way westward. The flatboat often ran aground on sandbars or was caught on underwater snags, and the men of the Corps of Discovery had to lift the boat or empty and reload its cargo in order to free the vessel. Along certain stretches of the river, the men had to use a technique called *cordelle,* in which they actually pulled the boats upstream with huge ropes that they dragged along the riverbanks.

The expedition made its way beyond the junction of the Platte River and, in so doing, officially entered Indian lands. By August 1804, the expedition had reached the camp of the Oto tribe, and there Lewis made his first speech to the Indians at a powwow. Lewis told the assembled chiefs that the party came in peace and that they wished for the Western tribes to remain at peace with one another. He also informed the Indians that the Spanish father was now gone, and hereafter the Great White Father in Washington would be their leader. He then smoked the calumet and distributed presents to the tribe.

Farther up the Missouri River, the Corps of Discovery would encounter another tribe that would not be as passive as the Oto. The Sioux were long considered to be the scourge of the Upper Missouri. They were located near enough to Canada to be under the economic spell of British presents and trade goods. The Sioux considered the Americans to be intruders into their established economic system, and they gave the Corps of Discovery a cold reception. The Sioux acted as though they were not satisfied with either the quality or quantity of presents that the Americans distributed among them. When it looked as if Sioux warriors might begin hostilities to prevent the further advance of the Americans, Lewis and Clark made clear that the Corps of Discovery would continue onward with its journey westward.

In addition to dealing with the Indians that the party encountered, Lewis and Clark also spent much of their time collecting samples of the flora and fauna of the West. Lewis found fossils and collected geological samples that were sent back to President Jefferson. Additionally, Lewis and Clark had the added responsibility of keeping order and maintaining discipline among the members of the corps. If anyone committed a violation of military posture, it was Lewis's responsibility to order and carry out the punishment in lashes.

As the winter of 1804 approached, the Corps of Discovery was nearing the village of the Mandan in the Dakota region. The American visitors were well received by the Mandan. Some believed (incorrectly) that these were the legendary "Welsh Indians"—the descendants of Welsh Prince Madoc whom some credit with the discovery of North America in 1170 C.E. The Mandan were rather free with their women, and the men of the Corps of Discovery appreciated greatly the attentions that were afforded them. It was here that Lewis and Clark met the French Canadian Toussaint Charbonneau and his pregnant squaw wife, Sacagawea. Both would join the Corps of Discovery when the group left the Mandan village with the spring thaw.

During the particularly cold winter of 1804, members

of the Corps of Discovery constructed a log fort near the site of the Mandan village. When food supplies ran low for both the corps and the Mandan, Lewis and Clark sent out some hunters to kill enough game to carry both groups through the winter. This action made the Mandan lasting friends of the Americans.

When the expedition departed on April 7, 1805, the lands west of the Mandan village were terra incognita to the men of the Corps of Discovery. The second phase of the expedition would take them into new lands and unknown hazards. The corps continued up the Missouri River using the geographical knowledge that had been acquired from the Mandan. When the river seemed to split, where the Marias and Missouri Rivers join, members of the expedition split into smaller groups, hoping to locate the Great Falls of the Missouri. Not finding this landmark within a day, they then determined that the South Fork of the Missouri River was the main branch that they should follow into the mountains.

The expedition continued on the Missouri until the party discovered the Great Falls. It would take the corps twenty-four days to portage eighty-five miles around the falls and the steep canyon country that followed. The party decided to leave behind, at this site, a pirogue containing specimens that had been collected, but unfortunately the cache of goods was in a ruined condition when the corps found them again on their return from the Pacific.

Once beyond the Great Falls, the Corps of Discovery would return to the river for transportation. Lewis and Clark were amazed that the Missouri River was still navigable so far upstream from St. Louis. At this point in the journey, Meriwether Lewis had to accept the unfortunate failure of his much-acclaimed collapsible iron and hide boat. The vessel failed miserably when it was tested. The group reached the three forks of the Missouri and named them the Jefferson, Madison, and Gallatin Rivers. As the expedition reached the headwaters of the Missouri River, members of the Corps of Discovery spotted Indian hunters from the Shoshoni tribe. These Indians advised the party as to the best route across the barrier of the Rocky Mountains, and the Lewis and Clark Expedition crossed the Continental Divide at Lemhi Pass (in present-day Montana) on August 12, 1805.

After the difficult crossing, the Corps of Discovery came upon the Shoshoni (or Snake) village. It was here that one of the true miracles of the expedition took place. Sacagawea, the Indian wife of Toussaint Charbonneau, suddenly realized that the chief of the Shoshoni was her brother Cameahwait, whom she had not seen in the four years since she had been kidnapped by the Hidatsa. Upon seeing his sister, who had been stolen into slavery, Cameahwait was touched, and he helped by providing horses and other necessary provisions that the Corps of Discovery would need for the next phase of the journey westward.

Once the party had crossed the Bitterroot Mountain range, the members of the corps followed the Snake River until they found themselves in the Columbia River basin, and the expedition was soon following the Columbia River westward to its junction with the Pacific Ocean. It was in this region that the expedition encountered the Flathead Indians, who were described as strange-looking and dirty, with lice-covered bodies. Several members of the expedition became ill after eating dried fish that had been offered by the Flathead; the Americans did not have a natural immunity to the bacteria that resided within the food. Despite these setbacks, the Corps of Discovery continued to travel down the Columbia River and soon began to encounter significant waves as they entered into the estuary of the Columbia basin. On November 8, 1805, Lewis and Clark and the members of their exploring party viewed the Pacific Ocean.

the feathers about its head pointed and stiff Some hairs the base of the beak. feathers fine and stiff about the ears. This is a faint likeness of the of the Plains or Heath the first of those fowls we met with was Missouri below in the neighbourhood of the Rocky and from which passes between and Rapids Gorgues and

The large Black & White Pheasant is peculiar to that portion of the Rocky Mountains watered by the Columbia River. at least we did not see them untill we reached the waters of that river, nor since we have left those mountains. They are about the size of a well grown hen. the contour of the bird is much that of the redish brown Pheasant common to our country. the tail is proportionably as long and is composed of 18 feathers of equal length, of a uniform dark brown tiped with black. the feathers of the body are of a dark brown black and white. the black

A page from William Clark's diary recorded during the Lewis and Clark Expedition (1804–1806). The page features a sketch of a "Cock of the Plains" that Clark observed. (North Wind Picture Archives)

The Americans constructed Fort Clatsop at the mouth of the Columbia River and spent the winter of 1805–1806 there. The party left written word at Fort

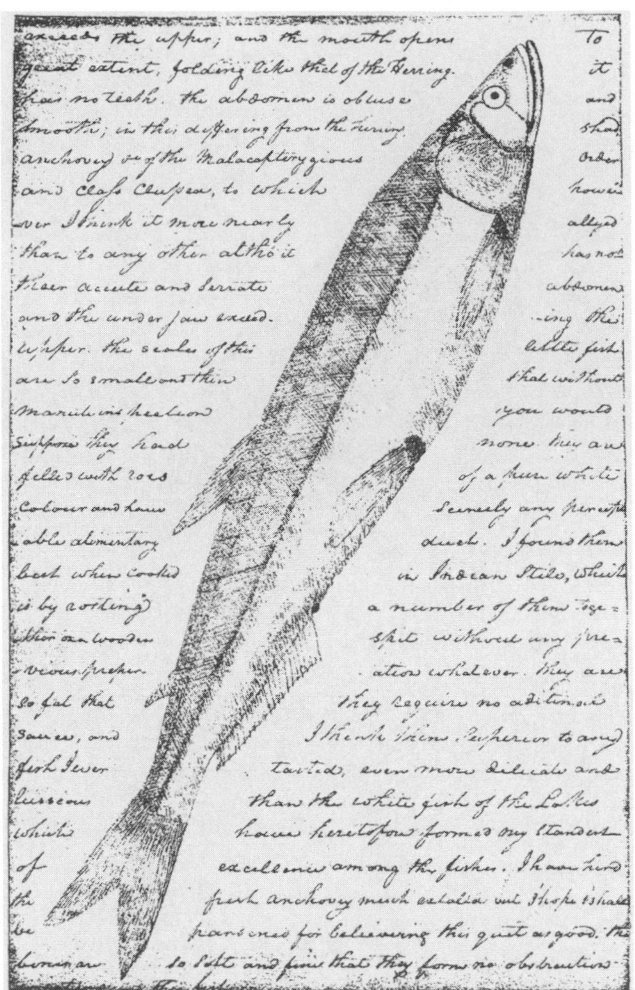

A page from William Clark's diary recorded during the Lewis and Clark Expedition (1804–1806). The page features a sketch of "A Trout" that Clark observed. (North Wind Picture Archives)

Clatsop that the Corps of Discovery had reached the Pacific Ocean, so that word of the expedition's success could be brought back to President Jefferson. When the spring thaw arrived in March 1806, it was time for the Corps of Discovery to begin its long journey home.

Members of the expedition remained together as a group until they reached the western base of the Rocky Mountains. At that point, they divided into two parties in order to explore a larger area and to find the easiest passage across the mountains. The two parties were to meet at the falls of the Missouri upon completing their journey across the mountains. It was during this phase of the expedition that Meriwether Lewis's party encountered a group of hostile Piegan Blackfoot who attempted to steal their guns and horses. During this struggle shots were fired, and two Indians were killed—the only Indian casualties of the entire expedition.

On August 11 an accident occurred during a hunting trip, when Private Peter Cruzatte fired into an area of bushes and wounded Meriwether Lewis. Although the flesh wound to his leg was certainly painful, it was not a mortal injury, and since the ball did not remain inside there was a lesser fear of infection. During the weeks while he recovered from this injury, Lewis requested that Clark assume command of the expedition.

On September 23, 1806, the Corps of Discovery made its triumphant return to St. Louis. The members of the expedition were feted as heroes, having achieved a monumental overland crossing to the Pacific that many had previously believed was unattainable.

The Lewis and Clark Expedition strengthened America's claim to the newly purchased Louisiana Territory, and it also provided a significant claim to the Oregon country that would be divided by a diplomatic agreement in 1846. The expedition provided a wealth of information about the flora, the fauna, and the ethnography of the West. The travels of Lewis and Clark also expanded our collective geographical sense of the West by providing more accurate maps that confirmed the vastness of the region. The expedition also disproved certain mythic falsehoods, such as the incredible hope that an easy, all-water route to the West might exist.

Perhaps the most perfect exploring journey in all of history, the Lewis and Clark Expedition ranks as a notable event in the history of the United States.

—Junius P. Rodriguez

See also

Cameahwait; Clark, William; Corps of Discovery; Flathead; Floyd, Charles; Jefferson, Thomas; Lewis, Meriwether; Mandan; Sacagawea; Shoshoni; York

For Further Reading

Allen, John Logan. 1975. *Passage through the Garden: Lewis and Clark and the Image of the American Northwest.* Urbana: University of Illinois Press; Chidsey, Donald Barr. 1970. *Lewis and Clark: The Great Adventure.* New York: Crown; Lavender, David. 1989. *Way to the Western Sea: Lewis and Clark across the Continent.* New York: Harper and Row; Ronda, James P. 1984. *Lewis and Clark among the Indians.* Lincoln: University of Nebraska Press.

LINCOLN, LEVI (1749–1820)

As President Thomas Jefferson's attorney general, Levi Lincoln offered his opinion of the constitutionality of the purchase of Louisiana, which provided for natural boundaries, unrestricted navigation of the Mississippi River, and a plan to ward off opposition from the Federalist Party.

Lincoln was a native of Massachusetts, Harvard educated, and was elected to several state positions following the American Revolution. He was a member of the Seventh Congress but resigned in March 1801, to accept Jefferson's appointment as attorney general, a post he filled from March 5, 1801, until late 1804. Lincoln also served as acting secretary of state from March to early May 1801. Considered by many to be a compromise choice for attorney general, Lincoln was a loyal Republican whose contributions to Jefferson's cabinet were minimal. Before Jefferson sent James Monroe to France to negotiate the purchase of Louisiana, the president asked cabinet members for their opinions on the legality of the acquisition of the new territory. Jefferson knew he would face difficult deadlines responding to any purchase offer, and any thought about calling a special session of Congress to seek approval was impossible. This led to his request for cabinet opinions and Lincoln's ensuing letter to Jefferson, dated January 10, 1803.

Lincoln's opinion set out a plan for the acquisition of new territory within the limits of the Constitution. Lincoln followed a strict construction of the constitutional right of acquiring lands but felt that the acquisition of New Orleans and the protection of navigation rights on the Mississippi were necessary and justified by any means. Geographically, Lincoln proposed acquiring land below a line just south of Natchez on the Mississippi River, east to the Chattahoochee River before it flows into the Apalachicola. From there, the territory ran along the Apalachicola to the river's mouth and then east to the Atlantic Ocean. By this plan, the southern boundary of Georgia would have run west from the old city of St. Augustine. The proposal would have added lands including present-day Alabama and Georgia. Lincoln felt his limited acquisition plan was logical because it added the port at New Orleans and Mississippi navigation rights—and it was constitutional. The constitutional basis of Lincoln's plan was that it acquired new lands without creating an independent territory, thus avoiding conflict with the Northeastern states over adding a new territory. This course of action would simply add new land to existing states under the authority of those states regulated by the federal government.

It is clear that, despite his Republican loyalties, Lincoln represented the New England view of territorial expansion, so much so that his biographer stated: "[He] forcefully set forth the opposition point of view" (Petroelje, 1969). Concluding that New England and New York would oppose any new states, he believed that the region would be less opposed to adding to existing states, therefore maintaining a balance of power in the Senate. In Lincoln's own words, his plan would "foreclose these objections," ward off Federalist objections, and avoid the necessity of a constitutional amendment.

Jefferson shared Lincoln's letter with his cabinet—all rejected it, primarily on the issue of Lincoln's strict construction of the constitutional power of acquiring territory. Secretary of the Treasury Albert Gallatin was especially harsh in his criticism of the Lincoln plan, spelling out the broad constructionist view. Gallatin carried no grudge against Lincoln, and had seen the man as a capable attorney and good scholar of sound judgment and discretion upon his initial appointment as attorney general. But Gallatin now treated Lincoln's plan with disfavor, responding that the United States had an inherent right to acquire new territory, notwithstanding the fact that, in Lincoln's opinion, no new lands could be added after the Constitution. Jefferson agreed with Gallatin, but Lincoln continued to express doubt as to the constitutionality of the purchase. He worked diligently on alternatives, including amendments to the Constitution, even after the Louisiana Purchase was announced to the nation. In another letter to Jefferson, dated August 30, 1803, Lincoln proposed granting citizenship to whites in Louisiana but not adding any new states to the Union until "an amendment of the Constitution shall be made for this purpose," and interestingly opted to maintain slavery in the area. Finally, Lincoln added that if no amendment were forthcoming, nothing should be said about the Constitutional issue, that it was best "to shut up the country." Once again Lincoln's plan was rejected, but Jefferson seriously considered amending the Constitution to avoid the precarious issue (Petroelje, 1969).

Ironically, as attorney general, Levi Lincoln would be involved in a variety of legal issues over land grants, boundaries, and government in the new territory. In an advisory letter to Jefferson (dated April 17, 1803), Lincoln also offered suggestions and support for the Lewis and Clark Expedition that Jefferson planned. Lincoln resigned his cabinet post at the end of 1804 but returned to politics in his native Massachusetts. He died on April 14, 1820.

—Boyd Childress

For Further Reading

Brown, Everett S. 1972. *The Constitutional History of the Louisiana Purchase, 1803–1812*. Edited by Herbert E. Bolton. Chevy Chase, MD: Beard Books. Petroelje, Marvin, Jr. 1969. "Levi Lincoln, Sr.: Jeffersonian Republican of Massachusetts." Unpublished dissertation, Michigan State University.

LISA, MANUEL (1772?–1820)

Famed merchant and fur trader Manuel Lisa was cofounder of the Missouri Fur Company and a pioneer of the Western fur trade. Lisa is thought to have been born September 8, 1772, in New Orleans. By 1796 he had become a merchant on the Mississippi River and had established a store at Vincennes. He soon married Polly Charles Chew and removed to St. Louis, where in 1802 he received a monopoly over the Osage Indian trade from the Spanish government.

Originally planning to enter the Santa Fe trade, Lisa opted instead for the upper Missouri's rich beaver country reported by the Lewis and Clark Expedition (which he had helped supply). In spring 1807, along with George

Drouillard, one of Lewis and Clark's men, Lisa organized the first trading and trapping expedition into the upper Missouri basin and the northern Rocky Mountains. In the fall 1807, his company established Fort Raymond, at the confluence of the Yellowstone and Bighorn Rivers. He sent John Colter, another veteran of the Lewis and Clark Expedition, on a winter mission to advertise the fort to the Indians of the region, and to urge them to bring in furs to trade. The epic trek took Colter up the Wind River, across the Tetons, and through the upper Yellowstone, where he made his discovery of the geyser basins that later became Yellowstone National Park. While Colter worked to drum up the Indian trade, Lisa's men spent the winter of 1807–1808 trapping in the areas around Fort Raymond.

Manuel Lisa returned to St. Louis to outfit another trip to the upper Missouri. He envisioned a grand plan for trade in the region, which included a series of forts and trading posts along the river. Upon his return to St. Louis, Lisa spent the winter of 1808–1809 organizing the Missouri Fur Company, with his former partners Menard and Morrison, and Benjamin Wilkinson, Pierre Chouteau, René Auguste Chouteau, Sylvestre Labbadie, Reuben Lewis, Andrew Henry, and William Clark.

In 1809, Lisa again ascended the river, establishing three trading posts as well as a company headquarters at Fort Mandan. During Lisa's absence, the Blackfoot Indians had driven his trappers out of the Three Forks country at the Missouri headwaters, an area considered the best beaver region in the West. In 1809, Andrew Henry undertook to re-enter the Three Forks country in force.

Lisa returned to St. Louis again in late 1809, to supply the 1810 outfit. Because President Jefferson's embargo had made manufactured good so scarce, Lisa had to cancel the 1810 expedition. Meanwhile, Andrew Henry and John Colter desperately needed resupply and reinforcement. Harassed by the Blackfoot, they abandoned their fort at the Three Forks. Accompanying these setbacks was the rise of competition, in the form of John Jacob Astor's Pacific Fur Company. The War of 1812 placed further impediments in Lisa's path. In 1812–1813, pro-British tribes in the upper Missouri forced Lisa and his men back downriver. When he returned to St. Louis, he learned that the Missouri Fur Company had ousted him from its board of directors. The company dissolved shortly thereafter, in 1814.

Unwilling to abandon his vision, Lisa joined with Theodore Hunt, of Kentucky, to return up the Missouri, re-establish his posts, and revive the trade. William Clark commissioned Lisa as Indian subagent for the Missouri tribes above the Kansas River, charging him with keeping the Sioux friendly to the United States. At Fort Hunt, Lisa married into the Omaha tribe and likewise enlisted the Teton and Yankton Sioux to fight the pro-British Santee. Lisa also brought several chiefs to St. Louis to sign treaties of peace and friendship. During the War of 1812, Lisa kept the Western tribes allied with the American side.

In 1817, Lisa terminated his partnership with Hunt and joined another trading venture, Cabanné and Company. But Lisa never could reach agreeable terms with the new partners, and the company dissolved. In 1819, Lisa hoped to organize a new Missouri Fur Company, and went upriver to prepare the way for the Stephen H. Long Expedition. Shortly after returning to St. Louis in the spring of 1820, Lisa grew sick and died.

Lisa made three significant contributions to the history of the Louisiana Purchase. He established and maintained friendly relations between the United States and the Missouri tribes during the War of 1812. His men gathered much of what was then known about the region's geography. Finally, although he met with limited financial success himself, his vision for opening the Missouri country fur trade made fortunes for those adventurers who followed him.

—*Douglas W. Dodd*

See also
Missouri Fur Company

For Further Reading

Goodrich, James W. 1999. "Manuel Lisa." In *American National Biography,* vol. 13. Edited by John A. Garraty and Mark C. Carnes. New York: Oxford University Press; Oglesby, Richard Edward. 1963. *Manuel Lisa and the Opening of the Missouri Fur Trade.* Norman: University of Oklahoma Press; Oglesby, Richard Edward. 1968. "Manuel Lisa." In *The Mountain Men and the Fur Trade of the Far West,* vol. 5. Edited by LeRoy Hafen. Glendale, CA: A. H. Clark.

LITERATURE, THE LOUISIANA PURCHASE IN

Literary works written during the period leading up to and immediately following the Louisiana Purchase largely fall into two categories: documentary materials, such as histories, letters, and travel narratives, and creative works such as poetry and novels. Until the late 1700s, narrative forms that recorded exploratory expeditions and personal experiences resulting from these expeditions and the resulting colonial settlements were the dominant literary genre. Much of the literature produced during this era was written in French, with many of the literary artists spending at least some of their time studying or writing in France. In addition, a substantial oral narrative tradition was firmly entrenched, especially among members of indigenous Native American communities.

The earliest writing from the colonial era of Louisiana came from the pens of diarists such as Henri de Tonti and Jacques de la Metairie, each of whom recorded his perceptions of events during La Salle's exploratory expeditions. Travel narratives were written by missionaries such as Father Paul du Ru and Father François-Xavier Charlevoix; Henry de Joutel penned a historical journal of La Salle's second expedition. André Pénicault produced a history of the Iberville colony spanning twenty-two years, and this work continues to provide scholars with a substantial portion of the primary source material available concerning Louisiana's early history. Further contributions were made by Ursline nuns Mare de Saint-Augustin Tranchepain and Marie Madeline Hachard. Tranchepain kept a journal describing her voyage to colonial Louisiana, and Hachard's letters to her family in France were later published, in part for the information they contained and in part because, as John Wilds points out, contemporary readers found their tone charming.

The first comprehensive history of Louisiana was written by Antoine Simon Le Page du Pratz in 1758. Du Pratz lived in Louisiana for a time, but colonial life was not to his liking, and he returned to France. Charles Gayarré also wrote a comprehensive discussion of the development of the territory, entitled *History of Louisiana: The French Domination.* Gayarré's three-volume *History* is still considered by many to be an authoritative history of the colonial period in Louisiana.

The first truly literary figure in Louisiana, Julien Poydras, a French poet and plantation owner, did not emerge until the late 1770s. Originally written in French, two of Poydras's three lengthy poems praised Governor Bernardo de Gálvez (1777). His masterpiece, "The God of the Mississippi," is especially noteworthy for its praise of both black and white soldiers during Gálvez's campaigns, and his treatments of people of color as equals in his work were somewhat unusual during this era. His third poem, entitled "A Prise du Morne du Baton Rouge," was written to commemorate the liberation of Baton Rouge from British control and demonstrates the suspicion with which intruders were viewed.

Following the cession of Louisiana to the United States through the period leading to the Civil War, much of the literature written in Louisiana continued to be written in French. Literary writers of this era included Creole poets Dominique and Adrien Rouquette, who were both greatly influenced by the French romanticism of Hugo and Chateaubriand, whom the poets met personally. Dominique published pieces such as *Meschacébéenes* (1839), and *Fleurs d'Amérique* (1857). Adrien published *Les Savanes* (1841) and *L'Antoniade* (1860), which served as precursors to his masterpiece, a narrative poem reflecting on the Native American, entitled *La Nouvelle Atala* (1879). According to John Wilds, this piece likely was derived from his experiences as a missionary to the Choctaw Indians in St. Tammany Parish. Further, Charles Testut Mercier's autobiographical novel, *L'Habitation Saint-Ybars,* details his experiences on an antebellum plantation.

Literary contributions were not limited to the white community, however, even during this era of racial inequality. *Les Cenelles* (1845), an anthology of poetry by free people of color living in the Louisiana Territory, has been called by Rayburn S. Moore the "most curious of all the volumes of antebellum Southern verse." The volume contained eighty-two poems by seventeen poets and was reputed to be the first anthology of African American poetry. Contributors to the volume included Victor Séjour, Nelson Debrosses, and Armand Lanusse, all of whom wrote in French. Victor Séjour, a free person of color who was born in New Orleans and later immigrated to Paris, became a successful playwright. His most important works included *Richard III: Drame en cinq actes, en prose* and *La Tireuse de Cartes,* both of which were published in Paris.

Out of the history and development of the Louisiana Territory grew a literary tradition that was rich and varied. The writers whose work appeared both before and immediately after the transfer of the territory to the United States—along with the cultural milieu that surrounded them—have continued to be influential upon later Louisiana writers, including Kate Chopin, George Washington Cable, Grace King, and Lafcadio Hearn.

—*Suzanne Disheroon-Green*

For Further Reading

Rubin, Louis D., et al. 1985. *The History of Southern Literature.* Baton Rouge: Louisiana State University Press; Wall, Bennett H., et al. 1997. *Louisiana: A History.* Wheeling, IL: Harlan Davidson; Wilds, John, et al. 1996. *Louisiana Yesterday and Today.* Baton Rouge: Louisiana State University Press.

LIVINGSTON, EDWARD (1764–1836)

Born in Clermont, New York, Edward Livingston grew up in a staunchly Federalist family. George Washington's failure to reward the Livingston family with patronage once he became the first president apparently compelled the Livingstons, including Edward, to switch their loyalties to Thomas Jefferson in the 1790s.

Edward used his educational background as a lawyer to gain public office in New York around the turn of the century. He served first as U.S. representative (1795–1801), then jointly held the positions of U.S. attorney for the district of New York and mayor of New York City (1801–1803). Financial improprieties that occurred during Livingston's term as mayor, while not involving him directly, forced his resignation from both posts in 1803. That same year, Edward's older brother Robert, in the position of U.S. minister to France, negotiated the purchase of the Louisiana Territory from Napoleon Bonaparte. Hounded by his acceptance of the debt incurred because of the financial scandal and perhaps lured by "newspaper accounts of the vast resources and the opportunities to amass a fortune in this new country," Edward set out for New Orleans in December 1803, arriving there in February 1804 (Hatcher, 1940).

Livingston started to make his fortune immediately, by establishing a legal practice. His clients included the infamous pirates the brothers Jean and Pierre Lafitte, Robert Fulton, and Robert Livingston (no relation). Whenever a client could not pay his fees, Edward accepted land instead. Livingston likely acquired this property in an attempt to obtain enough capital to pay off the substantial debt for which he had assumed responsibility during his time as mayor of New York City.

One particular land claim, the Batture Sainte Marie, caused Livingston further trouble. He represented a client, John Gravier, in his suit against the city of New Orleans for the batture. When the territorial court ruled in favor of Gravier, Livingston received half of the property as his fee. Incensed at Livingston, whom they blamed for initiating the legal action, the residents of New Orleans appealed to Governor William C. C. Claiborne for assistance in their fight. Claiborne in turn asked President Thomas Jefferson to intervene.

Jefferson opposed Livingston's claim, possibly because he viewed Livingston's actions as U.S. attorney as a discredit to the Jeffersonian political faction. A more likely reason for the president's repudiation of a former ally was Livingston's alleged involvement in the Burr conspiracy. Aaron Burr, one of Jefferson's chief rivals, attempted during this period to foment a rebellion among people of the southwestern territories. General James Wilkinson, a hero of the American Revolution and former territorial governor of Louisiana, alerted Jefferson to the conspiracy and accused Livingston of playing a part in Burr's scheme. Despite no direct evidence implicating Livingston in the abortive endeavor, Jefferson may have allowed the association to affect his actions.

Under Jefferson's directive, Secretary of State James Madison authorized the seizure of the disputed batture land. Livingston responded by bringing suit against the federal marshal who carried out the order and against Jefferson as well. The Supreme Court of Louisiana settled the contentious issue of the property in 1818, cutting Livingston's portion of the land. It was enough, however, to allow him eventually to pay off the debts sustained in New York. By 1830, the Treasury Department declared Livingston's debt paid.

In spite of his financial problems during these years, Livingston served Louisiana well in public positions. During the War of 1812, he acted as Andrew Jackson's aide. Historians have differed over how important Livingston was to Jackson's successful military campaigns, but none doubt that Jackson held him in high regard once the war ended, Livingston was elected to the lower house of the Louisiana state legislature in 1820. He served in the legislature until 1822, when he won election to the U.S. House of Representatives. Livingston served in the House from 1822 to 1829.

Livingston made his most important contributions to Louisiana during the 1820s, primarily in the area of legal reform. The Louisiana legislature had commissioned him to draw up a coherent legal code when he first moved to the territory in the early 1800s. Now the state legislature authorized him to reform the state's penal code. After a setback caused by a fire that destroyed his work in 1824, Livingston presented the state legislature his recommendations for revising the penal code in 1825. Although the legislature chose not to accept his reforms, Livingston's efforts on the penal code, as well as other suggested legal reforms, brought him worldwide recognition as a legal expert.

Following the rejection of his penal code revisions, Livingston appeared to disassociate himself from Louisiana. He lost re-election to the House in 1828, partly as a result of spending too much time in New York. However, the state legislature reaffirmed its support of Livingston by appointing him to the U.S. Senate. Livingston served there until 1831, when he replaced Martin Van Buren as secretary of state under his old friend Andrew Jackson. Livingston's main contributions in this office included his composition of a treaty with France regarding the spoliation claims of U.S. citizens and his assistance in the drafting of the Nullification Proclamation against South Carolina nullifiers. In 1833, Jackson appointed Livingston minister to France. Livingston continued to negotiate the spoliation claims against France and performed other diplomatic duties until he resigned in 1835 and retired to New York, where he died on May 23, 1836. Livingston viewed himself as an exile to Louisiana, yet he remained there for almost three decades. His contribution to the state materialized in his organization of the territorial legal code in 1805 and his attempted reform of the penal code in the 1820s. Strongly influenced by British jurist Jeremy Bentham, Livingston's proposals reflected a modern understanding of preventive measures against criminal acts.

—Mark R. Cheathem

See also

Claiborne, William Charles Cole; Wilkinson, James

For Further Reading

Hatcher, William B. 1940. *Edward Livingston: Jeffersonian Republican and Jacksonian Democrat.* Baton Rouge: Louisiana State University Press; Hunt, Charles H. 1864. *The Life of Edward Livingston.* New York: D. Appleton; Pound, Roscoe. 1950. *The Formative Era of American Law.* New York: Peter Smith; Tregle, Joseph G., Jr. 1999. *Louisiana in the Age of Jackson: A Clash of Culture and Personalities.* Baton Rouge: Louisiana State University Press.

LIVINGSTON, ROBERT R. (1746–1813)

Robert R. Livingston owed his diplomatic posting to France to his knowledge of French politics and diplomacy, as well as to his political support of Thomas Jefferson. Unfortunately, his appointment as minister to France in 1801 coincided with the rise of fresh tensions between the two countries, this time about New Orleans and the navigation of the Mississippi. Together with Monroe, he negotiated the May 3, 1803, treaty between France and the United States that ceded Louisiana to the United States.

A member of a prominent New York family and a signer of the Declaration of Independence, Robert R. Livingston served in the Continental Congress and in 1781 was put in charge of the diplomacy of the young nation. As secretary of foreign affairs, Livingston created an efficient foreign affairs department. He advised negotiators in Paris to cooperate with the French and urged the extension of U.S. boundaries to the Mississippi. But Congress retained most of the power, and a frustrated Livingston left office in 1783.

As political oppositions emerged in the 1790s between Federalists and Republicans, Livingston proved a consistent supporter of the Democratic-Republican Party, criticizing the Jay Treaty (1794) and campaigning for Jefferson in the 1800 elections. Thus both his political convictions and his past experience as a diplomat in France explain his being sent to Paris in the fall of 1801. His mission was to seek redress for the remaining U.S. grievances against France in the wake of the Convention of Mortefontaine (October 3, 1800); more specifically, Livingston was in charge of obtaining compensation for the damages sustained by the American merchant marine at the hands of French privateers during the Quasi-War (1798–1800). Inasmuch as the news of the retrocession of Louisiana was already rumored as he left, Livingston's instructions bore on that subject in great detail: if Louisiana had indeed been ceded to France, he was to secure the navigation of the Mississippi and try to purchase at least West Florida.

Soon after he arrived in France (November 12, 1801), General Leclerc's expedition, which was meant to reconquer the rebel French colony, St. Domingue, and thus create a future colonial market for the goods grown in now French Louisiana, sailed from Brest (November 22). This, and the general trend of conversations, convinced Livingston that the retrocession had indeed taken place, and he was urged to sound the French government on the possible sale of New Orleans and the Floridas.

Livingston's letters to the French minister for exterior relations, Talleyrand, remained unanswered. They grew more indignant as time passed. After he was officially informed that Spain had retroceded Louisiana, Livingston tried to convince the French that the Americans would be very hostile neighbors and that they could never keep the colony. Jefferson's now famous May 1802 letter to Livingston ("There is on the globe one single spot, the possessor of which is our enemy") prompted the minister to draft an essay entitled "Whether it will be advantageous to France to take possession of Louisiana?" which he circulated to key figures in the French government (Lyon). But that was of little avail, leading only to informal conversations with Joseph Bonaparte.

When he heard of the closure by Spain of the right of deposit that Americans had enjoyed in New Orleans (October 16, 1802), Livingston suggested in a memoir that France should cede northern Louisiana to the United States as a buffer zone against British Canada, being thus the first official ever to consider buying Louisiana. He also recommended that France sell West Florida and New Orleans to the United States. But the French government only told Livingston that General Bernadotte would be sent as minister to the United States, thus moving the discussions there. Livingston then penned another memoir, this time suggesting that New Orleans should be organized as an independent state, but to no avail. Only in March 1803, when Napoleon realized that the expedition to St. Domingue had been an utter failure and thus abandoned his American colonial ambitions in order to focus on Europe and Asia, did Talleyrand start answering Livingston.

By then, Thomas Jefferson had already decided to thwart Federalist demands for an unauthorized seizure of New Orleans by sending James Monroe as minister to France to assist Livingston, after sounding French authorities through the informal conduit of Du Pont de Nemours—two moves that revealed the administration's distrust of the American minister in Paris, whose arguments in various memoirs to the French government they considered unwise.

James Madison's instructions provided that the two ministers were to negotiate a treaty by which France would cede New Orleans and the Floridas to the United States. Meanwhile, Livingston had grown bitter and wary of the French (with whom he got on well, on a personal level), writing to Monroe on April 10 that he thought only war could solve the crisis; so the next day, when he was offered the whole of Louisiana by Talleyrand, he did not react enthusiastically. However, negotiations with François Barbé-Marbois, the minister of the treasury and a friend of the Americans, began immediately after Monroe arrived on April 11. The U.S. negotiators realized that they had to sign a treaty rapidly, on account of the political agitation on this issue in the United States and because of rapidly unfolding events in Europe. They thus disregarded their instructions and discussed the financial side of the transaction, which involved the United States taking over the long-awaited U.S. claims that Livingston had originally come to France to settle. The discussions were secret, and Livingston's role can be seen as central, as Monroe was still unwell.

The Louisiana Treaty and the convention regarding American claims are dated in the early days of May, but the real date of their signing was April 30: Livingston and Monroe had purchased Louisiana for sixty million francs, with twenty extra millions going to settle American claims ($15 million all together). The treaty was sent to the United States on May 13.

Livingston did not derive much personal benefit from the Louisiana Purchase. He tried to publicize his actions by having his latest correspondence with Talleyrand published in the United States immediately after the treaty was signed, perhaps in the hope of being selected as the next vice president. That unauthorized publication, along with other minor diplomatic disagreements, fully alienated the secretary of state against him and caused him to be called home. More seriously, because the claims commission did not apportion indemnities fairly among U.S. claimants, he had to fight accusations of corruption.

Before leaving, Livingston launched into new diplomatic efforts aimed at securing West Florida as part of the Louisiana Purchase. However Monroe, not Livingston, was entrusted with the specific task of negotiating for the Floridas.

After returning to the United States in 1805, Livingston no longer was involved in politics, turning to other pursuits. While in Paris, he had met Robert Fulton, the inventor whose steamboat project he started sponsoring, continuing to do so after coming back to his home state.

—Marie-Jeanne Rossignol

See also
Barbé-Marbois, François, Marquis de; Bonaparte, Joseph; Bonaparte, Napoleon; Jefferson, Thomas; Leclerc, Charles-Victor-Emmanuel; Madison, James; Monroe, James; Talleyrand-Perigord, Charles Maurice de

For Further Reading
Barbé-Marbois, François de. 1829. *Histoire de la Louisiane et de la cession de cette colonie par la France aux Etats-Unis de l'Amérique septentrionale.* Paris: Firmin Didot; Bemis, Samuel Flagg, ed. 1958. *The American Secretaries of State and Their Diplomacy.* New York: Pageant Books; Lyon, E. Wilson. 1974. *Louisiana in French Diplomacy: 1789–1804.* Norman: University of Oklahoma Press; Sprague, Marshall. 1974. *So Vast, So Beautiful a Land: Louisiana and the Purchase.* Boston: Little, Brown and Company.

LONDON, TREATY OF

See Jay's Treaty

LONG, JAMES (c. 1793–1822)

James Long was an American filibuster whose two attempts to wrest Texas from Spanish control ended in his capture and death in a Mexican prison. The Virginia-born Long grew up in Kentucky and Tennessee at a time when the region west of the Mississippi was coming under U.S. control. He served as a surgeon during the War of 1812, following which he practiced medicine in Port Gibson, Mississippi. By that time he had already married Jane Wilkinson. Long tried his hand as a planter in the Vicksburg area, but sold off the plantation in 1817 and turned to commerce, entering a partnership with W. W. Walker in Natchez.

The Adams-Onís Treaty (1819), in recognizing the Sabine River as the western boundary of the Louisiana Purchase, created considerable turmoil throughout the Western frontier, where the attitude among the Anglo-American population was that John Quincy Adams had given away Texas to Spain. At Natchez a large group of agitators, including Samuel Davenport and José Bernardo Gutiérrez de Lara, who had been involved in earlier insurrectionary activities in Texas, called for an expedition to liberate Texas from Spanish rule. Also among the group's members was Walker, Long's business partner, and it may have been because of his efforts that Long obtained command of the expedition after General John Adair declined the invitation.

Long's first expedition was underway by mid-1819. Recruits were attracted with promises of a league of land (approximately forty-five hundred acres) to each soldier, and in early June about 120 men crossed the Neutral Ground along with a printing press. Long followed with another 70 men later in the month and soon accepted the surrender of the Nacogdoches population. On June 23, 1819, Texas was declared a republic, with Long elected as its president of the supreme council and commander in chief of its armed forces. Long and his colleagues promptly revealed the real purpose for their undertaking, passing laws that granted each serviceman a league of land and calling for the survey and sale of public lands. He made contact with Jean and Pierre Lafitte, who maintained a base of operations at Galveston, and attempted to bring the privateers into the republic's fold. The Lafittes had no intention of allying themselves with the filibusters, and in fact conspired against them with the Spanish. The U.S. Army, in the meantime, made every effort to keep supplies from reaching the expeditionaries. By October 1819 Long's men were scattered in scavenging parties throughout east Texas and vulnerable to Spanish attack.

The Spanish authorities in Texas, while taxed to a state of extreme poverty, nevertheless mounted as vigorous a defense as possible against Long's expedition. The Lafittes handed over correspondence from Long that left no doubt in the minds of the royalist officers that the filibusters were working with the support of the U.S. government. In September a five-hundred-man force was placed under the command of San Antonio militia commander Ignacio Pérez, who marched to east Texas, rounding up as many of the scattered parties of Anglo-Americans as could be found. Poor communications among the filibusters caused Long not to get word of the royalists' approach until it was too late to do anything other than retreat to the Sabine. On October 28, 1819, Pérez entered Nacogdoches without opposition. At the end of the month he arrived at the Sabine, by which time he had thirty prisoners in hand, eighteen of whom he soon freed. By the end of November the remaining Anglo-Americans in east Texas, some of whom had begun building farms and houses, had been expelled, and Long's republic had collapsed.

Undaunted, Long attempted to reorganize his expedition around the few men who had made their way to Galveston Island, where they had gained the temporary assistance of the Lafittes. Long found that his financial situation was in shambles and that enthusiasm for the Texas enterprise had waned. When he arrived at Point Bolivar in early April 1820, Long found the Lafittes in the process of abandoning their stronghold there, under pressure from the U.S. Navy. He quickly returned to Louisiana to raise additional men and supplies, but managed to gather only about fifty recruits. Attempts to revive the Supreme Council and elect a new president filled the time left over from fighting off Karankawa Indians and building Fort Las Casas. For more than a year Long worked at building up a force sufficiently strong to undertake an offensive, but in the end all he could muster were three small ships and fifty men.

Oddly, Long's last attempt to liberate Texas came after Mexico had obtained its independence from Spain. Although he captured La Bahía without a fight in September 1821, Governor Antonio Martínez immediately sent Colonel Pérez against him, and on October 8, 1821, the last Texas filibuster surrendered. After a brief detention in San Antonio, Long was sent to Mexico City, where a prison guard shot him, according to Mexican authorities by accident, on April 8, 1822.

—Jesús F. de la Teja

See also

Gutierrez-Magee Expedition; Lafitte, Jean; Long (Stephen Harriman) Expedition; Nacogdoches; Neutral Ground; Texas; Transcontinental Treaty

For Further Reading

Chipman, Donald E. 1992. *Spanish Texas, 1519–1821*. Austin: University of Texas Press; Warren, Harris Gaylord. 1943. *The Sword Was Their Passport: A History of American Filibustering in the Mexican Revolution*. Baton Rouge: Louisiana State University Press.

LONG, STEPHEN HARRIMAN (1784–1864)

Stephen H. Long showed little interest in exploration or military service early in life, but his part-time work as a surveyor and experiments with machinery gained him the admiration of the army chief of engineers, General Joseph Swift. With the general's help and encouragement, Long gave up his job as a school principal and accepted an appointment to the army as a second lieutenant of engineers. In 1815 he served as assistant professor of mathematics at West Point and received a transfer to the Topographical Engineers the next year. Awarded the rank of brevet major, Long began his career as an explorer with this elite unit.

During the next two years, Long gained his first frontier experience. Working mostly in Illinois and Indiana, he inspected army garrisons, surveyed possible sites for new forts, and gathered information about the region. On an 1817 mission he assessed the portage between the Fox and Wisconsin Rivers and explored the upper Mississippi. These assignments served to train him as an explorer. As his interest in the West grew, Long urged his superiors to sponsor new explorations with emphasis on collecting scientific data.

In 1818, Long presented Secretary of War John C. Calhoun with an ambitious plan to use a steamboat for Western exploration. As part of the larger Yellowstone Expedition, Long set out in early May 1819 with a team of scientists and explorers from Pittsburgh with orders to survey the region between the Mississippi River and the Rocky Mountains. Government officials and the public held high hopes that this corps, which included a botanist, a geologist, and a zoologist, would make important discoveries, but the expedition fell short of expectations. Delayed by several illnesses and frequent mechanical breakdowns of the *Western Engineer*, a steamboat of Long's design, they made slow progress. The men reached the Platte River in September and encamped for the winter at Council Bluffs.

After a trip to Washington to report his progress, Long returned to the camp and set out again in 1820 along the Platte River. They headed west to the Rocky Mountains, where the corps discovered Long's Peak and became the first to reach the top of Pike's Peak. Turning south, Long then divided his company, personally leading one group to find the Red River, while the others moved east along the Arkansas River. Unfortunately, Long and his men mistakenly traveled along the Canadian, and, therefore, failed to survey the Red River, which had been their goal.

An 1823–1824 expedition was Long's last for the army. His team of scientists traveled up the Mississippi and Minnesota Rivers, and then into Canada along the Red River of the North. Making their way back east, the corps explored the northern shore of Lake Superior and crossed the Great Lakes to return to the United States. Their observations on this journey proved much less significant than the information that Long had gathered on the 1819–1820 mission.

Long's record as an explorer was mixed. Historians have faulted him for failure to accomplish specific goals, such as following the Arkansas River to its source. His harsh and mistaken description of the southern Plains helped create an image that this region was a "Great American Desert," unsuitable for settlement, although many of his contemporaries made similar assessments of the area. To his credit, Long organized his expeditions in a systematic fashion and recruited competent, well-trained men. His methods served as a model for future explorers. And he did in fact gather substantial data, adding to the scientific community's knowledge of geographical features, animal and plant life, and Native Americans in the unexplored regions of the frontier.

After his days as an explorer ended, Long became involved in improving the nation's infrastructure. Assigned by the army to aid in railroad planning, he became an expert on the subject and developed mathematical tables that sped the process of surveying routes for new railroad lines. In the 1840s, the War Department put Long to work on the problems of river obstructions, including the great raft of the Red River. Long spent the rest of his career attempting to improve navigation on the Midwestern river system, although he failed to find a permanent solution to the annually recurring snags and sandbars. He retired from the military in 1863 and died on September 4 of the following year.

—Christopher Dennis

See also

Great American Desert; Long (Stephen H.) Expedition

For Further Reading

Benson, Maxine, ed. 1988. *From Pittsburgh to the Rocky Mountains: Major Stephen Long's Expedition, 1819–1820.* Golden, CO: Fulcrum; Goetzmann, William. 1991. *Army Exploration in the American West, 1803–1863.* Austin: Texas State Historical Association; Nichols, Roger L., and Patrick L. Halley. 1980. *Stephen H. Long and American Frontier Exploration.* Newark: University of Delaware Press; Wood, Richard G. 1966. *Stephen Harriman Long, 1784–1864: Army Engineer, Explorer, Inventor.* Glendale, CA: Arthur Clark Company.

LONG (STEPHEN HARRIMAN) EXPEDITION (1820)

The Stephen H. Long Expedition of 1820 began from Engineer Cantonment near Council Bluffs on the Missouri River in June 1820. Because of transportation problems and funding reductions, the ambitious original mission of the expedition—to explore the upper Missouri, the upper Mississippi, and the Red River—had to be greatly reduced. The unrealistically high expectations placed upon the 1820 expedition, and its subsequent failure to meet them, caused the venture for a long time to be considered a failure. One nineteenth-century historian derided the 1820 journey to the Rocky Mountains as nothing more than a "sideshow" to distract attention from the failures of the 1819 venture to conduct a scientific investigation of the Missouri River. But more recent scholars have pointed to the significant achievements of the expedition: identification of several plant and animal species new to science, as well as the first systematic investigations of the large area of previously unexplored land in the Louisiana Purchase lying between the northerly route of the Lewis and Clark Expedition of 1804–1806 and Pike's southern explorations of 1806.

During the winter of 1819–1820, following his aborted attempt to ascend the Missouri to the mouth of the Yellowstone in the *Western Engineer,* Long returned to Washington, D.C. There he received word that the government had reduced the budget for his expedition and that he would have to undertake a more limited exploration as a result. He returned to Engineer Cantonment in May, and the party set out to the westward in June. The membership of the 1820 expedition was a much different group than that of the previous year. Only five of the original members remained. The new twenty-two-man party now consisted of Maj. Long, commanding; Capt. John R. Bell, the expedition's journalist; Lt. William H. Swift, assistant topographer (and in command of a seven-man rifle company); Dr. Edwin James, botanist, geologist, and physician; Thomas Say, zoologist and ethnologist; Titian Peale, assistant naturalist; and Samuel Seymour, an artist. Eight others served the party as hunters, interpreters, and baggage-handling *engagés.*

Heading west, the expedition traveled on foot and horseback across the Great Plains. By the end of June, the party had gained its first view of the Rocky Mountains, and notably, of the high, snowy summit that would later be named Long's Peak. In early July, they followed the South Platte River to reach the western edge of the Great Plains, at the foot of the Front Range. There they located the point where the South Platte issues from the mountains onto the plains, but did not seek to locate its source. Long then turned his men southward. They passed through the locations of present-day Denver and Colorado Springs in early July. On July 13–15, three of the party, including Dr. James and Lt. Swift, made the first documented ascent of 14,110-foot Pike's Peak. On July 16, the party located the Arkansas River, but made no attempt to seek its headwaters, and ascended the river no farther than the sheer-walled declivity of Royal Gorge. On July 19, the party began to descend the river, heading east. Long divided his party and led a group south to seek the Red River, while Capt. Bell had charge of a force that was to continue down the Arkansas. Upon striking the Canadian River, Long mistook it for the Red River and followed it—to his disappointment—back to the Arkansas. Long arrived at Fort Smith in September 1820, completing his sixteen-hundred-mile tour.

Long's exploration and his subsequent report helped to fix in the American mind the view of the Great Plains as the "Great American Desert." It was, he said, "almost wholly unfit for cultivation," and "uninhabitable by a people depending upon agriculture for their subsistence." Settlement of the High Plains eventually succeeded, but required adaptation to the semiarid environment.

From a scientific standpoint, the Long Expedition of 1820 yielded important contributions to knowledge, even though it fell short of its fulfilling its mission of geographic discovery. According to Howard Evans, Edwin

James returned with a large collection of Rocky Mountain and Great Plains plants, 140 of which botanists identified and described as new. Thomas Say identified several new animal species, including thirteen mammals, thirteen birds, twelve reptiles and amphibians, four arachnids and crustaceans, and more than 150 insects. Among the plants and animals discovered were such emblematically Western species as the coyote, mule deer, blue grouse, prairie rattlesnake, and Colorado blue columbine.

—Douglas W. Dodd

See also
Lewis and Clark Expedition; Long, Stephen Harriman; Pike Expedition

For Further Reading
Benson, Maxine. 1988. *From Pittsburgh to the Rocky Mountains: Major Stephen Long's Expedition, 1819–1820.* Golden, CO: Fulcrum; Evans, Howard Ensign. 1997. *A Natural History of the Long Expedition to the Rocky Mountains, 1819–1820.* New York: Oxford University Press; Goetzmann, William H. 1991. *Army Exploration in the American West, 1805–1863.* Austin: Texas State Historical Association; Nichols, Roger L., and Patrick L. Halley. 1980. *Stephen H. Long and American Frontier Exploration.* Newark: University of Delaware Press.

LOOSE CONSTRUCTION OF THE U.S. CONSTITUTION

Loose construction is the method of interpretation that broadly or permissively construes the meaning of the Constitution. Loose constructionists hold that the Constitution contains generous grants of power to the federal government. In particular, they argue that Article 1, Section 8 grants Congress wide discretionary powers over taxation and interstate commerce and power to enact all legislation judged necessary and proper for the general welfare of the nation. Opposed to this method of interpretation stands strict constructionism. Strict constructionists contend that the federal government can only rightfully exercise those powers that are expressly delegated to it by the Constitution, all other powers being reserved by the people or the states.

In his 1791 quarrel with Thomas Jefferson over the constitutionality of the bill to establish a national bank, Alexander Hamilton argued in favor of the bill from a loose constructionist perspective. Hamilton claimed that the delegation of certain specified powers to the federal government by the Constitution implied that the government also possessed the power to enact legislation deemed useful in carrying out the delegated powers. Jefferson, on the other hand, thought the establishment of a national bank was unconstitutional because it was not specifically authorized. Hamilton's doctrine of implied powers later received the endorsement of Chief Justice John Marshall in the case of *McCulloch v. Maryland* (1819). Likewise, in his 1792 *Report on Manufactures,* Hamilton favored a loose construction that allowed Congress to spend tax revenues on any project that promoted the general welfare. Again, Jefferson opposed him on strict constructionist grounds.

After purchasing Louisiana, President Jefferson fretted over the constitutionality of his decision. Being a strict constructionist, he was troubled by the thought that his actions exceeded those powers expressly delegated to the federal government. "The constitution has made no provision for our holding foreign territory, still less for incorporating foreign nations into our Union," he confessed to John C. Breckinridge on August 12, 1803 (Peterson, 1984). Therefore he proposed amending the Constitution so that it specifically granted the power he felt was lacking and to satisfy his strict constructionist scruples. "When an instrument admits two constructions, the one safe, the other dangerous, the one precise, the other indefinite, I prefer that which is safe & precise. I had rather ask an enlargement of power from the nation, where it is found necessary, than to assume it by a construction which would make our powers boundless," he wrote to Wilson Cary Nicholas on September 7, 1803 (ibid.). Congress, however, did not share Jefferson's constitutional doubts and saw little need for his proposed amendment.

Loose construction was also employed to justify the Alien and Sedition Acts of 1798, protective tariffs, and funding for internal improvements—all divisive issues in antebellum politics. Today, loose constructionism manifests itself in the notion that the Constitution is a living document needing to be adapted through interpretation to changing circumstances unforeseen by the Founders.

—Sean R. Busick

See also
Constitution of the United States; Federalist Party; Hamilton, Alexander; Marshall, John

For Further Reading
McDonald, Forrest. 1982. *Alexander Hamilton: A Biography.* New York: W. W. Norton; Peterson, Merrill D., ed. 1984. *Thomas Jefferson: Writings.* New York: Library of America.

LOS ADAES

Los Adaes was a mission-presidio complex that served as the first capital of Spanish Texas from 1717 to 1773. Los Adaes, named for the local tribe of Caddo Indians, was located on the outskirts of present-day Robeline, Louisiana, and was composed of Mission San Miguel de Linares de los Adaes (founded 1717) and Presidio Nuestra Señora del Pilar de los Adaes (founded 1721). Established to counter French westward expansion, the presidio became the official residence of Texas governors until the area was abandoned by the Spanish in the reorganization of frontier defenses following Louisiana's transfer to France.

In 1773, Governor Barón de Ripperdá directed the

evacuation of the hundreds of settlers and soldiers to San Antonio and forced the missionaries to close the moribund mission, but there is evidence that not all Spanish settlers left. After Nacogdoches was founded in 1779 by former Los Adaes residents, Spanish ranching, contraband, and Indian trading activities resumed in the Los Adaes area, particularly at a site called Bayou Pierre, which became the center for Spanish activities east of the Sabine in the last decade before the Adams-Onís Treaty (1819) permanently placed the area within the borders of the United States.

Despite its official abandonment, Spain never gave up its claim to Los Adaes as the eastern boundary of Texas. With the Louisiana Purchase, Spanish army officer Marqués de Casa Calvo undertook an inspection of the site to reinforce Spain's claim. In February 1806 a Spanish occupation force was driven out by the U.S. Army on its way to the Sabine. Under the agreement between General James Wilkinson and Colonel Simón de Herrera, Los Adaes became part of the Neutral Ground. Despite a clause prohibiting permanent settlement in the Neutral Ground, the Los Adaes area was quickly occupied by settlers from the United States, and the Spanish colonial population retreated to nearby Spanish Lake. The area's population was further reinforced by the arrival of Spanish and U.S. refugees from the disastrous Gutierrez-Magee Expedition. Although the mission site has yet to be worked, the presidio has received considerable attention from archaeologists and is today a Louisiana State Historical Monument.

—Jesús F. de la Teja

See also

Gutierrez-Magee Expedition; Herrera, Simón de; Nacogdoches; Natchitoches; Neutral Ground; Transcontinental Treaty; Wilkinson, James

For Further Reading

Bolton, Herbert E. 1970. *Texas in the Middle Eighteenth Century: Studies in Spanish Colonial History and Administration.* Austin: University of Texas Press; Castañeda, Carlos E. 1942. *Our Catholic Heritage in Texas, 1519–1936. Volume 5: The Mission Era: The End of the Spanish Regime, 1780–1810.* Austin: Von Boeckmann-Jones Company.

LOUISIANA

See **Orleans, Territory of**

LOUISIANA LAND LAW OF 1804

Passed by Congress on March 26, 1804, this measure concerning land grants in the Louisiana Territory stemmed from the dispute between Spain and the United States over the exact boundaries of certain areas included in the Louisiana Purchase. On March 10, 1804, the House of Representatives resolved that it was expedient to pass a law declaring null and void all land grants in the Louisiana Territory that had been issued by the Spanish government subsequent to the Treaty of San Ildefonso, which was signed on October 1, 1800. Under the terms of the treaty Spain ceded Louisiana back to the French, who then sold the territory to the United States under the Treaty of Paris signed April 30, 1803. According to the terms of this treaty, the United States claimed the land between the Iberville and Perdido Rivers. Spain argued that these lands had not been included in the cession to France and that the only territory involved in the Treaty of San Ildefonso consisted of the Isle of New Orleans and the lands that had originally been ceded to Spain by France west of the Mississippi.

The Spanish maintained that West Florida functioned as a separate administrative unit with its own governor. The Spanish argued that, although the boundaries of the Louisiana Territory had not been specifically defined, their intention to retain West Florida, along with the phrasing of the transfer back to France as a "recession," remained clear and should have been apparent to the United States. (The term "recession" denoted the transfer of title for the same territory the French had earlier given to Spain.) The Spanish position resulted in the granting of land east of the Mississippi to which the United States laid claim after the purchase.

Congressional members and senators debated the most appropriate method of handling the situation and decided that the best approach was to reject all claims to land in the disputed area except in certain limited situations. A proposed bill was introduced involving the government of Louisiana that dealt with the land issue. Congress debated the measure before finally referring the matter to the Committee of the Whole House that approved a bill entitled "An act erecting Louisiana into two Territories, and providing for the temporary Government thereof," and sent the piece of legislation on to the Senate. Article 14 of the act pertained to the issue of land grants. Congress declared null and void all claims but then recognized bona fide claims made by settlers who had obtained the grant by lawful means under the Spanish government and who had actually lived on the land prior to December 23, 1803. A limitation of one acre was placed on this proviso, with additional land allowed for wives and children. The provision eliminated opposition to the bill by senators and congressman who strongly believed in the protection of legally acquired property. The same article forbade U.S. citizens from settling, attempting to survey, or marking lands with boundary markers on trees or by other means, or committing any other act that would result in a claim upon any land owned by the U.S. government. Enforcement of the act included the imposition of a fine not to exceed $1,000 and twelve months imprisonment. Congress empowered the president to employ military force if necessary to remove any violators.

The passage of this act enabled the U.S. government to control the distribution of land in the newly acquired territory. Large land grants made by the Spanish government before the transfer of power back to France and then to the United States would have effectively reduced the amount of land accessible for sale by government land agents. In turn, the proceeds that would have been gained from the sale of the real estate would have been denied to the United States. Given the large dollar amount expended to acquire Louisiana, Congress sought to protect its right of ownership by passing this legislative act that became effective on October 31, 1803, and remained in effect for one year.

—*Cynthia Clark Northrup*

For Further Reading

Annals of Congress, 8th Congress, 1st Session.

LOUISIANA MEMORIAL (1804)

The Louisiana Memorial of 1804 (also known as the Louisiana Remonstrance) was signed by more than two hundred residents of the Territory of Orleans and sent to Congress at the end of 1804. It gave voice to the growing dissatisfaction of many of the local inhabitants with the administration of the first territorial governor, William C. C. Claiborne, and the disappointment with the manner in which Congress had organized its newest territory.

The event that prompted the drafting of the memorial was the March 26, 1804, act of Congress that organized the lands acquired by the Louisiana Purchase. This act divided the purchase lands and established the Territory of Orleans. It replaced the existing administrative and judicial systems in the territory, which were French and Spanish in origin, with U.S. institutions. Following the model for territorial development established by the Northwest Ordinance (1787), all offices in the territory were to be appointed by the president of the United States. Congress thereby limited the participation of the local residents in the administration of the territory. The act also restricted the slave trade, circumscribing the type and number of slaves allowed into the territory.

The provisions of this act were a profound disappointment for many of the white slave-owning residents of the territory. In a series of meetings held in New Orleans during the summer of 1804, opponents of the territorial administration gathered to discuss their grievances. The assembled Creoles and Americans agreed to compile their complaints in a memorial that would be sent to Congress. Edward Livingston, a prominent lawyer and politician recently arrived from New York, drafted the final memorial cataloguing their complaints.

Livingston, a skillful advocate and polemicist, produced a comprehensive manifesto. He argued that the Third Article of the Louisiana Treaty (1803) pledged the immediate admission of Louisiana into the Union as a state. He charged that Congress had established a territorial government lacking any semblance of self-government for the local inhabitants. By appointing government officials who failed to possess even rudimentary knowledge of the French or Spanish languages, institutions, and customs, Livingston argued, Congress had created a form of political despotism in which the local residents were deprived of political, and even cultural, self-determination.

For many white residents of the territory the most galling provision of the March 26 act, however, was the restriction that Congress had placed upon the slave trade. The act declared that only those slaves accompanying U.S. settlers would be allowed into the territory. Thus, white Creoles could not import more slaves to work on their plantations. This struck at the heart of their perceived property rights. Livingston argued in the memorial that slaves were a necessary prerequisite for the development and prosperity of the territory. Congressional restrictions on the slave trade, Livingston asserted, only reinforced the perception among the local white population that they had emerged from the Louisiana Purchase as colonial dependents rather than U.S. citizens.

The appropriate remedy to all of the objections outlined in the Louisiana Memorial, Livingston argued, was the admission of the Territory of Orleans as a state at the earliest possible date. Immediate statehood would fulfill the political strategy of the discontented Creole elite and their U.S. allies. Statehood and representative institutions would allow the white Creole population to dominate the legislature, to control the direction of the new state, to continue the slave trade, and to oust the politically unpopular governor.

The Louisiana Memorial was received by Congress on December 3, 1804. Members of Congress rejected Livingston's arguments. They denied that the Louisiana Treaty had provided for immediate statehood for any of the purchase lands. They also believed that they had fulfilled their responsibilities toward the local inhabitants by following the standard procedure for organizing new territories. However, members of Congress acknowledged that the form of government they had created for the Territory of Orleans needed modification. On March 2, 1805, Congress passed a new law that created a more representative form of government. Although the executive branch would remain appointive, the legislature would now be elected by the local white inhabitants.

The Louisiana Memorial failed in its primary goal of convincing Congress to grant the territory immediate statehood. It did, however, mobilize the political opponents of the territorial administration, and, in the election for the new Legislative Assembly held in 1805, Creoles won a majority of the seats. The Louisiana Memorial also highlighted the issues of cultural and linguistic diversity confronting the nation as it continued to expand and absorb new populations.

—*Christine Lambert*

See also

Claiborne, William Charles Cole; Livingston, Edward; Orleans, Territory of

For Further Reading

Dargo, George. 1975. *Jefferson's Louisiana: Politics and the Clash of Legal Traditions.* Cambridge: Harvard University Press; Gayarré, Charles. 1974. *History of Louisiana: The American Domination,* vol. 4. Gretna, LA: Pelican; Lambert, Christine. Forthcoming. "Citizens and Strangers: New Orleans and the New Nation after the Louisiana Purchase." Ph.D. dissertation, Emory University.

LOUISIANA PURCHASE INTERNATIONAL EXPOSITION (1904)

Between 1851 and World War I, world's fairs were important institutions of Western culture. They reflected a strong belief in technological innovation and commercial expansion and visualized the ideological core convictions of the time in an entertaining fashion. The United States hosted five major world's fairs between 1853 and World War I. Those "symbolic universes" exerted a formative influence on the way Americans have thought about themselves and the world.

The Louisiana Purchase Exposition that St. Louis hosted in 1904 was the largest world's fair ever held. It commemorated the centennial of the 1803 land purchase of a vast territory between the Mississippi River and the Rocky Mountains that had doubled the territory of the United States. The opening of the fair was originally planned for 1903 but was delayed for one year because of organizational reasons. By opening day, on April 30, 1904, the fair site consisted of more than fifteen hundred buildings on twelve hundred acres, representing sixty-two nations and forty-three states.

The vast proportions of the fair reflected a strong desire on the part of the organizers to outclass its competitor city, Chicago. (St. Louis had unsuccessfully tried to secure the Columbian Exposition, which opened in Chicago in 1893.) By 1896, German-born congressman Richard Bartholdt, who represented the St. Louis district, began to promote the fair idea anew to bolster a depressed local economy. Bartholdt, David R. Francis, governor of Missouri, and local businessmen emerged as driving forces behind the project. Their promotional activities successfully solicited extensive financial support for the project. Money came from fundraising among the Businessmen's League, a special city bond, and the commitment of the federal government for a loan subsidy. By May 1901 the Louisiana Purchase Exposition Company was formed under the presidency of Governor Wilson and ninety-three directors, chosen among business and civic leaders. Together with the reform-minded local mayor, Rolla Wells, they set out to improve the city of St. Louis substantially and thus create a beautiful, healthful, technologically advanced, and modern fair site.

Work began with the preparation of the fairgrounds, the western half of Forest Park, a forty-minute carriage ride from downtown. The exposition company also leased land and buildings from the as-yet unopened campus of Washington University, as well as additional land adjacent to the fairground to accommodate the enormous proportions and dimensions of the exposition. The city and local businesses began a substantial infrastructure improvement and beautification program. New transit facilities were created, streets repaired, new streets opened, air-pollution reduced, and water quality improved. Under the directorship of St. Louis architect Isaac Taylor, many famous architects and urban planners of the time—such as New York architect Cass Gilbert and Theodore Link—developed the elaborate design of the fair. The main exhibit palaces fanned out from the central Festival Hall atop Art Hill. Broad boulevards and spacious plazas with sunken gardens and parks structured the exhibit spaces. Most of the structures were built with colored staff, a mixture of plaster of Paris and hemp fiber. The main exhibits were housed in Renaissance revival style palaces, which were ornately detailed with massive columns and towers and illuminated at night by electric light.

The director of exhibits, F. J. V. Skift, director of Chicago's Field Museum and widely acclaimed authority on exhibitions, developed an elaborate classification scheme for the exposition. It structured the St. Louis fair in a sequential synopsis of the developments of human progress. As education was the key theme of the fair, Skiff planned the exposition as a portrayal of the evolution and development of individuals in their indigenous environments. The synchronic arrangement, which illustrated the ideal of the composite type of man, consisted of sixteen categories that corresponded to the exposition's departments.

At the top of the classification scheme stood the departments of Education, Arts, Liberal Arts, and Applied Sciences (including Manufactures, Machinery, Electricity, and Transportation). Those were followed by the departments that displayed raw materials: Agriculture, Horticulture, Mining, Forestry, and Fish and Game. The classification scheme was concluded by Anthropology, Social Economy, and Physical Culture.

The St. Louis Anthropology department was the most extensive of any world's fair. The anthropologists created an outdoor laboratory for anthropological fieldwork on the fairgrounds. They brought Pygmies from West Africa, giants from Patagonia, Native Americans, and others together in large ethnographic displays. An anthropological laboratory carried out experiments during the fair to introduce visitors to the pseudoscientific theories of the racial superiority of Anglo-Saxon civilization.

Visitors attending the Louisiana Purchase International Exposition in St. Louis in 1904 could visit anthropological exhibits where authentic Plains Indians were on public display.

Ethnographic villages formed an important part of the anthropology department's work. The villages served as an anthropologically calibrated yardstick for measuring the world's progress and projected racial notions and justifications of the emerging U.S. overseas empire. The Filipino exposition was particularly popular with the almost twenty million fairgoers who visited the exposition up to its close on December 1, 1904. This ethnographic display, officially known as the Philippine Reservation, consisted of several villages on a forty-seven-acre site and nearly twelve hundred Filipinos who lived on the reservation during the exhibit.

The elaborate displays of historical and anthropological exhibits were intended to emphasize the superiority of the Anglo-Saxon race over indigenous North American cultures and the civilizations of the newly acquired overseas possessions. Those exhibits fostered the creation of imperial mentalities and sustained racist attitudes to gather momentum and support for America's colonial enterprise.

In addition the fair also created and sustained enthusiasm for technological advances and the idea of progress. The fair impressed visitors with its extensive use of electricity, a novelty at the turn of the century. It staged the first successful demonstration of wireless telegraphy between ground and air in the United States and is also credited with mounting the first high-altitude meteorological experiments in North America. Visitors were also enchanted by novel modes of transportation as they enjoyed the illusion of a submarine ride or an airship flight over Paris.

Finally, the fair provided amusement and entertainment for millions of visitors. The third modern Olympiad, the first in North America, took place in St. Louis in conjunction with the fair. In addition, visitors enjoyed a giant ferris wheel and participated in the many attractions of the Pike, the amusement and concession area. There visitors could enjoy the Tyrolean Alps and a Parisian fashion show, or explore the North Pole. Fair folklore insists that ice cream cones were invented on the St. Louis Pike.

Unlike today's world's fairs, the St. Louis world exposition was an impressive financial success. Profits were used for substantial city beautification projects. The

A scene from the opening ceremonies of the 1904 Louisiana Purchase International Exposition, which was held in St. Louis

Louisiana Purchase Exposition served as an impressive reminder of the symbolic universe that world's fairs helped to create. It impressed upon the other nations the clear notion of America's rise to world power. The domestic audience was presented with the ideological parameters that reinforced racial stereotypes and technologically defined notions of progress and civilization. Above all, however, the fair served to reinforce and sustain imperial identities through the structure of the exhibit and, in particular, the racially charged ethnographic displays.

—Frank Schumacher

For Further Reading

Breitbart, Eric. 1997. *A World on Display: Photographs from the St. Louis World's Fair, 1904*. Albuquerque: University of New Mexico Press; Clevenger, Martha R., ed. 1996. *Indescribably Grand: Diaries and Letters from the 1904 World's Fair.* St. Louis: Missouri Historical Society Press; Condon, Yvonne. 1990. "St. Louis 1904: Louisiana Purchase International Exposition." In *Historical Dictionary of World's Fairs and Expositions, 1851–1988*. Edited by John E. Findling and Kimberly D. Pelle. Westport, CT: Greenwood Press; Rydell, Robert W. 1984. *All the World's a Fair: Visions of Empire at American International Expositions, 1876–1916*. Chicago: University of Chicago Press.

L'OUVERTURE, TOUSSAINT (c. 1743–1803)

Born a slave on the Bréda plantation, Toussaint received some education and developed a lifelong friendship with Bayou de Libertad, one of the plantation managers. Under Bayou de Libertad's tutelage, Toussaint moved into the upper level of slave society, becoming Libertad's coachman. He married Suzanne Simon-Baptiste and eventually received his freedom around 1781. As a free person of color, Toussaint lived as well as any former slave in St. Domingue prior to the slave revolt.

The society into which Toussaint was born had undergone tremendous economic growth over the course of the eighteenth century, making St. Domingue (located on the western half of the island of Hispaniola) France's richest Caribbean colony. The colony's economy, fueled by the exportation of sugar, indigo, and coffee, turned on a brutal system of slave labor and the importation of Africans as slaves. In 1789, the year of the French Revolution, St. Domingue's population consisted of approximately 40,000 white colonists, 30,000 free persons of color (both black and mulatto), and 500,000 slaves, two-thirds of whom were African-born.

At the close of the eighteenth century, social tensions inherent in a society based upon chattel slavery and racial difference were further aggravated by events in France. The outbreak of the French Revolution opened up divisions within the white ruling class, pitting the planter elite against the bourgeoisie, the republicans against the monarchists. In addition, the rhetoric of the revolution, which stressed "liberty, equality, fraternity" for all, became disseminated among *les affranchis* (free persons of color) and the slave population. This placed the white planters of St. Domingue in a contradictory position, because their economic and political power was based upon the lack of freedom of the vast majority of the colony's population.

A turning point came in 1790, when *les affranchis* demanded full citizenship rights as outlined by the French National Assembly in its Declaration of the Rights of Man and the Citizen (1789). St. Dominique's white planters refused this request, and, in response, the mulattos revolted in early 1791, led by Jacques Vincent Ogé, a former leader of the mulatto delegation to the French National Assembly. The revolt was brutally repressed; Ogé and the other conspirators were put to death. This, however, proved to be only a forerunner to the larger revolt by the slave majority several months later, in August 1791. This second revolt became a full-scale rebellion to end slavery and French rule in St. Domingue. Although the revolt was ultimately successful in that regard, it would last thirteen bloody years, devastating St. Domingue's economy and reducing the island's population by as much as 50 percent.

Like Toussaint, the leaders of the August 1791 conspiracy came largely from the upper echelons of slave society, having served as plantation *commandeurs* (overseers), coachmen, and domestic servants. Although Toussaint's role in the early days of the slave revolt of 1791 is unclear, historian Carolyn Fick has argued that he served as a go-between during the planning stages of the movement, because as a free person of color he was able to travel freely. Toussaint (then known as François Dominique Toussaint) left the Bréda plantation in the fall of 1791 and enlisted in the armies of generals Jean François and Georges Bissou, serving with Spanish forces in Santo Domingo, Spain's colony on the eastern half of the island of Hispaniola. Toussaint spent three years in the service of the Spanish, and it was during this time that he gained the surname "L'Ouverture," which some scholars believe refers to his military prowess at moving into openings on the battlefield. L'Ouverture was an adept military and political leader who rose quickly in the ranks, achieving the title "Doctor of the King's Armies," which placed him third in command after Jean François and Georges Bissou.

Toussaint was a complex figure, apparently motivated by a combination of his own personal desire for power and a desire to free the slaves of St. Domingue. Both of these objectives likely influenced his decision to leave the Spanish in May 1794, three months after the abolition of slavery by the French National Convention in February 1794. Toussaint initially allied himself with the French governor general Etienne Laveaux, whose forces were fighting offensives by both the British and the Spanish. From 1794 to 1798, rebel leaders André Rigaud and Toussaint L'Ouverture sought to defeat these outside threats and to neutralize local French control of the island while also engaging in a fierce struggle for power. During this period, Toussaint maneuvered himself into a dominant position both militarily and politically. In 1796, Etienne Laveaux, who had by then become Toussaint's puppet, appointed the black leader lieutenant governor. In 1799, Toussaint turned his attention to Rigaud's opposition mulatto armies in the south and launched the race war known as the War of the Knives (1799–1800). Toussaint eventually suppressed the mulattos and also conquered the Spanish colony of neighboring Santo Domingo.

Following the victories over the mulatto armies in the south and the Spanish forces in Santo Domingo, Toussaint became the de facto ruler of the entire island. He then set about establishing a new governmental structure that would stabilize St. Domingue society while also solidifying his own power. The Constitution of 1801 subsequently outlawed slavery and declared Toussaint governor for life. Napoleon Bonaparte, first consul and ruler of France, recognized Toussaint as captain general of St. Domingue; however, Toussaint proclaimed the new constitution without first receiving Napoleon's approval. Thus while Toussaint retained the pretense of French rule, he was veritably moving in a direction of independence from France.

In response to Toussaint's steps toward independence, as well as developments in Europe, Napoleon began to turn his attention toward France's overseas empire in the Western Hemisphere. By 1800 the first consul was triumphant in Europe and felt that he might reassert French dominion over Louisiana, French Guyana, and the French West Indies. The economic key to this plan was St. Domingue, since Napoleon envisioned making Louisiana and St. Domingue an allied economic unity. The French ruler also wanted to overturn the U.S. trade advantage that had developed in the French West Indies during the

French Revolution, a move that would allow him to strengthen the trading system of the French empire and challenge the economic position of the British. In 1800, France signed the Treaty of San Ildefonso, which arranged for the retrocession of Louisiana to France. The Peace of Amiens, signed in 1802, marked a brief truce in France's war with Great Britain. While the negotiations for the transfer of Louisiana continued with the Spanish through 1802, Napoleon made plans to retake possession of both St. Dominique and Louisiana.

Although Napoleon sought to reestablish French sovereignty in Louisiana and St. Domingue, France ultimately relinquished its claims on both the former colonies at the end of 1803. The U.S. acquisition of Louisiana and the independence of St. Domingue were the result of a convergence of events in Europe, North America, and St. Domingue. The U.S. policy toward St. Domingue combined both economic self-interest and political imperatives. Although willing to officially recognize French sovereignty over St. Domingue, the United States wished to retain lucrative trade links with the island. For this reason, the United States gave Toussaint L'Ouverture unofficial support as the de factor ruler of the former French colony. On the political front, President Thomas Jefferson maintained an equivocal position toward France, wary of French motives in the Western Hemisphere. In July 1801, Jefferson learned of the retrocession of Louisiana to France. This development was cause for serious concern, because a strong French presence in North America would hinder the westward expansion of the United States, which Jefferson believed essential to the future development of the young republic. In addition, Jefferson considered the Mississippi River a strategic interest of the United States, intrinsic to the country's natural right of navigation. With the French reacquisition of Louisiana, the president feared that France might block access to the Mississippi via the port of New Orleans.

Early in 1802, Napoleon sent troops to St. Domingue under the command of his brother-in-law, General Charles Leclerc. Leclerc's mission was to retake possession of St. Domingue, eliminate revolutionaries such as Toussaint L'Ouverture, and restore slavery and the plantation system. Initially it appeared that the French had gained the upper hand after Toussaint surrendered to General Leclerc in May 1802, following several months of conflict. Toussaint was arrested and sent to France, where he died in the French prison of Fort-de-Joux in the French Jura in April 1803. By 1803, however, the French forces had begun to falter, felled by yellow fever and the renewed efforts of rebel forces under the command of Henri Christophe. Britain and France returned to war in May 1803, which resulted in the French forces on St. Domingue facing external attacks from the British. In addition, Thomas Jefferson allowed U.S. traders to resupply the rebel forces rather than Leclerc's army.

In the spring of 1803, Napoleon's plans for an expedition to take possession of Louisiana foundered because of ice-bound ships in Holland, severe weather, and an English blockade in northern Europe. The setbacks in St. Domingue were also significant because, although not completely defeated, the French position on the island was severely weakened by that time. France needed St. Domingue for economic as well as strategic reasons to regain control of Louisiana. With a military success looking increasingly doubtful in St. Domingue and with France facing renewed hostilities with Britain, Napoleon renounced his quest for an expansive French empire in the Western Hemisphere. Rather than commit valuable resources to retain possession of Louisiana, Napoleon came to see the sale of the North American territory as a means to generate revenues for the fight against Great Britain in the European theater. The sale of Louisiana was negotiated in Paris in April 1803 and signed in May 1803. French troops withdrew from St. Domingue in November 1803. The revolutionaries subsequently named their newly independent nation Haiti, after the island's indigenous Arawak name.

Toussaint L'Ouverture's role in the U.S. acquisition of Louisiana had been significant. Although he did not live to see the final withdrawal of the French from St. Domingue, he had become the leading figure of the colony's slave revolt. In this respect he helped pave the way for the defeat of the French in 1803. More important, as the de facto ruler of St. Domingue, he was able to establish crucial trade links with the United States, links that ultimately worked against Napoleon's imperial interests in the Western Hemisphere.

—Melinda Marie Jetté

See also
Amiens, Peace of; Bonaparte, Napoleon; Jefferson, Thomas; San Ildefonso, Treaty of

For Further Reading
Fick, Carolyn. 1990. *The Making of the Revolution: The Saint Domingue Revolution from Below.* Knoxville: University of Tennessee Press; James, C. L. R. 1980. *The Black Jacobins: Toussaint L'Ouverture and the San Domingo Revolution.* Rev. ed. London: Allison and Busby; Ott, Thomas O. 1973. *The Haitian Revolution, 1789–1804.* Knoxville: University of Tennessee Press; Pluchon, Pierre. 1989. *Toussaint L'Ouverture.* Paris: Fayard.

LUNÉVILLE, TREATY OF (1801)

The Treaty of Lunéville was a significant diplomatic arrangement between the French Republic of First Consul Napoleon Bonaparte and Francis II, the Hapsburg monarch reigning as Holy Roman Emperor, Emperor and King of Austria-Hungary and Bohemia, and titular head of the German Body. Joseph Bonaparte, the emperor's brother, acted as the chief negotiator for France, while Louis Count Cobentzel was the primary diplomatic representative of the Germanic emperor. The treaty was negotiated and signed at the city of Lunéville, located in the department of Meurthe-et-Moselle in northeastern France, on February 9, 1801.

The Treaty of Lunéville was predicated upon two decisive defeats that Austrian forces had faced at the battles of Marengo (June 14, 1800) and Hohenlinden (December 3, 1800)—disastrous events that forced them to negotiate with the French. These defeats and the treaty arrangement that followed effectively ended the Second Coalition that had been allied against the French. Perhaps considering the gravity of the diplomatic sea change that was being effected, the terms that the French demanded in the treaty were exceptionally mild and were considered satisfactory to the Germanic cause. The French demanded that the Austrians reaffirm their previous commitment to the Treaty of Campo Formio (1797). France agreed to pay compensation to those princes of the Rhine region who had been dispossessed of their lands and hereditary titles. The French also agreed to return the King of Naples to his rightful throne.

The result of the redrawn boundaries outlined within the Treaty of Lunéville essentially involved the breakup of the Holy Roman Empire. The agreement effectively made real Voltaire's often-quoted assertion that the Holy Roman Empire was "neither holy, nor Roman, nor an empire." The Austrians agreed to cede the left (west) bank of the Rhine River to France, and they were also forced by both military circumstance and by the treaty to recognize the newly established Batavian, Helvetian, Cisalpine, and Ligurian Republics.

Article V of the Treaty of Lunéville contained provisions that had a direct influence upon the Louisiana Purchase negotiations that would take place between France and the United States in 1803. When the French demanded and received the retrocession of the Louisiana Territory in the secret Treaty of San Ildefonso (1800), France had committed itself to compensating Spain for the loss by providing a suitable kingdom for Fernando, the Duke of Parma. Spanish king Charles IV believed that exchanging "the vast wilderness of the Mississippi and of the Missouri" for Tuscany was a noble bargain, since that region was "the beautiful and learned home of Galileo, of Dante, of Petrarch, and other great men of letters and science" (DeConde, 1976).

Article V of the Treaty of Lunéville provided for the cession of Tuscany from the Holy Roman Empire. Thus, with the acquisition of Tuscany, Napoleon Bonaparte had satisfied an important precondition upon which the legality of the Treaty of San Ildefonso (1800) had been based. He could therefore consider himself the rightful owner of the Louisiana Territory, though the legality of his subsequent sale of that territory to the United States would be questioned by the Spanish as well as by other European powers.

It was not Napoleon Bonaparte's intention to offer Tuscany as a kingdom for Fernando, the Duke of Parma. Napoleon disliked the Duke of Parma and instead offered the newly named Kingdom of Etruria (formerly Tuscany) to Luis, the son of Fernando. Napoleon's younger brother Lucien, then serving as the French ambassador to the Spanish court, convinced King Charles IV to accept the modified arrangement.

—*Junius P. Rodriguez*

See also

Fernando, Duke of Parma; San Ildefonso, Treaty of

For Further Reading

DeConde, Alexander. 1976. *This Affair of Louisiana*. New York: Charles Scribner's Sons.

MACOMB, FORT

Within a decade of acquiring the Louisiana Purchase territory, the U.S. government began to realize the formidable difficulties associated with protecting the strategically important, yet vulnerable, city of New Orleans from the threat of foreign invasion. During the War of 1812, particularly in the weeks prior to the Battle of New Orleans, Louisiana militia and U.S. forces under the command of General Andrew Jackson worked feverishly to assemble a combined land and naval force that could repulse the British attack that was imminent. Although Jackson and the defenders of New Orleans were ultimately victorious on the plains of Chalmette, lessons learned at the time would influence future defensive readiness, especially with regard to the construction of coastal fortifications.

In the years following the War of 1812, during the so-called Era of Good Feeling, the United States experienced a rather euphoric sense of nationalism that saw itself expressed in many forms. One of the outcomes of this period, and a key policy of President James Monroe, was the outlay of federal funds to construct or renovate a series of forts along the Atlantic and Gulf coasts of the United States. In the eyes of many, a concerted policy of national defense aimed at protecting coastal assets was the most nationalistic, though not outwardly belligerent, policy that the United States could take. The construction costs associated with this building effort also had real economic implications, and the idea of distributing this federal largesse over a wide region won almost universal acclaim from senators and congressmen, regardless of ideology or political affiliation.

Fort Macomb was constructed to the east of New Orleans along the Chef Menteur Pass. The fort was built on the site of an earlier French fortification known previously as Fort Chef Menteur. In its early years, from 1815 to 1822, the new U.S. fort was called Fort Wood, but its name was changed in 1822 to honor Alexander Macomb (1782–1841), a hero of the War of 1812 who was, by 1822, a major general in the U.S. Army.

Fort Macomb was constructed nine miles west of Fort Pike, another coastal fortification that was created during the Era of Good Feeling. The French engineer Simon Bernard designed both of these forts, using the same general design for each. Both facilities were built to guard New Orleans at the Rigolets, the narrow strait that connects Lakes Borgne and Pontchartrain. With the combined effect of their heavy guns, sturdy walls, and marshy approaches, both forts were considered impregnable.

Fort Macomb was never used offensively for the purpose that necessitated its construction. The fort was manned only sporadically, when it was occasionally used as a staging area for military campaigns that occurred elsewhere during the Second Seminole War and the Mexican War. When the state of Louisiana seceded and joined the Confederate States of America, Fort Macomb was seized, but the site returned to Union hands when federal forces took New Orleans in April 1862. As the Confederates retreated from Fort Macomb, they burned some of the wooden barracks and destroyed the fort's heavy guns. Thereafter, Union forces occupied the fort and used it briefly as a training area for former slaves who were being trained as artillerymen for the U.S. Colored Troops (USCT).

—Junius P. Rodriguez

See also
Pike, Fort; New Orleans, Battle of

For Further Reading

Groene, Bertram H. 1988. *Pike: A Fortress in the Wetlands.* Hammond: Southeastern Louisiana University Press; Lewis, Emanuel Raymond. 1993. *Seacoast Fortifications of the United States: An Introductory History.* Annapolis: Naval Institute Press; Parkerson, Codman. 1990. *New Orleans: America's Most Fortified City.* New Orleans: The Quest.

MADISON, JAMES (1751–1836)

Founding Father and fourth president of the United States, James Madison, Jr., served as the secretary of state during the negotiations for the Louisiana Purchase.

Born on March 16, 1751, in Port Conway, Virginia, he was the eldest son of James Madison, Sr., and Nelly Conway Madison. Educated at the College of New Jersey (now Princeton University), Madison opposed the British policies that led to the American Revolution and was elected in 1776 to the Virginia Convention, where he helped write the Virginia Constitution and Declaration of Rights.

James Madison served as secretary of state in Thomas Jefferson's administration at the time that the United States purchased the Louisiana Territory from France.

Elected to the Continental Congress in 1779, he served throughout the American Revolution and returned to Virginia in 1783. Madison became one of the foremost advocates for a stronger constitution, and he played a leading role in the Constitutional Convention of 1787 in Philadelphia and the ratification process, during which he, together with Alexander Hamilton and John Jay, wrote the *Federalist Papers*. Elected as a member of the newly created House of Representatives, Madison largely wrote the first ten amendments to the Constitution—the Bill of Rights. Political differences with Alexander Hamilton, the secretary of treasury in George Washington's administration, led Madison into opposition with his friend Thomas Jefferson, with whom he helped create the Republican Party.

When Jefferson became the first Republican president, in March 1801, he appointed Madison secretary of state, an office he would occupy until March 1809. Madison, believing that the United States would eventually gain territory on the Gulf Coast, was initially content to allow Spain to remain in her colonies there; Spain's declining colonial power, he believed, would eventually lead to the acquisition of these colonies by the United States. When Robert Livingston, the U.S. minister in Paris, informed Madison in the spring of 1802 that rumors of a retrocession by Spain to France of Louisiana were true, Madison, who never entertained doubts that the United States could add to its territory by treaty, instructed Livingston in May of that year to attempt to negotiate the purchase of New Orleans and as much of West Florida territory as possible.

Following Western outrage and the public demands of Alexander Hamilton that New Orleans be seized when the Spanish intendant closed the city to U.S. commerce in October 1802, Madison dispatched James Monroe as a special envoy to Paris to aid Livingston in the negotiations for the purchase. During these negotiations Madison did his utmost to persuade Baron Pichon, the French chargé d'affaires in Washington, that the United States had an irrepressible right to the free navigation of the Mississippi River and that any attempt by France to regenerate its empire in the Mississippi Valley would lead to a U.S. alliance with Britain. Initially surprised at the news that Napoleon was prepared to sell the whole of Louisiana to the United States, Madison quickly endorsed the purchase, calling it a "truely noble acquisition." Remaining, like Jefferson and their representatives in Paris, unsure of the actual boundaries of the purchase, Madison busied himself with the practical issues of accepting the transfer of sovereignty, ignoring at first the constitutional "metaphysical subtleties" of the act itself.

In preparing negotiations for Monroe and Livingston in January 1803, Jefferson had expressed in the cabinet doubts regarding the constitutionality of the purchase; Madison, in deference to Jefferson, either kept his silence or made vague comments about the issue. However, when Jefferson proposed in the cabinet a draft constitutional amendment that would authorize the acquisition in July 1803, but which would imply a lack of power to acquire West Florida, Madison suggested two alternatives: that the amendment be broadened to say Louisiana "as ceded by France is made part of the United States" or, secondly, that "Congress may make part of the United States any other adjacent territories which shall be justly acquired." Although prepared to admit in private correspondence that West Florida did not seem to be part of the Purchase, Madison would constantly maintain in public that the boundaries of the new acquisition extended east to the Perdido River, thus including Mobile, and west to the Rio Bravo. In the congressional recess of the summer of 1803, Madison not only helped Jefferson to accept this position but was also able, because of Jefferson's confidence in Madison's grasp of constitutional issues, to persuade Jefferson to drop the amendment issue and ratify the treaty as quickly as possible.

Spain opposed the Louisiana Purchase and claimed that France had no right to sell the province to a third party. Madison rebuffed Spanish claims and tried to persuade the Spanish minister in Washington, the Marquis de Irujo, that a continued Spanish presence in the Floridas could only irritate Spanish-U.S. relations. On his part,

Irujo resisted the logic of Madison's claim, that if the earlier Spanish retrocession to France had included Louisiana as France had originally possessed it, then the Perdido River constituted the eastern boundary of the purchase. In February 1804, Madison suggested to Irujo that if Spain recognized U.S. claims to West Florida and allowed the United States to purchase East Florida, he would give up the U.S. claim that the western boundary of the purchase included Texas. A solution to this lingering boundary dispute would initially be made impossible when Spain broke off diplomatic relations in 1805. Spanish-U.S. relations became further strained when the Spanish in Texas began to send patrols across the Sabine River as far east as Natchitoches. War was averted in 1806, however, by the creation of a "neutral strip" between the Sabine River and the Arroyo Hondo, a dry gulch a few miles west of Natchitoches. Spain proved even more unwilling to discuss the boundaries of the Louisiana Purchase after 1808, when Britain, which became Spain's new ally against Napoleon, supported its position, especially regarding the Floridas. Elected president in 1809, Madison continued to pursue the same policy of national self-interest he had developed while secretary of state. In 1810, U.S.-born rebels under Philemon Thomas in West Florida attacked and captured Baton Rouge. When the Spanish withdrew from what are now called the Louisiana Florida Parishes, Madison, with congressional approval, seized the coastal strip of West Florida below the thirty-first parallel and proclaimed it part of the United States on October 27, 1810. Further U.S. encroachment into Florida was prevented in 1811 only by the presence of British warships at St. Augustine. The eastern boundary dispute of the Louisiana Purchase became something of a secondary issue when differences between the United States and Britain erupted into war on June 18, 1812. The decisive U.S. victory at New Orleans, in January 1815, would not only place the U.S. possession of Louisiana beyond question; it also weakened the Spanish possession of East Florida. The experiences of war, moreover, convinced Madison of the need for a new policy of economic and fiscal reform; the Madison Plan of 1816, attempted, by a policy of internal improvements, to tie the eastern and western parts of the United States closer together and promote the notion of sectional unity within the nation.

Madison returned to Virginia following the end of his presidency in 1817. He, like Jefferson, was alarmed at the Missouri Crisis of 1819–1821, and as an elder statesmen he continued to support the forces of compromise within the Union. Consequently, he opposed the attempt by South Carolina to nullify the Tariff of 1832. The last of the Founding Fathers, Madison died on June 28, 1836.

—Rory T. Cornish

For Further Reading

Brant, Irving. 1953. *James Madison: Secretary of State, 1800–1809*. Indianapolis: Bobbs-Merrill; Ketchum, Ralph. 1971. *James Madison: A Biography.* Charlottesville: University of Virginia Press; McCoy, Drew R. 1991. *The Last of the Fathers: James Madison and the Republic.* Cambridge and New York: Cambridge University Press; Smith, James Morton, ed. 1995. *The Republic of Letters: The Correspondence between Thomas Jefferson & James Madison, 1776–1826.* 3 vols. New York and London: Norton; Stagg, J. C. A. 1983. *Mr. Madison's War: Politics, Diplomacy and Warfare in the Early Republic, 1783–1830.* Princeton: Princeton University Press.

MAGRUDER, ALLAN BOWIE (1775–1822)

Louisiana land agent and one-term senator Allan Bowie Magruder wrote one of the earliest and most extensive accounts of the newly acquired Louisiana Territory. Magruder's analysis of the political, economic, and moral advantages of the Louisiana cession is the most comprehensive published treatment of the acquisition and a document generally ignored by historians of the Louisiana Purchase.

Allan Bowie Magruder was a native of Lexington, Kentucky. He was educated locally, studied law, and was admitted to the Kentucky bar in 1796. Magruder practiced law in Kentucky until about 1805, when he started a law practice in Opelousas, Louisiana. In July 1805 he was appointed a land agent for the western district of Orleans and Opelousas. Magruder was a chronic drunkard and was removed from the post by 1806.

In correspondence between Secretary of the Treasury Albert Gallatin and government officials, there are references to Magruder's intemperance, although Louisiana governor William C. C. Claiborne acknowledged Magruder's intelligence and knowledge of land affairs. From 1806 until 1812, he practiced law in Opelousas. He was a delegate to the state constitutional convention in 1812, where he was elected to a committee to draft the Louisiana constitution. Later that year, Magruder appeared in Washington to deliver the document to President James Madison.

Riding the wave of his success at the state level, Magruder was elected to the Senate in 1812, serving only one term. Following an uneventful stint in the Senate, he returned to his Opelousas law practice in 1813, where he died in 1822.

Magruder arrived in the Louisiana territory before 1805. His knowledge of the newly acquired land is obvious from his *Political, Commercial, and Moral Reflections on the Late Cession of Louisiana to the United States.* Published in1803 by D. Bradford in Lexington and dedicated to President Thomas Jefferson, this 150-page essay is laced with historical comparisons to the development of Western Europe. Magruder devotes more than half of his book to what he terms political advantages, including the avoidance of war. The removal of the

French threat in America eased tensions and eliminated the need for a standing army and the building of a strong navy, both of which would have increased the tax burden and created an immediate national debt. Those western regions would have suffered the most with hostilities and were the least able to pay for it.

In addition, the question of Mississippi navigation rights was solved. Magruder also warned of alliances with Great Britain. He wrote that the most singular advantage was that the cession "throws an additional weight in the agricultural scale of the nation," but closed the section on politics by asking serious questions about admitting the territory to the Union as a state and warned of treating Louisiana as a fief, similar to what Britain did with the Irish and Scotland.

Magruder next turned to the commercial advantages of adding Louisiana, and it is here where his knowledge of Louisiana's natural resources and potential for agricultural development is obvious. He outlines a blueprint for production, not missing the existing natural system of navigable waterways for increasing trade. Magruder points to the coastal trade with Pensacola and Mobile, and as well as with Native Americans, and its importance to the development of commerce. He even suggests that the government obtain Florida by purchase and further develop this coastal trade with Cuba. The fertile soil, Magruder argues, is ideal for growing sugar, cotton, rice, indigo, coffee, cocoa, and aloes. Louisiana was a natural habitat for furs and pelts, and for producing horses, cattle, and naval stores such as lumber, tar and pitch, and lead. The territory never had a better promoter for economic development.

The moral arguments that Magruder makes include using the land for civilizing the Indians by providing a means of relocation. He finally urges the abolition of slavery through colonization of blacks in Louisiana and the western regions. An advocate of emancipation, Magruder argued that by his plan the nation would be "delivered from its greatest misfortune." Considering the acuity of Magruder's reflections on the cession of Louisiana to the United States, his thoughts and reasoning are rather remarkable and insightful, yet few historians have turned to his book as a resource for writing the history of the expansion of the new nation.

Five years later, Magruder once again put his pen to work: his *A letter from Allan B. Magruder, Esq., of Opelousas, to his correspondent in the state of Virginia, dated 20th Nov. 1807* was printed in New Orleans. Time had not altered his optimism about the future of Louisiana, as he summarized commercial, governmental, transportation, and population developments since the cession. And, as in 1803, Magruder still insisted that Cuba would one day be a part of the United States. Ever looking into the future, Magruder was Louisiana's earliest salesman.

—Boyd Childress

For Further Reading

Carter, Clarence E. 1940. *Territorial Papers of the United States,* vol. IX. Washington, DC: Government Printing Office; Magruder, Allan Bowie. 1803. *Political, Commercial, and Moral Reflections on the Late Cession of Louisiana to the United States.* Lexington, KY: D. Bradford; Magruder, Allan Bowie. 1808. *A Letter from Allan B. Magruder, Esq., of Opelousas, to his Correspondent in the State of Virginia, dated 20th Nov. 1807.* New Orleans: Bradford and Anderson.

MANDAN

The Mandan, speakers of a Siouan language, figure prominently in the history of the American West. Like their fellow northern Plains villagers, the Mandan mixed hunting and seasonal gathering with a sophisticated agriculture, and resided in substantial villages along the Missouri River in the present-day Dakotas. Their location and the welcome they afforded to Indian, European, and American traders and travelers made the Mandan villages a regional center, and Europeans and Americans relied heavily on Mandan hospitality for the pursuit of their commercial, scientific, and political objects.

The Mandan were organized in two main divisions, the Nuitadi, or west-side Mandan, and the Nuptadi, or east-side Mandan, with a third division, the Awigaxa, absorbed by the Nuitadi during the eighteenth century. Although villages were autonomous political and economic entities, the Mandan maintained a larger, shared identity and a common defense. And with their migration to the Missouri River, the Mandan began a long history of association and exchange with the Hidatsa. So close was this association that archaeologists sometimes found Mandan and Hidatsa villages difficult to distinguish, and offer estimates of a combined pre-epidemic population of some sixteen thousand or more. Throughout the nineteenth century, disease diminished Mandan numbers, and Meriwether Lewis, William Clark, and the Corps of Discovery would find only two Mandan villages near the juncture of the Heart and the Missouri Rivers, with a total population of slightly less than two thousand, reduced from nine larger villages that had existed earlier.

Kinship is an essential element of Mandan life, with children born into their mother's clan. Clans often have specific duties, and clan membership provided ties to kin in other Mandan villages. Common observances of ceremonial life, such as the Okipa ceremony's dramatization of Lone Man's creation of the world and its animals, bound the Mandan community together and served as a time of collective and personal renewal. Physically, Mandan villages resembled Hidatsa and Arikara villages. Built on bluffs with the river and its heights as a natural defense, villages were augmented on landward sides by dry moats and pickets, and composed of several dozen

The Mandan were one of the larger tribes located along the Missouri River in present-day North Dakota. (Smithsonian American Art Museum/Art Resource)

domed earth-lodges, a change from an earlier rectangular-style of structure with similar wood, brush, and earth construction. Earth-lodges were home throughout much of the year, with temporary winter residences located on the floodplain. The situation of individual earth-lodges reflected social status, and prominent families were found near the village's central open space and a structure recalling Lone Man's willows, used to protect the Mandan people.

Mandan subsistence patterns and economic activities made extensive use of diverse environments surrounding the Missouri River. Although their ancestors may have been more oriented to gathering and hunting, the Mandan practiced a varied and successful agriculture centered on several varieties of corn, beans, and squash. A clear division of labor based on gender was maintained, with women engaged in agriculture, pottery, the construction and maintenance of homes and villages, and the care and feeding of families, while men engaged in hunting and warfare, often traveling far from their home villages to raid, trade, and conduct diplomatic affairs.

This mixed economy, combined with a fortuitous geographic location, led to Mandan participation in three regional trade networks. The Mandan traded to the west with peoples joined in a network extending to the Rocky Mountains and beyond; to the south with peoples joined in a network extending across the central and southern Plains to New Mexico; and, finally, to the north with peoples joined in a network extending to the parklands of Canada. After contact, these same networks would facilitate the exchange of non-native goods, while Europeans themselves would later follow these networks back to the Mandan villages.

The earliest recorded Mandan meeting with Europeans occurred in 1738, when a party of Assiniboine led Pierre Gaultier de Varennes de La Vérendrye and his party to vil-

This woodcut by a member of the Corps of Discovery shows how expedition members labored as they spent the winter of 1804–1805 living among the Mandan in present-day North Dakota. (North Wind Picture Archives)

lages near the Heart River. French traders likely continued a trade with the Mandan for decades, followed by English traders from the Hudson's Bay Company and North West Company during the late eighteenth and early nineteenth centuries. Beginning in the late eighteenth century, Spanish and U.S. traders arrived from St. Louis. Lewis, Clark, and the Corps of Discovery wintered with the Mandan in 1804–1805, and Mandan assistance played a vital role in the expedition's journey. The stream of visitors continued throughout the early nineteenth century, including the St. Louis trader Manuel Lisa, the English naturalist John Bradbury, the U.S. adventurer Henry Marie Brackenridge, the U.S. artist George Catlin, Prince Maximilian of Wied-Neuwied, and the prince's artist companion, Karl Bodmer, each recording, in words and images, the richness and complexity of Mandan life.

Traders and travelers would also chronicle a devastating smallpox epidemic among the Mandan in 1837–1838. Although accounts vary, most describe but 120 to 150 Mandan survivors, one of the most dramatic examples of the toll of alien disease in the indigenous Americas. But the epidemic did not lead, as is sometimes asserted, to Mandan extinction. In the ensuing years, the Mandan drew into still closer association with the Hidatsa for mutual support. In 1845 the two peoples would establish a common village with separate districts, known as Like-A-Fishhook, just below the junction of the Little Missouri and Missouri Rivers. There they were joined by the Arikara in 1862, and a common reservation was established in 1870.

Throughout the 1860s and 1870s, Sioux attacks continued to harry the three village tribes, even as the United States consolidated its control over the West. With the end of the Plains Wars, U.S. policymakers and politicians undertook a systematic assimilation program, suppressing traditional religious life, establishing compulsory education, and encouraging alien practices. In the mid-1880s, Mandan families moved to individual homesteads, leaving Like-A-Fishhook for the communities of Beaver Creek, Red Butte, and Charging Eagle, located south of the Missouri River. As it was for the Hidatsa and Arikara, the move challenged Mandan communal traditions. At the same time, efforts to cultivate the arid uplands of the Plains failed, as they did for non-Indian communities throughout the Dakotas. Other, more suitable endeavors, such as ranching, proved successful, and Fort Berthold Reservation became home to the modern Mandan community, which recast itself, with its Hidatsa and Arikara neighbors, as the Three Affiliated Tribes under terms of the Indian Reorganization Act of 1934.

—*J. Wendel Cox*

See also
Arikara; Catlin, George; Hidatsa; Maximilian, Prince Alexander Philipp zu Wied-Neuwied; Oglala Sioux

For Further Reading
Cash, Joseph H., and Gerald W. Wolff. 1974. *The Three Affiliated Tribes (Mandan, Arikara, and Hidatsa)*. Phoenix: Indian Tribal Series; Meyer, Roy W. 1977. *The Village Indians of the Upper Missouri: The Mandans, Hidatsas, and Arikaras*. Lincoln and London: University of Nebraska Press; Schneider, Mary Jane. 1986. *North Dakota Indians: An Introduction*. Dubuque, IA: Kendall Hunt.

MANDAN, FORT (1804–1805)

Noted as the 1804–1805 winter quarters of the Lewis and Clark Expedition, Fort Mandan was constructed on the Upper Missouri River in present-day North Dakota. The Lewis and Clark Expedition docked for its first winter in the northwestern Louisiana Territory near the Mandan and Hidatsa villages on October 25, 1804. The hospitality of the Mandan tribe, compounded by the freezing Missouri River, convinced Captains Meriwether Lewis and William Clark to construct their winter post and name it Fort Mandan.

The necessity of good relations with the local Indians caused the corps to build its fort a few miles between two Mandan and three Hidatsa villages, to avoid the intertribal politics of associating with one group over another. Cottonwood trees surrounded the expedition's new quarters, and construction began on November 3, 1804, in the Missouri River Valley, near where the Knife River flows into the Missouri from the west. Under the supervision of Sergeant Patrick Gass, a skilled Pennsylvania carpenter, the fort was erected in the snow. Gass designed a trapezoidal bastion with two converging rows of huts, set at an angle, with a gate on its longest side. The outer walls reached eighteen feet in height, and a palisade was constructed on the river side with a sentry post and a mounted swivel gun. The corps moved into the crude cottonwood fortress on November 20.

With Fort Mandan in full operation, Lewis and Clark looked to the necessities wanted to survive the winter and depart in the spring. Food became the immediate priority: the local game had thinned and its meat become leaner with nearly no fat, causing expedition members to be hungry. Luckily, the Mandan traded corn for metal tools, possibly saving the Lewis and Clark Expedition during their first winter at Fort Mandan. Captain Meriwether Lewis also hoped to find a guide and interpreter familiar with the land and languages of the West. In late November, Lewis found help in Toussaint Charbonneau, a French-Canadian fur trapper who was married to a Shoshone woman named Sacagawea. Although she was pregnant at the time, Sacagawea became an invaluable member of the expedition by guiding the corps over the mountains, easing hostility with other tribal groups, and acting as translator.

The five months at Fort Mandan allowed the corps to behave more freely than was possible on most military operations. Christmas at Fort Mandan was celebrated with rifle and cannon fire, and the U.S. flag was hoisted for the first time. On New Year's Day, the corps left their stronghold to travel to all of the Indian villages to dance and entertain. Captain Lewis frequently traveled to different camps, where his medical skills were of continued service. Lewis amputated frost-bitten toes, cured fevers with Rush's Thunderbolt pills, cured signs of venereal disease with mercury salve, and drew blood for other ailments. Lewis also delivered Sacagawea's son, Jean Baptiste, on February 11, 1805. Specified Indians were also permitted to spend the night inside Fort Mandan, and Corps of Discovery members were joined by Indian associates on hunting expeditions.

But the garrison at Fort Mandan continued with regular military security. Drills and the threat of attack, especially from the Sioux, kept the sentries on alert twenty-four hours a day despite a bitterly cold winter. Other duties at Fort Mandan included map making, collecting scientific data, canoe building, and preparing the keelboat for the spring. Lewis and Clark also found themselves useful as critically important consuls to Indian diplomatic conflicts and jealousies between various tribes in northwestern Louisiana. These sensitive matters were important for the expedition's safety and to the understanding that the tribes lived on newly acquired U.S. soil.

By late March the ice was no longer on the river and the corps prepared to continue westward. The Corps of Discovery left Fort Mandan on April 7, 1805, while Lewis and Clark sent a small detachment back to St. Louis to carry specimens, reports, and maps to President Thomas Jefferson about the Louisiana Territory. The Corps of Discovery left without a reported fight, desertion attempt, or direct assault on the fortification. The corps had spent five months at Fort Mandan, longer than any winter camp on the expedition, and left prepared for its journey to the Pacific Ocean. The Corps of Discovery would never return to the fort. The following winter Fort Mandan burned to the ground, leaving no remnants.

—*Nathan R. Meyer*

See also
Corps of Discovery; Lewis and Clark Expedition; Mandan; Sacagawea

For Further Reading
Clark, William. 1987. *The Journals of the Lewis and Clark Expedition: Volume III, August 25, 1804–April 6, 1805.*

Edited by Gary E. Moulton. Lincoln: University of Nebraska Press; MacGregor, Carol Lynn, ed. 1997. *The Journal and Account Book of Patrick Gass: Member of the Lewis and Clark Expedition.* Missoula, MT: Mountain Press.

MANIFEST DESTINY

As editor of the *United States Magazine and Democratic Review,* it is likely that John Louis O'Sullivan did not foresee that his phrase "Manifest Destiny"–borrowed from an 1845 editorial–would become synonymous with the historic territorial expansion of the United States. Yet, his proclamation that the United States possessed a "manifest destiny to overspread the continent allotted by Providence for the free development of our yearly multiplying millions" was a stirring call to action for millions who shared the insatiable desire of acquiring western land (Pratt, 1933). Although O'Sullivan is credited with coining the phrase, the notion of Manifest Destiny had existed previously in the hearts and minds of many early American expansionists.

O'Sullivan's boastful vision of the United States was that of a forward-looking nation that would not remain mired in its past. He wrote, "We have no interest in scenes of antiquity, only as lessons of avoidance of nearly all their examples. The expansive future is our arena. We are entering on its untrodden space with the truth of God in our minds, beneficent objects in our hearts, and with a clear conscience unsullied by the past. We are the nation of human progress, and who will, what can, set limits on our onward march? . . . The far-reaching, the boundless future will be the era of American greatness" (ibid.). Such haughty rhetoric may have been of recent vintage in the 1840s, but its origins were rooted in the nation's past.

One might argue that English claims to all of North America, predicated upon John Cabot's 1497 explorations, reveal an incipient understanding of America as a continental entity that could neither be subdivided nor shared. Such a unilateral notion, as both Britain, and later the United States, would come to understand, could only be realized through diplomacy and conquest. Whether obtained through either method, the acquisition of western land would come to reveal an imperialistic drive that characterized Anglo-American sensibilities and defined the territorial growth of the young American republic.

The expansion of the continental United States to extend from the Atlantic Ocean to the Pacific was achieved within a fifty-year spurt of territorial growth. The Mississippi River marked the western boundary of the United States when the Treaty of Paris (1783) defined the newly independent American republic. Through a combination of diplomacy and conquest, the young nation acquired additional lands as it grew westward. With the Louisiana Purchase (1803), the annexation of Texas (1845), the Oregon Country (1846), the Mexican Cession (1848), and the Gadsden Purchase (1853), the United States completed the territorial growth that made the young republic a continental power. Additionally, during this era the United States also acquired Florida (1819) after having sent an invading army across an international boundary.

The lure of the West in the American imagination loomed large. Even before he had acquired the Louisiana Purchase Territory in 1803, President Thomas Jefferson planned a scientific expedition to explore the northern parts of Louisiana and travel to the Pacific coast. Although the scientific value of such an expedition was immense, it is likely that Jefferson had other ideas in mind as he originated what eventually became the Lewis and Clark Expedition (1804–1806). Only a decade later, as war between the United States and Great Britain appeared imminent, a vocal faction within the Congress who were known as the War Hawks strongly supported a belligerent policy. It was the opinion of these congressmen, mostly from Western and Southern states, that the United States could acquire Canada by fighting a war with Britain. By 1846, the United States was involved in a war with Mexico. Opponents of that conflict charged that it was an immoral war that was a poorly veiled effort to grab territory from a weak neighbor.

To assert that Americans held a God-given right to obtain western land provided additional impetus for the notion of expansion. Much of the nineteenth century was characterized by prevailing ideas of Social Darwinism that found expression in both the missionary zeal and the certainty of Christian trusteeship, important moral obligations of the age. Like earlier conquerors who defined their sense of mission with the expression "Gold, Glory, and God," many advocates of nineteenth-century Manifest Destiny used the pretext of spreading the Gospel among heathen peoples as an altruistic subterfuge that might mask more nefarious aspirations. Gold and glory, along with other unforeseen blessings of America's continental bounty, were never far from the minds of those who advocated the territorial growth of the United States. Unfortunately, many who approached the issue of expansion as one of divine mission were also motivated by strongly held racist views that the Anglo-Saxon race was destined to govern "lesser" peoples. As a result of this ideology, the taking of land from Native American peoples was viewed by some as being divinely sanctioned.

In keeping with the heady nationalism of the time, few bothered to notice the double standard that existed in America's expansionist policy. When the United States issued the Monroe Doctrine (1823), the nations of Western Europe were warned that their former colonial domains of the Western Hemisphere, which had recently become independent republics, were effectively off-limits from any further European encroachment. Yet the self-proclaimed inviolability of territorial sovereignty did not seem to apply to U.S. interests as a vast expanse was

Americans moved westward in the 1840s as thousands of migrants journeyed overland to Oregon, Utah, and California. These hardy pioneers were the agents of Manifest Destiny.

taken from the Mexican republic in 1848 and the U.S. flag was planted along the Pacific.

Not all Americans supported the idea of territorial expansion. In New England especially there was tepid support for the Louisiana Purchase and subsequent territorial acquisitions. Many New England political leaders realized that their region's influence would only wane as additional states carved from western territories came into the Union. By the 1840s, abolitionists and other antislavery advocates began to suspect that a "slave power conspiracy" at the federal level was responsible for the nation's territorial expansion. Eventually the question of whether slavery would be allowed to spread into western lands would become an issue that paralyzed the nation and inextricably moved the United States to civil war by 1861.

According to the principle of environmental determinism, the economic power and prestige that the United States eventually enjoyed was attributable, in large measure, to Manifest Destiny. Vast deposits of yet undiscovered resources—including gold, silver, and oil—would contribute to the nation's wealth. Mineral deposits, such as coal and iron ore, would transform the United States as the blessings of the Industrial Revolution wrought the progress of modernity upon a nation so richly endowed.

In the late nineteenth century, much of the geopolitical attention of the world's great powers was focused upon the New Imperialism. During this period, the nations of Western Europe competed with one another in the so-called scramble for Africa, and in other efforts to acquire colonies in Asia and the Pacific Islands. The United States was conspicuously absent from this imperialistic rivalry. Many have argued that the situation in the United States, with reconstruction taking place in the South and settlement taking place in the West, provided an opportunity for internal colonization to occur. American industries, largely situated in the Northeast, were able to reap similar benefits from doing business with the states in the South and the West without having to bear the added costs entailed with trading to foreign ports. Inadvertently, Manifest Destiny, may have thus provided a special benefit to U.S. industrialists who would later compete on the world market.

The American author Ralph Waldo Emerson characterized the United States as a nation that had no past. It was his opinion that in this new land "all has an outward and prospective look." Whether for good or for ill, the American people seized upon the notion of Manifest Destiny in the nineteenth century to define a nation that was still a work in progress. In an age when growth was taken as a sign of progress—and stagnation of decay—the United States became a vibrant, dynamic nation and positioned itself for future greatness.

—*Junius P. Rodriguez*

For Further Reading
Johannsen, Robert W., and Sam W. Haynes. 1997. *Manifest Destiny and Empire: American Antebellum Expansionism.* College Station, TX: Texas A&M University Press; Jones, Howard. 1997. *Prologue to Manifest Destiny: Anglo-American Relations in the 1840s.* Wilmington, DE: Scholarly Resources; Owsley, Frank L., and Gene A. Smith. 1997. *Filibusters and Expansionists: Jeffersonian Manifest Destiny, 1800–1821.* Tuscaloosa: University of Alabama Press; Pratt, Julius W. 1933. "John L. O'Sullivan and Manifest Destiny." *New York History* 14(3): 214–234.

MARSHALL, JOHN (1755–1835)

In 1801, President John Adams appointed John Marshall chief justice of the United States. Marshall is credited with transforming the United States Supreme Court into an institution with respect and authority equal to the executive and legislative branches of government. By the end of Marshall's tenure, the Court enjoyed the power of judicial review and stood as the preeminent interpreter of the Constitution and the protector of contractual property rights. Reflecting Marshall's own nationalist beliefs, the Court affirmed in its rulings the supremacy of federal powers and rights over those of state governments. Some scholars believe that the decisions made by the Marshall Court facilitated the development of U.S. capitalism and helped give rise to a national market that incorporated the West.

The case of *Marbury v. Madison* (1803) established the Court's power of judicial review. In March 1801, John Adams made a number of "midnight appointments," granting Federalists various posts, including one that awarded William Marbury a judgeship. Marbury's commission, however, was not sent to him before Adams left office, and Republican president Thomas Jefferson's secretary of state, James Madison, refused to deliver it.

Marbury complained to the Court that he was entitled to the commission. The Court, with the Federalist Marshall writing the opinion, agreed with Marbury. Marshall, however, held that the Judiciary Act of 1789, which provided the Court the power to issue a writ requiring Madison to award Marbury his post, was unconstitutional because it gave the Court power beyond that prescribed in Article III of the Constitution. Thus the Court could not issue the writ that would provide Marbury his post. In addressing the Judiciary Act of 1789, the Court set the precedent of judicial review and carved out for itself the power to rule on the constitutionality of laws enacted by Congress.

Seven years later, in 1810, the Court moved to protect contractual property rights. In 1795 the Georgia legislature passed an act that granted the sale of thirty-five million acres of land along the Yazoo River to four companies. The companies had bribed legislators to secure the act. One year later, a new legislature, aware of the massive fraud under which the grant was made, repealed the 1795 act and declared that any sales made under it were null and void.

In *Fletcher v. Peck* (1810) the Court ruled that the Georgia legislature's repeal of the 1795 act violated the contract clause of the Constitution. Although fraud and bribery influenced the passage of the act, the grant itself was a legal and unbreakable contract that states did not have the power to nullify. Hence, contractual property rights in this case and others would be legally protected from interference by states.

Two other cases, *Dartmouth College v. Woodward,* and *McCulloch v. Maryland,* both decided in 1819, affirmed the sanctity of contracts and the supremacy of federal law over state law, respectively. The former case involved an attempt by the state of New Hampshire to revise Dartmouth College's original 1769 royal charter, effectively transforming the private institution into a public one. Marshall issued the Court's opinion protecting the school's charter as a contract that could not be altered without the consent of the college. The ruling's wider application protected private rights and privileges granted through charters or contracts.

In *McCulloch v. Maryland,* the state of Maryland challenged the supremacy of the national government by attempting to eliminate the Baltimore branch of the Second Bank of the United States through taxation. The Court ruled that Maryland's tax was unconstitutional, as a state could not exercise control over the federal government. The ruling further supported the supremacy of the federal government over the states.

Marshall's decision in *Gibbons v. Ogden* (1824) is credited with allowing trade to flow freely on America's rivers. *Gibbons,* regarded as the so-called emancipation proclamation of American commerce, guaranteed that the nation's rivers—including those in the Louisiana Purchase that would serve as highways to the West—were open to all who wished to navigate them and could not be restricted by state laws to grant monopolies to certain companies.

Two cases dealing with Native American issues came before the Supreme Court during Andrew Jackson's presidency, as Americans pushed farther west and south, toward valuable, productive land held by Indians in the southeastern United States. The Cherokee were the most advanced of the Southeastern tribes. They had developed their own constitution and alphabet, and as farmers they cultivated valuable agricultural land. In 1827, as whites encroached on their lands, they declared themselves an independent state. A year later, the state of Georgia enacted laws seizing Cherokee lands and subjecting the Indians to its laws.

The outcome of the first case, *Cherokee Nation v. Georgia* (1831), did nothing to stop Georgia from applying its laws to the Cherokee. A year later, in *Worcester v. Georgia,* the Court ruled favorably for the Cherokee. In this case, Vermont missionary Samuel A. Worcester, sympathetic to the Cherokee cause, established a mission in Cherokee territory. Georgia, however, had passed a law making it illegal for a white person to live among the Cherokee without a license from the state. Worcester was imprisoned and challenged the legality of the Georgia law.

The Court ruled in favor of Worcester, and hence the Cherokee. Marshall wrote that the laws of Georgia did not apply in the Cherokee Territory, therefore Worcester should be released. The Court, however, lacked enforcement powers. The federal government, under proremoval President Jackson, did nothing to protect the Indians. By 1838, under the Indian Removal Act of 1830, most of the Cherokee had been forced west of the Mississippi, onto the lands reserved for them in the southern Louisiana Purchase.

These cases and others reviewed by the Marshall Court strengthened the judiciary, protected contracts, and held the supremacy of federal government's rights and powers over those of the states. Cases such as *Worcester* v. *Georgia* and *Gibbons v. Ogden,* in particular, would have significant impact on the development of the Louisiana Purchase and the West.

—Alicia E. Rodriquez

See also
Indian Removal

For Further Reading

Hobson, Charles F. 1996. *The Great Chief Justice: John Marshall and the Rule of Law.* Lawrence: University of Kansas Press; Smith, Jean Edward. 1998. *John Marshall: Definer of a Nation.* New York: Henry Holt and Company; Stites, Francis N. 1981. *John Marshall: Defender of the Constitution.* Boston: Little, Brown, and Company; Swindler, William F. 1981. *The Constitution and Chief Justice Marshall.* New York: Dodd, Mead, and Company.

MAXIMILIAN, PRINCE ALEXANDER PHILIPP ZU WIED-NEUWIED (1782–1867)

Prince Maximilian, a seasoned explorer and ethnologist, arrived in the United States in July 1832 with Karl Bodmer, a Swiss-born artist, and David Dreidoppel, a German hunter and taxidermist, to chronicle the plants, animals, minerals, and American Indians of the region previously explored by Lewis and Clark. Following a lengthy visit with accomplished scientists in New Harmony, Indiana, the German prince and his companions traveled to St. Louis, Missouri. There William Clark, the superintendent of Indian affairs and famous veteran of the Corps of Discovery, shared his knowledge of the vast Louisiana Territory with his distinguished foreign visitors. Clark also helped Maximilian's party secure travel and lodging arrangements with officials of the Upper Missouri Outfit, the American Fur Company's most important subdivision.

In April 1833, Maximilian and his entourage, carrying maps from the Lewis and Clark expedition to guide them, boarded the *Yellow Stone,* the American Fur Company's steamboat, and began their journey up the Missouri River. Along the way Maximilian studied the appearance, artifacts, and customs of the Omahas and Yankton Sioux, while Bodmer sketched everything and made formal portraits of tribal leaders. After seven weeks of travel, the steamboat eventually reached Fort Pierre in present-day South Dakota. A short time later Maximilian's crew boarded another steamboat, the *Assiniboine,* and pushed on to Fort Clark, where they were greeted by several hundred Mandans and Hidatsas all dressed in their finest clothes. The hustle and bustle of James Kipp's trading post, adjacent to Mih-Tutta-Hang-Kusch, a thriving Mandan summer village of sixty-five earth-lodges, captivated Maximilian and Bodmer. Following a brief stay, the European adventurers returned to their steamboat and chugged along to Fort Union, an important fur trading post located near present-day Williston, North Dakota. Wanting to see more of Lewis and Clark's West, Maximilian, Bodmer, and Dreidoppel then boarded the *Flora,* a keelboat destined for Fort McKenzie, the American Fur Company's most remote wilderness outpost located twenty-five hundred miles from St. Louis in the heart of Blackfoot country. The keelboat's slow passage upstream afforded Maximilian the opportunity to collect new plant, animal, and mineral specimens. He also utilized the delay to compare his own impressions of the region with the notes recorded by Lewis and Clark.

During their stay at Fort McKenzie, Maximilian and Bodmer worked feverishly to record the daily routine of frontier life. Besides chronicling the protocol of the fur trade, Maximilian and Bodmer also documented life in a Piegan Blackfoot camp adjacent to the fort. The pair even witnessed an Assiniboine and Cree ambush on the unsuspecting Piegan camp. Unfortunately for the explorers who had hoped to see the Rocky Mountains, however, the threat of future Indian hostilities forced them to make their way back to Fort Union in September 1833. There, friendly Crees and Assiniboines posed for Bodmer while Maximilian searched for new plant and animal specimens to study. On November 8, 1833, the prince and his crew returned to Fort Clark, an outpost situated forty-five miles north of present-day Bismarck, North Dakota. A short time later Maximilian interviewed Toussaint Charbonneau, the aged French-Canadian guide who had accompanied Lewis and Clark. During their five-month stay at Fort Clark, Maximilian and Bodmer had the good fortune of witnessing several Mandan, Hidatsa, and Arikara ceremonies. Both men also established close relationships with several Indians, including Four Bears, a leading Mandan warrior chief, and Yellow Feather, a young Mandan warrior. During the bitterly cold winter of 1833–1834, a period when Maximilian succumbed to scurvy, game became scarce, and the fort's residents survived on a diet of cornmeal, biscuits, and maize broth.

On April 18, Maximilian, Bodmer, and Dreidoppel continued their journey down the Missouri, reaching St. Louis on May 27, 1834.

Following his return to Europe in August 1834, Maximilian spent the next four years editing his voluminous field journals. The English translation of Maximilian's two-volume account of his expedition, *Travels in the Interior of North America,* finally appeared in 1843. Bodmer's illustrations supplemented the prince's text as a separate folio, the *Atlas.* Maximilian's journals and Bodmer's 427 original watercolors and sketches were later discovered at Neuwied Castle following World War II. Today they form the basis of the Maximilian-Bodmer Collection at the Joslyn Art Museum in Omaha, Nebraska. The diaries, notebooks, correspondence, watercolors and sketches form an invaluable account of the Plains Indians before disease, warfare, and land encroachment nearly destroyed them.

—Jon L. Brudvig

For Further Reading

DeVoto, Bernard. 1947. *Across the Wide Missouri.* Boston: Houghton-Mifflin; Freedman, Russell. 1992. *An Indian Winter.* New York: Holiday House; Maximilian Prince of Wied. 1906 [1843]. *Travels in the Interior of North America, 1832–1834.* Translated by H. Evans Lloyd. London: Ackermann and Company. Reprinted as vols. 22–24 of Thwaites, Reuben Gold. *Early Western Travels, 1748–1846.* Cleveland: Arthur H. Clarke Co.; Robert, Henry Flood, Jr., ed. 1980. *The Art of Exploration: The Maximilian-Bodmer Expedition, 1832–34.* Omaha: Joslyn Art Museum; Thomas, David and Karin Ronnefeldt, eds. 1976. *People of the First Man.* New York: E. P. Dutton.

MCCLALLEN, JOHN (1772–1808)

The eldest son of an Albany, New York, mercantile family, John McClallen was born on June 29, 1772. At the age of twenty-two he was commissioned a lieutenant in the Corps of Artillery and Engineers. Four years later, during the military buildup during the Quasi-War with France (1798–1800), he was promoted to captain. In 1805, while commanding Fort McHenry at Baltimore, he was reassigned to the new Western frontier.

In a curiously intimate association with the commanding general of the army, James Wilkinson, McClallen took an assortment of goods to St. Louis to test the new business potential for the Baltimore capitalists James Calhoun & Sons. The Indian trade of the upper Missouri was dominated by British competitors, but McClallen, with Wilkinson's encouragement, focused on opening a commercial connection to Spanish Santa Fe. Returning to Baltimore and resigning his commission, McClallen arranged for a second stock, which he planned to carry overland from a point on the lower Platte River. On September 27, 1806, McClallen & Company was moving up the Missouri River when they encountered the returning Corps of Discovery.

From his former comrade-in-arms Captain Meriwether Lewis heard a firsthand relation of British encroachment along the northern frontier. Spanish intimidation of the Republican Pawnee frustrated McClallen's plan, and after wintering with the Yankton Dakota, the trader decided to penetrate New Mexico by the backdoor of the upper Yellowstone River. In passing the Mandan/Hidatsa villages on the upper Missouri, the party picked up about thirty former Canadian *engagés* set free after the recent merger of Montreal interests. This now sizable party ascended the Yellowstone. After hearing rumors of British plans to expand into the Pacific drainage, from a point on the upper Yellowstone on July 23, 1807, McClallen composed a circular letter setting out U.S. trading regulations, not only for northwestern Louisiana Territory but also for the drainage of the Columbia River. Lacking any official standing, McClallen signed with the alias Captain Zackery Perch.

To further confound the British expansion, he led a party of forty-two boatmen and trappers through the mountains to the vicinity of present-day Missoula, Montana. While the men scattered to trap, McClallen seconded the U.S. policy introduced by Lewis and Clark at a peace meeting between the mountain tribes. After intertribal jealousy aborted the peace treaty, McClallen followed the Clark Fork of the Columbia, completing a practical portage between the Missouri and Columbia that had been the primary mission of the Corps of Discovery. The presence of a second, larger party of Americans checked the activities of the British trader David Thompson, causing him to write that "we have perhaps arrived too late."

As the first U.S. officer in the West after Lewis and Clark, McClallen's remarkable initiative was the first statement of what was later known as "The Oregon Boundary Question." Most of the trappers returned to the Yellowstone in the spring and were absorbed into the Lisa/Drouillard operations. In the spring of 1808, hoping to renew the peace initiative, McClallen recrossed the mountains with a smaller party. Somewhere in the rolling downslope toward the great falls of the Missouri the party was intercepted by Northern Plains tribesmen hostile to the peace. According to Thompson, an "American officer and eight of twelve were killed." The date was May 22, 1808. Other survivors of this enigmatic adventure returned to the Salish Country and became the nucleus of the Western freemen, a swing faction in later U.S./British rivalry during the mountain man era.

—John C. Jackson

For Further Reading

Jackson, John C. 2000. *The Piikani Blackfeet: A Culture under Siege.* Missoula, MT: Mountain Press; Majors, Harry M. 1981. "John McClellan in the Montana Rockies, 1807." *Northwest Discovery: The Journal of Northwest History and Natural History* 2: 9; Nisbet, Jack. 1994. *Sources of the River: Tracking David Thompson across Western North America.* Seattle: Sasquatch Books.

MCKEAN, THOMAS (1734–1817)

Thomas McKean represented Delaware in the Continental Congress, served as chief justice of Pennsylvania, and was governor of Pennsylvania at the time of the Louisiana Purchase.

As a member of the Continental Congress, McKean initially voted with the radical bloc led by the Adamses and the Lees. He moved to the moderate bloc by the time of his presidency in 1781, as shown by his vote in favor of putting France in charge of the peace negotiations. If he was not a proponent of expansion, nor was he an enemy of the rising West. McKean supported making the free navigation of the Mississippi River a necessary article of peace. Unlike many of his colleagues from small states and states without Western claims, McKean did not make the cession of Western lands a precondition for supporting the Articles of Confederation. He believed that the larger states would simply bear a greater burden for the support of the Confederation.

McKean's connection to the diplomacy of the Louisiana Purchase began in his official capacity as chief justice of Pennsylvania and with a family connection to the Spanish minister to the United States, Don Carlos Martínez de Irujo. Irujo arrived in Philadelphia in 1797 and soon began courting McKean's youngest daughter, Sarah. Irujo and his country were attacked in the press by all sides, from the Republican Benjamin Franklin Bache to the Federalist William Cobbett. Irujo was not one to suffer what he saw as the insolence of the American press and sought a libel charge against Cobbett in federal court. Federal reluctance and slow progress led Irujo to seek a transfer to the state court, where he might expect a more sympathetic hearing. At McKean's prodding, Pennsylvania brought a bill for libel against Cobbett on November 18, 1797. The jury rebelled against McKean's heavy-handed action and refused to return a bill of indictment. The family connection between McKean and Irujo was sealed on April 10, 1798, when Sarah McKean converted to Catholicism and married Irujo. Cobbett continued to use Irujo as a vehicle to attack McKean.

McKean was elected governor of Pennsylvania in 1799, and re-elected in 1802 by such a wide margin that some suggested that McKean replace Burr on the Republican ticket in 1804. Irujo encouraged McKean to seek the vice presidential nomination, and a dissident Republican faction led by William Duane and Michael Lieb saw the chance to remove McKean from state politics. Such talk dissipated, however, by October 1803. The divisions that appeared in state politics over the vice presidency reappeared with the Louisiana Purchase. The Tammany Society and Republican Greens of Philadelphia, led by Duane and Lieb, celebrated the Louisiana Purchase on May 12, 1804, and pointedly avoided toasting McKean. The governor's supporters promised not to forget the slight. Irujo, as usual, managed to drag his father-in-law into difficulty. In the summer of 1804, Joseph Cabrera, Irujo's aide, cashed several checks in Irujo's name without authorization at the Bank of Pennsylvania. Irujo asked McKean to have Cabrera arrested. When the story became public in 1805, the *Aurora*, Duane's paper, accused McKean of violating the law of nations and opposing the Louisiana Purchase, both on Irujo's orders.

McKean became peripherally involved in the political aftermath of the Burr Conspiracy. Since the middle of 1805, Burr's movements in the West aroused concern and suspicion. McKean's enemies saw another chance to assault the governor. In January 1806 the *Aurora* charged that, like Burr, McKean planned to carve out an empire in the West ruled by his family, including Irujo. In the summer, the *Aurora* tried to link McKean and his supporters to Burr and the Yazoo land speculators. McKean's own conduct lent credence to the idea that at minimum he did not take Burr as seriously as he should have. In August 1806, Burr met with Colonel George Morgan at Morgan's estate outside Pittsburgh. Burr said that he expected the West to leave the Union, and boasted that he could take Washington with two hundred men and New York with five hundred. Morgan informed Jefferson of the meeting and met with several Pennsylvania leaders, including Chief Justice William Tilghman, on September 20, repeating Burr's tale. Tilghman informed McKean, but the governor saw no reason to report the meeting to the president. The dispute with Duane and Lieb, brought about in part by foreign affairs and the Louisiana Purchase, culminated in a motion to impeach McKean, introduced in 1807 and defeated in 1808. The next year McKean retired from politics.

—*Robert W. Smith*

See also
Burr, Aaron; Duane, William; Irujo, Carlos Martínez de (Marquis de Casa Irujo); Jefferson, Thomas

For Further Reading
Abernathy, Thomas Perkins. 1954. *The Burr Conspiracy.* New York: Oxford University Press; Henderson, H. James. 1974. *Party Politics in the Continental Congress.* New York: McGraw-Hill Book Company; Higginbotham, Sanford W. 1952. *The Keystone in the Democratic Arch: Pennsylvania Politics 1800–1816.* Harrisburg: Pennsylvania Historical and Museum Commission; Rowe, G. S. 1978. *Thomas McKean: The Shaping of an American Republicanism.* Boulder: Colorado Associated University Press.

MCLOUGHLIN, JOHN (1784–1857)

Honored as the "Father of Oregon" by that state's legislature in 1957, John McLoughlin was born October 19, 1784, in La Riviere du Loup, Quebec. Apprenticed to a doctor at age fourteen, he applied for his medical license in 1803, but signed a contract with the North West Company to serve as a clerk before the application was approved, possibly in order to avoid the repercussions of a recent conflict with a British officer. McLoughlin's contract specified his position as a "Surgeon and Apprentice Clerk," and he was paid a clerk's wages, suggesting he entered into the agreement with few alternatives. His first assignment was to the Lake Superior post of Fort Kaministiquia (later Fort William), where he entered into a seasonal arrangement, acting as physician at the fort in the summers and as a supervisor at frontier trading outposts in the winters. Over time he became more deeply involved with the trade and less engaged with medicine, signing a second contract in 1811 as a clerk on the promise of a future partnership in the company. He married Marguerite McKay, a métis woman widowed by the death of Alexander McKay at Fort Astoria, that same year.

When the North West Company merged with the Hudson's Bay Company in 1821, McLoughlin was made chief factor, entitling him to slightly less than a 1 percent share of the company's profits. Three years later he was given charge of the vast Columbia District, which had yet to yield substantial profits and where British and U.S. interests shared equal rights to the trade under an 1818 treaty. Upon his arrival in 1825, McLoughlin rejected the existing settlement of Fort George (formerly Astoria) as a suitable headquarters for the district, choosing instead to move inland and establish the new fort on the northern bank of the Columbia River, which he assumed would become the border when the region was divided permanently between the two countries. Fort Vancouver was thus located near the confluence of the Willamette and Columbia Rivers, offering easy access to the region's three primary trading routes as well as to the ocean, and McLoughlin was charged with fostering Hudson's Bay Company—and thus British—control over as much of the region as possible while also turning a profit.

McLoughlin soon earned the appellation "White-Headed Eagle" from the local Indians for his shock of white hair, and under his direction a stable peace was established with the local tribes who were an important source of trade for the company. As chief factor the doctor was the ultimate authority in the region, with complete control over his men and company policies. His success in building trade, as well as the construction of a fort that included mills, orchards, a dairy, and all the other necessities to support a significant settlement, would later serve as evidence to U.S. missionaries that settlement of the Pacific Northwest was possible and that the Indians were good subjects for their work. When Jason Lee, a Methodist minister, arrived in 1834 to establish his Willamette Mission south of Fort Vancouver, it was McLoughlin who welcomed his party to the area and provided the seeds for their first crops; he also collected donations in excess of $130 from the men of the fort to support the endeavor. Similar support was offered to Dr. Marcus Whitman and Henry Spalding when their missionary party arrived in 1836. The missionaries' reports, reprinted in Eastern papers, helped convince Americans of the settlement potential of the region and laid the foundation for the eventual end of British influence in the Oregon country. Although McLoughlin's generosity (in the form of credit) was extended to all emigrants, he did attempt to convince the Americans to settle south of the Columbia, in order to maintain British claims to the north.

U.S. emigrants, propelled by cries of Manifest Destiny, well outnumbered the men of Fort Vancouver by the 1840s, leading McLoughlin to petition for protection from the British government in 1843. Seeing the writing on the wall, though, he had laid claim to and platted out a town site to be called Oregon City at the falls of the Willamette, well south of Fort Vancouver, to which he retired when he left the company's service in 1846. McLoughlin's personal fortunes took a turn for the worse, though, as he was held liable by the company for the credit he had extended to settlers. Although he pledged allegiance to the United States when Oregon was organized as a territory in 1848, his land claims in Oregon City remained in dispute for the rest of his life. Following his death on September 5, 1857, McLoughlin was buried beneath a stone reading "The Pioneer and Friend of Oregon," and he was thereafter lionized as the representative of the first Anglo-European government established in the Pacific Northwest.

—Derek R. Larson

See also
Hudson's Bay Company

For Further Reading

Fogdall, Alberta Brooks. 1978. *Royal Family of the Columbia: Dr. John McLoughlin and His Family.* Fairfield, WA: Ye Galleon Press; Holman, Frederick V. 1907. *Dr. John McLoughlin: The Father of Oregon.* Cleveland: Arthur H. Clark Company; Morrison, Dorothy Nafus. 1999. *Outpost: John McLoughlin & the Far Northwest.* Portland: Oregon Historical Society Press; Rich, E. E. 1941–1944. *The Letters of John McLoughlin from Fort Vancouver to the Governor and Committee.* Toronto: Champlain Society.

MESABI RANGE

The Mesabi Range covers a strip of low hills over one hundred miles long and one to ten miles wide in northeastern Minnesota, containing significant deposits of iron ore and other minerals. Starting just west of Grand Rapids, Minnesota, on the west bank of the Mississippi River, the range extends northeastward roughly parallel to the Lake Superior shore toward Babbitt, Minnesota.

At the time of the purchase of the Louisiana Territory, the Mesabi Range, or "sleeping giant" in the Ojibwa language, was little more than pine forest and Indian trails.

British fur traders were active in the area, but because of the generally accepted interpretation of the Anglo-U.S. border defined in the Treaty of Paris (1783), the land was given to the United States. Without an accurate map of the region, treaty negotiators defined the border west of Lake Superior as running through "Long Lake" to the Lake of the Woods. Although the definition of "Long Lake" was not precise, British fur traders understood this to mean the Pigeon River.

Angered because of their betrayal by British negotiators, and fearing a U.S. takeover of Grand Portage and other posts south of the Pigeon River, fur trading merchants pressed British diplomats to throw the border definition into dispute and claim the St. Louis River as the true "Long Lake." Although the wealth of mineral resources in the Mesabi iron range would not be suspected until the 1820s, this British assertion of the border would have placed much of the mineral-rich land in Canadian territory.

A commission to survey the lands between Lake Superior and Lake of the Woods and to define the border was established in Article Seven of the Treaty of Ghent (1814). By 1826 work on the survey was complete, but Anglo-U.S. negotiations during the following two years failed to produce an acceptable compromise. Discussion on the matter was not resumed until 1838, and a clear definition of the present-day border between Minnesota and Ontario would not come until the ratification of the Webster-Ashburton Treaty (1842).

It was not until the late 1830s that the existence of large mineral deposits was confirmed. Surveyor Joseph N. Nicollet was the first to report the presence of iron sulfides in what he called the "Missabay Heights." Scientific surveys of the Mesabi Range by government surveyors were executed under the direction of David Dale Owen from 1848 to 1850 and were published by the U.S. Geological Survey in 1852.

—J. Brent Etzel

For Further Reading

Lass, William E. 1980. *Minnesota's Boundary with Canada: Its Evolution since 1763*. St. Paul: Minnesota Historical Society.

MICHAUX, ANDRÉ (1746–1802)

French botanist André Michaux first came to North America in 1785, when he was commissioned by the French monarchy to collect and study American trees and plants. Besides his studies of botany, Michaux was a renowned explorer. In 1792 he began organizing an expedition to cross the American continent. This plan was stopped short by rumors that Michaux was a French spy. A few years later, Lewis and Clark carried out this cross-continent expedition. Michaux's unaccomplished trip demonstrates the American desire, which predated Lewis and Clark's expedition, to explore Western territories.

The French government sent Michaux to North America in 1785, where he was to obtain "for the royal nurseries, all the young trees, shrubs and seeds he could possibly send" (Savage, 1986). More specifically, Michaux was supposed to find trees that could grow in France and be used to build ships. Michaux was accompanied by his son, François, who also became a distinguished botanist. His collecting expedition took him along the Atlantic seaboard and as far north as Hudson's Bay.

In 1786, Andre Michaux founded a botanical garden in New Jersey. He had already established his reputation as a botanist. Previously, he had collected plants in Great Britain, Spain, and Persia.

André Michaux proposed a transcontinental expedition to the American Philosophical Society in 1792. Meriwether Lewis was a contending applicant. At the time, Thomas Jefferson was the president of the society, and he favored Michaux for the position of expedition leader. The society accepted Michaux's proposal and collected $128.25. Both George Washington and Jefferson made personal pledges to the fund.

In July 1793, Michaux started west. The aim of the expedition was to explore the Far West by way of the Missouri. His journey ended when he reached the Mississippi River. Rumors of espionage forced the American Philosophical Society to cancel the expedition in the spring of 1794. Apparently André Michaux had another mission, which was to spy on the Spanish in behalf of the French Republic. Despite his family's political tradition, Michaux was a devout Republican. With hopes of improving their situation in North America, the French were trying to obtain information about the Spanish position in the West. Even before the Treaty of San Ildefonso (1800), the French hoped to regain the colony of Louisiana.

This expedition became a very sensitive issue for the American Philosophical Society. Jefferson feared that the Spanish would see this exploratory mission as a form of U.S. expansionism. When addressing Spanish officials, he was careful to emphasize the expedition's scholarly aims—most important, the advancement of geographic knowledge. For this reason, the accusation of espionage against Michaux was taken seriously and dealt with quickly. Jefferson did not want to damage Spanish-U.S. relations.

Shortly after the failure of his transcontinental voyage, André Michaux returned to France. Misfortune plagued the French botanist. During Michaux's return voyage in 1796, he was shipwrecked off the coast of Holland. His precious cargo, an extensive collection of plants and trees, was only partially salvaged. In October 1800, Michaux left France on Captain Nicolas Baudin's Australian expedition. Later, André Michaux decided to leave the group in order to explore Madagascar. There he caught a tropical fever and died on October 23, 1855.

André Michaux published a number of books on the flora and fauna of North America: *Flora boreali-americana* (Paris, 1803), *Histoire des Chênes de l'Amérique* (Paris, 1801), and "Mémoire sur les Dattiers," *Journal de Physique, de Chemie et d'Histoire Naturelle* (vol. LII, 1801).

—*Rachel Eden Black*

See also
Lewis and Clark Expedition
For Further Reading
Savage, Henry, Jr., and Elizabeth J. Savage. 1986. *André and François Michaux*. Charlottesville: University Press of Virginia.

MINNESOTA

As originally defined, the land acquired in the Louisiana Purchase included only the portion of the present-day state of Minnesota that drained into the Mississippi River valley system. This area was roughly the southern and western half of modern Minnesota. The northern portion of Minnesota, which drained northward through the Red River of the North, was technically a part of Canada until the region was effectively ceded to the United States by Great Britain in the Convention of 1818. This diplomatic agreement set the border between the United States and Canada along the Boundary Waters and at 49 degrees north latitude from Lake of the Woods westward to the Rocky Mountains. It was through this boundary adjustment that the United States acquired the mineral-rich Mesabi Range.

Much of the modern landscape of Minnesota is the product of glaciation from the time of the Ice Ages. Continental ice sheets both scoured the countryside and deposited their till as new landforms as glacial moraines became hills and ridges in the postglacial epoch. The eleven thousand lakes that are a characteristic feature of modern Minnesota owe their origin to Ice Age glaciation as well. The result of these events would produce over time a verdant environment of northwoods hardwood forests and fertile prairie grasslands as the well-watered environment, filled with numerous lakes and streams, became the natural habitat for abundant wildlife.

The beauty and natural bounty of the region attracted the Santee Sioux (Issati) and the Ojibwa when they migrated into the area nearly seven centuries ago. As the indigenous inhabitants of the region, these tribes occasionally quarreled between themselves; but the bounty of the land was sufficient to support both groups, and each settled within the headwaters region of the Mississippi River. Both of these groups cultivated small farm plots, fished, hunted, and trapped throughout the region.

The first Europeans to reach the lands of the Santee Sioux and the Ojibwa did so from the north as Canadian-based trappers and traders ventured southward and westward from their base of operations to search for new streams suitable for trapping in the Great Lakes region. Between 1654 and 1660, Pierre-Esprit Radisson and Médard Chouart Sieur des Groseilliers led two expeditions into the area of modern-day Minnesota as they scouted for lands that might be productive enough to support the expansion of the fur trade. The work of Radisson and Groseilliers led to the creation of the Hudson's Bay Company, and the expansive network of that enterprise eventually had the Santee Sioux and the Ojibwa within the economic sphere of the trappers and traders who worked for the company.

In subsequent years explorers operating out of New France penetrated farther into Minnesota and learned more about the geography and ethnography of the region. In 1679, Daniel Greysolon, Sieur du Luth, planted the French fleur-de-lis near the site of modern-day Duluth, where he had encountered the main village of the Santee Sioux. The following year, three French explorers, Father Louis Hennepin, Michel Accault, and Antoine Auguelle were captured by the Santee Sioux and held for a time near Mille Lacs. Upon their release, the three men explored the upper part of the Mississippi River Valley and discovered and named the Falls of St. Anthony. A series of forts soon followed, including Fort Antoine (1689), Fort L'Huillier (1700), and Fort Beauharnois (1727), as the French sought to establish economic hegemony in the region and protect their trappers and traders against any depredations that might befall them.

The Minnesota region would soon become one of many points of contention between Great Britain and France as they sought to maintain control of the fur trade and the colonial empire that had been established to sustain it. This rivalry over empire had generated a series of colonial wars between the two European powers, but it would be the French and Indian War that would bring an end to the French dream of a North American empire. In the Treaty of Paris (1763), the area of Minnesota that was to the east of the Mississippi River became a possession of the British, while the French ceded Minnesota lands west of the river to the Spanish as part of the Louisiana Territory.

Although the British legally held the region of Minnesota for only twenty years (1763–1783), they recognized the commercial value of the area and established a dominant presence in the region's fur trade. Even after the British ceded the area to the newly established United States in the Treaty of Paris (1783), Canadian-based British commercial interests were not yet prepared to surrender the exceedingly valuable fur trading monopoly that the North West Company enjoyed in the region. Despite the 1783 treaty terms, the British continued to hold forts in the Old Northwest; the bulk of traffic in animal pelts continued to flow northward into Canada; and the British used their economic suzerainty to persuade local Indian tribes to harass U.S. pioneers who entered the region.

U.S. interests in Minnesota improved gradually, but some of the problems associated with British treaty violations would not be effectually ended until the conclusion of the War of 1812. Nonetheless, there were improvements. In Jay's Treaty (1794), the British did agree to evacuate forts in the Old Northwest that they had continued to hold since the conclusion of the American Revolution. The U.S. government had taken the first steps to administer the region of Minnesota when that area was included in the Northwest Territory as defined by the Northwest Ordinance (1787). Stipulations included in that measure put Minnesota on track for future territorial status and eventual statehood once the area satisfied criteria outlined in the ordinance. When the United States purchased the Louisiana Territory from France in 1803, the Minnesota lands that lay west of the Mississippi River became part of the national domain of the United States. By 1805, the U.S. government had commissioned an official military expedition to explore the upper reaches of the Mississippi River. Lt. Zebulon M. Pike conducted this mission and was able to win treaty concessions from the Santee Sioux that permitted construction of army posts at the mouths of the Minnesota and St. Croix Rivers.

Upon the conclusion of the War of 1812, U.S. hegemony in Minnesota began to take shape. By 1815 the British had abandoned Prairie du Chien, the last garrison that they had held on U.S. soil. Economically, the story was similar. The fur trading monopoly that had been held by the British North West Company was assumed by the American Fur Company, which had been established by John Jacob Astor. Treaty negotiations with the Ojibwa and the Santee Sioux would soon lead to the reduction of their tribal lands, as U.S. officials desired to open vast areas of Minnesota to white settlement. Since the Minnesota tribes had fought in support of the British during the War of 1812, U.S. negotiators were not troubled by the treaty concessions that led to the dismemberment of Ojibwa and Santee Sioux tribal lands and provoked further Indian hostilities as these tribes encroached upon the lands of other indigenous peoples.

The beginnings of a stable U.S. presence in Minnesota were evident by 1820. Fort St. Anthony (later Fort Snelling) was established in that year at the mouth of the Minnesota River, and the presence of frontier regulars in the area encouraged the start of pioneer migration, albeit gradual, into the area. As settlement increased, there was a simultaneous diversification of the local economy that took place. The fur trade had always been a staple of the Minnesota economy, but by the 1820s other types of economic activity, including farming, logging, and mining, were starting to take shape. By 1837 the pressures caused by white settlement had become so great that in treaty negotiations the Santee Sioux were forced to cede all tribal lands east of the Mississippi River to the U.S. government.

The true "land rush" to Minnesota would take place in the 1850s. When the Seventh Census of the United States was completed in 1850, it recorded only 6,077 inhabitants; yet by 1856, the same territory had an unofficial population of 150,037 residents. A significant part of this story can be explained by the burgeoning national debate over the slavery question and the associated need to create new states in free territory to counter the political weight of what some called the "slave power conspiracy" that dominated antebellum political affairs. One must also consider the detrimental effect that such an intense period of migration had on Indian-white relations in the Minnesota Territory.

By the late 1850s this expansion was more than the Santee Sioux were willing to tolerate, and a resistance movement developed among a tribal band under the leadership of Inkpaduta ("Red Feather"). Enraged by encroaching white settlement near Lake Okoboji and Spirit Lake, Inkpaduta and his followers carried out the Spirit Lake Massacre (1857) through a series of attacks upon white squatters who had claimed areas of Santee territory.

The unrest continued even after Minnesota became a state on May 11, 1858. As the attention of the United States focused on the crisis of secession and civil war in the early 1860s, dissident elements of the Santee Sioux led by Little Crow rose in rebellion in the Sioux Uprising of 1862. So intense was the fighting in Minnesota that some within the federal government imagined that the conflict might have been fomented by Confederate sympathizers in order to draw the Union's attention and resources away from the Southern battlefields of the Civil War.

The suppression of this conflict would take a heavy toll on relations between the United States and not only the Sioux but also various other tribes of the Plains. In December 1862, thirty-eight Santee Sioux were hanged at Mankato by U.S. forces—the largest single-day execution toll in the entire history of the United States. Although Abraham Lincoln had commuted the death sentences of more than two hundred other warriors who had been captured, that act did not diminish the hatred that many Sioux had for the United States. In 1863 the United States broke all treaties that it had with the Santee Sioux and ordered the removal of the tribe to points in present-day South Dakota and Nebraska.

—Junius P. Rodriguez

See also

Mesabi Range; Ojibwa; Portage des Sioux, Treaty of; Santee Sioux; Snelling, Fort

For Further Reading

Blegen, Theodore C. 1975. *Minnesota: A History of the State.* Minneapolis: University of Minnesota Press; Giraud, Marcel. 1986. *The Metis in the Canadian West.* Lincoln: University of Nebraska Press.

MISSISSIPPI RIVER

Often called the "Father of Waters," the Mississippi River was discovered by Europeans in 1541 in the person of Spanish explorer Hernando De Soto. This North American river measures some 2,470 miles from its headwaters to mouth, and drains 1,257,000 square miles, nearly the entirety of land between the Appalachian and Rocky Mountains.

The city that commanded the Mississippi watershed is New Orleans—located about 105 miles northwest from the mouth of the river and surrounded by swamps, marshes, shallow lakes, and bayous. The river became the primary artery that connected New Orleans, Louisiana, and the interior of North America to the outside world. Moreover, in a very short time, the river had become essential to the growth and development of the fledgling United States.

With the ratification of the Treaty of Paris (1783), concluding the American Revolution, the river became the western boundary of the United States; Spain controlled lands south of the thirty-first parallel, the city of New Orleans, and land west of the Mississippi River. Britain, however, agreed to share with the United States the right to navigate the Mississippi River to its mouth, even though the lower portion of the river was entirely in Spanish territory. By March 1784 the Spanish, fearing growing settlements in Kentucky and Tennessee that used the Mississippi River system for transportation and communication, closed the river to U.S. commerce, which only intensified relations between the two countries. The following year the Spanish government sent Don Diego Gardoqui to negotiate with the U.S. secretary of foreign affairs John Jay and to settle the issues concerning the Mississippi River and the southern U.S. boundary. These negotiations solved nothing, and the issue remained unsettled until 1795. The U.S. finally gained full navigation rights to the Mississippi with the ratification of Pinckney's Treaty (the Treaty of San Lorenzo) with Spain in 1795. The Mississippi question appeared to be settled.

On October 16, 1802, the Spanish intendant at New Orleans—Juan Ventura Morales—acting under royal orders closed the river to all American commerce, blatantly violating the Pinckney Treaty and reopening the Mississippi question. This aggressive action prompted President Thomas Jefferson to send James Monroe to negotiate with both France and Spain to settle the issue. Anticipating that Monroe's mission might fail, Jefferson also prepared for war with Spain by asking Congress in early 1803 to begin constructing a naval flotilla that could be used on the inland rivers, including the Mississippi. The difficulties with Spain were short-lived, and by the spring of 1803, King Charles IV had disavowed Morales's act; the Spanish monarch renewed the right of deposit, thereby opening the river again to American commerce. Throughout this episode Jefferson took steps to ensure that the river would never again be closed. Monroe and Robert R. Livingston, minister to France, negotiated with François Marquis de Barbé-Marbois, French minister of finance, for the purchase of the Louisiana territory west of the Mississippi River. The subsequent purchase ensured U.S. control over this vital lifeline and thereby brought an end to the Mississippi saga. Moreover, the entire Mississippi River episode vividly demonstrated that Jefferson and the Republican Party strongly supported westward growth and expansion and understood that the river was essential to this development.

Even though the Louisiana Purchase seemed to have settled the Mississippi question, the river continued to play an important role in the daily lives of Western settlers as well as in the strategic vision of several different national governments, becoming an international concern during the latter stages of the War of 1812. In December 1814, British forces approached New Orleans, not directly by the river but rather via Lake Borgne, to the east of the city. After defeating the small U.S. gunboat flotilla stationed on Lake Borgne, British troops proceeded via Bayou Bienvenue to the eastern bank of the Mississippi River, some nine miles south of New Orleans. Master Commandant Daniel Todd Patterson, who commanded the New Orleans naval station, used the converted merchant sloop *Louisiana* and schooner *Carolina* in the Mississippi to cover British land attacks along the river, and prepared gunboats and fireships to discourage an assault via the river. Patterson's riverine operations supported General Andrew Jackson's position at the Rodriguez Canal and ultimately forced the English to funnel their forces along a narrow strip of land on the east bank that ran north toward the city. Jackson strengthened his defenses accordingly, placing the British at a severe disadvantage when they attacked on January 8, 1815.

The resultant Battle of New Orleans, which was a British disaster, demonstrated the unquestioned importance of the Mississippi River. Yet had the British won on the Plains of Chalmette, the circumstances could have been considerably different. British officers knew of the great quantities of cotton that had been stored in the city during the British blockade of the Mississippi River, and the possibilities for looting provided a strong incentive for the attack. Furthermore, the British government did not recognize the legality of the Louisiana Purchase. As such, had the British won the battle, the Louisiana Territory most likely would have been returned to Spain or kept by Britain; such a prospect would have prohibited, certainly for a time, future U.S. expansion and reopened the question over the Mississippi River.

The end of the War of 1812 and the corresponding postwar economic boom brought renewed prosperity and expansion. Moreover, the new economic growth, much of it based on cotton shipped from Mississippi River ports, greatly benefited the growing Southern states as well as the United States.

—Gene A. Smith

See also
Jay-Gardoqui Negotiations

For Further Reading

DeConde, Alexander. 1976. *This Affair of Louisiana*. New York: Scribner; Latour, Arsène Lacarrière. 1999 [1816]. *Historical Memoir of the War in West Florida and Louisiana in 1814–15: With an Atlas*. Edited by Gene A. Smith. Gainesville: Historic New Orleans Collection and the University Press of Florida; Owsley, Frank L., Jr. 1981. *Struggle for the Gulf Borderlands: The Creek War and the Battle of New Orleans, 1812–1815*. Gainesville: University Press of Florida; Stoddard, Amos. 1812. *Sketches, Historical and Descriptive, of Louisiana*. Philadelphia: Mathew Carey.

MISSOURI

Once the Louisiana Purchase territory had been turned over to the United States from French authorities in official ceremonies at New Orleans and St. Louis, the U.S. government began the process of administering and governing the vast territory. For administrative purposes, the region was divided into two territories: the Territory of Orleans and the Louisiana Territory. The Territory of Orleans corresponded roughly with the boundaries of the present-day state of Louisiana. The Louisiana Territory initially encompassed everything else that remained of the Louisiana Purchase lands above the line of 33 degrees north latitude.

The region that would eventually form the state of Missouri played a central role in the history of the Louisiana Purchase. Captain Amos Stoddard accepted the upper portion of the Louisiana Territory from the French in cession ceremonies held on May 10, 1804, at St. Louis. Just a few days later, the same location served as the departure point for Lewis and Clark and their Corps of Discovery as they began an expedition that would traverse the Missouri River Valley and take the explorers all the way to the Pacific Ocean.

Upon his return from the West in 1806, Meriwether Lewis was appointed second governor of the Louisiana Territory, but his administrative record in this position was rather poor. Lewis had tried to administer the territory as an absentee governor while he completed work on the official journals of his expedition in Washington, but that strategy did not work well. He also had a poor working relationship with the territorial secretary, and many political squabbles resulted. Lewis died in 1809 as he was traveling to the nation's capital to defend his controversial tenure as governor of the Louisiana Territory.

William Clark, coleader of the Lewis and Clark Expedition, was named governor of the Louisiana Territory in 1810, and he administered the Missouri Territory from St. Louis until the time of statehood in 1821. After the Territory of Orleans was admitted to the Union in 1812, using the name Louisiana, a portion of the old Louisiana Territory became known as the Missouri Territory. When a territorial legislature met for that newly defined region on October 1, 1812, there were delegates in attendance from the five original counties: Cape Girardeau, New Madrid, St. Charles, St. Louis, and Ste. Genevieve.

Much of the core region that became the Missouri Territory consisted of communities settled by the French in the mid-eighteenth century. Ste. Genevieve, the oldest settlement in the region, became a center of the early fur trade and also capitalized upon mining the abundant lead deposits in the region. Once it was established in 1764, the town of St. Louis was perfectly situated to become an interior way-station and outfitting and departure point for those individuals and companies willing to do business in the trans-Mississippi West. Located at the point where the Missouri River and the Mississippi River meet, St. Louis would eventually compete through much of the nineteenth century (with rival upstart Chicago), to be the commercial equivalent of New York City in the American interior.

Named in honor of the canonized French monarch Louis IX, St. Louis had a decidedly French atmosphere, as reflected by both its population and its early architecture. The outpost also faced the challenge of being a remote frontier village. From time to time the community was threatened by the Osage and the Sioux, who lived only a short journey upstream. Yet it was the maintenance of peace with the Western tribes, and the successful conclusion of commercial relationships with them, that would set St. Louis apart from other frontier towns. The town quickly grew into a commercial hub, making the transition to Spanish rule in 1770 and U.S. control in 1804.

Shortly after the Lewis and Clark Expedition ended in 1806, merchants in and around St. Louis became interested in forming large commercial enterprises that could harvest animal pelts from the Missouri River hinterland. Several notable businessmen, including Manuel Lisa, Rene Auguste Chouteau, and Pierre Chouteau, had formed the Missouri Fur Company by 1809. In time, the success of this company would lead to the establishment of many competitors, and those firms selected St. Louis as the center for their business operations.

In 1808 the U.S. Army established Fort Osage along the Missouri River, just west of St. Louis. The outpost was established for several reasons. Residents of St. Louis and other river towns wanted to make sure that hostilities with tribes like the Osage or Sioux would not threaten the communities that had been settled in the Missouri region. Additionally, the presence of the military along the frontier could keep the peace among Western tribes, which would greatly facilitate the development of the fur trade among these groups. A third factor that reflects the typical pattern of frontier settlement took place when the peace treaties that were arranged at Fort Osage and elsewhere led to the "opening" of vast tracts to white settlement.

A historic event of unparalleled proportions literally

shook the Missouri Territory during the winter of 1811–1812. The shifting of geological plates deep within the earth on the New Madrid Fault line resulted in a series of earthquakes that caused great damage and changed the landscape of some river communities. The force of the New Madrid earthquakes was reported as having caused the Mississippi River to flow upstream for a time, and the river actually changed its course in a few locations as the stream migrated, leaving the telltale oxbow lakes as silent indicators of its earlier channel.

During the second decade of the nineteenth century, it was clear that a farming frontier was being established in the northern half of the Missouri Territory in the fertile bottomland of the Missouri River Valley. Even the legendary frontiersman Daniel Boone was attracted by the quality of land available to those who were willing to relocate. Many pioneer settlers, some coming from as far away as Virginia and many from Kentucky, began to acquire homesteads on which they farmed—often with the use of slave labor. This pattern and the controversy that it would engender played a large role in the debates over Missouri's eventual quest for statehood.

When the Missouri Territory sought admission to the Union as a slave state on February 13, 1819, the action was challenged by New York representative James Tallmadge, Jr. Tallmadge proposed that two antislavery amendments be attached to the bill proposing Missouri statehood. The first would have prevented the further importation of slaves into Missouri, and the second would have emancipated all children born to slaves in Missouri, after its admission as a state, to be free at the age of twenty-five. Although the House of Representatives approved both of these amendments, the Senate defeated them. Nonetheless, from this point forward, it was clear that the admission of Missouri into the Union would be mired in controversy.

The question of Missouri statehood was eventually settled by the Missouri Compromise (1820), a political arrangement engineered by Henry Clay of Kentucky. According to Clay's compromise, the admission of Missouri was paired with the admission of Maine, so that there would be an equal number of slave states and free states. It was further agreed that, with the exception of Missouri, slavery would be prohibited north of 36 degrees 30 minutes north latitude.

Despite the political compromise, the path to Missouri statehood would still face an uncertain future. When the territorial legislature drafted a constitution for the proposed state of Missouri, the document included a discriminatory prohibition keeping mulattoes and free blacks from entering the future state. This controversial provision presented problems when the Congress reviewed the proposed constitution on November 14, 1820.

On March 2, 1821, Clay negotiated a last-minute caveat to the Missouri Compromise agreement as the Congress balked at discriminatory provisions in the proposed constitution. The Congress voted to approve statehood for Missouri provided that state officials did not attempt to limit the rights of citizens, especially free black citizens, as guaranteed by the U.S. Constitution. On June 26, 1821, the Missouri legislature approved this stipulation, and on August 10, 1821, Missouri entered the Union as the twenty-fourth state.

—Junius P. Rodriguez

See also

Chouteau, René Auguste; Clark, William; Missouri Compromise; New Madrid Earthquakes; Saint Genevieve; Saint Louis

For Further Reading

Foley, William E. 1989. *The Genesis of Missouri: From Wilderness Outpost to Statehood.* Columbia: University of Missouri Press; Houck, Louis. 1908. *History of Missouri from the Earliest Explorations and Settlements until the Admission of the State into the Union.* Chicago: R. R. Donnelley & Sons; Nasatir, A. P. 1990 [1952]. *Before Lewis and Clark: Documents Illustrating the History of Missouri, 1785–1804.* Lincoln: University of Nebraska Press.

MISSOURI COMPROMISE (1820)

During the particularly contentious era of 1819–1821, when the Missouri Territory sought the status of statehood, the U.S. Congress wrestled with the divisive issue of whether slavery would be permitted in states carved out of the Louisiana Purchase territory. The series of legislative measures enacted to remedy this situation and preclude further debate on the expansion of slavery became known as the Missouri Compromise (1820). The agreements reached in this compromise would be effectively overturned by passage of the Kansas-Nebraska Act (1854), and portions of the measure would be nullified by the U.S. Supreme Court's decision in *Dred Scott v. Sandford* (1857).

On January 26, 1819, Congress considered a measure to create the Arkansas Territory out of Arkansas County in the Missouri Territory. This action was approved, but not before the Congress had to defeat an amendment, proposed by New York representative John W. Taylor, that would have prohibited slavery from the Arkansas Territory. Nearly two weeks later, when the Missouri Territory sought admission to the Union as a slave state on February 13, 1819, the action was challenged by New York representative James Tallmadge, Jr. Tallmadge proposed that two antislavery amendments be attached to the bill proposing Missouri statehood. The first would have prevented the further importation of slaves into Missouri, and the second would have emancipated all children born to slaves in Missouri, after its admission as a state, to be free at the age of twenty-five. Although the House of Representatives approved both of these amendments, the Senate defeated them. Nonetheless, from this point forward, it was clear that the admission of Missouri into the Union would be mired in controversy.

The question of statehood for Missouri languished for an entire year as the Congress debated the merits of slave or free status for the region, should it be admitted as a state. On February 17, 1820, the U.S. Senate passed the measure that became known as the Missouri Compromise. In this legislation it was understood that Missouri would enter the Union as a slave state and Maine would enter as a free state, thus maintaining the delicate balance of votes that existed in the Senate chamber. Senator Jesse B. Thomas of Illinois introduced an amendment to this measure calling for the prohibition of slavery in those areas within the Louisiana Territory that lay above the line of 36 degrees 30 minutes north latitude. The measure passed as amended in the Senate.

The House of Representatives defeated the Senate version of the Missouri Compromise legislation on February 28. Members of the House attempted to pass a modified version of the bill that included the controversial Taylor Amendment, which would have barred slavery from any of the Western territories. (Taylor had first introduced this measure on January 26, 1819, but the proposal had been defeated at that time.)

By March 3, after effective cajoling by Speaker of the House Henry Clay, Congress agreed to the Missouri Compromise. Missouri entered the Union as a slave state and Maine as a free state, and slavery was prohibited from territories north of 36 degrees 30 minutes north latitude. (In developing the Missouri Compromise, the Thomas Amendment had been incorporated and the Taylor Amendment had been rejected.)

Despite Clay's success in getting the Congress to accept the compromise, the path to Missouri statehood would still face an uncertain future. The Missouri Territory drafted a constitution for the proposed state of Missouri, but the document included a discriminatory prohibition keeping mulattoes and free blacks from entering the future state. This controversial provision presented problems when the Congress reviewed the proposed constitution on November 14, 1820.

Finally, on March 2, 1821, Speaker of the House Henry Clay negotiated a last-minute caveat to the Missouri Compromise agreement. The Congress voted to approve statehood for Missouri provided that state officials did not attempt to limit the rights of citizens, especially free black citizens, as guaranteed by the U.S. Constitution. On June 26, 1821, the Missouri legislature approved of this stipulation.

On August 10, 1821, Missouri entered the Union as a slave state. At that point the United States consisted of twenty-four states that were evenly divided, with twelve free and twelve slave states. Despite the apparent solution to the question, the issue of permitting slavery to expand with the admission of new states was one that would continue to plague the nation up to the time of the Civil War. In 1820 the aged Thomas Jefferson, realizing the danger posed by the slavery controversy, described it as "a firebell in the night" that warned of potentially ominous times ahead in the life of the young nation (Moore, 1953).

—Junius P. Rodriguez

See also
Kansas-Nebraska Act; Missouri; 36 Degrees 30 Minutes North Latitude

For Further Reading
Moore, Glover. 1953. *The Missouri Controversy, 1819–1821.* Lexington: University of Kentucky Press.

MISSOURI FUR COMPANY (1809–1820)

The St. Louis Fur Company, better known as the Missouri Fur Company, was an early American attempt to capitalize on the reports returned by Merriwether Lewis and William Clark's Corps of Discovery, 1804–1806, on the large amounts of beaver in the Rocky Mountains. Formed in 1809 by Manuel Lisa, Andrew Henry, Pierre Chouteau, and William Clark, the company was the second substantial U.S. fur trading business to capitalize on the natural richness of the Louisiana Purchase. The Missouri Fur Company was founded only shortly after the organization of John Jacob Astor and Andrew Dripps's American Fur Company in 1808. Other competitors were the British Hudson's Bay Company and North West Company, which together gave Britain dominance of the Columbia River, northern Canada, and the Oregon Territory. Together, these companies competed for the beaver pelts that dominated men's fashion in the form of their top hats. Closer to midcentury silk became more popular for men's hats, and, by the time of America's great westward movement in the 1840s, the work of fur trading companies such as the Missouri Fur Company had trapped the beaver, once reported as so rich, to the point of extinction. At the founding of the Missouri Fur Company, St. Louis was the hub of the western fur trade and provided the home base for the company.

A leading mountain man of the company was John Colter. Having crossed the continent twice by 1806 as a member of the Corps of Discovery, Colter wanted to stay out West on Lewis and Clark's return voyage. He became the first white to see the geysers and springs of Yellowstone, and, in 1807, he joined Lisa on an expedition to the Rocky Mountains. George Drouillard, another member of the Corps of Discovery, also worked for Lisa. Colter and Drouillard are generally recognized as the first two mountain men. As a result of Lisa's trips up the Missouri River to the Rocky Mountains for beaver and trade with the Indians, people came to know him as the "Fur King." Lisa became established enough to help form the St. Louis Missouri Fur Company, capitalized with $40,000, which enjoyed good relations with the Indians.

A New Orleans–born Spaniard, Lisa settled in St. Louis in 1790. Before the Louisiana Purchase, he benefited from his Spanish heritage because Spanish officials in St. Louis gave him licenses to trade with the West. He became the first trapper to trade with the Osage and the driving force behind the Missouri Fur Company. He made the company move fast to establish forts and compete with Astor. As early as 1811, the company's trappers gave pursuit to an Astor expedition to Oregon, which Astor hoped would establish his Pacific Fur Company. Finally, Lisa's party overtook them. On this trip, the company established Fort Lisa at Point Lisa near Council Bluffs and Fort Manuel. Earlier, Colter and Lisa had established Fort Raymond (1807) in present-day Wyoming. Lisa's jealousy and rivalry with Astor showed his aggressive nature. Because of that nature other entrepreneurs did not like Lisa very much, and this was damaging for the Missouri Fur Company.

Despite the pioneering work done by the Missouri Fur Company, it saw little profit, and its owners dissolved it during the period of the War of 1812, when the American fur trade hit a dormant period. Shortly thereafter, William Ashley and Andrew Henry formed the more romantic and longer-lasting Rocky Mountain Fur Company, which was originally the Ashley-Henry Company. As Henry suggests with his later joint venture, the leading members of the Missouri Fur Company were more successful individually than collectively. With Merriwether Lewis, William Clark was a leader of the expedition exploring the Louisiana Purchase. Manuel Lisa was an early leader in white-Indian relations and assembled a boat crew for Lewis and Clark before their voyage of expedition. Pierre Chouteau was a member of the Chouteau family, whose members included his half-brother, René Auguste Chouteau, and stepfather, Pierre Laclède Liguest, founders of St. Louis as a fur-trading site in 1764. Pierre also brought the fur trade and the first permanent white settlement to Oklahoma.

—Christopher C. Strangeman

See also

Clark, William; Colter, John; Lisa, Manuel; Missouri; Saint Louis

For Further Reading

Burton, Harris. 1952. *John Colter, His Years in the Rockies.* New York: Scribner; Missouri Fur Company. 1812. *Articles of Association of the Missouri Fur Company.* St. Louis: n.p.; Oglesbey, Richard Edward. 1963. *Manuel Lisa and the Opening of the Missouri Fur Trade.* Norman: University of Oklahoma Press.

MONROE, JAMES (1758–1831)

The envoy-extraordinary to France during the negotiations for the Louisiana Purchase (January–May 1803) and fifth president of the United States, James Monroe was born in Virginia of a modest planting family in April 1758. He entered William and Mary College in 1774 but left his studies to fight in the American Revolution. Badly wounded at Trenton (1776), he achieved the rank of colonel in 1777. Dissatisfied with staff rank, he resigned his commission in 1778 and returned to Virginia to serve in the Virginia Line and study law under Thomas Jefferson, thus beginning a lifelong friendship.

Elected to the Virginia House of Delegates in 1782, Monroe later served in the Confederation Congress (1783–1786), taking a leading role in the opposition to the Jay-Gardoqui proposals that, in return for Spanish trade concessions, would have closed the Mississippi River to American commerce. He compounded his popularity in the West by helping to draft the terms of the Northwest Ordinance (1787). Following service in the Senate, he was appointed by the Washington administration as resident minister to France in 1794. His pro-French agenda, however, led to his recall in 1796, and, following a term as governor of Virginia (1799–1802), he returned to private life and his law practice in Virginia.

Somewhat surprised to be informed by President Jefferson in January 1803 that he had been named and confirmed as envoy-extraordinary to France, Monroe accepted the position after Jefferson had appealed to his sense of public duty. Following the closure of New Orleans to American commerce by Spain as a preliminary to the retrocession of Louisiana to France, both Jefferson and Secretary of State James Madison had become dissatisfied with the progress that Robert R. Livingston (1746–1818), the resident minister in France, had made in either establishing permanent trading rights at New Orleans or, at least, securing another site on the Gulf Coast as an American port of deposit. To counter increasing Western concerns and Federalist demands that New Orleans be seized, Monroe's appointment had emerged as something of a party political maneuver. However, he was dispatched to France with very specific instructions to purchase both New Orleans and West Florida and, if failing that, to proceed to London and seek an alliance with the Addington administration. Arriving to some local public acclaim at Le Havre on April 8, 1803, he arrived in Paris, where news of his instructions had proceeded him, on April 11, 1803.

Monroe's actual role in securing the Louisiana Purchase remains somewhat inconclusive: his appointment was resented by Livingston, and their mutual hostility has tended to generate partisanship among historians. It remains a matter of interpretation as to whether Monroe attempted to garnish all the credit for himself to further his political ambitions or whether Livingston later tampered with the evidence to magnify his own importance in the negotiations. It certainly is true, however, that Charles Maurice de Talleyrand-Perigord, the French foreign minister, did offer Livingston the purchase of the whole of Louisiana on April 10, before Monroe's arrival in Paris. However, whether he was authorized to do so remains a moot point. After his decision to sell Louisiana, Napoleon had appointed the finance minister, François, Marquis de Barbé-Marbois, to handle the negotiations after April 10. Although Barbé-Marbois repeated the offer to Livingston on the evening of April 13, from April 14, 1803, he treated both Monroe and Livingston as joint-equal envoys. Indeed, Monroe's arrival with new, forceful instructions may have acted as the necessary catalytic agent that helped make up Napoleon's mind to sell Louisiana, an action he hoped would perhaps forestall an Anglo-U.S. alliance.

Both envoys quickly decided to ignore their instructions and negotiate the sale of the whole province. These negotiations were begun in earnest on April 24, and after some haggling about price, terms were finally agreed upon and the treaty of cession signed on May 2, 1803, though dated April 30, 1803. Unlike Livingston, Monroe remained concerned regarding the boundaries of the purchase, especially regarding the question as to whether West Florida was included in the cession. Such questions would plague Spanish-U.S. diplomacy for the next sixteen years.

In July 1803, Monroe proceeded to London where he served as resident minister until 1807. Following continued disorder on the new Spanish-U.S. borders, he traveled to Madrid in January 1805, to try to persuade the Spanish to accept both the legality of the Louisiana Purchase and secure the transfer of West Florida to the United States. His negotiations with Pedro de Cevallos, the Spanish foreign minister, proved fruitless, and he returned to London in May 1805. Monroe was bitterly disappointed that his Anglo-U.S. treaty of 1806, which he had negotiated together with William Pinckney, was rejected by Jefferson. Although it removed some of Britain's restrictive trade practices against the United States, it had made no mention of ending the British impressment of U.S. seamen. Monroe blamed the failure to ratify the treaty on Madison, and, offended, he refused the administration's offer of the position of governor of Louisiana, a position he would again refuse in 1809. Jefferson finally managed to engineer a reconciliation between his two friends, and in May 1811, Monroe accepted the position of secretary of state in Madison's cabinet. Monroe fully supported Madison's wish for war against Britain in July 1812, and proving to be an able, trusted political ally to Madison, he succeeded him as president in 1816.

During Monroe's first administration, Spain's continued decline in the Americas once more focused his attention toward the boundaries of the Louisiana Purchase. Madison, by seizing a coastal strip of West Florida below the thirty-first parallel (October 1810) had helped destabilize Spain's grip on the Floridas, a process accelerated during the War of 1812. Continued frontier disorder promoted Andrew Jackson's invasion of the Floridian panhandle in 1818. Authorized by Monroe or not, it highlighted Spain's tenuous hold on the province, and Monroe, by refusing to censure Jackson, forced Spain to negotiate with the United States regarding the future of Florida. The negotiations between John Quincy Adams, Monroe's secretary of state, and Luis de Onís y Gonzales, Spain's resident minister, resulted in the Adams-Onís Treaty (1819), which not only ceded Florida to the United States but also regulated a western boundary line for the Louisiana Purchase northward to the forty-second parallel, and hence west to the Pacific coast. If the Louisiana Purchase had made Monroe a national figure, his administration's solution to a border problem that had bedeviled the republic for sixteen years delighted the nation.

Reelected in 1820, Monroe left the White House after the bitter election of 1824, to return to his estate at Oak Hill in Loudoun County, Virginia. Public service had left him in serious debt and in increasing ill health after 1827. He died on July 4, 1831, at his daughter's house in New York City. Originally buried in New York, he was reinterred in Richmond, Virginia, in 1858.

—*Rory T. Cornish*

See also
Jefferson, Thomas; Livingston, Robert R.

MONTANA

Montana is bordered by Canada to the north and Wyoming to the south. The Bitterroot Mountains divide the western reaches of Montana from Idaho, while North Dakota lies to the east. The fourth largest U.S. state boasts 147,138 square miles of rich and varied terrain. Dominated by the Rocky Mountains and the Bitterroot Range, western Montana is a spectacular landscape of rugged peaks and glacial lakes. Undulating plains and the tributaries of the Missouri River mark the eastern climes. Montana is noted for its climatic extremes. At Glendive in 1893 and Medicine Lake in 1937, temperatures rose to 117 degrees Fahrenheit, while in 1954, thermometers plummeted to minus 70 degrees Fahrenheit at Rogers Pass.

Paleo-Indians settled in Montana more than thirteen thousand years ago. Having migrated from Asia to North America using the Bering Strait land-bridge, prehistoric tribes typically traveled south along the Rocky Mountains, before dispersing across the continent. Paleo-Indian communities foraged the valleys of the Rockies for plants, and wandered onto the plains to hunt mammoth and bison. Kalispel, Salish, and Kutenai Tribes later ranged over a similar territory. In the 1600s and 1700s, Native Americans residing in eastern North America migrated west in response to European conquest. The Crow, Assiniboine, Blackfeet, and Gros Ventre crossed into eastern Montana, where they developed a distinctive Plains culture based upon bison hunting and horse trading. The Kutenai, Kalispel, and Salish retreated into westerly mountains.

In search of the elusive Northwest Passage linking Atlantic and Pacific waters, Europeans traveled westward during the late 1600s. Following an expedition led by French explorer Robert Cavelier de La Salle along the Mississippi River in 1682, France claimed eastern stretches of Montana as part of its Louisiana territory. British trappers employed by the Hudson's Bay Company and Montreal traders from the North West Company explored the drainage basins of the Missouri and Columbia Rivers in the late 1700s. With the purchase of Louisiana by the United States in 1803, eastern Montana passed into U.S. ownership. Hoping to circumscribe British claims to Oregon Country, President Thomas Jefferson instructed Lewis and Clark to survey Western lands carefully. On their journey through Montana, the intrepid explorers encountered formidable escarpments and rolling grasslands. Lewis and Clark named unfamiliar species of flora and fauna, while charting watercourses and mountain passes. Their journals provided Euro-Americans with the first detailed, written account of the region.

The pronouncement by Meriwether Lewis that the headwaters of the Missouri River were "richer in beaver and otter than any country on earth" inspired American fur trappers to journey to Montana. Manuel Lisa, a magnate from St. Louis, led a party of trappers up the Missouri in 1807, establishing Fort Raymond trading post at the confluence of the Bighorn and Yellowstone Rivers. John Colter, a veteran of the Lewis and Clark Expedition, also made extensive forays in the region. During the winter of 1807–1808, Colter explored the geyser basins of present-day Yellowstone National Park. Backed by Eastern capital, John Jacob Astor's American Fur Company constructed a line of forts along the upper Missouri River. American trappers expanded their operations into the Rocky Mountains, searching for beaver ponds in montane valleys. Furs were shipped via St. Louis to cities on the East Coast and abroad, tying developments in Montana to a global mercantile economy. The fur trade encouraged Americans to venture westward in search of profit. Travelers benefited from trails blazed by trapping parties. In the drive to harness Western resources, local Native American cultures were corrupted and the environment despoiled.

On their way from mines in Colorado to the goldfields of Idaho, John White and his compatriots discovered gold at Grasshopper Creek in western Montana in 1862. By the end of the summer, more than four hundred prospectors had set up camp. The haphazard mining community became Bannack City, the first of many boom towns to adorn Montana during the mineral rush era. Ramshackle abodes mushroomed around major gold strikes at Alder Gulch (1863), Last Chance Gulch (1864), and Confederate Gulch (1864). Gold-seekers panned streams and dug out shallow deposits, in a method known as placer mining. By the mid-1860s, most shallow seams had been exploited. Large corporations moved in with machinery capable of reaching deep quartz deposits. While local entrepreneurs Samuel Hauser and William A. Clark successfully tapped Montana's mineral resources, most mining operations were financed by East Coast or overseas investors.

The discovery of rich copper seams in Butte during the late 1870s spurred another mineral boom. Butte became known as "the richest hill on earth," with its "copper kings" dominating economic and political life in the region. The lure of precious metals attracted skilled Cornish miners to Montana, along with Yankees, African Americans, Chinese, and Irish. Although a number of women found employment in stores, boarding houses, saloons, and brothels, men dominated civic life. Little heed was paid to the social or environmental consequences of the Montanan mining boon. Hillsides were eroded, forests cut down, and streams polluted. Mining settlements suffered from poor sanitation, pungent fumes, and outbreaks of fire. According to Sarah Herndon, the mining town of Virginia City was marked by "great deep holes and high heaps of dirt" (Herndon, 1902).

Before becoming a territory in 1864, the region of Montana fell under various frontier dominions. Eastern Montana was allied to Indian Territory (up to 1805), Louisiana Territory (1805–1812), Missouri Territory (1812–1821), Indian Country (1821–1854), Nebraska Territory (1854–1861), and Dakota Territory (1861–1863). Lands west of the Rockies were part of Oregon Country (up to 1846), Oregon Territory (1848–1853), and Washington Territory (1853–1863). Hoping to oversee the escalation of mining activities in Western climes, members of Congress created Idaho Territory in 1863, encompassing the whole of present-day Idaho and Montana, and parts of Wyoming. However, the region proved too large to be administered effectively, and a second territory was inaugurated on May 26, 1864. Mining magnate Granville Stuart suggested that the new territory be called "To yabe-Shock up," meaning "mountainous country" in Shoshone. Legislators nevertheless chose "Montana," the Spanish word for mountains. Sidney Edgerton was elected first governor of Montana. Progress in territorial affairs proved slow, with Democrats and Republicans embroiled in broad debates concerning Unionism and slavery. Over a period of six years, the governorship of Montana changed hands several times. With the appointment of moderate Republican Benjamin Potts, regional politics gained a degree of stability. However, choosing a territorial capital remained contentious. The honor fell first to Bannack, then to Virginia City. Following a series of dubious elections, Helena was named the capital of Montana in 1875.

During the 1830s and 1840s, a few enterprising cattlemen ran herds close to fur trading posts. In 1850, Richard Grant, a former Hudson's Bay Company trapper, procured footsore cattle from Oregon-bound travelers near Fort Bridger. Grant drove the cattle north to rich Montana pastures for the winter, before selling them back to overlanders in the spring. Demand for beef rocketed during the mining era. Ranchers were drawn to the western valleys of Montana to supply mining camps with meat. William Orr and Philip Poindexter completed a drive from California to Montana in 1865, registering the first brand under the Square and Compass mark. The following year, Nelson Story drove the first longhorns to Montana from Texas. The cattle industry branched out onto the eastern plains during the 1870s. Montanan cattlemen embarked upon long drives, herding steers north to Canada and east to railheads. The Whoop-Up Trail became a bustling route used by ranchers to supply Albertan forts occupied by the Northwest Mounted Police. Aided by the westward progress of railroads in the early 1880s, Montanan livestock-raisers found ready markets in Eastern cities. By 1886, 664,000 head of cattle roamed the grasslands of Montana. However, overgrazing, depressed prices, and a severe winter in 1886–1887 decimated the ranching industry. The boom in homesteading after 1900 secured the end of the open range.

The demands of modern Americans for fresh soil and mineral resources led to constant reductions in Native American land holdings across Montana. Fervent desires for pastures, gold deposits, and agricultural spoils within Native territories accelerated the subjugation of Blackfoot, Crow, and Flathead Tribes. The *Montana Post,* the first newspaper in the territory, espoused a stereotypical view of Native Americans as corrupt and warlike inferiors, undeserving of legal protection. Treaties were renegotiated and local tribes hastened onto reservations. General Philip Sheridan applauded the decimation of bison herds as a way of breaking the resolve of Plains Indians, while idealizing a prairie home for "speckled cattle" and the "festive cowboy." The economic development of Montana fueled stately aspirations. From the 1860s onward Montanans clamored for statehood, in the hope of acquiring attendant voting and taxation privileges. Constitutional conventions in 1866 and 1884 made little headway, but the third convention, held on July 4, 1889, successfully drafted a legislative edict. The document was duly ratified by Congress, and Montana gained statehood on November 8, 1889. Joseph K. Toole became the first senator of Montana, and the forty-first state took the motto "Oro y Plata," with the insignia of a plow alongside a miner's pick and shovel.

—*Karen Jones*

For Further Reading

Herndon, Sarah. 1902. *Days on the Road: Crossing the Plains in 1865.* New York: Burr; Malone, Michael P., Richard B. Roeder, and William L. Lang. 1991. *Montana: A History of Two Centuries.* Seattle and London: University of Washington Press; Spence, Clark C. 1975. *Territorial Politics and Government in Montana, 1864–89.* Urbana: University of Illinois Press; Spence, Clark C. 1978. *Montana: A Bicentennial History.* New York: W. W. Norton.

MORALES, JUAN VENTURA

Juan Ventura Morales held numerous offices under the Spanish government of Louisiana. In 1791 he was selected as one of two *alcaldes ordinarios* by the voting members of the New Orleans Cabildo. As such, he held court over many of the simple judicial problems of the colony.

From 1796 to 1799, Morales served as intendant, the representative of the royal treasury, with jurisdiction over matters of justice and commerce. The position of intendant was especially important in Louisiana, which was dependent on subsidies from Madrid.

During his first term as intendant, Morales became involved in two controversial actions. The first concerned the creation of an American deposit at the port of New Orleans. The Treaty of Paris (1783) had given the right of navigation on the Mississippi River to the United States, but Spain refused Western farmers access to the port. Acquisition of a duty-free deposit for U.S. products became the goal of Western settlers. In 1795, Thomas Pinckney signed the Treaty of San Lorenzo for the United States, which granted the use of New Orleans as a place of deposit. Despite the treaty, no deposit was granted until 1798, when Spain went to war with Great Britain. On April 12, Intendant Morales issued regulations allowing American goods in transit to enter and leave New Orleans duty free. The American products could not, however, be legally sold in New Orleans. Immediately upon entry they had to be placed in storage and could be withdrawn only for re-export.

After the opening of the deposit, New Orleans merchant Daniel Clark petitioned Morales to allow U.S. ships to carry Louisiana products as well as U.S. goods from the deposit. Clark requested that the Louisiana merchandise bear the same duty in U.S. ships as in Spanish ships. Morales agreed, and he went even further in his June decree. To compensate Spanish shippers for the opening of the American deposit, export duty on Louisiana products shipped up the Mississippi River was ended. At this point, little produce moved upriver, but Morales believed that one day New Orleans would supply the entire Mississippi River Valley. The Spanish court tried to rescind Morales's order, but protests from the merchant community convinced Morales to continue the concessions.

The second controversy of Morales's first term as intendant involved land grants. In 1799 the Spanish colonial office decided that the intendant would share the governor's authority over the land office. Morales announced that the new regulation gave the intendant sole authority over land grants. The Spanish governor and the New Orleans Cabildo refused to acquiesce in the intendant's new powers. Eventually the Crown ruled in favor of the intendant, but Spanish governors consistently refused to enforce the order. The question of unconfirmed land titles, which constituted 70 percent of

Louisiana land grants, remained unresolved long after the cession of the province to the United States.

During his second term as intendant, Morales continued to be embroiled in controversy. Although the Treaty of San Ildefonso (1800) ceded Louisiana to France, Spain remained in control of the province until November 1803. On October 16, 1802, Intendant Morales announced the suspension of the American right of deposit at New Orleans. His action was in response to a secret order from the Spanish secretary of the treasury, Cayetano Soler. Soler instructed Morales not to divulge the source of his order. So secretive was Morales that his colleagues in the Spanish government of Louisiana were certain that he acted on his own authority. The Spanish minister in Washington, D.C., the Marques de Casa Irujo, ordered Morales to restore the deposit in New Orleans or assign another place of deposit. Morales did not respond.

The closure resulted in great consternation among the American merchants in New Orleans. Unlike Minister Irujo, Daniel Clark was certain that the intendant was executing an order from the Spanish Crown. Morales was, Clark wrote to Secretary of State Madison, "too rich, too sensible, and too cautious to take such responsibility on himself." Historian Arthur Whitaker calls the proclamation "one of the most provocative in the whole history of international rivalry in North America." From members of Congress and newspapers all over the country came a flood of criticism for Morales's decree. Federalists hoped that the Spanish action would provide the impetus to drive the Republicans from power, and for a few months the United States and Spain balanced on the point of war. Whitaker credits the closure of the deposit for Jefferson's decision to purchase New Orleans and ultimately all of Louisiana.

—Elizabeth Alexander

For Further Reading

Clark, John G. 1970. *New Orleans, 1718–1812: An Economic History.* Baton Rouge: Louisiana State University Press; "Documents: Despatches from the United States Consul in New Orleans, 1801–1803: Parts II." *American Historical Review* 33 (1928): 331–359; Kendall, John S. 1922. *History of New Orleans.* Chicago: Lewis; Whitaker, Arthur P. 1962. *The Mississippi Question, 1795–1803: A Study in Trade, Politics, and Diplomacy.* Gloucester, MA: Peter Smith.

MORMON ROAD

The Mormons were forced out of Missouri because of their religion, maybe their abolitionism, and their economic success based on communal effort. They were run out of Illinois for getting overly involved in state politics and for appearing a threat to the state. So they headed West to a place outside the United States, a place they could build their millennial Zion–Deseret. In 1846 the Mormons moved to Winter Quarters near Omaha, Nebraska. The next year they began a trek that would involve more than fifty thousand British, Scandinavian, and German converts among the sixty thousand total migrants before the road gave way to the transcontinental railroad in 1868.

The Mormon Trail wound from Nauvoo, Illinois, to Council Bluffs, Iowa, to Winter Quarters. The Mormon Road stretched 1,032 miles. It rambled to Salt Lake City along a path blazed by Indians, missionaries, and traders. It followed the Platte River Valley to Fort Laramie, merged with the Oregon and California Trails to just beyond South Pass, and proceeded to Fort Bridger near where the trail forked to Oregon and California. It went west from Fort Bridger through Echo, Weber, and East Canyons, then over the Wasatch Mountains to Salt Lake Valley over the route taken by the Donner-Reed party in 1846. Finally it crossed through Golden Pass, avoiding the Big and Little Mountains, and entered the Salt Lake Valley through Parley's Canyon.

Maybe ten thousand encamped in or near Winter Quarters. The number was well down from the twenty-five thousand Mormons who had met at a conference in Nauvoo in 1845. Brigham Young, who replaced the murdered Joseph Smith, led the first party. He knew that they had to reach the mountains by planting time, and they had to beat the Oregon-California migrants or lose the best of the trail. He set the pattern for migrations to follow.

Young organized his party into tens, fifties, and hundreds. They would take supplies and equipment stored beforehand at Winter Quarters. Aside from the three wives and two children taken by Lorenzo and Brigham Young and Heber Kimball, Young's party totaled 144 men and boys, seventy-two wagons, ninety-three horses, fifty-two mules, sixty-six oxen, nineteen cows, seventeen dogs, and some chickens. Each day there was a rotation of the lead wagon so that no single wagon had to break trail or eat dust all the time.

The tedious and dusty trip lasted for months. The Platte River Valley was ten to fifteen miles wide and, clear through most of its 650 miles, sloping imperceptibly upward, with occasional quicksand or bluffs crowding the river. Progress was marked at the end of each day's ten to fourteen miles. Then the trail left the river and entered terrain that was rugged, rocky, and arid. Finally came mountains.

The wagon count was 500 to 600 in 1849, 700 in 1850, 500 in 1851, and 1,300 to 1,400 in 1852. Annual migration was up to ten thousand people. A cheap means of moving the masses was the two-wheel Mormon carts used between 1856 and 1861 by nearly three thousand people, mostly English or Europeans. These travelers trekked up to fourteen hundred miles (over both the trail and the road), pushing or pulling their wooden carts, each a wagon's width and six to seven feet in length. Fully laden, the cart carried about five hundred pounds of

Facing hostility from those who opposed his religious beliefs and practices, Brigham Young led his fellow Mormons across the Great Plains to establish the Kingdom of Deseret. (North Wind Picture Archives)

foodstuffs, bedding, tent, and clothing. Some bore painted mottoes and inscriptions, such as "Truth Will Prevail" or "Zion's Express."

The trip was full of hardships. Exposure and malnutrition made travelers susceptible to malaria, cholera, whooping cough, tuberculosis, pleurisy, and asthma. Mormons avoided the smallpox and cholera that plagued the Oregon-California travelers because the trails were on opposite sides of the Platte. Both faced potentially dangerous encounters with Pawnee, Otoe, Omaha, Sioux, Crow, Shoshone, and Utah, some of whom were occasionally belligerent.

After 1861, Mormons sent trains to the Missouri River, picked up passengers and freight, and returned the same season. Mormons were considerate about identifying good camping areas, grass, water, and wood. They improved their road by building bridges and ferries and removing rocks and brush from rough spots. They were motivated by the idea that they were gathering at Zion to get their piece of the Kingdom.

Mormons could not escape the United States, however. They ran their own mail service to Independence from 1846; the government took over in 1850. Next came the stage, and trader cabins on the route. Permanent stage stations were in place by around 1857, and by 1860 the trail was just another route for the Forty-niners and those seeking homesteads in California and Oregon.

—*J. Herschel Barnhill*

For Further Reading

Arrington, Leonard, Jr., and Davis Bitton. 1979. *The Mormon Experience: A History of the Latter-Day Saints.* New York: Alfred A. Knopf; Billington, Ray Allen. 1974. *Westward Expansion: A History of the American Frontier.* New York: Macmillan; Kimball, Stanley B. 1991. *Historic Resource Study: Mormon Pioneer National Historic Trail.* Washington, DC: U.S. Department of Interior, National Park Service; Merk, Frederick. 1978. *History of the Westward Movement.* New York: Borzoi Books; Stegner, Wallace. 1964. *The Gathering of Zion.* New York: McGraw-Hill; Webb, Walter Prescott. 1972. *The Great Plains.* New York: Grosset and Dunlap.

MORTEFONTAINE, CONVENTION OF (1800)

Also known as the Convention of 1800, the Convention of Mortefontaine, which was initially signed on September 30, 1800, was a diplomatic arrangement that ended the undeclared naval war (the Quasi-War) fought between the United States and France since 1798. That conflict had resulted from the so-called XYZ Affair, in which U.S. diplomats had feigned indignation and refused to negotiate with French representatives who sought larger than expected tribute payments and other terms in order to begin the process of official negotiations. In addition to ending the undeclared naval war, the Convention of Mortefontaine also officially ended the Treaty of Alliance (1778) between the two nations and re-established a working relationship that redefined the state of Franco-American diplomacy. In this regard, the agreement can be viewed as the final act of the American Revolution and was certainly a critical turning point in U.S. diplomatic history. The arrangement also cleared the path for President Thomas Jefferson's subsequent purchase of Louisiana in 1803.

On July 31, 1801, U.S. negotiator William Vans

Murray, along with Oliver Ellsworth and William R. Davie, completed the final negotiation of the Convention of Mortefontaine by exchanging ratification in Paris with French commissioners representing the government headed by first consul Napoleon Bonaparte. In concluding the ratification process, Vans Murray acted without official instructions from the U.S. Senate, since the Sixth Congress was in conflict with members more inclined to spurn peace and undertake full-scale war with France.

The entire process of the momentous negotiations leading to the ratification of the Convention of Mortefontaine was difficult and tested the diplomatic skills of the novice U.S. negotiators and the courage and determination of President John Adams, who faced overwhelming political opposition from a Congress completely impatient with the pursuit of peace. Many have argued that Adams's pursuit of the unpopular convention with France cost him a second term and led to the collapse of the Federalist Party. Nonetheless, Adams's believed this to be the most important work of his presidency. Later in his life, Adams wrote: "I desire no other inscription over my gravestone than: 'Here lies John Adams, who took upon himself the responsibility of the peace with France in the year 1800'" (Bailey, 1974).

President Adams faced many problems during the final stages of the negotiations. The final ratification of the Convention of Mortefontaine was drawn out because of congressional efforts to weaken the treaty. President Adams did not support an effort by the Senate to place an eight-year limit on the time in which the convention would have effect. In Adams's opinion, any effort by the United States to add additional terms beyond those already negotiated would hinder the entire diplomatic effort. Additionally, Adams also had to face a delay in the final ratification when James A. Bayard, who had been ratified by the Senate as an official negotiator, refused to accept the appointment. As a result, the final negotiations of the Convention of Mortefontaine were conducted during the early months of Thomas Jefferson's administration.

All but the most belligerent could find satisfactory terms in the Convention of Mortefontaine. According to the agreement, the undeclared naval war (the Quasi-War) between the two nations was to come to an immediate end. The French government agreed to return all U.S. ships that had been captured during the two years of conflict. The United States agreed to compensate its own citizens for those damages inflicted by the French on U.S. shipping. (These damages totaled $20 million, of which the United States paid $3.9 million to the heirs of the original claimants in 1915.) The original Treaty of Alliance (1778) was terminated, but the United States and France re-established commercial relations on terms similar to those outlined in the earlier alliance. Additionally, the two countries granted each other most-favored-nation trading status.

Jefferson, having an appreciation of French diplomatic sensibilities, believed that the agreement was one that was in the best interests of the United States, and he supported the final efforts to obtain ratification. The Convention of Mortefontaine, among other things, guaranteed U.S. neutrality rights on the seas, which was especially important to the economic life of the young nation. Additionally, the establishment of more friendly relations between the United States and France made it easier to negotiate with the French once the Louisiana Territory was returned to them in the Treaty of San Ildefonso. In short, the Convention of Mortefontaine assisted the United States in its efforts to purchase the Louisiana Territory in 1803.

—*Junius P. Rodriguez*

See also
Jefferson, Thomas

For Further Reading
Bailey, Thomas. 1974. *A Diplomatic History of the American People.* Englewood Cliffs, NJ: Prentice-Hall; Bowman, Albert Hall. 1974. *The Struggle for Neutrality: Franco-American Diplomacy during the Federalist Era.* Knoxville: University of Tennessee Press; DeConde, Alexander. 1966. *The Quasi-War: The Politics and Diplomacy of the Undeclared War with France, 1797–1801.* New York: Charles Scribner's Sons; Lyon, E. Wilson. 1940. "The Franco-American Convention of 1800." *Journal of Modern History* 21: 305–333.

MOUNTAIN MEN

Men participating in the fur trade west of the Mississippi earned the distinctive appellation of "mountain men." They served as the vanguard of U.S. civilization in the Louisiana Territory. Mountain men explored, mapped, and carried the philosophy of national expansion across rivers and mountains to the Pacific coast. They blazed trails and established routes suitable for wagon travel across the mountains. Some, conscious of their historic role, recorded their observations and perceptions of the wilderness.

These bold adventurers often acted as guides for armies, missionary groups, Santa Fe trading parties, and emigrants. They helped the U.S. government establish territorial claims by assisting topographers and cartographers to chart the correct location of rivers, lakes, and mountain passes. Mountain men collected a vast amount of information about the location and movement of Indian tribes, the abundance or scarcity of game, the location of potable water, and the perils of mountain travel.

Rigorous mountain life brought physical deprivation and danger from wild animals and hostile Indians. The mountains challenged human endurance in bone-chilling blizzards, icy streams, and perilous mountain trails. Hard winters brought a scarcity of game and required innovative means to sustain life. As long as the fur trade was a lucrative business, however, many young men sought adventure in the mountains.

Men who chose to leave the populated areas east of the Mississippi for the mountain wilderness acquired a language, manner, and appearance peculiar to their occupation. The language they spoke was a mixed patois of English, French, and Indian. Animal skins and fur served as material for clothing. Few concerned themselves about personal grooming or hygiene, and most allowed their hair and beards to grow unkempt. Mountain men learned to subsist on meager diets and to enjoy foods that would have disgusted their Eastern brethren. They discovered that the hollowed-out carcass of their horse or pack animal could provide shelter from the snow and bitter cold; burying themselves in the sand could alleviate the searing heat of the Western desert.

Mountain men learned many of their survival skills from the Indians with whom they traded and often lived. They also witnessed, and learned to copy, the cruelty of Indian warriors. Trappers appreciated the skill and courage of the Indian, whether friend or foe. It was not unusual for mountain men to take Indian wives, sometimes temporarily, sometimes as lifelong companions. Indian wives brought increased trade opportunities with her family and tribe. The women also relieved the men of camp responsibilities and pelt preparation.

Some American fur trappers worked independently as free trappers, but most worked for privately owned companies. Many of the men who opened the Louisiana Territory to the U.S. fur trade worked for William Ashley's Rocky Mountain Fur Company. Most had come in response to Ashley's advertisement, published in the St. Louis newspapers, asking for enterprising young men willing to spend at least a year in the wilderness. As a result of the ad, men such as Jedediah Smith, Jim Bridger, Hugh Glass, Tom Fitzpatrick, James Clyman, Edward Rose, and the Sublette brothers signed on with the fur company. These men earned reputations as great adventurers and explorers. When Ashley recruited them, however, they were all entirely inexperienced in the ways of mountain life.

Mountain men came from a variety of backgrounds. John Colter had traveled with the Corps of Discovery; James Clyman and Joseph R. Walker had been surveyors. Jedediah Smith and William Sherley Williams ("Old Bill") came from religious backgrounds. Jim Bridger worked as an apprentice blacksmith, and William Sublette served as a local constable in Missouri. Many of the mountain men were former farmhands bored with the drudgery of the farm and fired with wanderlust. Others were too young to have done much of anything before joining the company. With few exceptions, the men were illiterate, hard drinking, rough talking, and superstitious. Contrary to long-held perceptions, these men did not seek to travel and work

Lured westward by the promise of profits in the fur trade, the trappers and traders who became known as mountain men were some of the earliest agents of Manifest Destiny. (North Wind Picture Archives)

alone. They traveled in groups, not only for safety but also because they enjoyed the camaraderie. From a group camp, individuals would branch out alone or with a companion to search for beaver.

Originally, at the end of a trapping season mountain men made their way to frontier forts situated along navigable rivers to trade their pelts and buy supplies. After 1824, at a yearly designated rendezvous, traders, trappers, and Indian bands met to buy and sell, to enjoy feasting, drinking, contests, and to swap tales of mountain adventures. Those tales compose the first chapter of the history of expansion into the Louisiana Territory.

—*Carol J. Terry*

See also

Bridger, James; Colter, John; Rendezvous System; Smith, Jedediah Strong; Williams, Bill

For Further Reading

Hafen, LeRoy R., ed. 1995. *Fur Traders, Trappers, and Mountain Men of the Upper Missouri.* Lincoln: University of Nebraska Press; Laycock, George. 1996. *The Mountain Men.* New York: Lyons and Burford; Utley, Robert M. 1997. *A Life Wild and Perilous: Mountain Men and the Paths to the Pacific.* New York: Henry Holt and Company.

La Salle's expedition, which traced the Mississippi River southward to its mouth, was the basis of French claims to all of the interior of North America.

MOUTHS OF THE MISSISSIPPI RIVER

Approximately ninety miles downstream from New Orleans, at the so-called Head of the Passes, the Mississippi River divides into four smaller outlets: North Pass, Pass a l'Outre, South Pass, and Southwest Pass. From the air, this final section of the river resembles a seagull's foot splayed out into the Gulf of Mexico. These four passes are the mouths of the Mississippi River, geological formations significant because they have represented both economic promise and environmental peril to people who have traded and settled in Louisiana.

Where the Mississippi meets the gulf, the river creates a watery obstacle course. Only small clumps of land break up the endless horizon of water found at the river's mouths, and prior to the middle of the nineteenth century, confused mariners often wondered if the four passes were the beginning of the continent, or just a cruel joke played by the sea. At the tail end of the seventeenth century, for instance, the explorer La Salle became so confused by the Mississippi's mouths on his second voyage to Louisiana that, instead of finding the river, he landed farther west on the Gulf Coast in what today is Texas.

For almost two more centuries, traders and travelers learned that a confusing landscape, wind, and unpredictable currents were not the only hazards impeding navigation at the river's mouths. Sandbars also threatened trade there. Because a river's ability to carry material in suspension is directly proportional to the speed of its current—the faster the current the more material can be carried—when the Mississippi divides at the Head of the Passes, the four channels take only a portion of the main stream's flow, diminishing the current in each. Then, where the four passes meet the gulf, the current decreases further when the confined river empties into open water. Consequently, at its four mouths the river no longer has the power to support the bulk of the sediment it has carried in suspension for thousands of miles along its valley. As a result, the river deposits a portion of its load, creating sandbars that can impede and endanger navigation.

Despite hazards at the river's mouths, people still traversed the Mississippi, because prior to the advent of railroads, automobiles, or airplanes—all technologies circumventing the vagaries of geography—the river was the most important commercial highway in the midcontinent. As a result, throughout the eighteenth and nineteenth centuries, people repeatedly attempted and failed to engineer the peril out of the river's mouths. For the most part, though, river traders recognized that they could do little to overcome the fickle passes, and they stood pat with the hand that geology had dealt them.

Finally, in the early 1870s, the mouths of the Mississippi became too grave a threat to commerce at the Port of New Orleans, prompting one of the great engineering controversies in the nation's history. Two men, Andrew Humphreys, the chief of the Army Corps of Engineers, and James Eads, an inventor, entrepreneur, and self-taught engineer, battled for the right to solve the problems at the river's mouths. Humphreys proposed a canal from near the Head of the Passes to the open water of the gulf. Eads insisted that a system of jetties—artificial riverbanks designed to narrow a stream, keeping its current powerful and channel deep—could pry open the river's mouths. After Eads offered to build his jetties and collect payment only if they maintained a channel deep enough to keep trade flowing (what he called a "no cure, no pay" deal), he won a contract from the federal government to build jetties at South Pass. By midsummer 1879, Eads and his crew of sun-baked, sweat-soaked laborers had succeeded in opening one of the river's mouths. Years later, the Corps of Engineers followed Eads's lead by constructing additional jetties at the larger Southwest Pass, rendering the original South Pass jetties obsolete.

—Ari Kelman

For Further Reading

Barry, John. 1996. *Rising Tide*. New York: Simon and Schuster; Corthell, E. L. 1881. *A History of the Jetties at the Mouth of the Mississippi River.* New York: John Wiley and Sons; Cowdrey, Albert E. 1977. *Land's End*. New Orleans: Corps of Engineers.

MURRAY, HUGH (1779–1846)

One of the United Kingdom's more prominent early geographers, Hugh Murray's writings included a three-volume encyclopedia of geography and a two-volume history of the United States. Murray was one of the first Europeans to detail the geographical and physical features of Louisiana for an international reading audience.

Scottish-born Hugh Murray was the son, grandson, and great-grandson of a line of ministers. He turned to life as an administrative clerk in the Edinburgh excise office but also devoted much of his time to writing. As early as 1804, Murray published a romance (*The Swiss Emigrants*) and, by 1834, had added two philosophical treatises, another novel, and a series of geographies covering the South Seas, the Polar Sea, India, China, Africa, and British America. In 1816, Murray was elected a fellow in the Royal Society of Edinburgh and later the Royal Geographical Society of London. He was briefly editor of the *Scots Magazine*. Thomas Constable described Murray as "an eminent geographer."

Murray's most significant contribution to the study of geography was the three-volume *Encyclopedia of Geography,* first published in 1834 in London. An American edition published by Lea and Blanchard was printed in 1839–1841, and a supplement in 1843. Murray collaborated with prominent scientists such as William Wallace (geology), Sir William Jackson Hooker (zoology), William W. Swainson (astronomy), and Robert Jameson (botany), but geography was the sole province of Murray. Although he had never traveled to America, Murray utilized secondary sources to provide details of the various U.S. states, including Louisiana. In five pages, he and the others described the land, the Mississippi and Red Rivers, waterways, harbors, agriculture, railroads, exploration, population, the value of lands, and several cities. The *Encyclopedia of Geography* was one of the first published works to include the details of so much of the new American nation, to say nothing of the rest of the world.

Murray turned to various printed sources to compile the state entries for his magnum opus. Two federal government surveys completed and published after 1827 provide much Louisiana material. Murray details the influences of the Mississippi River and the creation of four classes of lands: fertile soil covered with cane and timber; cypress swamps; sea marshes; and prairie lands. He describes the richest lands in Louisiana as those along the Mississippi, protected by six- to eight-foot levees and dominated by sugar cultivation. Murray also mentions the other rivers, such as the Red River, the Black, and the Vermillion. Cotton and sugar are the major crops of Louisiana, with rice, indigo, and timber also listed. Railroad construction is briefly mentioned. Murray's history of the state is sketchy and limited to one paragraph. He mentions school lands and three colleges—Louisiana College at Jackson, Franklin College, and Jefferson College, as well as a medical school in New Orleans. Murray included a population chart and a cursory section on the major cities, but his information on New Orleans runs over a full page. The present-day capital, at Baton Rouge, is barely mentioned. The Louisiana entry is typical of the coverage for each state—older states are generally treated in greater depth.

The encyclopedia was received as a remarkable work. Upon Murray's death in 1846, the *Gentleman's Magazine* called the work a "stupendous monument of reading, industry, and research," and mistakenly attributed the entire set to Murray, referring to the encyclopedia as "the united labors of a society of contributions, rather than the production of a single pen." Other reviews were just as praiseworthy, concluding that the work was "without a rival," "the most perfect book on its subject," and "full and minute." It certainly was the culmination of Murray's career as a geographer, although he continued to write of distant lands.

In the preface, Murray points to the value and importance of geography, especially in light of recent discoveries made and colonies established. He mentions a rigorous collection and analysis of data, recognizes the contributions of his colleagues, and credits J. R. McCulloch's *Dictionary, Practical, Theoretical, and Historical of Commerce and Commercial Navigation,* first published in 1832. Murray closed by taking responsibility for all errors or omissions. The U.S. edition dropped some of the material on Great Britain and generally included significant alterations on the United States, some of which was "written anew, the original being extremely imperfect and incorrect, as all European treatises on the subject are." Nevertheless, Murray's *Encyclopedia of Geography* represents one of the earliest comprehensive attempts to bring international geography to a popular reading audience.

In 1844, Murray completed a two-volume treatise on America, *The United States of America,* published in Edinburgh. Considering his lack of travel, Murray's writing reflects a keen synthesis of secondary sources describing Britain's former colonial empire. He briefly recounts the diplomatic and economic background of the Louisiana cession and perceptively reports the willingness of Congress to overlook any constitutional illegalities involved in the acquisition. Murray died in 1846 while visiting in London.

—Boyd Childress

For Further Reading

"Hugh Murray." 1917. In *Dictionary of National Biography.* Edited by George Smith. London: Oxford University Press; Murray, Hugh. 1839–1841. *Encyclopedia of Geography.* Philadelphia: Lea and Blanchard.

NAPOLEON

***See* Bonaparte, Napoleon**

NACOGDOCHES

Nacogdoches, a small city in Texas, is today the county seat of Nacogdoches County and has a population of over thirty-three thousand. Situated in east Texas, fifty miles west of the Sabine River and a hundred miles north of Beaumont, in the central part of the county, it was named for the Nacogdoche Indians, a Caddo group. In 1803, at the time of the Louisiana Purchase, Nacogdoches was at the western edge of a border area, long disputed in claims by Spain and France.

Archeological research has established that mounds found in the area date from approximately 1250 C.E., when Indian lodges are thought to have existed there. Spanish interest in Texas dates from the mapping of the Gulf of Mexico by Alonso Alvárez de Pineda in 1519. Spain's title to Texas remained uncontested until 1684, when René Robert Cavelier, Sieur de La Salle, appeared, with three French ships, off the Gulf coast. La Salle's exploratory expedition visited the Nacogdoches area in 1687. Later the French sent Louis Juchereau de St. Denis to establish trade with the Indians. He marked a trail through Nacogdoches to the Rio Grande that eventually became part of the Old San Antonio Road. In 1716, in an effort to discourage further French encroachment, the Spanish sent Domingo Ramón to east Texas to found Nuestra Señora de Guadalupe de los Nacogdoches, as well as five other missions in the vicinity. Then, in 1718, Spain founded San Antonio as its principal military garrison to rival the French in New Orleans.

Following the cession of Louisiana to Spain with the Treaty of Fontainebleau (1762), the Spanish forced European settlers to relocate to San Antonio. Relieved of the French threat on its borders, Spanish authorities determined to abandon the missions and presidios between the Trinity and Red Rivers. In 1779 some of these settlers, led by Antonio Gil Ibarvo (Ybarbo), returned to the abandoned mission site at Nacogdoches. Finally, recognized as a pueblo, Nacogdoches became a gateway for trade, mostly illicit, with the French and later Americans, from Natchitoches and New Orleans, Louisiana. Ibarvo constructed a house and trading post that later became well known as the "Old Stone Fort." Although demolished in 1902, a replica of this building has now been constructed on the campus of Stephen F. Austin State University. The location of Nacogdoches also gave it prominence in early military and political activities. During the 1790s, Philip Nolan, U.S. "mustanger" and "filibuster," often headquartered at Nacogdoches, which had become the major Spanish city in east Texas.

Soon after the United States secured the Louisiana Territory from France, boundary disputes with Spain, along the Texas border, followed. In 1806, Lt. Col. Símon de Herrera headquartered at Nacogdoches while negotiating the "Neutral Ground" agreement with General James Wilkinson of the United States. This "Neutral Ground" was the area between the Arroyo Hondo, near Natchitoches, Louisiana, and the Sabine River near Nacogdoches, Texas. The compact stated that neither country would exercise sovereignty over the land between the Sabine River and the Arroyo Hondo. Finally, in 1819, the Adams-Onís Treaty, ratified in 1821, fixed the northern boundary of Spanish Texas at the Sabine River.

—Richard H. Dickerson

See also

Fontainebleau, Treaty of; Herrera, Simón de; Natchitoches; Neutral Ground; Nolan, Philip; Texas

For Further Reading

Bolton, Herbert Eugene. 1970. *Texas in the Middle Eighteenth Century: Studies in Spanish Colonial History and Administration.* Austin: University of Texas Press; Ketz, Louise Bilebof, ed. 1976. "East Texas," "Neutral Ground," and "Texas." In *Dictionary of American History.* New York: Scribner's Sons; Marshall, Thomas Maitland. 1914. *A History of the Western Boundary of the Louisiana Purchase, 1819–1841.* Berkeley: University of California Press; Tyler, Ron, et al., eds. 1996. "Nacogdoches, Texas" and "Nacogdoches County." In *The New Handbook of Texas.* Austin: Texas State Historical Association.

NATCHEZ TRACE

The Natchez Trace has its origins in America's prehistory, when migrating game and aboriginal peoples created a network of trails and paths that connected the lower Mississippi River with the central Cumberland Plateau in modern-day Tennessee. Following along ridges and high ground to avoid bogs and swamps, these trails made possible trade and communications between the Natchez, Choctaw, Chickasaw, and various Native American groups in Mississippi, Alabama, and Tennessee. No one is certain when white settlers began to utilize these rudimentary paths, but their first recorded use by Europeans was in 1742, when a French explorer journeyed north from Fort Natchez to a French settlement near today's Nashville. Others probably followed, but as there was little political or economic need to connect these regions, the Trace's main travelers were Native Americans.

This situation changed in the late 1700s. American settlers flooding into Kentucky and Tennessee after the American Revolution sent their produce down the Mississippi River on primitive flatboats to Natchez or New Orleans. They were unable, however, to make their return home in the same manner, since the current of the Mississippi was too strong for upstream travel. Selling their boats for lumber or abandoning them if necessary, these "Kaintucks" would then make the arduous 450-mile trip overland using the Indian paths back to their homes in Tennessee and Kentucky.

Conditions along the Natchez Road (or Trace, as it was later known) were brutal, and many did not survive the month-long journey from Natchez to Nashville. Accommodations, called stands, were widely spaced, primitive, and expensive. Since the trail followed ridges as much as was possible, water was often in short supply. In other places, water was all too abundant. Many streams and rivers had to be forded, and what bridges existed were merely logs felled at convenient sites over creeks and streams. The paths were not clearly marked, so getting lost was always a danger for inexperienced travelers. Boatmen returning home with money were also easy targets for the many bandits who haunted the Trace, and the route soon gained an infamous reputation for murder and robbery.

America's acquisition of Natchez in the Treaty of San Lorenzo (1795) finally brought needed improvements to the crude trail snaking its way through the wilderness. Natchez was then America's only significant settlement on the southwestern frontier, and the U.S. government had to have a secure route to the outpost for both communications and defense purposes. In 1798, Governor Winthrop Sargent, the first governor of the Mississippi Territory, requested that the federal government begin regular mail service connecting Natchez with Tennessee, and in 1802 federal troops began improving and widening the route. Clearing a road that could be used by wagons, building causeways across swamps, and constructing bridges across streams for nearly five hundred miles through the wilderness proved a monumental undertaking for the fledgling nation, and work was not completed until 1809.

By the time that federal improvements to the Trace were completed, the route was serving a new purpose. Flatboatmen still continued to use the Trace as a return route to the north, but they began to encounter settlers coming south on the Trace. Rich cotton lands in the Mississippi Territory and, after 1803, in the territories of the Louisiana Purchase beckoned pioneers, and they began migrating down the Trace in large numbers. For those unable or unwilling to travel by water, the Natchez Trace provided the only ready access to these new American lands. The road remained difficult and dangerous, but thousands were willing to take the risk for the promise of a new start, and thus the Trace soon emerged as a major gateway to the western territories.

Use of the Trace peaked after 1810 and through the early 1820s. However, new technology and faster routes soon combined to render the Trace obsolete. The steamboat conquered the currents of the Mississippi River and made the lengthy land route unnecessary. Steamboats could make the trip from Natchez to Louisville in ten days, one-third the time required to walk the same distance. New post roads constructed to the east of the Trace connected Nashville with New Orleans along a much shorter and easier route, attracting travelers who soon forsook use of the Trace. By 1830 the Trace had been abandoned, and the few stands still in operation closed down as their clientele disappeared. Within a generation, the neglected road had largely disappeared, remembered only in legend and marked only by sunken tracks. In 1909 the Daughters of the American Revolution organized a program to mark the route of the Natchez Trace, and twenty-five years later, the National Park Service began a survey of the historic road. Today the Natchez Trace is a national park maintained and operated by the National Park Service.

—*James L. Sledge III*

See also
Lewis, Meriwether

For Further Reading

Daniels, Jonathan. 1962. *The Devil's Backbone: The Story of the Natchez Trace.* New York: McGraw-Hill Book Company; Davis, William C. 1995. *A Way through the Wilderness: The Natchez Trace and the Civilization of the Southern Frontier.* New York: Harper-Collins Publishers; Flemming, Alice. 1971. *Highways into History.* New York: St. Martin Press.

NATCHITOCHES

Founded in 1714, Natchitoches is considered the first permanent European settlement in the Louisiana Purchase; it is most certainly the oldest European town in the present-day state of Louisiana. Located in the Cane River region of northwest Louisiana, Natchitoches developed as a result of the Red River's changing its course. At one time, the Red River ran through the heart of Natchitoches, but in the 1760s the river diverged to the east, effectively isolating Natchitoches from the main traffic channel of the river and creating what is now called Cane River Lake.

Natchitoches was initially established to attract French traders to the area and rapidly developed as a center of trade with local Native American communities and the Spanish settlers in nearby Texas. Father Miguel Hidalgo y Costilla, a Catholic priest, was unable to secure the support of his native Spanish government for a mission on the eastern border of the Texas territory. As a result, in 1711, Father Hidalgo sent messages to Antoine de le Moth Cadillac, the governor of the Louisiana colony, offering trade incentives that the Frenchman Louis Juchereau de St. Denis could not refuse. St. Denis led a group of French and Native Americans to the area and established a military outpost, named St. Jean Baptiste, on the Red River. This military post grew into the city of Natchitoches.

Natchitoches operated under French control from the time that the post was established until the territory was ceded to Spain with the Treaty of Fontainebleau (1762). Many members of the surrounding Native American communities who conducted trade with the post, as well as the French settlers themselves, were distrustful of the Spanish. The Spanish government attempted to offset this distrust by appointing Athanase de Mezieres, the French former lieutenant-commander of the post, as its commandant during the Spanish regime. Natchitoches saw very little change in its government or way of life when the government changed from French to Spanish hands.

Despite the fact that the Louisiana territory was ceded back to France in 1800, news of this transaction did not reach Natchitoches until 1804, when the Americans arrived to take possession of the Natchitoches Post following the purchase of the Louisiana Territory in 1803. The U.S. Second Infantry arrived to find the Spanish flag still flying over the post. Accordingly, before the United States took full control of Natchitoches, the French flag flew over the post for two hours. These two hours represented the three years during which France had secretly owned the Louisiana Territory.

Like much of the Louisiana Territory, Natchitoches demonstrates significant French and Spanish influences. Even today, these influences are apparent in the architecture, folk traditions, religious and ethnic diversity, and culture of the city.

—Suzanne Disheroon-Green

See also
Creoles; Fontainebleau, Treaty of; Los Adaes

For Further Reading
Graves, Daniel. 1996. *Profiles of Natchitoches History.* Natchitoches, LA: Museum of Historic Natchitoches; Wall, Bennett H., et al. 1997. *Louisiana: A History.* Wheeling, IL: Harlan Davidson; Wilds, John, et al. 1996. *Louisiana Yesterday and Today.* Baton Rouge: Louisiana State University Press.

NEBRASKA

Nebraska is an Omaha or Otoe word translating roughly to "flat water" in English. The area once comprised a significant portion of the Louisiana Purchase territory north and west of the present states of Kansas and Missouri. In the context of the Louisiana Purchase and its territorial period (1854–1867), Nebraska served as an important highway across the continent, and its nineteenth-century history coincided with main currents of U.S. expansion and politics.

In the late 1980s, archaeological work at the La Sena Mammoth site in Frontier County, Nebraska, found evidence that humans may have hunted in the region as long as eighteen thousand years ago. Traditional theory holds that humans did not live in the area until about eight thousand years ago. By the late 1600s and early 1700s, at least two Indian cultures lived within the confines of present-day Nebraska. In the Sand Hills, people of the Dismal River culture hunted and farmed. In central Nebraska, people who were probably ancestors of the Pawnee lived in villages of earthen lodges where they planted corn and other crops and hunted and fished. In addition to the Pawnee, other Indian nations that called Nebraska home included the Omaha, Oto-Missouria, Ponca, Arapaho, Cheyenne, and some Lakota bands.

The U.S. government began extinguishing Indian title to land in the region in 1825, continuing for the next five decades. The Oto and Missouria, for instance, ceded part of their claim to Nebraska land in 1830 at Prairie du Chien. In subsequent cessions in 1833 and 1854, the groups gave up the remainder of their claims, except for a strip of fertile land along the Big Blue River. Mounting pressure from white settlers led Congress to sell part of that reservation during the 1870s and to remove the tribes to Indian Territory in 1881. The Pawnee, despite serving the United States by providing scouts for the Army, experienced a similar dispossession, ultimately leaving Nebraska in 1876. Nebraska currently houses reservations for the Omaha, Santee Sioux, Winnebago, Sac and Fox, and Ioway.

Almost immediately after the Louisiana Purchase, Nebraska became an important transit area for the United States, a distinction it has retained. The valley of the Platte River, the "flat water" described by the territory's name, provided an excellent natural overland highway from the Missouri River to the Rocky Mountains and beyond. Fur traders exploited the route in the early nineteenth century, bringing pelts from the mountains to trading posts on the Missouri's banks. Government sponsored expeditions yielded grim reports about Nebraska's interior, earning it and the rest of the Great Plains the label "Great American Desert." Although that estimation would be proved wrong, for decades it contributed to people passing through Nebraska rather than settling it.

The earliest white settlers included fur traders and soldiers along the Missouri River and missionaries who came to convert Nebraska's Indians starting in the 1830s. Travel across Nebraska increased during the early 1840s as Oregon missionaries spread word of great opportunities there. Hopeful settlers used the Platte Valley Road to reach Oregon and other points west. As emigration grew, so did demands for the government to protect the travelers. In 1848 the government built Fort Kearny on the Platte River at the confluence of the major overland trails. The fort opened just in time to serve California gold rush travelers in 1849. It watched over Colorado gold rushers a decade later, as well as Mormons headed for Utah and a wide variety of other travelers.

During the 1840s, politicians began laying the groundwork for another use of the Platte River Road, a transcontinental railroad. Stephen Douglas then first introduced legislation to create Nebraska Territory to provide government and infrastructure to support the railroad's construction. Political opposition delayed the bill for years. In 1854, Douglas finally ushered the Kansas-Nebraska Act through Congress, creating the Nebraska Territory. The act defined Nebraska Territory as land in the Louisiana Purchase north of Kansas to Canada (the fortieth parallel to the forty-ninth) and west of the Missouri River to the crest of the Rockies. For a time, Nebraska included parts of what eventually became Colorado, Wyoming, South Dakota, North Dakota, and most of Montana. The act also created Kansas Territory and called for the settlers in Kansas and Nebraska to determine their states' slave status by popular sovereignty, thereby overturning the Missouri Compromise (1820). Kansas experienced bloody conflict over the slavery issue, but Nebraska remained relatively calm. More important, perhaps, for the purpose at hand, the Kansas-Nebraska Act opened the remainder of the Louisiana Purchase to settlement.

Until creation of the Nebraska Territory, few whites had settled the area. A few squatters had cabins along the Missouri River, especially where ferries operated, and some settlers clung to Fort Kearny. Prospects looked dim when the first territorial governor, Francis Burt, became ill on his journey to Nebraska and died on October 18, 1854, two days after taking his oath of office from his sickbed. Thomas B. Cuming, a twenty-five-year-old Episcopal minister's son, rose from territorial secretary to replace Burt and quickly stamped the territory with his influence. The census he ordered showed 2,732 inhabitants, 1,818 of whom lived south of the Platte River, most very near the Missouri River. Despite the clear majority of population living south of the Platte, Cuming created a territorial government with a majority of representatives from the counties north of the Platte. Cuming clearly wished to establish the capital at Omaha (north of the Platte) in order to boost economic development and benefit his supporters from Council Bluffs, Iowa, located across the Missouri from Omaha. The North Platte–South Platte split dominated territorial politics and led South Platte residents to embark upon a short-lived campaign for annexation by Kansas. The sectional split ultimately influenced the state capital's location, which South Platte politicians wrested from Omaha with the establishment of Lincoln in 1867, south of the Platte. When it established a legal code, the territorial legislature adopted Iowa's.

Land speculation dominated the territory's early economy until the Panic of 1857 crushed banking and real estate ventures. With virtually no other options, many Nebraskans turned to agriculture, which they quickly identified as a viable enterprise. The 1860 census identified three thousand farmers, and in 1862 the value of agricultural goods exported from Nebraska exceeded the value of goods imported. Newspaper editors and other boosters trumpeted Nebraska's agricultural virtues, hoping to draw settlers. The German-language *Nebraska Deutsche Zeitung*, for instance, sent copies to German-speaking areas of Europe with hopes that farmers there would relocate to Nebraska. The territorial legislature joined the recruiting effort by passing measures encouraging timber cultivation. It hoped to show that tree cultivation would provide building materials and fuel and to overcome the "Great American Desert" stereotype by showing the region fit for agriculture.

Thanks to the Platte River Road, transportation and communications became and remained important businesses for territorial Nebraska. Steamboats brought supplies and overland travelers to ports such as Omaha, Bellevue, and Nebraska City. River traffic grew throughout the 1850s, reaching its peak in 1859 with the Colorado gold rush. Overland freighting—by firms such as Wells, Fargo and Company and Russell, Majors, and Waddell—became one of the territory's biggest businesses, shipping supplies from river ports to inland customers. Along the trails, entrepreneurs established road ranches to supply travelers with food and other goods. Russell, Majors, and Waddell ran weekly mail service through the Platte Valley to Colorado by the late 1850s, which helped spawn a famous but short-lived venture in fast mail service: the Pony Express. Although the Pony Express lasted only eighteen months, in 1860 and 1861, and contributed to the financial destruction of Russell, Majors, and Waddell, it showed the year-round feasibility of using a central route across the country, a route later adopted by the transcontinental railroad.

Even as the Pony Express demonstrated Nebraska's importance linking the nation, its competitor and successor, the telegraph, reached across the territory and the nation. Telegraph lines reached Omaha in September 1860, and Fort Kearny by November. When the cross-country lines linked at Salt Lake City in October 1861, the Pony Express died, but the Platte Valley continued to provide a crucial transcontinental link.

The transcontinental railroad brought the next innovation to Nebraska as it began construction through the Platte Valley. Track reached Fort Kearny by August 1866, spelling that institution's demise, and it reached North Platte by the end of the year. In addition to linking the nation, the railroad also brought economic development to Nebraska Territory. Work camps sprang up along the line. Some, such as Fremont, Kearney, North Platte, and Sidney, became permanent and profitable towns. The railroad, as it sought to dispose of land granted to it along the right-of-way by the federal government, recruited settlers and offered them access to national and international markets.

Democrats dominated the territorial government and helped delay statehood. When first considered seriously in 1860, both major parties cluttered the statehood question with sectional issues, which postponed action. When the issue resurfaced in 1864, Democrats argued that statehood would bring higher taxes and that their party's true leadership was absent from Congress and from the territorial legislature. Again, statehood waited. In 1866, Republican territorial officials pushed a constitution through the legislature and submitted it to residents, who approved it 3,938 to 3,838. Congress, dominated by Republicans, bridled at the Nebraska constitution's limitation of suffrage to free white males. Republican senator George Edmunds of Vermont proposed an amendment to overcome the race restriction. Congress approved the amended constitution, and, after President Andrew Johnson vetoed it, overrode his veto to make Nebraska a state, conditional upon its accepting the modified constitution. After Nebraska officials agreed, Johnson signed a proclamation on March 1, 1867, admitting Nebraska as the thirty-seventh state.

—Todd M. Kerstetter

See also

Kearny, Fort; Sand Hills

For Further Reading

Luebke, Frederick C. 1995. *Nebraska: An Illustrated History.* Lincoln: University of Nebraska Press; Olson, James C., and Ronald C. Naugle. 1997. *History of Nebraska.* 3d ed. Lincoln: University of Nebraska Press; Tate, Michael L. 1995. *Nebraska History: An Annotated Bibliography.* Westport, CT: Greenwood Press; Wishart, David J. 1994. *An Unspeakable Sadness: The Dispossession of the Nebraska Indians.* Lincoln: University of Nebraska Press.

NEUTRAL GROUND

The Neutral Ground was a disputed area running north-south, roughly between the Sabine River and the Calcasieu River and Natchitoches, Louisiana, created by the lack of specific boundaries in the Louisiana Purchase agreement between the French and the United States. Spanish claims to what is now western Louisiana, beginning at Los Adaes, dated back to 1716, when Spain occupied the area to counter French occupation of Natchitoches. Following the transfer of Louisiana to Spain at the conclusion of the French and Indian War, Spain reorganized its frontier defenses and decided to abandon Los Adaes as a cost saving measure. Although Spanish colonials continued to conduct Indian trade, smuggling, and livestock raising in the area in the last quarter of the eighteenth century, the closest substantial Spanish settlement in Texas was Nacogdoches, west of the Sabine River; by the turn of the century, however, an informal settlement of about two hundred residents had formed at Bayou Pierre, a site close to Los Adaes.

At the turn of the century, Anglo-American westward expansion, renewed French imperial aspirations in North America, and Spanish efforts to maintain an effective frontier buffer produced mounting tensions along the Louisiana-Texas border region. Philip Nolan's mustang capturing–Indian trade expeditions deep into Texas came to be considered spying by Spanish authorities in both Louisiana and Texas, and led to a confrontation in the spring of 1801 in which Nolan was killed and his men captured. As Louisiana moved, first to French control, then to that of the United States, both nations began moving troops into the Texas border region. The Spanish reinforced Nacogdoches, reoccupied Los Adaes, and began construction of new posts on the coast and along the Camino Real under the aggressive leadership of Governor Manuel Antonio Cordero y Bustamente. The Americans were no less active, quickly occupying Natchitoches, establishing contact with the local Indian peoples, and laying claim to all territory to the Rio Grande as part of the purchase. Incidents were not long in coming, including complaints from Natchitoches-area residents of being accosted by Spanish soldiers while traveling in the area.

As both the United States and Spain moved to assert their rights in the border region in 1804 and 1805, the area became increasingly militarized. In early 1806 confrontations between U.S. forces under Major Moses Porter and Spanish troops under the command of Sebastián Rodríguez at the various Spanish posts within the disputed territory led to the withdrawal of the latter beyond the Sabine. At the same time the Spanish were in retreat, Nemecio Salcedo, commandant general on the Spanish frontier, first proposed that both sides evacuate the disputed territory until the two governments could reach agreement on the issue. The U.S. rejection of the proposal forced Salcedo to take a more active approach, and at his orders Colonel Simón de Herrera, commander of troops in Texas, reoccupied Bayou Pierre and the region to Arroyo Hondo by June 1806. The Spanish actions triggered a reinforcement of Natchitoches. In late August, Louisiana territorial governor William C. C. Claiborne demanded the withdrawal of the Spanish troops and an explanation for the Spanish treatment of the Red River expedition and the detention of three U.S. residents who were sent to San Antonio for questioning.

The arrival on the border of General James Wilkinson with orders from the U.S. War Department to expel all Spanish forces from territory east of the Sabine marked the height of the crisis. Speculation regarding his motive for attempting to provoke an incident with Herrera's forces centers on his relationship with Aaron Burr. On September 24, 1806, Wilkinson issued an ultimatum to Governor Cordero declaring that although the Louisiana Purchase extended as far as the Rio Grande, the U.S. government was concerned with extending its jurisdiction only to the Sabine; Spanish forces should withdraw west of that river or face forced expulsion. Whether intentionally or not, with his statement that the United States viewed the Sabine as the border of Spanish Texas, Wilkinson undermined the bargaining position of the United States, which had been trying to turn all of Texas into the subject of negotiations with Spain. Although Cordero replied that he had no authority to abandon the territory between the Sabine and Arroyo Hondo, and that the matter had been forwarded to Commandant General Salcedo, Colonel Herrera decided to take action. Recognizing the untenable position of Spanish forces in east Texas, he assumed responsibility for accepting Wilkinson's offer. On November 5, 1806, operating under Herrera's orders, Francisco Viana, the inspector of troops in east Texas, signed what has come to be known as the Neutral Ground Agreement with Wilkinson.

For fifteen years the region between the Calcasieu and Sabine Rivers remained outside the effective control of either nation. The lawless district became home to smugglers, filibusters, and criminals. Runaway slaves and squatters also settled in the area. Periodically, when conditions deteriorated on either side of its boundaries, patrols were sent into the region to deal with the specific problem at hand. Only with the ratification of the Adams-Onís Treaty (1819), which established the permanent boundary between Louisiana and Texas along the Sabine River, and from 32 degrees north latitude due northward to the Red River, did the Neutral Ground cease to exist.

—Jesús F. de la Teja

See also

Burr, Aaron; Camino Real, El; Herrera, Simón de; Los Adaes; Nacogdoches; Natchitoches; Transcontinental Treaty; Wilkinson, James

For Further Reading

Castañeda, Carlos E. 1942. *Our Catholic Heritage in Texas, 1519–1936*. Volume 5: *The Mission Era: The End of the Spanish Regime, 1780–1810*. Austin, TX: Von Boeckmann-Jones; Haggard, J. Villasana. 1945. "The Neutral Ground between Louisiana and Texas, 1806–1821." *Louisiana Historical Quarterly* 28, no. 4: 1001–1128.

NEW MADRID EARTHQUAKES (1811–1812)

In the early hours of December 16, 1811, two earthquakes hit the central-Mississippi River Valley. The first, which occurred at 2:00 A.M., was the more powerful. These shocks were matched in strength by two more earthquakes in less than two months. The second occurred on January 23, 1812, and the third on February 7, 1812. The latter was, in fact, the most powerful of all the earthquakes.

The fault line, later called the New Madrid fault, running slightly northeast to southwest, was nearly parallel to the Mississippi River. The region most affected by the earthquakes covered southeastern Missouri, northeastern Arkansas, southwestern Kentucky, and northwestern Tennessee. The shocks, however, were felt all the way to the Gulf and Atlantic coasts, and to Canada. The strongest convulsions covered an area two to three times larger than the 1964 Alaska earthquake and ten times larger than the 1906 San Francisco earthquake.

The rivers, the Mississippi especially, churned in the turmoil created by the earthquakes. Islands and banks sank into the Mississippi. Fissures, which opened in the riverbeds, created water spouts and waves that tossed boats on the river. Little Prairie was destroyed as a result of flooding caused by the December earthquakes. Near New Madrid, the February 7 earthquake redirected the river for a short time and created a falls similar to the Falls of the Ohio (located near Louisville, Kentucky). The famous notion that the Mississippi ran backward was probably a result of the waves created by fissuring and falling banks. The force of the waves pushed boats moored at New Madrid up the mouth of the St. John Bayou, and the receding water stranded them.

There was a very real human dimension to the catastrophe. The mild fall and winter had increased traffic on the rivers. Many boatmen were able to survive, but some boats on the river were capsized and members of some crews were lost.

New sections of river channel were formed and old channels cut off. Travel upriver to New Madrid had usually gone through the St. Francis River, which had a weaker current than the Mississippi, followed by a short portage to New Madrid. After the earthquakes, the St. Francis was nearly impassable because of the sunken lands, sunken forests, and other obstructions. Boats were forced to take the more time-consuming route up the Mississippi. Slower transportation made Arkansas Post even more isolated from the governmental centers in New Madrid and St. Louis. A year after the quakes, Arkansas County was formed to correct the problem.

The St. Francis had been known as the sunken country before the earthquakes, but the shocks changed the course of the river and created swamps and bogs. Uprooted trees and sunken forests further obstructed travel.

The earthquakes did not only cause river courses to change. They also caused land subsidence deep enough to create new lakes, such as Reelfoot Lake in Tennessee and Lake St. Francis in Arkansas. Reelfoot Lake was created by a subsidence of 1.5 to 6 meters and possibly by the rising of land around the lake. Lake St. Francis was formed by a stretch of sunken land 64 kilometers long and 1 kilometer wide. At the same time, fissures in the swamps along the river spewed forth coal and sand, and the water level rose eight to nine meters.

In some places, the land was raised so much that domes were created and river and lake beds were raised and drained. The Pemiscot River, a tributary of the St. Francis, was said to have exploded and was covered in sand.

On land, log cabins and similar buildings withstood the earthquakes better than the masonry and stone structures in the towns. Even log cabins, however, were not immune to the earthquakes. Buildings toppled in New Madrid during the earthquakes of December 11 as people fled the town. Those first shocks caused chimneys to collapse in Louisville, Kentucky.

Several shocks occurred on February 7, the last of which was the fourth and largest earthquake of the series. It destroyed the town of New Madrid and damaged homes and buildings in St. Louis.

Sand blows (the eruption of sand from underground), fissures, and land subsidence destroyed farmland in the region. In 1815, Congress passed legislation giving 160 acres to settlers who lost one or more acres of land to the earthquakes. As was often the case in early America, many claims were obtained fraudulently, and land speculators acquired claims on the cheap from the original claimants.

—Joseph Patrick Key

For Further Reading
Fuller, Myron. 1912. "The New Madrid Earthquake." *United States Geological Survey Bulletin 494*. Washington, DC: Government Printing Office; Logsdon, David R., ed. 1990. *"I Was There!" In the New Madrid Earthquakes of 1811–1812*. Nashville: Kettle Mills Press; Penick, James J., Jr. 1976. *The New Madrid Earthquakes of 1811–1812*. Columbia: University of Missouri Press; Ross, Margaret. 1968. "New Madrid Earthquake." *Arkansas Historical Quarterly* 27: 104.

NEW MEXICO

It is likely that the first white man to enter into what would become known as New Mexico was Alvar Nunez Cabeza de Vaca, one of the survivors of the ill-fated expedition of Panfilo Narvaez, 1528–1536. Equally important was the reconnaissance of Fray Marcos de Niza in 1539, which led directly to the expedition commanded by Francisco Vasquez Coronado, then governor of the Province of Nueva Galicia.

Coronado left Compestella in February 1540 with some two hundred horsemen, seventy foot-soldiers, and nearly one thousand Indian allies and servants. The expedition was equipped at royal expense with a thousand horses, fine trappings, pack-mules, several cannon, and with droves of cattle, sheep, goats, and swine for food.

By July, Coronado had reached the Zuni pueblos, which he conquered with little difficulty. Hearing of the Moqui pueblos to the north of Zuni, Coronado sent Lieutenant Tobar to find them, which he succeeded in doing. The expedition wintered at Tiguex above Isleta. It was there that the Indians in New Mexico first revolted, and they were put down with great severity.

Coronado had heard rumors of a rich country far to the north called Gran Quivira, and in April 1541, he set out to find it. Crossing the mountains and descending the Pecos River, he marched out into the limitless buffalo plains, the Llano del Cibola, inhabited only by the roving Apache. Near the upper Brazos River he turned north, crossed the Texas Panhandle and Oklahoma, and reached Quivira in eastern Kansas. The Indian villages were poor and certainly did not have the wealth that he sought. These Indians were probably the Wichita. Urged now by his men, who were tired and had not found their fortunes, he turned southeasterly toward Mexico. Three fearless missionaries remained to preach the Gospel and soon achieved "the crown of martyrdom."

Coronado found that Indians who dwelt in substantial towns and possessed a civilization similar to that of the Aztecs inhabited large parts of New Mexico and adjacent regions. Their terraced dwellings, which were also fortifications, were constructed of stone or adobe and were several stories high. The inhabitants lived a settled life, practiced agriculture by means of irrigation, and raised cotton for clothing. They were constantly beset by the more warlike tribes who surrounded them and were already declining under the effect of those tribes' incursions. At the time of the Spanish conquest, it was estimated that there were some seventy inhabited pueblos, whose total population may have been as much as sixty thousand. The principal regions were the upper Rio Grande, the upper Pecos, Acoma, and the Zuni and Moqui towns. Some of these still exist and are important archaeological sites.

In 1581, a party of nine soldier-colonists and three missionaries led by Captain Francisco Sanchez and Fray Augustin Rodriguez entered into the Pueblo country from the Rio Grande Valley and explored most of the area in which the Pueblo Indians lived.

In 1598, Juan de Onate, the newly appointed governor of the Province of New Mexico, proceeded up the Rio Grande Valley to the Chama River, where he established his capital at San Juan de los Caballeros. The capital was relocated to nearby San Gabriel the following year. Ornate also failed to find the wealth that he was seeking. He maintained his authority with difficulty, inasmuch as his soldiers wanted their share of the gold and silver that was supposed to be there—as it had been in Mexico. He resigned in 1607. His successor, Pedro de Peralta, the new governor, founded a new capital at the Villa de Santa Fe in 1610.

Spain's rule was not seriously challenged until 1680. In that year, an Indian rebellion virtually emptied the province of all white settlers. Diego de Vargas, Marquis of Brazinas, was appointed governor in 1692 and was successful in re-establishing control. Santa Fe again became the capital, the Spanish missionaries returned, and Albuquerque was founded (1706), as were several other settlements.

Throughout the Spanish period, the province was subject to attack from several militant Indian tribes, including Navajo, Apache, Comanche, and Ute. After 1700 there were continual rumors of French invaders. In later years, rumors that an Anglo-American alliance might form in order to seize northern Mexico's rich silver mines caused consternation throughout the region.

When the United States purchased the Louisiana Territory in 1803, the western boundary of that territory was uncertain, and Mexico's control over the province of New Mexico was weak until the Americans arrived. The first of these was Lieutenant Zebulon M. Pike, in 1806–1807. William Becknell, founder of the Santa Fe Trade, arrived in 1821. Spanish rule ended in 1821, with Mexico's independence, after which New Mexico was governed from Mexico City. More and more Americans participated in trading with Santa Fe; many settled there and became Mexican citizens and Roman Catholics, as the law required.

During the Mexican War (1846–1848) the province of New Mexico fell easily before the invasion by General Stephen Watts Kearny, who occupied Santa Fe on August 10, 1846. New Mexico became a part of the United States as a result of the Treaty of Guadeloupe Hidalgo in 1848. Military rule continued there until New Mexico became a territory by the Compromise of 1850.

New Mexico Territory was invaded by Confederate troops operating out of Fort Bliss in Texas during the early part of the American Civil War. General Henry Hopkins Sibley and Colonel Robert R. Baylor led both Confederate regulars and irregulars called the Texas Second Mounted Rifles into the territory, with the objective of opening a window on the Pacific. Baylor established the Confederate Territory of Arizona and set up a rebel government at Messila. The Texas troops were defeated at battles including Apache Pass in 1861, Valverde in February 1862, and Glorieta Pass in early April. The Union troops were under the command of Colonel Edward Richard S. Canby, Fifth U.S. Cavalry. Canby had been appointed department commander upon the resignation of Colonel William Cloud Loring, who, with several other officers and enlisted men, had joined the Confederacy. Canby was successful, and the Confederates left the territory never to return.

The U.S. troops that were victors over the Confederates in New Mexico were redeployed to fight in the eastern theaters of the war, leaving a vacuum of which the Indians quickly took advantage. Navajo, Apache, and Comanche took this opportunity to lay waste to small settlements and remote ranches. Their depredations sorely threatened the Santa Fe trade, which was continuing under great hardships. Troops arrived from California (the California Column) to take the place of those sent East. Led by General James Henry Carleton, they successfully invaded the Indians' home country, subdued them, and relocated the tribes to a new reservation in eastern New Mexico. The Bosque Redondo Reservation was established east of the Pecos River and a new military post built to oversee them. That post was designated Fort Sumner, to honor Major General Edward Vose Sumner. The Navajo Indians remained at the Bosque Redondo until 1868, when they were returned to their own country in the Canyon de Chelly area. This set the federal government's policy of establishing reservations solely for Indians, located far from white settlements.

After a number of unsuccessful tries at achieving statehood, New Mexico finally became a state in 1912, along with Arizona, to complete the continental forty-eight.

—Henry H. Goldman

See also

Becknell, William; Pike Expedition; Santa Fe Trail; Taos

For Further Reading

Bancroft, Hubert Howe. 1889. *History of Arizona and New Mexico, 1530–1888.* San Francisco: History Company; Bolton, Herbert Eugene, and Thomas Maitland Marshall. 1932. *The Colonization of North America, 1492–1783.* New York: Macmillan Company; Forbes, Jack D. 1960. *Apache, Navajo, and Spaniard.* Norman: University of Oklahoma Press; Lowery, Woodbury. 1959. *The Spanish Settlements within the Present Limits of the United States, 1513–1561.* New York: Russell and Russell.

NEW ORLEANS

New Orleans, the final capital of the French colony of Louisiana, was founded in 1718 by Jean Baptiste le Moyne, Sieur de Bienville. Dissatisfied with the earlier capitals of Biloxi and Mobile, neither of which provided control over the Mississippi River, the directors of the company dispatched Bienville and fifty colonists to build a settlement one hundred miles upriver from the Gulf of Mexico, on the first piece of high ground. In addition to controlling the river, this spot also had ready access to the Gulf through Lakes Pontchartrain and Borgne. Its strategic location was one of the few factors working in its favor; the site was swampy, mosquito infested, and vulnerable to floods and hurricanes. Undeterred, Bienville's men began work; by the end of the year, a few roughly constructed thatch huts had been built, all of which were destroyed in a hurricane the following year. Bienville was unwilling to abandon the site, and in 1720 additional workers under the colony's assistant engineer, Adrien de Pauger, arrived to rebuild the city. Pauger designed a layout for the new settlement based on a typical late-medieval French town, a gridwork of forty blocks surrounding a central square, the Place d'Armes (renamed Jackson Square in 1849), all

Andrew Jackson's victory in the Battle of New Orleans was of great consequence because it guaranteed that America would remain in possession of the Louisiana Territory.

of which was to be surrounded by fortifications. In time Pauger's original plan was enlarged to seventy-seven blocks, and it now forms the French Quarter (Vieux Carre) of modern New Orleans. Envisioning great promise in this city emerging by the river, the directors of the colony moved its capital to New Orleans in 1722.

New Orleans and the entire Louisiana territory grew slowly under French authority, despite its great potential. In 1721, New Orleans had a population of only 372, living in muddy squalor. Disease, the humid climate, lack of trade, and horror stories filtering back to France made it impossible to recruit new settlers. The colony's directors were reduced to shipping criminals, prostitutes, slaves, and kidnapped persons to the colony in a feeble attempt to increase the population. Exacerbating this problem were the French government's strict immigration policies and financial difficulties, which rendered them unwilling and unable to provide the colony with the necessary money and leadership. Deprived of the necessary human and economic resources, New Orleans and the Louisiana colony remained a white elephant, consuming resources that the French government could scarcely afford.

Following years of frustration, France secretly transferred New Orleans and the Louisiana colony west of the Mississippi to Spain in the Treaty of Fontainebleau (1762), with the first Spanish governor, Don Antonio de Ulloa, arriving in New Orleans in 1766. Ulloa found New Orleans a disaster: buildings in disrepair, fortifications in ruins, and the church so dilapidated that the sacrament had been moved to a guardhouse. The Creole inhabitants of New Orleans proved equally disappointing, resenting and ultimately resisting their new masters. Spain moved quickly to establish firm control, putting down revolts and implementing policies to provide effective government, such as the establishment of the Cabildo (town council) in New Orleans in 1769. Under the effective leadership of Spanish governors O'Reilly, Galvez, Miro, and Carondelet, New Orleans flourished and grew to more than eight thousand inhabitants by 1801. The Spanish were also responsible for New Orleans's characteristic architecture; disastrous fires in 1788 and 1794 destroyed all traces of the earlier French structures, and new, mostly brick buildings reflecting Spanish tastes were built as replacements.

The Spanish government could claim credit for some of the city's vitality, encouraging immigration and integrating New Orleans into the greater Spanish colonial world, but much of the city's burgeoning growth stemmed from external events. U.S. expansion into the Mississippi and Ohio River Valleys in the late 1700s finally provided the city with the economic hinterland necessary for development as a commercial entrepôt. American settlers moving across the Appalachians found the Mississippi River and New Orleans, which controlled the river, their sole outlet to the larger world. As trade with American settlers in the West exploded and U.S. influence in the city grew, Spanish authorities attempted to arrest this growth by restricting the right of deposit by American traders. This policy did little to stem the tide of American trade and, by demonstrating the crucial role that New Orleans played in America's economic growth, created a strong sentiment in the United States for outright seizure of the city. Faced with this threat, Spain signed the Treaty of San Lorenzo (1795), guaranteeing Americans the right of deposit in New Orleans for three years. The importance of New Orleans to the new American nation had proven to be the city's economic salvation, but from the Spanish perspective, it was also its greatest weakness.

New Orleans and the entire Louisiana Territory prospered under Spain's guardianship. Louisiana's population grew by 500 percent, and New Orleans emerged as a substantial settlement. Events in Europe, however, soon made Spain relinquish control of her territory. Napoleon Bonaparte, dreaming of a worldwide empire, forced Spain to return Louisiana to France. For the Americans, this was a potentially devastating blow. An aggressive Napoleon controlling New Orleans and America's Western trade was unthinkable. If France blocked American use of the Mississippi, Western settlement would become impossible. President Thomas Jefferson, in a letter to the U.S. minister to France, Robert Livingston, declared that French control of Louisiana "works most sorely on the United States," and that whoever controlled New Orleans "is our natural and habitual enemy." Livingston was instructed to open negotiations with Napoleon to purchase New Orleans, and in 1803 the U.S. Senate passed a series of resolutions authorizing the president to arm eighty thousand militiamen, ostensibly to seize the city by force. Faced with potential U.S. hostility, the futility of building a New World empire, and an inability to defend the territory from Britain, the French government opened negotiations with Livingston and special representative James Monroe. By early May, Napoleon had agreed to sell New Orleans and the entire French territory to the United States. In New Orleans, the French did not resume control of the territory from Spain until November 30 (seven months after the sale to the United States), and just twenty days later, W. C. C. Claiborne (later appointed governor of the territory) and General James Wilkinson arrived in New Orleans to formalize U.S. possession of the city.

Now that New Orleans was politically united with its hinterland, the city grew rapidly. By 1810 its population expanded to 24,522, making it the country's fifth largest city, and the largest city west of the Appalachian mountains. The old city designed by Pauger could no longer contain this explosive growth, and a new American Section developed across Canal Street, with other suburbs rapidly following. As the most important settlement in the new territory, New Orleans was made the capital of the Territory of Orleans, and after Louisiana achieved statehood in 1812, New Orleans served as the state capital until 1846. Extensive expansion of cotton production upriver provided New Orleans with an abundance of business, and it emerged as one of the leading ports of the United States. By the 1850s, when the cotton boom was at its peak, nearly one-third of all U.S. exports were shipped out of New Orleans, and its population had swelled to nearly 170,000. The disruptions of the Civil War and Reconstruction did not significantly harm New Orleans's position as one of America's leading commercial sites, and throughout the late 1800s and early 1900s it remained the financial and business hub of the South. In the twentieth century, New Orleans was eclipsed in size and importance by the growth of other Southern cities, yet it still today retains its position of prominence as one of America's most important ports. More important, New Orleans has emerged as a leading center of tourism, drawing on its uniquely European charm that is the heritage of its early French and Spanish settlers.

—*James L. Sledge III*

See also

Carondelet, Louis Francisco Hector de; Claiborne, William Charles Cole; Creoles; Laussat, Pierre Clément de; New Orleans, Battle of; Orleans, Territory of; Right of Deposit; Wilkinson, James

For Further Reading

Clark, John G. 1970. *New Orleans, 1718–1812: An Economic History.* Baton Rouge: Louisiana State University Press; Garvey, Joan B., and Mary Lou Widmer. 1988. *Beautiful Crescent: A History of New Orleans.* New Orleans: Garner Press; Kendall, John Smith. 1922. *History of New Orleans.* 3 vols. Chicago: Lewis.

NEW ORLEANS, BATTLE OF (JANUARY 8, 1815)

The Battle of New Orleans was the climactic engagement of a military campaign fought along the Gulf Coast between the United States and Great Britain from September 14, 1814, until February 12, 1815. Since the beginning of the War of 1812 there had been rumors that the British planned to land on the Gulf Coast to prosecute a Southern war, and New Orleans was obviously the primary objective.

British plans called for using Indian allies and runaway slaves as military supplements during operations in the South. Yet the prospect of these two groups fomenting an uprising and joining with the British greatly threatened white Southerners, who demanded that the U.S. government take action to curtail them. When the Creek Indian War (1813–1814) started, it seemed that British plans were being realized. By the time British operations in the Gulf had begun, in the late summer of 1814, the Indians had already been defeated. General Andrew Jackson had crushed the hostile Creeks at Horseshoe Bend (Tohopeka) on March 27, 1814, and before the end of the summer he had forced them to surrender nearly twenty-three million acres of land in the Treaty of Fort Jackson. The Southern Indians' military power had been broken even before they could assist the British; thereafter, the Creeks would drain rather than assist Britain's war effort.

During the late summer of 1814, British naval vessels landed advance forces on the Apalachicola River and at the Spanish city of Pensacola, establishing bases for their campaign. The British soon reinforced Pensacola and Fort San Carlos de Barrancas, which guarded its harbor, without Spanish permission. On September 14–15, British naval and land forces attacked U.S. Fort Bowyer on Mobile Bay; during the unsuccessful attack the British lost the sloop *Hermes*. Meanwhile Jackson advanced against Pensacola in early November with four thousand men, and after a short fight on November 7, the Spanish governor surrendered the city. Disgusted by the Spanish action, the British destroyed Fort Barrancas and its powder magazine—rendering the city useless as a U.S. base—before retreating to the Apalachicola River. Jackson, discovering that New Orleans was the true British objective on the Gulf, immediately left Pensacola for the Crescent City, where he arrived on December 1, 1814.

Jackson found New Orleans inadequately defended, which made him realize that he needed more time, men, and supplies before meeting the British attack. He also realized after surveying the area that the city was exposed to many avenues of attack, of which Lake Borgne was the most obvious. The Lake Borgne approach was confirmed on December 14, 1814, when forty barges and more than a thousand British men commanded by Vice Admiral Sir Alexander F. I. Cochrane attacked Lieutenant Thomas ap Catesby Jones's five U.S. gunboats. For more than two hours Jones and his small flotilla, unable to retreat because of unfavorable tide and winds, fought a desperate contest before each of the vessels succumbed to British numerical superiority. Although the U.S. flotilla had been defeated, Jones's defense had provided Jackson with time and valuable information concerning the proposed British invasion route.

Cochrane's army soon landed at Bayou Bienvenu, which drained the area east of New Orleans and stretched from Lake Borgne to within a mile of the Mississippi River. Major General John Keene moved British forces north along the river levee—a narrow strip of land through the region's sugar plantations—and by December 23 had established a base at the Villeré Plantation. Not knowing how many Americans he faced or their disposition, Keene chose to wait for the arrival of Lieutenant General Sir Edward Pakenham and reinforcements.

Although Jackson was unaware of British strength or intentions, he nevertheless ambushed the unprepared British troops at Villeré Plantation on the evening of December 23. Supported by naval gunfire from the Mississippi River, Jackson's army drove the British back; the following morning Louisiana militia attacked the rear of Keene's line, further demoralizing the British troops. The British had held their position, but Jackson's attacks won time for the American defense effort. The attacks also reassured the British that they needed Pakenham, additional troops, and heavy artillery if they expected to take New Orleans.

During the next week the British transported heavy guns from the fleet some sixty-two miles away as U.S. naval vessels harassed Keene's operations near New Orleans. Meanwhile Jackson occupied a defensive position on the north side of the Rodriguez Canal and established four batteries that stretched from a cypress swamp in the east to the Mississippi River in the west, where the navy provided additional artillery support. On December 28 and again on January 1, 1815, Pakenham boldly attacked Jackson's entrenched position, without gaining any advantage. Finally, Pakenham planned for Colonel William Thornton to cross to the west side of the Mississippi River on the night of January 7, move north to capture naval batteries the following morning, and then turn the guns on Jackson's line. On the morning of January 8, Major General John Lambert would lead an eight-thousand-man frontal assault into the teeth of Jackson's line. If Thornton was successful, Pakenham believed that Lambert would have little difficultly breaching Jackson's defenses.

Pakenham's plans were too complicated and called for too much precision and cooperation. Moreover, once the fighting started on the morning of January 8, 1815, the British plan crumbled. Pakenham's army met stiff opposition at the Rodriguez Canal, and within thirty minutes some two thousand Redcoats had been killed, wounded, or captured. The dead included Pakenham. Thornton's operations on the west bank had fared better, but the disaster on the Plains of Chalmette effectively determined the outcome of the Battle of New Orleans, as well as the British Southern campaign.

Beginning on January 9, British ships bombed Fort St. Philip to the south on the Mississippi River, in the hopes of clearing a water approach to the city. Yet after nine unsuccessful days of bombing, the British gave up their quest for New Orleans and evacuated Louisiana. The last military operation of the campaign occurred a month later (February 8–11, 1815) at Fort Bowyer. Yet two days after the British victory at Fort Bowyer, news of the Treaty of Ghent—ending the war—reached the Gulf Coast, which ended all operations.

The British disaster at the Battle of New Orleans settled once and for all the question of the Louisiana Purchase. Neither the British nor the Spanish government had recognized the legality of the transfer, and, as such, the British had planned either to retain the region or return Louisiana to Spain had they won the battle. Jackson's victory, however, provided military force to the argument that Louisiana had been legally purchased, developed, and defended by the United States—thus it was unquestionably U.S. territory. The Battle of New Orleans ensured that the United States would retain Louisiana, which in turn guaranteed future westward expansion for a growing American republic.

—Gene A. Smith

See also
War of 1812

For Further Reading

Brown, Wilburt S. 1969. *The Amphibious Campaign for West Florida and Louisiana, 1814–1815.* Tuscaloosa: University of Alabama Press; Latour, Arsène Lacarrière. 1999 [1816]. *Historical Memoir of the War in West Florida and Louisiana in 1814–15: With an Atlas.* Edited by Gene A. Smith. Gainesville: Historic New Orleans Collection and the University Press of Florida; Owsley, Frank L., Jr. 1981. *Struggle for the Gulf Borderlands: The Creek War and the Battle of New Orleans, 1812–1815.* Gainesville: University Press of Florida; Remini, Robert V. 1999. *The Battle of New Orleans: Andrew Jackson and America's First Military Victory.* New York: Viking Press.

NEWSPAPERS (INTERNATIONAL) AND THE LOUISIANA PURCHASE

News of the Louisiana Purchase appeared in print primarily in the countries affected directly by the acquisition of the territory by the United States. French papers, fearing retribution or the loss of their privilege to publish, offered scant accounts concerning the transfer of Louisiana, based entirely on fact with no editorials. The Spanish government refused to recognize the legitimacy of the transaction, therefore any printed information focused on Spain's displeasure with the affair. British newspapers offered information concerning the purchase primarily through quoting U.S. newspapers. On occasion the publishers interjected limited editorial comments.

The Spanish government contested the treaty that transferred power over Louisiana from the French to the U.S. government. Spanish newspapers indicated that the disagreement specifically involved the apparent inclusion of West Florida as part of the actual purchase. Arguing that their country had conquered both East and West Florida from the British in 1730 and that West Florida had remained a separate government that formed no part of Louisiana at any time, the Spanish press contended that the transfer of Louisiana back to the French and subsequently to the United States could not include any territory east of the Mississippi as far as the River Perdido. Inasmuch as the Treaty of Paris, which ceded Louisiana to the United States, omitted any reference to West Florida, the Spanish court stated that the U.S. position remained "untenable." Letters from Spain published in U.S. papers indicated that Spain would not be willing to relinquish the disputed territory unless duly compensated. Other accounts indicated that the French never fulfilled the provision of the Treaty of San Ildefonso (1800) by which the territory would revert back to the Spanish, thereby bringing the whole issue of the purchase into question. A letter republished in the British papers signed by Vizente Tolch from Pensacola on May 1, 1804, indicated that the Spanish would be willing to resist, by force of arms if necessary, any U.S. attempt to occupy and control West Florida. When U.S. minister Charles Pinckney attempted to confer with the Spanish government concerning the matter, the King of Spain refused to meet with him. Pinckney subsequently returned to the United States without official recognition of the purchase from the Spanish court.

British newspapers, dealing with more important stories, such as the progress of the war against Napoleon, included a limited number of stories concerning the Louisiana Purchase. Upon learning of the proposed purchase, the *Times* carried a brief reference to Lord Hawkesbury's discussing papers before the House of Commons concerning events at the Cape of Good Hope and also involving Louisiana. The next reference simply stated that the newspaper had learned that the convention between the United States and France had been ratified by the French government on May 22, 1803, and that West Florida, but not East Florida, was included in the territory to be transferred. At this point the editors raised the issue of British commercial rights under the terms of the treaty. According to the terms of the purchase, New Orleans remained a free port for both the French and the Spanish. The United States had already concluded a treaty establishing most favored nation status with Great Britain. The editor noted that a difficulty between the two countries could possibly arise over the issue. He then noted that dissension had developed within the United States over the acquisition of Louisiana by purchase and that the upcoming presidential elections were being conducted with much acrimony. The next reference discussed a "curious statement" printed in the *Daily Advertiser* (New York) which stated that dispatches from England contained references to the British government's taking possession of Louisiana and warning President Thomas Jefferson not to pay the French government the agreed-upon price. No further editorial comment accompanied the report.

With rumors abounding concerning the possibility of Spanish resistance to the transfer, stories appeared in the *Times* concerning the matter. The newspaper reprinted a letter from an American in New Orleans dated December 18, 1802, in which he claimed to have a copy of the instructions given to the Spanish intendant's office. The orders stated that the Colony of Louisiana was to be turned over to the French commission at the pleasure of the King of Spain. Another letter to the intendant of Louisiana from the legislature of New York reprinted on the same page warned that the people of that state hoped that the issue between the United States and Spain could be resolved peacefully, but that barring any diplomatic solution they would be willing to defend the nation's honor and rights. The editor noted that Jefferson was under pressure from the Western states to take control of the territory before it reverted back to France, thereby ensuring control over the region by military force. In late November 1803 the *Times* published another article in which a reference was made to a Philadelphia paper that discussed the continued dissatisfaction over the measure and the anticipation of armed resistance to the transfer. The editor then noted that the first consul [Napoleon] had sold Louisiana both for the money and to prevent Great Britain from acquiring the territory militarily. With the Americans preparing to take possession, the British newspapers ran a rather lengthy article concerning the continued use of the French language in Louisiana. The editors argued that the diffusion of the French language would lead to all vernacular material being read in that dialect. Subsequently, the population would become Frenchified, resulting in a state within the United States tied to France that could become an enemy of the Senate and the House. As the time of U.S. possession approached, several articles appeared reporting the formation of troops from Ohio, Kentucky, and Tennessee that would march from Fort Adams to New Orleans. After chronicling the departure of the French from the port city, the British newspapers dropped the story.

—*Cynthia Clark Northrup*

For Further Reading

London Times. January 8, 1803–February 24, 1804.

NEWSPAPERS (U.S.) AND THE LOUISIANA PURCHASE

Newspaper reaction to the Spanish cession of Louisiana to France and Jefferson's purchase of the territory ran predictably along party lines. Both Republican and Federalist papers strongly opposed extended French presence in America, but, once the purchase had been announced, Federalist editors rose in near unison against the administration's liberal spending and what party leaders considered unconstitutional treaty terms.

America's newspaper industry at the turn of the nineteenth century was as unstable as the political arena and economic markets. Newspapers appeared one day and went out of business within weeks or months. Although several survived for years, most were short-lived. The average paper was of four folio pages and dominated by advertisements. For example, the New York *Evening Post,* one of the strongest papers of the early nineteenth century, carried only advertisements on the front page. The news was dominated by European affairs, and the local news that was published was primarily reprinted material from some of the major papers and other well-established sources. It was common, during the congressional session on the Louisiana treaty, for all newspapers to reprint Senate and House debates over issues such as monies paid France or the constitutionality of the treaty. Not all papers, however, regurgitated news—again the *Evening Post* included a daily opinion on a current issue such as the disposition of Louisiana. These newspapers were primarily weeklies, and distribution was irregular. Most newspapers were circulated and recirculated through informal networks such as libraries, clubs, reading rooms, and taverns. Few had a lengthy subscription list, and payments were often in arrears. If not for advertising and political patronage, most newspapers would not have remained in publication for very long.

Some of the finest minds of the early Republic found careers in newspaper editing. These included Samuel Harrison Smith of the *National Intelligencer,* William Duane of the Philadelphia *Aurora,* William Coleman of the *Evening Post,* and Enos Bronson of the *Gazette of the United States* in Philadelphia. Men such as these followed party affiliations in their editorials and seldom strayed from the party line on national issues. The press reaction to the Louisiana Purchase, with a few exceptions, fits this description.

The leading administration newspapers of the day included the *Aurora,* Washington's *National Intelligencer,* the Richmond *Enquirer,* and Boston's *Independent Chronicle.* Jefferson's close ally Thomas Ritchie was editor of the *Enquirer,* and Abijah Adams edited the Boston newspaper. Among prominent Federalist papers were Coleman's *Evening Post;* the *Columbian Centinel* of Boston, edited by Benjamin Russell; the Richmond *Recorder;* and the *Gazette of the United States.* One of the most outspoken and controversial figures of the early American press, James Thomson Callender, operated the *Recorder.* Collectively, these and other newspapermen played significant roles in the nation's public reaction to the Louisiana Purchase, yet objectivity was never certain in the press—party loyalty was much more important.

In early March 1802, the opposition newspapers began covering Spain's cession to France. With the *Aurora* stating the Republican position that a cession had occurred, various Federalist papers questioned any ceding of territory, and a press war over Louisiana ensued. The next issue to be widely debated in the press was rumors of the closing of the port at New Orleans and what course the administration intended to follow. On

November 26, 1802, the *National Intelligencer* announced the closing, an event that brought diplomatic relations between the United States, Spain, and France to a loggerhead. Typical of the Federalist stance was the *Recorder* (April 3, 1802), in which Callender commented: "The French are now masters of the Western water. Tennessee and Kentucky cannot send a single barrel of flour to the West Indies, if the first consul chuses [*sic*] to forbid them." He and other Federalist editors continued attacking Jefferson over access to New Orleans, but when Jefferson announced James Monroe's appointment as special envoy to France and Spain, the *Evening Post* (February 8, 1803) termed the appointment "the weakest measure that ever disgraced the administration of any country." The Federalist newspapers took turns offering wild speculation on pending conflict over the territory, the closing of New Orleans, and the administration's ineptness in dealing with Napoleon. The Republican press countered with what they thought was sound argument and calming words, indicating that in the end diplomacy would address U.S. concerns favorably.

On June 30, 1803, the *Independent Chronicle's* headline blared forth: "LOUISIANA CEDED TO THE UNITED STATES!" With an "I told you so" attitude, Adams reminded readers that "the wise, seasonable and politic negotiation of the President . . . has gloriously terminated to the immortal honor of the friends of peace and good government, and to the utter disappointment of the factious and turbulent throughout the Union." On July 4, the *National Intelligencer* followed in a less assertive manner, and the *Aurora* announced the treaty on July 7. Newspapers around the country reprinted the news, hailed as a "highly brilliant event," from these Republican papers. The Federalist press, however, responded predictably, calling into question the secrecy of the details of the treaty, only to follow with concerns over constitutionality.

The potential to upset the balance in the Senate was noted by the *Columbian Centinel,* which called the region (July 13, 1803): "a great waste, a wilderness unpeopled with any beings except wolves and wandering Indians." On July 5, the *Evening Post* noted surprisingly that Louisiana was an "important acquisition" not so much for the territory as for "being essential for the peace and prosperity of our Western country." But Coleman never ceased his attacks upon Jefferson and his character, stating in the same column that the acquisition was the result of political entanglements in Europe, "and not to any wise or vigorous measures on the part of the American government." Other Federalist papers followed the *Evening Post*'s lead attacking Jefferson, but some did not agree that acquiring Louisiana was essential. The *Columbian Centinel* continued to question the cost: "It rises daily," Russell quipped on August 10, 1803, a price that all Federalists considered exorbitant. The Republican press ardently defended the purchase, those who arranged it (most notably, Robert Livingston and Monroe), Jefferson, and eventually the constitutionality of the Louisiana treaty.

Another common newspaper practice in the early nineteenth century was to offer criticism of opposing newspapers by reprinting their editorials with an especially sharp attack. Both Federalist and Republican newspapers were littered with reprinted segments of an opposition paper's editorials followed by a biting critique on the author's logic. An example is a column in Coleman's *Evening Post,* which refers to Duane, one of Coleman's favorite targets, as "[t]he poleman who edits the *Aurora.*"

The Louisiana treaty dominated the press during the first six months of 1803 and beyond. But other issues replaced party divisions over Louisiana, such as a yellow fever epidemic that hit New York City in the summer of 1803. Yet the escalating cost of acquiring the territory, its unsettled lands and exploration, and congressional representation were all issues freely discussed in print, all with the same party thrust and parry so common to Federalists and Republicans of the new republic.

—*Boyd Childress*

For Further Reading

Knudson, Jerry W. 1969. "Newspaper Reaction to the Louisiana Purchase: 'This New, Immense, Unbounded World.'" *Missouri Historical Review* 63: 182–215; Knudson, Jerry W. 1962. "The Jefferson Years: Response by the Press, 1801–1809." Unpublished dissertation, University of Virginia.

NOLAN, PHILIP (1771–1801)

Philip Nolan was the first Anglo-American to pursue a systematic horse-trading operation in Texas, making four journeys into the region. His efforts garnered the interest of Thomas Jefferson and the wrath of Spanish officials. By 1778 the native of Belfast, Ireland, resided in Kentucky and served as the clerk for General James Wilkinson. Through that nefarious leader, Nolan gained significant insight into Western lands and learned to speak Spanish. His occupation enabled him to witness the lack of horses for the booming U.S. cattle industry. The promise of riches and the long, poorly defended border lured Nolan to Texas.

Nolan first entered Texas in 1791 after receiving permission from the governor of Louisiana. Officials in the area, however, objected to his activities and confiscated his trade goods after accusing Nolan of spying. Once freed he remained in Texas, living among the Comanche for two years. In 1793, Governor Luis Hector, Baron de Carondelet, of Louisiana granted Nolan a pass to return to Texas. After traveling as far south as La Bahía, Nolan returned to Natchez and sold 250 mustangs. He also provided a detailed account to Wilkinson that deemed the region fertile and extremely conducive to collecting large numbers of horses.

Despite serious apprehensions about Americans in general, and Nolan in particular, Spanish officials granted him a third passport in 1799. Nolan gathered more than twelve hundred mustangs and successfully conducted extensive trade with the Indians. Again he passed on information to Wilkinson, which the general used to make the first American map of Louisiana and Texas. His motives, ties to Wilkinson, and friendly relations with the Comanche convinced the Spanish commander for the region, Pedro de Nava, to order the arrest and interrogation of Nolan, if the mustanger returned to Texas. In Natchez, Governor Manuel Gayoso de Lemos concurred, charging that Nolan worked directly for Wilkinson and was a significant threat to the Spanish. In 1799, Gayoso warned Nava that Nolan should be prevented from reconnoitering Spanish territory in the future.

Although aware of his sullied reputation, Nolan prepared for his most ambitious enterprise. In October 1800 he departed Natchez with twenty-seven men, enraging Gayoso, who alerted the frontier to the hostile intentions of the expedition. The mustangers entered Texas north of Nacogdoches and proceeded to cross the Trinity River before continuing on to the Brazos River (near the present-day Hill County town of Blum). There the men constructed a crude fort and horse pens. Spanish troops from Nacogdoches converged on the mustangers on March 21, 1801. Outnumbered six to one, Nolan and his followers mounted a meager defense, but a cannon ball killed Nolan and the remaining men surrendered. The captives languished in prisons until 1807, when Spanish officials ordered the remaining eight men to cast dice to determine which one of their party would be executed for firing on the king's soldiers. Ephrium Blackburn's total of four, the smallest sum, resulted in his execution. With relative ease, the Spanish blunted Nolan's effort and temporarily secured the region from U.S. interference. His purpose was commercial in nature and only partially successful. He had no intention of attempting to wrest control of Texas from the Spanish like the Burr Conspiracy, the Long Expedition, or the Gutierrez-Magee invasion.

Nolan's efforts, however, had a significant impact. His four expeditions into the region demonstrated the lack of Spanish preparedness in Texas. Spanish officials muted the incursion only because of Nolan's poor planning and paucity of numbers. After eliminating the perceived threat, the Spanish failed to assess accurately or make changes in the region. Nolan's expeditions continued to color Spanish perceptions of Americans until the Mexican Revolution (1821). Spanish officials believed that Americans were either outlaws or intriguers who wanted to take control of the area. The Louisiana Purchase in 1803 heightened these feelings as Texas became a strategically significant area, rather than an isolated outpost. Nolan's death and the treatment of the remaining prisoners also intensified U.S.-Spanish relations. Throughout the expanding American west, Nolan became a symbol of U.S. ambition. Writer Edward Everett Hale selected Nolan as the hero for his popular story "The Man without a Country." As a result, he earned a patriotic reputation as an early agent of Manifest Destiny. Nolan's most vital contribution to the area, however, came in identifying the first great industry of Texas—cattle and horses.

—*Dallas Cothrum*

See also
Manifest Destiny; Texas; Wilkinson, James

For Further Reading
Wilson, Maurie T., and Jack Jackson. 1987. *Philip Nolan and Texas: Experience into the Unknown Land, 1791–1801.* Waco: Texian Press.

NOOTKA SOUND CRISIS (1789)

The Nootka Sound crisis opened the eyes of American political leaders, including Secretary of State Thomas Jefferson, to the potential dangers to American security of a British attack on Florida and Louisiana. The incident helped many political leaders to reach the conclusion that the United States should possess those territories. Therefore, when rumors of Louisiana's retrocession to France through the Treaty of San Ildefonso (1800) reached Washington, it was only natural for Jefferson to take steps to purchase Louisiana from the French in 1803. Certainly, therefore, the Nootka Sound crisis was an antecedent leading to the purchase of the territory.

The crisis had its genesis in the centuries-old colonial and commercial rivalry between Catholic Spain and Protestant England. The Spanish claimed the territory in contention, Nootka Sound, on the western coast of Vancouver Island in present-day British Columbia. Although the Spanish had visited the area as early as 1774, Captain James Cook, an Englishman, was perhaps the first European to go ashore in 1778. Cook found out that Nootka was an excellent source of sea otter skins. After his journals were published, Nootka Sound immediately became a destination for Europeans and Americans seeking furs and profits.

The Spaniards in Mexico became alarmed at the intense fur trade at Nootka, and they decided to fortify the area to protect their interests. Having established a settlement there, the Spaniards decided to dislodge others from the area, including the British, by seizing their ships. The British attempt to set up a post was scuttled, and some of the British settlers were captured and deported to Mexico. Exaggerated accounts of Spanish aggrandizement reached Great Britain. The British government demanded that Spain release its ships and their crews, pay compensation for Spanish infringement upon British sovereignty, and allow the British to establish settlements on areas unoccupied by the Spanish. Spain demanded that

Great Britain apologize for the conduct of its nationals. Britain threatened to go to war against Spain. Once again, Europe was on the verge of a crisis and war appeared imminent throughout the summer of 1790 as Prime Minister William Pitt made preparations for war.

During the crisis, it was rumored that the British might attack and occupy Spanish territories in Florida and Louisiana. The Washington administration was alarmed about the prospects of the British taking over those territories in case of a war with Spain. President Washington believed that it was undesirable to allow the British to encircle the United States both on the east and west of the country. Washington sought the advice of his cabinet in dealing with a potential British threat. Pro-British Alexander Hamilton and Pro-French Thomas Jefferson were unanimous in their opinion that, at least in the long run, the United States should possess both the Florida and Louisiana Territories. Jefferson suggested intervention in the war to see that Britain did not occupy both Florida and Louisiana. He believed that Spain should be pressured to surrender those territories to the United States.

The United States had hoped to mediate the conflict between Spain and Britain. That, however, did not materialize. At this time Spain was without allies in Europe because its traditional ally, France, was in the throes of a revolution. Therefore, the Spanish backed down and signed the Convention of 1790. The convention settled the dispute between the two countries and opened the area for British exploitation. However, since Britain and France remained deadlocked in a deadly war between 1793 and 1815, Britain was unable to exploit this concession fully. That allowed the United States to expand without British opposition. The crisis enabled the Spaniards to realize the seriousness of American intentions toward the Spanish colonial territories in North America. The Spanish, however, had no intention to give any of their territories to the United States because Spain's policy after America gained independence was to contain the United States and keep it from expanding, especially in the direction of Spanish territories.

The American leaders realized the perils for the United States of European rivalry in areas around the Mississippi River. Jefferson became aware of the Louisiana Territory's value in the development of the country. It was therefore, no wonder that Jefferson, during his first term as president, became disturbed over the rumored retrocession of Louisiana to the French and took immediate steps to purchase New Orleans.

—*George Thadathil*

For Further Reading

Bemis, Samuel Flagg, ed. 1963. *The American Secretaries of State and Their Diplomacy.* New York: Cooper Square; DeConde, Alexander. 1976. *This Affair of Louisiana.* New York: Charles Scribner's Sons; Whitaker, Arthur Preston. 1949. *The Mississippi Question, 1795–1803: A Study in Trade, Politics and Diplomacy.* New York: Foreign Policy Association.

NORTH DAKOTA

Present-day North Dakota is the geographical center of North America with points practically equidistant between the Atlantic and Pacific Oceans, as well as being situated midway between the Arctic Ocean and the Gulf of Mexico. The western two-thirds of the state is situated within the Missouri-Mississippi drainage basin and therefore was acquired by the United States when it purchased the Louisiana Territory from France in 1803. The eastern portion of the state, which drains northward into Canada through the Mouse River and the Red River of the North, came into American possession once the United States and Great Britain signed the Convention of 1818 and set the U.S.-Canadian border at 49 degrees north latitude.

The prairies and woodlands of North Dakota were home to indigenous peoples for thousands of years prior to the arrival of Europeans into the region. The presence of these native communities and the sophistication of the culture that they formed is evidenced by impressive artifacts of material culture that survive, such as the complex burial and ceremonial site at Jamestown mounds. In the early seventeenth century, just prior to the arrival of Europeans in the region, many of the indigenous peoples of North Dakota were on the move. Many among the Cheyenne, the Hidatsa, and the Sioux were migrating from the eastern woodlands setting where they had lived as agriculturalists to the Missouri River Valley where they became more nomadic hunters of the Northern Plains.

For many years, this pattern of life was undisturbed, but by the mid-eighteenth century, changes began to occur as European visitors arrived in the Dakota region. The elusive search for a Northwest Passage to the Pacific first brought Europeans to the region, but it was the trapping potential of the streams within what is now the state of North Dakota that impressed the early explorers. As early as 1738, an expedition from New France led by Pierre Gaultier de Varennes, Sieur de La Vérendrye, and his brothers Francois and Louis Joseph, traveled through much of the Missouri Valley and claimed it for France. These French explorers were the first Europeans to make contact with the Mandan villages that were located along the Missouri River. Similar expeditions that sought to determine the value of the region to the fur trade were led by Jonathan Carver in 1768 and by David Thompson in 1797.

The potential value of North Dakota's rivers and streams attracted many agents of empire who used the pretext of the fur trade to extend territorial claims. In time, the French, the Spanish, and the British would all investigate the wealth borne by beaver and other fur-bearing animals that inhabited the Dakota streams. By 1781 trappers associated with the North West Company had established a fur trading post along the Souris River, but the facility was soon abandoned when Sioux living in the region showed little support for the venture. By 1801 there were four fur trading posts established in the area—along the Knife River, at Pembina, at Park River, and at Grand Forks.

The multinational interest in North Dakota subsided as the French were removed from North America under terms of the Treaty of Paris (1763), and again in 1803, when the United States acquired the Louisiana Territory. Still, a rivalry between British and American fur interests persisted in the area since both nations did possess legal claims to territory within present-day North Dakota. The presence of American explorers, merchants, and traders would become increasingly familiar in the region as the Missouri River Valley soon became the favored corridor of transit and commerce for U.S. expeditions that traveled through North Dakota.

By 1804, the United States government had authorized a federally funded expedition to explore the upper reaches of the Louisiana Territory and to travel overland to the Pacific Ocean. On both their trip to and from the Pacific, Lewis and Clark and their Corps of Discovery would traverse the region of North Dakota as they followed the path of the Missouri River. Along the route, the expedition held council with the Arikara and lived among the Mandan, near present-day Washburn during the winter of 1804–1805.

In spite of the volume of traffic that passed through present-day North Dakota, there were very few white settlements established in the area. By 1812 the region around Pembina, located along the Red River of the North, had become a nucleus of farm settlements, but few pioneers ventured beyond the well-watered bottomlands to settle upon and attempt to cultivate the sod of the vast prairie. The U.S. Army created a number of frontier outposts in North Dakota in order to protect the fur trade, but these locations did little to foster creation of towns.

The U.S. government conducted surveying and mapping expeditions in the region generally under the auspices of the army. In 1839 much of the east-central portion of present-day North Dakota was explored by John C. Frémont and Jean Nicollet. In 1853 Issac I. Stevens traveled through the region conducting topographic surveying that was associated with efforts to find the most practical route for constructing a transcontinental railroad. Much of Stevens's route would later be used by entrepreneur James J. Hill when he created the Great Northern Railroad. By 1861 the U.S. government established the Dakota Territory—the region that encompasses modern North and South Dakota—and named William Jayne as the first territorial governor.

White settlement in North Dakota began to increase after the passage of the Homestead Act (1862), but it remained rather limited. Later, in the 1870s, large numbers of Scandinavian immigrants and others from Northern Europe were recruited to settle in the area as the tracks of the Northern Pacific and the Great Northern Railroads were built. This immigration pattern persisted for nearly four decades and helped to create a unique cultural population in the area.

As a result of the Sioux Uprising (1862) in neighboring Minnesota, large numbers of Santee Sioux were relocated to reservation land in the Dakotas. By 1870 the U.S. government had established the Fort Berthold Indian Reservation, which became home to many Sioux and Ojibwa who had been relocated from Minnesota.

The presence of two transcontinental railroads in the region made much of North Dakota accessible to Eastern markets. As a result, settlers began to settle the rich prairies and cultivate wheat. With the exaggeration of self-promotion, some Dakota wheat farmers maintained that the fertile topsoil in the region was four feet deep. In other regions, where water scarcity made agriculture less practical, large portions of the Dakota prairie became prime ranch land. The lure of profits in wheat and cattle, and for some, the adventurous chance to live upon America's last frontier, attracted many to the region. By the late 1870s, the area experienced a bit of a land rush. Even a young Theodore Roosevelt left the East to live and work as a ranch hand in the Dakota Badlands, near Medora, from 1883 to 1886.

The 1880 census recorded 98,000 residents in the Dakota Territory, which then included both present-day North and South Dakota, and by 1890, the population had reached 349,000. The two states of North Dakota and South Dakota entered the Union—simultaneously—on November 29, 1889, becoming the thirty-ninth and fortieth states.

—Junius P. Rodriguez

See also
Mandan; Santee Sioux; South Dakota

For Further Reading

Robinson, Elwyn B. 1966. *History of North Dakota.* Lincoln: University of Nebraska Press.

NUTTALL, THOMAS (1786–1859)

Thomas Nuttall was a leading naturalist in the United States during the first half of the nineteenth century. During his career, he explored and collected plant specimens in much of the region that composed the Louisiana Purchase. He published his observations in numerous works, helping to disseminate information about the natural history of the area and identifying plant species never before recorded. Nuttall also essentially changed the way that naturalists, and especially botanists, conducted their work. Prior to his career, botanists tended to study the specimen collected by others, generally explorers with little or no training, such as Meriwether Lewis. With Nuttall, fieldwork became standard practice for botanists, along with time spent in herbariums and museums.

Thomas Nuttall was born in England on January 5, 1786. After apprenticing as a printer in Liverpool, he left to pursue his first love—botany. Having arrived in Philadelphia in 1808, Nuttall took up the study of his chosen field with Dr. Benjamin Smith Barton of the Medical College of Philadelphia, a noted naturalist and physician who had trained Meriwether Lewis in the basic principles of natural history in preparation for the Lewis and Clark expedition. It is likely that some of Nuttall's earliest botanical studies involved specimens collected during that famous journey, for Thomas Jefferson had ordered the first shipment of such items sent to Barton for study and cataloging. By 1810, the massive project still barely underway, Barton turned to his young protégé, Nuttall, for assistance. He charged Nuttall with retracing Lewis and Clark's journey in order to collect additional plant specimens, to verify and extend the knowledge acquired on the first expedition.

Nuttall set out in 1810, taking a circuitous route through the Great Lakes region in order to study its flora. He then journeyed down the Mississippi to St. Louis. From there, in the spring of 1811, he joined a party exploring the regions around the Missouri River, through the heart of the Louisiana Territory, collecting plants and other specimens along the way. The threat of war with England in late 1811 forced Nuttall to return to his homeland. While in England, Nuttall wrote descriptions of many of the plant specimens that he had collected in the Louisiana Territory. Some of Nuttall's specimens were listed in a leaflet published by Fraser's Nursery, Chelsea, entitled *A Catalogue of New and Interesting Plants, Collected in Upper Louisiana, and Principally on the River Missouri, North America* (1813). Frederick Pursh, another disciple of Barton's who was also in England at the time, wrote scientific descriptions of some of Nuttall's specimens and included them in his *Flora Americae Septentrionalis* (1814). While he was in England, the prestigious Linnaean Society of London honored Nuttall's work as a naturalist by electing him to its membership.

At the war's conclusion, Nuttall returned to the United States and began his most prolific years as a naturalist. From 1815 to 1817 he traveled through the southeastern United States studying its flora and collecting specimens. In 1817 the Academy of Natural Sciences of Philadelphia and the American Philosophical Society each honored Nuttall by electing him to membership. In 1818, drawing on all of his observations since he began botanical studies in 1808, Nuttall published his first major work, the two-volume *Genera of North American Plants with a Catalogue of the Species through 1817* (Philadelphia: D. Heartt, 1818).

From 1818 to 1820, Nuttall explored the southwestern portion of the Louisiana Purchase (the Arkansas Territory, then comprising what is now Oklahoma). His *Journal of Travels into the Arkansas Territory during the Year 1819* offered for a general audience the first detailed account of the flora and fauna of that region. He did not, however, produce scientific descriptions of the specimens he gathered there until 1837.

In 1822, Nuttall began an eleven-year career as curator of the botanic gardens and lecturer in natural history at Harvard University. During that time he published his first textbook, the *Introduction to Systematic and Physiological Botany* (1827). In 1833, Boston merchant Nathaniel Wyeth brought Nuttall some plant samples from the Rocky Mountain regions in order to tempt him to resign his university position and once again venture into the vast regions of the Louisiana Purchase. Wyeth was funding an expedition to the Columbia River in the far Northwest and wanted Nuttall to join the team in the capacity of naturalist. Wyeth's persuasion successful, Nuttall departed from St. Louis in 1834. In 1834 and 1835, Nuttall explored, collected plant specimens, and studied birds in what are now Wyoming, Idaho, Oregon, California, and Hawaii.

Late in 1835, Nuttall returned to Philadelphia. From 1836 to 1841, he was affiliated with the Academy of Natural Sciences of Philadelphia (est. 1812), one of the most distinguished scientific organizations in North America. Although he took some shorter collecting trips during this period, he devoted most of his time to writing descriptions of the hundreds of plant species he had discovered during his travels in the regions of the Louisiana Purchase. Some of those descriptions appeared in *Flora of North America,* by John Torrey and Asa Gray.

Nuttall retired from active field work in 1841, returning to England to satisfy the conditions of a recent inheritance the terms of which stipulated that he reside in that country for at least a part of each year. Between 1842 and 1852, he produced his last major work, a revision of François André Michaux's *Histoire des arbres forestiers de l'Amérique septentrionale* (two volumes, Paris, 1810–1813). Drawing on many years of fieldwork, Nuttall completed a three-volume supplement and added illustrations. The resulting work, *North American Sylva; or a Description of the Forest Trees of the United States, Canada, and Nova Scotia,* took seven years to complete and appeared in three volumes, the last published in 1849. Nuttall died in England in 1859.

—Lisa J. Pruitt

See also

Flora of the Louisiana Purchase; Michaux, André

For Further Reading

Beidleman, Richard G. 1960. "Some Biographical Sidelights on Thomas Nuttall, 1786–1859." *Proceedings of the American Philosophical Society* 104, no. 1: 86–100; Graustein, Jeannette E. 1967. *Thomas Nuttall, Naturalist: Explorations in America, 1808–1841.* Cambridge: Harvard University Press; Lottinville, Savoie, ed. 1980. "Editor's Introduction." In *A Journal of Travels into the Arkansas Territory during the Year 1819.* Norman: University of Oklahoma Press; Merritt, John I., III. 1977. "Naturalists across the Rockies: The 1834 Journey of John Kirk Townsend and Thomas Nuttall." *s* 14, no. 2: 4–9, 62–63.

OGLALA SIOUX

The Sioux (Lakota/Dakota/Nakota) nation consists of several different groups who were the original inhabitants of much of the northern portion of the Louisiana Purchase Territory. The name Sioux was first applied by French trappers and traders who mispronounced the derogatory term *Nadowesioux* (meaning "little snake" or "enemy") that the Ojibwa used to describe their neighbors. When American settlers first encountered the Lakota, they also used the name Sioux.

The Oglala (meaning "Scatter Their Own") Sioux were members of the Tetonwan division of the Lakota Nation—an ethnic subdivision that included the Brule, Hunkpapa, Blackfoot, Minnecoujou, No Bows, and Two Kettle bands. The Yankton and the Isanti constitute the two other major divisions of the Lakota.

Perhaps the most representative of the tribes of the Northern Plains, the Sioux were a nomadic group of hunters who relied almost exclusively upon the presence of the bison. (Smithsonian American Art Museum/Art Resource)

Archaeological evidence suggests that the Lakota arrived in Minnesota around 1200 C.E. and established farming villages. In addition to farming, the group also fished in the numerous lakes and streams of the region and hunted the wild game that abounded in the woodlands. By the sixteenth century, around the time that the Oglala Sioux first encountered French trappers and traders, the group had extended themselves into portions of present-day South Dakota. The Oglala had migrated westward because the better-armed Ojibwa had forced them out of contested terrain in Minnesota. In time, the Oglala adapted to their new environment and became expert horsemen and buffalo hunters of the Great Plains. They became known by surrounding tribes as Pte Oyate (the "Buffalo People").

Newly arrived in the Dakota region and settled along the Missouri River, the Oglala Sioux soon became notorious among Western trappers and traders for disrupting river commerce. Most problematic to the St. Louis merchants, who were unable to reach the Mandan because of the Sioux, was that the British trappers of the North West Company were reaching the Mandan by way of Lake Winnipeg. In the eyes of the merchants and pioneers from the United States who hoped to make the Missouri River a safe avenue on which to facilitate commerce and westward settlement, the Sioux would either have to be pacified or otherwise removed from their Missouri River villages.

The U.S. government negotiated with the Oglala Sioux and other tribes in the Treaty of Fort Laramie (1851) and again in the Treaty of Fort Laramie (1868). The result of these agreements was the gradual resettlement of the Sioux in the Black Hills region of southwestern South Dakota, which became, in time, the spiritual center of the Oglala Sioux nation. Gold was discovered in the Black Hills in 1874, and shortly thereafter the United States again sought to relocated the Sioux, to more restrictive reservation lands. The Sioux began to fashion a resistance campaign that would culminate at the Battle of Little Big Horn in 1876.

Even though the Sioux won a tremendous victory when they defeated General George A. Custer and the Seventh Cavalry, in the end the superior weapons and the determination of the U.S. government would lead to the reduction of the tribe and its relocation to reservation plots. Still, the Sioux would not make the task an easy one. With the "Sell or Starve Bill," the Agreement of 1877, U.S. government took the Black Hills from the Sioux after the tribe collectively refused to sell its sacred lands. Subsequent legislation relocated the remaining Sioux to reservations.

By the late 1880s, with their lands much reduced by treaties and federal legislation and with their numbers decimated by the combined effects of war, disease, relocation, and malnutrition, the Sioux had become a subject people. Further humiliation took place on December 15, 1890, when Hunkpapa chief Sitting Bull was killed while being arrested by Indian Police at the Standing Rock Reservation.

It was during this era that the Sioux, like many other Western tribes, placed their hope in the Ghost Dance. This messianic religious movement had spread rapidly from Nevada to the Dakotas and had inspired many by its other-worldly focus upon a return to the best elements of the past. As Western tribes longed for the much-anticipated day when the ancestors, the buffalo, and the land would be restored, U.S. government officials contemplated how they might stop the movement that they did not understand, but which they feared. The end would come at Wounded Knee—the December 29, 1890, massacre that marked the end of the Plains Indian Wars.

—Junius P. Rodriguez

See also
Black Hills; Wounded Knee

For Further Reading

Price, Catherine. 1996. *The Oglala People, 1841–1879: A Political History.* Lincoln: University of Nebraska Press.

OJIBWA

At the time of the Louisiana Purchase, the Ojibwa were one of the native peoples living within the territory. They occupied land to the south and north of Lakes Superior, Michigan, and Huron, and as far west as the western bank of the Mississippi River and its headwaters. A woodland Algonquian language culture, the Ojibwa had migrated west some four hundred years before, with the Ottawa and Potawatomi, from the mouth of the St. Lawrence River. Because of this alliance, these tribes were called the "Three Fires." Migrations led to battles with the Iroquois, Fox, and Sioux. Partial peace came with the 1825 Treaty of Prairie du Chien, which created a "no-man's land" between the Ojibwa and Sioux, and the 1826 Treaty of Fond du Lac. Even so, fighting continued into the 1850s. Referred to in treaties as the Chippewa, the Ojibwa called themselves Anishinabe, the First or Original People. "Ojibwa," may refer to the distinctive puckered seam used on moccasins or to a pictographic writing style.

Ojibwa communities were organized into clans or family lineages. Clans were denoted by animal, bird, fish, or reptile totems, or by symbols that provided spiritual guidance and specific attributes and predestined contributions. Families moved with the seasons from the spring maple sugar bush and fish camps to summer berry-picking and fall fishing and gathering of wild rice. The Ojibwa raised small gardens of squash, beans, corn, potatoes, and melons. Families were often isolated in winter, subsisting on food caches, hunting, and ice fishing. They traveled on foot, by birchbark canoe, or snow shoe. Ojibwa lived in easily constructed dome-shaped wigwams, frames of bent saplings covered with bark and woven rush mats. They fashioned birchbark containers and left birchbark pictographic scrolls with painted records of religious ceremonies and songs connected with the Midewiwin religion. In this Grand Medicine Society practitioners achieved expertise in medical treatments through study and initiation. Individual families gathered in the summers for socializing and trading. The traditional gathering place was first the Straits of Mackinac, where the Three Fires separated from each other, and, as the Ojibwa moved farther west, Madeleine Island. The Ojibwa leadership model included a hereditary elected civil chief who coordinated decisions through consensus. A war chief served in times of crisis with enough military support. Orators who participated in treaty negotiations were also valued. The Ojibwa were guided by dream interpretation, personal visions, and moral instruction through storytelling. Stories often featured Nanabush, a half-human, half-spirit culture-hero and shape changer whose often humorous or poignant struggles illustrated how the frailty of humankind attracted the benevolence of the universal spirit. The Ojibwa identified other manitou or spirits, both benign and, like the cannibalistic windigo, ferocious. Ojibwa decorated their deerskin clothing with dyed porcupine quills and later, through trading with Euro-Americans, colored glass beads, often sewn in floral designs.

The first contact with Europeans, French Jesuit missionaries, was in the 1640s, and, soon after, with French traders. Ojibwa culture was heavily influenced by the fur trade industry, which provided them with firearms. Contact with Euro-Americans also brought illness and death, through disease, easy access to alcohol, and abuse by unscrupulous traders. The General Allotment Act (1887) brought the establishment of reservations and individual land parcels, resulting in loss of tribal land. Assimilation was attempted through boarding schools, in which Indian children were educated in environments that discouraged cultural expression. The attempted removal of all Minnesota Ojibwa people to a newly created reservation, White Earth, in the late 1890s resulted in greater loss of tribal land. The Indian Reorganization Act (1934) enabled Ojibwa reservations to incorporate, and a short-lived culturally responsive educational model was introduced. This movement was stalled with the 1950s relocation movement but revitalized with the passage of the Self-Determination and Educational Assistance Act (1975).

The 1990, U.S. Census listed fifty thousand Ojibwa, ranking them one of the top ten tribal groups in terms of population size. About a third live on some one hundred reservations and reserves in the United States and Canada, including the seven reservations in Minnesota, as well as smaller numbers of reservations in Wisconsin, North Dakota, and Montana. Other Ojibwa live near reservations or in urban areas. Treaties reduced the Ojibwa homelands. The Ojibwa are currently undergoing a cultural reclamation movement, with governing models following a philosophy of self-determination, language recovery, land recovery, economic initiatives, and the exercising of treaty rights to hunt and fish. Some of these improvements are the result of casinos and other gaming enterprises.

—Loriene Roy

See also

Fox; Fur Trapping; Manifest Destiny; Minnesota; Mississippi River; Potawatomi

For Further Reading

Danziger, Edmund Jefferson, Jr. 1990. *The Chippewas of Lake Superior.* Norman, London: University of Oklahoma Press; Johnston, Basil. 1990. *Ojibway Heritage.* Toronto: McClelland and Stewart, 1976. Reprint: Lincoln: University of Nebraska Press; Tanner, Helen Hornbeck. 1992. *The Ojibwa.* New York, Philadelphia: Chelsea House; Tanner, John. *The Falcon: A Narrative of the Captivity and Adventures of John Tanner.* 1994 [1830]. New York: G. and C. H. Carvill. Reprint: New York: Penguin.

OKLAHOMA

Thomas Jefferson set aside Indian Territory beyond the 100-degree west meridian to be the "Home of the Red Man" (in Choctaw, "Oklahoma") forever. After the formation of the Kansas and Nebraska Territories before the Civil War, Southerners pressed for a transcontinental railroad route through southern Indian Territory. Agricultural expansion around the Great American Desert added pressure for settlement of part if not all of Indian Territory.

Because some Indians supported the Confederacy during the Civil War, the federal government ruled that their nations had abrogated their treaties. After the war, the government reduced reservations and attempted to bring the unoccupied lands onto the market. But the Indians stood firm against breaking up their lands into individual plots, and the government was unable to force them into allotment until the 1880s. Whites eager for new lands saw the western hunting area of the civilized tribes and Southern Plains Indians as unoccupied, and they wanted to settle there. They claimed that the Indians were allowing white cattlemen to use grazing lands anyway. And pressure for the southern transcontinental railroad grew. After the Civil War, the strong Eastern desire for Texas beef led to cattle drives through Indian Territory to the westward-moving railhead. The Chisholm Trail cut through Indian Territory west of the Indian meridian. Cattle drovers noticed that western Indian Territory was good cattle-raising country.

Sooners from Kansas pressured the government by moving onto Indian Territory and establishing camp on Stillwater Creek several times during the 1880s. Repeatedly, under the leadership of David Payne and William L. Couch, they entered; and repeatedly the army removed them. Each time, the size of the encroaching party grew. Finally Congress authorized the opening of the unassigned lands, the area remaining after the Dawes Act (1887) broke up tribal common lands into 160-acre tracts and induced the Indians to take allotment. That led to the run of 1889, in which fifty thousand claimants vied for ten thousand sites that were too small for viable plains agriculture.

Indian Territory developed a satellite, dependent, extractive economy of timber, tenancy, and coal. J. H. McAlester typified the Eastern railroad and coal owners. After leasing Choctaw coal lands, he arranged for the building of a railroad to the mines. Then he imported European miners because the Indians refused to work in the mines, among the most dangerous in the world. Most of the money from the mines went out of the territory to the Eastern railroad companies.

In Oklahoma Territory, wheat and petroleum dominated. Wheat farming attracted railroads, which attracted farmers, and the mutually beneficial exchange allowed the area to develop after the initial dusting out of the undercapitalized; on occasion the railroads would even provide free seed to encourage wheat planting. For oil, the Eastern giants could not establish the control that the coal barons had in Indian Territory. There was too much, and too many small players (wildcatters) could strike it rich from Cushing in the north to Healdton in the south—and seemingly everywhere in between.

White outlawry was a problem, because the U.S. government failed to give the Indians effective government or courts; Indian Territory became a hiding place for notorious outlaws such as Bill Doolin and Belle Starr, the horse thief. Hanging judge Parker hanged eighty-nine criminals between 1875 and 1895. Other white people co-opted dishonest Indians into joint ventures in poaching, smuggling, bootlegging, and cattle rustling.

Land runs occurred six times between 1889 and 1895. Among those coming to Oklahoma were Poles, Germans, Irish, and Slavs. Oklahoma began taking on an ethnic identity distinct from that of Indian Territory, where ownership still remained in the hands of the Indians, whether black or red. African Americans, either on the run or as independent freedmen, founded Taft, Boley, Langston, Arcadia, and other towns.

Too many people came in the land runs, and the original homestead was too small. The flurry of building in Tulsa and Oklahoma City fizzled. Many Sooners were undercapitalized; many were poor, including those who had lost their land in Kansas or Texas, and others were blacklisted miners or unemployed laborers. Tornadoes and drought were severe enough, but, in addition, capital was needed to prevent foreclosure. The dispossessed and poor of the West moved into Indian Territory, which saw a population increase from 70,000 in 1889 to 258,657 in 1890. Many became tenants, because land ownership by non-Indians was still barred.

The Organic Act (1890) organized Oklahoma as a territory with an appointed governor and secretary as well as patronage positions as judges, marshals, attorneys, and postmasters. In Indian Territory there was federal oversight of five republican governments with legislatures, courts, and various town governments. Both sides had Republicans, Democrats, Populists, and Socialists. Elections filled the territorial legislature, multitudes of local and regional offices, and one representative to the U.S. Congress. Electoral turnout in the 1890s averaged 75 percent. African Americans constituted about 5 percent of the electorate. Republicans dominated as the party of Union, Emancipation, the land run of 1889, and the Free Homes Bill (1900), which lifted the $15 million owed by settlers to the federal government.

Indian Territory politics were tribal, with only a handful of intermarried or adopted whites allowed to own property or to engage in politics. White politics focused on the hundreds of federal patronage positions. Although most officeholders were Republicans, the majority in Indian Territory were probably Democrat because of Southern migration patterns. Territorial government was a struggle between the governor and congressional delegate for patronage. Politics was issueless and ineffective in both Oklahoma and Indian Territory.

At the turn of the century, trusts and corporations such as U.S. Steel and International Harvester took over competitors and dominated the economy. After twenty-five years of deflation, prices rose 35 percent between 1897 and 1909. Food rose 36 percent and fuel rose 53 percent. Trusts abused their power. In Indian Territory, railroads shipped contaminated and rotting wheat. In Muskogee, the milk contained half a dozen dangerous drugs, boric acid, and bacteria. Territorial merchants sometimes sold foods that were outlawed in the surrounding states. Protest of an unsafe railroad bridge went nowhere for eight years; finally the span collapsed, and one hundred people died. Individuals were powerless, as the kerosene and book trusts bribed the territorial legislature. And corporations, when they paid taxes at all, paid a small fraction of the individual rate.

Progressive forces in Oklahoma and Indian Territories reacted. From 1903 farmers joined the Farmers' Educational and Co-operative Union. Labor created the Twin Territories Federation of Labor in 1903 (the United Mine Workers of America had seven thousand members at statehood). People such as Charles N. Haskell, the first state governor, worried about the class gap between producers and parasites. Reformer Kate Barnard, known as "Our Good Angel, Kate," organized a union of the poor. She advocated banning child labor, taxing inequitable wealth, and improving the lot of working men and women.

With statehood imminent, Indian Territory Democrats roused themselves from their lethargy in 1905. At Sequoyah, the supposed last effort to create an Indian state, Charles Haskell and "Alfalfa Bill" Murray stepped forward as progressive leaders to take the state from the political time-servers. The Sequoyah constitution outlawed trusts and tightly regulated corporations. It included tax reform, consumer protection, advanced labor laws, and humanitarian measures for the underprivileged. Approved by 86 percent of the voters, it was rejected outright by Congress.

The Enabling Act (1906) set in place the machinery for a constitutional convention. The Democrats met at Shawnee to write their platform. When Republicans ran a whites-only campaign, they alienated blacks and their vote plummeted. Democrats controlled the convention of 1907 and the state that followed. Led by Alfalfa Bill and Pete Hanraty of the coal miners, the convention produced a constitution that contained every progressive idea. Voters supported it by a margin of five-to-two. The first legislature, dominated by Democrats, enacted prohibition and Jim Crow laws, which remained in force for half a century.

Oklahoma was more than Boomers and Sooners. There were cowboys and Indians, black, white, and red—and coal miners who fought the absentee owners and made 1907 Oklahoma a model of progressivism. And there were the radicals, from the populists of the 1890s to 1907 to the IWW (International Workingmen of the World, a radical union) and the Socialists who, until World War I, were stronger in Oklahoma than anywhere else in the United States. But it all came crashing down after 1918. The last hurrah of the neopopulist coalition came in 1922 with the election of Jack Walton. After that, ownership of the state lay securely in the hands of the capitalist bankers, landlords, and oilmen who understood the national market economy and Oklahoma's subordinate role in it. Oklahomans either resisted the New Deal or accepted assistance only with great reluctance during the Great Depression; they staked their economic well-being on oil and gas into the 1980s, and they persisted as conservative Democrats or Republicans.

—J. Herschel Barnhill

For Further Reading

Gibson, Arrell. 1965. *Oklahoma: A History of Five Centuries.* Norman, OK: Harlow; Green, James R. 1978. *Grass-Roots Socialism: Radical Movements in the Southwest, 1895–1943.* Baton Rouge: Louisiana State University Press; Hines, Gordon. 1932. *Alfalfa Bill: An Intimate Biography.* Oklahoma City: Oklahoma Press; Joyce, Davis D. 1994. *An Oklahoma I Had Never Seen Before: Alternative Views of Oklahoma History.* Norman: University of Oklahoma Press; McReynolds, Edwin C. 1964. *Oklahoma: A History of the Sooner State.* Norman: University of Oklahoma Press; Morgan, Anne Hodges, and H. Wayne Morgan, eds. 1982. *Oklahoma: New Views of the Forty-Sixth State.* Norman: University of Oklahoma Press; Otis, D. S. 1973. *The Dawes Act and the Allotment of Indian Lands.* Norman: University of Oklahoma Press; Scales, James R., and Danney Goble. 1982. *Oklahoma Politics: A History.* Norman: University of Oklahoma Press; Thompson, John. 1986. *Closing the Frontier: Radical Response in Oklahoma, 1889–1923.* Norman: University of Oklahoma Press; Thurman, Melvena, ed. 1982. *Women in Oklahoma: A Century of Change.* Oklahoma City: Oklahoma Historical Society.

OREGON COUNTRY

The Oregon Country was the name attached to the vast and resource-rich region lying to the northwest of the Louisiana Purchase. The Oregon Country held the shortest land passage from the Missouri River to the Pacific Ocean, and was in a strategic location for trade between China, Spanish California, Russian Alaska, and America.

Although for much of its history the Oregon Country's boundaries were ambiguous and disputed, between 1819 and 1846 they became more firmly established. The Oregon Country's boundaries were the Continental Divide, on the east; the Pacific Ocean, on the west; the boundary of Russian Alaska at 54 degrees 40 minutes north latitude, on the north; and the boundary with Mexico at 42 degrees north latitude, on the south. The Oregon Country contained a great variety of terrain. Abundant rain from the northern Pacific Ocean created a temperate forest climate in the coastal mountain ranges, the Willamette Valley, Puget Sound, and the western Cascade Mountains. East of the Cascade crest were the semiarid sagebrush steppes of the Columbia Plateau and Snake River Plain, and several well-timbered interior mountain ranges. The Columbia River and its tributaries drained the majority of the region. Not all rivers drained to the Columbia, however. Several smaller rivers headed in the coastal ranges or northern Cascades and flowed directly into the Pacific Ocean or Puget Sound. Some southern sections of the Oregon Country were located in the Great Basin, and the streams there ended in large interior lakes, rather than the ocean.

The Oregon Country was a remote region, among the last places in North America visited by explorers of European heritage. The Spanish, seeking to block Russian expansion south from Alaska, were the first to explore and map the coast of the Oregon Country. In 1774, Juan Pérez sailed as far north as Nootka Sound on present-day Vancouver Island. During his expedition of 1789–1794, Alejandro Malaspina undertook scientific surveys of the coastal Oregon Country and southern Alaska. As a result, the Spanish sought to claim the Oregon Country, which bordered their northern territory of Alta California. Of course, Russia laid claim to the region as well.

The British based their claims to the region upon the northwest coastal explorations of Captain James Cook in 1778. In 1792, Captain George Vancouver made a more extensive survey of Vancouver Island, Puget Sound, and the Columbia River, which his subordinate, Lieutenant Broughton, sailed up aboard the H.M.S. *Chatham* in October 1792. The imperial aspirations of the European powers had clashed in 1789, when the Spanish seized a British vessel and trading post on Nootka Sound. The Nootka controversy sparked the first foreign policy crisis for the United States, and Americans feared a war in which the British would seize Louisiana from Spain. Such fears, however, were never realized.

Drawn westward by so-called Oregon Fever, thousands of American pioneers took the perilous overland journey to settle Oregon's rich Willamette Valley.

Acquisition of the Louisiana Purchase in 1803 stimulated U.S. interest in the Oregon Country. The U.S. government pressed its claim to the territory, citing the efforts of its explorers. In 1792, Captain Robert Gray, a U.S. merchant, had been the first to cross the treacherous bar at the mouth of the Columbia River, just months before Broughton. Gray named the river for his ship, the *Columbia Rediviva.* In 1805 the Lewis and Clark expedition crossed the Bitterroot Range into the Oregon Country. Navigating down the Columbia, they reached the Pacific Ocean in November of that year.

Both the United States and Great Britain lay claim to the region and competed for its natural resources. The maritime fur trade, which brought American and British traders in search of sea otter pelts, thrived between 1790 and 1812. With the collapse of the sea otter population, attention turned to the fur-bearing mammals of the interior, principally the beaver. In 1811, American fur traders representing John Jacob Astor's Pacific Fur Company arrived at the mouth of the Columbia and established Fort Astoria.

During the War of 1812, the British seized the Oregon Country and the American outpost at Astoria, which they renamed Fort George. The Treaty of Ghent, which ended the war in 1814, restored Astoria to the Americans. The Convention of 1818 established the forty-ninth parallel as the international boundary between the United States and Canada, but that line ran only from the Lake of the Woods, on the east, to the Continental Divide, on the west. It did not resolve the question of a boundary in the Oregon Country. Instead, it called for Anglo-American joint occupancy until a boundary could be settled. In 1819 the Spanish abandoned their claims north of the forty-second parallel in the Adams-Onís Treaty. In 1825 the Russians agreed that the southern boundary of their holdings in Alaska would be 54 degrees 40 minutes north latitude.

Although Americans had the right to occupy the Oregon Country, it was Britain, through its fur trading companies, that would effectively dominate the region until the 1840s. After it absorbed the North West Company of Montreal in 1821, the Hudson's Bay Company (HBC) was for twenty years the most powerful and influential force in the Oregon Country. Operating from its departmental headquarters at Fort Vancouver on the Columbia River, the Hudson's Bay Company, under the leadership of chief factor John McLoughlin, managed an enormous enterprise. HBC was engaged in trapping, trading, farming, and fishing. It also served as Britain's civil government in the Northwest. HBC posts stretched from Fort Vancouver deep into the hinterland, including Fort Walla Walla, Fort Colville, Fort Boise, and Fort Hall. To keep rival U.S. fur trappers from crossing over the Rockies from the Missouri River basin, the company dispatched Peter Skene Ogden and his "Snake Brigades" of trappers to deplete the beaver populations of the interior, creating a "fur desert" that would make the area unattractive to the Americans.

The Hudson's Bay Company had located Fort Vancouver on the north bank of the Columbia River because it hoped that the river might eventually become the international boundary. In the late 1830s and early 1840s, however, that outcome appeared less likely, as American settlers began pouring into the region. The first Americans into the Willamette Valley were Methodist missionaries led by Jason Lee in 1834. Subsequent American missions were established by the Whitmans, near present-day Walla Walla, and the Spaldings, at Lapwai, in 1836. Overland emigration of settlers over the Oregon Trail began in 1840. The "Great Migration" of 1843 brought more than nine hundred settlers, and signaled the coming flood.

To protect the interests of Britain and the HBC, John McLoughlin did what he could to encourage them to settle south of the Columbia River. He was largely successful, but the influx of Americans and the declining fortunes of the fur trade led Britain to loosen its hold on the southern part of the region. By 1845 there were 5,000 Americans in Oregon, compared with a British population of only 750. Americans, too, were exerting their political independence. Far beyond the reach of the U.S. government, and unwilling to submit to the rule of HBC, Oregonians created their own laws. In 1843, at Champoeg on the Willamette River, American settlers established a provisional government for the Oregon Country. Although HBC did not recognize its legitimacy, these laws, and subsequent amendments to them, would govern Americans in Oregon until it achieved territorial status in 1848.

The Oregon Country, along with Texas and the Southwest, played a role in the presidential election of 1844. James K. Polk became president after waging an expansionist campaign that offered his solution for settling the Oregon Question: "Fifty-four Forty or Fight!" After taking office, however, Polk agreed to resolve the dispute without a war with Britain. In 1846 the Oregon Treaty between Britain and the United States extended the existing international boundary along the forty-ninth parallel from the Continental Divide to the Pacific Ocean.

In 1848, Congress organized the Oregon Territory, encompassing all of the American portion of the Oregon Country. In 1853 it divided the territory at the Columbia River, creating the new Washington Territory to the north. Overland emigrants continued to pour into the region in the 1850s, drawn by the promises of the Oregon Donation Land Act, in which the federal government offered to grant up to 640 acres of land per family. By 1860 more than fifty-three thousand people had immigrated overland to Oregon.

The Oregon Country gave rise to three new states and parts of two others, as well as one Canadian province. The area north of the international boundary became British Columbia. Oregon Territory became a state in 1859. In the 1860s, mining rushes to the interior Northwest spurred population growth, industry, and the creation of new territories. In 1863, Washington Territory was divided to create the Idaho Territory, east of the Snake River, and Oregon's eastern border. The northeastern and southeastern sections of the Idaho Territory later became parts of Montana Territory (1864) and Wyoming Territory (1868), respectively. These territories developed more slowly than Oregon, and did not achieve statehood until thirty years later. Washington and Montana became states in 1889, followed by Idaho and Wyoming in 1890.

—Douglas W. Dodd

See also

Lewis and Clark Expedition; Hudson's Bay Company; Oregon Trail

For Further Reading

Johnson, David Alan. 1992. *Founding the Far West: California, Oregon, and Nevada, 1840–1890.* Berkeley: University of California Press; Merk, Frederick. 1967. *The Oregon Question: Essays in Anglo-American Diplomacy and Politics.* Cambridge: Harvard University Press; Pletcher, David M. 1973. *The Diplomacy of Annexation: Texas, Oregon, and the Mexican War.* Columbia: University of Missouri Press; Schwantes, Carlos A. 1989. *The Pacific Northwest: An Interpretive History.* Lincoln: University of Nebraska Press.

OREGON TRAIL

The Louisiana Purchase (1803) and Lewis and Clark Expedition (1804–1806) encouraged Americans to regard all land west of the Mississippi as destined for acquisition. During the 1820s, Hall Jackson Kelley, a Boston schoolteacher, fervently promoted the idea of settling the Oregon Country. With British and U.S. diplomats locked in disputes over the Pacific Northwest, settlement offered a practical means of solving the nagging question of sovereignty. While experienced fur trappers blazed trails across the Louisiana Territory and into the Far West in the 1820s and 1830s, a two-thousand-mile trek through unfamiliar country posed significant hazards to the average traveler. Dr. John McLoughlin, of the Hudson's Bay Company, commented that emigrants could as easily "undertake to go to the moon" as travel overland to Oregon. However, in 1834 a small party of Methodists led by Rev. Jason Lee crossed the West with Nathaniel Wyeth, an entrepreneur from Massachusetts (Wyeth had first journeyed to Oregon in 1832). The missionaries settled in the beautiful

The steady stream of wagons heading westward along the Oregon Trail symbolized the heady spirit of Manifest Destiny that characterized American expansionism.

Willamette Valley. Other caravans traveled westward, following a similar route. By the early 1840s, the "Oregon Trail" had emerged.

Reeling from the Panic of 1837 and disenchanted with their lot, Missourian farmers were impressed by the rhetoric of Oregon boosters such as Hall Kelley. For restless Americans, a journey westward promised adventure, a fresh start, and rich, fertile land. An outbreak of "Oregon Fever" resulted in the "Great Migration" of 1843, whereby a caravan of nearly nine hundred Americans left for the Far West, led by trail veteran Dr. Marcus Whitman. Twenty-five hundred emigrants took to the Oregon Trail in 1845. Two years later, the annual number of overlanders exceeded four thousand. Families gathered to form trail parties at Independence, Missouri, in early spring, hoping to reach Oregon in the fall. Travelers felt secure in large groups, while well-organized parties pooled resources to ease river crossings and mountain climbs. However, arguments flared over slow wagons, leadership, and petty crimes. The ease with which wagons and oxen traversed the early stretches of the Oregon Trail, covering up to twenty miles a day, gave a false impression of the journey ahead. For three weeks parties followed the Platte River across the Great Plains, resting at Fort Laramie to stock up on supplies. After traveling 838 miles along the trail, emigrants paused to sign "the register of the desert" at Independence Rock, before ascending to the South Pass, whereupon the trail crossed the Rockies. At Fort Hall, 1,288 miles from Independence, emigrants gained valuable respite before tackling the final and most taxing stages of the Oregon Trail. Parties struggled on the cliffs above the Snake River, and winched their belongings across ravines in the treacherous Blue Mountains. The final stretch entailed a one-hundred-mile-long journey on the Columbia River. While foolhardy overlanders took their chances on the river wilds, others trusted Native Americans to ferry them by canoe toward the Willamette Valley and Oregon.

Winding across mountains, rivers, and plains, the Oregon Trail introduced pioneers to the epic diversity of the Western landscape. Travelers were forced to adapt to dramatic changes in climate, water supply, and vegetation. Parties struggled with cholera, scurvy, and mountain fever, while drownings and firearm mishaps proved commonplace. Men usually made the decision to move westward, yet much of the preparation and sacrifice fell on their female partners. While husbands rested during evenings and relished sport-hunting, women rarely escaped the confines of the wagon, or their duties of cooking and washing. Although many families feared Indian attack, Native Americans served as trail-guides and traded food for trinkets. More Native Americans died because of emigrant malice and misjudgment than the number of overlanders killed in "Indian massacres."

By the 1850s, the Oregon Trail had become a popular route across Louisiana and the far-Western territories. Oregon-bound families encountered eastbound Americans, federal soldiers, gold-seekers, and overzealous traders along the trail. Overlanders complained of traffic congestion and pricey provisions. Dust clouds billowed from well-worn tracks. Dead oxen, wagon axles, and goods considered too heavy to haul up mountain passes littered the trailside. Pastures suffered from overgrazing, while gunfire scattered local wildlife. Oregon fever hastened the demise of Native American tribes. Westerly travelers spread smallpox to indigenous communities, and appropriated ancestral Indian lands.

By 1860, more than fifty thousand Americans had immigrated to Oregon. The success of overland routes heralded the development of the United States as a continent-spanning nation. While it was also used for sheep and cattle drives to Eastern markets in the 1880s, the lasting image of the Oregon Trail is one of cloth-covered prairie schooners carrying pioneer families westward.

—*John Wills*

See also

Laramie, Fort; Independence Rock; South Pass

For Further Reading

Faragher, John Mack. 1979. *Women and Men on the Overland Trail.* New Haven: Yale University Press; Lavender, David. 1963. *Westward Vision: The Story of the Oregon Trail.* Lincoln: University of Nebraska Press; Parkman, Francis. 1994 [1849]. *The Oregon Trail.* Lincoln: University of Nebraska Press; Unruh, John D., Jr. 1993. *The Plains Across: The Overland Emigrants and the Trans-Mississippi West, 1840–1860.* Urbana: University of Illinois Press.

ORLEANS, TERRITORY OF

Once the Louisiana Purchase territory had been turned over to the United States from French authorities in official ceremonies at New Orleans and St. Louis, the U.S. government began the process of administering and governing the vast territory. For administrative purposes, the region was divided into two territories: the Territory of Orleans and the Louisiana Territory. The Territory of Orleans was that portion of the purchase lands on the western side of the Mississippi River that were south of 33 degrees north latitude, plus the Isle of Orleans—roughly the area of the modern-day state of Louisiana minus the "Florida Parishes" region. After the West Florida Rebellion (1810), the United States annexed that region and added portions of it to the Territory of Orleans and the Mississippi Territory. The Louisiana Territory initially encompassed everything else that remained of the Louisiana Purchase lands above the 33 degree north latitude line.

One of the key issues that troubled the Territory of Orleans was the lack of a clearly defined western boundary for the territory. The Louisiana Purchase territory was generally understood as being the western half of the drainage basin formed by the Mississippi River system plus the Isle of Orleans. If the United States used a strict interpretation of that definition, the valley of the Red River, being a tributary of the Mississippi River, would have been included in the Louisiana Purchase. Inasmuch as the Spanish held Mexico and maintained that their province of Texas included portions of the Red River Valley, there was a section of western land in the Territory of Orleans that remained contested by the United States and Spain until the matter was settled in the Adams-Onís Treaty (1819).

This disputed territory produced an uneasy relationship between U.S. authorities in the Territory of Orleans and Spanish officials in east Texas. Moreover, since only a few miles separated the early French colonial town of Natchitoches, the oldest town in the Louisiana Purchase, from Los Adaes, the Spanish capital of Texas and Couhila, the international tensions created by the boundary dispute were real; many believed that hostilities were imminent. U.S. general James Wilkinson negotiated with Spanish authorities and established the so-called Neutral Zone between the Territory of Orleans and Texas. The area was a veritable no-man's land that came to be associated with its own brand of anarchy and vice. The Neutral Zone attracted outlaws, thieves, renegade Indians, fugitive slaves, and other assorted undesirables who felt themselves beyond the reach of either Spanish or U.S. law.

The Territory of Orleans also consisted of a population that was quite cosmopolitan. For years Louisiana had been a colony of France (1699–1762), and after its cession in the Treaty of Fontainebleau (1762) it had been a Spanish possession for nearly four decades. As a result, the region's inhabitants in 1803 were primarily of French or Spanish descent, were predominantly Roman Catholic, and were accustomed to monarchial-based colonial governance. In addition, there were other aspects of the region's ethnography that were unique. Among the French inhabitants there were differences between the Creole population (that is, those born in the colony) and the Acadians ("Cajuns"), who had begun migrating to the colony in 1765 after their expulsion from Nova Scotia. A population of Rhinelanders had settled just west of New Orleans on the "German Coast" (Cote des Allemands) of St. Charles and St. John the Baptist Parishes. There were also Portuguese *Islenos* who had settled east of New Orleans in St. Bernard Parish after migrating from the Canary Islands. Additionally, a significant number of exiles from St. Domingo, who were later expelled from Cuba in 1809, were given special permission by the U.S. Congress to settle in the Territory of Orleans with their slaves, some of whom had been exposed to the slave revolt that had occurred in St. Domingo.

With such a diverse population, and a citizenry that was largely distrustful of and unprepared for governance by the new Anglo-Saxon, Protestant Americans, who boasted the yet-unseen blessings of democracy and republican government, many viewed the Territory of Orleans as a social and cultural tinderbox that would require effective stewardship from its new leaders. Thomas Jefferson appointed William Charles Cole Claiborne, then serving as the territorial governor of Mississippi, to be the governor of the Territory of Orleans, with administrative headquarters at New Orleans. Governor Claiborne's demeanor was initially viewed by territorial residents as being somewhat cold and distant, but after marrying into a French Creole family, the governor found himself more accepted by the populace. Still, most of the political squabbles that took place within the Territory of Orleans were based upon the often baseless notion that favoritism was being shown toward one clique or another. With such a diverse population, Claiborne had to navigate the shoals of social diplomacy within the Territory of Orleans carefully, as he sought to keep peace among the factions and tutor the region toward the possibility of statehood.

Much of the history of the Territory of Orleans was characterized by intrigue. U.S. general James Wilkinson, as commander of the Southern District, spent much of his time in New Orleans and the surrounding region. Despite being one of the highest ranking officers in the U.S. Army, Wilkinson was also a nefarious opportunist who, in earlier years, had been a secret agent of Spain, hired to try to encourage the secession of the trans-Appalachian West. By 1805–1807, Wilkinson had become involved in a conspiracy with former vice president Aaron Burr that likely involved the seizure of Spanish Texas. When word arrived in the Territory of Orleans that Burr was traveling down the Mississippi to begin his misadventure, a hysteria developed, and Wilkinson found himself in the strange position of protecting the region's security by arresting his former partner when he arrived within the Territory of Orleans. Wilkinson would later testify against Burr at his treason trial.

Further intrigue occurred in 1810, when residents of West Florida revolted against Spanish colonial authority. President James Madison used the opportunity to order U.S. troops to occupy the disputed area, which was then incorporated into the Territory of Orleans and the Mississippi Territory. The Spanish maintained that this was an illegal seizure of their sovereign territory, but they did little, besides their diplomatic protests, to reclaim the territory. Like the settlement of the western boundary question, the disposition of the West Florida question would finally be settled by the Adams-Onís Treaty (1819), in which Spain ceded both East and West Florida to the United States.

Despite these challenges, U.S. authorities did a good job in preparing the Territory of Orleans for eventual statehood. One of the most challenging aspects of this transformation was the creation of a unified code of law that blended elements of the *Code Napoleon*, the French legal code, within the framework of an American legal system that was largely predicated upon English Common Law. Edward Livingston deserves the credit for developing this unified code that still, to this day, characterizes the law in Louisiana courts. Governor Claiborne realized the importance of this work and recognized that the success of convincing residents of the Territory of Orleans to accept the imposition of U.S. governance would be largely determined by their perception and appreciation of fair and equitable treatment in the territorial courts.

The Territory of Orleans also figured prominently in national affairs because the port facilities of New Orleans were of central importance to the success of Western trade and commerce. As the "queen city" of the Mississippi River, New Orleans found itself attracting a steady stream of flatboat men from the Ohio River Valley and northern parts of the Mississippi Valley who brought their produce downriver for sale at New Orleans. As a booming commercial center, the city would eventually have a number of banks and counting houses. In later years, the federal government would even establish a branch of the U.S. Mint at New Orleans.

Perhaps the greatest crisis that faced the Territory of Orleans took place in January 1811, when a massive slave revolt began in the German Coast parishes just thirty-five miles west of New Orleans. New Orleans was threatened as an army of slave rebels, estimated to number as many as five hundred, burned several sugar plantations and killed three planters as they advanced toward the territorial capital. A contingent of U.S. Army troops, acting in concert with local militia and vigilantes, set upon the rebels and, with superior firepower, brutally ended the revolt.

In 1812 the Territory of Orleans petitioned the U.S. Congress to establish the region as a state with the name Louisiana. Although the debates were contentious, with some New England Federalists questioning whether the region was ready—or would ever be ready—for statehood, the Congress would eventually grant Louisiana its statehood on April 30, 1812. Governor Claiborne, who had served as territorial governor throughout the entire history of the Territory of Orleans, was elected the first governor of the new state of Louisiana.

—Junius P. Rodriguez

See also

Claiborne, William Charles Cole; Isle of Orleans; Los Adaes; Natchitoches; Neutral Ground; New Orleans; Transcontinental Treaty; West Florida; Wilkinson, James

For Further Reading
Clark, John G. 1970. *New Orleans, 1718–1812: An Economic History.* Baton Rouge: Louisiana State University Press; Gayarré, Charles. 1965. *A History of Louisiana.* Gretna, LA: Pelican Publishing; Hirsch, Arnold R., and Joseph Logsdon, eds. 1992. *Creole New Orleans: Race and Americanization.* Baton Rouge: Louisiana State University Press; Ingersoll, Thomas N. 1999. *Mammon and Manon in Early New Orleans: The First Slave Society in the Deep South, 1718–1819.* Knoxville: University of Tennessee Press.

OSAGE

The Osage tongue evolved from the Siouan branch of the Hokan-Siouan language group. The name Osage came from European interpretations of the name Wazhazhe, which referred to one of the major divisions of the people, the meat-eaters. Another division, the Tsishu, was a vegetarian group.

Together, the groups formed the NiuKonska, or "Little Ones of the Middle Waters." Legend links the Osage with the millennia-old Mississippian, or Mound-builder, culture that thrived in the heart of North America and left significant architectural remains. Osage myth explains that the Osage came from the stars and named all of the features of the earth, sky, and water. The people's purpose, so the legend goes, was to understand the Wah'Kon, or mysterious life-force, that animates the world, and to learn to harness it.

By the time of first contact with the French in the seventeenth century, the Osage lived near the Missouri and Osage Rivers in what today are the states of Missouri, Kansas, Oklahoma, and Arkansas. Like other native nations, the Osage lived in permanent villages along the rivers and also maintained hunting camps across the Great Plains. The buffalo and deer supplemented crops of corn, pumpkin, and squash. Unlike some neighbors, however, the Osage had a unified and complex system of institutions, the chief of which was the organized priesthood. The Osage believed that their society's structure reflected the order of the universe, and that they could unravel the mysteries of the cosmos by finding the perfect balance within their own people. Sacred numbers such as four and seven became guiding forces in the government of the people.

To this end, they divided their society into groups representing the sky, water, and land. Within these divisions were housed from seven to twenty-one (eventually changed to twenty-four) "fireplaces," or clans. The names of these fireplaces ranged from the concrete "White Water" to the abstract "Men of Mystery."

At various times, Osage peoples broke away from the main nation and developed an independent tribe. The Kansa, Omaha, Quapaw, and Ponca all began as Osage. The Osage remained, however, the central tribe among the Southern Siouan-speaking native peoples.

After their discovery by the French, the Osage allied with the Europeans to fight other neighboring tribes. Their fierce protection of their territory and their early use of firearms enhanced their reputation as a warlike people. The Osage warred against the Caddoan people (Tawehash, Tawakoni, Yscani, Waco, and Kichai) in particular, but also had many other enemies. European contact brought some changes, however. Their strategic position between the Europeans to the east and Amerindians to the west made them de facto power brokers in the great intercultural trade exchange and brought the Osage substantial power in the region.

By the time that the Osage were contacted by the Lewis and Clark Expedition, the people had developed three loose divisions: the Great Osage, along the Osage River; the Little Osage, above them on the Missouri River; and the Arkansas band, on the Vermilion River. Estimates placed their combined number at fifty-five hundred.

By 1808 the Osage recognized the westward movement of U.S. settlers brought about by the Louisiana Purchase, and they ceded more than one hundred million acres of territory in what is today Arkansas, Missouri, and Oklahoma. They agreed to relocate to present-day Oklahoma.

In 1872 the Osage purchased their present reservation from the Cherokee. This land was formerly Osage hunting area at the east of the so-called Cherokee Outlet. There the Osage divided again into three groups and settled in Pawhuska, Hominy, and Gray Horse. The Osage capital remains today in Pawhuska.

The move also brought fulfillment to a legendary prophecy that the Osage would find great wealth. Since the voluntary move, the Osage received the right to own land individually. The discovery of oil on Osage land, coupled with the amount of property the people control, has made the Osage the most wealthy tribal community in the United States. Since 1897, oil and gas revenues alone have brought the Osage more than one billion dollars. Today the Osage have more than tripled their population from what it was at the time of the Louisiana Purchase. Their numbers had fallen to 2,228 by 1906, but they are now estimated to be over 18,000.

—*Amy H. Sturgis*

See also
Ponca; Quapaw

For Further Reading
Baird, W. David. 1972. *The Osage People.* Phoenix, AZ: Indian Tribal Series; La Flesche, Francis. 1970 [1921]. *The Osage Tribe: Rite of the Chiefs; Sayings of the Ancient Men.* New York: Johnson Reprint Corporation; La Flesche, Francis. 1939. *War Ceremony and Peace Ceremony of the Osage Indians.* Washington, DC: Government Printing Office; Mathews, John Joseph. 1961. *The Osages, Children of the Middle Waters.* Norman: University of Oklahoma Press; Rollings, Willard. 1992. *The Osage: An Ethnohistorical Study of Hegemony on the Prairie-Plains.* Columbia: University of Missouri Press; Wilson, Terry P. 1985. *Bibliography of the Osage.* Metuchan, NJ: Scarecrow Press.

OSAGE, FORT

For more than a decade, Fort Osage on the Missouri River served as the westernmost military fortification and Indian agency in the Louisiana Purchase. Because of Fort Bellefontaine's poor location for the Indian trade, and upon hearing recommendations from Indian agent William Clark, the War Department agreed to close the Bellefontaine factory and construct two new government factories, Fort Osage and Fort Madison, to serve the Indians on the Missouri and Mississippi Rivers. In order to establish a U.S. presence near the influential Osage nation to help quell Indian depredations on the Louisiana Territory frontier, Governor Meriwether Lewis ordered Clark to establish a government Indian factory/military fortification to serve and protect the Osage. Lewis and Clark agreed on a site three hundred miles from St. Louis on the Fire Prairie, a location overlooking the Missouri River that they had noted during their Western expedition.

Clark personally oversaw the construction of Fort Osage, the largest, most expensive, most western, and most profitable of the twenty-eight government factories. Two groups proceeded upriver toward the Fire Prairie. George C. Sibley, the post factor and Indian agent, recorded the month-long water voyage of the six keelboats commanded by Captain Eli B. Clemson, bringing eighty-one men and $20,000 worth of goods from Fort Bellefontaine to supply the factory. During August and September 1808, Clark kept a diary of the 250-mile land expedition, which included an escort party of eighty volunteers from the St. Charles Dragoons guided by Captain Nathan Boone. On September 4, 1808, at the south bank of the Missouri River about forty miles below the mouth of the Kansas River and near the present town of Sibley, Clark ordered the men to begin construction on a bluff almost one hundred feet above the river.

Also called Clark's Fort, Fort Clark, Fire Prairie Fort, and Fort Sibley, the fort/factory complex was built in an odd pentagonal shape consisting of four blockhouses, officers' quarters, barracks, stockade, factory house, a blockade on a point, and a separate house for traders enclosed by a stockade. Constructed out of white oak logs on a prominent overlook of the Missouri, the site easily controlled the Missouri River trade, since all passing craft fell within gun range of the fort on the bluffs—thus deterring Indian raiding parties from venturing unopposed downriver and preventing unlicensed traders from proceeding upriver. Fort Osage provided a place for the friendly portion of the Osage to trade, negotiate treaties, and receive supplies and annuities.

Clark sent Nathan Boone and interpreter Paul Loise to summon the Osage to the fort. Wearied of hostile Osage bands that plundered settlers and warred with the Cherokee, Clark informed them that he would invite other Indian nations to make war on those Osage who did not respond to the call to come to the fort. Upon their arrival, Clark negotiated and signed a treaty with Osage leaders White Hair and Walking Rain, who ceded thirty million acres of the Osage homeland in Missouri and Arkansas to the United States. In return, the Great Osage were promised $1,000 annually and the Little Osage $500. Both would retain hunting privileges on the ceded land and receive the benefits of a blacksmith, farm implements, military protection at the fort, and an Indian factory for trading purposes.

Leaving Fort Osage in the able hands of Sibley and Indian subagent Reuben Lewis, Clark returned to St. Louis with the treaty. Unfortunately, some seventy Osage had been in St. Louis during Clark's absence, and they refused to accept the treaty. Governor Lewis took the treaty, modified a few of the articles, and sent it back to the fort with the Osages' agent, Pierre Chouteau. On November 10 the tribal majority reluctantly agreed to the new treaty's terms, and by the following August the last Osage signers finally gave their consent.

Fort Osage provided a military presence in Louisiana Territory until the War of 1812, counteracting Spanish and British influence on the middle and lower Missouri and courting favor with Indian tribes by offering merchandise at the government factory. Although temporarily abandoned during the War of 1812, Fort Osage was reoccupied after the 1814 Treaty of Ghent. Internal tension existing between the military garrison and the factory escalated with the removal of the Cherokee and other Eastern Indians to the Missouri and Arkansas territorial frontiers. In 1819 the majority of the military personnel moved upriver to Fort Atkinson near Council Bluffs, though the factory remained. The factory closed down in 1822, when the government factory system was abandoned altogether; however, travelers, garrisons, surveyors, and military escorts on the Santa Fe Trail continued to use the facilities. The army abandoned Fort Osage after it constructed Fort Leavenworth upstream in 1827 to protect the trail. Through the efforts of Fort Osage Restoration, the fortification was partially reconstructed following World War II. The National Park Service maintains the fort today as a tourist attraction.

—Jay H. Buckley

For Further Reading

Clark, William. 1937. *Westward with Dragoons: The Journal of William Clark on His Expedition to Establish Fort Osage, August 25 to September 22, 1808.* Edited by Kate L. Gregg. Fulton, MO: Ovid Bell Press; Gregg, Kate L. 1940. "The History of Fort Osage." *Missouri Historical Review* 24: 439–488; Grove, Nettie T. 1921. "Fort Osage, First Settlement in Jackson County." *Missouri Valley Historical Society* 1: 56–70; Jones, Charles T., Jr. 1970. *George Champlain Sibley: The Prairie Puritan, 1782–1863.* Independence, MO: Jackson County Historical Society.

PAINE, THOMAS (1737–1809)

A political writer and one of the Founding Fathers, Thomas Paine supported the purchase of the Louisiana Territory and entered the debate over what to do with the inhabitants of the land. Born in Thetford, England, Paine developed compassion for the struggles of ordinary people while he worked as a revenue officer. With a deeply felt commitment to liberalism and republican government, he never found a place in England.

After immigrating to Philadelphia in 1774, Paine obtained the position of editor at the *Pennsylvania Magazine.* As the struggle between the American colonies and Great Britain accelerated, he argued for the inevitability of liberty in the 1776 best-selling pamphlet *Common Sense.* In this immensely influential work, Paine not only called for American independence but also attacked hereditary rule. For the next several years, Paine pursued the cause of liberty. Besides reviving American morale with *The American Crisis,* he served in the militia and joined the forces of George Washington. In the 1780s, Paine's writings increasingly concerned themselves with the economic policies of the new nation and the need to strengthen national authority.

Thomas Paine urged U.S. president Thomas Jefferson to attempt to purchase Louisiana from France in order to solve the vexing "Mississippi Question" that plagued the nation.

A man of letters and of science, Paine sought financing for a wrought-iron bridge that he designed. Unable to gather funds in the United States, he traveled to England and France in 1787. He remained in Europe for several years, finding time to publish a 1791 defense of the French Revolution, *Rights of Man.* With the publication of this work, Paine became a French hero and found himself elected to the National Convention. Unfortunately, Paine spoke little French and quickly ran afoul of the Jacobins, who imprisoned him for nearly a year. While jailed, Paine completed the *Age of Reason* (1794), an attack on organized religion that destroyed his reputation among devout Christians. In 1802, at the invitation of President Thomas Jefferson, Paine set sail for the United States.

On Christmas Day 1802, Paine wrote to Jefferson about the vexing problem of American exclusion from New Orleans and from navigation along the Mississippi River. Declaring that the French government required money to finance Napoleon's military ambitions, Paine recommended that the United States buy the territory that France had received from Spain. Paine's suggestion was in accord with Jefferson's thinking, as the president had already planned to make the purchase. After the papers for Louisiana were signed, Paine worried whether the Federalists in Congress could obstruct the purchase attempt, since the Senate had to ratify the treaty. Paine wrote to Senator John C. Breckinridge of Kentucky, a leading advocate of westward expansion, and asked him whether the Senate would have to ratify the agreement to make the purchase, as if it were a treaty rather than an executive order by Jefferson. Observing that the Constitution itself accommodated the addition of territory, Paine argued that a Senate wrestling match should be avoided, and that the only ratification needed was the payment of money.

Once the purchase agreement was completed, the question arose of what to do with the inhabitants of Louisiana. Paine regarded the Louisianans as dangerously undemocratic, since most were Roman Catholic with cultural ties to Spain or France. Assuming that they had little knowledge of elections and democratic government, Paine proposed to Jefferson that the Louisianans be given lessons in participatory democracy. He recommended the establishment of a provisional government formed by Congress that would last from three to seven years, during which the new Americans would be initiated into democracy by electing their municipal government.

The Louisiana Purchase made the threat of war with France moot, but Paine did not let up on his attack on John Adams and the Federalists during the rest of 1803. The quarrel with the conservatives had begun when Paine supported the French Revolution despite its bloodshed; the publication of the *Age of Reason* had simply exacerbated those tensions. Paine complained in a letter that Adams had sought war against France, and that showed that the Adams administration posed an expensive menace to the nation. America was not a barbaric nation, Paine stated, and while the territory in question could have been easily seized, it could only have been taken at the expense of the nation's reputation.

His words did not receive much of an audience. Many of Jefferson's supporters were evangelical Christians, and the pamphleteer had become a political liability. Paine retired to his farm and gradually sank into poverty and obscurity. By the time of his death in 1809 in New York, he had been largely forgotten.

—*Caryn E. Neumann*

For Further Reading

Fruchtman, Jack, Jr. 1994. *Thomas Paine: Apostle of Freedom.* New York: Four Walls Eight Windows.

PARIS, TREATY OF (1763)

Negotiated by the Duc de Choiseul, the French foreign minister; the Marquis de Grimaldi, the Spanish ambassador to France; and the Duke of Bedford, the British ambassador, the Treaty of Paris was the culmination of lengthy negotiations first opened in May 1761. The peace preliminaries were signed on November 23, 1762, and the final treaty agreed to on February 10, 1763. The treaty ended the American hostilities of these three colonial powers, as well as their participation in the Seven Years' War (1756–1763). The war was officially ended when Prussia and Austria agreed to the Treaty of Hubertsburg on February 15, 1763.

The British colonial victories of 1759–1760 initiated the first move toward peace when they prompted French king Louis XV, in March 1761, to appeal formally for a European convention to end the war. Britain and France formally exchanged envoys, and the early negotiations between May and September 1761—the unsuccessful Stanley-Bussey talks—floundered upon the unacceptably high British colonial demands. British opinion, heightened by the domestic Canada-Guadeloupe debate that had begun in December 1759, was reflected in William Pitt's demands that Britain retain Canada in exchange for the return of Guadeloupe or Cape Breton and that France be excluded from the Newfoundland fisheries, a right extended to France by the Treaty of Utrecht (1713). Determined to rebuild the French colonial trade devastated by the war, Choiseul refused to accept French exclusion from the Newfoundland fisheries, an economic activity that brought to France more money annually than the whole of the Canadian fur trade. The British demand for Canada also focused attention on the future of Louisiana, a province long ignored by France.

If Choiseul was willing to accept the loss of Canada, he attempted to lessen this loss by claiming an extended northern boundary of Louisiana. Experts in Paris assured him that its north-south boundary began on a line extending from the Perdido River, passing Fort Toulouse in the Alabama country, then to the western end of Lake Erie, thence to the eastern end of Lake Huron to the high ground south of Hudson Bay toward Lake Abitibi. British ministers, fearful of a massive Canadian immigration to Louisiana and aware of the importance of the trans-Appalachian region to their own colonial security, resisted the redrawing of Louisiana's boundaries and in turn demanded the cession of the Ohio-Illinois country as well as eastern Louisiana.

During these early negotiations Choiseul exhibited an ambiguous attitude toward the future of Louisiana because of his secret negotiations with the anti-English Spanish king Charles III, who had ascended to the Spanish throne following the death of the more pro-English Ferdinand VI on August 10, 1759. Hoping to create a new Franco-Spanish alliance, Choiseul was then unwilling to upset Spanish sensibilities regarding Louisiana, a territory also claimed by Spain. Following the signing of the anti-English Third Family Compact between France and Spain on August 15, 1761, Choiseul broke off negotiations. When the British cabinet refused to endorse Pitt's demand for an immediate declaration of war against Spain, Pitt resigned from office on October 5, 1761. Pitt's fall from power may have made the possibility of a peace treaty more likely, but Spain's disastrous entry into the war in January 1762, and continued British colonial military success, only complicated later peace negotiations, especially those concerning the status of Louisiana.

Lord Bute, Pitt's successor, was eager to terminate the costly war, and in December 1761 he opened negotiations with Choiseul. Initially these talks were kept secret from Charles III, but by August 1762, Franco-British negotiations had almost agreed upon preliminary terms. When the Marquis de Grimaldi was made aware of the terms, he strongly voiced opposition to them. In return for the recently captured St. Lucia and Martinique, Britain reiterated its demand for eastern Louisiana. A British occupation of that area would violate a basic tenet of Spanish colonial policy—of keeping Britain away from the coast of the Gulf of Mexico and, by extension, Spanish trade with Cuba and South America. Grimaldi argued that France had no right to dispose of any part of Louisiana without Spanish consent, and he suggested instead that a neutral Native American buffer zone be created between Georgia and the Mississippi River. In return, Spain would officially recognize the British in Georgia and the French possession of western Louisiana. The Duke of Bedford brushed aside Spanish objections, and by September 1762, even Choiseul, frustrated by his ally's obstinacy, warned Madrid that France would not allow the negotiations to founder over the question of Louisiana. Two developments would eventually persuade Spain to come to terms.

In a stroke of great diplomatic genius, Choiseul persuaded the British that the Iberville River (Bayou Manchac) and Lakes Maurepas and Pontchartrain formed one of the mouths of the Mississippi River; in granting the British free navigation on the Mississippi, he persuaded Bedford to give up the British demand for New Orleans. Henceforth, New Orleans and the "island" on which it stood were associated with the right bank of the Mississippi. This made the occupation of western Louisiana more valuable, and Choiseul made it known to Grimaldi that France was willing to sacrifice it to Spain in return for their agreeing to the peace. Spain finally relented when news of the British capture of Havana arrived in Madrid in September 1761. Lord Bute's willingness, much against the wishes of some of his colleagues, to exchange Havana for Spanish Florida made a British entry upon the Gulf of Mexico something of an academic question. On November 23, 1762, all three powers accepted the preliminary terms of the Peace of Paris, and two days later France formally transferred New Orleans and western Louisiana to Spain by the Treaty of Fontainebleau, to compensate her for the loss of Florida. On December 2, 1762, Charles sent a personal letter of gratitude to his French cousin, Louis XV.

By the terms of the Peace of Paris, Britain retained Canada, Cape Breton, eastern Louisiana, three of the Neutral Islands, and Florida; Manila was returned to a grateful Spain without further compensation. In the face of almost total defeat, Choiseul managed to persuade Britain to return St. Lucia, Guadeloupe, and Martinique, and to guarantee French rights to continue to fish off the coast of Newfoundland. To facilitate that activity, Britain ceded to France the two small islands of St. Pierre and Miquela.

The Peace of Paris originated the question that was later to dominate the early years of the United States—the free navigation of the Mississippi. It was also the first chapter in a sequence of events that led to the purchase of Louisiana by the United States in 1803. Following the Peace of Paris, Britain took formal control of its new territories on the Gulf of Mexico at Mobile on October 30, 1763. Her creation of the province of West Florida, which included eastern Louisiana, would bedevil the later negotiations for the Louisiana Purchase. Following its defeat in the War of Independence, Britain ceded the trans-Appalachian region to the new United States but returned both East and West Florida to Spain by the Treaty of Versailles (1783). These events would form the basis of Spain's later claim that eastern Louisiana was not an integral part of the Louisiana Territory included in the retrocession made to Napoleon in 1800.

—*Rory T. Cornish*

For Further Reading

Aiton, Arthur S. 1931. "The Diplomacy of the Louisiana Cession." *American Historical Review* 36: 701–720; Anderson, Fred. 2000. *Crucible of War: The Seven Years' War and the Fate of Empire in British North America, 1754–1766.* New York: Alfred A. Knopf; Christelow, Allan. 1941. "French Interest in the Spanish Empire during the Ministry of the Duc de Choiseul, 1759–1771." *Hispanic American Historical Review* 21: 515–537; Davenport, Frances G., and Charles O. Paullin, eds. 1917–1937. *European Treaties Bearing on the History of the United States and Its Dependencies.* 4 vols. Washington, DC: Carnegie Institution; Gipson, Lawrence Henry. 1966. *The Great War for the Empire: The Culmination, 1760–1763: The British Empire before the American Revolution.* Vol. 8. New York: Alfred A. Knopf; Hotblack, Kate. 1908. "The Peace of Paris, 1763." *Royal Historical Society Transactions* 11 (3d series): 235–267; Lyon, E. Wilson. 1974. *Louisiana in French Diplomacy, 1759–1804.* Norman: University of Oklahoma Press; Rashed, Zenab E. 1951. *The Peace of Paris, 1767.* Liverpool: Liverpool University Press; Wall, Helen. 1960. "Transfer of Louisiana from France to Spain." M.A. thesis, Louisiana State University.

PAWNEE

The Pawnee are a Native American group of Caddoan-speaking peoples of Hokan-Siouan linguistic origin who are culturally related to the Wichita, Arikara, and Caddo. During the fourteenth century C.E., the ancestors of the Pawnee settled the interior plains of North America in the region between the Missouri River and the Rocky Mountains from the Niobrara to the Arkansas River. Archaeological evidence indicates that they may have inhabited lands as far south as present-day Texas. After several centuries on the Plains, the Pawnee divided into four bands: the Skidi (Wolf), the Grand, the Republican, and the Tapage (Noisy). All four groups eventually moved northward, where they settled the Platte River Valley in the southern part of present-day Nebraska.

The Pawnee first encountered Europeans during the

expedition of the Spanish conquistador Francisco Coronado in 1541 as he searched for the legendary cities of Cibola, traveling as far as modern-day Kansas. By the eighteenth century, the Pawnee had become acquainted with the French, with whom they engaged in the fur trade. The Pawnee would first encounter representatives from the United States when members of Zebulon M. Pike's Expedition in 1806 traveled through Pawnee lands as they traced the origins of the Arkansas River.

Scholars are not sure of the exact origins of the name "Pawnee." One theory is that the name comes from the Sioux word *pani* (*pányi*), which meant "red bird," and may have made reference to the Pawnee's use of brilliant feathers for adornment. Others believe that the name was derived from the Caddoan term *pariki* (meaning "horn"), which referred to a style of hair that was typical among tribal members. The Pawnee called themselves the Chahiksichakihs ("men of men").

Although they lived on the Great Plains, the Pawnee do not fall into the typical pattern of Plains Indian culture—namely, being nomadic hunters. The Pawnee lived in small villages that consisted of semipermanent dome-shaped, earth-covered lodges that could each house several families. The women generally farmed small plots, rather intensively raising corn, beans, and squash, while Pawnee men were responsible for hunting. The Pawnee were quite adept at making pottery and used the earthenware containers for food storage and cooking.

The Pawnee were one of the first tribes of the Great Plains to become expert horsemen. That skill, combined with the use of bows made of Osage orange, made the Pawnee excellent hunters and warriors. The Pawnee were known to be hostile to the Sioux and the Cheyenne, but they remained friendly toward the Oto. They never warred against the United States. Several Pawnee scouts served the U.S. Army during the Indian wars, while others assisted during the construction of the first transcontinental railroad.

Despite being considered "friendly Indians" by the United States, the Pawnee suffered immensely from their encounters with American settlement of the West. The Pawnee saw their numbers decimated during the early nineteenth century by epidemics of smallpox and cholera, to which they had no natural immunity. The Pawnee also suffered great losses in attacks by the Sioux, their hereditary enemies on the central plains. A series of treaties (1833, 1848, and 1857) negotiated with the United States resulted in the gradual reduction of tribal lands until the Pawnee were left with limited reservation lands in Oklahoma.

—*Junius P. Rodriguez*

See also
Oglala Sioux; Wichita

For Further Reading

Hyde, George. E. 1973. *The Pawnee Indians*. Norman: University of Oklahoma Press; Linton, Ralph. 1922. *The Sacrifice to the Morning Star by the Skidi Pawnee*. Chicago: Field Museum of Natural History; Wedel, Waldo R. 1936. *An Introduction to Pawnee Archeology*. Washington, DC: Government Printing Office; Weltfish, Gene. 1965. *The Lost Universe*. New York: Basic Books.

PEACE OF . . .

***See* individual treaties listed by location**

PICHON, LOUIS-ANDRÉ (1771–1854)

Born in humble circumstances, Louis-André Pichon rose through the ranks of the French diplomatic service and then of the French civil service, to be created a hereditary baron by Charles X in 1830. As the French chargé d'affaires in Washington between 1801 and 1804, he tried to promote French-U.S. friendship and faithfully reported, in his many dispatches to his foreign minister, Talleyrand, American fears of any future repossession of Louisiana.

The major part of Pichon's diplomatic career was spent dealing with French-U.S. relations. Between 1793 and 1796 he was employed at the French legation in Philadelphia, soon reaching the position of second secretary. Back in Paris, he was instrumental in 1798 and 1799 in bringing about a reconciliation between the two countries, which was made official with the Convention of Mortefontaine (October 3, 1800).

Pichon was sent to Philadelphia again, this time holding the rank of general officer (*commissaire général*) for commercial relations, together with that of chargé d'affaires to the U.S. government. As the foremost representative of France in the United States, Pichon met regularly with Thomas Jefferson and Secretary of State James Madison after he arrived in Washington on March 7, 1801. Although he was instructed to secure the adherence of the United States to the pro-French armed neutrality, Pichon immediately insisted on respecting the independent type of U.S. neutrality that Jefferson had advocated in his inaugural address. He thought that friendship with the United States was to be cultivated, as Anglo-American maritime frictions would necessarily urge the new nation to find other markets and allies in Europe, and as French colonies in the New World could be preserved only with the support of American trade and regained with the consent of the U.S. government.

When the first rumors on the retrocession of Louisiana surfaced in the United States, Pichon informed his minister that it would be a very delicate undertaking, as most Americans viewed New Orleans and the Floridas as necessary outlets for Western trade. He reported Madison's menacing remarks on any future French occupation of Louisiana, and constantly portrayed the United States as a future great power with expansionist ambitions. The arrival of General Leclerc's army in St. Domingue in January 1802, confirming France's policy of regaining control of its colonial empire, made Pichon's position very uncomfortable; yet he informed his government that he found no excuse for Leclerc's arrogant manner toward American traders. Pichon's frankness led to the young general's refusal to correspond any longer with him, in spite of the frantic efforts by the chargé d'affaires to provide Leclerc's fleet with provisions.

Another cause of worry for Pichon was the reports that Robert R. Livingston had not been warmly received in Paris, and that his messages to the French government remained unanswered. Pichon advised his government to accede to U.S. demands about New Orleans and the Floridas, echoing Jefferson's argument that the United States would seize those territories as soon as war broke out again between France and Britain. He reported the indignation and threats that were voiced by the press, by politicians, and by the administration, as well as his private conviction that France could not retain the territory long. American anger grew when it was learned that the Spanish intendant had stopped the American right of deposit in New Orleans on October 1, 1802—so much so that Pichon felt compelled to write a note reassuring the U.S. government. Just before Monroe was sent to Paris as a special envoy in March 1803, he confided in Pichon that, if his mission failed, the next step would be alliance with Great Britain, a confidence of which the chargé d'affaires dutifully informed his minister. Fortunately, by the summer of 1803, Pichon could rejoice at the sale of Louisiana, which seemed to him the best way to ensure U.S. neutrality as war between France and Great Britain loomed again on the horizon.

Relations between France and the United States remained complex, owing to the situation in St. Domingue and U.S. refusal to interrupt its trade with that former colony. However, Pichon was peremptorily recalled on September 15, 1804, a decision that put an end to his career in the imperial diplomatic service. The often given reason for his dismissal is his not having prevented the marriage of Napoleon's brother, Jerome, to a young American woman, Miss Elizabeth Patterson. Jerome was not ungrateful and offered prestigious civil service positions to Pichon in Westphalia, a state of which he had been made king. Another reason was the diplomat's forcefulness in voicing his own opinions, which often ran against official policy on Louisiana and St. Domingue.

Pichon made his criticism of the empire more vocal and public in the last years of Napoleon's declining reign, which allowed him to continue his brilliant career in the French civil service after the Bourbon kings returned to power.

—Marie-Jeanne Rossignol

See also
Bonaparte, Joseph; Haiti; Leclerc, Charles-Victor-Emmanuel; Livingston, Robert R.; Madison, James; Monroe, James; Mortefontaine, Convention of; Talleyrand-Perigord, Charles Maurice de

For Further Reading
DeConde, Alexander. 1966. *The Quasi-War: The Politics and Diplomacy of the Undeclared War with France, 1797–1801*. New York: Charles Scribner's Sons; Veyrier, Henri. 1990. *Dictionnaire des diplomates de Napoléon*. Paris: Kronos.

PICKERING, TIMOTHY (1745–1829)

Timothy Pickering, the third secretary of state and a Federalist senator from Massachusetts, played peripheral, albeit important, roles in the history of the Louisiana Purchase against the backdrop of the French Revolutionary and Napoleonic Wars (1792–1815). During his tenure as secretary of state, Thomas Pinckney and Manuel de Godoy successfully concluded the Treaty of San Lorenzo (1795). Pickering was involved in heated diplomatic exchanges with Spain's minister to the United States, Carlos Martínez de Irujo, over the implementation of Pinckney's Treaty. The XYZ Affair (1797) and Quasi-War (1798–1800) with France took place during Pickering's term of office. Secretary of State Pickering strongly advocated strengthening American defenses and pursuing a foreign policy independent of French or British designs. After entering the Senate, Pickering, a member of the Essex Junto, denounced the Louisiana Purchase as part of a broad Jeffersonian conspiracy aimed at establishing a Republican dictatorship over the United States.

Secretary of War Pickering engineered Secretary of State Edmund Randolph's resignation in 1795, following questions that arose over possible French subsidies for Pennsylvania Republicans during the Whiskey Rebellion (1794), and was named in his stead. Shortly thereafter, Pinckney's Treaty was concluded. Godoy, however, delayed the evacuation of specific lands following news of Jay's Treaty (1794) because he and Baron de Carondelet suspected that it was part of an Anglo-American alliance aimed at seizing Louisiana. Spanish suspicions increased following the Blount Conspiracy, a plot by Senator William Blount, Republican of Tennessee, for invading and seizing land in Louisiana. This, coupled with a 1797 rebellion by American settlers and sympathizers in Natchez, increased the tension between Pickering and Irujo, who had been quarreling over the Spanish delays in evacuating the specified territory. Moreover, the treaty raised French suspicions of an Anglo-American alliance against France.

Spain's continued presence in Louisiana mattered greatly; Pickering feared that if the province were ceded to France, it would pose a threat to the republic. He believed that France would instigate a Western secessionist movement among American settlers and a slave rebellion in the South as it re-established its American empire and dominance over the United States. He predicted that such an event would result in an alliance with Great Britain and war against France.

France reacted to Jay's Treaty (1794), and an earlier contention that the United States had not fulfilled its 1778 treaty commitments of amity, commerce, and alliance, by seizing U.S. ships, which contributed to the Quasi-War, an undeclared naval war. Meanwhile, Pickering arranged James Monroe's recall from France and his replacement by Charles Cotesworth Pinckney of South Carolina in 1797. The revolutionary Directory refused Pinckney's credentials and threatened him with arrest. Hoping to avoid a complete break in relations, President John Adams dispatched Pinckney, John Marshall, and Elbridge Gerry to France. French foreign minister Charles Maurice de Talleyrand-Périgord hoped that the budding conflict would force U.S. compliance with the 1778 Franco-American treaties. French agents, identified as X, Y, and Z, approached the Americans soliciting a bribe for Talleyrand and a loan for France in exchange for negotiations. The Americans rebuffed the French advances and returned home as heroes for having refused the French agents.

Pickering viewed the Republican ascendancy as a plot for undermining the accomplishments of the American Revolution, overthrowing the Federalist political order, and making Thomas Jefferson president for life. As a senator, Pickering resisted the purchase of Louisiana because it seemed a part of the Republican plot that had already removed from office Federalist members of the judiciary and ratified the Twelfth Amendment. Pickering understood the purchase of Louisiana as a move toward increasing the number of slave states in the Union. By doing this, Jefferson's adherents would overturn Federalist and New England influence in national affairs. Earlier in Pickering's career he had favored acquiring Louisiana, but now, with the Federalists in decline, he opposed the purchase. Following Pickering's retirement from political life, he moved to Salem, Massachusetts, and devoted his time to agronomy.

—Ricardo A. Herrera

See also

Carondelet, Louis Francisco Hector de; Essex Junto; Federalist Party; Godoy, Manuel de; Irujo, Carlos Martínez de (Marquis de Casa Irujo); Jay's Treaty; Pinckney, Thomas; Right of Deposit; San Lorenzo, Treaty of

For Further Reading

Clarfield, Gerard H. 1969. *Timothy Pickering and American Diplomacy.* Columbia: University of Missouri Press; Clarfield, Gerard H. 1980. *Timothy Pickering and the American Republic.* Pittsburgh: University of Pittsburgh Press; De Conde, Alexander. 1976. *This Affair of Louisiana.* New York: Charles Scribner's Sons; Pickering, Octavius, and Charles W. Upham. 1867–1873. *Life of Timothy Pickering.* 4 vols. Boston: Little, Brown, and Company.

PIKE EXPEDITION (1805–1806)

The explorations of Zebulon Montgomery Pike helped to establish the boundaries of the Louisiana Purchase and to acquire knowledge of its geography, natural productions, and native inhabitants. Pike, a native of New Jersey and son of Revolutionary War veteran Zebulon Pike, matured on the frontier outposts of the Ohio River Valley, where his father was stationed during the Indian wars of the 1790s. Young Pike, as a teenager in 1794, saw action at the Battle of Fallen Timbers. During the few years preceding the Louisiana Purchase, Lieutenant Pike supervised supply routes along the Ohio River, married, and was assigned to Fort Knox in Indiana Territory. Pike, whose drive to achieve fame was equaled by his adherence to the military code of honor, was a natural choice to lead men in search of the sources of the Mississippi, Arkansas, and Red Rivers. Zebulon Pike revealed, on two separate expeditions, that he had the right mix of arrogance, confidence, and patience to lead motley groups of soldiers, hunters, ne'er-do-wells, adventurers, and explorers into the wilderness extremes of the Louisiana Territory.

In 1805, at the same time that Meriwether Lewis and William Clark were making their way across the Continental Divide, Lieutenant Pike set out from St. Louis up the Mississippi River in a keelboat that measured seventy feet in length, leading an exploring party of twenty men. Their orders were to explore the Mississippi to its source, taking latitudes, gauging distances, and mapping the terrain along the way; to befriend, learn the customs of, and gain the trust of the Indians; to make note of whatever natural and mineral resources would prove useful to the United States in general and new settlers in particular; and to collect specimens and report at length on his experiences and observations. Pike was equal to all of these tasks, notwithstanding that the soldiers journeyed north as winter approached, the keelboat would eventually prove useless, the men were not as rugged and determined as their commander, and their supplies gave out. The Mississippi, never a river to accommodate anyone, challenged Pike and his men with sawyers and planters, sandbars and erratic currents, and water of varying depths that would freeze and thaw at the most inopportune moments. But Pike had an excellent hunter in Fraser, and he would find more useful modes of transport—birch-bark canoes and pirogues. Pike turned out to be a resourceful leader, exercising strict command and achieving the obedience of his men and the respect of such tribes as the Sioux. He was also a sensitive observer of human behavior and natural history. Even amid the challenge of the wilderness, he could discover the romantic beauty inherent in the Louisiana Territory.

—Russell M. Lawson

For Further Reading

Coues, Elliott, ed. 1965. *The Expeditions of Zebulon*

Montgomery Pike. Minneapolis: Ross and Haines; Terrell, John Upton. 1968. *Zebulon Pike: The Life and Times of an Adventurer.* New York: Weybright and Talley.

PIKE EXPEDITION (1806–1807)

The vast Louisiana Territory captured the curiosity of many Americans and necessarily invited speculation regarding what exactly the nation had acquired. Lewis and Clark's Expedition (1804–1806) encouraged even more questions. Lieutenant Zebulon Montgomery Pike (1779–1813) set out to find answers. On two separate expeditions, Pike sought to explore portions of the newly acquired territory in order to map the headwaters of various rivers, negotiate peace with Indians, and make clear to foreign trappers that they were on U.S. soil.

Beginning his second, sometimes called the Southwest, expedition on July 15, 1806, Pike left St. Louis with twenty-two men bound for the headwaters of the Arkansas and Red Rivers. His journey brought him to the Osage and Pawnee tribes with whom Pike was to negotiate treaties. Contact with the Osage went well, but the Pawnee were another matter. The area of the Louisiana Purchase explored by Pike was extremely close to Spanish territory. Indeed, there existed no clear boundary line between the two territories. Thus when Pike arrived at the Pawnee villages he learned that a formidable Spanish force had visited the Indians a month before and ensured a cool reception for the Americans. Pike traded what he could but was unable to impress upon the Pawnee the greater importance of the U.S. government.

After leaving the Pawnee, Pike ascended the Arkansas River and in November reached the Rocky Mountains, where he attempted to ascend what he called "Grand Peak," later to become known as Pike's Peak. The men were wholly unequipped for such a venture, and the brutal climb took them through waist-deep snow and subzero temperatures. Still, Pike reveled in the spectacle: "The unbounded prairie was overhung with clouds, which appeared like the ocean in a storm, wave piled on wave and foaming, while the sky was perfectly clear where we were" (Quaife, 1925).

Pike spent two months in the Colorado area in a failed attempt to locate the headwaters of the Red River. He then crossed the Sangre de Cristo Mountains and ultimately reached the Rio Grande, where his men erected a stockade to protect themselves from the bitter February weather. Pike later asserted that he thought they had once again reached the Red River. The explorer must, however, have surmised that they were perilously close to Spanish territory. If he did not consider this possibility, Pike soon found out the hard way. After a member of the expedition, Dr. John Robinson, left the party and arrived in Santa Fe on business, Spanish officials were quickly apprised of Pike's location, and on February 26, 1807, Spanish cavalry arrived at the explorers' shelter and escorted the party to Santa Fe.

Suspicious of U.S. intrusion, Spanish officials questioned the reason for Pike's presence on the Rio Grande. Even though Pike maintained that he thought the party was in U.S. territory, Spanish governor Allencaster believed Pike to be a spy. After seizing a trunk with various maps and papers, Allencaster was even more certain and sent Pike and his men to Chihuahua for questioning by higher officials. Although the Americans had little choice but to comply with Spanish dictates, Pike and his men were hardly prisoners. Pike noted that they stopped in many villages and were often welcomed by town officials with banquets and balls.

After arriving in Chihuahua, Pike waited two months while Spanish and American diplomats debated the intent of Pike's expedition. Although unsatisfied with U.S. claims that Pike was not a spy, Spain nevertheless released the explorers but retained the majority of Pike's documents. A keen observer, however, Pike took note of his travels in Spanish territory and also managed to conceal some written documentation. He was later able to provide information on the number and types of Spanish troops in Northern Mexico. Pike ultimately traveled to San Antonio, then Natchitoches and the Louisiana border, where he was turned over to U.S. troops on July 1, 1807.

Three years later, in 1810, Pike published an account of his expedition, and it was from this source that Americans came to believe that the western Plains were a "Great Desert." The publication also lifted Pike to national fame as a great explorer. There is little doubt that Zebulon Montgomery Pike's exploration of the new Louisiana Territory both encouraged and represented an American restlessness and willingness to forge ahead.

—Matthew Warshauer

For Further Reading

Elliot Coues, ed. 1895. *The Expeditions of Zebulon Montgomery Pike.* New York: Francis P. Harper; Hollon, Eugene. 1949. *The Lost Pathfinder: Zebulon Montgomery Pike.* Norman: University of Oklahoma Press; Quaife, Milo Milton, ed. 1925. *The Southwestern Expedition of Zebulon M. Pike.* Chicago: R. R. Donnelley and Sons.

PIKE, FORT

Within a decade of acquiring the Louisiana Purchase territory, the U.S. government began to realize the formidable difficulties associated with protecting the strategically important, yet vulnerable, city of New Orleans from the threat of foreign invasion. During the War of 1812, particularly in the weeks prior to the Battle of New Orleans, Louisiana militia and U.S. forces under the command of General Andrew Jackson worked feverishly to assemble a combined land and naval force that could repulse the British attack that was imminent. Although Jackson and the defenders of New Orleans were ultimately victorious on the plains of Chalmette, lessons learned at the time would influence future defensive readiness, especially with regard to the construction of coastal fortifications.

In the years following the War of 1812, during the so-called Era of Good Feeling, the United States experienced a rather euphoric sense of nationalism that saw itself expressed in many forms. One of the outcomes of this period, and a key policy of President James Monroe, was the outlay of federal funds to construct or renovate a series of forts along the Atlantic and Gulf coasts of the United States. In the eyes of many, a concerted policy of national defense aimed at protecting coastal assets was the most nationalistic, though not outwardly belligerent, policy that the United States could take. The construction costs associated with this building effort also had real economic implications, and the idea of distributing this federal largesse over a wide region won almost universal acclaim from senators and congressmen, regardless of ideology or political affiliation.

Fort Pike was constructed to the east of New Orleans along the Chef Menteur Pass. The fort was built on the site of an earlier French fortification named Fort Petite Coquilles. Fort Pike was constructed between 1819 and 1826, and it was named in honor of Brigadier General Zebulon Montgomery Pike, the Western explorer who had discovered Pike's Peak.

Fort Pike was one of six masonry forts built along the Louisiana coast, and it was constructed just nine miles east of Fort Macomb, another coastal fortification that was created during the Era of Good Feeling. The French engineer Simon Bernard designed both of these forts, using the same general design. Both were built to guard New Orleans at the Rigolets, the narrow strait that connects Lakes Borgne and Pontchartrain. With the combined effect of their heavy guns, sturdy walls, and marshy approaches, both forts were considered impregnable.

Fort Pike was never used offensively for the purpose that necessitated its construction. The fort was manned only sporadically when it was occasionally used as a staging area for military campaigns that occurred elsewhere, during the Second Seminole War and the Mexican War. When the state of Louisiana seceded and joined the Confederate States of America, Fort Pike was seized, but the site returned to Union hands when federal forces took New Orleans in April 1862. As the Confederates retreated from Fort Pike they burned some of the wooden barracks and destroyed the fort's heavy guns. Thereafter, Union forces occupied the fort and used it briefly as a training area for former slaves who were being trained as artillerymen for the U.S. Colored Troops (USCT).

—Junius P. Rodriguez

See also

Macomb, Fort; New Orleans, Battle of

For Further Reading

Groene, Bertram H. 1988. *Pike: A Fortress in the Wetlands.* Hammond: Southeastern Louisiana University Press; Lewis, Emanuel Raymond. 1993. *Seacoast Fortifications of the United States: An Introductory History.* Annapolis: Naval Institute Press; Parkerson, Codman. 1990. *New Orleans: America's Most Fortified City.* New Orleans: The Quest.

PIKE, ZEBULON MONTGOMERY (1779–1813)

Zebulon M. Pike followed his father, a Revolutionary War veteran, into the army in 1794. Earning the rank of first lieutenant by the age of twenty, Pike served at numerous posts in the West. The young, ambitious soldier sought difficult assignments, hoping for a chance to earn promotion. This opportunity arose when General James Wilkinson selected him to lead an expedition up the Mississippi River. Pike eagerly accepted the command and set out on his first exploration from St. Louis on August 9, 1805.

In an effort to strengthen the U.S. claim to recently purchased territory, Wilkinson set multiple assignments for the mission. Besides mapping and making scientific observations, he also ordered Pike to find the source of the Mississippi, establish friendly relations with the local Indians, and investigate the activities of British fur traders. Pike and his party of twenty men traveled more than five thousand miles in nine months but accomplished few of those goals. They incorrectly identified Leech Lake as the source of the Mississippi River, and the maps and journals the corps produced were filled with errors, adding little to geographic or scientific knowledge. Although they met with various tribes, peace with the Native Americans had not been won. Nor were the British persuaded to end their illegal trade or schemes with the Indians. Despite these failures, the expedition did help to establish Minnesota as part of the Louisiana Purchase and prepared Pike for his future duties.

Pike received the assignment that would earn him his place in history from General Wilkinson soon after returning to St. Louis in April 1806. He hastily compiled his notes and journal for a report of the Mississippi expedition and set out west along the Missouri River on July 15, 1806. His party of twenty-one soldiers, an interpreter, and a surgeon had orders to explore the southwestern region of the Louisiana Purchase and to establish friendly relations with area Indians. Wilkinson instructed Pike to proceed with great care as he neared New Mexico, so as not to offend Spanish officials, but some historians speculate that spying on Spanish settlements was the secret objective of the mission.

On the first leg of the journey, the party escorted a

group of Indians, ransomed by the federal government from the Potawatomi, to their homes at Grand Osage. From there the explorers continued west to the Republican River, where they encamped among Pawnee settlements. Pike met with several tribes but found some of them reluctant to make any agreement that might offend the Spanish. One chief even threatened to stop any Americans attempting to cross the Plains, but Pike was not intimidated. He replied that his men could not be turned back with words and proceeded south without incident along what later became the Santa Fe Trail.

Once they reached the Arkansas, a group of five men were instructed to descend the river to the Mississippi while Pike led the rest of the corps in the opposite direction up the Arkansas. The men were not equipped for the Colorado winter, and the journey became increasingly difficult as they approached the Rocky Mountains. In November, Pike sighted the famous mountain that now bears his name, Pike's Peak, although he failed to climb it. They advanced north to the South Platte River before turning south in an unsuccessful search for the Red River. With some of the party members now suffering from frostbite and unable to travel, Pike constructed a small stockade for them and continued south with the others to find a more hospitable campsite across the Sangre de Cristo Mountains. They selected a location along the Rio Conejos, a branch of the Rio Grande, in Spanish Territory. After building a new stockade, five soldiers volunteered to return for the men they had left behind.

The Spanish had known of Pike's expedition from the beginning and had dispatched troops to intercept it. Thus far they had failed, but now Pike apparently decided to make his whereabouts known to his pursers. John H. Robinson, a civilian doctor who had joined the party in St. Louis, departed for Santa Fe where he met with Governor Joaquin del Real Alencaster and revealed the location of the Conejos camp. One hundred Spanish soldiers arrived at the stockade on February 26 to demand its surrender. Pike denied that he had intentionally trespassed into foreign territory, claiming that he thought he had encamped along the Red River, not the Rio Grande. He offered no resistance and agreed to be escorted to Santa Fe, because the explorer planned to use his capture as an opportunity to survey New Mexico.

At Santa Fe, Pike was unable to convince his captors that he was not a spy. Governor Alencaster decided to send the corps to Chihuahua, where they would be questioned further. The Americans were treated well, but after seizing and translating Pike's papers, officials doubted Pike's story even more. Nevertheless, in order not to provoke the U.S. government, the Spanish only issued a strongly worded protest and allowed Pike to return home. The men crossed Texas and arrived at Natchitoches, Louisiana, nearly one year after the expedition had departed St. Louis.

Upon his return, Pike faced allegations that his expedition had actually been part of Aaron Burr and General Wilkinson's intrigues in the Southwest. And indeed, many historians find the circumstantial evidence that Wilkinson had ulterior motives for sending the explorers West convincing. Secretary of War Henry Dearborn cleared Pike of involvement in the conspiracy, but it remains uncertain to what extent, if any, Pike might have known of Wilkinson's plans.

Zebulon Pike led an expedition that traveled up the Arkansas River Valley toward the Rocky Mountains in 1806.

The publication of Pike's journal in 1810 brought him international fame. Although poorly edited and filled with errors and contradictions, it was popular and reprinted in several languages. His account of the Plains helped create the "Great American Desert" myth of the Midwest. Still, even without the benefit of his papers, still held by the Spanish, Pike managed to relate important data about the lands he explored and provided Americans with the first account of the southwestern region of the Louisiana Purchase territory.

Pike remained in the army. He became a major in 1808 and reached the rank of brigadier general by 1813. A capable commander, he participated in several battles during the War of 1812. After leading a successful assault on York (present-day Toronto), Canada, Pike was killed by an exploding powder magazine on April 27, 1813.

—*Christopher Dennis*

See also

Pike Expedition (1805–1806); Pike Expedition (1806–1807); Wilkinson, James

For Further Reading
Coues, Elliott, ed. 1965. *The Expeditions of Zebulon Montgomery Pike.* Minneapolis: Ross and Haines; Hollon, W. Eugene. 1949. *The Lost Pathfinder: Zebulon Montgomery Pike.* Norman: University of Oklahoma Press; Jackson, Donald, ed. 1966. *Journals of Zebulon Montgomery Pike.* Norman: University of Oklahoma Press; Terrell, John Upton. 1968. *Zebulon Pike: The Life and Times of an Adventurer.* New York: Weybright and Talley.

PINCKNEY, CHARLES COTESWORTH (1746–1825)

Charles Cotesworth Pinckney was the U.S. minister to France (1796–1798) and head of mission during the XYZ Affair (1797–1798). Pinckney, a South Carolinian, was the brother of diplomat Thomas Pinckney, who negotiated the Treaty of San Lorenzo (1795). Pinckney was appointed as tension between France and the United States rose following Jay's Treaty (1794). Politically independent at first, Pinckney refused affiliation with either the Federalist or Republican Party in the 1790s. He was an early admirer of the French Revolution and republic, and he publicly welcomed and feted Edmond Charles Genêt on his 1793 visit to Charleston. Pinckney's experiences in France, however, embittered him toward France and its revolutionary regime. He was thereafter a Federalist.

Despite Pinckney's political independence, he recognized the need for an active federal government and supported George Washington's administration (1789–1797), including its insistence on neutrality during the French Revolutionary Wars (1792–1800). Washington, looking to bolster Southern support, thrice offered Pinckney Supreme Court or cabinet appointments (1791, 1794, and 1795), but Pinckney, because of tenuous personal finances, refused. Later, once his finances were in order, Pinckney accepted appointment as minister to France, replacing James Monroe, who was discredited in Federalist eyes because of his overtly pro-French stance. The appointment came at a time of rising tensions between the countries over French suspicions of Jay's Treaty (1794) as an Anglo-American alliance and U.S. neutrality. Pinckney owed his appointment to his support for Washington's policies, his influence in South Carolina, and the fact that he was not opposed to the French Revolution; thus the Directory might consider him an acceptable replacement.

Pierre Auguste Adet, French minister to the United States, denounced Pinckney to the Directory as hostile to the Revolution and republicanism before the South Carolinian's arrival in France. While Pinckney was en route, the Directory suspended diplomatic relations with the United States and authorized the navy to search and seize U.S. ships and their cargoes if they were bound for Great Britain.

The Directory refused Pinckney's diplomatic credentials and threatened him with arrest. Despite this, Pinckney waited until French authorities ordered him out of the country, leaving for Amsterdam in 1797. He believed that a voluntary withdrawal would surrender U.S. diplomatic standing and diminish national honor. The Directory's preference for Monroe and anti-French letters from Secretary of State Timothy Pickering led Pinckney to believe that Republicans bent on destroying the Federalist administration had engineered French hostility. From this point onward, Pinckney began a turn toward Federalist politics and showed a decided enmity toward France.

In response to this and French provocations at sea, John Adams appointed Federalist John Marshall of Virginia and Republican Elbridge Gerry of Massachusetts to join Pinckney, to open negotiations with France, and to settle the countries' differences so as to avoid war. Conrad Hottinguer ("X"), a Swiss banker representing Charles Maurice Duc de Talleyrand and the Directory, approached the mission. Hottinguer explained that before any negotiations, the United States would have to pay a 1,200,000-livre ($250,000) bribe, or *doucer* ("sweetener"), to Talleyrand, make a substantial loan to the French government, and reimburse French claims against the United States. Pinckney and Marshall decided against the French demands, whereas Gerry believed that they might be considered a starting point in negotiations.

Talleyrand hoped to avoid a war while also convincing the Adams government of abrogating Jay's Treaty (1794). War, he believed, would only drive the United States closer to Great Britain, weaken Spain, and dash his hope for a new American empire. Talleyrand envisioned re-establishing French sovereignty in Louisiana and checking U.S. and British expansion with strategically placed colonies throughout the Mississippi River Valley. Besides blocking Anglo-American expansion, the French colonies might also supply the French sugar colonies with foodstuffs and thus decrease their dependence on the United States.

A second French representative, Lucien Hauteval ("Z"), informed the Americans that Talleyrand would meet with them unofficially; however, Pinckney and Marshall refused and would meet only following an official invitation. Pierre Bellamy ("Y") later approached Marshall and intimated that Great Britain was close to collapse and that France might then turn its military power against the United States. On October 27, 1797, Hottinguer once more broached the topic with the Americans, reiterating Bellamy's threat. The Americans were intransigent; the bribe had assumed central importance. Pinckney was not opposed to paying Talleyrand; he was against paying the minister without having achieved anything. Thus, for Pinckney, the payment was a reward or recognition in the wake of successful negotiations, not a precursor to them. Furthermore Pinckney preferred that negotiations take place openly and honestly. By having approached the Americans as he did, Talleyrand signaled to Pinckney that he preferred engaging in subterfuge. Moreover, Pinckney believed that the loan would violate U.S. neutrality. With this in mind Pinckney replied to Hottinguer's demand for the *doucer* with "no, no, not a sixpence." Pinckney returned to the United States in 1798, his mission having failed.

Ironically, Americans hailed Pinckney as a hero for having resisted French entreaties. In the short term, the XYZ Affair strengthened the Federalists and eliminated Republican opposition in foreign and domestic affairs. The Federalists were able, albeit temporarily, to increase the army, create a navy department, and pass the Alien and Sedition Acts. An undeclared naval war, the Quasi-War (1798–1800), followed on the heels of the Pinckney mission. The XYZ Affair and resulting hostility effectively ended U.S. use of France as an effective counterweight to British diplomacy. Pinckney, a hero, was made a major general in the newly raised army, and later stood unsuccessfully for vice president in 1800 and for president in 1804 and 1808, as a Federalist.

—Ricardo A. Herrera

See also
Adet, Pierre Auguste; Genêt, Edmond Charles; Jay's Treaty; Marshall, John; Monroe, James; Pickering, Timothy; Pinckney, Thomas; San Lorenzo, Treaty of; Talleyrand-Perigord, Charles Maurice de

For Further Reading
DeConde, Alexander. 1966. *The Quasi-War: The Politics and Diplomacy of the Undeclared War with France, 1797–1801.* New York: Charles Scribner's Sons; Stinchcombe, William. 1980. *The XYZ Affair.* Westport, CT: Greenwood; Zahniser, Marvin R. 1967. *Charles Cotesworth Pinckney: Founding Father.* Chapel Hill: University of North Carolina, Institute of Early American History.

PINCKNEY, THOMAS (1750–1828)

The noted soldier and statesman Thomas Pinckney was born in Charleston, South Carolina, the son of Charles Pinckney and Eliza Lucas Pinckney, members of the South Carolina low-country aristocracy. The Pinckneys were a particularly distinguished family: Eliza Pinckney had introduced indigo production to the South; Charles Pinckney had served in London as South Carolina's agent (1754–1756); and Thomas's elder brother, Charles Cotesworth Pinckney (1746–1825), had followed a political career and was a Founding Father and the Federalist presidential candidate in 1804 and 1808. Their cousin, Charles Pinckney (1757–1824), was also a Founding Father and later served as the U.S. minister to Spain (1802–1805).

Educated at the Westminister School, London, and Christ Church College, Oxford, Pinckney later studied for the English bar at Middle Temple, London. Following extensive travel in Europe, he returned to South Carolina to practice law in 1774. Like his elder brother, he had a distinguished military career during the American Revolution, being seriously wounded at Camden (1780) and later serving at Yorktown. A Federalist, he later served two consecutive terms as governor of South Carolina (1787–1788) and somewhat reluctantly accepted the Washington administration's appointment as minister to Great Britain (1792–1796). Well liked as an educated man of liberal manners, Pinckney was a success in London, although, as a loyal patriot, he constantly complained about the British policy of impressment, a practice that increased after the outbreak of war between Britain and France in 1793. Following the negotiations that resulted in the Jay Treaty (1794), Pinckney was dispatched to Madrid by the Washington administration as a special envoy to negotiate a settlement regarding the riverine disputes over the Mississippi and the dangerous situation on the border between the United States and Spanish Louisiana.

By the Treaty of Paris (1783), the British government had ceded to the United States all of its territory east of the Mississippi River except the two provinces of East and West Florida, which were returned to Spain. In an attempt to slow down U.S. movement into what is now Mississippi and Alabama, Spanish authorities encouraged the Native American tribes to defend their sovereignty. To further slow down American westward movement, the government at New Orleans also occasionally attempted to close the city, and hence the Mississippi River, to American commerce, thus threatening the economic interests of thousands of settlers in Ohio, Kentucky, and Tennessee. In 1794, Spanish authorities actually encroached upon U.S. sovereignty by crossing the Mississippi and constructing a fort at the present site of Memphis, Tennessee.

Pinckney arrived in Madrid at the end of June 1795, when Spain was finishing its negotiated peace treaty with France, the Treaty of Basel. Expecting to experience, as a consequence, the full wrath of Great Britain, the Spanish minister of state, Manuel de Godoy, was concerned that the Jay Treaty could be the beginning of a new anti-Spanish, Anglo-American realignment and was thus ready to negotiate. Initially he offered Pinckney liberal terms that would have fulfilled U.S. demands if, in return, he would accept an alliance with Spain, or a triple alliance that included France, mutually guaranteeing Spanish and U.S. territory. When Pinckney declined both alliances, Godoy countered with a revised offer, one that conceded the free navigation of the Mississippi and a fixed boundary with West Florida on the thirty-first parallel north latitude, but which denied the future right of American deposit at New Orleans. When Pinckney declined and demanded his passports Godoy relented, and the negotiations held at the royal monastery of San Lorenzo del Escorial concluded with the signing of the Treaty of San Lorenzo, or "Pinckney's Treaty," on October 27, 1795.

This was a diplomatic coup for Pinckney. He had secured the free navigation of the Mississippi, a fixed southern boundary, a three-year renewable right of tax-free deposit at New Orleans for Americans, and a mutual agreement to control the Native Americans within each party's respective territories. The treaty marked the final abandonment of Spain's long-standing policy of keeping the United States as far away as possible from Louisiana, and Pinckney's achievement was greeted with great enthusiasm when the news reached the United States in February 1796. Spain's later refusal to renew the right of American deposit at New Orleans would generate the negotiations that eventually led to the Louisiana Purchase itself.

Following his resignation from his London post in 1796, Pinckney was nominated as John Adams's Federalist running mate while he was on his way home. He lost that election to Jefferson in the Electoral College but was elected to the House of Representatives in March 1797, where he served until his retirement from public life in 1801. With the outbreak of the War of 1812, however, his military training and command experience led to his being commissioned a brigadier general. In 1813 he was promoted major general and given command of the Sixth Military District, which included North Carolina, South Carolina, and Georgia.

Generally, Pinckney had a quiet war; yet he proved to be an able administrator, and his determination to keep General Andrew Jackson unselfishly supplied helped lead to the crushing defeat of the Creek Redsticks in the battle of Horseshoe Bend (March 27, 1814). Jackson's victory, and the harsh land confiscations that followed, stimulated an acceleration in the settlement of the then southwest, a process initially stimulated by Pinckney's Treaty itself. Although Pinckney remained active in South Carolina politics, he never again held public office. He died in Charleston in November 1828 and was buried in St. Phillip's churchyard, Charleston.

—*Rory T. Cornish*

See also
Godoy, Manuel de; Right of Deposit; San Lorenzo, Treaty of

PINCKNEY'S TREATY

See San Lorenzo, Treaty of

PONCA

The Ponca belonged to the Siouan branch of the Hokan-Siouan linguistic group. The group was at one time a member of the greater Osage people. Eventually they, the Omaha, and the Iowa left the Osage River area and migrated to present-day Minnesota in a move that began in approximately 1500 C.E. War with the Sioux led to another relocation, this time to the Black Hills, in what is now South Dakota, and later to the mouth of the Niobrara, in what would become Nebraska. There they joined the Pawnee, Otoe, Omaha, Cheyenne, and Arapaho.

Unlike the nomadic Sioux, Cheyenne, and Arapaho, the Ponca lived in settled agricultural villages and moved to hunting camps only when they needed buffalo to supplement their crops. Many of the clashes with the Sioux came from disputes over hunting areas and buffalo herds. Like their neighbors, they supplemented their diets with crops of beans, squash, and corn.

Culturally, the Ponca resembled their close cousins the Omaha. Social custom permitted polygamy—men could take up to three wives, for example—and political power rested with two chiefs and a council. They also practiced the so-called Sun Dance, which took its name from an English translation of the Sioux term for the event. This famous summer ritual brought Great Plains tribes together for social and religious activities such as fasting, dancing, and singing. It is perhaps the best known of the Amerindian celebrations, and has been documented for centuries in writing and art. In 1883 the U.S. Courts of Indian Offenses made observing the Sun Dance festival a punishable offense, but the ban was lifted in 1934. The Sun Dance survives in some forms to this day.

The semipermanent communities and society of the Ponca supported a high tolerance for warfare, and a system of alliances and enemies developed (with the Omaha chief among the former, and the Sioux chief among the latter). European traders often became entangled in the hostilities, and the reputation of the Ponca as a warlike people grew.

The Ponca were not to be a formidable enemy or ally for long, however. As the United States negotiated the Louisiana Purchase with France, smallpox and cholera hit the Omaha and soon spread through the Ponca villages. By the time the Lewis and Clark Expedition reached the Ponca in 1804, their numbers had been reduced by the epidemic to approximately two hundred. The Ponca people rallied, however. They had more than doubled their size once again by 1842.

With the Sioux on one side and the encroaching United States on the other, the Omahas and their defense of their homeland were eventually worn down. They ceded their land in 1854. The Ponca, however, continued to hold out until 1858, when they surrendered all of their lands to the United States with the exception of a small reserve along the Niobrara River. There they continued to experience trouble with the Sioux and faced new agricultural difficulties as well. The United States forcibly removed the Poncas in 1877 and relocated them in Indian Territory in a violent removal that is now known as the Ponca Trail of Tears.

This terrible event has been credited with being the catalyst for a new national concern for Native American rights. Eastern philanthropists, in particular, responded to the disturbing images of the Ponca ordeal with new concern for and interest in the plight of the American Indian. Ponca leader Chief Standing Bear also made his mark on the American consciousness. The celebrated case *Standing Bear v. Crook* (1879) brought the Ponca new fame as the U.S. Supreme Court declared that American Indians were, in fact, to be considered people under U.S. laws.

In the wake of this triumph, the Ponca pressed their land claims against the United States and eventually received a hearing in 1880 under a commission organized under President Rutherford B. Hayes. As a result of the commission's report, most of the Ponca remained in Oklahoma. A small number, approximately two hundred, however, were allowed to return to their former Nebraska home. In 1962, at the request of the Ponca, this Nebraska reservation was terminated. The Ponca Tribe of Nebraska has only recently regained official recognition from the U.S. federal government. Today the Ponca tribes continue to exist separately and rarely reunite.

—*Amy H. Sturgis*

See also
Arapaho; Black Hills; Cheyenne; Iowa; Oglala Sioux; Osage; Pawnee

For Further Reading
Howard, James Henri. 1965. *The Ponca Tribe*. Washington, DC: Government Printing Office; Jablow, Joseph. 1974. *Ethnohistory of the Ponca: Commission Findings [on the Ponca Indians]*. New York: Garland; Skinner, Alanson. 1915. *Societies of the Iowa, Kansa, and Ponca Indians*. New York: The Trustees; Tibbles, Thomas Henry. 1972. *The Ponca Chiefs: An Account of the Trial of Standing Bear*. Edited by Kay Graber. Lincoln: University of Nebraska Press.

PONTALBA, JOSEPH XAVIER DE (1764–1834)

In 1801, Joseph Xavier de Pontalba wrote a memoir on the political and economic situation in Louisiana as the nineteenth century began. Napoleon and Captain General Claude Perrin Victor used the document to plan the intended expedition to occupy and defend the Louisiana colony for France, and it may have influenced Napoleon's eventual decision to sell the territory.

Pontalba was born in New Orleans in 1764. He was educated in France, then served in the French army, distinguishing himself during the siege of Savannah in 1772. After retiring from the army in 1784 with the rank of captain, he returned to Louisiana, where he became commander of the militia companies along the Cote des Allemands (the German Coast) and rose to the rank of lieutenant colonel in the Regiment of Louisiana. Returning to France around 1800, he received a commission in the French army as adjutant commandant in 1802, and was ordered to accompany Victor on his expedition to Louisiana.

Pontalba's experience in Louisiana gave him a unique perspective. In his *Memoir* he wrote: "This is the information that I have acquired, during a residence of eighteen years attached to the government as a superior officer, on the situation of Louisiana and her natural enemies, the means of improving the colony so that it may defend itself, its commerce, and its actual products . . . to give a perfect knowledge of that immense country, and its dangerous neighbors" (Pontalba, 1801).

The dangerous neighbors to whom Pontalba was referring were Americans living on the western frontier. Because of the enormous cost of transportation across the Alleghenies, the only reasonable outlet for their agricultural products was via the Mississippi River. This dependency made navigation rights on the river essential for their prosperity and placed Louisiana—considering its state of development—in an uncomfortable situation. Pontalba believed that Kentucky and Tennessee had sufficient population and means to launch an attack against Louisiana. Because of the rapid river currents, he thought that the Americans could quickly descend upon New Orleans with a force of twenty or thirty thousand armed men. For this reason, he believed that it was essential to maintain good communications and to grant river privileges until Louisiana was in a position to defend itself.

Pontalba noted that U.S. newspaper articles frequently referred to Louisiana as the "road to the conquest of Mexico." He noted that France would be better able to protect Mexico from invasion than Spain. And as payment for such protection, France could obtain from Spain freedom of commerce for Louisiana with the ports on the Gulf of Mexico. He believed that this arrangement would give Louisiana an opportunity to develop and become an economic asset for France.

A significant portion of the *Memoir* is devoted to an economic analysis of the colony. Pontalba indicated that Louisiana was operating at a substantial deficit, and if for some reason Spain should close to Louisiana the ports on the Gulf of Mexico, that deficit would be even greater. He concluded that the colony would be a financial liability to France for several years. One of the biggest problems was the high cost of labor. He strongly advised against the liberation of slaves, noting that "their freedom would destroy all fortunes, annihilate all means of existence, and be an omen of the greatest misfortunes" (ibid.).

Pontalba saw that strong alliances with Indian tribes were necessary for defending the colony because they served as a barrier against the United States. Spain had maintained these alliances, and Pontalba advised that France do the same until the colony were better prepared to defend itself. The cost of these alliances, however, was very high. According to Pontalba's calculations, it represented nearly one-fifth of the colony's deficit.

The major theme throughout the *Memoir* is Louisiana's vulnerability to U.S. expansion. Although

Pontalba did seem to advocate the French acquisition of Louisiana and its eventual economic benefits to France, his realistic thoughts on the difficulty and expense of defending it may have encouraged Napoleon's decision to sell the territory.

—*Mark Cave*

See also
Victor, Claude Perrin

For Further Reading

Pontalba, Joseph Xavier de. 1801. "Memoir of Colonel Joseph Xavier Delfau de Pontalba, as translated and found in Alcée Fortier." 1904. *The History of Louisiana, Volume II: The Spanish Domination and the Cession to the United States.* New York: Goupil and Company of Paris.

POPULAR SOVEREIGNTY

The notion of popular sovereignty asserts that ultimate political power rests entirely with the masses. A reaction against royal absolutism based on the theory of divine right, popular sovereignty is understood as the natural right of the people to establish, alter, or abolish government. Although the concept may be radical or idealistic in theory, in practice popular sovereignty is representative government. For example, the first three words of the Preamble to the U.S. Constitution—"We the People"—are followed by the outline of a complex governmental system. The state is regarded as the political unit of the people because universal suffrage allows the people to delegate their authority to representatives who conduct the business of the state.

The ideas from which popular sovereignty originated are primarily rooted in Enlightenment philosophy and Reformation politics, although Aristotle's *Politics* has been cited for ethical justification. The Protestant Reformation was very significant because it provided instances of successful rebellion against established authority, both ecclesiastical and civil. The French philosophers Montesquieu and Voltaire contributed to the notion of popular will by condemning despotic systems. However, Rousseau went further by declaring that sovereignty belongs to the people as a whole. Tocqueville, describing America of the nineteenth century, observed: "The people . . . are the cause and the aim of all things; everything comes from them, and everything is absorbed in them."

American ideas about popular sovereignty, however, have not been unanimous. A major issue has been a contradiction of vision, the federalist versus the antifederalist. A federalist belief was based on the view that the entire nation must act together, whereas the antifederalists identified with the uniqueness of local communities. As the land composing the Louisiana Purchase came to be settled, this debate lingered. The slavery question was the major source of friction between the two camps. The nonfederalists associated popular sovereignty with the settlers' right to decide whether or not the institution of slavery should be permitted. They argued that the people living in a federal territory, not Congress, have the right to determine the slavery question. (Of course, back then the dominant culture did not permit people of color to contribute their say in this matter.) Opponents of the spreading of slavery dubbed this expression of self-determinism "squatter sovereignty." Lewis Cass and Stephen A. Douglas, U.S. senators and leading figures of the Democratic Party, endorsed the principle of "squatter sovereignty" because they favored limiting the power of the federal government.

The debate over the issue of slavery in the western territories led to many legislative actions, including the Missouri Compromise (1820), the Compromise of 1850, and the Kansas-Nebraska Act (1854). The Missouri Compromise established a precedent for the settling of the North-South argument over slavery, as it declared a permanent prohibition of slavery in the Louisiana Purchase above 36 degrees 30 minutes north latitude, except in Missouri. In 1850, Congress voted California's entrance into the Union as a free state, while allowing slavery south of the fortieth parallel in the remainder of the land once owned by Mexico. However, the Kansas-Nebraska Act partially repealed the Missouri Compromise, as it authorized the settlers of the present-day states of Kansas, Nebraska, Montana, South Dakota, and North Dakota to decide for themselves whether or not slavery would be allowed in those territories. The North-South polarization of the nation became all the more acute after the Dred Scott decision of 1857, which ruled, in part, that Congress was not authorized to prohibit slavery in the federal territories.

The Kansas-Nebraska Act accented the North-South political polarization of the nation, and it led to the founding of the Republican Party. The famous 1858 Lincoln-Douglas debates in Illinois significantly focused on the question of the expansion of slavery in the Western territories. Abraham Lincoln strongly argued against "squatter sovereignty," as he felt that the Western territories should be inhabited by free white labor, and he feared that slavery would depress wages overall. In 1860, Lincoln and Douglas were opponents in the presidential election, and the question of popular sovereignty was the major campaign issue. The subsequent Civil War pitted against one another the two opposing views of popular sovereignty, the federalist versus the antifederalist, and settled the issue of slavery.

Today popular sovereignty remains a cogent factor in U.S. politics. In the twentieth century, distorted views of popular sovereignty led to many political and social abuses, including public lynchings, mob rule, demagoguery, and McCarthyism. The tyranny of the majority, often asserted by popular referenda, has in recent times declared war on illegal aliens and curbed needed spending for local school districts. In the name of the people, some elected officials have decimated welfare assistance and scuttled affirmative action programs. On the other hand, globalization has inspired a radicalized view of popular sovereignty in an international context, of which the mass protests against the World Bank and World Trade Organization are representative.

—*Roger Chapman*

For Further Reading

Dippel, Horst. 1996. "The Changing Idea of Popular Sovereignty in Early American Constitutionalism: Breaking Away from European Patterns." *Journal of the Early Republic* 16: 21–45; Epstein, David F. 1984. *The Political Theory of the Federalist.* Chicago: University of Chicago Press; Hinsley, F. H. 1986. *Sovereignty.* 2d ed. London and New York: Cambridge University Press; Hoffman, John. 1998. *Sovereignty.* Minneapolis: University of Minnesota Press; Laski, Harold J. 1921. *The Foundations of Sovereignty and Other Essays.* London: George Allen and Unwin; Levin, Daniel Lessard. 1999. *Representing Popular Sovereignty: The Constitution in American Political Culture.* Albany: State University of New York Press; Morgan, Edmund S. 1988. *Inventing the People: The Rise of Popular Sovereignty in England and America.* New York: W. W. Norton and Company.

PORTAGE DES SIOUX, TREATY OF (1815)

Negotiated with more than a dozen tribes and bands in the summer of 1815, the Treaty of Portage des Sioux sought to end hostilities associated with the War of 1812 as provided for in the Treaty of Ghent (1814). Actually a series of all but identical agreements, the treaty focused on making peace and did not address the grievances of individual communities or questions of territorial cession.

In the spring of 1815, William Clark, governor of the Missouri Territory; Ninian Edwards, governor of the Illinois Territory; and Auguste Chouteau, notable St. Louis fur trader, were selected to lead the American delegation. They immediately set to the difficult task of locating emissaries willing to travel into Indian country and inform bands and tribes, some of whom continued to engage in hostilities and depredations, of the pending council.

Portage des Sioux was chosen for its location on the west bank of the Mississippi River, near both the Missouri River and the Illinois River. In rather short order, a thriving community began to emerge at the council site. In addition to a sizable U.S. military presence, perhaps as many as two thousand Native Americans were in attendance, including various delegates from the invited tribes and bands, along with their advisors and families, as well as individuals from other tribes on friendly terms with the United States. Throughout the summer an array of curious, entrepreneurial, and concerned citizens came to witness the events, learn of the progress of the talks, and profit from the assembled.

Against this backdrop, negotiations began in earnest on July 6, 1815, and concluded on September 16, 1815. Individually and collectively the representatives of the federal government held talks with delegations from the Iowa, Kansa, Kickapoo, Osage, Piankashaw, the Potawotomi residing on the Illinois River, the Sac and Fox of Missouri, the Teton Sioux, Sioux of the lakes, Sioux residing on the St. Peter's River, and the Yankton Sioux. These talks hinged on securing peace. To facilitate this process and demonstrate the good intentions of the United States, in accordance with custom, gifts were given to the leaders of the various native nations in attendance. In fact, the Department of War apportioned $20,000 for this purpose at Portage des Sioux. Complementing the exchange of wealth, U.S. delegates made threats and promises in dramatic oratory. Clark, for instance, remarked to the assembled Kickapoo: "You have a choice: say you wish for war, and we are ready; say you wish for peace and it shall be so" (Fisher, 1933).

The treaties negotiated at Portage des Sioux concerned themselves with peace and reconciliation. They declared "perpetual peace and friendship" among the parties. They called for the mutual forgiving of past transgressions, including the return of any prisoners taken during the conflict. They affirmed previous agreements entered into by individual native nations and the United States. They brought the signatory tribes and bands not previous tied by treaties "under the protection of the United States." They also stipulated that all lands previously ceded to Britain, France, or Spain were transferred to the United States.

The first treaties were signed on July 18, 1815, with the Piankashaw and the Potawatomi of the Illinois River. Two days later, an additional five treaties were signed with the Teton Sioux, the Sioux of the Lakes, the Sioux of St. Peter's River, the Yankton Sioux, and the Maha. Following an adjournment of the talks, agreements were reached nearly two months later, on September 16, 1815, with the Kickapoo, the Big and Little Osage, the Missouri River Sac and Fox, and the Iowa. The U.S. Congress ratified all of these pacts on December 26, 1815.

The Treaty of Portage des Sioux marked an important turning point. It marked an end to organized resistance to U.S. expansion and the suspension (if only temporarily) of hostilities in the upper Mississippi Valley. It opened large portions of the Louisiana Territory to migration. In turn, pacification prompted a shift in federal Indian policy, which increasingly emphasized land cession and the removal of indigenous peoples.

—*C. Richard King*

See also

Chouteau, René Auguste; Clark, William

For Further Reading

Fisher, Robert L. 1933. "The Treaties of Portage des Sioux." *Mississippi Valley Historical Review* 19, no. 4: 495–508; Prucha, Francis Paul. 1994. *American Indian Treaties: The History of a Political Anomaly.* Berkeley: University of California Press.

POTAWATOMI

The Potawatomi ("People of the Place of Fire") had first contact with Europeans in the mid–seventeenth century as French traders and Jesuit missionaries visited the area of present-day Green Bay, Wisconsin. Pushed west by the Iroquois, at the time of the Louisiana Purchase the Potawatomi were south of Lake Michigan, occupying an area now located in four states: Michigan, Indiana, Illinois, and Wisconsin. The Ojibwa, Ottawa, and Potawatomi constituted the Three Fires, tribes that traveled together from the East Coast and separated at the Straits of Michilimackinac. Legends call them brothers, each with an assigned responsibility: the Ojibwa were the Keepers of the Faith; the Ottawa were the Keepers of the Trade; and the Potawatomi were the Keepers of the Council Fire.

By the early nineteenth century, there were multiple bands of Potawatomi, grouped into two major divisions. The Potawatomi who left the woodlands of Wisconsin to live in the prairie lands of Illinois and Indiana were called the Prairie Potawatomi. Those who stayed north were the Forest Potawatomi, Potawatomi of the Woods, or, later, Mission or Citizen Potawatomi.

The Potawatomi long illustrated split allegiances. Some supported the British during the Revolutionary War, others supported the American colonists. Some backed the British during the War of 1812. A number of Prairie Potawatomi joined Tenskwatawa, the Shawnee Prophet, and his brother Tecumseh in attacking Americans. A few Potawatomi joined Black Hawk during the Black Hawk War (1832), but most chose not to support or harbor Black Hawk and his followers.

The Potawatomi signed forty-two treaties with the United States between 1789 and 1867, more than ten of which were cession treaties. These treaties followed a pattern whereby the Indians received annuities in exchange for land, were unable to sustain themselves, went into debt to traders, then were forced to sell the smaller allotted lands to pay their debts. Landless, they then were moved to more isolated lands to the west after the passage of the Indian Removal Act (1830). Some communities avoided removal by traveling north and even escaping into Canada; these bands still remain in or close to their cultural homelands.

The Potawatomi signed a treaty in Chicago in 1833, ceding five million acres and expediting their removal west. The Prairie Potawatomi were first removed, in 1834, to Missouri's Platte Country, then in 1837 they were removed once again to southwestern Iowa, near Council Bluffs.

The Trail of Death occurred in 1838 with the enforced removal of 850 Potawatomi of the Woods from Indiana to the Osage River in eastern Kansas. More than 140 died along the way. This event is now remembered by a pilgrimage called the Commemorative Caravan, which traces the removal along the Trail of Death Regional Historic Trail.

In 1846 the Iowa and Osage River reservations were eliminated. The two groups of Potawatomi were united on a single reservation near Topeka, Kansas, in 1846 and briefly called the United Band. In the 1860s, the segment of Forest Potawatomi now called the Citizen Band, because of their acceptance of Christianity and abandonment of traditional culture, decided to exchange their communal land holdings for individual allotments while the remaining members, the Prairie Band, elected to stay on the reservation on tribally owned land. By 1867 the Citizen Band had lost its land to non-Indian citizens. In 1870 the Citizen Band then accepted a move to a new reservation in Indian Territory (Oklahoma) near Shawnee, where they again lost much of their land to allotment in 1889.

The Prairie Band opted to stay in Kansas when the reservation was divided in 1861. They were given land in Jackson County, Kansas, near Mayetta, where they continue to live.

Traditionally, the Potawatomi men were fishermen and hunters, and the women tended gardens of beans, potatoes, pumpkin, squash, and medicinal plants. They gathered wild rice, seasoned their food with maple sugar or syrup, and lived in bark and mat-covered wigwams in the winter and in larger, rectangular dwellings during the summer. They referred to themselves as Nishnabek, or "The People," and spoke an Algonquian language.

Today there are at least twenty-four thousand Potawatomi living in Kansas, Oklahoma, Wisconsin, Michigan, and Ontario, Canada. The Pokagon and Nottawaseppi Bands of Potawatomi received federal recognition in 1994 and 1996, respectively. Other Potawatomi bands include the Hannahville Indian Community, the Gun Lake Tribe, and the Forest County Potawatomi Community in Wisconsin. Bands inside Canada include the Stoney Point and Kettle Point Bands and the Walpole Island First Nation.

—Loriene Roy

See also
Black Hawk; Black Hawk War; Indian Removal; Indian Territory; Iowa; Kansas; Manifest Destiny; Missouri; Ojibwa; Oklahoma

For Further Reading
Clifton, James A. 1977. *The Prairie People: Continuity and Change in Potawatomi Indian Culture, 1665–1965.* Lawrence: Regents Press of Kansas; Clifton, James A. 1984. *The Pokagons, 1683–1983: Catholic Potawatomi Indians of the St. Joseph River Valley.* New York, London: Lanham; Edmunds, R. David. 1978. *The Potawatomis: Keepers of the Fire.* Norman, London: University of Oklahoma Press.

PREEMPTION ACT (1841)

Signed into law on September 4, 1841, the Preemption Act encouraged the settlement of the former Louisiana Purchase lands by providing easier access to land. The act also represented an attempt by the Whig and Democratic Parties to court the growing political power of the Western states. In regard to public lands, the act accommodated squatters who settled on lands prior to government surveys by legalizing early settlement on unsurveyed land. This was important because it recognized squatting as a legitimate means of establishing a land claim and it decriminalized a widespread practice among settlers in this period. The law allowed a settler, or squatter, to buy up to 160 acres of land for a minimum payment of $1.25 per acre, provided that the settler file a preemption in the local land office. The preemption process consisted of two parts.

First, the settler made a declaratory statement. This sworn statement indicated that the squatter had settled on a tract of land and intended to claim it. This had to be done within three months of settlement, if it was on surveyed land. On unsurveyed land, the claimant had to file at the time of settlement or three months after the government survey. To qualify for a preemption, claimants had to be U.S. citizens who were single men twenty-one years of age, a head of a household, or a widow. Aliens were eligible for a preemption upon declaring their intention to become citizens. The second part of the process required the claimant to prove occupation and improvement of the land and to pay for it. The law required the preemptor to return to the land office thirty days after filing a preemption with two witnesses to testify that the claimant had occupied the land for the prescribed period of time and that improvements had been made. Claimants were required to pay for their land eighteen months after making a declaration.

The law intended to benefit squatters by preventing subsequent claims against a tract of land and by distributing land before the public auction convened. The act also allowed settlers to possess land twenty-two months prior to actually purchasing it. The statute further favored small landholders over speculators by stipulating that any one that owned more than 320 acres in any state or territory could not file for a preemption, nor could they abandon land they owned in the same state or territory for preempted lands. The law also allowed payment for the land in cash, military bounty warrants, or agricultural college scrip.

The furious debate in Congress that surrounded the Preemption Act (1841) reflected the growing influence of the West at this time, and the highly partisan and sectional nature of U.S. politics. Champions of preemption, such as Democratic senators Thomas Hart Benton of Missouri and Robert J. Walker of Mississippi, fought constantly to include the right of preemption in the nation's land policy. Preemption was a popular issue in the West, and after the panic of 1837 agitation for it increased. However, powerful politicians like Henry Clay, defending Eastern interests and fears, rallied support repeatedly to defeat it. Easterners believed that the migration West would cause wages to rise and that subsequent agricultural competition would lower the value of Eastern farmers' lands and produce. The election of 1840 changed the situation of preemption in the political landscape.

In the Log Cabin campaign of William Henry Harrison, Whigs appealed to Western interests in their successful bid for the presidency. After their victory, Democrats, led by Benton, pushed a new preemption bill to expose the hypocrisy of their political foes. To save face and make the bill more palatable to Whig interests, Clay introduced a distribution provision that required revenues from land sales to be divided among the other states, a measure fervently opposed by Democrats. The compromise bill weathered the storm and passed the House 166 to 108, and the Senate 22 to 18. The compromise, however, was short lived. In 1842, Congress passed a tariff bill that negated the distribution clause. Also, the measure did not satisfy Westerners that increasingly desired free land.

Although effectively replaced by the Homestead Act (1862), the law existed until 1891, when it was finally repealed. Not very pleased with the law, Western interests did, however, win in the political struggle. But the benefits to potential small farmers were unclear, because the pace of land sales remained roughly the same. Regardless, the act marked an important shift in the U.S. government's policy toward Western lands.

—Peter S. Genovese, Jr.

For Further Reading

Dick, Everett. 1970. *The Lure of the Land: A Social History of the Public Lands from the Articles of Confederation to the New Deal.* Lincoln: University of Nebraska Press; Hibbard, Benjamin Horace. 1965. *A History of the Public Land Policies.* Madison: University of Wisconsin Press; Robbins, Roy M. 1960. *Our Landed Heritage: The Public Domain, 1776–1936.* Gloucester, MA: Peter Smith; Stephenson, George M. 1967. *The Political History of the Public Lands from 1840 to 1862: From Preemption to Homestead.* New York: Russell and Russell.

QUAPAW

The Quapaw Indians were first observed in 1673 by Father Jacques Marquette. They lived in four villages: three along the Mississippi River near the mouth of the Arkansas River and the fourth on the Arkansas. By the time of the Louisiana Purchase, disease and war had reduced the Quapaw to a population of 575 who were concentrated in three villages on the Arkansas River. They intermarried with French during the colonial period, and had been strong allies of the French and later the Spanish when they acquired Louisiana in 1762.

The Quapaws' involvement in local and regional trade continued into the territorial period. Corn, raised by Quapaw women, and horses, raised by both men and women, were traded to their white neighbors, as well as to hunters. Quapaw men also continued to hunt and to trade animal products.

As the U.S. population grew, the Quapaws' economic role diminished and their land became more desirable. The Quapaw were not a priority for the United States as they had been for the French and Spanish. As long as the Mississippi River was a boundary and travel on it could be contested, the Quapaw were important to colonial diplomacy and defense. Once the United States united both banks of the Mississippi River with the Louisiana Purchase, however, the Quapaw no longer held a strategic position.

In an 1818 treaty, the Quapaw agreed to a reservation of one million acres running northeast to southwest between the Arkansas and Ouachita Rivers. They relinquished their claims to forty-three million acres south of the Arkansas and to the west in exchange for $4,000 in goods and an annual payment of $1,000 worth of goods.

The 1818 treaty was not enough for settlers and territorial officials, who coveted valuable Quapaw land on the Arkansas River. These groups put pressure on the Quapaw, who signed the Treaty of 1824 and ceded their reservation to the United States. In return they received land among the Caddo on the Red River in northwestern Louisiana, $4,000 in goods, and a $2,000 annual annuity for eleven years. The treaty also reserved land along the Arkansas River for eleven mixed-blood families.

The Quapaw moved to Caddo country in early 1826 but met with disaster. Floods destroyed crops; starvation killed sixty people, including members of Sarasin's family; and bureaucratic confusion undermined the Quapaws' confidence in the federal government's agents. After six months there, Sarasin broke with Heckaton, the principal chief, and led one-fourth of the nation back to the land reserved for him on the Arkansas River.

The federal government responded by awarding one-fourth of the Quapaws' annuity to the Arkansas band, but in hopes of persuading Sarasin and his band to leave Arkansas again, prohibited them from using the annuity money to buy land. Many Quapaw became squatters on land near Pine Bluff, farming and hiring themselves out to pick cotton and hunt game for white families. The Quapaw began to use the annuity to lay the foundation for a Quapaw future in Arkansas. They persuaded Governor George Izard to buy agricultural implements with the annuity and paid for ten Quapaw boys to go to school.

By 1830 all of the Quapaw had returned to Arkansas. Heckaton abandoned the Red River settlement and led the remnant of the nation back to the Arkansas River. Sarasin rejected government suggestions that his people join the Cherokee or the Osage. (The latter he considered enemies of the Quapaw.) He and Heckaton pleaded with federal and territorial officials to allow the Quapaw to remain in Arkansas. Only Sarasin was promised that he could remain in the territory.

In 1832 the Quapaw finally received annuity payments that had been denied them for years. It was too little and too late. Unable to buy land, many Quapaw were pushed off their farms by white settlers, and some found refuge only in the swamps. With their situation becoming more desperate, the Quapaw signed the treaty of 1833 by which they agreed to move to 150 acres in the northeastern corner of the Indian Territory.

To the chagrin of government officials, many did not go to the new reservation. Instead, Sarasin led three hundred Quapaw back to the Red River, where the annuity had been sent. He soon returned to Arkansas and lived in Jefferson County until his death. Heckaton and the rest of the Quapaw, meanwhile, started the process of rebuilding their nation in the Indian Territory.

—Joseph Patrick Key

For Further Reading

Arnold, Morris. 2000. *The Rumble of a Distant Drum: The Quapaws and Old World Newcomers, 1673–1804.* Fayetteville: University of Arkansas Press; Baird, W. David. 1980. *The Quapaws: A History of the Downstream People.* Norman: University of Oklahoma Press; Sabo, George, III. 1992. *Paths of Our Children: Historic Indians of Arkansas*. Fayetteville: Arkansas Archeological Survey.

QUIDS

See Tertium Quids

RANDOLPH, JOHN (1773–1833)

The leader of the Jeffersonian Republicans, John Randolph served as majority leader in the House of Representatives during Thomas Jefferson's first presidential term. Subsequently, he became the administration's sharpest critic. Randolph initially favored Western expansion, but he came to regret deeply its effect on American politics.

John Randolph began his national political career as a Jeffersonian stalwart in the 1790s. Dedicated to the principle of majority rule and self-government for a liberty-loving people, Randolph took every opportunity to attack Federalist policies. His services and his veracious political eccentricities propelled him to the position of majority leader after Thomas Jefferson's presidential victory in 1800. A primary articulator of Jeffersonian policies, few were clever enough, or brave enough, to challenge Randolph in open debate. His leadership style, as detrimental to the Federalists as it may have been, alienated several Republican followers who took a more nationalistic approach to federal politics. Randolph always believed the federal government to be constitutionally limited in power and restrained from exercising jurisdiction over matters best left to local majorities.

Randolph initially supported the Louisiana Purchase as well as Western expansion. Cooperating with Albert Gallatin, he introduced legislation on October 22, 1803, to carry the treaties of cession into effect, and in November of that year he sponsored a bill known as the Mobile Act, which extended federal revenue laws to Louisiana. Randolph and the administration began to differ when boundary negotiations deteriorated in 1805. Randolph condemned the tactics of secretly placating Spain with money while publicly claiming that force might be necessary to stop Spanish aggression. When he pushed the administration to finally reveal its tactics, the president was humiliated.

Since those normally associated with a "strict interpretation" of the Constitution (men such as Randolph, John Taylor of Caroline, William B. Giles, and Nathaniel Macon) favored annexation, their reputation for constitutional principles is often questioned. However, federal land purchases and admission of new states was not a matter of strict versus loose interpretation of the Constitution, but centered on differing beliefs about the national compact. Federalists thought the compact theory implied that only those that were a party to ratification in 1787–1789 could admit new territory. Thus, the original thirteen states had to agree to admission; otherwise, the compact enlarged and was diversified at the expense of social order. But as Randolph showed, the Jeffersonian compact theory was synonymous with limited federal power. Although Randolph and his distant cousin, Thomas Jefferson, did not always share common concerns during the years between 1800 and 1820, their fears about the Louisiana Purchase were quite similar. Both men thought that the purchase conferred too much power to the president despite the fact that Randolph did not favor a constitutional amendment to justify annexation. Randolph hoped that posterity would cherish their self-government and rely on constitutional principles rather than federal precedents that might evolve from the purchase.

Randolph placed great faith in a free people to govern themselves as long as proper safeguards were in place that forced them to protect their interests. For example, he thought that constitutions served as a guide to focus popular attention on the first principles of republicanism rather than empowerment texts for governments. At the time Louisiana was acquired, Randolph still believed that the American people would always seek to protect their liberty, which he defined as their traditional customs and economic habits. Americans would journey westward and settle down to create their own interests and defend them. But when it became apparent that Westerners were going to mimic Eastern customs while gradually adopting national rather than local attitudes, Randolph began seriously to question Western expansion and his early support for taking Louisiana.

Having split from the administration with other Tertium Quids over the Yazoo Land controversy and measures deemed too nationalistic, Randolph's opposition to Jefferson peaked when the president pushed for an economic embargo in 1807. His position in that difficult time was not always clear-cut, but it appears that Randolph's opposition to the embargo and the War of 1812 rested on two propositions. First, the embargo severely affected the Virginia plantation interests he represented by depressing prices and motivating further migration to newly opened Western lands. Second, he realized that the embargo directed nationalism on the frontier toward intensive protectionism. At the time, Western supporters of protection and internal improvements attacked New England commerce for making the United States dependent upon foreign production. But Randolph knew that such sentiment would be used against other local interests in the future.

Randolph reserved his greatest animosity for the leading proponent of frontier nationalism, Henry Clay. One of the few politicians capable of corralling Randolph's political and rhetorical maneuvers, Clay represented everything Randolph despised. Clay's American System, so Randolph believed, distracted Westerners from their local interests, focusing their attention on the national government, aggrandizing federal power, and loosening their commitment to self-government. By the 1820s, when support for the American System was at its highest, Randolph and other "Old Republicans" underwent a serious transition as they jettisoned their earlier commitments to majority rule and constitutionalism. Such things worked, they thought, only when people defended their local interests. However, coalition governments, religious revivalism on the frontier, and abstract ideas such as progress and nationalism distracted people from their local customs and prevented interest-based majorities from forming at the federal level. Randolph's last public service occurred in the Virginia Constitutional Convention of 1829–1830, where his finest political speeches were delivered, all of which illustrated how Western expansion transformed Jeffersonian political theory.

Randolph died during the nullification controversy of the early 1830s, opposing nullification in favor of secession. Losing hope that a liberty-loving majority could ever be formed at the national level, Randolph insisted on being buried head-up, facing west, so he could keep his eyes on Henry Clay and the demagoguery he believed destroyed interest-based politics.

—Carey M. Roberts

See also
Federalist Party; Gallatin, Albert; Jefferson, Thomas; Loose Construction of the U.S. Constitution; Louisiana Memorial; *Tertium Quids*

For Further Reading
Dawidoff, Robert. 1979. *The Education of John Randolph.* New York: Norton; Garland, Hugh A. 1850. *Life of Randolph of Roanoke.* New York: D. Appleton and Company; Kirk, Russell. 1997. *Randolph of Roanoke.* Indianapolis: Liberty Fund; Malone, Dumas. 1970. *Jefferson the President: First Term, 1801–1805.* Boston: Little, Brown, and Company.

RELF, RICHARD (1776–1857)

One of the most successful American merchants in early Louisiana, Richard Relf was born in Philadelphia, Pennsylvania, in 1776. When he was sixteen years old, Relf relocated to the Spanish colony of Louisiana and settled at New Orleans.

By 1801, Relf and Beverly Chew became partners in a mercantile house with Daniel Clark. As a result of Clark's prominent position in early Louisiana, particularly his service as U.S. consul and as a member of the House of Representatives, both Relf and Chew found themselves well situated in the New Orleans business community. Relf and Chew would eventually become executors of Clark's will when he died on August 16, 1813, but the controversial settlement of that will would become one of the most celebrated legal cases of nineteenth-century America. Clark's daughter, Myra Clark Whitney Gaines, contested her father's 1811 will, and the case lingered in Louisiana courts until a final settlement was reached in May 1883.

In addition to their legal business ventures, the firm of Chew and Relf also engaged in enterprises that circumvented the law. After the importation of Africans as slaves was outlawed by federal law in 1808, Chew and Relf often acted as middlemen for other firms, some as distant as Charleston, South Carolina, that wished to import Africans into North America. Chew and Relf used their business contacts with Spanish officials in West Florida to facilitate the landing of slave ships and the distribution of their cargoes at the port of Mobile.

In 1818, Relf was appointed cashier of the Louisiana State Bank, and he held that position until his death in 1857. In addition to his work with the Louisiana State Bank, Relf also held the position of Steamship Debenture clerk at the New Orleans customhouse for many years.

Richard Relf was actively involved with the founding of the Canal Bank in New Orleans. He also served as a vestry and senior warden of Christ Church, the main Episcopalian congregation in nineteenth-century New Orleans.

Relf died in 1857 and was buried in the Girod Street Cemetery in New Orleans.

—Junius P. Rodriguez

See also
Clark, Daniel

For Further Reading
Gaines, Edmund Pendleton. 1845. *The Case of General Gaines and Wife versus Richard Relf and Beverly Chew, in the Circuit Court of the United States for the State of Louisiana: Answer, &c., of the Defendants, Relf, Chew, Ferrier, and Barnes and Wife.* New Orleans: Joseph Cohn.

RENDEZVOUS SYSTEM

The Rocky Mountain fur trade enjoyed considerable success due in large part to the rendezvous system, in which trappers and traders met yearly at designated sites to transact their business. The fur trade in the Louisiana Territory began almost immediately after the Lewis and Clark Expedition. The vast expanse of the newly purchased region offered immense possibilities for men interested in the lucrative business. Previously, from 1806 until 1823, the fur trade had focused on the area of the Upper Missouri, and those involved had relied on major waterways to transport pelts and supplies to trading posts or military forts. Hostile Indian tribes, however, resenting the advancement of the white man, made it difficult to maintain frontier outposts and increased the trappers' danger in traveling to sell their cache. The search for beaver then shifted from the Upper Missouri to the Rocky Mountains, and traders began to travel overland to the mountains.

The Ashley-Henry Fur Company initiated the rendezvous system in 1824 after a party of their trappers met with disaster at the hands of the Arikara Indians on the Upper Missouri. Suffering loss of life and property, Ashley turned from the use of permanent posts to overland travel. He informed his men that he would bring supplies from St. Louis to a designated rendezvous point in the mountains. The trappers were to meet at the rendezvous with their cache. Mountain men, most of whom regretted the trek to settled areas, could then remain in the mountain wilderness.

Circumstances and improvisation characterized the first rendezvous. Ashley scheduled the rendezvous to be held the following summer, the end of the trapping season. Winter and early spring provided the best conditions for trapping, and summer made travel easier for the supply trains. Ashley arranged to meet with his men at Henry's Fork on the Green River (near present-day Burntfork, Wyoming) in late June 1825. Ashley arrived on July 1 to find 120 men ready to trade. The first rendezvous officially lasted only one day, but many, enjoying the camaraderie, stayed on after Ashley left for St. Louis.

To the first rendezvous, Ashley brought supplies of sugar, flour, coffee, tobacco, lead, powder, knives, bar iron, and Indian trinkets. Although he brought no rum, demand for it made it a future staple. Other goods brought by the suppliers were silk, needles, ribbons, combs, earrings, and soap, as well as ammunition and traps. Mountain men paid $2.50 each for knives, $1.50 a pound for coffee and sugar, and $6.00 a yard for cloth. Traders paid up to $3.00 a pound for fur. Each trapper brought in from 100 to 136 pounds of fur. Ashley left the first mountain rendezvous with 8,829 pounds of fur. The system proved so successful for Ashley that he retired a wealthy man after the second annual event.

The rendezvous, open to anyone involved in the fur trade, became an annual event for the next fifteen years. Their mules laden with the season's rich cache, trappers joined the supply wagons from St. Louis. Indians also attended the rendezvous to barter furs or just to participate in the festivities. Entire tribes often attended, setting up their camps near the main site. By both mountain man and Indian, it was an eagerly awaited social event. Each rendezvous provided an opportunity for shooting matches, horse racing, gambling, and contests of skill and physical strength, as well as occasion for drinking and

Before the annual rendezvous began, fur trappers and traders returned eastward each year to deliver their pelts to the company and obtain necessary goods for the coming season. (North Wind Picture Archives)

carousing. Men shared information on the location of hostile Indians, the fate of acquaintances, and the habits of the beaver. It was also a time for swapping tall tales and exaggerated adventures.

Occasionally, serious conflicts occurred, as in 1827 when a party of hostile Blackfoot Indians attacked a group of Shoshone camped near the rendezvous. Trappers joined the skirmish in aid of their allies. Another time the Blackfoot attacked a party of mountain men bound for the yearly event. In spite of this, it became common for more than a thousand trappers, traders, and Indians to gather for a time of abandonment and carousing. The yearly gathering became one of the most exciting and colorful episodes in the American experience.

The annual event took place in spectacular surroundings. Key participants at each event chose the location for the next year's gathering. Most frequently, they selected a site along the Green River in Wyoming or Utah. Although Pierre's Hole (near present-day Riggs, Idaho) twice provided the necessary amenities for the concourse, rivers and streams in Utah or Wyoming hosted all other annual events. The often-traveled routes to the rendezvous sites later became the Overland Trail. By the second rendezvous, pack-animal supply trains had given way to wagon caravans, demonstrating the possibility of westward expansion across the Louisiana Territory.

—*Carol J. Terry*

See also
Ashley, William Henry; Mountain Men

For Further Reading
Gowen, Fred R. 1976. *Rocky Mountain Rendezvous: A History of the Fur Trade Rendezvous, 1825–1840*. Provo, UT: Brigham Young University; Wishart, David J. 1979. *Fur Trade of the American West, 1807–1840*. Lincoln: University of Nebraska Press.

RIGHT OF DEPOSIT

The Right of Deposit was a diplomatic concession granted by Spanish colonial authorities to the United States as part of Pinckney's Treaty (1795), allowing Americans to land with cargo in New Orleans. The Right of Deposit was important because it emerged from and later shaped the fight for free navigation of the Mississippi River, which ultimately led to the Louisiana Purchase.

In the 1780s and 1790s, for settlers in what was then called the West, an open Mississippi promised economic advance; a closed river spelled ruin. Consequently, when John Jay, negotiating a commercial treaty with Spain in the wake of the Revolutionary War, suggested that the United States give up the river's navigation in exchange for other diplomatic objectives, Westerners erupted in outrage, scuttling Jay's efforts. Although Thomas Jefferson served in Paris at the height of Jay's negotiations with Spain, he was aware of the turmoil surrounding the proposed treaty. The controversy crystallized the Mississippi's importance for the future president.

In 1790, when Jefferson became secretary of state, he demonstrated that he had learned from Jay's errors, arguing not only for free use of the Mississippi but also access to markets in New Orleans. In short, the nation needed to secure an open Mississippi and the right to land on its banks in New Orleans. In support of his arguments for why the United States had a right to use the Mississippi, Jefferson articulated a kind of ecological diplomacy, pointing to the will of "Nature." As for why Western settlers should be allowed to land in New Orleans, he cleverly explained: "The right to use a thing comprehends a right to the means necessary to its use" (Whitaker, 1934).

Twin themes—the will of "Nature" and the public character of the river and its banks—continued driving Jefferson's foreign policy, but Westerners still fumed as the Mississippi remained in Spanish hands. After some settlers began threatening to secede in the early 1790s, Thomas Pinckney averted that disaster by securing free use of the river and an American deposit in New Orleans when, in 1795, he signed the treaty that bore his name.

For six years after that, Western settlers navigated the Mississippi freely, landing with cargo at New Orleans. American commerce in the city boomed, and traders grew increasingly dependent on the river. In 1802, James Madison summed up the river's significance for Westerners, noting that "the Mississippi to them is everything. It is the Hudson, the Delaware, the Potomac, and all the navigable rivers of the Atlantic States, formed into one stream" (Ogg, 1904). And so, Westerners were outraged when Spain closed the American deposit in New Orleans on October 16, 1802. In the days following, Westerners again threatened to secede. President Jefferson, observing the rising tide of protest, responded by redoubling efforts, already under way, to acquire New Orleans.

—*Ari Kelman*

For Further Reading
Ogg, Frederic Austin. 1904. *The Opening of the Mississippi*. New York, London: Macmillan Company; Whitaker, Arthur Preston. 1934. *The Mississippi Question*. New York: D. Appleton Company.

RILEY, FORT

Established in 1853 as Camp Center, Fort Riley became an important military reserve, and it remains so to the present. The fort is located where the Republican River merges into the Kansas River, approximately sixty miles west of Topeka, Kansas. A special board of army officers recommended the site in 1852. The original purpose for Fort Riley was to protect Kansas settlers from raids by Plains Indians. The post was named for Major General Bennett Riley (d. 1853).

Major E. A. Ogden was the fort's initial commander and supervised the construction of Fort Riley's first buildings. The first significant problem faced at the garrison was not Indian trouble, but an outbreak of cholera that occurred in 1855, taking several lives, including Major Ogden's. Fifteen persons died on August 3, with more than seventy dying as the cholera epidemic ran its course. Most of the garrison, however, was away from the fort on campaigns in the western territory, subduing Plains Indians.

In addition to protecting settlers from Indians, as in the campaign against the Cheyenne in 1857, the cavalry from Fort Riley became involved in the internal warfare of "Bleeding Kansas," as proslavery and antislavery forces battled in that territory. On several occasions the cavalry was mustered out to protect communities from marauding raiders, especially proslavery forces from Missouri. Consequently, dragoons from Fort Riley were called upon to "police" the Kansas Territory. Fort Riley dragoons also protected mail trains, travel routes, and trade routes—most notably, the Santa Fe Trail. As a result of these patrols, several minor campaigns were carried out in the West in a region from present-day Colorado to Texas.

Perhaps the most famous man to spend time at Fort Riley in the nineteenth century was George Armstrong Custer. The legendary Seventh Cavalry was organized at Fort Riley in 1866, with the goal of protecting the railroad lines being laid across western Kansas. (It was formed under the command of Colonel Andrew J. Smith, Lieutenant Colonel George A. Custer serving as second-in-command.) It was at Fort Riley that Custer organized a regimental band and adopted "Gerry Owen" as the regimental song.

In 1867 the Seventh Cavalry participated in a campaign against Indians on the High Plains. The Seventh Cavalry joined other troops under the command of General Winfield Scott Hancock. The combined forces then marched westward to Fort Larned, where Hancock held council with several Cheyenne, Arapaho, and Kiowa leaders. After the meeting failed, Hancock ordered Custer to take the Seventh Cavalry and pursue the Indians. In the meantime, Hancock's infantry burned several Indian encampments, including the tepees and all Indian possessions. Instead of preventing a frontier war, as originally intended, Hancock had foolishly angered the Indians by his haughty, dictatorial approach and impossible demands.

General Philip Sheridan took command of the Kansas forts in 1866–1867 and ordered Custer to destroy all Indian villages. As a consequence, Custer and the Seventh Cavalry descended upon Black Kettle's village on an early November morning. Hoping to avoid another Sand Creek massacre, Black Kettle mounted his pony, and giving the sign of peace, went to meet the U.S. Cavalry. Black Kettle was shot dead in his saddle as he gave the peace gesture. While destroying Black Kettle's village, the Seventh Cavalry killed 103 Cheyenne, of whom only eleven were warriors. The sounds of fighting brought nearby Arapaho (who wiped out a platoon of soldiers), and later Kiowa and Commanches arrived. Custer, seeing the odds shifting dramatically against him, took his troops back to Camp Supply on the Canadian River, along with more than fifty captives—mostly women and children. The campaign continued into the following summer, and Lieutenant Colonel Custer, wanting to tend to personal business, abandoned his command. As a result he was court-martialed and suspended for a year without pay.

Two other famed units were stationed at Fort Riley in the nineteenth century—the Ninth and Tenth Cavalry Regiments, more commonly known as the Buffalo Soldiers. The Tenth Cavalry was stationed at Fort Riley in 1868 and again in 1913.

Following the end of the Plains Indian Wars, Fort Riley became headquarters for the U.S. Cavalry. Troops were trained at Fort Riley to serve the nation in World War I, World War II, the Korean War, the Vietnam War, and Desert Storm. Concerning the fort in the twentieth century, General George S. Patton, Jr., described it as "the most strictly army place I have ever been in" (Pride, 1997).

Fort Riley remains an active post. There are museums and historic sites on the military reserve, including an outstanding U.S. Cavalry Museum that attracts many visitors.

—Gene Mueller

See also
Buffalo Soldiers; Cheyenne; Kansas

For Further Reading
Brown, Dee. 1970. *Bury My Heart at Wounded Knee.* New York: Holt, Rinehart and Winston; Pride, W. F. 1997. *The History of Fort Riley.* Fort Riley, KS: U.S. Cavalry Museum.

ROCKY MOUNTAIN FUR COMPANY (1822–1835)

After the dormancy of the American fur trade from 1814 to 1819 because of the War of 1812, William Henry Ashley and his partner, Andrew Henry, became American entrepreneurs in the trade by establishing the Ashley-Henry Fur Company in St. Louis. This company would become the Rocky Mountain Fur Company and the last of the major American companies formed based on the reports of beaver in the Rocky Mountains by Meriwether Lewis and William Clark's Corps of Discovery, 1804–1806. With an 1822 advertisement in the St. Louis *Gazette and Public Advertiser,* they called for "Enterprising young men . . . to ascend the Missouri to its source, there to be employed for one, two, or three years" (Berry, 1961). Responses came from Jedediah Smith, Etienne Provost, Jim Bridger, Thomas Fitzpatrick, and Hugh Glass, among others. Although not as administratively powerful as either the merged British Hudson's Bay Company and North West Company or John Jacob Astor's American Fur Company, the Ashley-Henry Company quickly developed a reputation for being more romantic and adventuristic than other fur companies.

During the course of their careers, many of the Rocky Mountain Fur Company mountain men became trailblazers of the Louisiana Purchase and the western United States. Jedediah Smith became the first white man to travel from the Great Salt Lake to California by two different routes and was the first man to enter the Mojave from the east and come out alive on the west. Only eighteen years old when he signed on with Ashley, Jim Bridger became the first white man to discover the Great Salt Lake; he established Fort Bridger as a supply station on the Oregon and Mormon Trails. Thomas Fitzpatrick inspired the first treaties with the Plains Indians at Fort

Laramie in 1851 and Fort Atkinson in 1853, working for the Upper Platte and Arkansas Indian agency.

People did not officially call the Ashley-Henry Company the Rocky Mountain Fur Company until 1830, by which time it was out of the hands of both men. After the first call for mountain men in 1822, Jedediah Smith quickly became a leader of company parties between 1823 and 1830. In 1826 he bought out Ashley with some associates, including William Sublette and David Jackson, for control of the company. Henry had retired earlier, in 1824. Before 1825, Ashley lost a fortune in attempting to establish his trapping business on the upper Missouri River. Nevertheless, with a new plan to trap to the south, he became rich on the beaver found in the valley of the Green River. Possibly the most successful of the mountain men, he retired to politics after being bought out. In 1831, Ashley was elected to the U.S. House of Representatives from Missouri and took action after Smith's death that year to make Smith's papers become Senate document 39 of the Second Session of the 21st Congress of the United States. These papers became a fair presentation of the West's potential and inspired others to go westward. In 1830 the company officially took the name of the Rocky Mountain Fur Company after a group including Fitzpatrick and Bridger bought it out. By 1835 the Rocky Mountain Fur Company yielded to the American Fur Company.

As well as its romantic and adventuristic reputation, the Rocky Mountain Fur Company was also innovative in its use of the "free-trapper system" and the rendezvous. Although other companies helped the trapper operate by providing an economic system for the fur trade and initial capital for the trapper, they controlled him almost to the point of company slavery. In contrast, the Rocky Mountain Fur Company used free-trappers. Free-trappers were at the top of the social pyramid and not controlled by any company, trapping wherever and with whomever they pleased and outfitting themselves.

The Rocky Mountain Fur Company was innovative in its use of the annual rendezvous for its trappers. The rendezvous allowed the company and the mountain men to meet in the wilderness, rather than dragging the men back to St. Louis or to trading posts. The original rendezvous was held in July of 1825, still under the supervision of Ashley, at Henry's Fork of the Sidskadee (Green) River in northeastern Utah. The sixteenth and last rendezvous was held in 1840. During the in-between years, the company held the rendezvous during the summer, when the trapping was slow in present-day Utah, Montana, and Wyoming. At rendezvous sites, mountain men traded beaver pelts for supplies, as Indians, trappers, and company men gathered for companionship and business. Once the buyers had purchased the trappers' furs, they would haul them by mule train and wagon to the city to sell them. In return, the mountain men were able to stay in the wilderness all year.

—*Christopher C. Strangeman*

See also

Ashley, William Henry; Bridger, James; Fitzpatrick, Thomas; Rendezvous System; Smith, Jedediah Strong

For Further Reading

Berry, Don. 1961. *A Majority of Scoundrels: An Informal History of the Rocky Mountain Fur Company.* New York: Harper; Dale, Clifford. 1910. *The Ashley-Smith Explorations and the Discovery of a Central Route to the Pacific, 1822–1829, with the Original Journals.* Cleveland: Arthur H. Clark Company; Smith, Henry Nash. 1970. *Virgin Land.* Cambridge, MA: Cambridge University Press.

ROCKY MOUNTAINS

The Rocky Mountains stretch from the Liard River, in northern Canada, to Santa Fe, New Mexico, and consist of two parallel ranges running north-south. Formed sixty million years ago by the uplifting of sedimentary beds and volcanic activity, the Rockies are young by geological standards. Mountain topography is extremely diverse, encompassing alpine peaks exceeding fourteen thousand feet, glaciers, high desert plateaus, geothermal basins, forests, and meadows. The American Rocky Mountains can be divided into three zones. The Northern Rockies reach from the Canadian border to the Wasatch and Uinta Mountains, Utah, while the Southern Rockies extend from Santa Fe to southern Wyoming. The area between these branches is known as the Middle Rockies and the Wyoming Basin.

Some fifteen thousand years ago, paleo-Indians traveled along the eastern slopes of the Rocky Mountains before dispersing across America. Native Americans spoke proudly of the journey taken by their ancestors on the "Great North Trail." The Shoshone used the trail to supply Albertan tribes with horses. Meanwhile, Nez Perce and Flathead hunters blazed paths across the Continental Divide to reach bison grounds on the eastern plains. The forested slopes and stony features of the Rockies fed the material and spiritual needs of the local populace. The Ute of southern Colorado gathered berries and seeds from valleys. The Blackfeet of northeastern Montana referred to the Rocky Mountains as the "Backbone of the World," home of the powerful spirits Wind-Maker and Thunder.

Despite British, French, and Spanish penetration of the Rocky Mountains during the 1700s, information on the region remained dubious at the time of the Louisiana Purchase (1803). Maps of North America portrayed the Rockies as an ill-defined range of mountains, west of their true location. Mistaking shimmering glaciers for mineral-encrusted peaks, explorer Jonathan Carver labeled the Rockies "the Shining Mountains." Errors aside, the crest of the Rockies demarcated the official western boundary of the United States under the terms of the Louisiana Purchase. With hopes of further westward expansion, the Lewis and Clark Expedition (1804–1806)

In this idealized print, the sylvan image of the Rocky Mountain region belied the difficult crossing that many pioneers faced when they journeyed westward.

set out to locate suitable passage over the Rocky Mountains for the purposes of trade in the Far West and Orient. However, an easy route across the continent failed to materialize as Lewis and Clark struggled across the unforgiving mountain terrain. After eleven days in montane wilderness, Lewis commented in his journal: "[T]he pleasure I now felt in having tryumphed over the rockey Mountains and descending once more to a level and fertile country where there was every rational hope of finding a comfortable subsistence for myself and party can be more readily conceived than expressed" (Thwaites, 1904–1905). The explorers nonetheless amassed a wealth of information regarding the geography, flora, and fauna of the Rockies.

Expedition reports of streams filled with beaver inspired trappers to take to the Rockies. The severe climate and inhospitable terrain tested the survival skills of opportunistic fur seekers. During their search for beaver ponds, mountain men developed an intimate knowledge of their surroundings. In 1824, Jedediah Smith learned of the South Pass from Crow Indians. The High Plain in the Middle Rockies, where the mountains recede to form the Wyoming Basin, provided easy passage over the Continental Divide. The pass became a vital crossing point for Mormons, Oregon settlers, and gold prospectors in the 1840s. Fur traders encouraged Americans to think of the Rockies as a storehouse of resources. The discovery of gold at Pikes Peak, Colorado, in 1858, together with major strikes in Idaho and Montana in the early 1860s, bolstered the reputation of the region as laden with natural riches. Butte, Montana, was described as "the richest hill on earth" because of its copper deposits. Miners flocked to the mountains, setting up ramshackle and ephemeral camps in valleys and on hillsides. Mining companies exploited laborers and despoiled pristine environments.

Other Americans traveled to the Rockies for aesthetic enrichment. Monumental peaks and tranquil lakes garnered glorious overtures from writers and artists. Isabella Bird lauded the "romantic ravines" of Estes Park, Colorado, while Albert Bierstadt depicted grand Western landscapes on appropriately large canvases. Nature-lovers lamented the loss of Rocky Mountain wilderness to industry and settlement. Historian Francis Parkman bemoaned that the "untrodden mountains" had been colonized by mining camps, with "hotels and gambling-houses among the haunts of the grizzly bear" (Parkman, 1872). The need to conserve montane environmental treasures was recognized in the creation of Yellowstone National Park (1872), a plateau in northwestern Wyoming. Resource exploiters and preservationists contested the fate of the Rocky Mountains throughout the twentieth century.

—*Karen Jones*

See also
Colorado; Fur Trapping; Montana; Wyoming
For Further Reading
Conzen, M. P., ed. 1990. *The Making of the American Landscape.* New York and London: Routledge; Meinig, D. W. 1993. *The Shaping of America: A Geographical Perspective on 500 Years of History, Vol. 2: Continental America 1800–67.* New Haven and London: Yale University Press; Parkman, Francis. 1872. *The Oregon Trail: Sketches of Prairie and Rocky Mountain Life.* Boston: Little, Brown; Thwaites, Reuben G. 1904. *The Journals of Lewis and Clark.* 8 vols. New York: Dodd, Mead.

ROSS, JAMES (1762–1847)

As a Federalist senator from Pennsylvania, James Ross submitted a series of resolutions in February 1803 that would have permitted the president to seize New Orleans.

Ross served in the Senate from 1794 to 1803 and was particularly concerned with the free navigation of the Mississippi. He favored the Jay Treaty (1794) and closer relations with Great Britain as a hedge against a French seizure of Louisiana and occlusion of the Mississippi to American shipping. The Spanish intendant of New Orleans, Juan Ventura Morales, suspended the American right of deposit on October 18, 1802, confirming Ross's worst fears. Ross demanded immediate action when the Senate convened in February 1803.

Ross addressed the Senate on the Mississippi question on February 14, 1803. He did not at first attack Jefferson's policy of negotiation but proposed to enhance the president's position by authorizing the use of force. Ross asserted an "undoubted right from nature" to the Mississippi and condemned the Spanish intendant for suspending the right of deposit without cause (*Annals,* 1834). Ross then moved on to the specific injuries done to the West. As a resident of the Pittsburgh area, Ross was one of the few Federalists who could credibly present himself as a defender of Western interests. Ross noted that half a million Westerners were deprived of a livelihood. They demanded action, and if Congress took none it might force the West to act on its own, and look elsewhere, probably France, for protection. Turning to the retrocession of Louisiana to France, Ross believed that France was unlikely to sell Louisiana to the United States without a threat of force.

Ross returned to the Mississippi question on February 16, and showed less patience for negotiation than even the little he had had two days before. No nation, Ross argued, had suffered such an insult as Spain had given without response. Yet the United States was still unarmed and unprepared to offer any substantial response. "Negotiation alone, under such circumstances, must be hopeless," Ross maintained (ibid.). Ross believed that preparation would prevent rather than cause war.

At the conclusion of his speech, Ross submitted his resolutions to the Senate. First, the United States had a natural right to the navigation of the Mississippi and to deposit goods at New Orleans. Second, the Spanish suspension of the right of deposit was an act of aggression contrary to U.S. honor and interest. Third, the United States could not allow its right to the Mississippi to rest on uncertain grounds. Fourth, the security and prosperity of the West depended on an unrestricted access to the Mississippi. Fifth, the president would be authorized to seize the Isle of New Orleans if he deemed it necessary. Sixth, the president should be authorized to call up fifty thousand militiamen from South Carolina, Georgia, Ohio, Kentucky, Tennessee, and the Mississippi territory to secure New Orleans. Seventh, that Congress would appropriate $5 million to implement the previous resolutions.

Ross's fellow Federalists supported his resolutions, while the Republicans believed the resolutions were a trick to create an army and embarrass the president. In response, John Breckinridge of Kentucky submitted a milder set of resolutions, which authorized the president to raise a militia of eighty thousand men and construct a series of forts and arsenals in the West.

On February 24, Ross took credit for the action the Republicans were willing to take, noting that they had not proposed any action before the Ross resolutions, but that afterward they were willing to raise a militia and build forts. Ross also observed that the Republicans agreed with the premise of his resolutions, that the United States had a right to navigate the Mississippi and deposit goods at New Orleans. The only dispute was over when and how the United States should act. Ross reiterated that the Spanish action harmed national honor and interest, and that the West might not wait for negotiations.

Two days later the Senate rejected the Ross resolutions by a party-line vote of 15 to 11, and unanimously approved the Breckinridge resolutions as a substitute. Jefferson and Madison, like the Senate Republicans, condemned the Ross resolutions as warlike and unconstitutional, but they used the resolutions in negotiation. Louis Pichon, the French minister to the United States, feared that if France did not cede New Orleans, war would follow. Robert R. Livingston, the U.S. minister to France, told Napoleon of the resolutions, and was disappointed that they had failed. In 1817, President Monroe paid tribute to Ross's efforts, telling an audience in Pittsburgh that Ross had "made Pittsburgh the Gateway of the West" (Brownson, 1910).

—*Robert W. Smith*

See also

Bonaparte, Napoleon; Breckinridge, John; Diplomacy of the Louisiana Purchase; Federalist Party; Jefferson, Thomas; Madison, James; Mississippi River; Monroe, James; Morales, Juan Ventura; Mouths of the Mississippi River; New Orleans; Pichon, Louis-André; Right of Deposit; Seventh Congress

For Further Reading

Brownson, James I. 1910. *The Life and Times of Senator James Ross.* Washington, PA: Washington County Historical Society; *Debates and Proceedings in the Congress of the United States (Annals of Congress).* 42 vols. 1834–1856. Washington, DC: Gales and Seaton; DeConde, Alexander. 1976. *This Affair of Louisiana.* New York: Charles Scribner's Sons; Jefferson, Thomas. 1903. *The Complete Annals of Thomas Jefferson.* Edited by Franklin B. Sawvel. New York: Round Table Press.

RUTLEDGE, JOHN (1739–1800)

John Rutledge's nomination to the chief justiceship of the Supreme Court was defeated by the Federalist-controlled Senate because of his outspoken opposition to Jay's Treaty (1794).

Born in Charles Town (now Charleston) in 1739, Rutledge served South Carolina as a lawyer, judge, governor, and delegate to the Continental Congress and the Constitutional Convention. Rutledge was a famous speaker; indeed, Patrick Henry called him the greatest orator in the Continental Congress. In 1776 he was elected president of the newly organized Republic of South Carolina. Two years later he resigned that position because he felt that revisions made to the state constitution were too democratic. In January 1779, with the state facing invasion, he was elected governor under the new, more democratic constitution. After the fall of Charleston to the British in 1780, the Assembly adjourned for two years and Rutledge was the de facto government of South Carolina. An influential delegate at the Philadelphia Convention of 1787, Rutledge served as chairman of the important Committee of Detail, which was charged with the actual writing of the Constitution. Upon the formation of the federal government, he was appointed senior associate justice of the Supreme Court, but he soon resigned the position to accept the chief justiceship of South Carolina.

On June 12, 1795, Rutledge wrote to President Washington to apprise him of his willingness to serve as chief justice upon John Jay's resignation of the post. The very day after receiving the letter, Washington decided to offer him the chief justiceship, effective the day of Jay's official resignation, July 1, 1795. Rutledge thus took over as chief justice, awaiting Senate confirmation. Meanwhile, the public received their first glimpse of Jay's Treaty when it was published in the Philadelphia *Aurora* on June 29. Following publication of the treaty widespread public opposition erupted, especially among Republicans. In cities and towns across the nation, including Charleston, public meetings were called to express dissatisfaction.

In Charleston a public meeting was held on Jay's Treaty at St. Michael's Church on July 16. At the meeting, Federalist chief justice Rutledge gave the keynote address, a long, bitter, point-by-point denunciation of the treaty that was enthusiastically received by the audience. According to the chief justice, the treaty's wording was dangerously careless and it amounted to a surrender of the rights of American freemen to the British monarch. Specifically, he objected to the provision for the appointment of commissioners to settle the debts owed by Americans to British creditors. Jurisdiction over those claims, he argued, properly belonged to the U.S. Supreme Court. He also asserted that Jay should have demanded the abandonment of Western posts by the British as a prerequisite to any negotiations. In short, Rutledge expressed a partiality for France over England and said that he would prefer war rather than the treaty. After the meeting, an election was held to choose fifteen men to form a committee to consider the treaty. Among those elected were Rutledge and Charles C. Pinckney. However, Pinckney, whom Washington would appoint minister to France in 1796, judiciously declined to serve.

When news spread of Rutledge's verbal assault on the treaty, the High Federalists led by Alexander Hamilton were infuriated by what they considered the chief justice's act of treason against his party. Hamilton questioned Rutledge's sanity in the press and advised Federalists in the Senate against confirming his appointment. Rutledge's lack of party loyalty cost him dearly. When his appointment finally came before the Senate for confirmation on December 15, 1795, he was rejected after a heated debate by a vote of 14 to 10, with eight senators absent. The vote followed party lines. Among those voting in favor of confirmation, the lone Federalist was Jacob Read of South Carolina.

Humiliated by his political defeat, Rutledge attempted suicide two days after Christmas of 1795, thereby lending credibility to those who previously had questioned his sanity. He survived the attempted suicide and quietly lived out the remainder of his life in Charleston. On July 18, 1800, John Rutledge died and was buried at St. Michael's, site of his speech against Jay's Treaty five years earlier.

—Sean R. Busick

See also

Constitution of the United States; Federalist Party; Jay's Treaty; Pinckney, Charles Cotesworth

For Further Reading

McCowan, George S., Jr. 1961. "Chief Justice Rutledge and the Jay Treaty." *South Carolina Historical Magazine* 62: 10–23; Rogers, George C., Jr. 1969. *Charleston in the Age of the Pinckneys.* Norman: University of Oklahoma Press.

S

SAC AND FOX

The first written histories record that the Sac and Fox Tribes originally settled in eastern Michigan. Having started out as friendly neighbors, the two tribes became close allies and finally joined together. Both descended from the Algonquian branch of the Algonquian-Wakashan language group. By the mid–seventeenth century, sixty-five hundred Sac and Fox lived in present-day Wisconsin. When Europeans, mostly the French in the 1730s, forced Eastern Indians westward, the Sac and Fox headed northwesterly and settled west of Lake Michigan and south of Lake Superior. The Sac built villages near Green Bay, and the Fox along the Wolf River. They ranged as far as Lake Superior in the north, to Lake Michigan in the east, and the headwaters of the Mississippi River in the south. By the mid–eighteenth century, the Sac and Fox had migrated to Ohio and Illinois, as well as Michigan.

After the 1803 Louisiana Purchase, the U.S. government moved quickly to sign treaties with the indigenous tribes in the newly acquired lands. The government did not want open warfare and urged the Indians to sign treaties. The Sac and Fox could either resist the white intruders or abandon their homeland.

In 1804 four Sac representatives met with William Henry Harrison, governor of the Illinois and Indiana Territories. Harrison unscrupulously had the tribal members agree to sign a treaty by which they lost the rights to their land east of the Mississippi River in the present-day states of Illinois and Wisconsin, and also some lands in Missouri. The government guaranteed the Sac their remaining lands west of the Mississippi in perpetuity and $600 per year for an unspecified length of time. The catch in the treaty was that the tribe would live on "government land" only until the government sold the lands to individual settlers. The Sac, however, did not understand English, and, in addition, the translators were often purposefully inaccurate. Troubles quickly arose. The major chiefs declared the treaty was unjust and insisted that the four Sac signers did not have the authority to sell their people's land. The government did nothing.

In 1806 seven Sac delegates traveled to Washington, D.C., to protest settlers who were pouring into their lands and local authorities who did nothing to stop it. Jefferson spoke kindly and talked of justice for all; nevertheless, no action was taken to stop white intrusion or settlers' attacks on Indians.

During the War of 1812, the Sac fought mainly with the British. A British colonel conferred the rank of general on the Sac war chief Black Hawk. After the war the Sac, like many Western tribes, suffered the fate of British abandonment. The whites poured into Western Indian lands. Instead of worrying about the settlers' advances causing problems, the government appealed to the impoverished Indians to give up their lands without a fight.

In 1824 a treaty between the Sac and United States ceded a tract of land west of the Mississippi River for a paltry sum of money. In the spring of 1830, when the Sac returned to their village after winter hunting expeditions, they found American settlers living there. This was the time when Congress, with the support of President Andrew Jackson, passed the Indian Removal Act (1830), forcing Indians west. In an effort to avoid war, the majority of the Sac, led by Chief Keokuk, relocated to territory in present-day Iowa and Missouri.

Promises of aid to the Sac from the British in Canada and various Indian tribes encouraged some six hundred warriors and their families under Chief Black Hawk to try to return to their abandoned village, Saukenuk, within their lost territory. In response, the U.S. Army commander in the region, Major General Alexander Macomb, and Illinois governor John Reynolds issued a call for volunteers to take up arms against the Sac. Initially Black Hawk attempted to parlay, but the thirteen-hundred-man white force was out for blood. These untrained and undisciplined volunteers under the command of Henry Atkinson caused indiscriminate slaughter of the Indians at the Battle of Bad Axe River. This marked the end of the war and the end of Sac resistance.

Repeatedly, the Sac's treaties had given settlers land, gaining little in return. The Sac made their final relocation to Indian Territory that was poor for farming or buffalo hunting. In these new surroundings, many of the Sac could not survive on their own, became dependent on government rations and supplies, and contracted European diseases. Nevertheless, the Sac managed to follow their own religious beliefs, maintain clan ceremonies, and retain their native language. The populations of the three Sac and Fox reservations in Iowa, Nebraska, Kansas, and Oklahoma grew steadily in the twentieth century.

The Sac and Fox take part in a ritual war dance.

According to the 1990 census, Oklahoma had more than four thousand Sac and Fox tribal members living on reservations.

—*Scott L. Stabler*

See also
Black Hawk; Black Hawk War; Fox

For Further Reading
Bonvillain, Nancy. 1995. *The Sac and Fox*. Edited by Frank W. Porter III. New York: Chelsea House; Hagan, William T. 1958. *The Sac and Fox Indians*. Norman: University of Oklahoma Press.

SACAGAWEA (1786?1788?–?)

Sacagawea—a Lemhi Shoshone woman known in fact and persisting in legend—was born in the Lemhi River Valley of present-day Idaho, between 1786 and 1788. The daughter of a chief, she was captured around 1800 by a Hidatsa raiding party who sold her to the Mandan. Her Hidatsa name, Tsi-Ki-Ka-Wi-As, meant Bird Woman, but she is remembered for her Shoshone name, which meant "Boat Pusher" or "Boat Launcher." Within a few years, she, along with her friend, Otter Woman, became one of the wives of Toussaint Charbonneau, a French-Canadian trapper/trader who "won" Sacagawea through gambling. Unlike most Indian women of the nineteenth century, Sacagawea (also spelled Sacajawea and Sakakawea) became well known, largely through her involvement with Lewis and Clark's Corps of Discovery. She met the expedition party during that first winter of 1804–1805 at Fort Mandan, near the present site of Bismarck, North Dakota. When Charbonneau was hired as one of its interpreters, she joined the expedition as it headed west in April 1805. She was accompanied by her two-month-old son, Jean Baptiste, nicknamed Pomp (Pompey or Pompei), Shoshone for "first born." Sacagawea was featured prominently in the journal of William Clark, who depicted her as a valued member of the expedition and who called her Janey. Her presence, along with that of her son, signaled the expedition's peaceful purpose to other native peoples. Even though she did not serve as a leader or guide, she provided useful assistance as an interpreter and helped locate edible and medicinal plants. With her calm and uncomplaining nature, she boosted morale and provided a level head during tense moments, including an episode when she calmly rescued diaries and instruments after her boat nearly capsized. Sacagawea recognized the site of her previous capture as the place were three rivers flowed into the Missouri. In August 1805, Sacagawea interceded during negotiations with the Shoshone. Sacagawea became reunited with her family when it became apparent that the band chief was her brother, Cameahwait. Cameahwait provided thirty horses, drafted a map for their progress across the Bitterroot Mountains, and loaned the services of a guide. That guide, Old Tom, accompanied the expedition to the land of the Nez Perce, where they could once again proceed by water. Sacagawea made only one special request during the expedition: that, in November 1805, she be allowed to see the Pacific Ocean and the remains of a whale. Sacagawea continued with Lewis and Clark through the next twelve months, departing from them when the party arrived again at Fort Mandan on its return trip east. During the journey she had experienced a serious illness, had nearly drowned, and had endured the day-to-day hardship associated with traveling four thousand miles while tending to the needs of an infant.

There are several versions of Sacagawea's subsequent life. She and her family joined Clark for a brief time in St. Louis. She and Charbonneau returned to the Dakotas, leaving Pomp with Clark, who would provide him with schooling. Several written accounts place her death, due to fever, on December 20, 1812, or between 1825 and 1828. She may also have been survived by an infant daughter, identified as Lizette, who was left in the care of John Luttig, a clerk at Fort Manuel, South Dakota. Lizette remains a shadowy figure, but Jean Baptiste is known to have accompanied various trading and exploration parties. He served as a guide and trapper with Jim Bridger (1832) and Kit Carson (1839). Jean Baptiste traveled to Europe with Prince Paul of Wurttemberg and resided in Germany for several years. His death date is also disputed: some place it at 1866, while tribal oral history indicates that he lived until 1885. His grave site in Danner, Oregon, was rededicated in 2000. Native oral histories also account that Sacagawea may have lived to nearly one hundred, dying on April 9, 1884. These stories note that she left Charbonneau within a few years after returning to Fort Mandan and acquired the name of Porivo. She moved among tribal groups, married into the Comanches, and started a new family. Finally, after being widowed, she returned to the Shoshone at the Wind River Reservation, where some claim she was buried in the Fort Washakie Cemetery.

Although Charbonneau was compensated for his services to the Corps of Discovery with $500 and land near St. Louis, Sacagawea received no payment. Yet Sacagawea is well commemorated in monuments, geographic place names, legends, and, most recently, by being portrayed in 2000, along with her son, on a gold-tinted one-dollar coin. Her actual physical appearance is not known.

—Loriene Roy

See also

Cameahwait; Charbonneau, Toussaint; Corps of Discovery; Hidatsa; Lewis and Clark Expedition; Mandan; North Dakota; Shoshoni

For Further Reading

Ambrose, Stephen E. 1996. *Undaunted Courage: Meriwether Lewis, Thomas Jefferson, and the Opening of the American West.* New York: Simon and Schuster; Bruchac, Joseph. 2000. *Sacagawea.* Orlando, FL: Harcourt.

SAINT DOMINGUE

***See* Haiti**

SAINT GENEVIEVE

The historic community of Ste. Genevieve, recognized as the first permanent white settlement established in what constitutes the present-day state of Missouri, is located forty-six miles southeast of St. Louis on the right descending (west) bank of the Mississippi River. The community is situated along the historic River Road (Highway 61) and is located midway between the towns of St. Mary's and Bloomsdale. Today the town of Ste. Genevieve serves as the county seat of Ste. Genevieve County and has an estimated population of fifty-eight hundred residents.

Nicknamed "Miserere" by its French founders, the community of Ste. Genevieve has survived for at least 250 years, enduring both the periodic ravages of Mississippi River flooding and the peculiar uncertainties of geopolitical diplomacy. Historians debate the actual year in which the frontier river settlement was founded, and the debate seems to be centered upon which primary sources are used to make the determination. Many of the descendants of early settlers claim that the town was established in 1735, and this date is accepted in *History of Southeast Missouri* (1888). In a more recent monograph, however, *Colonial Ste. Genevieve* (1996), historian Carl J. Ekberg claims that the founding likely occurred around 1750. Ekberg's interpretation of early documents including letters, maps, and Roman Catholic church records forms the basis of his claim.

Regardless of the exact year of the town's founding, it was established as a French outpost within what was then considered the Illinois Country. Ste. Genevieve was to be one of a series of French locations established between and theoretically connecting New France (French Canada) and the Louisiana colony that had been established near the mouth of the Mississippi River. When the French faced defeat at the end of the French and Indian War and the likelihood that all French lands claimed in North America were soon to be lost to their British rivals, the French leadership engineered a method whereby they might be able to preserve a portion of their empire. In the Treaty of Fontainebleau (1762), the French Bourbon monarch delivered the western portion of the Louisiana Territory to his Spanish Bourbon cousin. In this swap, the community of Ste. Genevieve and its surrounding region became a part of the Spanish colonial empire.

The region was one considered rich in natural resources. Both the French and later the Spanish exploited the deposits of salt, marble, and lead that were located in the area. In addition to the mining and quarrying, the area also became the center of an active fur trade. Additionally, the region's soil was quite fertile, and agriculture soon developed in and around Ste. Genevieve as foodstuffs were produced to feed both the town's residents as well as other French settlers in nearby outposts such as Cahokia, Prairie du Rocher, St. Philippe, Fort de Chartres and Kaskaskia.

The town grew in size and influence as it became a center of regional trade and commerce. Its importance was noted as the initial settlement of Ste. Genevieve was relocated to higher ground after severe flooding took place in 1785. By 1800 there was a commercial ferry in operation at Ste. Genevieve. Some American settlers began settling around Ste. Genevieve around 1788, and by the time of the Louisiana Purchase (1803), there was a strong American presence already established in the region.

—Junius P. Rodriguez

See also
Chartres, Fort de; Kaskaskia
For Further Reading
Ekberg, Carl J. 1996. *Colonial Ste. Genevieve: An Adventure on the Mississippi Frontier.* Tucson, AZ: Patrice Press; Franzwa, Gregory M. 1967. *The Story of Old Ste. Genevieve: An Account of an Old French Town in Upper Louisiana.* Tucson, AZ: Patrice Press.

SAINT LOUIS

Few cities in all of North America are as perfectly located by geographical circumstance to be major entrepôts of trade and commerce as is St. Louis, Missouri. While New Orleans was undoubtedly the queen city of the Mississippi River Valley, occupying a commanding presence with its port facilities near the mouth of the Mississippi River, the site that became St. Louis was perfectly situated to become an interior way-station and outfitting and departure point for those individuals and companies willing to do business in the trans-Mississippi West. Located at the point where the Missouri River and the Mississippi River meet, St. Louis competed through much of the nineteenth century (with rival upstart Chicago) to be the commercial equivalent of New York City in the American interior.

When the French and Indian War ended in 1763, New Orleans merchant Pierre Laclède Liguest (of Maxent, Laclède and Company) moved upriver to the Illinois Country, where he planned to become involved in frontier trade and commerce as an agent of the Louisiana Fur Trade Company. The previous year, Laclède had obtained an eight-year monopoly for conducting the Missouri region fur trade. He had initially hoped to use Fort de Chartres as his primary trading post, but the transfer of that site to Britain in the Treaty of Paris (1763) forced him to change his plans. In 1764, Laclède and his stepson, René Auguste Chouteau, began work on establishing a fur trading center on the western bank of the Mississippi River near the point where the Missouri River joined. This was the beginning of St. Louis.

Named in honor of the canonized French monarch Louis IX, the early community that Laclède founded had a decidedly French atmosphere, as reflected by both its population and its early architecture. The outpost also faced the challenge of being a remote frontier village. From time to time the community was threatened by the Osage and the Sioux who lived only a short journey upstream. Yet it was the maintenance of peace with the Western tribes, and the successful conclusion of commercial relationships with them, that would set St. Louis apart from other frontier towns. The village quickly grew into a commercial hub, making the transition to Spanish rule in 1770 and U.S. control in 1804.

Meriwether Lewis and William Clark and their Corps of Discovery witnessed the formal exchange of the upper portion of the Louisiana Territory at St. Louis on March 10, 1804. During the ceremony, the Spanish flag was lowered and replaced by the French tricolor, and shortly thereafter, that flag was lowered and replaced by the U.S. flag. Captain Amos Stoddard accepted the Louisiana Territory from the French on behalf of the U.S. government. Only days after observing this historic event, the Lewis and Clark Expedition set out from St. Louis, on May 14, 1804, on its journey to the Pacific.

St. Louis became the commercial center of the trans-Mississippi fur trade with a hinterland that included the entire Missouri Valley and vast parts of the Rocky Mountain interior. While geographical determinists would point out its supremacy of location, St. Louis also benefited from having the commercial infrastructure that could support the fur trade—one of the most significant economic activities in early-nineteenth-century America. The city boasted of its banks and counting houses, along with its packing sheds, warehouses, and docks—all of which played vital roles in accumulating wealth as investors and boosters alike shared the wealth of the fur trade's bounty. Within time, virtually all of the major fur trading companies had headquarters for their trapping operations in St. Louis.

Besides its role as an economic center, St. Louis also served as an administrative center from which the vast reaches of Upper Louisiana were governed. In addition to being the home of the territorial governor (1812–1821), the city also contained Jefferson Barracks (constructed in 1826) for frontier regulars who stood ready to defend the city and the surrounding countryside should hostilities arise. As the largest city in the Missouri Territory, St. Louis also was the site of a federal land office, and as such, the city attracted a large number of itinerant, westward-bound pioneers who wished to obtain legal title to tracts of government land.

The combination of an old French-colonial aristocracy, a burgeoning U.S. presence, frontier regulars, backwoodsmen, pioneers, rough-hewn trappers and traders, rowdy boatmen, and slaves gave the city of St. Louis a unique cultural atmosphere. It was, in many respects, the one spot in America where the culture and values of the East and West met. And not unexpectedly, the wealth of the city was often matched only by its vices.

As the main commercial center that was associated with the western fur trade, St. Louis, Missouri, was the place where the East met the West in early nineteenth century America. (North Wind Picture Archives)

Heralded as the "Gateway to the West," St. Louis was central to the story of the Louisiana Purchase and the development of nineteenth-century America. Not surprisingly, when a site was sought to hold a world's fair to commemorate the centennial of the Louisiana Purchase, it was St. Louis that was selected to host the 1904 Louisiana Exposition. Today, as host to the Jefferson National Expansion Memorial and its signature Gateway Arch, the vibrant modern city of St. Louis reminds the nation of the central place that it played in the formative years of the nation's history.

—*Junius P. Rodriguez*

See also

Chouteau, René Auguste; Fur Trapping; Gateway Arch; Louisiana Purchase International Exposition

For Further Reading

Gore, S. Joseph. 1964. *Heritage of St Louis.* St. Louis: St. Louis Public Library; Peters, Frank. 1989. *A Guide to the Architecture of St. Louis.* Columbia: University of Missouri Press; Scharf, J. Thomas. 1883. *History of St. Louis and St. Louis County, from Earliest Periods to the Present Day: Including Biographical Sketches of Representative Men.* Philadelphia: L. H. Everts and Company; Thomas, William Lyman. 1911. *History of St. Louis County, Missouri.* St. Louis: S. J. Clarke

SAN ILDEFONSO, TREATY OF (1800)

The Treaty of San Ildefonso (1800) was an agreement between Spain and France that called for the retrocession of Louisiana to France and its new Napoleonic regime, which had assumed power in November 1799. As a result of the Seven Years' War (known in the Americas as the French and Indian War) and the Treaty of Paris (1763), the French colony of Louisiana was ceded to the Spanish kingdom for its assistance in the futile battle for empire with the British. The Spanish, who had to relinquish their longstanding colony of Florida, in turn, were "rewarded" with a Mississippi River colony adjacent to Mexico and claimed Oregon territory. In reality this treaty was the second one signed at the palace of San Ildefonso, for the first had enunciated an alliance between revolutionary France and Spain.

The arrival of the Spanish in New Orleans and the rest of the colony left its mark both architecturally and sociologically. However, the establishment of the adjacent United States by 1783 created significant problems both economic and diplomatic. The Treaty of Paris (1783) recognized the Mississippi River as its western border, but the influx of settlers west of the Appalachians in the postbellum era posed a threat to Spanish control of its new trans-Mississippi colony. Not only was the riverine border indefensible, but the demands of the new frontier republic and its economic requirements made the position of New Orleans near the mouth of the great river difficult to maintain. The natural geographic route from the trans-Appalachian West—the Ohio River system—led through the Mississippi River Valley to New Orleans. The commercial viability of the region depended directly on special tariff arrangements with the Spanish, and indeed the new republic successfully arranged what is traditionally called Pinckney's Treaty (1795), which secured for Americans the right of deposit without tariff at New Orleans and with the right of trans-shipment to other countries. Nonetheless, the colony remained a burden on the strained Spanish economy even after the retrocession of Florida following the War for American Independence. By 1800 its fifty thousand non-Indian inhabitants were spread over a region that stretched from Ste. Genevieve south of modern St. Louis to the mouth of the Mississippi. The fur trade remained the most important factor in the economy, and even the recently arrived Acadians (later known as Cajuns), dispossessed forcefully from Nova Scotia, had not yet developed their economic potential. Talleyrand, minister of foreign affairs, most probably surmised, based on his year-and-a-half sojourn in the United States during the Reign of Terror, that although the situation of the colony was virtually untenable, a "last ditch effort" might work, because he and his European colleagues desired additional opportunities for land speculation. His assessment even offered the French a possibility of success in colonizing underpopulated Louisiana. And when he coupled this with his financial acumen and hopefulness, he agreed to reassess the political situation of the colony and encourage retrocession.

In order to persuade King Charles IV to relinquish Louisiana, Napoleon employed the dynastic and familial aspirations of the reigning Spanish Bourbons to further his designs. The king's cousin (and simultaneously brother-in-law) was the Duke of Parma, a region coveted by Napoleon, who seized power in France in November 1799. The Spanish monarch, despite his close blood relationship with the guillotined Louis XVI, admired Napoleon and his government and willingly created an alliance with revolutionary France in the first Treaty of Ildefonso, following the Treaty of Basel (1795). He and his consort, Maria Luisa, as well as their favorite, Manuel Godoy, enthusiastically supported Napoleon's designs to redraw the boundaries of northern Italy when it became apparent that he planned a new kingdom named Etruria, centered on historic Florence and Tuscany. Duke Ferdinand of Parma was not submissive to the new designs and died in 1801 without recognizing the new political arrangements. During the duke's failing months, Napoleon organized another coup by naming the duke's epileptic son, Louis, as the King of Etruria with the Spanish infanta, his spouse, Maria Luisa Josefina, as sovereigns. Napoleon crowned this political victory by having the new monarchs visit Paris before assuming official "control" of Etruria. It must be noted that only eight years earlier, their kinsman Louis XVI had been guillotined by the revolutionary French. Nonetheless, the Spanish royal family was ecstatic that their daughter gained the title of queen. An important force in the negotiations for this treaty was Napoleon's brother Lucien, who acted as his plenipotentiary in Madrid and developed a close relationship with Godoy and through him direct access to the monarchs.

When completed in 1800 after intense negotiations, the Treaty of Ildefonso focused primarily on two areas—northern Italy and Louisiana. Charles IV and Maria Luisa, of course, secured royal status for their daughter and son-in-law in Tuscany, to which neighboring Piombino was added—the new configuration was renamed Etruria, a classical allusion to its pre-Roman settlers. The colony of Louisiana was transferred or retroceded to France, but only on the condition that the Etrurian kingdom be established and recognized by the powers of Europe. Although that did not occur, the transfer of the colony did take place, but only belatedly—in fact, some two years later.

By the transfer of Louisiana to the French, Napoleon hoped to begin a rejuvenation of the empire, which had been decimated by the Seven Years' War, the Treaty of Paris (1763), and the slave rebellion in the lucrative colony of St. Domingue (modern Haiti). In the latter, the charismatic Toussaint L'Ouverture had led a successful revolt against the white French minority and created a political entity that acknowledged French suzerainty without direct control. Before 1789, this was by far the wealthiest colony in the French Empire. Napoleon in his grand scheme wanted to reinstate the colony under its old repressive form and use the regained Louisiana as its major source of food, so that the island could produce its cash crop, sugar, without interference. The first consul also looked forward to an end of hostilities with the British—a situation that would ensure success of his colonial ventures because their navy always remained a threat to French aspirations outside of Continental Europe.

This (second) Treaty of San Ildefonso (1800) did create some panic on the international scene and surprised not only the British but especially the Americans. Of course, it negated Pinckney's Treaty (1795) and changed dramatically the colonial organization of the Caribbean Sea. However, the Spanish did not willingly relinquish their control of the colony because of developments in northern Italy. Charles IV was confident that Napoleon was sincere in his promises, yet he required in the treaty that the colony return to Spain should the French not want to keep it. Nonetheless, some eight months after the official transfer of the colony to the French,

Napoleon offered it to the United States for sixty million francs. As a result, the retrocession of 1800 led indirectly to the dramatic expansion of the fledgling United States of America.

—*Thomas C. Sosnowski*

See also
Tuscany
For Further Reading
Chastenet, Jacques. 1972. *Godoy: Master of Spain, 1792–1808*. Translated by J. F. Huntington. London: Batchworth Press; Hilt, Douglas. 1987. *The Troubled Trinity: Godoy and the Spanish Monarchs*. Tuscaloosa: University of Alabama Press; Lyon, E. Wilson. 1974. *Louisiana in French Diplomacy, 1730–1804*. Norman: University of Oklahoma Press; Whitaker, Arthur Preston. 1949. *The Mississippi Question, 1795–1803*. New York: Foreign Policy Association.

SAN LORENZO, TREATY OF (1795)

Also called Pinckney's Treaty, the Treaty of San Lorenzo was signed on October 27, 1795, between the United States and Spain. By this treaty Spain granted the United States the right of free navigation on the Mississippi River, the right to ship goods originating in American ports through the mouth of the Mississippi without paying duty, and also a three-year right of deposit of American goods for trans-shipment at the port of New Orleans, with the possibility of an extension of that right after three years. The southern boundary of the United States and that of Spanish Florida was fixed at 31 degrees north latitude, and Spain recognized the western boundary of the United States at the Mississippi River. Both nations agreed to restrain the Indians within their respective borders from attacks on the other. There were some provisions for the freedom of the seas, and Spain also recognized the neutral rights of the United States. The treaty was negotiated by Thomas Pinckney for the United States and Manuel de Godoy for Spain.

At the end of the American Revolution, Spain was concerned with unrestricted U.S. advancement of the frontier toward the Mississippi and Spanish Florida. Following the end of the war, thousands of American settlers had crossed the Appalachian Mountains and settled in the American West, primarily in Kentucky, and they clamored for commercial rights on the Mississippi for the shipment of their goods. Madrid, however, closed the Mississippi River, the primary channel for the commerce of the rapidly growing American West, and even laid claim to territory as far north and east as the Ohio River and the Appalachians. Many settlers called for war with Spain, and there were even separatist movements that appeared in Kentucky over the issue of use of the Mississippi. Spain also promoted Indian hostility toward the new nation in order to challenge U.S. expansion. All that changed in the 1790s, however, when revolutionary France threatened the status quo in Europe. The resulting crises gave the United States the opportunity to gain favorable concessions from Madrid regarding boundaries and commercial rights.

Spain had been an ally of Great Britain in the coalition against revolutionary France that had been formed in 1793, but she was rapidly moving toward a separate peace with her traditional ally, France, in 1794–1795. Realizing that such a shift in alliance would most likely involve war with her traditional enemy Great Britain, Spain considered the likelihood of a British move against her colonies in North America. When Spanish minister Manuel de Godoy became aware of John Jay's mission to London in July 1794, which ultimately resulted in Jay's Treaty, Spain became fearful of an alliance between the United States and Great Britain that could result in an Anglo-American move upon Louisiana and Florida. Upon intimations from Madrid about possible concessions in the West, President Washington appointed minister to Great Britain Thomas Pinckney as minister to Spain. Pinckney replaced William Short, just as Jay had replaced Pinckney in London.

Upon his arrived in Madrid at the end of June 1795, Pinckney found that circumstances were most favorable for the interests of the United States. Peace negotiations between France and Spain were proceeding rapidly, and were ultimately concluded on July 22 with the Treaty of Basel. Meanwhile, news that Jay's Treaty had been signed between the United States and Great Britain reached Madrid. Godoy most likely did not know the exact terms of the treaty, and probably thought that the Anglo-American commercial treaty might be a disguised alliance. Had he known for certain, however, that it was merely a commercial alliance, and among many Americans a very unpopular one, it is unlikely that Godoy would have been willing to concede so much to the Americans. Nevertheless, there was the fear in Madrid that the United States, regardless of Jay's Treaty and the crisis in Europe, was ultimately desirous of the acquisition of Louisiana and probably Spanish Florida, by force if not by treaty. Godoy knew that once Spain was at war with Great Britain, the United States might take the opportunity to seize Louisiana and Florida while Spain was preoccupied in Europe and without fear of a British reprisal for an attack on her ally. Godoy hoped, therefore, that by signing a treaty with the United States, he could soften her alliance with Great Britain and, at the same time, satisfy her desires concerning the Mississippi, New Orleans, and the border with Spanish Florida, thus avoiding the possibility of war with the United States and Great Britain simultaneously.

Negotiations between Pinckney and Godoy began with Pinckney's arrival on June 28 and continued through October 1795. During the course of the negotiations Pinckney refused both an offer of a triple alliance with Spain and Great Britain and an alliance with Spain only, in exchange for the desired commercial rights and boundary definitions. Washington approved of this avoidance of an entangling alliance. At one point Pinckney threatened to leave the negotiations over the issue of the right of deposit at New Orleans, and Godoy eventually capitulated. After weeks of negotiation, the treaty was signed at San Lorenzo on October 27, 1795. The Senate ratified the treaty virtually without opposition.

The concessions granted the United States in the Treaty of San Lorenzo were crucial to the infant nation's economic well-being. The Eastern ports of the United States shared in the prosperity that followed the opening of the Mississippi. Upon the ratification of the treaty, the separatist conspiracies among American settlers in Kentucky fell apart. Peaceful American settlement of Louisiana followed. The United States defined its western and southern boundaries with Spain, just as it had defined its northwestern boundaries with Great Britain in Jay's Treaty (1794). Thus the United States took advantage of Europe's preoccupation with revolutionary France to improve its political and economic circumstances in the West. Similar political conditions in Europe would in another five years lead to the Spanish retrocession of Louisiana to France, and in a further three years, the sale of Louisiana by France to the United States.

—Scott D. Wignall

See also

Diplomacy of the Louisiana Purchase; Jay's Treaty; Mississippi River; New Orleans; Pinckney, Thomas; Right of Deposit

For Further Reading

Bemis, Samuel Flagg. 1960. *Pinckney's Treaty: America's Advantage from Europe's Distress, 1783–1800,* New Haven: Yale University Press; Ferrell, Robert H. 1969. *American Diplomacy: A History.* New York: W. W. Norton; Ogg, Frederic Austin. 1904. *The Opening of the Mississippi: A Struggle for Supremacy in the American Interior.* New York: Greenwood Press; Pratt, Julius W. 1965. *A History of United States Foreign Policy.* Englewood Cliffs, NJ: Prentice-Hall.

SAND HILLS

The roughly twenty thousand square miles (Massachusetts, Connecticut, and Rhode Island could fit inside, with room to spare) of sand dunes north of the Platte River in what is now north-central Nebraska constitutes the largest sand-dune region in the Western Hemisphere and one of the largest grass-stabilized dune areas worldwide. Drastic weather patterns range from bitter cold and blizzards to blazing heat. Average annual precipitation ranges from twenty-three inches in the east to less than seventeen inches in the west, yet interdunal valleys contain marshes, ponds, and lakes.

Human presence in the Sand Hills dates to at least 11,500 years ago and may extend as far back as 20,000 years. The earliest human occupants chiefly hunted in the region, lured by game animals thriving on the excellent range. Archaeological evidence indicates that between 500 and 1,000 years ago people, probably the ancestors of the Pawnee and Arikara, began living in seasonal (May–October) villages in stream valleys and along lakeshores where they practiced some horticulture. Plains Apache and Comanche occupied the Sand Hills, perhaps for a fifty-year period, during the late 1600s and early 1700s. Among historic Indian nations, the Skidi Pawnee hunted in the Sand Hills well into the 1800s, as did the Ponca, Omaha, Cheyenne, Arapaho, Crow, and some Lakota bands. Although these people gathered plant resources such as wild rice, bison provided the main attraction. Human utilization of the Sand Hills shifted from almost exclusively Indian use in 1850 to almost exclusively white use by 1880.

Settlers of European stock perceived the Sand Hills as desolate, in some cases feared the region, and took decades to embrace and exploit it. Early white explorers discouraged interest by describing the area as an uninhabitable desert. The importance of the Platte River trails and the 1854 Kansas-Nebraska Act triggered construction of military forts near the Sand Hills and the removal of Nebraska Indians to reservations. The forts created economic opportunity and perceptions of increased safety for whites, which drew new settlers. Demand for beef at forts and Indian reservations gave incentive for cattle raising along the periphery of the Sand Hills, which received further encouragement with the end of the Civil War and the expansion of railroads into Nebraska. The Treaty of Fort Laramie (1868) placed the western Sand Hills in the Great Sioux Reservation, and the Lakota hunted in the region into the 1870s. Lakota hunting rights and settlement restrictions from the treaty discouraged whites from entering the area. As the U.S. Land Survey moved across the Sand Hills during the early 1870s, its grim descriptions did little to encourage white settlement. In 1875 and 1876, government negotiations with the Lakota stripped them of hunting rights in the Sand Hills. In the late 1870s, ranchers discovered that the forage, water, and shelter of the interior Sand Hills provided excellent cattle range, especially during the harsh winters, which spurred additional settlement and growth in the area's ranching industry, still its economic mainstay. The Black Hills gold rush helped create overland routes from the Platte River Road through the Sand Hills, such as the Grand Island Black Hills Road and the Kearney Black Hills Road, which increased human traffic through the region and boosted settlement. The human population of the Sand Hills peaked with the 1920 census and has been declining ever since.

—Todd M. Kerstetter

See also

Arikara; Cheyenne; Comanche; Crow; Nebraska; Pawnee; Ponca

For Further Reading
Bleed, Ann S., and Charles A. Flowerday, eds. 1998. *An Atlas of the Sand Hills*. 3d ed. Lincoln: Conservation and Survey Division, Institute of Agriculture and Natural Resources, University of Nebraska; Johnsgard, Paul A. 1995. *This Fragile Land: A Natural History of the Nebraska Sandhills*. Lincoln: University of Nebraska Press; McIntosh, Charles Barron. 1996. *The Nebraska Sand Hills: The Human Landscape*. Lincoln: University of Nebraska Press.

SANTA FE TRAIL

The Santa Fe Trail was an important commercial route for the fifty-nine years between 1821 and 1880. Since most of the trail lay over the High Plains and avoided river crossings, inasmuch as possible, wagons could be employed over the route. Toward the middle of the nineteenth century, the trail was extended for an additional thousand miles beyond Santa Fe through El Paso, Chihuahua, and Durango.

Initial attempts to open trade with Santa Fe by U.S. citizens were met with open hostility by the Spanish authorities, who viewed all Americans with suspicion. Members of Lieutenant Zebulon Pike's expedition of 1806 to the Arkansas River were captured and maps were taken from the group. A party of twelve from St. Louis was arrested in 1812 and imprisoned for nine years. Auguste Chouteau's St. Louis fur brigade of 1815 was stopped while trapping beaver on the upper Arkansas. His property, valued at $30,000, was confiscated, but the party was released after forty-eight days.

The first serious trader on what was to become the Santa Fe Trail was William Becknell in 1821. He reached Santa Fe on November 16 and sold his Indian trade goods at from ten to twenty times St. Louis prices. Becknell had learned about Mexico's independence from Spanish control while en route. Two additional trading parties arrived later and were also warmly received. These were led by Thomas James of St. Louis and Hugh Glenn, a trader with the Osage Indians.

There was no well-defined trail prior to Becknell's journey. Previous groups had followed various routes. The Mallet brothers, Baptiste La Lande, and James Purcell followed the Platte River to the mountains. Chouteau and Glenn used the Osage Trail from southwest Missouri to the Arkansas. Thomas James crossed present-day Arkansas and Oklahoma on his way from the Mississippi.

Becknell started from Franklin, Missouri, followed the prairie divide between the tributaries of the Kansas and Arkansas Rivers to the Great Bend of the Arkansas, then the Arkansas River almost to the mountains before turning south toward Santa Fe. His route became the Santa Fe Trail of history. In 1822, on his second trading expedition, he carried part of his merchandise in wagons.

The Missouri terminus was first at Franklin, then Independence, and finally, Westport Landing (now Kansas City, Missouri). At the trail's western end it turned south toward Santa Fe from the Arkansas by three different routes. The Taos Trail left the Arkansas at the confluence of the Huerfano River, southeast of present-day Pueblo, Colorado. A middle course branched from the Arkansas west of the mouth of the Purgatory River to cross Raton Pass. The shortest and, later, the most traveled route was the Cimarron Cutoff. This trail departed the Arkansas near present-day Cimarron, Kansas, and proceeded southwest across the Cimarron Valley.

The routes themselves were laid out by the U.S. government. Because of increasing Indian hostility toward the traders by 1824, Senator Thomas Hart Benton of Missouri read into the record (January 3, 1825) the reports of Indian problems along the road to Santa Fe. A bill was drafted to survey and build a road from Fort Osage on the Kansas River to the Arkansas. The bill was quickly passed with a majority of 30 in the House, and by 30 to 12 in the Senate; a sum of $30,000 was appropriated for that purpose. President John Quincy Adams signed the bill into law.

The law provided for the appointment of a board of commissioners to oversee the survey of the route and to treat with the Indians whose lands lay along the road. These commissioners included Benjamin H. Reeves and George Champlain Sibley of Missouri. The negotiations for the road through Mexican territory represented one of the first diplomatic issues to be discussed between the United States and the newly created Republic of Mexico.

The trade with Santa Fe brought into the United States much needed silver, gave to America the "Missouri" mule, and led to the conquest of the Southwest in the Mexican War (1846–1848). Federal mail service by stagecoach to Santa Fe was begun in 1849. Completion of the final section of the rail line from Topeka to Santa Fe in 1880 ended the importance of the trail and the wagon route.

—*Henry H. Goldman*

For Further Reading
Bancroft, Hubert Howe. 1889. *History of Arizona and New Mexico, 1530–1888*. San Francisco: History Company; George Champlain Sibley Papers. Missouri Historical Society, St. Louis; Gregg, Josiah. 1905. *Commerce on the Prairies*. 2 vols. Cleveland, OH: Arthur H. Clark; Hayes, A. A., Jr. 1880. "The Santa Fe Trail." *Harper's New Monthly Magazine* 61: 185–196.

SANTEE SIOUX

The Sioux (Lakota/Dakota/Nakota) nation consists of several different groups who were the original inhabitants of much of the northern portion of the Louisiana Purchase territory. The Santee Sioux form the Dakota (meaning "allies" or "friends") division of the Sioux and consist of four bands: Mdewakantonwan, Wahpeton, Sissetonwan, and the Wahpekute. The Santee Sioux generally referred to themselves as the Isanti ("Stone Knife People"). Occasionally called the Eastern Sioux or the Woodland Sioux, the Santee Sioux were initially a group of woodlands inhabitants who practiced farming in semipermanent villages scattered throughout the headwaters region of the Mississippi River in present-day Minnesota. Today the remaining Santee Sioux live in a wide area including reservation lands in Minnesota (Granite Falls, Morton, Prior Lake, Prairie Island), South Dakota (Flandreau, Crow Creek), and Nebraska (Santee of Nebraska).

Archaeological evidence suggests that the Santee Sioux arrived in Minnesota around 1200 C.E. and established farming villages. In addition to farming, the group fished in the numerous lakes and streams of the region and also hunted wild game that abounded in the woodlands. By the sixteenth century, around the time that the Santee Sioux first encountered French trappers and traders, the group had extended themselves into portions of present-day Iowa, establishing villages in the headwaters region of the Des Moines River and along the course of the Big Sioux River. Ever leery of the European trespassers, the Santee viewed themselves as the "frontier guardians" of the entire Sioux nation.

The expansion southward into Iowa meant that the Santee were competing with other tribes, particularly the Sauk and the Ioway, who had inhabited the region previously. As a result, the expansion of the Santee Sioux fomented intertribal conflicts that discouraged settlement in the disputed region by Americans who had acquired the Louisiana Territory in 1803. For the first two decades after the Louisiana Purchase, much of Minnesota and Iowa remained de facto "Indian Country" because of the hostilities that existed in the region. In 1825 the Santee Sioux agreed to a peace treaty with their southern neighbors, but while the agreement brought peace it also brought the arrival of American settlers. Despite protestations of peace, the dislike between the Santee Sioux and the Sauk was so great that during the Black Hawk War (1832), the Santee allied themselves with the U.S. forces and were involved in the massacre at the Battle of Bad Axe.

Beginning in the 1830s and into the 1850s, the homeland of the Santee Sioux was reduced by a series of treaties with the U.S. government. Each of the treaties was followed by the expansion (or encroachment) of white settlement into lands that had historically belonged to the Sioux. By the late 1850s this expansion was more than the "frontier guardians" were willing to tolerate, and a resistance movement developed among some elements of the Santee Sioux. A band under the leadership of Inkpaduta ("Red Feather") was enraged by white settlement near Lake Okoboji and Spirit Lake in Minnesota, and in 1857 they carried out the Spirit Lake Massacre through a series of attacks upon white squatters who had claimed areas of Santee territory.

The unrest continued even after Minnesota became a state in 1858. As the attention of the United States focused on the crisis of secession and civil war in the early 1860s, dissident elements of the Santee Sioux led by Little Crow rose in rebellion, in the Sioux Uprising of 1862. So intense was the conflict in Minnesota that some within the federal government imagined that the conflict might have been fomented by Confederate sympathizers in order to draw the Union's attention and resources away from the Southern battlefields of the Civil War.

The suppression of this conflict would take a heavy toll on relations between the United States and not only the Sioux but also various other tribes of the Plains. In December 1862, thirty-eight Santee Sioux were hanged at Mankato by U.S. forces—the largest single-day execution in the entire history of the United States. Although Abraham Lincoln had commuted the death sentences of more than two hundred other warriors who had been captured, that fact did not diminish the hatred that many Sioux had for the United States. In 1863 the United States broke all treaties that it had with the Santee Sioux and ordered the removal of the tribe to points in present-day South Dakota and Nebraska. The forced migration caused great hardship and resulted in many deaths. Years later, when General George A. Custer and the men of the Seventh Cavalry were massacred at the Little Big Horn in Montana, some surviving members of the Santee Sioux, including Inkpaduta, participated in the encounter.

Although the Santee Sioux were initially a mainly sedentary woodlands people who farmed and fished the region of Minnesota, their forced migration to reservation lands involved not merely physical relocation but also a tremendous cultural disconnection. The Santee Sioux were forced, by circumstance, to adopt the ways of the Plains Indians in the Dakota Territory and in Nebraska while struggling to maintain the traditions, beliefs, and history that were their own.

—Junius P. Rodriguez

See also
Ioway; Oglala Sioux; Sauk
For Further Reading

Bonvillain, Nancy, and Frank W. Porter III, eds. 1997. *The Santee Sioux.* Philadelphia: Chelsea House.

SAUK

The Sauk, sometimes referred to as Sac, are from the Algonquian family of Woodlands culture. Living along the boundary between forest and plains, the Sauk are sometimes classified as Prairie Algonquian. Historically allied with the Fox (Meskwaki), the tribes collectively were known to the U.S. government as the "Sac and Fox," with disastrous consequences.

The name Sauk comes from "Asakiwaki," an Algonquian term meaning "Yellow Earth People," the color of the soil around the original Sauk villages. (The Fox are the "Red Earth People.") Both tribes are related to the Kickapoo; all three may have been one group that later split.

Sauk culture and religion are traditionally based on a clan system. A council of sacred clan chiefs heads the Sauk tribe. When appropriate, a war chief would join in deliberations. Representative clans include Fish, Ocean, Thunder, Bear, Fox, Potato, and Snow, clearly demonstrating the broad scope of Sauk life. Clan feasts are held in honor of, for example, the naming of children, adoptions, and burials.

In oral tradition, the Sauk once lived in Canada, along the Saint Lawrence River. When Europeans pushed into North America's interior, the Sauk lived on the lower peninsula of Michigan, near Saginaw Bay. The Sauk moved into Wisconsin in the 1640s, perhaps prompted by epidemics. The new Sauk homeland, near Green Bay, was once Winnebago territory. The largest villages were along the Wisconsin River.

The Sauk farmed during warm months, occupying permanent villages. They lived in multifamily, bark-covered houses. They raised corn, their primary food crop, as well as squash, beans, pumpkins, and tobacco. In winter they became nomads, lived in portable, reed-covered wigwams, and hunted buffalo and other large game. The Sauk were active in the fur trade with the French.

When war broke out for control of the fur trade, the Sauk defended their territory, but the Fox were nearly destroyed by the Ojibwa and their French allies. The Sauk and Fox allied in 1734, and members of each tribe lived among the other's villages. Intermarriage was common, with children retaining their mother's tribal affiliation.

In 1769 the Sauk and Fox attacked the Illinois, and moved slowly into territory along both banks of the Mississippi. The main Sauk village, Saukenuk ("River of the Rock"), was established where the Rock River joined the Mississippi. During the American Revolution, the Sauk fought against American forces. When Continental forces under George Rogers Clark dominated the region, the Sauk became neutral.

Following the Louisiana Purchase, the situation changed rapidly. In 1804, Sauk elders, primarily from Missouri, signed a treaty with the U.S. government that ceded all Sauk land in Illinois, though the tribes were allowed to remain until the area was officially opened to settlement. Because villages like Saukenuk were not represented in the delegation, the treaty essentially split the tribe into factions: those ready to fight to retain their land and those willing to relocate to avoid bloodshed. The issue lasted for thirty years.

During the War of 1812, those who disputed the treaty, led by Black Hawk, fought for the British. Having picked the losing side, the Sauk were in no position to negotiate with the United States afterward. In 1829, when the Sauk left for the winter, settlers occupied Sauk fields and lodges. When the Sauk returned in the spring, they faced militia determined to keep them from retaking their former land. Half of the tribe, under Keokuk, moved across the Mississippi into eastern Iowa to avoid conflict. The rest, under Black Hawk, remained; an uneasy truce lasted a year.

Images of Indians and scenes of the western landscape fascinated the imagination of many Americans in nineteenth-century America. This print captured both of these ideals.

Open warfare broke out in 1832. Black Hawk's band put up spirited resistance to the local militia and created havoc along the frontier. Once federal troops arrived, however, the war proved short-lived. The Sauk were battered and hounded. Once Black Hawk was in federal hands, Sauk resistance evaporated.

The postwar settlement moved the Sauk into Iowa. In 1842, under pressure from settlement, the Sauk ceded their land and moved into Kansas. Encroachment further pressured many Sauk to move later to Indian Territory in Oklahoma, where land "runs" on Native American land further squeezed the Sauk. The Sauk, still legally combined with the Fox as a single entity, live on tribal land and trust properties in Iowa, Kansas, and Oklahoma. Black Hawk and Keokuk aside, the most famous Sauk was Jim Thorpe, perhaps the greatest athlete of the twentieth century.

—*Michael S. Casey*

See also
Black Hawk; Fox; Kickapoo; Ojibwa

For Further Reading

Black Hawk. 1999. *Black Hawk: An Autobiography.* Edited by Roger L. Nichols. Ames: Iowa State University Press; Hagan, William Thomas. 1958. *The Sac and Fox Indians.* Norman: University of Oklahoma Press; Stevens, Frank E. 1903. *The Black Hawk War.* Chicago: F. E. Stevens.

SCOTT, FORT

Following the Indian Removal Act (1830), Congress established an Indian Frontier to separate Indian peoples from the states and territories of the United States. Consequently, Indians were to move west of the Mississippi River, excluding the regions already settled—Missouri, Louisiana, and the Arkansas Territory.

Built on bluffs above the Marmaton River in what is present-day Kansas, Fort Scott was constructed as one in a series of forts on the Indian Frontier to protect both white settlers and Indian tribes. The fort was located four miles west of the Missouri border, ninety miles south of Kansas City, and 125 miles north of Fort Smith, Arkansas.

In 1837, Colonel Zachary Taylor appointed a military board of commissioners whose orders were to build a fort midway between Fort Coffey in the Cherokee Nation, and Fort Leavenworth, Kansas. Stephen W. Kearny and Captain Nathan Boone, First U.S. Dragoons, selected the site on the Marmaton River. General Winfield Scott personally approved the site in January 1841. The fort was initially called Camp Scott, and the first soldiers arrived in May 1842, led by Captain William B. D. Moore. Their first task, when time allowed, was to build a sawmill and begin making bricks. With significant construction projects completed in 1844, notably the infantry barracks and dragoon barracks, the post was officially named Fort Scott. The garrison's first commander was Captain Moore, who was succeeded by Major William M. Graham.

Life at Fort Scott was, for the most part, uneventful. The nearby Osage Indians were mostly peaceful though poor. Alcoholism was the most pressing problem among tribal members. Considerable game could be found in the region. George A. McCall wrote in a letter on March 3, 1844, that there were deer, geese, ducks, swans, and sand-hill cranes, all in prodigious numbers. Perhaps the most perilous times were when fever spread among the troops (for example, there were 1,717 malarial fever cases between 1842 and 1849). Besides training at Fort Scott, the soldiers' military duties took them deep into Indian Territory in the west and into Missouri in the east.

Fulfilling their duties to maintain the frontier line, dragoons rode into Missouri in 1842 and 1844 to force Indians to return to their homes in the Indian Territory. In turn, dragoons also evicted white settlers who unlawfully constructed homes on the Osage reservation, such as one John Mathews. However, much of the dragoons' time was spent guiding missionaries, protecting the Santa Fe Trail trade route, and serving on expeditions into Indian Territory.

Company A from Fort Scott, commanded by William Eustes and assisted by Richard H. Ewell, joined Colonel Stephen W. Kearny's expedition in 1845 to the Rocky Mountains. The expedition was in response to America's drive to the west—Manifest Destiny. The very next year, the United States was at war with Mexico, and dragoons from Fort Scott were called to serve. Company A served under General Zachary Taylor in northern Mexico, while Company C served under Colonel Kearny in New Mexico and California, where Captain Moore died in the Battle of San Pasqual.

The U.S. victory in the Mexican War (1846–1848) and Mexico's subsequent cession of vast territories to the United States ended the concept of an Indian Frontier. As a result the number of troops at Fort Scott was considerably reduced, and in 1850, Congress ordered further construction to cease. Finally, after the Kansas Territory was opened to increased permanent white settlement, Fort Scott was abandoned—left in the hands of a caretaker sergeant. Troops returned in late 1857 to bring order to southeastern Kansas, where proslavery forces and abolitionists were fighting. When peace was restored in early 1859, the troops once again left Fort Scott.

There would be two additional periods when Fort Scott would reopen: during the Civil War (1861–1865) and again in 1869–1873, to protect railroad rights-of-way. During the Civil War, Fort Scott served as a proving ground for inducting Indian and black soldiers into the military. In the spring of 1873 the last of the federal troops left Fort Scott by rail. The fort's brief history—upholding the integrity of the Indian Frontier, protecting a "Bleeding Kansas" from internal rebellion, serving as an outpost in the Civil War, and guarding railroad expansion—had finally come to an end.

—*Gene Mueller*

See also
Kansas; Leavenworth, Fort

For Further Reading

Holcombe, R. I. 1887. *History of Vernon County Missouri.* St. Louis: Brown and Co.; Olivia, Leo. 1984. *Fort Scott on the Indian Frontier.* Topeka: Kansas State Historical Society; Robley, T. F. 1894. *History of Bourbon County, Kansas to the Close of 1865.* Fort Scott, KS: Press of the Monitor Book and Print Co.; Shoemaker, Earl Arthur. 1986. *The Permanent Indian Frontier: The Reason for the Construction and Abandonment of Fort Scott, Kansas, during the Dragoon Era.* Washington, DC: National Park Service.

SEDELLA, ANTONIO DE (1748–1829)

Antonio de Sedella was the controversial pastor of St. Louis Cathedral in New Orleans during the chaotic period following the Louisiana Purchase. The transfer fundamentally altered church-state relations in a colony in which many of the religious officials owed as much loyalty to the Spanish king, who continued to pay their salaries even after 1803, as they did to the pontiff.

Affection for Sedella has remained constant among New Orleanians for three centuries, but his reputation waxed and waned among his peers and superiors during his lifetime, and among historians ever since. Although some nineteenth-century writers considered Sedella a saint, most twentieth-century historians have portrayed him as a troubling example of shameful and rebellious clerical ambition. Only recently have writers begun to suggest that Sedella's career and reputation ought to be reassessed in light of the profound confusion created in the Catholic community of New Orleans following the Louisiana Purchase.

Born in Sedella, Spain, and christened Francisco Antonio Idelfonso Moreno y Arce, the priest later attached his place of birth to his Christian name. Father Antonio de Sedella, who would later be known by the affectionate French nickname Père Antoine, first came to Louisiana in 1781. By the mid-1780s he was acting pastor of the St. Louis Cathedral and was also appointed local commissioner of the Inquisition. In 1790, Bishop Cirillo de Barcelona charged Sedella with a variety of clerical infractions and, with Governor Miro's assistance, had him deported to Spain. The priest spent the next five years gathering evidence and defending his conduct of office. Ultimately he was exonerated and returned to New Orleans in 1795, this time working effectively with his superior, Bishop Luis Peñalver y Cardenas, who was appointed the first Bishop of Louisiana and the Floridas in 1793. After Peñalver was promoted to the see of Guatemala in 1801, his office remained vacant until 1815, creating a power vacuum in the colony's church hierarchy.

Patrick Walsh, formerly Peñalver's vicar general, assumed authority in Louisiana following the bishop's departure and the death of his other superiors in the territory. Sedella contested Walsh's claim to authority, and, in response, Walsh attempted to suspend the popular priest, without success. In early 1804, Sedella resigned and Walsh named himself pastor of the St. Louis Cathedral. Apparently having second thoughts, Sedella withdrew his resignation, and chaos ensued. The cathedral's parishioners sided with Sedella and, in the course of an unruly meeting held in the cathedral on March 14, 1805, asked him to remain their pastor. This so-called schism of 1805 was caused, at least in part, by the political and religious uncertainty introduced into the region following the Louisiana Purchase.

Although priests like Sedella continued to be paid by the Spanish Crown for several years after the purchase, the Vatican charged the Bishop of Baltimore, John Carroll, with overseeing developments in Louisiana. Although the official stance of the new United States was separation between church and state, Carroll consulted with Secretary of State James Madison about what issues ought to be considered in naming an appropriate bishop for Louisiana. Priests like Sedella, who had economic ties and longstanding loyalty to European monarchs, were suspect. Local authorities, including Governor William C. C. Claiborne, were also suspicious of Sedella and believed, probably rightly, that his personal loyalties remained tied to the King of Spain, who had been both his patron and protector. In 1806, in response to such concerns, Claiborne forced Sedella to take an oath of loyalty to the United States.

Sedella remained pastor of the St. Louis Cathedral until his death on January 22, 1829. Most of the city's population, including the Freemasons and others from a variety of religious denominations, attended his funeral and procession.

Although he has been widely criticized by scholars as rebellious and power-grabbing, recent scholarship has not only tried to reconstruct and re-evaluate the role that Sedella played in church politics but has also celebrated his well-known embrace of Louisiana's culturally and racially diverse peoples. The confusion created by the Louisiana Purchase, and the introduction of the separation of church and state, a situation that was completely unfamiliar to Sedella and most of his fellow prelates, certainly help to account for the chaos that ensued in the Catholic Church in New Orleans following the Louisiana Purchase.

Alecia P. Long

For Further Reading

Baudier, Roger. 1939. *The Catholic Church in Louisiana.* New Orleans: Baudier; Bruns, J. Edgar. 1988. "Sedella, Antonio de." In *Dictionary of Louisiana Biography.* Edited by Glenn R. Conrad. Lafayette: Louisiana Historical Association and the Center for Louisiana Studies; O'Neill, Charles Edwards. 1990. "'A Quarter Marked by Sundry Peculiarities': New Orleans, Lay Trustees, and Père Antoine." *Catholic Historical Review* 76: 235–277.

SEVEN YEARS' WAR

***See* French and Indian War**

SEVENTH CONGRESS (MARCH 4, 1801, TO MARCH 3, 1803)

The first Congress to meet under the administration of newly elected President Thomas Jefferson, the Seventh Congress was dominated by Jeffersonian Republicans and issues such as the judiciary, financial matters, and Spain's ceding Louisiana to France.

As the new American nation moved into the nineteenth century, the legislative branch of the federal government experienced a decided shift in political power and influence. The days of the Federalist Party were in decline and the Jeffersonian Republicans, headed by newly elected President Thomas Jefferson, were in ascendance. Jefferson's close victory over the ubiquitous Aaron Burr was a less than clear mandate to Jefferson's colleagues in Congress to implement the president's program, but Congress moved rapidly to displace Federalist conservatism with an aggressive financial policy, judicial reform, and, by chance, a remarkable land acquisition. Yet expansion into Louisiana was preceded by an alarming development when Spain ceded the territory to France and Napoleon—French presence in North America was of considerable concern to the Seventh Congress.

The first session of the Seventh Congress convened on December 7, 1801. Republicans outnumbered Federalists in both houses—by 69 to 36 in the House and 18 to 13 in the Senate. For the second session (December 6, 1802–March 3, 1803), these numbers increased dramatically, as Republicans in the House increased to 102 to only 39 Federalists. The Senate experienced an even more dramatic shift, as Republicans added six seats and the Federalists dropped four. The administration's congressional leadership fell to Virginia's John Randolph of Roanoke in the House, although North Carolina's venerable Nathaniel Macon was speaker. Another Virginian, William Branch Giles, was Jefferson's House floor leader. In the Senate, Republican Abraham Baldwin of Georgia and, for the second session, Stephen R. Bradley of Vermont, also a Jeffersonian, filled the post of president pro tempore. Samuel Mitchell of New York sounded still another powerful Republican voice on the House floor, but the true Republican leader of the Senate was John Breckinridge of Kentucky. Stevens T. Mason of Virginia was the equal of any Senate Federalist in debate. Jeffersonians had a stranglehold on Congress. By the middle of 1803, Jefferson's grasp on offices under presidential appointment was also tightened, as only 130 of 316 officeholders were Federalists.

Federalist House leadership fell to the gifted James A. Bayard of Delaware and the often arrogant and offensive Roger Griswold of Connecticut. Federalists of note in the Senate included Connecticut's Uriah Tracy and the incomparable Gouverneur Morris of New York, complete with wooden leg, command of French, remarkable gift of oratory, and admiration of all around him. To a man the Federalists had a bitter hatred and distrust of democracy, and, while as talented a group of individuals as ever sat in Congress, they were simply outnumbered in voting strength.

When the Seventh Congress met in December 1801, there was little hint of trouble brewing on the frontier. Jefferson's message to Congress focused on trouble with the Barbary states, the need for budget management, military posts and harbor fortifications, and the president's personal concerns about naturalization laws. He did not mention Louisiana, France, or Spain. By the Treaty of San Ildefonso (1800), Spain had ceded the Louisiana Territory to France, but word did not reach Washington until May 1801. Until then, Congress had been concerned mainly with the Judiciary Act. In his message to the second congressional session (December 15, 1802), Jefferson implied that the cession of Louisiana to France would "make a change in the aspect of our foreign relations, which will doubtless have just weight in any deliberations of the Legislature connected with that subject" (Smelser, 1968). On January 5, discussions on how to proceed over Mississippi River navigation and the cession issue began, with Griswold and Randolph leading their respective party's stance. Griswold unsuccessfully pressed the administration to supply the House with documentation of the cession to France. In turn, on January 11 (the same day that Jefferson sent the message to the Senate), the entire discussion immediately became moot, when the president and Randolph successfully orchestrated a $2 million appropriation "for the purposes of intercourse between the United States and foreign nations" (*Debates,* 1851). Jefferson's motive was political—he feared that Federalists might push for war on the frontier over navigation rights and gain support among Western interests in Congress. By appointing James Monroe to join Robert Livingston, already negotiating with the French in Paris, Jefferson thwarted the Federalists, as Monroe's appointment would ease the tensions shared by the Westerners. At this point, the Seventh Congress moved on to matters of finance, land claims, and naval yards, and the affair of Louisiana fell to the diplomats.

—Boyd Childress

For Further Reading

Smelser, Marshall. 1968. *The Democratic Republic: 1801–1815.* New York: Harper and Row; U.S. Congress. 1851. *The Debates and Proceedings in the Congress of the United States.* Seventh Congress. Washington, DC: Gales and Seaton.

SHOSHONI

In the early nineteenth century, the Shoshoni homeland stretched from the Great Basin in the west, across the Rocky Mountains, and onto the Great Plains in the east. This territory now composes parts of Idaho, Montana, Wyoming, Nevada, Utah, and Colorado. Straddling physical and cultural boundaries, the Shoshoni are a varied people, incorporating elements of Plateau, Plains, and Great Basin cultures. No pan-Shoshonean "tribe" as such exists, but a shared Uto-Aztecan language is a common thread between peoples variably spelled "Shoshoni," "Shoshone," or "Shoshonie."

Once Lewis and Clark and the Corps of Discovery crossed the Continental Divide at Lemhi Pass in present-day Montana, they entered the territory of the Shoshoni.

During the seventeenth century, the northward- and eastward-expanding Shoshoni began their gradual separation from those pressing toward the south. The Comanche, though linguistically related, became a distinct people on the southern Great Plains. The migrating Great Basin peoples, later called the Northern and Eastern Shoshoni, adopted Plains cultural traits.

Eastern and Northern Shoshoni relied on a combination of buffalo hunting and gathered foods. For those in the Snake River watershed, salmon was an important resource. The first buffalo hunt of the season was in early spring, followed by fishing through early summer. During the fishing season, horse herds increased in strength in preparation for longer journeys in the late summer and, in fall, a second season of buffalo hunting. Over winter, many bands divided into smaller units to sustain themselves through the season.

As the first group in the region to obtain horses from the south, the Shoshoni rapidly rose to a position of power in relation to nearby peoples. Many bands participated in a horse culture from the early eighteenth century forward. As mounted hunters, they were able to traverse vast distances and dominated the trade of the region. The Blackfoot in particular appear to have borne the brunt of Shoshoni expansion as they pushed northward to the Saskatchewan River. However, with the appearance of British trade goods, the Blackfoot gained the gun and ascendance and forced their rivals southward by the 1750s. Smallpox epidemics in 1781, and again in 1800, further weakened the Shoshoni as they withdrew from the Great Plains.

Eighteenth-century French and British traders regarded the Shoshoni as raiders of Plains tribes with whom they traded. Referred to as "Gens du Serpent" or "Snake Indians," they were purportedly so named for their practice of carrying sticks painted to resemble snakes. A more likely explanation may derive from a misunderstood sign language weaving motion referring to the Great Basin "Grass-House People." Regardless, speculative Euro-American geography placed the Shoshoni/Snake as the most important tribe between the Pacific Ocean and the Great Plains.

Under these circumstances, in August 1805, the Lewis and Clark Expedition encountered the Shoshoni in their homeland. Just west of the Continental Divide, this American party met a people coalesced against the encroachment of other tribes. The Americans had been desperately seeking the Shoshoni and their horses, knowing that these people held the knowledge and the means for any link to the Pacific. For their part, the Shoshoni welcomed the appearance of potential new trading partners, and Lemhi band leader Cameahwait supplied horses and much-needed guides for the journey into the Columbia River basin.

The role of the Shoshoni as guides and escorts through the confusing geography between the Mississippi-Missouri and Columbia-Snake river systems continued during the fur trapping era. In 1810–1812, John Jacob Astor's representatives traversed Shoshoni lands in an attempt to extend American fur trade to the mouth of the Columbia. Eastbound Astorians relied on Shoshoni knowledge to become the first Euro-Americans to traverse through South Pass in 1812.

The Montreal-based North West Company entered the Snake River plain in 1818. Although a few small parties (John Colter in 1807 and Andrew Henry in 1810) had trapped Shoshoni streams previously, the St. Louis–based Rocky Mountain Fur Company's arrival in 1824 triggered many more "mountain men" to follow. The Shoshoni largely welcomed the opportunity to trade and counter the advantage held by both Blackfoot and Crow. The "rendezvous system" attributed to William Ashley was quite familiar to the Shoshoni, having long organized such trade fairs. The difference was the Americans' direct trade with the Shoshoni and their Salish (Flathead) allies. Together, the two tribes were able to increase pressure on the Blackfoot and achieve a military balance. That in turn curtailed Blackfoot raiding and brought the Shoshoni a resurgence of power in the region.

The reduction in Blackfoot raids also allowed American and British trappers relatively safe passage. Trappers and nations engaged in severe competition with each other within Shoshoni lands. Trappers worked streams themselves, departing from the previous post-based fur trade that relied upon Indians to supply pelts. Finding themselves in competition with newcomers, obtaining surplus fur and hides to participate in the new trade drove the native economy. Trappers often intermarried with Shoshoni families, and parties "wintered over" with or near Shoshoni camps, contending for game as well as fodder for their horses. The fur traders' Green River rendezvouses and Fort Hall co-opted Shoshoni trade fairs, further incorporating the Shoshoni into a new trade system.

As the fur trade declined in the 1840s, emigrants on the Oregon and California Trails began to pour through South Pass and across Shoshoni lands. Within the Shoshoni homeland, pressure from Mormon settlement (1847) and expansion, the regularly used transcontinental route, and periodic gold rushes created an increasingly untenable situation. Often forced to traverse Crow lands to hunt buffalo, the Shoshoni found tribal conflict increasing as well. Tribal leaders such as Washakie attempted to navigate between these various influences. Other bands, under Pocatello and Sagwitch, engaged in armed conflict. The 1863 Bear River Massacre proved that Americans could and would inflict severe casualties on Shoshoni men, women, and children.

Within a few years, many Eastern Shoshoni accepted a reservation at Wind River in Wyoming. The Northern Shoshoni were allotted both a short-lived reservation centered on the Lemhi River in Idaho and another at Fort Hall, Idaho. Today, Shoshoni culture centers on their two largest reservations, at Fort Hall and Wind River, as well as other colonies and reservations scattered across the northern Great Basin. As one of the largest and most widespread tribes in the Western states, Shoshoni ranchers and farmers find themselves at the center of many land and water issues.

—Steven M. Fountain

See also

Blackfoot; Cameahwait; Lewis and Clark Expedition; Rendezvous System; Sacagawea; South Pass

For Further Reading

Calloway, Colin G. 1991. "Snake Frontiers: The Eastern Shoshones in the Eighteenth Century." *Annals of Wyoming* 63: 82–92; Heaton, John W. 1995. "'No Place to Pitch Their Teepees': Shoshone Adaptation to Mormon Settlers in Cache Valley 1855–70." *Utah Historical Quarterly* 63, no. 2: 158–171; Liljeblad, Sven. 1972. *The Idaho Indians in Transition 1805–1960.* Pocatello: Idaho State University Museum; Madsen, Brigham D. 1979. *The Lemhi: Sacajawea's People.* Caldwell, ID: Caxton; Madsen, Brigham D. 1980. *The Northern Shoshoni.* Caldwell, ID: Caxton; Madsen, Brigham D. 1986. *The Shoshoni Frontier and the Bear River Massacre.* Salt Lake City: University of Utah; Malouf, Carling I., and Åke Hultkrantz, eds. 1974. *Shoshone Indians.* New York: Garland; Murphy, Robert F., and Yolanda Murphy. 1959. "Shoshone-Bannock Subsistence and Society." *University of California Anthropological Records* 16, no. 7: 293–338; Murphy, Robert F., and Yolanda Murphy. 1986. "Northern Shoshone and Bannock." In *Handbook of North American Indians, Volume 11: Great Basin.* Edited by Warren L. d'Azevedo. Washington, DC: Smithsonian Institution; Shimkin, Demitri B. 1947. "Wind River Shoshone Ethnogeography." *University of California Anthropological Records* 5, no. 4: 245–288; Stamm, Henry E. IV. 1999. *People of the Wind River: The Eastern Shoshones 1825–1900.* Norman: University of Oklahoma Press; Trenholm, Virginia Cole, and Maurine Carley. 1964. *The Shoshonis: Sentinels of the Rockies.* Norman: University of Oklahoma Press; Walker, Deward. 1978. *Indians of Idaho.* Moscow, ID: University Press of Idaho.

SIBLEY, JOHN (1757–1837)

Dr. John Sibley was best known as an Indian agent and informant in the Louisiana Territory from 1803 to 1815. The Massachusetts-born doctor participated in the American Revolution as a surgeon's mate. After the war he opened a private practice in Great Barrington, Massachusetts, and later moved to Fayetteville, North Carolina, with his wife, Elizabeth, and their two sons. After his wife's death he remarried, this time to a widow named Mary Winslow. After losing his personal fortune, Sibley fled to Louisiana, leaving his wife and children, an act that later resulted in questions being raised about his character.

Sibley reached Spanish Louisiana in September 1802, and within the next year he settled at Natchitoches, where he would live the rest of his life. From this frontier outpost he traveled throughout the territory, learning what he could about the Spanish in both Louisiana and Texas as well as the Indians of the Red River area. During his expeditions he kept a journal describing the country and its inhabitants. In 1803, after the United States purchased Louisiana from the French, Sibley wrote several letters to officials in Washington, D.C., in which he discussed the land, resources, Indians, and local conditions. The U.S. press published many of his letters drawing attention to both the newly acquired territory and Sibley himself. As a reward for services rendered, Sibley received an appointment as the contract surgeon to Fort Claiborne. By December 1804 he began acting as the "occasional" Indian agent for Louisiana, and W. C. C. Claiborne, the governor of the new Territory of Orleans, introduced Sibley to President Thomas Jefferson. The following year Sibley forwarded a report to the president entitled "Historical Sketches of the Several Tribes in Louisiana South of the Arkansas River and between the Mississippi and the River Grand." He also forwarded a copy of the 1803 journal of his Red River expedition to the secretary of war. For this valuable information, gleaned from firsthand knowledge as well as second-hand accounts of French-Caddo hunters, Jefferson appointed Sibley as the permanent "Indian Agent of Orleans Territory and the region South of the Arkansas River."

In his capacity as Indian agent, Sibley strengthened relations with the Indians at the expense of the Spanish in Texas. The U.S. government provided him with $1,000 per year for his salary, along with $3,000 in goods to be distributed to the Indians as he saw fit. He advocated friendly relations with the Indians in Texas and persuaded many of them to trade with the Americans instead of the Spanish. He established a factory at Natchitoches where they came from around the entire region to trade their goods, instead of going to the Spanish factory at Nacogdoches. He also licensed American traders to undercut the Spanish and to sell guns in exchange for horses and furs. The Indians, already dissatisfied with Spanish traders, readily accepted the Americans. In 1807, Sibley arranged a Grand Council in Natchitoches that was attended by more than thirty Indian nations of the near southwest. Sibley's aggressive policies ensured the support of Indians from Louisiana west to Matagorda Bay and, when the French occupied Spain in 1808, helped initiate a series of revolutions in Mexico and Texas. Hoping to influence the outcome of the revolution in Texas, Sibley backed the Gutierrez-Magee expedition, led by the Mexican revolutionist Jose Bernardo Gutierrez and a former U.S. Army lieutenant, William Augustus Magee, with its goal of liberating Texas from Spanish rule. Friendly relations with the Indians also prevented the British from forming an alliance with them during the War of 1812 and using Indian territory as a base against the United States in the western part of the country, especially the port of New Orleans.

Throughout his term as Indian agent, Sibley continued to provide information to officials in the nation's capital. Then on January 25, 1815, the secretary of war replaced him with a less politically active successor, Thomas Gale. Protesting that he had received no notification or explanation for his removal, Sibley continued to live in Natchitoches and remained active in public and private life until his death. He held the position of justice of the peace, judge, and state senator. He acquired a large amount of property on both sides of the Red River, grew cash crops such as cotton, raised cattle, manufactured salt from the nearby salt springs, and settled down with his third wife, Eudalie Malige, in 1813. Having witnessed some of the major events of his times, Sibley died at his home in 1837.

—*Cynthia Clark Northrup*

See also
Gutierrez-Magee Expedition; Natchitoches
For Further Reading
DeConde, Alexander. 1976. *This Affair of Louisiana.* New York: Charles Scribner's Sons.

SIOUX

***See* Oglala Sioux; Santee Sioux.**

SLAVERY

Enslaved people of African descent were already present in the Louisiana Territory in 1803, when the United States purchased it from France. French and Spanish colonizers had failed to create a captive labor force by enslaving Native Americans, so whites had turned next to enslaved Africans. Many were brought from the Caribbean, but the majority came from West Africa. While colonial governments failed to create a West Indian-styled economic regime of sugarcane and superprofits in Lower Louisiana, the French imposed the same set of laws that governed their Caribbean colonies. Their *Code Noir* mandated harsh labor requirements and brutal punishments, but it also mandated conversion of the enslaved to Catholicism and prohibited slaveowners from dividing mothers and children by sale. Following French Caribbean practices, slaveowning fathers in colonial Louisiana freed many of their children with enslaved women, producing a large free, "mixed-race" population. And after the outbreak of the Haitian Revolution (1791), white and mulatto slaveowners came in large numbers to New Orleans from St. Domingue, bringing enslaved people from that island. All these factors created a regime of slavery different from those that prevailed in the southeastern

United States in 1803, one characterized by both great cruelty and relative cultural openness.

After the United States purchased the western Mississippi basin from France in 1803, slavery as an institution, and as the subject of debate, dominated the settlement of both Lower Louisiana and the territories to its north for sixty years. By the late 1790s, the French colonists had finally refined techniques for producing sugar in Louisiana. Anglo-American settlers hoped to reap the profits of that most desired crop. Although Creole and English-speaking whites sometimes disagreed in Louisiana, they formed alliances based on their common desire for slave-made wealth early and strengthened them over time. Especially important was the access of the new migrants to large numbers of slaves from the Chesapeake region. New Orleans became the focal point of an interstate trade in human beings. African Americans were brought by ship from Virginia and Maryland, and even from New Jersey. Others came overland or down the river, and by 1861 hundreds of thousands had been sold in the markets of New Orleans.

Some were taken on to Missouri and Arkansas. Arkansas delta lands became a vast cotton field in which slaves worked in the 1830s, and Missouri played a unique role in the political history of slavery in the United States. By 1819 migrants from Kentucky, Tennessee, and Virginia, clamored for Missouri's admission to the United States. Northern Congressmen, however, balked at the idea of adding another slave state to the Union. They proposed a ban on further importation of slaves to Missouri and the gradual emancipation of those already there. After lengthy debates, Congress worked out a compromise that admitted Missouri as a slave state but mandated that any other states created in the Purchase north of Missouri's southern border—thirty-six degrees and thirty minutes north latitude—would be free.

Huge plantations never characterized Missouri, where hemp, grain, tobacco, and livestock were the main products, but slavery continued to be the chief source of prestige and wealth for whites there. Indeed, the massive southwestward forced migration of enslaved African Americans was the single largest demographic, economic, and cultural force shaping the Louisiana Purchase and its settlers prior to the Civil War. This was true most of all for the enslaved, who faced daunting changes. Those sent to the sugar plantations and bayous of Louisiana struggled to adjust to new customs, language, and work regimes and were subjected to new diseases. Plantation owners held the prospect of sale "down the river" to the sugar country of south Louisiana over the heads of the enslaved.

Yet enslaved migrants gradually knit together a common culture. The rich folk traditions of black New Orleans and Louisiana are a product of that process. Family, religion, and music helped many to see life as worth living, but the hope of freedom and the desperation of slavery made others believe that life was worth risking. The 1811 German Coast rebellion in St. John the Baptist Parish (Louisiana) was one of the largest in North American history. The execution of at least eighty-two rebels did not quell whites' fears, but planters and merchants could not bring themselves to stop the influx of slaves. Instead, in 1817 the state of Louisiana banned the importation of slaves "of bad character." Later, in the panic generated by the 1831 outbreak of Nat Turner's rebellion in Virginia, Louisiana legislators tried to shut out the professional slave traders entirely. But with the massive cotton boom of the mid-1830s, Louisiana whites swept their own laws away, and New Orleans filled once more with traders, slaves, and buyers.

The national debate over slavery never disappeared after 1819, but the Missouri Compromise line proved a workable compromise. The expansion of slavery in the Louisiana Purchase itself was not at issue until Senator Stephen A. Douglas of Illinois introduced his Kansas-Nebraska bill in 1854. This opened the possibility that these two territories could become slave states, even though they lay north of thirty-six degrees and thirty minutes north latitude, the boundary set by the Missouri Compromise. Kansas soon became the site of armed confrontation between proslavery "Border ruffians" from Missouri and Free Soil Movement from the North. The latter group was more numerous and thus victorious, in part because slaveowners feared moving valuable slaves into a battleground.

Events in Kansas foreshadowed slaveholders' secession and the Civil War. Slavery would end in the Louisiana Purchase as it did in other parts of the South after the Civil War. As soon as the Union Army seized a key point like New Orleans, enslaved people flocked to Northern-held territory. These newly freed slaves helped to force changes in Northern war aims, first at the level of local policy, and then influenced the policies of President Lincoln. The war became one against slavery, and one in which the "slavery chain broke at last," to use the words of the newly free. Although the struggles of Reconstruction that followed did not produce full freedom, the Louisiana Purchase—meant as a haven for a white yeomanry—became first the place where slavery met its expansionist peak, and then, where slaveowners overreached and brought the whole structure crashing down.

—Edward E. Baptist

See also

Creoles; Haiti; Kansas-Nebraska Act; Missouri Compromise; Popular Sovereignty

For Further Reading

Hall, Gwendolyn Midlo. 1992. *Africans in Colonial Louisiana: The Development of Afro-Creole Culture in the Eighteenth Century.* Baton Rouge: Louisiana State University Press; Johnson, Walter. 1999. *Soul By Soul: Life Inside the Antebellum Slave Market.* Cambridge: Harvard University Press; Malone, Ann Patton. 1992. *Sweet Chariot: Slave Family and Household Structure in Nineteenth-Century Louisiana.* Chapel Hill: University of North Carolina Press; McNeilly, Donald. 2000. *The Old South Frontier: Cotton Plantations and the Formation of Arkansas Society, 1819–1860.* Fayetteville: University of Arkansas Press; Russell, Sarah P. 2000. "Cultural Conflicts and Common Interests: The Making of the Sugar Planter Class in Louisiana, 1795–1853." Ph.D. dissertation, University of Maryland, College Park, Maryland; Taylor, Joe Gray. 1963. *Negro Slavery in Louisiana.* Baton Rouge: Louisiana Historical Association.

SMITH, FORT

Fort Smith served as a frontier outpost from 1817 until 1896. Major William Bradford, a veteran of the War of 1812, established the fort on the Belle Point site at the juncture of the Arkansas and Poteau Rivers. Fort Smith, located on what is the present-day Arkansas and Oklahoma border, became the first U.S. military installation in the primitive wilderness of the Southwest. The fort guarded U.S. interests and assisted in opening the vast expanse of the Louisiana Purchase. Fort Smith, actively occupied for almost eighty years, served the federal government longer than most frontier military settlements.

The history of Fort Smith began in 1817, when General Andrew Jackson received orders to oversee the establishment of a federal outpost on the southwestern frontier. Advised to select experienced and skillful men to carry out this mission, Jackson chose the Rifle Regiment, a crack infantry unit skilled in scouting and patrol duty. Members of Rifle Regiments from Baton Rouge and Natchitoches joined Major William Bradford's company at Belle Fontaine, a post just north of St. Louis on the Missouri River. Major Stephen H. Long and a five-man engineering party accompanied Bradford and his troops to select a site and to sketch construction plans.

Major Long chose a site on the Arkansas River that offered a well-watered, healthy-looking, and strategic location. He named the post Camp Smith. Leaving two men and the construction plans with Bradford, Long and the other members of his party became the first of many exploration groups to use Fort Smith as the springboard for discovery and mapping expeditions. Major Long's party explored the surrounding country, accumulating valuable information for use in future developments. They traveled along the Poteau River, through the Kiamichi Mountains, and along the north bank of the Red River. They continued north from the "thirty thermal springs" and forded the Arkansas near present-day Little Rock. Long explored his way back to St. Louis while Bradford set his men to work in putting the engineers' plans into action.

By 1818 the War Department had designated Camp Smith a permanent post in the system of Western defenses and named it Fort Smith. The new fort played a significant role in paving the way for the emergence of civilian settlements in the Southwest. The men stationed in this frontier outpost opened roads, established lines of communication, explored, and mapped the surrounding country. They settled disputes between feuding Native American tribes and between Indians and settlers. Through Fort Smith funneled soldiers, mountain men, government explorers, Texas-bound immigrants, the U.S. mail, and passengers on the Butterfield Overland Stage.

Because of the energy and resourcefulness of those involved in its development and maintenance, Fort Smith frequently received orders to send men and supplies to build other outposts on the frontier. The Arkansas fort became known as the "mother post for the Southwest."

Fort Smith troops increasingly faced frontier violence. Relocation programs brought increasing numbers of Cherokee to territory traditionally belonging to the Osage Indians. Encroaching settlers also added to the volatile situation. Fort Smith's officers and troops struggled to maintain order and security in the face of horse stealing, the slaughter of buffalo, the effects of frontier whisky, and the virulent animosity between the three groups.

The Battle of Claremore Mound in October 1817 presented the new, and as yet unfinished, fort with its first formidable task. Cherokee chief Tick-e-Toke led a raid against an Osage village. Most of the young men were away hunting, and, virtually unhindered, the Cherokees ravished the village. Tick-e-Toke's warriors killed sixty-nine men, women, and children and carried away more than one hundred captives. Bradford managed to negotiate a treaty and prevent an all-out war.

Being the westernmost outpost in the region, it fell also to Bradford's troops to watch and protect the border from illegal Spanish activity. Trappers often brought word of Spanish troops camped within U.S. territory. Information also filtered in concerning Spanish traders who encouraged renegade Indians to harass white settlers along the border. The nebulous boundary of the Louisiana Purchase complicated Bradford's task until the Adams-Onís Treaty (1819) established definite borders.

Even after Arkansas became a state, in 1836, Fort Smith continued to serve the federal government in westward expansion. Men from the fort aided in the Mexican War (1846–1848), the post served as a point of departure for the Gold Rush, and it housed first Confederate and then Union troops during the Civil War. In March 1871, Fort Smith became home of the federal district court. From within the walls of the fort, Judge Isaac Parker fought to maintain law and order in Indian Territory from 1875 until his death, and the end of the fort's career, in 1896. It is now a National Historic Site.

—*Carol J. Terry*

See also
Arkansas; Gibson, Fort; Long, Stephen Harriman; Oklahoma; Osage; Towson, Fort

For Further Reading
Bearss, Edwin. 1969. *Fort Smith, Little Gibraltar on the Arkansas.* Norman: University of Oklahoma Press; Shirley, Glenn. 1957. *Law West of Fort Smith.* New York: Henry Holt and Company.

SMITH, JEDEDIAH STRONG (1799–1831)

Jedediah Smith, more than any man of his time, acquired a comprehensive idea of the nature of the West. As a fur trapper he became intimately familiar with the region, from the Missouri River to the Pacific and from Mexico to Canada. In his pursuit of beaver he rediscovered Wyoming's South Pass and ascertained that it was an open corridor through the Rocky Mountains to the Pacific. He was the first white man to cross the Sierra Nevada Mountains and the first to make the land journey from California to Oregon. From the Great Salt Lake he had cut two different routes to the Pacific. Although Smith traveled primarily in search of beaver, he consciously observed his surroundings, kept careful journals, and mapped much of the vast expanse of the Louisiana Territory.

Smith's first twenty-two years are hidden to history. Early on, however, Jedediah appears to have set his sights on exploration. He wrote of his early desire, to view a country upon which no white man's eyes had gazed, and to travel uncharted rivers. His first step toward the realization of that dream occurred in 1822 as he entered the St. Louis office of William H. Ashley and became part of the fur trade west of the Mississippi.

Jedediah was not the typical mountain man. Those who knew him described him as modest, unassuming, and quiet. They called him a moral and honorable man. Jedediah did not conform to the mountain man's habit of neglecting daily ablutions or of allowing hair and beard to grow. He did not use tobacco or coarse language, and he did not adopt the drunken and uncouth manners of his mountain companions. He seldom drank alcoholic beverages, and he did not seek the company of women. Intelligent and obviously well educated, Jedediah kept a journal that reveals his contemplative and philosophic turn of mind.

Although unlike his contemporaries in character and appearance, Jedediah Smith exemplified the best and the most necessary qualities of a successful mountain man. He demonstrated incredible courage, perseverance, and endurance. He adapted to the unfamiliar and unfriendly environment of the wilderness during searing summer heat and bitterly cold winters. Jedediah faced angry grizzlies and war-painted Indians with equal bravery. His keen sense of the significant equipped him to map and record the character of the Louisiana Territory.

Other momentous contributions to American expansion can be added to Jedediah's record. He is given credit for initiating and mastering the technique of moving large parties to and from the mountains and for development of the yearly rendezvous system used by trappers and traders. His arrival in California's San Bernadino Valley alerted Mexican authorities that the formidable barrier of the southwestern desert could no longer hold back the inevitable tide of American settlers.

Smith met adversity with calm and innovative action, whether it was the harshness of nature or the violence of human enemies. He proved his mettle during an attack by the Arikara on the Missouri, a massacre by Mojave Indians in the Southwest, and the Umpqua massacre in the Pacific Northwest. For nine years Jedediah fought and survived against terrible odds, bringing his men and his furs through time after time.

A favorite story of those who talk of Smith illustrates his courage. In one of his first expeditions he confronted an angry grizzly nose-to-nose and received a severe mauling. With his head torn from ear to ear, and bleeding profusely from numerous wounds, Jedediah coolly instructed his reluctant companion to sew him back together with what was at hand. Weak with loss of blood from wounds that should have rendered him prostrate with pain, Jedediah managed to mount his horse and ride to camp. Amazing his companions, he survived to complete the season's trapping expedition and numerous other life-threatening experiences.

Jedediah made his last trek westward leading a trading venture to Santa Fe. Having traveled for more than two days without water, Smith's party of eighty-three men and numerous wagons of trade goods faced potential disaster on the dry plains between the Arkansas and the Cimarron Rivers. Jedediah and one companion left the main party to scout ahead for water. Leaving his companion at a disappointingly dry hole, Smith continued the search. It was the last that any saw of the intrepid mountain man. His body was never recovered. Apparently he had been set upon by a war party, for some of his effects turned up in the possession of Comanche warriors.

—Carol J. Terry

See also

Ashley, William Henry; Mountain Men; Rendezvous System

For Further Reading

Goetzmann, William H. 1995. *New Lands, New Men.* Austin: Texas State Historical Association; Morgan, Dale L. 1953. *Jedediah Smith and the Opening of the West.* Lincoln: University of Nebraska Press.

SNELLING, FORT

Located at the mouth of the St. Peter (now Minnesota) River near present-day St. Paul and Minneapolis, Fort Snelling was the northernmost U.S. military post on the Mississippi River at the time of its construction. It served to establish a U.S. military presence in the northern portion of the Louisiana Purchase, maintain peace between the Sioux and Ojibwa (Chippewa) Indians, and to protect settlers entering the region.

Lieutenant Zebulon M. Pike was given the commission by Thomas Jefferson to explore the northern Mississippi, identify the location and size of local Indian tribes, and find potential sites for military posts. Before his departure from St. Louis on August 9, 1805, Pike also received orders from General James Wilkinson to gain Indian consent for the Americans to build military forts and trading posts in the area of the mouth of the Minnesota River, the Falls of St. Anthony (at present-day Minneapolis), and other strategic locations.

Pike and a detachment of twenty soldiers reached the junction of the Minnesota and Mississippi Rivers in September 1805. At that time the Dakota Sioux, who occupied most of the land that is now northern and western Minnesota, and the Ojibwa (Chippewa), who occupied lands east of the Mississippi, were regular traders with the British, and had not yet come into contact with the U.S. military. Given the task to establish U.S. control of the northern portion of the Louisiana Purchase, Pike succeeded in gaining from the Sioux nine square miles of land, including the confluence of the Minnesota and Mississippi and the Falls of St. Anthony. Although the land was valued at $200,000, Pike exchanged just $200 worth of trade goods to the Sioux in the purchase.

Movement to begin construction of a U.S. military post in the region would not resume for a dozen years. In the time after Pike's voyage the resident Indian tribes remained loyal to the British and were familiar only with British successes in the War of 1812.

In 1817, Major Stephen H. Long was sent to survey the land acquired through Pike's treaty and to find a suitable site for the erection of a military post. From his findings, as well as Pike's, the War Department chose to build a post at the confluence of the Minnesota and Mississippi Rivers.

In August 1819, Lieutenant Colonel Henry Leavenworth and nearly a hundred soldiers from the U.S. Fifth Infantry arrived at the mouth of the Minnesota River. These first troops, along with an additional attachment that arrived the following month, established a camp south of the Minnesota River near present-day Mendota, Minnesota. That base, given the name "Cantonment New Hope," suffered through a severe first winter that saw at least forty enlisted men die of scurvy.

Cantonment New Hope was abandoned in the spring for a site north of the river. The new camp was more appropriately named "Coldwater," after a spring near the site. However, because of lingering illness among many of the troops, construction of the new camp was slow.

Colonel Josiah Snelling was sent to relieve Leavenworth of his command in the fall of 1820. Soon after, Snelling selected a site atop a bluff immediately to the west of the confluence of the rivers for the construction of a stone fortress. From this position his troops could monitor activity on both the Mississippi to the north and south, and on the Minnesota to the west. As it was being constructed, Snelling chose to name the structure Fort St. Anthony.

In the summer of 1824, General Winfield Scott visited the fortress and was so pleased by the progress of the regiment and the performance of its commanding officer that he recommended the name of the post to be changed to Fort Snelling. A general order issued on January 7, 1825, gave Fort Snelling the name it holds to this day. Construction of the fortress was completed later that year.

In addition to its barracks and officer's quarters, the Fort Snelling featured a schoolhouse, workshops for blacksmiths and other craftsmen, and a bakehouse. As early as 1823, Snelling's men had cultivated 210 acres of land outside the fort. Upriver, at the Falls of St. Anthony, a stone gristmill and sawmill were constructed.

In the years prior to the establishment of Minnesota Territory in 1849, Fort Snelling served its mission to maintain peace among the Indian tribes in the northern Mississippi Valley. Much of this success can be attributed to the work of Major Lawrence Taliaferro, who served as the fort's Indian agent from 1819 until his resignation in 1839. No major incidents of war occurred in the area during his tenure. His efforts gained him respect from the Ojibwa (Chippewa) and Sioux as a friend and defender, while gaining him adversaries among local traders and the American Fur Company.

As the frontier moved farther west, Fort Snelling was relegated to the role of a supply depot in 1851. When Minnesota became a state in 1858, the fort was sold and was charted to be the site of a town. Those plans were abandoned with the onset of the American Civil War.

—*J. Brent Etzel*

See also

Minnesota; Ojibwa; Pike Expedition; Santee Sioux

For Further Reading

Jones, Evan. 2001. *Citadel in the Wilderness: The Story of Fort Snelling and the Northwest Frontier.* Minneapolis: University of Minnesota Press.

SOUTH DAKOTA

Practically all of present-day South Dakota was included in the Louisiana Purchase Territory that the United States acquired from France in 1803. Only a small section of the northeast corner of South Dakota—near present-day Aberdeen—was not included since it was a part of the drainage basin of the Red River of the North and not the Mississippi River system. That region became American territory when the United States and Great Britain agreed to the Convention of 1818 that set the Canadian border at 49 degrees north latitude and thereby made adjustments to the northern boundary of the Louisiana Territory.

Long before Europeans or Anglo-Americans ever visited the area, the Dakota region had become home to several Native American groups. The Arikara, Mandan, and, eventually, several bands of the Sioux, inhabited the Dakota plains. So central were the Sioux to the story

Water scarcity in some parts of the High Plains was a perennial problem. An oasis in the South Dakota Badlands provided welcomed relief and temporary respite in the forbidding landscape.

of the region that the name Dakota, the indigenous name of the Oglala Sioux, was adopted as the name for the entire region. In Sioux religion the Black Hills were seen as the navel of the earth, and Sioux mythology and folklore maintained that they had always lived in the region, which they viewed as the spiritual center of tribal identity. Archaeological evidence suggests that they migrated westward into the Dakota region in the mid-eighteenth century.

The indigenous inhabitants of the Dakota region maintained a sustainable existence by utilizing the natural resources of the land. They practiced intensive agriculture in those well-watered bottomlands that were adjacent to the region's rivers and streams. Farming by Indian peoples, usually the responsibility of women within the tribes, produced harvests of corn, beans, and squash that were essential dietary components among indigenous inhabitants. Men conducted the hunting that provided meat for the tribe as well as hides and bone that could be made into needed household items. The fall hunt was always one of the essential expeditions since the survival of the tribe through the winter months would depend upon the success of that event.

For centuries this pattern of life was undisturbed, but by the mid–eighteenth century, changes began to occur as European visitors arrived in the Dakota region. The elusive search for a Northwest Passage to the Pacific first brought Europeans to the region, but it was the trapping potential of the streams within what is now the state of South Dakota that impressed the early explorers. As early as 1743, an expedition from New France led by Pierre Gaultier de Varennes, Sieur de La Vérendrye, and his brothers Francois and Louis Joseph, traveled through much of the Missouri Valley and claimed it for France. The Vérendrye brothers made this claim as they buried an engraved lead marker at the site of modern-day Pierre.

Despite French interest in the region, the verities of war and international diplomacy would limit French control of the region, as tenuous as it was, to only two more decades after the initial visit by the Vérendrye brothers. During that time, a few French trappers operating out of Quebec and frontier outposts like Ste. Genevieve and Kaskaskia began to make expeditions into the Dakota country to ply their trade. These early trappers conducted business with the Arikara and Mandan, but once the Santee Sioux began to relocate into the Dakota region around 1750, many of the recently established trading connections became disrupted. For the fifty years that followed, most of the Missouri River trappers considered the Sioux to be a hostile presence since they restricted access to Arikara and Mandan villages that had shown an early eagerness to trade.

The Spanish acquired the Louisiana Territory from Spain in 1762 and held the region for nearly four decades. The Spanish showed very little interest in the far reaches of upper Louisiana—practically considering the region a wasteland—and concentrated their attention elsewhere within their empire. French trappers operating out of Ste. Genevieve, Kaskaskia, and the newly established town of St. Louis, continued to practice a somewhat sporadic trading relationship with the tribes of the upper Missouri basin.

The United States purchased the Louisiana Territory from France in 1803 and thereby acquired the vast wilderness that included much of the Dakota lands. By 1804, the U.S. government had authorized a federally funded expedition to explore the upper reaches of the Louisiana Territory and to travel overland to the Pacific Ocean. On both their trip to and from the Pacific, Lewis and Clark and their Corps of Discovery would traverse the region of South Dakota as they followed the path of the Missouri River. Along the route, the expedition would hold council with the Arikara and lived among the Mandan, in present-day North Dakota, during the winter of 1804–1805.

In the years following the Lewis and Clark Expedition only a limited number of trappers and traders from the United States lived and worked within the Dakota region. Since the fur trade concentrated primarily on the Rocky Mountain region, interest in the Dakota trade was of secondary importance. Additionally, since pioneer trails that ran westward did not travel through the Dakota region, there was very little pioneer settlement in the area. The first American settlement in South Dakota was not established until 1856, at Sioux Falls, and the Sioux Uprising in Minnesota (1862) would eventually lead to the abandonment of that frontier community.

Still, despite the lack of trappers working in the Dakota region or settlers establishing homesteads there, it was important to the U.S. government to keep the region secure since the Missouri River route connected the commercial interests of St. Louis-based companies with their trappers who lived and worked in the Rocky Mountain region. For this reason there were military outposts established in the region and negotiations with Indian tribes to remove them from lands adjacent to the Missouri River where they might harass river commerce.

The story of the Dakota region was largely determined by a series of measures taken by the U.S. government. In the Treaty of Fort Laramie (1851) the U.S. government attempted to hold a general council with major tribal groups of the upper plains to end intertribal conflict and to prevent depredations against overland or riverbound travelers. Delegations of Sioux, Crow, Cheyenne, and Arapaho attended the negotiations and ended up with a reduction in their lands. In 1861, the U.S. Congress created the Dakota Territory, defining the region as everything west of Minnesota to the Rocky Mountains. Generally, the creation of such an officially recognized territory was the prelude to white settlement of an area. In the Treaty of Fort Laramie (1868) the reservation land that had been guaranteed to the Sioux was further reduced, and they were promised the Black Hills of present-day South Dakota as a permanent home. That promise would also be broken within six years.

The discovery of gold along French Creek in the Black Hills in 1874 had consequences that would affect the history of both the Sioux Nation and the United States for many years to come. When the U.S. government ordered General George A. Custer and the Seventh Cavalry to remove the Sioux from the Black Hills land the Indians had been promised under treaty, the Sioux set into motion an organized campaign of resistance. Two years later, on the high plains of Montana at the Little Big Horn River, an army of Sioux warriors would exact punishment upon Custer and the Seventh Cavalry for the failure of the U.S. government to keep its treaty promises.

The success of the Sioux at Little Big Horn was a pyrrhic victory. Within a year the United States had seized the tribal lands of the Black Hills and limited the surviving members of the tribe to isolated reservation lands. The lure of gold in the Black Hills prompted speculators and settlers to flock to South Dakota in unprecedented numbers. Many flocked to mining camps in the Black Hills like Deadwood, which quickly became one of the most notorious settlements of the West. The 1880 census recorded 98,000 residents in the Dakota Territory, which then included both present-day North and South Dakota, and by 1890, the population had reached 349,000. The two states of North Dakota and South Dakota entered the Union on November 29, 1889.

—*Junius P. Rodriguez*

See also
Badlands; Black Hills; Mandan; Mandan, Fort; Oglala Sioux; Santee Sioux

For Further Reading
Robinson, Doane. 1904. *History of South Dakota*. Logansport: IN: B. F. Bowen.

SOUTH PASS

South Pass through the Rocky Mountains was the most celebrated route through the mountains to the Pacific Ocean. Geographically inauspicious, South Pass "is barely 7,500 feet high, and is situated in open valley of gentle slopes in either direction, with little to mark it as a crossing of the main chain of the Rocky mountains [*sic*]. But as a gateway between the Atlantic slope and the Pacific, it became the most noted pass in the mountains" (Chittenden, 1954).

There is much controversy over the question of who

was the principal discoverer of South Pass. There were claims that John Colter, of Yellowstone fame and the Lewis and Clark Expedition, discovered South Pass in 1807 or 1808. Others claimed that Robert Stuart and the returning Astorians crossed through South Pass from west to east in 1812. Thomas Fitzpatrick, a fur trader and mountain man, made the effective discovery in 1824. Fitzpatrick was associated with Jedediah S. Smith and was traveling with him. Some writers have given Smith the credit of "rediscovering" South Pass and the emigrant route.

Captain Benjamin L. E. Bonneville took wagons through the pass in 1832, that being the first time that wagons were used in the mountains. From the 1830s until after the Civil War, South Pass became the principal route over which passed the Oregon Trail.

John C. Fremont and Kit Carson used the South Pass route on their way to California in 1845. About the pass, Fremont wrote: "[T]he traveler, without being reminded of any change by toilsome ascents, suddenly finds himself on the waters which flow to the Pacific Ocean."

South Pass is located in the southwestern portion of the modern state of Wyoming, 947 miles west of Independence, Missouri (Fremont counted it as 962 miles).

—*Henry Goldman*

For Further Reading

Chittenden, Hiram Martin. 1954. *A History of the American Fur Trade of the Far West.* 2 vols. Stanford, CA: Academic Reprints; DeVoto, Bernard. 1947. *Across the Wide Missouri.* Boston: Houghton Mifflin Company; Unruh, John D., Jr. 1993. *The Plains Across: The Overland Emigrants and the Trans-Mississippi West, 1840–1860.* Urbana: University of Illinois Press; Utley, Robert M. 1997. *A Life Wild and Perilous: Mountain Men and the Paths to the Pacific.* New York: Henry Holt; Young, Otis E. 1955. *The West of Philip St. George Cooke, 1809–1895.* Glendale, CA: Arthur H. Clark.

SQUATTER'S RIGHTS

Once the territory acquired in the Louisiana Purchase became a part of the national domain, there were unique problems that arose in determining who had first purchase rights to land within the territory. The government's solution was defined by the notion of preemption, a concept more commonly identified by the phrase "squatter's rights."

By legal definition, the term "squatter's rights" refers to one's legal allowance to use the property of another in the absence of an attempt by the true owner to force eviction from the land. In some situations, this right can be converted into actual title to the property if state law recognizes the notion of adverse possession (that is, through actual, continuous, open occupancy) of the property in question. After the Louisiana Purchase (1803) was concluded, the windfall in new territory within the national domain proved to be a bonanza that many potential squatters were unable to ignore. In the eyes of many, the risk involved in staking a claim, albeit an illegal one, in such a land-rich environment was a chance worth taking. Many pioneers who settled upon the lands of the Louisiana Purchase territory were willing to hedge their bets as they skirted the land law policies of the day.

The U.S. Congress had always been reluctant to enact any legislation that gave official title to individuals who occupied and made improvements to land, because establishing such a precedent would legitimize the claims of those Indians and mixed-blood offspring to the lands of their ancestors. A special clause that was included in the Louisiana Purchase Treaty (1803) was designed to protect the rights of people who lived on the land at the time of the purchase and give land title to them under English common law. To protect these people, the Congress of the United States passed a series of measures leading up to the Preemption Act (1841), which gave official title to those settlers who lived on the land. This legislation gave rise to the concept of squatter's rights and was supported by many who subscribed to the notion that God had created the land for them and that they could legally hold it despite any contrary land law.

Squatters generally selected a location to their liking, constructed a rude cabin, cleared a few acres of brush, and sometimes planted crops. Their understanding was that this action was supposed to give them legal claim to the land, or at least, the right to sell their improvements, or trade their claim to the land. This differed from English common law principles, in which land ownership was established by buying it from the government or claiming it under law, living on it, improving it, and, after a period, patent could be obtained by paying a fee. This difference of interpretation resulted in much controversy and many ejection suits.

In many cases the individuals identified as squatters were not trying to avoid obtaining their land legally, but rather were trying to obtain it quickly. Quite often settlers were moving into territory before official government surveying was completed. This problem accelerated in the 1830s, when the number of pioneer families seeking Western lands exceeded the ability of government surveyors to complete their tasks. Since the true value of land was often determined by its ready access to water, squatters often sought property that was adjacent to creeks and other streams. It was the investment in time and improvements upon the land that squatters sought to protect, and the notion of "preemption"—the first right to buy the land—was viewed by many pioneers as a fair course of action.

There were several preemption measures passed by the Congress in the 1830s that dealt specifically with lands within the Louisiana Purchase territory. According to these measures, those squatters who had lived upon lands and made improvements to the same prior to February 19, 1816, were granted first purchase rights when those properties were offered for sale by the regional land office. The Preemption Act (1841) would later allow squatters to purchase up to 160 acres of land, provided they could document that they had lived upon the land for a period of years and made improvements to it. For an era that glorified the role of the common man as an integral element within the notion of Jacksonian Democracy, the concept of preemption, or squatter's rights, was both egalitarian and politically astute.

—*Junius P. Rodriguez*

See also
Preemption Act

For Further Reading

Gates, Paul W., and Robert W. Swenson. 1968. *History of Public Land Law Development*. Washington, DC: Public Land Law Review Commission; Hibbard, Benjamin H. 1924. *A History Public Land Policies*. New York: Macmillan; Rohrbough, Malcom J. 1968. *The Land Office Business: The Settlement and Administration of American Public Lands, 1789–1837*. New York: Oxford University Press; Treat, Payson, J. 1967. *The National Land System, 1785–1820*. New York: Russell and Russell; White, C. Albert. 1982. *A History of the Rectangular Survey System*. Washington, DC: Government Printing Office.

STODDARD, AMOS (1762–1813)

Amos Stoddard began his military career in the Continental Army during the Revolutionary War. In 1779 he joined the infantry under Baron Friedrich von Steuben and later transferred to the artillery. After serving for the duration of the war, Stoddard left the army. In the years following the war he studied law and worked as an assistant clerk for the Massachusetts Supreme Court. He also participated in the suppression of Shays' Rebellion in that state. He was admitted to the bar in 1793 and later served as a state legislator, but Stoddard soon returned to the military. He joined the militia in 1796 and accepted a commission two years later as captain of engineers and artillery in the U.S. Army. He was selected to handle the transfer of Upper Louisiana to the United States while on assignment in the West.

Acting as the agent and commissioner for France, the captain traveled to St. Louis and accepted from the Spanish governor formal possession of Upper Louisiana for the French government. The next day, March 10, 1804, he took control of the territory in the name of the U.S. government and assumed the position of civil and military commandant.

Stoddard had orders to conciliate and win the friendship of the people of Louisiana. Accordingly, he changed the government and administration of the territory as little as possible. The commandant left existing laws in place and reappointed local officials to their posts in several districts. Being fluent in French helped him gain the trust of the new Americans. He entertained members of leading families and did all he could to make the transfer go as smoothly as possible. Stoddard introduced the inhabitants to republicanism. He reassured them that their customs and manners would be respected, and that as citizens of the United States, their liberty, property, and religious freedom would all be protected. He also promised that Congress was making arrangements for a new territorial government and that the advantages of statehood were not far off. His efforts helped ensure the native residents' cooperation with the new government.

During his brief administration, Stoddard also organized militia units in numerous settlements, met with local Indian tribes, and investigated land claims. Quite successful in these duties, he was roundly praised for evenhandedness and sound judgment. On October 1, 1804, the government of the District of Louisiana assumed control of the territory, and Stoddard was relieved of his duties.

Assigned to Orleans Territory, Stoddard spent much of the next five years traveling throughout the district. He preserved archives, gathered records, and made careful observations regarding history, geography, and culture. At first he may have collected this information to satisfy his own curiosity, but with public interest in Louisiana growing he decided to publish a description of the region. *Sketches, Historical and Descriptive, of Louisiana* (1812) was one of the first popularly printed English-language accounts of Louisiana. Stoddard addressed the reservations that some Americans had concerning the acquisition of Louisiana and the issue of statehood. He praised the region's economic and agricultural potential and assured readers that the native inhabitants would eventually assimilate into U.S. culture and make loyal citizens. He also strongly encouraged emigration as the best way to develop the region. The book remains a valuable resource for historians of early Louisiana.

Stoddard served under General William Henry Harrison during the War of 1812. Having been promoted to deputy quartermaster shortly after the conflict began, he oversaw preparations for the defense of Fort Meigs on the Maumee River in Ohio and directed the artillery during British general Henry Procter's siege of the fort. Wounded by an exploding shell, he died of tetanus on May 11, 1813.

—*Christopher Dennis*

See also
Saint Louis; Orleans, Territory of

For Further Reading

Houck, Louis. 1908. *A History of Missouri from the Earliest Explorations and Settlements until the Admission of the State into the Union*, vol. 2. Chicago: R. R. Donnelly & Sons; Jacobs, James Ripley. 1947. *The Beginning of the U.S. Army, 1783–1812*. Princeton: Princeton University Press; Newton, Craig A., and James M. Newton. 1966. "Not an Enemy of Cession Will Remain." *Louisiana Studies* 5: 37–49; Stoddard, Amos. 1973. *Sketches, Historical and Descriptive, of Louisiana*. New York: AMS Press.

TALLEYRAND-PERIGORD, CHARLES MAURICE DE (1754–1838)

On April 11, 1803, the French foreign minister, Charles Maurice de Talleyrand, opened negotiations for the sale of Louisiana to the United States.

The life of Charles Maurice de Talleyrand coincides with one of the most turbulent periods in the history of the Western world. Although Talleyrand's life was closely linked to the many revolutionary changes taking place on the French political landscape, he remained nonetheless a product of the *ancien regime.* The eldest son of minor Parisian nobility, Talleyrand received an adequate education before embarking on a notorious career in the Roman Catholic Church. Despite frequent bouts of atheism and a tendency to espouse revolutionary doctrine, he was made Bishop of Autun in 1788. Soon after his meteoric rise to the rank of bishop, Talleyrand forswore religion for a career in the French diplomatic corps. Following stints in both Great Britain and the United States, he returned to France during the Directory and served as foreign minister (1797–1799). In recognition of both his abilities and his support during the coup d'état of Brumaire, First Consul Napoleon Bonaparte maintained Talleyrand's services as foreign minister under the Consulate government. As foreign minister, Talleyrand was responsible for carrying out Napoleon's vision for the future of France in the New World. The U.S. ambassador, Robert Livingston, once summed up the Napoleonic government in an 1802 letter to James Madison: "There never was a government in which less could be done by negotiation than here. There are no people, no legislature, no counsellors. One man is everything. He seldom asks advice, and never hears it unasked. His ministers are mere clerks; and his legislature and counsellors parade officers." Fortunately, the new foreign minister shared Napoleon's views on Louisiana—that is, France must make every effort to return to the Mississippi Valley or else risk leaving the world stage to the British and Americans. As foreign minister for the Directory government, Talleyrand failed in his early attempts to return North America to France by acquiring the Louisiana Territory from Spain. Under the Consulate, however, Talleyrand's efforts were rewarded as France regained Louisiana through the Treaty of San Ildefonso on October 1, 1800.

The return of Louisiana to French control marked a dramatic shift in consular foreign policy. The re-establishment of France on the Mississippi River not only stimulated a renewed French presence in North America but also energized Napoleon to pursue an ambitious policy toward the entire Caribbean region. To that end, Talleyrand worked to gather area support by offering "only sentiments of friendship for the United States" and by forming loose alliances with both the area Spanish and Native American tribes. The foreign minister realized that Bonaparte's plan to integrate the Louisiana Territory and Caribbean possessions into a New World empire depended on: the passivity of the United States, a temporary peace with Great Britain, and the pacification of Caribbean revolutionaries. These conditions however, proved impossible to achieve. Subsequent defeats at the hands of rebellious Caribbean slaves forced France to abandon the island of Hispaniola in 1802. The French defeat in the Caribbean provided an opportunity for both the United States and Great Britain to pursue more aggressive foreign policies toward French interests in North America. This effectively meant the end of all French colonial ventures in North America, since the loss of Saint Domingo made Louisiana virtually impossible to maintain.

After learning in 1803 that another war with Great Britain was a virtual certainty and that the U.S. Senate was contemplating war against France, the first consul instructed Talleyrand to sell the Louisiana Territory to the United States. In an abrupt turn of fortunes, Talleyrand made the best of a potentially disastrous situation by placating the Americans and denying the British the opportunity to invade the Louisiana Territory. Ultimately it was Talleyrand working at the behest of the first consul that accomplished the sale of Louisiana. In his typically Machiavellian style, Talleyrand successfully used the sale of Louisiana to restore the depleted French treasury with U.S. currency, to rehabilitate the French image in the United States, and to place Great Britain in the role of potential enemy of the United States.

—*Christopher Blackburn*

For Further Reading

Brinton, Crane. 1963. *The Lives of Talleyrand.* New York:

Norton; Lyon, E. Wilson. 1974. *Louisiana in French Diplomacy 1759–1804*. Norman: University of Oklahoma Press; Lyon, E. Wilson. 1942. *The Man Who Sold Louisiana: The Career of Francois Barbe-Marbois*. Norman: University of Oklahoma Press.

TALLMADGE AMENDMENT

The Louisiana Purchase of 1803 had been opposed by Northern Federalists, and they would later oppose the admission of Louisiana as a state in April 1812. Sectional concern over the growth of the South, and by extension, slavery, would explode when Missouri, part of the Louisiana Purchase that had been organized as a territory in 1817, applied for admission to the Union as a slave state in January 1819. John Scott, the Missouri congressional territorial delegate, argued that the third article of the Louisiana Purchase Treaty prevented Congress from prohibiting slavery in any state that might be carved out of the territory. Northern concern that slavery would now cross the Mississippi and contaminate the West prompted James Tallmadge (1778–1853), a one-term New York Republican congressman, to propose his amendment in two clauses on February 13, 1819.

The son of a Revolutionary patriot, James Tallmadge had served as a brigadier general of New York militia in the War of 1812. Elected to Congress in June 1817, he was considered by his peers as able but something of an opportunist. He had helped the passage of the New York Emancipation Act that would free all slaves within the state ten years hence. In November 1818, he had voiced concern in Congress that the new state constitution of Illinois had not expressly prohibited slavery in the state, and he demanded that Congress should scrupulously guard against slavery's passing into territory where it had the power to prevent its entrance. Furthermore, like many other Northern politicians, Tallmadge was concerned with Article 1, Section 2 of the Constitution, the Three-fifths Clause, which gave the South disproportionate congressional representation, fourteen extra presidential electors, and, by extension, too dominant an influence in the Republican Party itself.

The first clause of his amendment barred the future importation of slaves into Missouri, thus keeping the state's black population limited to approximately ten thousand, about 16 percent of the population. Tallmadge hoped that without an increasing black population the new state, like New York itself, would eventually confront the need for emancipation. The second clause of the amendment, he hoped, would create just such a situation: it proposed the postnatal emancipation of all Missouri slaves born after 1819 at the age of twenty-five. In a moderate emancipation measure, one that would not free any slave born before 1819 nor any slave at all before 1844, the Tallmadge Amendment challenged the Southern belief that the states, and not Congress, should decide the future of slavery.

This amendment to the Missouri State Bill passed the House by a vote of 87 to 76, but it was defeated in the Senate by 22 to 16, a number of Northern senators allying themselves with the South. In the same congressional session similar antislavery requirements, attached to a bill to organize the Arkansas territory, which also later encompassed the state of Oklahoma, were defeated in the House by a vote of 89 to 87, as well as in the Senate by 19 to 14. With the question of Missouri undecided, Congress adjourned in March 1819, and the question of slavery was hotly debated in the nation. Led by South Carolina spokesmen, many Southerners for the first time defended slavery as a positive, moral good, and many Northerners began to announce publicly the belief that it was a national shame.

When Congress reconvened, a final compromise to the growing crisis was successfully suggested by Senator Jesse B. Thomas of Illinois (formerly of Maryland). On February 16, 1820, he moved that the admission of Maine to the Union be linked with Missouri and that the linkage bill ignore the previous vote on the Tallmadge Amendment. This would maintain the sectional balance in the Senate, and, to pacify Northern opinion, he further suggested the passage of a bill outlawing slavery in the Louisiana Purchase north of 36 degrees 30 minutes, the southern state line of Missouri. This, at least, it was argued, would secure the admission of Missouri as a slave state, and, if the vast bulk of the Louisiana Purchase were to be closed to slavery, the South could at least look toward the eventual admission of both Arkansas and Oklahoma as slave states. The linked compromise bills passed the Senate by a vote of 24 to 20. In the House of Representatives, Henry Clay skillfully marshaled the forces of compromise to pass each bill separately, and Missouri was admitted to the Union without the restrictive Tallmadge Amendment conditions. Although the amendment had failed to restrict slavery in Missouri, it had prompted Congress to close the vast part of the Louisiana Purchase north of 36 degrees 30 minutes to its extension.

Tallmadge had refused to run for re-election in 1818, and he returned to New York, where he was unsuccessful in a bid for a state senate seat in 1819. Becoming part of the Tammany faction in New York City, he briefly served as lieutenant governor in 1825–1826 but never regained the national prominence he had enjoyed over the Tallmadge Amendment. He died in New York City in September 1853.

—*Rory T. Cornish*

See also

Missouri; Missouri Compromise; Slavery

For Further Reading

Freehling, William W. 1990. *The Road to Disunion: Secessionists at Bay, 1776–1854*. New York: Oxford University Press; Moore, Glover. 1953. *The Missouri Controversy,*

1819–1821. Louisville: University of Kentucky Press; Talmadge, Arthur. 1909. *The Talmadge, Tallmadge and Talmage Genealogy*. New York: Grafton Press.

TAOS

Surrounded by the Sangre de Cristo Mountains approximately seventy miles north of Santa Fe, Taos was the northernmost settlement in Spain's North American empire at the time of the Louisiana Purchase. The original inhabitants of the area, the Tiwa Indians, descended from the Anasazi culture, and they lived in the multilevel adobe structure known as Taos Pueblo. Indeed, Taos Pueblo has been continuously settled for eight centuries, and the pueblo is the oldest continually inhabited structure in the United States. The Spanish first arrived in the area when Francisco Vasquez Coronado reached the pueblo in 1540 while searching for the Cities of Gold, and Spanish settlement began in 1598 with the arrival of Don Juan de Oñate. The Spanish infused Taos with much of their own culture. The realms of art, architecture, and religion are the most obvious examples, but the Spanish also brought less obvious aspects of their civilization, such as irrigation and government.

Because of its extreme northern position in the Spanish empire, Taos became an important trading center in the eighteenth century. The annual Taos Fair attracted a variety of traders. Several Native American tribes, French fur trappers, and even government officials from Santa Fe would attend. These fairs occurred every July, and traders bartered for all sorts of items, ranging from horses and guns to furs and clothing. With the establishment of permanent stores near the beginning of the nineteenth century, the huge annual fairs stopped, but Taos remained an important trading center. Caravans destined for Santa Fe, Chihuahua, and eventually Mexico City regularly headed southward out of Taos.

The Louisiana Purchase did little to change the role of Taos at first. Since 1723, Spain had denied New Mexico the right to trade with the United States. Certainly, American merchants still attempted to trade and sent expeditions, and the expedition of Baptiste La Lande serves as an example for Taos. La Lande was a French Canadian sent by Illinois merchants to New Mexico in 1804. He sold his goods for a handsome profit upon reaching the Spanish territory, but the Spanish government refused to allow him to leave. Apparently, keeping the profits and remaining in New Mexico did not prove much of a dilemma for La Lande, and he eventually married and settled in Taos as one of its wealthier residents.

When Mexico claimed independence from Spain in 1821, the trade situation quickly changed. The Mexican government ended the prohibition on trade, and the Santa Fe Trail subsequently connected Santa Fe with Missouri. Traders in covered wagons moved in and out of Santa Fe, but Taos became the center of the fur trade and a headquarters for the mountain men. The most famous of these mountain men residents was Christopher "Kit" Carson, who settled in Taos from 1826 until his death in 1868. Taos provided a convenient trading post where the trappers could unload their goods, and merchants would then carry those goods down to Santa Fe before transporting them east.

—John K. Franklin

See also

Carson, Christopher "Kit"; New Mexico; Santa Fe Trail

For Further Reading

Baptista Pino, Don Pedro. 1995. *The Exposition on the Province of New Mexico, 1812*. Translated and edited by Adrian Bustamante and Marc Simmons. Santa Fe: University of New Mexico Press; Grant, Blanche C. 1934. *When Old Trails Were New: The Story of Taos*. New York: Press of the Pioneers.

TAYLOR AMENDMENT

Introduced on January 26, 1820, the Taylor Amendment was part of the political debate that resulted in the Missouri Compromise (1820). Proposed by Congressman John W. Taylor of New York, the amendment declared that in the new state of Missouri "there shall be neither slavery nor involuntary servitude." This amendment was similar to the Tallmadge Amendment of the previous Congress, which had passed the House but failed in the Senate. The Senate also rejected the Taylor Amendment, so Illinois senator Jesse B. Thomas offered another alternative amendment instead. The Thomas Amendment forbade the extension of slavery to that part of the Louisiana Purchase above 36 degrees 30 minutes north latitude, except in Missouri.

The Missouri Compromise was possible because of the application of Maine for admission as a new state. A conference committee between the House and the Senate chose not to reconcile the differences between the Taylor and Thomas Amendments, but reported bills that admitted both Maine and Missouri to the Union as states. The Thomas Amendment was part of the Missouri statehood legislation, which in essence rendered it a slave state. With Maine as a free state, the political balance of power between North and South would be maintained (for a time).

Although the Taylor Amendment was a stand against the spread of slavery in the land composing the Louisiana Territory, it nevertheless endorsed the notion that slaves are property. Thus there was a clause in the amendment declaring that slave fugitives may be lawfully reclaimed in Missouri even though it would have been a free state.

Had it passed, the Taylor Amendment would have amended the fourth section of the Missouri Statehood bill to read as follows: "And shall ordain and establish that there shall be neither slavery nor involuntary servitude in the said State, otherwise than in the punishment of crimes, whereof the party shall have been duly convicted: *Provided, always,* That any person escaping into the same, from whom labor or service is lawfully claimed in any other State, such fugitive may be lawfully reclaimed, and conveyed to the person claiming his or her labor or service as aforesaid: *And provided, also,* That the said provision shall not be construed to alter the condition or civil rights of any person now held to service or labor in the said Territory" (Commager, 1973).

Ten months after the introduction of his amendment, John W. Taylor was chosen to serve as speaker of the House of Representatives. He replaced the absent Henry Clay and served in that position during the period when the Missouri Compromise was passed.

—Roger Chapman

See also
Missouri Compromise; Slavery; Tallmadge Amendment

For Further Reading
Commager, Henry Steele, ed. 1973. *Documents of American History,* vol. 1. Englewood Cliffs, NJ: Prentice-Hall; Fehrenbacher, Don E. 1995. *Sectional Crisis and Southern Constitutionalism.* Baton Rouge: Louisiana University State Press.

TERRITORY OF . . .

***See* individual territories**

TERTIUM QUIDS

Tertium Quid is a Latin term, sometimes used as an epithet, signifying a "third something" between the Federalists and Republicans. It was first commonly used in the United States to designate a political faction of the Republican Party in Pennsylvania that officially called itself the Society of Constitutional Republicans. The Pennsylvania *Quids* emerged around 1804 as united Federalist and Republican supporters of Republican governor Thomas McKean, who was opposed by the majority faction within his own party. The Pennsylvania *Quids* were liberal, democratic capitalists who feared political and social convulsion. A group of Federalists and Republicans united under the name *Tertium Quids* in New York as well, to support Morgan Lewis for governor in 1807 against the candidate of the majority of the Republican Party, DeWitt Clinton.

However, the name *Tertium Quids* is most frequently used to refer to the small, informal group of conservative, mostly Southern, Old Republicans who were followers of John Randolph of Roanoke. These Old Republicans had little in common with the *Quids* in New York and Pennsylvania. Although few in number and consisting chiefly of North Carolinians and Virginians, Randolph's faction included some of the ablest political leadership in the nation. In addition to Randolph, who was considered far and away the best orator in the House, the *Quids* counted among their number Speaker of the House Nathaniel Macon and Richard Stanford of North Carolina, Joseph Bryan and Thomas Spalding of Georgia, and Joseph Hopper Nicholoson of Maryland.

In general, Randolph's *Tertium Quids* favored the old opposition ideals of the Republican Party before it took over the reigns of government following Jefferson's election in the Revolution of 1800. The *Tertium Quids* were opposition men, faithful adherents to the Jeffersonian "Principles of '98." They felt that these ideals of strict constructionism, states' rights, agrarianism, economy in government, and avoidance of foreign entanglements were being eroded by electoral success and that the administration and the majority of Republicans in Congress were too willing to compromise their out-of-power principles for the sake of political expediency or personal aggrandizement. The *Quids* believed that the chief culprit in the Republican declension was James Madison.

The decisive issue in splitting the *Tertium Quids* from the administration and the Republican majority was the Jefferson administration's planned acquisition of West Florida. The status of Spanish-ruled West Florida was left intentionally unclear in the treaty for the purchase of Louisiana. Jefferson and Secretary of State James Madison had insisted since 1803 that Louisiana had always included this strip of land along the Gulf of Mexico, but in 1804 France denied that West Florida had been sold to the United States. To settle the issue without resorting to war, Jefferson and his secretary of state determined in December 1805 to offer France $2 million in return for recognition of the U.S. claim to West Florida.

As far as Randolph was concerned, the offer of $2 million was the same sort of bribery that made the XYZ Affair so obnoxious. He was certain that it was a symptom of Federalist corruption and decaying Republican morals. Randolph and his followers vociferously denounced Madison and the bribery scheme, and succeeded in delaying but were unable to prevent passage of the Two Million Dollar Bill by administration supporters in Congress in February 1806. However, by delaying and publicizing the measure, they were able to impact the negotiations with France and thereby prevent the purchase of West Florida.

In 1808 the *Tertium Quids* unsuccessfully supported James Monroe for the presidency over James Madison. By 1810 the schism within the Republican Party was largely healed. Although the *Tertium Quids* had failed to elect Monroe in 1808, failed to prevent passage of the "Two Million Act" in 1806, and did not form a lasting third party, their influence was felt long after 1810. Their schism gave voice to a strong conservative undercurrent among Southern Republicans that would continue to grow in power and influence throughout the antebellum years.

—*Sean R. Busick*

See also
Randolph, John
For Further Reading
Cunningham, Noble E., Jr. 1963. "Who Were the Quids?" *Mississippi Valley Historical Review* 50: 252–263; Risjord, Norman K. 1965. *The Old Republicans: Southern Conservatism in the Age of Jefferson.* New York: Columbia University Press; Shankman, Andrew. 1999. "Malcontents and Tertium Quids: The Battle to Define Democracy in Jeffersonian Pennsylvania." *Journal of the Early Republic* 19: 43–72.

TEXAS

After the United States purchased the Louisiana Territory from France in 1803, there arose a controversy between the United States and Spain over what constituted the western boundary of the purchased lands with regard to Spanish Texas. The Spanish maintained that Texas, being a sovereign province of the colony of Mexico, was inviolable terrain—that it could not be included, in all or in part, in any real estate transfer conducted between the United States and France. Some individuals within the United States believed that a portion of Texas might well have been a part of the Louisiana Purchase, since the Red River was a tributary of the Mississippi River system. Since the French had historically defined Louisiana according to Robert Cavelier, Sieur de LaSalle's 1682 claim that the territory was defined by the drainage basin of the Mississippi River, there was some merit in the U.S. position. What weakened the position was the extravagant claim by some that all of Texas was part of the Louisiana Purchase territory.

The Spanish claim to Texas was based upon the doctrine of discovery, which was historically solid, but Spain's actual level of possession (or occupancy) of the province was quite tenuous. It was for this reason that the Spanish authorities in Mexico were always fearful that a foreign power might have designs upon the sparsely populated and weakly defended province of Texas. For example, when the French explorer LaSalle established Fort St. Louis at Matagorda Bay in 1685, the Spanish responded to the perceived threat by beginning construction of *El Camino Real* (the King's Highway), to link the isolated missions and presidios of eastern Texas with the seat of vice-royal authority in Mexico City. The Camino Real also symbolized Spanish authority to the various Native American groups, including the Caddo and the Commanche, who inhabited portions of eastern Texas.

Although the threat from LaSalle's colony was short-lived, the Spanish kept a guarded eye on the French colony of Louisiana, which was first established in 1699 on the central Gulf Coast. Fortunately for the Spanish, the early Louisiana colony was not in a position whereby it could threaten Texas. Spanish anxiety lessened after the Treaty of Utrecht (1713) was signed, officially ending the War of the Spanish Succession, as Bourbon monarchs who were cousins sat upon the thrones of France and Spain. When the French monarch ceded the Louisiana Territory to his Spanish cousin in 1762, fears of a Louisiana-based seizure of Texas vanished, since the Spanish now possessed the two contiguous territories. Even after the United States became an independent nation in the Treaty of Paris (1783), the Spanish authorities in Mexico City felt confident that Texas remained safe because they believed that the trans-Appalachian West was too vast to permit rapid expansion by the Americans.

Although the French and Spanish Bourbons had a working relationship, they did not completely trust each other. When the French explorer St. Denis established a settlement in northwestern Louisiana at Natchitoches on the Red River, the Spanish immediately responded in kind. The community of Los Adaes was created by the Spanish just a few miles west of Natchitoches, and this new outpost—at the easternmost extremity of Texas (in present-day Louisiana)—was made to be the capital of Texas and Couhila. For the century that followed, the boundary line between Louisiana and Texas would be an amorphous one, and the borderlands region assumed an atmosphere of frontier anarchy that characterized its status as disputed turf.

The Spanish would soon learn that they had made a strategic mistake by incorrectly predicting the rapidity of American expansion into the trans-Appalachian West. By being in possession of New Orleans, the Spanish found themselves bedeviled by the requests of U.S. authorities to permit Western frontiersmen to use the Mississippi River and to warehouse their goods at New Orleans. Much of the early diplomacy between the United States and Spain centered upon this question, and the issue remained a key one until the time of the retrocession of Louisiana from Spain back to France in 1800. In the end, it would be U.S. persistence on this question that would encourage President Thomas Jefferson to begin the negotiations with France in 1803 that resulted in the Louisiana Purchase.

Even before the United States acquired the Louisiana Territory, a series of filibustering expeditions had begun to take place as men of destiny conducted themselves into Texas, and that pattern continued after the United States acquired Louisiana. Philip Nolan used the pretext of being a horse trader when he entered Texas on four occasions from 1791 to 1801 to purchase mustangs, but Spanish authorities did not believe his story. Many believe that, shortly after the Louisiana Purchase was concluded, General James Wilkinson and former vice president Aaron Burr engaged in a conspiracy that may have involved the conquest of Texas. Much more serious was the effort by Jose Bernardo Gutierrez and William

Augustus Magee, who in 1812 used the instability created by the failed Hidalgo Revolt (1810) led by Father Miguel Hidalgo y Costilla as the opportune time to enter Texas with a private army of 130 men. In 1819, James Long led an expedition inspired by Natchez planters who wanted to seize Texas, but the expedition ended in failure and Long's execution by Mexican authorities.

In the Adams-Onís Treaty (1819), the United States and Spain settled some of the diplomatic questions that had lingered for years between the two nations. Two particular points of the treaty related to Texas. The United States gave up any right to claim Texas as having been part of the Louisiana Purchase territory. In exchange, the Spanish gave up their claim to the Oregon Country and also agreed that the Sabine River would serve as the boundary between Louisiana and Texas.

By 1821, Spanish rule in Mexico had come to a bloodless end as a new cadre of leaders who were Mexican creole gentry began to govern the vast territory that had formerly been Spanish Mexico. One of the greatest challenges that the new leaders of Mexico faced was how they might strengthen their authority in the more sparsely populated areas like Texas. Mexican leaders were also interested in fiscal policies that might generate revenue to offset an inherited deficit. The idea of encouraging immigration to Texas coupled with the sale of land in that province seemed to be the ideal answer. Mexican authorities began to issue contracts to individuals, known as *empresarios,* who promised to serve as agents and deliver a prescribed number of individuals or families for resettlement in Texas. Moses Austin may be one of the most famous of those immigration brokers in all of Texas history.

A large number of U.S. citizens immigrated to Texas in the 1820s, as did many Europeans who hoped to make a new life for themselves in Texas. On occasion one could purchase prime farmland in eastern Texas at the price of ten cents per acre, while the cheapest price that one might pay for comparable property in the United States at the time was $1.25 per acre. In the eyes of small farmers in the United States, Texas was a multiplication table that could generate great wealth for those who simply had the determination to relocate and work hard. For many who hoped to become large planters, such a dream was possible only on eastern Texas farmland.

The relationship between the Mexican authorities and the new emigrant guests in Texas began to unravel after a decade. In 1829, Mexico abolished slavery. For those who had moved to Texas in the hope of becoming planters, and slave owners, the 1829 law seemed to threaten their livelihood as well as their dreams. By 1830, Mexican officials halted further immigration into Texas, as they began to suspect that the burgeoning immigrant population might harbor too much of an independent spirit. Since the settlers in Texas were largely U.S. citizens who had moved into the Mexican province, officials in Mexico City feared that the United States might find a way to annex Texas should the foreign nationals living in Texas rise in rebellion.

Skirmishes began early in Texas—well before the Texas Revolution (1835–1836). The first blood was shed on June 26, 1832, when Mexicans under Domingo de Ugartechea were forced to surrender because they ran out of ammunition. Texan residents used the political system as well to try to redress their grievances, but conventions that were held in 1832 and again in 1833 did not achieve satisfactory outcomes. By October 2, 1835, when Texans turned back a group of Mexican cavalry in the Battle of Gonzales, a true revolution had begun.

Texans eventually won their independence from Mexican authority. The conflict included setbacks that only served to strengthen the resolve of the Texans. After a group of Texans under the command of Col. William B. Travis died when an overwhelming Mexican force stormed the Alamo in San Antonio on March 6, 1836, the stirring cry "Remember the Alamo" challenged Texans to continue the struggle. Even after nearly four hundred Texans were massacred at Goliad on March 27, 1836, the rebels pressed forward with their cause. Finally, at the Battle of San Jacinto, near modern-day Houston, the Texans under General Sam Houston defeated Mexican forces on April 21, 1836, and effectively won their independence.

From 1836 to 1845 the Republic of Texas was an independent nation. Every U.S. president from Andrew Jackson through John Tyler wrestled with the question of whether or not to annex Texas to the United States. Tyler's decision to annex Texas, an action taken during the final days of his administration, set the stage for an eventual war with Mexico that occurred during the administration of President James K. Polk.

—Junius P. Rodriguez

See also

Camino Real, El; Gutierrez-Magee Expedition; Los Adaes; Nacogdoches; Nolan, Philip; Transcontinental Treaty

For Further Reading

Calvert, Robert A., and Arnoldo DeLeon. 1996. *The History of Texas.* Wheeling, IL: Harlan Davidson; Richardson, Rupert N., Ernest Wallace, and Adrian Anderson. 1997. *Texas, The Lone Star State.* Upper Saddle River, NJ: Prentice Hall; Weber, David J. 1992. *The Spanish Frontier in North America.* New Haven: Yale University Press.

TEXTBOOKS: THE LOUISIANA PURCHASE IN HIGH SCHOOL TEXTBOOKS

High school history textbooks in the United States present the Louisiana Purchase in a vacuum, as if the United States really bought the land from France. A recent example, *The American Journey* by Joyce Appleby, Alan Brinkley, and James

McPherson, echoes earlier textbooks: "With the signing of the treaty, the size of the United States doubled." Of the fifteen textbooks surveyed for this article, not one points out that the Louisiana Territory was not France's to sell—it was Indian land. The French never consulted with native owners before selling it; Native Americans did not even know of the sale. If they had, they would have been outraged.

Of course, France did not really sell Louisiana for $15 million. Charles Maurice de Talleyrand, France's foreign minister, could not even tell the U.S. negotiators its boundaries. France merely sold *its claim* to the land. To put it another way, the United States really bought from France the right to deal with the Native American peoples in the area, and the concession from the French not to do so.

The United States was still paying Native American tribes for Louisiana throughout the nineteenth century. But the United States was also fighting them for it: the *Army Almanac* lists more than fifty Indian wars in the Louisiana Purchase territory from 1819 to 1890. To treat France as the seller, as all our textbooks do, is Eurocentric.

Eurocentrism also prevails in the maps of the Louisiana Purchase included in almost every textbook. Native Americans are invisible; the maps imply that the United States bought vacant land from the French. A good example of this can be seen in the map of the Louisiana Purchase that appears in John Garraty's *American History.* Like the maps in fourteen other high school textbooks surveyed, it shows only European occupiers of North America. Most of these Louisiana Purchase maps also show the Lewis and Clark Expedition route. Although Lewis and Clark made their way from Indian nation to Indian nation during their stirring two-year trek, the maps again make American Indians invisible. During the winter of 1804–1805 the expedition stayed with the Mandans in what is now North Dakota, but the Mandans disappear, replaced by Fort Mandan. The next winter, Lewis and Clark camped near the Clatsops, who likewise disappear in favor of Fort Clatsop. Thus the Lewis and Clark Expedition is transformed into a "man against the elements" narrative, like Shackleton at the South Pole, instead of the exercise in intergroup relations that it was.

Why was France willing to sell its claims to this huge area? Partly because Haitians had just defeated the French and declared independence. Shortly after taking office in 1801, Thomas Jefferson reversed U.S. policy toward Haiti and secretly gave France the go-ahead to reconquer the island. In so doing, the United States not only betrayed its own revolutionary heritage, it also acted against its own self-interest. For if France had indeed been able to retake Haiti, Napoleon would have maintained his dream of an American empire. But the Haitian Revolution scared planters in the United States, including Jefferson. They thought it might inspire slave revolts here (which it did). Haiti won despite the U.S. change of policy, and eight of the fifteen textbooks surveyed do mention how Haitian resistance led France to sell its claim to Louisiana to the United States. None tells of Jefferson's reversal in the Haitian Revolution, however. Indeed, few textbooks ever make any connection between slavery and U.S. foreign policy.

When it comes to how the United States took Louisiana, most textbooks do include the Plains Wars, especially the Battle of the Little Bighorn (1876), Geronimo's Apache War (1885), and the Wounded Knee massacre (1890). The first and last of these took place in Louisiana Purchase land. But these incidents were late mopping-up operations. *The American People,* by Gary Nash et al., tells how white pressure increased war among native groups in the 1840s in Louisiana Purchase land. *Life and Liberty,* a textbook intended for pre–high schoolers or slower readers, tells how America's westward movement triggered alcoholism and disease. It also pays attention to the Dakota Uprising (1862), which killed more whites than any other Indian war west of the Mississippi, and the Colorado conflicts that included the Sand Creek Massacre (1864). Joy Hakim's *A History of US,* a maverick textbook intended for pre–high schoolers, includes a map of the West, particularly focusing on Louisiana Purchase land, showing "when lands were ceded or taken." But even these three books do not allow their superior handling of Indian issues in Louisiana Purchase land to inform their earlier treatment of the purchase itself.

Instead of analyzing the importance of the Louisiana Purchase to conflict between whites and natives, the issue on which textbooks dwell lay within the mind of Thomas Jefferson: "Once again the two Jeffersons wrestled with each other in private: the theorist and former strict constructionist versus the realist and public official," in the words of *The American Pageant,* by Thomas Bailey and David M. Kennedy. Jefferson did question whether his act was constitutional, but later he agonized whether the acquisition would lead to civil war over the expansion of slavery, including his famous "fire bell in the night" letter.

That is the other crucial conflict occasioned by the Louisiana Purchase: between pro- and antislavery Americans. The purchase made more salient the issue of whether slavery should expand. Since the impact of the Civil Rights movement in about 1970, textbooks treat slavery and the Civil War much more accurately. They now admit that slavery and its expansion was the primary cause of the conflict. Before 1970 many textbooks had held that almost anything else—differences over tariffs and internal improvements, blundering politicians, economic conflict between the agrarian South and the industrial North—caused the war.

Under those interpretations, the Louisiana Purchase was unrelated to this conflict. Although recent textbooks do not refer to the Louisiana Purchase as a cause of the war, they do make the purchase the first in a series, followed by the Missouri Compromise, the independence of

Texas, the Mexican War and Wilmot Proviso, the Compromise of 1850, the Kansas-Nebraska Act, and the Dred Scott decision. Authors note that the Missouri Compromise permitted slavery in Missouri while outlawing it from the rest of the Louisiana Purchase that lay north of 36 degrees 30 minutes north latitude. Beginning with the purchase itself, each step gave slave owners more room to expand and more national legitimacy. As the series went on, Northerners and Southerners were invited to infer that slavery was becoming national, making freedom sectional. The result was the growth of the Republican Party, emphasizing "free soil" in the West, and the triumph of the Southern "Fire Eaters" during the 1850s. Viewed from 1861 (or today), the conflict looks inevitable, triggered initially by the expansion of the United States, in turn triggered by the Louisiana Purchase.

—*James W. Loewen*

36 DEGREES 30 MINUTES NORTH LATITUDE

The boundary established at 36 degrees 30 minutes north latitude, which separated Missouri (except for the so-called boot heel region) from the Arkansas Territory, became one of the most significant borders within the United States during the antebellum era. Through the Missouri Compromise (1820), this line of demarcation limited slavery's expansion in the Louisiana Purchase territory to points south of the line, while lands above it became free territory that prohibited slavery. Within the Louisiana Purchase territory, the Missouri Compromise allowed slavery to exist only above the line of 36 degrees 30 minutes north latitude in Missouri, which was admitted to the Union as the twenty-second state in 1821. The decision issued by the U.S. Supreme Court in the *Dred Scott v. Sandford* (1857) case effectively nullified the portion of the Missouri Compromise that had created the line of demarcation between slave and free territory.

From the point of its inception in the Missouri Compromise, the line of 36 degrees 30 minutes north latitude by design would have allowed slavery to expand only into the territory that eventually formed the states of Arkansas and Oklahoma. This restriction, coupled with the South's desire for additional territory where cotton and slavery might expand, encouraged Southern interest in Texas and other lands of the Southwest that belonged to Mexico. When the United States and Mexico went to war in 1846, Congressman David Wilmot of Pennsylvania introduced an unsuccessful resolution (known as the Wilmot Proviso) that sought to prohibit the expansion of slavery into any territory that might be acquired from Mexico. In 1848, after the United States defeated Mexico and acquired the huge Mexican Cession territory in the Treaty of Guadalupe Hidalgo, some Northern political leaders hoped that the north latitude boundary of 36 degrees 30 minutes might be extended westward to the Pacific Ocean.

By 1848, Northern Democrats like Lewis Cass of Michigan and Stephen A. Douglas of Illinois believed that the answer to the slavery controversy could be settled best not by an inflexible line of demarcation, but rather by an ingenious new concept, which they termed popular sovereignty. According to this new policy, the people of a territory seeking statehood would have the opportunity to vote for or against slavery in a popular referendum. The Kansas-Nebraska Act (1854), which included a specific provision for popular sovereignty, ran counter to the decision reached in the Missouri Compromise by allowing the possibility that slavery might become established in lands north of 36 degrees 30 minutes north latitude if such were the will expressed by territorial residents. The Kansas-Nebraska Act thus reignited the largely sectional debate over slavery's expansion into the territories, and in so doing, furthered the resolve of the Free Soil movement in the United States, inspired the creation of the Republican Party, and led the nation, many would argue, much closer to civil war.

Protests for and against the line of 36 degrees 30 minutes north latitude became moot in 1857 when the Supreme Court ruled that slavery could exist anywhere within the United States. More than an ordinary boundary between states, the line of 36 degrees 30 minutes north latitude assumed a much larger meaning in the sectional debate over slavery's expansion into the territories.

—*Junius P. Rodriguez*

See also
Kansas-Nebraska Act; Missouri Compromise; Popular Sovereignty; Slavery; Tallmadge Amendment; Taylor Amendment

For Further Reading

Fehrenbacher, Don E. 1995. *Sectional Crisis and Southern Constitutionalism.* Baton Rouge: Louisiana State University Press; Ray, Perley Orman. 1909. *Repeal of the Missouri Compromise, Its Origin and Authorship.* Cleveland: A. H. Clark Company.

TOUSSAINT L'OUVERTURE

See **L'Ouverture, Toussaint**

TOWSON, FORT

Fort Towson was a frontier outpost established near the confluence of the Kiamichi and Red Rivers, a site that is in present-day southeastern Oklahoma. Founded by Major William Bradford in 1824, the post was named for Nathan Towson, paymaster general of the U.S. Army and hero of the War of 1812. Located near the Mexican province of Texas, the fort was built to control whites and Indians along the U.S. border with Mexico. It was shut down in 1829 but reopened in 1830 as an arrival and supply post at the end of the Trail of Tears. The U.S. military abandoned it permanently in 1854. Subsequently, it served as the capital of the Choctaw nation and the headquarters of the Confederate Indian Brigade.

The impetus for the establishment of Fort Towson was conflict between the Osage people and white and Indian hunters, including Cherokee, who had moved onto Osage lands. More generally, the post was intended to keep the peace between the parts of the Louisiana Purchase that Anglo-Americans had settled (Louisiana, Arkansas, and Missouri) and their dangerous neighbors—Mexicans to the south and Plains Indians to the west. In addition to protecting white settlements, the post's orders were to keep whites from settling upon Indian lands. This dual mission led to conflicts with Anglo-American settlers who wanted to push Indians farther west. Understaffed and charged with an impossible mission, the troops at Cantonment Towson were unable to prevent Indian-white conflicts. After the U.S. military abandoned the fort in 1829, white settlers burned it down.

Fort Towson was rebuilt in 1830 in response to the enactment of the Indian Removal Act, which implemented Thomas Jefferson's concept of using part of the Louisiana Purchase as an Indian country. As one of the two main arrival points in Indian Territory, Fort Towson received many thousands of Indians from the Five Civilized Tribes forcibly removed from the Southeast. First came some fifteen thousand Choctaw who traveled from Mississippi, across Arkansas, to Indian Territory. The removal was poorly organized, so the emigrants were forced to travel in winter on bad roads, often on foot, and short of supplies. They arrived at Fort Towson starving and cold. Thousands died from cholera and exposure to the elements along the route. In the late 1830s, thousands of Chickasaw were brought up the Red River to Fort Towson, and from there to their lands in Indian territory.

The fort continued to serve as an instrument of Indian control and westward expansion. Its troops attempted to keep the peace among Indian peoples native to the region, such as the Osage, and the Southeastern emigrants—Cherokee, Choctaw, Chickasaw, Creek, and Seminole. It was a central point for distributing supplies from New Orleans that were destined for Indian Territory. The road built between Fort Towson and Fort Smith in 1832 was one of the first military roads in Indian Territory. The fort's jurisdiction continued to witness border conflicts between Mexico and the United States. Commanders at the fort in the late 1830s regularly received reports of Mexican emissaries attempting to recruit Indian allies on the U.S. side of the border.

After the Mexican War (1846–1848), the frontier moved west and south, and Fort Towson declined in importance for U.S. security. The U.S. military permanently abandoned the fort in 1854, but this time the fort remained in use. The Choctaw nation took possession of it and made it the Choctaw capital. During the Civil War, the fort was the headquarters for the Confederate Indian Brigade. Cherokee general Stand Watie (De-ga-ta-ga) surrendered there in June 1865, the last Confederate general to accept Northern victory.

—Kathleen DuVal

See also

Indian Removal; Indian Territory; Osage

For Further Reading

Frazer, Robert W. 1965. *Forts of the West: Military Forts and Presidios and Posts Commonly Called Forts West of the Mississippi River to 1898.* Norman: University of Oklahoma Press; Gibson, Arrell M. 1981. *Oklahoma: A History of Five Centuries.* Norman: University of Oklahoma Press; McGuigan, Patrick B. 1978. "Bulwark of the American Frontier: A History of Fort Towson." In *Early Military Forts and Posts in Oklahoma.* Edited by Odie B. Faulk, Kenny A. Franks, and Paul F. Lambert. Oklahoma City: Oklahoma Historical Society; Morris, John W., Charles R. Goins, and Edwin C. McReynolds. 1986. *Historical Atlas of Oklahoma.* Norman: University of Oklahoma Press.

TRACY, URIAH (1755–1807)

Leader of Federalist opposition to the Louisiana Purchase in the U.S. Senate, Uriah Tracy was an outspoken critic of the Jefferson administration and a skilled debater who used sarcasm and satire in attacking Republican actions and policies on the Senate floor and in the press. Finally, Tracy was a leader of an ill-fated, Northern secession movement over the purchase and ensuing treaty acquiring Louisiana.

A native of Connecticut, 1778 graduate of Yale, experienced lawyer, and elected state official, Uriah Tracy served in the U.S. House (1793–1796) and was elected to the Senate in 1796, serving until his death from dropsy in 1807. A stout Federalist, Tracy was a gifted speaker and shrewd political strategist. He was closely allied with the leading Federalists of his day, including Alexander Hamilton, Rufus King, and John Quincy Adams. Tracy was an irascible cynic who led the Senate opposition against Republican leadership once Jefferson was elected. Respected by his Federalist colleagues, Tracy was revered by many. Fisher Ames once compared him to the biblical Goliath, trusting there were no Davids to slay him. Tracy despised democratic principles but supported the Constitution, predicting that a monarchy would grow out of "the madness democracy was fastening upon us" (Deutsch, 1967).

Tracy's opposition to the treaty approving the addition of Louisiana centered on the constitutionality of the third and seventh articles, which he deemed unconstitutional. The third article, one that even the administration realized would create havoc, provided for citizenship for inhabitants of the Louisiana Territory. The irascible Tracy did not believe that the president (with Senate consent) had unlimited power to act in such a manner, insisting that by a fair reading of the Constitution, "the President and Senate have not the power of thus obtruding upon us Louisiana" (*Debates,* 1852). Article seven, Tracy contended, would give the port of New Orleans a commercial preference over the ports of the several states by admitting ships from France and Spain into the port duty-free. But Tracy's real reason for opposing the treaty was the serious threat to New England and Eastern importance. The treaty as proposed "would be absorbing the Northern States and rendering them as insignificant to the Union as they ought to be, if, by their own consent, the measure should be adopted" (ibid.). Senator Tracy argued vehemently that neither treaty, legislation, nor amendment could admit territorial inhabitants and create states—such had to be accomplished "by universal consent of all the States or partners to our political association" (ibid.). Tracy's thoughts and words were echoed in debate by Senator Samuel White of Delaware and the outspoken Senator William Plummer of New Hampshire, who himself referred to Massachusetts senator Timothy Pickering's threat of disunion. Tracy also appealed to his constituency in Connecticut when he charged that the state's financial burden for the Louisiana Territory would be three-quarters of a million dollars. He was one of five Senate Federalists to vote against the treaty. Never one to admit defeat or back down from a challenge, he retorted "that the quiver of malice has been exhausted of its last arrow, to wound me," in defending the Federalist Party in his native state in an 1803 address (Deutsch, 1967).

It was this same 1803 address, *To the Freemen of Connecticut,* that rapidly incited many Federalists to talk of disunion. Over dinners and long evenings during late-1803 and into 1804 in the Washington boarding house frequented by several party loyalists, prominent Federalists such as James Hillhouse (senator from Connecticut), Plumer, the outspoken secessionist Pickering, and party House leader Roger Griswold (Connecticut) conspired to secede from the existing republic. Their plans called for the New England states of Massachusetts, Connecticut, and New Hampshire to lead the movement, with New York to follow. New Jersey would surely follow New York's lead, and eastern Pennsylvania was also likely to join secession. The Federalist leadership was sure that their plans would include New York because of the presence of the vice president, New Yorker Aaron Burr. The Essex Junto of Massachusetts Federalists were also among the conspirators. All were united around two primary beliefs—their hatred of democracy and utter distrust of Jefferson. Although several members of the conspiracy expressed doubts about the timing of plans to secede, even Hamilton and King were included in secession plans. The key was Burr's election in New York's gubernatorial race, but when the cunning and resourceful Burr was defeated, secession plans faltered.

Tracy, resolute as ever, remained a thorn in Jefferson's side, but the Federalist Party was in full decline after the vote on the Louisiana Territory and the failed secession plot. True to Federalist principles until the end, Tracy died at the height of the *Chesapeake* Affair (July 19, 1807) and was the first person buried in Washington's new Congressional Cemetery.

—*Boyd Childress*

See also
Essex Junto; Federalist Party

For Further Reading

Deutsch, Eberhard P. 1967. "The Constitutional Controversy over the Louisiana Purchase." *American Bar Association Journal* 53: 50–57; U.S. Congress. 1852. *The Debates and Proceedings in the Congress of the United States.* Eighth Congress. Washington, DC: Gales and Seaton.

TRANSCONTINENTAL TREATY (1819)

Also called the Adams-Onís Treaty or the Purchase of Florida, the Transcontinental Treaty was signed on February 22, 1819, between the United States and Spain. The principal negotiators were Secretary of State John Quincy Adams and Spanish minister to the United States Luís de Onís y Gonzales. The treaty ceded all of Spanish Florida to the United States and set the boundaries between the Louisiana Purchase and Spanish Mexico and California. Moreover, it strengthened the claims of the United States to lands between the Rocky Mountains and the Pacific Ocean.

The Transcontinental Treaty dealt with three important issues: the Floridas, Texas, and the western boundaries of the Louisiana Purchase. The United States laid claim to West Florida, territory that it claimed was part of the Louisiana Purchase, and East Florida. West Florida extended from the Mississippi River in the west to the Perdido River in the east. East Florida comprised the territory east of the Perdido and south of the thirty-first parallel—most of the present-day state of Florida. Because this territory had passed between three different nations in the century preceding the Transcontinental Treaty, and because the language of the Louisiana Purchase Treaty was ambiguous, there were uncertainties about what the United States had actually purchased in 1803.

The language of the Louisiana Purchase Treaty included a definition of the "colony or province of Louisiana, with the same extent that it now has in the hands of Spain, and that it had when France possessed it." Except for the two decades after the French and Indian War when Britain possessed the Floridas, the land that became known as West Florida had been part of Louisiana. In 1719, Spain and France had agreed that the boundary between French Louisiana and Spanish Florida would be the Perdido River. When Spain acquired Louisiana from France and Spanish Florida passed to Great Britain at the end of the French and Indian War, the British took possession of the territory between the Perdido and Mississippi and named it West Florida. In 1783, Spain reacquired the Floridas and incorporated West Florida into the administrative structure of Louisiana, of which it remained a part until the retrocession of 1800. The United States, however, was ignorant of this administrative change, knowledge of which would have strengthened its claim to the land. Nevertheless, the United States argued that "historic Louisiana"—that is, the Louisiana of 1719–1763—was the Louisiana purchased in the treaty of 1803. Napoleon, for his part, purposely left the boundaries of the sale vague, and instructed Talleyrand, the chief French negotiator of the Louisiana treaty, to tell the Americans to make the most of the bargain. Consequently, Congress passed the Mobile Act (1804), which organized West Florida as a U.S. customs district.

As for East Florida, U.S. claims were based not on the Louisiana Purchase Treaty but were nonetheless ingenious. Adams argued that East Florida should pass to the United States because Spain had violated the Treaty of San Lorenzo (1795) by failing to restrain the Indians in East Florida from raiding U.S. territory. Adams also claimed that because Spanish and French ships based in Spanish ports in East Florida had seized U.S. commercial vessels during the Napoleonic Wars, cession of East Florida to the United States would satisfy claims of compensation for those seizures. Additionally, Adams maintained that possession of East Florida would compensate for commercial losses incurred when Spain withheld the American right of deposit in New Orleans in 1802.

Negotiations between Adams and Onís had begun in 1818. Meanwhile, events on the border between Florida and the United States changed the context of the talks. President James Monroe had ordered General Andrew Jackson and three thousand troops to the border to stop Seminole attacks on American settlements. Jackson, never a moderate in his actions, marched into East Florida, destroyed several Seminole villages, and even executed two British citizens who had been inciting Indian violence against the United States. Jackson then advanced to West Florida's capital, Pensacola, and captured it on May 28, 1818. He appointed one of his officers as military and civil governor and announced the immediate enforcement of the revenue laws of the United States. President Monroe was shocked, but Adams defended Jackson's actions. He argued that because the two British subjects were obviously at fault and because Britain did not want war with the United States, they should not fear any retaliation from London. Onís lodged complaints in Washington, but Spain had no diplomatic support. The British advised Onís to yield. Neither did Onís receive backing from France or Russia. Spain did not want war with the United States, as it was preoccupied with rebellion in its Latin American colonies; it was therefore compelled to agreed to the cession of Florida.

The Spanish failed in their efforts to pursue a strong diplomacy in Florida, but in the second important issue, the matter of Texas, they were more successful. At least it appeared so in 1819; two years later Mexico would achieve independence, making possible both the Texas Revolution and the Mexican War, in which Mexico would lose much more than Texas to the United States. Onís had instructions from Madrid to cede Texas if necessary, but the Spanish minister proved stubborn in the negotiations. Adams, unaware of Onís's instructions regarding Texas, tried to get it, but the cabinet, who considered Florida more important than Texas, did not back him, and he was forced to accept the Sabine River as the border between the Louisiana Purchase and Spanish Mexico.

The negotiations on the third important issue settled by the Transcontinental Treaty, the trans-Mississippi boundary between Spanish possessions and the territory of the United States, are what made the treaty a transcontinental one. Adams first suggested extending the Spanish-U.S. border to the Pacific during the negotiations for Florida. In the same year, 1818, the United States and Great Britain had concluded an agreement concerning Oregon, the vast territory that included present-day Oregon, Washington, Idaho, and parts of Montana, Wyoming, and British Columbia. In the Convention of 1818, the Anglo-American border was set from the Lake of the Woods to the Rocky Mountains, and then to the Pacific in a "joint occupation." Perhaps Adams thought that by fixing the southern boundary of Oregon with Spain, future U.S. claims to that territory would be strengthened. Onís was responsive to Adams's suggestion, and a boundary composed of rivers and parallels was settled. From the east, the border would follow the Red River to the meridian of 100 degrees longitude, following that line north to the Arkansas River, then west to the source of that river, then north to the forty-second parallel, then west to the Pacific. During the negotiations over the river boundaries, Adams's tenacity was most apparent. Although it was customary in diplomacy to set river boundaries at midchannel, the secretary of state pressed for the farthest edge. In the face of this stubbornness, Onís was compelled to acquiesce. Adams agreed, however, that the United States would assume $5 million in damage claims by U.S. citizens against the Spanish government.

The Transcontinental Treaty was signed on February 22, 1819. The Senate quickly and unanimously approved it after some grumbling about the matter of Texas. President Monroe ratified it on February 25. Spain, however, delayed ratification for more than a year, as Ferdinand VII had deeded most of the public land in East Florida to three members of the Spanish court. Although Adams showed that one of these deeds had been granted after the treaty was signed, the other two were good. Furthermore, Spain attempted to obtain a promise from the United States not to recognize the independence of Spain's rebellious Latin American colonies—a promise that the United States would not give. These hurdles were finally overcome when a revolution in Spain in 1820 resulted in the establishment of a liberal constitution. Ratification of the treaty must now come from the new legislative body, the Cortes. The new government nullified the land grants, accepted the treaty, and the king ratified it in October 1820. It became effective when final ratifications were exchanged between Spain and the United States on February 22, 1821, exactly two years from the signing of the treaty.

The Transcontinental Treaty has been called the greatest diplomatic victory won by a single individual in the history of the United States. John Quincy Adams successfully took advantage of Spain's diplomatic isolation and preoccupation with revolution in its Latin American colonies to acquire the whole of Spanish Florida for virtually nothing. The future president also helped define the western and southern boundaries of the Louisiana Purchase and, at the same time, strengthened the claims of the United States to the Oregon Country. Although he failed to acquire Texas, it was probably for the best; that region would eventually embroil the United States in a war with Mexico that yielded territory destined to become all of present-day California, Nevada, and Utah, and parts of New Mexico, Arizona, and Colorado. Thus the Transcontinental Treaty played a crucial role in determining the modern boundaries of the United States.

—*Scott D. Wignall*

See also
Adams, John Quincy; Convention of 1818; Diplomacy of the Louisiana Purchase; French and Indian War; West Florida

For Further Reading
Bemis, Samuel Flagg. 1959. *A Short History of American Foreign Policy and Diplomacy.* New York: Holt, Rinehart, and Winston; Ferrell, Robert H. 1969. *American Diplomacy: A History.* New York: W. W. Norton; Pratt, Julius W. 1965. *A History of United States Foreign Policy.* Englewood Cliffs, NJ: Prentice-Hall.

TREATY OF . . .
***See* individual treaties listed by location**

TUCKER, ST. GEORGE (1752–1827)

Virginia jurist, legal educator, and author, St. George Tucker wrote *Reflections on the Cession of Louisiana to the United States* (1803), in which he set out the advantages of acquiring the Louisiana Territory to the new United States. Published under the pseudonym "Sylvestris," the pamphlet-length publication presented several conservative ideas for the future settlement of the vast regions acquired from France.

Born in Bermuda, St. George Tucker attended the College of William and Mary in Virginia and studied law under the esteemed attorney George Wythe. After a brief start on a career as a lawyer, he returned to Bermuda, where he joined his family in the illegal trade of weapons to Virginia colonists. Tucker returned to Virginia in 1777 to operate the stateside business for the family. He married in 1778, joined the Virginia militia, and fought in the Revolution at Guilford Court House and Yorktown. He also managed his own agricultural interests. After the Revolution, Tucker began an illustrious career on the bench until his final retirement from the judiciary in 1825 due to illness.

Tucker was a supporter of the administration of Thomas Jefferson, and, though he sought no political appointments, he wrote several pamphlets supporting Jefferson's policies. Among his more noteworthy publications was *A Dissertation on Slavery* (1796), a call for a gradual end to slavery and the removal of freed slaves to the West. Tucker also published an American edition of Sir William Blackstone's *Commentaries on the Laws of England* (1803), an effort that earned him the nickname of "the American Blackstone." He wrote some loose fiction and assorted books of verse. Tucker's sons included two noted Virginia legal figures and jurists, Nathaniel Beverley Tucker and Henry St. George Tucker. The Tucker name was destined to become one of the FFVs, or "First Families of Virginia."

Although never a close political ally of Jefferson, Tucker was a strong advocate of the Republican political position. Some of his early writings were both critical and satirical of Federalist politics, but in his 1803 pamphlet, *Reflections on the Cession of Louisiana to the United States,* Tucker supported the acquisition and reflected on the advantages the territory presented to the new republic. Dated August 10, 1803, the twenty-five-page pamphlet was initially advertised for sale for a quarter in the *National Intelligencer* for October 17, 1803, an advertisement that ran in subsequent issues. Samuel Harrison Smith, the newspaper's editor and publisher, also published the pamphlet, and ran a very brief excerpt in the newspaper on October 19. The original was signed as a product of the pen of "Sylvestris," and mystery surrounded the authorship until 1935, when a collector located Tucker's own copy, which identified the judge as author.

Despite Tucker's strong allegiance to Jefferson, the brief volume avoided excessive praise for the cession and detailed what the author saw as the advantages of acquiring Louisiana. The author termed the acquisition a good bargain, then quickly moved to the long- and short-term advantages to the United States. First and foremost was the immediate removal of the real French threat, but the long-term elimination of the French was welcome relief for a still vulnerable nation. Tucker also thought that gaining navigation rights to the Mississippi and the port of New Orleans "without bloodshed" was an advantage not to be overlooked. He further saw the region as a barrier against any invasion, and concluded that Louisiana "may be regarded as the most momentous object which has been achieved" since independence from Great Britain. He deemed the barriers "incalculable" and reflected: "I am almost led to break out into strains of rapture and enthusiasm." "Sylvestris" thought that acquiring Louisiana helped to preserve the Union and secured the nation against the threat of the sale of Western lands located east of the Mississippi, as well as providing security against depopulation in the Western states. Tucker's logic was simple: the French could have offered bounties to Americans living in frontier states and others with a promise of unlimited land. Immigrants would also be attracted, thus creating a loss of both land and population for the fledgling American nation, what the author termed "objects of the first importance."

Tucker then advised against ignoring the advantages gained, calling Louisiana a "treasure in the bank." He warned of inflated land prices and unscrupulous land agents, and endorsed settling and cultivating the states east of the Mississippi River before moving west—a policy he termed settle, cultivate, and populate. Fearing a race to settle the "howling wilderness of Louisiana," Tucker compared the region to a colony, and wanted to keep the treasure "locked up; and, wonderful to behold." Predicting national policy, he suggested settling the frontier lands with Indians. More radically, Tucker favored settling Louisiana with slaves if slavery were abolished; he was a strong advocate of abolition. Finally, Tucker recommended using the lands as an exile for criminals, where they could "repent, and become useful members of society."

Judge Tucker died in November 1827, while living with his daughter.

—Boyd Childress

See also
Colony for Freed Slaves
For Further Reading
Cullen, Charles T. 1971. "St. George Tucker and Law in Virginia, 1772–1804." Unpublished dissertation, University of Virginia; Scott, Robert Morton. 1991. "St George Tucker and the Development of American Culture in Early Federal Virginia, 1790–1824." Unpublished dissertation, George Washington University; Sylvestris [St. George Tucker]. 1803. *Reflections on the Cession of Louisiana to the United States.* Washington, DC: Samuel Harrison Smith.

TURNER, FREDERICK JACKSON (1861–1932)

The foremost interpreter of the history and process of Western expansion, Frederick Jackson Turner was born in Portage, Wisconsin, on November 14, 1861, and witnessed firsthand the transition of his hometown from a virtual frontier settlement into a model American community. The young Turner worked in his father's newspaper office before attending the University of Wisconsin, where he studied history under William F. Allen, who favored a scientific approach to the field and applied a developmental model to economic and cultural history that would have great impact on Turner's intellectual development. After completing his bachelor's degree in 1884, Turner worked as a newspaper correspondent for two years before returning to Madison to pursue the master of arts under Allen, which he earned in 1888; he then enrolled in the doctoral program in history at Johns Hopkins University. Prior to completing a dissertation entitled *The Character and Influence of the Indian Trade in Wisconsin* under the well-known historian Herbert Baxter Adams, Turner accepted an appointment as assistant professor of history at the University of Wisconsin and returned there in 1889 to teach while completing the requirements for the degree.

Turner quickly became a popular teacher and valued member of the Madison faculty, replacing his mentor, Allen, as chairman of the Department of History in 1890. His graduate seminars in particular illustrated his fascination with the westward progression of settlement and the development of American culture in its wake, a topic central to his intellectual interests and the subject of a paper entitled "The Significance of the Frontier in American History," which he read before the American Historical Association at the Columbian Exposition in Chicago in 1893. Although it met with little immediate interest, this paper and the "frontier thesis" it incorporated would dramatically impact Americans' understanding of their national character in the years that followed. Noting that the Census Bureau had been unable to identify a clear line demarcating a Western frontier in 1890, as it had done in previous decades, Turner's paper offered an interpretation of American history that presented the frontier experience as the critical element in the development of U.S. institutions and identity. The frontier experience, he argued, differentiated the United States from Europe and provided an effective means of both Americanizing immigrants and fostering democracy. Although the paper received little notice in Chicago, Turner continued to advance the thesis to broader audiences as an explanation for the political and social turbulence of the 1890s, in the process turning himself into an academic celebrity and his thesis into a topic of popular discussion that informed a new nationalistic identity.

In the years following the publication of his frontier thesis, Turner continued to teach at the University of Wisconsin, making the history of Western expansion his signature course and planning extensive writing projects. He became a powerful figure in campus politics and frequently received offers from other universities who wanted the prominent historian to join their faculties. Despite this acclaim, however, Turner was unable to produce the book-length studies that others expected of him, preferring instead to continue writing essays expanding on his frontier theory and the broader issue of sectionalism in American history. His only book, *The Rise of the New West, 1819–1829* (1906), was followed years later by a collection of essays under the title *The Frontier in American History* (1920), but the great books expected by his contemporaries never appeared.

In 1910, Turner accepted an offer from Harvard University and taught there until his retirement in 1924, when he returned briefly to lecture in Madison until health problems led him to relocate to Pasadena, California, where he died on March 14, 1932. Turner's final acclaim came in the form of the Pulitzer Prize, awarded for his collection of essays entitled *The Significance of Sections in American History* (1932), published soon after his death. Based on the importance of the frontier thesis alone, Turner remains the single most influential interpreter of the history of Western expansion, and although his thesis has waxed and waned in popularity, it is still considered a critical element of American historiography and emblematic of its era.

—*Derek R. Larson*

For Further Reading

Bennett, James D. 1975. *Frederick Jackson Turner.* Boston: Twayne Publishers; Billington, Ray Allen. 1973. *Frederick Jackson Turner: Historian, Scholar, Teacher.* New York: Oxford University Press; Bogue, Allan G. 1998. *Frederick Jackson Turner: Strange Roads Going Down.* Norman: University of Oklahoma Press; Jacobs, Wilbur R. 1968. *The Historical World of Frederick Jackson Turner.* New Haven: Yale University Press.

TUSCANY

Tuscany is a region of north-central Italy with Florence as its nucleus and the Arno River as a noted geographic feature. From the Middle Ages and throughout the Renaissance, it was an area noted for its superior craftsmanship and intense commercial activity. Its central financial role was undercut by the development of new trade routes by the Portuguese and Spanish, especially in the sixteenth century. Nonetheless, by 1800 it boasted a population of one million and still remained a significant focus of French political and economic interests.

At the end of the eighteenth century, the dynastic aspirations of the Spanish Bourbons and the imperialistic schemes of the wily Napoleon were brought together in north-central Italy with Parma and later Tuscany acting as diplomatic pawns. Napoleon's hope to re-create the French empire, a project encouraged by his minister of foreign affairs, Talleyrand, involved retrocession of Louisiana and the suppression of the successful slave revolt on St. Domingue (Haiti). The Grand Duchy of Tuscany was ruled by scions of the Austrian Hapsburg family and sometimes acted as a steppingstone to more significant roles in their grand court at Vienna. For example, the emperor Leopold II was its grand duke prior to the death of his celibate brother Joseph II in 1790. The neighboring duchy of Parma was designated for the Spanish Bourbon family and indeed was considered diplomatically as a secundogeniture (that is, a region that was given to the second oldest or younger members of the royal family). Its Duke Ferdinand was the first cousin of Charles IV of Spain and brother of his wife, Maria Luisa. Later he became the father-in-law of his third daughter, Maria Luisa Josefina, because of her marriage to the sickly son of the Parmese duke. The colony of Louisiana, a recent addition to the Spanish diadem, was a "gift" from the French for assistance, albeit futile, during the Seven Years' War (known in the Americas as the French and Indian War). This region did not hold the same status for the king as did traditional domains such as Mexico and Peru and was therefore considered expendable. In addition, the colony was never a financial success. With only fifty thousand non-Indian inhabitants and a lengthy border with the United States, the crown deemed it burdensome, if not useless to Spanish fortunes.

Napoleon, who assumed power in France after his coup d'état in November 1799, had been involved militarily in northern Italy since the mid-1790s. His defeat of the Austrians inspired his megalomania, especially after his successful Treaty of Campo Formio (1797). Not dampened by his defeat and military isolation in Egypt in 1798–1799, he apparently planned another takeover of Italy, expecting longer-lasting effects than those of his predecessors, such as Charles VIII and Francis I in the sixteenth century. Napoleon was never interested in sharing power and demanded obedience from the conquered as well as from the underlings in his government. At the same time, he presented himself publicly as the son of the Revolution and the savior of its liberties. He projected the same image in the areas he conquered, such as Italy. Nonetheless, during his renewed struggles with the Austrians after his assumption of power in France, the position of Parma became more tenuous, inasmuch as it could act as a geographic bridge to the pro-Austrian Papal States and the anglophilic Kingdom of Naples. Ferdinand, the Duke of Parma, was not compliant, while his sister, the Spanish queen and her principal favorite, the Prince of the Peace, Manuel Godoy, were. Despite the executions of the French Louis XVI and Marie Antoinette, their relatives only several degrees removed, Charles IV admired Napoleon and agreed to work with the revolutionary French in the Treaty of Basel (1795). Napoleon understood their malleability and used it successfully while appealing to their dynastic and familial desires.

In the resulting Treaty of San Ildefonso (1800), the Duke of Parma was transferred to the newly created Kingdom of Etruria, the geographic base of which was Tuscany with the noticeable addition of adjacent Piombino. In return, the Spanish offered to retrocede the colony of Louisiana. Duke Ferdinand was unwilling to succumb to Napoleon's diplomacy and refused to leave the ducal palace. As a result of his intransigence, he was deposed by Napoleon, who in turn appointed Ferdinand's son as the King of Etruria with the blessings of the Spanish monarchs and their advisor, Godoy. This new arrangement was guaranteed in the Convention of Aranjuez (1801). Until then, Charles IV and Queen Maria Luisa never believed that their Infanta Maria Luisa Josefina would become queen, thinking that she would remain only a duchess. However, the unscrupulous Napoleon employed those familial emotions to further his own ambitions in northern Italy and North America. The treaty itself, as well as the resulting Convention of Aranjuez, coupled the retrocession of Louisiana with the de facto takeover of the newly constituted Etruria by the Infanta and her husband and its recognition by the powers of Europe. These minutiae did not disturb the first consul, who continued to maintain close control over the new kingdom despite the presumed assumption of power by its new monarchs. Nevertheless, Tuscany provided a convenient excuse for Napoleon to gain Louisiana, which at the time seemed advantageous. His vision of a French empire was nourished simultaneously by a growing British war fatigue and his underestimation of the determination of the former slaves of St. Domingue (Haiti) to maintain their freedom. The new Etruscan monarchs who visited Paris and Napoleon within a decade of their cousins' executions did not realize how little power they were to assume and how transitory were their new positions, which depended on the vagaries of Napoleon's military and diplomatic actions. In sum, Tuscany provided Napoleon with a pawn with which to gain his desired Louisiana and thereby re-create a worldwide French empire that had been decimated in the recent past.

—Thomas C. Sosnowski

See also

Aranjuez, Convention of; Fernando, Duke of Parma; San Ildefonso, Treaty of

For Further Reading

Chastenet, Jacques. 1972. *Godoy: Master of Spain, 1792–1808.* Translated by J. F. Huntington. London: Batchworth Press; Fugier, André. 1947. *Napoléon et l'Italie.* Paris: Dijon; Hilt, Douglas. 1987. *The Troubled Trinity: Godoy and the Spanish Monarchs.* Tuscaloosa: University of Alabama Press; Lyon, E. Wilson. 1974. *Louisiana in French Diplomacy, 1730–1804.* Norman: University of Oklahoma Press; Villa-Urrutia, Marques de. 1923. *La Reina de Etruria, Doña Maria Luisa de Borbon, Infanta de España.* Madrid: F. Beltrán; Whitaker, Arthur Preston. 1949. *The Mississippi Question, 1795–1803.* New York: Foreign Policy Association.

UNITED STATES CONSTITUTION

See Constitution of the United States

VALLÉ, JEAN-BAPTISTE (1760–1849)

Jean-Baptiste Vallé was born in the French colonial settlement of Kaskaskia (located in the Illinois Country) on September 25, 1760. He was the son of Francois and Marianne [Billeron] Vallé. On January 7, 1783, Jean-Baptiste Vallé married Marie Jeanne Barbeau of Prairie du Rocher in the Illinois Country. The marriage took place in Ste. Genevieve. The couple raised four sons: Jean-Baptiste II, Francois-Baptiste, Louis, and Felix.

The family Vallé, which owned more than one hundred slaves, was a prosperous merchant family in the Ste. Genevieve region and had found success in both the mercantile business and in early lead mining operations. Francois Vallé had established the Vallé Mining Company when he arrived in the Missouri region in 1749 (the company is still in operation today). The wealth associated with the Vallé family helped to make Francois Vallé and his heirs influential members of the local political establishment.

The original French settlers who established Ste. Genevieve continued to thrive after the region fell under Spanish control following the Treaty of Fontainebleau (1762) and the Treaty of Paris (1763). The individuals who had been politically connected during the French reign continued to wield power and influence under the new Spanish regime.

The Spanish quickly realized the power and influence of the Vallé family. In a letter dated January 15, 1798, the lieutenant-governor of Spanish Illinois, Zenon Trudeau, wrote to Governor-General Gayoso de Lemos in New Orleans that the inhabitants of Ste. Genevieve were united by the Vallé family bond—almost all of them being related in some way. Trudeau continued: "Don Francisco Valle, who is their commandant at present, is, at the same time, the head of the most numerous and notable families. . . . Not only is he esteemed by those habitants, but he is their true friend and protector" (Nasatir, 1952). Perhaps not surprisingly, Francisco Vallé served the Spanish as commandant at Ste. Genevieve for more than a decade.

Jean-Baptiste Vallé, following in the footsteps of his father, served as the last commandant of Ste. Genevieve during the final days of Spanish rule before the French took back the Louisiana Territory and subsequently sold it to the United States in 1803. Despite the international diplomatic intrigue as the Louisiana Territory changed hands several times, the region that the Vallé family controlled in and around Ste. Genevieve did not witness a tremendous amount of change. The colonial French heritage of the community was so strong that the Spanish interlude did not effect any real changes in the economy and society of the region. Jean-Baptiste Vallé and his heirs would eventually serve the United States as local leaders because of the hereditary positions of authority that they held. The Vallé family would continue its lead mining in the region and would use its wealth to invest in other economic enterprises, such as the fur trade and commercial agriculture.

Considered the grand old man of the French colonial era, Jean-Baptiste Vallé died on August 3, 1849, and was buried in Ste. Genevieve, Missouri.

—Junius P. Rodriguez

See also
Saint Genevieve
For Further Reading
Drury, John. 1947. *Historic Midwest Houses.* New York: Bonanza Books; Franzwa, Gregory M. 1973. *The Story of Old Ste. Genevieve: An Account of an Old French Town in Upper Louisiana; Its People and Their Homes.* Gerald, MO: Patrice Press; Hamilton, M. Colleen. 1990. "French Colonial Land Use: The Felix Valle House, a State Historic Site." Master's thesis, Department of History, University of Missouri-St. Louis; Nasatir, Abraham B., ed. 1952. *Before Lewis and Clark, 1785–1804.* St. Louis: St. Louis Historical Documents Foundation.

VICTOR, CLAUDE PERRIN (1764–1841)

In the summer of 1802, Napoleon appointed Claude Perrin Victor captain-general of a military force that was to occupy Louisiana. Delicate and sometimes frustrating diplomatic negotiations had led to the retrocession of the colony from Spain back to France, but France held the colony in word alone. By 1802 extensive preparations for the French occupation and administration of the colony were underway. Under the direction of Victor, the occupation forces, which included both military and administrative personnel, were to be assembled at the Dutch port of Helvoet Sluys. Bad luck repeatedly delayed the expedition until April 1803, and it was finally abandoned when news arrived from Paris that Napoleon had abruptly sold the Louisiana Territory to the United States.

Victor had distinguished himself in 1793 at the siege of Toulon and had risen to lieutenant general when Napoleon placed him in charge of the Louisiana expedition. The assignment was a complicated one, and preparations had to anticipate various scenarios. The problem was that no one knew exactly what the expedition would encounter when it arrived. Some intelligence was gleaned from the memoirs of General Victor Collot and Joseph Xavier de Pontalba, both of whom were very familiar with Louisiana. Both Collot and Pontalba encouraged immediate action by the French for fear of U.S. encroachment into the territory.

Containing U.S. expansion was central to Victor's mission once he arrived in Louisiana. The port of New Orleans was to be secured firmly, and close attention was to be paid to British and U.S. use of the Mississippi River. Victor was also to assume and maintain Spanish-Indian alliances for France. While he was creating a French-Indian alliance against U.S. expansion into the territory, Victor was also expected to maintain friendly relations with the United States and discourage Indian attacks against Americans on the frontier. To secure these complex and delicate alliances, great quantities of trinkets, intended as presents for the Indians, were included with the supplies for the expedition, along with two hundred medals that were to be distributed among the various Indian chiefs.

The expedition was scheduled to sail in December 1802, but a shortage of transport ships delayed its departure. As a result it was decided to send the civilian administrator Pierre Clement Laussat ahead to make preparations for the arrival of the main body of the expedition in hopes of smoothing the transfer of power. His vessel left France on January 10, 1803. The planned route was via Cuba then to Santo Domingo, but in reality he went straight to New Orleans. When he arrived, he set out, without much cooperation from Spanish officials, to secure supplies and build barracks for the rest of the expedition, which he believed would arrive soon. Even when the ships did not arrive, Laussat was diligent in writing reports to Victor regarding the status of his preparations and the political situation in the colony.

The expedition was delayed further because of repairs needed on several ships damaged by strong winds, but by the time those repairs were made the ships were icebound. It was not until mid-March that the weather improved enough for departure. This delay was perhaps the final blow for the expedition, for by this time the British navy, well aware of the purpose of Victor's expedition, had established a blockade off the Dutch coast. In April, when the expedition was finally ready to sail, Victor received word that the project had been abandoned and that Napoleon had sold Louisiana to the United States. Victor demanded an explanation and was told that Napoleon was concerned that the expedition would damage the current peace he was maintaining with England.

Although this grand scheme to re-establish a French stronghold in America was never realized, the resources and energy expended in preparation demonstrate just how serious Napoleon was in redeveloping a New World empire. It is likely that if Victor's expedition had sailed as scheduled and successfully fulfilled its mission, once in Louisiana, Napoleon's decision regarding the sale of Louisiana might have been different.

—Mark Cave

See also

Bonaparte, Napoleon; Pontalba, Joseph Xavier de

For Further Reading

Claude Perrin Victor Papers 1802–1804. MSS 94. Williams Research Center. New Orleans, Louisiana; Smith, Ronald D. 1971. "Napoleon and Louisiana: Failure of the Proposed Expedition to Occupy and Defend Louisiana, 1801–1803." *Louisiana History* 12, no. 1: 21–41.

WAR HAWKS

The War Hawks were a vociferous group of U.S. congressmen who, during the presidency of James Madison, persistently called for war with Great Britain. Historians identify myriad reasons for the War Hawks' discontent with Great Britain, but most agree that British policies that violated U.S. neutrality and commercial rights assumed the greatest importance. In particular, the British use of impressment, the blockading of American ports, and the interruption of U.S. trade with the European continent during Great Britain's conflict with Napoleonic France drew the ire of the War Hawks and the nation at large. Ironically, in calling for war with Great Britain, the War Hawks downplayed the violations of U.S. neutrality and commercial rights that resulted from France's wartime trade policies. Some historians argue that the War Hawks' emphasis on British violations indicates that they possessed ulterior motives in calling for war with Great Britain alone. The recent acquisition of the Louisiana Purchase perhaps had inspired expansionist-minded legislators to increase further U.S. territory by seizing Canada and Florida in a war with Great Britain. Western and Southern representatives also held suspicions about British involvement in frontier conflicts with Native Americans, a belief supported by the retreat of Shawnee chief Tecumseh into Canada in 1811. A war with Britain could therefore provide the opportunity to secure peace and territory on the newly expanded frontier by allowing the United States to attack Native Americans who were perceived to be British allies. Others argue that the War Hawks merely had grown frustrated by President Madison's unsuccessful attempts to end British violations through economic coercion and negotiation. Supporters of this interpretation assert that the War Hawks simply believed that war was the only way to preserve the honor and independence of the United States. Partisan politics may also have fired the War Hawks' enthusiasm, as the June 4, 1812, vote for war with Great Britain passed without a single Federalist supporting the measure. More specifically, in the 79 to 49 House of Representatives vote for a declaration of war, all of the ayes cast came from Democratic Republicans, most of whom were from the South and West.

In the congressional elections of 1810, nearly half of all incumbents met defeat or did not attempt a return to Congress. Some of the more talented and notable War Hawks, such as Henry Clay, John C. Calhoun, and Felix Grundy, entered the House of Representatives during this election. This influx of new congressmen allowed the War Hawks to assume prominent positions within the House leadership. For example, the House membership elected Henry Clay of Kentucky as speaker, even though he was only thirty-four years of age and a freshman congressman. Clay's election as speaker of the house for the Twelfth Congress reflects not only his well-documented leadership abilities but also the growing political influence and war interest of the young nation's rapidly increasing Western and Southern states. Clay used his appointment powers as speaker to place War Hawks in key House committee positions. War Hawks Peter Porter, Langdon Cheves, David Williams, and Ezekiel Bacon chaired the important Foreign Relations, Naval, Military Affairs, and Ways and Means Committees. Joining Porter on the Foreign Relations Committee were fellow War Hawks John C. Calhoun, Joseph Desha, Felix Grundy, and John Harper. Such well-placed allies allowed Clay and the War Hawks to pursue effectively President Madison's desire for military preparations and to deliver the votes necessary to declare war on Great Britain.

—Daniel L. Fountain

See also
War of 1812

For Further Reading

Fritz, Harry W. 1977. "The War Hawks of 1812: Party Leadership in the Twelfth Congress." *Capital Studies* 5: 25–42; Hatzenbuehler, Ronald L. 1976. "The War Hawks and the Question of Congressional Leadership in 1812." *Pacific Historical Review* 45: 1–22; Horsman, Reginald. 1964. "Who Were the War Hawks?" *Indiana Magazine of History* 60: 122–136; Stagg, J. C. A. 1983. *Mr. Madison's War Politics, Diplomacy and Warfare in the Early American Republic, 1783–1830.* Princeton: Princeton University Press.

WAR OF 1812

The War of 1812, also known as the Second War for American Independence, or the War for American Economic Independence, was a North American outgrowth of the Napoleonic Wars fought between the United States and Great Britain. Declared by the U.S. Congress on June 18, 1812, the war concluded with the Treaty of Ghent on December 24, 1814; sporadic fighting continued until February 1815. The war's notable highlights included: the failed invasions of Canada by U.S. Generals William Hull, Stephen Van Rensselaer, and Henry Dearborn in the fall of 1812; U.S. naval victories on Lake Erie by Oliver Hazard Perry in 1813 and Lake Champlain by Thomas Macdonough in 1814; British general Robert Ross's August 1814 raid and burning of Washington, D.C., and his unsuccessful September 1814 attack against Baltimore, Maryland; and Andrew Jackson's spring 1814 defeat of the Creek Indians at Horseshoe Bend and his dramatic victory against the British at the Battle of New Orleans in January 1815.

Historians have debated the causes of the conflict since the end of the war, yet there has been little consensus. There were several immediate causes, however, whose antecedents can be traced back to 1789. The beginning of the French Revolution initiated a generation of warfare between Great Britain and France, and the fighting placed all neutral nations, especially the new republic of the United States, in a precarious position. As war escalated between the two European powers, both France and Britain violated U.S. neutral rights by seizing ships and sailors—Americans viewed this as an insult to their national honor and a threat to their sovereignty. From 1798 to 1800 the United States fought an undeclared naval conflict—the Quasi-War—with France in the Caribbean to redress U.S. rights and honor. Although the Treaty of Mortefontaine (1800), signed between the United States and France, and the subsequent Louisiana Purchase reduced tensions between the two countries, it did not completely redress the grievances. The renewal of hostilities between France and Great Britain in 1803 again placed neutral nations like the United States in a predicament.

Both Britain and France tried to prevent the United States from supplying the needs of their enemy, and both countries indiscriminately seized ships and sailors. The United States responded to these violations with a series of legislative restrictions—Embargo Act (1807), Non-Intercourse Act (1809), and Macon's Bill No. 2 (1810)—but these did little to change the prevailing relationships. During the summer of 1807 the H.M.S. *Leopard* fired upon the U.S. frigate *Chesapeake* off the coast of Virginia. Although the affair produced great consternation in the United States, it still did not drive the two countries to war.

Increased tensions between Britain and the United States, combined with an uncompromising British government, ultimately prompted President James Madison in June 1812 to ask Congress for a declaration of war. Madison's message listed the major reasons for the conflict: (a) British impressment of U.S. seamen; (b) Violation of U.S. neutral rights on the high seas and in U.S. territorial waters; (c) British blockade of U.S. ports; and (d) British refusal to revoke or modify their Orders in Council. These have been considered the official justification, but other important causes included the British encouragement of Indian attacks along the U.S. frontier; Manifest Destiny, or the desire by U.S. War Hawks to acquire Canadian and indigenous Western tribal lands, or perhaps even Spanish East and West Florida; an agricultural depression, which prompted some Southern congressmen to view war as a means of reviving the sagging U.S. economy; and lastly, an intense U.S. Anglophobia created by years of humiliation at the hands of Great Britain.

Most of the war occurred along the Canadian-U.S. border, especially in the Niagara region, and along the mid-Atlantic coast. The lands encompassing the Louisiana Purchase saw little fighting. The Missouri Territory, a far-removed and isolated Western frontier, experienced British-sponsored and -supported Indian raids that did little damage. Otherwise, the most significant action occurred in early June 1814, when territorial governor William Clark led a squadron of gunboats, militia, and regulars up the Mississippi River to Prairie du Chien, an undefended British post and settlement located on the east bank of the Mississippi River just north of its confluence with the Wisconsin River. Clark's force easily captured the British base and hastily constructed and armed Fort Shelby. Yet before the end of July a contingent of British regulars and Indians had recaptured the position. Two subsequent U.S. attempts to regain Prairie du Chien failed, and the post remained in British hands until the end of the war.

The most important military action that occurred in the Louisiana Purchase was the Battle of New Orleans—a series of engagements fought between the United States and Britain from September 14, 1814, until February 12, 1815. British war plans during the fall of 1814 called for a series of diversionary activities along the southern Atlantic coast to support a major assault against the city of New Orleans; British army and naval officers understood that the city commanded the Mississippi River watershed, and that gaining control over it would provide them with an important foothold, one that could further demoralize the U.S. war effort as well as limit the future growth and development of the United States. The climactic engagement of the campaign occurred on January 8, 1815, when British lieutenant general Sir Edward Pakenham's regulars attacked Major General Andrew Jackson's entrenched ragtag force on the plains of Chalmette, south of the city; within thirty minutes some two thousand British redcoats had been killed, wounded, or captured. The campaign against New Orleans had ended as a British disaster.

The Battle of New Orleans settled once and for all the question over the Louisiana Purchase. Neither the British nor the Spanish government had recognized the legality of the transfer, and, as such, the British planned either to retain the region or return Louisiana to Spain had they won the battle. Jackson's victory, however, added military force to the argument that Louisiana had been legally purchased, developed, and defended by the United States—thus, it was unquestionably U.S. territory. The end of the War of 1812, and the retention of Louisiana, guaranteed future westward expansion for a growing United States.

—*Gene A. Smith*

For Further Reading

Hickey, Donald R. 1989. *The War of 1812: A Forgotten Conflict.* Urbana: University of Illinois Press; Horsman, Reginald. 1962. *The Causes of the War of 1812.* Philadelphia: University of Pennsylvania Press; Latour, Arsène Lacarrière. 1999 [1816]. *Historical Memoir of the War in West Florida and Louisiana in 1814–15: With an Atlas.* Edited by Gene A. Smith. Gainesville: Historic New Orleans Collection and the University Press of Florida; Stagg, J. C. A. 1983. *Mr. Madison's War: Politics, Diplomacy, and Warfare in the Early Republic.* Princeton: Princeton University Press.

WASHITA, FORT

Fort Washita was established in 1841 by General Zachary Taylor, the commander of the Second Military Department in the Southwest. The fort was located about eighteen miles north of the Red River on the Washita River in Indian Territory (present-day Oklahoma), about eighty miles west of Fort Towson. Remains of the fort can be seen between the present-day towns of Madill and Durant, Oklahoma.

General Taylor wanted to build a military outpost to protect the Choctaw and Chickasaw Indians from raiding parties of the Plains tribes, particularly the Comanche. Construction of the fort began in the spring of 1842, and immediately the building was hindered by supply difficulties. Because of its location deep in the frontier, local materials had to be used for construction and food had to be obtained in the area. Manufactured goods from St. Louis and New Orleans were shipped to Doaksville, located near Fort Towson, eighty miles to the east, and then moved west on the Red River to the Washita.

Companies A and F of the Second Dragoons participated in most of the construction. Temporary log barracks were built in 1842 and served until larger barracks were built in 1850. The fort was almost abandoned before completion. In March 1843, Taylor learned that the War Department in Washington was considering abandoning the new fort. The department reconsidered, however, after hearing Taylor's convincing arguments about the value of the fort's location.

To protect the Choctaw and Chickasaw, troops at the fort regularly participated in forays west against raiding Plains tribes. The most consistent enemy of the Washita garrison were the Comanche. Fort Washita had an extensive corral and stable area, as well as blacksmith and farrier shops, to serve the cavalry and dragoons who operated in this sector of the Southwestern frontier. In 1842 the fort was ordered to protect the frontier of Texas against Indian attacks so that Texans could leave their homes to protect their country from an anticipated Mexican invasion.

In spite of Washington's early reluctance to maintain Fort Washita, it eventually grew to cover an extensive area. The parade ground was enclosed on the south by the South Barracks, the enlisted men's quarters. On the west were the West Barracks, also for enlisted men. The commanding officer's quarters were to the north, and to the east were the Bachelor Officers' Quarters. Married Officers' Quarters and the hospital were located behind the commanding officer's quarters.

A number of prominent men served at Fort Washita. General Zachary Taylor founded the fort. Captains Randolph B. Marcy and George B. McClellan, and General William G. Belknap also served at the post. In 1854, Colonel Braxton Bragg, later a general in the Confederate Army, commanded the Second Artillery Regiment stationed at the fort.

Shortly after the fall of Fort Sumter in South Carolina in 1861, federal forces abandoned Fort Washita. Confederate forces from Texas occupied the fort, and it became a major supply depot for Confederate troops in Indian Territory. Confederate general Douglas Cooper commanded the fort briefly after the Battle of Honey Springs, the largest battle fought in Indian Territory. General Albert Pike served at the fort for a short period, and commanded nearby Fort McCulloch, named for Confederate general Ben McCulloch. Stand Watie, a Cherokee who was a Confederate brigadier general, was one of the officers commanding the Southern occupation forces. The fort was also a regional headquarters and hospital facility for Southern troops operating in the area.

After the Civil War, the frontier bypassed Fort Washita. The War Department transferred the fort to the Department of the Interior in 1870. It was never reactivated, as it had become militarily obsolete with the increased frontier expansion. The Department of the Interior turned the land over to Abbie Davis Colbert and her son, a Chickasaw family. The remaining structures of the fort served as farm buildings well into the twentieth century. In 1962, Ward S. Merrick, Sr., of Ardmore, contributed money to the Oklahoma Historical Society for the fort's purchase. Five years later the state legislature appropriated money for restoration under the guidance of the Oklahoma Historical Society.

—*John David Rausch, Jr.*

See also

Gibson, Fort; Indian Territory; Smith, Fort; Towson, Fort

For Further Reading

Corbett, William P. 1982. "Rifles and Ruts: Army Road Builders in Indian Territory." *Chronicles of Oklahoma* 60: 294–309; Dyer, Brainerd. 1946. *Zachary Taylor.* Baton Rouge: Louisiana State University Press; Fowler, Jack D.

1997. "Amid Bedbugs and Drunken Secessionists." *Civil War Times Illustrated* 36: 44–50; Holcomb, Raymond L. 1990. *The Civil War in the Western Choctaw Nation, 1861–1865*. Atoka, OK: Atoka County Historical Society.

WEST FLORIDA

During the late eighteenth century, some of the most contentious debates in international diplomacy surrounded the exact definition and the actual disposition of the region known as West Florida. The major European powers of the day—Great Britain, France, and Spain—along with the newly established United States, found themselves at odds over a rather small section of real estate along the northern coast of the Gulf of Mexico.

When the French and Indian War officially ended with the terms of the Treaty of Paris (1763), Great Britain received Florida from Spain, and obtained from France that portion of the Louisiana Territory lying between the Mississippi and Perdido Rivers (except for the region known as the Isle of Orleans). During the twenty years (1763–1783) that they possessed Florida, the British organized the territory into two provinces: East Florida (roughly equivalent to the present-day state of Florida) and West Florida (the Gulf Coastal strip that forms portions of present-day Florida, Alabama, Mississippi, and Louisiana). The British used the Apalachicola River to mark the boundary between the Floridas. The two regions prospered during the two decades of British control as a significant number of emigrants, largely Loyalists from the former Atlantic seaboard colonies, relocated to the Floridas during the years of the American Revolution. In 1764, as the British controlled the eastern half of the North American continent, they arbitrarily changed West Florida's northern boundary from 31 degrees north latitude to the so-called Yazoo Line at 32 degrees 28 minutes north latitude, so that West Florida would include the Natchez District.

By the terms of the Treaty of Paris (1783) that ended the American Revolution, Great Britain ceded Florida back to Spain, but the specifics of its boundaries were not made clear by the language of the treaty. The dispute over whether 31 degrees north latitude or 32 degrees 28 minutes north latitude was the northern boundary of West Florida would put the United States and Spain at odds with each other. The Jay-Gardoqui negotiations would prove unsuccessful at solving the impasse, but the Treaty of San Lorenzo (1795) would finally settle the question in a manner favorable to U.S. interests.

Prior to the negotiation of the Louisiana Purchase, President Thomas Jefferson had instructed U.S. minister Robert R. Livingston to attempt to purchase New Orleans from the French, and possibly, to have the French convince the Spanish to sell West Florida to the United States as well. Jefferson realized that there were many eager expansionists along the Southern and Western frontiers who were hinting that the seizure of West Florida was not inconceivable.

When the United States purchased the Louisiana Territory from France in 1803, there arose a new dispute with Spain concerning West Florida's boundaries. The treaty of cession with France was purposefully vague—not specifying the boundaries of the Louisiana Purchase—and the Americans claimed that a portion of West Florida (the region lying between the Perdido and the Mississippi Rivers) was a part of the Louisiana Purchase territory, inasmuch as it had been part of Louisiana before 1763. The Spanish denied this claim.

Residents of West Florida revolted against Spanish authority in 1810. President James Madison used the opportunity to order U.S. troops to occupy the disputed area, which was incorporated into the Territory of Orleans and the Mississippi Territory. The Spanish maintained that this was an illegal seizure of their sovereign territory, but they did little, besides their diplomatic protests, to reclaim the territory. During the War of 1812, the United States seized the remaining West Florida lands up to the Perdido River (in 1813) and held onto the territory after the war, despite the "status quo antebellum" stipulation of the Treaty of Ghent (1814), which ended the conflict. The West Florida question was finally settled by the Adams-Onís Treaty (1819), negotiated between U.S. secretary of state John Quincy Adams and the Spanish minister Luis de Onís, whereby Spain renounced all claims to West Florida and ceded East Florida to the United States as well.

—Junius P. Rodriguez

For Further Reading

Cox, I. J. 1967. *The West Florida Controversy, 1798–1813*. Gloucester, MA: Peter Smith.

WEST FLORIDA REBELLION (1810–1811)

On September 23, 1810, English-speaking settlers in the territory of West Florida staged a rebellion that overthrew Spanish rule and later resulted in the territory's annexation by the United States. West Florida, which encompassed a strip of territory along the Gulf of Mexico east of the Mississippi River and west of the Perdido River, eventually became part of Louisiana, Mississippi, and Alabama.

During the colonial era, the territory attracted the interests of various European powers. Although inhabited by Choctaw and later Creek Indians, Spain claimed the region from early sixteenth-century explorations, and from 1699 to 1763, France possessed it as part of Louisiana. The white population in the region, however, remained small until Great Britain obtained control in

1763 and named the area West Florida. During the American Revolution hundreds of Loyalists used it as a place of refuge, and hundreds of Georgians and Kentuckians came to the territory in the following years. When Spain obtained control of West Florida from Great Britain in 1783, most of the residents in the region spoke English, and many had once been U.S. citizens. U.S. interest in the region grew during the early republic as runaway slaves and hostile Indians increasingly found refuge there.

In 1803, President Thomas Jefferson and the United States claimed West Florida and its strategically valuable coastline and rivers as part of the Louisiana Purchase. The ensuing negotiations between the United States and Spain could not resolve the boundary dispute. Spain asserted that the U.S. claim was illegitimate because France could not cede that which it did not possess, and Spain kept her colonial government intact. The United States read the treaty differently. In 1804, Congress authorized President Jefferson to use military force to seize the disputed area, but Jefferson refrained from direct actions because of Spanish protests. Spanish control of the region, however, hardly prevented residents of West Florida from thinking that they would soon be included as part of the rapid territorial expansion of the United States. They believed, much like some U.S. officials, that the Spanish territory had been included in the purchase from France.

The insurgency against Spanish rule began on June 23, 1810, when nearly five hundred citizens of Spanish West Florida met at the Egypt Plantation to "secure themselves against foreign invasion and domestic disturbance" (Arthur, 1935). They organized a government council that contained four representatives from each district of West Florida and declared that Spanish authorities could maintain their offices as long as they submitted to the council. A month later, on July 25, sixteen delegates convened at St. John's Plains near Baton Rouge to form a new government. They formed a legislature, named John Rhea its chairman, and believed that annexation by the United States was in their immediate future.

The political protest turned into a military struggle on September 23, when eighty men attacked and captured Baton Rouge. They stated their grievances against Spain and on September 26 declared West Florida "a free and independent State, absolved from all allegiance to a Government which no longer protects us" (ibid.). Soon after, Chairman Rhea requested annexation by the United States, a $100,000 loan, and a reservation of public lands for those who orchestrated the West Florida Rebellion. President James Madison, who privately supported the insurgents' designs against Spain, initially rejected the request and did not recognize the new nation's independence. Instead, on October 27, 1810, Madison repeated U.S. claims to the territory as part of the Louisiana Purchase and occupied the territory up to the Pearl River. British threats on the region, Madison publicly claimed, made this military action necessary.

Although Great Britain protested, Congress met in a secret session of January 15, 1811, and passed a resolution that claimed authority over the West Florida territory. Seven years after the Louisiana Purchase and seventy-four days after West Florida declared itself a free and independent nation, the United States annexed the disputed lands. The controversy over the territory continued until Spain and the United States finally agreed to a resolution in the Adams-Onís Treaty (1819), which ended the dispute.

—*Andrew K. Frank*

See also
West Florida

For Further Reading
Arthur, Stanley Clisby. 1935. *The Story of the West Florida Rebellion.* St. Francisville, LA: St. Francisville Democrat; Cox, Isaac John. 1918. *West Florida Controversy, 1798–1813: A Study in American Diplomacy.* Baltimore: Johns Hopkins Press; Waciuma, Manjoni. 1976. *Intervention in Spanish Floridas, 1810–1813: A Study in Jeffersonian Foreign Policy.* Boston: Branden Press.

WICHITA

Prior to the Wichita's removal, a direct result of the U.S. purchase of Louisiana in 1803, the tribe occupied the south-central plains from the Arkansas River of Kansas to the Brazos River of Texas. Once a confederacy of between thirty-eight thousand and fifty thousand people, the tribe now occupies allotted reservation lands and numbers between eight hundred and one thousand, a reduction largely attributable to smallpox epidemics that struck in the early 1800s and consumed approximately half of the existing population.

The U.S. policy of westward expansion relied heavily on a belief in Indian compression and containment. President Thomas Jefferson predicted in 1803: "Our settlements will gradually circumscribe and approach the Indians, and they will in time either incorporate with us as citizens of the United States, or remove beyond the Mississippi" (Drinnon, 1980). This region beyond the Mississippi, according to Jefferson, could be described as "a great deal of land unoccupied by any red men." But as Richard Drinnon has noted in his effort to draw attention to the blindness inherent in nation-building, this region was as "unoccupied as the wilderness Bradford and the Pilgrims came to was unpeopled" (ibid.). And the Wichita, unfortunately, were among those people invisible to Jefferson and his army of nation-builders.

A Plains tribe, the Wichita had historically relied on bison, corn, beans, squash, and tobacco (some native-grown and some the result of trade with the Europeans) for subsistence, so that camps were at times villagelike and at other times camplike. Because hunting required a great deal of mobility, being hemmed in suddenly by settlers forcibly altered the Wichita ways of life. Too, because of this mobility, the Wichita could not prove satisfactorily their claims of residency to a settlement-oriented U.S. government, which in turn left room for government justification of the reservation system. In fact, when the Wichita attempted in 1939 to recover some of their land that Jefferson had thought "unpeopled by red men," the Indian Commission decided that "[t]he record in this case does not establish as a fact that the Wichitas and affiliated bands of Indians at any time prior to 1859 ever possessed or occupied, to the exclusion of other tribes or bands of Indians, an area, within the territory which they claim, greater than the reservation within that territory of 743,257.19 acres which was set aside for and given to them by the United States for their absolute use and occupancy" (Washburn, 1973).

Prior to the Louisiana Purchase and the struggles for residency tied to it, the Wichita had interacted with both French and Spanish explorers. They traded with the French but maintained a very tension-fraught relationship with the Spanish: when Spanish forces tried to overtake the main Wichita town, they were forced to retreat by a well-fortified group of Indians who flew a French flag. Similarly, post-Purchase contact with American settlers often prompted hostility on both sides, particularly when the Wichita attempted to maintain residency within the Republic of Texas. In 1835 the Wichita signed a treaty with the United States, promising to coexist peacefully with already-present neighboring tribes and those recently removed to the area as a result of the Louisiana Purchase. This peace did not survive long, however, for settlers encroaching on the lands west of the Mississippi had little patience for Indian neighbors. Much of that tension remains, the by-product of forced relocation and its accompanying paternalism.

American history posits the beginning of Wichita existence as the time of contact with Spanish explorer Coronado in 1541. According to Wichita mythology, though, the world as it exists now actually emerged when Star That Is Always Moving heard a voice telling him to shoot the last of three deer that were going to leap from the water. The first deer was white, the second was black, and the third was both white and black. Star That Is Always Moving managed only to wound the third deer and so followed him and the other two into the sky, where they remain even today. After the deer became a constellation and the man who spoke to Star That Is Always Moving became the sun, villages appeared and people learned to live by hunting and planting corn. Star That Is Always Moving still chases those three deer, and when he catches up with them and retrieves his arrow, the stars and sun will become human—and it is said that a whole new world will be created.

—Lisa R. Williams

See also
Indian Removal; Jefferson, Thomas

For Further Reading

American Indian Publishers. 1995. *Dictionary of Indian Tribes of the Americas,* vol. 3. Newport Beach, CA: American Indian Publishers; Bierhorst, John. 1985. *The Mythology of North America.* New York: Quill William Morrow; Drinnon, Richard. 1980. *Facing West: The Metaphysics of Indian-Hating & Empire-Building.* Norman: University of Oklahoma Press; Washburn, Wilcomb E. 1973. *The American Indian and the United States: A Documentary History.* New York: Random House.

WILKINSON, JAMES (1757–1825)

James Wilkinson was born in Calvert County, Maryland, in 1757. In 1777, during the Revolutionary War, he received a brevet commission as brigadier general and was appointed secretary of the Board of War. Wilkinson held that position until 1778, when his involvement in the Conway Cabal against General Washington forced his resignation from the army.

In 1783, Wilkinson moved his family to Kentucky, where he became a leader of the faction seeking statehood. In 1787, Wilkinson sent a cargo of tobacco and other Kentucky products down the Mississippi River to the Spanish port of New Orleans. By convincing Spanish governor Miró that Kentuckians were willing to separate from the United States and join with Spain if they could use the port, Wilkinson persuaded Miró to change the Spanish policy of confiscation and grant Wilkinson and his partners a monopoly over Western trade with Louisiana. Wilkinson also agreed to serve as a source of information for Spain and signed a declaration of allegiance to Spain. His First Memorial to Miró presented a picture of conditions in Kentucky that played on Spanish fears of invasion. Wilkinson threatened that disgruntled Americans in Kentucky might ally with the British in Canada and attack Louisiana. Allowing Kentucky farmers to ship produce through New Orleans would promote disunion and ultimate alignment with Spain.

In the various meetings concerning the selection of Kentucky delegates to the Virginia convention to ratify the new U.S. Constitution, Wilkinson did propose independence for Kentucky under the protection of Spain. But made aware of the lack of support for his position, he abandoned his advocacy of separation. He did not, however, inform Miró of his failure. For the next ten years Wilkinson continued to write the Spanish governors of Louisiana, hinting that Kentucky might abandon the United States for Spain. The Spanish assigned Wilkinson the title Secret Agent #13, and promised him a pension for his efforts.

In 1791, Wilkinson rejoined the U.S. Army. In August 1803, President Jefferson selected Wilkinson and William C. C. Claiborne (governor of the Territory of Mississippi) as joint commissioners to receive the province of

Louisiana from the French, according to the terms of the Louisiana Purchase. Rumors were rife in New Orleans that the populace would not submit peacefully to the transfer to U.S. rule. Regular troops and volunteers from militia units in Tennessee and Kentucky assembled at Natchez under Wilkinson's command and prepared to march on New Orleans. Whether because of Wilkinson's army or because the rumors were untrue, the transfer of Louisiana to the United States proceeded without incident. On December 20, 1803, General Wilkinson received the keys to the city from the French representative, Pierre de Laussat, and he and Governor Claiborne watched as the French flag was lowered and the U.S. flag raised.

After Congress divided the province of Louisiana into two territories, Jefferson rewarded Wilkinson's service in 1805 with an appointment as governor of the Territory of Louisiana based in St. Louis. Wilkinson provided Jefferson with an extensive report on the geography and resources of the portion of Louisiana west and north of New Orleans. Knowing of the president's interest in exploring the new territory, Wilkinson sent Captain Zebulon Pike in 1805 to explore the upper Mississippi River Valley. After Pike's return to St. Louis, Wilkinson sent him off on another expedition to the headquarters of the Arkansas and Red Rivers. Wilkinson subsequently negotiated the Neutral Ground Treaty with Spanish Texas.

During this period, Wilkinson also renewed his correspondence with the Spanish officials remaining in New Orleans and sought payment of his promised pension. At the same time, he conferred with Aaron Burr. Wilkinson's complicity in Burr's schemes is uncertain. His report of the unsettled conditions in New Orleans and the desires of Western farmers to extend the frontier into Spanish territory may have suggested to Burr the possibility of a filibustering expedition in the Southwest. In a meeting at Four Massac on the Ohio River in June 1805, Wilkinson gave Burr letters of introduction to Governor Claiborne and other leading citizens of New Orleans. Informed by Daniel Clark, the city's leading merchant and former vice-consul, that Wilkinson was called Burr's right-hand man in the "absurd and wild reports" circulating in the city, Wilkinson asserted his ignorance of Burr's plans. But in September 1806, Burr's messenger, Samuel Swartwout, arrived at Wilkinson's headquarters with a letter from Burr announcing that his plans for an invasion of Louisiana and Mexico were ready. Two weeks later, in an apparent attempt to save himself, Wilkinson wrote President Jefferson exposing Burr's plot. Hastening to New Orleans, Wilkinson declared martial law in the city, an action opposed by many residents as an abuse of power.

Wilkinson testified against Burr at the former vice president's trial in Richmond, thus gaining for himself the support and protection of President Jefferson. Burr's allies attempted to discredit Wilkinson by resurrecting the charge that he had spied for Spain. In 1811, President James Madison ordered a court martial, which declared Wilkinson not guilty of treason. The general's Spanish conspiracy was not proved until long after his death by researchers in the Spanish archives taken in Havana after the Spanish-American War.

During the War of 1812 forces commanded by Wilkinson occupied Mobile, establishing U.S. control over the territory east to the Perdido River, and fought with General Wade Hampton in the campaign against Montreal. The failure of U.S. forces to take the Canadian city resulted in another court martial for Wilkinson, and he was again acquitted.

In the final years of his life, General Wilkinson published his memoirs defending his actions during his army career and in conjunction with the Burr plot. His years as adventurer, pioneer settler and trader, Western expansionist, army commander, Indian negotiator, and military administrator were over. His biographers, Thomas Hay and M. R. Werner, describe the general as an "enigmatic, resourceful, aggressive and sometimes unscrupulous personality," whose faith in America's Manifest Destiny was usually expressed in terms of his personal welfare. In his final years, Wilkinson hoped to recoup his fortunes by obtaining an *empressario* grant to settle a colony in Texas. He was living in Mexico City awaiting approval of his grant when he died on December 28, 1825. He is buried in the cemetery of the church of Archangel San Miguel.

—Elizabeth U. Alexander

For Further Reading

Clark, Daniel. 1970 [1809]. *Proofs of the Corruption of General James Wilkinson* . . . . Freeport, NY: Books for Libraries Press; Hay, Thomas, and M. R. Werner. 1941. *The Admirable Trumpeter: A Biography of General James Wilkinson.* New York: Doubleday, Doran and Company; Shepherd, William R. 1904. "Papers Bearing on James Wilkinson's Relations with Spain, 1787–1789" together with "Wilkinson's Second Memorial, New Orleans, September 17, 1789," and "Wilkinson and the Beginnings of the Spanish Conspiracy." *American Historical Review* 9: 490–506, 748–766; Whitaker, Arthur P. 1928. "James Wilkinson's First Descent to New Orleans in 1787." *Hispanic-American Historical Review* 8: 82–97; Wilkinson, James. 1811. *Aaron Burr's Conspiracy Exposed and General Wilkinson Vindicated* . . . . Washington, DC: Printed for the Author; Wilkinson, James. 1816. *Memoirs of My Own Time.* 3 vols. Philadelphia: Abraham Small.

WILLIAMS, BILL (1787–1849)

Mountain man, preacher, interpreter, guide, trapper, Indian trader, Indian fighter, trickster, and figure of Western legend, Bill Williams began his career in Spanish Louisiana.

Born in North Carolina, Williams moved west with his parents and siblings in 1794. Wanting to attract settlers to Louisiana, the Spanish government had offered land grants to Anglo-American families. The Williams grant lay on the Missouri River above St. Louis. Williams attended school for a few years but spent much of his time trapping in the woods and getting to know the neighboring Osage, Delaware, and Shawnee Indians.

Williams left home when he was sixteen or seventeen, about the time of the Louisiana Purchase. He was an itinerant preacher in Upper Louisiana until about 1807, when he settled among the Osage as a missionary. Williams lived with them for nearly fifteen years, but it does not appear that he made any converts to Christianity. Rather, the Osage adopted him and gave him an Osage name. Williams married an Osage woman with whom he had two children.

As the United States extended its influence over the trans-Mississippi West, Williams found that his knowledge of the region and its peoples created opportunities for employment. He scouted for Captain James Callaway's Mounted Rangers during the War of 1812. Subsequently, he carried dispatches for the U.S. Army. He was an interpreter at the Fort Osage trading post and the Osage factory at Marais des Cygnes, Missouri. In 1820, Christian missionaries settled near the Osage, and Williams interpreted for them in their conversations with the Indians and in their religious services. He gave the missionaries lessons in the Osage language and helped them to write a two-thousand-word Osage-English dictionary and to construct an Osage grammar book.

Besides working for the U.S. government and the missionaries, Williams also interpreted for the Osage in their diplomatic and legal relations with other tribes and with the United States. He interpreted at the Osage-Cherokee peace treaty at Fort Smith in 1822, and he was a translator and adviser for Mad Buffalo and other Osage men accused of murdering U.S. citizens in 1824. Williams was an interpreter and negotiator at the Osage treaty with the United States in 1825, but he may have worked more for his family's interests than for the Osage people at large. The treaty ceded almost all Osage lands in Missouri and Arkansas but reserved lands there for Williams's mixed-blood daughters.

By the mid-1820s, Williams began to move away from the Osage and the Louisiana Purchase. In 1822, Congress ended the factory system, which had provided official trade to Indians. Missouri had become a state, greatly increased its white population, and pushed its native population west. Williams's wife had died, and it is likely that his actions at the 1825 treaty had decreased his status among the Osage. As Williams's options in Missouri declined, opportunities farther west beckoned. Trade with Santa Fe was growing, and the U.S. government was sending exploratory and military missions to the Far West. There was plenty of work for an independent trader, interpreter, and guide. Williams followed the course of U.S. expansion, leaving the Louisiana region and heading for the Rockies. He was a guide and interpreter for Major George Sibley's survey of the Santa Fe Trail in 1825 and later hunted with Kit Carson and other mountain men. After the Mexican War, Williams guided the disastrous Frémont expedition through the Rockies, in which ten men died. Bill Williams Mountain in Arizona and the Bill Williams Fork of the Colorado River are named after him.

Williams is equally important as a figure of Western myth and legend. During his lifetime and after his death, countless anecdotes spread about his wild nature. The New Orleans *Daily Picayune* reported in 1844 that one cold winter day Williams shot and scalped a wolf in order to cover his head with the still-warm skin. He earned the nicknames "Old Bill," "Old Solitaire," and "Parson Williams." He was known for his bright red hair and beard, Indian dress, and a reputation for mysticism. He was renowned for his knowledge of many Indian languages, as well as English, French, Spanish, and, according to some, Greek and Latin. The typical mountain man, he was described as eccentric and curmudgeonly but also honest and generous. His reputation as both a romantic Indianlike figure and a patriotic U.S. Indian fighter embodies nineteenth-century Anglo-Americans' contradictory feelings about Indians. Williams's life reflects the westward movement of the frontier and the multicultural nature of the American West.

—Kathleen DuVal

See also
Carson, Christopher "Kit"; Mountain Men; Osage; Santa Fe Trail

For Further Reading
Favour, Alpheus H. 1936. *Old Bill Williams, Mountain Man.* Chapel Hill: University of North Carolina Press; Graves, W. W. 1949. *The First Protestant Osage Missions, 1820–1837.* Oswego, KS: Carpenter Press; Hill, Joseph J. 1930. "Free Trapper: The Story of Old Bill Williams, One of the Southwest's Most Mythical and Legendary Frontiersmen, Now Completely Recounted for the First Time." *Touring Topics* 22: 18–27; Voelker, Frederic E. 1971. "William Sherley (Old Bill) Williams." In *The Mountain Men and the Fur Trade of the Far West,* vol. 8. Edited by LeRoy R. Hafen. Glendale, CA.: Arthur H. Clark.

WINNEBAGO

The name "Winnebago" came from the Fox word *Ouinipegouek,* which meant "people of the stinking water." This referred to the waters of the Fox River and Lake Winnebago, both rich in algae, near which the Winnebago people lived. The Winnebago called themselves *Horogi* ("fish eaters") or *Hochungarra* ("trout nation").

The Winnebago spoke a Siouan tongue closely related to the language of the Iowa and Missouri. For ages the Winnebago inhabited what is today Wisconsin, and they may be descendants of the prehistoric mound-building Mississippian, Hopewell, and Adena peoples. Their power extended from what is today northern Michigan down to the Mississippi.

They dwelled in wigwams and practiced sophisticated agriculture, growing three types of corn as well as tobacco, squash, and beans. They hunted buffalo and fished using dugout canoes. Wild rice from the nearby lakes also supplemented their diet in the fall. They maintained their villages year-round and did not separate to hunting villages in the winter as did many of their neighbors.

Like that of many central Algonquins, the Winnebago religion revolved around the Manuna, or earth-maker deity. The people maintained Siouan myths about five individuals created by the central spirit to free the world from monsters and other forces of evil. Other legends included those of a great flood, a paradise in the sky, and a pathway for ascending souls of the dead, thought to be the Milky Way. They organized their society around twelve patrilineal clans, four representing the air and eight representing the earth, with one clan producing the hereditary chief.

The two major ceremonies of the Winnebago were the Mankani (medicine) dance, a secret and mysterious rite meant to prolong life, and the Wagigo feast, intended to appease the gods with offerings and celebration. The former was practiced by an elite, while the latter included the entire tribe.

The Winnebago first encountered Europeans in the form of Jesuit missionaries. In 1671, some of these Frenchmen reported that the Winnebago people had once been captured en masse by the Illinois but were then later released. The Winnebago later fought with the French and other allies against the Illinois.

They had the luxury of being on the fringe of colonial and later U.S. settlement until the Louisiana Purchase, which then placed Winnebago territory in the middle of the United States. Zebulon Pike's northern expedition made contact with the group in 1805 with little incident. Fort Madison followed four years later, the first U.S. fort on the upper Mississippi. It was a sign that things would change for the Winnebago.

At this time, the tribe was recovering from a smallpox epidemic that had nearly destroyed it. The population had fallen from approximately twenty thousand in the mid–seventeenth century to something like five thousand in the early nineteenth century. At one point in the eighteenth century, the numbers were believed to have plunged to a mere five hundred. The Winnebago faced the challenges of the encroaching United States, then, while climbing back from near-extinction.

In 1836 one of every four remaining Winnebago succumbed to another smallpox epidemic. The once-dominant nation ceded its Wisconsin land to the United States, and many members relocated to an area near Fort Atkinson in present-day Iowa to seek shelter from Fox and Sauk attacks. In 1845 the Winnebago exchanged Iowa lands for a reserve in Minnesota, but this move placed them between the Sioux and Ojibwa and left them with poor soil and harsh conditions for agriculture. The dwindling and besieged Winnebago moved again in 1856, to another reserve in southern Minnesota.

The United States forcibly removed the Winnebago from Minnesota after a Sioux attack on U.S. settlers in 1862. Although the Winnebago were not involved, the climate became dangerous. The terrible conditions in the South Dakota reservation where the United States had deposited the Winnebago survivors prompted them to flee and ask the eastern Nebraska Omaha for sanctuary. In 1865 the move became official, and forty thousand acres of Omaha land were purchased for the use of the Winnebago.

Eventually, most of the Winnebago returned to their native Wisconsin. The United States eventually stopped trying to fight the self-relocation and purchased Wisconsin homesteads for the determined tribespeople. Today both the Nebraska and Wisconsin Winnebago are recognized by the U.S. federal government (the Wisconsin tribe delayed this until 1963). Together they number over twelve thousand, making them one of the larger Amerindian communities in the United States.

—Amy H. Sturgis

See also

Fox; Ojibwa; Pike, Zebulon Montgomery; Santee Sioux; Sauk

For Further Reading

Radin, Paul. 1970. *The Winnebago Tribe*. Lincoln: University of Nebraska Press; Smith, David Lee. 1997. *Folklore of the Winnebago Tribe*. Norman: University of Oklahoma Press.

WORLD'S FAIR OF 1904

See **Louisiana Purchase International Exposition**

WOUNDED KNEE

Wounded Knee, a creek and village on the Pine Ridge Sioux Reservation in South Dakota, was the site of two famous events in Native American history: the massacre of Lakota Sioux by the U.S. Army in 1890 and the seizure of the village by members of the American Indian Movement (AIM) in 1973.

The Wounded Knee massacre was the last major military engagement of the Indian wars. This military confrontation had accompanied the Euro-American settlement of North America since the early seventeenth century and resulted in the complete military defeat of the indigenous societies. The warfare was characterized by the technological superiority of the invaders, who justified their military expansion through social Darwinist ideologies of Manifest Destiny. Particularly in the decades

The December 1890 massacre at Wounded Knee in South Dakota is often considered to be the final event of the Plains Indian Wars.

after the American Civil War, the fighting increased in frequency, and the dehumanization and brutalization, inherent in any war, reached new highs. Fostered by racism and derogatory stereotyping of Indians as savages, the Indian fighters embarked on a strategy of annihilation that further obscured the division between combatants and noncombatants and highlighted the totality of warfare as carried out by both sides. Instructive in this context was the Wounded Knee engagement.

As life on the reservation became desperate for the Sioux, they began to turn to the millenarian vision of a Paiute prophet named Wovoka. Through the Ghost Dance the tribes hoped to return to the days before the invasion of their homelands. Thousands of Lakota, Oglala, and Sincagu camped in the Badlands of South Dakota to escape temporarily the reservation system. The U.S. government considered this millenarian movement a serious threat and sent a large number of troops to the Badlands. The commander of the Military Division of the Missouri, General Nelson A. Miles, ordered the arrest of two important tribal chiefs, Big Foot and Sitting Bull.

An already tense situation threatened to worsen when Lakota chief Sitting Bull was killed in December 1890. Fearing for their safety, Big Foot and his band moved toward the Pine Ridge Agency and surrendered on December 28 to the Seventh Cavalry, Custer's old regiment, now under the command of Colonel James Forsyth.

The band camped along Wounded Knee Creek and agreed to be escorted to the railhead for transfer to Omaha. The 106 warriors were separated from the approximately 250 women and children, and the camps were surrounded by troops armed with four rapid-fire Hotchkiss field pieces. As the Indians were disarmed on the morning of December 29 a scuffle broke out, and fighting immediately commenced. The troops utilized their superior firepower and fired round after round into the melee with their canons. Bodies of women and children were found scattered for miles from the camp.

Estimates of Indian dead vary between 150 and 300. Another fifty of Big Foot's band were wounded. Twenty-five soldiers were killed and another thirty-nine wounded. On New Year's Day the soldiers dug a pit to bury the Indians, but not before many had stripped the dead bodies of the ghost shirts that they later sold as relics.

General Miles was outraged, as he considered the massacre an unnecessary blunder. Consequently, Colonel Forsyth was relived of command. He was reinstated later by the War Department and rose to the rank of major general. A number of enlisted men and officers received the Medal of Honor for their participation in the last major engagement of the Indian wars.

Wounded Knee ended more than two centuries of military confrontation between Native Americans and Euro-American settlers. The military defeat threatened the very

Bodies of dead Sioux remained unburied in the snow in the aftermath of the infamous Wounded Knee Massacre of December 1890.

survival of Indian nations and ended tribal control over the trans-Mississippi West.

The Wounded Knee Massacre has had a lasting symbolic significance for the Indian nations. In 1973 a young Sioux, Wesley Bad Heart Bull, was killed. In the ensuing emotionally charged and violent debate on the potential punishment for the suspected murderer, two hundred Sioux led by the American Indian Movement (AIM) seized control of a church, museum, and trading post on the Pine Ridge Reservation near the gravesite of the killed Lakotas. The goal of the seventy-one day occupation was to focus international media attention on what AIM perceived as a miscarriage of justice. Wounded Knee remained a symbol for the plight of the North American Indians.

—*Frank Schumacher*

For Further Reading

Brown, Dee. 1981. *Bury My Heart at Wounded Knee.* New York: Pocket Books; Coleman, William S. E. 2000. *Voices of Wounded Knee.* Lincoln: University of Nebraska Press; Mooney, James. 1991. *The Ghost Dance Religion and the Sioux Outbreak of 1890.* Lincoln: University of Nebraska Press; Utley, Robert M. 1963. *The Last Days of the Sioux.* New Haven: Yale University Press.

WYOMING

Land in the eastern two-thirds of the present-day state of Wyoming was included in the original Louisiana Purchase Territory. The Continental Divide that runs along the highest crests of the Rocky Mountains transected the Wyoming region dividing it between the Louisiana Territory and the Oregon Country. Since both of these early territories were points of contention between major world powers and their control often depended upon actual possession as well as diplomatic sanction, the early Wyoming region attracted many interested observers from Spain, France, Great Britain, and the United States.

Once the United States became the influential power in the region, practically all of the major trails that brought American pioneers into the Far West traveled through Wyoming. Whether one followed the Oregon Trail, the California Trail, or the Mormon Road, all of these corridors of expansion brought settlers through Wyoming, and early forts and settlements served as way stations and break-of-bulk points for pioneers who prepared for the transmountain crossing that lay shortly down the trail. Later, Wyoming would keep its preeminent position in the history of the American West by being the home to long stretches of the transcontinental telegraph line, the Pony Express route, and the first transcontinental railroad.

Before Europeans arrived in North America, the Wyoming region was home to a number of Native American groups who had settled on the high plains and in the valley bottoms of the Bighorn, Laramie, Medicine Bow, Absaroka, and Teton mountain ranges. Bands of Crow, Arapaho, Cheyenne, Sioux, and Assiniboine shared the bounty of the plains while the Flathead and other mountain-dwelling tribes who made occasional hunting forays into the region, were often contested as trespassers in the region. Bison herds were abundant on the high plains, and most tribes in the region had a culture and economy that was largely centered upon the success of the hunt. Additionally, many of Wyoming's rivers and streams contained a bounty of fish, and the waterways also provided an ideal environment for beaver, which were trapped.

The vast number of beaver pelts that could be taken from the Wyoming region is what first attracted Europeans to the region. As early as 1743, an expedition from New France led by Pierre Gaultier de Varennes, Sieur de La Vérendrye traveled through much of the Missouri Valley and claimed it for France. The Vérendrye exploring party became the first white men to enter Wyoming, and they traversed the region far enough to sight the Bighorn Mountains. For the next two decades, French trappers and traders operating out of the Lake Winnipeg region in Canada would work to bring the Wyoming fur trade into the French-Canadian economic orbit, but the vast distances involved limited the success of the endeavor. The Spanish acquired the Louisiana Territory from Spain in 1762 and held the region for nearly four decades. The Spanish showed very little interest in the far reaches of upper Louisiana—practically considering the region a wasteland—and concentrated their attention elsewhere within their empire.

When the United States purchased the Louisiana Territory in 1803, it soon became clear that American interest in the region would surpass that of the French and the benign neglect of the Spanish. Members of the Lewis and Clark Expedition inadvertently bypassed all of Wyoming on their excursion to and from the Pacific, but the glowing reports that they delivered about the potential of the Far West—in its entirety—was strong enough to create an almost insatiable interest in the West on the part of many American trappers and traders. John Colter, credited with being the first U.S. citizen to enter Wyoming, arrived in the region and began trapping in 1806. Within a short period others, including Ezekiel Williams and Edward Rose, followed Colter's lead. Despite the long distances involved, the solitude of the trapper's lifestyle, and the dangers of facing the uncertainties of frontier existence, the trappers who arrived in Wyoming realized that they had found a rich region that, as of yet, was virtually untapped.

Besides their obvious role as trappers and traders, the Americans who made their way into Wyoming also performed another important service as they became some of the most expert cartographers of the region's rugged terrain. In later years when the golden age of the fur trade would fade, many of these former trappers and traders, or mountain men, became guides to government expeditions and parties of emigrants who sought to follow the trails westward to new opportunities and adventure. Many of the fur trappers and traders were young men who were often unschooled in a classical sense, but they learned to read nature and survive the adversity of a frontier environment and thus gained a worldly knowledge that kept them prosperous and alive. In their ever-expanding search to find new streams to trap, the mountain men advanced the geographical knowledge of the West, discovering, for example, South Pass, which countless emigrant trains used as a relatively easy passage over the Continental Divide.

When the Rocky Mountain fur trade began in earnest, fur trading companies that operated out of St. Louis sent parties of trappers up the Missouri River to reach the mountain valleys. Each year, after conducting a successful season of trapping, these trappers were responsible for making a return trip to St. Louis to deliver the cache of pelts that they had taken in the previous year. This process was both tiresome and inefficient. During the 1820s, the St. Louis fur companies began the process of holding an annual rendezvous in a predetermined mountain valley to collect the pelts that had been trapped by the mountain men employed by the company. This business model made the mountain men permanent residents of the regions that they trapped, and the necessity of finding safe passage for valuable cargoes improved the quality of trails in portions of the Far West. When the company of Smith, Jackson, and Sublette delivered supplies to the 1829 rendezvous near the mouth of the Popo Agie River, they introduced the first mule-drawn wagon train in Wyoming history. By the early 1830s these trails westward were becoming better marked and soon the construction of U. S. military garrisons along these routes would bring an added dimension of security to overland travel and commerce.

The presence of the mountain men trapping and trading in the Far West did not provoke the Indian tribes that inhabited the region into widespread hostilities. Although skirmishes did occur from time to time, the overall record of the economic and social relationship between the mountain men and the Indian population of the area was tolerable and somewhat symbiotic. The two groups engaged one another in trade, and as such, each group needed something that the other possessed. Many of the mountain men adopted Indian women as wives, and while some of these were arrangements of convenience, in many cases the relationships endured for a lifetime. There certainly were negative consequences of the trade that was conducted. Mountain men often attempted to cheat Indians who traded animal pelts for American-made trade goods. In many cases, Indians were supplied with alcohol before a trade was conducted so that they might be less likely to protest unfair trade practices that were used against them.

The frequency and number of Indian attacks increased proportionally as larger and larger numbers of emigrant pioneers began to travel the Oregon Trail after 1832. The pioneer wagon trains were often poorly defended and they were supply-rich, which made them attractive targets to many of the tribes who inhabited the high plains. It increasingly became the role of frontier regulars from places like Fort Bridger and Fort Laramie to police the overland trails and try to prevent Indian attacks on pioneer groups. In time, the U. S. military installations in the West would become the sites of treaty negotiations as the U.S. government began the process of removing tribal groups from their homelands to other locations where they would be less likely to disrupt commerce or navigation along the western trails.

In the Treaty of Fort Laramie (1851) the U. S. government attempted to hold a general council with major tribal groups of the upper plains to end intertribal conflict and to prevent depredations against overland travelers. Delegations of Sioux, Crow, Cheyenne, and Arapaho attended the negotiations and ended up with a reduction in their lands. In the Treaty of Fort Laramie (1868) the reservation land that had been guaranteed to the Sioux was further reduced and they were promised the Black Hills of present-day South Dakota as a permanent home. That promise would also be broken within six years.

Throughout the early history of Wyoming, the region always had many people passing through, but few remained to become permanent residents. To many the forbidding arid landscape of the high plains was an unattractive option while places like Oregon, which was described as a veritable Eden, beckoned. The U.S. Congress officially created the Territory of Wyoming on July 25, 1868, but the name was more impressive than the reality. In the 1870 census, the Territory of Wyoming contained only 9,118 residents. The Territory made history in 1869 when it became the first region in the United States to grant the right to vote to women. Even though the population had doubled by the end of the decade, Wyoming was still perceived by many as a region that was land-rich, but people-poor. The 1890 census recorded the population of the Territory of Wyoming at 62,553 residents—just far enough beyond the legislative stipulation to be considered for statehood. Wyoming achieved statehood on July 10, 1890, when it became the forty-fourth state in the Union.

—Junius P. Rodriguez

See also

Bonneville, Benjamin L. E.; Colter, John; Dry Farming; Fur Trapping; Hunt, Wilson Price; Laramie, Fort; Rendezvous System; Smith, Jedediah Strong; South Pass

For Further Reading

Bartlett, I. S., ed. 1918. *History of Wyoming*. Chicago: S. J. Clarke Publishing Company; Coutant, Charles G. 1899. *The History of Wyoming from the Earliest Known Discoveries*. 3 vols. Laramie, WY: Chaplin, Spafford and Mathison.

YORK
(c. 1770–1831)

York, the lone black slave who participated in the Lewis and Clark Expedition, was a member of the Corps of Discovery from 1803 to 1806. His invaluable manpower and his courage toward his owner, Captain William Clark, and the entire corps helped the expedition through Louisiana to the Pacific Ocean and to its safe return to the East. Despite his slave status, he voted when decisions were made, eased Indian relations, and had responsibilities similar to those of other corps members on the expedition.

Bequeathed to his son in John Clark's will dated July 24, 1799, York became property of William Clark. York and William Clark were roughly the same age and had been childhood companions on Clark's family plantations in Virginia and Kentucky. When Meriwether Lewis asked his former military leader, William Clark, to be co-commander of the expedition in 1803, York became an immediate member. The two lived together on the north bank of the Ohio River, opposite Louisville, where they met Lewis's keelboat on October 29 and headed west.

The corps wintered near St. Louis and voyaged up the Missouri River in 1804, where York's duties included preparing the captains' meals, manning the keelboat and pirogues, and hunting. As a slave in the East, York had been prohibited by statute from handling firearms without special license, but he became a resourceful hunter in the plains of the Louisiana Territory by killing buffalo and other game.

Indian encounters on the Missouri River and at the 1805 winter camp with the Mandan only reinforced York's importance. Tribes considered him a novelty and took dirt or water to try to rub the black off his skin, because the Indians had not seen a person of African descent before. York's immense size and skin color made him a favorite among the Indian men, women, and children. His status allowed him the opportunity to have intimate relations with Indian women because many tribes believed that York's power and spirit would be given to their wives and back to their husbands through intercourse. The Arikara Indians, who at first could not tell if he was man, beast, or spirit being, dubbed him "Big Medicine." His significance allowed him to dance freely and play practical jokes on the Indians, sometimes to the dismay of his owner.

Unfortunately, there remain long periods of the expedition without information on York. He is scarcely mentioned after wintering at Fort Mandan until the expedition reached the Pacific, when he joined Clark and others to walk nineteen miles to see the "main ocean." He also helped to build Fort Clatsop, the expedition's 1805–1806 winter camp, and helped prepare for the journey home. On the return trip, he was entrusted with trade goods and was a member of Clark's detachment exploring the Yellowstone River. Despite the slave and master relationship, York risked his life in a flood for his owner. Clark named a small tributary "York's Dry River," and also doctored his sick slave to health on the expedition.

The Corps of Discovery returned to St. Louis on September 23, 1806, and all the members, including York, were eagerly greeted. The transition back to "civilized society" in the East was difficult. On the expedition, York had acted freely, but by returning to the East, he again became a slave and his opportunities were limited by that status. Afterward, York asked for his freedom, or to be hired out near Louisville to be closer to his wife, who was also a slave. The initial request infuriated Clark, but in 1809 he sent York to Kentucky. Nearly ten years after the expedition, Clark granted York his freedom. York lived as a free black man in a slave-based society and went to work in an unsuccessful freight business in Kentucky and Tennessee. The former member of the Corps of Discovery and the first black man to cross the North American continent north of Mexico died of cholera in 1831.

—Nathan R. Meyer

See also
Clark, William; Corps of Discovery; Lewis and Clark Expedition

For Further Reading
Betts, Robert B. 1985. *In Search of York: The Slave Who Went to the Pacific with Lewis and Clark*. Boulder: Colorado Association University Press; DeVoto, Bernard. 1953. *The Journals of Lewis and Clark*. New York: Houghton Mifflin; Gibbs, Carroll R. 1992. *Black Explorers*. Silver Spring, MD: Three Dimensional Publishing.

CHRONOLOGY

1497–1498
The Venetian navigator John Cabot [Giovanni Caboto], and his son Sebastian, explore North America for England. Cabot sailed the *Matthew* from Bristol in search of a northwestern route to Asia. Finding no such passage, Cabot's party landed on Cape Breton Island for fifty-two days, sailed southward until reaching 38 degrees north latitude and then returned to England. It is upon the basis of this voyage that the English King Henry VII lays claim to all lands of the North American continent.

c. 1500
French fishermen from the Norman and Breton coasts visit the waters off of Newfoundland. They make no effort to establish a settlement in the region.

1524
The Florentine navigator Giovanni da Verrazano explores the coast of North America for the French. Verrazano sails from Cape Fear to Cape Breton during his expedition and becomes the first European to view the future harbor site of New York.

1535
French explorer Jacques Cartier discovers the St. Lawrence River and claims Canada for France.

1540–1542
An expedition led by Spanish *conquistador* Francisco Vásquez de Coronado searches in vain to find the legendary seven lost cities of Cibola. Drawn onward by the lure of gold and hoping to duplicate the success of other conquerors, such as Hernán Cortés and Francisco Pizarro, Coronado and his party wander through much of the present-day southwestern United States, reaching territory as far interior as the site of present-day Kansas.

1541 May 8
Members of the Hernando DeSoto expedition become the first Europeans to reach and cross the Mississippi River. This magnificent waterway, called the "Father of Waters" by the indigenous peoples who lived in its valley, would become in time the primary commercial artery of much of North America.

1541–1542
Jacques Cartier and Jean-François de la Rocque de Roberval attempt to establish a colony at the site of present-day Quebec. It was the first attempt by Europeans to establish a settlement in North America (outside of Mexico).

1542
Members of the Juan Rodriquez Cabrillo expedition become the first Europeans to reach the Pacific coast of what eventually became the United States. The group lands near what is now San Diego, California.

1543 July 19
Survivors of the DeSoto expedition, led by Luis de Moscoso, become the first white men to descend the Mississippi River all the way to the Gulf of Mexico.

1562 April 30
French settlers led by Jean Ribaut establish a settlement at Port Royal on Parris Island, just off the coast of present-day South Carolina. The Huguenot [French Calvinist] settlers abandoned the Port Royal colony in 1564, when the French failed to resupply it.

1564
A group of Huguenots [French Calvinists] led by René Goulaine de Laudonnière found a short-lived colony at Fort Caroline along the St. John's River in present-day Florida. It was destroyed by the Spanish, who established St. Augustine the following year.

1565 September 8
The Spanish establish a settlement at St. Augustine, Florida. The community is noted as being the oldest town established by Europeans in what eventually became the United States.

1603
French explorer Samuel de Champlain establishes a French colonial settlement in Acadia.

1604
Pierre du Guast, Sieur de Monts, establishes a French settlement of Port Royal on Neutral Island in the St. Croix River, in what is present-day Maine.

1607
The London Company founds an English settlement at Jamestown, Virginia. This was the first permanent English settlement in North America, and it became the

nucleus of the thirteen Atlantic seaboard colonies that were eventually established by the English.

1608
Samuel de Champlain founds a French settlement at Quebec. This fortified city became, in time, the center of New France, and it served as the commercial entrepôt for much of the fur trapping that took place in the North American interior. Rivalry between New France and the English seaboard colonies would eventually result in warfare between the two European powers.

1609–1613
Traveling into the Canadian interior with Algonquian and Huron Indian guides, French explorer Samuel de Champlain seeks out fur trapping areas in the region of Georgian Bay.

1610
The Dutch explorer Henry Hudson discovers Hudson's Bay in Canada. The region of Hudson's Bay would become the center of fur trapping operations in North America during the seventeenth century. When the Dutch leave their North American possessions in 1664, the English assume control and become participants in the region's fur trade.

1613
English forces led by Samuel Argall destroy the French colonial settlement at Port Royal.

1627
The administrators of the colony of New France grant a charter to the commercial enterprise Compagnie des Cent-Associes (also called the Company of One Hundred, or the Company of New France).

1629
French-Canadian explorer and guide Étienne Brulé becomes a traitor to his countrymen when he leads a force of Englishmen who capture Quebec and take Samuel de Champlain prisoner. Three years later, Brulé was murdered and eaten by a group of Huron Indians with whom he had quarreled.

1629–1632
For a brief period, the French colonial areas of Acadia and Quebec fall under control by England, but the colonies revert back to French control in 1632.

1634
French explorer Jean Nicolet searches in vain to find the fabled Northwest Passage across the continent. He crosses the Great Lakes and discovers Lake Michigan.

1638
The American log cabin, initially a structure of Finnish design, is introduced to the New World by Swedish settlers of Delaware. This quintessential "American" dwelling soon became the mainstay of frontier dwellers. The log cabin would later appear in those areas of the Louisiana Purchase territory that were well endowed with forests.

1642
The Canadian city of Montreal is founded. It quickly becomes the primary base of operations for French fur trappers and traders who are operating in the St. Lawrence River Valley.

1654–1661
French explorers and fur trappers Pierre Esprit Radisson and Médart Chouart, Sieur des Groseilliers, lead expeditions west of the Great Lakes and north of Lake Superior. When officials in New France angered them, they offered their discoveries of new trapping areas to the English. This led to the establishment of the Hudson's Bay Company.

1663
French King Louis XIV declares Canada to be a royal province and establishes its capital at Quebec. Operating under the economic system of mercantilism, France would reap huge profits from Canada's fur trade.

1664
The French government charters the Compagnie des Indes Occidentales to control all aspects of trade related to French colonial possessions.

1670
After forcing the Dutch to abandon their North American colonial assets in September 1664, the English establish the Hudson's Bay Company to compete in the fur trade with the French.

1673
Jesuit Father Jacques Marquette and fur trapper Louis Joliet explore the upper portion of the Mississippi River Valley. Their journey takes them through the Great Lakes and along the Wisconsin, Illinois, and Mississippi Rivers. Their expedition traveled as far southward on the Mississippi River as the mouth of the Arkansas River.

1675
The French establish the frontier settlement of Kaskaskia in the Illinois Country.

1675–1676
King Philip's War in New England is the bloodiest of all the Indian wars experienced in colonial New England. Half of the English settlements in New England were destroyed during this conflict, and one of every sixteen white settlers of military age was killed. Thousands of Narraganset were killed, and many of those captured were either driven away as refugees or sold into slavery.

The conflict set the tone for subsequent relations between Euro-American settlers and Native American groups.

1679
French explorer Daniel Greysoln, Sieur DuLuth, claims Lake Superior and the upper portion of the Mississippi River basin for France.

1680
Father Louis Hennepin, Michel Accault, and Antoiné Auguelle are sent by La Salle to explore the upper part of the Mississippi River Valley. They are captured and temporarily held hostage by the Santee Sioux.

1681
The French establish a trading license (*congé*) system to regulate the fur trade in New France.

1682 April 9
French explorer Robert Cavelier, Sieur de La Salle, reaches the mouth of the Mississippi River after traversing much of the length of that stream. Standing near the end of the river, La Salle claimed the river and all the lands that it drained for France. He named the territory Louisiana in honor of French King Louis XIV. In making this proclamation, La Salle claimed for France nearly two-thirds of the territory that constitutes the present-day United States. Virtually all of the territory between the Appalachian and Rocky Mountains was defined as Louisiana by La Salle's action. This French land claim would come into conflict with the English claim based upon John Cabot's voyage (1497).

1687
Leaders of England and France sign the Peace of Whitehall. In this document, both nations declare that they will never fight each other over their colonial possessions in the New World. Despite their promise, the nations would be at war with one another within two years.

1689
French trapper and explorer Nicolas Perrot takes formal possession of the upper Louisiana region for France. Perrot had been instrumental in forging an alliance with the Algonquian Indians to oppose the Iroquois, who were allies of the English.

1689–1697
King William's War [known as the War of the Grand Alliance in Europe] was the first of a series of colonial wars that pitted England against France. Control of North American territory was the key objective of both sides in these conflicts. The war was concluded by the Treaty of Ryswick (1697).

1699
French Sulpician missionaries establish a mission at Cahokia in the Illinois Country.

The LeMoyne brothers [Iberville and Bienville] found the Louisiana colony for France. The initial settlement was established near the site of present-day Mobile, Alabama. The long-range goal of the French crown was to link the Quebec-based New France settlement with the new Louisiana colony situated along the Gulf of Mexico. Key to linking these regions would be the Mississippi River.

1699 March 2
Iberville becomes the first European to find the Mississippi River from the Gulf of Mexico.

1701 July 24
Antoine de la Mothe Cadillac founds a French settlement at Detroit, Michigan. Located at the strategic point where Lake Erie and Lake Huron meet, the outpost was founded to protect French fur interests in the Illinois Country.

1702–1713
Queen Anne's War represents the North American phase of the War of the Spanish Succession (1701–1714). The conflict concluded with the Treaty of Utrecht (1713). At the end of the war, the French cede Acadia, Newfoundland, and Hudson's Bay to the English.

1703
The French soldier and author Louis Armand de Lom d'Arce, Baron de Lahontan, publishes *Nouveaux Voyages* (1703), which popularized the idea of the American Indian as the "noble savage." Lahontan's descriptions of the Canadian wilderness and the people who inhabited the region would become a stereotype to many European readers of the Enlightenment Era.

1704 February 29
The Deerfield Massacre takes place in Massachusetts, as French colonial settlers and their Indian allies burn a New England town, killing forty-seven and taking 109 individuals as captives.

1709
Jacques Raudot, the intendant of New France, declares the ownership of African or Indian slaves to be legal within the province.

1714
Natchitoches is founded by Louis St. Denis, who establishes Fort St. Jean Baptiste along the Red River. It is the oldest European settlement in the entire Louisiana Purchase territory. The Spanish would respond to this action by establishing the town of Los Adaes.

1717
John Law's Company of the West is given an exclusive charter by the French government for the development of the Louisiana colony.

1718 February
New Orleans is founded by the French. It becomes the capital of the Louisiana colony.

1721
The Lords of Trade petition British king George I to "fortify the passes in the back of Virginia" in an effort to disrupt French expansion efforts in the Ohio country.

1724
The French build Fort Vincennes on the lower Wabash River in the Ohio country.

French trapper Etienne de Bourgmont builds Fort Orleans on the north bank of the Missouri River, in present-day Carroll County, Missouri. The site was abandoned in 1730.

1726
The French build a fort at the junction of the Illinois and Mississippi Rivers.

1728
Arrival of the "casket girls" in New Orleans. They are sent to North America to become wives of French colonial settlers.

1729
The Natchez Rebellion occurs in colonial Louisiana. The Natchez Indians kill 250 people at Fort Rosalie.

The French send Chaussegros de Léry to fortify the Ohio River Valley down to the Miami River in the Ohio country.

1742–1743
French explorers of the LaVérendrye family conduct an expedition into the Dakota region. They travel as far west as the Black Hills region. The explorers claim the Missouri River Valley for France.

1745–1748
King George's War is the North American phase of the War of the Austrian Succession (1740–1748). The conflict concluded with the Treaty of Aix-la-Chapelle [Aachen].

1747
In the colony of Virginia, the Ohio Company of Virginia is established to promote settlement of the Ohio River Valley by American colonists.

1749 June
An expedition sets out from Montreal in New France to gain control of the Ohio River Valley. Pierre Joseph de Céloron de Blainville leads a group of French-Canadian frontiersmen and their Indian allies into the Ohio Valley to convince tribes in that region that their region belongs to France. The expedition traveled for thirteen hundred miles and buried inscribed lead plates to verify French ownership of the region.

c. 1750
Several bands of Sioux begin to migrate into the Dakota region.

Founding of Ste. Genevieve, in present-day Missouri. The community became the first permanent white settlement in Missouri. It was a center for fur trapping and lead mining.

1750
Dr. Thomas Walker discovers Cumberland Gap. This passageway through the Appalachian Mountains, located near the point where the modern-day states of Virginia, Kentucky, and Tennessee meet, would be the place where thousands would cross the mountains into the trans-Appalachian West.

Maryland-born American colonial explorer Christopher Gist became the first Anglo-American to visit the Ohio River Valley. Gist had been commissioned by the Ohio Company of Virginia to conduct a reconnaissance mission into the trans-Appalachian region.

1751
A variety of St. Dominque sugar cane is introduced into Louisiana by the Jesuits. Sugar would eventually become the cash crop of the Louisiana colony.

1752
A group of Indians who are allies of the French attack a trading post that the British had established at Pickawillany, in the Ohio Valley, to conduct the business of the fur trade.

1754–1763
The French and Indian War [Seven Years War] is fought. It is concluded with the Treaty of Paris (1763). France will lose her North American empire as a result of being defeated by the British in this conflict.

1755
British forces expel the Acadians from Nova Scotia. Believing that these former French colonial residents of Acadia [Nova Scotia] would act in a fashion contrary to British interests during the war with France, the British government uses forced removal to remedy the problem. Significant numbers of Acadians would eventually settle in south Louisiana, where they became known as Cajuns.

1761
The "Family Compact" is signed between the Bourbon monarchs of France and Spain.

1762 November 3
The Treaty of Fontainebleau is negotiated between France and Spain. The French turn the western half of the Louisiana Territory over to the Spanish.

1763 February 10
In the Treaty of Paris (1763), France cedes to Great Britain all of Louisiana east of the Mississippi River.

1763 May 7
Ottawa chief Pontiac leads a rebellion in the Ohio River Valley against British settlers who have entered the region. The British Parliament passes the Proclamation of 1763, which prohibits American colonists from entering the trans-Appalachian West.

1764 February 15
St. Louis, Missouri, is founded by Pierre Laclede Liguest.

1764
Some of the first Acadians begin to arrive in Louisiana.

1769
In what is present-day Missouri, the city of St. Charles is first established as a trading post by Louis Blanchette.

1769 August 17
Spanish take effective control of Louisiana with the arrival of Governor O'Reilly.

1774–1770
The Indian leader Tahgahjute of the Mingo tribe, who has adopted the name John Logan, leads a campaign of sustained warfare against American pioneer settlers who have moved into the Ohio River Valley.

1775–1783
British colonists in the thirteen Atlantic seaboard colonies rise in rebellion against Great Britain and seek independence from their mother country.

1778 February 6
France and the United States sign the Treaty of Alliance. France agrees to support America's effort to win independence from Great Britain.

1779
During the American Revolution, General George Rogers Clark captures the frontier outpost of Vincennes in the name of the Continental Army, thereby ensuring that the United States will have a strong claim to the trans-Appalachian West in subsequent treaty negotiations with the British.

1781 March 1
The U.S. government begins to operate under the Articles of Confederation.

1783 September 3
The Treaty of Paris officially ends the American Revolution. Great Britain recognizes the independence of the United States of America.

1784
The North West Company is established in Canada to challenge the supremacy of the Hudson's Bay Company in the fur trade.

1785
The Land Ordinance is enacted by Congress under the Articles of Confederation government. The measure establishes a system of land units called townships that are defined by a grid of township and range lines. The goal of the measure is to create an orderly process by which Western lands can be sold to settlers who hope to move into the trans-Appalachian West.

1786–1787
The Jay-Gardoqui negotiations take place between the United States and Spain. The Spanish are willing to offer the United States trading concessions if the Americans will agree to postpone the demands of Western frontiersmen, who desire the right to use the Mississippi River, for a period of twenty-five years. The United States does not accept the treaty proposal.

1787 July 13
The Northwest Ordinance is enacted by the Congress under the Articles of Confederation government. Lands north of the Ohio River are designated as the Northwest Territory, and slavery is prohibited from the region.

1789 April
Upon ratification of the U.S. Constitution, a new and stronger federal system of government is adopted by the United States. George Washington is elected to serve as the first president of the United States under the new constitutional arrangement.

1789 July 14
In Paris, mobs storm the Bastille, marking the start of the French Revolution.

1789–1790
The Nootka Sound crisis occurs in the Pacific Northwest. Territorial rivalry between Spain and Great Britain leads to the threat of war between the two nations. Many in the United States fear that such a war might threaten the territorial integrity of the young American republic should British forces march across U.S. territory to attack Spanish possessions.

1791
A massive slave insurrection begins in the French colony of St. Domingue. In the end, slaves led by Toussaint L'Ou-

verture will overthrow French colonial authority and establish an independent black republic. By 1804, the area will become known as Haiti.

1792
U.S. sea captain Robert Gray reaches the mouth of the Columbia River in the Pacific Northwest and gives the United States a partial claim to the Oregon Country.

Spanish colonial officials in Louisiana restrict the importation of slaves into the colony from any of the French Caribbean colonies for fear that ideas of slave insurrection might spread.

1793
Scottish-born Canadian explorer Alexander Mackenzie becomes the first European to cross the Rocky Mountains and reach the Pacific Ocean by traveling overland across North America.

Citizen Edmond Genêt arrives in Charleston, South Carolina, after being appointed French minister to the United States. Over the course of several months, the brash young diplomat encourages U.S. citizens to honor the Treaty of Alliance (1778) and support the French people in their time of need. Genêt also conspires to try to recover Spanish Louisiana for the French Republic.

1793 April 25
Pope Pius VI establishes the Diocese of Louisiana and the Floridas.

1793
President George Washington issues his Neutrality Proclamation and says that the United States will not become involved in the European war between France and Great Britain.

1794
The French National Assembly outlaws slavery in the French colonies.

1794 November 19
Jay's Treaty is concluded between the United States and Great Britain. The United States did not win the concessions that it had sought in the negotiations.

1795 October 20
Pinckney's Treaty [Treaty of San Lorenzo] is concluded between the United States and Spain. Both parties agree to a Florida boundary line at 31 degrees north latitude. The United States also acquires the "right of deposit" at New Orleans for a period of three years.

1797 October
In Europe, France and Austria agree to terms of a truce with the Peace of Campo Formio.

1798
Lieutenant Governor Zenon Trudeau of Spanish Louisiana invites U.S. frontiersman Daniel Boone to settle in the Louisiana Territory by offering him one thousand arpents of territory. Boone would immigrate to what is present-day Missouri and establish a homestead.

1798–1800
The United States and France fight an undeclared naval war (the Quasi-War). The conflict is the U.S. response to the diplomatic event known as the XYZ Affair, when French diplomats tried to exact a bribe from U.S. negotiators.

1799
The Russian American Fur Company is chartered under impetus of the traders Gregory Shelikov and Alexander Baranov.

Morales, the Spanish intendant of Louisiana, discontinues the "right of deposit" at New Orleans that had been granted to American frontiersmen in the Treaty of San Lorenzo (1795). The king reverses the ruling of the intendant in 1800.

1799 November 9
Napoleon Bonaparte stages the coup d'état of 18 Brumaire and comes to power as first consul of France.

1800
Convention of 1800 [Treaty of Mortefontaine] is signed with France. This document officially ends the undeclared naval war (Quasi-War) that the nations had been fighting since 1798.

1800 October 1
The secret second Treaty of San Ildefonso is negotiated between France and Spain. In this agreement, the Spanish planned to retrocede the Louisiana Territory to France as soon as certain treaty stipulations were met. The final transfer would be effected after the Convention of Aranjuez (1801) was signed.

1801 February
In the Treaty of Lunéville the French Republic makes peace with the Austrian leaders of the old Holy Roman Empire. The French acquire the Italian kingdom of Tuscany in this agreement.

1801 March 21
The Convention of Aranjuez completes the treaty negotiations between France and Spain over the retrocession of the Louisiana Territory.

1802
King-Hawkesbury negotiations take place between the United States and Great Britain. The United States is unwilling to join an alliance with the British.

1802 March 25
With the Treaty of Amiens, the French Republic and Great Britain agree to a temporary truce.

1802 April 18
Thomas Jefferson writes a letter to Robert Livingston, U.S. minister to France, describing how critical New Orleans is to American commercial independence.

1802 May
Napoleon Bonaparte names himself consul for life.

1802 October 16
Morales, the Spanish intendant of Louisiana, again discontinues the "right of deposit" at New Orleans that had been granted to American frontiersmen in the Treaty of San Lorenzo (1795).

1802 December 15
Thomas Jefferson's Second Message to Congress acknowledges concern about what the retrocession of Louisiana from Spain to France will mean for U.S. commercial interests.

1803 January 11
Jefferson's Message to the Senate calls for the appointment of Robert Livingston and James Monroe to negotiate with First Consul Napoleon Bonaparte to remedy the commercial difficulty that the United States faces along the Mississippi River, and specifically at New Orleans.

1803 March 26
Colonial Prefect Pierre Laussat arrives at New Orleans and makes the first public announcement that the Louisiana Territory has been retroceded to the French.

1803 April 30
The Louisiana Purchase is concluded. First Consul Napoleon Bonaparte decides to sell the entire Louisiana Territory and the Isle of Orleans to the United States.

1803 May 2
The main Louisiana Purchase treaty document is signed.

1803 May 23
Talleyrand sends a letter to Duc Denis Decres, French minister to the United States, informing him of the sale of Louisiana to the United States.

1803 June 20
Thomas Jefferson's letter to Meriwether Lewis describes the objectives that are to be carried out by the Corps of Discovery as it travels overland to the Pacific Ocean.

1803 August 17
French colonial prefect Lassaut writes a letter to Decres, French minister to the United States, informing him that word about the sale of Louisiana to the United States has arrived at New Orleans.

1803 October 17
Thomas Jefferson's Third Message to Congress urges the immediate ratification of the Louisiana Purchase Treaty documents.

1803 October 19
The U.S. Senate ratifies the Louisiana Purchase Treaty.

1803 October 21
Jefferson's Message to the Senate and House asks for implementation of the special conditions that are outlined in the Louisiana Purchase Treaty documents, so that the legal transfer of the territory can take place.

1803 October 31
The U.S. Congress approves of enabling legislation that authorizes President Jefferson to take possession of Louisiana.

1803 November 2
Senator Samuel White's speech criticizing the Jefferson administration for its purchase of Louisiana is delivered in the U.S. Senate.

1803 November 10
The final treaty details of the Louisiana Purchase are enacted by the U.S. Congress as it creates necessary stock to fund the purchase and writes provisions to make Louisiana citizens U.S. citizens.

1803 November 30
Colonial Prefect Lassaut issues a proclamation as he takes formal possession of Louisiana. The period of French control would last for twenty days.

1803 December 20
The cession of Louisiana from France to the United States takes place at New Orleans.

1804–1806
The Lewis and Clark Expedition takes place. The Corps of Discovery travels from St. Louis to the Pacific following the Missouri River and the Snake and Columbia Rivers.

1804
The Dunbar-Hunter Expedition takes place in the Arkansas River Valley.

1804 January 16
President Thomas Jefferson's Message to the Senate and House describes his plans for the administration of the Louisiana Purchase Territory.

1804 February 24

Congress makes provisions for the collection of duties and imports at New Orleans.

1804 March 26

The Land Law of 1804 is enacted by the Congress, specifying how territory within the national domain is to be sold through federal land offices.

1804 March 26

Two governments are created in the Louisiana Purchase territory: the Territory of Orleans and the Louisiana Territory.

1804 November 8

President Jefferson's Fourth Message to Congress reports upon the progress made in bringing the Louisiana Purchase territory into the U.S. system.

1805

Citizens of Louisiana issue the Louisiana Memorial to Congress, calling for the recognition of the rights that they enjoyed under previous French and Spanish colonial administrations.

1805–1806

Lieutenant Zebulon M. Pike leads a military expedition to discover the source of the Mississippi River.

1806

John Colter, a former member of the Lewis and Clark Expedition, returns to the valley of the Yellowstone River with a group of trappers.

The Thomas Freeman Expedition sets out to explore the Red River Valley. General James Wilkinson informs Spanish officials of the pending expedition, and the Freeman Party is stopped and forced to turn around.

The Office of Superintendent of Indian Trade is established in the War Department under the secretary of war, to administer federal Indian trading houses.

1806–1807

Lieutenant Zebulon M. Pike leads an expedition to the Southwest designed to follow the Arkansas River to its headwaters. Pike and his men were arrested and jailed by Spanish authorities for trespassing into Spanish Mexico.

Former vice president Aaron Burr plots a conspiracy involving the seizure of Western lands. Although his co-conspirator, General James Wilkinson, testified against Burr at his 1807 treason trial, Burr was acquitted.

1807

Manuel Lisa builds a fort at the mouth of the Big Horn River in Crow country. This location becomes the first post for the Rocky Mountain fur trade.

U.S. engineer Robert Fulton demonstrates the first commercially successful steamboat, the *Clermont*. Within a decade steamboats would ply Western rivers as commerce carriers, and they would be used by exploring parties in the West.

1807–1808

John Colter travels the West, visiting Jackson's Hole, Yellowstone Park, Pierre's Hole, and adjacent territory.

1808

John Jacob Astor establishes the American Fur Company.

Under the direction of William Clark, the U.S. Army establishes Fort Osage on the Missouri River.

1809

The St. Louis Missouri Fur Company is charted. Its partners include Manuel Lisa, William Clark, Pierre Chouteau, Sr., and Andrew Henry.

1810

Andrew Henry ascends the Missouri River to the Three Forks and builds a fort there among the Blackfoot.

1810 September 24

The West Florida Rebellion takes place. President James Madison annexes West Florida and attaches the region to the Territory of Orleans and the Mississippi Territory.

1811 January

A slave insurrection along the German Coast region just west of New Orleans threatens the security of the Territory of Orleans. The revolt is suppressed by a local vigilante force supported by territorial militia and U.S. Army forces.

1811 May

Astoria, Oregon, is founded by John Jacob Astor and his Pacific Fur Company, a subsidiary of the American Fur Company. Wilson Price Hunt led the overland expedition that joined the other Astorians at the mouth of the Columbia River.

1811 December–1812 January

A series of earthquakes occur at New Madrid, in present-day Missouri. The tremors are strong enough to change the course of the Mississippi River in some areas.

1812 April 30

Louisiana is admitted into the Union as the eighteenth state, the first to be admitted from territory acquired from the Louisiana Purchase.

1812–1813

One of the Astorian fur trappers, Robert Stuart, makes a

trip eastward, likely making the first trip by a white man through South Pass in Wyoming.

The Guiterrez-Magee Expedition takes place as American adventurers try to establish control of part of east Texas.

1813
Fort Astoria is surrendered to the North West Company, and the site is renamed Fort George.

1815 January 8
Andrew Jackson defeats British forces at the Battle of New Orleans.

1815
The Treaty of Portage des Sioux restricts the territory of several tribes in the upper Mississippi River Valley. Several of the affected tribes had supported the British during the War of 1812.

1816
In a nationalistic measure of the "Era of Good Feelings," the U.S. Congress enacts a measure that prohibits British fur trappers and traders from operating upon U.S. territory.

1817
The United States and Great Britain sign the Rush-Bagot Agreement and jointly declare that the Great Lakes will be demilitarized.

1817–1820
The pirate Jean Lafitte occupies Galveston Island along the Texas coast and uses it as his base of operations for smuggling and privateering.

1818
In the "Convention of 1818" the United States and Great Britain establish an official boundary line between Canada and the United States. From the Great Lakes westward to Lake of the Woods, the boundary will fall upon the Boundary Waters. From Lake of the Woods westward, the boundary will run along the line of 49 degrees north latitude up to the Rocky Mountains. The United States and Great Britain also agree on "joint occupancy" for the Oregon Country.

A "cotton boom" in the Southwest brings large numbers of settlers into the Arkansas Territory.

1819
Encouraged by a group of Natchez, Mississippi, planters who seek to establish control over eastern Texas, James Long leads an expedition that creates a short-lived Texan republic. Long was killed by Mexican authorities in 1822.

1819 February 22
The Transcontinental Treaty [Adams-Onís Treaty] is signed between the United States and Spain. The United States acquired Florida from Spain. The United States gave up its claims to Texas, and the Spanish gave up their claim to the Oregon Country. The boundary of Texas and Louisiana was set at the Sabine River.

1820
With the Land Law of 1820, the U.S. Congress further clarifies the process that will be used to sell portions of the national domain through federal land offices.

Henry Clay develops the Missouri Compromise agreement, which will allow both Missouri and Maine to enter the Union, as slave and free states, respectively. The line of 36 degrees 30 minutes is set as the boundary between slave and free territory for the remaining portion of the Louisiana Purchase territory.

The Stephen H. Long Expedition explores the headwaters of the Arkansas River in present-day Colorado.

1820–1821
William Becknell conducts trading expeditions from Franklin, Missouri, to the Mexican city of Santa Fe. Becknell's route became known as the Santa Fe Trail.

1821 August 10
Missouri is admitted into the Union as the twenty-fourth state, the second to be admitted from territory acquired from the Louisiana Purchase.

1821
The Merger of the North West Company and the Hudson's Bay Company takes place. Previously, these had been Canada's two largest rivals in the fur trade.

Mexico receives its independence from Spain.

1822
The Office of Indian Trade and all Indian trading houses (the so-called factory system) are abolished by congressional action.

William Ashley establishes the Rocky Mountain Fur Company.

1823
A fur trading expedition led by William Ashley is halted by the Arikara when they attack the river-borne trappers and traders.

1824
The Bureau of Indian Affairs is organized as part of the War Department. In 1832 it is formally recognized by a law of Congress.

1823–1824
"Mountain men" Jedediah Smith and Thomas Fitzpatrick cross the Continental Divide at South Pass, in what is now Wyoming. Countless emigrant pioneers would cross the Rocky Mountains at South Pass as pioneer trails westward converged at that location.

1823–1829
Canadian-born explorer Peter Skene Ogden explores parts of present-day Idaho, Nevada, Utah, California, Oregon, and Montana while conducting expeditions on behalf of the Hudson's Bay Company.

1825
John McLoughlin, chief factor of the Columbia District for the Hudson's Bay Company, constructs Fort Vancouver on the north bank of the Columbia and uses it as his headquarters.

1826
The Fredonian Revolt takes place in east Texas.

1828
American Insurance Co. v. Canter is decided by the U.S. Supreme Court. The case recognizes the legality of the United States to govern and administer territory acquired through treaty or purchase.

1830
The Indian Removal Act passes Congress, calling for relocation of Eastern Indians to an Indian territory west of the Mississippi River. Cherokees contest it in court, and in 1832, the Supreme Court decides in their favor, but Andrew Jackson ignores the decision. From 1831 to 1839, the Five Civilized tribes of the Southeast are relocated to the Indian Territory. The Cherokee "Trail of Tears" takes place in 1838–1839.

A particularly harsh influenza epidemic is noted among tribes of British Columbia. In 1830–1833, there are similar outbreaks of European diseases in California and Oregon.

1830–1836
Famed artist George Catlin travels among and paints the Plains Indians.

1831
American inventor Cyrus Hall McCormick invents the mechanical reaper. This device would be used by pioneer farmers to harvest crops throughout the Louisiana Purchase territory.

1832
American explorer and ethnologist Henry R. Schoolcraft traces the Mississippi River northward to its source at Lake Itasca, in present-day Minnesota.

The Bureau of Indian Affairs is created as an agency of the U.S. government. It is housed in the War Department.

The Black Hawk War is fought in Illinois and Wisconsin between combined Sauk and Fox tribes and the United States.

The Black Hawk Purchase Treaty takes place upon the conclusion of the Black Hawk War.

1832–1835
Captain Benjamin L. E. de Bonneville leads a military exploring party into the West. The expedition produced the first authoritative maps of the Rocky Mountain and Far West region.

1833–1834
The Missouri River Expedition of two Europeans, Prince Maximilian and the painter Karl Bodmer, takes place.

1834
Congress reorganizes the Indian offices, creating the U.S. Department of Indian Affairs (still within the War Department). The Trade and Intercourse Act redefines the Indian Territory and Permanent Indian Frontier, and gives the army the right to quarantine Indians.

Pierre Chouteau of St. Louis becomes a part-owner of the Western Department of John Jacob Astor's American Fur Company. This company would dominate the fur trade of the Missouri and Mississippi River Valleys until 1865.

1835
The Treaty of Camp Holmes is negotiated with the Comanche and Wichita and other tribal bands in Indian Country (present-day Oklahoma).

Texas declares itself a republic, independent from Mexico. The Texas Rangers are organized to campaign against the Comanches.

1836
Marcus and Narcissa Whitman and other missionaries establish missions among the Indians. Mrs. Whitman and the other missionary wives become the first white women to cross the Continental Divide.

1836 March 6
Mexican forces overrun the Texan defenders of the Alamo in San Antonio. Despite their defeat, the Texans would later inspire forces to ultimate victory in the Texas Revolution using the rallying cry "Remember the Alamo."

1836 June 15
Arkansas is admitted into the Union as the twenty-fifth

state, the third to be admitted from territory acquired from the Louisiana Purchase.

1837
A smallpox epidemic occurs among Mandan, Hidatsa, and Arikara tribes of the upper Missouri. From 1837 to 1870, at least four different smallpox epidemics ravage Western tribes.

Illinois blacksmith John Deere invents the steel-blade plow. Deere was mass-producing his product by 1847, and it was later credited with helping to "break" the plains.

American artist Alfred Jacob Miller travels through the West with a group of American Fur Company trappers. Miller sketches and chronicles the final days of the Rocky Mountain fur trade.

1838
Jesuit missionary Father Pierre Jean DeSmet founds a mission at Council Bluffs, in present-day Iowa, where he begins his ministry to various tribes in the region. DeSmet would later travel the Oregon Trail to the Pacific Northwest, where he continued his missionary endeavors among the Indians.

1838–1839
Some fifteen thousand Cherokee are ordered removed from their ancestral lands in the southeastern United States. They were removed to Indian Territory in present-day Oklahoma, following the "Trail of Tears" to the site. Four thousand Cherokee died during the journey to Oklahoma.

1841
The U.S. Congress adopts the Preemption Act of 1841. The measure is an effort to adopt some of the views of "squatter's rights" into government land policy.

The first emigrant party to travel the Oregon Trail, the Bidwell-Bartleson party, heads for California with one hundred farmers and their families. En route, some of them change their minds and opt for Oregon.

1841–1842
John Charles Frémont conducts a U.S. military expedition into the Far West with Kit Carson as a guide.

1842
Fort Bridger is established by fur trappers and traders in what is present-day Wyoming. It would later become a military outpost.

1843
The first emigrant wagon train reaches the Oregon Country via the Oregon Trail.

1844
Four major wagon trains along the Oregon Trail bring two thousand farmers, merchants, mechanics, and lawyers to Oregon. One party each leaves Independence, Westport, St. Joseph, and Bellevue (near Council Bluffs).

1845
Newspaper editor John L. O'Sullivan first uses the expression "manifest destiny" in the *United States Magazine and Democratic Review*. O'Sullivan's editorial comments were written in support of the annexation of Texas by the United States.

1846 December 28
Iowa is admitted into the Union as the twenty-ninth state, the fourth to be admitted from territory acquired from the Louisiana Purchase.

1846
The United States and Great Britain agree to divide the Oregon country at the forty-ninth parallel. Hudson's Bay Company headquarters are moved from Fort Vancouver to Fort Victoria on Vancouver Island.

Paul Kane travels among and paints Indians of southern Canada and the American Northwest.

1846–1848
The United States fights against Mexico in the Mexican War. The conflict is viewed by many as an effort provoked by the United States to acquire the vast Mexican landholdings of the American southwest.

1847 July 24
Brigham Young and the Mormon settlers, having blazed the Mormon Road, reach the site of present-day Salt Lake City.

1848 January 24
James W. Marshall discovers gold at Sutter's Mill in California, starting the California Gold Rush and the attrition of the California and Plains Indians. Thousands of gold-seekers would trek across the lands of the Louisiana Purchase Territory to make their way to California.

1849
Establishment of the U.S. Department of Interior.

The Bureau of Indian Affairs, first established in 1832, is transferred from the War Department to the Department of the Interior.

The Courthouse Rebellion takes place in Canada, involving the métis population of the Red River of the North.

American historian Francis Parkman publishes *The California and Oregon Trail*.

1850
The first of a series of treaties between Canada and Canadian tribes is enacted, a policy that continued until 1923.

1850–1860
A terrible cholera epidemic occurs among the Indians of the Great Basin and Southern Plains.

1851
The Treaty of Fort Laramie between the U.S. government and several tribes of the Northern Plains leads to the reduction of Indian lands.

1852
Wells, Fargo and Company is established to bring mail and banking services to the West.

1853–1856
The United States acquires 174 million acres of Indian lands through fifty-two treaties, all of which are subsequently broken by the government.

1854
The Commissioner of Indian Affairs calls for an end to the Indian removal policy.

The Graduation Act is passed by the Congress. The measure offers some parcels of land in the national domain at a reduced price per acre.

The U.S. Congress enacts the Kansas-Nebraska Act. The measure will cause the liquidation of northern portions of the Indian Territory when the Kansas and Nebraska Territories are established.

1855
The firm of Russell, Majors and Waddell is established. As the major freight and stagecoach firm of the trans-Mississippi West, the company held a monopoly on freight hauling to military outposts in the West from 1855 to 1862.

Amana Community starts in Iowa. This experiment in Christian communism was begun by Christian Metz, who led the Community of True Inspiration. Metz and his German immigrant followers established seven villages in east-central Iowa.

1856 May 24
The abolitionist John Brown and his sons carry out the Potawatomi Creek Massacre in the Kansas Territory. Five proslavery settlers were killed in the event.

1857 March
Speaking for the majority, Supreme Court chief justice Roger B. Taney issues a ruling in the case of *Dred Scott v. Sandford.* The ruling states that the U.S. Congress does not have the authority to prohibit slavery from the Western territories.

1858
Albert Bierstadt first visits the Rockies and begins to paint images of Western landscapes that have broad popular impact.

1858–1859
The Colorado Gold Rush (Pike's Peak Gold Rush) begins as gold is discovered at Cherry Creek, near present-day Denver.

1858 May 11
Minnesota is admitted into the Union as the thirty-second state, the fifth to be admitted from territory acquired from the Louisiana Purchase.

1860 April–1861 October
The Pony Express is in operation, providing mail service between Missouri and California. The need for this service ended when the transcontinental telegraph line was completed in 1861.

1861 January 29
Kansas is admitted into the Union as the thirty-fourth state, the sixth to be admitted from territory acquired from the Louisiana Purchase.

1862
The Homestead Act opens up Western land to pioneer settlers, who are guaranteed their 160-acre plots for free after inhabiting them for five years and making improvements to the land.

1862–1863
Santee Sioux stage an uprising in Minnesota under Chief Little Crow. In 1863–1864, it spreads to North Dakota and involves the Teton Sioux as well. Thirty-eight Indians are sentenced and hanged.

1864–1865
The Cheyenne-Arapaho War is fought in Colorado and Kansas. On November 29, 1864, Colonel John M. Chivington's Colorado Volunteers kill more than three hundred Indians in the infamous Sand Creek Massacre.

1864
George Perkins Marsh publishes *Man and Nature, or Physical Geography as Modified by Human Action*. The publication of this book is often recognized as marking the origin of the U.S. conservation movement.

1865
In Chicago, Illinois, the Union Stock Yards open for business. This enterprise would soon be associated with the great "cattle drives" of the West, as Texas longhorns were

brought to Northern railheads and then shipped eastward to Chicago to be slaughtered.

1865–1869
Meat hunters hired by the Union Pacific Railroad destroy herds of bison on the Great Plains as they feed the laborers who are constructing the first transcontinental railroad through the region.

1865–1866
Jesse Chisholm, a mixed-blood Western guide, opens the Chisolm Trail.

1866
The word *ecology* is coined by the German biologist Ernst Haeckel.

Jim Bridger, working as a scout for the U.S. government, maps the 967 miles of the Bozeman Trail from Missouri to Montana.

1866–1868
War is fought for the Bozeman Trail in Wyoming and Montana, involving the Sioux, Cheyenne, and Arapaho, under the leadership of Chief Red Cloud. A second Fort Laramie Treaty resolves the conflict in 1868.

1867
Inspired by the idea of Joseph G. McCoy, the first of the great "cattle drives" from Texas arrives at the railhead in Abilene, Kansas.

In the British Parliament, the British North American Act establishes the Confederation of Canada. The First Dominion Parliament is assembled. In 1868, an Indian Act shapes new administrative machinery for Indian affairs in Canada.

The Treaty of Medicine Lodge is signed, in which Plains tribal leaders accept permanent lands within the Indian Territory.

The government-sponsored "Indian Peace Commission" makes a survey of Indian affairs and recommends that the current treaty process be abandoned. This commission and the Nez Percé Indians negotiate the last of 370 treaties between the federal government and tribes.

1867 March 1
Nebraska is admitted into the Union as the thirty-seventh state, the seventh to be admitted from territory acquired from the Louisiana Purchase.

1868
The commissioner of Indian Affairs estimates that the Indian Wars in the West are costing the U.S. government $1 million per Indian killed.

1868–1869
The Southern Plains War (also called the Sheridan Campaign) takes place. This conflict involved the Cheyenne, Sioux, Arapaho, Kiowa, and Comanche.

1869 May 10
The first transcontinental railroad is completed. The Union Pacific and Central Pacific link at Promontory Point, in present-day Utah.

1869
Hudson's Bay Company sells its vast holdings of land (Rupert's Land) to the Dominion of Canada.

1872
The famed Chiricahua Apache warrior Cochise surrenders to U.S. general Oliver O. Howard.

The U.S. Congress establishes Yellowstone National Park.

1873
The U.S. Congress enacts the Timber Culture Act, which grants additional acreage in the Great Plains to those homesteaders who promise to plant trees. The measure was repealed by the Congress in 1891.

1874
Gold is discovered in the Black Hills of South Dakota. Treaties protecting Indian lands are ignored by miners.

Illinois inventor Joseph Glidden receives a patent for barbed wire. This invention would transform much of the West and lead to the end of the open range.

American engineer James Buchanan Eads constructs the first steel-arch bridge, across the Mississippi River at St. Louis, Missouri. Later in 1874, Eads worked to construct rock jetties at the mouth of the Mississippi River that helped to deepen the channels there, which previously would fill with silt.

1874–1875
The Red River War on the Southern Plains is fought. It involved the Comanche, Kiowa, and Cheyenne, under Quanah Parker.

1876–1877
The Sioux War for the Black Hills is fought, involving the Sioux, Cheyenne, and Arapaho, under Sitting Bull and Crazy Horse. On June 25, 1876, U.S. general George Armstrong Custer and the men of the Seventh Cavalry were defeated in the Battle of Little Big Horn.

1876 August 1
Colorado is admitted into the Union as the thirty-eighth state, the eighth to be admitted from territory acquired from the Louisiana Purchase.

1877
The U.S. Congress enacts the Desert Land Act. This measure permitted Western settlers to purchase up to 640 acres (one square mile) of arid lands within the national domain. The individual landowners would be responsible for irrigating the land that they purchased. This legislation was a greater benefit to Western cattlemen than it was to homesteaders who had hoped to farm.

1877 October 5
Chief Joseph and his band of Nez Percé surrender to General Oliver O. Howard after having avoided capture for months by attempting to escape into the Canadian Rockies.

1880
Completion of the Atchison, Topeka and Santa Fe Railroad, another transcontinental line, marks the end of overland traffic on the Santa Fe Trail.

1881
Marcus Daly establishes the Anaconda Copper Mining Company in Butte, Montana.

Helen Hunt Jackson publishes *A Century of Dishonor*. The book is the first by a white author to challenge the U.S. government's Indian policy as being built upon fraud and deceit.

1883
William Frederick "Buffalo Bill" Cody first organizes and performs his famous Wild West Show. Cody would perform until 1916 in tours that took place throughout the United States and Europe.

1884 June–1886 October
Future president of the United States Theodore Roosevelt works on a cattle ranch in the Dakota Territory.

1887
The U.S. Congress passes the General Allotment Act (the Dawes Severalty Act), in which reservation lands are given to individual Indians in parcels. Indian tribes lost millions of acres of land. The measure had been intended to help Indians integrate into U.S. life by encouraging them to farm on private homesteads.

The U.S. Congress enacts the Hatch Act as a further extension of the Morrill Act (1862), which had created land-grant colleges and universities. According to the Hatch Act, federal dollars could be expended to support state agricultural experimental stations. The research in the agricultural and mechanical arts conducted at these locations was instrumental in changing the landscape of the American West.

1889 April 22
The Oklahoma "Land Rush" begins as thousands of settlers pour into the territory to claim land that had previously been Indian Territory, unavailable to white homesteaders.

1889 November 2
North Dakota is admitted into the Union as the thirty-ninth state, the ninth to be admitted from territory acquired from the Louisiana Purchase.

1889 November 2
South Dakota is admitted into the Union as the fortieth state, the tenth to be admitted from territory acquired from the Louisiana Purchase.

1889 November 8
Montana is admitted into the Union as the forty-first state, the eleventh to be admitted from territory acquired from the Louisiana Purchase.

1890
The Ghost Dance Movement led by the Paiute prophet Wovoka gains influence among Western Indians. Sitting Bull is murdered on December 15. At Wounded Knee, U.S. troops massacre 350 Sioux Indians en route to a Ghost Dance celebration on December 28.

1890 July 10
Wyoming is admitted into the Union as the forty-fourth state, the twelfth to be admitted from territory acquired from the Louisiana Purchase.

1891
U.S. naturalist John Muir is instrumental in having the U.S. Congress create the National Forest System with passage of the Forest Reserve Act.

1892
The Sierra Club is founded by U.S. naturalist John Muir.

1893
U.S. historian Frederick Jackson Turner presents the essay "The Significance of the Frontier in American History" at the annual convention of the American Historical Association meeting in Chicago.

1894
After an estimated thirteen million bison have been slaughtered on the Great Plains, the U.S. government takes its first action to protect the animals. Yellowstone National Park becomes the first refuge with lands specifically set aside for the bison.

The U.S. Congress enacts the Carey Desert Land Grant Act. Settlers are allowed to purchase Western lands that are classified as desert at the price of fifty cents per acre.

1899
Considered one of the earliest pieces of environmental legislation passed by the U.S. Congress, the Rivers and Harbors Act (Refuse Act) of 1899 prohibits the dumping of refuse into navigable waterways.

1899 January 10
Representatives of all the Louisiana Purchase states meet in St. Louis at the Southern Hotel and decide that a World's Fair would best commemorate the event, and that it should be held in St. Louis in 1903.

1900
A monument is built in Iowa honoring Sergeant Charles Floyd, the only member of Lewis and Clark's Corps of Discovery to die on the expedition.

1900 June 4
Congress passes the Sundry Civil Appropriation Bill, carrying an amendment pledging the national government's support of the World's Fair project, together with an appropriation of $5 million, conditioned on the raising of another $5 million by popular subscription and the appropriation of $5 million by the city of St. Louis.

1901
President William McKinley issues a proclamation supporting the choice of St. Louis to host the World's Fair Exposition.

1902
During President Theodore Roosevelt's administration the Congress enacts the Newlands Reclamation Act. This measure authorized federal funding to support irrigation projects in Western areas that had been too expensive for states or individuals to do on their own. As a result of this measure, twenty million acres of once-marginal or desert land will be turned into farmland.

American author Owen Wister publishes the novel *The Virginian*. This work is credited with popularizing the genre of cowboy fiction that became common in the twentieth century.

1903
President Theodore Roosevelt speaks at the dedication of the Louisiana Purchase Exposition in St. Louis, Missouri.

1905
The American Bison Society is founded to promote the survival of the species.

1907 November 16
Oklahoma is admitted into the Union as the forty-sixth state, the thirteenth to be admitted from territory acquired from the Louisiana Purchase.

1911 April 11
The ground-breaking ceremony is held for the Jefferson Memorial in St. Louis.

1911 May 1
The cornerstone is laid for the Jefferson Memorial in St. Louis.

1913
The U.S. Treasury introduces the "buffalo nickel," which features the likeness of an American Indian on one side and a buffalo on the other. The coins were minted every year until 1938, with the exceptions of 1922, 1932, and 1933. During the years that it was in production, 1.2 billion coins were minted.

1913 April 30
The Jefferson Memorial is dedicated in St. Louis.

1916 November
Jeanette Rankin of Montana becomes the first woman elected to serve in the U.S. House of Representatives.

1928
Several states hold ceremonies to commemorate the 125th anniversary of the Louisiana Purchase.

1928 November
Herbert Clark Hoover of Iowa becomes the first American born west of the Mississippi River to be elected president of the United States of America. Hoover's vice president, Charles Curtis of Kansas, was the first vice president with Native American ancestry.

1930
American artist Grant Wood paints "American Gothic."

1931
American historian Walter Prescott Webb publishes *The Great Plains*.

1934
The U.S. Congress enacts the Wheeler-Howard Act. This measure restores the ownership of Indian lands to the tribes rather than to individual members of tribes.

1934 June 26
Congress creates the Thomas Jefferson Memorial Commission, to create a suitable memorial to commemorate the nation's third president.

1939 November 15
The cornerstone is laid for the Jefferson Memorial in Washington, D.C.

1943 April 13
The Jefferson Memorial in Washington, D.C., is dedicated on the bicentennial of Jefferson's birth.

1947
Historian Bernard A. DeVoto publishes the Pulitzer Prize–winning *Across the Wide Missouri.*

1953
Several states hold ceremonies to commemorate the 150th anniversary of the Louisiana Purchase.

President Dwight D. Eisenhower speaks in New Orleans, Louisiana, to commemorate the sesquicentennial of the Louisiana Purchase.

1954
The U.S. Postal Service issues a commemorative postage stamp in honor of Lewis and Clark's 150th anniversary celebration.

1958
A replica of Fort Clatsop, built in approximately the same place that Lewis and Clark had built it 150 years earlier, is formally recognized by the U.S. National Park Service.

1964
Congress establishes the Lewis and Clark National Trail.

1967
The Gateway Arch opens in St. Louis, Missouri.

1968 May 25
The Gateway Arch is dedicated.

1969
The Lewis and Clark Trail Heritage Foundation, Inc., is established.

1973
Members of the American Indiana Movement (AIM) take control of the Wounded Knee site on the Pine Ridge Reservation in South Dakota. AIM members held the site for two months.

1974
The Lewis and Clark Trail Heritage Foundation begins publication of the quarterly magazine *We Proceeded On.*

1976
Historian Alexander DeConde publishes *This Affair of Louisiana.*

1978
The Bureau of Outdoor Recreation adds the word *historic* to the newly renamed Lewis and Clark National Historic Trail.

Several states hold ceremonies to commemorate the 175th anniversary of the Louisiana Purchase.

2000
The U.S. Treasury introduces into circulation a new one-dollar coin bearing the image of Sacagawea and her child.

President Bill Clinton grants William Clark posthumous captain's commission.

2002 April 3
The U.S. Mint announces plans to reduce production of the Sacagawea dollar coin as public use of the coin fails to meet expectations.

DOCUMENTS

DOCUMENT 1
TREATY OF FONTAINEBLEAU (1762)

Le Roi Très Chretien etant dans la ferme resolution de reserrer de plus en plus et de perpetuer les liens de la tendre amitié qui l'unissent au Roi Catholique son cousin, se propose d'agir en conséquence en tout temps et à tous egards avec sa Majesté Catholique dans une parfaite uniformité de principes, relativement à la gloire commune de leur maison, et à l'interêt réciproque de leurs monarchies.

Dans cette vue sa, véritablement sensible aux sacrifices que le Roy Catholique a bien voulu faire généreusement pour concourir avec elle au rétablissement de la paix, a désiré de lui donner à cette occasion une preuve du vif interêt qu'elle prend à sa satisfaction et aux avantages de sa couronne.

Pour cet effet, le Roi Très Chretien a autorisé le Duc de Choiseul son ministre à delivrer dans la forme la plus autentique au Marquis de Grimaldi ambassadeur extraordinaire du Roy Catholique, un acte par lequel sa Majesté Très Chretien cede en toute proprieté, purement et simplement, et sans aucune exception, à sa Majesté Catholique et à ses successeurs à perpetuité, tout le pays connu sous le nom de la Louisiane, ainsy que la nouvelle Orleans et l'isle dans la quelle cette ville est située.

Mais le Marquis de Grimaldi n'etant pas assez esactement informé des intentions de sa Majesté Catholique, a cru ne devoir accepter la dite cession, que conditionellement et sub spe rati, en attendant les ordres qu'il recevra du Roi son maitre, lesquels s'ils sont conformes aux desirs de sa Majesté Très Chretienne, comme elle l'espère, seront immediatement suivis de l'acte formel et autentique de la cession don't il s'agit, dans lesquels seront stipulées les mesures à prendre et l'epoque à fixer d'un commun accord, tant pour l'evacuation, de la Louisiane et de la nouvelle Orleans par les sujets de sa Majesté Chretienne, que pour la prise de posesion des dits pays et ville par sujets de sa Majesté Catholique.

En témoignage de quoi, nous ministres respectifs avons signé le présent acte preliminaire, et y avons fait apposer le cachet de nos armes.

Fait à Fontainebleau le trois novembre mille sptecent soixante deux.

The Most Christian King being of firm resolution to strengthen and perpetuate the ties of friendship which unite him with the Catholic King, his cousin, consequently proposes to act for all time and in every aspect with his Catholic Majesty in a perfect uniformity of principles relating to the common glory of their dominions and in the mutual interests of their monarchies.

In this view, his Most Christian Majesty, being truly sensitive to the sacrifices that the Catholic King has generously been willing to make in order to cooperate with him towards the re-establishment of peace, desired on this occasion to give him proof of his sincere interest in the satisfaction and honor of his crown.

To this effect, The Most Christian King has authorized his Minister the Duc de Choiseul to deliver in the most authentic form to the Marquis de Grimaldi, Ambassador Extraordinary of the Catholic King, an act by which his Most Christian Majesty renounces all pretentions, purely and simply, and without exception, to all the land known under the name of Louisiana as well as the town of New Orleans and the island in which it is situated, to his Catholic Majesty and to his successors for all perpetuity.

But the Marquis de Grimaldi not being precisely informed of the intentions of his Catholic Majesty, believed himself obliged only to accept the said cessions conditionally and sub spe rati, while awaiting the orders which he will receive from the King his master, which, if they conform to the desires of his Most Christian Majesty, as he expects, will be followed immediately by the formal and authentic act of the transfer in question, in which the measures to follow and the fixed epoch for a common accord will be stipulated, as much as for the emigration from Louisiana and New Orleans by the subjects of His Christian Majesty as for the taking of possession of the said lands and town by the subjects of his Catholic Majesty.

In witness whereof, we the underwritten ministers have signed the current preliminary act and have caused the seal of our arms to be put thereto.

Done at Fontainebleau the third day of November, 1762.

El Marques de Grimaldi
Le Duc de Choiseul

Source: Paullin, Charles Oscar, ed. 1967. *European Treaties Bearing on the History of the United States and Its Dependencies.* Translated by Elizabeth Field. Vol. 4. Gloucester, MA: Peter Smith.

DOCUMENT 2

JAY'S TREATY (TREATY OF LONDON) (1794)

TREATY OF AMITY COMMERCE AND NAVIGATION

His Britannic Majesty and the United States of America, being desirous, by a treaty of amity, commerce and navigation, to terminate their difference in such a manner, as, without reference to the merits of their respective complaints and pretentions, may be the best calculated to produce mutual satisfaction and good understanding; and also to regulate the commerce and navigation between their respective countries, territories and people, in such a manner as to render the same reciprocally beneficial and satisfactory; they have, respectively, named their Plenipotentiaries, and given them full powers to treat of, and conclude the said treaty, that is to say:

His Britannic Majesty has named for his Plenipotentiary, the Right Honorable William Wyndham Baron Grenville of Wotton, one of His Majesty's Privy Council, and His Majesty's Principal Secretary of State for Foreign Affairs; and the President of the said United States, by and with the advice and consent of the Senate thereof, hath appointed for their Plenipotentiary, the Honorable John Jay, Chief Justice of the said United States, and their Envoy Extraordinary to His Majesty; Who have agreed on and concluded the following articles:

ART. I.
There shall be a firm, inviolable and universal peace, and a true and sincere friendship between His Britannic Majesty, his heirs and successors, and the United States of America; and between their respective countries, territories, cities, towns and people of every degree, without exception of persons or places.

ART. II.
His Majesty will withdraw all his troops and garrisons from all posts and places within the boundary lines assigned by the treaty of peace to the United States. This evacuation shall take place on or before the first day of June, one thousand seven hundred and ninety six, and all the proper measures shall in the interval be taken by concert between the Government of the United States and His Majesty's Governor-General in America for settling the previous arrangements which may be necessary respecting the delivery of the said posts:

The United States in the mean time, at their discretion, extending their settlements to any part within the said boundary line, except within the precincts or jurisdiction of any of the said posts. All settlers and traders, within the precincts or jurisdiction of the said posts, shall continue to enjoy, unmolested, all their property of every kind, and shall be protected therein. They shall be at full liberty to remain there, or to remove with all or any part of their effects; and it shall also be free to them to sell their lands, houses or effects, or to retain the property thereof, at their discretion; such of them as shall continue to reside within the said boundary lines, shall not be compelled to become citizens of the United States, or to take any oath of allegiance to the Government thereof; but they shall be at full liberty so to do if they think proper, and they shall make and declare their election within one year after the evacuation aforesaid. And all persons who shall continue there after the expiration of the said year, without having declared their intention of remaining subjects of His Britannic Majesty, shall be considered as having elected to become citizens of the United States.

ART. III.
It is agreed that it shall at all times be free to His Majesty's subjects, and to the citizens of the United States, and also to the Indians dwelling on either side of the said boundary line, freely to pass and repass by land or inland navigation, into the respective territories and countries of the two parties, on the continent of America, (the country within the limits of the Hudson's Bay Company only excepted.) and to navigate all the lakes, rivers and waters thereof, and freely to carry on trade and commerce with each other. But it is understood that this article does not extend to the admission of vessels of the United States into the seaports, harbours, bays or creeks of His Majesty's said territories; nor into such parts of the rivers in His Majesty's said territories as are between the mouth thereof, and the highest port of entry from the sea, except in small vessels trading bona fide between Montreal and Quebec, under such regulations as shall be established to prevent the possibility of any frauds in this respect. Nor to the admission of British vessels from the sea into the rivers of the United States, beyond the highest ports of entry for foreign vessels from the sea.

The river Mississippi shall, however, according to the treaty of peace, be entirely open to both parties; and it is further agreed, that all the ports and places on its eastern side, to whichsoever of the parties belonging, may freely be resorted to and used by both parties, in as ample a manner as any of the Atlantic ports or places of the United States, or any of the ports or places of His Majesty in Great Britain All goods and merchandize whose importation into His Majesty's said territories in America shall not be entirely prohibited, may freely, for the purposes of commerce, be carried into the same in the manner aforesaid, by the citizens of the United States, and such goods and merchandize shall be subject to no higher or other duties than would be payable by His Majesty's subjects on the importation of the same from Europe into the said territories.

And in like manner all goods and merchandize whose importation into the United States shall not be wholly prohibited, may freely, for the purposes of commerce, be carried into the same, in the manner aforesaid, by His Majesty's subjects, and such goods and merchandize shall be subject to no higher or other duties than would be payable by the citizens of the United States on the importation of the same in American vessels into the Atlantic ports of the said States.

And all goods not prohibited to be exported from the said territories respectively, may in like manner be carried out of the same by the two parties respectively, paying duty as aforesaid. No duty of entry shall ever be levied by either party on peltries brought by land or inland navigation into the said territories respectively, nor shall the Indians passing or repassing with their own proper goods and effects of whatever nature, pay for the same any impost or duty whatever.

But goods in bales, or other large packages, unusual among Indians, shall not be considered as goods belonging bona fide to Indians.

No higher or other tolls or rates of ferriage than what are or shall be payable by natives, shall be demanded on either side; and no duties shall be payable on any goods which shall merely be carried over any of the portages or carrying places on either side, for the purpose of being immediately reembarked and carried to some other place or places.

But as by this stipulation it is only meant to secure to each party a free passage across the portages on both sides, it is agreed that this exemption from duty shall extend only to such goods as are carried in the usual and direct road across the portage, and are not attempted to be in any manner sold or exchanged during their passage across the same, and proper regulations may be established to prevent the possibility of any frauds in this respect.

As this article is intended to render in a great degree the local advantages of each party common to both, and thereby to promote a disposition favorable to friendship and good neighborhood, it is agreed that the respective Governments will mutually promote this amicable intercourse, by causing speedy and impartial justice to be done, and necessary protection to be extended to all who may be concerned therein.

ART. IV.

Whereas it is uncertain whether the river Mississippi extends so far to the northward as to be intersected by a line to be drawn due west from the Lake of the Woods, in the manner mentioned in the treaty of peace between His Majesty and the United States:

It is agreed that measures shall be taken in concert between His Majesty's Government in America and the Government of the United States, for making a joint survey of the said river from one degree of latitude below the falls of St. Anthony, to the principal source or sources of the said river, and also of the parts adjacent thereto; and that if, on the result of such survey, it should appear that the said river would not be intersected by such a line as is above mentioned, the two parties will thereupon proceed, by amicable negotiation, to regulate the boundary line in that quarter, as well as all other points to be adjusted between the said parties, according to justice and mutual convenience, and in conformity to the intent of the said treaty.

ART. V.

Whereas doubts have arisen what river was truly intended under the name of the river St. Croix, mentioned in the said treaty of peace, and forming a part of the boundary therein described; that question shall be referred to the final decision of commissioners to be appointed in the following manner. viz.:

One commissioner shall be named by His Majesty, and one by the President of the United States, by and with the advice and consent of the Senate thereof, and the said two commissioners shall agree on the choice of a third; or if they cannot so agree, they shall each propose one person, and of the two names so proposed, one shall be drawn by lot in the presence of the two original Commissioners.

And the three Commissioners so appointed shall be sworn, impartially to examine and decide the said question, according to such evidence as shall respectively be laid before them on the part of the British Government and of the United States. The said Commissioners shall meet at Halifax, and shall have power to adjourn to such other place or places as they shall think fit.

They shall have power to appoint a Secretary, and to employ such surveyors or other persons as they shall judge necessary. The said Commissioners shall, by a declaration, under their hands and seals, decide what river is the river St. Croix, intended by the treaty.

The said declaration shall contain a description of the said river, and shall particularize the latitude and longitude of its mouth and of its source.

Duplicates of this declaration and of the statements of their accounts, and of the journal of their proceedings, shall be delivered by them to the agent of His Majesty, and to the agent of the United States, who may be respectively appointed and authorized to manage the business on behalf of the respective Governments. And both parties agree to consider such decision as final and conclusive, so as that the same shall never thereafter be called into question, or made the subject of dispute or difference between them.

ART. VI.

Whereas it is alleged by divers British merchants and others His Majesty's subjects, that debts, to a considerable amount, which were bona fide contracted before the peace, still remain owing to them by citizens or inhabitants of the United States, and that by the operation of various lawful impediments since the peace, not only the full recovery of the said debts has been delayed, but also the value and security thereof have been, in several instances, impaired and lessened, so that, by the ordinary course of judicial proceedings, the British creditors cannot now obtain, and actually have and receive full and adequate compensation for the losses and damages which they have thereby sustained: It is agreed, that in all such cases, where full compensation for such losses and damages cannot, for whatever reason, be actually obtained, had and received by the said creditors in the ordinary course of justice, the United States will make full and complete compensation for the same to the said creditors: But it is distinctly understood, that this provision is to extend to such losses only as have been occasioned by the lawful impediments aforesaid, and is not to extend to losses occasioned by such insolvency of the debtors or other causes as would equally have operated to produce such loss, if the said impediments had not existed; nor to such losses or damages as have been occasioned by the manifest delay or negligence, or wilful omission of the claimant.

For the purpose of ascertaining the amount of any such losses and damages, five Commissioners shall be appointed and authorized to meet and act in manner following, viz.: Two of them shall be appointed by His Majesty, two of them by the President of the United States by and with the advice and consent of the Senate thereof, and the fifth by the unanimous voice of the other four; and if they should not agree in such choice, then the Commissioners named by the two parties shall respectively propose one person, and of the two names so proposed, one shall be drawn by lot, in the presence of the four original Commissioners. When the five Commissioners thus appointed shall first meet, they shall, before they proceed to act, respectively take the following oath, or affirmation, in the presence of each other; which oath, or affirmation, being so taken and duly attested, shall be entered on the record of their proceedings, viz.:

I, A.B., one of the Commissioners appointed in pursuance of the sixth article of the Treaty of Amity, Commerce and Navigation, between His Britannic Majesty and the United States of America, do solemnly swear (or affirm) that I will honestly, diligently, impartially and carefully examine, and to the best of my judgment, according to justice and equity, decide all such complaints, as under the said article shall be preferred to the said Commissioners: and that I will forbear to act as a Commissioner, in any case in which I may be personally interested.

Three of the said Commissioners shall constitute a board, and shall have power to do any act appertaining to the said Commission, provided that one of the Commissioners named on each side, and the fifth Commissioner shall be present, and all decisions shall be made by the majority of the voices of the Commissioners than present.

Eighteen months from the day on which the said Commissioners shall form a board, and be ready to proceed to business, are assigned for receiving complaints and applications; but they are nevertheless authorized, in any particular cases in which it shall appear to them to be reasonable and just, to extend the said term of eighteen months for any term not exceeding six months, after the expiration thereof.

The said Commissioners shall first meet at Philadelphia, but they shall have power to adjourn from place to place as they shall see cause.

The said Commissioners in examining the complaints and applications so preferred to them, are empowered and required in pursuance of the true intent and meaning of this article to take into their consideration all claims, whether of principal or interest, or balances of principal and interest and to determine the same respectively, according to the merits of the several cases, due regard being had to all the circumstances thereof, and as equity and justice shall appear to them to require.

And the said Commissioners shall have power to examine all such persons as shall come before them on oath or affirmation, touching the premises; and also to receive in evidence, according as they may think most consistent with equity and justice, all written depositions, or books, or papers, or copies, or extracts thereof, every such deposition, book, or paper, or copy, or extract, being duly authenticated either according to the legal form now respectively existing in the two countries, or in such other manner as the said Commissioners shall see cause to require or allow.

The award of the said Commissioners, or of any three of them as aforesaid, shall in all cases be final and conclusive both as to the justice of the claim, and to the amount of the sum to be paid to the creditor or claimant; and the United States undertake to cause the sum so awarded to be paid in specie to such creditor or claimant without deduction; and at such time or times and at such place or places, as shall be awarded by the said Commissioners; and on condition of such releases or assignments to be given by the creditor or claimant, as by the said Commissioners may be directed: Provided always, that no such payment shall be fixed by the said Commissioners to take place sooner than twelve months from the day of the exchange of the ratifications of this treaty.

ART. VII.

Whereas complaints have been made by divers merchants and others, citizens of the United States, that during the course of the war in which His Majesty is now engaged, they have sustained considerable losses and damage, by reason of irregular or illegal captures or condemnations of their vessels and other property, under color of authority or commissions from His Majesty, and that from various circumstances belonging to the said cases, adequate compensation for the losses and damages so sustained cannot now be actually obtained, had, and received by the ordinary course of judicial proceedings; it is agreed, that in all such cases, where adequate compensation cannot, for whatever reason, be now actually obtained, had, and received by the said merchants and others, in the ordinary course of justice, full and complete compensation for the same will be made by the British Government to the said complainants.

But it is distinctly understood that this provision is not

to extend to such losses or damages as have been occasioned by the manifest delay or negligence, or wilful omission of the claimant.

That for the purpose of ascertaining the amount of any such losses and damages, five Commissioners shall be appointed and authorized to act in London, exactly in the manner directed with respect to those mentioned in the preceding article, and after having taken the same oath or affirmation, (mutatis mutandis,) the same term of eighteen months is also assigned for the reception of claims, and they are in like manner authorized to extend the same in particular cases.

They shall receive testimony, books, papers and evidence in the same latitude, and exercise the like discretion and powers respecting that subject; and shall decide the claims in question according to the merits of the several cases, and to justice, equity and the laws of nations.

The award of the said Commissioners, or any such three of them as aforesaid, shall in all cases be final and conclusive, both as to the justice of the claim, and the amount of the sum to be paid to the claimant; and His Britannic Majesty undertakes to cause the same to be paid to such claimant in specie, without any deduction, at such place or places, and at such time or times, as shall be awarded by the said Commissioners, and on condition of such releases or assignments to be given by the claimant, as by the said Commissioners may be directed.

And whereas certain merchants and others, His Majesty's subjects, complain that, in the course of the war, they have sustained loss and damage by reason of the capture of their vessels and merchandise, taken within the limits and jurisdiction of the States and brought into the ports of the same, or taken by vessels originally armed in ports of the said States:

It is agreed that in all such cases where restitution shall not have been made agreeably to the tenor of the letter from Mr. Jefferson to Mr. Hammond, dated at Philadelphia, September 5, 1793, a copy of which is annexed to this treaty; the complaints of the parties shall be and hereby are referred to the Commissioners to be appointed by virtue of this article, who are hereby authorized and required to proceed in the like manner relative to these as to the other cases committed to them; and the United States undertake to pay to the complainants or claimants in specie, without deduction, the amount of such sums as shall be awarded to them respectively by the said Commissioners, and at the times and places which in such awards shall be specified; and on condition of such releases or assignments to be given by the claimants as in the said awards may be directed: And it is further agreed, that not only the now existing cases of both descriptions, but also all such as shall exist at the time of exchanging the ratifications of this treaty, shall be considered as being within the provisions, intent and meaning of this article.

ART. VIII.

It is further agreed that the Commissioners mentioned in this and in the two preceding articles shall be respectively paid in such manner as shall be agreed between the two parties such agreement being to be settled at the time of the exchange of the ratifications of this treaty.

And all other expenses attending the said Commissions shall be defrayed jointly by the two parties, the same being previously ascertained and allowed by the majority of the Commissioners.

And in the case of death, sickness or necessary absence, the place of every such Commissioner respectively shall be supplied in the same manner as such Commissioner was first appointed, and the new Commissioners shall take the same oath or affirmation and do the same duties.

ART. IX.

It is agreed that British subjects who now hold lands in the territories of the United States, and American citizens who now hold lands in the dominions of His Majesty, shall continue to hold them according to the nature and tenure of their respective estates and titles therein; and may grant, sell or devise the same to whom they please, in like manner as if they were natives and that neither they nor their heirs or assigns shall, so far as may respect the said lands and the legal remedies incident thereto, be regarded as aliens.

ART. X.

Neither the debts due from individuals of the one nation to individuals of the other, nor shares, nor monies, which they may have in the public funds, or in the public or private banks, shall ever in any event of war or national differences be sequestered or confiscated, it being unjust and impolitic that debts and engagements contracted and made by individuals having confidence in each other and in their respective Governments, should ever be destroyed or impaired by national authority on account of national differences and discontents.

ART. XI.

It is agreed between His Majesty and the United States of America, that there shall be a reciprocal and entirely perfect liberty of navigation and commerce between their respective people, in the manner, under the limitations, and on the conditions specified in the following articles.

ART. XII.

His Majesty consents that it shall and may be lawful, during the time hereinafter limited, for the citizens of the United States to carry to any of His Majesty's islands and ports in the West Indies from the United States, in their own vessels, not being above the burthen of seventy tons, any goods or merchandizes, being of the growth, manufacture or produce of the said States, which it is or may be lawful to carry to the said islands or ports from the said States in British vessels; and that the said American vessels shall be subject there to no other or higher tonnage duties or charges than shall be payable by British vessels in the ports of the United States; and that the cargoes of the said American vessels shall be subject there to no other or higher duties or charges than shall be payable on the like articles if imported there from the said States in British vessels.

And His Majesty also consents that it shall be lawful for the said American citizens to purchase, load and carry away in their said vessels to the United States, from the said islands and ports, all such articles, being of the growth, manufacture or produce of the said islands, as may now by law be carried from thence to the said States in British vessels, and subject only to the same duties and charges on exportation, to which British vessels and their cargoes are or shall be subject in similar circumstances.

Provided always, that the said American vessels do carry and land their cargoes in the United States only, it being expressly agreed and declared that, during the continuance of this article, the United States will prohibit and restrain the carrying any molasses, sugar, coffee, cocoa or cotton in American vessels, either from His Majesty's islands or from the United States to any part of the world except the United States, reasonable seastores excepted. Provided, also, that it shall and may be lawful, during the same period, for British vessels to import from the said islands into the United States, and to export from the United States to the said islands, all articles whatever, being of the growth, produce or manufacture of the said islands, or of the United States respectively, which now may, by the laws of the said States, be so imported and exported.

And that the cargoes of the said British vessels shall be subject to no other or higher duties or charges, than shall be payable on the same articles if so imported or exported in American vessels. It is agreed that this article, and every matter and thing therein contained, shall continue to be in force during the continuance of the war in which His Majesty is now engaged; and also for two years from and after the date of the signature of the preliminary or other articles of peace, by which the same may be terminated. And it is further agreed that, at the expiration of the said term, the two contracting parties will endeavour further to regulate their commerce in this respect, according to the situation in which His Majesty may then find himself with respect to the West Indies, and with a view to such arrangements as may best conduce to the mutual advantage and extension of commerce.

And the said parties will then also renew their discussions, and endeavour to agree, whether in any and what cases, neutral vessels shall protect enemy's property; and in what cases provisions and other articles, not generally contraband, may become such.

But in the mean time, their conduct towards each other in these respects shall be regulated by the articles hereinafter inserted on those subjects.

ART. XIII.

His Majesty consents that the vessels belonging to the citizens of the United States of America shall be admitted and hospitably received in all the seaports and harbors of the British territories in the East Indies.

And that the citizens of the said United States may freely carry on a trade between the said territories and the said United States, in all articles of which the importation or exportation respectively, to or from the said territories, shall not be entirely prohibited. Provided only, that it shall not be lawful for them in any time of war between the British Government and any other Power or State whatever, to export from the said territories, without the special permission of the British Government there, any military stores, or naval stores, or rice.

The citizens of the United States shall pay for their vessels when admitted into the said ports no other or higher tonnage duty than shall be payable on British vessels when admitted into the ports of the United States. And they shall pay no other or higher duties or charges, on the importation or exportation of the cargoes of the said vessels, than shall be payable on the same articles when imported or exported in British vessels. But it is expressly agreed that the vessels of the United States shall not carry any of the articles exported by them from the said British territories to any port or place, except to some port or place in America, where the same shall be unladen and such regulations shall be adopted by both parties as shall from time to time be found necessary to enforce the due and faithful observance of this stipulation.

It is also understood that the permission granted by this article is not to extend to allow the vessels of the United States to carry on any part of the coasting trade of the said British territories; but vessels going with their original cargoes, or part thereof, from one port of discharge to another, are not to be considered as carrying on the coasting trade. Neither is this article to be construed to allow the citizens of the said States to settle or reside within the said territories, or to go into the interior parts thereof, without the permission of the British Government established there; and if any transgression should be attempted against the regulations of the British Government in this respect, the observance of the same shall and may be enforced against the citizens of America in the same manner as against British subjects or others transgressing the same rule. And the citizens of the United States, whenever they arrive in any port or harbour in the said territories, or if they should be permitted, in manner aforesaid, to go to any other place therein, shall always be subject to the laws, government and jurisdiction of what nature established in such harbor, port or place, according as the same may be.

The citizens of the United States may also touch for refreshment at the island of St. Helena, but subject in all respects to such regulations as the British Government may from time to time establish there.

ART. XIV.

There shall be between all the dominions of His Majesty

in Europe and the territories of the United States a reciprocal and perfect liberty of commerce and navigation.

The people and inhabitants of the two countries, respectively, shall have liberty freely and securely, and without hindrance and molestation, to come with their ships and cargoes to the lands, countries, cities, ports, places and rivers within the dominions and territories aforesaid, to enter into the same, to resort there, and to remain and reside there, without any limitation of time.

Also to hire and possess houses and warehouses for the purposes of their commerce, and generally the merchants and traders on each side shall enjoy the most complete protection and security for their commerce; but subject always as to what respects this article to the laws and statutes of the two countries respectively. It is agreed that no other or high duties shall be paid by the ships or merchandise of the one party in the ports of the other than such as are paid by the like vessels or merchandize of all other nations.

Nor shall any other or higher duty be imposed in one country on the importation of any articles the growth, produce or manufacture of the other, than are or shall be payable on the importation of the like articles being of the growth, produce or manufacture of any other foreign country.

Nor shall any prohibition be imposed on the exportation or importation of any articles to or from the territories of the two parties respectively, which shall not equally extend to all other nations. But the British Government reserves to itself the right of imposing on American vessels entering into the British ports in Europe a tonnage duty equal to that which shall be payable by British vessels in the ports of America; and also such duty as may be adequate to countervail the difference of duty now payable on the importation of European and Asiatic goods, when imported into the United States in British or in American vessels The two parties agree to treat for the more exact equalization of the duties on the respective navigation of their subjects and people, in such manner as may be most beneficial to the two countries.

The arrangements for this purpose shall be made at the same time with those mentioned at the conclusion of the twelfth article of this treaty, and are to be considered as a part thereof. In the interval it is agreed that the United States will not impose any new or additional tonnage duties on British vessels, nor increase the nowsubsisting difference between the duties payable on the importation of any articles in British or in American vessels.

ART. XV.

It is agreed that no other or high duties shall be paid by the ships or merchandise of the one party in the ports of the other than such as are paid by the like vessels or merchandize of all other nations. Nor shall any other or higher duty be imposed in one country on the importation of any articles the growth, produce or manufacture of the other, than are or shall be payable on the importation of the like articles being of the growth, produce or manufacture of any other foreign country. Nor shall any prohibition be imposed on the exportation or importation of any articles to or from the territories of the two parties respectively, which shall not equally extend to all other nations.

But the British Government reserves to itself the right of imposing on American vessels entering into the British ports in Europe a tonnage duty equal to that which shall be payable by British vessels in the ports of America; and also such duty as may be adequate to countervail the difference of duty now payable on the importation of European and Asiatic goods, when imported into the United States in British or in American vessels. The two parties agree to treat for the more exact equalization of the duties on the respective navigation of their subjects and people, in such manner as may be most beneficial to the two countries.

The arrangements for this purpose shall be made at the same time with those mentioned at the conclusion of the twelfth article of this treaty, and are to be considered as a part thereof. In the interval it is agreed that the United States will not impose any new or additional tonnage duties on British vessels, nor increase the nowsubsisting difference between the duties payable on the importation of any articles in British or in American vessels.

ART. XVI.

It shall be free for the two contracting parties, respectively, to appoint Consuls for the protection of trade, to reside in the dominions and territories aforesaid; and the said Consuls shall enjoy those liberties and rights which belong to them by reason of their function.

But before any Consul shall act as such, he shall be in the usual forms approved and admitted by the party to whom he is sent; and it is hereby declared to be lawful and proper that, in case of illegal or improper conduct towards the laws or Government, a Consul may either be punished according to law, if the laws will reach the case, or be dismissed, or even sent back, the offended Government assigning to the other their reasons for the same. Either of the parties may except from the residence of Consuls such particular places as such party shall judge proper to be so excepted.

ART. XVII.

It is agreed that in all cases where vessels shall be captured or detained on just suspicion of having on board enemy's property, or of carrying to the enemy any of the articles which are contraband of war, the said vessels shall be brought to the nearest or most convenient port; and if any property of an enemy should be found on board such vessel, that part only which belongs to the enemy shall be made prize, and the vessel shall be at liberty to proceed with the remainder without any impediment. And it is agreed that all proper measures shall be taken to prevent delay in deciding the cases of ships or cargoes so brought in for adjudication, and in the payment or recovery of any indemnification, adjudged or agreed to be paid to the masters or owners of such ships.

ART. XVIII.
In order to regulate what is in future to be esteemed contraband of war, it is agreed that under the said denomination shall be comprised all arms and implements serving for the purposes of war, by land or sea, such as cannon, muskets, mortars, petards, bombs, grenades, carcasses, saucisses, carriages for cannon, musketrests, bandoliers, gunpowder, match, saltpetre, ball, pikes, swords, headpieces, cuirasses, halberts, lances, javelins, horsefurniture, holsters, belts, and generally all other implements of war, as also timber for shipbuilding, tar or rozin, copper in sheets, sails, hemp, and cordage, and generally whatever may serve directly to the equipment of vessels, unwrought iron and fir planks only excepted, and all the above articles are hereby declared to be just objects of confiscation whenever they are attempted to be carried to an enemy.

And whereas the difficulty of agreeing on the precise cases in which alone provisions and other articles not generally contraband may be regarded as such, renders it expedient to provide against the inconveniences and misunderstandings which might thence arise: It is further agreed that whenever any such articles so becoming contraband, according to the existing laws of nations, shall for that reason be seized, the same shall not be confiscated, but the owners thereof shall be speedily and completely indemnified; and the captors, or, in their default, the Government under whose authority they act, shall pay to the masters or owners of such vessels the full value of all such articles, with a reasonable mercantile profit thereon, together with the freight, and also the demurrage incident to such detention.

And whereas it frequently happens that vessels sail for a port or place belonging to an enemy without knowing that the same is either besieged, blockaded or invested, it is agreed that every vessel so circumstanced may be turned away from such port or place; but she shall not be detained, nor her cargo, if not contraband, be confiscated, unless after notice she shall again attempt to enter, but she shall be permitted to go to any other port or place she may think proper; nor shall any vessel or goods of either party that may have entered into such port or place before the same was besieged, blockaded, or invested by the other, and be found thereinafter the reduction or surrender of such place, be liable to confiscation, but shall be restored to the owners or proprietors there.

ART. XIX.
And that more abundant care may be taken for the security of the respective subjects and citizens of the contracting parties, and to prevent their suffering injuries by the menofwar, or privateers of either party, all commanders of ships of war and privateers, and all others the said subjects and citizens, shall forbear doing any damage to those of the other party or committing any outrage against them, and if they act to the contrary they shall be punished, and shall also be bound in their persons and estates to make satisfaction and reparation for all damages, and the interest thereof, of whatever nature the said damages may be.

For this cause, all commanders of privateers, before they receive their commissions, shall hereafter be obliged to give, before a competent judge, sufficient security by at least two responsible sureties, who have no interest in the said privateer, each of whom, together with the said commander, shall be jointly and severally bound in the sum of fifteen hundred pounds sterling, or, if such ships be provided with above one hundred and fifty seamen or soldiers, in the sum of three thousand pounds sterling, to satisfy all damages and injuries which the said privateer, or her officers or men, or any of them, may do or commit during their cruise contrary to the tenor of this treaty, or to the laws and instructions for regulating their conduct; and further, that in all cases of aggressions the said commissions shall be revoked and annulled. It is also agreed that whenever a judge of a court of admiralty of either of the parties shall pronounce sentence against any vessel or goods or property belonging to the subjects or citizens of the other party, a formal and duly authenticated copy of all the proceedings in the cause, and of the said sentence, shall, if required, be delivered to the commander of the said vessel, without the smallest delay, he paying all legal fees and demands for the same.

ART. XX.
It is further agreed that both the said contracting parties shall not only refuse to receive any pirates into any of their ports, havens or towns, or permit any of their inhabitants to receive, protect, harbor, conceal or assist them in any manner, but will bring to condign punishment all such inhabitants as shall be guilty of such acts or offences. And all their ships, with the goods or merchandizes taken by them and brought into the port of either of the said parties, shall be seized as far as they can be discovered, and shall be restored to the owners, or their factors or agents, duly deputed and authorized in writing by them (proper evidence being first given in the court of admiralty for proving the property) even in case such effects should have passed into other hands by sale, if it be proved that the buyers knew or had good reason to believe or suspect that they had been piratically taken.

ART. XXI.
It is likewise agreed that the subjects and citizens of the two nations shall not do any acts of hostility or violence against each other, nor accept commissions or instructions so to act from any foreign Prince or State, enemies to the other party; nor shall the enemies of one of the parties be permitted to invite, or endeavor to enlist in their military service, any of the subjects or citizens of the other party; and the laws against all such offences and aggressions shall be punctually executed.

And if any subject or citizen of the said parties respectively shall accept any foreign commission or letters of marque for arming any vessel to act as a privateer against the other party, and be taken by the other party, it is hereby declared to be lawful for the said party to treat and punish the said subject or citizen having such commission or letters of marque as a pirate.

ART. XXII.

It is expressly stipulated that neither of the said contracting parties will order or authorize any acts of reprisal against the other, on complaints of injuries or damages, until the said party shall first have presented to the other a statement thereof, verified by competent proof and evidence, and demanded justice and satisfaction, and the same shall either have been refused or unreasonably delayed.

ART. XXIII.

The ships of war of each of the contracting parties shall, at all times, be hospitably received in the ports of the other, their officers and crews paying due respect to the laws and Government of the country. The officers shall be treated with that respect which is due to the commissions which they bear, and if any insult should be offered to them by any of the inhabitants, all offenders in this respect shall be punished as disturbers of the peace and amity between the two countries.

And His Majesty consents that in case an American vessel should, by stress of weather, danger from enemies, or other misfortune, be reduced to the necessity of seeking shelter in any of His Majesty's ports, into which such vessel could not in ordinary cases claim to be admitted, she shall, on manifesting that necessity to the satisfaction of the Government of the place, be hospitably received, and be permitted to refit and to purchase at the market price such necessaries as she may stand in need of, conformably to such orders and regulations at the Government of the place, having respect to the circumstances of each case, shall prescribe.

She shall not be allowed to break bulk or unload her cargo, unless the same should be bona fide necessary to her being refitted. Nor shall be permitted to sell any part of her cargo, unless so much only as may be necessary to defray her expences, and then not without the express permission of the Government of the place. Nor shall she be obliged to pay any duties whatever, except only on such articles as she may be permitted to sell for the purpose aforesaid.

ART. XXIV.

It shall not be lawful for any foreign privateers (not being subjects or citizens of either of the said parties) who have commissions from any other Prince or State in enmity with either nation to arm their ships in the ports of either of the said parties, nor to sell what they have taken, nor in any other manner to exchange the same; nor shall they be allowed to purchase more provisions than shall be necessary for their going to the nearest port of that Prince or State from whom they obtained their commissions.

ART. XXV.

It shall be lawful for the ships of war and privateers belonging to the said parties respectively to carry whithersoever they please the ships and goods taken from their enemies, without being obliged to pay any fee to the officers of the admiralty, or to any judges whatever; nor shall the said prizes, when they arrive at and enter the ports of the said parties, be detained or seized, neither shall the searchers or other officers of those places visit such prizes, (except for the purpose of preventing the carrying of any of the cargo thereof on shore in any manner contrary to the established laws of revenue, navigation, or commerce,) nor shall such officers take cognizance of the validity of such prizes; but they shall be at liberty to hoist sail and depart as speedily as may be, and carry their said prizes to the place mentioned in their commissions or patents, which the commanders of the said ships of war or privateers shall be obliged to show.

No shelter or refuge shall be given in their ports to such as have made a prize upon the subjects or citizens of either of the said parties; but if forced by stress of weather, or the dangers of the sea, to enter therein, particular care shall be taken to hasten their departure, and to cause them to retire as soon as possible. Nothing in this treaty contained shall, however, be construed or operate contrary to former and existing public treaties with other sovereigns or States. But the two parties agree that while they continue in amity neither of them will in future make any treaty that shall be inconsistent with this or the preceding article.

Neither of the said parties shall permit the ships or goods belonging to the subjects or citizens of the other to be taken within cannon shot of the coast, nor in any of the bays, ports or rivers of their territories, by ships of war or others having commission from any Prince, Republic or State whatever. But in case it should so happen, the party whose territorial rights shall thus have been violated shall use his utmost endeavors to obtain from the offending party full and ample satisfaction for the vessel or vessels so taken, whether the same be vessels of war or merchant vessels.

ART. XXVI.

If at any time a rupture should take place (which God forbid) between His Majesty and the United States, and merchants and others of each of the two nations residing in the dominions of the other shall have the privilege of remaining and continuing their trade, so long as they behave peaceably and commit no offence against the laws; and in case their conduct should render them suspected, and the respective Governments should think proper to order them to remove, the term of twelve months from the publication of the order shall be allowed them for that purpose, to remove with their families, effects and property, but this favor shall not be extended to those who shall act contrary to the established laws; and for greater certainty, it is declared that such rupture shall not be deemed to exist while negociations for accommodating differences shall be depending, nor until the respective Ambassadors or Ministers, if such there shall be, shall be recalled or sent home on account of such differences, and not on account of personal misconduct, according to the nature and degrees of which both parties retain their rights, either to request the recall, or immediately to send home the Ambassador or Minister of the other, and that without prejudice to their mutual friendship and good understanding.

ART. XXVII.
It is further agreed that His Majesty and the United States, on mutual requisitions, by them respectively, or by their respective Ministers or officers authorized to make the same, will deliver up to justice all persons who, being charged with murder or forgery, committed within the jurisdiction of either, shall seek an asylum within any of the countries of the other, provided that this shall only be done on such evidence of criminality as, according to the laws of the place, where the fugitive or person so charged shall be found, would justify his apprehension and commitment for trial, if the offence had there been committed. The expence of such apprehension and delivery shall be borne and defrayed by those who made the requisition and receive the fugitive.

ART. XXVIII.
It is agreed that the first ten articles of this treaty shall be permanent, and that the subsequent articles, except the twelfth, shall be limited in their duration to twelve years, to be computed from the day on which the ratifications of this treaty shall be exchanged, but subject to this condition. That whereas the said twelfth article will expire by the limitation therein contained, at the end of two years from the signing of the preliminary or other articles of peace, which shall terminate the present war in which His Majesty is engaged, it is agreed that proper measures shall by concert be taken for bringing the subject of that article into amicable treaty and discussion, so early before the expiration of the said term as that new arrangements on that head may by that time be perfected and ready to take place.

But if it should unfortunately happen that His Majesty and the United States should not be able to agree on such new arrangements, in that case all the articles of this treaty, except the first ten, shall then cease and expire together.

Lastly.

This treaty, when the same shall have been ratified by His Majesty and by the President of the United States, by and with the advice and consent of their Senate, and the respective ratifications mutually exchanged, shall be binding and obligatory on His Majesty and on the said States, and shall be by them respectively executed and observed with punctuality and the most sincere regard to good faith; and whereas it will be expedient, in order the better to facilitate intercourse and obviate difficulties, that other articles be proposed and added to this treaty, which articles, from want of time and other circumstances, cannot now be perfected, it is agreed that the said parties will, from time to time, readily treat of and concerning such articles, and will sincerely endeavor so to form them as that they may conduce to mutual convenience and tend to promote mutual satisfaction and friendship; and that the said articles, after having been duly ratified, shall be added to and make a part of this treaty.

In faith whereof we, the undersigned Ministers Plenipotentiary of His Majesty the King of Great Britain and the United States of America, have signed this present treaty, and have caused to be affixed thereto the seal of our arms.

Done at London this nineteenth day of November, one thousand seven hundred and ninety four.

(SEAL) GRENVILLE
(SEAL) JOHN JAY

Source: Malloy, William M., ed. 1910. *Treaties, Conventions, International Acts, Protocols and Agreements Between the United States of America and Other Powers, 1776–1909*. Vol. 1. Washington: Government Printing Office.

DOCUMENT 3

PINCKNEY'S TREATY (TREATY OF SAN LORENZO) (1795)

His Catholic Majesty and the United States of America desiring to consolidate on a permanent basis the Friendship and good correspondence which happily prevails between the two parties, have determined to establish by a convention several points, the settlement whereof will be productive of general advantage and reciprocal utility to both Nations.

With this intention his Catholic Majesty has appointed the most Excellent Lord, Don Manuel de Godoy, and Alvarez de Faria, Rios, Sanchez Zarzosa, Prince de la Paz, Duke de la Alcudia, Lord of the Soto de Roma and of the State of Albalá, Grandee of Spain of the first class, perpetual Regidor of the City of Santiago, Knight of the illustrious Order of the Golden Fleece, and Great Cross of the Royal and distinguished Spanish order of Charles the III. Commander of Valencia del Ventoso, Rivera, and Acenchal in that of Santiago; Knight and Great Cross of the religious order of St. John; Counsellor of State; First Secretary of State and Despacho; Secretary to the Queen; Superintendent General of the Posts and High Ways; Protector of the Royal Academy of the Noble Arts, and of the Royal Societies of natural history, Botany, Chemistry, and Astronomy: Gentleman of the King's Chamber in employment: Captain General of his Armies: Inspector and Major of the Royal Corps of Body Guards &. a., &. a., &.a., and the President of the United States, with the advice and consent of their Senate, has appointed Thomas Pinckney a Citizen of the United States, and their Envoy Extraordinary to his Catholic Majesty. And the said Plenipotentiaries have agreed upon and concluded the following Articles.

ART. I
There shall be a firm and inviolable Peace and sincere Friendship between His Catholic Majesty his successors and subjects, and the United States and their Citizens without exception of persons or places.

ART. II
To prevent all disputes on the subject of the boundaries which separate the territories of the two High contracting Parties, it is hereby declared and agreed as follows: to wit: The Southern boundary of the United States which divides their territory from the Spanish Colonies of East and West Florida, shall be designated by a line beginning on the River Mississippi at the northernmost part of the thirty first degree of latitude North of the Equator, which from thence shall be drawn due East to the middle of the River Apalachicola or Catahouche, thence along the middle thereof to its junction with the Flint, thence straight to the head of St. Mary's River, and thence down the middle thereof to the Atlantic Ocean. And it is agreed that if there should be any troops, Garrisons or settlements of either Party in the territory of the other according to the above mentioned boundaries, they shall be withdrawn from the said territory within the term of six months after the ratification of this treaty or sooner if it be possible and that they shall be permitted to take with them all the goods and effects which they possess.

ART. III
In order to carry the preceding Article into effect one Commissioner and one Surveyor shall be appointed by each of the contracting Parties who shall meet at the Natchez on the left side of the River Mississippi before the expiration of six months from the ratification of this convention, and they shall proceed to run and mark this boundary according to the stipulations of the said Article. They shall make Plats and keep journals of their proceedings which shall be considered as part of this convention, and shall have the same force as if they were inserted therein. And if on any account it should be found necessary that the said Commissioners and Surveyors should be accompanied by Guards, they shall be furnished in equal proportions by the Commanding Officer of his Majesty's troops in the two Floridas, and the Commanding Officer of the troops of the United States in their Southwestern territory, who shall act by common consent and amicably, as well with respect to this point as to the furnishing of provisions and instruments and making every other arrangement which may be necessary or useful for the execution of this article.

ART. IV
It is likewise agreed that the Western boundary of the United States which separates them from the Spanish Colony of Louisiana, is in the middle of the channel or bed of the River Mississippi from the Northern boundary of the said States to the completion of the thirty first degree of latitude North of the Equator; and his Catholic Majesty has likewise agreed that the navigation of the said River in its whole breadth from its source to the Ocean shall be free only to his Subjects, and the Citizens of the United States, unless he should extend this privilege to the Subjects of other Powers by special convention.

ART. V
The two High contracting Parties shall by all the means in their power maintain peace and harmony among the several Indian Nations who inhabit the country adjacent to the lines and Rivers which by the preceding Articles form the boundaries of the two Floridas; and the better to obtain this effect both Parties oblige themselves expressly to restrain by force all hostilities on the part of the Indian Nations living within their boundaries: so that Spain will not suffer her Indians to attack the Citizens of the United States, nor the Indians inhabiting their territory; nor will the United States permit these last mentioned Indians to commence hostilities against the Subjects of his Catholic Majesty, or his Indians in any manner whatever.

And whereas several treaties of Friendship exist between the two contracting Parties and the said Nations of Indians, it is hereby agreed that in future no treaty of alliance or other whatever (except treaties of Peace) shall be made by either Party with the Indians living within the boundary of the other; but both Parties will endeavour to make the advantages of the Indian trade common and mutualy [sic] beneficial to their respective Subjects and Citizens observing in all things the most complete reciprocity: so that both Parties may obtain the advantages arising from a good understanding with the said Nations, without being subject to the expence which they have hitherto occasioned.

ART. VI
Each Party shall endeavour by all means in their power to protect and defend all Vessels and other effects belonging to the Citizens or Subjects of the other, which shall be within the extent of their jurisdiction by sea or by land, and shall use all their efforts to recover and cause to be restored to the right owners their Vessels and effects which may have been taken from them within the extent of their said jurisdiction whether they are at war or not with the Power whose Subjects have taken possession of the said effects.

ART. VII
And it is agreed that the Subjects or Citizens of each of the contracting Parties, their Vessels, or effects shall not be liable to any embargo or detention on the part of the

other for any military expedition or other public or private purpose whatever; and in all cases of seizure, detention, or arrest for debts contracted or offenses committed by any Citizen or Subject of the one Party within the jurisdiction of the other, the same shall be made and prosecuted by order and authority of law only, and according to the regular course of proceedings usual in such cases. The Citizens and Subjects of both Parties shall be allowed to employ such Advocates, Sollicitors, Notaries, Agents, and Factors, as they may judge proper in all their affairs and in all their trials at law in which they may be concerned before the tribunals of the other Party, and such Agents shall have free access to be present at the proceedings in such causes, and at the taking of all examinations and evidence which may be exhibited in the said trials.

ART. VIII
In case the Subjects and inhabitants of either Party with their shipping whether public and of war or private and of merchants be forced through stress of weather, pursuit of Pirates, or Enemies, or any other urgent necessity for seeking of shelter and harbor to retreat and enter into any of the Rivers, Bays, Roads, or Ports belonging to the other Party, they shall be received and treated with all humanity, and enjoy all favor, protection and help, and they shall be permitted to refresh and provide themselves at reasonable rates with victuals and all things needful for the sustenance of their persons or reparation of their Ships, and prosecution of their voyage; and they shall no ways be hindered from returning out of the said Ports, or Roads, but may remove and depart when and whither they please without any let or hindrance.

ART. IX
All Ships and merchandise of what nature soever which shall be rescued out of the hands of any Pirates or Robbers on the high seas shall be brought into some Port of either State and shall be delivered to the custody of the Officers of that Port in order to be taken care of and restored entire to the true proprietor as soon as due and sufficient proof shall be made concerning the property thereof.

ART. X
When any Vessel of either Party shall be wrecked, foundered, or otherwise damaged on the coasts or within the dominion of the other, their respective Subjects or Citizens shall receive as well for themselves as for their Vessels and effects the same assistance which would be due to the inhabitants of the Country where the damage happens, and shall pay the same charges and dues only as the said inhabitants would be subject to pay in a like case: and if the operations of repair should require that the whole or any part of the cargo be unladen they shall pay no duties, charges, or fees on the part which they shall relade and carry away.

ART. XI
The Citizens and Subjects of each Party shall have power to dispose of their personal goods within the jurisdiction of the other by testament, donation, or otherwise; and their representatives being Subjects or Citizens of the other Party shall succeed to their said personal goods, whether by testament or ab intestato and they may take possession thereof either by themselves or others acting for them, and dispose of the same at their will paying such dues only as the inhabitants of the Country wherein the said goods are shall be subject to pay in like cases, and in case of the absence of the representatives, such care shall be taken of the said goods as would be taken of the goods of a native in like case, until the lawful owner may take measures for receiving them. And if question shall arise among several claimants to which of them the said goods belong the same shall be decided finally by the laws and Judges of the Land wherein the said goods are. And where on the death of any person holding real estate within the territories of the one Party, such real estate would by the laws of the Land descend on a Citizen or Subject of the other were he not disqualified by being an alien, such subject shall be allowed a reasonable time to sell the same and to withdraw the proceeds without molestation, and exempt from all rights of detraction on the part of the Government of the respective states.

ART. XII
The merchant Ships of either of the Parties which shall be making into a Port belonging to the enemy of the other Party and concerning whose voyage and the species of goods on board her there shall be just grounds of suspicion shall be obliged to exhibit as well upon the high seas as in the Ports and havens not only her passports but likewise certificates expressly showing that her goods are not of the number of those which have been prohibited as contraband.

ART. XIII
For the better promoting of commerce on both sides, it is agreed that if a war shall break out between the said two Nations one year after the proclamation of war shall be allowed to the merchants in the Cities and Towns where they shall live for collecting and transporting their goods and merchandizes, and if any thing be taken from them, or any injury be done them within that term by either Party, or the People or Subjects of either, full satisfaction shall be made for the same by the Government.

ART. XIV
No subject of his Catholic Majesty shall apply for or take any commission or letters of marque for arming any Ship or Ships to act as Privateers against the said United States or against the Citizens, People, or inhabitants of the said United States, or against the property of any of the inhabitants of any of them, from any Prince or State with which the said United States shall be at war.

Nor shall any Citizen, Subject, or Inhabitant of the said United States apply for or take any commission or letters of marque for arming any Ship or Ships to act as Privateers against the subjects of his Catholic Majesty or the property of any of them from any Prince or State with which the said King shall be at war. And if any person of either Nation shall take such commissions or letters of marque he shall be punished as a Pirate.

ART. XV
It shall be lawful for all and singular the Subjects of his Catholic Majesty, and the Citizens People, and inhabitants of the said United States to sail with their Ships with all manner of liberty and security, no distinction being made who are the proprietors of the merchandizes laden thereon from any Port to the Places of those who now are or hereafter shall be at enmity with his Catholic Majesty or the United States. It shall be likewise lawful for the Subjects and inhabitants aforesaid to sail with the Ships and merchandizes aforementioned, and to trade with the same liberty and security from the Places, Ports, and Havens of those who are Enemies of both or either Party without any opposition or disturbance whatsoever, not only directly from the Places of the Enemy aforementioned to neutral Places but also from one Place belonging to an Enemy to another Place belonging to an Enemy, whether they be under the jurisdiction of the same Prince or under several, and it is hereby stipulated that Free Ships shall also give freedom to goods, and that every thing shall be deemed free and exempt which shall be found on board the Ships belonging to the Subjects of either of the contracting Parties although the whole lading or any part thereof should appertain to the Enemies of either; contraband goods being always excepted. It is also agreed that the same liberty be extended to persons who are on board a free Ship, so that, although they be Enemies to either Party they shall not be made Prisoners or taken out of that free Ship unless they are Soldiers and in actual service of the Enemies.

ART. XVI
This liberty of navigation and commerce shall extend to all kinds of merchandizes excepting those only which are distinguished by the name of contraband; and under this name of contraband or prohibited goods shall be comprehended arms, great guns, bombs, with the fusees, and other things belonging to them, cannon ball, gun powder, match, pikes, swords, lances, speards, halberds, mortars, petards, grenades, salpetre, muskets, musket ball, bucklers, helmets, breast plates, coats of mail, and the like kind of arms proper for arming soldiers, musket rests, belts, horses with their furniture and all other warlike instruments whatever. These merchandizes which follow shall not be reckoned among contraband or prohibited goods; that is to say, all sorts of cloths and all other manufactures woven of any wool, flax, silk, cotton, or any other materials whatever, all kinds of wearing aparel [sic] together with all species whereof they are used to be made, gold and silver as well coined as uncoined, tin, iron, latton, copper, brass, coals, as also wheat, barley, oats, and any other kind of corn and pulse: tobacco and likewise all manner of spices, salted and smoked flesh, salted fish, cheese and butter, beer, oils, wines, sugars, and all sorts of salts, and in general all provisions which serve for the sustenance of life. Furthermore all kinds of cotton, hemp, flax, tar, pitch, ropes, cables, sails, sail cloths, anchors, and any parts of anchors, also ships masts, planks, wood of all kind, and all other things proper either for building or repairing ships, and all other goods whatever which have not been worked into the form of any instrument prepared for war by land or by sea, shall not be reputed contraband, much less such as have been already wrought and made up for any other use: all which shall be wholly reckoned among free goods, as likewise all other merchandizes and things which are not comprehended and particularly mentioned in the foregoing enumeration of contraband goods: so that they may be transported and carried in the freest manner by the subjects of both parties, even to Places belonging to an Enemy, such towns or Places being only excepted as are at that time besieged, blocked up, or invested. And except the cases in which any Ship of war or Squadron shall in consequence of storms or other accidents at sea be under the necessity of taking the cargo of any trading Vessel or Vessels, in which case they may stop the said Vessel or Vessels and furnish themselves with necessaries, giving a receipt in order that the Power to whom the said ship of war belongs may pay for the articles so taken according to the price thereof at the Port to which they may appear to have been destined by the Ship's papers: and the two contracting Parties engage that the Vessels shall not be detained longer than may be absolutely necessary for their said Ships to supply themselves with necessaries: that they will immediately pay the value of the receipts: and indemnify the proprietor for all losses which he may have sustained in consequence of such transaction.

ART. XVII
To the end that all manner of dissensions and quarrels may be avoided and prevented on one side and the other, it is agreed that in case either of the Parties hereto should be engaged in a war, the ships and Vessels belonging to the Subjects or People of the other Party must be furnished with sea letters or passports expressing the name, property, and bulk of the Ship, as also the name and place of habitation of the master or commander of the said Ship, that it may appear thereby that the Ship really and truly belongs to the Subjects of one of the Parties; which passport shall be made out and granted according to the form annexed to this Treaty. They shall likewise be recalled every year, that is, if the ship happens to return home within the space of a year. It is likewise agreed that such ships being laden, are to be provided not only with

passports as above mentioned but also with certificates containing the several particulars of the cargo, the place whence the ship sailed, that so it may be known whether any forbidden or contraband goods be on board the same; which certificates shall be made out by the Officers of the place whence the ship sailed in the accustomed form; and if any one shall think it fit or adviseable to express in the said certificates the person to whom the goods on board belong he may freely do so: without which requisites they may be sent to one of the Ports of the other contracting Party and adjudged by the competent tribunal according to what is above set forth, that all the circumstances of this omission having been well examined, they shall be adjudged to be legal prizes, unless they shall give legal satisfaction of their property by testimony entirely equivalent.

ART. XVIII
If the Ships of the said subjects, People or inhabitants of either of the Parties shall be met with either sailing along the Coasts on the high Seas by any Ship of war of the other or by any Privateer, the said Ship of war or Privateer for the avoiding of any disorder shall remain out of cannon shot, and may send their boats aboard the merchant Ship which they shall so meet with, and may enter her to number of two or three men only to whom the master or Commander of such ship or vessel shall exhibit his passports concerning the property of the ship made out according to the form inserted in this present Treaty: and the ship when she shall have shewed such passports shall be free and at liberty to pursue her voyage, so as it shall not be lawful to molest or give her chace in any manner or force her to quit her intended course.

ART. XIX
Consuls shall be reciprocally established with the privileges and powers which those of the most favoured Nations enjoy in the Ports where their consuls reside, or are permitted to be.

ART. XX
It is also agreed that the inhabitants of the territories of each Party shall respectively have free access to the Courts of Justice of the other, and they shall be permitted to prosecute suits for the recovery of their properties, the payment of their debts, and for obtaining satisfaction for the damages which they may have sustained, whether the persons whom they may sue be subjects or Citizens of the Country in which they may be found, or any other persons whatsoever who may have taken refuge therein; and the proceedings and sentence of the said Court shall be the same as if the contending parties had been subjects or Citizens of the said Country.

ART. XXI
In order to terminate all differences on account of the losses sustained by the Citizens of the United States in consequence of their vessels and cargoes having been taken by the Subjects of his Catholic Majesty during the late war between Spain and France, it is agreed that all such cases shall be referred to the final decision of Commissioners to be appointed in the following manner. His Catholic Majesty shall name one Commissioner, and the President of the United States by and with the advice and consent of their Senate shall appoint another, and the said two Commissioners shall agree on the choice of a third, or if they cannot agree so they shall each propose one person, and of the two names so proposed one shall be drawn by lot in the presence of the two original Commissioners, and the person whose name shall be so drawn shall be the third Commissioner, and the three Commissioners so appointed shall be sworn impartially to examine and decide the claims in question according to the merits of the several cases, and to justice, equity, and the laws of Nations. The said Commissioners shall meet and sit at Philadelphia and in the case of the death, sickness, or necessary absence of any such commissioner his place shall be supplied in the same manner as he was first appointed, and the new Commissioner shall take the same oaths, and do the same duties. They shall receive all complaints and applications, authorized by this article during eighteen months from the day on which they shall assemble. They shall have power to examine all such persons as come before them on oath or affirmation touching the complaints in question, and also to receive in evidence all written testimony authenticated in such manner as they shall think proper to require or admit. The award of the said Commissioners or any two of them shall be final and conclusive both as to the justice of the claim and the amount of the sum to be paid to the claimants; and his Catholic Majesty undertakes to cause the same to be paid in specie without deduction, at such times and Places and under such conditions as shall be awarded by the said Commissioners.

ART. XXII
The two high contracting Parties hoping that the good correspondence and friendship which happily reigns between them will be further increased by this Treaty, and that it will contribute to augment their prosperity and opulence, will in future give to their mutual commerce all the extension and favor which the advantage of both Countries may require; and in consequence of the stipulations contained in the IV. article his Catholic Majesty will permit the Citizens of the United States for the space of three years from this time to deposit their merchandize and effects in the Port of New Orleans, and to export them from thence without paying any other duty than a fair price for the hire of the stores, and his Majesty promises either to continue his permission if he finds during that time that it is not prejudicial to the interests of Spain, or if he should not agree to continue it there, he will assign to them on another part of the banks of the Mississippi an equivalent establishment.

ART. XXIII
The present Treaty shall not be in force until ratified by the Contracting Parties, and the ratifications shall be exchanged in six months from this time, or sooner if possible.

In Witness whereof We the underwritten Plenipotentiaries of His Catholic Majesty and of the United States of America have signed this present Treaty of Friendship, Limits and Navigation and have thereunto affixed our seals respectively.

Done at San Lorenzo el Real this seven and twenty day of October one thousand seven hundred and ninety five.

THOMAS PINCKNEY [SEAL]
EL PRINCIPE DE LA PAZ [SEAL]

Source: Malloy, William M., ed. 1910. *Treaties, Conventions, International Acts, Protocols and Agreements between the United States of America and Other Powers, 1776–1909*. Vol. 2. Washington: Government Printing Office.

DOCUMENT 4

TREATY OF SAN ILDEFONSO (OCTOBER 1, 1800)

Preliminary and Secret Treaty between the French Republic and His Catholic Majesty the King of Spain, Concerning the Aggrandizement of His Royal Highness the Infant Duke of Parma in Italy and the Retrocession of Louisiana.

His Catholic Majesty having always manifested an earnest desire to procure for His Royal Highness the Duke of Parma an aggrandizement which would place his domains on a footing more consonant with his dignity; and the French Republic on its part having long since made known to His Majesty the King of Spain its desire to be again placed in possession of the colony of Louisiana; and the two Governments having exchanged their views on these two subjects of common interest, and circumstances permitting them to assume obligations in this regard which, so far as depends on them, win assure mutual satisfaction, they have authorized for this purpose the following: the French Republic, the Citizen Alexandre Berthier General in Chief, and His Catholic Majesty, Don Mariano Luis de Urquijo, knight of the Order of Charles III, and of that of St. John of Jerusalem, a Counselor of State, his Ambassador Extraordinary and Plenipotentiary appointed near the Batavian Republic, and his First Secretary of State ad interim, who, having exchanged their powers, have agreed upon the following articles, subject to ratification.

ARTICLE 1
The French Republic undertakes to procure for His Royal Highness the Infant Duke of Parma an aggrandizement of territory which shall increase the population of his domains to one minion inhabitants, with the title of King and with all the rights which attach to the royal dignity; and the French Republic undertakes to obtain in this regard the assent of His Majesty the Emperor and King and that of the other interested states' so that His Highness the Infant Duke of Parma may be put into possession of the said territories without opposition upon the conclusion of the peace to be made between the French Republic and His Imperial Majesty.

ARTICLE 2
The aggrandizement to be given to His Royal Highness the Duke of Parma may consist of Tuscany, in case the present negotiations of the French Government with His Imperial Majesty shall permit that Government to dispose thereof; or it may consist of the three Roman legations or of any other continental provinces of Italy which form a rounded state.

ARTICLE 3
His Catholic Majesty promises and undertakes on his part to retrocede to the French Republic, six months after the fun and entire execution of the above conditions and provisions regarding His Royal Highness the Duke of Parma, the colony or province of Louisiana, with the same extent that it now has in the hands of Spain and that it had when France possessed it, and such as it ought to be according to the treaties subsequently concluded between Spain and other states.

ARTICLE 4
His Catholic Majesty will give the necessary orders for the occupation of Louisiana by France as soon as the territories which are to form the aggrandizement of the Duke of Parma shall be placed in the hands of His Royal Highness. The French Republic may, according to its convenience, postpone the taking of possession; when that is to be executed, the states directly or indirectly interested will agree upon such further conditions as their common interests and the interest of the respective inhabitants require.

ARTICLE 5
His Catholic Majesty undertakes to deliver to the French Republic in Spanish ports in Europe, one month after the execution of the provision with regard to the Duke of Parma, six ships of war in good condition built for seventy-four guns, armed and equipped and ready to receive French crews and supplies.

ARTICLE 6
As the provisions of the present treaty have no prejudicial object and leave intact the rights of all, it is not to be supposed that they win give offense to any power. However, if the contrary shall happen and if the two states, because of the execution thereof, shall be attacked or threatened, the two powers agree to make common cause not only to repel the aggression but also to take conciliatory measures properfor the maintenance of peace with all their neighbors.

ARTICLE 7
The obligations contained in the present treaty derogate in no respect from those which are expressed in the Treaty of Alliance signed at San Ildefonso on the 2d Fructidor, year 4 (August 19, 1796); on the contrary they unite anew the interests of the two powers and assure the guaranties stipulated in the Treaty of Alliance for all cases in which they should be applied.

ARTICLE 8
The ratifications of these preliminary articles shall be effected and exchanged within the period of one month, or sooner if possible, counting from the day of the signature of the present treaty.

In faith whereof we, the undersigned Ministers Plenipotentiary of the French Republic and of His Catholic Majesty, in virtue of our respective powers, have signed these preliminary articles and have affixed thereto our seals.

Done at San Ildefonso the 9th Vendemiaire, 9th year of the French Republic (October 1, 1800)

[Seal] ALEXANDRE BIRTHIER

[Seal] MARIANO LUIS DE URQUIJO

Source: *American State Papers: Documents, Legislative and Executive, of the Congress of the United States.* Editorship varies. Washington: Gales and Seaton, 1832–1861. 38 vols.

DOCUMENT 5

TREATY OF LUNEVILLE (1801)

Treaty of Peace concluded at Luneville, Feb. 9, 1801, between the French Republic, and the Emperor and the Germanic Body.

His majesty, the emperor and the king of Hungary and Bohemia, and the first consul of the French Republic, in the name of the French people, having equally at heart to put an end to the miseries of war, have resolved to proceed to the conclusion of a definite treaty of peace and amity.

His said imperial and royal majesty, not less anxiously desirous of making the Germanic empire participate in the blessings of peace, and the present conjecture not allowing the time necessary for the empire to be consulted, and to take part by its deputies in the negotiation; his said majesty having, besides, regard to what has been agreed upon by the deputation of the empire at he preceding congress at Rastadt, has resolved, in conformity with the precedent of what has taken place in familiar circumstances, to stipulate in the name of the Germanic body.

In consequence of which the contracting parties have appointed as their plenipotentiaries, to it,

His imperial and royal majesty, the Sieur Louis Cobentzel, count of the holy Roman empire, knight of the golden fleece, grand cross of the royal order of St Stephen and of the order of St. John of Jerusalem, chamberlain, and privy counsellor of his imperial and royal majesty, his minister for the conference, and vice-chancellor of the court of state;

And the first consul of the French Republic, in the name of the French people, has appointed citizen Joseph Bonaparte, counsellor of state; who, after having exchanged their full powers, have agreed to the following articles:

ART. I
There shall be henceforth and forever, peace, amity, and good understanding, between his majesty the emperor, king of Hungary and Bohemia, stipulating, as well in his own name as that of the Germanic empire, and the French Republic, is said majesty engaging to cause the empire to give ratification in good and due form to the present treaty. The greatest attention shall be paid on both sides to the maintenance of perfect harmony, to preventing all hostilities by land and by sea, for whatever cause, or on whatever pretence, and to carefully endeavouring to maintain the union happily established. No assistance or protection shall be given, either directly or indirectly, to those who would do any thing to the prejudice of either of the contracting parties.

ART. II
The cession of the ci-devant Belgic provinces to the French Republic, stipulated by the 3rd article of the treaty of Campo Formio, is renewed there in the most formal manner, so that his imperial and royal majesty, for himself and his successors, as well in his own name as that of the Germanic empire, renounces all his right and title to the said provinces, which shall be possessed henceforth as its sovereign right and property by the French Republic, with all the territorial property dependant on it. There shall also be given up to the French Republic by his imperial and royal majesty, and with the formal consent of the empire:

1st, The comté of Falkenstein, with its dependencies.

2d, The Frickthall, and all belonging to the house of Austria in the left bank of the Rhine, between Zarsach and Basle; the French Republic reserving to themselves the right of ceding the latter country to the Helvetic republic.

ART. III
In the same manner, in renewal and confirmation of the 6th article of the treaty of Campo Formio, his majesty the emperor and the king shall possess in sovereignty, and as his right, the countries below enumerated, viz. Istria, Dalmatia, and the Venetian isles in the Adriatic dependant upon those countries, the Bocca de Cattaro, the city of Venice, the canals and the country included between the hereditary state of his majesty the emperor and king; the Adriatic sea, and the Adige, form its leaving the Tyrol to the mouth of the said sea; the towing path of the Adige serving as the line of limitation. And as by this line the cites of Verona and of Porto Legnano will be divided, there shall be established, on the middle bridges of the said cities, drawbridges to mark the separation.

ART. IV
The 18th article of the treaty of Campo Formio is also renewed thus far, that his majesty the emperor and king binds himself to yield to the Duke of Modena, as an indemnity for the countries which this prince and his heirs had in Italy, the Brisgau, which he shall hold on the same terms as those by virtue of which he possesses the Modenese.

ART. V
It is moreover agreed, that his royal highness the grand duke of Tuscany shall renounce, for himself and his successors, having any right to it, the grand dutchy of Tuscany, and that part of the isle of Elba which is dependant upon it, as well as all right and title resulting from his rights on the said states, which shall be henceforth possessed in complete sovereignty, and as his own property, by his royal highness the infant duke of Parma. The grand duke shall obtain in Germany a full and complete indemnity for his Italian states. The grand duke shall dispose at pleasure of the goods and property which he possesses in Tuscany, either by personal acquisition, or by descent from his late father, the emperor Leopold II, or from his grandfather the emperor Francis I. It is also agreed, that other property of the grand dutchy, as well as the debts secured on the country, shall pass to the new grand duke.

ART. VI
His majesty the emperor and king, as well as in his own name as in that of the Germanic empire, consents that the French Republic shall possess henceforth in complete sovereignty, and as their property, the country and domains situated on the left bank of the Rhine, and which formed part of the Germanic empire: so that, in conformity with what had been expressly consented to at the congress of Rastadt, by the deputation of the empire, and approved by the emperor, the towing path of the Rhine will henceforth be the limit between the French Republic and the Germanic empire; that is to say, from the place where the Rhine leaves the Helvetic territory, to that where it enters the Batavian territory.

In consequence of this, the French Republic formally renounces all possession whatever on the right bank of the Rhine, and consents to restore to those whom it may belong, the fortresses of Dusseldorff, Ehrenbreitstein, Philipsburgh, the fort of Cassel, and other fortification opposite to Mentz, on the right bank, the fort of Kehl, and Old Brisach, on the express condition that these places and fortresses shall continue and remain in the state in which they were at the time of their evacuation.

ART. VII
And as, in consequence of the cession which the empire makes to the French Republic, several princes and states of the empire will be dispossessed, either altogether or in part, whom it is incumbent upon the Germanic empire collectively to support, the losses resulting from the stipulations in the present treaty, it is agreed between his majesty the emperor and king, as well in his own name as in that of the Germanic empire, and the French Republic, that in conformity with the principles formally established at the congress of Rastadt, the empire shall be bound to give to the hereditary princes who shall be dispossessed on the left bank of the Rhine, an indemnity, which shall be taken from the whole of the empire, according to arrangements which on these bases shall be ultimately determined upon.

ART. VIII
In all the ceded countries, acquired or exchanged by the present treaty, it is agreed, as had already been done by the 4th and 10th articles of the treaty of Campo Formio, that those to whom they shall belong shall take them, subject to the debts charged on the said countries; but considering the difficulties which have arisen in this respect, with regard to the interpretation of the said articles of the treaty of Campo Formio, it is expressly understood, that the French Republic will not take upon itself any thing more that the debts resulting from the loans formally agreed to by the state to the ceded countries, or by the actual administrations of such countries.

ART. IX
Immediately after the change of the ratifications of the present treaty, the sequestration imposed on the property, effects, and revenues of the inhabitants or proprietors, shall be taken off. The contracting parties oblige themselves to pay all they may owe for money lent them by individuals, as well as by the public establishments of the said countries and to pay and reimburse all annuities created for their benefit on every one of them. In consequence of this, it is expressly admitted, that the holders of stock in the bank of Vienna, become French subjects, shall continue to enjoy the benefit of their funds, and shall receive the interest accrued, or to accrue, not withstanding the infringement which the holders aforesaid, become French subjects, sustained by not being able to pay the 30 and 100 percent. Demanded by him imperial and royal majesty, of all creditors of the bank of Vienna.

ART. X
The contracting parties shall also cause all the sequestrations to be taken off, which have been imposed on account of the war, on the property, the rights, and revenues of the emperor, or of the empire, in the territory of the French Republic, and of the French citizens in the states of the said majesty or the empire.

ART. XI
The present treaty of peace, and particularly the 8th, 9th, 10th and 15th articles, are declared to extend to, and to be common to the Batavian, Helvetic, Cisalpine and Ligurian republics. The contracting parties mutually guaranty the independence of the said republics, and the right

of the people who inhabit them to adopt what form of government they please.

ART. XII
His imperial and royal majesty renounces for himself and his successors, in favour of the Cisalpine republic, all rights and titles arising from those rights, which his majesty might claim on the countries of the 8th article of the treaty of Campo Formio, now form part of the Cisalpine republic, which shall possess them as their sovereignty and property, with all the territorial property dependant upon it.

ART. XIII
His imperial and royal majesty, as well in his own name as in that of the Germanic empire, confirms the agreement already entered into by the treaty of Campo Formio, for the union of ci-devant imperial fiefs to the Ligurian republic, and renounces all rights and titles arising from these rights on the said fiefs.

ART. XIV
In conformity with the 2d article of the treaty of Campo Formio, the navigation of the Adige, which serves as the limits between his majesty the emperor and king, and the navigation of the rivers in the Cisalpine republic, shall be free, nor shall any toll be imposed, nor any ship of war kept there.

ART. XV
All prisoners of war on both sides, as well as hostages given or taken during the war, who shall not be yet restored, shall be so within forty days from the time of the signing of the present treaty.

ART. XVI
The real and personal property unalienated to this royal highness the archduke Charles, and of the heirs of her royal highness the archduchess Christina, deceased, situated in the countries ceded to the French Republic, shall be restored to them on condition of their selling them within three years. The same shall be the case also with the landed and personal property of their royal highnesses the archduke Ferdinand and the archduchess Beatrice, his wife, in the territory of the Cisalpine republic.

ART. XVII
The 12th, 13th, 15th, 16th 17th, and 23d articles of the treaty of Campo Formio, are particularly renewed, and are to be executed according to their form and effect, as if they were here repeated verbatim.

ART. XVIII
The contributions, payments, and war impositions, of whatever kind, shall cease from the day of the exchange of the ratifications of the present treaty on the one hand, by his imperial majesty and the Germanic empire, and on the other by the French Republic.

ART. XIX
The present treaty shall be ratified by his majesty the emperor and king, by the empire, and by the French Republic, in the space of thirty days or sooner if possible; and it is agreed that the armies of the two powers shall remain in the present positions, both in Germany and in Italy, until the ratification shall be respectively, and at the same moment, exchanged at Luneville.

It is also agreed, that ten days after the exchange of ratifications, the armies of this imperial and royal majesty shall enter the hereditary possessions, which shall, within the same space of time, be evacuated by the French armies; and thirty days after the said ratifications shall be exchanged, the French armies shall evacuate the whole of the territory of the said empire.

Executed at Luneville, Feb. 9, 1801
Louis Count Cobentzel
Joseph Bonaparte

Source: *The Annual Register, or, A View of the History, Politics, and Literature for the Year 1801.* London: Printed by R. Wilks for W. Otridge and Sons, et al. (Publisher varies by year.) 1758–1837. 80 vols.

DOCUMENT 6
TREATY OF AMIENS (1802)

Definitive Treaty of Peace between the French Republic, his Majesty the King of Spain and the Indies, and the Batavian Republic (on the one Part); and his Majesty, the King of the United Kingdom of Great Britain and Ireland (on the other Part).

The first consul of the French Republic, in the name of the French people, and his majesty the king of the united kingdom of Great Britain and Ireland, being equally animated with a desire to put an end to the calamities of war, have laid the foundation of peace, by the preliminary articles, which were signed in London the 9th Vendemaire, (or the first of October 1801).

And as by the 15th article of the preliminaries it has been agreed on, *"that plenipotentiaries should be named on the part of each government, who should repair to Amiens, and there proceed to arrange a definitive treaty, in concert with the allies of the contracting powers."*

The first consul of the French Republic, in the name of the French people, has named as plenipotentiary the citizen Joseph Buonaparte, counsellor of state:

His majesty the king of the united kingdom of Great Britain and Ireland has named the marquis Cornwallis, knight of the most noble order of the garter, one of his majesty's privy council, general in his majesty's army, &c. &c.

His majesty the king of Spain and the Indies, and the

government of the Batavian republic, have appointed the following plenipotentiaries, to wit, his catholic majesty has named Don Joseph Nicolas d'Azara, his counsellor of state, grand cross of the order of Charles III. ambassador extraordinary of his majesty to the French Republic &c. &c. :

And the government of the Batavian republic, Jean Schimmelpennick its ambassador extraordinary to the French Republic, &c.:

Which said plenipotentiaries having duly communicated to each other their respective Powers, which are transcribed at the conclusion of the present treaty, have agreed the following articles:

ART. I

There shall be peace, friendship, and good understanding between the French Republic, his majesty the king of Spain, his heirs and successors, and the Batavian republic, on the one part, and his majesty the king of the united kingdom of Great Britain and Ireland, his heirs and successors, on the other part.

The contracting parties shall use their utmost efforts to preserve a perfect harmony between their respective countries, without permitting any act of hostility whatever by sea or by land, for any cause, or under any pretext.

They shall carefully avoid every thing which might for the future disturb the happy union now re-established between them, and stall not give any succour or protection, directly or indirectly, to those who wish to injure any of them.

ART. II

All the prisoners made on one side and the other, as well by land as by sea, and the hostages carried off, or delivered up during the war, and up to the present day, shall be restored without ransom in six weeks at the latest, to be reckoned from the day when the ratifications of the present treaty are exchanged, and on paying the debts which they shall have contracted during their captivity. Each of the contracting parties shall respectively discharge the advances which shall have been made by any of the contracting parties, for the support and maintenance of prisoners in the countries where they have been detained. There shall be appointed by mutual consent for this purpose a commission, especially empowered to ascertain and determine the compensation which may be due to any one of the contracting parties. The time and the place shall likewise be fixed, by mutual consent, for the meeting of the commissioners, who shall be entrusted with the execution of this article, and who shall take into account, not only the expenses incurred on account of the prisoners of the respective nations, but likewise on account of the foreign troops, who, before being taken, were in the pay, and at the disposal of one of the contracting parties.

ART. III

His Britannic majesty restores to the French Republic and its allies, viz. his Catholic majesty and the Batavian republic, all the possessions and colonies which respectively belonged to them, and which have been either occupied or conquered by the British forces, during the course of the present war, with the exception of the island of Trinidad, and of the Dutch possessions on the island of Ceylon.

ART. IV

His Catholic majesty cedes and guarantees, in full property and sovereignty, the island of Trinidad to his Britannic majesty.

ART. V

The Batavian republic cedes and guarantees, in full property and sovereignty, to his Britannic majesty, all the possessions and establishments in the island of Ceylon, which previous to the war belonged to the republic of the united provinces, or to the Dutch East India company.

ART. VI

The port of the Cape of Good Hope remains to the Batavian republic in full sovereignty, in the same manner as it did previous to the war.

The ships of every kind belonging to the other contracting parties, shall be allowed to enter the said ports, and there to purchase what provisions they may stand in need of heretofore, without being liable to pay any other imposts than such as the Batavian republic compels the ships of its own nation to pay.

ART. VII

The territories and possessions of his most Faithful majesty are maintained in their integrity, such as they were antecedent to the war. However the boundaries of French and Portuguese Guiana are fixed by the river Arrowary, which empties itself into the ocean above Cape North, near the islands Nuovo and Penetentia, about a degree and a third of north latitude. These boundaries shall run along the river Arrowary, from its mouth, the most distant from Cape North, to its source, and afterwards on a right line, drawn from that source, to the Rio Brunco, towards the west.

In consequence, the northern bank of the river Arrowary, from its said mouth to its source, and the territories that lie to the north of the line of boundaries laid down as above, shall belong in full sovereignty to the French Republic.

The southern bank of the said river, from the same mouth, and all the territories to the south of the said line, shall belong to her most Faithful majesty.

The navigation of the river Arrowary, along the whole of its course, shall be common to both nations.

The arrangements which have been agreed upon between the courts of Madrid and Lisbon, respecting the settlement of their boundaries in Europe, shall nevertheless be adhered to conformably to the stipulations of the treaty of Badajos.

ART. VIII
The territories, possessions, and rights of the sublime Porte, are maintained in their integrity, as they were before the war.

ART. IX
The republic of the Seven Islands is recognised.

ART. X
The islands of Malta, Gozo, and Comino, shall be restored to the order of St. John of Jerusalem to be held on the same conditions, on which it possessed them before the war, and under the following stipulations.

1. The knights of the order whose Langues shall continue to subsist after the exchange of the ratification of the present treaty, are invited to return to Malta, as soon as the exchange shall have taken place. They shall there form a general chapter, and proceed to the election of a grand master, chosen from among the natives of those nations which are to preserve their Langues, unless that election has been already made since the exchange of the preliminaries.

2. It is understood that an election made subsequent to that epoch, shall alone be considered valid, to the exclusion of any other that have taken place at any period prior to that epoch.

3. The governments of the French Republic, and of Great Britain, desiring to place the order and island of Malta in a state of entire independence with respect to themselves, agree that there shall not be in future either a French or an English Langue; and that no individual belonging to either the one or to the other of these powers shall be admitted into the order.

4. There shall be established a Maltese Langue, which shall be supported by the territorial revenues and commercial duties of the island. This Langue shall have its peculiar dignities, an establishment and a mansion-house. Proofs of nobility shall not be necessary for the admission of knights of the Langue; and they shall be moreover admissible to all offices, and shall enjoy all privileges, in the same manner as the knights of the other Langues. At least half of the municipal, administrative, civil, judicial, and other employments depending on the government, shall be filled by inhabitants of the islands of Malta, Gozo, and Comino.

5. The forces of his Britannic majesty shall evacuate the island, and its dependencies, within three months from the exchange of the ratifications, or sooner if possible. At that epoch it shall be given up to the order in its present state, provided the grand master, or commissaries, fully authorized according to the statutes of the order, shall be in the island to take possession, and that the force which is to be provided by his Sicilian majesty, as is hereafter stipulated, shall have arrived there.

6. One half of the garrison at least shall always be composed of native Maltese; for the remainder, the order may levy recruits in those countries only which continue to possess the Langues. The Maltese troops shall have Maltese officers. The commandership in chief of the garrison, as well as the nomination of the officers, shall pertain to the grand master, and this right he cannot resign even temporarily, except in favour of a knight, and in concurrence with the advice of the council of the order.

7. The independence of the isles Malta, of Gozo, and Comino, as well as the present arrangement, shall be placed under the protection and guarantee of France, Great Britain, Austria, Spain, Russia, and Prussia.

8. The neutrality of the order and of the island of Malta, with its dependencies, is hereby proclaimed.

9. The ports of Malta shall be opened to the commerce and the navigation of all nations, who shall there pay equal and moderate duties: these duties shall be applied to the maintenance of the Maltese Langue, as specified in paragraph 3, to that of the civil and military establishments of the island, as well as to that of a general lazaret, open to all colours.

10. The states of Barbary are excepted from the conditions of the preceding paragraphs, until, by means of an arrangement to be procured by the contracting parties, the system of hostilities, which subsists between the states of Barbary, and the order of St. John, or the powers possessing the Langue, or concurring in the composition of the order, shall have ceased.

11. The order shall be governed, both with respect to spirituals and temporals, by the same statutes which were in force when the knights left the isle, as far as the present treaty does not abrogate them.

12. The regulations contained in the paragraphs 3, 5, 7, 8, and 10, shall be converted into laws, and perpetual statutes of the order, in the customary manner; and the grand master, or, if he shall not be in the island, at the time of its restoration to the order, his representative, as well as his successors, shall be bound to take an oath for their punctual observance.

13. His Sicilian majesty shall be invited to furnish 2000 men, natives of his states, to serve as a garrison in the different fortresses of the said islands. That force shall remain one year, to bear date from their restitution to the knights; and if, at the expiration of this term, the order should not have raised a force sufficient, in the judgement of the guarantying powers to garrison the island and its dependencies, as is specified in the 5th paragraph, the Neapolitan troops shall continue there until they shall be replaced by a force deemed sufficient by the said powers.

14. The different powers designated in the 6th paragraph, to wit, France, Great Britain, Austria, Spain, Russia, and Prussia, shall be invited to accede to the present stipulations.

ART. XI
The French troops shall evacuate the kingdom of Naples and the Roman states; the English forces shall also evacuate Porto Ferrajo, and generally all the ports and islands, that they occupy in the Mediterranean or the Adriatic.

ART. XII
The evacuations, cessions, and restitutions, stipulated by the present treaty, shall be executed in Europe within a month; on the continent and seas of America and Africa in three months; on the continent and seas of Asia in six months, which shall follow the ratification of the present definitive treaty, except in case of a special reservation.

ART. XIII
In all cases of restitution, agreed upon by the present treaty, the fortifications shall be restored in the condition they were in at the time of signing the preliminiaries; and all the works which shall have been constructed since their occupation shall remain untouched.

It is agreed besides that in all the stipulated cases of cessions, there shall be allowed to the inhabitants, of whatever rank or nation they may be, a term of three years, reckoning from the notification of the present treaty, to dispose of all their properties, whether acquired by them before or during the continuance of the present war; during which term of three years, they shall have free and entire liberty to exercise their religion, and to enjoy their fortunes. The same power is granted in the countries that are hereby restored, to all persons, whether inhabitants or not, who shall have formed any establishments there, during the time that those countries were in the possession of Great Britain.

As to the inhabitants of the countries restored or ceded, it is hereby agreed, that no person shall, under any pretence, be prosecuted, disturbed, or molested, either in person or property, on account of his political conduct or opinion, or for his attachment to any of the contracting parties, on any account whatever except for debts contracted with individuals, or for acts subsequent to the present treaty.

ART. XIV
All the sequestrations laid on either side on funds, revenues, and credits, of what nature soever they may be, belonging to any of the contracting powers, or to their citizens or subjects, shall be taken off immediately after the signature of this definitive treaty.

The decision of all chains among the individuals of the respective nations, for debts, property, effects, or rights, of any nature whatsoever, which should, according to received usages, and the law of nations, be preferred at the epoch of the peace shall be referred to the competent tribunals: in all those cases speedy and complete justice shall be done in the countries wherein those claims shall be respectively preferred.

ART. XV
The fisheries on the coasts of Newfoundland, and of the adjacent islands, and in the gulf of St. Laurence, are placed on the same footing as they were before the war.

The French fishermen of Newfoundland, and the inhabitants of the islands of St. Pierre and Miquelon, shall have liberty, to cut such wood as may be necessary for them in the bays of Fortune and Despair during the first year, reckoning from the ratification of the present treaty.

ART. XVI
To prevent all grounds of complaint and disputes which might arise on account of captures which may have been made at sea subsequent to the signing of the preliminaries, is reciprocally agreed that the ships and property which may have been taken in the channel, and in the north seas, after a space of twelve days, reckoning from the exchange of the ratifications of the preliminary articles, shall be restored on the one side and the other; that the term shall be one month for the space, from the channel and the north seas, as far as the Canary islands inclusively, as well in the ocean as in the Mediterranean; two months from the Canary island to the equator; and, finally five months in all other parts of the world, without any further exceptions or distinction of time or place.

ART. XVII
The ambassadors, ministers, and other agents of the contracting powers, shall enjoy respectively in the states of the said powers the same rank, privileges, prerogative, and immunities, which were enjoyed before the war by agents of the same class.

ART. XVIII
The branch of the house of Nassau, which was established in the ci-devant republic of the united provinces, now the Batavian republic, having experienced some losses, as well with respect to private property as by the change of constitution adopted in those countries, an equivalent compensation shall be procured for the losses which it shall be proved to have sustained.

ART. XIX
The present definitive treaty of Peace is declared common to the sublime Ottoman Porte, the ally, of his Britannic majesty; and the sublime Porte shall be invited to transmit its act of accession as soon as possible.

ART. XX
It is agreed that the contracting parties, upon requisitions made by them respectively, or by their ministers, or officers duly authorized for that purpose, shall be bound to deliver up to justice persons accused of' murder, forgery, or fraudulent bankruptcy, committed within the jurisdiction of the requiring party, provided that this shall only be done in cases in which tile evidence of the crime shall be such, that the laws of the place in which the accused persons shall be discovered, would have authorized the detaining and bringing him to trial, had the offence been committed there. The expenses of the arrest and prosecution shall be defrayed by the party making the requisition; but this article has no sort of reference to crimes of

murder, forgery, or fraudulent bankruptcy, committed before the conclusion of this definitive treaty.

ART. XXI
The contracting parties promise to observe sincerely and faithfully all the articles contained in the present treaty, and will not suffer any sort of counteraction, direct or indirect, to be made to it by their citizens, or respective subjects; and the contracting parties guaranty, generally and reciprocally, all the stipulations of the present treaty.

ART. XXII
The present treaty shall be ratified by the contracting parties, as soon as possible, and the ratifications shall be exchanged in due form in Paris.

In testimony whereof, we, the undersigned plenipotentiaries, have signed with our hands, and in virtue of our respective full powers, the present definitive treaty, causing it to be sealed with our respective seals.

Done at Amiens, the 4th Germinal, in the year 10 (March 25, 1802)

Bonaparte.
Cornwallis.
Azara.
Schimmelpennick.

Source: *The Annual Register, or, A View of the History, Politics, and Literature from the Year 1802.* London: Printed by R. Wilks for W. Otridge and Sons, et al. (Publisher varies by years.) 1758–1802, 80 vols.

DOCUMENT 7

LETTER FROM THOMAS JEFFERSON TO ROBERT LIVINGSTON (APRIL 18, 1802)

Excerpts:

"The cession of Louisiana and the Floridas by Spain to France works most sorely on the United States. On this subject the Secretary of State has written to you fully. Yet I cannot forbear recurring to it personally, so deep is the impression it makes in my mind. It completely reverses all the political relations of the United States and will form a new epoch in our political course. Of all nations of any consideration, France is the one which hitherto has offered the fewest points on which we could have any conflict of right and the most points of a communion of interests. From these causes, we have ever looked to her as our *natural friend,* as one with which we never could have an occasion of difference. Her growth, therefore, we viewed as our own, her misfortunes ours. There is on the globe one single spot, the possessor of which is our natural and habitual enemy. It is New Orleans, through which the produce of three-eighths of our territory must pass to market, and from its fertility it will ere long yield more than half of our whole produce and contain more than half our inhabitants. France placing herself in that door assumes to us the attitude of defiance. Spain might have retained it quietly for years. Her pacific dispositions, her feeble state, would induce her to increase our facilities there, so that her possession of the place would be hardly felt by us, and it would not perhaps be very long before some circumstance might arise which might make the cession of it to us the price of something of more worth to her. Not so can it ever be in the hands of France. The impetuosity of her temper, the energy and restlessness of her character placed in a point of eternal friction with us, and our character, which though quiet and loving peace and the pursuit of wealth, is high-minded, despising wealth in competition with insult or injury, enterprising and energetic as any nation on earth—these circumstances render it impossible that France and the United States can continue long friends when they meet in so irritable a position. They as well as we must be blind if they do not see this; and we must be very improvident if we do not begin to make arrangements on that hypothesis. The day that France takes possession of New Orleans fixes the sentence which is to restrain her forever within her low water mark. It seals the union of two nations who, in conjunction, can maintain exclusive possession of the ocean. From that moment we must marry ourselves to the British fleet and nation. We must turn all our attentions to a maritime force, for which our resources place us on very high grounds: and having formed and cemented together a power which may render reinforcement of her settlements here impossible to France, make the first cannon which shall be fired in Europe the signal for tearing up any settlement she may have made and for holding the two continents of America in sequestration for the common purposes of the united British and American nations. This is not a state of things we seek or desire. It is one which this measure, if adopted by France, forces on us as necessarily as any other cause, by the laws of nature, brings on its necessary effect. It is not from a fear of France that we deprecate this measure proposed by her. For however greater her force is than ours compared in the abstract, it is nothing in comparison of ours when to be exerted on our soil. But it is from a sincere love of peace and a firm persuasion that, bound to France by the interests and the strong sympathies still existing in the minds of our citizens and holding relative positions which ensure their continuance, we are secure of a long course of peace. Whereas, the change of friends which will be rendered necessary if France changes that position embarks us necessarily as a belligerent power in the first war of Europe. In that case, France will have held possession of New Orleans during the interval of a peace, long or short, at the end of which it will be wrested from her. Will this short-lived possession have been an equivalent to her for the transfer of such a weight into the scale of her enemy? Will not the amalgamation of a young, thriving nation continue to that enemy the health and force which are at present so evidently on the decline? And will a few years possession of New Orleans add equally to the strength of France? She may say she needs Louisiana for the supply of her West Indies. She does not need it in time of peace. And in war she could not depend on them because they would be so easily intercepted. I should suppose that all these considerations might in some proper form be brought into view of the government of France. Though stated by us, it ought not to give offense because we do not bring them forward as a menace, but as consequences not controllable by us but inevitable from the course of things. We mention them not as things which we desire by any means, but as things we deprecate; and we beseech a friend to look forward and to prevent them for our common interests ..."

"I have no doubt you have urged these considerations on every proper occasion with the government where you are. They are such as must have effect if you can find the means of producing thorough reflection on them by that government. The idea here is that the troops sent to St. Domingo were to proceed to Louisiana after finishing their work in that island. If this were the arrangement, it will give you time to return again and again to the charge, for the conquest of St. Domingo will not be a short work. It will take considerable time to wear down a great number of soldiers. Every eye in the United States is now fixed on this affair of Louisiana. Perhaps nothing since the revolutionary war has produced more uneasy sensations through the body of the nation. Notwithstanding temporary bickerings have taken place with France, she has still a strong hold on the affections of our citizens generally. I have thought it not amiss, by way of supplement to the letters of the Secretary of State, to write you this private one to impress you with the importance we affix to this transaction. I pray you to cherish Dupont. He has the best disposition for the continuance of friendship between the two nations, and perhaps you may be able to make a good use of him."

Source: April 18, 1802. Jefferson, Thomas. *Writings: Autobiography, Notes on the State of Virginia, Public and Private Papers, Addresses, Letters.* (Library of America). Merrill D. Peterson, ed. New York: Viking Press, 1984.

DOCUMENT 8

THOMAS JEFFERSON'S SECOND ANNUAL MESSAGE TO THE CONGRESS (DECEMBER 15, 1802)

To the Senate and House of Representatives of the United States:

When we assemble together, fellow-citizens, to consider the state of our beloved country, our just attentions are first drawn to those pleasing circumstances which mark the goodness of that Being from whose favor they flow and the large measure of thankfulness we owe for His bounty. Another year has come around, and finds us still blessed with peace and friendship abroad; law, order, and religion at home; good affection and harmony with our Indian neighbors; our burthens lightened, yet our income sufficient for the public wants, and the produce of the year great beyond example. These, fellow-citizens, are the circumstances under which we meet, and we remark with special satisfaction those which under the smiles of Providence result from the skill, industry, and order of our citizens, managing their own affairs in their own way and for their own use, unembarrassed by too much regulation, unoppressed by fiscal exactions.

On the restoration of peace in Europe that portion of the general carrying trade which had fallen to our share during the war was abridged by the returning competition of the belligerent powers. This was to be expected, and was just. But in addition we find in some parts of Europe monopolizing discriminations, which in the form of duties tend effectually to prohibit the carrying thither our own produce in our own vessels. From existing amities and a spirit of justice it is hoped that friendly discussion will produce a fair and adequate reciprocity. But should false calculations of interest defeat our hope, it rests with the Legislature to decide whether they will meet inequalities abroad with countervailing inequalities at home, or provide for the evil in any other way.

It is with satisfaction I lay before you an act of the British Parliament anticipating this subject so far as to authorize a mutual abolition of the duties and countervailing duties permitted under the treaty of 1794. It shows on their part a spirit of justice and friendly accommodation which it is our duty and our interest to cultivate with all nations. Whether this would produce a due equality in the navigation between the two countries is a subject for your consideration.

Another circumstance which claims attention as directly affecting the very source of our navigation in the defect or the evasion of the law providing for the return of seamen, and particularly of those belonging to vessels sold abroad. Numbers of them, discharged in foreign ports, have dangers into which their distresses might plunge them and save them to their country, have found it necessary in some cases to return them at the public charge.

The cession of the Spanish Province of Louisiana to France, which took place in the course of the late war, will if carried into effect, make a change in the aspect of our foreign relations which will doubtless have just weight in any deliberations of the Legislature connected with that subject.

There was reason not long since to apprehend that the warfare in which we were engaged with Tripoli might be taken up by some other of the Barbary Powers. A reenforcement, therefore, was immediately ordered to the vessels already there. Subsequent information, however has removed these apprehensions for the present. To secure our commerce in that sea with the smallest force competent, we have supposed it best to watch strictly the harbor of Tripoli. Still, however, the shallowness of their coast and the want of smaller vessels on our part has permitted some cruisers to escape unobserved, and to one of these an American vessel unfortunately fell a prey. The captain, one American seaman, and two others of color remain prisoners with them unless exchanged under an agreement formerly made with the Bashaw, to whom, on the faith of that, some of his captive subjects had been restored.

The convention with the State of Georgia has been ratified by their legislature, and a repurchase from the Creeks has been consequently made of a part of the Talasscee country. In this purchase has been also comprehended a part of the lands within the fork of Oconee and Oakmulgee rivers. The particulars of the contract will be laid before Congress so soon as they shall be in a state for communication.

In order to remove every ground of difference possible with our Indian neighbors, I have proceeded in the work of settling with them and marking the boundaries between us. That with Choctaw Nation is fixed in one part and will be through the whole within a short time. The country to which their title had been extinguished before the Revolution is sufficient to receive a very respectful population, which Congress will probably see the expediency of encouraging so soon as the limits shall be declared. We are to view this position as an outpost of the United States, surrounded by strong neighbors and distant from its support; and how far that monopoly which prevents population should here be guarded against and actual habitation made a condition of the continuance of title will be for your consideration. A prompt settlement, too, of all existing rights and claims within this territory presents itself as a preliminary operation.

In that part of the Indian Territory which includes Vicennes the lines settled with neighboring tribes fix the extinction of their title at a breadth of 24 leagues from east to west and about the same length parallel with and including the Wabash. They have also ceded a tract of 4 miles square, including the salt springs near the mouth of that river.

In the Department of Finance it is with pleasure I inform you that the receipts of external duties for the last twelve months have exceeded those of any former year, and that the ratio of increase has been also greater than usual. This has enabled us to answer all the regular exigencies of Government, to pay from the Treasury within one year upward of $8,000,000, principal and interest, of the public debt, exclusive of upward of one million paid by the sale of bank stock, and making in the whole a reduction of nearly five millions and a half of principal, and to have now in the Treasury $4,500,000, which are in a course of application to the further discharge of debt and current demands. Experience, too, so far, authorizes us to believe, if no extraordinary event supervenes, and the expenses which will be actually incurred shall not be greater than were contemplated by Congress at their last session, that we shall not be disappointed in the expectations then formed. But nevertheless, as the effect of peace on the amount of duties is not yet fully ascertained, it is the more necessary to practice every useful economy and to incur no expense which may be avoided without prejudice.

The collection of the internal taxes having been retarded, it will be some time before the system is closed. It is not yet been thought necessary to employ the agent authorized by an act of the last session for transacting business in Europe relative to debts and loans. Nor have we used the power confided by the same act of prolonging the foreign debt by reloans, and of redeeming instead thereof an equal sum of domestic debt. Should, however, the difficulties of remittance on so large a scale render it necessary at any time, the power shall be executed and the money thus unemployed abroad shall, in conformity with that law, be faithfully applied here in equivalent extinction of domestic debt. When effects do salutary result from the plans you have already sanctioned; when merely by avoiding false objects of expense we are able, without a direct tax, without internal taxes, and without borrowing to make large and effectual payments toward the discharge of public debt and the emancipation of our posterity from that mortal canker, it is an encouragement, fellow-citizens, of the highest order to proceed as we have begun in substituting economy for taxation, and in pursuing what is useful for a nation placed as we are, rather than what is practiced by others under different circumstances. And whensoever we are destined to meet events which shall call forth all the energies of our countryman, we have the firmest reliance on those energies and the comfort of leaving for calls like these the extraordinary resources of loans and internal taxes. In the meantime, by payments of the principal of our debt, we are liberating annually portions of the external taxes and forming from them a growing fund still further to lessen the necessity of recurring to extraordinary resources.

The usual account of receipts and expenditures for the last year, with an estimate of the expenses of the ensuing one, will be laid before you by the Secretary of Treasury.

No change being deemed necessary in our military establishment, an estimate of its expenses for the ensuing year on its present footing, as also sums to be employed in fortifications and other objects within that department, has been prepared by the Secretary of War, and will make a part of the general estimates which will be presented you.

Considering that our regular troops are employed for local purposes, and that the militia our general reliance for great and sudden emergencies, you will doubtless think this institution worth of a review, and give those improvements of which you find susceptible.

Estimates for the Naval Department, prepared by the Secretary of the Navy, for another year will in like manner be communicated with general estimates. A small force in the Mediterranean will still be necessary to restrain the Tripoline cruisers, and the uncertain tenure of peace with some other of the Barbary Powers may eventually require that force to be augmented. The necessity of procuring some smaller vessels for that service will raise the estimate, but the difference in their maintenance will soon make it a measure of economy.

Presuming it will be deemed expedient to expend annually a convenient sum toward providing the naval defense which our situation may require. I can not but recommend that the first appropriations for that purpose may go to the saving what we already possess. No cares, no attentions, can preserve vessels from rapid decay which lie in water exposed to the sun. These decays require great and constant repairs and will consume, if continues, a great portion of the moneys destined to naval purposes. To avoid this waste of our resources it is proposed to add to our navy-yard here a dock within which our present vessels may be laid up dry and cover from the sun. Under these circumstances experience proves that works of wood will remain scarcely at all affected by time. The great abundance of running water which this situation possess, at heights far above the level of the tide, if employed as is practiced for lock navigation, furnishes the means for raising and laying up our vessels on a dry and sheltered bed. And should the measure be found useful here, similar depositories for laying up as well as for building and repairing vessel may hereafter be undertaken at other navy-yards offering the same means. The plans and estimates of the work, prepared by a person of skill and experience, will be presented to you without delay, and from this it will be seen that scarcely more than has been the cost of one vessel is necessary to save the whole, and that the annual sum to be employed toward its completion may be adapted to the views of the Legislature as to naval expenditure.

To cultivate peace and maintain commerce and navigation in all their lawful enterprises; to foster our fisheries as nurseries of navigation and for the nurture of man, and protect the manufactures adapted to our circumstances; to preserve the faith of the nation by an exact discharge of its debts and contracts, expend the public money with same care and economy we would practice with our own, and impose on our citizens no unnecessary burthens; to keep in all of safety-these, fellow-citizens, are the landmarks by which we are to guide ourselves in all our proceedings. By continuing to make these the rule of our action we shall endear to our countrymen the true principles of their Constitution and promote an union of sentiment an of action equally auspicious to their happiness and safety. On my part, you may count on a cordial concurrence in every measure for the public good and on all the information I possess which may enable you to discharge to advantage the high functions with which you are invested by your country.

Source: Richardson, James D., ed. 1897. *A Compilation of the Messages and Papers of the Presidents Prepared under the Direction of the Joint Committee on Printing, of the House and Senate Pursuant to an Act of the Fifty-Second Congress of the United States*. New York: Bureau of National Literature.

DOCUMENT 9

THOMAS JEFFERSON'S MESSAGE TO THE SENATE (JANUARY 11, 1803)

Gentlemen of the Senate:

The cession of the Spanish Province of Louisiana to France, and perhaps of the Floridas, and the late suspension of our right of deposit at New Orleans are events of primary interest to the United States. On both occasions such measures were promptly taken as were thought most likely amicably to remove the present and to prevent future causes of inquietude. The objects of these measures were to obtain the territory on the left bank of the Mississippi and eastward of that, if practicable, on conditions to which the proper authorities of our country would agree, or at least to prevent any changes which might lessen the secure exercise of our rights. While my confidence in our minister plenipotentiary at Paris is entire and undiminished, I still think that these objects might be promoted by joining with him a person sent from hence directly, carrying with him the feelings and sentiments of the nation excited on the late occurrence, impressed by full communications of all the views we entertain on this interesting subject, and thus prepared to meet and to improve to an useful result the counter propositions of the other contracting party, whatsoever form their interests may give to them, and to secure to us the ultimate accomplishment of our object.

I therefore nominate Robert R. Livingston to be minister plenipotentiary and James Monroe to be minister extraordinary and plenipotentiary, with full powers to both jointly, or to either on the death of the other, to enter into a treaty or convention with the First Consul of France for the purpose of enlarging and more effectually securing our rights and interests in the river Mississippi and in the Territories eastward thereof.

But as the possession of these provinces is still in Spain, and the course of events may retard or prevent the cession to France being carried into effect, to secure our object it will be expedient to address equal powers to the Government of Spain also, to be used only in the event of its being necessary.

I therefore nominate Charles Pinckney to be minister plenipotentiary, and James Monroe, of Virginia, to be minister extraordinary and plenipotentiary, with full powers to both jointly, or to either on the death of the other, to enter into a treaty or convention with His Catholic Majesty for the purpose of enlarging and more effectually securing our rights and interests in the river Mississippi and in the Territories eastward thereof.

TH. JEFFERSON

Source: Richardson, James D., ed. 1897. *A Compilation of the Messages and Papers of the Presidents Prepared under the Direction of the Joint Committee on Printing, of the House and Senate Pursuant to an Act of the Fifty-Second Congress of the United States*. New York: Bureau of National Literature.

DOCUMENT 10

JEFFERSON'S MESSAGE TO SENATE AND HOUSE (JANUARY 18, 1803)

TUESDAY, January 18.

Two Messages were received from the PRESIDENT OF THE UNITED STATES, the first a confidential Message, which was read, as follows:

Gentlemen of the Senate, and of the House of Representatives:

As the continuance of the act for establishing trading houses with the Indian tribes will be under the consideration of the Legislature at its present session, I think it my duty to communicate the views which have guided me in the execution of that act, in order that you may decide on the policy of continuing it, in the present, or any other form, or discontinue it altogether, if that shall on the whole, seem most for the public good.

The Indian tribes residing within the limits of the United States, have, for a considerable time, been growing more and more uneasy at the constant diminution of the territory they occupy, although effected by their own voluntary sales; and the policy has long been. gaining strength with them, of refusing absolutely all further sale, on any conditions; insomuch that, at this time, it hazards their friendship, and excites dangerous jealousies and perturbations in their minds to make any overture for the purchase of the smallest portions of their land. A very few tribes only are not yet obstinately in these dispositions. In order peaceably to counteract this policy of theirs, and to provide an extension of territory, which the rapid increase of our numbers will call for, two measures are deemed expedient. First, to encourage them to abandon hunting, to apply to the raising stock, to agriculture, and domestic manufacture; and thereby prove to themselves that less land and labor will maintain them in this, better than in their former mode of living. The extensive forests necessary in the hunting life, will then become useless; and they will see advantage in exchanging them for the means of improving their farms, and of increasing their domestic comforts. Secondly, to multiply trading houses among them, and place within their reach those things which will contribute more to their domestic comfort, than the possession of extensive, but uncultivated wilds. Experience and reflection will develope to them the wisdom of exchanging what they can spare and we want, for what we can spare, and they want. In leading them thus to agriculture, to manufactures, and civilization; in bringing together their and our settlements, and in preparing them ultimately to participate in the benefits of our Government, I trust and believe we are acting for their greatest good. At these trading-houses we have pursued the principles of the, act of Congress, which directs that the commerce shall be carried on liberally, and requires only that the capital stock shall not be diminished. We, consequently, undersell private traders, foreign and domestic, drive them from the competition; and thus, with the good will of the Indians, rid ourselves of a description of men who are constantly endeavoring to excite in the Indian mind suspicions, fears, and irritations, towards us. A letter now enclosed, shows the effect of our competition on the operations of the traders, while the Indians, perceiving the advantage of purchasing from us, are soliciting, generally, our establishment of trading houses among them. In one quarter this is particularly interesting. The Legislature, reflecting on the late occurrences on the Mississippi, must be sensible how desirable it is to possess a respectable breadth of country on that river, from our Southern limit to the Illinois, at least; so that we may present as firm a front on that as on our Eastern border. We possess what is below the Yazoo, and can, probably, acquire a certain breadth from the Illinois and Wabash to the Ohio; but between the Ohio and Yazoo, the country all belongs to the Chickasaws, the most friendly tribe within our limits, but the most decided against the alienation of lands. The portion of our country most important for us, is exactly that which they do not inhabit. Their settlements are not on the Mississippi, but in the interior country. They have lately shown a desire to become agricultural; and this leads to the desire of buying implements and comforts. In the strengthening and gratifying of these wants, I see the only prospect of planting on the Mississippi itself, the means of its own safety. Duty has required me to submit these views to the judgment of the Legislature; but, as their disclosure might embarrass and defeat their effect, they are committed to the special confidence of the two Houses.

While the extension of the public commerce among the Indian tribes may deprive of that source of profit such of our citizens as are engaged in it, it might be worthy the attention of Congress, in their care of individual as well as of the general interest, to point, in another direction, the enterprise of these citizens, as profitably for themselves, and more usefully for the public. The river Missouri, and the Indians inhabiting it, are not as well known as is rendered desirable by their connexion with the Mississippi, and consequently with us. It is, however, understood, that the country on that river is inhabited by numerous tribes, who furnish great supplies of furs and peltry to the trade of another nation, carried on in a high latitude, through an infinite number of portages and lakes, shut up by ice through a long season. The commerce on that line could bear no competition with that of the Missouri, traversing a moderate climate, offering, according to the best accounts, a continued navigation from its source, and possibly with a single portage, from the Western ocean, and finding to the Atlantic a choice of channels through the Illinois, or Wabash, the lakes and Hudson, through the Ohio and

Susquehanna, or Potomac or James rivers, and through the Tennessee and Savannah rivers. An intelligent officer, with ten or twelve chosen men, fit for the enterprise, and willing to undertake it, taken from our posts, where they may be spared without inconvenience, might explore the whole line, even to the Western ocean, have conferences with the natives on the subject of commercial intercourse, get admission among them for our traders, as others are admitted, agree on convenient deposits for an interchange of articles, and return with the information acquired, in the course of two summers. Their arms and accoutrements, some instruments of observation, and light, and cheap presents for the Indians, would be all the apparatus they could carry, and with an expectation of a soldier's portion of land on their return, would contribute the whole expense. Their pay would be going on, whether here or there. While other civilized nations have encountered great expense to enlarge the boundaries of knowledge, by undertaking voyages of discovery, and for other literary purposes, in various parts; and directions, our nation seems to owe to the same object, as well an to its own interests, to explore this, the only line of easy communication across the continent and so directly traversing our own part of it. The interests of commerce place the principal object within the Constitutional powers and care of Congress, and that it should incidentally advance the geographical knowledge of our continent, cannot but be an additional gratification. The nation claiming the territory, regarding this as a literary pursuit, which it is in the habit of permitting within its dominions, would not be disposed to view it with jealousy, even if the expiring state of its interests there did not render it a matter of indifference. The appropriation of two thousand five hundred dollars, "for the purpose of extending the external commerce of the United States," while understood and considered by the Executive as giving the Legislative sanction, would cover the undertaking from notice, and prevent the obstructions which interested individuals might otherwise previously prepare in its way.

TH. JEFFERSON.

Source: *Annals of Congress*, Seventh Congress, Second Session, 24–26.

DOCUMENT 11

ON THIS QUESTION OF WHETHER IT BE ADVANTAGEOUS FOR FRANCE TO TAKE POSSESSION OF LOUISIANA

Presented to the French Government By Mr. Livingston, the American Minister at Paris

(Translated by Mr. Nancrede)

This question presents itself in two points of view:—First, in the relation of commerce and manufactures: Secondly, in those of the positive or relative force of France.

Colonies do not excite interest for their own fate, but only as respects the influence they may have on a nation; & and one man alone is more useful by remaining at home, than two by removing at a distance, a wise nation does not seek to colonize, until she has a superabundance of population, which they usefully can not employ in any other way.

Though very considerable, the population of France is very far from having reached the term which renders colonies necessary: Her solid, climate, and local situation give her, as a commercial, and especially as a manufacturing nation, great advantages over all the nations of Europe. The spirit of invention, the taste and industry of its inhabitants, place her in the first rank. But those advantages are wonderfully abridged by the want of capitals sufficient to make use of them. A rival nation, greatly inferior in every one of these particulars, has, by the effect alone of an immense capital, obtained the superiority, not only in commerce, but also in manufactures; and these advantages, by increasing the national fortune, furnish it with the means of maintaining that very superiority.

Capitals increase the number of manufactures, by the introduction of machines, by the regular payment of workmen, by the reduction of the interest money, and especially by the possession of new markets.

None but rich individuals can undertake those slow and expensive speculations, which often give the superiority to a manufacture. A poor merchant cannot undertake long voyages, returns from which are slow; They are reserved for the wealthy, who can give credits long enough to tempt foreign nations to give his articles the preference over those of other nations, which expect a quick return for theirs. The want of capitals in France, is such that no manufacturer has at his command a quantity of articles sufficient to answer demands; And consequently no foreigner can be sure to obtain from his French correspondent wherewith to make his returns without retarding his vessel in port, or, at least, without being obliged to take a considerable quantity of articles of inferior quality, picked up in a number of different manufacturers; so that he commits any fraud, no one can be charged with it. This renders the character of of manufacture of very little importance in the eyes of a French workman.

Hence when a foreign vessel, especially if owned at a great distance, sells her cargo in France, she is ordered to take nothing but wines or brandies, because they are the only articles which the owner is sure to procure in sufficient quantities, in the fixed time.

In England, on the contrary, he will find all sorts of goods, in one hour, from one manufacture, the reputation of which would suffer, if the whole supply were not of the same quality with the sample. This consideration will ever induce a foreigner to apply to an English, in preference to a French merchant, for a purchase of goods of the same kind. Hence cargoes are sold in France, and the proceeds carried to England, there to be sold for articles which France might supply, if her manufacturers were rich enough to answer every demand, in a short time, without compelling the purchaser to have recourse to a number of manufacturers.

This inconvenience can only be removed by increasing the capitals of manufacturers. It would be too great a deviation from my subject to point out that the means of obtaining those capitals; but it is evident, that they must be considerably lessened by the forming of a Navy at the expense of a manufactures, or by using the capitals of the nation in distant countries. it is beyond doubt, that capitals open new channels; for nothing is more natural for merchants whose capital is small, than to content themselves with acting the part of Broker or Commission-Merchants, to those who can supply them with goods on no credit; and for this very reason, England lost nothing by the independence of America. Her immense capitals have created a monied dependence, which in a commercial relation, replaced the supremacy she had lost in the government. The increase of capital in America frees it in some degree from that dependency, and by furnishing her with the means of extending her commerce, and even to offer capitals to other nations which know how to calculate the value of the markets which the offers to manufacturers and to the luxury of Europe.

It will be readily granted, that Colonies seas add nothing to the force of a nation, there are, on the contrary, weak points, which are guarded at a very great expense, both in men and money, especially if they be in hot and unhealthy climates.

The question, therefore, is reduced to this: Has France a superiority of men and money great enough to supply the settling of a new colony?

Those which France already possesses in the West Indies and at Cayenne are more than sufficient for her wants, and even the wants of all Europe, if they were cultivated so as to produce all they were capable of. But how are they to be cultivated? Experience has proved that the inhabitants of hot climates never work from want: Force alone can supply the two great spurs to labour in Northern climates, hunger and cold, which nature has placed in those severe climates. Hence, slavery alone can fertilize those colonies, and slaves can not be procured but at a great expense.

The Spanish port of Hispaniola was almost uncultivated for want of slaves. It is now possessed by France; and to render it of advantage, it will be necessary to lay out immense capitals in slaves, in buildings, and in improvements of uncultivated lands. Others will be necessary to make up for the losses of the French part of that, not to mention the Islands. Where are those capitals to be found? Men who travel into distant and unhealthy climates are seldom wealthy. Those riches must therefore be found in France, or in some country that has a superfluity of capital. If they are found in France, it can only be, to a certain degree, at the expense of internal manufactures. It may, however, appear advantageous, in a national point of view, to encourage the use of the riches of France for that object; considering the extreme fertility of the French West Indies, and their present situation of culture, those funds which soon yield a profit. But so long as money will command so high an interest; so long as the interior of the Republic shall offer monied men a source of speculations, and property shall lie in so few hands, it will be difficult to induce the majority of them to dispossess themselves of this capital to send it at a distance, and run the risk of the integrity of their agents, and all those whom recent examples have taught them to dread.

The United States possess considerable capitals to money, and productions necessary to the restoration of the Islands. No great credit, in money, will probably be given to the planters; but with suitable encouragements, there is no doubt they will be able to obtain those productions which must, were it not for circumstance, be paid for in cash and the commercial speculations of the United States will extend to the French Islands, when the public and private credit of France shall have been restored, and when experience shall have convinced unwise it is to establish a revenue upon foreign trade, while it is in fact collected from their own citizens. At Hispaniola, a duty of 20 percent is paid upon articles introduced by strangers. This duty is in fact paid by strangers, and it happens that fraud, and the bad administration of Custom-Houses is, as usual, a force of vexation for foreign merchants. But it is the planter who furnishes the money, for this tax is always added to the price, and even an interest is advanced upon it as compensation for the vexations which the Captains experience in their commerce. What then is the effect of that operation, if not to take from the planter one-fourth part of the money which he had so much difficulty to get from France? Or otherwise to stop, by that means, partly the re-establishment of the capitals which alone can render the Islands productive? I say finally, for it is folly to believe that they will yield to France, a compensation for her actual outlets, unless it be after a good many years. I will even say that unless the ports of Hispaniola are open to every vessel loaded with articles of necessity, unless the inhabitants have the right of buying cheap and selling dear, by encouraging the rivalry between the sellers and and the purchasers, unless every sort of vexation is removed, and strangers receive every possible security for their capitals in the Islands, ages will pass away before Hispaniola will cease draining France of its riches and strength without offering her any equivalent return.

It is, therefore, evident that if France had no other possession beyond the seas, except her islands, it might finally place all the capital of which she now can and probably hereafter will be able to dispose in a long series of years.

But if to all this, we add the immense possessions of Guyana, her productions, and the capitals necessary to carry the whole of it to its full value; if we add the settlements necessary to be made in India, if the design be to bring into the ports of France, that variety of articles which invite exchanges, and give commerce its due activity, we shall find that one century at least will pass away before France may want possessions of that kind.

But as France has, like other countries, but a confined capital, the only question is where shall this capital be placed? Shall it be here? In the West Indies? At Cayenne? In India, or at Louisiana? For it is obvious that what will be placed in one of those settlements will be at the expense of another; it is equally so, that the national expenditures will increase with her colonies; and that, in case of war, the points of attack and defense will be multiplied in the same ratio.

Able statesmen have mentioned whether colonies are useful to a country situated like France but my design is not to examine this theory. France has colonies;—she has invited her citizens to go and carry those riches to them; honor requires that she keep and protect them; but she is under no obligation to create new ones; to multiply points of defense; to squander away the capitals she wants at home and abroad. How could the possession of Louisiana be useful to her? In the first place, its cultivation is to be carried on, as in all warm countries, by slaves; the capitals spent in buying them, or the slaves themselves, would have been carried to the islands, if this new channel had not been opened. This rivalry will rise the price of slaves for the planters, and thus much retard the settlement.

On their arrival at Louisiana, the slaves will be employed in the barren occupation of the felling of large forests with which this immense country is covered, a labour but little suited for slaves, for it requires being long accustomed to the ax; and force and activity are seldom found in slaves. They must be clothed, fed and maintained during whole years before profit can be derived from them. What I am about to relate may serve to determine that period. In the Northern and Middle States in America, the usual term of a quit-rent lease in the new hands is ten years free from rent, and after this the lease pays 12 bushels of wheat for every 100 acres forever. It is therefore obvious that the first ten years are considered as a time of expense, during which term the owner requires no payment. But in the Southern States, new hands can not be given out on those terms, because the White planter sets a higher value on his labour, and the clearing of forests requires too great outsets for any one but the owner of the land.

Who then will cultivate Louisiana with slaves? When is the citizen willing to bestow large capitals upon so precarious a property with the prospect of distant return?

It may be asked, why does it not happen in Southern States? It is answered, first because none are southerly enough enough to be wholly free from the colds of winter, which renders savage life very difficult to man, born in hot climates; and secondly, because the Southern States, are mostly surrounded by the sea, and by mountains the whole population of which is white, and which cut off the communications between the slaves and the vast forests of the interior parts.

But let us suppose that these difficulties overcome, what commercial advantages can France derive from the settlement of this colony?—The productions of Louisiana being the same as the whole West Indies, no advantage is to be reaped, for the islands, being well cultivated, will suffice for the wants of France, and even all of Europe. The introduction of those from Louisiana, would only lessen the price without adding anything to the value, and France would be obliged, to prevent the ruin of those who had employed their funds in the colonies, to imitate the Dutch, who destroy their spices and teas, when the quantity of these commodities in Europe is large enough to cause a depreciation of their value.

The productions of Louisiana, which do not grown in the West Indies, are only lumber, and perhaps rice; but it is certain that those productions, considering their difficulties procuring them in a hot climate, will not cover the outsets, or, at least, will not yield the same profits as would be procured raising them in the Islands, in procuring the same or other more valuable articles.

The proof of this is found in the United States. It is not from Georgia, nor South Carolina, that the West Indies are supplied with lumber, but chiefly from the Northern States, where forests are more scarce and more valuable in the South. The cause of this is, that the supplying of lumber, the mills necessary to prepare them for sale, all these are the work of free hands, which are satisfied with a moderate price.

I shall presume to further lay down, however paradoxical it may seem, that it is not advantageous for France to supply itself with lumber, even if she could procure it from Louisiana.—I have two reasons to offer—What lumber the Northern States supply her colonies is paid for in molasses and some rum. The first article costs the planter nothing, for were it not for that, this would be an useless production of his sugar, and the second is but a very moderate expense for distillation. If it were consumed in America, molasses would be thrown away as useless, and this was the case when America was a British colony, because French commerce does not offer any other market for that commodity.

It may, therefore, be said that colonies have from the United States, lumber for nothing. Should, on the contrary, a settlement be formed in Louisiana for the supplying of that article, every expense and outset of this establishment, all the labour necessary to cut, saw, and transport to the place where it is to be sold, would be a real loss for the nation, even admitting that the cutters and other men employed, should take, as payment, molasses and rum; because their labor would produce nothing for the nation.

But it is certain that Louisiana could not furnish a market for molasses or rum. It is only in New England (Northern States) that those articles are consumed.—The inhabitants of the South prefer ardent spirits, distilled from grain, apples, and peaches, to those distilled from molasses.

On the supposition, therefore, that the planters supply themselves with lumber in a French colony, exclusively at

Louisiana, they would be forced to pay for it in money or objects of real value. If the right of supply is not exclusive, it is null, because the labourer of a southern climate cannot work as cheap as the robust son of the North.

It might be thought that molasses would still find a market in New England, though it will still no longer the price of lumber.—It would be an error. They have no other reason to take it, than its being offered to them in exchange for an article which they have few other markets. Let the colonies refuse lumber, from the North, spirits from grain, apples, &c. will immediately be substituted to those from sugar, because the price of rum would immediately be higher. Then it will be that every fort of commerce between them and the colonies will cease unless it be for provisions which will only be paid for in money, or in which pass in foreign markets, for money.

The second reason why France might not get her lumber from Louisiana, even though she might do it, is, that in case of war, supposing England should preserve her naval superiority, no sure calculations could be made upon receiving provisions; and they could not be supplied from the United States, for that commerce, having being abandoned since the peace, those whom it then employed have sought other objects of industry; and saw mills, erected to prepare that lumber, are out of use, and will not easily be set up again, at the renewal of hostilities, so that the misfortunes which are the consequence of it would be doubly distressing to the colonies.

It is, therefore very evident the colonizing of Louisiana would, in a commercial point of view, be very injurious to France, because it would employ capitals which would be more usefully employed in the other colonies; because those capitals would lie dormant for several years, and admitting they should become productive for individuals, they would add nothing to the national mass, and would have no other effect than to lower the price of colonial produce, and lessen the profits of their labor.

It might however be thought that the possession of Louisiana would afford one more market to French manufactures, and thus compensate the expense of the nation for its settlement. This question deserves a particular examination, and the provisioning or the consumption of French manufactures may relate either to the free or bond population.

Source: Livingston, Robert R., *The Letters of Robert R. Livingston: The Diplomatic Story of the Louisiana Purchase.* Worcester, MA: American Antiquarian Society, 1943.

DOCUMENT 12

LOUISIANA PURCHASE TREATY (APRIL 30, 1803)

Treaty Between the United States of America and the French Republic

The President of the United States of America and the First Consul of the French Republic in the name of the French People desiring to remove all Source of misunderstanding relative to objects of discussion mentioned in the Second and fifth articles of the Convention of the 8th Vendémiaire on 9/30 September 1800 relative to the rights claimed by the United States in virtue of the Treaty concluded at Madrid the 27 of October 1795, between His Catholic Majesty & the Said United States, & willing to Strengthen the union and friendship which at the time of the Said Convention was happily reestablished between the two nations have respectively named their Plenipotentiaries to wit The President of the United States, by and with the advice and consent of the Senate of the Said States; Robert R. Livingston Minister Plenipotentiary of the United States and James Monroe Minister Plenipotentiary and Envoy extraordinary of the Said States near the Government of the French Republic; And the First Consul in the name of the French people, Citizen Francis Barbé Marbois Minister of the public treasury who after having respectively exchanged their full powers have agreed to the following Articles.

Article I

Whereas by the Article the third of the Treaty concluded at St Ildefonso the 9th Vendémiaire on 1st October 1800 between the First Consul of the French Republic and his Catholic Majesty it was agreed as follows.

"His Catholic Majesty promises and engages on his part to cede to the French Republic six months after the full and entire execution of the conditions and Stipulations herein relative to his Royal Highness the Duke of Parma, the Colony or Province of Louisiana with the Same extent that it now has in the hand of Spain, & that it had when France possessed it; and Such as it Should be after the Treaties subsequently entered into between Spain and other States."

And whereas in pursuance of the Treaty and particularly of the third article the French Republic has an incontestible title to the domain and to the possession of the said Territory—The First Consul of the French Republic desiring to give to the United States a strong proof of his friendship doth hereby cede to the United States in the name of the French Republic for ever and in full Sovereignty the said territory with all its rights and appurtenances as fully and in the Same manner as they have been acquired by the French Republic in virtue of the above mentioned Treaty concluded with his Catholic Majesty.

Article II

In the cession made by the preceeding article are included the adjacent Islands belonging to Louisiana all public lots and Squares, vacant lands and all public buildings, fortifications, barracks and other edifices which are not private property.The Archives, papers & documents relative to the domain and Sovereignty of Louisiana and its dependances will be left in the possession of the Commissaries of the United States, and copies will be afterwards given in due form to the Magistrates and Municipal officers of such of the said papers and documents as may be necessary to them.

Article III
The inhabitants of the ceded territory shall be incorporated in the Union of the United States and admitted as soon as possible according to the principles of the federal Constitution to the enjoyment of all these rights, advantages and immunities of citizens of the United States, and in the mean time they shall be maintained and protected in the free enjoyment of their liberty, property and the Religion which they profess.

Article IV
There Shall be Sent by the Government of France a Commissary to Louisiana to the end that he do every act necessary as well to receive from the Officers of his Catholic Majesty the Said country and its dependances in the name of the French Republic if it has not been already done as to transmit it in the name of the French Republic to the Commissary or agent of the United States.

Article V
Immediately after the ratification of the present Treaty by the President of the United States and in case that of the first Consul's shall have been previously obtained, the commissary of the French Republic shall remit all military posts of New Orleans and other parts of the ceded territory to the Commissary or Commissaries named by the President to take possession—the troops whether of France or Spain who may be there shall cease to occupy any military post from the time of taking possession and shall be embarked as soon as possible in the course of three months after the ratification of this treaty.

Article VI
The United States promise to execute Such treaties and articles as may have been agreed between Spain and the tribes and nations of Indians until by mutual consent of the United States and the said tribes or nations other Suitable articles Shall have been agreed upon.

Article VII
As it is reciprocally advantageous to the commerce of France and the United States to encourage the communication of both nations for a limited time in the country ceded by the present treaty until general arrangements relative to commerce of both nations may be agreed on; it has been agreed between the contracting parties that the French Ships coming directly from France or any of her colonies loaded only with the produce and manufactures of France or her Said Colonies; and the Ships of Spain coming directly from Spain or any of her colonies loaded only with the produce or manufactures of Spain or her Colonies shall be admitted during the Space of twelve years in the Port of New-Orleans and in all other legal ports-of-entry within the ceded territory in the Same manner as the Ships of the United States coming directly from France or Spain or any of their Colonies without being Subject to any other or greater duty on merchandize or other or greater tonnage than that paid by the citizens of the United. States.

During that Space of time above mentioned no other nation Shall have a right to the Same privileges in the Ports of the ceded territory—the twelve years Shall commence three months after the exchange of ratifications if it Shall take place in France or three months after it Shall have been notified at Paris to the French Government if it Shall take place in the United States; It is however well understood that the object of the above article is to favour the manufactures, Commerce, freight and navigation of France and of Spain So far as relates to the importations that the French and Spanish Shall make into the Said Ports of the United States without in any Sort affecting the regulations that the United States may make concerning the exportation of the produce and merchandize of the United States, or any right they may have to make Such regulations.

Article VIII
In future and for ever after the expiration of the twelve years, the Ships of France shall be treated upon the footing of the most favoured nations in the ports above mentioned.

Article IX
The particular Convention Signed this day by the respective Ministers, having for its object to provide for the payment of debts due to the Citizens of the United States by the French Republic prior to the 30th Sept. 1800 (8th Vendémiaire an 9) is approved and to have its execution in the Same manner as if it had been inserted in this present treaty, and it Shall be ratified in the same form and in the Same time So that the one Shall not be ratified distinct from the other.

Another particular Convention Signed at the Same date as the present treaty relative to a definitive rule between the contracting parties is in the like manner approved and will be ratified in the Same form, and in the Same time and jointly.

Article X
The present treaty Shall be ratified in good and due form and the ratifications Shall be exchanged in the Space of Six months after the date of the Signature by the Ministers Plenipotentiary or Sooner if possible.

In faith whereof the respective Plenipotentiaries have Signed these articles in the French and English languages; declaring nevertheless that the present Treaty was originally agreed to in the French language; and have thereunto affixed their Seals.

Done at Paris the tenth day of Floreal in the eleventh year of the French Republic; and the 30th of April 1803.

Robt R Livingston [seal] Jas. Monroe [seal] Barbé Marbois [seal]

Source: Miller, Hunter, ed. 1931. *Treaties and Other International Acts of the United States of America*. Vol. 2. Washington: Government Printing Office.

DOCUMENT 13

LOUISIANA PURCHASE: FIRST CONVENTION (1803)

A Convention Between the United States of America and the French Republic

The President of the United States of America and the First Consul of the French Republic in the name of the French people, in consequence of the treaty of cession of Louisiana which has been Signed this day; wishing to regulate definitively every thing which has relation to the Said cession have authorized to this effect the Plenipotentiaries, that is to say the President of the United States has, by and with the advice and consent of the Senate of the Said States, nominated for their Plenipotentiaries, Robert R. Livingston, Minister Plenipotentiary of the United States, and James Monroe, Minister Plenipotentiary and Envoy-Extraordinary of the Said United States, near the Government of the French Republic; and the First Consul of the French Republic, in the name of the French people, has named as Pleniopotentiary of the Said Republic the citizen Francis Barbé Marbois: who, in virtue of their full powers, which have been exchanged this day, have agreed to the followings articles:

Article 1
The Government of the United States engages to pay to the French government in the manner Specified in the following article the sum of Sixty millions of francs independant of the Sum which Shall be fixed by another Convention for the payment of the debts due by France to citizens of the United States.

Article 2
For the payment of the Sum of Sixty millions of francs mentioned in the preceeding article the United States shall create a Stock of eleven millions, two hundred and fifty thousand Dollars bearing an interest of Six per cent: per annum payable half yearly in London, Amsterdam or Paris amounting by the half year to three hundred and thirty Seven thousand five hundred Dollars, according to the proportions which Shall be determined by the French Govenment to be paid at either place: The principal of the Said Stock to be reimbursed at the treasury of the United States in annual payments of not less than three millions of Dollars each; of which the first payment Shall commence fifteen years after the date of the exchange of ratifications:—this Stock Shall be transferred to the government of France or to Such person or persons as Shall be authorized to receive it in three months at most after the exchange of ratifications of this treaty and after Louisiana Shall be taken possession of the name of the Government of the United States.

It is further agreed that if the French Government Should be desirous of disposing of the Said Stock to receive the capital in Europe at Shorter terms that its measures for that purpose Shall be taken So as to favour in the greatest degree possible the credit of the United States, and to raise to the highest price the Said Stock.

Article 3
It is agreed that the Dollar of the United States Specified in the present Convention shall be fixed at five francs 3333/100000 or five livres eight Sous tournois.

The present Convention Shall be ratified in good and due form, and the ratifications Shall be exchanged the Space of Six months to date from this day or Sooner it possible.

In faith of which the respective Plenipotentiaries have Signed the above articles both in the French and English languages, declaring nevertheless that the present treaty has been originally agreed on and written in the French language; to which they have hereunto affixed their Seals.

Done at Paris the tenth of Floreal eleventh year of the French Republic 30th April 1803.

Robt. R. Livingston [seal]
Jas. Monroe [seal]
Barbé Marbois [seal]

Source: Miller, Hunter, ed. 1931. *Treaties and Other International Acts of the United States of America.* Vol. 2. Washington: Government Printing Office.

DOCUMENT 14

LOUISIANA PURCHASE: SECOND CONVENTION (1803)

Convention Between the United States of America and the French Republic

The President of the United States of America and the First Consul of the French Republic in the name of the French People having by a Treaty of this date terminated all difficulties relative to Louisiana, and established on a Solid foundation the friendship which unites the two nations and being desirous in complyance with the Second and fifth Articles of the Convention of the 8th Vendémiaire ninth year of the French Republic (30th September 1800) to Secure the payment of the Sums due by France to the citizens of the United States have respectively nominated as Plenipotentiaries that is to Say The President of the United States of America by and with the advise and consent of their Senate Robert R. Livingston Minister Plenipotentiary and James Monroe Minister Plenipotentiary and Envoy Extraordinary of the Said States near the Government of the French Republic: and the First Consul in the name of the French People the Citizen Francis Barbé Marbois Minister of the public treasury; who after having exchanged their full powers have agreed to the following articles:

Article 1
The debts due by France to citizens of the United States contracted before the 8th Vendémiaire ninth year of the French Republic (30th September 1800) Shall be paid according to the following regulations with interest at Six

per Cent; to commence from the period when the accounts and vouchers were presented to the French Government.

Article 2
The debts provided for by the preceeding Article are those whose result is comprised in the conjectural note annexed to the present Convention and which, with the interest cannot exceed the Sum of twenty millions of Francs. The claims comprised in the Said note which fall within the exceptions of the following articles, Shall not be admitted to the benefit of this provision.

Article 3
The principal and interests of the Said debts Shall be discharged by the United States, by orders drawn by their Minister Plenipotentiary on their treasury, these orders Shall be payable Sixty days after the exchange of ratifications of the Treaty and the Conventions Signed this day, and after possession Shall be given of Louisiana by the Commissaries of France to those of the United States.

Article 4
It is expressly agreed that the preceding articles Shall comprehend no debts but Such as are due to citizens of the United States who have been and are yet creditors of France for Supplies for embargoes and prizes made at Sea, in which the appeal has been properly lodged within the time mentioned in the Said Convention 8th Vendémiaire ninth year, (30th Sept 1800)

Article 5
The preceding Articles Shall apply only, First: to captures of which the council of prizes Shall have ordered restitution, it being well understood that the claimant cannot have recourse to the United States otherwise than he might have had to the Government of the French republic, and only in case of insufficiency of the captors—2d the debts mentioned in the Said fifth Article of the Convention contracted before the 8th Vendémiaire an 9/30th September 1800 the payment of which has been heretofore claimed of the actual Government of France and for which the creditors have a right to the protection of the United States;—the Said 5th Article does not comprehend prizes whose condemnation has been or Shall be confirmed: it is the express intention of the contracting parties not to extend the benefit of the present Convention to reclamations of American citizens who Shall have established houses of Commerce in France, England or other countries than the United States in partnership with foreigners, and who by that reason and the nature of their commerce ought to be regarded as domiciliated in the places where Such house exist.—All agreements and bargains concerning merchandize, which Shall not be the property of American citizens, are equally excepted from the benefit of the said Conventions, Saving however to Such persons their claims in like manner as if this Treaty had not been made.

Article 6
And that the different questions which may arise under the preceding article may be fairly investigated, the Ministers Plenipotentiary of the United States Shall name three persons, who Shall act from the present and provisionally, and who shall have full power to examine, without removing the documents, all the accounts of the different claims already liquidated by the Bureaus established for this purpose by the French Republic, and to ascertain whether they belong to the classes designated by the present Convention and the principles established in it or if they are not in one of its exceptions and on their Certificate, declaring that the debt is due to an American Citizen or his representative and that it existed before the 8th Vendémiaire 9th year/30 September 1800 the debtor shall be entitled to an order on the Treasury of the United States in the manner prescribed by the 3d Article.

Article 7
The Same agents Shall likewise have power, without removing the documents, to examine the claims which are prepared for verification, and to certify those which ought to be admitted by uniting the necessary qualifications, and not being comprised in the exceptions contained in the present Convention.

Article 8
The Same agents shall likewise examine the claims which are not prepared for liquidation, and certify in writing those which in their judgement ought to be admitted to liquidation.

Article 9
In proportion as the debts mentioned in these articles Shall be admitted they Shall be discharged with interest at Six per Cent: by the Treasury of the United States.

Article 10
And that no debt shall not have the qualifications above mentioned and that no unjust or exorbitant demand may be admitted, the Commercial agent of the United States at Paris or such other agent as the Minister Plenipotentiary or the United States Shall think proper to nominate shall assist at the operations of the Bureaus and cooperate in the examinations of the claims; and if this agent Shall be of the opinion that any debt is not completely proved, or if he shall judge that it is not comprised in the principles of the fifth article above mentioned, and if notwithstanding his opinion the Bureaus established by the french Government should think that it ought to be liquidated, he shall transmit his observations to the board established by the United States, who, without removing documents, shall make a complete examination of the debt and vouchers which Support it, and report the result to the Minister of the United States.—The Minister of the United States Shall transmit his observations in all Such cases to the Minister of the treasury of the French Repub-

lic, on whose report the French Government Shall decide definitively in every case.

The rejection of any claim Shall have no other effect than to exempt the United States from the payment of it, the French Government reserving to itself, the right to decide definitively on Such claim So far as it concerns itself.

Article 11
Every necessary decision Shall be made in the course of a year to commence from the exchange of ratifications, and no reclamation Shall be admitted afterwards.

Article 12
In case of claims for debts contracted by the Government of France with citizens of the United States Since the 8th Vendémiaire 9th year/30 September 1800 not being comprised in this Convention may be pursued, and the payment demanded in the Same manner as if it had not been made.

Article 13
The present convention Shall be ratified in good and due form and the ratifications Shall be exchanged in Six months from the date of the Signature of the Ministers Plenipotentiary, or Sooner if possible.

In faith of which, the respective Ministers Plenipotentiary have signed the above Articles both in the French and English languages, declaring nevertheless that the present treaty has been originally agreed on and written in the French language, to which they have hereunto affixed their Seals.

Done at Paris, the tenth of Floreal, eleventh year of the French Republic. 30th April 1803.

Robt. R. Livingston [seal]
Jas. Monroe [seal]
Barbé Marbois [seal]

Source: Miller, Hunter, ed. 1931. *Treaties and Other International Acts of the United States of America*. Vol. 2. Washington: Government Printing Office.

DOCUMENT 15

TALLEYRAND'S LETTER TO DECRÉS (MAY 23, 1803)

CITIZEN MINISTER: I have the honor to send you a copy of the treaty by which France cedes Louisiana to the United States.

The desire to spare the continent of North America from the war that threatened it, of settling various points of litigation between the Republic and the United States, and to remove all new causes for misunderstanding that their competition and neighborhood would have given rise to between them; the position of the French colonies, their need of men, agriculture, and aid; and finally, the force of circumstances, foresight for the future, and the intention of compensating by an advantageous arrangement for the inevitable loss of a country which war was about to place at the mercy of another nation: all these reasons have decided the government to cause all the rights that it had acquired from Spain to the sovereignty and to the possession of Louisiana to pass to the United States.

Citizen Minister, please take measures so that that country, where it suffices henceforth to send a French commissioner, who may take possession of it, may be transferred by that agent to the disposition of the United States, in the same condition in which it was ceded to us by Spain, and under the reservation of the advantages assured to our navigation and to our commerce by the treaty of which I have the honor to inform you. I have the honor to salute you,

TALLEYRAND

Source: Robertson, James Alexander, ed. 1911. *Louisiana under Spain, France and the United States, 1785–1807: Social, Economic, and Political Conditions of the Territory Represented in the Louisiana Purchase*. Vol. 2. Cleveland, OH: Arthur H. Clark Co.

DOCUMENT 16

LETTER FROM THOMAS JEFFERSON TO MERIWETHER LEWIS (JUNE 20, 1803)

To Meriwether Lewis, esquire, captain of the first regiment of infantry of the United States of America:

Your situation as Secretary of the President of the United States, has made you aquainted with the objects of my confidential message of January 18, 1803, to the legislature; you have seen the act they passed, which, though expressed in general terms, was meant to sanction those objects, and you are appointed to carry them to execution.

Instruments for ascertaining, by celestial observations, the geography of the country through which you will pass, have already been provided. Light articles for barter and presents among the Indians, arms for your attendants, say from ten to twelve men, boats, tents, and other traveling apparatus, with ammunition, medicine, surgical instruments and provisions, you will have prepared, with such aids as the secretary at war can yield in his department; and from him also you will receive authority to engage among our troops, by voluntary agreement, the attendants abovementioned; over whom you, as their commanding officer, are invested with all the powers the laws give in such a case.

As your movements, while within the limits of the United States, will be better directed by occasional communications, adapted to circumstances as they arise, they will not be noticed here. What follows will respect your proceedings after your departure from the United States.

Your mission has been communicated to the ministers here from France, Spain, and Great Britain, and through them to their governments; and such assurances given them as to its objects, as we trust will satisfy them. The country of Louisiana having ceded by Spain to France, the passport you have from the minister of France, the representative of the present sovereign of the country, will be a protection with all its subjects; and that from the Minister of England will entitle you to the friendly aid of any traders of that allegiance with whom you may happen to meet.

The object of your mission is to explore the Missouri River, and such principal streams of it, as, by its course and communication with the waters of the Pacific Ocean, whether the Columbia, Oregan [sic], Colrado [sic], or any other river, may offer the most direct and practible water-communication across the continent, for the purposes of commerce.

Beginning at the mouth of the Missouri, you will take observations of latitude and longitude, at all remarkable points on the river, and especially at the mouths of rivers, at rapids, at islands, and other places and objects distinguished by such natural marks and characters, of a durable kind, as that they may with certainty be recognised hereafter. The courses of the river between these points of observation may be supplied by the compass, the log-line, and by time, corrected by the observations themselves. The variations of the needle, too, in different places, should be noticed.

The interesting points of the portage between the heads of the Missouri, and of the water offering the best communication with the Pacific ocean, should also be fixed by observation; and the course of that water to the ocean, in the same manner as that of the Missouri.

Your observations are to be taken with great pains and accuracy; to be entered distinctly and intelligibly for others as well as yourself; to comprehend all the elements necessary, with the aid of the usual tales, to fix the latitude and longitude of the places at which they were taken; and are to be rendered to the war-office, for the purpose of having the calculations made concurrently by proper persons within the United States. Several copies of these, as well as of your other notes, should be made at leisure times, and put into the care of the most trust worthy of your attendants to guard, by multiplying them against the accidental losses to which they will be exposed. A further guard would be, that one of these copies be on the cuticular membranes of the paper-birch, as less liable to injury from damp than common paper.

The commerce which may be carried on with the people inhabiting the line you will pursue, renders a knowledge of those people important. You will therefore endeavour to make yourself acquainted, as far as a diligent pursuit of your journey shall admit, with the names of the nations and their numbers;

The extent and limits of their possessions;
Their relations with other tribes or nations;
Their language, traditions, monuments;
Their ordinary occupations in agriculture, fishing, hunting, war, arts, and the implements for these;
Their food, clothing, and domestic accommodations:
The diseases prevalent among them, and the remedies they use;
Moral and physical circumstances which distinguish them from the tribes we know;
Peculiarities in their laws, customs, and dispositions;
And articles of commerce they may need or furnish, and to what extent.

And, considering the interest which every nation has in extending and strengthening the authority of reason and justice among the people around them, it will be useful to acquire what knowledge you can of the state of morality, religion, and information amoung them; as it may better enable those who may endeavour to civilize and instruct them, to adapt their measures to the existing notions and practices of those on whom they are to operate.

Other objects worthy of notice will be;
The soil and face of the country, its growth and vegetable productions, especially those not of the United States;
The animals of the country generally, and especially those not known in the United States;
The remains and accounts of any which may be deemed rare or extinct;
The mineral productions of every kind, but more particularly metals, lime-stone, pit-coal, and saltpetre; salines and mineral waters, noting the temperature of the last, and such circumstances as may indicate their character;
Volcanic appearances;
Climate, as characterized by the thermometer, by the proportion of rainy, cloudy, and clear days; by lightning, hail, snow, ice; by the access and recess of frost; by the winds prevailing at different seasons; the dates at which particular plants put forth, or lose their flower or leaf; times of appearance of particular birds, reptiles or insects.

Although your route will be along the channel of the Missouri, yet you will endeavour to inform yourself, by inquiry, of the character and extent of the country watered by its branches, and especially on its southern side. The North river, or Rio Bravo, which runs into the gulf of Mexico, and the North river, or Rio Colorado, which runs into the gulf of California, are understood to be the principal streams heading opposite to the waters of the Missouri, and running southwardly. Whether the dividing grounds between the Missouri and them are mountains or flat lands, what are their distance from the Missouri, the character of the intermediate country, and the people inhabiting it, are worthy of particular inquiry. The northern waters of the Missouri are less to be inquired after, because they have been ascertained to a considerable degree, and are still in a course of ascertainment by English traders and travellers; but if you can learn any thing certain of the most northern source of the Mississippi, and of its position relatively to the Lake of the Woods, it will be interesting to us. Some account too of the path of the Canadian traders from the Missisippi, at the mouth of the

Ouisconsing to where it strikes the Missouri, and of the soil and rivers in its course, is desireable.

In all your intercourse with the natives, treat them in the most friendly and conciliatory manner which their own conduct will admit; allay all jealousies as to the object of your journey; satisfy them of its innocence; make them acquainted with the position, extent, character, peaceable and commercial dispositions of the United States; of our wish to be neighbourly; friendly, and useful to them, and of our dispositions to a commercial intercourse with them; confer with them on the points most convenient as mutual emporiums, and the articles of most desirable interchange for them and us. If a few of their influential chiefs, within practicable distance, wish to visit us, arrange such a visit with them, and furnish them with authority to call on our officers on their entering the United States, to have them conveyed to this place at the public expense. If any of them should wish to have some of their young people brought up with us, and taught such arts as may be useful to them, we will receive, instruct, and take care of them. Such a mission, whether of influential chiefs, or of young people, would give some security to your own party. Carry with you some matter of the kine-pox; inform those of them with whom you may be of its efficacy as a preservative from the small-pox, and instruct and encourage them in the use of it. This may be especially done wherever you winter.

As it is impossible for us to foresee in what manner you will be received by those people, whether with hospitality or hostility, so is it impossible to prescribe the exact degree of perseverance with which you are to pursue your journey. We value too much the lives of citizens to offer them to probable destruction. Your numbers will be sufficient to secure you against the unauthorized opposition of individuals, or of small parties; but if a superior force, authorized, or not authorized, by a nation, should be arrayed against your further passage, and inflexibly determined to arrest it, you must decline its further pursuit and return. In the loss of yourselves we should lose also the information you will have acquired. By returning safely with that, you may enable us to renew the essay with better calculated means. To your own discretion, therefore, must be left the degree of danger you may risk, and the point at which you should decline, only saying, we wish you to err on the side of your safety, and to bring back your party safe, even if it be with less information.

As far up the Missouri as the white settlements extend, an intercourse will probably be found to exist between them and the Spanish post of St. Louis opposite Cahokia, or St. Genevieve opposite Kaskaskia. From still further up the river the traders may furnish a conveyance for letters. Beyond that you may perhaps be able to engage Indians to bring letters for the government to Cahokia, or Kaskaskia, on promising that they shall there receive such special compensation as your shall have stipulated with them. Avail yourself of these means to communicate to us, at seasonable intervals, a copy of your journal, notes and observations of every kind, putting into cypher whatever might do injury if betrayed.

Should you reach the Pacific ocean, inform yourself of the circumstances which may decide whether the furs of those parts may not be collected as advantageously at the head of the Missouri (convenient as is supposed to the waters of the Colorado and Oregan [sic] or Columbia) as at Nootka Sound, or any other point of that coast; and that trade be consequently conducted through the Missouri and United States more beneficially than by the circumnavigation now practised.

On your arrival on that coast, endeavour to learn if there be any port within your reach frequented by the sea vessels of any nation, and to send two of your trusty people back by sea, in such way as shall appear practicable, with a copy of your notes; and should you be of opinion that the return of your party by the way they went will be imminently dangerous, then ship the whole, and return by sea, by the way either of Cape Horn, or the Cape of Good Hope, as you shall be able. As you will be without money, clothes, or provisions, you must endeavour to use the credit of the United States to obtain them; for which purpose open letters of credit shall be furnished you, authorizing you to draw on the executive of the United States, or any of its officers, in any part of the world, on which draughts can be disposed of, and to apply with our recommendations to the consuls, agents, merchants, or citizens of any nation with which we have intercourse, assuring them, in our name, that any aids they may furnish you shall be honourably repaid, and on demand. Our consuls, Thomas Hewes, at Batavia, in Java, William Buchanan, in the Isles of France and Bourbon, and John Elmslie, at the Cape of Good Hope, will be able to supply your necessities, by draughts on us.

Should you find it safe to return by the way you go, after sending two of our party round by sea, or with your whole party, if no conveyance by sea can be found, do so; making such observations on your return as may serve to supply, correct, or confirm those made on your outward journey.

On reentering the United States and reaching a place of safety, discharge any of your attendants who may desire and deserve it, procuring for them immediate payment of all arrears of pay and clothing which may have incurred since their departure, and assure them that they shall be recommended to the liberality of the legislature for the grant of a soldier's portion of land each, as proposed in my message to congress, and repair yourself, with your papers, to the seat of government.

To provide, on the accident of your death, against anarchy, dispersion, and the consequent danger to your party, and total failure of the enterprise, you are hereby authorized, by any instrument signed and written in your own hand, to name the person among them who shall succeed to the command on your decease, and by like instruments to change the nomination, from time to time, as further experience of the characters accompanying you shall point out superior fitness; and all the powers and authorities given to yourself are, in the event of your death, transferred to, and vested in the successor so named, with further power to him and his successors, in like manner to name each his successor, who, on the death of his predecessor, shall be invested with all the powers and authorities given to yourself. Given under my hand at the city of Washington, this twentieth day of June, 1803.

TH. JEFFERSON

Source: Ford, Paul Leicester, ed. 1897. *The Writings of Thomas Jefferson.* Vol. 3. New York: G.P. Putnam's Sons.

DOCUMENT 17

LAUSSAT'S LETTER TO DECRÉS (AUGUST 17, 1803)

CITIZEN MINISTER: The courier sent overland from Washington City [United States] brought here the day before yesterday, the printed bulletin herewith enclosed. It is the official news of the cession of Louisiana to the United States by a treaty signed at Paris, 10 Floréal last [April 30].

This bulletin which has been scattered about profusely and is accompanied by letters setting forth the conditions and other details of that arrangement has produced a considerable sensation here. The Anglo-Americans are extravagant in their joy. Most of the Spaniards, between joy at seeing this colony escape French domination and the regret of losing it themselves, have the stupidity to show themselves satisfied. The French, that is to say, nine-tenths of the population, are stupified and disconsolate; they speak only of selling out and fleeing far from this country.

For my part, I am quieting them and telling them (as I believe) that this news, in whatever character it be viewed, is an improbable and impudent lie. I see in it only a matter for cabal on the part of the party in power which, at this moment of the elections in the United States and on the eve of the expiration of Jefferson's presidency, has thought to throw this news suddenly into the midst of the electoral college in order to create more favor for the partisans of the present president.

The effect that results from it is to electrify the heads of the Anglo-Americans more and more for the possession of Louisiana and to discourage French affections for it.

Under this point of view, these lies are productive of much evil. Salutation and respect.

LAUSSAT

Source: Robertson, James Alexander, ed. 1911. *Louisiana under Spain, France and the United States, 1785–1807: Social, Economic, and Political Conditions of the Territory Represented in the Louisiana Purchase.* Vol. 2. Cleveland, OH: Arthur H. Clark Co.

DOCUMENT 18

THOMAS JEFFERSON'S THIRD ANNUAL MESSAGE TO THE CONGRESS (OCTOBER 17, 1803)

To the Senate and House of Representatives of the United States:

In calling you together, fellow citizens, at an earlier day than was contemplated by the act of the last session of Congress, I have not been insensible to the personal inconveniences necessarily resulting from an unexpected change in your arrangements. But matters of great public concernment have rendered this call necessary, and the interests you feel in these will supersede in your minds all private considerations.

Congress witnessed, at their late session, the extraordinary agitation produced in the public mind by the suspension of our right of deposit at the port of New Orleans, no assignment of another place having been made according to treaty. They were sensible that the continuance of that privation would be more injurious to our nation than any consequences which could flow from any mode of redress, but reposing just confidence in the good faith of the Government whose officer had committed the wrong, friendly and reasonable representations were resorted to, and the right of deposit was restored.

Previous, however, to this period, we had not been unaware of the danger to which our peace would be perpetually exposed whilst so important a key to the commerce of the Western country remained under foreign power. Difficulties, too, were presenting themselves as to the navigation of other streams, which, arising within our territories, pass through those adjacent. Propositions had, therefore, been authorized for obtaining, on fair conditions, the sovereignty of New Orleans, and of other possessions in that quarter interesting to our quiet, to such extent as was deemed practicable; and the provisional appropriation of $2,000,000 to be applied and accounted for by the President of the United States, intended as part of the price, was considered as conveying the sanction of Congress to the acquisition proposed. The enlightened Government of France saw, with just discernment, the importance to both nations of such liberal arrangements as might best and permanently promote the peace, friendship, and interests of both; and the property and sovereignty of all Louisiana, which had been restored to them, have on certain conditions been transferred to the United States by instruments bearing date the 30th of April last. When these shall have received the constitutional sanction of the Senate, they will without delay be communicated to the Representatives also, for the exercise of their functions, as to those conditions which are within the powers vested by the Constitution in Congress.

Whilst the property and sovereignty of the Mississippi

and its waters secure an independent outlet for the produce of the Western States, and an uncontrolled navigation through their whole course, free from collision with other powers and the dangers to our peace from that source, the fertility of the country, its climate and extent, promise in due season important aids to our Treasury, an ample provision for our posterity, and a wide spread field for the blessings of freedom and equal laws.

With the wisdom of Congress it will rest to take those ulterior measures which may be necessary for the immediate occupation and temporary government of the country; for its incorporation into our Union; for rendering the change of government a blessing to our newly adopted brethren; for securing to them the rights of conscience and of property: for confirming to the Indian inhabitants their occupancy and self-government, establishing friendly and commercial relations with them, and for ascertaining the geography of the country acquired. Such materials for your information, relative to its affairs in general, as the short space of time has permitted me to collect, will be laid before you when the subject shall be in a state for your consideration.

Another important acquisition of territory has also been made since the last session of Congress. The friendly tribe of Kaskaskia Indians with which we have never had a difference, reduced by the wars and wants of savage life to a few individuals unable to defend themselves against the neighboring tribes, has transferred its country to the United States, reserving only for its members what is sufficient to maintain them in an agricultural way. The considerations stipulated are, that we shall extend to them our patronage and protection, and give them certain annual aids in money, in implements of agriculture, and other articles of their choice. This country, among the most fertile within our limits, extending along the Mississippi from the mouth of the Illinois to and up the Ohio, though not so necessary as a barrier since the acquisition of the other bank, may yet be well worthy of being laid open to immediate settlement, as its inhabitants may descend with rapidity in support of the lower country should future circumstances expose that to foreign enterprise. As the stipulations in this treaty also involve matters within the competence of both Houses only, it will be laid before Congress as soon as the Senate shall have advised its ratification.

With many other Indian tribes, improvements in agriculture and household manufacture are advancing, and with all our peace and friendship are established on grounds much firmer than heretofore. The measure adopted of establishing trading houses among them, and of furnishing them necessaries in exchange for their commodities, at such moderated prices as leave no gain, but cover us from loss, has the most conciliatory and useful effect upon them, and is that which will best secure their peace and good will.

The small vessels authorized by Congress with a view to the Mediterranean service, have been sent into that sea, and will be able more effectually to confine the Tripoline cruisers within their harbors, and supersede the necessity of convoy to our commerce in that quarter. They will sensibly lessen the expenses of that service the ensuing year.

A further knowledge of the ground in the northeastern and northwestern angles of the United States has evinced that the boundaries established by the treaty of Paris, between the British territories and ours in those parts, were too imperfectly described to be susceptible of execution. It has therefore been thought worthy of attention, for preserving and cherishing the harmony and useful intercourse subsisting between the two nations, to remove by timely arrangements what unfavorable incidents might otherwise render a ground of future misunderstanding. A convention has therefore been entered into, which provides for a practicable demarcation of those limits to the satisfaction of both parties.

An account of the receipts and expenditures of the year ending 30th September last, with the estimates for the service of the ensuing year, will be laid before you by the Secretary of the Treasury so soon as the receipts of the last quarter shall be returned from the more distant States. It is already ascertained that the amount paid into the Treasury for that year has been between $11,000,000 and $12,000,000, and that the revenue accrued during the same term exceeds the sum counted on as sufficient for our current expenses, and to extinguish the public debt within the period heretofore proposed.

The amount of debt paid for the same year is about $3,100,000, exclusive of interest, and making, with the payment of the preceding year, a discharge of more than $8,500,000 of the principal of that debt, besides the accruing interest; and there remain in the Treasury nearly $6,000,000. Of these, $880,000 have been reserved for payment of the first instalment due under the British convention of January 8, 1802, and two millions are what have been before mentioned as placed by Congress under the power and accountability of the President, toward the price of New Orleans and other territories acquired, which, remaining untouched, are still applicable to that object, and go in diminution of the sum to be funded for it.

Should the acquisition of Louisiana be constitutionally confirmed and carried into effect, a sum of nearly $13,000,000 will then be added to our public debt, most of which is payable after fifteen years; before which term the present existing debts will all be discharged by the established operation of the sinking fund. When we contemplate the ordinary annual augmentation of imposts from increasing population and wealth, the augmentation of the same revenue by its extension to the new acquisition, and the economies which may still be introduced into our public expenditures, I cannot but hope that Congress in reviewing their resources will find means to meet the intermediate interests of this additional debt without recurring to new taxes, and applying to this object only the ordinary progression of our revenue. Its extraordinary increase in times of foreign war will be the proper and sufficient fund for any measures of safety or precaution which that state of things may render necessary in our neutral position.

Remittances for the instalments of our foreign debt having been found impracticable without loss, it has not been thought expedient to use the power given by a former act of Congress of continuing them by reloans, and of redeeming instead thereof equal sums of domestic debt, although no difficulty was found in obtaining that accommodation.

The sum of $50,000 appropriated by Congress for providing gun-boats, remains unexpended. The favorable and peaceful turn of affairs on the Mississippi rendered an immediate execution of that law unnecessary, and time was desirable in order that the institution of that branch of our force might begin on models the most approved by experience. The same issue of events dispensed with a resort to the appropriation of $1,500,000 contemplated for purposes which were effected by happier means.

We have seen with sincere concern the flames of war lighted up again in Europe, and nations with which we have the most friendly and useful relations engaged in mutual destruction. While we regret the miseries in which we see others involved let us bow with gratitude to that kind Providence which, inspiring with wisdom and moderation our late legislative councils while placed under the urgency of the greatest wrongs, guarded us from hastily entering into the sanguinary contest, and left us only to look on and to pity its ravages. These will be heaviest on those immediately engaged. Yet the nations pursuing peace will not be exempt from all evil. In the course of this conflict, let it be our endeavor, as it is our interest and desire, to cultivate the friendship of the belligerent nations by every act of justice and of incessant kindness; to receive their armed vessels with hospitality from the distresses of the sea, but to administer the means of annoyance to none; to establish in our harbors such a police as may maintain law and order; to restrain our citizens from embarking individually in a war in which their country takes no part; to punish severely those persons, citizen or alien, who shall usurp the cover of our flag for vessels not entitled to it, infecting thereby with suspicion those of real Americans, and committing us into controversies for the redress of wrongs not our own; to exact from every nation the observance, toward our vessels and citizens, of those principles and practices which all civilized people acknowledge; to merit the character of a just nation, and maintain that of an independent one, preferring every consequence to insult and habitual wrong. Congress will consider whether the existing laws enable us efficaciously to maintain this course with our citizens in all places, and with others while within the limits of our jurisdiction, and will give them the new modifications necessary for these objects. Some contraventions of right have already taken place, both within our jurisdictional limits and on the high seas. The friendly disposition of the governments from whose agents they have proceeded, as well as their wisdom and regard for justice, leave us in reasonable expectation that they will be rectified and prevented in the future; and that no act will be countenanced by them which threatens to disturb our friendly intercourse. Separated by a wide ocean from the nations of Europe, and from the political interests which entangle them together, with productions and wants which render our commerce and friendship useful to them and theirs to us, it cannot be the interest of any to assail us, nor ours to disturb them. We should be most unwise, indeed, were we to cast away the singular blessings of the position in which nature has placed us, the opportunity she has endowed us with of pursuing, at a distance from foreign contentions, the paths of industry, peace, and happiness; of cultivating general friendship, and of bringing collisions of interest to the umpirage of reason rather than of force. How desirable then must it be, in a Government like ours, to see its citizens adopt individually the views, the interests, and the conduct which their country should pursue, divesting themselves of those passions and partialities which tend to lessen useful friendships, and to embarrass and embroil us in the calamitous scenes of Europe. Confident, fellow citizens, that you will duly estimate the importance of neutral dispositions toward the observance of neutral conduct, that you will be sensible how much it is our duty to look on the bloody arena spread before us with commiseration indeed, but with no other wish than to see it closed, I am persuaded you will cordially cherish these dispositions in all discussions among yourselves, and in all communications with your constituents; and I anticipate with satisfaction the measures of wisdom which the great interests now committed to *you* will give you an opportunity of providing, and *myself* that of approving and carrying into execution with the fidelity I owe to my country.

TH. JEFFERSON

Source: Richardson, James D., ed. 1897. *A Compilation of the Messages and Papers of the Presidents Prepared under the Direction of the Joint Committee on Printing, of the House and Senate Pursuant to an Act of the Fifty-Second Congress of the United States.* New York: Bureau of National Literature.

DOCUMENT 19

THOMAS JEFFERSON'S MESSAGE TO THE SENATE (OCTOBER 17, 1803)

Gentlemen of the Senate:

In my message of this day to both Houses of Congress I explained the circumstances which had led to the conclusion of conventions with France for the cession of the Province of Louisiana to the United States. Those conventions are now laid before you with such communications relating to them as may assist in deciding whether you will advise and consent to their ratification.

The ratification of the First Consul of France is in the

hands of his chargé d'affaires here, to be exchanged for that of the United States whensoever, before the 30th instant, it shall be in readiness.

TH. JEFFERSON

Source: Richardson, James D., ed. 1897. *A Compilation of the Messages and Papers of the Presidents Prepared under the Direction of the Joint Committee on Printing, of the House and Senate Pursuant to an Act of the Fifty-Second Congress of the United States*. New York: Bureau of National Literature.

DOCUMENT 20

THOMAS JEFFERSON'S MESSAGE TO THE SENATE AND THE HOUSE (OCTOBER 21, 1803)

To the Senate and House of Representatives of the United States:

In my communication to you of the 17th instant I informed you that conventions had been entered into with the Government of France for the cession of Louisiana to the United States. These, with the advice and consent of the Senate, having now been ratified and my ratification exchanged for that of the First Consul of France in due form, they are communicated to you for consideration in your legislative capacity. You will observe that some important conditions can not be carried into execution but with the aid of the Legislature, and that time presses a decision on them without delay.

The ulterior provisions, also suggested in the same communication, for the occupation and government of the country will call for early attention. Such information relative to its government as time and distance have permitted me to obtain will be ready to be laid before you within a few days; but as permanent arrangements for this object may require time and deliberation, it is for your consideration whether you will not forthwith make such temporary provisions for the preservation in the meanwhile of order and tranquillity in the country as the case may require.

TH. JEFFERSON

Source: Richardson, James D., ed. 1897. *A Compilation of the Messages and Papers of the Presidents Prepared under the Direction of the Joint Committee on Printing, of the House and Senate Pursuant to an Act of the Fifty-Second Congress of the United States*. New York: Bureau of National Literature.

DOCUMENT 21

PRESIDENT JEFFERSON GIVEN AUTHORITY TO TAKE POSSESSION OF THE LOUISIANA PURCHASE TERRITORY

An Act to enable the President of the United States to take possession of the territories ceded by France to the United States, by the treaty concluded at Paris, on the thirtieth of April last; and for the temporary government thereof.

Be it enacted by the Senate and House of Representatives of the United States of America in Congress assembled, That the President of the United States be, and he is hereby authorized to take possession of, and occupy the territory ceded by France to the United States, by the treaty concluded at Paris, on the thirtieth day of April last, between the two nations; and that he may for that purpose, and in order to maintain in the said territories the authority of the United States, employ any part of the army and navy of the United States, and of the force authorized by an act passed the third day of March last, entitled "An act directing a detachment from the militia of the United States, and for erecting certain arsenals," which he may deem necessary: and so much of the sum appropriated by the said act as may be necessary, is hereby appropriated for the purpose of carrying this act into effect; to be applied under the direction of the President of the United States.

SEC. 2. *And be it further enacted*, That until the expiration of the present session of Congress, unless provision for the temporary government of the said territories be sooner made by Congress, all the military, civil and judicial powers, exercised by the officers of the existing government of the same, shall be vested in such person and persons, and shall be exercised in such manner, as the President of the United States shall direct for maintaining and protecting the inhabitants of Louisiana in the free enjoyment of their liberty, property and religion.

APPROVED, October 31, 1803

Source: *United States Statutes at Large*. Vol. 2 Edited by Richard Peters. Boston: Charles C. Little and James Brown, 1845.

DOCUMENT 22

SENATE OPPOSITION TO THE LOUISIANA PURCHASE (NOVEMBER 2, 1803)

Mr. [Samuel] WHITE rose and made the following remarks:

Mr. President, by the provisions of the bill before us, and which are thus far in conformity with the words of the treaty, we have until three months after the exchange of ratifications and the delivery of possession to pay this money in. Where then, is the necessity for such haste on this subject? It seems to me to be anticipating our business unnecessarily, and perhaps unwisely; it is showing on our part a degree of anxiety that may be taken advantage of and operate to our injury, and that may serve to retard the accomplishment of the very object that gentlemen seem to have so much at heart. It is not at present altogether certain that we shall ever have occasion to use this stock, and it will be time enough to provide it when the occasion arises, when we see ourselves in the undisturbed possession of this mighty boon, or wherefore are we allowed these three months credit after the delivery of possession? The ratifications have been already exchanged; the French officer who is to make the cession is said to be at New Orleans, and previous to the adjournment of Congress we shall know with certainty whether the First Consul will or can carry this treaty faithfully into operation. We have already passed a bill authorizing the President to take possession, for which I voted, and it will be time enough to create this stock and to make the other necessary arrangements when we find ourselves in possession of the territory, or when we ascertain with certainty that it will be given to us.

But, Mr. President, it is now a well known fact, that Spain considers herself injured by this treaty, and if it should be in her power to prevent it, will not agree to the cession of New Orleans and Louisiana to the United States. She considers herself absolved from her contract with France, in consequence of the latter having neglected to comply with certain stipulations in the Treaty of St. Ildefonso, to be performed on her part, and of having violated her engagement never to transfer this country into other hands. Gentlemen may say this money is to be paid upon the responsibility of the President of the United States, and not until after the delivery of possession to us of the territory; but why cast from ourselves all the responsibility upon this subject and impose the whole weight upon the President, which may hereafter prove dangerous and embarrassing to him? Why make the President the sole and absolute judge of what shall be a faithful delivery of possession under the treaty? What he may think a delivery of possession sufficient to justify the payment of this money, we might not; and I have no hesitation in saying that if, in acquiring this territory under the treaty, we have to fire a single musket, to charge a bayonet, or to lose a drop of blood, it will not be such a cession on the part of France as should justify to the people of this country the payment of any, and much less so enormous a sum of money. What would the case be, sir? It would be buying of France authority to make war upon Spain; it would be giving the First Consul fifteen millions of dollars to stand aloof until we can settle our differences with His Catholic Majesty. Would honorable gentlemen submit to the degradation of purchasing even his neutrality at so inconvenient a price? We are told that there is in the hands of the French Prefect at New Orleans a royal order of His Catholic Majesty, founded upon the Treaty of St. Ildefonso, for the delivery of possession of this territory to France; but which has never been done–the precedent conditions not having been performed on the part of France. This royal order, it is probable, will be handed over to our Commissioner, or to whoever may be sent down to receive possession. We may then be told that we have the right of France, as she acquired it from Spain, which is all she is bound by her treaty to transfer to us; we may be shown the Spaniards, who yet claim to be the rightful owners of the country, and be told that we have the permission of the First Consul to subdue or drive them out, and according to the words of the treaty, to take possession. Of our capacity to do so I have no doubt; but this we could have done, sir, six months ago, and with one-sixth of fifteen millions of dollars, when they had wantonly violated the sacred obligations of a treaty, had insulted our Government, and prostrated all the commerce of our Western country. Then we had, indeed, a just cause for chastising them; the laws of nations and of honor authorized it, and all the world would have applauded our conduct. And it is well known that if France had been so disposed she could not have brought a single man or ship to their relief; before the news could have reached Europe, she was blockaded in her own ports by the British fleets. But that time was permitted to go by unimproved, and instead of regretting the past, let us provide for the future.

Admitting then, Mr. President, that His Catholic Majesty is hostile to the cession of this territory to the United States, and no honorable gentlemen will deny it, what reasons have we to suppose that the French Prefect, provided the Spaniards should interfere, can give us to peaceable possession of the country? He is acknowledged there in no public character, is clothed with no authority, nor has he a single soldier to enforce his orders. I speak now, sir, from mere probabilities. I wish not to be understood as predicting that the French will not cede to us the actual and quiet possession of the territory. I hope to God they may, for possession of it we must have–I mean of New Orleans, and of such other positions on the Mississippi as may be necessary to secure to us forever the complete and uninterrupted navigation of that river. This I have ever been in favor of; I think it essential to the peace of the United States, and to the prosperity of our Western country. But as to Louisiana, this new, immense, unbounded world, if it should ever be incorporated into this Union, which I have no idea can be done but by altering the Constitution, I believe it will be the greatest curse that could at present befall us; it may be productive of innumerable evils, and especially of one that I fear even to look upon. Gentlemen on all sides, with very few exceptions, agree that the settlement of this country will be highly injurious and dangerous to the United states; but as to what has been suggested of removing the Creeks and other nations of Indians from the eastern to the western banks of the Mississippi, and of making the fertile regions of Louisiana a howling wilderness, never to be trodden by the foot of civilized man, it is impracticable. The gentleman from Tennessee (Mr. [William] COCKE) has shown his usual candor on this subject, and I believe with him to use his strong language, that you had as well pretend to inhibit the fish from swimming in the sea as to prevent the population of that country after its sovereignty shall become ours. To every man acquainted with the adventurous, roving, and enterprising temper of our people, and with the manner in which our Western country has been settled, such and idea must be chimerical.

The inducements will be so strong that it will be impossible to restrain our citizens from crossing the river. Louisiana must and will become settled, if we hold it, and with the very population that would otherwise occupy part of our present territory. Thus our citizens will be removed to the immense distance of two or three thousand miles from the capital of the Union, where they will scarcely ever feel the rays of the General Government; their affections will become alienated; they will gradually begin to view us as strangers; they will form other commercial connexions [sic], and our interests will become distinct.

These, with other causes that human wisdom may not now foresee, will in time effect a separation, and I fear our bounds will be fixed nearer to our houses than the waters of the Mississippi. We have already territory enough, and when I contemplate the evils that may arise to these States, from this intended incorporation of Louisiana into the Union, I would rather see it given to France, to Spain, or to any other nation of the earth, upon the mere condition that no citizen of the United States should ever settle within its limits, than to see the territory sold for an hundred millions of dollars, and we retain the sovereignty. But however dangerous the possession of Louisiana might prove to us, I do not presume to say that the retention of it would not have been very convenient to France, and we know that at the time of the mission of Mr. Monroe, our Administration had never thought of the purchase of Louisiana, and that nothing short of the fullest conviction on the part of the First Consul that he was on the very eve of a war with England; that this being the most defenceless point of his possessions, if such they could be called, was the one at which the British would first strike, and that it must inevitably fall into their hands, could ever have induced his pride and ambition to make the sale. He judged wisely, that he had better sell it for as much as he could get than lose it entirely. And I do say that under existing circumstances, even supposing that this extent of territory was a desirable acquisition, fifteen missions of dollars was a most enormous sum to give. Our Commissioners were negotiating in Paris–they must have known the relative situation of France and England–they must have known at the moment that a war was unavoidable between the two countries, and they knew the pecuniary necessities of France and the naval power of Great Britain. These imperious circumstances should have been turned to our advantage, and if we were to purchasc, should have lessened the consideration. Viewing, Mr. President, this subject in any point of light–either as it regards the territory purchased, the high consideration to be given, the contract itself, or any of the circumstances attending it, I see no necessity for precipitating the passage of this bill; and if this motion for postponement should fail, and the question of the final passage of the bill be taken now, I shall certainly vote against it.

Source: United States Congress. 1834–1856. Seventh Congress, Second Session. *Annals of the Congress of the United States*. Washington: Gales and Seaton.

DOCUMENT 23

STOCK ISSUED BY CONGRESS TO IMPLEMENT THE TREATY WITH THE FRENCH REPUBLIC

An Act authorizing the creation of a stock, to the amount of eleven millions two hundred and fifty thousand dollars, for the purpose of carrying into effect the convention of the thirtieth of April, one thousand eight hundred and three, between the United States of America and the French Republic; and making provision for the payment of the same.

Be it enacted by the Senate and House of Representatives of the United States of America in Congress assembled, That for the purpose of carrying into effect the convention of the thirtieth day of April, one thousand eight hundred and three, between the United States of America and the French Republic, the Secretary of the Treasury be, and he is hereby authorized, to cause to be constituted, certificates of stock, signed by the register of the treasury, in favour of the French Republic, or of its assignees, for the sum of eleven millions two hundred and fifty thousand dollars, bearing an interest of six per centum per annum, from the time when possession of Louisiana shall have been obtained, in conformity with the treaty of the thirtieth day of April, one thousand eight hundred and three, between the United States of America and the French Republic, and in other respects conformable with the tenor of the convention aforesaid; and the President of the United States is authorized to cause the said certificates of stock to be delivered to the government of France, or to such person or persons as shall be authorized to receive them, in three months at most, after the exchange of the ratifications of the treaty aforesaid, and after Louisiana shall be taken possession of in the name of the government of the United States; and credit, or credits, to the proprietors thereof, shall thereupon be entered and given on the books of the treasury, in like manner as for the present domestic funded debt, which said credits or stock shall thereafter be transferable only on the books of the treasury of the United States, by the proprietor or proprietors of such stock his, her or their attorney: and the faith of the United States is hereby pledged for the payment of the interest, and for the reimbursement of the principal of thc said stock, in conformity with the provisions of the said convention: Provided however, that the Secretary of the Treasury may, with the approbation of the President of the United States, consent to discharge the said stock in four equal annual instalments, and also shorten the periods fixed by the convention for its reimbursement: And provided also, that every proprietor of the said stock may, until otherwise directed by law, on surrendering his certificate of such stock, receive another to the same amount, and bearing an interest of six per centum per annum, payable quarter-yearly at the treasury of the United States.

SEC. 2. *And be it further enacted*, That the annual interest accruing on the said stock, which may, in conformity with the convention aforesaid, be payable in Europe, shall be paid at the rate of four shillings and sixpence sterling for each dollar, if payable in London, and at the rate of two Guilders and one half of a guilder, current money of Holland, for each dollar, if payable in Amsterdam.

SEC. 3. *And be it further enacted*, That a sum equal to what will be necessary to pay the interest which may accrue on the said stock to the end of the present year, be, and the same is hereby appropriated for that purpose, to be paid out of any monies in the treasury not otherwise appropriated.

SEC. 4. *And be it further enacted*, That from and after the end of the present year, (in addition to the annual sun of seven millions three hundred thousand dollars yearly appropriated to the sinking fund, by virtue of the act, intituled "An act making provision for the redemption of the whole of the public debt of the United States,") a further annual sum of seven hundred thousand dollars, to be paid out of the duties on merchandise and tonnage, be, and the same hereby is, yearly appropriated to the said fund, making in the whole, an annual sum of eight millions of dollars, which shall be vested in the commissioners of the sinking fund in the same manner, shall be applied by them for the same purposes, and shall be, and continue appropriated, until the whole of the present debt of the United States, inclusively of the stock created by virtue of this act, shall be reimbursed and redeemed, under the same limitations as have been provided by the first section of the above-mentioned act, respecting the annual appropriation of seven millions three hundred thousand dollars, made by the same.

SEC. 5. *And be it further enacted*, That the Secretary of the Treasury shall cause the said further sum of seven hundred thousand dollars to be paid to the commissioners of the sinking fund, in the same manner as was directed by the above-mentioned act respecting the annual appropriation of seven millions three hundred thousand dollars; and it shall be the duty of the commissioners of the sinking fund to cause to be applied and paid out of the said fund, yearly, and every year, at the treasury of the United States, such sum and sums as may be annually wanted to discharge the annual interest and charges accruing on the stock created by virtue of this act, and the several instalments, or parts of principal of the said stock, as the same shall become due and may be discharged, in conformity to the terms of the convention aforesaid, and of this act.

APPROVED, November 10, 1803

Source: *United States Statutes at Large*. Vol. 2. Edited by Richard Peters. Boston: Charles C. Little and James Brown, 1845.

DOCUMENT 24

PROVISION FOR CLAIMS OF UNITED STATES CITIZENS ON THE GOVERNMENT OF FRANCE

An Act making provision for the payment of claims of citizens of the United States on the government France, the payment of which has been assumed by the United States, by virtue of the convention of the thirtieth of April, one thousand eight hundred and three, between the United States and the French Republic.

Be it enacted by the Senate and House of Representatives of the United States of America in Congress assembled, That a sum, not exceeding three millions seven hundred and fifty thousand dollars, (inclusive of a sum of two millions of dollars, appropriated by the act of the twenty-sixth day of February, one thousand eight hundred and three, entitled "An act making further provision for the expenses attending the intercourse between the United States and foreign nations,") to be paid out of any monies in the treasury not otherwise appropriated, be, and the same hereby is appropriated, for the purpose of discharging the claims of citizens of the United States against the government of France, the payment of which has been assumed by the government of the United States, by virtue of a convention made the thirtieth day of April one thousand eight hundred and three, between the United States of America and the French Republic, respecting the said claims.

SEC. 2. *And be it further enacted*, That the Secretary of the Treasury shall cause to be paid, at the treasury of the United States, in conformity to the convention aforesaid, the amount of such claims, abovementioned, as, under the provisions of the said convention, shall be awarded to the respective claimants; which payments shall be made on the orders of the minister plenipotentiary of the United States for the time being, to the French Republic, in conformity with the convention aforesaid, and the said minister shall be charged on the treasury books with the whole amount of such payments, until he shall have exhibited satisfactory proof to the accounting officers of the treasury, that his orders, thus paid, have been issued in conformity with the provisions of the said convention.

SEC. 3. *And be it further enacted*, That the President of the United States be, and he hereby is authorized to borrow, on the credit of the United States, to be applied to the purposes authorized by this act, a sum not exceeding one million seven hundred and fifty thousand dollars, at a rate of interest, not exceeding six per centum per annum; reimbursable out of the appropriation made by virtue of the first section of this act, at the pleasure of the United States, or at such period, not exceeding five years from the time of obtaining the loan, as may be stipulated by contract; and it shall be lawful for the Bank of the United States to lend the same.

SEC. 4. *And be it further enacted*, That so much of the duties on merchandise and tonnage as may be necessary, be, and the same hereby is appropriated for the purpose of paying the interest which shall accrue on the said loan.

SEC. 5. *And be it further enacted*, That for defraying the expense incident to the investigation of the claims above mentioned, there be appropriated a sum not exceeding eighteen thousand five hundred and seventy-five dollars, to be paid out of any monies in the treasury not otherwise appropriated: Provided, that the compensation to be made to any of the commissioners appointed, or to be appointed, in pursuance of the above-mentioned convention, shall not exceed the rate of four thousand four hundred and fifty dollars per annum; that the compensation of their secretary shall not exceed the rate of two thousand two hundred and twenty-five dollars per annum; and that the compensation of the agent shall not exceed the rate of one thousand dollars per annum.

APPROVED, November 10, 1803

Source: *United States Statutes at Large*. Vol. 2. Edited by Richard Peters. Boston: Charles C. Little and James Brown, 1845.

DOCUMENT 25

LAUSSAT'S PROCLAMATION (NOVEMBER 30, 1803)

Pierre Clément Laussat, Colonial Prefect, Commissioner of the French Republic, To the Louisianians.

LOUISIANIANS: The Mission which brought me across 2500 leagues of sea to your midst, that mission in which I have for a long time placed so many honorable hopes & so many wishes for your happiness, is changed today: that of which I am at this time the minister & the executer, less pleasing, though equally flattering to me, offers me one consolation, that is, that in general it is much more advantageous to you.

In virtue of the powers & the respective orders, the Commissioners of H.C.M. have just turned the country over to me, & you see the standards of the French Republic floating & you hear the repeated sound of its cannons announce to you on all sides on this day the return of its sovereignty over these shores: it will be, Louisianians, only for a short time, & I am on the eve of transferring them to the United States Commissioners charged with taking possession of them, in the name of their Federal Government: they are about to arrive; I am awaiting them.

The approach of a war begun under bloody & terrible auspices & threatening the four quarters of the globe has led the French Government to turn its attention and its thoughts to these regions: views of prudence & humanity, allied with views of a broader and firmer policy, worthy, in brief, of the genius who at this very hour is swaying such great destinies among the Nations, have then given a new turn to France's beneficent intentions toward Louisiana: she has ceded it to the United States of America.

Thus you become, Louisianians, the cherished pledge of a friendship between these two Republics that can not fail to keep on getting stronger from day to day & that must contribute so strongly towards their common tranquility and their common prosperity.

Article III of the Treaty will not escape you: "The inhabitants, it is said in that article, of the ceded territories shall be incorporated into the union of the United States, & admitted, as soon as possible, according to the principles of the Federal Constitution, to the enjoyment of all the rights, advantages & immunities of Citizens of the United States; &, while waiting, they shall be maintained & protected in the enjoyment [of] their liberties and possessions & in the practice of the religions that they profess."

Thus, Louisianians, you are at one stroke invested with an acquired right to the prerogatives of a constitution & of a free government, erected by might, cemented by treaties, & tested by experience & years.

You are going to form part of a People already numerous & powerful, renowned also for its activity, its industry, its patriotism and its enlightenment, & which, in its rapid advance, promises to fill one of the most splendid places that a people has ever occupied on the face of the globe.

Its position is, at the same time, so fortunate, that neither its successes nor its splendor can for long detract from its felicity.

However benevolent and pure the wishes for a mother country may have been (you understand, do you not?), an immense distance is an impregnable rampart favoring oppression, exactions & abuses: frequently the very facility & certainty of covering them up will corrupt a man who first viewed them with the greatest hate & fear.

From this time on you cease to be exposed to that fatal and disheartening drawback.

By the nature of the government of the United States & the guaranties into the enjoyment of which you enter immediately, you will have, even under a provisional system, popular leaders, subject with impunity to your protests and your censure, & who will have permanent need of your esteem, your votes & your affections.

Public affairs & interests, far from being prohibited to you, will be your own affairs & interests, over which wise & impartial opinions will be sure to obtain preponderant influence in the long run, & to which even you could not remain indifferent without experiencing bitter repentance.

The time will soon come when you will give yourselves a special form of government which, while respecting the sacred maxims recorded in the constitution of the federal union, will be adapted to your manners, your usages, your climate, your soil and your location.

But in particular you will not be long in experiencing the precious benefits of full, impartial and incorruptible justice, where uniform procedure, publicity, and the restrictions carefully placed on injustice in the application of the laws will contribute, with the high & national character of the judges & juries, toward effectively being responsible to the citizens for their safety and their property; for that is one of the attributes peculiarly characteristic of the government under which you are passing.

Its principles, its legislation, its conduct, its care, its vigilance, its encouragement, to the interests of agriculture & commerce, & the progress which they have made are well known to you, Louisianians, by the very share you have derived from them with so much profit during these last few years.

There is not & can not be a mother country without a more or less exclusive colonial monopoly: on the contrary, you have to expect from the United States only unbounded freedom of exportation, & import duties devised solely to suit your public needs or your domestic industry: through unlimited competition, you can buy cheaply, you will sell at high prices and will also receive the benefits of an immense market: the Nile of America, this Mississippi, which bathes, not deserts of burning sand, but the most extensive, the most fertile, the most fortunately situated plains in the New World, will shortly be seen to be covered, along the wharves of this other Alexandria, with thousands of vessels of all nations.

Among them your glances, Louisianians, will, I hope, always pick out with gratification the French flag, & the sight of it will not fail to rejoice your hearts: such is our firm hope; I profess it formally here in the name of my country & my Government.

Bonaparte, in stipulating by Article VII of the treaty that Frenchmen should be permitted for twelve years to trade on your shores under the same conditions as & without paying other charges than the citizens of the United States themselves, had as one of his principal aims that of giving opportunity and time for the old ties between the French people of Louisiana and the French people of Europe to be renewed, reenforced, perpetuated. A new correspondence of relations is going to be established between us, from one continent to the other, all the more satisfactory and lasting as it will be based purely on constant reciprocity of feelings, services & advantage. Your children, Louisianians, will be our children, & our children will become yours: you will see them perfecting their knowledge & their talents amongst us, & we shall see them amongst you increasing your powers, your labor, your industry, & wresting with you their tribute from a still unconquered Nature.

I am pleased, Louisianians, to contrast rather fully this picture with the touching reproaches of abandonment & the tender regrets which the ineffaceable attachment of a multitude among you to the country of their ancestors has made them breathe forth under these circumstances: France and her Government will listen to the recital of them with love & gratitude; but you will do them before long, from your own experience, this justice that they have distinguished themselves with respect to you by the most eminent & the most memorable of benefits.

The French Republic in this event, the first in modern times, traces the example of a colony which she herself voluntarily emancipates, the example of one of those colonies the image of which we discover with charm in the fine ages of antiquity: so in our days & in the future may a Louisianian and a Frenchman never meet, anywhere in the world, without feeling affected and giving each other the sweet name of brother; may that title alone be capable of representing from this time on the idea of their eternal attachments & their free dependence!

New Orleans, Frimaire 8, Year XII of the French Republic & November 30, 1803.

[Signed] LAUSSAT.

By the Colonial Prefect, Commissioner of the French Government,

[Signed] DAUGEROT. Secretary of the Commission

Source: Carter, Clarence E., ed. 1940. *Territorial Papers of the United States.* Vol. 9, *The Territory of Orleans, 1803–1812.* Washington: Government Printing Office.

DOCUMENT 26

ARTICLES OF EXCHANGE OF POSSESSION

CITY OF NEW ORLEANS, *December 20, 1803*

SIR: We have the satisfaction to announce to you that the Province of Louisiana was this day surrendered to the United States by the Commissioner of France; and to add, that the flag of our country was raised in this city amidst the acclamations of the inhabitants.

The enclosed is a copy of an instrument of writing, which was signed and exchanged by the Commissioners of the two Governments, and is designed as a record of this interesting transaction.

Accept assurances of our respectful consideration.

WM. C.C. CLAIBORNE.

JAMES WILKINSON.

JAMES MADISON.

Secretary of State

The undersigned, William C.C. Claiborne and James Wilkinson, commissioners or agents of the United States, agreeably to the full powers they have received from Thomas Jefferson, President of the United States, under date of the 31st October, 1803, and twenty-eighth year of the independence of the United States of America, (8th Brumaire, 12th year of the French Republic,) countersigned by the Secretary of State, James Madison, and Citizen Peter Clement Laussat, Colonial Prefect and Commissioner of the French Government, for the delivery, in the name of the French Republic, of the country, territories, and dependencies of Louisiana, to the commissioners or agents of the United States, conformably to the powers, commission, and special mandate which he has received, in the name of the French people, from citizen Bonaparte, First Consul, under date of the 6th June 1803, (17th Prairial, eleventh year of the French Republic,) countersigned by the Secretary of State, Hugues Maret, and by his Excellency the Minister of Marine and Colonies, Decres, do certify by these presents, that on this day, Tuesday, the 20th December, 1803, of the Christian era, (28th Frimaire, twelfth year of the French Republic,) being convened in the hall of the Hotel de Ville of Orleans, accompanied on both sides by the Chiefs and Officers of the Army and Navy, by the municipality and divers respectable citizens of their respective Republics, the said William C.C. Claiborne and James Wilkinson, delivered to the said citizen Laussat their aforesaid full powers, by which it evidently appears that full power and authority has been given them jointly and severally to take possession of, and to occupy the territories ceded by France to the United States by the treaty concluded at Paris on the 30th day of April last past, (10th Floreal,) and for that purpose to repair to the said Territory, and there to execute and perform all such acts and things, touching the premises, as may be necessary for fulfiling their appointment conformably to the said treaty and the laws of the United States; and thereupon the said citizen Laussat declared that, in virtue of, and in the terms of the powers, commission, and special mandate dated at St. Cloud, 6th June, 1803, of the Christian era, (17th Prairial, 11th year of the French Republic,) he put from that moment the said Commissioners of the United States in possession of the country, territories, and dependencies of Louisiana, conformably to the first, second, fourth, and fifth articles of the treaty and two conventions, concluded and signed the 30th April, 1803, (10th Floreal, 11th year of the French Republic,) between the French Republic and the United States of America, by citizen Barbé Marbois, Minister of the Public Treasury, and Messrs. Robert R. Livingston and James Monroe, Ministers Plenipotentiary of the United States, all three furnished with full powers, of which treaty and two conventions the ratifications, made by the First Consul of the French Republic on the one part, and by the President of the United States, by and with the advice and consent of the Senate, on the other part, have been exchanged and mutually received at the City of Washington, the 21st October, 1803, (28th Vendemiaire, 12th year of the French Republic,) by citizen Louis André Pichon, chargé des affaires of the French Republic near the United States, on the part of France, and by James Madison, Secretary of State of the United States, on the part of the United States, according to the *procès verbal* drawn up on the same day; and the present delivery of the country is made to them, to the end that, in conformity with the object of the said treaty, the sovereignty and property of the colony or province of Louisiana may pass to the said United States, under the same clauses and conditions as it had been ceded by Spain to France, in virtue of the treaty concluded at St. Ildefonso, on the 1st October, 1800, (9th Vendemiaire, 9th year,) between these two last Powers, which has since received its execution by the actual re-entrance of the French Republic into possession of the said colony or province.

And the said citizen Laussat in consequence, at this present time, delivered to the said Commissioners of the United States, in this public sitting, the keys of the City of New Orleans, declaring that he discharges from their oaths of fidelity towards the French Republic, the citizens and inhabitants of Louisiana, who shall chose to remain under the dominion of the United States.

And that it may forever appear, the undersigned have signed the *procès verbal* of this important and solemn act, in the French and English languages, and have sealed it with their seals, and have caused it to be countersigned by the secretaries of commission, the day, month, and year above written.

[Signed] WM. C.C. CLAIBORNE
[Signed] JAMES WILKINSON
[Signed] LAUSSAT

Source: United States Government. 1903. *State Papers and Correspondence Bearing upon the Purchase of the Territory of Louisiana*. Washington: Government Printing Office.

DOCUMENT 27

GOVERNOR'S ADDRESS TO THE CITIZENS OF LOUISIANA

The following address was delivered by the Undersigned to a large Assemblage of Citizens in the Grand Salee of the City Hall, on the 20th day of December 1803.

Fellow Citizens of Louisiana!
On the great and interesting event which is now finally consummated;—An event so advantageous to yourselves, and so glorious to United America, I cannot forbear offering you my warmest congratulations.—The wise Policy of the Consul of France, has by the Cession of Louisiana to the United States secured to you a connection *beyond the reach of change,* and to your posterity the sure inheritance of Freedom. The American people receive you as Brothers, and will hasten to extend to you a participation in those invaluable rights which have formed the basis of their own unexampled prosperity. Under the Auspices of the American Government, you may confidently rely upon the security of your Liberty, your property and the religion of your choice;—You may with equal certainty rest assured that your commerce will be promoted, and your agriculture cherished; in a word that your interest will be among the principal cares of the National Legislature. In return for these benefits the United States will be amply remunerated, if your growing attachment to the *Constitution* of our Country, and your veneration for the principles on which it is founded, be duly proportioned to the blessings which they will confer.

Among your first duties therefore you should cultivate with assiduity among yourselves the advancement of Political information; you should guide the rising generation in the paths of republican economy and virtue: you should encourage Literature, for without the advantages of education, your descendants will be unable sufficiently to appreciate the intrinsic worth of the Government transmitted to them.

As for myself fellow Citizens, receive a sincere assurance that during my continuance in the situation in which the President of the United States has been pleased to place me, every exertion will be made on my part, to foster your internal happiness, and to promote your general welfare, for it is by such measures alone, that I can Secure to myself the approbation of those great and just men who preside in the Council of our nation.

[Signed] Wm. C. C. Claiborne

Source: United States Government. 1903. *State Papers and Correspondence Bearing upon the Purchase of the Territory of Louisiana*. Washington: Government Printing Office.

DOCUMENT 28

GOVERNOR CLAIBORNE'S PROCLAMATION (DECEMBER 20, 1803)

PROCLAMATION BY HIS EXCELLENCY, WILLIAM C. C. CLAIBORNE, GOVERNOR OF THE MISSISSIPPI TERRITORY, EXERCISING THE POWERS OF GOVERNOR-GENERAL AND INTENDANT OF THE PROVINCE OF LOUISIANA.

Whereas, by stipulation between the Governments of France and Spain, the latter ceded to the former the colony and province of Louisiana, with the same extent which it had at the date of the abovementioned treaty in the hands of Spain, and that it had when France possessed it, and such as it ought to be after the treaties subsequently entered into between Spain and other States; and whereas the Government of France has ceded the same to the United States by a treaty duly ratified, and bearing date the 30th of April in the present year, and the possession of the said colony and province is now in the United States, according to the tenor of the last-mentioned treaty; and whereas the Congress of the United States on the 31st day of October in the present year, did enact that, until the expiration of the session of Congress then sitting, (unless provisions for the temporary government of the said territories be made by Congress,) all the military, civil, and judicial powers exercised by the then existing government of the same, shall be vested in such person or persons, and shall be exercised in such manner as the President of the United States shall direct, for the maintaining and protecting the inhabitants of Louisiana in the free enjoyment of their liberty, property, and religion; and the President of the United States has, by his commission, bearing date the same 31st day of October, invested me with all the powers, and charged me with the several duties heretofore held and exercised by the Governor-General and Intendant of the Province.

I have, therefore, thought fit to issue this, my proclamation, making known the premises, and to declare, that the government heretofore exercised over the said Province of Louisiana, as well under the authority of Spain as the French Republic has ceased, and that of the United States of America is established over the same; that the inhabitants thereof will be incorporated in the Union of the United States, and admitted as soon as possible, according to the principles of the Federal Constitution, to the enjoyment of all the rights, advantages, and immunities of citizens of the United States; that, in the meantime, they shall be maintained and protected in the free enjoyment of their liberty, property, and the religion which they profess; that all laws and municipal regulations which were in existence at the cessation of the late government, remain in full force; and all civil officers charged with their execution, except those whose powers have been specially vested in me, and except, also, such officers as have been intrusted with the collection of the revenue, are continued in their functions, during the pleasure of the Governor for the time being, or until provision shall otherwise be made.

And I do hereby exhort and enjoin all the inhabitants, and other persons within the said province, to be faithful and true in their allegiance to the United States, and obedient to the laws and authorities of the same, under full assurance that their just rights will be under the guardianship of the United States, and will be maintained from all force or violence from without or within.

In testimony whereof I have hereunto set my hand.

Given at the city of New Orleans, the 20th day of December, 1803, and of the independence of the United States of America, the twenty-eighth.

[Signed] Wm. C. C. CLAIBORNE.

Source: United States Government. 1903. *State Papers and Correspondence Bearing upon the Purchase of the Territory of Louisiana*. Washington: Government Printing Office.

DOCUMENT 29

THOMAS JEFFERSON'S MESSAGE TO THE SENATE AND THE HOUSE (JANUARY 16, 1804)

To the Senate and House of Representatives of the United States:

In execution of the act of the present session of Congress for taking possession of Louisiana, as ceded to us by France, and for the temporary government thereof, Governor Claiborne, of the Mississippi Territory, and General Wilkinson were appointed commissioners to receive possession. They proceeded with such regular troops as had been assembled at Fort Adams from the nearest posts and with some militia of the Mississippi Territory to New Orleans. To be prepared for anything unexpected which might arise out of the transaction, a respectable body of militia was ordered to be in readiness in the States of Ohio, Kentucky, and Tennessee, and a part of those of Tennessee was moved on to the Natchez. No occasion, however, arose for their services. Our commissioners, on their arrival at New Orleans, found the Province already delivered by the commissioners of Spain to that of France, who delivered it over to them on the 20th day of December, as appears by their declaratory act accompanying this. Governor Claiborne, being duly invested with the powers heretofore exercised by the governor and intendant of

Louisiana, assumed the government on the same day, and for the maintenance of law and order immediately issued the proclamation and address now communicated.

On this important acquisition, so favorable to the immediate interests of our Western citizens, so auspicious to the peace and security of the nation in general, which adds to our country territories so extensive and fertile and to our citizens new brethren to partake of the blessings of freedom and self-government, I offer to Congress and our country my sincere congratulations.

TH. JEFFERSON

Source: Richardson, James D., ed. 1897. *A Compilation of the Messages and Papers of the Presidents Prepared under the Direction of the Joint Committee on Printing, of the House and Senate Pursuant to an Act of the Fifty-Second Congress of the United States.* New York: Bureau of National Literature.

DOCUMENT 30

COLLECTION OF DUTIES AND IMPORTS WITHIN THE LOUISIANA TERRITORY

Be it enacted by the Senate and House of Representatives of the United States of America in Congress assembled, That the same duties which by lay, now are, or hereafter may be laid on goods, wares, and merchandise imported into the United States, on the tonnage of vessels, and on the passports and clearances of vessels, shall be laid and collected on goods, wares, and merchandise imported into the territories ceded to the United States, by the treaty of the thirtieth of April, one thousand eight hundred and three, between the United States and the French Republic; and on vessels arriving in, or departing from the said territories: and the following acts, that is to say, the act, entitled,

"An act to establish the treasury department."

"An act concerning the registering and recording of ships and vessels."

"An act for enrolling and licensing ships or vessels to be employed in the coasting trade and fisheries."

"An act to regulate the collection of duties on imports and tonnage."

"An act to establish the compensations of officers employed in the collection of the duties on imports and tonnage, and for other purposes."

"An act for the more effectual recovery of debts due from individuals to the United States."

"An act to provide more effectually for the settlement of accounts between the United States and receivers of public money."

"An act to authorize the sale and conveyance of lands in certain cases, by the marshals of the United States, and to confirm former sales," and

"An act to provide for mitigating or remitting the forfeitures, penalties and disabilities accruing in certain cases therein mentioned."

"An act to establish a mint and to regulate the coins of the United States."

"An act regulating foreign coins, and for other purposes."

And the act supplementary to, and amendatory of the two last-mentioned acts, or so much of the said acts as is now in force, and also so much of any other act or acts of the United States as is now in force, or may be hereafter enacted, for laying any duties on imports, tonnage, seamen or shipping, for regulating and securing the collection of the same, and for regulating the compensations of the officers employed in the collection of the same; for granting and regulating drawbacks, bounties and allowances in lieu of drawbacks: concerning the registering, recording, enrolling and licensing of ships and vessels; to provide for the settlement of accounts between the United States and individuals; for the recovery of debts due to the United States; and for remitting forfeitures, penalties and disabilities, shall extend to, and have full force and effect in the above-mentioned territories: *Provided however, and it is hereby further enacted,* That ships or vessels, which on the twentieth day of December last, were owned by persons then residing in the above mentioned territories, and who, either were citizens of the United States, or had resided in the said territories, during five years next preceding, shall be entitled to the benefits and privileges of ships or vessels of the United States, whilst they shall continue to be wholly owned by such persons, or by citizens of the United States: *Provided nevertheless,* that the persons claiming such privileges for their ships or vessels, shall in every other respect, comply with the provisions of the acts for registering, recording, enrolling and licensing of ships or vessels, and who, if not citizens of the United States, shall have previously taken an oath of allegiance to the United States, which oath the collector of the port is hereby authorized to administer.

SEC. 2. *And be it further enacted,* That so much of any act or acts of the United States, now in force, or which may be hereafter enacted, concerning the Bank of the United States, and for the punishment of frauds committed on the same; for the relief of sick and disabled seamen; for the protection of American seamen; for the government and of regulation of seamen in the merchant service; and for preventing the exportation of goods not duly inspected; shall extend to and have full force and effect in the above-mentioned territories.

SEC. 3. *And be it further enacted,* That so much of

any law or laws, laying any duties on the importation into the United States of goods, wares and merchandise from the said territories (or allowing drawbacks on the importation of the same from the United States to the said territories), or respecting the commercial intercourse between the United States and the said territories, or between the several parts of the United States through the said territories, which is inconsistent with the provisions of the preceding section, be, and the same hereby is repealed; and all duties on the exportation of goods, wares and merchandise from the said territories, as well as all duties on the importation of goods, wares and merchandise into the said territories, on the transfer of ships or vessels, and on the tonnage of vessels, other than those laid by virtue of the laws of the United States, shall, from the time when this act shall commence to be in force, cease and determine: *Provided however,* that nothing herein contained, shall be construed to affect the fees and other charges usually paid in the said territories on account of pilotage, wharfage, or the right of anchoring by the levy of the city of New Orleans, which several fees and charges shall, until otherwise directed, continue to be paid and applied to the same purposes as heretofore.

SEC. 4. *And be it further enacted,* That, to the end that the laws providing for the collection of the duties imposed, by law, on goods, wares and merchandise, imported into the United States, and on the tonnage of ships and vessels, and the laws respecting the revenue and navigation of the United States, may be carried into effect within the said territories, the territories ceded to the United States by the treaty above mentioned, and also all the navigable waters, rivers, creeks, bays, and inlets, lying within the United States, which empty into the Gulf of Mexico, east of the river Mississippi, shall be annexed to the Mississippi district, and shall, together with the same, constitute one district, to be called the "District of Mississippi." The city of New Orleans shall be the sole port of entry in the said district, and the town of Bayou St. John shall be a port of delivery, a collector, naval officer, and surveyor shall be appointed to reside at New Orleans, and a surveyor shall be appointed to reside at the port of Bayou St. John; and the President of the United States is hereby authorized to appoint, not exceeding three surveyors, to reside at such other places, within the said district, as he shall deem expedient, and to constitute each, or either of such places ports of delivery only. And so much of any law or laws, as establishes a district on the river Mississippi, south of the river Tennessee, is hereby repealed, except as to the recovery and receipt of such of duties on goods, wares and merchandise, and on the tonnage of ships or vessels, as shall have accrued, and as to the recovery and distribution of fines, penalties, and forfeitures, which shall have been incurred before the commencement of the operation of this act.

SEC. 5. *And be it further enacted,* That the shores and waters of the town of Natchez, shall be one district, to be called the district of Natchez, and a collector shall be appointed who shall reside at Natchez, which shall be the only port of entry or delivery within the said district, of any goods, wares and merchandise, not the growth or manufacture of the United States: *Provided nevertheless,* that it shall be the duty of every master or commander of any ship or vessel destined for the said port of Natchez, to stop at New Orleans, and there deliver to the collector of said port a manifest of the cargo on board such ship or vessel agreeably to law, on penalty of five thousand dollars. And it shall be the duty of said collector to transmit a certified copy of such manifest to the collector of the said port of Natchez, and to direct an inspector to go on board such ship or vessel, and proceed therewith to the port of Natchez, and there report such ship or vessel to the collector of said port of Natchez, Immediately after his arrival, when the duty of said inspector shall cease.

SEC. 6. *And be it further enacted,* That foreign ships or vessels shall be admitted to unlace at the port of New Orleans, and at no other port within the district of Mississippi; and ships or vessels belonging to citizens of the United States, coming directly from France or Spain, or any of their colonies, shall not be admitted to unlace at any port within the district of Mississippi, other than New Orleans: and ships or vessels arriving from the Cape of Good Hope, or from any place beyond the same, shall be admitted to make entry at the port of New Orleans, and at no other port within the district of Mississippi: *Provided however,* that nothing in this act contained, shall authorize the allowing of drawbacks on the exportation of any goods, wares and merchandise from the said port of New Orleans, other than on those which shall have been imported directly into the same, from a foreign port or place.

SEC. 7. *And be it further enacted,* That the master or commander of every ship or vessel, bound to a port of delivery only, other than the port of Bayou St. John, in the district of Mississippi, shall first come to at the port of New Orleans with his ship or vessel, and there make report and entry, in writing, and pay, or secure to be paid, all legal duties, port fees, and charges, in manner provided by law, before such ship or vessel shall proceed to her port of delivery; and any ship or vessel, bound to the port of Bayou St. John, may first proceed to the said port, and afterwards make report and entry at the port of New Orleans, within the time by law limited; and the master of every ship or vessel, arriving from a foreign port or place, or having goods on board of which the duties have not been paid or secured, and bound to any port within the district of Mississippi, (other than New Orleans, or Bayou St. John,) shall take an inspector on board at New Orleans, before proceeding to such port; and if any master of a ship or vessel shall proceed to such port of delivery, contrary to the directions aforesaid, he shall forfeit and pay five hundred dollars, to be recovered in any court of competent jurisdiction, with the costs of suit.

SEC. 8. *And be it further enacted,* That during the term of twelve years, to commence three months after the exchange of the ratifications of the above-mentioned treaty shall have been notified, at Paris, to the French government, French ships or vessels, coming directly from France, or any of her colonies, laden only with the produce or manufactures of France, or any of her said colonies; and Spanish ships or vessels, coming directly from Spain, or any of her colonies, laden only with the produce or manufactures of Spain, or any of her said colonies, shall be admitted into the port of New Orleans, and into all other ports of entry which may hereafter be established by law, within the territories ceded to the United States by the above-mentioned treaty, in the same manner as ships or vessels of the United States, coming directly from France or Spain, or any of their colonies, and without being subject to any other, or higher duty on the said produce or manufacture, than by law now is, or shall, at the time, be payable, by citizens of the United States on similar articles, imported from France or Spain, or any of their colonies, in vessels of the United States, into the said port of New Orleans, or other ports of entry in the territories above mentioned; or to any other, or higher tonnage duty, than by law now is, or shall at the time be, laid on the tonnage of vessels of the United States coming from France, or Spain, or from any of their colonies, to the said port of New Orleans, or other ports of entry within the territories above mentioned.

SEC. 9. *And be it further enacted,* That the collector of the district of Mississippi, shall give bond for the true and faithful discharge of his duties, in the sum of fifteen thousand dollars, and shall be allowed in addition to the fees and emoluments of his office, in lieu of all other commissions, one and a half per cent on all monies by him received, on account of the duties arising from goods, wares and merchandise imported into the said district, and on the tonnage of ships and vessels; and the naval officers and surveyors of the said district shall, respectively, receive an annual compensation of two hundred and fifty dollars, in addition to their other fees and emoluments.

SEC. 10. *And be it further enacted,* That the President of the United States be, and he hereby is authorized, to cause to be built and equipped, one revenue cutter in addition to those heretofore authorized by law, which cutter may be officered, manned and employed, in the same manner, and the expense thereof shall be paid out of the same fund, as is provided for defraying the expense of the revenue cutters heretofore authorized by law.

SEC. 11. *And be it further enacted,* That the President of the United States be, and he hereby is authorized, whenever he shall deem it expedient, to erect the shores, waters and inlets of the bay and river Mobile, and of the other rivers, creeks, inlets and bays emptying into the Gulf of Mexico, east of the said river Mobile, and west thereof to the Pascaguola inclusive into a separate district, and to establish such place within the same, as he shall deem expedient, to be the port of entry and delivery for such district; and to designate such other places, within the same district, not exceeding two, to be ports of delivery only. Whenever such separate district shall be erected, a collector shall be appointed, to reside at the port of entry, and a surveyor shall likewise be appointed to reside at each of the ports of delivery which may be established. And such collector and surveyor shall be entitled to receive, in addition to their other fees and emoluments, an annual salary of two hundred and fifty dollars. And the said collector shall give bond for the faithful discharge of the duties of his office, in the sum of five thousand dollars.

SEC. 12. *And be it further enacted,* That this act shall commence thirty days after the passing thereof.

APPROVED, February 24, 1804

Source: *United States Statutes at Large*. Vol. 2. Edited by Richard Peters. Boston: Charles C. Little and James Brown, 1845.

DOCUMENT 31

LAND LAW
(1804)

An Act making provision for the disposal of the public lands in the Indiana territory, and for other purposes.

Be it enacted by the Senate and House of Representatives of the United States of America in Congress assembled, That the powers vested by law in the surveyor-general, shall extend over all the public lands of the United States to which the Indian title has been or shall hereafter be extinguished, north of the river Ohio, and east of the river Mississippi; and it shall be the duty of the said surveyor-general to cause the said lands to be surveyed into townships, six miles square, and divided in the same manner and under the same regulations, and to do and perform all such other acts in relation to the said lands, as is provided by law in relation to the lands of the United States, situate northwest of the river Ohio and above the mouth of Kentucky river: *Provided*, that the whole expense of surveying and marking the lines shall not exceed three dollars for every mile that shall be actually run, surveyed and marked: *And provided also*, that such tracts of land as are lawfully claimed by individuals within the said boundaries, and the title whereto has been or shall be recognized by the United States, shall be laid out and surveyed at the expense of the parties respectively, in conformity with the true boundaries of such tracts. And it shall also be the duty of the said surveyor-general to cause to be run, surveyed and marked such of the Indian boundary lines of the said lands, as have not yet been surveyed; and with the approbation of the President of the United States to ascertain by astronomical observations the positions of such places north of the river Ohio and east of the river Mississippi, as may be deemed necessary for the correctness of the surveys, and to be the most important points of the geography of the country.

SEC. 2. *And be it further enacted*, That for the disposal of the lands of the United States, north of the river Ohio and east of the river Mississippi, in the Indiana territory, three land-offices shall be established in the same, one at Detroit for the lands lying north of the state of Ohio to which the Indian title has been extinguished; one at Vincennes for the lands to which the Indian title has been extinguished, and which are included within the boundaries fixed by the treaty lately held with the Indian tribes of the Wabash; and one at Kaskaskia, for so much of the lands included within the boundaries fixed by the treaty of the thirteenth of August, one thousand eight hundred and three, with the Kaskaskia tribe of Indians, as is not claimed by any other Indian tribe: and for each of the said offices a register and a receiver of public monies shall be appointed, who shall give security in the same manner, in the same sums, and whose compensation, emoluments and duties, and authority, shall, in every respect, be the same in relation to the lands which shall be disposed of at their offices, as are or may be by law provided, in relation to the registers and the receivers of public monies in the several offices established for the disposal of the lands of the United States north of the river Ohio, and above the mouth of Kentucky river.

SEC. 3. *And be it further enacted*, That every person claiming lands within any of the three tracts of land described in the preceding section, by virtue of any legal grant made by the French government, prior to the treaty of Paris, of the tenth of February, one thousand seven hundred and sixty-three, or of any legal grant made by the British government, subsequent to the said treaty, and prior to the treaty of peace between the United States and Great Britain, of the third of September, one thousand seven hundred and eighty-three, or of any resolution, or act of Congress, subsequent to the said treaty of peace, shall, on or before the first day of January, one thousand eight hundred and five, deliver to the register of the land-office, within whose district the land may lie, a notice in writing, stating the nature and extent of his claims, together with a plot of the tract or tracts claimed, and may also, on or before that day, deliver to the said register, for the purpose of being recorded, every grant, order of survey, deed, conveyance, or other written evidence of his claim; and the same shall be recorded by the said register, in books to be kept for that purpose, on receiving from the parties at the rate of twelve and a half cents, for every hundred words contained in such written evidence of their claim; and if such person shall neglect to deliver such notice, in writing, of his claim, or to cause to be recorded such written evidence of the same, all his right, so far as the same is derived from any resolution or act of Congress, shall become void, and for ever be barred.

SEC. 4. *And be it further enacted*, That the register, and receiver of public monies, of the three above mentioned land-offices, shall, for the lands respectively lying within their districts, be commissioners for the purpose of examining the claims of persons claiming lands by virtue of the preceding sections. Each of the said commissioners shall, previous to entering on the duties of his appointment, respectively, take and subscribe the following oath or affirmation, before some person qualified to administer the same: "I, do solemnly swear, (or affirm,) that I will impartially exercise and discharge the duties imposed upon me, as commissioner for examining the claims to land, by an act of Congress, entitled An act making provision for the disposal of the public lands in the Indiana territory, and for other purposes."

It shall be the duty of the said commissioners to meet at the places where the said land-offices are by this act established, respectively, on or before the first day of January, one thousand eight hundred and five; and each board shall, in their respective districts, have power to bear in a summary manner all matters respecting such claims; also to compel the attendance of witnesses, to administer oaths, and examine witnesses, and such other testimony as may be adduced, and to decide thereon according to justice and equity, which decision shall be laid before Congress in the manner herein after directed, and be subject to their decision thereon. The said boards, respectively, shall have power to appoint a clerk, whose duty it shall be to enter in a book to be kept for that purpose, full and correct minutes of their proceedings and decisions, together with the evidence on which such decisions are made; which books and papers, on the dissolution of the boards, shall be deposited in the respective offices of the registers of the land-offices; and the said clerk shall prepare two transcripts of all the decisions made by the said commissioners in favour of the claimants to land, both of which shall be signed by the said commissioners, and one of which shall be transmitted to the surveyor-general, and the other to the Secretary of the Treasury; and the lands, the claims to which shall have been thus affirmed by the commissioners, shall not be otherwise disposed of, until the decision of Congress thereupon shall have been made. It shall likewise be the duty of the said commissioners to make to the Secretary of the Treasury a full report of all the claims filed with the register of the proper land-office, as above directed, which they may have rejected, together with the substance of the evidence adduced in support thereof, and such remarks thereon as they may think proper: which reports, together with the transcripts of the decisions of the commissioners in favour of claimants, shall be laid by the Secretary of the Treasury before Congress at their next ensuing session. Each of the commissioners and clerks aforesaid, shall be allowed a compensation of five hundred dollars in full for his services as such; and each of the said clerks shall, previous to his entering on the duties of his office, take and subscribe the following oath or affirmation, to wit: "I, do solemnly swear, (or affirm,) that I will truly and faithfully discharge the duties of a clerk to the board of commissioners for examining the claims to land, as enjoined by an act of Congress, entitled An act making provision for the disposal of the public lands in the Indiana territory, and for other purposes."

SEC. 5. *And be it further enacted*, That all the lands aforesaid, not excepted by virtue of the preceding section, shall, with the exception of the section "number sixteen," which shall be reserved in each township for the support of schools within the same, with the exception also of an entire township in each of the three above-described tracts of country or districts, to be located by the Secretary of the Treasury, for the use of a seminary of learning, and with the exception also of the salt springs and lands reserved for the use of the same as herein after directed, be offered for sale to the highest bidder, under the direction of the surveyor-general, or governor of the Indiana territory, of the register of the land-office, and of the receiver of public monies, at the places respectively, where the land-offices are kept, and on such day or days as shall, by a public proclamation of the President of the United States, be designated for that purpose. The sales shall remain open at each place for three weeks and no longer: the lands shall not be sold for less than two dollars an acre, and shall in every other respect, be sold in tracts of the same size and on the same terms and conditions as have been or may be by law provided for the lands sold north of the river Ohio, and above the mouth of Kentucky river. All lands, other than the reserved sections and those excepted as above mentioned, remaining unsold at the closing of the public sales, may be disposed of at private sale, by the registers of the respective land-offices, in the same manner, under the same regulations, for the same price, and on the same terms and conditions, as are or may be provided by law for the sale of the lands of the United States north of the river Ohio, and above the mouth of Kentucky river. And patents shall be obtained for all lands granted or sold in the Indiana territory, in the same manner and on the same terms as is or may be provided by law for lands sold in the state of Ohio, and in the Mississippi territory.

SEC. 6. *And be it further enacted*, That all the navigable rivers, creeks and waters, within the Indiana territory, shall be deemed to be and remain public highways; and the several salt springs in the said territory, together with as many contiguous sections to each, as shall be deemed necessary by the President of the United States, shall be reserved for the future disposal of the United States: and any grant which may hereafter be made for a tract of land, containing a salt spring which had been discovered previous to the purchase of such tract from the United States, shall be considered as fraudulent and null.

SEC. 7. *And be it further enacted*, That the several provisions made in favour of persons who have contracted for lands with John Cleves Symmes and his associates, by an act entitled "An act to extend and continue in force the provisions of an act entitled An act giving a right of pre-emption to certain persons, who have contracted with John Cleves Symmes or his associates, for lands lying between the Miami rivers in the territory northwest of the Ohio, and for other purposes," shall be and the same are hereby continued in force until the first day of June next: *Provided*, that the register of the land-office and receiver of public monies at Cincinnati shall perform the same duties, exercise the same powers, and enjoy the same emoluments, which by the last-recited act were enjoined on or vested in the commissioners designated by the said act: *And provided also*, that no certificate for a right of pre-emption shall be granted, except in favour of persons who had, before the first day of January, one thousand eight hundred, made contracts in writing with John Cleves Symmes or with any of his associates, and who had made to him or them any payment or payments of money for the purchase of such lands; nor unless at least one twentieth part of the purchase money of the land claimed, shall have previously been paid to the receiver of public monies, or shall be paid prior to the first day of January next. And every person who shall obtain a certificate of pre-emption, shall be allowed until the first day of January, one thousand eight hundred and six, to complete the payment of his first instalment: *And provided also*, that where any person or persons shall, in virtue of a contract entered into with John Cleves Symmes, have entered and made improvements on any section or half section prior to the first day of April last (having conformed with all the foregoing provisions in this section), which improvements by the running of the lines subsequently thereto shall have fallen within any section, or half section other than the one purchased as aforesaid, and other than section number sixteen, such section or half section shall in that case be granted to the person or persons who shall have so entered, improved and cultivated the same, on payment of the purchase money agreeably to the provisions made by law for lands sold at private sale: but nothing herein contained shall be construed to give to any such person or persons a greater number of acres than he or they had contracted for, with John Cleves Symmes as aforesaid.

SEC. 8. *And be it further enacted*, That every person who may have heretofore obtained from the commissioners, a certificate of a right of pre-emption for lands lying between the two Miami rivers, on account of contracts with, or purchase from John Cleves Symmes or his associates, and who has paid his first instalment; and every person, who may obtain a similar certificate by virtue of the preceding section, and shall, on or before the first day of January, one thousand eight hundred and six, pay his first instalment, be permitted to pay the residue of the purchase money in six annual equal payments.

SEC. 9. *And be it further enacted*, That fractional sections of the public lands of the United States, either north of the river Ohio, or south of the state of Tennessee, shall, under the directions of the Secretary of the Treasury, be either sold singly, or by uniting two or more together; any act to the contrary, notwithstanding: *Provided*, that no fractional sections shall be sold in that manner until after they shall have been offered for sale to the highest bidder, in the manner herein after directed.

SEC. 10. *And be it further enacted*, That all the public lands of the United States, the sale of which is authorized by law, may, after they shall have been offered for sale to the highest bidder in quarter sections, as herein after directed, be purchased at the option of the purchaser, either in entire sections, in half sections, or in quarter sections; in which two last cases the sections shall be divided into half sections by lines running due north and south, and the half sections shall be divided into quarter sections by lines running due east and west. And in every instance in which a subdivision of the lands of the United States, as surveyed in conformity with law, shall be necessary to ascertain the boundaries or true contents of the tract purchased, the same shall be done at the expense of the purchaser.

SEC. 11. *And be it further enacted*, That no interest shall be charged on any instalment which may hereafter become due, in payment for any of the public lands of the United States, wherever situated, and which have been sold in pursuance of the act, entitled "An act to amend the act entitled An act providing for the sale of the lands of the United States, in the territory northwest of the Ohio, and above the mouth of Kentucky river," or which may hereafter be sold by virtue of that, or of any other act of Congress: *Provided*, that such instalments shall be paid on the day on which the same shall become due; but the interest shall be charged and demanded in conformity with the provisions heretofore in force, from the date of the purchase on each instalment which shall not be paid on the day on which the same shall become due: *Provided however*, that on the instalments which are, or may become due before the first day of October next, interest shall not be charged, except from the time they became due until paid, but in failure to pay the said instalments on the said first day of October, interest shall be charged thereon, in conformity with the provisions heretofore in force, from the date of the purchase.

SEC. 12. *And be it further enacted*, That the sections which have been heretofore reserved, and are by this act directed to be sold, also, the fractional sections, classed as is by the ninth section of this act directed, and all the other lands of the United States, north of the Ohio, and above the mouth of Kentucky river, shall be offered for sale in quarter sections, to the highest bidder, under the directions of the register of the land-office, and of the receiver of public monies, at the places, respectively, where the land-offices are kept, that is to say; the lands in the districts of Chilicothe, on the first Monday of May; the lands in the district of Marietta, on the second Monday of May; the lands in the district of Zanesville, on the third Monday of May; the, lands in the district of Steubenville, on the second Monday of June; and the lands in the district of Cincinnati, on the first Monday of September. The sales shall remain open at each place no longer than three weeks; the lands which may be thus sold, shall not be sold for less than two dollars per acre, and shall, in every other respect be sold on the same terms and conditions, as is provided for the sale of lands sold at private sale. And all the other public lands of the United States, either north of the Ohio, or south of the state of Tennessee, which are directed to be sold at public sale, shall be offered for sale to the highest bidder, in quarter sections: *Provided however*, that section number twenty-six of the third township of the second fractional range within the grant made by the United States to John Cleves Symmes, on which is erected a mill-dam, is hereby granted to Joseph Vanhorne, the proprietor of the said dam; and also, that section number twenty-nine of the second township of the fourth entire range, be granted to James Sutton; and also, that section number twenty-one of the ninth township of the twenty-first range, be granted to Christian Van Gundy, on their payment of the purchase money, agreeably to the provisions made by law, for lands sold at private sale.

SEC. 13. *And be it further enacted*, That whenever any of the public lands shall have been surveyed in the manner directed by law, they shall be divided by the Secretary of the Treasury into convenient surveying districts, and a deputy surveyor shall, with the approbation of the said secretary, be appointed by the surveyor-general for each district, who shall take an oath or affirmation truly and faithfully to perform the duties of his office; and whose duty it shall be to run and mark such lines as may be necessary for subdividing the lands surveyed as aforesaid, into sections, half sections or quarter sections, as the case may be; to ascertain the true contents of such subdivisions; and to record in a book to be kept for that purpose, the surveys thus made. The surveyor-general shall furnish each deputy surveyor with a copy of the plat of the townships and fractional parts of townships contained in his district, describing the subdivisions thereof, and the marks of the corners. Each deputy surveyor shall be entitled to receive from the purchaser of any tract of land, of which a line or lines shall have been run and marked by him, at the rate of three dollars for every mile thus surveyed and marked, before he shall deliver to him a copy of the plat of such tract, stating its contents. The fees payable by virtue of former laws for surveying expenses shall, after the first day of July next, be no longer demandable from, and paid by the purchasers. And no final certificate shall thereafter be given by the register of any land-office to the purchaser of any tract of land, all the lines of which shall not have been run, and the contents ascertained by the surveyor-general or his assistants, unless such purchaser shall lodge with the said register a plat of such tract, certified by the district surveyor.

SEC. 14. *And be it further enacted*, That from and after the first day of April next, each of the registers and receivers of public monies of the several land-offices established by law, either north of the river Ohio, or south of the state of Tennessee, shall, in addition to the commission heretofore allowed, receive one half per cent on all the monies paid for public lands sold in their respective offices, and an annual salary of five hundred dollars, the register and receiver of the land-office at Marietta excepted, the annual salary of whom shall be two hundred dollars. And from and after the same day the fees payable by virtue of former laws, to the registers of the several land-offices, for the entry of lands and for certificates of monies paid, shall no longer be demandable from nor paid by the purchasers of public lands. And it shall be the duty of the Secretary of the Treasury to cause, at least once every year, the books of the officers of the land-offices to be examined, and the balance of public monies in the hands of the several receivers of public monies of the said offices, to be ascertained.

SEC. 15. *And be it further enacted*, That from and after the first day of April next, the fees heretofore payable for patents for lands, shall no longer be paid by the purchasers. And it shall be the duty of every register of a land office on application of the party, to transmit, by mail, to the register of the treasury, the final certificate granted by such register to the purchaser of any tract of land sold at his office: and it shall be the duty of the register of the treasury, on receiving any such certificate, to obtain and transmit, by mail, to the register of the proper land-office, the patent to which such purchaser is entitled; but, in every such instance, the party shall previously pay to the proper deputy postmaster, the postage accruing on the transmission of such certificate and patent.

SEC. 16. *And be it further enacted*, That the President of the United States shall have full power to appoint and commission the several registers and receivers of public monies of the land-offices established by this act, in the recess of Congress; and their commissions shall continue in force until the end of the session of Congress next ensuing such appointment.

SEC. 17. *And be it further enacted*, That the several superintendents of the public sales directed by this act, shall receive six dollars each, for each day's attendance on the said sales.

SEC. 18. *And be it further enacted*, That a sum not exceeding twenty thousand dollars be, and the same is hereby appropriated, for the purpose of carrying this act into effect; which sum shall be paid out of any unappropriated monies in the treasury.

APPROVED, March 26, 1804.

Source: *United States Statutes at Large*. Vol. 2. Edited by Richard Peters. Boston: Charles C. Little and James Brown, 1845.

DOCUMENT 32

LOUISIANA ERECTED INTO TWO TERRITORIES AND TEMPORARY GOVERNMENTS ESTABLISHED

An Act erecting Louisiana into two territories, and providing for the temporary government thereof.

Be it enacted by the Senate and House of Representatives of the United States of America in Congress assembled, That all that portion of country ceded by France to the United States, under the name of Louisiana, which lies south of the Mississippi territory, and of an east and west line to commence on the Mississippi river, at the thirty-third degree of north latitude, and to extend west to the western boundary of the said cession, shall constitute a territory of the United States, under the name of the territory of Orleans; the government whereof shall be organized and administered as follows:

SEC. 2. The executive power shall be vested in a governor, who shall reside in the said territory, and hold his office during the term of three years, unless sooner removed by the President of the United States. He shall be commander in chief of the militia of the said territory; shall have power to grant pardons for offenses against the said territory, and reprieves for those against the United States, until the decision of the President of the United States thereon, shall be made known; and to appoint and commission all officers civil and of the militia, whose appointments are not herein otherwise provided for, and which shall be established by law. He shall take care that the laws be faithfully executed.

SEC. 3. A secretary of the territory shall also be appointed, who shall hold his office during the term of four years, unless sooner removed by the President of the United States, whose duty it shall be, under the direction of the governor, to record and preserve All the papers and proceedings of the executive, and all the acts of the governor and legislative council and transmit authentic copies of the Proceedings of the Governor in his executive department, every six months, to the President of the United States. In case of the vacancy of the office of governor, the government of the said territory shall devolve on the secretary.

SEC. 4. The legislative powers shall be vested in the governor, and in thirteen of the most fit and discreet persons in the territory, to be called the legislative council, who shall be appointed annually by the President of the United States from among those holding real estate therein, and who shall have resided one year at least, in the said territory, and hold no office of profit under the territory or the United States. The governor, by and with advice and consent of the said legislative council, or of a majority of them, shall have power to alter, modify, or repeal the laws which may be in force at the commencement of this act. Their legislative powers shall also extend to all the rightful subjects of legislation; but no law shall be valid which is inconsistent with the constitution and laws of the United States, or which shall lay any person under restraint, burthen, or disability, on account of his religious opinions, professions or worship; in all which he shall be free to maintain his own, and not burthened for those of another. The governor shall publish throughout the said territory, all the laws which shall be made, and shall from time to time, report the same to the President of the United States, to be laid before Congress; which, if disapproved of by Congress, shall thenceforth be of no force. The governor or legislative council shall have no power over the primary disposal of the soil, nor to tax the lands of the United States, nor to interfere with the claims to and within the said territory. The governor shall convene and prorogue the legislative council, whenever he may deem it expedient. It shall be his duty to obtain all the information in his power, in relation to the customs, habits, and dispositions of the inhabitants of the said territory and communicate the same from time to time, to the President of the United States.

SEC. 5. The judicial power shall be vested in a superior court, and in such inferior courts, and justices of the peace, as the legislature of the territory may from time to time establish. The judges of the superior court and the justices of the peace, shall hold their offices for the term of four years. The superior court shall consist of three judges, any one of whom shall constitute a court; they shall have jurisdiction in all criminal cases, and exclusive jurisdiction in all those which are capital; and original and appellate jurisdiction in all civil cases of the value of one hundred dollars. Its sessions shall commence on the first Monday of every month, and continue till all the business depending before them shall be disposed of. They shall appoint their own clerk. In all criminal prosecutions which are capital, the trial shall be by a jury of twelve good and lawful men of the vicinage: and in all cases criminal and civil in the superior court, the trial shall be by a jury, if either of the parties require it. The inhabitants of the said territory shall be entitled to the benefits of the writ of habeas corpus; they shall be bailable, unless for capital offenses where the proof shall be evident, or the presumption great; and no cruel and unusual punishments shall be inflicted.

SEC. 6. The governor, secretary, judges, district attorney, marshal, and all general officers of the militia, shall be appointed by the President of the United States, in the recess of the Senate; but shall be nominated at their next meeting for their advice and consent. The governor, secretary, judges, members of the legislative council, justices of the peace, and all other officers, civil and of the militia, before they enter upon the duties of their respective offices, shall take an oath or affirmation to support the constitution of the United States, and for the faithful discharge of the duties of their office; the governor, before the President of the United States, or before a judge of the supreme or district court of the United States, or before such other person as the President of the United States shall authorize to administer the same; the secretary, judges, and members of the legislative council, before the governor; and all other officers before such persons as the governor shall direct. The governor shall receive an annual salary of five thousand dollars; the secretary of two thousand dollars, and the judges of two thousand dollars each, to be paid quarter yearly out of the revenues of impost and tonnage, accruing within the said territory. The members of the legislative council shall receive four dollars each per day, during their attendance in council.

SEC. 7. *And be it further enacted*, That the following acts, that is to say:

An act for the punishment of certain crimes against the United States.

An act, in addition to an act, for the punishment of certain crimes against the United States.

An act to prevent citizens of the United States from privateering against nations in amity with, or against citizens of the United States.

An act for the punishment of certain crimes therein specified.

An act respecting fugitives from justice, and persons escaping from service of their masters.

An act to prohibit the carrying on the slave trade from the United States to any foreign place or country.

An act to prevent the importation of certain persons into certain states, where by the laws thereof, their admission is prohibited.

An act to establish the post-office of the United States.

An act further to alter and establish certain post roads, and for the more secure carriage of the mail of the United States.

An act for the more general promulgation of the laws of the United States.

An act, in addition to an act, intituled an act for the more general promulgation of the laws of the United States.

An act to promote the progress of useful arts, and to repeal the act heretofore made for that purpose.

An act to extend the privilege of obtaining patents for useful discoveries and inventions to certain persons therein mentioned, and to enlarge and define the penalties for violating the rights of patentees.

An act for the encouragement of learning, by securing the copies of maps, charts, and books, to the authors and proprietors of such copies, during the time therein mentioned.

An act, supplementary to an act, intituled An act for the encouragement of learning, by securing the copies of maps, charts, and books, to the authors and proprietors of such copies, during the time therein mentioned; and extending the benefits thereof to the arts of designing, engraving, and etching historical and other prints.

An act providing for salvage in cases of recapture.

An act respecting alien enemies.

An act to prescribe the mode in which the public acts, records, and judicial proceedings in each state shall be authenticated, so as to take effect in every other state.

An act for establishing trading houses with the Indian tribes.

An act for continuing in force a law, entitled An act for establishing trading houses with the Indian tribes. And

An act making provision relative to rations for Indians, and to their visits to the seat of government, shall extend to, and have full force and effect in the above mentioned territories.

SEC. 8. There shall be established in the said territory a district court, to consist of one judge, who shall reside therein, and be called the district judge, and who shall hold, in the city of Orleans, four sessions annually; the first to commence on the third Monday in October next, and the three other sessions, progressively, on the third Monday of every third calendar month thereafter. He shall, in all things, have and exercise the same jurisdiction and powers, which are by law given to, or may be exercised by the judge of Kentucky district; and shall be allowed an annual compensation of two thousand dollars, to be paid quarter yearly out of the revenues of impost and tonnage accruing within the said territory. He shall appoint a clerk for the said district, who shall reside, and keep the records of the court, in the city of Orleans, and shall receive for the services performed by him, the same fees to which the clerk of Kentucky district is entitled for similar services.

There shall be appointed in the said district, a person learned in the law, to act as attorney for the United States, who shall, in addition to his stated fees, be paid six hundred dollars, annually, as a full compensation for all extra services. There shall also be appointed a marshal for the said district, who shall perform the same duties, be subject to the same regulations and penalties, and be entitled to the same fees to which marshals in other districts are entitled for similar services; and shall moreover be paid two hundred dollars, annually, as a compensation for all extra services.

SEC. 9. All free male white persons, who are housekeepers, and who shall have resided one year, at least, in the said territory, shall be qualified to serve as grand or petit jurors, in the courts of the said territory; and they shall, until the legislature thereof shall otherwise direct, be selected in such manner as the judges of the said courts, respectively, shall prescribe, so as to be most conducive to an impartial trial, and to be least burthensome to the inhabitants of the said territory.

SEC. 10. It shall not be lawful for any person or persons to import or bring into the said territory, from any port or place without the limits of the United States, or cause or procure to be so imported or brought, or knowingly to aid or assist in so importing or bringing any slave or slaves. And every person so offending, and being thereof convicted before any court within said territory, having competent jurisdiction, shall forfeit and pay for each and every slave so imported or brought, the sum of three hundred dollars; one moiety for the use of the United States, and the other moiety for the use of the person or persons who shall sue for the same; and every slave so imported or brought, shall thereupon become entitled to, and receive his or her freedom. It shall not be lawful for any person or persons to import or bring into the said territory, from any port or place within the limits of the United States, or to cause or procure to be so imported or brought, or knowingly to aid or assist in so importing or bringing any slave or slaves, which shall have been imported since the first day of May, one thousand seven hundred and ninety-eight, into any port or place within the limits of the United States, or which may hereafter be so imported, from any port or place without the limits of the United States; and every person so offending, and being thereof convicted before any court within said territory, having competent jurisdiction, shall forfeit and pay for each and every slave so imported or brought, the sum of three hundred dollars, one moiety for the use of the United States, and the other moiety for the use of the person or persons who shall sue for the same; and no slave or slaves shall directly or indirectly be introduced into said territory, except by a citizen of the United States, removing into said territory for actual settlement, and being at the time of such removal bona fide owner of such slave or slaves; and every slave imported or brought into the said territory, contrary to the provisions of this act, shall thereupon be entitled to, and receive his or her freedom.

SEC. 11. The laws in force in the said territory, at the commencement of this act, and not inconsistent with the provisions thereof, shall continue in force, until altered, modified, or repealed by the legislature.

SEC. 12. The residue of the province of Louisiana, ceded to the United States, shall be called the district of Louisiana, the government whereof shall be organized and administered as follows:

The executive power now vested in the governor of the Indiana territory, shall extend to, and be exercised in the said district of Louisiana. The governor and judges of the Indiana territory shall have power to establish, in the said district of Louisiana, inferior courts, and prescribe their jurisdiction and duties, and to make all laws which they may deem conducive to the good government of the inhabitants thereof: Provided however, that no law shall be valid which is inconsistent with the constitution and laws of the United States, or which shall lay any person under restraint or disability on account of his religious opinions, profession, or worship; in all of which he shall be free to maintain his own, and not burthened for those of another: And provided also, that in all criminal prosecutions, the trial shall be by a jury of twelve good and lawful men of the vicinage, and in all civil cases of the value of one hundred dollars, the trial shall be by jury, if either of the parties require it. The judges of the Indiana territory, or any two of them, shall hold annually two courts within the said district, at such place as will be most convenient to the inhabitants thereof in general, shall possess the same jurisdiction they now possess in the Indiana territory, and shall continue in session until all the business depending before them shall be disposed of. It shall be the duty of the secretary of the Indiana territory to record and preserve all the papers and proceedings of the governor, of an executive nature, relative to the district of Louisiana, and transmit authentic copies thereof every six months to the President of the United States. The governor shall publish throughout the said district, all the laws which may be made as aforesaid, and shall from time to time report the same to the President of the United States, to be laid before Congress, which, if disapproved of by Congress, shall thenceforth cease, and be of no effect.

The said district of Louisiana shall be divided into districts by the governor, under the direction of the President, as the convenience of the settlements shall require, subject to such alterations hereafter as experience may prove more convenient. The inhabitants of each district, between the ages of eighteen and forty-five, shall be formed into a militia, with proper officers, according to their numbers, to be appointed by the governor, except the commanding officer, who shall be appointed by the President, and who whether a captain, a major or a colonel, shall be the commanding officer of the district, and as such, shall, under the governor, have command of the regular officers and troops in his district, as well as of the militia, for which he shall have a brevet commission, giving him such command, and the pay and emoluments of an officer of the same grade in the regular army; he shall be specially charged with the employment of the military and militia of his district, in cases of sudden invasion or insurrection, and until the orders of the governor can be received, and at all times with the duty of ordering a military patrol, aided by militia if necessary, to arrest unauthorized settlers in any part of his district, and to commit such offenders to jail to be dealt with according to law.

SEC. 13. The laws in force in the said district of Louisiana, at the commencement of this act, and not inconsistent with any of the provisions thereof, shall continue in force until altered, modified or repealed by the governor and judges of the Indiana territory, as aforesaid.

SEC. 14. And be it further enacted, That all grants for lands within the territories ceded by the French Republic to the United States, by the treaty of the thirtieth of April, in the year one thousand eight hundred and three, the title whereof was, at the date of the treaty of St. Ildefonso, in the crown, government or nation of Spain, and every act and proceeding subsequent thereto, of whatsoever nature, towards the obtaining any grant, title, or claim to such lands, and under whatsoever authority transacted, or pretended, be, and the same are hereby declared to be, and to have been from the beginning, null, void, and of no effect in law or equity. Provided nevertheless, that anything in this section contained shall not be construed to make null and void any bona fide grant, made agreeably to the laws, usages and customs of the Spanish government to an actual settler on the lands so granted, for himself, and for his wife and family; or to make null and void any bona fide act or proceeding done by an actual settler agreeably to the laws, usages and customs of the Spanish government, to obtain a grant for lands actually settled on by the person or persons claiming title thereto, if such settlement in either case was actually made prior to the twentieth day of December, one thousand eight hundred and three: And provided further, that such grant shall not secure to the grantee or his assigns more than one mile square of land, together with such other and further quantity as heretofore hath been allowed for the wife and family of such actual settler, agreeably to the laws, usages and customs of the Spanish government. And that if any citizen of the United States, or other person, shall make a settlement on any lands belonging to the United States, within the limits of Louisiana, or shall survey, or attempt to survey, such lands, or to designate boundaries by marking trees, or otherwise, such offender shall, on conviction thereof, in any court of record of the United States, or the territories of the United States, forfeit a sum not exceeding one thousand dollars, and suffer imprisonment not exceeding twelve months; and it shall, moreover, be lawful for the President of the United States to employ such military force as he may judge necessary to remove from lands belonging to the United States any such citizen or other person, who shall attempt a settlement thereon.

SEC. 15. The President of the United States is hereby authorized to stipulate with any Indian tribes owning lands on the east side of the Mississippi, and residing thereon, for an exchange of lands, the property of the United States, on the west side of the Mississippi, in case the said tribes shall remove and settle thereon; but in such stipulation, the said tribes shall acknowledge themselves to be under the protection of the United States, and shall agree that they will not hold any treaty with any foreign power, individual state, or with the individuals of any state or power; and that they will not sell or dispose of the said lands, or any part thereof, to any sovereign power, except the United States, nor to the subjects or citizens of any other sovereign power, nor to the citizens of the United States. And in order to maintain peace and tranquillity with the Indian tribes who reside within the limits of Louisiana, as ceded by France to the United States, the act of Congress, passed on the thirtieth day of March, one thousand eight hundred and two, entitled "An act to regulate trade and intercourse with the Indian tribes, and to preserve peace on the frontiers," is hereby extended to the territories erected and established by this act; and the sum of fifteen thousand dollars of any money in the treasury not otherwise appropriated by law, is hereby appropriated to enable the President of the United States to effect the object expressed in this section.

SEC. 16. The act, passed on the thirty-first day of October, one thousand eight hundred and three, entitled "An act to enable the President of the United States to take possession of the territories ceded by France to the United States, by the treaty concluded at Paris, on the thirtieth day of April last, and for the temporary government thereof," shall continue in force until the first day of October next, any thing therein to the contrary notwithstanding; on which said first day of October, this act shall commence, and have full force, and shall continue in force for and during the term of one year, and to the end of the next session of Congress which may happen thereafter.

APPROVED, March 26, 1804

Source: *United States Statutes at Large*. Vol. 2. Edited by Richard Peters. Boston: Charles C. Little and James Brown, 1845.

DOCUMENT 33

THOMAS JEFFERSON'S FOURTH ANNUAL MESSAGE TO THE CONGRESS (NOVEMBER 8, 1804)

To the Senate and House of Representatives of the United States:

To a people, fellow-citizens, who sincerely desire the happiness and prosperity of other nations; to those who justly calculate that their own well-being is advanced by that of the nations with which they have intercourse, it will be a satisfaction to observe that the war which was lighted up Europe a little before our last meeting has not yet extended its flames to other nations, nor been marked by the calamities which sometimes stain the footsteps of war. The irregularities, too on the ocean, which generally harass the commerce of neutral nations, have in distant parts, disturbed ours less than on former occasions; but in the American seas they have been greater from peculiar causes, and even within our harbors and jurisdiction infringements on the authority of the laws have been committed which have called for serious attention The friendly conduct of the Governments from whose officers and subjects these acts have proceeded, in other respects and in places more under their observation and control, gives us confidence that our representations on this subject will have been completely regarded.

While noticing the irregularities committed on the ocean by others, those on our own part should not be omitted nor left unprovided for. Complaints have been received that persons residing within the United States have taken on themselves to arm merchant vessels and to force a commerce into certain ports and countries in defiance of the laws of those countries in defiance of the laws of those countries. That individuals should undertake to wage private war, independently of the authority of their country, can not be permitted in a well-ordered society. Its tendency to produce aggression on the laws and rights of other nations and to endanger the peace of our own is so oblivious that I doubt not you will adopt measures for restraining it effectually in future.

Soon after the passage of the act of the last session authorizing the establishment of a district and a port of entry on the waters of the Mobile we learnt that its object was misunderstood on the part of Spain. Candid explanations were immediately given and assurances that, reserving our claims in that quarter as a subject of discussion and arrangement with Spain, no act was mediated in the meantime inconsistent with peace and friendship existing between the two nations, and that conformably to these intentions would be the execution of the law. That Government had, however, thought proper to suspend the ratification of the convention of 1802; but the explanations which would reach them soon after, and still more the confirmation of them by the tenor of the instrument establishing the port and district, may reasonably be expected to replace them in the dispositions and views of the whole subject which originally dictated the convention.

I have the satisfaction to inform you that the objections which had been urged by that Government against the validity of our title to the country of Louisiana have been withdrawn, its exact limits, however, remaining still to be settled between us; and to this is to be added that having prepared and delivered the stock created in execution of the convention of Paris of April 30, 1803. In consideration of the cession of that country, we have received from the Government of France an acknowledgment in due form, of the fulfillment of that stipulation.

With the nations of Europe in general our friendship and intercourse are undisturbed, and from the Governments of the belligerent powers especially we continue to receive those friendly manifestations which are justly due to an honest neutrality and to such good offices consistent with that as we have opportunities of rendering.

The activity and success of the small force employed in the Mediterranean in the early part of the present year, the reenforcements sent into that sea, and the energy of the officers having command in the several vessels will, I trust, by the sufferings of war, reduce the barbarians of Tripoli to the desire of peace on proper terms. Great injury, however, ensues to ourselves, as well as to others interested, from the distance to which prizes must be brought for adjudication and from the impracticability of bringing hither such as are not seaworthy.

The Bey of Tunis having made requisitions unauthorized by our treaty, their rejection has produced from him some expressions of discontent. But to those who expect us to calculate whether a compliance with unjust demands will not cost us less than a war we must leave as a question of calculation for them also whether to retire from unjust demands will not cost them less than a war. We can do to each other very sensible injuries by war, but mutual advantages of peace make that the best interest of both.

Peace and intercourse with other powers on the same coast continue on the footing on which they are established by treaty.

In pursuance of the act providing for the temporary government of Louisiana, the necessary officers for the Territory of Orleans were appointed in due time to commence the exercise of their functions on the 1st. day of October. The distance, however, of some of them and indispensable previous arrangements may have retarded its commencement in some of its parts. The form of government thus provided having been considered but as temporary, and open to such future improvements as further information of the circumstances of our brethren there might suggest, it will of course be subject to your consideration.

In the District of Louisiana it has been thought best to adopt the division into subordinate districts which had been established under its former government. These being five in number, a commanding officer has been appointed to each, according to the provisions of the law, and so soon as they can be at their stations that district will also be in its due state of organization. In the meantime their places are supplied by the officers commanding there. And the functions of the governor and judges of Indiana having commenced, the government, we presume is preceding in its new form. The lead mines in that district offer so rich a supply of that metal as to merit attention. The report now communicated will inform you of their state and of the necessity of immediate inquiry into their occupation and titles.

With the Indian tribes established within our newly acquired limits, I have deemed it necessary to open conferences for the purpose of establishing a good understanding and neighborly relations between us. So far as we have yet learned, we have reason to believe that their dispositions on their part, we have in our own hands means which can not fail us for preserving their peace and friendship. By pursuing an uniform course of justice toward them, by aiding them in all the improvements which may better their condition, and especially by establishing a commerce on terms which shall be advantageous to them and only not losing to us, and so regulated as that no incendiaries of our own or any other nation may be permitted to disturb the natural effects of our just and friendly offices, we may render ourselves so necessary to their comfort and prosperity that the protection of our citizens from their disorderly members will become their interest and their voluntary care. Instead, therefore, of an augmentation of military force proportioned to our extension of frontier, I propose a moderate enlargement of the capital employed in that commerce as a more effectual, economical, and humane instrument for preserving peace and good neighborhood with them.

On this side of the Mississippi an important relinquishment of native title has been received from the Delawares. That tribe, desiring to extinguish in their people the spirit of hunting and to convert superfluous lands into the means of improving what they retain, has ceded to us all the country between Wabash and Ohio south of and including the road from the rapids toward Vincennes, for which they are to receive annuities in animals and implements for agriculture and in other necessaries. This acquisition is important, not only for its extent and fertility, but as fronting 300 miles on the Ohio, and near half that on the Wabash. The produce of the settled country descending those rivers will no longer pass in review of the Indian frontier but in a small portion, and, with the cession heretofore made by the Kaskaskias, nearly consolidates our possessions north of the Ohio, in a very respectful breadth-from Lake Erie to the Mississippi. The Piankeshaws having some claim to the country ceded by the Delawares, it has been thought best to keep quiet that by fair purchase also. So soon as the treaties on this subject shall have received their constitutional sanctions they shall be laid before both Houses.

The act of Congress of February 28, 1803, for building and employing a number of gunboats, is now in a course of execution to the extent there provided for. The obstacle to naval enterprise which vessels of this construction offer for our seaport towns, their utility toward supporting within our waters the authority of the laws, the promptness with which they will be manned by the seamen and militia of the place in the moment they are wanting, the facility of their assembling from different parts of the coast to any point where they are required in greater force than ordinary, the economy of their maintenance and preservation from decay when not in actual service, and the competence of our finances to this defensive provision without any new burthen are considerations which will have due weight with Congress in deciding on the expediency of adding to their number from year to year, as experience shall test their utility, until all our important harbors, by these and auxiliary means, shall be secured against insult and opposition to the laws.

No circumstance has arisen since your last session which calls for any augmentation of our regular military force. Should any improvement occur in militia system, that will be always seasonable.

Accounts of the receipts and expenditures of the last year, with estimates for the ensuing one, will as usual be laid before you.

The state of our finances continues to fulfill our expectations. Eleven millions and a half of dollars, received in the course of the year ending the 30th of September last, have enabled us, us, after meeting all the ordinary expenses of the year, to pay upward of $3,600,000 of the public debt, exclusive of interest. This payment, with those of the two preceding years, has extinguished upward of twelve millions of the principle and a greater sum of interest within that period, and by a proportionate diminution of interest renders already sensible the effect of the growing sum yearly applicable to the discharge of the principle.

It is also ascertained that the revenue accrued during the last year exceeds that of the preceding, and the probable receipts of the ensuing year may safely be relied on as sufficient, with the sum already in the Treasury, to meet all the current demands of the year, to discharge upwards of three millions and a half of the engagements incurred under the British and French conventions, and to advance in the further redemption of the funded debt as rapidly as had been contemplated. These, fellow-citizens, are the principle matters which I have thought it necessary at this time to communicate for your consideration and attention. Some others will be laid before you in the course of the session; but in the discharge of the great duties confided to you by our country you will take a broader view of the field of legislation. Whether the great interests of agriculture, manufactures, commerce, or navigation can within the pale of your constitutional powers be aided in any of their relations; whether laws are provided in all cases where they are wanting; whether those provided are exactly what they should be; whether any abuses take place in their administration, or in that of the public revenues; whether the organization of the public agents or of the public force is perfect in all its parts; in fine, whether anything can be done to advance the general good, are questions within the limits of your functions which will necessarily occupy your attention. In these and all other matters which you in your wisdom may propose for the good of our country you may count with assurance on my hearty cooperation and faithful execution.

TH. JEFFERSON

Source: Richardson, James D., ed. 1897. *A Compilation of the Messages and Papers of the Presidents Prepared under the Direction of the Joint Committee on Printing, of the House and Senate Pursuant to an Act of the Fifty-Second Congress of the United States*. New York: Bureau of National Literature.

DOCUMENT 34

THE UNITED STATES ANNEXES WEST FLORIDA (1810)

By the President of the United States of America.

A PROCLAMATION.

Whereas the territory south of the Mississippi Territory and eastward to the river Mississippi, and extending to the river Perdido, of which possession was not delivered to the United States in pursuance of the treaty concluded at Paris on the 30th of April 1803, has, at all times, as is well known, been considered and claimed by them, as being within the colony of Louisiana conveyed by the said treaty, in the same extent that it had in the hands of Spain, and that it had when France originally possessed it;

And whereas the acquiescence of the United States in the temporary continuance of the said Territory under the Spanish authority was not the result of any distrust of their title, as has been particularly evinced by the general tenor of their laws, and by the distinction made in the application of those laws between that Territory and foreign countries, but was occasioned by their conciliatory views, and by a confidence in the justice of their cause, and in the success of candid discussion and amicable negotiation with a just and friendly Power;

And whereas a satisfactory adjustment, too long delayed, without the fault of the United States, has for some time been entirely suspended by events over which they had no control; and whereas a crisis has at length arrived subversive of the order of things under the Spanish authorities, whereby a failure of the United States to take the said Territory into its possession may lead to events ultimately contravening the views of both parties, whilst, in the mean time, the tranquility and security of our adjoining Territories are endangered, and new facilities given to violators of our revenue and commercial laws, and of those prohibiting the introduction of slaves:

Considering, moreover, that under these peculiar and imperative circumstances, a forbearance on the part of the United States to occupy the Territory in question, and thereby guard against the confusions and contingencies which threaten it, might be construed into a dereliction of their title, or an insensibility to the importance of the stake: Considering that in the hands of the United States it will not cease to be a subject of fair and friendly negotiation and adjustment: Considering, finally, that the acts of Congress, though contemplating a present possession by a foreign authority, have contemplated also an eventual possession of the said Territory by the United States, and are according so framed as, in that case, to extend in their operation to the same:

Now, be it known, that I, JAMES MADISON, President of the United States of America, in pursuance of these weighty and urgent considerations, have deemed it right and requisite that possession should be taken of the said Territory, in the name and behalf of the United States. William C.C. Claiborne, Governor of the Orleans Territory, of which the said Territory is to be taken as part, will accordingly proceed to execute the same, and to exercise over the said Territory the authorities and functions legally appertaining to his office. And the good people inhabiting the same are invited and enjoined to pay due respect, to him in that character, to be obedient to the laws, to maintain order, to cherish harmony, and in every manner to conduct themselves as peaceable citizens, under full assurance that they will be protected, in the enjoyment of their liberty, property, and religion.

In testimony whereof, I have caused the seal of the United States to be hereunto affixed, and signed the same with my hand.

Done at the City of Washington, the twenty-seventh day of October, A.D. 1810, and in the thirty-fifth year of the independence of the said United States.

JAMES MADISON
United States.
By the President: [seal]
R. SMITH, *Secretary of State*

Source: *Annals of Congress,* 11th Cong., 3rd sess. Washington: Gales and Seaton, 1856.

DOCUMENT 35

PETITION FROM WEST FLORIDA RESIDENTS TO THE CONGRESS

[Communicated to the House, November 20, 1811.]
To the Honorable the Senate and House of Representatives of the United States:

We, the inhabitants of West Florida, your petitioners, represent to your honorable body, that, while we rejoice in the late event which has brought about our emancipation from the iron shackles of despotism, or rather released us from the more horrid calamities of anarchy, we still labor under the painful apprehension that your enlightened body will either continue us a separate Territory, or attach as to the Territory of New Orleans, instead of incorporating us with the Mississippi Territory, which we most ardently wish, for the following reasons:

The geographical and relative situation of West Florida and the Mississippi Territory plead powerfully in favor of the measure. The climate, the soil, the peoples. the manners, and the politics of both countries, are the same, being only divided by an ideal boundary. We are all Americans by birth, and in principle; but if we are united with the Territory of Orleans, we will be subjected to all the inconveniences and miseries resulting from a difference of people, language, manners, custom, and politics. The safety, and, indeed, the political salvation of the Government of the United States, entirely depend on the unanimity of all its parts, which is best insured by combining persons and things homogeneous in their nature. If this be true, and if West Florida and the Territory of Orleans differ in every material respect, (of which there can be no doubt,) it. follows that a coalition of the two countries would be productive of discord, the evil genius of republican Governments.

Your petitioners are aware of the policy suggested by some, of adding us, who are all Americans, to the people of the Territory of Orleans, who are chiefly French, in order to counteract the French influence. This may be sound policy, but to make us the instruments of effecting that object, at the same time that it might be advantageous to the United States in general, it would be destructive to our individual happiness; a sacrifice too great, we trust, to be required of us to make by a Government wise in its Constitution, and just in its Administration.

If, to counteract French influence, and subvert French politics, by populating the country with Americans, be the policy of the Government, your petitioners conceive that object will be shortly effected by the very great emigration of Americans from all parts of the United States. If those emigrants are subjected to all the inconveniences which we deprecate from a similar connexion, the case is not so hard with them as, it would be with us, because they have voluntarily chosen that situation.

But, waiving all objection on the score of dissimilarity betwixt us and the people of Orleans, nature herself seems to have thrown a barrier in the way to oppose the union. The city of New Orleans is, and in all probability will continue to be, the seat of government of that country; where, of course, all public business must be transacted, and which will, therefore, induce the necessity of the personal attendance of a great proportion of the people within the jurisdiction of that government, at the city of New Orleans; which will be extremely inconvenient to the inhabitants of West Florida on account of the largeness and difficult navigation of Lake Pontchartrain, which completely insulates us from the city of New Orleans.

If, however, your honorable body should deem it unadvisable to attach us to the Territory of Orleans, in order to prevent a measure calculated to continue us under a separate Territorial government, we beg leave to state that, owing to the local situation of our country, it is not susceptible of a thick settlement; that, if it were settled with as many persons as the nature of the country will admit, yet we do not believe there would be wealth enough among us to defray the expenses of a government, without operating a very serious injury to us. But, admitting we are able to bear the expenses of a Territorial government, if the Mississippi Territory, and the Territory of Orleans should become States, independent of us, we would forever remain a Territory; for, neither in point of numbers nor in point of extent of country would we ever arrive at the proud magnitude of claiming an admission into the Union as a free, sovereign and independent State. Our only hope of participating with the rest of our brethren on the Continent in the rights and blessings of State sovereignty, is built upon the pleasing anticipation of becoming a part of the Mississippi Territory: By that means, independent of our own individual interests, the Mississippi Territory will derive the advantage of an extensive seacoast, of which she will otherwise be deprived.

For the foregoing reasons, we humbly trust that your honorable body will grant our request, by adding all that tract of country now in possession, by virtue of the President's proclamation of 1810, to the Mississippi Territory.

There is also another subject in which your petitioners are deeply interested to which we beg leave to call your attention. Your petitioners have generally emigrated to this country since the cession of Louisiana to the United States. When possession of New Orleans, and that of the country west of the Mississippi was taken, and the Province of West Florida left in possession and under the exclusive jurisdiction of Spain, we took it for granted that the Government of the United States either did not claim, or, if they did, meant not to insist upon their claim to West Florida; we, therefore, have made settlements on lands, under the rules and forms of the Spanish Government, expecting to hold our lands to ourselves and our heirs forever. We, therefore, pray your honorable body to confirm to us our settlement rights, made between the time of the cession of Louisiana, until the time of taking possession of West Florida, wherever they have been made bona fide, and not with an intention to monopolize unreasonable quantities of lands, under such regulations as may best comport with the wisdom and justice of Congress.

We humbly trust that your enlightened body will grant this request, when you take into view all the circumstances which it involves. The consequences to us and our families are all important. If we are deprived of our possessions we are deprived of our property; and consequently, will be reduced to the extremes of want and wretchedness.

GEORGE PATTERSON

And four hundred and ten others.

Source: *Annals of Congress,* 12th Cong., 1st sess. Washington: Gales and Seaton, 1856.

DOCUMENT 36

TREATY OF PORTAGE DES SIOUX (1815)

A TREATY OF PEACE AND FRIENDSHIP,

Made and concluded between William Clark, Ninian Edwards, and Auguste Chouteau, Commissioners Plenipotentiary of the United States of America, on the part and behalf of the said States, of the one part; and the undersigned Chiefs and Warriors of the Siouxs of the Lakes, on the part and behalf of their Tribe, of the other part.

The parties being desirous of re-establishing peace and friendship between the United States and the said tribe, and of being placed in all things, and in every respect, on the same footing upon which they stood before the late war between the United States and Great Britain, have agreed to the following articles:

ARTICLE 1. Every injury, or act of hostility, committed by one or either of the contracting parties against the other, shall be mutually forgiven and forgot.

ARTICLE 2. There shall be perpetual peace and friendship between all the citizens of the United States of America and all the individuals composing the said tribe of the Lakes, and all the friendly relations that existed between them before the war, shall be, and the same are hereby renewed.

ARTICLE 3. The undersigned chiefs and warriors, for themselves and their said tribe, do hereby acknowledge themselves and their aforesaid tribe to be under the protection of the United States, and of no other nation, power, or sovereign, whatsoever.

In witness whereof the said William Clark, Ninian Edwards, and Auguste Chouteau, Commissioners aforesaid, and the Chiefs and Warriors of the aforesaid tribe, have hereunto subscribed their names and affixed their seals, this nineteenth day of July, in the year of our Lord one thousand eight hundred and fifteen, and of the independence of the United States the fortieth.

WILLIAM CLARK,
NINIAN EDWARDS,
AUGUSTE CHOUTEAU.
Tatangamanie, the walking buffaloe,
Haisanwee, the horn,
Aampahaa, the speaker,
Nareesagata, the hard stone,
Haibohaa, the branching horn.

Done at Portage des Sioux, in the presence of R. Wash, Secretary to the Commission. John Miller, col. 3d. inf. T. Paul, C.T. of the C. Edmund Hall, lieut. Late 28th inf. J.B. Clark, adj. 3d. inf. Manuel Lisa, agent. Thomas Forsyth, I. Agent. Jno. W. Johnson, U.S.F. and I. Agent. Maurice Blondeaux. Lewis Decouagne. Louis Doiron. John A. Cameron. Jacques Mettee. John Hay.

[To the Indian names are subjoined a mark and seal.]

Source: *United States Statutes at Large*. Vol. 7. Edited by Richard Peters. Boston: Charles C. Little and James Brown, 1846.

DOCUMENT 37

CONVENTION OF 1818

The United States of America, and His Majesty The King of the United Kingdom of Great Britain and Ireland, desirous to cement the good Understanding which happily subsists between them, have, for that purpose, named their respective Plenipotentiaries, that is to say: The President of the United States, on his part, has appointed, Albert Gallatin, Their Envoy Extraordinary and Minister Plenipotentiary to the Court of France; and Richard Rush, Their Envoy Extraordinary and Minister Plenipotentiary to the Court of His Britannic Majesty: And His Majesty has appointed The Right Honorable Frederick John Robinson, Treasurer of His Majesty's Navy, and President of the Committee of Privy Council for Trade and Plantations; and Henry Goulburn Esquire, One of His Majesty's Under Secretaries of State: Who, after having exchanged their respective Full Powers, found to be in due and proper Form, have agreed to and concluded the following Articles.

ART. I

Whereas differences have arisen respecting the Liberty claimed by the United States for the Inhabitants thereof, to take, dry, and cure Fish on certain Coasts, Bays, Harbours, and Creeks of His Britannic Majesty's Dominions in America, it is agreed between The High Contracting Parties, that the Inhabitants of the said United States shall have for ever, in common with the Subjects of His Britannic Majesty, the Liberty to take Fish of every kind on that part of the Southern Coast of Newfoundland which extends from Cape Ray to the Rameau Islands, on the Western and Northern Coast of Newfoundland, from the said Cape Ray to the Quirpon Islands on the Shores of the Magdalen Islands, and also on the Coasts, Bays, Harbours, and Creeks from Mount Joly on the Southern Coast of Labrador, to and through the Streights of Belleisle and thence Northwardly indefinitely along the Coast, without prejudice however, to any of the exclusive Rights of the Hudson Bay Company: and that the American Fishermen shall also have liberty for ever, to dry and cure Fish in any of the unsettled Bays, Harbours, and Creeks of the Southern part of the Coast of Newfoundland hereabove described, and of the Coast of Labrador; but so soon as the same, or any Portion thereof, shall be settled, it shall not be lawful for the said Fishermen to dry or cure Fish at such Portion so settled, without previous Agreement for such purpose with the Inhabitants, Proprietors, or Possessors of the Ground. And the United States hereby renounce for ever, any Liberty heretofore enjoyed or claimed by the Inhabitants thereof, to take, dry, or cure Fish on, or within three marine Miles of any of the Coasts, Bays, Creeks, or Harbours of His Britannic Majesty's Dominions in America not included within the above mentioned Limits; provided however, that the American Fishermen shall be admitted to enter such Bays or Harbours for the purpose of Shelter and of repairing Damages therein, of purchasing Wood, and of obtaining Water, and for no other purpose whatever. But they shall be under such Restrictions as may be necessary to prevent their taking, drying or curing Fish therein, or in any other manner whatever abusing the Privileges hereby reserved to them.

ART. II
It is agreed that a Line drawn from the most North Western Point of the Lake of the Woods, along the forty ninth Parallel of North Latitude, or, if the said Point shall not be in the forty ninth Parallel of North Latitude, then that a Line drawn from the said Point due North or South as the Case may be, until the said Line shall intersect the said Parallel of North Latitude, and from the Point of such Intersection due West along and with the said Parallel shall be the Line of Demarcation between the Territories of the United States, and those of His Britannic Majesty, and that the said Line shall form the Northern Boundary of the said Territories of the United States, and the Southern Boundary of the Territories of His Britannic Majesty, from the Lake of the Woods to the Stony Mountains.

ART. III
It is agreed, that any Country that may be claimed by either Party on the North West Coast of America, Westward of the Stony Mountains, shall, together with its Harbours, Bays, and Creeks, and the Navigation of all Rivers within the same, be free and open, for the term of ten Years from the date of the Signature of the present Convention, to the Vessels, Citizens, and Subjects of the Two Powers: it being well understood, that this Agreement is not to be construed to the Prejudice of any Claim, which either of the Two High Contracting Parties may have to any part of the said Country, nor shall it be taken to affect the Claims of any other Power or State to any part of the said Country; the only Object of The High Contracting Parties, in that respect, being to prevent disputes and differences amongst Themselves.

ART. IV
All the Provisions of the Convention "to regulate the Commerce between the Territories of the United States and of His Britannic Majesty" concluded at London on the third day of July in the Year of Our Lord One Thousand Eight Hundred and Fifteen, with the exception of the Clause which limited its duration to Four Years, & excepting also so far as the same was affected by the Declaration of His Majesty respecting the Island of St. Helena, are hereby extended and continued in force for the term of ten Years from the date of the Signature of the present Convention, in the same manner, as if all the Provisions of the said Convention were herein specially recited.

ART. V
Whereas it was agreed by the first Article of the Treaty of Ghent, that "All Territory, Places, and Possessions whatsoever taken by either Party from the other during the War, or which may be taken after the signing of this Treaty, excepting only the Islands hereinafter mentioned, shall be restored without delay; and without causing any destruction, or carrying away any of the Artillery or other public Property originally captured in the said Forts or Places which shall remain therein upon the Exchange of the Ratifications of this Treaty, or any Slaves or other private Property"; and whereas under the aforesaid Article, the United States claim for their Citizens, and as their private Property, the Restitution of, or full Compensation for all Slaves who, at the date of the Exchange of the Ratifications of the said Treaty, were in any Territory, Places, or Possessions whatsoever directed by the said Treaty to be restored to the United States, but then still occupied by the British Forces, whether such Slaves were, at the date aforesaid, on Shore, or on board any British Vessel lying in Waters within the Territory or Jurisdiction of the United States; and whereas differences have arisen, whether, by the true intent and meaning of the aforesaid Article of the Treaty of Ghent the United States are entitled to the Restitution of, or full Compensation for all or any Slaves as above described, the High Contracting Parties hereby agree to refer the said differences to some Friendly Sovereign or State to be named for that purpose; and The High Contracting Parties further engage to consider the decision of such Friendly Sovereign or State, to be final and conclusive on all the Matters referred.

ART. VI
This Convention, when the same shall have been duly ratified by The President of the United States, by and with the Advice and Consent of their Senate, and by His Britannic Majesty, and the respective Ratifications mutually exchanged, shall be binding and obligatory on the said United States and on His Majesty; and the Ratifications shall be exchanged in Six Months from this date, or sooner, if possible.

In witness whereof the respective Plenipotentiaries have signed the same, and have hereunto affixed the Seal of their Arms.

Done at London this Twentieth day of October, in the Year of Our Lord One Thousand Eight Hundred and Eighteen.

ALBERT GALLATIN [Seal]
RICHARD RUSH. [Seal]
FREDERICK JOHN ROBINSON [Seal]
HENRY GOULBURN [Seal]

Source: Malloy, William M., ed. 1910. *Treaties, Conventions, International Acts, Protocols and Agreements between the United States of America and Other Powers, 1776–1909.* Vol. 1. Washington: Government Printing Office.

DOCUMENT 38

ADAMS-ONÍS TREATY [TRANSCONTINENTAL TREATY] (1819)

Treaty of Amity, Settlement and Limits Between the United States of America, and His Catholic Majesty

The United States of America and His Catholic Majesty desiring to consolidate on a permanent basis the friendship and good correspondence which happily prevails between the two Parties, have determined to settle and terminate all their differences and pretensions by a Treaty, which shall designate with precision the limits of their respective bordering territories in North America.

With this intention the President of the United States has furnished with their full Powers John Quincy Adams, Secretary of State of the said United States; and His Catholic Majesty has appointed the Most Excellent Lord Don Luis de Onís, Gonzales, Lopez y Vara, Lord of the Town of Rayaces, Perpetual Regidor of the Corporation of the City of Salamanca, Knight Grand Cross of the Royal American Order of Isabella, the Catholic, decorated with the Lys of La Vendee, Knight Pensioner of the Royal and distinguished Spanish Order of Charles the Third, Member of the Supreme Assembly of the said Royal Order; of the Council of His Catholic Majesty; his Secretary with Exercise of Decrees, and his Envoy Extraordinary and Minister Plenipotentiary near the United States of America.

And the said Plenipotentiaries, after having exchanged their Powers, have agreed upon and concluded the following articles.

ART. 1
There shall be a firm and inviolable peace and sincere friendship between the United States and their Citizens, and His Catholic Majesty, his Successors and Subjects, without exception of persons or places.

ART. 2
His Catholic Majesty cedes to the United States, in full property and sovereignty, all the territories which belong to him, situated to the Eastward of the Mississippi, known by the name of East and West Florida. The adjacent Islands dependent on said Provinces, all public lots and squares, vacant Lands, public Edifices, Fortifications, Barracks and other Buildings, which are not private property, Archives and Documents, which relate directly to the property and sovereignty of said Provinces, are included in this article. The said Archives and Documents shall be left in possession of the Commissaries, or Officers of the United States, duly authorized to receive them.

ART. 3
The Boundary Line between the two Countries, West of the Mississippi, shall begin on the Gulph of Mexico, at the mouth of the River Sabine in the Sea, continuing North, along the Western Bank of that River, to the 32d degree of Latitude; thence by a Line due North to the degree of Latitude, where it strikes the Rio Roxo of Nachitoches, or Red-River, then following the course of the Rio-Roxo Westward to the degree of Longitude, 100 West from London and 23 from Washington, then crossing the said Red-River, and running thence by a Line due North to the River Arkansas, thence, following the Course of the Southern bank of the Arkansas to its source in Latitude, 42 North and thence by that parallel of Latitude to the South-Sea. The whole being as laid down in Melish's Map of the United States, published at Philadelphia, improved to the first of January 1818. But if the Source of the Arkansas River shall be found to fall North or South of Latitude 42, then the Line shall run from the said Source due South or North, as the case may be, till it meets the said Parallel of Latitude 42, and thence along the said Parallel to the South Sea: all the Islands in the Sabine and the Said Red and Arkansas Rivers, throughout the Course thus described, to belong to the United States; but the use of the Waters and the navigation of the Sabine to the Sea, and of the said Rivers, Roxo and Arkansas, throughout the extent of the said Boundary, on their respective Banks, shall be common to the respective inhabitants of both Nations. The Two High Contracting Parties agree to cede and renounce all their rights, claims and pretensions to the Territories described by the said Line: that is to say.——The United States hereby cede to His Catholic Majesty, and renounce forever, all their rights, claims, and pretensions to the Territories lying West and South of the above described Line; and, in like manner, His Catholic Majesty cedes to the said United States, all his rights, claims, and pretensions to any Territories, East and North of the said Line, and, for himself, his heirs and successors, renounces all claim to the said Territories forever.

ART. 4
To fix this Line with more precision, and to place the Landmarks which shall designate exactly the limits of both Nations, each of the Contracting Parties shall appoint a Commissioner, and a Surveyor, who shall meet before the termination of one year from the date of the Ratification of this Treaty, at Nachitoches on the Red River, and proceed to run and mark the said Line from the mouth of the Sabine to the Red River, and from the Red River to the River Arkansas, and to ascertain the

Latitude of the Source of the said River Arkansas, in conformity to what is above agreed upon and stipulated, and the Line of Latitude 42 to the South Sea: they shall make out plans and keep Journals of their proceedings, and the result agreed upon by them shall be considered as part of this Treaty, and shall have the same force as if it were inserted therein. The two Governments will amicably agree respecting the necessary articles to be furnished to those persons, and also as to their respective escorts, should such be deemed necessary.

ART. 5
The Inhabitants of the ceded Territories shall be secured in the free exercise of their Religion, without any restriction, and all those who may desire to remove to the Spanish Dominions shall be permitted to sell, or export their Effects at any time whatever, without being subject, in either case, to duties.

ART. 6
The Inhabitants of the Territories which His Catholic Majesty cedes to the United States by this Treaty, shall be incorporated in the Union of the United States, as soon as may be consistent with the principle of the Federal Constitution, and admitted to the enjoyment of all the privileges, rights and immunities of the Citizens of the United States.

ART. 7
The Officers and Troops of His Catholic Majesty in the Territories hereby ceded by him to the United States shall be withdrawn, and possession of the places occupied by them shall be given within six months after the exchange of the Ratifications of this Treaty, or sooner if possible, by the Officers of His Catholic Majesty, to the Commissioners or Officers of the United States, duly appointed to receive them; and the United States shall furnish the transports and escort necessary to convey the Spanish Officers and Troops and their baggage to the Havana.

ART. 8
All the grants of land made before the 24th of January 1818 by His Catholic Majesty or by his lawful authorities in the said Territories ceded by His Majesty to the United States, shall be ratified and confirmed to the persons in possession of the lands, to the same extent that the same grants would be valid if the Territories had remained under the Dominion of His Catholic Majesty. But the owners in possession of such lands, who by reason of the recent circumstances of the Spanish Nation and the Revolutions in Europe, have been prevented from fulfilling all the conditions of their grants, shall complete them within the terms limited in the same respectively, from the date of this Treaty; in default of which the said grants shall be null and void—all grants made since the said 24th of January 1818 when the first proposal on the part of His Catholic Majesty, for the cession of the Floridas was made, are hereby declared and agreed to be null and void.

ART. 9
The two High Contracting Parties animated with the most earnest desire of conciliation and with the object of putting an end to all the differences which have existed between them, and of confirming the good understanding which they wish to be forever maintained between them, reciprocally renounce all claims for damages or injuries which they, themselves, as well as their respective citizens and subjects may have suffered, until the time of signing this Treaty.

The renunciation of the United States will extend to all the injuries mentioned in the Convention of the 11th of August 1802.

2.[sic] To all claims on account of Prizes made by French Privateers, and condemned by French consuls, within the Territory and Jurisdiction of Spain.

3. To all claims of indemnities on account of the suspension of the right of Deposit at New Orleans in 1802.

4. To all claims of Citizens of the United States upon the Government of Spain, arising from the unlawful seizures at Sea, and in the ports and territories of Spain or the Spanish Colonies.

5. To all claims of Citizens of the United States upon the Spanish Government, statements of which, soliciting the interposition of the Government of the United States have been presented to the Department of State, or to the Minister of the United States in Spain, since the date of the Convention of 1802, and until the signature of this Treaty.

The renunciation of His Catholic Majesty extends,

1. To all the injuries mentioned in the Convention of the 11th of August 1802.

2. To the sums which His Catholic Majesty advanced for the return of Captain Pike from the Provincias Internas.

3. To all injuries caused by the expedition of Miranda that was fitted out and equipped at New York.

4. To all claims of Spanish subjects upon the Government of the United States arizing from unlawful seizures at Sea or within the ports and territorial Jurisdiction of the United States.

Finally, to all the claims of subjects of His Catholic Majesty upon the Government of the United States, in which the interposition of His Catholic Majesty's Government has been solicited before the date of this Treaty, and since the date of the Convention of 1802, or which may have been made to the Department of Foreign Affairs of His Majesty, or to His Minister in the United States.

And the High Contracting Parties respectively renounce all claim to indemnities for any of the recent events or transactions of their respective Commanders and Officers, in the Floridas.

The United States will cause satisfaction to be made

for the injuries, if any, which by process of Law, shall be established to have been suffered by the Spanish Officers, and individual Spanish inhabitants, by the late operations of the American Army in Florida.

ART. 10
The Convention entered into between the two Governments on the 11 of August 1802, the Ratifications of which were exchanged the 21st December 1818, is annulled.

ART. 11
The United States, exonerating Spain from all demands in future, on account of the claims of their Citizens, to which the renunciations herein contained extend, and considering them entirely cancelled [sic], undertake to make satisfaction for the same, to an amount not exceeding Five Millions of Dollars. To ascertain the full amount and validity of those claims, a Commission, to consist of three Commissioners, Citizens of the United States, shall be appointed by the President, by and with the advice and consent of the Senate; which Commission shall meet at the City of Washington, and within the space of three years, from the time of their first meeting, shall receive, examine and decide upon the amount and validity of all the claims included within the descriptions above mentioned.

The said Commissioners shall take an oath or affirmation, to be entered on the record of their proceedings, for the faithful and diligent discharge of their duties; and in case of the death, sickness, or necessary absence of any such Commissioner, his place may be supplied by the appointment, as aforesaid, or by the President of the United States during the recess of the Senate, of another Commissioner in his stead. The said Commissioners shall be authorized to hear and examine on oath every question relative to the said claims, and to receive all suitable authentic testimony concerning the same. And the Spanish Government shall furnish all such documents and elucidations as may be in their possession, for the adjustment of the said claims, according to the principles of Justice, the Laws of Nations, and the stipulations of the Treaty between the two Parties of 27th October 1795; the said Documents to be specified, when demanded at the instance of the said Commissioners.

The payment of such claims as may be admitted and adjusted by the said Commissioners, or the major part of them, to an amount not exceeding Five Millions of Dollars, shall be made by the United States, either immediately at their Treasury or by the creation of Stock bearing an interest of Six per Cent per annum, payable from the proceeds of Sales of public lands within the Territories hereby ceded to the United States, or in such other manner as the Congress of the United States may prescribe by Law.

The records of the proceedings of the said Commissioners, together with the vouchers and documents produced before them, relative to the claims to be adjusted and decided upon by them, shall, after the close of their transactions, be deposited in the Department of State of the United States; and copies of them or any part of them, shall be furnished to the Spanish Government, if required, at the demand of the Spanish Minister in the United States.

ART. 12
The Treaty of Limits and Navigation of 1795 remains confirmed in all and each one of its articles, excepting the 2, 3, 4, 21 and the second clause of the 22d article, which, having been altered by this Treaty, or having received their entire execution, are no longer valid.

With respect to the 15th article of the same Treaty of Friendship, Limits and Navigation of 1795, in which it is stipulated, that the Flag shall cover the property, the Two High Contracting Parties agree that this shall be so understood with respect to those Powers who recognize this principle; but if either of the two Contracting Parties shall be at War with a Third Party, and the other Neutral, the Flag of the Neutral shall cover the property of Enemies, whose Government acknowledge this principle, and not of others.

ART. 13
Both Contracting Parties, wishing to favour their mutual Commerce, by affording in their ports every necessary Assistance to their respective Merchant Vessels, have agreed, that the Sailors who shall desert from their Vessels in the ports of the other, shall be arrested and delivered up, at the instance of the Consul——who shall prove nevertheless, that the Deserters belonged to the Vessels that claim them, exhibiting the document that is customary in their Nation: that is to say, the American Consul in a Spanish Port, shall exhibit the Document known by the name of articles, and the Spanish Consul in American Ports, the Roll of the Vessel; and if the name of the Deserter or Deserters, who are claimed, shall appear in the one or the other, they shall be arrested, held in custody and delivered to the Vessel to which they shall belong.

ART. 14
The United States hereby certify, that they have not received any compensation from France for the injuries they suffered from her Privateers, Consuls, and Tribunals, on the Coasts and in the Ports of Spain, for the satisfaction of which provision is made by this Treaty; and they will present an authentic statement of the prizes made, and of their true value, that Spain may avail herself of the same in such manner as she may deem just and proper.

ART. 15
The United States to give to His Catholic Majesty, a proof of their desire to cement the relations of Amity subsisting between the two Nations, and to favour the Commerce of the Subjects of His Catholic Majesty, agree that Spanish Vessels coming laden only with productions of Spanish

growth, or manufactures directly from the Ports of Spain or of her Colonies, shall be admitted for the term of twelve years to the Ports of Pensacola and St. Augustine in the Floridas, without paying other or higher duties on their cargoes or of tonnage than will be paid by the Vessels of the United States. During the said term no other Nation shall enjoy the same privileges within the ceded Territories. The twelve years shall commence three months after the exchange of the Ratifications of this Treaty.

ART. 16
The present Treaty shall be ratified in due form by the Contracting Parties, and the Ratifications shall be exchanged in Six Months from this time or sooner if possible.

In Witness whereof, We the Underwritten Plenipotentiaries of the States of America and of His Catholic Majesty, have signed, by virtue of Our Powers, the present Treaty of Amity, Settlement and Limits, and have thereunto affixed our Seals respectively.

Done at Washington, this Twenty-Second day of February, One Thousand Eight Hundred and Nineteen.

JOHN QUINCY ADAMS [SEAL]
LUIS DE ONÍS [SEAL]

Source: Malloy, William M., ed. 1910. *Treaties, Conventions, International Acts, Protocols and Agreements between the United States of America and Other Powers, 1776–1909*. Vol. 2. Washington: Government Printing Office.

DOCUMENT 39
LAND LAW
(1820)

An Act making further provision for the sale of the public lands.

Be it enacted by the Senate and House of Representatives of the United States of America, in Congress assembled, That from and after the first day of July next, all the public lands of the United States, the sale of which is, or may be authorized by law, shall when offered at public sale, to the highest bidder, be offered in half quarter sections; and when offered at private sale, may be purchased at the option of the purchaser, either in entire sections, half sections, quarter sections, or half quarter sections; and in every case of the division of a quarter section, the line for the division thereof, shall run north and south, and the corners and contents of half quarter sections which may thereafter be sold, shall be ascertained in the manner, and on the principles directed and prescribed by the second section of an act entitled, "An act concerning the mode of surveying the public lands of the United States," passed on the eleventh day of February, eighteen hundred and five; and fractional sections, containing one hundred and sixty acres, or upwards, shall in like manner, as nearly as practicable, be sub-divided into half quarter sections, under such rules and regulations as may be prescribed by the Secretary of the Treasury; but fractional sections, containing less than one hundred and sixty acres, shall not be divided, but shall be sold entire: *Provided*, That this section shall not be construed to alter any special provision made by law for the sale of land in town lots.

SEC. 2. *And be it further enacted*, That credit shall not be allowed for the purchase money on the sale of any of the public lands which shall be sold after the first day of July next, but every purchaser of land sold at public sale thereafter, shall, on the day of purchase, make complete payment therefor; and the purchaser at private sale shall produce, to the register of the land office, a receipt from the treasurer of the United States, or from the receiver of public moneys of the district, for the amount of the purchase money on any tract, before he shall enter the same at the land office; and if any person, being the highest bidder, at public sale, for a tract of land, shall fail to make payment therefor, on the day on which the same was purchased, the tract shall be again offered at public sale, on the next day of sale, and such person shall not be capable of becoming the purchaser of that or any other tract offered at such public sales.

SEC. 3. *And be it further enacted*, That from and after the first day of July next, the price at which the public lands shall be offered for sale, shall be one dollar and twenty-five cents an acre; and at every public sale, the highest bidder, who shall make payment as aforesaid, shall be the purchaser; but no land shall be sold, either at public or private sale, for a less price than one dollar and twenty-five cents an acre; and all the public lands which shall have been offered at public sale before the first day of July next, and which shall then remain unsold, as well as the lands that shall thereafter be offered at public sale before the first day of July next, and which shall then remain unsold, as well as the lands that shall thereafter be offered at public sale, according to law, and remain unsold at the close of such public sales, shall be subject to be sold at private sale, by entry at the land office, at one dollar and twenty-five cents an acre, to be paid at the time of making such entry as aforesaid; with the exception, however, of the lands which may have reverted to the United States, for failure in payment, and of the heretofore reserved sections for the future disposal of Congress, in the states of Ohio and Indiana, which shall be offered at public sale, as hereinafter directed.

SEC. 4. *And be it further enacted*, That no lands which have reverted, or which shall hereafter revert, and become forfeited to the United States for failure in any manner to make payment, shall, after the first day of July next, be subject to entry at private sale nor until the same shall have been first offered to the highest bidder at public sale; and all such lands which shall have reverted before the said first day of July next, and which shall then belong to the United States, together with the sections, and parts of sections, heretofore reserved for the future disposal of Congress, which shall, at the time aforesaid, remain unsold, shall be offered at public sale to the highest bidder, who shall make payment therefor, in half quarter sections, at the land office for the respective districts, on such day or days as shall, by proclamation of the President of the United States, be designated for that purpose; and all lands which shall revert and become forfeited for failure of payment after the said first day of July next, shall be offered in like manner at public sale, at such time, or times, as the President shall by his proclamation designate for the purpose: *Provided*, That no such lands shall be sold at any public sales hereby authorized, for a less price than one dollar and twenty-five cents an acre, offered at such public sales, and which shall remain unsold at the close thereof, shall be subject to entry at private sale, in the same manner, and at the same price with the other lands sold at private sale, at the respective land offices.

SEC. 5. *And be it further enacted*, That the several public sales authorized by this act, shall, respectively, be kept open for two weeks, and no longer; and the registers of the land office and the receivers of public money shall each, respectively, be entitled to five dollars for each day's attendance thereon.

SEC. 6. *And be it further enacted*, That, in every case hereafter, where two or more persons shall apply for the purchase, at private sale, of the same tract, at the same time, the register shall determine the preference, by forthwith offering the tract to the highest bidder.

APPROVED, April 24, 1820

Source: *United States Statutes at Large*. Vol. 3. Edited by Richard Peters. Boston: Charles C. Little and James Brown, 1846.

DOCUMENT 40

AMERICAN INSURANCE COMPANY VS. CANTER (1828)

Excerpts from the majority opinion, written by Chief Justice John Marshall:

The plaintiffs filed their libel in this cause in the District Court of South Carolina to obtain restitution of 356 bales of cotton ... which had been insured by them on a voyage from New Orleans to Havre de Grace, in France. The *Point a Petre* was wrecked on the coast of Florida, the cargo saved by the inhabitants, and carried into Key West, where it was sold for the purpose of satisfying the salvers; by virtue of a decree of a court, consisting of a notary and five jurors, which was erected by an act of the territorial Legislature of Florida. The owners abandoned to the underwriters, who proceeded against the property; alleging that the sale was not made by order of a court competent to change the property ...

David Canter claimed the cotton as a *bona fide* purchaser, under the decree of a competent court ...

The district judge pronounced the decree of the Territorial Court a nullity, and awarded restitution to the libelants ...

The libelants and claimant both appealed ...

The cause depends mainly on the question whether the property in the cargo saved, was changed, by the sale at Key West.... Its validity has been denied, on the ground, that it was ordered by an incompetent tribunal. The tribunal was constituted by an act of the territorial legislature of Florida, passed on the 4th July, 1823, which is inserted in the record. That act purports to give the power which has been exercised; consequently, the sale is valid, if the territorial legislature was competent to enact the law.

The course which the argument has taken, will require, that, in deciding this question, the court should take into view the relation in which Florida stands to the United States.

The Constitution confers absolutely on the government of the Union the powers of making war and of making treaties; consequently, that government possesses the power of acquiring territory, either by conquest or by treaty. The usage of the world is, if a nation be not entirely subdued, to consider the holding of conquered territory as a mere military occupation, until its fate shall be determined at the treaty of peace. If it be ceded by the treaty, the acquisition is confirmed, and the ceded territory becomes a part of the nation to which it is annexed; either on the terms stipulated in the treaty of cession, or on such as its new master shall impose. On such transfer of territory, it has never been held that the relations of the inhabitants with each other undergo any change. Their relations with their former sovereign are dissolved, and new relations are created between them and the government which has acquired their territory. The same act which transfers their country transfers the allegiance of those who remain in it; and the law which may be denominated political is necessarily changed, although that which regulates the intercourse and general conduct of individuals remains in force, until altered by the newly created power of the state.

On the 2d of February, 1819, Spain ceded Florida to the United States. The 6th article of the treaty of cession contains the following provision: "The inhabitants of the territories which his Catholic Majesty cedes to the United States by this treaty shall be incorporated in the Union of the United States, as soon as may be consistent with the principles of the federal Constitution; and admitted to the enjoyment of the privileges, rights, and immunities of the citizens of the United States."

This treaty is the law of the land, and admits the inhabitants of Florida to the enjoyment of the privileges, rights and immunities of the citizens of the United States. It is unnecessary to inquire whether this is not their condition, independent of stipulation. They do not, however, participate in political power; they do not share in the government till Florida shall become a State. In the meantime Florida continues to be a territory of the United States, governed by virtue of that clause in the Constitution which empowers Congress "to make all needful rules and regulations respecting the territory or other property belonging to the United States."

Perhaps the power of governing a territory belonging to the United States which has not by becoming a State acquired the means of self-government may result necessarily from the facts that it is not within the jurisdiction of any particular State, and is within the power and jurisdiction of the United States. The right to govern may be the inevitable consequence of the right to acquire territory. Whichever may be the source whence the power is derived, the possession of it is unquestioned. In execution of it Congress, in 1822, passed "An Act for the Establishment of a Territorial Government in Florida;" and on the 3d of March, 1823, passed another act to amend the act of 1822. Under this act the territorial legislature enacted the law now under consideration ...

It has been contended that, by the Constitution, the judicial power of the United States extends to all cases of admiralty and maritime jurisdiction; and that the whole of this judicial power must be vested "in one supreme court, and in such inferior courts as Congress shall from time to time ordain and establish." Hence, it has been argued that Congress cannot vest admiralty jurisdiction in courts created by the territorial legislature.

We have only to pursue this subject one step further, to perceive that this provision of the Constitution does not apply to it. The next sentence declares, that "the judges both of the supreme and inferior courts, shall hold their offices during good behavior." The judges of the superior courts of Florida hold their offices for four years. These courts, then, are not constitutional courts in which the judicial power conferred by the Constitution on the general government can be deposited. They are incapable of receiving it. They are legislative courts, created in virtue of the general right of sovereignty which exists in the government, or in virtue of that clause which enables Congress to make all needful rules and regulations, respecting the territory belonging to the United States. The jurisdiction with which they are invested, is not a part of that judicial power which is defined in the third article of the Constitution but is conferred by Congress, in the execution of those general powers which that body possesses over the territories of the United States. Although admiralty jurisdiction can be exercised in the States, in those courts only which are established in pursuance of the third article of the Constitution; the same limitation does not extend to the territories. In legislating for them, Congress exercises the combined powers of the general, and of a state government.

We think, then, that the act of the territorial legislature erecting the court by whose decree the cargo of the *Point a Petre* was sold, is not "inconsistent with the laws and Constitution of the United States," and is valid. Consequently, the sale made in pursuance of it changed the property, and the decree of the circuit court, awarding restitution of the property to the claimant, ought to be affirmed, with costs.

Decree affirmed.

Source: 1 Peters 511; 7 L. Ed. 242 (1828).

DOCUMENT 41

BLACK HAWK PURCHASE TREATY (SEPTEMBER 21, 1832)

Proclamation: February 13, 1833

Articles of a Treaty of Peace, Friendship and Cession, concluded at Fort Armstrong, Rock Island, Illinois, between the United Sates of America, by their Commissioners, Major General Winfield Scott, of the United States Army, and his Excellency John Reynolds, Governor of the State of Illinois, and the confederated tribes of Sac and Fox Indians, represented, in general Council, by the undersigned Chiefs, Headmen and Warriors

WHEREAS, under certain lawless and desperate leaders, a formidable band, constituting a large portion of the Sac and Fox nation, left their country in April last, and, in violation of treaties, commenced an unprovoked war upon unsuspecting and defenseless citizens of the United States, sparing neither age nor sex; and whereas, the United States, at a great expense of treasure, have subdued the said hostile band, killing or capturing all its principal Chiefs and Warriors the said States, partly as indemnity for the expense incurred, and partly to secure the future safety and tranquillity of the invaded frontier, demand of the said tribes, to the use of the United States, a cession of a tract of the Sac and Fox country, bordering on said frontier, more than proportional to the numbers of the hostile band who have been so conquered and subdued.

ART. 1

Accordingly, the confederated tribes of Sacs and Foxes hereby cede to the United States forever, all the lands to which the said tribes have title, or claim, (with the exception of the reservation hereinafter made) included within the following bounds, to wit: Beginning on the Mississippi river, at the point where the Sac and Fox northern boundary line, as established by the second article of the treaty of Prairie du Chien, of the fifteenth of July, one thousand eight hundred and thirty, strikes said river; thence, up said boundary line to a point fifty miles from the Mississippi, measured on said line; thence, in a right line to the nearest point on the Red Cedar of the Ioway, forty miles from the Mississippi river; thence, in a right line to a point in the northern boundary line of the State of Missouri, fifty miles, measured on said boundary, from the Mississippi river; thence, by the last mentioned boundary to the Mississippi river, and by the western shore of said river to the place of beginning.

And the said confederated tribes of Sacs and Foxes hereby stipulate and agree to remove from the lands herein ceded to the United States, on or before the first day of June next; and, in order to prevent any future misunderstanding, it is expressly understood, that no band or party of the Sac or Fox tribes shall reside, plant, fish, or hunt on any portion of the ceded country after the period just mentioned.

ART. 2
Out of the cession made in the preceding article, the United States agree to a reservation for the use of the said confederated tribes, of a tract of land containing four hundred square miles, to be laid off under the directions of the President of the United States, from the boundary line crossing the Ioway river, in such manner that nearly an equal portion of the reservation may be on both sides of said river, and extending downwards, so as to include Ke-o-kuck's principal village on its right bank, which village is about twelve miles from the Mississippi river.

ART. 3
In consideration of the great extent of the foregoing cession, the United States stipulate and agree to pay to the said confederated tribes, annually, for thirty successive years, the first payment to be made in September of the next year, the sum of twenty thousand dollars in specie.

ART. 4
It is further agreed that the United States shall establish and maintain within the limits, and for the use and benefit of the Sacs and Foxes, for the period of thirty years, one additional black and gun smith shop, with the necessary tools, iron and steel; and finally make a yearly allowance for the same period, to the said tribes, of forty kegs of tobacco, and forty barrels of salt, to be delivered at the mouth of the Ioway river.

ART. 5
The United States, at the earnest request of the said confederated tribes, further agree to pay to Farnham and Davenport, Indian traders at Rock island, the sum of forty thousand dollars without interest, which sum will be in full satisfaction of the claims of the said traders against the said tribes, and by the latter was, on the tenth day of July, one thousand eight hundred and thirty-one, acknowledged to be justly due, for articles of necessity, furnished in the course of the seven preceding years, in an instrument of writing of said date, duly signed by the Chiefs and Headmen of said tribes, and certified by the late Felix St. Vrain, United States' agent, and Antoine Le Claire, United States' Interpreter, both for the said tribes.

ART. 6
At the special request of the said confederated tribes, the United States agree to grant, by patent, in fee simple, to Antoine Le Claire, Interpreter, a part Indian, one section of land opposite Rock Island, and one section at the head of the first rapids above said Island, within the country herein ceded by the Sacs and Foxes.

ART. 7
Trusting to the good faith of the neutral bands of Sacs and Foxes, the United States have already delivered up to those bands the great mass of prisoners made in the course of the war by the United States, and promise to use their influence to procure the delivery of other Sacs and Foxes, who may still be prisoners in the hands of a band of Sioux Indians, the friends of the United States; but the following named prisoners of war, now in confinement, who were Chiefs and Headmen, shall be held, as hostages for the future good conduct of the late hostile bands, during the pleasure of the President of the United States, viz: Muk-ka-ta-mish-a-ka-kaik (or Black Hawk) and his two sons; Wau-ba-kee-shik (the Prophet) his brother and two sons; Na-pope; We-sheet Ioway; Pamaho; and Cha-kee-pa-Shi-pa-ho (the little stabbing Chief).

ART. 8
And it is further stipulated and agreed between the porties to this treaty, that there shall never be allowed in the confederated Sac and Fox nation, any separate band, or village, under any chief or warrior of the late hostile bands; but that the remnant of the said hostile bands shall be divided among the neutral bands of the said tribes according to blood the Sacs among the Sacs, and the Foxes among the Foxes.

ART. 9
In consideration of the premises, peace and friendship are declared, and shall be perpetually maintained between the United States and the whole confederated Sac and Fox nation, excepting from the latter the hostages before mentioned.

ART. 10
The United States, besides the presents, delivered at the signing of this treaty, wishing to give a striking evidence of their mercy and liberality, will immediately cause to be issued to the said confederated tribes, principally for the use of the Sac and Fox women and children, whose husbands, fathers and brothers, have been killed in the late war, and generally for the use of the whole confederated tribes, articles of subsistence as follows: thirty-five beef cattle; twelve bushels of salt; thirty barrels of pork; and fifty barrels of flour, and cause to be delivered for the same purposes, in the month of April next, at the mouth of the lower Ioway, six thousand bushels of maize or Indian corn.

ART. 11
At the request of the said confederated tribes, it is agreed that a suitable present shall be made to them on their pointing out to any United States agent, authorized for the purpose, the position or positions of one or more mines, supposed by the said tribes to be of a metal more valuable than lead or iron.

ART. 12
This treaty shall take effect and be obligatory on the contracting parties, as soon as the same shall be ratified by the President of the United States, by and with the advice and consent of the Senate thereof.

Done at Fort Armstrong, Rock Island, Illinois, this twenty-first day of September, in the year of our Lord one thousand eight hundred and thirty-two, and of the independence of the United States the fifty-seventh.

Winfield Scott John Reynolds

Sacs:
Kee-o-kuck, or he who has been every where, his x mark Pa-she-pa-ho, or the stabber, his x mark Pia-tshe-noay, or the noise maker, his x mark Wawk-kum-mee, or clear water, his x mark O-sow-wish-kan-no, or yellow bird, his x mark Pa-ca-tokee, or wounded lip, his x mark Winnewun-quai-saat, or the terror of man, his x mark Mau-noa-tuck, or he who controls many, his x mark Wau-we-au-tun, or the curling wave, his x mark

Foxes:
Wau-pel-la, or he who is painted white, his x mark Tay-wee-mau, or medicine man, (strawberry) his x mark Pow-sheek, or the roused bear, his x mark An-nau-mee, or the running fox, his x mark Ma-tow-e-qua, or the jealous woman, his x mark Me-shee-wau-quaw, or the dried tree, his x mark May-kee-sa-mau-ker, or the wampum fish, his x mark Chaw-co-saut, or the prowler, his x mark Kaw-kaw-kee, or the crow, his x mark Mau-que-tee, or the bald eagle, his x mark Ma-she-na, or cross man, his x mark Kaw-kaw-ke-monte, or the pouch, (running bear) his x mark Wee-she-kaw-k-a-skuck, or he who steps firmly, his x mark., Wee-ca-ma, or good fish, his x mark Paw-qua-nuey, or the runner, his x mark Ma-hua-wai-be, or the wolf skin, his x mark Mis-see-quaw-kaw, or hairy neck, his x mark Waw-pee-shaw-kaw, or white skin, his x mark Mash-shen-waw-pee-tch, or broken tooth, his x mark Nau-nah-que-kee-shee-ko, or between two days, his x mark Paw-puck-ka-kaw, or stealing fox, his x mark Tay-e-sheek, or the falling bear, his x mark Wau-pee-maw-ker, or the white loon, his x mark Wau-co-see-nee-me, or fox man, his x mark

In presence of:
R. Bache, captain ordnance, secretary to the commission Abrm. Eustis Alex. Cummings, lieutenant-colonel Second Infantry Alex. R. Thompson, major U. S. Army Sexton G. Frazer P. H. Galt, Assistant Adjutant-General Benj. F. Pike Wm. Henry James Craig John Aukeney J. B. F. Russell Isaac Chambers John Clitz, adjutant infantry John Pickell, lieutenant Fourth Artillery A. G. Miller, lieutenant First Infantry Geo. Davenport, assistant quartermaster-general Illinois Militia A. Drane Aeneas Mackay, captain U. S. Army J. R. Smith, first lieutenant Second Infantry Wm. Maynadier, lieutenant and aid-de-camp J. S. Gallagher, first lieutenant, acting commissary subsistence N. B. Bennett, lieutenant Third Artillery B. Riley, major U. S. Army H. Dodge, major W. Campbell Hy. Wilson, major Fourth U. S. Infantry Donald Ward Thos. Black Wolf Horatio A. Wilson, lieutenant Fourth Artillery H. Day, lieutenant Second Infantry Jas. W. Penrose, lieutenant Second Infantry J. E. Johnston, lieutenant Fourth Artillery S. Burbank, lieutenant First Infantry J. H. Prentiss, lieutenant First Artillery L. J. Beall, lieutenant First Infantry Addison Philleo Thomas L. Alexander, lieutenant Sixth Infantry Horace Beale, acting surgeon U. S. Army Oliver W. Kellogg Jona Leighton, acting surgeon U. S. Army Robt. C. Buchanan, lieutenant Fourth Infantry Jas. S. Williams, lieutenant Sixth Infantry John W. Spencer Antoine Le Claire, interpreter.

Source: Kappler, Charles J., ed. 1904. *Indian Affairs. Laws and Treaties.* Vol. 2. Washington: Government Printing Office.

DOCUMENT 42
TREATY OF CAMP HOLMES
(1835)

With the Comanche and Witchetaw Indians and their associated Bands.

For the purpose of establishing and perpetuating peace and friendship between the United States of America and the Comanche and Witchetaw nations, and their associated bands or tribes of Indians, and between these nations or tribes, and the Cherokee Muscogee, Choctaw, Osage, Seneca and Quapaw nations or tribes of Indians, the President of the United States has, to accomplish this desirable object, and to aid therein, appointed Governor M. Stokes, M. Arbuckle Brigdi. Genl. United States army, and F.W. Armstrong, Actg. Supdt. Western Territory, commissioners on the part of the United States: and the said Governor M. Stokes and M. Arbuckle, Brigdi. Genl. United States army, with the chiefs and representatives of the Cherokee, Muscogee, Choctaw, Osage, Seneca, and Quapaw nations or tribes of Indians, have met the chiefs, warriors, and representatives of the tribes first above named at Camp Holmes, on the eastern border of the Grand Prairie, near the Canadian river, in the Muscogee nation, and after full deliberation, the said nations or tribes have agreed with the United States, and with one another upon the following articles:

ARTICLE 1. There shall be perpetual peace and friendship between all the citizens of the United States of America, and all the individuals composing the Comanche and Witchetaw nations and their associated bands or tribes of Indians, and between these nations or tribes and the Cherokee, Muscogee, Choctaw, Osage, Seneca and Quapaw nations or tribes of Indians.

ARTICLE 2. Every injury or act of hostility by one or either of the contracting parties on the other, shall be mutually forgiven and forever forgot.

ARTICLE 3. There shall be a free and friendly intercourse between all the contracting parties hereto, and it is distinctly understood and agreed by the Comanche and Witchetaw nations and their associated bands or tribes of Indians, that the citizens of the United States are freely permitted to pass and repass through their settlements or hunting ground without molestation or injury on their way to any of the provinces of the Republic of Mexico, or returning therefrom, and that each of the nations or tribes named in this article, further agree to pay the full value for any injury their people may do to the goods or property of the citizens of the United States taken or destroyed, when peaceably passing through the country they inhabit, or hunt in, or elsewhere. And the United States hereby guaranty to any Indian or Indians of either of the said Comanche or Witchetaw nations, and their associated bands or tribes of Indians, a full indemnification for any horses or other property which may be stolen from them: *Provided*, that the property so stolen cannot be recovered, and that sufficient proof is produced that it was actually stolen by a citizen of the United States, and within the limits thereof.

ARTICLE 4. It is understood and agreed by all the nations or tribes of Indians parties to this treaty, that each and all of the said nations or tribes have free permission to hunt and trap in the Great Prairie west of the Cross Timber, to the western limits of the United States.

ARTICLE 5. The Comanche and Witchetaw nations and their associated bands or tribes of Indians, severally agree and bind themselves to pay full value for any injury their people may do to the goods or other property of such traders as the President of the United States may place near to their settlements or hunting ground for the purpose of trading with them.

ARTICLE 6. The Comanche and Witchetaw nations and their associated bands or tribes of Indians, agree, that in the event any of the red people belonging to the nations or tribes residing south of the Missouri river and west of the State of Missouri, not parties to this treaty, should visit their towns or be found on their hunting ground, that they will treat them with kindness and friendship and do no injury to them in any way whatever.

ARTICLE 7. Should any difficulty hereafter unfortunately arise between any of the nations or tribes of Indians parties hereunto, in consequence of murder, the stealing of horses, cattle, or other cause, it is agreed that the other tribes shall interpose their good offices to remove such difficulties, and also that the Government of the United States may take such measures as they may deem proper to effect the same object, and see that full justice is done to the injured party.

ARTICLE 8. It is agreed by the commissioners of the United States, that in consequence of the Comanche and Witchetaw nations and their associated bands or tribes of Indians having freely and willingly entered into this treaty, and it being the first they have made with the United States or any of the contracting parties, that they shall receive presents immediately after signing, as a donation from the United States; nothing being asked from these nations or tribes in return, except to remain at peace with the parties hereto, which their own good and that of their posterity require.

ARTICLE 9. The Comanche and Witchetaw nations and their associated bands or tribes, of Indians, agree, that their entering into this treaty shall in no respect interrupt their friendly relations with the Republic of Mexico, where they all frequently hunt and the Comanche nation principally inhabit; and it is distinctly understood that the Government of the United States desire that perfect peace shall exist between the nations or tribes named in this article and the said republic.

ARTICLE 10. This treaty shall be obligatory on the nations or tribes parties hereto from and after the date hereof, and on the United States from and after its ratification by the Government thereof.

Done and signed and sealed at Camp Holmes on the eastern border of the Grand Prairie near the Canadian river in the Muscogee nation, this twenty-fourth day of August, one thousand eight hundred and thirty-five, and of the independence of the United States the sixtieth.

MONTFORT STOKES,
M. ARBUCKLE,
Brigr. Genl. U.S. Army.

Comanches.

Ishacoly, or the wolf.
Qeenashano, or the war eagle.
Tabaqeena, or the big eagle.
Pohowetowshah, or the brass man.
Shabbakasha, or the roving wolf.
Neraquassi, or the yellow horse.
Toshapappy, or the white hare.
Pahohsareya, or the broken arm.
Pahkah, or the man who draws the bow.
Witsitony, or he who sucks quick.
Leahwiddikah, or one who stirs up water.
Esharsotsiki, or the sleeping wolf.
Pahtrisula, or the dog.
Ettah, or the gun.
Tennowikah, or the boy who was soon a man.
Kumaquoi, or the woman who cuts buffalo meat.
Taqquanno, or the amorous man.
Kowa, or the stinking tobacco box.
Soko, or the old man.

Witchetaws.

Kanostowah, or the man who don't speak.
Kosharoka, or the man who marries his wife twice.
Terrykatowatix, or the riding chief.
Tahdaydy, or the traveller.
Hahkahpillush, or the drummer.
Lachkah, or the first man in four battles.
Learhehash, the man who weans children too soon.
Lachhardich, the man who sees things done in the wrong way.
Noccuttardaditch, the man who tries to excel the head chief.
Katardedwadick, or the man who killed an enemy in the water.
Losshah, or the twin.
Taytsaaytah, or the ambitious adulturer.
Tokaytah, or the summer.
Musshakratsatady, or the man with the dog-skin cap.
Kipsh, or the man with one side of his head shaved.

Cherokees.
Dutch.
David Melton.
Muscogees.
Roley McIntosh.
Chily McIntosh.
Cho-co-te-tuston-nogu, or Marshal of the Cho-co-te clan.
Tus-ca-ne-ha, or the marshal.
Tulsy Harjoe, or Crazy town.
Alexander Lasley.
Neha Harjoe, or Crazy marshal.
Tustunucke Harjoe, or Crazy warrior.
Powes Emarlo, or Marshal of Powes clan.
Cosa Yehola, or Marshal of Cosa clan.
Powes Yehola, or Marshal of Powes clan.
Toma Yehola, or Marshal of Toma clan.
Cosado Harjoe, or Crazy Cosada.
Neha Harjoe, or Crazy marshal.
Cosada Tustonnogee, or the Cosada warrior.
Octiyachee Yehola, or Marshal of Octiyachee clan.
Nulthcup Tustonnogee, or the middle warrior.
Ufala Harjoe, or Crazy Ufala.
Cholafixico, or a fox without a heart.
Joseph Miller.
Samuel Brown.
Archi Kennard.
Towannay, or the slender man.
Saccasumky, or to be praised.
Shah Hardridge.
Warrior Hardridge.
George Stedham.
Itchhas Harjoe, or Crazy beaver.
Itchofake Harjoe, or Crazy deer's heart.
Satockhaky, or the broad side.
Semehechee, or Hide it away.
Hoyane, or Passed by.
Melola, or Waving.
Matcter, or the man who missed it.
Billy.
Tuskia Harjoe, or Crazy brave.
Aussy, or the pursuer.
Tohoithla, or Standing upon.
John Hambly.
K. Lewis.
John Wynn.
David McKillap.
Choctaws.
Musha-la-tubbee, or the man killer.
Na-tuck-a-chee, or Fair day.
Par-chee-ste-cubbee, or the scalp-holder.
To-pi-a-chee-hubbee, or the painted face.
Ya-cha-a-ho-poy, or the leader of the warriors.
Tus-qui-hola-tah, or the traveling warrior.
Tic-eban-jo-hubbee, or the first for war.
Nucke Stubbee, or the bullet that has killed.
Toqua, or What you say.
Po-sha-ma-stubbee, or the killer.
Nuck-ho-ma-harjoe, or the bloody bullet.
Thomas Mickie.
Halam-be-sha, or the bat.
Ok-chia, or Life.
Tus-ca-homa-madia, or the red warrior.
Tun-up-me-a-homa, or the red man who has gone to war.
Par-homa, or the red hoop.
No-wah-ba, or the man who kills the enemy when he meets him.
Hisho-he-meta, or a young waiter.
Cho-ma-la-tubbee, or the man who is sure his enemy is dead.
Hokla-no-ma, or the traveler in the town.
William.
Measho Nubbee, or he who knows where the enemy was killed.
Jim.
Eu-eck-Harma, or the man who is never tired.
Nat-la Homa, or the bloody man.
Pia-o-sta, or to whoop four times.
Pa-sha-oa-cubbee, or the man who puts his foot on the scalp.
La-po-na, or the man who killed the enemy.
A-mo-na-tubbee, or lying in wait to kill.
A-fa-ma-tubbee, or the man who kills every thing he meets.
Osages.
Tah-ha-la, or the leaping deer.
Shone-ta-sah-ba, or the black dog.
Wah-shin-pee-sha, or the wicked man.
Tun-wan-le-he, or the town mover.
Whoa-har-tee, or the war eagle.
Me-tah-ne-gah, or the crazy robe.
Wah-she-sho-ee, or the smart spirit.
Ah-ke-tah, or the soldier.
Weir-sah-bah-sha, or the hidden black.
Ne-ko-jah, or the man hunter.
Hor-tea-go, or like night.
Wah-hah-tah-nee, or the fast runner.
Wah-nah-shee, or the taker away.
Ces-sah-ba, or the man in black.
Es-kah-she-la, or the white horn.
Kou-sah-she-la, or walking together.
Tcha-to-kah, or the buffalo.
O-ke-sah, or the man aside.
Wah-she-wah-ra, or the stopper.
Wah-ho-ba-shungee, or the idolater.
Tone-ba-wah-tcha-la, or hard to look at the sun rising.
Shoe-chem-mo-nee, or the elk whistler.
Wash-kah-cha, or the tumbler.
Wah-ha, or the Pawnee chief's namesake.
Wah-kee-bah-nah, or the hard runner.
War-tcha-sheen-gah, or the scalp-carrier.
O-shaun-ga-tun-ga, or the big path.
Wah-hee-no-pee, or the bone necklace.

Lee-sap-kah-pee, or the man who missed his enemy.
Wah-to-ke-kah, or raw meat.
Wah-wah-shee, or quick runner.
Kah-he-ka-sara, or chief killer.
O-lash-tah-ba, or plate-licker.
Mah-ne-nah-shee, or the walker.
Shaun-ga-mo-nee, or the fall chief.
Tee-sha-wah-ra, or dry grass.
Ne-kah-wah-shee-tun-gah, or the brave spirit.
Senecas.
Thomas Brant.
Small Crout Spicier.
Isaac.
Mingo Carpenter.
John Sky.
Henry Smith.
Little Town Spicier.
Young Henry.
Peter Pork.
William Johnston.
Big Bone.
Big Isaac.
Civil Jack.
Ya-ga-ha, or the water in the apple.
Cau-ya-que-neh, or the snow drift.
Ya-ta-ato, or the little lake.
Douglass.
George Herring.
Quapaws.
Hi-ka-toa, or the dry man.
Wa-ga-de-tone, or the maggot.
Wa-to-va, or the spider.
Ca-ta-hah, or the tortoise.
Ma-towa-wah-cota, or the dug out.
Wa-go-dah-hou-kah, or the plume.
Ma-com-pa, or the doctor of the nose.
Cas-sa, or the black tortoise.
Haw-tez-chee-ka, or the little cedar.
Ma-sa-goda-toah, or the hawk.
Wa-ka-toa-nosa, or the standing man.
Motosa, or the black bear.
Mor-bre-tone, or the little hawk.
Mor-to-ho-ga, or the white bear.
To-se-ca-da, or he who shows his track.
Tah-tah-ho-sa, or the wind.
Hi-da-khe-da-sa, or the panther eagle.
O-tene-cah-chee-ka, or he who struck the enemy.
Me-ki-wah-kotah, or the star.
Ka-ti-mo-ne, or clear weather.
Vet-he-ka-ne, or thunder.
Ne-to-sa-mo-ne, or the black freshet.

In presence of R.B. Mason, Major of Dragoons. G. Birch, Major U.S. Army. Francis Lee, Captain 7th Infantry. Samuel G. DeCamp, Surgeon. W. Seawell, Lieut. And Aid-de-Camp; Sec'y to the Comm'rs. Thomas B. Ballard. Augustine A. Chouteau. John Hambly, U.S. Interpreter to the Creeks. George Herron. Leonard C. McPhail, Ass't Surgeon U.S. Army Robert M. French.

[To the Indian names are subjoined marks.]

Source: *Indian Affairs: Laws and Treaties.* Vol. 2. Compiled and Edited by Charles J. Kappler. Washington: Government Printing Office, 1904.

DOCUMENT 43

PRE-EMPTION ACT
(1841)

An Act to appropriate the proceeds of the sales of the public lands, and to grant pre-emption rights.

Be it enacted by the Senate and House of Representatives of the United States of America in Congress assembled, That from and after the thirty-first day of December, in the year of our Lord one thousand eight hundred and forty-one, there be allowed and paid to each of the States of Ohio, Indiana, Illinois, Alabama, Missouri, Mississippi, Louisiana, Arkansas, and Michigan, over and above what each of the said States is entitled to by the terms of the compacts entered into between them and the United States, upon their admission into the Union, the sum of ten per centum upon the nett proceeds of the sales of the public lands, which, subsequent to the day aforesaid, shall be made within the limits of each of said States respectively: *Provided,* That the sum so allowed to the said States, respectively, shall be in no wise affected or diminished on account of any sums which have been heretofore, or shall be hereafter, applied to the construction or continuance of the Cumberland road, but that the disbursements for the said road shall remain, as heretofore, chargeable on the two per centum fund provided for by compacts with several of the said States.

SEC. 2. And be it further enacted, That after deducting the said ten per centum, and what, by the compacts aforesaid has heretofore been allowed to the States aforesaid, the residue of the nett proceeds, which nett proceeds shall be ascertained by deducting from the gross proceeds all the expenditures of the year for the following objects: salaries and expenses on account of the General Land Office, expenses for surveying public lands; salaries and expenses in the surveyor general's offices; salaries, commissions, and allowances to the registers and receivers; the five per centum to new States, of all the public lands of the United States, wherever situated, which shall be sold subsequent to the said thirty-first day of December, shall be divided among the twenty-six States of the Union and the District of Columbia, and the Territories of Wisconsin, Iowa, and Florida, according to their respective federal representative population as ascertained by the last census, to be applied by the Legislatures of the said States to such purposes as the said Legislatures may direct: *Provided,* That the distributive share to which the District of Columbia shall be entitled, shall he applied to free schools, or education in some other form, as Congress may direct: *And Provided, also,* That nothing herein contained shall be construed to the prejudice of future applications for a reduction of the price of the public lands, or to the prejudice of applications for a transfer of the public lands, on reasonable terms, to the States within which they lie, or to make such future disposition of the public lands, or any part thereof, as Congress may deem expedient.

SEC. 3. *And be it further enacted*, That the several sums of money received in the Treasury as the nett proceeds of the sales of the public, lands shall be paid at the Treasury half yearly on the first day of January and July in each year, during the operation of this act, to such person or persons as the respective Legislatures of the said States and Territories, or the Governors thereof, in case the Legislatures shall have made no such appointment, shall authorize and direct to receive the same.

SEC. 4. *And be it further enacted*, That any sum of money, which at any time may become due, and payable to any State of the Union, or to the District of Columbia, by virtue of this act, as the portion of the said State or District, of the proceeds of the sales of the public lands, shall be first applied to the payment of any debt, due, and payable from the said State or District, to the United States: *Provided*, That this shall not be construed to extend to the sums deposited with the States under the act of Congress of twenty-third June, eighteen hundred and thirty-six, entitled "an act to regulate the deposites of the public money," nor to any sums apparently due to the United States as balances of debts growing out of the transactions of the Revolutionary war.

SEC. 5. *And be it further enacted*, That this act shall continue and be in force until otherwise provided by law, unless the United States shall become involved in war with any foreign Power, in which event, from the commencement of hostilities, this act shall be suspended during the continuance of such war: *Provided, nevertheless*, That if, prior to the expiration of this act, any new State or States shall be admitted into the Union, there be assigned to such new State or States, the proportion of the proceeds accruing after their admission into the Union, to which such State or States may be entitled, upon the principles of this act, together with what such State or States may be entitled to by virtue of compacts to be made on their admission into the Union.

SEC. 6. *And be it further enacted*, That there shall be annually appropriated for completing the surveys of said lands, a sum not less than one hundred and fifty thousand dollars; and the minimum price at which the public lands are now sold at private sale shall not be increased, unless Congress shall think proper to grant alternate sections along the line of any canal or other internal improvement, and at the same time to increase the minimum price of the sections reserved; and in case the same shall be increased by law, except as aforesaid, at any time during the operation of this act, then so much of this act as, provides that the nett proceeds of the sales of the public lands shall be distributed among the several States, shall, from and after the increase of the minimum price thereof, cease and become utterly null and of no effect, any thing in this act to the contrary notwithstanding: *Provided*, That if, at any time during the existence of this act, there shall be an imposition of duties on imports inconsistent with the provisions of the act of March second one thousand eight hundred and thirty-three, entitled, "An act to modify the act of the fourteenth of July one thousand eight hundred and thirty-two, and all other acts imposing duties on imports," and beyond the rate of duty fixed by that act, to wit: twenty per cent on the value of such imports, or any of them then the distribution provided in this act shall be suspended and shall so continue until this cause of its suspension shall be removed, and when removed, if not, prevented by other provisions of this act, such distribution shall be resumed.

SEC. 7. *And be it further enacted*, That the Secretary of the Treasury may continue any land district in which is situated the seat of government of any one of the States, and may continue the land office in such district, notwithstanding the quantity of land unsold in such district may not amount to one hundred thousand acres, when, in his opinion, such continuance may be required by public convenience, or in order to close the land system in such State at a convenient point, under the provisions of the act on that subject, approved twelfth June, one thousand eight hundred and forty.

SEC. 8. *And be it further enacted*, That there shall be granted, to each State specified in the first section of this act five hundred thousand acres of land for purposes of internal improvement: *Provided*, that to each of the said States which has already received grants for said purposes, there is hereby granted no more than a quantity of land which shall, together with the amount such State has already received as aforesaid, make five hundred thousand acres, the selections in all of the said States, to be made within their limits respectively in such manner as the Legislatures thereof shall direct; and located in parcels conformably to sectional divisions and subdivisions, of not less than three hundred and twenty acres in any one location, on any public land except such as is or may be reserved from sale by an law of Congress or proclamation of the President of the United States, which said locations may be made at any time after the lands of the United States in said States respectively, shall have been surveyed according to existing laws. And there shall be and hereby is granted to each new State that shall be hereafter admitted into the Union, upon such admission, so much land as, including such quantity as may have been granted to such State before its admission and while under a Territorial Government, for purposes of internal improvement as aforesaid, as shall make five hundred thousand acres of land, to be selected and located as aforesaid.

SEC. 9. *And be it further enacted*, That the lands herein granted to the States above named shall not be disposed of at a price less than one dollar and twenty-five cents per acre, until otherwise authorized by a law of the United

States; and the nett proceeds of the sales of said lands shall be faithfully applied to objects of internal improvement within the States aforesaid, respectively, namely: Roads, railways, bridges, canals and improvement of watercourses, and draining of swamps; and such roads, railways, canals, bridges and watercourses, when made or improved, shall be free for the transportation of the United States mail, and munitions of war, and for the passage of their troops, without the payment of any toll whatever.

SEC. 10. *And be it further enacted*, That from and after the passage of this act, every person being the head of a family, or widow, or single man, over the age of twenty-one years, and being a citizen of the United States, or having filed his declaration of intention to become a citizen as required by the naturalization laws, who since the first day of June, A.D. eighteen hundred and forty, has made or shall hereafter make a settlement in person on the public lands to which the Indian title had been at the time of such settlement extinguished, and which has been, or shall have been, surveyed prior thereto, and who shall inhabit and improve the same, and who has or shall erect a dwelling thereon, shall be, and is hereby, authorized to enter with the register of the land office for the district in which such land may lie, by legal subdivisions, any number of acres not exceeding one hundred and sixty, or a quarter section of land, to include the residence of such claimant, upon paying to the United States the minimum price of such land, subject, however, to the following limitations and exceptions: No person shall be entitled to more than one pre-emptive right by virtue of this act; no person who is the proprietor of three hundred and twenty acres of land in any State or Territory of the United States, and no person who shall quit or abandon his residence on his own land to reside on the public land in the same State or Territory, shall acquire any right of pre-emption under this act; no lands included in any reservation by any treaty, law, or proclamation of the President of the United States or reserved for salines, or for other purposes; no lands reserved for the support of schools, nor the lands acquired by either of the two last treaties with the Miami tribe of Indians in the State of Indiana, or which may be acquired of the Wyandot tribe of Indians in the State of Ohio, or other Indian reservation to which the title has been or may be extinguished by the United States at any time during the operation of this act; no sections of land reserved to the United States alternate to other sections granted to any of the States for the construction of any canal, railroad, or other public improvement; no sections or fractions of sections included within the limits of any incorporated town; no portions of the public lands which have been selected as the site for a city or town; no parcel or lot of land actually settled and occupied for the purposes of trade and not agriculture; and no lands on which are situated any known salines or mines, shall be liable to entry under and by virtue of the provisions of this act. And so much of the proviso of the act of twenty-second of June, eighteen hundred and thirty-eight, or any order of the President of the United States, as directs certain reservations to be made in favor of certain claims under the treaty of Dancing-rabbit creek, be, and the same is hereby, repealed: Provided, That such repeal shall not affect any title to any tract of land secured in virtue of said treaty.

SEC. 11. *And be it further enacted*, That when two or more persons shall have settled on the same quarter section of land, the right of pre-emption shall be in him or her who made the first settlement provided such persons shall conform to the other provisions of this act; and all questions as to the right of pre-emption arising between different settlers shall be settled by the register and receiver of the district within which the land is situated, subject to an appeal to and a revision by the Secretary of the Treasury of the United States.

SEC. 12. *And be it further enacted*, That prior to any entries being made under and by virtue of the provisions of this act, proof of the settlement and improvement thereby required, shall be made to the satisfaction of the register and receiver of the land district in which such lands may lie, agreeably to such rules as shall be prescribed by the Secretary of the Treasury, who shall each be entitled to receive fifty cents from each applicant for his services to be rendered as aforesaid; and all assignments and transfers of the right hereby secured prior to the issuing of the patent, shall be null and void.

SEC. 13. *And be it further enacted*, That before any person claiming the benefit of this act shall be allowed to enter such lands, he or she shall make oath before the receiver or register of the land district in which the land is situated, (who are hereby authorized to administer the same,) that he or she has never had the benefit of any right of pre-emption under this act; that he or she is not the owner of three hundred and twenty acres of land in any State or Territory of the United States, nor hath he or she settled upon and improved said land to sell the same on speculation, but in good faith to appropriate it to his or her own exclusive use or benefit; and that he or she has not, directly or indirectly, made any agreement or contract, in any way or manner, with any person or persons whatsoever by which the title which he or she might acquire from the Government of the United States should enure in whole or in part, to the benefit of any person except himself or herself; and if any person taking such oath shall swear falsely in the premises, he or she shall be subject to all the pains and penalties of perjury, and shall forfeit the money which he or she may have paid for said land, and all right and title to the same; and any grant or conveyance which he or she may have made, except in the hands of bona fide purchasers, for a valuable consideration, shall be null and void. And it shall be the duty of the officer administering such oath to file a certificate thereof in the public land office of such district, and to transmit a duplicate copy to the General Land Office, either of which shall be good and sufficient evidence that such oath was administered according to law.

SEC. 14. *And be it further enacted,* That this act shall not delay the sale of any of the public lands of the United States beyond the time which has been or may be, appointed by the proclamation of the President, nor shall the provisions of this act be available to any person or persons who shall fail to make the proof and payment, and file the affidavit required before the day appointed for the commencement of the sales as aforesaid.

SEC. 15. *And be it further enacted,* That whenever any person has settled or shall settle and improve a tract of land, subject at the time of settlement to private entry, and shall intend to purchase the same under the provisions of this act, such person shall in the first case, within three months after the passage of the same, and in the last within thirty days next after the date of such settlement, file with the register of the proper district a written statement, describing the land settled upon, and declaring the intention of such person to claim the same under the provisions of this act; and shall, where such settlement is already made, within twelve months after the passage of this act, and hereafter be made, within the same period after the date of such settlement, make the proof, affidavit, and payment herein required; and if he or she shall fail to file such written statement as aforesaid, or shall fail to make such affidavit, proof, and payment, within the twelve months aforesaid, the tract of land so settled and improved shall be subject to the entry of any other purchaser.

SEC. 16. *And be it further enacted*, That the two per cent of the nett proceeds of the lands sold, or that may hereafter be sold, by the United States in the State of Mississippi, since the first day of December, eighteen hundred and seventeen, and by the act entitled "An act to enable the people of the western part of the Mississippi Territory to form a constitution and State government, and for the admission of such State into the Union on an equal footing with the original States," and all acts supplemental thereto reserved for the making of a road or roads leading to said State, be, and the same is hereby relinquished to the State of Mississippi, payable in two equal instalments; the first to be paid on the first of May, eighteen hundred and forty-two, and the other on the first of May, eighteen hundred and forty-three, so far as the same may then have accrued, and quarterly, as the same may accrue after said period: *Provided*, That the Legislature of said State shall first pass an act, declaring their acceptance of said relinquishment in full of said fund, accrued and accruing, and also embracing a provision, to be unalterable without the consent of Congress, that the whole of said two per cent fund shall be faithfully applied to the construction of a railroad, leading from Brandon, in the State of Mississippi, to the eastern boundary of said State, in the direction, as near as may be of the towns of Selma, Cahaba, and Montgomery, in the State of Alabama.

SEC. 17. *And be it further enacted*, That the two per cent of the nett proceeds of the lands sold by the United States, in the State of Alabama, since the first day of September, eighteen hundred and nineteen and reserved by the act entitled "An act to enable the people of the Alabama Territory to form a constitution and State government, and for the admission of such State into the Union on an equal footing with the original States," for the making of a road or roads leading to the said State, be, and the same is hereby, relinquished to the said State of Alabama, payable in two equal instalments, the first to be paid on the first day of May, eighteen hundred and forty-two, and the other on the first day of May, eighteen hundred and forty-three, so far as the same may then have accrued, and quarterly, as the same may thereafter accrue: *Provided*, That the Legislature of said State shall first pass an act, declaring their acceptance of said relinquishment, and also embracing a provision, to be unalterable without the consent of Congress, that the whole of said two per cent fund shall be faithfully applied, under the direction of the Legislature of Alabama, to the connection, by some means of internal improvement, of the navigable waters of the bay of Mobile with the Tennessee river, and to the construction of a continuous line of internal improvements from a point on the Chattahoochie river, opposite West Point, in Georgia, across the State of Alabama, in a direction to Jackson in the State of Mississippi.

APPROVED, September 4, 1841.

Source: *United States Statutes at Large.* Vol. 5. Edited by Richard Peters. Boston: Little, Brown and Company, 1856. Pp. 453–458.

DOCUMENT 44

KANSAS-NEBRASKA ACT (1854)

An Act to Organize the Territories of Nebraska and Kansas.

Be it enacted by the Senate and House of Representatives of the United States of America in Congress assembled, That all that part of the territory of the United States included within the following limits, except such portions thereof as are hereinafter expressly exempted from the operations of this act, to wit: beginning at a point in the Missouri River where the fortieth parallel of north latitude crosses the same; then west on said parallel to the east boundary of the Territory of Utah, the summit of the Rocky Mountains; thence on said summit northwest to the forty-ninth parallel of north latitude; thence east on said parallel to the western boundary of the territory of Minnesota; thence southward on said boundary to the Missouri River; thence down the main channel of said river to the place of beginning, be, and the same is hereby, created into a temporary government by the name of the Territory Nebraska; and when admitted as a State or States, the said Territory or any portion of the same, shall be received into the Union with or without slavery, as their constitution may prescribe at the time of the admission: Provided, That nothing in this act contained shall be construed to inhibit the government of the

United States from dividing said Territory into two or more Territories, in such manner and at such times as Congress shall deem convenient and proper, or from attaching a portion of said Territory to any other State or Territory of the United States: *Provided further*, That nothing in this act contained shall be construed to impair the rights of person or property now pertaining to the Indians in said Territory so long as such rights shall remain unextinguished by treaty between the United States and such Indians, or include any territory which, by treaty with any Indian tribe, is not, without the consent of said tribe, to be included within the territorial line or jurisdiction of any State or Territory; but all such territory shall excepted out of the boundaries, and constitute no part of the Territory of Nebraska, until said tribe shall signify their assent to the President of the United States to be included within the said Territory of Nebraska. or to affect the authority of the government of the United States make any regulations respecting such Indians, their lands, property, or other rights, by treaty, law, or otherwise, which it would have been competent to the government to make if this act had never passed.

SEC. 2. *And Be it further enacted*, That the executive power and authority in and over said Territory of Nebraska shall be vested in a Governor who shall hold his office for four years, and until his successor shall be appointed and qualified, unless sooner removed by the President of the United States. The Governor shall reside within said Territory, and shall be commander-in-chief of the militia thereof. He may grant pardons and respites for offences against the laws of said Territory, and reprieves for offences against the laws of the United States, until the decision of the President can be made known thereon; he shall commission all officers who shall be appointed to office under the laws of the said Territory, and shall take care that the laws be faithfully executed.

SEC. 3. *And Be it further enacted*, That there shall be a Secretary of said Territory, who shall reside therein, and hold his office for five years, unless sooner removed by the President of the United States; he shall record and preserve all the laws and proceedings of the Legislative Assembly hereinafter constituted, and all the acts and proceedings of the Governor in his executive department; he shall transmit one copy of the laws and journals of the Legislative Assembly within thirty days after the end of each session, and one copy of the executive proceedings and official correspondence semi-annually, on the first days of January and July in each year to the President of the United States, and two copies of the laws to the President of the Senate and to the Speaker of the House of Representatives, to be deposited in the libraries of Congress, and in or case of the death, removal, resignation, or absence of the Governor from the Territory, the Secretary shall be, and he is hereby, authorized and required to execute and perform all the powers and duties of the Governor during such vacancy or absence, or until another Governor shall be duly appointed and qualified to fill such vacancy.

SEC. 4. *And be it further enacted*, That the legislative power and authority of said Territory shall be vested in the Governor and a Legislative Assembly. The Legislative Assembly shall consist of a Council and House of Representatives. The Council shall consist of thirteen members, having the qualifications of voters, as hereinafter prescribed, whose term of service shall continue two years. The House of Representatives shall, at its first session, consist of twenty-six members, possessing the same qualifications as prescribed for members of the Council, and whose term of service shall continue one year. The number of representatives may be increased by the Legislative Assembly, from time to time, in proportion to the increase of qualified voters: *Provided*, That the whole number shall never exceed thirty-nine. An apportionment shall be made, as nearly equal as practicable, among the several counties or districts, for the election of the council and representatives, giving to each section of the Territory representation in the ratio of its qualified voters as nearly as may be. And the members of the Council and of the House of Representatives shall reside in, and be inhabitants of, the district or county, or counties for which they may be elected, respectively. Previous to the first election, the Governor shall cause a census, or enumeration of the inhabitants and qualified voters of the several counties and districts of the Territory, to be taken by such persons and in such mode as the Governor shall designate and appoint; and the persons so appointed shall receive a reasonable compensation therefor. And the first election shall be held at such time and places, and be conducted in such manner, both as to the persons who shall superintend such election and the returns thereof, as the Governor shall appoint and direct; and he shall at the same time declare the number of members of the Council and House of Representatives to which each of the counties or districts shall be entitled under this act. The persons having the highest number of legal votes in each of said council districts for members of the Council, shall be declared by the Governor to be duly elected to the Council; and the persons having the highest number of legal votes for the House of Representatives, shall be declared by the Governor to be duly elected members of said house: *Provided*, That in case two or more persons voted for shall have an equal number of votes, and in case a vacancy shall otherwise occur in either branch of the Legislative Assembly, the Governor shall order a new election; and the persons thus elected to the Legislative Assembly shall meet at such place and on such day as the Governor shall appoint; but thereafter, the time, place, and manner of holding and conducting all elections by the people, and the apportioning the representation in the several counties or districts to the Council and House of Representatives, according to the number of qualified voters, shall be prescribed by law, as well as the day of the commencement of the regular sessions of the Legislative Assembly: *Provided*, That no session in any one year shall exceed the term of forty days, except the first session, which may continue sixty days.

SEC. 5. *And be it further enacted*, That every free white male inhabitant above the age of twenty-one years who shall be an actual resident of said Territory, and shall possess the qualifications hereinafter prescribed, shall be entitled to vote at the first election, and shall be eligible to any office within the said Territory; but the qualifications of voters, and of holding office, at all subsequent elections, shall be such as shall be prescribed by the Legislative Assembly: *Provided*, That the right of suffrage and of holding office shall be exercised only by citizens of the United States and those who shall have declared on oath their intention to become such, and shall have taken an oath to support the Constitution of the United States and the provisions of this act: And provided further, That no officer, soldier, seaman, or marine, or other person in the army or navy of the United States, or attached to troops in the service of the United States, shall be allowed to vote or hold office in said Territory, by reason of being on service therein.

SEC. 6. *And Be it further enacted*, That the legislative power of the Territory shall extend to all rightful subjects of legislation consistent with the Constitution of the United States and the provisions of this act; but no law shall be passed interfering with the primary disposal of the soil; no tax shall be imposed upon the property of the United States; nor shall the lands or other property of non-residents be taxed higher than the lands or other property of residents. Every bill which shall have passed the Council and House of Representatives of the said Territory shall, before it become a law, be presented to the Governor of the Territory; if he approve, he shall sign it; but if not, he shall return it with his objections to the house in which it originated, who shall enter the objections at large on their journal, and proceed to reconsider it. If, after such reconsideration two thirds of that house shall agree to pass the bill, it shall be sent, together with the objections, to the other house, by which it shall likewise be reconsidered, and if approved by two thirds of that house, it shall become a law. But in all such cases the votes of both houses shall be determined by yeas and nays, to be entered on the journal of each house respectively. If any bill shall not be returned by the Governor within three days (Sundays excepted) after it shall have been presented to him, the same shall be a law in like manner as if he had signed it, unless the Assembly, by adjournment, prevents its return, in which case it shall not be a law.

SEC. 7. *And be it further enacted*, That all township, district, and county officers, not herein otherwise provided for, shall be appointed or elected, as the case may be, in such manner as shall be provided by the Governor and Legislative Assembly of the Territory of Nebraska. The Governor shall nominate, and, by and with the advice and consent of the Legislative Council, appoint all officers not herein otherwise provided for; and in the first instance the Governor alone may appoint all said officers, who shall hold their offices until the end of the first session of the Legislative Assembly; and shall lay off the necessary districts for members of the Council and House of Representatives, and all other officers.

SEC. 8. *And be it further enacted*, That no member of the Legislative Assembly shall hold, or be appointed to, any office which shall have been created, or the salary or emoluments of which shall have been increased, while he was a member, during the term for which he was elected, and for one year after the expiration of such term; but this restriction shall not be applicable to members of the first Legislative Assembly; and no person holding a commission or appointment under the United States, except Postmasters, shall be a member of the Legislative Assembly, or hold any office under the government of said Territory.

SEC. 9. *And be it further enacted*, That the judicial power of said Territory shall be vested in a Supreme Court, District Courts, Probate Courts, and in Justices of the Peace. The Supreme Court shall consist of a chief justice and two associate justices, any two of whom shall constitute a quorum, and who shall hold a term at the seat of government of said Territory annually, and they shall hold their offices during the period of four years, and until their successor shall be appointed and qualified. The said Territory shall be divided into three judicial districts, and a district court shall be held in each of said districts by one of the justices of the Supreme Court, at such times and places as may be prescribed by of law; and the said judges shall, after their appointments, respectively, reside in the districts which shall be assigned them. The jurisdiction of the several courts herein provided for, both appellate and original, and that of the probate courts and of justices of the peace, shall be as limited by law: *Provided*, That justices of the peace shall not have jurisdiction of any matter in controversy when the title or boundaries of land may be in dispute, or where the debt or sum claimed shall exceed one hundred dollars; and the said supreme and districts courts, respectively, shall possess chancery as well as common law jurisdiction. Each District Court, or the judge thereof, shall appoint its clerk, who shall also be the register in chancery, and shall keep his office at the place where the court may, be held. Writs of error, bills of exception, and appeals, shall be allowed in all cases from the final decisions of said district courts to the Supreme Court, under such regulations as may be prescribed by law; but in no case removed to the Supreme Court shall trial by jury be allowed in said court. The Supreme Court, or the justices thereof, shall appoint its own clerk, and every clerk shall hold his office at the pleasure of the court for which he shall have been appointed. Writs of error, and appeals from the final decisions of said Supreme Court, shall be allowed, and may be taken to the Supreme Court of the United States, in the same manner and under the same regulations as from the circuit courts of the United States, where the value of the property, or the amount in controversy, to be ascertained by the oath or affirmation of either party, or other competent witness, shall exceed one thousand dollars; except only that in all cases involving title to slaves, the said writs of error, or appeals shall be allowed and decided by the said Supreme Court, without regard to the value of the matter, property, or title in controversy; and except also that a writ of error or appeal shall also be allowed to the Supreme Court of the United States, from the decision of the said Supreme Court created by this act, or of any judge thereof, or of the district courts created by this act, or of any judge thereof, upon any writ of habeas corpus, involving the question of personal freedom: *Provided*, that nothing herein contained shall be construed to apply to or affect the provisions to the "act respecting fugitives from justice, and persons escaping from the service of their masters," approved February twelfth, seventeen hundred and ninety-three, and the "act to amend and supplementary to the aforesaid act," approved September eighteen, eighteen hundred and fifty; and each of the said district courts shall have and exercise the same jurisdiction in all cases arising under the Constitution and Laws of the United States as is vested in the Circuit and District Courts of the United States; and the said Supreme and District Courts of the said Territory, and the respective judges thereof, shall and may grant writs of habeas corpus in all cases in which the same are granted by the judges of the United States in the District of Columbia; and the first six days of every term of said courts, or so much thereof as shall be necessary, shall be appropriated to the trial of causes arising under the said constitution and laws, and writs of error and appeal in all such cases shall be made to the Supreme Court of said Territory, the same as in other cases. The said clerk shall receive in all such cases the same fees which the clerks of the district courts of Utah Territory now receive for similar services.

SEC. 10. *And Be it further enacted*, That the provisions of an act entitled "An act respecting fugitives from justice, and persons escaping from the service of their masters," approved February twelve, seventeen hundred and ninety-three, and the provisions of the act entitled "An act to amend, and supplementary to, the aforesaid act," approved September eighteen, eighteen hundred and fifty, be, and the same are hereby, declared to extend to and be in full force within the limits of said Territory of Nebraska.

SEC. 11. *And be it further enacted*, That there shall be appointed an Attorney for said Territory, who shall continue in office for four years, and until his successor shall be appointed and qualified, unless sooner removed by the President, and who shall receive the same fees and salary as the Attorney of the United States for the present Territory of Utah. There shall also be a Marshal for the Territory appointed, who shall hold his office for four years, and until his successor shall be appointed and qualified, unless sooner removed by the President, and who shall execute all processes issuing from the said courts when exercising their jurisdiction as Circuit and District Courts of the United States; he shall perform the duties, be subject to the same regulation and penalties, and be entitled to the same fees, as the Marshal of the District Court of the United States for the present Territory of Utah, and shall, in addition, be paid two hundred dollars annually as a compensation for extra services.

SEC. 12. *And be it further enacted*, That the Governor, Secretary, Chief Justice, and Associate Justices, Attorney and Marshal, shall be nominated, and, by and with the advice and consent of the Senate, appointed by the President of the United States. The Governor and a Secretary to be appointed as aforesaid, shall, before they act as such, respectively take an oath or affirmation before the District Judge or some Justice of the Peace in the limits of said Territory, duly authorized to administer oaths and affirmations by the laws now in force therein, or & before the Chief Justice, or some Associate Justice of the Supreme Court of the United States, to support the Constitution of the United States, and faithfully to discharge the duties of their respective offices, which said oaths, when so taken, shall be certified by the person by whom the same shall have been taken; and such certificates shall be received and recorded by the said Secretary among the Executive proceedings; and the Chief Justice and Associate Justices, and all other civil officers in said Territory, before they act as such, shall take a like oath or affirmation before the said Governor or Secretary, or some Judge or Justice of the Peace of the Territory, who may be duly commissioned and qualified, which said oath or affirmation shall be certified and transmitted by the person taking the same to the Secretary, to be by him recorded as aforesaid; and, afterwards, the like oath or affirmation shall be taken, certified, and recorded, in such manner and form as may be prescribed by law. The Governor shall receive an annual salary of two thousand five hundred dollars. The Chief Justice and Associate Justices shall each receive an annual salary of two thousand dollars. The Secretary shall receive an annual salary of two thousand dollars. The said salaries shall be paid quarter-yearly, from the dates of the respective appointments, at the Treasury of the United States; but no such payment shall be made until said officers shall have entered upon the duties of their respective appointments. The members of the Legislative Assembly shall be entitled to receive three dollars each per day during their attendance at the sessions thereof, and three dollars each for every twenty miles' travel in going to and returning from the said sessions, estimated according to the nearest usually travelled route; and an additional allowance of three dollars shall be paid to the presiding officer of each house for each day he shall so preside. And a chief clerk, one assistant clerk, a sergeant-at-arms, and doorkeeper, may be chosen for each house; and the chief clerk shall receive four dollars per day, and the said other officers three dollars per day, during the session of the Legislative Assembly; but no other officers shall be paid by the United States: *Provided*, That there shall be but one session of the legislature annually, unless, on an extraordinary occasion, the Governor shall think proper to call the legislature together.

There shall be appropriated, annually, the usual sum, to be expended by the Governor, to defray the contingent expenses of the Territory, including the salary of a clerk of the Executive Department; and there shall also be appropriated, annually, a sufficient sum, to be expended by the Secretary of the Territory, and upon an estimate to be made by the Secretary of the Treasury of the United States, to defray the expenses of the Legislative Assembly, the printing of the laws, and other incidental expenses; and the Governor and Secretary of the Territory shall, in the disbursement of all moneys intrusted to them, be governed solely by the instructions of the Secretary of the Treasury of the United States, and shall, semi-annually, account to the said Secretary for the manner in which the aforesaid moneys shall have been expended; and no expenditure shall be made by said Legislative Assembly for objects not specially authorized by the acts of Congress, making the appropriations, nor beyond the sums thus appropriated for such objects.

SEC. 13. *And be it further enacted*, That the Legislative Assembly of the Territory of Nebraska shall hold its first session at such time and place in said Territory as the Governor thereof shall appoint and direct; and at said first session, or as soon thereafter as they shall deem expedient, the Governor and Legislative Assembly shall proceed to locate and establish the seat of government for said Territory at such place as they may deem eligible; which place, however, shall thereafter be subject to be changed by the said Governor and Legislative Assembly.

SEC. 14. *And be it further enacted*, That a delegate to the House of Representatives of the United States, to serve for the term of two years, who shall be a citizen of the United States, may be elected by the voters qualified to elect members of the Legislative Assembly, who shall be entitled to the same rights and privileges as are exercised and enjoyed by the delegates from the several other Territories of the United States to the said House of Representatives, but the delegate first elected shall hold his seat only during the term of the Congress to which he shall be elected. The first election shall be held at such time and places, and be conducted in such manner, as the Governor shall appoint and direct; and at all subsequent elections the times, places, and manner of holding the elections, shall be prescribed by law. The person having the greatest number of votes shall be declared by the Governor to be duly elected; and a certificate thereof shall be given accordingly. That the Constitution, and all Laws of the United States which are not locally inapplicable, shall have the same force and effect within the said Territory of Nebraska as elsewhere within the United States, except the eighth section of the act preparatory to the admission of Missouri into the Union approved March sixth, eighteen hundred and twenty, which, being inconsistent with the principle of non-intervention by Congress with slaves in the States and Territories, as recognized by the legislation of eighteen hundred and fifty, commonly called the Compromise Measures, is hereby declared inoperative and void; it being the true intent and meaning of this act not to legislate slavery into any Territory or State, nor to exclude it therefrom, but to leave the people thereof perfectly free to form an regulate their domestic institutions in their own way, subject only to the Constitution of the United States: *Provided*, That nothing herein contained shall be construed to revive or put in force any law or regulation which may have existed prior to the act of sixth March, eighteen hundred and twenty, either protecting, establishing, prohibiting, or abolishing slavery.

SEC. 15. *And Be it further enacted*, That there shall hereafter be appropriated, as has been customary for the Territorial governments, sufficient amount, to be expended under the direction of the said Governor of the Territory of Nebraska, not exceeding the sums heretofore appropriated for similar objects, for the erection of suitable public buildings at the seat of government, and for the purchase of a library, to be kept at the seat of government for the use of the Governor, Legislative Assembly, Judges of the Supreme Court, Secretary, Marshal, and Attorney of said Territory, and such other persons, and under such regulations as shall be prescribed by law.

SEC. 16. *And be it further enacted*, That when the lands in the said Territory shall be surveyed under the direction of the government of the United States, preparatory to bringing the same into market, section; numbered sixteen and thirty-six in each township in said Territory shall be, and the same are hereby, reserved for the purpose of being applied to schools in said Territory, and in the States and Territories hereafter to be erected out of the same.

SEC. 17. *And be it further enacted*, That, until otherwise provided by law, the Governor of said Territory may define the Judicial Districts of said Territory, and assign the judges who may be appointed for said Territory to the several districts; and also appoint the times and places for holding courts in the several counties or subdivisions in each of said Judicial Districts by proclamation, to be issued by him; but the Legislative Assembly, at their first or any subsequent session, may organize, alter, or modify such Judicial Districts, and assign the judges, and alter the times and places of holding the courts, as to them shall seem proper and convenient.

SEC. 18. *And be it further enacted*, That all officers to be appointed by the President, by and with the advice and consent of the Senate, for the Territory of Nebraska, who, by virtue of the provisions of any law now existing, or which may be enacted during the present Congress, are required to give security for moneys that may be intrusted with them for disbursement, shall give such security, at such time and place, and in such manner, as the Secretary of the Treasury may prescribe.

SEC. 19. *And be it further enacted*, That all that part of the Territory of the United States included within the following limits, except such portions thereof as are hereinafter expressly exempted from the operations of this act, to wit, beginning at a point on the western boundary of the State of Missouri, where the thirty-seventh parallel of north latitude crosses the same; thence west on said parallel to the eastern boundary of New Mexico; thence north on said boundary to latitude thirty-eight; thence following said boundary westward to the east boundary of the Territory of Utah, on the summit of the Rocky Mountains; thence northward on said summit to the fortieth parallel of latitude, thence east on said parallel to the western boundary of the State of Missouri; thence south with the western boundary of said State to the place of beginning, be, and the same is hereby, created into a temporary government by the name of the Territory of Kansas; and when admitted as a State or States, the said Territory, or any portion of the same, shall be received into the Union with or without slavery, as their Constitution may prescribe at the time of their admission: *Provided*, That nothing in this act contained shall be construed to inhibit the government of the United States from dividing said Territory into two or more Territories, in such manner and at such times as Congress shall deem convenient and proper, or from attaching any portion of said Territory to any other State or Territory of the United States: *Provided* further, That nothing in this act contained shall be construed to impair the rights of person or property now pertaining to the Indians in said Territory, so long as such rights shall remain unextinguished by treaty between the United States and such Indians, or to include any territory which, by treaty with any Indian tribe, is not, without the consent of said tribe, to be included within the territorial limits or jurisdiction of any State or Territory; but all such territory shall be excepted out of the boundaries, and constitute no part of the Territory of Kansas, until said tribe shall signify their assent to the President of the United States to be included within the said Territory of Kansas, or to affect the authority of the government of the United States to make any regulation respecting such Indians, their lands, property, or other rights, by treaty, law, or otherwise, which it would have been competent to the government to make if this act had never passed.

SEC. 20. *And be it further enacted*, That the executive power and authority in and over said Territory of Kansas shall be vested in a Governor, who shall hold his office for four years, and until his successor shall be appointed and qualified, unless sooner removed by the President of the United States. The Governor shall reside within said Territory, and shall be commander-in-chief of the militia thereof. He may grant pardons and respites for offences against the laws of said Territory, and reprieves for offences against the laws of the United States, until the decision of the President can be made known thereon; he shall commission all officers who shall be appointed to office under the laws of the said Territory, and shall take care that the laws be faithfully executed.

SEC. 21. *And be it further enacted*, That there shall be a Secretary of said Territory, who shall reside therein, and hold his office for five years, unless sooner removed by the President of the United States; he shall record and preserve all the laws and proceedings of the Legislative Assembly hereinafter constituted, and all the acts and proceedings of the Governor in his Executive Department; he shall transmit one copy of the laws and journals of the Legislative Assembly within thirty days after the end of each session, and one copy of the executive proceedings and official correspondence semi-annually, on the first days of January and July in each year, to the President of the United States, and two copies of the laws to the President of the Senate and to the Speaker of the House of Representatives, to be deposited in the libraries of Congress; and, in case of the death, removal, resignation, or absence of the Governor from the Territory, the Secretary shall be, and he is hereby, authorized and required to execute and perform all the powers and duties of the Governor during such vacancy or absence, or until another Governor shall be duly appointed and qualified to fill such vacancy.

SEC. 22. *And be it further enacted*, That the legislative power and authority of said Territory shall be vested in the Governor and a Legislative Assembly. The Legislative Assembly shall consist of a Council and House of Representatives. The Council shall consist of thirteen members, having the qualifications of voters, as hereinafter prescribed, whose term of service shall continue two years. The House of Representatives shall, at its first session, consist of twenty-six members possessing the same qualifications as prescribed for members of the Council, and whose term of service shall continue one year. The number of representatives may be increased by the Legislative Assembly, from time to time, in proportion to the increase of qualified voters: *Provided*, That the whole number shall never exceed thirty-nine. An apportionment shall be made, as nearly equal as practicable, among the several counties or districts, for the election of the Council and Representatives, giving to each section of the Territory representation in the ratio of its qualified voters as nearly as may be. And the members of the Council and of the House of Representatives shall reside in, and be inhabitants of, the district or county, or counties, for which they may be elected, respectively. Previous to the first election, the Governor shall cause a census, or enumeration of the inhabitants and qualified voters of the several counties and districts of the Territory, to be taken by such persons and in such mode as the Governor shall designate and appoint; and the persons so appointed shall receive a reasonable compensation therefor. And the first election shall be held at such time and places, and be conducted in such manner, both as to the persons who shall superintend such election and the returns thereof, as the Governor shall appoint and direct; and he shall at the same time declare the number of members of the Council and House of Representatives to which each of the counties or districts shall be entitled under this act. The persons having the highest number of legal votes in each of said Council Districts for members of the Council, shall be declared by the Governor to be duly elected to the Council; and the persons having the highest number of legal votes for the House of Representatives, shall be declared by the Governor to be duly elected members of said house: Provided, That in case two or more persons voted for shall have an equal number of votes, and in case a vacancy shall otherwise occur in either branch of the Legislative Assembly, the Governor shall order a new election; and the persons thus elected to the Legislative Assembly shall meet at such place and on such day as the Governor shall appoint; but thereafter, the time, place, and manner of holding and conducting all elections by the people, and the apportioning the representation in the several counties or districts to the Council and House of Representatives, according to the number of qualified voters, shall be prescribed by law, as well as the day of the commencement of the regular sessions of the Legislative Assembly: *Provided*, That no session in any one year shall exceed the term of forty days, except the first session, which may continue sixty days.

SEC. 23. *And be it further enacted*, That every free white male inhabitant above the age of twenty-one years, who shall be an actual resident of said Territory, and shall possess the qualifications hereinafter prescribed, shall be entitled to vote at the first election, and shall be eligible to any office within the said Territory; but the qualifications of voters, and of holding office, at all subsequent elections, shall be such as shall be prescribed by the Legislative Assembly: *Provided*, That the right of suffrage and of holding office shall be exercised only by citizens of the United States, and those who shall have declared, on oath, their intention to become such, and shall have taken an oath to support the Constitution of the United States and the provisions of this act: And, provided further, That no officer, soldier, seaman, or marine, or other person in the army or navy of the United States, or attached to troops in the service of the United States, shall be allowed to vote or hold office in said Territory by reason of being on service therein.

SEC. 24. *And be it further enacted*, That the legislative power of the Territory shall extend to all rightful subjects of legislation consistent with the Constitution of the United States and the provisions of this act; but no law shall be passed interfering with the primary disposal of the soil; no tax shall be imposed upon the property of the United States; nor shall the lands or other property of non-residents be taxed higher than the lands or other property of residents. Every bill which shall have passed the Council and House of Representatives of the said Territory shall, before it become a law, be presented to the Governor of the Territory; if he approve, he shall sign it; but if not, he shall return it with his objections to the house in which it originated, who shall enter the objections at large on their journal, and proceed to reconsider it. If, after such reconsideration, two thirds of that house shall agree to pass the bill, it shall be sent, together with the objections, to the other house, by which, it shall likewise be reconsidered, and, if approved by two thirds of that house, it shall become a law. But in all such cases the votes of both houses shall be determined by yeas and nays, to be entered on the journal of each house, respectively. If any bill shall not be returned by the Governor within three days (Sundays excepted) after it shall have been presented to him, the same shall be a law in like manner as if he had signed it, unless the Assembly, by adjournment, prevent its return, in which case it shall not be a law.

SEC. 25. *And be it further enacted*, That all township, district, and county officers, not herein otherwise provided for, shall be appointed or elected as the case may be, in such manner as shall be provided by the Governor and Legislative Assembly of the Territory of Kansas. The Governor shall nominate, and, by and with the advice and consent of the Legislative Council, appoint all officers not herein otherwise provided for; and, in the first instance, the Governor alone may appoint all said officers, who shall hold their offices until the end of the first session of the Legislative Assembly; and shall lay off the necessary districts for members of the Council and House of Representatives, and all other officers.

SEC. 26. *And be it further enacted*, That no member of the Legislative Assembly shall hold, or be appointed to, any office which shall have been created, or the salary or emoluments of which shall have been increased, while he was a member, during the term for which he was elected, and for one year after the expiration of such term; but this restriction shall not be applicable to members of the first Legislative Assembly; and no person holding a commission or appointment under the United States, except postmasters, shall be a member of the Legislative Assembly, or shall hold any office under the government of said Territory.

SEC. 27. *And be it further enacted*, That the judicial power of said Territory shall be vested in a supreme court, district courts, probate courts, and in justices of the peace. The Supreme Court shall Consist of chief justice and two associate justices, any two of whom shall constitute a quorum, and who shall hold a term at the seat of government of said Territory annually; and they shall hold their offices during the period of four years, and until their successors shall be appointed and qualified. The said Territory shall be divided into three judicial districts, and a district court shall be held in each of said districts by one of the justices of the Supreme Court, at such times and places as may be prescribed by law; and the said judges shall, after their appointments, respectively, reside in the districts which shall be assigned them. The jurisdiction of the several courts herein provided for, both appellate and original, and that of the probate courts and of justices of the peace, shall be as limited by law: *Provided*, That justices of the peace shall not have jurisdiction of any matter in controversy when the title or boundaries of land may be in dispute, or where the debt or sum claimed shall exceed one hundred dollars; and the said supreme and district courts, respectively, shall possess chancery as well as common law jurisdiction. Said District Court, or the judge thereof, shall appoint its clerk, who shall also be the register in chancery, and shall keep his office at the place where the court may be held. Writs of error, bills of exception, and appeals shall be allowed in all cases from the final decisions of said district courts to the Supreme Court, under such regulations as may be prescribed by law; but in no case removed to the Supreme Court shall trial by jury be allowed in said court. The Supreme Court, or the justices thereof, shall appoint its own clerk, and every clerk shall hold his office at the pleasure of the court for which he shall have been appointed. Writs of error, and appeals from the final decisions of said supreme court, shall be allowed, and may be taken to the Supreme Court of the United States, in the same manner and under the same regulations as from the Circuit Courts of the United States, where the value of the property, or the amount in controversy, to be ascertained by the oath or affirmation of either party, or other competent witness, shall exceed one thousand dollars; except only that in all cases involving title to slaves, the said writ of error or appeals shall be allowed and decided by said supreme court, without regard to the value of the matter, property, or title in controversy; and except also that a writ of error or appeal shall also be allowed to the Supreme Court of the United States, from the decision of the said supreme court created by this act, or of any judge thereof, or of the district courts created by this act, or of any judge thereof, upon any writ of habeas corpus, involving the question of personal freedom: *Provided*, That nothing herein contained shall be construed to apply to or affect the provisions of the "act respecting fugitives from justice, and persons escaping from the service of their masters," approved February twelfth, seventeen hundred and ninety-three, and the "act to amend and supplementary to the aforesaid act," approved September eighteenth, eighteen hundred and fifty; and each of the said district courts shall have and exercise the same jurisdiction in all cases arising under the Constitution and laws of the United States as is vested in the Circuit and District Courts of the United States; and the said supreme and district courts of the said Territory, and the respective judges thereof, shall and may grant writs of habeas corpus in all cases in which the same are granted by the judges of the United States in the District of Columbia; and the first six days of every term of said courts, or so much thereof as may be necessary, shall be appropriated to the trial of causes arising under the said Constitution and laws, and writs of error and appeal in all such cases shall be made to the Supreme Court of said Territory, the same as in other cases. The said clerk shall receive the same fees in all such cases, which the clerks of the district courts of Utah Territory now receive for similar services.

SEC. 28. *And be it further enacted*, That the provisions of the act entitled "An act respecting fugitives from justice, and persons escaping from the service of their masters," approved February twelfth, seventeen hundred and ninety-three, and the provisions of the act entitled "An act to amend, and supplementary to, the aforesaid act," approved September eighteenth, eighteen hundred and fifty, be, and the same are hereby, declared to extend to and be in full force within the limits of the said Territory of Kansas.

SEC. 29. *And be it further enacted*, That there shall be appointed an attorney for said Territory, who shall continue in office for four years, and until his successor shall be appointed and qualified, unless sooner removed by the President, and who shall receive the same fees and salary as the Attorney of the United States for the present Territory of Utah. There shall also be a marshal for the Territory appointed, who shall hold his office for four years, and until his successor shall be appointed and qualified, unless sooner removed by the President, and who shall execute all processes issuing from the said courts where exercising their jurisdiction as Circuit and District Courts of the United States; he shall perform the duties, be subject to the same regulations and penalties, and be entitled to the same fees, as the Marshal of the District Court of the United States for the present Territory of Utah, and shall, in addition, be paid two hundred dollars annually as a compensation for extra services.

SEC. 30. *And be it further enacted*, That the Governor, Secretary, Chief Justice, and Associate Justices, Attorney, and Marshal, shall be nominated, and, by and with the advice and consent of the Senate, appointed by the President of the United States. The Governor and Secretary to be appointed as aforesaid shall, before they act as such, respectively take an oath or affirmation before the district judge or some justice of the peace in the limits of said Territory, duly authorized to administer oaths and affirmations by the laws now in force therein, or before the Chief Justice or some Associate Justice of the Supreme Court of the United States, to support the Constitution of the United States, and faithfully to discharge the duties of their respective offices, which said oaths, when so taken, shall be certified by the person by whom the same shall have been taken; and such certificates shall be received and recorded by the said secretary among the executive proceedings; and the Chief Justice and Associate Justices, and all other civil officers in said Territory, before they act as such, shall take a like oath or affirmation before the said Governor or Secretary, or some Judge or Justice of the Peace of the Territory who may be duly commissioned and qualified, which said oath or affirmation shall be certified and transmitted by the person taking the same to the Secretary, to be by him recorded as aforesaid; and, afterwards, the like oath or affirmation shall be taken, certified, and recorded, in such manner and form as may be prescribed by law. The Governor shall receive an annual salary of two thousand five hundred dollars. The Chief Justice and Associate Justices shall receive an annual salary of two thousand dollars. The Secretary shall receive an annual salary of two thousand dollars. The said salaries shall be paid quarter-yearly, from the dates of the respective appointments, at the Treasury of the United States; but no such payment shall be made until said officers shall have entered upon the duties of their respective appointments. The members of the Legislative Assembly shall be entitled to receive three dollars each per day during their attendance at the sessions thereof, and three dollars each for every twenty miles' travel in going to and returning from the said sessions, estimated according to the nearest usually travelled route; and an additional allowance of three dollars shall be paid to the presiding officer of each house for each day he shall so preside. And a chief clerk, one assistant clerk, a sergeant at-arms, and door-keeper, may be chosen for each house; and the chief clerk shall receive four dollars per day, and the said other officers three dollars per day, during the session of the Legislative Assembly; but no to other officers shall be paid by the United States: Provided, That there shall be but one session of the Legislature annually, unless, on an extraordinary occasion, the Governor shall think proper to call the Legislature together. There shall be appropriated, annually, the usual sum, to be expended by the Governor, to defray the contingent expenses of the Territory, including the salary of a clerk of the Executive Department and there shall also be appropriated, annually, a sufficient sum, to be expended by the Secretary of the Territory, and upon an estimate to be made by the Secretary of the Treasury of the United States, to defray the expenses of the Legislative Assembly, the printing of the laws, and other incidental expenses; and the Governor and Secretary of the Territory shall, in the disbursement of all moneys intrusted to them, be governed solely by the instructions of the secretary of the Treasury of the United States, and shall, semi-annually, account to the said secretary for the manner in which the aforesaid moneys shall have been expended; and no expenditure shall be made by said Legislative Assembly for objects not specially authorized by the acts of Congress making the appropriations, nor beyond the sums thus appropriated for such objects.

SEC. 31. *And be it further enacted*, That the seat of government of said Territory is hereby located temporarily at Fort Leavenworth; and that such portions of the public buildings as may not be actually used and needed for military purposes, may be occupied and used, under the direction of the Governor and Legislative Assembly, for such public purposes as may be required under the provisions of this act.

SEC. 32. *And be it further enacted*, That a delegate to the House of Representatives of the United States, to serve for the term of two years, who shall be a citizen of the United States, may be elected by the voters qualified to elect members of the Legislative Assembly, who shall be entitled to the same rights and privileges as are exercised and enjoyed by the delegates from the several other Territories of the United States to the said House of Representatives, but the delegate first elected shall hold his seat only during the term of the Congress to which he shall be elected. The first election shall be held at such time and places, and be conducted in such manner, as the Governor shall appoint and direct; and at all subsequent elections, the times, places, and manner of holding the elections shall be prescribed by law. The person having the greatest number of votes shall be declared by the Governor to be duly elected, and a certificate thereof shall be given accordingly. That the Constitution, and all laws of the United States which are not locally inapplicable, shall have the same force and effect within the said Territory of Kansas as elsewhere within the United States, except the eighth section of the act preparatory to the admission of Missouri into the Union, approved March sixth, eighteen hundred and twenty, which, being inconsistent with the principle of non-intervention by Congress with slavery in the States and Territories, as recognized by the legislation of eighteen hundred and fifty, commonly called the Compromise Measures, is hereby declared inoperative and void; it being the true intent and meaning of this act not to legislate slavery into any Territory or State, nor to exclude it therefrom, but to leave the people thereof perfectly free to form and regulate their domestic institutions in their own way, subject only to the Constitution of the United States: *Provided*, That nothing herein contained shall be construed to revive or put in force any law or regulation which may have existed prior to the act of sixth of March, eighteen hundred and twenty, either protecting, establishing, prohibiting, or abolishing slavery.

SEC. 33. *And be it further enacted*, That there shall hereafter be appropriated, as has been customary for the territorial governments, a sufficient amount, to be expended under the direction of the said Governor of the Territory of Kansas, not exceeding the sums heretofore appropriated for similar objects, for the erection of suitable public buildings at the seat of government, and for the purchase of a library, to be kept at the seat of government for the use of the Governor, Legislative Assembly, Judges of the Supreme Court, Secretary, Marshal, and Attorney of said Territory, and such other persons, and under such regulations, as shall be prescribed by law.

SEC. 34. *And be it further enacted*, That when the lands in the said Territory shall be surveyed under the direction of the government of the United States, preparatory to bringing the same into market, sections numbered sixteen and thirty-six in each township in said Territory shall be, and the same are hereby, reserved for the purpose of being applied to schools in said Territory, and in the States and Territories hereafter to be erected out of the same.

SEC. 35. *And be it further enacted*, That, until otherwise provided by law, the Governor of said Territory may define the Judicial Districts of said Territory, and assign the judges who may be appointed for said Territory to the several districts; and also appoint the times and places for holding courts in the several counties or subdivisions in each of said judicial districts by proclamation, to be issued by him; but the Legislative Assembly, at their first or any subsequent session, may organize, alter, or modify such judicial districts, and assign the judges, and alter the times and places of holding the courts as to them shall seem proper and convenient.

SEC. 36. *And be it further enacted*, That all officers to be appointed by the President, by and with the advice and consent of the Senate, for the Territory of Kansas, who, by virtue of the provisions of any law now existing, or which may be enacted during the present Congress, are required to give security for moneys that may be intrusted with them for disbursement, shall give such security, at such time and place, and in such manner as the Secretary of the Treasury may prescribe.

SEC. 37. *And be it further enacted*, That all treaties, laws, and other, engagements made by the government of the United States with the Indian tribes inhabiting the territories embraced within this act, shall be faithfully and rigidly observed, notwithstanding any thing contained in this act; and that the existing agencies and superintendencies of said Indians be continued with the same powers and duties which are now prescribed by law, except that the President of the United States may, at his discretion, change the location of the office of superintendent.

Approved, May 30, 1854

Source: *United States Statutes at Large.* Vol. 10. Edited by George Minot. Boston: Little, Brown and Company, 1855.

DOCUMENT 45

GRADUATION ACT
(1854)

An Act to Graduate and Reduce the Price of the Public Land, to actual Settlers and Cultivators.

Be it enacted by the Senate and House of Representatives of the United States of America in Congress assembled, That all of the public lands of the United States which shall have been in market for ten years or upwards, prior to the time of application to enter the same under the provisions of this act, and still remaining unsold, shall be subject to sale at the price of one dollar per acre; and all of the lands of the United States that shall have been in market for fifteen years or upwards, as aforesaid, and still remaining unsold, shall be subject to sale at seventy-five cents per acre; and all of the lands of the United States that shall have been in market for twenty years or upwards, as aforesaid, and still remaining unsold, shall be subject to sale at fifty cents per acre; and all of the lands of the United States that shall have been in market for twenty-five years and upwards, as aforesaid, and still remaining unsold, shall be subject to sale at twenty-five cents per acre; and all lands of the United States that shall have been in market for thirty years or more, shall be subject to sale at twelve-and-a-half cents per acre; *Provided,* This section shall not be so construed as to extend to lands reserved to the United States, in acts granting land to States for railroad or other internal improvements, or to mineral lands held at over one dollars and twenty-five cents per acre.

SEC. 2. *And be it further enacted,* That upon every reduction in price under the provisions of this act, the occupant and settler upon the lands shall have the right of pre-emption at such graduated price, upon the same terms, conditions, restrictions, and limitations, upon which the public lands of the United States are now subject to the right of pre-emption, until within thirty days preceding the next graduation or reduction that shall take place; and if not so purchased, shall again be subject to right of pre-emption for eleven months as before, and so on from time to time, as reductions take place: *Provided,* That nothing in this act shall be so construed as to interfere with any right which has or may accrue by virtue of any act granting pre-emption to actual settlers upon public lands.

SEC. 3. *And be it further enacted*, That any person applying to enter any of the aforesaid lands shall be required to make affidavit before the register or receiver of the proper land-office, that he or she enters the same for his or her own use, and for the purpose of actual settlement and cultivation, or for the use of an adjoining farm or plantation, owned or occupied by him or herself, and together with said entry, he or she has not acquired from the United States, under the provisions of this act, more than three hundred and twenty acres, according to the established surveys and if any person or persons taking such oath or affidavit shall swear falsely in the premises, he or she shall be subject to all the pains and penalties of perjury.

APPROVED, August 4, 1854.

Source: *United States Statutes at Large.* Vol. 10. Edited by George Minot. Boston: Little, Brown and Company, 1855.

DOCUMENT 46

HOMESTEAD ACT
(1862)

An Act to secure Homesteads to actual Settlers on the Public Domain.

Be it enacted by the Senate and House of Representatives of the United States of America in Congress assembled, That any person who is the head of a family, or who has arrived at the age of twenty-one years, and is a citizen of the United States, or who shall have filed his declaration of intention to become such, as required by the naturalization laws of the United States, and who has never borne arms against the United States Government or given aid and comfort to its enemies, shall, from and after the first January, eighteen hundred and sixty-three, be entitled to enter one quarter section or a less quantity of unappropriated public lands, upon which said person may have filed a preemption claim, or which may, at the time the application is made, be subject to preemption at one dollar and twenty-five cents, or less, per acre; or eighty acres or less of such unappropriated lands, at two dollars and fifty cents per acre, to be located in a body, in conformity to the legal subdivisions of the public lands, and after the same shall have been surveyed: *Provided*, That any person owning and residing on land may, under the provisions of this act, enter other land lying contiguous to his or her said land, which shall not, with the land so already owned and occupied, exceed in the aggregate one hundred and sixty acres.

SEC. 2. *And be it further enacted*, That the person applying for the benefit of this act shall, upon application to the register of the land office in which he or she is about to make such entry, make affidavit before the said register or receiver that he or she is the head of a family, or is twenty-one years or more of age, or shall have performed service in the army or navy of the United States, and that he has never borne arms against the Government of the United States or given aid and comfort to its enemies, and that such application is made for his or her exclusive use and benefit, and that said entry is made for the purpose of actual settlement and cultivation, and not either directly or indirectly for the use or benefit of any other person or persons whomsoever; and upon filing the said affidavit with the register or receiver, and on payment of ten dollars, he or she shall thereupon be permitted to enter the quantity of land specified: *Provided, however*, That no certificate shall be given or patent issued therefor until the expiration of five years from the date of such entry; and if, at the expiration of such time, or at any time within two years thereafter, the person making such entry; or, if he be dead, his widow; or in case of her death, his heirs or devisee; or in case of a widow making such entry, her heirs or devisee, in case of her death; shall prove by two credible witnesses that he, she, or they have resided upon or cultivated the same for the term of five years immediately succeeding the time of filing the affidavit aforesaid, and shall make affidavit that no part of said land has been alienated, and that he has borne true allegiance to the Government of the United States; then, in such case, he, she, or they, if at that time a citizen of the United States, shall be entitled to a patent, as in other cases provided for by law: *And provided, further*, That in case of the death of both father and mother, leaving an infant child, or children, under twenty-one years of age, the right and fee shall enure to the benefit of said infant child or children; and the executor, administrator, or guardian way, at any time within two years after the death of the surviving parent and in accordance with the laws of the State in which such children for the time being have their domicile sell said land for the benefit of said infants, but for no other purpose; and the purchaser shall acquire the absolute title by the purchase, and be entitled to a patent from the United States, on payment of the office fees and sum of money herein specified.

SEC. 3. *And be it further enacted*, That the register of the land office shall note all such applications on the tract books and plats of his office and keep a register of all such entries, and make return thereof to the General Land Office, together with the proof upon which they have been founded.

SEC. 4. *And be it further enacted*, That no lands acquired under the provisions of this act shall in any event become liable to the satisfaction of any debt or debts contracted prior to the issuing of the patent therefor.

SEC. 5. *And be it further enacted*, That if, at any time after the filing of the affidavit, as required in the second section of this act, and before the expiration of the five years aforesaid, it shall be proven, after due notice to the settler, to the satisfaction of the register of the land office that the person having filed such affidavit shall have actually changed his or her residence, or abandoned the said land for more than six months at any time, then and in that event the land so entered shall revert to the government.

SEC. 6. *And be it further enacted*, That no individual shall be permitted to acquire title to more than one quarter section under the provision of this act; and that the Commissioner of the General Land Office is hereby required to prepare and issue such rules and regulations, consistent with this act, as shall be necessary and proper to carry its provisions into effect; and that the registers and receivers of the several land offices shall be entitled to receive the same compensation for any lands entered under the provisions of this act that they are now entitled to receive when the same quantity of land is entered with money, one half to be paid by the person making the application at the time of so doing, and the other half on the issue of the certificate by the person to whom it may be issued; but this shall not be construed to enlarge the maximum of compensation now prescribed by law for any register or receiver: *Provided*, That nothing contained in this act shall be so construed as to impair or interfere in any manner whatever with existing preemption rights: *And provided, further*, That all persons who may have filed their applications for a preemption right prior to the passage of this act, shall be entitled to all privileges of this act: *Provided, further*, That no person who has served, or may hereafter serve, for a period of not less than fourteen days in the army or navy of the United States, either regular or volunteer, under the laws thereof, during the existence of an actual war, domestic or foreign, shall be deprived of the benefits of this act on account of not having attained the age of twenty-one years.

SEC. 7. *And be it further enacted*, That the fifth section of the act entitled "An act in addition to an act more effectually to provide for the punishment of certain crimes against the United States, and for other purposes," approved the third of March, in the year eighteen hundred and fifty-seven, shall extend to all oaths, affirmations, and affidavits, required or authorized by this act.

SEC. 8. *And be it further enacted*, That nothing in this act shall be so construed as to prevent any person who has availed him or herself of the benefits of the first section of this act, from paying the minimum price, or the price to which the same may have graduated, for the quantity of land so entered at any time before the expiration of the five years, and obtaining a patent therefor from the government, as in other cases provided by law, on making proof of settlement and cultivation as provided by existing laws granting preemption rights.

APPROVED, May 20, 1862.

Source: *United States Statutes at Large*. Vol. 12. Edited by George P. Sanger. Boston: Little, Brown and Company, 1863.

DOCUMENT 47

PRESIDENT WILLIAM MCKINLEY'S PROCLAMATION (AUGUST 20, 1901)

BY THE PRESIDENT OF THE UNITED STATES OF AMERICA.

A PROCLAMATION.

Whereas notice has been given me by the Louisiana Purchase Exposition Commission, in accordance with the provisions of section 9 of the act of Congress, approved March 3, 1901, entitled "An act to provide for celebrating the one hundredth anniversary of the purchase of the Louisiana territory by the United States by holding an international exhibition of arts, industries, manufactures, and the products of the soil, mine, forest and sea, in the city of St. Louis, in the State of Missouri," that provision has been made for grounds and buildings for the uses provided for in the said act of Congress:

Now, therefore, I, William McKinley, President of the United States, by virtue of the authority vested in me by said act, do hereby declare and proclaim that such International Exhibition will be opened in the city of St. Louis, in the State of Missouri, not later than the first day of May, 1903, and will be closed not later than the first day of December thereafter. And in the name of the Government and of the people of the United States, I do hereby invite all the nations of the earth to take part in the commemoration of the Purchase of the Louisiana Territory, an event of great interest to the United States and of abiding effect on their development, by appointing representatives and sending such exhibits to the Louisiana Purchase Exposition as will most fitly and fully illustrate their resources, their industries and their progress in civilization.

In testimony whereof, I have hereunto set my hand and caused the seal of the United States to be affixed.

Done at the city of Washington, this 20th day of August, A.D. 1901, and of the Independence of the United States, the one hundred and twenty-sixth.

[SEAL]
WILLIAM McKINLEY.
By the President:
JOHN HAY,
Secretary of State.

Source: Richardson, James D., ed. 1897–1921. *A Compilation of the Messages and Papers of the Presidents Prepared under the Direction of the Joint Committee on Printing, of the House and Senate Pursuant to an Act of the Fifty-Second Congress of the United States*. Vol. 14. New York: Bureau of National Literature.

DOCUMENT 48

PRESIDENT THEODORE ROOSEVELT'S ADDRESS AT THE DEDICATION CEREMONIES OF THE LOUISIANA PURCHASE EXPOSITION (1903)

Mr. President, ladies, and gentlemen:

At the outset of my address let me recall to the minds of my hearers that the soil upon which we stand, before it was ours, was successively the possession of two mighty empires, Spain and France, whose sons made a deathless record of heroism in the early annals of the New World. No history of the Western country can be written with out paying heed to the wonderful part played therein in the early days by the soldiers, missionaries, explorers, and traders, who did their work for the honor of the proud banners of France and Castile. While the settlers of English-speaking stock, and those of Dutch, German, and Scandinavian origin who were associated with them, were still clinging close to the Eastern seaboard, the pioneers of Spain and of France had penetrated deep into the hitherto unknown wilderness of the West, and had wandered far and wide within the boundaries of what is now our mighty country. The very cities themselves—St. Louis, New Orleans, Santa Fe—bear witness by their titles to the nationalities of their founders. It was not until the Revolution had begun that the English-speaking settlers pushed west across the Alleghenies, and not until a century ago that they entered in to possess the land upon which we now stand.

We have met here today to commemorate the hundredth anniversary of the event which more than any other, after the foundation of the Government and always excepting its preservation, determined the character of our national life—determined that we should be a great expanding nation instead of relatively a small and stationary one.

Of course it was not with the Louisiana Purchase that our career of expansion began. In the middle of the Revolutionary War the Illinois region, including the present States of Illinois and Indiana, was added to our domain by force of arms, as a sequel to the adventurous expedition of George Rogers Clarke and his frontier riflemen. Later the treaties of Jay and Pinckney materially extended our real boundaries to the west. But none of these events was of so striking a character as to fix the popular imagination. The old thirteen colonies had always claimed that their rights stretched westward to the Mississippi, and vague and unreal though these claims were until made good by conquest, settlement, and diplomacy, they still served to give the impression that the earliest westward movements of our people were little more than the filling in of already existing national boundaries.

But there could be no illusion about the acquisition of the vast territory beyond the Mississippi, stretching westward to the Pacific, which in that day was known as Louisiana. This immense region was admittedly the territory of a foreign power, of a European kingdom. None of our people had ever laid claim to a foot of it. Its acquisition could in no sense be treated as rounding out any existing claims. When we acquired it we made evident once for all that consciously and of set purpose we had embarked on a career of expansion, that we had taken our place among those daring and hardy nations who risk much with the hope and desire of winning high position among the great powers of the earth. As is so often the case in nature, the law of development of a living organism showed itself in its actual workings to be wiser than the wisdom of the wisest.

This work of expansion was by far the greatest work of our people during the years that intervened between the adoption of the Constitution and the outbreak of the Civil War. There were other questions of real moment and importance, and there were many which at the time seemed such to those engaged in answering them; but the greatest feat of our forefathers of those generations was the deed of the men who, with pack-train or wagon-train, on horseback, on foot, or by boat upon the waters, pushed the frontier ever westward across the continent.

Never before had the world seen the kind of national expansion which gave our people all that part of the American continent lying west of the thirteen original States; the greatest landmark in which was the Louisiana Purchase. Our triumph in this process of expansion was indissolubly bound up with the success of our peculiar kind of federal government; and this success has been so complete that because of its very completeness we now sometimes fail to appreciate not only the all-importance but the tremendous difficulty of the problem with which our nation was originally faced.

When our forefathers joined to call into being this nation, they undertook a task for which there was but little encouraging precedent. The development of civilization from the earliest period seemed to show the truth of two propositions: In the first place, it had always proved exceedingly difficult to secure both freedom and strength in any government; and in the second place, it had always proved well-nigh impossible for a nation to expand without either breaking up or becoming a centralized tyranny. With the success of our effort to combine a strong and efficient national union, able to put down disorder at home and to maintain our honor and interest abroad, I have not now to deal. This success was signal and all-important, but it was by no means unprecedented in the same sense that our type of expansion was unprecedented. The history of Rome and of Greece illustrates very well the two types of expansion which had taken place in ancient time and which had been universally accepted as the only possible types up to the period when as a nation we ourselves began to take possession of this continent. The Grecian states performed remarkable feats of colonization, but each colony as soon as created became entirely independent of the mother state, and in after years was almost as apt to prove its enemy as its friend. Local self-government, local independence, was secured, but only by the absolute sacrifice of anything resembling national unity. In consequence, the Greek world, for all its wonderful brilliancy and the extraordinary artistic, literary, and philosophical development which has made all mankind its debtors for the ages, was yet wholly unable to withstand a formidable foreign foe, save spasmodically. As soon as powerful, permanent empires arose on its outskirts, the Greek states in the neighborhood of such empires fell under their sway. National power and greatness were completely sacrificed to local liberty.

With Rome the exact opposite occurred. The imperial city rose to absolute dominion over all the peoples of Italy and then expanded her rule over the entire civilized world by a process which kept the nation strong and united, but gave no room whatever for local liberty and self-government. All other cities and countries were subject to Rome. In consequence this great and masterful race of warriors, rulers, road-builders, and administrators stamped their indelible impress upon all the after life of our race, and yet let an over-centralization eat out the vitals of their empire until it became an empty shell; so that when the barbarians came they destroyed only what had already become worthless to the world.

The underlying viciousness of each type of expansion was plain enough and the remedy now seems simple enough. But when the fathers of the Republic first formulated the Constitution under which we live this remedy was untried and no one could foretell how it would work. They themselves began the experiment almost immediately by adding new States to the original thirteen. Excellent people in the East viewed this initial expansion of the country with great alarm. Exactly as during the colonial period many good people in the mother country thought it highly important that settlers should be kept out of the Ohio valley in the interest of the fur companies, so after we had become a nation many good people on the Atlantic coast felt grave apprehension lest they might somehow be hurt by the westward growth of the nation. These good people shook their heads over the formation of States in the fertile Ohio valley which now forms part of the heart of our nation; and they declared that the destruction of the Republic had been accomplished when through the Louisiana Purchase we acquired nearly half of what is now that same Republic's present territory. Nor was their feeling unnatural. Only the adventurous and the far-seeing can be expected heartily to welcome the process of expansion, for the nation that expands is a nation which is entering upon a great career, and with greatness there must of necessity come perils which daunt all save the most stout-hearted.

We expanded by carving the wilderness into Territories and out of these Territories building new States when once they had received as permanent settlers a sufficient number of our own people. Being a practical nation we have never tried to force on any section of our new territory an unsuitable form of government merely because it was suitable for another section under different conditions. Of the territory covered by the Louisiana Purchase a portion was given statehood within a few years. Another portion has not been admitted to statehood, although a century has elapsed—although doubtless it soon will be. In each case we showed the practical governmental genius of our race by devising methods suitable to meet the actual existing needs; not by insisting upon the application of some abstract shibboleth to all our new possessions alike, no matter how incongruous this application might sometimes be.

Over by far the major part of the territory, however, our people spread in such numbers during the course of the nineteenth century that we were able to build up State after State, each with exactly the same complete local independence in all matters affecting purely its own domestic interests as in any of the original thirteen States—each owing the same absolute fealty to the Union of all the States which each of the original thirteen States also owes,—and finally each having the same proportional right to its share in shaping and directing the common policy of the Union which is possessed by any other State, whether of the original thirteen or not.

This process now seems to us part of the natural order of things, but it was wholly unknown until our own people devised it. It seems to us a mere matter of course, a matter of elementary right and justice, that in the deliberations of the national representative bodies the representatives of a State which came into the Union but yesterday stand on a footing of exact and entire equality with those of the Commonwealths whose sons once signed the Declaration of Independence. But this way of looking at the matter is purely modern, and in its origin purely American. When Washington during his Presidency saw new States come into the Union on a footing of complete equality with the old, every European nation which had colonies still administered them as dependencies, and every other mother country treated the colonist not as a self-governing equal but as a subject.

The process which we began has since been followed by all the great peoples who were capable both of expansion and of self-government, and now the world accepts it as the natural process, as the rule; but a century and a quarter ago it was not merely exceptional, it was unknown.

This, then, is the great historic significance of the movement of continental expansion in which the Louisiana Purchase was the most striking single achievement. It stands out in marked relief even among the feats of a nation of pioneers, a nation whose people have from the beginning been picked out by a process of natural selection from among the most enterprising individuals of the nations of western Europe. The acquisition of the territory is a credit to the broad and far-sighted statesmanship of the great statesmen to whom it was immediately due, and above all to the aggressive and masterful character of the hardy pioneer folk to whose restless energy these statesmen gave expression and direction, whom they followed rather than led. The history of the land comprised within the limits of the Purchase is an epitome of the entire history of our people. Within these limits we have gradually built up State after State until now they many times over-surpass in wealth, in population, and in many-sided development the original thirteen States as they were when their delegates met in the Continental Congress. The people of these States have shown themselves mighty in war with their fellow-man, and mighty in strength to tame the rugged wilderness. They could not thus have conquered the forest and the prairie, the mountain and the desert, had they not possessed the great fighting virtues, the qualities which enable a people to overcome the forces of hostile men and hostile nature. On the other hand, they could not have used aright their conquest had they not in addition possessed the qualities of self-mastery and self-restraint, the power of acting in combination with their fellows, the power of yielding obedience to the law and of building up an orderly civilization. Courage and hardihood are indispensable virtues in a people; but the people which possesses no others can never rise high in the scale either of power or of culture. Great peoples must have in addition the governmental capacity which comes only when individuals fully recognize their duties to one another and to the whole body politic, and are able to join together in feats of constructive statesmanship and of honest and effective administration.

The old pioneer days are gone, with their roughness and their hardship, their incredible toil and their wild half-savage romance. But the need for the pioneer virtues remains the same as ever. The peculiar frontier conditions have vanished; but the manliness and stalwart hardihood of the frontiersmen can be given even freer scope under the conditions surrounding the complex industrialism of the present day. In this great region acquired for our people under the Presidency of Jefferson, this region stretching from the Gulf to the Canadian border, from the Mississippi to the Rockies, the material and social progress has been so vast that alike for weal and for woe its people now share the opportunities and bear the burdens common to the entire civilized world. The problems before us are fundamentally the same east and west of the Mississippi, in the new States and in the old, and exactly the same qualities are required for their successful solution.

We meet here today to commemorate a great event, an event which marks an era in statesmanship no less than in pioneering. It is fitting that we should pay our homage in words; but we must in honor make our words good by deeds. We have every right to take a just pride in the great deeds of our forefathers; but we show ourselves unworthy to be their descendants if we make what they did an excuse for our lying supine instead of an incentive to the effort to show ourselves by our acts worthy of them. In the administration of City, State, and Nation, in the management of our home life and the conduct of our business and social relations, we are bound to show certain high and fine qualities of character under penalty of seeing the whole heart of our civilization eaten out while the body still lives.

We justly pride ourselves on our marvelous material prosperity, and such prosperity must exist in order to establish a foundation upon which a higher life can be built; but unless we do in very fact build this higher life thereon, the material prosperity itself will go for but very little. Now, in 1903, in the altered conditions, we must meet the changed and changing problems with the spirit shown by the men who in 1803 and in the subsequent years gained, explored, conquered, and settled this vast territory, then a desert, now filled with thriving and populous States.

The old days were great because the men who lived in them had mighty qualities; and we must make the new days great by showing these same qualities. We must insist upon courage and resolution, upon hardihood, tenacity, and fertility in resource; we must insist upon the strong virile virtues; and we must insist no less upon the virtues of self-restraint, self-mastery, regard for the rights of others; we must show our abhorrence of cruelty, brutality, and corruption, in public and in private life alike. If we come short in any of these qualities we shall measurably fail; and if, as I believe we surely shall, we develop these qualities in the future to an even greater degree than in the past, then in the century now beginning we shall make of this Republic the freest and most orderly, the most just and most mighty, nation which has ever come forth from the womb of time.

Source: Roosevelt, Theodore. 1904. *Addresses and Presidential Messages of Theodore Roosevelt, 1902–1904*. New York: G. P. Putnam's Sons.

DOCUMENT 49

PRESIDENT DWIGHT D. EISENHOWER'S ADDRESS IN NEW ORLEANS AT THE CEREMONY MARKING THE 150TH ANNIVERSARY OF THE LOUISIANA PURCHASE (OCTOBER 7, 1953)

Mr. Chairman, Your Excellency the Ambassador of France, Your Excellencies the Ambassadors from other countries here represented, Governor Kennon, Mayor Morrison, Your Excellency the Archbishop, other distinguished guests—and my fellow Americans:

Before I shall try to expose to you the thoughts that I believe appropriate to this occasion, might I have a moment to express a personal word of thanks, not only on my behalf, but I am sure they would want me to speak for them—the other guests of your city today—on behalf of all of us, our thanks for the cordiality, the hospitality this city has displayed to us. We have been privileged to take part not only in an historically significant occasion, but in a most colorful one, and for my part, I owe a special debt of gratitude to Your Majesties King Rex and King Comus, for graciously allowing a part of this parade—your traditional parade—to take part in this ceremony this morning. It is the first time I have had the honor of seeing it, and I thoroughly appreciate it. Thank you.

My friends, we are today observing the anniversary of an event which ranks with the most important in our history.

The Louisiana Purchase effectively doubled the area of our young nation, brought this country unimagined wealth, and gave us strength and international influence beyond the dreams of our nation's founders just 25 years earlier.

We are observing the anniversary of an act which, though born of other nations' conflicts, involved the death of not a single American soldier. It was, for the United States, an act of peace. It was also an act of vision and of daring.

It was daring for a new-born nation, lacking all modern communications making for unity, to venture into a huge, unexplored area of unknown natural hazards and little-known inhabitants. It was daring for such a nation to accept so heavy a debt as this unique purchase imposed upon it. It was daring for our two negotiators in Paris—Livingston and Monroe—to decide to accept Napoleon's surprising offer without fear of repudiation by their national leaders separated from them by the breadth of an ocean. It was daring for our President, Thomas Jefferson, to support their decision instantly and to face squarely the opposition not only of foreign powers but of political critics of great passion and small vision.

That daring, typically American, has been justified in rare measure. It has been justified to an extent which staggers the mind; to an extent which, mathematically, is almost incalculable.

What once was the Louisiana Territory, today embraces six of our forty-eight states and large parts of seven others. It was 900 thousand square miles. It is bordered by a river almost unmatched in length and unsurpassed in majesty.

The bounty of this area has been even more phenomenal than its size. Its total cost, after all other increments were added to the 15 million dollars, was 23 million dollars—the cost today of a single Navy cargo ship. For this outlay, what did America get?

Let me give you one interesting example:

One single state—of the thirteen originally involved in the Purchase—recently reported the value of one single crop in one single year.

The state was Iowa. The crop was corn. The value was

over 700 million dollars. This sum is thirty times as much as was paid for the entire Louisiana Territory.

Only one other example shall I give you. It concerns this city of New Orleans, and, specifically, one part of this city—the Port of New Orleans. During the first four months of this year, there passed from the fields and cities of America, through the port of this city, exports valued at more than 250 million dollars. And this is a sum eleven times greater than the cost of the whole Territory.

Now I find this last example singularly meaningful—not to New Orleans alone but to all America. For here we see dramatically highlighted one of the critical facts of our national life—our dependence on foreign trade.

We all know that New Orleans has always been a vital American port. As you well remember, it was closure of this port that sharpened our nation's anxiety to buy from France the area around this city—to insure our frontiersmen this essential gateway to the open sea.

The passage of a century and a half has decisively underscored the need of that day. For today our whole economy turns and depends upon the commerce of the world through such ports as this.

Through such ports as this on this Gulf, on two oceans, on the Great Lakes, come almost all the tungsten used in our tool steel, almost all the nickel and practically all the chromite used in stainless steel.

The tin used in canning our food, the columbite and the cobalt that are needed in the manufacture of high alloys, the manganese that goes into our American steel, the hemp for our ropes and hawsers, all of these come, almost exclusively, from foreign markets.

This dependence of our industry is certain to increase as the tempo of our industry increases. It highlights the most compelling practical reason why we must have friends in the world. We know that nations of hostile intent would not trade with us except as it suited their own convenience. And this means that hostile rule of areas supplying us essential imports would place the American production line at the mercy of those who hope for its destruction.

But foreign trade means much more than the obtaining of vital raw materials from other nations. It means effectively strengthening our friends in the world at large—strengthening them not only to fortify their own economies—not only to be independent of direct financial aid from wealthier nations—but also to buy from us what we must sell to the world.

By making it possible for our friends to sell their products to us, we thus at once help them to be strong and enable them to earn the dollars by which they can, in turn, help our economy to be healthy and progressive. Clearly, we need these friends abroad, just as they need us. Consider some of our agricultural products which demand foreign markets—many of those products coming from the land originally involved in the Louisiana Purchase and much of them flowing through this port.

In the crop year 1951–52:

Of all the barley produced in this year, more than 12 percent was paid for outside our borders.

Almost 50 percent of all our wheat was paid for in foreign markets.

Almost 60 percent of our entire rice crop was bought by other nations.

With non-agricultural products, the facts are much the same. Half a million of our refrigerators and home-type freezers, more than 30 million dollars' worth of our sulphur, more than 250 million dollars' worth of our machine tools and our agricultural machinery, more than a quarter of all the lubricating oil, and almost half of all our copper sulphate—all these were paid for in foreign countries.

Now, these facts and figures affect every American, no matter who he is: all who work on our farms, all who labor in our industries. They can signify for our whole economy the difference between productive profit and paralyzing loss.

This is a partial measure of the material meaning of foreign trade to America.

And this dramatizes, with sharp clarity, the role that New Orleans has played in helping this country form and sustain the international friendships which we need and cherish. Through such gateways as New Orleans, we have been able to trade with these friends on a fair and mutually profitable basis. We have been able to cooperate with them in projects developing their physical resources. There has been for a century and a half a stream of visitors flowing in both directions—from other countries to this, and from this to other countries. Through the knowledge and mutual understanding gained and spread by these people, there have been built friendships based upon mutual respect, mutual liking, and mutual need. Such friendships are many.

But there must be more. They must be stronger. They must be deeper. I think that almost any American traveling abroad these days experiences occasionally a sense of shock when he recalls an opinion about Americans in general held abroad, that seems to that American visitor to be so far from the truth. He finds himself considered immature diplomatically—impulsive—too proud of their strength—ready to fight—wanting war. He is shocked. He is considered rude. Even his deportment is not admired, because of unfortunate incidents on the part of individuals.

These friendships of which I speak, my friends, are so vital to us, that no American, no matter how exalted or how lowly may be his station, can afford to ignore them.

Each of us, whether bearing a commission from his Government or traveling by himself for pleasure or for business is a representative of the United States of America, and he must try to portray America as he believes it in his heart to be: a peace-loving nation, living in the fear of God, but in the fear of God only, and trying to be partners with our friends—and we accept for a friend anyone who genuinely holds out the hand of friendship to us, as we do to them.

And now this great port must meet the challenge of the coming decades. It offers foreign shippers 40 miles of river front. It is enhanced by a foreign trade zone. Its modern facilities are daily being enlarged and improved. It is manned by workers celebrated for their skill, their enthusiasm, and their vigor. It is an inspiring symbol not only of the vastly prosperous area whose anniversary we are this year celebrating, but of the nation it has served for the past 150 years. And with every item of commerce that comes in, with every one that goes out, let us strive to see that it is packaged in understanding, and handled in friendship.

Here, in the Port of New Orleans, we see reflected America's strength, her vitality, her confidence, her irrepressible desire for improvement, her magnificent ability to meet resourcefully the demands of changing times.

It has been thus—in New Orleans, in the Louisiana Territory, throughout the United States—during the past century-and-a-half.

With God's help, with our friends in the world, and with unity among ourselves, it will continue to be so, throughout all the years that lie ahead.

Thank you, my friends.

Source: Eisenhower, Dwight. D. 1995. *Public Papers of the Presidents: Dwight D. Eisenhower 1953–61.* 8 vols. CD-ROM edition. Oakman, AL: H-Bar Enterprises.

BIBLIOGRAPHY

Abbot, Carl, Stephen J. Leonard, and David McComb. 1994. *Colorado: A History of the Centennial State*. Boulder: University Press of Colorado.

Aberbach, Alan D. 1971. "A Search for an American Identity." *Canadian Review of American Studies* 2, no. 2: 77–88.

Abernathy, Thomas Perkins. 1954. *The Burr Conspiracy*. New York: Oxford University Press.

Adams, Henry. 1986. *History of the United States of America during the Administrations of Jefferson and Madison*. New York: Literary Classics of America.

———. 1887. *Documents Relating to New-England Federalism, 1800–1815*. New York: Burt Franklin.

Agnew, Brad. 1980. *Fort Gibson: Terminal on the Trail of Tears*. Norman: University of Oklahoma Press.

Ahler, Stanley A., Thomas D. Thiessen, and Michael K. Trimble. 1991. *People of the Willows: The Prehistory and Early History of the Hidatsa Indians*. Grand Forks: University of North Dakota Press.

Aiton, Arthur S. 1931. "The Diplomacy of the Louisiana Cession." *American Historical Review* 36: 701–720.

Alexander, Elizabeth U. 2001. *Notorious Woman: The Celebrated Case of Myra Clark Gaines*. Baton Rouge: Louisiana State University Press.

Allen, John Logan. 1975. *Passage through the Garden: Lewis and Clark and the Image of the American Northwest*. Urbana: University of Illinois Press.

Alter, J. Cecil. 1962 [1925]. *Jim Bridger*. Norman: University of Oklahoma Press.

Alvord, Clarence W. 1965. *The Illinois Country*. Chicago: Loyola University Press.

Ambrose, Stephen E. 1996. *Undaunted Courage: Meriwether Lewis, Thomas Jefferson and the Opening of the American West*. New York: Simon and Schuster.

American Indian Publishers. 1995. *Dictionary of Indian Tribes of the Americas*, vol. 3. Newport Beach, CA: American Indian Publishers.

Ames, Fisher. 1835. *The Influences of Democracy on Liberty, Property, and the Happiness of Society, Considered*. London: J. W. Parker.

———. 1969 [1854]. *Works of Fisher Ames: With a Selection from His Speeches and Correspondence*. Edited by Seth Ames. New York: DaCapo Press.

Anderson, Fred. 2000. *Crucible of War: The Seven Year's War and the Fate of Empire in British North America, 1754–1766*. New York: Alfred A. Knopf.

Anderson, Irving W. 1992. *A Charbonneau Family Portrait: Biographical Sketches of Sacagawea, Jean Baptiste, and Toussaint Charbonneau*. Astoria, OR: Fort Clatsop Historical Society.

Andrist, Ralph K. 1964. *The Long Death: The Last Days of the Plains Indians*. New York: Macmillan

Annals of Congress, Eighth Congress, 1st Session.

Annals of Congress, Sixteenth Congress, 1st Session.

Arnold, Morris. 1991. *Colonial Arkansas, 1686–1804: A Social and Cultural History*. Fayetteville: University of Arkansas Press.

———. 2000. *The Rumble of a Distant Drum: The Quapaws and Old World Newcomers, 1673–1804*. Fayetteville: University of Arkansas Press.

Arrington, Leonard J., and Davis Bitton. 1979. *The Mormon Experience: A History of the Latter-Day Saints*. New York: Alfred A. Knopf.

Arthur, Stanley Clisby. 1935. *The Story of the West Florida Rebellion*. St. Franciscille, LA: St. Francisville Democrat.

Athearn, Robert G. 1967. *Forts on the Upper Missouri*. Lincoln: University of Nebraska Press.

Augur, Helen. 1946. *Passage to Glory: John Ledyard's America*. Garden City, NY: Doubleday.

Bacarisse, Charles A. 1955. "Baron de Bastrop." *Southwestern Historical Quarterly* 58, no. 3: 319–330.

Bailey, Thomas. 1974. *A Diplomatic History of the American People*. Englewood Cliffs, NJ: Prentice-Hall.

Baird, W. David. 1972. *The Osage People*. Phoenix: Indian Tribal Series.

———. 1980. *The Quapaws: A History of the Downstream People*. Norman: University of Oklahoma Press.

Bakeless, John. 1947. *Lewis and Clark: Partners in Discovery*. New York: William Morrow.

———. 1965. *Daniel Boone*. Harrisburg, PA: Stackpole Company.

Bancroft, Hubert Howe. 1889. *History of Arizona and New Mexico, 1530–1888*. San Francisco: History Company.

Banner, James M., Jr. 1970. *To the Hartford Convention: The Federalists and the Origins of Party Politics in Massachusetts*. New York: Alfred A. Knopf.

Banning, Lance. 1978. *The Jeffersonian Persuasion: Evolution of a Party Ideology*. Ithaca: Cornell University Press.

Baptista Pino, Don Pedro. 1995. *The Exposition on the Province of New Mexico, 1812*. Translated and edited by Adrian Bustamante and Marc Simmons. Santa Fe: University of New Mexico Press.

Barbé-Marbois, M. 1829. *Histoire de la Louisiane et de la cession de cette colonie par la France aux Etats-Unis de l'Amérique septentrionale*. Paris: Firmin Didot.

Barry, John. 1996. *Rising Tide*. New York: Simon and Schuster.

Bartel, Diane. 1984. *Amana: From Pietist Sect to American Community*. Lincoln: University of Nebraska Press.

Bartlett, I. S., ed. 1918. *History of Wyoming*. Chicago: S. J. Clarke.

Barton, Sir Dunbar Plunkett. 1929. *The Amazing Career of Bernadotte, 1763–1844*. London: John Murray.

Baudier, Roger. 1939. *The Catholic Church in Louisiana*. New Orleans: Baudier.

Bearss, Edwin. 1969. *Fort Smith, Little Gibraltar on the Arkansas*. Norman: University of Oklahoma Press.

Bechdolt, Frederick Ritchie. 1969. *Giants of the Old West*. Freeport, NY: Books for Libraries Press.

Becknell, Thomas. 1910. "The Journals of Thomas [William] Becknell from Boone's Lick to Santa Fe and from Santa Cruz to Green River." *Missouri Historical Review* 4: 76–79.

Beidleman, Richard G. 1960. "Some Biographical Sidelights on Thomas Nuttall, 1786–1859." *Proceedings of the American Philosophical Society* 104, no. 1: 86–100.

Belting, Natalia Maree. 1948. *Kaskaskia under the French Regime*. Urbana: University of Illinois Press.

Bemis, Samuel Flagg. 1923. *Jay's Treaty: A Study in Commerce and Diplomacy.* New York: Macmillan.

———. 1959. *A Short History of American Foreign Policy and Diplomacy.* New York: Holt, Rinehart, and Winston.

———. 1960 [1926]. *Pinckney's Treaty: A Study of America's Advantage from Europe's Distress*. Baltimore: Johns Hopkins Press. Reprint: New Haven: Yale University Press.

Bemis, Samuel Flagg, 1963. *The American Secretaries of State and Their Diplomacy*. New York: Cooper Square.

Ben-Atar, Doron, and Barbara B. Oberg, eds. 1998. *Federalist Reconsidered*. Charlottesville: University Press of Virginia.

Bennett, James D. 1975. *Frederick Jackson Turner*. Boston: Twayne Publishers.

Benson, Maxine, ed. 1988. *From Pittsburg to the Rocky Mountains: Major Stephen Long's Expedition, 1819–1820*. Golden, CO: Fulcrum.

Benton, Thomas Hart. 1854–1856. *Thirty Years' View; or, A History of the Working of the American Government for Thirty Years, from 1820 to 1850*. New York: Appleton.

Bergamini, John D. 1974. *The Spanish Bourbons: The History of a Tenacious Dynasty*. New York: G. P. Putnam's Sons.

Bernhard, Winfred E. A. 1965. *Fisher Ames: Federalist and Statesman, 1758–1808*. Chapel Hill: University of North Carolina Press.

Berry, Don. 1961. *A Majority of Scoundrels: An Informal History of the Rocky Mountain Fur Company*. New York: Harper.

Berthrong, Donald J. 1976. *The Cheyenne and Arapaho Ordeal: Reservation and Agency Life in the Indian Territory*. Norman: University of Oklahoma Press

Bertrand, Louis, and Sir Charles Petrie. 1956. *The History of Spain, Part II*. London: Eyre and Spottiswoode.

Betts, Robert B. 1985. *In Search of York: The Slave Who Went to the Pacific with Lewis and Clark*. Boulder: Colorado Association University Press.

Bierhorst, John. 1985. *The Mythology of North America.* New York: Quill William Morrow.

Billington, Ray Allen. 1973. *Frederick Jackson Turner: Historian, Scholar, Teacher*. New York: Oxford University Press.

———. 1974. *Westward Expansion: A History of the American Frontier*. New York: Macmillan.

Black Hawk. 1999 [1834]. *Life of Ma-Ka-Tai-Me-She-Kia-Kiak or Black Hawk*. Boston: Russell, Odiorne and Metcalf. Reprint: *Black Hawk's Autobiography*. Edited by Roger L. Nichols. Ames: Iowa State University Press.

Blaine, Martha Royce. 1995. *The Ioway Indians*. Norman: University of Oklahoma Press.

Bleed, Ann S., and Charles A. Flowerday, eds. 1998. *An Atlas of the Sand Hills*. 3d ed. Lincoln: Conservation and Survey Division, Institute of Agriculture and Natural Resources, University of Nebraska.

Blegen, Theodore C. 1975. *Minnesota: A History of the State*. Minneapolis: University of Minnesota Press.

Bloch, E. Maurice. 1986. *The Paintings of George Caleb Bingham: A Catalogue Raisonné*. Columbia: University of Missouri Press.

Blue, Fredrick J. 1973. *The Free Soilers: Third Party Politics, 1848–54*. Urbana: University of Illinois Press.

Bogue, Allan G. 1998. *Frederick Jackson Turner: Strange Roads Going Down*. Norman: University of Oklahoma Press.

Bolton, Herbert Eugene. 1970. *Texas in the Middle Eighteenth Century: Studies in Spanish Colonial History and Administration*. Austin: University of Texas Press.

Bolton, Herbert Eugene, and Thomas Maitland Marshall. 1932. *The Colonization of North America, 1492–1783*. New York: Macmillan Company.

Bolton, S. Charles. 1993. *Territorial Ambition: Land and Society in Arkansas, 1800–1840*. Fayetteville: University of Arkansas Press.

———. 1998. *Arkansas, 1800–1860: Remote and Restless*. Fayetteville: University of Arkansas Press.

Bonvillain, Nancy. 1995. *The Sac and Fox*. Edited by Frank W. Porter III. New York: Chelsea House.

Bonvillain, Nancy, and Frank W. Porter III, eds. 1997. *The Santee Sioux*. Philadelphia: Chelsea House.

Bowman, Albert Hall. 1974. *The Struggle for Neutrality: Franco-American Diplomacy during the Federalist Era*. Knoxville: University of Tennessee Press.

Branagan, Thomas. 1805. *Serious remonstrances, addressed to the citizens of the northern states, and their representatives microform....* Philadelphia: T. T. Stiles.

Brandon, William. 1968. "Wilson Price Hunt." In *The Mountain Men and the Fur Trade of the Far West.* Edited by Le Roy Hafen, vol. 6. Glendale, CA: Arthur H. Clark.

Brandt, Penny S. 1988. "A Letter of Dr. John Sibley, Indian Agent." *Louisiana History* 29, no. 4: 365–387.

Brant, Irving. 1953. *James Madison. Secretary of State, 1800–1809*. Indianapolis: Bobbs-Merrill.

Brasseaux, Carl. 1987. *The Founding of New Acadia: The Beginnings of Acadian Life in Louisiana, 1765–1803*. Baton Rouge: Louisiana State University Press.

———. 1992. *Acadian to Cajun: Transformation of a People, 1803–1877.*Jackson: University Press of Mississippi.

Breitbart, Eric. 1997. *A World on Display: Photographs from the St. Louis World's Fair, 1904*. Albuquerque: University of New Mexico Press.

Brent, Robert. 1968. "Puncturing Some Jeffersonian Mythology." *Southern Quarterly* 6, no. 2: 175–190.

Brierly, J. L. 1963. *The Law of Nations: An Introduction to the International Law of Peace*. 6th ed. Edited by Humphrey Waldock. New York and Oxford: Oxford University Press.

Brinton, Crane. 1963. *The Lives of Talleyrand*. New York: Norton.

Brookhiser, Richard. 1999. *Alexander Hamilton, American*. New York: Free Press.

Brown, Dee. 1970. *Bury My Heart at Wounded Knee*. New York: Holt, Rinehart and Winston.

Brown, Everett S. 1972. *The Constitutional History of the Louisiana Purchase, 1803–1812*. Edited by Herbert E. Bolton. Chevy Chase, MD: Beard Books.

Brown, Margaret K. 1977. "Uncovering the Mystery of the Three Forts de Chartres." *Illinois Magazine* 16(9): 23–29.

Brown, Margaret K., and Lawrie Cena Dean. 1995. *The French Colony in the Mid-Mississippi Valley.* Carbondale, IL.: American Kestral Books.

Brown, Sharon. 1980. "Jefferson National Expansion Memorial: The 1947–48 Competition." *Gateway Heritage: The Quarterly Journal of the Missouri Historical Society* 1, no. 3: 40–48.

———. 1985. *Administrative History: Jefferson National Expansion Memorial National Historic Site.* St. Louis: National Park Service, Jefferson National Expansion Memorial National Historic Site.

Brown, Wilburt S. 1969. *The Amphibious Campaign for West Florida and Louisiana, 1814–1815.* Tuscaloosa: University of Alabama Press.

Brownson, James I. 1910. *The Life and Times of Senator James Ross.* Washington, PA: Washington County Historical Society.

Bruchac, Joseph. 2000. *Sacajawea.* Orlando, FL: Harcourt.

Bruns, J. Edgar. 1988. "Sedella, Antonio de." In *Dictionary of Louisiana Biography.* Edited by Glenn R. Conrad. Lafayette: Louisiana Historical Association and the Center for Louisiana Studies.

Buckley, Jay H. 2001. "William Clark: Superintendent of Indian Affairs at St. Louis, 1813–1838." Ph.D. diss., Department of History, University of Nebraska, Lincoln.

Burton, Harris. 1952. *John Colter, His Years in the Rockies.* New York: Scribner.

Bush, Robert D. 1977. "Documents on the Louisiana Purchase: The Laussat Papers." *Louisiana History* 18, no. 1: 104–107.

Caesar, Gene. 1961. *King of the Mountain Men: The Life of Jim Bridger.* New York: E. P. Dutton Company.

Calloway, Colin G. 1991. "Snake Frontiers: The Eastern Shoshones in the Eighteenth Century." *Annals of Wyoming* 63: 82–92.

Calvert, Robert A., and Arnoldo DeLeon. 1996. *The History of Texas.* Wheeling, IL: Harlan Davidson.

Campbell, Charles S. 1974. *From Revolution to Rapproachment: The United States and Great Britain, 1783–1900.* New York: John Wiley and Son.

Campbell, Eugene E. 1988. *Establishing Zion: The Mormon Church in the American West, 1847–1869.* Salt Lake City: Signature Books.

Carson, David A. 1992. "Blank Paper of the Constitution: The Louisiana Purchase Debates." *Historian* 54, no. 3: 477–490.

———. 1998. "The Role of Congress in the Acquisition of the Louisiana Territory." In *The Louisiana Purchase and Its Aftermath.* Edited by Dolores Egger Labbe. Lafayette: Center for Louisiana Studies.

Carter, Clarence E., ed. 1934–1975. *The Territorial Papers of the United States.* Washington, DC: Government Printing Office.

Carter, Harvey Lewis. 1968. *Dear Old Kit: The Historical Christopher Carson.* Norman: University of Oklahoma Press.

———. 1969. "William H. Ashley." In *The Mountain Men and the Fur Trade of the Far West.* Edited by LeRoy R. Hafen, vol. 7. Glendale, CA: A. H. Clark.

Cash, Joseph H., and Gerald W. Wolff. 1974. *The Three Affiliated Tribes (Mandan, Arikara, and Hidatsa).* Phoenix: Indian Tribal Series.

Castañeda, Carlos E. 1942. *Our Catholic Heritage in Texas, 1519–1936, vol. 5: The Mission Era: The End of the Spanish Regime, 1780–1810.* Austin: Von Boeckmann-Jones Company.

Cava, María Jesús, and Begoña Cava. 1992. *Diego María de Gardoqui: Un Bilbaino en la Diplomacia del Siglo XVIII.* Bilbao, Spain: Bilbao Bizkaia Kutxa.

Chambers, William N. 1956. *Old Bullion Benton: Senator from the New West.* Boston: Little, Brown and Co.

Chancellor, John. 1978. *Audubon.* New York: Viking Press.

Chastenet, Jacques. 1972. *Godoy: Master of Spain, 1792–1808.* Translated by J. F. Huntington. London: Batchworth Press.

Chidsey, Donald Barr. 1967. *The Great Conspiracy: Aaron Burr and His Strange Doings in the West.* New York: Crown Publishers.

———. 1970. *Lewis and Clark: The Great Adventure.* New York: Crown.

Chipman, Donald E. 1992. *Spanish Texas, 1519–1821.* Austin: University of Texas Press.

Chittenden, Hiram Martin. 1954. *A History of the American Fur Trade of the Far West.* 2 vols. Stanford, CA: Academic Reprints.

Christ-Janer, Albert. 1940. *George Caleb Bingham of Missouri.* New York: Dodd, Mead and & Company.

Christelow, Allan. 1941. "French Interest in the Spanish Empire during the Ministry of the Duc de Choiseul, 1759–1771." *Hispanic American Historical Review* 21: 515–537.

———. 1946. "Economic Background of the Anglo-Spanish War of 1762." *Journal of Modern History* 18: 22–36.

Claiborne, W. C. C. 1917. *The Official Letter Books of W. C. C. Claiborne.* Edited by Dunbar Rowland. Jackson: Mississippi Department of Archives and History.

Claiborne, Nathaniel Herbert. 1819. *Notes on the War in the South; with Biographical Sketches of the Lives of Montgomery, Jackson, Sevier, and Late Gov. Claiborne, and Others.* Richmond: William Ramsay.

Clarfield, Gerard H. 1969. *Timothy Pickering and American Diplomacy.* Columbia: University of Missouri Press.

———. 1980. *Timothy Pickering and the American Republic.* Pittsburgh: University of Pittsburgh Press.

Clark, Daniel. 1970 [1809]. *Proofs of the Corruption of General James Wilkinson, and of his connexion with Aaron Burr ....* Freeport, NY: Books for Libraries Press.

Clark, John G. 1970. *New Orleans, 1718–1812: An Economic History.* Baton Rouge: Louisiana State University Press.

Clark, William. 1937. *Westward with Dragoons: The Journal of William Clark on His Expedition to Establish Fort Osage, August 25 to September 22, 1808.* Edited by Kate L. Gregg. Fulton, MO: Ovid Bell Press.

———. 1987. *The Journals of the Lewis and Clark Expedition, vol. 3: August 25, 1804–April 6, 1805.* Edited by Gary E. Moulton. Lincoln: University of Nebraska Press.

Claude Perrin Victor Papers. 1802–1804. MSS 94. Williams Research Center, New Orleans, Louisiana.

Clevenger, Martha R., ed. 1996. *Indescribably Grand: Diaries and Letters from the 1904 World's Fair.* St. Louis: Missouri Historical Society Press.

Clifton, James A. 1977. *The Prairie People: Continuity and Change in Potawatomi Indian Culture, 1665–1965.* Lawrence: Regents Press of Kansas.

———. 1984. *The Pokagons, 1683–1983: Catholic Potawatomi Indians of the St. Joseph River Valley*. New York, London: Lanham.

Clokey, Richard M. 1980. *William H. Ashley: Enterprise and Politics in the Trans-Mississippi West*. Norman: University of Oklahoma Press.

Coleman, William S. E. 2000. *Voices of Wounded Knee*. Lincoln: University of Nebraska Press.

Collot, Georges Henri Victor. 1974 [1826]. *Journey in North America*. New York: AMS Press.

Commager, Henry Steele, ed. 1973. *Documents of American History*, vol. 1. Englewood Cliffs, NJ: Prentice-Hall.

Condon, Yvonne. 1990. "St. Louis 1904: Louisiana Purchase International Exposition." In *Historical Dictionary of World's Fairs and Expositions, 1851–1988*. Edited by John E. Findling and Kimberly D. Pelle. Westport, CT: Greenwood Press.

Conzen, M. P., ed. 1990. *The Making of the American Landscape*. New York, & London: Routledge.

Corbett, William P. 1982. "Rifles and Ruts: Army Road Builders in Indian Territory." *Chronicles of Oklahoma* 60: 294–309.

Corle, Edwin. 1949. *The Royal Highway: El Camino Real*. New York: Bobbs-Merrill.

Cornish, Rory T. 1986. "A Vision of Empire: The Development of British Opinion regarding the American Colonial Empire, 1730–1770." Ph.D. diss., University of London.

Corthell, E. L. 1881. *A History of the Jetties at the Mouth of the Mississippi River*. New York: John Wiley & Sons.

Coues, Elliot, ed. 1965. *The Expeditions of Zebulon Montgomery Pike*. Minneapolis: Ross and Haines.

Coutant, Charles G. 1899. *The History of Wyoming from the Earliest Known Discoveries*. 3 vols. Laramie, WY: Chaplin, Spafford and Mathison.

Cowdrey, Albert E. 1977. *Land's End*. New Orleans: Corps of Engineers.

Cox, Isaac John. 1967. *The West Florida Controversy, 1798–1813: A Study in American Diplomacy*. Glouster, MA: Peter Smith.

Crouse, Nellis M. 1956. *La Verendrye: Fur Trader and Explorer.* Ithaca: Cornell University Press.

Cullen, Charles T. 1971. "St. George Tucker and Law in Virginia, 1772–1804." Ph.D. diss., University of Virginia.

Cunningham, Noble E., Jr. 1963. "Who Were the Quids?" *Mississippi Valley Historical Review* 50: 252–263.

Dale, Clifford. 1910. *The Ashley-Smith Explorations and the Discovery of a Central Route to the Pacific, 1822–1829, with the Original Journals*. Cleveland: Arthur H. Clark.

Daniels, Jonathan. 1962. *The Devil's Backbone: The Story of the Natchez Trace*. New York: McGraw-Hill.

Danziger, Edmund Jefferson, Jr. 1990. *The Chippewas of Lake Superior*. Norman, London: University of Oklahoma Press.

Dargo, George. 1975. *Jefferson's Louisiana: Politics and the Clash of Legal Traditions*. Cambridge: Harvard University Press.

Davenport, Frances G., and Charles O. Paullin, eds. 1917–1937. *European Treaties Bearing on the History of the United States and Its Dependencies*. 4 vols. Washington DC: Carnegie Institution.

Davis, W. N. 1971. "The Sutler at Fort Bridger." *Western Historical Quarterly* 2: 37–54.

Davis, William C. 1995. *A Way through the Wilderness: The Natchez Trace and the Civilization of the Southern Frontier*. New York: Harper-Collins Publishers.

Dawidoff, Robert. 1979. *The Education of John Randolph*. New York: Norton.

De Grummond, Jane Lucas. 1961. *The Baratarians and the Battle of New Orleans*. Baton Rouge: Louisiana State University Press.

———. 1983. *Renato Beluche: Smuggler, Privateer and Patriot, 1780–1860*. Baton Rouge: Louisiana State University Press.

De Laussat, Pierre Clément. 1978. *Memoirs of My Life to My Son during the Years 1803 and After ....* Edited by Robert D. Bush. Translated by Sister Agnes-Josephine Pastwa, Order of St. Francis. Baton Rouge: Published for the Historic New Orleans Collection by the Louisiana State University Press.

de Morembert, Tribout. 1958. "Une famille d'ancienne bourgeoisie messine et ses alliances: Barbé et Barbé de Marbois." *Cahiers lorrains*.

Debates and Proceedings in the Congress of the United States (Annals of Congress). 42 vols. 1834–1856. Washington, DC: Gales and Seaton.

DeConde, Alexander. 1958. *Entangling Alliance: Politics & Diplomacy under George Washington*. Durham: Duke University Press.

———. 1966. *The Quasi-War: The Politics and Diplomacy of the Undeclared War with France, 1797–1801*. New York: Charles Scribner's Sons.

———. 1976. *This Affair of Louisiana*. New York: Charles Scribner's Sons.

Delderfield, Ronald F. 1962. *The March of the Twenty-Six: The Story of Napoleon's Marshals*. London: Hodder and Stoughton.

Dempsey, Hugh A. 1972. *Crowfoot, Chief of the Blackfeet*. Norman: University of Oklahoma Press.

Denig, Edwin Thompson. 1975. *Five Indian Tribes of the Upper Missouri: Sioux, Arickaras, Assiniboines, Crees, Crows*. Edited by John C. Ewers. Norman, London: University of Oklahoma Press.

Descola, Jean. 1963. *A History of Spain*. New York: Alfred A. Knopf.

Deutsch, Eberhard P. 1967. "The Constitutional Controversy over the Louisiana Purchase." *American Bar Association Journal* 53: 50–57.

DeVoto, Bernard. 1947. *Across the Wide Missouri*. Boston: Houghton Mifflin.

———. 1983. *The Course of Empire*. Lincoln: University of Nebraska Press.

DeVoto, Bernard, ed. 1953. *The Journals of Lewis and Clark*. Boston: Houghton Mifflin Company.

Dick, Everett. 1970. *The Lure of the Land: A Social History of the Public Lands from the Articles of Confederation to the New Deal*. Lincoln: University of Nebraska Press.

———. 1975. *Conquering the Great American Desert: Nebraska*. Omaha: Nebraska State Historical Society.

Dicken-Garcia, Hazel. 1991. *To Western Woods: The Breckinridge Family Moves to Kentucky in 1793*. Rutherford, NJ: Fairleigh Dickinson University Press.

Dillon, Richard H. 1988. *Meriwether Lewis: A Biography*. Santa Cruz, CA: Western Tanager Press.

Din, Gilbert C. 1990. "Francisco Bouligny, Marqués de Casa-Calvo, Manuel Juan de Salcedo, Pierre Clément, Baron de

Laussat, Colonial Governors, 1799–1803." In *The Louisiana Governors, from Iberville to Edwards*. Edited by Joseph G. Dawson III. Baton Rouge: Louisiana State University Press.

Dippel, Horst. 1996. "The Changing Idea of Popular Sovereignty in Early American Constitutionalism: Breaking Away from European Patterns." *Journal of the Early Republic* 16: 21–45.

"Documents: Despatches from the United States Consul in New Orleans, 1801–1803: Parts II." *American Historical Review* 33 (1928): 331–359.

Domínguez, Virginia. 1986. *White by Definition: Social Classification in Creole Louisiana*. New Brunswick, NJ: Rutgers University Press.

Drinnon, Richard. 1980. *Facing West: The Metaphysics of Indian-Hating & Empire-Building*. Norman: University of Oklahoma Press.

Drury, John. 1947. *Historic Midwest Houses*. New York: Bonanza Books.

Dunbar, Jean. 2001. *Omaha, Council Bluffs, and Bellevue in the Nineteenth Century: A Photographic History*. Chicago: Arcadia Publishing.

Dunn, J. P. 1886. *Massacres of the Mountains: A History of the Indian Wars of the Far West, 1815–1875*. New York: Archer House.

Dwight, Theodore. 1970. *History of the Hartford Convention: With A Review of the Policy of the United States Government which Led to the War of 1812*. New York: DaCapo.

Dyer, Brainerd. 1946. *Zachary Taylor*. Baton Rouge: Louisiana State University Press.

Eby, Cecil. 1973. *"That Disgraceful Affair," the Black Hawk War*. New York: W. W. Norton.

Eccles, W. J. 1972. *France in America*. New York: Harper Torchbooks.

Echeverria, Durand, trans. 1952. "General Collot's Plan for a Reconnaissance of the Ohio and Mississippi Valleys, 1796." *William and Mary Quarterly* 9, no. 3: 518.

Edmunds, R. David. 1978. *The Potawatomis: Keepers of the Fire*. Norman, London: University of Oklahoma Press.

———. 1993. *The Fox Wars: The Mesquakie Challenge to New France*. The Civilization of the American Indian, vol. 211. Norman: University of Oklahoma Press.

Egan, Clifford L. 1983. *Neither Peace nor War: Franco-American Relations, 1803–1812*. Baton Rouge: Louisiana State University Press.

Ekberg, Carl J. 1996. *Colonial Ste. Genevieve: An Adventure on the Mississippi Frontier*. Tucson, AZ: Patrice Press.

Elliot, T. C. 1931. "Wilson Price Hunt." *Oregon Historical Quarterly* 32: 130–135.

Ellison, Robert S. 1981 [1931]. *Fort Bridger: A Brief History*. Cheyenne: Wyoming State Archives, Museums and Historical Department.

Engelbert, Ernest A., ed. 1985. *Water Scarcity Impacts on Western Agriculture*. Berkley: University of California Press.

Epstein, David F. 1984. *The Political Theory of the Federalist*. Chicago: University of Chicago Press.

Erney, Richard A. 1979. *The Public Life of Henry Dearborn*. New York: Arno Press.

Ernst, Robert. 1968. *Rufus King: American Federalist*. Chapel Hill: University of North Carolina Press.

Evans, Howard Ensign. 1997. *A Natural History of the Long Expedition to the Rocky Mountains, 1819–1820*. New York: Oxford University Press.

Everett, Dianna. 1990. *The Texas Cherokees: A People between Two Fires, 1819–1840*. Norman: Oklahoma University Press.

Ewan, Joseph, ed. 1969. *A Short History of Botany in the United States*. New York: Hofner Publishing Company.

Ewers, John C. 1967. *The Blackfeet: Raiders on the Northwestern Plains*. Norman: University of Oklahoma Press.

———. 1982. *Artists of the Old West*. New York: Promontory Press.

Ewing, Frank. 1959. *America's Forgotten Statesman: Albert Gallatin*. New York: Vantage Press.

Faragher, John Mack. 1979. *Women and Men on the Overland Trail*. New Haven: Yale University Press.

———. 1992. *Daniel Boone: The Life and Times of an American Pioneer*. New York: Henry Holt and Company.

Farnham, Thomas J. 1965. "The Federal-State Issue and the Louisiana Purchase." *Louisiana History* 6, no. 1: 5–25.

Favour, Alpheus H. 1936. *Old Bill Williams, Mountain Man*. Chapel Hill: University of North Carolina Press.

Faye, Stanley. 1940. "The Great Stroke of Pierre Laffite." *Louisiana Historical Quarterly* 23: 733–826.

Fehrenbacher, Don E. 1995. *Sectional Crisis and Southern Constitutionalism*. Baton Rouge: Louisiana University State Press.

Ferguson, E. James, ed. 1967. *Selected Writings of Albert Gallatin*. Indianapolis: Bobbs-Merrill Company.

Ferrell, Robert H. 1969. *American Diplomacy: A History*. New York: W. W. Norton.

Fick, Carolyn. 1990. *The Making of the Revolution: The Saint Dominigue Revolution from Below*. Knoxville: University of Tennessee Press.

Fischer, David Hackett. 1964. "The Myth of the Essex Junto." *William and Mary Quarterly* 21: 191–235.

———. 1965. *The Revolution of American Conservatism: The Federalist Party in the Era of Jeffersonian Democracy*. New York: Harper & Row.

Fisher, Robert L. 1933. "The Treaties of Portage des Sioux." *Mississippi Valley Historical Review* 19, no. 4: 495–508.

Fleming, Thomas. *Duel. 1999. Alexander Hamilton, Aaron Burr, and the Future of America*. New York: Basic Books.

Flemming, Alice. 1971. *Highways into History*. New York: St. Martin's Press.

Flores, Dan L. 1984. "The Ecology of the Red River in 1806: Peter Custis and Early Southwestern Natural History." *Southwestern Historical Quarterly* 88: 1–42.

Flores, Dan L., ed. 1984. *Jefferson and Southwestern Exploration: The Freeman and Custis Accounts of the Red River Expedition of 1806*. Norman: University of Oklahoma Press.

Fogdall, Alberta Brooks. 1978. *Royal Family of the Columbia: Dr. John McLoughlin and His Family*. Fairfield, WA: Ye Galleon Press.

Foley, William E. 1989. *The Genesis of Missouri: From Wilderness Outpost to Statehood*. Columbia: University of Missouri Press.

Foner, Eric. 1970. *Free Soil, Free Labor, Free Men: The Ideology of the Republican Party before the Civil War*. New York: Oxford University Press.

Forbes, Jack D. 1960. *Apache, Navajo, and Spaniard.* Norman: University of Oklahoma Press.

Foreman, Grant. 1976. *Indian Removal.* Norman: University of Oklahoma Press.

Fort Jesup Collection. Microfilm Collection #206, reel 4. Northwestern State University Archives. Natchitoches, LA.

Fortier, Alcée. 1904. *A History of Louisiana, vol. 3: The American Domination, Part I, 1803–1861.* New York: Goupil and Company.

Fowler, Jack D. 1997. "Amid Bedbugs and Drunken Secessionists." *Civil War Times Illustrated* 36: 44–50.

Fowler, Loretta. 1989. *The Arapaho.* New York: Chelsea House

———. 1987. *Shared Symbols, Contested Meanings: Gros Ventre Culture and History, 1778–1984.* Ithaca: Cornell University Press.

Franchère, Gabriel. 1969. *Journal of a Voyage on the North West Coast of North America during the Years 1811, 1812, 1813, and 1814.* Toronto: Champlain Society.

Franzwa, Gregory M. 1967. *The Story of Old Ste. Genevieve: An Account of an Old French Town in Upper Louisiana.* Tucson, AZ: Patrice Press.

———. 1973. *The Story of Old Ste. Genevieve: An Account of an Old French Town in Upper Louisiana; Its People and Their Homes.* Gerald, MO: Patrice Press.

Frazer, Robert W. 1965. *Forts of the West: Military Forts and Presidios and Posts Commonly Called Forts West of the Mississippi River to 1898.* Norman: University of Oklahoma Press.

Freedman, Russell. 1992. *An Indian Winter.* New York: Holiday House.

Freehling, William W. 1990. *The Road to Disunion: Secessionists at Bay, 1776–1854.* New York: Oxford University Press.

Fritz, Harry W. 1977. "The War Hawks of 1812: Party Leadership in the Twelfth Congress." *Capital Studies* 5: 25–42.

Froiland, Sven. 1990. *Natural History of the Black Hills and Badlands.* Sioux Falls, SD: Center for Western Studies.

Fruchtman, Jack, Jr. 1994. *Thomas Paine: Apostle of Freedom.* New York: Four Walls Eight Windows.

Fugier, André. 1947. *Napoléon et l'Italie.* Paris: Dijon.

Fuller, Myron. 1912. "The New Madrid Earthquake." *United States Geological Survey Bulletin 494.* Washington, DC: Government Printing Office.

Gaines, Edmund Pendleton. 1845. *The Case of General Gaines and Wife versus Richard Relf and Beverly Chew, in the Circuit Court of the United States for the State of Louisiana: Answer, &c., of the Defendants, Relf, Chew, Ferrier, and Barnes and Wife.* New Orleans: Joseph Cohn.

Garland, Hugh A. 1850. *Life of Randolph of Roanoke.* New York: D. Appleton & Company.

Garvey, Joan B., and Mary Lou Widmer. 1988. *Beautiful Crescent: A History of New Orleans.* New Orleans: Garner Press.

Gash, Norman. 1984. *Lord Liverpool: The Life and Political Career of Robert Banks Jenkinson, Second Earl of Liverpool, 1770–1828.* Cambridge: Harvard University Press.

Gates, Paul W. 1979. *History of Public Land Law Development.* New York: Arno Press.

Gates, Paul W., and Robert W. Swenson. 1968. *History of Public Land Law Development.* Washington, DC: Public Land Law Review Commission.

Gayarré, Charles. 1883. "Historical Sketch of Pierre and Jean Lafitte: The Famous Smugglers of Louisiana." *Magazine of American History* 10: 284–298, 389–396.

———. 1903. *History of Louisiana: The Spanish Domination.* New Orleans: F. F. Hansell & Brothers.

———. 1965. *A History of Louisiana.* Gretna, LA: Pelican Publishing.

———. 1974. *History of Louisiana: The American Domination,* vol. 4. Gretna, LA: Pelican Publishing.

Genovese, Eugene D. 1976. *Roll, Jordan, Roll: The World the Slaves Made.* New York: Vintage.

George Champlain Sibley Papers. Missouri Historical Society, St. Louis, MO.

Gibbs, Carroll R. 1992. *Black Explorers.* Silver Spring, MD: Three Dimensional Publishing.

Gibson, Arrell Morgan. 1963. *The Kickapoos: Lords of the Middle Border.* Norman: University of Oklahoma Press.

———. 1965. *Oklahoma: A History of Five Centuries.* Norman, OK: Harlow.

Gienapp, William E. 1987. *The Origins of the Republican Party, 1852–1856.* New York: Oxford University Press.

Gilman, Carolyn, and Mary Jane Schneider. 1987. *The Way to Independence: Memories of a Hidatsa Indian Family, 1840–1920.* St. Paul: Minnesota Historical Society Press.

Gipson, Lawrence Henry. 1966. *The Great War for the Empire: The Culmination, 1760–1763. The British Empire before the American Revolution,* vol. 8. New York: Alfred A. Knopf.

Giraud, Marcel. 1986. *The Metis in the Canadian West.* Lincoln: University of Nebraska Press.

Gittinger, Roy. 1917. *The Formation of the State of Oklahoma: 1803–1906.* Berkeley: University of California Press.

Goetzmann, William H. 1966. *Exploration and Empire: The Explorer and the Scientist in the Winning of the American West.* New York: Alfred A. Knopf.

———. 1991. *Army Exploration in the American West, 1803–1863.* Austin: Texas State Historical Association.

———. 1995. *New Lands, New Men.* Austin: Texas State Historical Association.

Goetzmann, William, et al. 1985. *Karl Bodmer's America.* Lincoln: Joslyn Art Museum and the University of Nebraska Press.

Goodrich, James W. 1999. "Manuel Lisa." In *American National Biography.* Edited by John A. Garraty and Mark C. Carnes, vol. 13. New York: Oxford University Press.

Goodyear Freehling, Alison. 1982. *Drift toward Dissolution: The Virginia Slavery Debate of 1831–1832.* Baton Rouge, London: Louisiana State University Press.

Gore, S. Joseph. 1964. *Heritage of St Louis.* St. Louis: St. Louis Public Library.

Gowans, Fred R., and Eugene E. Campbell. 1975. *Fort Bridger: Island in the Wilderness.* Provo, UT: Brigham Young University Press.

Gowen, Fred R. 1976. *Rocky Mountain Rendezvous: A History of the Fur Trade Rendezvous, 1825–1840.* Provo, UT: Brigham Young University.

Grant, Blanche C. 1934. *When Old Trails Were New: The Story of Taos.* New York: Press of the Pioneers.

Graustein, Jeannette E. 1967. *Thomas Nuttall, Naturalist: Explorations in America, 1808–1841.* Cambridge: Harvard University Press.

Graves, Daniel. 1996. *Profiles of Natchitoches History.* Natchitoches, LA: Museum of Historic Natchitoches.

Graves, W. W. 1949. *The First Protestant Osage Missions, 1820–1837.* Oswego, KS: Carpenter Press.

Green, James R. 1978. *Grass-Roots Socialism: Radical Movements in the Southwest, 1895–1943.* Baton Rouge: Louisiana State University Press.

Greene, Jerome A. 1994. *Lakota and Cheyenne: Indian Views of the Great Sioux War, 1876–1877.* Norman: University of Oklahoma Press.

Gregg, Josiah. 1905. *Commerce on the Prairies.* 2 vols. Cleveland: Arthur H. Clark.

Gregg, Kate L. 1936. "Building of the First American Fort West of the Mississippi." *Missouri Historical Review* 30: 345–364.

———. 1940. "The History of Fort Osage." *Missouri Historical Review* 24: 439–488.

Grinnell, G. B. 1956. *The Fighting Cheyennes.* Norman: University of Oklahoma Press.

———. 1972. *The Cheyenne Indians,* 2 vols. Lincoln: University of Nebraska Press

Groene, Bertram H. 1988. *Pike: A Fortress in the Wetlands.* Hammond: Southeastern Louisiana University Press.

Grove, Nettie T. 1921. "Fort Osage, First Settlement in Jackson County." *Missouri Valley Historical Society* 1: 56–70.

Haeger, John Denis. 1991. *John Jacob Astor: Business and Finance in the Early Republic.* Detroit: Wayne State University Press.

Hafen, LeRoy R. 1929. "Tom Fitzpatrick and the First Indian Agency in Colorado." *Colorado Magazine* 6: 53–62.

Hafen, LeRoy R., ed. 1995. *Fur Traders, Trappers, and Mountain Men of the Upper Missouri.* Lincoln: University of Nebraska Press.

Hafen, LeRoy R., and W. J. Ghent. 1981 [1931]. *Broken Hand: The Life Story of Thomas Fitzpatrick, Mountain Man, Guide, and Indian Agent.* Lincoln: University of Nebraska Press.

Hafen, LeRoy R., and Ann W. Hafen. 1969. "Thomas Fitzpatrick." In *The Mountain Men and the Fur Trade of the Far West.* 10 vols. Edited by Hafen, 7: 87–105. Glendale, CA: Arthur H. Clark Co.

Hagan, William Thomas. 1958. *The Sac and Fox Indians.* Norman: University of Oklahoma Press.

Haggard, J. Villasana. 1945. "The Neutral Ground between Louisiana and Texas, 1806–1821." *Louisiana Historical Quarterly* 28, no. 4: 1001–1128.

Haggerty, Richard A., ed. 1989. *Haiti: A Country Study.* Washington, DC: Federal Research Division, Library of Congress.

Hall, Gwendolyn Midlo. 1992. *Africans in Colonial Louisiana: The Development of Afro-Creole Culture in the Eighteenth Century.* Baton Rouge: Louisiana State University Press.

Hall, Philip S. 1993. *Reflections on the Badlands.* Vermillion: University of South Dakota Press.

Hamilton, Alexander. 1963–. *The Papers of Alexander Hamilton.* Edited by Harold Syrett. New York: Columbia, University Press.

Hamilton, M. Colleen. 1990. "French Colonial Land Use: The Felix Valle House, a State Historic Site." Master's thesis, Department of History, University of Missouri-St. Louis.

Hargreaves, Mary W. M. 1993. *Dry Farming in the Northern Great Plains: Years of Readjustment, 1920–1990.* Lawrence: University Press of Kansas.

Harlan, Edgar Rubey. 1931. *A Narrative History of the People of Iowa.* New York: American Historical Society.

Harmon, Nolan B. 1946. *The Famous Case of Myra Clark Gaines.* Baton Rouge: Louisiana State University Press.

Harris, Burton. 1993 [1952]. *John Colter, His Years in the Rockies.* New York: Scribner. Reprint: Lincoln: University of Nebraska Press.

Harrison, Lowell H. 1969. *John Breckinridge: Jeffersonian Republican.* Louisville: Filson Club.

Hatcher, William B. 1940. *Edward Livingston: Jeffersonian Republican and Jacksonian Democrat.* Baton Rouge: Louisiana State University Press.

Hatfield, Joseph T. 1976. *William Claiborne: Jeffersonian Centurion in the American Southwest.* Lafayette: University of Southwestern Louisiana.

Hatzenbuehler, Ronald L. 1976. "The War Hawks and the Question of Congressional Leadership in 1812." *Pacific Historical Review* 45: 1–22.

Hauk, Joy K. 1987. *Badlands: Its Life and Landscape.* Interior, SD: Badlands Natural History Association.

Hauser, Raymond. 1993. "The Fox Raid of 1752: Defensive Warfare and the Decline of the Illinois Indian Tribe." *Illinois Historical Journal* 86, no. 4: 210–224.

Hay, Thomas, and M. R. Werner. 1941. *The Admirable Trumpeter: A Biography of General James Wilkinson.* New York: Doubleday, Doran and Company.

Hayes, A. A., Jr. 1880. "The Santa Fe Trail." *Harper's New Monthly Magazine* 61: 185–196.

Heathcote, T. A. 1987. "Bernadotte: Serjent Belle Jambe." In *Napoleon's Marshals.* Edited by David G. Chandler. New York: Macmillan Publishing.

Heaton, John W. 1995. "'No Place to Pitch Their Teepees': Shoshone Adaptation to Mormon Settlers in Cache Valley 1855–70." *Utah Historical Quarterly* 63, no. 2: 158–171.

Heidenreich, Virginia L., ed. 1990. *The Fur Trade in North Dakota.* Bismarck: State Historical Society of North Dakota.

Heinl, Robert Debs, Jr., and Nancy Gordon Heinl. 1996. *Written in Blood: The Story of the Haitian People 1492–1971.* Lanham, MD: University Press of America.

Henderson, H. James. 1974. *Party Politics in the Continental Congress.* New York: McGraw-Hill Book Company.

Herndon, Sarah. 1902. *Days on the Road: Crossing the Plains in 1865.* New York: Burr.

Hibbard, Benjamin H. 1924. *A History of Public Land Policies.* New York: Macmillan.

———. 1965. *A History of the Public Land Policies.* Madison: University of Wisconsin Press.

Hickey, Donald R. 1989. *The War of 1812: A Forgotten Conflict.* Urbana: University of Illinois Press.

Hidy, Ralph W. 1949. *The House of Baring in American Trade and Finance: English Merchant Bankers at Work, 1763–1861.* Cambridge: Harvard University Press.

Higginbotham, Sanford W. 1952. *The Keystone in the Democratic Arch: Pennsylvania Politics, 1800–1816.* Harrisburg: Pennsylvania Historical and Museum Commission.

Hill, Joseph J. 1930. "Free Trapper: The Story of Old Bill Williams, One of the Southwest's Most Mythical and

Legendary Frontiersmen, Now Completely Recounted for the First Time." *Touring Topics* 22: 18–27

Hilt, Douglas. 1987. *The Troubled Trinity: Godoy and the Spanish Monarchs*. Tuscaloosa: University of Alabama Press.

Hines, Gordon. 1932. *Alfalfa Bill: An Intimate Biography*. Oklahoma City: Oklahoma Press.

Hinsley, F. H. 1986. *Sovereignty*. 2d ed. London, New York: Cambridge University Press.

Hirsch, Arnold R., and Joseph Logsdon, eds. 1992. *Creole New Orleans: Race and Americanization*. Baton Rouge: Louisiana State University Press.

Hobson, Charles F. 1996. *The Great Chief Justice: John Marshall and the Rule of Law*. Lawrence: University of Kansas Press.

Hoebel, E. Adamson 1960. *The Cheyennes*. New York: Holt

Hoffman, John. 1998. *Sovereignty*. Minneapolis: University of Minnesota Press.

Holcomb, Raymond L. 1990. *The Civil War in the Western Choctaw Nation, 1861–1865*. Atoka, OK: Atoka County Historical Society.

Holcombe, R. I. 1887. *History of Vernon County Missouri*. St. Louis: Brown and Co.

Hollon, W. Eugene. 1949. *The Lost Pathfinder: Zebulon Montgomery Pike*. Norman: University of Oklahoma Press.

Holman, Frederick V. 1907. *Dr. John McLoughlin: The Father of Oregon*. Cleveland: Arthur H. Clark Company.

Holmes, Jack D. L. 1964. "Showdown on the Sabine: General James Wilkinson vs. Lieutenant-Colonel Simón de Herrera." *Louisiana Studies* 3: 46–76.

———. 1965. *Gayoso: The Life of a Spanish Governor in the Mississippi Valley, 1789–1799*. Baton Rouge: Louisiana State University Press.

———. 1966. "The Marqués de Casa-Calvo, Nicolás deFiniels, and the 1805 Spanish Expedition through East Texas and Louisiana." *Southwestern Historical Quarterly* 69: 324–339.

Holt, Michael F. 1978. *The Political Crisis of the 1850s*. New York: W. W. Norton.

———. 1999. *The Rise and Fall of the American Whig Party: Jacksonian Politics and the Onset of the Civil War*. New York: Oxford University Press.

Horse Capture, George P. 1992. *The Seven Visions of Bull Lodge*. Lincoln: University of Nebraska Press.

Horsman, Reginald. 1962. *The Causes of the War of 1812*. Philadelphia: University of Pennsylvania Press.

———. 1964. "Who Were the War Hawks?" *Indiana Magazine of History* 60: 122–136.

Hosmer, James Kendall. 1902. *A History of the Louisiana Purchase*. New York: D. Appleton.

Hotblack, Kate. 1908. "The Peace of Paris, 1763." *Royal Historical Society Transactions* (3d series) 11: 235–267.

Houck, Louis. 1908. *A History of Missouri from the Earliest Explorations and Settlements until the Admission of the State into the Union*, vol. 2. Chicago: R. R. Donnelly & Sons.

Howard, James Henri. 1965. *The Ponca Tribe*. Washington, DC: Government Printing Office.

"Hugh Murray." 1917. In *Dictionary of National Biography*. Edited by George Smith. London: Oxford University Press.

Hunt, Charles H. 1864. *The Life of Edward Livingston*. New York: D. Appleton.

Hunt, Elvid. 1937. *History of Fort Leavenworth, 1827–1927*. Fort Leavenworth, KS: General Staff School.

Hyde, George E. 1968. *A Life of George Bent, Written from His Letters*. Norman: University of Oklahoma Press.

———. 1973. *The Pawnee Indians*. Norman: University of Oklahoma Press.

Ingersoll, Thomas N. 1999. *Mammon and Manon in Early New Orleans: The First Slave Society in the Deep South, 1718–1819*. Knoxville: University of Tennessee Press.

Irving, Washington. 1837. *The Adventures of Captain Bonneville Or Scenes, Incidents, and Adventure in the Far West*. Philadelphia: Carey, Lea, and Blanchard.

Isenberg, Andrew C. 2000. *The Destruction of the Bison: An Environmental History, 1750–1920*. Cambridge: Cambridge University Press.

Jablow, Joseph. 1974. *Ethnohistory of the Ponca: Commission Findings on the Ponca Indians*. New York: Garland.

Jackson, Donald. 1966. *Custer's Gold: The United States Cavalry Expedition*. New Haven: Yale University Press.

Jackson, Donald, ed. 1955. *Black Hawk (Ma-Ka-Tai-Me-She-Kia-Kiak): An Autobiography*. Urbana: University of Illinois Press.

———. 1966. *Journals of Zebulon Montgomery Pike*. Norman: University of Oklahoma Press.

———. 1978. *Letters of the Lewis and Clark Expedition, with Related Documents: 1783–1854*. Urbana: University of Illinois Press.

Jackson, John C. 2000. *The Piikani Blackfeet: A Culture under Siege*. Missoula, MT: Mountain Press.

Jacobs, James Ripley. 1947. *The Beginning of the U.S. Army, 1783–1812*. Princeton: Princeton University Press.

Jacobs, Wilbur R. 1968. *The Historical World of Frederick Jackson Turner*. New Haven: Yale University Press.

James, C. L. R. 1980. *The Black Jacobins: Toussaint L'Ouverture and the San Domingo Revolution*. Rev. ed. London: Allison and Busby.

James, James Alton. 1928. *The Life of George Rogers Clark*. Chicago: University of Chicago Press.

Jefferson, Thomas. 1903. *The Complete Annals of Thomas Jefferson*. Edited by Franklin B. Sawvel. New York: Round Table Press.

Jennings, Francis. 1998. *Empire of Fortune: Crowns, Colonies and Tribes in the Seven Years War in America*. New York: W. W. Norton.

Johannsen, Robert W., and Sam W. Haynes. 1997. *Manifest Destiny and Empire: American Antebellum Expansionism*. College Station, TX: Texas A&M University Press.

Johnsgard, Paul A. 1995. *This Fragile Land: A Natural History of the Nebraska Sandhills*. Lincoln: University of Nebraska Press.

Johnson, David Alan. 1992. *Founding the Far West: California, Oregon, and Nevada, 1840–1890*. Berkeley: University of California Press.

Johnson, Olga Weydemeyer. 1969. *Flathead and Kootenay: The Rivers, the Tribes, and the Region's Traders*. Glendale, CA: A. H. Clark Company.

Johnson, Walter. 1999. *Soul By Soul: Life Inside the Antebellum Slave Market*. Cambridge: Harvard University Press.

Johnston, Basil. 1990. *Ojibway Heritage*. Toronto: McClelland and Stewart, 1976. Reprint: Lincoln: University of Nebraska Press.

Jones, Charles T., Jr. 1970. *George Champlain Sibley: The*

Prairie Puritan, 1782–1863. Independence, MO: Jackson County Historical Society.

Jones, Douglas C. 1966. *The Treaty of Medicine Lodge*. Norman: University of Oklahoma Press.

Jones, Evan. 2001. *Citadel in the Wilderness: The Story of Fort Snelling and the Northwest Frontier.* Minneapolis: University of Minnesota.

Jones, Howard. 1997. *Prologue to Manifest Destiny: Anglo-American Relations in the 1840s*. Wilmington, DE: Scholarly Resources.

Jorgensen, Joseph G. 1969. *Salish Language and Culture: A Statistical Analysis of Internal Relationships, History, and Evolution*. Bloomington: Indiana University Press.

Josephy, Alvin. 1958. *The Patriot Chiefs: A Chronicle of Indian Resistance*. New York: Viking Press.

Joyce, Davis D. 1994. *An Oklahoma I Had Never Seen Before: Alternative Views of Oklahoma History.* Norman: University of Oklahoma Press.

Judge Jones Collection. Folder 39. Northwestern State University Archives, Natchitoches, LA.

Kaminski, John P. 1993. *George Clinton: Yeoman Politician of the New Republic*. Madison, WI: Madison House.

Kaplan, Lawrence S. 1999. *Thomas Jefferson: Westward the Course of Empire*. Wilmington, DE: Scholarly Resources.

Keats, John. 1973. *Eminent Domain: The Louisiana Purchase and the Making of America*. New York: Charterhouse.

Kelly, Alfred H., and Winfred A. Harbison. 1970. *The American Constitution: Its Origins and Development*. New York: W. W. Norton.

Kendall, John S. 1922. *History of New Orleans*. Chicago: Lewis Publishing Company.

Kenner, Charles. 1999. *Buffalo Soldiers and Officers of the Ninth Cavalry*. Norman: University of Oklahoma.

Kern, Robert W., ed. 1990. *Historical Dictionary of Modern Spain*. New York: Greenwood Press.

Ketchum, Ralph. 1971. *James Madison: A Biography.* Charlottesville: University of Virginia Press.

Ketz, Louise Bilebof, ed. 1976. "East Texas," "Neutral Ground," and "Texas." In *Dictionary of American History*. New York: Scribner's Sons.

Kimball, Stanley B. 1991. *Historic Resource Study: Mormon Pioneer National Historic Trail*. Washington, DC: United States Department of Interior, National Park Service.

King, Charles R., ed. 1971. *The Letters and Correspondence of Rufus King*. New York: DaCapo Press.

Kirk, Russell. *Randolph of Roanoke*. Indianapolis: Liberty Fund.

Kivett, Marvin, and Sally Johnson. 1959. "Fort Atkinson on the Council Bluffs." Lincoln: University of Nebraska Press.

Klier, Betje B. 1998. *Tales of the Sabine Borderlands*. College Station: Texas A&M University Press.

Klime, Mary-Jo, ed. 1983. *Political Correspondence and Public Papers of Aaron Burr*. 2 vols. Princeton: Princeton University Press.

Knudson, Jerry W. 1962. "The Jefferson Years: Response by the Press, 1801–1809." Ph.D. diss., University of Virginia.

———. 1969. "Newspaper Reaction to the Louisiana Purchase: 'This New, Immense, Unbounded World.'" *Missouri Historical Review* 63: 182–215.

Kracht, Benjamin. 1996. "Kiowa." In *Encyclopedia of North American Indians*. Edited by Frederick Hoxie. Boston: Houghton Mifflin.

Kukla, Jon, ed. 1993. *A Guide to the Papers of Pierre Clément Laussat, Napoleon's Prefect for the Colony of Louisiana, and of General Claude Perrin Victor at the Historic New Orleans Collection*. Baton Rouge: Louisiana University Press.

La Flesche, Francis. 1939. *War Ceremony and Peace Ceremony of the Osage Indians*. Washington, DC: Government Printing Office.

———. 1970 [1921]. *The Osage Tribe: Rite of the Chiefs; Sayings of the Ancient Men*. New York: Johnson Reprint Corporation.

Lambert, Christine. Forthcoming. "Citizens and Strangers: New Orleans and the New Nation after the Louisiana Purchase." Ph.D. diss., Emory University.

Laski, Harold J. 1921. *The Foundations of Sovereignty and Other Essays*. London: George Allen & Unwin.

Lass, William E. 1980. *Minnesota's Boundary with Canada: Its Evolution since 1763*. St. Paul: Minnesota Historical Society.

Latorre, Felipe A., and Dolores L. Latorre. 1976. *The Mexican Kickapoo Indians*. Austin: University of Texas Press.

Latour, Arsène Lacarrière. 1999 [1816]. *Historical Memoir of the War in West Florida and Louisiana in 1814–15: With an Atlas*. Edited by Gene A. Smith. Gainesville: Historic New Orleans Collection and the University Press of Florida.

Lavender, David. 1963. *Westward Vision: The Story of the Oregon Trail*. Lincoln: University of Nebraska Press.

———. 1964. *The Fist in the Wilderness*. Garden City, NY: Doubleday & Company.

———. 1982. *Ft. Laramie*. Tucson, AZ: Patrice Printing.

———. 1989. *Way to the Western Sea: Lewis and Clark across the Continent*. New York: Harper and Row.

Laycock, George. 1996. *The Mountain Men*. NY: Lyons Press.

Leckie, William. 1967. *The Buffalo Soldiers: A Narrative of the Negro Cavalry in the West*. Norman: University of Oklahoma.

Leclerc, V.-L. 1937. *Lettres de Saint-Domingue*. Paris: Sociéte de l'histoire des colonies françaises.

Lefebvre, Georges. 1969. *Napoleon: From 18 Brumaire to Tilsit, 1799–1807*. New York: Columbia University Press.

LeRoy, Reuben Hafen. 1984. *Ft. Laramie and the Pageant of the West*. New York: Bison Books.

Levin, Daniel Lessard. 1999. *Representing Popular Sovereignty: The Constitution in American Political Culture*. Albany: State University of New York Press.

Lewis, Emanuel Raymond. 1993. *Seacoast Fortifications of the United States: An Introductory History*. Annapolis: Naval Institute Press.

Liljeblad, Sven. 1972. *The Idaho Indians in Transition 1805–1960*. Pocatello: Idaho State University Museum.

Limerick, Patricia. 1987. *Legacy of Conquest: The Unbroken Past of the American West*. New York: W. W. Norton.

Linton, Ralph. 1922. *The Sacrifice to the Morning Star by the Skidi Pawnee*. Chicago: Field Museum of Natural History.

Lodge, Henry Cabot. 1878. *Life and Letters of George Cabot*. Boston: Little, Brown.

Logsdon, David R., ed. 1990. *"I Was There!" In the New Madrid Earthquakes of 1811–1812*. Nashville: Kettle Mills Press.

Lokke, Carl Ludwig. 1943. "Secret Negotiations to Maintain the Peace of Amiens." *American Historical Review* 49: 55–64.

Lomask, Milton. 1982. *Aaron Burr.* 2 vols. New York: Farrar, Straus and Giroux.
London Times. January 8, 1803–February 24, 1804.
Loos, John L. 1953. "A Biography of William Clark, 1770–1813." Ph.D. diss., Washington University, St. Louis, MO.
Lottinville, Savoie, ed. 1980. "Editor's Introduction." In *A Journal of Travels into the Arkansas Territory during the Year 1819.* Norman: University of Oklahoma Press.
Louisiana Legislature. 1816. "1803 Treaty of Cession." In *A General Digest of the Acts of the Legislatures of the Late Territory of Orleans and of the State of Louisiana.* New Orleans: Peter K. Wagner.
Lowery, Woodbury. 1959. *The Spanish Settlements within the Present Limits of the United States, 1513–1561.* New York: Russell and Russell.
Luebke, Frederick C. 1995. *Nebraska: An Illustrated History.* Lincoln: University of Nebraska Press.
Luettenegger, Benedict, trans. 1978. "Puelles' Report of 1827 on the Texas-Louisiana Boundary." Translated by Benedict Luettenegger. *Louisiana History* 19, no. 2: 133–180.
Lyman, Edward Leo. 1986. *Political Deliverance: The Mormon Quest for Utah Statehood.* Urbana: University of Illinois Press.
Lynch, John. 1989. *Bourbon Spain, 1700–1808.* Oxford: Basil Blackwell.
Lyon, E. Wilson. 1940. "The Franco-American Convention of 1800." *Journal of Modern History* 21: 305–333.
———. 1942. *The Man Who Sold Louisiana: The Career of Francois Barbe-Marbois.* Norman: University of Oklahoma Press.
———. 1974. *Louisiana in French Diplomacy, 1759–1804.* Norman: University of Oklahoma Press.
MacDonell, Archibald G. 1934. *Napoleon and His Marshals.* London: Macmillan and Company.
MacGregor, Carol Lynn, ed. 1997. *The Journal and Account Book of Patrick Gass: Member of the Lewis and Clark Expedition.* Missoula, MT: Mountain Press Publishing Company, Inc.
Madsen, Brigham D. 1979. *The Lemhi: Sacajawea's People.* Caldwell, ID: Caxton.
———. 1980. *The Northern Shoshoni.* Caldwell, ID: Caxton.
———. 1986. *The Shoshoni Frontier and the Bear River Massacre.* Salt Lake City: University of Utah.
Magnaghi, Russell M. 1981. "The Belle Fontaine Indian Factory, 1805–1808." *Missouri Historical Review* 75: 396–416.
Magruder, Allan Bowie. 1803. *Political, Commercial, and Moral Reflections on the Late Cession of Louisiana to the United States.* Lexington: D. Bradford.
———. 1808. *A Letter from Allan B. Magruder, Esq., of Opelousas, to His Correspondent in the State of Virginia, dated 20th Nov. 1807.* New Orleans: Bradford and Anderson.
Majors, Harry M. 1981. "John McClellan in the Montana Rockies, 1807." *Northwest Discovery: Journal of Northwest History and Natural History* 2: 9.
Malone, Ann Patton. 1992. *Sweet Chariot: Slave Family and Household Structure in Nineteenth-Century Louisiana.* Chapel Hill: University of North Carolina Press.
Malone, Dumas. 1948–1962. *Jefferson and His Time.* 6 vols. Boston: Little, Brown.
———.1970. *Jefferson the President: First Term, 1801–1805.* Boston: Little, Brown, and Company.
Malone, Dumas, ed. 1932. *Dictionary of American Biography*, vol. 8. New York: Charles Scribner's Sons.
Malone, Michael P., Richard B. Roeder, and William L. Lang. 1991. *Montana: A History of Two Centuries.* Seattle, London: University of Washington Press.
Malouf, Carling I., and Åke Hultkrantz, eds. 1974. *Shoshone Indians.* New York: Garland.
Mantor, Lyle E. 1948. "Fort Kearny and the Westward Movement." *Nebraska History* 29: 175–207.
Markham, Felix Maurice Hippisley. 1975. *The Bonapartes.* London: Weidenfeld and Nicolson.
Marks, Frederick W. 1973. *Independence on Trial: Foreign Affairs and the Making of the Constitution.* Baton Rouge: Louisiana University Press.
Marshall, Thomas Maitland. 1914. *A History of the Western Boundary of the Louisiana Purchase, 1819–1841.* Berkeley: University of California Press.
Martin, Henri. 1866. *History of France from the Most Remote Period to 1789*, vol. 15. Translated by Mary L. Booth. Boston: Walker, Fuller, and Company.
Martineau, Gilbert. 1989. *Lucien Bonaparte, Prince de Canino.* Paris: Editions France-Empire.
Mason, Leonard. 1967. *The Swampy Cree: A Study in Acculturation.* Ottawa: Queen's Printer.
Masters, Joseph G. 1935. *Stories of the Far West: Heroic Tales of the Last Frontier.* Boston: Ginn and Company.
Mathews, John Joseph. 1961. *The Osages, Children of the Middle Waters.* Norman: University of Oklahoma Press.
Mattes, Merrill J. 1955. "Chimney Rock on the Oregon Trail." *Nebraska History* 36: 1–26.
———. 1969. *The Great Platte River Road: The Covered Wagon Mainline via Fort Kearny to Fort Laramie.* Lincoln: Nebraska State Historical Society.
Maximilian Prince of Wied. 1906 [1843]. *Travels in the Interior of North America, 1832–1834.* Translated by H. Evans Lloyd. London: Ackermann & Co. Reprint: Vols. 22–24 of Reuben Gold Thwaites, *Early Western Travels, 1748–1846.* Cleveland: Arthur H. Clarke Co.
May, Dean L. 1987. *Utah: A People's History.* Salt Lake City: University of Utah Press.
Mayfield, John. 1980. *Rehearsal for Republicanism: Free Soil and the Politics of Anti-Slavery.* Port Washington, WA: Kennikat Press.
Mayhall, Mildred. 1962. *The Kiowas.* Norman: University of Oklahoma Press.
———. 1965. *Indian Wars of Texas.* Waco, TX: Texian Press.
Mayo, Bernard, ed. 1971. *Instructions to the British Ministers to the United States, 1791–1812.* New York: DaCapo Press.
McCall, Henry. 1899. *History of Evan Hall Plantation.* Chapel Hill: Southern Historical Collection, University of North Carolina.
McCaughty, Robert A. 1974. *Josiah Quincy, 1772–1864: the Last Federalist.* Cambridge: Harvard University Press.
McCowan, George S., Jr. 1961. "Chief Justice Rutledge and the Jay Treaty." *South Carolina Historical Magazine* 62: 10–23.
McCoy, Drew R. 1991. *The Last of the Fathers: James Madison and the Republic.* Cambridge, New York: Cambridge University Press.

McDermott, John Francis, ed. 1965. *Audubon in the West.* Norman: University of Oklahoma Press.
McDonald, Forrest. 1976. *The Presidency of Thomas Jefferson.* Lawrence: University Press of Kansas.
———. 1982. *Alexander Hamilton: A Biography.* New York: W. W. Norton.
McFee, Malcolm. 1972. *Modern Blackfeet; Montanans on a Reservation.* New York: Holt, Rinehart and Winston.
McGuigan, Patrick B. 1978. "Bulwark of the American Frontier: A History of Fort Towson." In *Early Military Forts and Posts in Oklahoma.* Edited by Odie B. Faulk, Kenny A. Franks, and Paul F. Lambert. Oklahoma City: Oklahoma Historical Society.
McIntosh, Charles Barron. 1996. *The Nebraska Sand Hills: The Human Landscape.* Lincoln: University of Nebraska Press.
McKay, Douglas. 1937. *The Honourable Company: A History of the Hudson's Bay Company.* London: Cassell and Company.
McKelvey, Susan Delano. 1991 [1956]. *Botanical Exploration of the Trans-Mississippi West, 1790–1850.* Corvallis: Oregon State University Press.
McNeil, John Robert. 1985. *Atlantic Empires of France and Spain: Louisbourg and Havana, 1700–1763.* Chapel Hill: University of North Carolina Press.
McNeilly, Donald. 2000. *The Old South Frontier: Cotton Plantations and the Formation of Arkansas Society, 1819–1860.* Fayetteville: University of Arkansas Press
McPherson, James M. 1988. *Battle Cry of Freedom: The Civil War Era.* New York: Oxford University Press.
McReynolds, Edwin C. 1964. *Oklahoma: A History of the Sooner State.* Norman: University of Oklahoma Press.
Meigs, William M. 1904. *The Life of Thomas Hart Benton.* Philadelphia: J. B. Lippincott.
Meinig, D. W. 1993. *The Shaping of America: A Geographical Perspective on 500 Years of History, Vol. 2: Continental America, 1800–67.* New Haven, & London: Yale University Press.
Merk, Frederick. 1967. *The Oregon Question: Essays in Anglo-American Diplomacy and Politics.* Cambridge: Harvard University Press.
———. 1978. *History of the Westward Movement.* New York: Borzoi Books.
Merritt, John I., III. 1977. "Naturalists across the Rockies: The 1834 Journey of John Kirk Townsend and Thomas Nuttall." *American West* 14, no. 2: 4–9, 62–63.
Meyer, Roy W. 1977. *The Village Indians of the Upper Missouri: The Mandans, Hidatsas, and Arikaras.* Lincoln, London: University of Nebraska Press.
Millard, Joseph. 1964. *The Cheyenne Wars.* Derby, CT: Monarch Books
Mills, Gary B. 1977. *The Forgotten People: Cane River's Creoles of Color.* Baton Rouge: Louisiana State University Press.
Missouri Fur Company. 1812. *Articles of Association of the Missouri Fur Company.* St. Louis, MO.
Mitchell, Broadus. 1957–1962. *Alexander Hamilton.* 2 vols. New York: Macmillan.
———. 1976. *Alexander Hamilton: A Concise Biography.* New York: Oxford University Press.
Mooney, James. 1979 [1898]. *Calendar History of the Kiowa Indians. Seventeenth Annual Report of the Bureau of American Ethnology, 1895–1896, Part 1.* Washington, DC: Government Printing Office. Reprint: Washington: Smithsonian Institution Press.
———. 1991. *The Ghost Dance Religion and the Sioux Outbreak of 1890.* Lincoln: University of Nebraska Press.
Moore, Glover. 1953. *The Missouri Controversy, 1819–1821.* Louisville: University of Kentucky Press.
Moore, J. H. 1987. *The Cheyenne Nation.* Lincoln: University of Nebraska.
Moore, Richard W. 1948. "The Role of the Baron de Bastrop in the Anglo-American Settlement of the Spanish Southwest." *Louisiana Historical Quarterly* 31, no. 3: 606–681.
Moore, Robert J. 1997. *Native Americans: The Art and Travels of Charles Bird King, George Catlin, and Karl Bodmer.* New York: Stewart, Tabori, and Chang.
Morgan, Anne Hodges, and H. Wayne Morgan, eds. 1982. *Oklahoma: New Views of the Forty-Sixth State.* Norman: University of Oklahoma Press.
Morgan, Dale L. 1953. *Jedediah Smith and the Opening of the West.* Lincoln: University of Nebraska Press.
———. 1987. *The State of Deseret.* Logan: Utah State University Press.
Morgan, Edmund S. 1988. *Inventing the People: The Rise of Popular Sovereignty in England and America.* New York: W. W. Norton.
Morison, Samuel Eliot. 1913. *The Life and Letters of Harrison Gray Otis, Federalist, 1765–1848.* 2 vols. Boston: Houghton Mifflin Company.
Morris, John W., Charles R. Goins, and Edwin C. McReynolds. 1986. *Historical Atlas of Oklahoma.* Norman: University of Oklahoma Press.
Morrison, Dorothy Nafus. 1999. *Outpost: John McLoughlin & the Far Northwest.* Portland: Oregon Historical Society Press.
Moulton, Gary E., ed. 1983–2001. *The Journals of the Lewis and Clark Expedition.* 13 vols. Lincoln: University of Nebraska Press.
———.*Herbarium of the Lewis and Clark Expedition: The Journals of the Lewis and Clark Expedition, vol. 12.* Lincoln: University of Nebraska Press.
———. 1987. *The Journals of the Lewis and Clark Expedition*, vol. 3. Lincoln: University of Nebraska Press.
Munford, James Kenneth, ed. 1963. *John Ledyard's Journal of Captain Cook's Last Voyage.* Corvallis: Oregon State University.
Munkres, Robert. 1978. "Broken Hand and the Indians: A Case Study of Mid-19th Century White Attitudes." *Annals of Wyoming* 50, no. 1: 157–171.
Murat, Ines. 1981. *Napoleon and the American Dream.* Baton Rouge: Louisiana State University Press.
Murphy, Robert F., and Yolanda Murphy. 1959. "Shoshone-Bannock Subsistence and Society." *University of California Anthropological Records* 16, no. 7: 293–338.
———. 1986. "Northern Shoshone and Bannock." In *Handbook of North American Indians, vol. 11: Great Basin.* Edited by Warren L. d'Azevedo. Washington, DC: Smithsonian Institution.
Murray, Hugh. 1839–1841. *Encyclopedia of Geography.* Philadelphia: Lea and Blanchard.
Nabokov, Peter. 1967. *Two Leggings: The Making of a Crow*

Warrior. New York: Thomas Y. Crowell Co.
Nabonne, B. 1963. *Pauline Bonaparte*. Paris: Hachette.
Nadeau, Remi. 1967. *Fort Laramie and the Sioux Indians*. Englewood Cliffs, NJ: Prentice Hall.
Nasitir, Abraham P. 1952. *Before Lewis and Clark: Documents Illustrating the History of the Missouri, 1785–1804*. St. Louis: St. Louis Historical Documents Foundation. Reprint: Lincoln: University of Nebraska Press.
———. 1976. *Borderland in Retreat: From Spanish Louisiana to the Far Southwest*. Albuquerque: University of New Mexico Press.
National Park Service. 1963. *Soldier and Brave: Indian and Military Affairs in the Trans-Mississippi West*. New York: Harper and Row.
———. 1967. *Founders and Frontiersmen: Historic Places Commemorating Early Nationhood and the Westward Movement, 1783–1828*. Washington, DC: United States Department of the Interior.
Nettl, Bruno. 1989. *Blackfoot Musical Thought: Comparative Perspectives*. Kent, OH: Kent State University Press
Newton, Craig A., and James M. Newton. 1966. "Not an Enemy of Cession Will Remain." *Louisiana Studies* 5: 37–49.
Ney, Virgil. 1977. "Daily Life at Fort Atkinson on the Missouri 1820–1827." Parts 1 and 2. *Military* Review 57 (I/2): 1:36–48; 2:50–66
Nichols, Roger L. 1992. *Black Hawk and the Warrior's Path*. Arlington Heights, IL: Harlan Davidson.
Nichols, Roger L., and Patrick L. Halley. 1980. *Stephen H. Long and American Frontier Exploration*. Newark: University of Delaware Press.
Nisbet, Jack. 1994. *Sources of the River: Tracking David Thompson across Western North America*. Seattle: Sasquatch Books.
Norton, W. T. 1911. "Old Fort Belle Fontaine." *Journal of the Illinois State Historical Society* 4: 334–339.
Nye, Wilbur S. 1962. *Bad Medicine and Good: Tales of the Kiowas*. Norman: University of Oklahoma Press.
O'Neill, Charles Edwards. 1990. "'A Quarter Marked by Sundry Peculiarities': New Orleans, Lay Trustees, and Père Antoine." *Catholic Historical Review* 76: 235–277.
Ogg, Frederic Austin. 1904. *The Opening of the Mississippi: A Struggle for Supremacy in the American Interior*. New York, London: Macmillan Company.
Oglesbey, Richard Edward. 1963. *Manuel Lisa and the Opening of the Missouri Fur Trade*. Norman: University of Oklahoma Press.
———. 1968. "Manuel Lisa." In *The Mountain Men and the Fur Trade of the Far West*, vol. 5. Edited by LeRoy Hafen. Glendale, CA: A. H. Clark.
Oliva, Leo E. 1967. *Soldiers on the Santa Fe Trail*. Norman: University of Oklahoma Press.
———. 1984. *Fort Scott on the Indian Frontier*. Topeka: Kansas State Historical Society.
Olson, James C., and Ronald C. Naugle. 1997. *History of Nebraska*. 3d ed. Lincoln: University of Nebraska Press.
Opie, John. 1987. *The Law of the Land: Two Hundred Years of American Farmland Policy*. Lincoln: University of Nebraska Press.
Otis, D. S. 1973. *The Dawes Act and the Allotment of Indian Lands*. Norman: University of Oklahoma Press.
Ott, Thomas O. 1973. *The Haitian Revolution, 1789–1804*. Knoxville: University of Tennessee Press.
Owsley, Frank L., Jr. 1981. *Struggle for the Gulf Borderlands: The Creek War and the Battle of New Orleans, 1812–1815*. Gainesville: University Press of Florida.
Owsley, Frank L., and Gene A. Smith. 1997. *Filibusters and Expansionists: Jeffersonian Manifest Destiny, 1800–1821*. Tuscaloosa: University of Alabama Press.
Parkerson, Codman. 1990. *New Orleans: America's Most Fortified City*. New Orleans: The Quest.
Parkman, Francis. 1994 [1849]. *The Oregon Trail*. Lincoln: University of Nebraska Press.
Parks, Douglas R. 1996. *Myths and Traditions of the Arikara Indians*. Lincoln, London: University of Nebraska Press.
Partin, John W., ed. 1983. *A Brief History of Fort Leavenworth, 1827–1983*. Fort Leavenworth, KS: U.S. Army Command and General Staff College.
Peckham, Howard H. 1964. *The Colonial Wars, 1689–1762*. Chicago: University of Chicago Press.
Pellew, George. 1847. *The Life and Correspondence of the Rt. Hon. Henry Addington, First Viscount Sidmouth*. 3 vols. London: Murray and Company.
Penick, James J., Jr. 1976. *The New Madrid Earthquakes of 1811–1812*. Columbia: University of Missouri Press.
Perkins, Bradford. 1967. *The First Rapprochement: England and the United States, 1795–1805*. Berkeley: University of California Press.
Perkins, William Rufus. 1975. *History of the Amana Society*. New York: Arno Press.
Peters, Frank. 1989. *A Guide to the Architecture of St. Louis*. Columbia: University of Missouri Press.
Peterson, Merrill D. 1960. *The Jefferson Image in the American Mind*. New York: Oxford University Press.
———. 1970. *Thomas Jefferson and the New Nation: A Biography*. London: Oxford University Press.
———. 1998. "Louisiana!" In *The Louisiana Purchase Bicentennial Series in Louisiana History*, vol. 3. Edited by Dolores Egger Labbe. Lafayette: Center for Louisiana Studies.
Peterson, Merrill D., ed. 1984. *Thomas Jefferson: Writings*. New York: Library of America.
Petrie, Sir Charles. 1956. *The History of Spain: Part II: From the Death of Philip II to 1945*. London: Eyre & Spottiswoode.
Petroelje, Marvin, Jr. 1969. "Levi Lincoln, Sr.: Jeffersonian Republican of Massachusetts." Ph.D. diss., Michigan State University.
Philips, Kimberly T. 1968. "William Duane, Revolutionary Editor." Ph.D. diss., University of California-Berkeley.
Phillips, Paul Chrisler, and J. W. Smurr. 1967. *The Fur Trade*. Norman: University of Oklahoma Press.
Pickering, Octavius, and Charles W. Upham. 1867–1873. *Life of Timothy Pickering*. 4 vols. Boston: Little, Brown, and Company.
Pletcher, David M. 1973. *The Diplomacy of Annexation: Texas, Oregon, and the Mexican War*. Columbia: University of Missouri Press.
Pluchon, Pierre. 1989. *Toussaint L'Ouverture*. Paris: Fayard.
Pontalba, Joseph Xavier de. 1801. "Memoir of Colonel Joseph Xavier Delfau de Pontalba." As translated and found in Alcée Fortier. 1904. *The History of Louisiana, vol. 2: The Spanish Domination and the Cession to the United States*. New York: Goupil and Company.

Pound, Roscoe. 1950. *The Formative Era of American Law.* New York: Peter Smith.
Pratt, Julius W. 1933. "John L. O'Sullivan and Manifest Destiny." *New York History* 14(3): 214–234.
———. 1965. *A History of United States Foreign Policy.* Englewood Cliffs, NJ: Prentice-Hall.
Price, Catherine. 1996. *The Oglala People, 1841–1879: A Political History.* Lincoln: University of Nebraska Press.
Pride, W. F. 1997. *The History of Fort Riley.* Fort Riley, KS: U.S. Cavalry Museum.
Prucha, Francis Paul. 1969. *The Sword of the Republic: The United States Army on the Frontier, 1783–1846.* New York: Macmillan.
———. 1984. *The Great Father.* 2 vols. Lincoln: University of Nebraska Press.
———. 1994. *American Indian Treaties: The History of a Political Anomaly.* Berkeley: University of California Press.
Quaife, Milo Milton, ed. 1925. *The Southwestern Expedition of Zebulon M. Pike.* Chicago: R. R. Donnelley and Sons.
Radin, Paul. 1970. *The Winnebago Tribe.* Lincoln: University of Nebraska Press.
Rashed, Zenab E. 1951. *The Peace of Paris, 1767.* Liverpool: Liverpool University Press.
Rawley, James A. 1969. *Race and Politics: Bleeding Kansas and the Coming of the Civil War.* Philadelphia: J. B. Lippincott.
Ray, Arthur J. 1974. *Indians in the Fur Trade: Their Role as Trappers, Hunters, and Middlemen in the Lands Southwest of Hudson Bay, 1660–1870.* Toronto, Buffalo: University of Toronto Press.
Ray, Perley Orman. 1909. *Repeal of the Missouri Compromise, Its Origin and Authorship.* Cleveland: A. H. Clark.
Remini, Robert V. 1999. *The Battle of New Orleans: Andrew Jackson and America's First Military Victory.* New York: Viking Press.
Reveal, James L. 1992. *Gentle Conquest: The Botanical Discovery of North America with Illustrations from the Library of Congress.* Washington, DC: Starwood Publishing.
Rich, E. E. 1941–1944. *The Letters of John McLoughlin from Fort Vancouver to the Governor and Committee.* Toronto: Champlain Society.
Richardson, Rupert Norval. 1933. *The Comanche Barrier to South Plains Settlement.* Glendale, CA: Arthur H. Clark.
Richardson, Rupert Norval, Ernest Wallace, and Adrian Anderson. 1997. *Texas, The Lone Star State.* Upper Saddle River, NJ: Prentice Hall.
Risjord, Norman K. 1965. *The Old Republicans: Southern Conservatism in the Age of Jefferson.* New York: Columbia University Press.
Robbins, Roy M. 1960. *Our Landed Heritage: The Public Domain, 1776–1936.* Gloucester, MA: Peter Smith.
Robert, Henry Flood, Jr., ed. 1980. *The Art of Exploration: The Maximilian-Bodmer Expedition, 1832–34.* Omaha: Joslyn Art Museum.
Robertson, James Alexander, ed. 1911. *Louisiana under the Rule of Spain, France and the United States, 1785–1807.* Cleveland: Arthur C. Clark.
Robinson, Doane. 1904. *History of South Dakota.* Logansport, IN: B. F. Bowen.
Robinson, Elwyn B. 1966. *History of North Dakota.* Lincoln: University of Nebraska Press.
Robley, T. F. 1894. *History of Bourbon County, Kansas.* Fort Scott, Kansas: Press of the Monitor Book & Printing Co.
Rock Island Arsenal Historical Branch. 1966. *A Short History of Fort Armstrong.* Rock Island, IL: Rock Island Arsenal Historical Branch.
Rogers, George C., Jr. 1969. *Charleston in the Age of the Pinckneys.* Norman: University of Oklahoma Press.
Rohrbough, Malcom J. 1968. *The Land Office Business: The Settlement and Administration of American Public Lands, 1789–1837.* New York: Oxford University Press.
Rollings, Willard. 1992. *The Osage: An Ethnohistorical Study of Hegemony on the Prairie-Plains.* Columbia: University of Missouri Press.
Ronda, James P. 1984. *Lewis and Clark among the Indians.* Lincoln: University of Nebraska Press.
———. 1990. *Astoria and Empire.* Lincoln: University of Nebraska Press.
———. 1998. *Voyages of Discovery: Essays on the Lewis and Clark Expedition.* Helena: Montana Historical Society Press.
Roosevelt, Theodore. 1886. *Thomas Hart Benton.* Boston: Houghton Mifflin.
Ros, Martin. 1994. *Night of Fire: The Black Napoleon and the Battle for Haiti.* New York: Sarpedon Publishers.
Ross, Margaret. 1968. "New Madrid Earthquake." *Arkansas Historical Quarterly* 27: 104.
Rousséve, Charles Barthelemy. 1937. *The Negro in Louisiana: Aspects of His History and His Literature.* New Orleans: Xavier University Press.
Rowe, G. S. 1978. *Thomas McKean: The Shaping of an American Republicanism.* Boulder: Colorado Associated University Press.
Rowland, Mrs. Dunbar, ed. 1930. *Life, Letters and Papers of William Dunbar.* Jackson: Press of the Mississippi Historical Society.
Rubin, Louis D., et al. 1985. *The History of Southern Literature.* Baton Rouge: Louisiana State University Press.
Rushton, William Faulkner. 1979. *The Cajuns: From Acadia to Louisiana.* New York: Farrar Straus Giroux.
Russell, Osborne. 1965. *Journal of a Trapper.* Lincoln: University of Nebraska Press.
Russell, Sarah P. 2000. "Cultural Conflicts and Common Interests: The Making of the Sugar Planter Class in Louisiana, 1795–1853." Ph.D. dissertation, University of Maryland, College Park, Maryland.
Ruth Cross Collection. Box 2, Folder 47. Northwestern State University Archives, Natchitoches, LA.
Rydell, Robert W. 1984. *All the World's a Fair: Visions of Empire at American International Expositions, 1876–1916.* Chicago: University of Chicago Press.
Sabo, George, III. 1992. *Paths of Our Children: Historic Indians of Arkansas.* Fayetteville: Arkansas Archeological Survey.
Sage, Leland L. 1974. *A History of Iowa.* Ames: Iowa State University Press.
Saricks, Ambrose. 1965. *Pierre Samuel Du Pont de Nemours.* Lawrence: University of Kansas Press.
Savage, Henry, Jr., and Elizabeth J. Savage. 1986. *André and François Michaux.* Charlottesville: University Press of Virginia.
Scales, James R., and Danney Goble. 1982. *Oklahoma Politics: A History.* Norman: University of Oklahoma Press.

1801–1803." *Louisiana History* 12, no. 1: 21–40.
Scharf, J. Thomas. 1883. *History of St. Louis and St. Louis County, from Earliest Periods to the Present Day: Including Biographical Sketches of Representative Men.* Philadelphia: L. H. Everts and Company.
Schneider, Mary Jane. 1986. *North Dakota Indians: An Introduction.* Dubuque, IA: Kendall Hunt Publishing Company.
Schom, Alan. 1997. *Napoleon Bonaparte.* New York: New York: HarperCollins.
Schwantes, Carlos A. 1989. *The Pacific Northwest: An Interpretive History.* Lincoln: University of Nebraska Press.
Scott, Robert Morton. 1991. "St George Tucker and the Development of American Culture in Early Federal Virginia, 1790–1824." Ph.D. diss., George Washington University.
Shambaugh, Bertha M. H. 1971. *Amana that Was and Amana that Is.* New York: Benjamin Blom.
Shankman, Andrew. 1999. "Malcontents and Tertium Quids: The Battle to Define Democracy in Jeffersonian Pennsylvania." *Journal of the Early Republic* 19: 43–72.
Sheehan, Bernard W. 1973. *Seeds of Extinction: Jeffersonian Philanthropy and the American Indian.* Chapel Hill: University of North Carolina Press.
Sheidley, Harlow. 1998. *Sectional Nationalism.* Cambridge: Harvard University Press.
Shepherd, William R. 1904. "Papers Bearing on James Wilkinson's Relations with Spain, 1787–1789," "Wilkinson's Second Memorial, New Orleans, September 17, 1789," and "Wilkinson and the Beginnings of the Spanish Conspiracy." *American Historical Review* 9: 490–506, 748–766.
Shimkin, Demitri B. 1947. "Wind River Shoshone Ethnogeography." *University of California Anthropological Records* 5, no. 4: 245–288.
Shirley, Glenn. 1957. *Law West of Fort Smith.* New York: Henry Holt and Company.
Shoemaker, Earl Arthur. 1986. *The Permanent Indian Frontier: The Reason for the Construction and Abandonment of Fort Scott, Kansas, during the Dragoon Era.* Washington, DC: National Park Service.
Shuler, Jay. 1987. *A Revelation Called the Badlands: Building a Nation Park, 1909–1939.* Interior, SD: Badlands Natural History Association.
Skeen, C. Edward. 1981. *John Armstrong, Jr., 1758–1843: A Biography.* Syracuse, NY: Syracuse University Press.
Skinner, Alanson. 1915. *Societies of the Iowa, Kansa, and Ponca Indians.* New York: The Trustees.
Smelser, Marshall. 1968. *The Democratic Republic: 1801–1815.* New York: Harper and Row.
Smith, David Lee. 1997. *Folklore of the Winnebago Tribe.* Norman: University of Oklahoma Press.
Smith, Elbert B. 1958. *Magnificent Missourian: The Life of Thomas Hart Benton.* Philadelphia: J. B. Lippincott.
Smith, James Morton, ed. 1995. *The Republic of Letters: The Correspondence between Thomas Jefferson & James Madison, 1776–1826.* 3 vols. New York, London: Norton.
Smith, Jean Edward. 1998. *John Marshall: Definer of a Nation.* New York: Henry Holt and Company.
Smith, Henry Nash. 1970. *Virgin Land.* Cambridge, MA: Cambridge University Press.
Smith, Ronald D. 1971. "Napoleon and Louisiana: Failure of the Proposed Expedition to Occupy and Defend Louisiana,
Sparks, Jared. 1828. *The Life of John Ledyard, The American Traveler; Comprising Selections from His Journals and Correspondence.* Cambridge, MA: Hilliard and Brown.
Spaulding, Ernest W. 1938. *His Excellency George Clinton: Critic of the Constitution.* New York: Macmillan.
Spence, Clark C. 1975. *Territorial Politics and Government in Montana, 1864–89.* Urbana: University of Illinois Press.
———. 1978. *Montana: A Bicentennial History.* New York: W. W. Norton.
Sprague, Marshall. 1974. *So Vast, So Beautiful a Land: Louisiana and the Purchase.* Boston: Little, Brown and Company.
———. 1976. *Colorado: A Bicentennial History.* New York: W. W. Norton.
Stagg, J. C. A. 1983. *Mr. Madison's War: Politics, Diplomacy and Warfare in the Early American Republic, 1783–1830.* Princeton: Princeton University Press.
Stamm, Henry E., IV. 1999. *People of the Wind River: The Eastern Shoshones, 1825–1900.* Norman: University of Oklahoma Press.
Staudenraus, P. J. 1961. *The African Colonization Movement, 1816–1865.* New York: Columbia University Press.
Steele, Ian. 1990. *Fort William Henry and the "Massacre."* New York: Oxford University Press.
Stegner, Wallace. 1964. *The Gathering of Zion.* New York: McGraw-Hill.
Steffen, Jerome O. 1977. *William Clark: Jeffersonian Man on the Frontier.* Norman: University of Oklahoma Press.
Stephenson, George M. 1967. *The Political History of the Public Lands from 1840 to 1862: From Pre-emption to Homestead.* New York: Russell & Russell.
Stevens, Frank E. 1903. *The Black Hawk War.* Chicago: F. E. Stevens.
Stinchcombe, William. 1980. *The XYZ Affair.* Westport, CT: Greenwood.
Stites, Francis N. 1981. *John Marshall: Defender of the Constitution.* Boston: Little, Brown, and Company.
Stoddard, Amos. 1973 [1812]. *Sketches, Historical and Descriptive, of Louisiana.* New York: AMS Press.
Streshinsky, Shirley. 1993. *Audubon: Life and Art in the American Wilderness.* New York: Villard Books.
Stuart, Reginald. 1988. *United States Expansion and British North America, 1775–1871.* Charlotte: University of North Carolina Press.
Sunder, John E. 1965. *The Fur Trade on the Upper Missouri, 1840–1865.* Norman: University of Oklahoma Press.
Swindler, William F. 1981. *The Constitution and Chief Justice Marshall.* New York: Dodd, Mead, & Company.
Sylvestris [St. George Tucker]. 1803. *Reflections on the Cession of Louisiana to the United States.* Washington, DC: Samuel Harrison Smith.
Talmadge, Arthur. 1909. *The Talmadge, Tallmadge and Talmage Genealogy.* New York: Grafton Press.
Tanner, Helen Hornbeck. 1992. *The Ojibwa.* New York, Philadelphia: Chelsea House.
Tanner, John. 1994 [1830]. *The Falcon: A Narrative of the Captivity and Adventures of John Tanner.* New York: G. & C. H. Carvill. Reprint: New York: Penguin.
Tate, Michael L. 1995. *Nebraska History: An Annotated Bibliography.* Westport, CT: Greenwood Press.
Taylor, Joe Gray. 1963. *Negro Slavery in Louisiana.* Baton

Rouge: Louisiana Historical Association.
Terrell, John Upton. 1968. *Zebulon Pike, The Life and Times of an Adventurer*. New York: Weybright and Talley.
Tharp, Louise Hall. 1946. *Company of Adventurers: The Story of the Hudson's Bay Company*. Boston: Little Brown and Company.
Thomas, David, and Karin Ronnefeldt, eds. 1982. *People of the First Man: Life among the Plains Indians in Their Final Days of Glory*. New York: Promontory Press.
Thomas, William Lyman. 1911. *History of St. Louis County, Missouri*. St. Louis: S. J. Clarke.
Thompson, John. 1986. *Closing the Frontier: Radical Response in Oklahoma, 1889–1923*. Norman: University of Oklahoma Press.
Thurman, Melvena, ed. 1982. *Women in Oklahoma: A Century of Change*. Oklahoma City: Oklahoma Historical Society.
Thwaites, Reuben G. 1904. *The Journals of Lewis and Clark*. 8 vols. New York: Dodd, Mead.
Tibbles, Thomas Henry. 1972. *The Ponca Chiefs: An Account of the Trial of Standing Bear*. Edited by Kay Graber. Lincoln: University of Nebraska Press.
Tillinghast, B. F. 1898. *Rock Island Arsenal in Peace and War*. Rock Island, IL: B. F. Tillinghast.
Treat, Payson, J. 1967. *The National Land System, 1785–1820*. New York: Russell and Russell.
Tregle, Joseph G., Jr. 1999. *Louisiana in the Age of Jackson: A Clash of Culture and Personalities*. Baton Rouge: Louisiana State University Press.
Trenholm, Virginia Cole, and Maurine Carley. 1964. *The Shoshonis: Sentinels of the Rockies*. Norman: University of Oklahoma Press.
———. 1970. *The Arapahoes, Our People*. Norman: University of Oklahoma Press.
Troccoli, Joan Carpenter. 1993. *First Artist of the West: George Catlin Paintings and Watercolors from the Collection of Gilcrease Museum*. Tulsa: Thomas Gilcrease Museum Association.
Truettner, William H., ed. 1991. *The West as America*. Washington, DC: Smithsonian Institution Press for the National Museum of Art.
Tucker, Robert W., and David C. Hendrickson. 1990. *Empire of Liberty: The Statecraft of Thomas Jefferson*. New York: Oxford University Press.
Tucker, St. George. 1803. *Reflections on the Cession of Louisiana to the United States*. Washington, DC: Samuel Harrison Smith.
Tulard, Jean, ed. 1989. *Dictionnaire Napoléon*. Paris: Fayard.
Turner, Frederick Jackson. 1894 *The Significance of the Frontier in American History*. Washington, DC: American Historical Association.
———. 1904. *Correspondence of the French Ministers to the United States, 1791–1797*. In *American Historical Association Annual Report: 1903*, vol. 2. Washington, DC: Government Printing Office.
Tyler, Ron C., et al., eds. 1996. *New Handbook of Texas*. Austin: Texas State Historical Association.
Unrau, William E. 1971. *The Kansa Indians: A History of the Wind People, 1673–1873*. Norman: University of Oklahoma Press.
Unruh, John D., Jr. 1993. *The Plains Across: The Overland Immigrants and the Trans-Mississippi West, 1840–1860*. Urbana: University of Illinois Press.
U.S. Arsenal, Rock Island, IL. 1954. *A History of Rock Island and the Rock Island from the Earliest Times to 1954*. Rock Island, IL: U.S. Army, Rock Island Arsenal.
U.S. Congress. 1851. *The Debates and Proceedings in the Congress of the United States*. Seventh Congress. Washington, DC: Gales and Seaton.
U.S. Congress. 1852. *The Debates and Proceedings in the Congress of the United States*. Eighth Congress, First session. Washington, DC: Gales and Seaton.
U.S. Congress. 1851. *Annals of the Congress of the United States*, vol. 12. Washington, DC: Gales and Seaton.
U.S. Government. 1903. *State Papers and Correspondence Bearing upon the Purchase of the Territory of Louisiana*. Washington, DC: Government Printing Office.
Utley, Robert M. 1963. *The Last Days of the Sioux*. New Haven: Yale University Press.
———. 1984. *The Indian Frontier of the American West, 1846–1890*. Albuquerque: University of New Mexico Press.
———. 1997. *A Life Wild and Perilous: Mountain Men and the Paths to the Pacific*. New York: Henry Holt and Company.
Vestal, Stanley. 1946. *Jim Bridger: Mountain Man*. Lincoln: University of Nebraska Press.
Veyrier, Henri. 1990. *Dictionnaire des diplomates de Napoléon*. Paris: Kronos.
Vifquain, Sally. 2000. "Public History: A Case Study and Annotated Bibliography of Fort Kearny, 1848–1999." Master's thesis, University of Nebraska-Kearney.
Villa-Urrutia, Marques de. 1923. *La Reina de Etruria, Doña Maria Luisa de Borbon, Infanta de España*. Madrid: F. Beltrán.
Vinton, Stallo. 1926. *John Colter, Discoverer of Yellowstone Park; an account of his exploration in 1807 and of his further adventures as hunter; trapper; Indian fighter; pathfinder; and member of the Lewis and Clark Expedition*. New York: E. Eberstadt.
Voelker, Frederic E. 1971. "William Sherley (Old Bill) Williams." In *The Mountain Men and the Fur Trade of the Far West*, vol. 8. Edited by LeRoy R. Hafen. Glendale, CA.: Arthur H. Clark.
Waciuma, Manjoni. 1976. *Intervention in Spanish Floridas, 1810–1813: A Study in Jeffersonian Foreign Policy*. Boston: Branden Press.
Walker, Deward. 1978. *Indians of Idaho*. Moscow: University Press of Idaho.
Wall, Bennett H., et al. 1997. *Louisiana: A History*. Wheeling, IL: Harlan Davidson.
Wall, Helen. 1960. "Transfer of Louisiana from France to Spain." M.A. thesis, Louisiana State University.
Wallace, Ernest, and E. Adamson Hoebel. 1964. *The Comanches: Lords of the South Plains*. Norman: University of Oklahoma Press.
Wallace, Earnest, David M. Vigness, and George B. Ward, eds. 1994. "The Neutral Ground Agreement: October 29 and November 4, 1806." In *Documents in Texas History*. Austin: State House Press
Walters, Raymond, Jr. 1957. *Albert Gallatin: Jeffersonian Financier and Diplomat*. New York: Macmillan Company.
Walton, George. 1973. *Fort Leavenworth and the American West*. Edgewood Cliffs, NJ: Prentice Hall.

Warren, Harris Gaylord. 1943. *The Sword Was Their Passport: A History of American Filibustering in the Mexican Revolution*. Baton Rouge: Louisiana State University Press.

Washburn, Wilcomb E. 1973. *The American Indian and the United States: A Documentary History*. New York: Random House.

Watrous, Stephen D. 1966. *John Ledyard's Journey through Russia and Siberia, 1787–1788*. Madison: University of Wisconsin.

Webb, Walter Prescott. 1972. *The Great Plains*. New York: Grosset and Dunlap.

Weber, David J. 1992. *The Spanish Frontier in North America*. New Haven: Yale University Press.

Wedel, Waldo R. 1936. *An Introduction to Pawnee Archeology*. Washington, DC: Government Printing Office.

Weltfish, Gene. 1965. *The Lost Universe*. New York: Basic Books.

Wesley, Edgar. 1935. *Guarding the Frontier*. Minneapolis: University of Minnesota Press.

———. 1939. "Life at a Frontier Post: Fort Atkinson, 1823–1826." *Journal of the American Military History Foundation* 3: 202–209.

West, C. W. 1974. *Fort Gibson: Gateway to the West*. Muskogee, OK: Muskogee Publishing Company.

Whitaker, Arthur P. 1928. "James Wilkinson's First Descent to New Orleans in 1787." *Hispanic-American Historical Review* 8: 82–97.

———. 1962. *The Mississippi Question, 1795–1803: A Study in Trade, Politics and Diplomacy*. Glouster, MA: Peter Smith.

———. 1962 [1927]. *The Spanish Frontier, 1783–1795: The Westward Movement and Spanish Retreat in the Mississippi Valley*. Lincoln: University of Nebraska Press. Reprint: Gloucester, MA: Peter Smith.

White, C. Albert. 1982. *A History of the Rectangular Survey System*. Washington, DC: Government Printing Office.

White, Lonnie J. 1964. *Politics on the Southwestern Frontier: Arkansas Territory, 1819–1838*. Memphis: Memphis State University Press.

White, Phillip M., ed. 1999. *The Kickapoo Indians, Their History and Culture: An Annotated Bibliography*. Westport, CT: Greenwood Press.

Wilds, John, et al. 1996. *Louisiana Yesterday and Today*. Baton Rouge: Louisiana State University Press.

Wilkinson, James. 1811. *Aaron Burr's Conspiracy Exposed and General Wilkinson Vindicated ....* Washington, DC: Printed for the Author.

———. 1816. *Memoirs of My Own Time*. 3 vols. Philadelphia: Abraham Small.

Williams, Kenneth H. 1999. "Du Pont, Elèuthere Irénée." In *American National Biography*. Edited by John A. Garraty and Mark C. Carnes. New York: Oxford University Press.

Wilson, Maurie T., and Jack Jackson. 1987. *Philip Nolan and Texas: Experience into the Unknown Land, 1791–1801*. Waco: Texian Press.

Wilson, Terry P. 1985. *Bibliography of the Osage*. Metuchan, NJ: Scarecrow Press.

Winkler, Ernest William. 1903. "The Cherokee Indians in Texas." *Quarterly of the Texas State Historical Association* 7, no. 2: 95–165.

Winsor, Justin. 1895. *The Mississippi Basin: The Struggle in America between England and France, 1697–1763*. Boston, New York: Houghton, Mifflin, and Company.

Wishart, David J. 1979. *The Fur Trade of the American West, 1807–1840: A Geographical Synthesis*. London: Croom Helm.

———. 1994. *An Unspeakable Sadness: The Dispossession of the Nebraska Indians*. Lincoln: University of Nebraska Press.

———. 1999. "William Henry Ashley." In *American National Biography*, vol. 1. Edited by John A. Garraty and Mark Carnes. New York: Oxford University Press.

Wood, Richard G. 1966. *Stephen Harriman Long, 1784–1864: Army Engineer, Explorer, Inventor*. Glendale, CA: Arthur Clark.

Woodcock, George. 1970. *The Hudson's Bay Company*. New York: Crowell-Collier Press.

Wooldridge, Rhoda. 1975. *Chouteau and the Founding of Saint Louis*. Independence, MO: Independence Press.

Wright, J. Leita, Jr. 1975. *Britain and the American Frontier, 1783–1815*. Athens: University of Georgia Press.

Young, Peter. 1973. *Napoleon's Marshals*. London: Hippocrene Books.

Young, Otis E. 1955. *The West of Philip St. George Cooke, 1809–1895*. Glendale, CA: Arthur H. Clark.

Zahniser, Marvin R. 1967. *Charles Cotesworth Pinckney: Founding Father*. Chapel Hill: University of North Carolina, Institute of Early American History.

Zegler, Philip. 1988. *The Sixth Great Power: Barings, 1762–1929*. London: Collins.

Ziegler, Philip. 1965. *Addington: A Life of Henry Addington, First Viscount Sidmouth*. New York: John Day & Company.

INDEX

ABOUT THE EDITOR

Junius P. Rodriguez is an associate professor of history at Eureka College in Eureka, Illinois. He is the author of *Chronology of World Slavery* (ABC-CLIO, 1999) and general editor of the award-winning *The Historical Encyclopedia of World Slavery* (ABC-CLIO, 1997).